Wilde p. xvi
"A truth in art is that whose
Contradiction is also true."

A BARTHES READER

A
BARTHES
READER

EDITED, AND WITH AN INTRODUCTION, BY
Susan Sontag

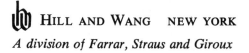 HILL AND WANG   NEW YORK
A division of Farrar, Straus and Giroux

Library of Congress Cataloging in Publication Data
Barthes, Roland.
A Barthes reader.
1. Arts—Articles, essays, lectures. I. Sontag, Susan. II. Title.
NX65.B37   700   80–26762

CONTENTS

v

Writing Itself: On Roland Barthes

> *"The best poetry will be rhetorical criticism . . ."*
> —WALLACE STEVENS (in a journal of 1899)
>
> *"I rarely lose sight of myself."*
> —PAUL VALÉRY, *Monsieur Teste*

TEACHER, man of letters, moralist, philosopher of culture, connoisseur of strong ideas, protean autobiographer . . . of all the intellectual notables who have emerged since World War II in France, Roland Barthes is the one whose work I am most certain will endure. Barthes was in full flow, incessantly productive as he had been for over three decades, when he was struck by a van as he started across a street in Paris in early 1980—a death felt by friends and admirers to be excruciatingly untimely. But along with the backward look of grief comes the awareness that confers upon his large, chronically mutating body of writing, as on all major work, its retroactive completeness. The development of Barthes's work now seems logical; more than that, exhaustive. It even begins and falls silent on the same subject—that exemplary instrument in the career of consciousness, the writer's journal. As it happens, the first essay Barthes ever published celebrates the model consciousness he found in the *Journal* of André Gide, and what turned out to be the last essay published before he died offers Barthes's musings on his own journal-keeping. The symmetry, however adventitious, is an utterly appropriate one, for Barthes's writing, with its prodigious variety of subjects, has finally one great subject: writing itself.

His early themes were those of the freelance partisan of

letters, on the occasions afforded by cultural journalism, literary debate, theater and book reviews. To these were added topics that originated and were recycled in seminars and from the lecture platform, for Barthes's literary career was run concurrently with a (very successful) academic one, and in part *as* an academic one. But the voice was always singular, and self-referring; the achievement is of another, larger order than can be had even by practicing, with thrilling virtuosity, the most lively and many-tracked of academic disciplines. For all his contributions to the would-be science of signs and structures, Barthes's endeavor was the quintessentially literary one: the writer organizing, under a series of doctrinal auspices, the theory of his own mind. And when the current enclosure of his reputation by the labels of semiology and structuralism crumbles, as it must, Barthes will appear, I think, as a rather traditional *promeneur solitaire*, and a greater writer than even his more fervent admirers now claim.

He always wrote full out, was always concentrated, keen, indefatigable. This dazzling inventiveness seems not just a function of Barthes's extraordinary powers as a mind, as a writer. It seems to have almost the status of a position—as if this is what critical discourse *must* be. "Literature is like phosphorous," he says in his first book, which came out in 1953, *Writing Degree Zero*; "it shines with its maximum brilliance at the moment when it attempts to die." In Barthes's view, literature is already a posthumous affair. His work affirms a standard of vehement brilliance that is indeed one ideal of a cultural moment which believes itself to be having, in several senses, the last word.

Its brilliance aside, Barthes's work has some of the specific traits associated with the style of a late moment in culture— one that presumes an endless discourse anterior to itself, that presumes intellectual sophistication: it is work that, strenuously unwilling to be boring or obvious, favors compact assertion, writing that rapidly covers a great deal of ground. Barthes was an inspired, ingenious practitioner of the essay and the anti-essay—he had a resistance to long forms. Typically, his sentences are complex, comma-ridden and colon-prone, packed with densely worded entailments of ideas deployed as if these were the materials of a supple prose. It is a style of exposition, recognizably French, whose parent tradition is to be found in the tense, idiosyncratic essays published between the two world wars in the *Nouvelle Revue Française*—a perfected version of the *NRF*'s house style which can deliver more ideas per page while retaining the brio of that style, its acuteness of timbre. His vocabulary is large, fastidious, fearlessly mandarin. Even Barthes's less fleet, more jargon-haunted writings—most of them from the 1960s—are full of flavor; he manages to make an exuberant use of neologisms. While exuding straight-ahead energy, his prose constantly reaches for the summative formulation; it is irrepressibly aphoristic. (Indeed, one could go through Barthes's work extracting superb bits—epigrams, maxims—to make a small book, as has been done with Wilde and Proust.) Barthes's strengths as an aphorist suggest a sensibility gifted, before any intervention of theory, for the perception of structure. Being a method of condensed assertion by means of symmetrically counterposed terms, the maxim or aphorism inevitably displays the symmetries and complementarities of situations or ideas—that design, their shape. Like a markedly greater feeling for drawings than for paintings, a talent for aphorism is one of the signs of what could be called the formalist temperament.

The formalist temperament is just one variant of a sensibility shared by many who speculate in an era of hypersaturated awareness. What characterizes such a sensibility more generally is its reliance on the criterion of taste, and its proud refusal to propose anything that does not bear the stamp of subjectivity.

Confidently assertive, it nevertheless insists that its assertions
are no more than provisional. (To do otherwise would be . . .
bad taste.) Indeed, adepts of this sensibility usually make a
point of claiming and reclaiming amateur status. "In linguistics
I have never been anything but an amateur," Barthes told an
interviewer in 1975. Throughout his late writings Barthes
repeatedly disavows the, as it were, vulgar roles of system-
builder, authority, mentor, expert, in order to reserve for himself the privileges and freedoms of delectation: the exercise
of taste for Barthes means, usually, to praise. What makes the
role a choice one is his unstated commitment to finding
something new and unfamiliar to praise (which requires having
the right dissonance with established taste); or to praising a
familiar work differently.

An early example is his second book—it appeared in 1954—
which is on Michelet. Through an inventory of the recurrent
metaphors and themes in the great nineteenth-century historian's epic narratives, Barthes discloses a more intimate
narration: Michelet's history of his own body and the "lyric
resurrection of past bodies." Barthes is always after another
meaning, a more eccentric—often utopian—discourse. What
pleased him was to show insipid and reactionary works to be
quirky and implicitly subversive; to display in the most extravagant projects of the imagination an opposite extreme—in
his essay on Sade, a sexual ideal that was really an exercise in
delirious rationality; in his essay on Fourier, a rationalist ideal
that was really an exercise in sensual delirium. Barthes did take
on central figures of the literary canon when he had something
polemical to offer: in 1960 he wrote a short book on Racine,
which scandalized academic critics (the ensuing controversy
ended with Barthes's complete triumph over his detractors);
he also wrote on Proust and Flaubert. But more often, armed
with his essentially adversary notion of the "text," he applied
his ingenuity to the marginal literary subject: an unimportant

"work"—say, Balzac's *Sarrasine,* Chateaubriand's *Life of Rancé*—could be a marvelous "text." Considering something as a "text" means for Barthes precisely to suspend conventional evaluations (the difference between major and minor literature), to subvert established classifications (the separation of genres, the distinctions among the arts).

Though work of every form and worth qualifies for citizenship in the great democracy of "texts," the critic will tend to avoid the texts that everyone has handled, the meaning that everyone knows. The formalist turn in modern criticism—from its pristine phase, as in Shklovsky's idea of defamiliarizing, onward—dictates just this. It charges the critic with the task of discarding worn-out meanings for fresh ones. It is a mandate to scout for new meanings. *Etonne-moi.*

The same mandate is supplied by Barthes's notions of "text" and "textuality." These translate into criticism the modernist ideal of an open-ended, polysemous literature; and thereby make the critic, just like the creators of that literature, the inventor of meaning. (The aim of literature, Barthes asserts, is to put "meaning" into the world but not "a meaning.") To decide that the point of criticism is to alter and to relocate meaning—adding, subtracting, multiplying it—is in effect to base the critic's exertions on an enterprise of avoidance, and thereby to recommit criticism (if it had ever left) to the dominion of taste. For it is, finally, the exercise of taste which identifies meanings that are familiar; a judgment of taste which discriminates against such meanings as too familiar; an ideology of taste which makes of the familiar something vulgar and facile. Barthes's formalism at its most decisive, his ruling that the critic is called on to reconstitute not the "message" of a work but only its "system"—its form, its structure— is perhaps best understood thus, as the liberating avoidance of the obvious, as an immense gesture of good taste.

For the modernist—that is, formalist—critic, the work with

its received valuations already exists. Now, what *else* can be said? The canon of great books has been fixed. What can we add or restore to it? The "message" is already understood, or is obsolete. Let's ignore it.

Of a variety of means Barthes possessed for giving himself something to say—he had an exceptionally fluent, ingenious generalizing power—the most elementary was his aphorist's ability to conjure up a vivacious duality: anything could be split either into itself and its opposite, or into two versions of itself; and one term then fielded against the other to yield an unexpected relation. The point of Voltairean travel, he remarks, is "to manifest an immobility"; Baudelaire "had to protect theatricality from the theater"; the Eiffel Tower "makes the city into a kind of Nature"—Barthes's writing is seeded with such ostensibly paradoxical, epigrammatic formulas as these, whose point is to sum something up. It is the nature of aphoristic thinking to be always in a state of concluding; a bid to have the final word is inherent in all powerful phrase-making.

Less elegant, indeed making a point of dogged explicitness, and far more powerful as an instrument for giving himself something to say, are the classifications that Barthes lays out in order to topple himself into a piece of argument—dividing into two, three, even four parts the matter to be considered. Arguments are launched by announcing that there are two main classes and two subclasses of narrative units, two ways in which myth lends itself to history, two facets of Racinean eros, two musics, two ways to read La Rochefoucauld, two kinds of writers, two forms of his own interest in photographs. That there are three types of corrections a writer makes, three Mediterraneans and three tragic sites in Racine, three levels on which to read the plates of the *Encyclopedia*, three areas of spectacle and three types of gesture in Japanese puppet theater, three attitudes toward speech and writing, equivalent to three vocations: writer, intellectual, and teacher. That there are four kinds of readers, four reasons for keeping a journal . . . And so on. This is the codifying, frontal style of French intellectual discourse, a branch of the rhetorical tactics that the French call, not quite accurately, Cartesian. Although a few of the classifications Barthes employs are standard, such as semiology's canonical triad of signified, signifier, and sign, many are inventions devised by Barthes in order to *make* an argument, such as his assertion in a late book, *The Pleasure of the Text*, that the modern artist seeks to destroy art, "this effort taking three forms." The aim of this implacable categorizing is not just to map the intellectual territory: Barthes's taxonomies are never static. Often the point is precisely for one category to subvert the other, as do the two forms, which he calls *punctum* and *studium*, of his interest in photographs. Barthes offers classifications to keep matters open—to reserve a place for the uncodified, the enchanted, the intractable, the histrionic. He was fond of bizarre classifications, of classificatory excess (Fourier's, for example), and his boldly physical metaphors for mental life stress not topography but transformation. Drawn to hyperbole, as all aphorists are, Barthes enlists ideas in a drama, often a sensual melodrama or a faintly Gothic one. He speaks of the quiver, thrill, or shudder of meaning, of meanings that themselves vibrate, gather, loosen, disperse, quicken, shine, fold, mutate, delay, slide, separate, that exert pressure, crack, rupture, fissure, are pulverized. Barthes offers something like a poetics of thinking, which identifies the meaning of subjects with the very mobility of meaning, with the kinetics of consciousness itself; and liberates the critic as artist. The uses that binary and triadic thinking had for Barthes's imagination were always provisional, available to correction, destabilization, condensation.

As a writer he preferred short forms, and had been planning

to give a seminar on them; he was particularly drawn to miniature ones, like the haiku and the quotation; and, like all true writers, what enthralled him was "the detail" (his word) —experience's model short form. Even as an essayist, Barthes mostly wrote short, and the books he did write tend to be multiples of short forms rather than "real" books, itineraries of topics rather than unified arguments. His *Michelet*, for example, keys its inventory of the historian's themes to a large number of brief excerpts from Michelet's prolific writings. The most rigorous example of the argument as an itinerary by means of quotation is *S/Z*, published in 1970, his model exegesis of Balzac's *Sarrasine*. From staging the texts of others, he passed inevitably to the staging of his own ideas. And, in the same series on great writers (*"Ecrivains de toujours"*) to which he contributed the Michelet volume, he eventually did one on himself in 1975: that dazzling oddity in the series, *Roland Barthes* by Roland Barthes. The high-velocity arrangements of Barthes's late books dramatize both his fecundity (insatiability *and* lightness) and his desire to subvert all tendencies to system-making.

An animus against the systematizers has been a recurrent feature of intellectual good taste for more than a century; Kierkegaard, Nietzsche, Wittgenstein are among the many voices that proclaim, from a superior if virtually unbearable burden of singularity, the absurdity of systems. In its strong modern form, scorn for systems is one aspect of the protest against Law, against Power itself. An older, milder refusal is lodged in the French sceptic tradition, from Montaigne to Gide: writers who are epicures of their own consciousness are likely to decry "the sclerosis of systems," a phrase Barthes used in his first essay, on Gide. And along with these refusals a distinctive modern stylistics has evolved, the prototypes of which go back at least to Sterne and the German Romantics— the invention of anti-linear forms of narration: in fiction, the

destruction of the "story"; in nonfiction, the abandon
linear argument. The presumed impossibility (or irrel
of producing a continuous systematic argument has l
remodeling of the standard long forms—the treatise, tl...ung
book—and a recasting of the genres of fiction, autobiography,
and essay. Of this stylistics, Barthes is a particularly inventive
practitioner.

The Romantic and post-Romantic sensibility discerns in
every book a first-person performance: to write is a dramatic
act, subject to dramatic elaboration. One strategy is to use
multiple pseudonyms, as Kierkegaard did, concealing and
multiplying the figure of the author. When autobiographical,
the work invariably includes avowals of reluctance to speak
in the first person. One of the conventions of *Roland Barthes*
is for the autobiographer to refer to himself sometimes as "I,"
sometimes as "he." All this, Barthes announces on the first
page of this book about himself, "must be considered as if
spoken by a character in a novel." Under the meta-category
of performance, not only the line between autobiography and
fiction is muted, but that between essay and fiction as well.
"Let the essay avow itself almost a novel," he says in *Roland Barthes*. Writing registers new forms of dramatic stress,
of a self-referring kind: writing becomes the record of com-
pulsions and of resistances to write. (In the further extension
of this view, writing itself becomes the writer's subject.)

For the purpose of achieving an ideal digressiveness and an
ideal intensity, two strategies have been widely adopted. One
is to abolish some or all of the conventional demarcations or
separations of discourse, such as chapters, paragraphing, even
punctuation, whatever is regarded as impeding formally the
continuous production of (the writer's) voice—the run-on
method favored by writers of philosophical fictions such as
Hermann Broch, Joyce, Stein, Beckett. The other strategy is
the opposite one: to multiply the ways in which discourse is

segmented, to invent further ways of breaking it up. Joyce and
Stein used this method, too; Shklovsky in his best books, from
the 1920s, writes in one-sentence paragraphs. The multiple
openings and closures produced by the start-and-stop method
permit discourse to become as differentiated, as polyphonous,
as possible. Its most common shape in expository discourse is
that of short, one- or two-paragraph units separated by spaces.
"Notes on . . ." is the usual literary title—a form Barthes uses
in the essay on Gide, and returns to often in his later work.
Much of his writing proceeds by techniques of interruption,
sometimes in the form of an excerpt alternating with a disjunctive commentary, as in *Michelet* and *S/Z*. To write in fragments or sequences or "notes" entails new, serial (rather than
linear) forms of arrangements. These sequences may be staged
in some arbitrary way. For example, they may be numbered—
a method practiced with great refinement by Wittgenstein. Or
they may be given headings, sometimes ironic or overemphatic
—Barthes's strategy in *Roland Barthes*. Headings allow an
additional possibility: for the elements to be arranged alpha-
betically, to emphasize further the arbitrary character of their
sequence—the method of *A Lover's Discourse* (1977), whose
real title evokes the notion of the fragment; it is *Fragments
d'un discours amoureux*.

Barthes's late writing is his boldest formally: all major work
was organized in a serial rather than linear form. Straight
essay writing was reserved for the literary good deed (pref-
aces, for example, of which Barthes wrote many) or journalistic whim. However, these strong forms of the late writing
only bring forward a desire implicit in all of his work—
Barthes's wish to have a superior relation to assertion: the
relation that art has, of pleasure. Such a conception of writing
excludes the fear of contradiction. (In Wilde's phrase: "A
truth in art is that whose contradiction is also true.") Barthes
repeatedly compared teaching to play, reading to eros, writing

to seduction. His voice became more and more personal, more full of grain, as he called it; his intellectual art more openly a performance, like that of the other great anti-systematizers. But whereas Nietzsche addresses the reader in many tones, mostly aggressive—exulting, berating, coaxing, prodding, taunting, inviting complicity—Barthes invariably performs in an affable register. There are no rude or prophetic claims, no pleadings with the reader, and no efforts *not* to be understood. This is seduction as play, never violation. All of Barthes's work is an exploration of the histrionic or ludic; in many ingenious modes, a plea for savor, for a festive (rather than dogmatic or credulous) relation to ideas. For Barthes, as for Nietzsche, the point is not to teach us something in particular. The point is to make us bold, agile, subtle, intelligent, detached. And to give pleasure.

Writing is Barthes's perennial subject—indeed, perhaps no one since Flaubert (in his letters) has thought as brilliantly, as passionately as Barthes has about what writing is. Much of his work is devoted to portraits of the vocation of the writer: from the early debunking studies included in *Mythologies* (1957) of the writer as seen by others, that is, the writer as fraud, such as "The Writer on Holiday," to more ambitious essays on writers writing, that is, the writer as hero and martyr, such as "Flaubert and the Sentence," about the writer's "agony of style." Barthes's wonderful essays on writers must be considered as different versions of his great apologia for the vocation of the writer. For all his admiration for the self-punishing standards of integrity set by Flaubert, he dares to conceive of writing as a kind of happiness: the point of his essay on Voltaire ("The Last Happy Writer"), and of his portrait of Fourier, unvexed by the sense of evil. In his late work he speaks directly of his own practice, scruples, bliss.

Barthes construes writing as an ideally complex form of

consciousness: a way of being both passive and active, social and asocial, present and absent in one's own life. His idea of the writer's vocation excludes the sequestration that Flaubert thought inevitable, would appear to deny any conflict between the writer's necessary inwardness and the pleasures of worldliness. It is, so to speak, Flaubert strongly amended by Gide: a more well-bred, casual rigor, an avid, guileful relation to ideas that excludes fanaticism. Indeed, the ideal self-portrait—the portrait of the self as writer—that Barthes sketched throughout his work is virtually complete in the first essay, on Gide's "work of egoism," his *Journal*. Gide supplied Barthes with the patrician model for the writer who is supple, multiple; never strident or vulgarly indignant; generous . . . but also properly egotistical; incapable of being deeply influenced. He notes how little Gide was altered by his vast reading ("so many self-recognitions"), how his "discoveries" were never "denials." And he praises the profusion of Gide's scruples, observing that Gide's "situation at the intersection of great contradictory currents has nothing facile about it . . ." Barthes subscribes as well to Gide's idea of writing that is elusive, willing to be minor. His relation to politics also recalls Gide's: a willingness in times of ideological mobilization to take the right stands, to be political—but, finally, not: and thereby, perhaps, to tell the truth that hardly anybody else is telling. (See the short essay Barthes wrote after a trip to China in 1974.) Barthes had many affinities with Gide, and much of what he says of Gide applies unaltered to himself. How remarkable to find it all laid out—including the program of "perpetual self-correction"—well before he embarked on his career. (Barthes was twenty-seven, a patient in a sanatorium for tubercular students, when he wrote this essay in 1942 for the sanatorium's magazine; he did not enter the Paris literary arena for another five years.)

When Barthes, who began under the aegis of Gide's doctrine

of psychic and moral availability, started writing regularly,
Gide's important work was long over, his influence already
negligible (he died in 1951); and Barthes put on the armor of
postwar debate about the responsibility of literature, the terms
of which were set up by Sartre—the demand that the writer be
in a militant relation to virtue, which Sartre described by the
tautological notion of "commitment." Gide and Sartre were,
of course, the two most influential writer-moralists of this
century in France, and the work of these two sons of French
Protestant culture suggests quite opposed moral and aesthetic
choices. But it is just this kind of polarization that Barthes,
another Protestant in revolt against Protestant moralism,
seeks to avoid. Supple Gidean that he is, Barthes is eager to
acknowledge the model of Sartre as well. While a quarrel with
Sartre's view of literature lies at the heart of his first book,
Writing Degree Zero (Sartre is never mentioned by name),
an agreement with Sartre's view of the imagination, and its
obsessional energies, surfaces in Barthes's last book, *Camera
Lucida* (written "in homage" to the early Sartre, the author
of *L'Imaginaire*). Even in the first book, Barthes concedes a
good deal to Sartre's view of literature and language—for
example, putting poetry with the other "arts" and identifying
literature with prose, with argument. Barthes's view of literature in his subsequent writing was more complex. Though he
never wrote on poetry, his standards for literature approached
those of the poet: language that has undergone an upheaval,
has been displaced, liberated from ungrateful contexts; that,
so to speak, lives on its own. Although Barthes agrees with
Sartre that the writer's vocation has an ethical imperative, he
insists on its complexity and ambiguity. Sartre appeals to the
morality of ends. Barthes invokes "the morality of form"—
what makes literature a problem rather than a solution; what
makes literature.

To conceive of literature as successful "communication"

and position-taking, however, is a sentiment that must inevitably become conformist. The instrumental view expounded in Sartre's *What Is Literature?* (1948) makes of literature something perpetually obsolete, a vain—and misplaced—struggle between ethical good soldiers and literary purists, that is, modernists. (Contrast the latent philistinism of this view of literature with the subtlety and acuity of what Sartre had to say about visual images.) Riven by his love of literature (the love recounted in his own perfect book, *The Words*) and an evangelical contempt for literature, one of the century's great *littérateurs* spent the last years of his life insulting literature and himself with that indigent idea, "the neurosis of literature." His defense of the writer's project of commitment is no more convincing. Accused of thereby reducing literature (to politics), Sartre protested that it would be more correct to accuse him of overestimating it. "If literature isn't *everything*, it's not worth a single hour of someone's trouble," he declared in an interview in 1960. "That's what I mean by 'commitment.'" But Sartre's inflation of literature to "everything" is another brand of depreciation.

Barthes, too, might be charged with overestimating literature—with treating literature as "everything"—but at least he made a good case for doing so. For Barthes understood (as Sartre did not) that literature is first of all, last of all, language. It is language that is everything. Which is to say that all of reality is presented in the form of language—the poet's wisdom, and also the structuralist's. And Barthes takes for granted (as Sartre, with his notion of writing as communication, did not) what he calls the "radical exploration of writing" undertaken by Mallarmé, Joyce, Proust, and their successors. That no venture is valuable unless it can be conceived as a species of radicalism, radicalism thereby unhinged from any distinctive content, is perhaps the essence of what we call modernism.

Barthes's work belongs to the sensibility of modernism in the extent to which it assumes the necessity of the adversary stance: literature conceived by modernist standards but not necessarily a modernist literature. Rather, all varieties of counterposition are available to it.

Perhaps the most striking difference between Sartre and Barthes is the deep one, of temperament. Sartre has an intellectually brutal, *bon enfant* view of the world, a view that wills simplicity, resolution, transparence; Barthes's view is irrevocably complex, self-conscious, refined, irresolute. Sartre was eager, too eager, to seek confrontation, and the tragedy of this great career, of the use he made of his stupendous intellect, was just his willingness to simplify himself. Barthes preferred to avoid confrontation, to evade polarization. He defines the writer as "the watcher who stands at the crossroads of all other discourses"—the opposite of an activist or a purveyor of doctrine.

Barthes's utopia of literature has an ethical character almost the opposite of Sartre's. It emerges in the connections he makes between desire and reading, desire and writing—his insistence that his own writing is, more than anything, the product of appetite. The words "pleasure," "bliss," "happiness" recur in his work with a weight, reminiscent of Gide, that is both voluptuous and subversive. As a moralist—Puritan or anti-Puritan—might solemnly distinguish sex for procreation from sex for pleasure, Barthes divides writers into those who write *something* (what Sartre meant by a writer) and the real writers, who do not write something but, rather, *write.* This intransitive sense of the verb "to write" Barthes endorses as not only the source of the writer's felicity but the model of freedom. For Barthes, it is not the commitment that writing makes to something outside of itself (to a social or moral goal) that makes literature an instrument of opposition and subversion but a certain practice of writing itself: excessive, playful, intricate, subtle, sensuous—language which can never be that of power.

Barthes's praise of writing as a gratuitous, free activity is, in one sense, a political view. He conceives of literature as a perpetual renewal of the right of individual assertion; and all rights are, finally, political ones. Still, Barthes is in an evasive relation to politics, and he is one of the great modern refusers of history. Barthes started publishing and mattering in the aftermath of World War II, which, astonishingly, he never mentions; indeed, in all his writings he never, as far as I recall, mentions the word "war." Barthes's friendly way of understanding subjects domesticates them, in the best sense. He lacks anything like Walter Benjamin's tragic awareness that every work of civilization is also a work of barbarism. The ethical burden for Benjamin was a kind of martyrdom; he could not help connecting it with politics. Barthes regards politics as a kind of constriction of the human (and intellectual) subject which has to be outwitted; in *Roland Barthes* he declares that he likes political positions "lightly held." Hence, perhaps, he was never gripped by the project that is central for Benjamin, as for all true modernists: to try to fathom the nature of "the modern." Barthes, who was not tormented by the catastrophes of modernity or tempted by its revolutionary illusions, had a post-tragic sensibility. He refers to the present literary era as "a moment of gentle apocalypse." Happy indeed the writer who can pronounce such a phrase.

Much of Barthes's work is devoted to the repertoire of pleasure—"the great adventure of desire," as he calls it in the essay on Brillat-Savarin's *Physiology of Taste*. Collecting a model of felicity from each thing he examines, he assimilates intellectual practice itself to the erotic. Barthes called the life of the mind desire, and was concerned to defend "the plurality of desire." Meaning is never monogamous. His joyful wisdom or gay science offers the ideal of a free yet capacious, satisfied consciousness; of a condition in which one does not have to choose between good and bad, true and false, in which it is not necessary to justify. The texts and enterprises that engaged Barthes tend to be those in which he could read a defiance of these antitheses. For example, this is how Barthes construes fashion: as a domain, like eros, where contraries do not exist ("Fashion seeks equivalences, validities—not verities"); where one can allow oneself to be gratified; where meaning—and pleasure—is profuse.

To construe in this way, Barthes requires a master category through which everything can be refracted, which makes possible the maximum number of intellectual moves. That most inclusive category is language, the widest sense of language— meaning form itself. Thus, the subject of *Système de la mode* (1967) is not fashion but the language of fashion. Barthes assumes, of course, that the language of fashion *is* fashion; that, as he said in an interview, "fashion exists only through the discourse on it." Assumptions of this sort (myth is a language, fashion is a language) have become a leading, often reductive convention of contemporary intellectual endeavor. In Barthes's work the assumption is less a reductive one than it is proliferative—embarrassment of riches for the critic as artist. To stipulate that there is no understanding outside of language is to assert that there is meaning *everywhere*.

By so extending the reach of meaning, Barthes takes the notion over the top, to arrive at such triumphant paradoxes as the empty subject that contains everything, the empty sign to which all meaning can be attributed. With this euphoric sense of how meaning proliferates, Barthes reads that "zero degree of the monument," the Eiffel Tower, as "this pure— virtually empty—sign" that (his italics) *"means everything."* (The characteristic point of Barthes's arguments-by-paradox is to vindicate subjects untrammeled by utility: it is the uselessness of the Eiffel Tower that makes it infinitely useful as a sign, just as the uselessness of genuine literature is what makes it morally useful.) Barthes found a world of such liberating absences of meaning, both modernist and simply non-Western, in Japan; Japan, he noted, was full of empty signs. In place of moralistic antitheses—true versus false, good versus bad—Barthes offers complementary extremes. "Its form is empty but present, its meaning absent but full," he writes about myth in an essay in the 1950s. Arguments about many subjects have this identical climax: that absence is really presence, emptiness repletion, impersonality the highest achievement of the personal.

Like that euphoric register of religious understanding which discerns treasures of meaning in the most banal and meaningless, which designates as the richest carrier of meaning one vacant of meaning, the brilliant descriptions in Barthes's work bespeak an ecstatic experience of understanding; and ecstasy—whether religious, aesthetic, or sexual—has perennially been described by the metaphors of being empty and being full, the zero state and the state of maximal plentitude: their alternation, their equivalence. The very transposing of subjects into the discourse about them is the same kind of move: emptying subjects out to fill them up again. It is a method of understanding that, presuming ecstasy, fosters detachment. And his very idea of language also supports both aspects of Barthes's sensibility: while endorsing a profusion of meaning, the Saussurean theory—that language *is* form (rather than substance) —is wonderfully congruent with a taste for elegant, that is, reticent, discourse. Creating meaning through the intellectual equivalent of negative space, Barthes's method has one never talking about subjects in themselves: fashion is the language of fashion, a country (Japan) is "the empire of signs"—the ultimate accolade. For reality to exist *as* signs conforms to a maximum idea of decorum: all meaning is deferred, indirect, elegant.

Barthes's ideals of impersonality, of reticence, of elegance, are set forth most beautifully in his appreciation of Japanese culture: in the book called *Empire of Signs* (1970) and in his essay on the Bunraku puppets. This essay, "Lesson in Writing," recalls Kleist's "On the Puppet Theater," which similarly celebrates the tranquillity, lightness, and grace of beings free of thinking, of meaning—free of "the disorders of consciousness." Like the puppets in Kleist's essay, the Bunraku puppets are seen as incarnating an ideal "impassivity, clarity, agility, subtlety." To be both impassive and fantastic, inane and profound, unselfconscious and supremely sensuous —these qualities that Barthes discerned in various facets of Japanese civilization project an ideal of taste and deportment, the ideal of the aesthete in its larger meaning that has been in general circulation since the dandies of the late eighteenth century. Barthes was hardly the first Western observer for whom Japan has meant an aesthete's utopia, the place where one finds aesthete views everywhere and exercises one's own at liberty. The culture where aesthete goals are central—not, as in the West, eccentric—was bound to elicit a strong response. (Japan is mentioned in the Gide essay written in 1942.)

Of the available models of the aesthetic way of looking at the world, perhaps the most eloquent are French and Japanese. In France it has largely been a literary tradition, though with annexes in two popular arts, gastronomy and fashion. Barthes did take up the subject of food as ideology, as classification, as taste—he talks often of savoring; and it seems inevitable that he found the subject of fashion congenial. Writers from Baudelaire to Cocteau have taken fashion seriously, and one of the founding figures of literary modernism, Mallarmé, edited a fashion magazine. French culture, where aesthete ideals have been more explicit and influential than in any other European culture, allows a link between ideas of vanguard art and of fashion. (The French have never shared the Anglo-American conviction that makes the fashionable the opposite of the serious.) In Japan, aesthete standards appear to imbue the whole culture, and long predate the modern ironies; they were formulated as early as the late tenth century, in Sei Shōnagon's *Pillow Book*, that breviary of consummate dandy attitudes, written in what is for us an astonishingly modern, disjunctive form—notes, anecdotes, and lists. Barthes's interest in Japan expresses the attraction to a less defensive, more innocent, and far more elaborated version of the aesthete sensibility: emptier and prettier than the French, more straightforward (no beauty in ugliness, as in Baudelaire); pre-apocalyptic, refined, serene.

In Western culture, where it remains marginal, the dandy attitude has the character of an exaggeration. In one form, the older one, the aesthete is a willful exclusionist of taste, holding attitudes that make it possible to like, to be comfortable with, to give one's assent to the smallest number of things; reducing things to the smallest expression of them. (When taste distributes its plusses and minuses, it favors diminutive adjectives, such as—for praise—happy, amusing, charming, agreeable, suitable.) Elegance equals the largest amount of refusal. As language, this attitude finds its consummate expression in the rueful quip, the disdainful one-liner. In the other form, the aesthete sustains standards that make it possible to be pleased with the largest number of things; annexing new, unconventional, even illicit sources of pleasure. The literary device that best projects this attitude is the list (*Roland Barthes* has many)—the whimsical aesthete polyphony that juxtaposes things and experiences of a starkly different, often incongruous nature, turning them all, by this technique, into artifacts, aesthetic objects. Here elegance equals the wittiest acceptances. The aesthete's posture alternates between *never* being satisfied and *always* finding a way of being satisfied, being pleased with virtually everything.[1]

Although both directions of dandy taste presuppose detachment, the exclusivist version is cooler. The inclusivist version can be enthusiastic, even effusive; the adjectives used for praise tend to be over- rather than understatements. Barthes, who had much of the high exclusivist taste of the dandy, was more inclined to its modern, democratizing form: aesthete leveling —hence his willingness to find charm, amusement, happiness, pleasure in so many things. His account of Fourier, for example, is finally an aesthete's appraisal. Of the "little details" that, he says, make up the "whole of Fourier," Barthes writes: "I am carried away, dazzled, convinced by a sort of charm of expressions . . . Fourier is swarming with these felicities . . . I cannot resist these pleasures; they seem 'true' to me." Similarly: what another *flâneur*, less committed to finding pleasure everywhere, might experience as the oppressive overcrowdedness of streets in Tokyo signifies for Barthes "the transformation of quality by quantity," a new relation that is "a source of endless jubilation."

Many of Barthes's judgments and interests are implicitly affirmations of the aesthete's standards. His early essays championing the fiction of Robbe-Grillet, which gave Barthes the misleading reputation as an advocate of literary modernism, were in effect aesthete polemics. The "objective," the "literal"—these austere, minimalist ideas of literature are in fact Barthes's ingenious recycling of one of the aesthete's principal theses: that surface is as telling as depth. What Barthes discerned in Robbe-Grillet in the 1950s was a new,

[1] The version of the aesthete sensibility I once tried to include under the name "camp" can be regarded as a technique of taste for making the aesthete taste less exclusionary (a way of liking more than one really wants to like) and as part of the democratizing of dandy attitudes. Camp taste, however, still presupposes the older, high standards of discrimination—in contrast to the taste incarnated by, say, Andy Warhol, the franchiser and mass marketer of the dandyism of leveling.

high-tech version of the dandy writer; what he hailed in
Robbe-Grillet was the desire "to establish the novel on the
surface," thereby frustrating our desire to "fall back on a
psychology." The idea that depths are obfuscating, demagogic,
that no human essence stirs at the bottom of things, and
that freedom lies in staying on the surface, the large glass
on which desire circulates—this is the central argument of
the modern aesthete position, in the various exemplary forms
it has taken over the last hundred years. (Baudelaire. Wilde.
Duchamp. Cage.)

Barthes is constantly making an argument against depth,
against the idea that the most real is latent, submerged.
Bunraku is seen as refusing the antinomy of matter and soul,
inner and outer. "*Myth hides nothing,*" he declares in "Myth
Today" (1956). The aesthete position not only regards the
notion of depths, of hiddenness, as a mystification, a lie, but
opposes the very idea of antitheses. Of course, to speak of
depths and surfaces is already to misrepresent the aesthetic
view of the world—to reiterate a duality, like that of form
and content, it precisely denies. The largest statement of
this position was made by Nietzsche, whose work constitutes
a criticism of fixed antitheses (good versus evil, right versus
wrong, true versus false).

But while Nietzsche scorned "depths," he exalted "heights."
In the post-Nietzschean tradition, there are neither depths
nor heights; there are only various kinds of surface, of spectacle. Nietzsche said that every profound nature needs a mask,
and spoke—profoundly—in praise of intellectual ruse; but he
was making the gloomiest prediction when he said that the
coming century, ours, would be the age of the actor. An ideal
of seriousness, of sincerity, underlies all of Nietzsche's work,
which makes the overlap of his ideas and those of a true
aesthete (like Wilde, like Barthes) so problematic. Nietzsche
was a histrionic thinker but not a lover of the histrionic.

His ambivalence toward spectacle (after all, his criticism of Wagner's music was finally that it was a seduction), his insistence on the authenticity of spectacle, means that criteria other than the histrionic are in effect. In the aesthete's position, the notions of reality and spectacle precisely reinforce and infuse each other, and seduction is always something positive. In this respect, Barthes's ideas have an exemplary coherence. Notions of the theater inform, directly or indirectly, all his work. (Divulging the secret, late, he declares in *Roland Barthes* that there was no single text of his "which did not treat of a certain theater, and the spectacle is the universal category through whose forms the world is seen.") Barthes explains Robbe-Grillet's empty, "anthological" description as a technique of theatrical distancing (presenting an object "as if it were in itself a spectacle"). Fashion is, of course, another casebook of the theatrical. So is Barthes's interest in photography, which he treats as a realm of pure haunted spectatorship. In the account of photography given in *Camera Lucida* there are hardly any photographers—the subject is photographs (treated virtually as found objects) and those who are fascinated by them: as objects of erotic reverie, as *memento mori*.

What he wrote about Brecht, whom he discovered in 1954 (when the Berliner Ensemble visited Paris with their production of *Mother Courage*) and helped make known in France, has less to do with the theatrical than does his treatment of some subjects as *forms* of the theatrical. In his frequent use of Brecht in seminars of the 1970s, he cited the prose writings, which he took as a model of critical acuity; it was not Brecht the maker of didactic spectacles but Brecht the didactic intellectual who finally mattered to Barthes. In contrast, with Bunraku what Barthes valued was the element of theatricality as such. In Barthes's early work, the theatrical is the domain of liberty, the place where identities are only roles and one can *change* roles, a zone where meaning itself may be refused.

(Barthes speaks of Bunraku's privileged "exemption from meaning.") Barthes's talk about the theatrical, like his evangelism of pleasure, is a way of proselytizing for the attenuating, lightening, baffling of the Logos, of meaning itself.

To affirm the notion of the spectacle is the triumph of the aesthete's position: the promulgation of the ludic, the refusal of the tragic. All of Barthes's intellectual moves have the effect of voiding work of its "content," the tragic of its finality. That is the sense in which his work is genuinely subversive, liberating—playful. It is outlaw discourse, in the great aesthete tradition, which often assumes the liberty of rejecting the "substance" of discourse in order better to appreciate its "form": outlaw discourse turned respectable, as it were, with the help of various theories known as varieties of formalism. In numerous accounts of his intellectual evolution, Barthes describes himself as the perpetual disciple—but the point that he really wants to make is that he remains, finally, untouched. He spoke of his having worked under the aegis of a succession of theories and masters. In fact, Barthes's work has altogether more coherence, and ambivalence. For all his connection with tutelary doctrines, Barthes's submission to doctrine was superficial. In the end, it was necessary that all intellectual gadgetry be discarded. His last books are a kind of unraveling of his ideas. *Roland Barthes*, he says, is the book of his resistance to his ideas, the dismantling of his own authority. And in the inaugural lecture that marked his acceding to a position of the highest authority—the Chair of Literary Semiology at the Collège de France in 1977—Barthes chooses, characteristically enough, to argue for a soft intellectual authority. He praises teaching as a permissive, not a coercive, space where one can be relaxed, disarmed, floating.

Language itself, which Barthes called a "utopia" in the euphoric formulation that ends *Writing Degree Zero*, now comes under attack, as another form of "power," and his very effort to convey his sensitivity to the ways in which language is "power" gives rise to that instantly notorious hyperbole in his Collège de France lecture: the power of language is "quite simply fascist." To assume that society is ruled by monolithic ideologies and repressive mystifications is necessary to Barthes's advocacy of egoism, post-revolutionary but nevertheless antinomian: his notion that the affirmation of the unremittingly personal is a subversive act. This is a classic extension of the aesthete attitude, in which it becomes a politics: a politics of radical individuality. Pleasure is largely identified with unauthorized pleasure, and the right of individual assertion with the sanctity of the asocial self. In the late writings, the theme of protest against power takes the form of an increasingly private definition of experience (as fetishized involvement) and a ludic definition of thought. "The great problem," Barthes says in a late interview, "is to outplay the signified, to outplay law, to outplay the father, to outplay the repressed—I do not say to explode it, but to outplay it." The aesthete's ideal of detachment, of the selfishness of detachment, allows for avowals of passionate, obsessed involvement: the selfishness of ardor, of fascination. (Wilde speaks of his "curious mixture of ardour and of indifference . . . I would go to the stake for a sensation and be a sceptic to the last.") Barthes has to keep affirming the aesthete's detachment, and undermining it—with passions.

Like all great aesthetes, Barthes was an expert at having it both ways. Thus he identifies writing both with a generous relation to the world (writing as "perpetual production") and with a defiant relation (writing as "a perpetual revolution of language," outside the bounds of power). He wants a politics and an anti-politics, a critical relation to the world and one beyond moral considerations. The aesthete's radicalism is the radicalism of a privileged, even a replete, consciousness —but a genuine radicalism nonetheless. All genuine moral views are founded on a notion of refusal, and the aesthete's view, which can be conformist, does provide certain potentially powerful, not just elegant, grounds for a great refusal.

The aesthete's radicalism: to be multiple, to make multiple identifications; to assume fully the privilege of the personal. Barthes's work—he avows that he writes by obsessions—consists of continuities and detours; the accumulation of points of view; finally, their disburdenment: a mixture of progress and caprice. For Barthes, liberty is a state that consists in remaining plural, fluid, vibrating with doctrine; whose price is being indecisive, apprehensive, fearful of being taken for an impostor. The writer's freedom that Barthes describes is, in part, flight. The writer is the deputy of his own ego—of that self in perpetual flight before what is fixed by writing, as the mind is in perpetual flight from doctrine. "Who *speaks* is not who *writes*, and who *writes* is not who *is*." Barthes wants to move on—that is one of the imperatives of the aesthete's sensibility.

Throughout his work Barthes projects himself into his subject. He is Fourier: unvexed by the sense of evil, aloof from politics, "that necessary purge"; he "vomits it up." He is the Bunraku puppet: impersonal, subtle. He is Gide: the writer who is ageless (always young, always mature); the writer as egoist—a triumphant species of "simultaneous being" or plural desire. He is the subject of all the subjects that he praises. (That he must, characteristically, praise may be connected with his project of defining, creating standards for himself.) In this sense, much of what Barthes wrote now appears autobiographical.

Eventually, it became autobiographical in the literal sense. A brave meditation on the personal, on the self, is at the center of his late writings and seminars. Much of Barthes's work, especially the last three books with their poignant themes of loss, constitutes a candid defense of his sensuality (as well as his sexuality)—his flavor, his way of tasting the world. The books are also artfully anti-confessional. *Camera Lucida* is a meta-book: a meditation on the even more personal auto-biographical book that he planned to write about photographs of his mother, who died in 1978, and then put aside. Barthes starts from the modernist model of writing that is superior to any idea of intention or mere expressiveness; a mask. "The work," Valéry insists, "should not give the person it affects anything that can be reduced to an idea of the author's person and thinking."[2] But this commitment to impersonality does not preclude the avowal of the self; it is only another variation on the project of self-examination: the noblest project of French literature. Valéry offers one ideal of self-absorption—impersonal, disinterested. Rousseau offers another ideal—passionate, avowing vulnerability. Many themes of Barthes's work lie in the classic discourse of French literary culture: its taste for elegant abstraction, in particular for the formal analysis of the sentiments; its disdain for mere psychology; and its coquetry about the impersonal (Flaubert declaring *"Madame Bovary, c'est moi"* but also insisting in letters on his novel's "impersonality," its lack of connection with himself).

Barthes is the latest major participant in the great national literary project, inaugurated by Montaigne: the self as vocation, life as a reading of the self. The enterprise construes the self as the locus of all possibilities, avid, unafraid of contradiction (nothing need be lost, everything may be gained), and the exercise of consciousness as a life's highest aim, be-

---

[2] This modernist dictum that writing is, ideally, a form of impersonality or absence underlies Barthes's move to eliminate the "author" when considering a book. (The method of his *S/Z*: an exemplary reading of a Balzac novella as virtually an authorless text.) One of the things Barthes does as a critic is to formulate the mandate for one kind of modernism (Flaubert, Valéry, Eliot) for the writer as a general program for *readers*. Another is to contravene that mandate in practice—for most of Barthes's writing is precisely devoted to personal singularity.

cause only through becoming fully conscious may one be free. The distinctive French utopian tradition is this vision of reality redeemed, recovered, transcended by consciousness; a vision of the life of the mind as a life of desire, of full intelligence and pleasure—so different from, say, the traditions of high moral seriousness of German and of Russian literature.

Inevitably, Barthes's work had to end in autobiography. "One must choose between being a terrorist and being an egoist," he once observed in a seminar. The options seem very French. Intellectual terrorism is a central, respectable form of intellectual practice in France—tolerated, humored, rewarded: the "Jacobin" tradition of ruthless assertion and shameless ideological about-faces; the mandate of incessant judgment, opinion, anathematizing, overpraising; the taste for extreme positions, then casually reversed, and for deliberate provocation. Alongside this, how modest egoism is!

Barthes's voice became steadily more intimate, his subjects more inward. An affirmation of his own idiosyncrasy (which he does not "decipher") is the main theme of *Roland Barthes*. He writes about the body, taste, love; solitude; erotic desolation; finally, death, or rather desire and death: the twin subjects of the book on photography. As in the Platonic dialogues, the thinker (writer, reader, teacher) and the lover—the two main figures of the Barthesian self—are joined. Barthes, of course, means his erotics of literature more literally, as literally as he can. (The text *enters*, *fills*, it *grants* euphoria.) But finally he seems fairly Platonic after all. The monologue of *A Lover's Discourse*, which obviously draws on a story of disappointment in love, ends in a spiritual vision in the classic Platonic way, in which lower loves are transmuted into higher, more inclusive ones. Barthes avows that he "wants to unmask, no longer to interpret, but to make of consciousness itself a drug, and thus accede to a vision of irreducible reality, to the great drama of clarity, to prophetic love."

As he divested himself of theories, he gave less weight to the modernist standard of the intricate. He does not want, he says, to place any obstacles between himself and the reader. The last book is part memoir (of his mother), part meditation on eros, part treatise on the photographic image, part invocation of death—a book of piety, resignation, desire; a certain brilliance is being renounced, and the view itself is of the simplest. The subject of photography provided the great exemption, perhaps release, from the exactions of formalist taste. In choosing to write about photography, Barthes takes the occasion to adopt the warmest kind of realism: photographs fascinate because of what they are about. And they may awaken a desire for a further divestment of the self. ("Looking at certain photographs," he writes in *Camera Lucida*, "I wanted to be a primitive, without culture.") The Socratic sweetness and charm become more plaintive, more desperate: writing is an embrace, a being embraced; every idea is an idea reaching out. There is a sense of disaggregation of his ideas, and of himself—represented by his increasing fascination with what he calls "the detail." In the preface to *Sade/Fourier/Loyola,* Barthes writes: "Were I a writer, and dead, how pleased I would be if my life, through the efforts of some friendly and detached biographer, were to reduce itself to a few details, a few preferences, a few inflections, let us say: to 'biographemes' whose distinction and mobility might travel beyond the limits of any fate, and come to touch, like Epicurean atoms, some future body, destined to the same dispersion." The need to touch, even in the perspective of his own mortality.

Barthes's late work is filled with signals that he has come to the end of something—the enterprise of the critic as artist—and was seeking to become another kind of writer. (He announced his intention to write a novel.) There were exalted avowals of vulnerability, of being forlorn. Barthes more and more entertained an idea of writing which resembles the mystical idea of *kenosis*, emptying out. He acknowledged that not only systems—his ideas were in a state of melt—but the "I" as well has to be dismantled. (True knowledge, says Barthes, depends on the "unmasking of the 'I.' ") The aesthetics of absence—the empty sign, the empty subject, the exemption from meaning—were all intimations of the great project of depersonalization which is the aesthete's highest gesture of good taste. Toward the close of Barthes's work, this ideal took on another inflection. A spiritual ideal of depersonalization—that is perhaps the characteristic terminus of every serious aesthete's position. (Think of Wilde, of Valéry.) It is the point at which the aesthete's view self-destructs: what follows is either silence —or becoming something else.

Barthes harbored spiritual strivings that could not be supported by his aesthete's position. It was inevitable that he pass beyond it, as he did in his very last work and teaching. At the end, he had done with the aesthetics of absence, and now spoke of literature as the embrace of subject and object. There was an emergence of a vision of "wisdom" of the Platonic sort—tempered, to be sure, by wisdom of a worldly kind: skeptical of dogmatisms, conscientious about gratification, wistfully attached to utopian ideals. Barthes's temperament, style, sensibility, had run its course. And from this vantage point his work now appears to unfold, with more grace and poignancy and with far greater intellectual power than that of any other contemporary, the considerable truths vouchsafed to the aesthete's sensibility, to a commitment to intellectual adventure, to the talent for contradiction and inversion— those "late" ways of experiencing, evaluating, reading the world; and surviving in it, drawing energy, finding consolation (but finally not), taking pleasure, expressing love.

SUSAN SONTAG

Note

This selection of Barthes's work was devised over a year before death closed the canon, and without consulting the author.

The ordering is chronological, and has three parts, corresponding to the three decades in which Barthes did the bulk of his work. Part One, which starts with the first text Barthes published, in 1942, includes work that appeared in the 1950s. Part Two includes work from the 1960s. Part Three, the work from the 1970s, ends with the last essay published before he died. So conventional a grouping is not meant to suggest a notion about how, if at all, Barthes's work falls into periods; it is just a formal way of taking a breath.

These are the first English translations of the opening and closing essays in the Reader. The Inaugural Lecture, which Barthes gave when he was elected to a chair at the Collège de France in 1977, appears here in English for the first time in book form.

Most selections, being essays, are of course complete. Whole sections from several larger works, such as *Writing Degree Zero*, are given uncut. In the case of the short sections drawn from different parts of *The Pleasure of the Text* and *Roland Barthes*, the jumps in the text are indicated by three dots.

Some writings were chosen because they seemed so representative of Barthes's work, or have been so influential. Mostly I chose writings that I find particularly fortifying; or, in a few cases, that seem to me irresistibly odd.

Barthes is such a glorious writer that there has to be a problem about what to exclude. It seemed unwise to try to make a larger, more compendious volume than this. But, inevitably, I have had some afterthoughts. How I wish now that I had included Barthes's essay on La Rochefoucauld, his "From Work to Text," and "The Death of the Author," his preface to Brillat-Savarin's *The Physiology of Taste*, and "Change the Object Itself," his second thoughts on mythology (from 1971). As my admiration for and pleasure in Barthes's work is unending, the list is actually longer, but I cannot resist these few rueful commendations. And, obviously, no excerpts can do justice to Barthes's last and deepest books, the three installments of one of the most intelligent, subtle, and gallant of autobiographical projects: *Roland Barthes, A Lover's Discourse*, and *Camera Lucida*. I implore readers of this Reader to go on, or back, to them.

S.S.

December 1981

PART ONE

On Gide and His Journal

R ELUCTANT to enclose Gide in a system I knew would never content me, I was vainly trying to find some connection among these notes. Finally I decided it would be better to offer them as such—notes—and not try to disguise their lack of continuity. Incoherence seems to me preferable to a distorting order.

I. THE JOURNAL

I doubt that the *Journal* has much interest, if reading the work has not awakened some initial curiosity as to the man.

In Gide's *Journal* the reader will find his ethic—the genesis and the life of his books—his readings—the basis for a critique of his work—silences—exquisite instances of wit—trivial avowals which make him man par excellence, another Montaigne.

"Notes sur André Gide et son Journal" was published in July 1942 in *Existences*, the magazine of the Sanatorium des Etudiants de France at Saint-Hilaire-du-Touvet (Isère). Barthes, who had tuberculosis, was a patient there in 1942 and 1943–5.
Translated by Richard Howard.

3

Many entries in the *Journal* will doubtless irritate those who have some prejudice, secret or otherwise, against Gide. These same entries will delight those who have some reason, secret or otherwise, to believe themselves like Gide. This is true of any personality which *compromises itself.*

The *Journal* is not an explanatory, an external work; it is not a chronicle (though actuality is often caught in its web). It is not like Jules Renard's journals, or like Saint-Simon, and those who scan it for important judgments on the work of some contemporary (Valéry or Claudel, of whom Gide often speaks) will certainly be disappointed. It is a work of *egoism,* in fact, and especially when it speaks of others. Though Gide's aim is always good, it is valid only because of its reflexive force, turning back on Gide himself.

"What must appear here is precisely what is too insignificant to have been retained by the sieve of any *work*. Here I must write, and without prearrangement, *details* (1929)." Hence we must not suppose that the *Journal* is in opposition to the work and not itself a work of art. There are sentences which are halfway between confession and creation; they require only to be inserted into a novel and are already less sincere (or rather: their sincerity counts less than something else, which is the pleasure we take in reading them). I should prefer to say this: it is not "Edouard's Journal" which resembles Gide's; on the contrary, many entries in Gide's *Journal* have the autonomy of "Edouard's Journal." They are no longer completely Gide; they begin to be outside him, en route for some unspecified work in which they want to appear, which they summon into being.

Nietzsche writes: "Far from being superficial, a great Frenchman has his superficies to the extreme degree, a natural envelope which surrounds his depths" (*Dawn*, aphorism 192).

Gide's work constitutes his depths; let us say that his *Journal* is his superficies; he draws his contours and juxtaposes his extremes; readings, reflections, narratives show how distant these extremes are, how enormous is Gide's superficies.

II. *DAS SCHAUDERN*

Goethe, quoted by Gide: "Fear and trembling (*das Schaudern*) is the best of man."

Goethe's *Schaudern* is very much like Montaigne's "marvelously supple man." I don't know if we have accorded enough importance to Gide's Goethean aspect; the same is also true of his affinities with Montaigne (Gide's predilections indicate not an influence but an identity); it is never without a reason that Gide writes a critical work. His preface to selections from Montaigne, indeed his very choice of texts, tells us as much about Gide as about Montaigne.

The Dialogues. Nothing more characteristic of French literature, nothing more precious than these duets which occur, from century to century, between writers of the same class: Pascal and Montaigne, Rousseau and Molière, Hugo and Voltaire, Valéry and Descartes, Montaigne and Gide. Nothing offers better proof of the perenniality of this literature, and also, precisely, of its *Schaudern*, its suppleness, by which it manages to escape the sclerosis of systems, by which its remotest past is renewed upon contact with a present intelligence. If the great classics of French literature are eternal, it is because they can still be modified. The stream is more durable than marble . . .

A critic of Gide must not attempt to produce a portrait of him in terms of good and evil, as biographers are in the habit of doing; his role should be to keep us from misjudging—out of ignorance, or even worse, out of preterition, deliberate or otherwise—certain of his works, or of his expressions. It is a matter of being "infinitely respectful of personality," as Gide himself was of others'. Indeed, the *Journal* is often written to correct some notion of Gide we might have arrived at because of quotations out of context, false reports, inexact words. It is a perpetual self-correction; like a scrupulous *projector*, Gide constantly adjusts his image to counteract the public's lazy or spiteful vision. "They want to make me into a dreadfully anxious being. My only anxiety is to find my thoughts misinterpreted" (*Journal*, 1927).

Let those who blame Gide for his contradictions (his refusal to choose among them) remember this page of Hegel: "For common sense, an opposition between true and false is something fixed; common sense expects us to approve or to reject an existing system *en bloc*. It does not conceive the difference among philosophical systems as the gradual development of truth; for common sense diversity means only contradiction . . . The mind which grasps contradiction cannot release it and keep it in its unilateralness and recognize (in the form of what seems to oppose and contradict itself) mutually necessary moments."

Gide is a simultaneous being. To a greater or lesser degree, Nature has posited him as complete, from the very first. He has merely taken the time to reveal the various aspects of himself in succession, but we must always remember that these aspects are in fact contemporaries of each other, as are his works: "It is still hard for them to admit that these books have cohabited, and cohabit even now in my mind. They succeed each other only on paper and because it was impossible to write them simultaneously. Whatever book I am writing, I never give myself up to it altogether, and the subject which next demands me most insistently is even now developing at the other end of myself" (*Journal*, 1909). Whence: fidelity and contradictions. *Fidelity*: All of Gide is in André Walter, and André Walter is still in Gide's 1939 *Journal*. It follows that Gide is ageless; he is always young, always mature; he is always sage, always fervent. Perhaps the latter half of his life, because of his great age, has assumed a darker tonality, in the manner of the Greek tragic poets. But he has been able to incarnate certain of his tendencies—or certain aspects—in young men quite as well as in old (Gide's characters are never objective without being purely himself), in Lafcadio as well as in La Pérouse. Gide has a loyal heart, a loyal soul. Indeed, it is odd how little his vast reading has altered his physiognomy. His discoveries have never been denials. When he read Nietzsche, Dostoevsky, Whitman, Blake, or Browning (except for Goethe, whose influence he admits), these encounters were so many self-recognitions, hence so many reasons for continuity. Gide's situation at the intersection of great contradictory currents has nothing facile about it. Which makes his perseverance admirable: indeed, it is his very *raison d'être*, the thing that makes him great. How many would have made a conversion into an ending? This fidelity to the truth of his life is heroic. "How much easier to proceed according to a given aesthetic and a given ethic! Writers who subscribe to a recognized religion advance confidently enough. I must invent everything. Sometimes this results in endless groping toward an almost imperceptible light. And sometimes I whisper to myself: What's the use?" (*Journal*, 1930).

Contradictions. In what direction, then, could this loyal nature move, though each of his works leaves an impression of iridescence and transformation—so that he has often been accused of inconsistency and evasion? Here we must dissipate the prejudice of rigidity: certain minds seem consistent because they are forever harping on one and the same quality;

they spirit away their hesitations and present only the hardened surface of their new opinion, which they solidify by doing violence to a great many others. Gide's attitude, confronted with such minds, is humbler and more measured. Possessing a conscience which ordinary morality has the odd habit of calling sickly, Gide explains himself, surrenders himself, delicately retracts or asserts himself bravely enough, but never abuses the reader as to his mutations; Gide puts everything in the *movement* of his thought and not in its brutal profession. I see several reasons for this attitude: (1) the impulses of a soul are the mark of its authenticity (Gide's entire effort is to render himself and others "authentic"); (2) the aesthetic pleasure he takes in slowly revealing the infinitesimal changes of his nature (*movement* remaining for Gide the best of man); (3) the profusion of his scruples in the search for truth, pursued through the finest nuances (truth is never brutal); (4) lastly, the moral importance accorded to states of conflict, perhaps because they are warrants of humility.

In Japan, where the conflict between Catholicism and Protestantism, between Hellenism and Christianity, may not have much meaning, Gide is nonetheless widely read. What is it that is admired in this writer? The image of a conscience which honestly pursues its truth.

The only point where we can speak of Gide's *development* is this: at a certain moment the social question assumed a larger importance for him than the ethical one. In 1901, he wrote: "Social questions? Of course. But the ethical ones come first. Man is more interesting than men: it is *he* and not *them* whom God created in His image. Each is more precious than all" (*Journal*). Then, in 1934, when world revolutions take him from the world of art: ". . . I feel almost nothing but sympathy. Wherever I look, I see nothing but distress. To remain contemplative today, a spectator, is to give evidence of an inhuman philosophy or a monstrous blindness" (*Journal*). But does this represent a true development? At most, in Gide, a recrudescence of the evangelical ferment to which he surrenders all the more freely, no longer bearing the shackles of his youth; and also the weight of actuality which he has always felt in human terms.

Some choose a path and keep to it; others change paths, each time with the same conviction. Gide has remained at an intersection, constantly, loyally, at the most important, the most populous one, where the two greatest roads of the West cross—the Greek and the Christian; he has preferred this *total* situation, where he could receive both lights, both energies. In this heroic situation, protected by nothing but also enclosed by nothing, he has subjected himself to every attack, offered himself to every affection. For him to endure in so perilous a situation, this man required a certain hardness, out of which masterpieces are made . . .

Yet this cannot be denied: "He who loveth his life shall lose it." This saying of Christ's is the basis of every one of Gide's works. His entire output can be considered as a certain mythology of pride. Pride, for him, is the capital moral phenomenon. Every critic must insist on this and show the place this subject occupies, from *Dostoevsky* to *Numquid et tu?* and the diptych of *The Immoralist* and *Strait Is the Gate*. It is no use claiming to know Gide to any degree if we do not have a clear conception of the importance of this evangelical saying.

In the last hundred years, there have been three men who have had the most intense, the most intimate, and even what I

might call the most fraternal attraction to Christ's person—
outside of a dogmatic or mystical knowledge: Nietzsche (as a
frère ennemi), Rozanov, and Gide.

"Confronting this Asiaticism," Gide writes (he is talking
about Renan, Barrès, Loti, Lemaître), "how Dorian I feel!"
(*Journal*, 1932). Gide's Hellenism is fulfilled during his old
age. From the time of *Fruits of the Earth* there was always
something Hellenistic about him: Pierre Louÿs was not far
away. But of late he has become truly Greek, i.e., tragic. In
the last years of the *Journal*, there are admirable pages to
which wisdom and suffering give an extraordinary resonance
of purity and proximity. Now the difficult thing, so successfully achieved by the fifth-century Greeks, is to be wise without necessarily being reasonable, to be happy without necessarily renouncing suffering. In Gide's ultimate wisdom, there is
no assurance, but always that trembling (*das Schaudern*); the
demons are not frozen out, and his eyelid, drooping with age,
does not stare at God with an insulting serenity. In the last
Journal pages I seem to be seeing Oedipus, but Oedipus at
Colonus, and no longer Oedipus the King.

III. THE WORK OF ART

"It is from the point of view of art that what I write should
be judged, a point of view never taken, or almost never taken
by the critics . . . Moreover, it is the only point of view which
is not exclusive of any other" (*Journal*, 1918).

"I first regarded myself as a mere artist, and concerned
myself, à la Flaubert, with nothing but the good quality of my
work. Its profound meaning, strictly speaking, escaped me altogether" (*Journal*, 1931). Gide became aware of this profound meaning of his work only when confronted with others'
reactions; and he systematized it in his critical works. Books

like *Fruits of the Earth* would not be so fine, so lasting, if he had consciously assigned them an intention antecedent to the work, of which the work would be no more than a convenient scaffolding. These are specifically poetic books, in which the author is, like the Latin *vates*, no more than an interpreter; his message transcends him and indeed he may not understand it very well himself; it proceeds from something stronger than himself, from something or someone that inhabits him, from a god. Once created, his work almost surprises him; it is already to such a degree not himself that he can fall in love with it, as Pygmalion with the statue.

The Legitimate Excuse. Let us make no mistake about Gide's critical labors; it is here that he preserves the deepest part of himself. These are his systematic books—admitting that Gide has a system; the others are too much works of art, too gratuitous. It is only at second hand, illuminated by these critical works, but so to speak in spite of himself, that *Fruits of the Earth* or *Oedipus* can assume the contour of gospels and their message be discerned as that of a new ethic. Gide's work is a net of which no mesh can be dropped. I believe it is quite futile to divide it up by chronological or methodical slices. It almost requires to be read in the fashion of certain Bibles, with a synoptic table of references, or even like those pages of the *Encyclopedia* where marginal notes gave the text its explosive value. Gide is often his own scholiast. This was necessary in order to permit the work to retain its gratuitousness, its freedom. Gide's version of the work of art is deliberately evasive; it escapes—God be thanked—any annexation of parties or dogmas, even if they were revolutionary. If anything else were the case, it would not be a work of art. But from this to infer that Gide's *thought* is evasive is a mistake. Gide permits us to grasp and define him very clearly in his critical works, in his *Journal.* When we know this latter Gide, there emanates

from his poetic work certain new resonances, a courageously
systematic view of man.

"I wanted to indicate in this *'tentative amoureuse'* the
book's influence on the person who is writing it, and during the
writing itself. For as it leaves us, it changes us, it modifies the
movement of our life . . . Our actions have a retroaction upon
us" (*Journal*, 1893). Compare these words with Michelet's:
"History, in the march of time, makes the historian much
more than it is made by him. My book has created me. I am
its work" (Preface of 1869). If we admit that the work is an
expression of Gide's will (Lafcadio's life, Michel's, Edouard's), the *Journal* is actually the converse of the work, its
contrary complement. The work: Gide as he should (would)
be. The *Journal*: Gide as he is, or more exactly: as Edouard,
Michel, and Lafcadio have made him (any number of fine
passages from the *Journal* on this subject) . . .

It is because at a certain moment he wanted to be someone
that he summoned up Ménalque, Lafcadio, Michel, or Edouard, that Gide wrote *Fruits of the Earth, The Immoralist*,
and *The Counterfeiters*. "The desire to portray characters one
has encountered is, I believe, quite common. But the creation
of new characters becomes a natural need only in those tormented by an imperious complexity and whom their own gesture does not exhaust" (*Journal*, 1924).

Novels and Récits. Gide's aesthetic includes two currents
which exhaust, on the one hand, the importance he assigns to
man's moral nature, and on the other the organic pleasure he
takes in imagining himself in someone else's skin.

Récits (*André Walter, The Pastoral Symphony, The Immoralist, Strait Is the Gate*). Fictionalization—if that—of a

case, of a theme, of a pathology. Were it not for Gide's extraordinary art, this would be virtually an apology, but an apology attached to no particular theory. In short, these narratives are almost so many myths. There is a Gidean mythology (a Promethean and not an Olympian mythology), each of whose characters does not fear to reproduce the others somewhat, and which, like any mythology, tends toward allegory, toward the symbol, or at least which can be so interpreted. Each hero engages the reader, promulgates example or iconoclasm. Mythology, as in these récits of Gide's, proves nothing: it is a work of art in which a great deal of faith circulates; a fine fiction in which one agrees to believe because it explains life and at the same time is a little stronger, a little larger than life (it affords the image of an ideal; every mythology is a dream). And these récits of Gide's, like every myth, are an equivalence between an abstract reality and a concrete fiction. All these books are Christian works.

Novels (*Lafcadio's Adventures, The Counterfeiters*). Characteristic of these novels is their utter gratuitousness; they are games. (The game in relation to the obligation is what is done "for nothing.") They prove nothing and are not even psychological except insofar as they present an imbroglio and an incoherence quite proper to life itself. They are born of the superior pleasure of imagining stories into which one introduces oneself under the most numerous and piquant aspects possible (everything which one cannot be). It is the same instinct of fabulation as is found among children which imparts so much lightness, so much sparkling irreverence to *Lafcadio's Adventures*, and to *The Counterfeiters* so much unlikely complexity. That Gide conceived his characters with a deep pleasure and that it was his desire to *be* them, that in them he is incarnated, I see proved in any number of humble details which cannot deceive us: Lafcadio's pleasure in wearing new clothes, scrupulously described (as a child details a toy he wants, especially when it is imaginary); Edouard's attitude to Olivier. As in children's games, reality suddenly spills over into the fantastic: real episodes are inserted into the novel, without Gide's bothering to change the names: the episode of the old La Pérouse, Georges's theft, etc.

The Counterfeiters. "What do I want this novel to be? A crossroads—a rendez-vous of problems" (*Journal*, 1923). It would be of a certain interest to criticism, no doubt, to consider this book as a great Russian novel conceived and executed by a great French writer. The tone, the spirit of the episode of the boys in *The Brothers Karamazov* recurs almost entirely in the first scene of *The Counterfeiters.* Like all of Dostoevsky's novels (except perhaps *The Eternal Husband*), *The Counterfeiters* is a knot of discrepant stories, whose connections are not immediately apparent. (It was on Martin du Gard's advice that Gide gathered these independent plots into a single sheaf.) Like *Lafcadio's Adventures, The Counterfeiters* is a diabolic novel; I mean that unity of action is dissolved for the sake of unpredictable and frequently unexploited perspectives, so that we rediscover here an infernal fantasy. A proof *a contrario*: Gide's récits are evangelical works; their tone and plot have the simplicity of angels.

Onomastics of Gide's characters: We can distinguish the heroes with a first name from the characters with a family name. The patronyms are most often characteristic or ironic (though chosen with such finesse!): Baraglioul, Profitendieu, Fleurissoire. By their family names, Gide mocks what most people are proudest of but what in his eyes keeps them from being authentic. The first names, on the contrary, are always vague, impersonal: Edouard, Michel, Bernard, Robert. They are loose garments which betray nothing; the personality of these heroes is in something else than their name (i.e.: their family, their society), for which they are not responsible. There are also the mythological or exotic first names (also chosen quite simply because they are splendid): Ménalque, Lafcadio, whose historical or geographic eccentricity declasses or dislocates the hero, warns us that we will not encounter him in our time or our place, and—perhaps ironically—justifies the strangeness of his ethic or his actions. They seem to say: "Rest easy, you will find no Ménalque, no Lafcadio among us; but that may be too bad."

Gide's novels. Note that the habitual aspect of novels (observations, atmosphere, psychology) is passed over in silence. All this is regarded as *given*. The novel has been written *beyond*, starting from the ordinary warp and woof; it relies on the reader's quality.

Our period, in several of its greatest writers (as a matter of fact, since Poe), might well be defined by this, that the artist himself dismantles the procedures of creation and is interested in them almost as much as in his work itself. This is because we have realized that art is a game, a technique (this dates from the French invention of the formula *l'Art pour l'Art*. See Nietzsche's *Beyond Good and Evil*, aphorism 254). I do not think I misinterpret Valéry when I say he made himself a poet to be able to afford an exact account of the procedures of poetics. Whence Edouard's astonishing Journal, and also many passages of Gide's own *Journal*.

Natural Sciences. The *Journal* will lead the future critic to consider Gide's affection for the Natural Sciences. ". . . I missed my vocation; I wanted to be a naturalist, and should have been one" (*Journal*, 1938). This affection has permitted him to regard the formal world most attentively. Scratch a poet and you will always find a naturalist. The Natural Sciences afforded Gide many comparisons, even whole sectors of demonstration (in *Corydon*, in his attacks on Maeterlinck's scientific books). This is because nothing raises the ontological problem better than such analogies. Many great minds make use of Science to render this problem explicit, at first to themselves, then to their readers. The attention that Valéry gives to epistemology, that Gide gives to the Natural Sciences, should make us reflect . . .

Commonplaces. Sometimes, in Gide, we meet the shadow of a commonplace, but clothed in that always admirable style, which perhaps at this moment has somewhat led him on, deceived him. But I am not at all sure that this "neutral" thought was not deliberate, in order to contrast all the more vividly with the grace of his expression or even out of humility; i.e., out of that conscience which makes him explain at such length (in the *Journal*) the minor problems of translation. With this man, you never know; he has put himself in a position to forestall you in the estimation of his weaknesses, so that you are hard put to impute them to him. You cannot be certain he does not yield them up deliberately, but without warning, without informing us whether or not he is conscious of them.

Coquetry of the uniform. This consists in the fact that it is harder to shine where everyone possesses equal and ordinary weapons; the victory is only the more valuable. For Gide, too, there is a certain coquetry of the commonplace, of the uniform. With the same ideas and the same words as everyone else, he manages to say something valid. This is the classical rule: to have the courage of saying splendidly what is obvious, so that it is never on a first reading that a classical author delights us; he actually seduces us by what he has not said, but which we will be quite naturally led to discover, so clearly drawn are the essential lines. But furthermore the accessory lines are suppressed. This is characteristic of all art (see in this regard certain significant drawings by Picasso). As Montesquieu said: "We do not describe without omitting the intermediate notions." And Gide adds: "There is no work of art without foreshortenings." This does not occur without an initial obscurity, or an extreme simplicity, which makes a mediocre mind say that it does not "understand." In this sense, the Classics are the great masters of the obscure, even of the equivocal; i.e., of the preterition of the superfluous (that superfluous of which the vulgar mind is so fond), or if you prefer, masters of the shadow propitious to meditation and to individual discovery. To oblige us to think for ourselves, that is a possible definition of classical culture; whereby it is no longer the monopoly of a century, but of all rigorous minds, whether they are called Racine, Stendhal, Baudelaire, or Gide.

1942

The World of Wrestling

"The grandiloquent truth of gestures on life's great occasions."
—BAUDELAIRE

T<small>HE</small> virtue of all-in wrestling is that it is the spectacle of excess. Here we find a grandiloquence which must have been that of ancient theaters. And in fact wrestling is an open-air spectacle, for what makes the circus or the arena what they are is not the sky (a romantic value suited rather to fashionable occasions), it is the drenching and vertical quality of the flood of light. Even hidden in the most squalid Parisian halls, wrestling partakes of the nature of the great solar spectacles, Greek drama and bullfights: in both, a light without shadow generates an emotion without reserve.

There are people who think that wrestling is an ignoble sport. Wrestling is not a sport, it is a spectacle, and it is no more ignoble to attend a wrestled performance of Suffering than a performance of the sorrows of Arnolphe or Andromaque.[1] Of course, there exists a false wrestling, in which the participants unnecessarily go to great lengths to make a show of a fair fight; this is of no interest. True wrestling, wrongly called amateur wrestling, is performed in second-rate

From *Mythologies*, translated by Annette Lavers (New York: Hill and Wang, 1972).

[1] In Molière's *L'École des Femmes* and Racine's *Andromaque.*

halls, where the public spontaneously attunes itself to the spectacular nature of the contest, like the audience at a suburban
cinema. Then these same people wax indignant because wrestling is a stage-managed sport (which ought, by the way, to
mitigate its ignominy). The public is completely uninterested
in knowing whether the contest is rigged or not, and rightly so;
it abandons itself to the primary virtue of the spectacle, which
is to abolish all motives and all consequences: what matters is
not what it thinks but what it sees.

This public knows very well the distinction between wrestling and boxing; it knows that boxing is a Jansenist sport,
based on a demonstration of excellence. One can bet on the
outcome of a boxing match: with wrestling, it would make no
sense. A boxing match is a story which is constructed before
the eyes of the spectator; in wrestling, on the contrary, it is
each moment which is intelligible, not the passage of time. The
spectator is not interested in the rise and fall of fortunes; he
expects the transient image of certain passions. Wrestling
therefore demands an immediate reading of the juxtaposed
meanings, so that there is no need to connect them. The logical conclusion of the contest does not interest the wrestling
fan, while on the contrary a boxing match always implies a
science of the future. In other words, wrestling is a sum of
spectacles, of which no single one is a function: each moment
imposes the total knowledge of a passion which rises erect and
alone, without ever extending to the crowning moment of a
result.

Thus the function of the wrestler is not to win; it is to go
exactly through the motions which are expected of him. It is
said that judo contains a hidden symbolic aspect; even in the
midst of efficiency, its gestures are measured, precise but restricted, drawn accurately but by a stroke without volume.
Wrestling, on the contrary, offers excessive gestures, exploited
to the limit of their meaning. In judo, a man who is down is

hardly down at all, he rolls over, he draws back, he eludes defeat, or, if the latter is obvious, he immediately disappears; in wrestling, a man who is down is exaggeratedly so, and completely fills the eyes of the spectators with the intolerable spectacle of his powerlessness.

This function of grandiloquence is indeed the same as that of ancient theater, whose principle, language and props (masks and buskins) concurred in the exaggeratedly visible explanation of a Necessity. The gesture of the vanquished wrestler signifying to the world a defeat which, far from disguising, he emphasizes and holds like a pause in music, corresponds to the mask of antiquity meant to signify the tragic mode of the spectacle. In wrestling, as on the stage in antiquity, one is not ashamed of one's suffering, one knows how to cry, one has a liking for tears.

Each sign in wrestling is therefore endowed with an absolute clarity, since one must always understand everything on the spot. As soon as the adversaries are in the ring, the public is overwhelmed with the obviousness of the roles. As in the theater, each physical type expresses to excess the part which has been assigned to the contestant. Thauvin, a fifty-year-old with an obese and sagging body, whose type of asexual hideousness always inspires feminine nicknames, displays in his flesh the characters of baseness, for his part is to represent what, in the classical concept of the *salaud*, the "bastard" (the key concept of any wrestling match), appears as organically repugnant. The nausea voluntarily provoked by Thauvin shows therefore a very extended use of signs: not only is ugliness used here in order to signify baseness, but in addition ugliness is wholly gathered into a particularly repulsive quality of matter: the pallid collapse of dead flesh (the public calls Thauvin *la barbaque*, "stinking meat"), so that the passionate condemnation of the crowd no longer stems from its judgment, but instead from the very depth of its humors. It will thereafter let itself be frenetically embroiled in an idea of Thauvin which will conform entirely with this physical origin: his actions will perfectly correspond to the essential viscosity of his personage.

It is therefore in the body of the wrestler that we find the first key to the contest. I know from the start that all of Thauvin's actions, his treacheries, cruelties, and acts of cowardice, will not fail to measure up to the first image of ignobility he gave me; I can trust him to carry out intelligently and to the last detail all the gestures of a kind of amorphous baseness, and thus fill to the brim the image of the most repugnant bastard there is: the bastard octopus. Wrestlers therefore have a physique as peremptory as those of the characters of the *Commedia dell'Arte*, who display in advance, in their costumes and attitudes, the future contents of their parts: just as Pantaloon can never be anything but a ridiculous cuckold, Harlequin an astute servant, and the Doctor a stupid pedant, in the same way Thauvin will never be anything but an ignoble traitor, Reinières (a tall blond fellow with a limp body and unkempt hair) the moving image of passivity, Mazaud (short and arrogant like a cock) that of grotesque conceit, and Orsano (an effeminate teddy boy first seen in a blue-and-pink dressing gown) that, doubly humorous, of a vindictive *salope*, or bitch (for I do not think that the public of the Elysée-Montmartre, like Littré, believes the word *salope* to be a masculine).

The physique of the wrestlers therefore constitutes a basic sign, which like a seed contains the whole fight. But this seed proliferates, for it is at every turn during the fight, in each new situation, that the body of the wrestler casts to the public the magical entertainment of a temperament which finds its natural expression in a gesture. The different strata of meaning throw light on each other, and form the most intelligible of spectacles. Wrestling is like a diacritic writing: above the fundamental meaning of his body, the wrestler arranges comments which are episodic but always opportune, and constantly help the reading of the fight by means of gestures, attitudes, and mimicry which make the intention utterly obvious. Sometimes the wrestler triumphs with a repulsive sneer while kneeling on the good sportsman; sometimes he gives the crowd a conceited smile which forebodes an early revenge; sometimes, pinned to the ground, he hits the floor ostentatiously to make evident to all the intolerable nature of his situation; and sometimes he erects a complicated set of signs meant to make the public understand that he legitimately personifies the ever-entertaining image of the grumbler, endlessly confabulating about his displeasure.

We are therefore dealing with a real Human Comedy, where the most socially inspired nuances of passion (conceit, rightfulness, refined cruelty, a sense of "paying one's debts") always felicitously find the clearest sign which can receive them, express them, and triumphantly carry them to the confines of the hall. It is obvious that at such a pitch, it no longer matters whether the passion is genuine or not. What the public wants is the image of passion, not passion itself. There is no more a problem of truth in wrestling than in the theater. In both, what is expected is the intelligible representation of moral situations which are usually private. This emptying out of interiority to the benefit of its exterior signs, this exhaustion of the content by the form, is the very principle of triumphant classical art. Wrestling is an immediate pantomime, infinitely more efficient than the dramatic pantomime, for the wrestler's gesture needs no anecdote, no decor, in short no transference in order to appear true.

Each moment in wrestling is therefore like an algebra which instantaneously unveils the relationship between a cause and its represented effect. Wrestling fans certainly experience a kind of intellectual pleasure in *seeing* the moral mechanism function so perfectly. Some wrestlers, who are great comedians, entertain as much as a Molière character, because they succeed in imposing an immediate reading of the inner nature: Armand Mazaud, a wrestler of an arrogant and ridiculous character (as one says that Harpagon[2] is a character), always delights the audience by the mathematical rigor of his transcriptions, carrying the form of his gestures to the furthest reaches of their meaning, and giving to his manner of fighting the kind of vehemence and precision found in a great scholastic disputation, in which what is at stake is at once the triumph of pride and the formal concern with truth.

What is thus displayed for the public is the great spectacle of Suffering, Defeat, and Justice. Wrestling presents man's suffering with all the amplification of tragic masks. The wrestler who suffers in a hold which is reputedly cruel (an arm lock, a twisted leg) offers an excessive portrayal of Suffering; like a primitive Pietà, he exhibits for all to see his face, exaggeratedly contorted by an intolerable affliction. It is obvious, of course, that in wrestling reserve would be out of place, since it is opposed to the voluntary ostentation of the spectacle, to this Exhibition of Suffering which is the very aim of the fight. This is why all the actions which produce suffering are particularly spectacular, like the gesture of a conjurer who holds out his cards clearly to the public. Suffering which appeared without intelligible cause would not be understood; a concealed action that was actually cruel would transgress the unwritten rules of wrestling and would have no more sociological efficacy than a mad or parasitic gesture. On the contrary, suffering appears as inflicted with emphasis and conviction, for everyone must not only see that the man suffers but also and above all understand why he suffers. What wrestlers call a hold, that is, any figure which allows one to immobilize the adversary indefinitely and to have him at one's mercy, has precisely the function of pre-

[2] In Molière's *L'Avare*.

paring in conventional, therefore intelligible, fashion the spectacle of suffering, of methodically establishing the conditions of suffering. The inertia of the vanquished allows the (temporary) victor to settle in his cruelty and to convey to the public this terrifying slowness of the torturer who is certain about the outcome of his actions; to grind the face of one's powerless adversary or to scrape his spine with one's fist with a deep and regular movement, or at least to produce the superficial appearance of such gestures: wrestling is the only sport which gives such an externalized image of torture. But here again, only the image is involved in the game, and the spectator does not wish for the actual suffering of the contestant; he only enjoys the perfection of an iconography. It is not true that wrestling is a sadistic spectacle: it is only an intelligible spectacle.

There is another figure, more spectacular still than a hold; it is the forearm smash, this loud slap of the forearm, this embryonic punch with which one clouts the chest of one's adversary, and which is accompanied by a dull noise and the exaggerated sagging of a vanquished body. In the forearm smash, catastrophe is brought to the point of maximum obviousness, so much so that ultimately the gesture appears as no more than a symbol; this is going too far, this is transgressing the moral rules of wrestling, where all signs must be excessively clear, but must not let the intention of clarity be seen. The public then shouts, "He's laying it on!", not because it regrets the absence of real suffering, but because it condemns artifice: as in the theater, one fails to put the part across as much by an excess of sincerity as by an excess of formalism.

We have already seen to what extent wrestlers exploit the resources of a given physical style, developed and put to use in order to unfold before the eyes of the public a total image of Defeat. The flaccidity of tall white bodies which collapse with one blow or crash into the ropes with arms flailing, the inertia

of massive wrestlers rebounding pitiably off all the elastic surfaces of the ring, nothing can signify more clearly and more
passionately the exemplary abasement of the vanquished. Deprived of all resilience, the wrestler's flesh is no longer anything but an unspeakable heap spread out on the floor, where
it solicits relentless reviling and jubilation. There is here a
paroxysm of meaning in the style of antiquity, which can only
recall the heavily underlined intentions in Roman triumphs. At
other times, there is another ancient posture which appears in
the coupling of the wrestlers, that of the suppliant who, at the
mercy of his opponent, on bended knees, his arms raised
above his head, is slowly brought down by the vertical pressure of the victor. In wrestling, unlike judo, Defeat is not a
conventional sign, abandoned as soon as it is understood; it is
not an outcome, but quite the contrary, it is a duration, a
display, it takes up the ancient myths of public Suffering and
Humiliation: the cross and the pillory. It is as if the wrestler is
crucified in broad daylight and in the sight of all. I have heard
it said of a wrestler stretched on the ground: "He is dead, little
Jesus, there, on the cross," and these ironic words revealed the
hidden roots of a spectacle which enacts the exact gestures of
the most ancient purifications.

But what wrestling is above all meant to portray is a purely
moral concept: that of justice. The idea of "paying" is essential to wrestling, and the crowd's "Give it to him" means
above all else "Make him pay." This is therefore, needless to
say, an immanent justice. The baser the action of the "bastard,"
the more delighted the public is by the blow which he justly
receives in return. If the villain—who is of course a coward—
takes refuge behind the ropes, claiming unfairly to have a right
to do so by a brazen mimicry, he is inexorably pursued there
and caught, and the crowd is jubilant at seeing the rules broken
for the sake of a deserved punishment. Wrestlers know very
well how to play up to the capacity for indignation of the

public by presenting the very limit of the concept of Justice, this outermost zone of confrontation where it is enough to infringe the rules a little more to open the gates of a world without restraints. For a wrestling fan, nothing is finer than the revengeful fury of a betrayed fighter who throws himself vehemently not on a successful opponent but on the smarting image of foul play. Naturally, it is the pattern of Justice which matters here, much more than its content: wrestling is above all a quantitative sequence of compensations (an eye for an eye, a tooth for a tooth). This explains why sudden changes of circumstances have in the eyes of wrestling habitués a sort of moral beauty: they enjoy them as they would enjoy an inspired episode in a novel, and the greater the contrast between the success of a move and the reversal of fortune, the nearer the good luck of a contestant to his downfall, the more satisfying the dramatic mime is felt to be. Justice is therefore the embodiment of a possible transgression; it is from the fact that there is a Law that the spectacle of the passions which infringe it derives its value.

It is therefore easy to understand why out of five wrestling matches, only about one is fair. One must realize, let it be repeated, that "fairness" here is a role or a genre, as in the theater: the rules do not at all constitute a real constraint; they are the conventional appearance of fairness. So that in actual fact a fair fight is nothing but an exaggeratedly polite one: the contestants confront each other with zeal, not rage; they can remain in control of their passions, they do not punish their beaten opponent relentlessly, they stop fighting as soon as they are ordered to do so, and congratulate each other at the end of a particularly arduous episode, during which, however, they have not ceased to be fair. One must of course understand here that all these polite actions are brought to the notice of the public by the most conventional gestures of fairness: shaking hands, raising the arms, ostensibly avoiding a fruitless hold which would detract from the perfection of the contest.

Conversely, foul play exists only in its excessive signs: administering a big kick to one's beaten opponent, taking refuge behind the ropes while ostensibly invoking a purely formal right, refusing to shake hands with one's opponent before or after the fight, taking advantage of the end of the round to rush treacherously at the adversary from behind, fouling him while the referee is not looking (a move which obviously only has any value or function because in fact half the audience can see it and get indignant about it). Since Evil is the natural climate of wrestling, a fair fight has chiefly the value of being an exception. It surprises the aficionado, who greets it when he sees it as an anachronism and a rather sentimental throwback to the sporting tradition ("Aren't they playing fair, those two"); he feels suddenly moved at the sight of the general kindness of the world, but would probably die of boredom and indifference if wrestlers did not quickly return to the orgy of evil which alone makes good wrestling.

Extrapolated, fair wrestling could lead only to boxing or judo, whereas true wrestling derives its originality from all the excesses which make it a spectacle and not a sport. The ending of a boxing match or a judo contest is abrupt, like the full stop which closes a demonstration. The rhythm of wrestling is quite different, for its natural meaning is that of rhetorical amplification: the emotional magniloquence, the repeated paroxysms, the exasperation of the retorts can only find their natural outcome in the most baroque confusion. Some fights, among the most successful kind, are crowned by a final charivari, a sort of unrestrained fantasia where the rules, the laws of the genre, the referee's censuring and the limits of the ring are abolished, swept away by a triumphant disorder which overflows into the hall and carries off pell-mell wrestlers, seconds, referee, and spectators.

It has already been noted that in America wrestling represents a sort of mythological fight between Good and Evil (of a quasi-political nature, the "bad" wrestler always being supposed to be a Red). The process of creating heroes in French wrestling is very different, being based on ethics and not on politics. What the public is looking for here is the gradual construction of a highly moral image: that of the perfect "bastard." One comes to wrestling in order to attend the continuing adventures of a single major leading character, permanent and multiform like Punch or Scapino, inventive in unexpected figures and yet always faithful to his role. The "bastard" is here revealed as a Molière character or a "portrait" by La Bruyère, that is to say, as a classical entity, an essence, whose acts are only significant epiphenomena arranged in time. This stylized character does not belong to any particular nation or party, and whether the wrestler is called Kuzchenko (nicknamed Mustache after Stalin), Yerpazian, Gaspardi, Jo Vignola or Nollières, the aficionado does not attribute to him any country except "fairness"—observing the rules.

What then is a "bastard" for this audience composed in part, we are told, of people who are themselves outside the rules of society? Essentially someone unstable, who accepts the rules only when they are useful to him and transgresses the formal continuity of attitudes. He is unpredictable, therefore asocial. He takes refuge behind the law when he considers that it is in his favor, and breaks it when he finds it useful to do so. Sometimes he rejects the formal boundaries of the ring and goes on hitting an adversary legally protected by the ropes, sometimes he re-establishes these boundaries and claims the protection of what he did not respect a few minutes earlier. This inconsistency, far more than treachery or cruelty, sends the audience beside itself with rage: offended not in its morality but in its logic, it considers the contradiction of arguments as the basest of crimes. The forbidden move becomes dirty only when it destroys a quantitative equilibrium and disturbs the rigorous reckoning of compensations; what is condemned by the audience is not at all the transgression of insipid official rules, it is the lack of revenge, the absence of a punishment. So that there is nothing more exciting for a crowd than the grandiloquent kick given to a vanquished "bastard"; the joy of punishing is at its climax when it is supported by a mathematical justification; contempt is then unrestrained. One is no longer dealing with a *salaud* but with a *salope*—the verbal gesture of the ultimate degradation.

Such a precise finality demands that wrestling should be exactly what the public expects of it. Wrestlers, who are very experienced, know perfectly how to direct the spontaneous episodes of the fight so as to make them conform to the image which the public has of the great legendary themes of its mythology. A wrestler can irritate or disgust, he never disappoints, for he always accomplishes completely, by a progressive solidification of signs, what the public expects of him. In wrestling, nothing exists except in the absolute, there is no symbol, no allusion, everything is presented exhaustively. Leaving nothing in the shade, each action discards all parasitic meanings and ceremonially offers to the public a pure and full signification, rounded like Nature. This grandiloquence is nothing but the popular and age-old image of the perfect intelligibility of reality. What is portrayed by wrestling is therefore an ideal understanding of things; it is the euphoria of men raised for a while above the constitutive ambiguity of everyday situations and placed before the panoramic view of a univocal Nature, in which signs at last correspond to causes, without obstacle, without evasion, without contradiction.

When the hero or the villain of the drama, the man who was seen a few minutes earlier possessed by moral rage, magnified into a sort of metaphysical sign, leaves the wrestling hall, impassive, anonymous, carrying a small suitcase and arm-in-arm with his wife, no one can doubt that wrestling holds that power of transmutation which is common to the Spectacle and to Religious Worship. In the ring, and even in the depths of their voluntary ignominy, wrestlers remain gods because they are, for a few moments, the key which opens Nature, the pure gesture which separates Good from Evil, and unveils the form of a Justice which is at last intelligible.

1952

from *Writing Degree Zero*

WHAT IS WRITING?

W E know that a language is a corpus of prescriptions and habits common to all the writers of a period. Which means that a language is a kind of natural ambience wholly pervading the writer's expression, yet without endowing it with form or content: it is, as it were, an abstract circle of truths, outside of which alone the solid residue of an individual *logos* begins to settle. It enfolds the whole of literary creation much as the earth, the sky, and the line where they meet outline a familiar habitat for mankind. It is not so much a stock of materials as a horizon, which implies both a boundary and a perspective; in short, it is the comforting area of an ordered space. The writer literally takes nothing from it; a language is for him rather a frontier, to overstep which alone might lead to the linguistically supernatural; it is a field of action, the definition of, and hope for, a possibility. It is not the locus of a social commitment, but merely a reflex response involving no choice, the undivided property of men, not of writers; it remains outside

Writing Degree Zero, translated by Annette Lavers and Colin Smith (New York: Hill and Wang, 1977).

the ritual of Letters; it is a social object by definition, not by option. No one can without formalities pretend to insert his freedom as a writer into the resistant medium of language because, behind the latter, the whole of History stands unified and complete in the manner of a Natural Order. Hence, for the writer, a language is nothing but a human horizon which provides a distant setting of *familiarity*, the value of which, incidentally, is entirely negative: to say that Camus and Queneau speak the same language is merely to presume, by a differential operation, all languages, archaic and futuristic, that they do not use. Suspended between forms either disused or as yet unknown, the writer's language is not so much a fund to be drawn on as an extreme limit; it is the geometrical *locus* of all that he could not say without, like Orpheus looking back, losing the stable meaning of his enterprise and his essential gesture as a social being.

A language is therefore on the hither side of Literature. Style is almost beyond it: imagery, delivery, vocabulary spring from the body and the past of the writer and gradually become the very reflexes of his art. Thus under the name of style a self-sufficient language is evolved which has its roots only in the depths of the author's personal and secret mythology, that subnature of expression where the first coition of words and things takes place, where once and for all the great verbal themes of his existence come to be installed. Whatever its sophistication, style has always something crude about it: it is a form with no clear destination, the product of a thrust, not an intention, and, as it were, a vertical and lonely dimension of thought. Its frame of reference is biological or biographical, not historical: it is the writer's "thing," his glory and his prison, it is his solitude. Indifferent to society and transparent to it, a closed personal process, it is in no way the product of a choice or of a reflection on Literature. It is the private portion of the ritual, it rises up from the writer's myth-laden depths

Isn't this logocentric
meaning transcendent?

and unfolds beyond his area of control. It is the decorative voice of hidden, secret flesh; it works as does Necessity, as if, in this kind of floral growth, style were no more than the outcome of a blind and stubborn metamorphosis starting from a sub-language elaborated where flesh and external reality come together. Style is properly speaking a germinative phenomenon, the transmutation of a Humor. Hence stylistic overtones are distributed in depth; whereas speech has a horizontal structure, its secrets are on a level with the words in which they are couched, and what it conceals is revealed by the very duration of its flow. In speech, everything is held forth, meant for immediate consumption, and words, silences, and their common mobility are launched toward a meaning superseded: it is a transfer leaving no trace and brooking no delay. Style, on the other hand, has only a vertical dimension, it plunges into the closed recollection of the person and achieves its opacity from a certain experience of matter; style is never anything but metaphor, that is, equivalence of the author's literary intention and carnal structure (it must be remembered that structure is the residual deposit of duration). So that style is always a secret; but the occult aspect of its implications does not arise from the mobile and ever-provisional nature of language; its secret is recollection locked within the body of the writer. The allusive virtue of style is not a matter of speed, as in speech, where what is unsaid nevertheless remains as an interim of language, but a matter of density, for what stands firmly and deeply beneath style, brought together harshly or tenderly in its figures of speech, are fragments of a reality entirely alien to language. The miracle of this transmutation makes style a kind of supra-literary operation which carries man to the threshold of power and magic. By reason of its biological origin, style resides outside art, that is, outside the pact which binds the writer to society. Authors may therefore be imagined who prefer the security of art to the loneliness of style. The very type of an author without a style is Gide, whose craftsmanlike approach exploits the pleasure the moderns derive from a certain classical ethos, just as Saint-Saëns has composed in Bach's idiom, or Poulenc in Schubert's. In contrast, modern poetry—such as Hugo's, Rimbaud's or Char's—is saturated with style and is *art* only by virtue of an intention to be Poetry. It is the Authority of style, that is, the entirely free relationship between language and its fleshly double, which places the writer above History as the freshness of Innocence.

A language is therefore a horizon, and style a vertical dimension, which together map out for the writer a Nature, since he does not choose either. The language functions negatively, as the initial limit of the possible, style is a Necessity which binds the writer's humor to his form of expression. In the former, he finds a familiar History, in the latter, a familiar personal past. In both cases he deals with a Nature, that is, a familiar repertory of gestures, a gestuary, as it were, in which the energy expended is purely operative, serving here to enumerate, there to transform, but never to appraise or signify a choice.

Now every Form is also a Value, which is why there is room, between a language and a style, for another formal reality: writing. Within any literary form, there is a general choice of tone, of ethos, if you like, and this is precisely where the writer shows himself clearly as an individual because this is where he commits himself. A language and a style are data prior to all problematics of language, they are the natural product of Time and of the person as a biological entity; but the formal identity of the writer is truly established only outside the permanence of grammatical norms and stylistic constants, where the written continuum, first collected and enclosed within a perfectly innocent linguistic nature, at last becomes a total sign, the choice of a human attitude, the affirmation of a certain Good. It thus commits the writer to manifest and communicate a state of happiness or malaise, and links the form of his utterance, which is at once normal and singular, to the vast History of the Others. A language and a style are blind forces; a mode of writing is an act of historical solidarity. A language and a style are objects; a mode of writing is a function: it is the relationship between creation and society, the literary language transformed by its social finality, form considered as a human intention and thus linked to the great crises of History. Mérimée and Fénelon, for instance, are separated by linguistic phenomena and contingent features of style; yet they make use of a language charged with the same intentionality, their ideas of form and content share a common framework, they accept the same type of conventions, the same technical reflexes work through both of them. Although separated by a century and a half, they use exactly the same instrument in the same way: an instrument perhaps a little changed in outward appearance, but not at all in the place and manner of its employment. In short, they have the same mode of writing. In contrast, writers who are almost contemporaries, Mérimée and Lautréamont, Mallarmé and Céline, Gide and Queneau, Claudel and Camus, who have shared or who share our language at the same stage of its historical development use utterly different modes of writing. Everything separates them: tone, delivery, purpose, ethos, and naturalness of expression: the conclusion is that to live at the same time and share the same language is a small matter compared with modes of writing so dissimilar and so sharply defined by their very dissimilarity.

These modes of writing, though different, are comparable, because they owe their existence to one identical process,

namely the writer's consideration of the social use which he
has chosen for his form, and his commitment to this choice.
Placed at the center of the problematics of literature, which
cannot exist prior to it, writing is thus essentially the morality
of form, the choice of that social area within which the writer
elects to situate the nature of his language. But this social area
is by no means that of an actual consumption. It is not a
question for the writer of choosing the social group for which
he is to write: well he knows that, save for the possibility of a
Revolution, it can only be for the self-same society. His choice
is a matter of conscience, not of efficacy. His writing is a way
of conceiving Literature, not of extending its limits. Or better
still: it is because the writer cannot modify in any way the
objective data which govern the consumption of Literature
(these purely historical data are beyond his control even if he
is aware of them) that he voluntarily places the need for a
free language at the sources of this language and not in its
eventual consumption. So that writing is an ambiguous reality:
on the one hand, it unquestionably arises from a confrontation
of the writer with the society of his time; on the other hand,
from this social finality, it refers the writer back, by a sort of
tragic reversal, to the sources, that is to say, the instruments of
creation. Failing the power to supply him with a freely consumed language, History suggests to him the demand for one
freely produced.

Thus the choice of, and afterward the responsibility for, a
mode of writing point to the presence of Freedom, but this
Freedom has not the same limits at different moments of History. It is not granted to the writer to choose his mode of
writing from a kind of non-temporal store of literary forms. It
is under the pressure of History and Tradition that the possible
modes of writing for a given writer are established; there is a
History of Writing. But this History is dual: at the very mo-

ment when general History proposes—or imposes—new problematics of the literary language, writing still remains full of the recollection of previous usage, for language is never innocent: words have a second-order memory which mysteriously persists in the midst of new meanings. Writing is precisely this compromise between freedom and remembrance, it is this freedom which remembers and is free only in the gesture of choice, but is no longer so within duration. True, I can today select such and such mode of writing, and in so doing assert my freedom, aspire to the freshness of novelty or to a tradition; but it is impossible to develop it within duration without gradually becoming a prisoner of someone else's words and even of my own. A stubborn after-image, which comes from all the previous modes of writing and even from the past of my own, drowns the sound of my present words. Any written trace precipitates, as inside a chemical at first transparent, innocent and neutral, mere duration gradually reveals in suspension a whole past of increasing density, like a cryptogram.

Writing as Freedom is therefore a mere moment. But this moment is one of the most explicit in History, since History is always and above all a choice and the limits of this choice. It is because writing derives from a meaningful gesture of the writer that it reaches the deeper layers of History, much more palpably than does any other cross-section of literature. The unity of classical writing, which remained uniform for centuries, the plurality of its modes in modern times, increased in the last hundred years until it came near to questioning the very fact of literature, this kind of disintegration of French writing does indeed correspond to a great crisis in general History, which is noticeable in literary History proper, only much more confusedly. What separates the "thought" of a Balzac from that of a Flaubert is a variation within the same school; what contrasts their modes of writing is an essential break, at the precise moment when a new economic structure is joined on to an older one, thereby bringing about decisive changes in mentality and consciousness.

POLITICAL MODES OF WRITING

All modes of writing have in common the fact of being "closed" and thus different from spoken language. Writing is in no way an instrument for communication, it is not an open route through which there passes only the intention to speak. A whole disorder flows through speech and gives it this self-devouring momentum which keeps it in a perpetually suspended state. Conversely, writing is a hardened language which is self-contained and is in no way meant to deliver to its own duration a mobile series of approximations. It is on the contrary meant to impose, thanks to the shadow cast by its system of signs, the image of a speech which had a structure even before it came into existence. What makes writing the opposite of speech is that the former always *appears* symbolical, introverted, ostensibly turned toward an occult side of language, whereas the second is nothing but a flow of empty signs, the movement of which alone is significant. The whole of speech is epitomized in this expendability of words, in this froth ceaselessly swept onward, and speech is found only where language self-evidently functions like a devouring process which swallows only the moving crest of the words. Writing, on the contrary, is always rooted in something beyond language, it develops like a seed, not like a line, it manifests an essence and holds the threat of a secret, it is an anti-communication, it is intimidating. All writing will therefore contain the ambiguity of an object which is both language and coercion: there exists fundamentally in writing a "circumstance" foreign to language, there is, as it were, the weight of a gaze conveying an intention which is no longer linguistic. This gaze may well express a passion of language, as in literary modes of writing;

it may also express the threat of retribution, as in political ones: writing is then meant to unite at a single stroke the reality of the acts and the ideality of the ends. This is why power, or the shadow cast by power, always ends in creating an axiological writing, in which the distance which usually separates fact from value disappears within the very space of the word, which is given at once as description and as judgment. The word becomes an alibi, that is, an elsewhere and a justification. This, which is true of the literary modes of writing, in which the unity of the signs is ceaselessly fascinated by zones of infra- or ultra-language, is even truer of the political ones, in which the alibi stemming from language is at the same time intimidation and glorification: for it is power or conflict which produces the purest types of writing.

We shall see later that classical writing was a ceremonial which manifested the implantation of the writer into a particular political society, and that to speak like Vaugelas meant in the first place to be connected with the exercise of power. The Revolution did not modify the norms of this writing, since its force of thinkers remained, all things considered, the same, having merely passed from intellectual to political power; but the exceptional conditions of the struggle nevertheless brought about, within the great Form of classicism, a revolutionary mode of writing proper, defined not by its structure (which was more conventional than ever) but by its closed character and by its counterpart, since the use of language was then linked, as never before in history, to the Blood which had been shed. The Revolutionaries had no reason to wish to alter classical writing; they were in no way aware of questioning the nature of man, still less his language, and an "instrument" they had inherited from Voltaire, Rousseau, or Vauvenargues could not appear to them as compromised. It was the singularity of the historical circumstances which produced the identity of the revolutionary mode of writing. Baudelaire spoke somewhere of the "grandiloquent truth of gestures on life's great occasions." The Revolution was in the highest degree one of those great occasions when truth, through the bloodshed that it costs, becomes so weighty that its expression demands the very forms of theatrical amplification. Revolutionary writing was the one and only grand gesture commensurate with the daily presence of the guillotine. What today appears turgid was then no more than life-size. This writing, which bears all the signs of inflation, was an exact writing: never was language more incredible, yet never was it less spurious. This grandiloquence was not only form modeled on drama; it was also the awareness of it. Without this extravagant pose, typical of all the great revolutionaries, which enabled Guadet, the Girondin, when arrested at Saint-Emilion, to declare without looking ridiculous, since he was about to die: "Yes, I am Guadet. Executioner, do your duty. Go take my head to the tyrants of my country. It has always turned them pale; once severed, it will turn them paler still," the Revolution could not have been this mythical event which made History fruitful, along with all future ideas on revolution. Revolutionary writing was so to speak the entelechy of the revolutionary legend: it struck fear into men's hearts and imposed upon them a citizen's sacrament of Bloodshed.

Marxist writing is of a different order. Here the closed character of the form does not derive from rhetorical amplification or from grandiloquence in delivery, but from a lexicon as specialized and as functional as a technical vocabulary; even metaphors are here severely codified. French revolutionary writing always proclaimed a right founded on bloodshed or moral justification, whereas from the very start Marxist writing is presented as the language of knowledge. Here, writing is univocal, because it is meant to maintain the cohesion of a Nature; it is the lexical identity of this writing which allows it to impose a stability in its explanations and a permanence in its method; it is only in the light of its whole linguistic system that Marxism is perceived in all its political implications. Marxist writing is as much given to understatement as revolutionary writing is to grandiloquence, since each word is no longer anything but a narrow reference to the set of principles which tacitly underlie it. For instance, the word "imply," frequently encountered in Marxist writing, does not there have its neutral dictionary meaning; it always refers to a precise historical process, and is like an algebraical sign representing a whole bracketed set of previous postulates.

Being linked to action, Marxist writing has rapidly become, in fact, a language expressing value judgments. This character, already visible in Marx, whose writing however remains in general explanatory, has come to pervade writing completely in the era of triumphant Stalinism. Certain outwardly similar notions, for which a neutral vocabulary would not seek a dual designation, are evaluatively parted from each other, so that each element gravitates toward a different noun: for instance, "cosmopolitanism" is the negative of "internationalism" (already in Marx). In the Stalinist world, in which *definition*, that is to say, the separation between Good and Evil, becomes the sole content of all language, there are no more words without values attached to them, so that finally the function of writing is to cut out one stage of a process: there is no more lapse of time between naming and judging, and the closed character of language is perfected, since in the last analysis it is a value which is given as explanation of another value. For instance, it may be alleged that such and such a criminal has engaged in activities harmful to the interests of the state; which boils down to saying that a criminal is someone who commits a crime. We see that this is in fact a tautology, a device constantly used in Stalinist writing. For the latter no longer aims at founding a Marxist version of the facts, or a revolutionary rationale of actions, but at presenting reality in a prejudged form, thus imposing a reading which involves immediate condemnation: the objective content of the word "deviationist" puts it into a penological category. If two deviationists band together, they become "fractionists," which does not involve an objectively different crime but an increase in the sentence imposed. One can enumerate a properly Marxist writing (that of Marx and Lenin) and a writing of triumphant Stalinism; there certainly is as well a Trotskyist writing and a tactical writing, for instance that of the French Communist Party with its substitution of "people," then of "plain folk," for "working class," and the willful ambiguity of terms like "democracy," "freedom," "peace," etc.

There is no doubt at all that each regime has its own writing, no history of which has yet been written. Since writing is the spectacular commitment of language, it contains at one and the same time, thanks to a valuable ambiguity, the reality and the appearance of power, what it is, and what it would like to be thought to be: a history of political modes of writing would therefore be the best of social phenomenologies. For instance, the French Restoration evolved a class writing by means of which repression was immediately given as a condemnation spontaneously arising from classical "Nature": workers claiming rights were always "troublemakers," strike-breakers were "good workmen," and the subservience of judges became, in this language, the "paternal vigilance of magistrates" (it is thanks to a similar procedure that Gaullism today calls Communists "separatists"). We see that here the function of writing is to maintain a clear conscience and that its mission is fraudulently to identify the original fact with its remotest subsequent transformation by bolstering up the justification of actions with the additional guarantee of its own reality. This fact about writing is, by the way, typical of all authoritarian regimes; it is what might be called police-state writing: we know, for example, that the content of the word "Order" always indicates repression.

The spreading influence of political and social facts into the literary field of consciousness has produced a new type of scriptor, halfway between the party member and the writer, deriving from the former an ideal image of committed man, and from the latter the notion that a written work is an act. Thus while the intellectual supersedes the writer, there appears in periodicals and in essays a militant mode of writing entirely freed from stylistic considerations, and which is, so to speak, a professional language signifying "presence." In this mode of writing, nuances abound. Nobody will deny that there is such a thing, for instance, as a writing typical of *Esprit* or of *Les Temps Modernes*.[1] What these intellectual modes of writing have in common is that in them language, instead of being a privileged area, tends to become the sufficient sign of commitment. To come to adopt a closed sphere of language under the pressure of all those who do not speak it, is to proclaim one's act of choosing, if not necessarily one's agreement with that choice. Writing here resembles the signature one affixes at the foot of a collective proclamation one has not written oneself. So that to adopt a mode of writing—or, even better, to make it one's own—means to save oneself all the preliminaries of a choice, and to make it quite clear that one takes for granted the reasons for such a choice. Any intellectual writing is therefore the first of the "leaps of the intellect." Whereas an ideally free language never could function as a sign of my own person and would give no information whatsoever about my history and my freedom, the writing to which I entrust myself already exists entirely as an institution; it reveals my past and my choice, it gives me a history, it blazons forth my situation,

---

[1] *Esprit* and *Les Temps Modernes* are two prominent monthlies, the first left-wing Catholic and the second directed by J.-P. Sartre.

it commits me without my having to declare the fact. Form thus becomes more than ever an autonomous object, meant to signify a property which is collective and protected, and this object is a trouble-saving device: it functions as an economy signal whereby the scriptor constantly imposes his conversion without ever revealing how it came about.

This duplicity of today's intellectual modes of writing is emphasized by the fact that in spite of the efforts made in our time, it has proved impossible successfully to liquidate Literature entirely: it still constitutes a verbal horizon commanding respect. The intellectual is still only an incompletely transformed writer, and unless he scuttles himself and becomes forever a militant who no longer writes (some have done so, and are therefore forgotten), he cannot but come back to the fascination of former modes of writing, transmitted through Literature as an instrument intact but obsolete. These intellectual modes of writing are therefore unstable, they remain literary to the extent that they are powerless, and are political only through their obsession with commitment. In short, we are still dealing with ethical modes of writing, in which the conscience of the scriptor (one no longer ventures to call him a writer) finds the comforting image of collective salvation.

But just as, in the present state of History, any political mode of writing can only uphold a police world, so any intellectual mode of writing can only give rise to a para-literature, which no longer dares to speak its name. Both are therefore in a complete blind alley, they can lead only to complicity or impotence, which means, in either case, to alienation.

WRITING AND THE NOVEL

The Novel and History have been closely related in the very century which witnessed their greatest development. Their link in depth, that which should allow us to understand at once Balzac and Michelet, is that in both we find the construction of an autarkic world which elaborates its own dimensions and limits, and organizes within these its own Time, its own Space, its population, its own set of objects and its myths.

This sphericity of the great works of the nineteenth century found its expression in those long recitatives, the Novel and History, which are, as it were, plane projections of a curved and organic world of which the serial story which came into being at that precise moment, presents, through its involved complications, a degraded image. And yet narration is not necessarily a law of the form. A whole period could conceive novels in letters, for instance; and another can evolve a practice of History by means of analyses. Therefore Narration, as a form common to both the Novel and to History, does remain, in general, the choice or the expression of a historical moment.

Obsolete in spoken French, the preterite, which is the cornerstone of Narration, always signifies the presence of Art; it is a part of a ritual of Letters. Its function is no longer that of a tense. The part it plays is to reduce reality to a point of time, and to abstract, from the depth of a multiplicity of experiences, a pure verbal act, freed from the existential roots of knowledge, and directed toward a logical link with other acts, other processes, a general movement of the world: it aims at maintaining a hierarchy in the realm of facts. Through the preterite, the verb implicitly belongs with a causal chain, it partakes of a set of related and orientated actions, it functions as the algebraic sign of an intention. Allowing as it does an ambiguity between temporality and causality, it calls for a sequence of events, that is, for an intelligible Narrative. This is why it is the ideal instrument for every construction of a world; it is the unreal time of cosmogonies, myths, History, and Novels. It presupposes a world which is constructed, elaborated, self-sufficient, reduced to significant lines, and not one which has been sent sprawling before us, for us to take or leave. Behind the preterite there always lurks a demiurge, a God, or a reciter. The world is not unexplained since it is told like a story; each one of its accidents is but a circumstance, and the preterite is precisely this operative sign whereby the narrator reduces the exploded reality to a slim and pure logos, without density, without volume, without spread, and whose sole function is to unite as rapidly as possible a cause and an end. When the historian states that the duc de Guise died on December 23, 1588, or when the novelist relates that the Marchioness went out at five o'clock,[2] such actions emerge from a past without substance; purged of the uncertainty of existence, they have the stability and outline of an algebra, they are a recollection, but a useful recollection, the interest of which far surpasses its duration.

So that finally the preterite is the expression of an order, and consequently of a euphoria. Thanks to it, reality is neither mysterious nor absurd; it is clear, almost familiar, repeatedly gathered up and contained in the hand of a creator; it is sub-jected to the ingenious pressure of his freedom. For all the great storytellers of the nineteenth century, the world may be full of pathos but it is not derelict, since it is a grouping of coherent relations, since there is no overlapping between the written facts, since he who tells the story has the power to do away with the opacity and the solitude of the existences which made it up, since he can in all sentences bear witness to a communication and a hierarchy of actions and since, to tell the truth, these very actions can be reduced to mere signs.

The narrative past is therefore a part of a security system for Belles-Lettres. Being the image of an order, it is one of those numerous formal pacts made between the writer and society for the justification of the former and the serenity of the latter. The preterite *signifies* a creation: that is, it pro-

---

[2] The sentence which for Valéry epitomized the conventions of the novel.

claims and imposes it. Even from the depth of the most somber realism, it has a reassuring effect because, thanks to it, the verb expresses a closed, well-defined, substantival act, the Novel has a name, it escapes the terror of an expression without laws: reality becomes slighter and more familiar, it fits within a style, it does not outrun language. Literature remains the currency in use in a society apprised, by the very form of words, of the meaning of what it consumes. On the contrary, when the Narrative is rejected in favor of other literary genres, or when, within the narration, the preterite is replaced by less ornamental forms, fresher, more full-blooded and nearer to speech (the present tense or the present perfect), Literature becomes the receptacle of existence in all its density and no longer of its meaning alone. The acts it recounts are still separated from History, but no longer from people.

We now understand what is profitable and what is intolerable in the preterite as used in the Novel: it is a lie made manifest, it delineates an area of plausibility which reveals the possible in the very act of unmasking it as false. The teleology common to the Novel and to narrated History is the alienation of the facts: the preterite is the very act by which society affirms its possession of its past and its possibility. It creates a content credible, yet flaunted as an illusion; it is the ultimate term of a formal dialectics which clothes an unreal fact in the garb first of truth then of a lie denounced as such. This has to be related to a certain mythology of the universal typifying the bourgeois society of which the Novel is a characteristic product; it involves giving to the imaginary the formal guarantee of the real, but while preserving in the sign the ambiguity of a double object, at once believable and false. This operation occurs constantly in the whole of Western art, in which the false is equal to the true, not through any agnosticism or poetic duplicity, but because the true is supposed to contain a germ of the universal, or to put it differently, an essence capa-

ble of fecundating by mere reproduction, several orders of
things among which some differ by their remoteness and some
by their fictitious character.

It is thanks to an expedient of the same kind that the triumphant bourgeoisie of the last century was able to look upon
its values as universal and to carry over to sections of society
which were absolutely heterogeneous to it all the Names which
were parts of its ethos. This is strictly how myths function, and
the Novel—and within the Novel, the preterite—are mythological objects in which there is, superimposed upon an immediate intention, a second-order appeal to a corpus of dogmas, or
better, to a pedagogy, since what is sought is to impart an
essence in the guise of an artifact. In order to grasp the significance of the preterite, we have but to compare the Western art
of the novel with a certain Chinese tradition, for instance, in
which art lies solely in the perfection with which reality is
imitated. But in this tradition no sign, absolutely nothing, must
allow any distinction to be drawn between the natural and the
artificial objects: this wooden walnut must not impart to me,
along with the image of a walnut, the intention of conveying to
me the art which gave birth to it. Whereas, on the contrary,
this is what writing does in the novel. Its task is to put the
mask in place and at the same time to point it out.

This ambiguous function disclosed in the preterite is found
in another fact relating to this type of writing: the third person
in the Novel. The reader will perhaps recall a novel by Agatha
Christie in which all the invention consisted in concealing the
murderer beneath the use of the first person of the narrative.
The reader looked for him behind every "he" in the plot: he
was all the time hidden under the "I." Agatha Christie knew
perfectly well that, in the novel, the "I" is usually a spectator,
and that it is the "he" who is the actor. Why? The "he" is a
typical novelistic convention; like the narrative tense, it signi-

fies and carries through the action of the novel; if the third person is absent, the novel is powerless to come into being, and even wills its own destruction. The "he" is a formal manifestation of the myth, and we have just seen that, in the West at least, there is no art which does not point to its own mask. The third person, like the preterite, therefore performs this service for the art of the novel, and supplies its consumers with the security born of a credible fabrication which is yet constantly held up as false.

Less ambiguous, the "I" is thereby less typical of the novel: it is therefore at the same time the most obvious solution, when the narration remains on this side of convention (Proust's work, for instance, purports to be a mere introduction to Literature), and the most sophisticated, when the "I" takes its place beyond convention and attempts to destroy it, by conferring on the narrative the spurious naturalness of taking the reader into its confidence (such is the guileful air of some stories by Gide). In the same way the use of the "he" in a novel involves two opposed systems of ethics: since it represents an unquestioned convention, it attracts the most conformist and the least dissatisfied, as well as those others who have decided that, finally, this convention is necessary to the novelty of their work. In any case, it is the sign of an intelligible pact between society and the author; but it is also, for the latter, the most important means he has of building the world in the way that he chooses. It is therefore more than a literary experiment: it is a human act which connects creation to History or to existence.

In Balzac, for instance, the multiplicity of "he's," this vast network of characters, slight in terms of solid flesh, but consistent by the duration of their acts, reveals the existence of a world of which History is the first datum. The Balzacian "he" is not the end product of a development starting from some transformed and generalized "I"; it is the original and crude element of the novel, the material, not the outcome, the creative activity: there is no Balzacian history prior to the history of each third person in the novels of Balzac. His "he" is analogous to Caesar's "he": the third person here brings about a kind of algebraic state of the action, in which existence plays the smallest possible part, in favor of elements which connect, clarify, or show the tragedy inherent in human relationships. Conversely—or at any rate previously—the function of "he" in the novel can be that of expressing an existential experience. In many modern novelists the history of the man is identified with the course of the conjugation: starting from an "I" which is still the form which expresses anonymity most faithfully, man and author little by little win the right to the third person, in proportion as existence becomes fate, and soliloquy becomes a Novel. Here the appearance of the "he" is not the starting point of History, it is the end of an effort which has been successful in extracting from a personal world made up of humors and tendencies, a form which is pure, significant, and which therefore vanishes as soon as it is born, thanks to the totally conventional and ethereal decor of the third person. This certainly was the course displayed in the first novels of Jean Cayrol, whose case can be taken as an exemplar. But whereas in the classics—and we know that where writing is concerned classicism lasts until Flaubert—the withdrawal of the biological person testifies to the establishment of essential man, in novelists such as Cayrol, the invasion of the "he" is a progressive conquest over the profound darkness of the existential "I": so true it is that the Novel, identified as it is by its most formal signs, is a gesture of sociability; it establishes Literature as an institution.

Maurice Blanchot has shown, in the case of Kafka, that the elaboration of the impersonal narrative (let us notice, apropos of this term, that the "third person" is always presented as a negative degree of the person) was an act of fidelity to the essence of language, since the latter naturally tends toward its own destruction. We therefore understand how "he" is a victory over "I," inasmuch as it conjures up a state at once more literary and more absent. Nonetheless this victory is ceaselessly threatened: the literary convention of the "he" is necessary to the belittling of the person, but runs at every moment the risk of encumbering it with an unexpected density. For Literature is like phosphorus: it shines with its maximum brilliance at the moment when it attempts to die. But as, on the other hand, it is an act which necessarily implies a duration—especially in the Novel—there can never be any Novel independently of Belles-Lettres. So that the third person in the Novel is one of the most obsessive signs of this tragic aspect of writing which was born in the last century, when under the weight of History, Literature became dissociated from the society which consumes it. Between the third person as used by Balzac and that used by Flaubert, there is a world of difference (that of 1848): in the former we have a view of History which is harsh but coherent and certain of its principles, the triumph of an order; in the latter, an art which in order to escape its pangs of conscience either exaggerates conventions or frantically attempts to destroy them. Modernism begins with the search for a Literature which is no longer possible.

Thus we find, in the Novel too, this machinery directed toward both destruction and resurrection, and typical of the whole of modern art. What must be destroyed is duration, that is, the ineffable binding force running through existence: for order, whether it be that of poetic flow or of narrative signs, that of Terror or plausibility, is always a murder in intention. But what reconquers the writer is again duration, for it is impossible to develop a negative within time, without elaborating a positive art, an order which must be destroyed anew. So that the greater modern works linger as long as possible, in a sort of miraculous stasis, on the threshold of Literature, in this anticipatory state in which the breadth of life is given, stretched but not yet destroyed by this crowning phase, an order of signs. For instance, we have the first person in Proust, whose whole work rests on a slow and protracted effort toward Literature. We have Jean Cayrol, whose acquiescence to the Novel comes only as the very last stage of soliloquy, as if the literary act, being supremely ambiguous, could be delivered of a creation consecrated by society, only at the moment when it has at last succeeded in destroying the existential density of a hitherto meaningless duration.

The Novel is a Death; it transforms life into destiny, a memory into a useful act, duration into an orientated and meaningful time. But this transformation can be accomplished only in full view of society. It is society which imposes the Novel, that is, a complex of signs, as a transcendence and as the History of a duration. It is therefore by the obviousness of its intention, grasped in that of the narrative signs, that one can recognize the path which, through all the solemnity of art, binds the writer to society. The preterite and the third person in the Novel are nothing but the fateful gesture with which the writer draws attention to the mask which he is wearing. The whole of Literature can declare *Larvatus prodeo*,[3] As I walk forward, I point out my mask. Whether we deal with the inhuman experience of the poet, who accepts the most momentous of all breaks, that from the language of society, or with the plausible untruth of the novelist, sincerity here feels a need of the signs of falsehood, and of conspicuous falsehood in order to last and to be consumed. Writing is the product, and ultimately the source, of this ambiguity. This specialized language, the use of which gives the writer a glorious but none the less superintended function, evinces a kind of servitude, invis-

[3] *Larvatus prodeo* was the motto of Descartes.

ible at first, which characterizes any responsibility. Writing, free in its beginnings, is finally the bond which links the writer to a History which is itself in chains: society stamps upon him the unmistakable signs of art so as to draw him along the more inescapably in its own process of alienation.

IS THERE ANY POETIC WRITING?

In the classical period, prose and poetry are quantities, their difference can be measured; they are neither more nor less separated than two different numbers, contiguous like them, but dissimilar because of the very difference in their magnitudes. If I use the word prose for a minimal form of speech, the most economical vehicle for thought, and if I use the letters a, b, c for certain attributes of language, which are useless but decorative, such as meter, rhyme or the ritual of images, all the linguistic surface will be accounted for in M. Jourdain's[4] double equation:

$$Poetry = Prose + a + b + c$$
$$Prose = Poetry - a - b - c$$

whence it clearly follows that Poetry is always different from Prose. But this difference is not one of essence, it is one of quantity. It does not, therefore, jeopardize the unity of language, which is an article of classical dogma. One may effect a different dosage in manner of speech, according to the social occasion: here, prose or rhetoric, there, poetry or precosity, in accordance with a whole ritual of expression laid down by good society, but there remains everywhere a single language, which reflects the eternal categories of the mind. Classical poetry is felt to be merely an ornamental variation of prose, the fruit of an *art* (that is, a technique), never a different language, or the product of a particular sensibility. Any poetry

[4] Molière's *Bourgeois Gentilhomme*.

is then only the decorative equation, whether allusive or forced, of a possible prose which is latent, virtually and potentially, in any conceivable manner of expression. "Poetic," in the days of classicism, never evokes any particular domain, any particular depth of feeling, any special coherence, or separate universe, but only an individual handling of a verbal technique, that of "expressing oneself" according to rules more artistic, therefore more sociable, than those of conversation, in other terms, the technique of projecting out an inner thought, springing fully armed from the Mind, a speech which is made more socially acceptable by virtue of the very conspicuousness of its conventions.

We know that nothing of this structure remains in modern poetry, which springs not from Baudelaire but from Rimbaud, unless it is in cases where one takes up again, in a revised traditional mode, the formal imperatives of classical poetry: henceforth, poets give to their speech the status of a closed Nature, which covers both the function and the structure of language. Poetry is then no longer a Prose either ornamental or shorn of liberties. It is a quality *sui generis* and without antecedents. It is no longer an attribute but a substance, and therefore it can very well renounce signs, since it carries its own nature within itself, and does not need to signal its identity outwardly: poetic language and prosaic language are sufficiently separate to be able to dispense with the very signs of their difference.

Furthermore, the alleged relations between thought and language are reversed; in classical art, a ready-made thought generates an utterance which "expresses" or "translates" it. Classical thought is devoid of duration, classical poetry has it only in such degree as is necessary to its technical arrangement. In modern poetics, on the contrary, words produce a kind of formal continuum from which there gradually emanates an intellectual or emotional density which would have been impossible without them; speech is then the solidified time of a more spiritual gestation, during which the "thought" is prepared, installed little by little by the contingency of words. This verbal luck, which will bring down the ripe fruit of a meaning, presupposes therefore a poetic time which is no longer that of a "fabrication" but that of a possible adventure, the meeting point of a sign and intention. Modern poetry is opposed to classical art by a difference which involves the whole structure of language, without leaving between those two types of poetry anything in common except the same sociological intention.

The economy of classical language (Prose and Poetry) is relational, which means that in it words are abstracted as much as possible in the interest of relationships. In it, no word has a density by itself, it is hardly the sign of a thing, but rather the means of conveying a connection. Far from plunging into an inner reality consubstantial to its outer configuration, it extends, as soon as it is uttered, toward other words, so as to form a superficial chain of intentions. A glance at the language of mathematics will perhaps enable us to grasp the relational nature of classical prose and poetry: we know that in mathematical language, not only is each quantity provided with a sign, but also that the relations between these quantities are themselves transcribed, by means of a sign expressing operative equality or difference. It may be said that the whole movement of mathematical flow derives from an explicit reading of its relations. The language of classicism is animated by an analogous, although of course less rigid, movement: its "words," neutralized, made absent by rigorous recourse to a tradition which desiccates their freshness, avoid the phonetic or semantic accident which would concentrate the flavor of language at one point and halt its intellectual momentum in the interest of an unequally distributed enjoyment. The classical flow is a succession of elements whose density is even; it is exposed to the same emotional pressure, and relieves those elements of any tendency toward an individual meaning appearing at all invented. The poetic vocabulary itself is one of usage, not of invention: images in it are recognizable in a body; they do not exist in isolation; they are due to long custom, not to individual creation. The function of the classical poet is not therefore to find new words, with more body or more brilliance, but to follow the order of an ancient ritual, to perfect the symmetry or the conciseness of a relation, to bring a thought exactly within the compass of a meter. Classical conceits involve relations, not words: they belong to an art of expression, not of invention. The words, here, do not, as they later do, thanks to a kind of violent and unexpected abruptness, reproduce the depth and singularity of an individual experience; they are spread out to form a surface, according to the exigencies of an elegant or decorative purpose. They delight us because of the formulation which brings them together, not because of their own power or beauty.

True, classical language does not reach the functional perfection of the relational network of mathematics: relations are not signified, in it, by any special signs, but only by accidents of form and disposition. It is the restraint of the words in itself, their alignment, which achieves the relational nature of classical discourse. Overworked in a restricted number of ever-similar relations, classical words are on the way to becoming an algebra where rhetorical figures of speech, clichés, function as virtual linking devices; they have lost their density and gained a more interrelated state of speech; they operate in the manner of chemical valences, outlining a verbal area full of symmetrical connections, junctions and networks from which arise, without the respite afforded by wonder, fresh intentions towards signification. Hardly have the fragments of classical discourse yielded their meaning than they become messengers or harbingers, carrying ever further a meaning which refuses to settle within the depths of a word, but tries instead to spread widely enough to become a total gesture of intellection, that is, of communication.

Now the distortion to which Hugo tried to subject the alexandrine, which is of all meters the most interrelational, already contains the whole future of modern poetry, since what is attempted is to eliminate the intention to establish relationships and to produce instead an explosion of words. For modern poetry, since it must be distinguished from classical poetry and from any type of prose, destroys the spontaneously functional nature of language, and leaves standing only its lexical basis. It retains only the outward shape of relationships, their music, but not their reality. The Word shines forth above a line of relationships emptied of their content, grammar is bereft of its purpose, it becomes prosody and is no longer anything but an inflection which lasts only to present the Word. Connections are not properly speaking abolished, they are merely reserved areas, a parody of themselves, and this void is necessary for the density of the Word to rise out of a magic vacuum, like a sound and a sign devoid of background, like "fury and mystery."

In classical speech, connections lead the word on, and at once carry it toward a meaning which is an ever-deferred project; in modern poetry, connections are only an extension of the word, it is the Word which is "the dwelling place," it is rooted like a *fons et origo* in the prosody of functions, which are perceived but unreal. Here, connections only fascinate, and it is the Word which gratifies and fulfills like the sudden revelation of a truth. To say that this truth is of a poetic order is merely to say that the Word in poetry can never be untrue, because it is a whole; it shines with an infinite freedom and prepares to radiate toward innumerable uncertain and possible connections. Fixed connections being abolished, the word is left only with a vertical project, it is like a monolith, or a pillar which plunges into a totality of meanings, reflexes, and recollections: it is a sign which stands. The poetic word is here an act without immediate past, without environment, and which holds forth only the dense shadow of reflexes from all sources which are associated with it. Thus under each Word in modern poetry there lies a sort of existential geology, in which is gathered the total content of the Name, instead of a chosen content as in classical prose and poetry. The Word is no longer guided *in advance* by the general intention of a socialized discourse; the consumer of poetry, deprived of the guide of selective connections, encounters the Word frontally, and receives it as an absolute quantity, accompanied by all its possible associations. The Word, here, is encyclopedic, it contains simultaneously all the acceptations from which a relational discourse might have required it to choose. It therefore achieves a state which is possible only in the dictionary or in poetry— places where the noun can live without its article—and is reduced to a sort of zero degree, pregnant with all past and future specifications. The word here has a generic form; it is a category. Each poetic word is thus an unexpected object, a Pandora's box from which fly out all the potentialities of language; it is therefore produced and consumed with a peculiar curiosity, a kind of sacred relish. This Hunger of the Word, common to the whole of modern poetry, makes poetic speech terrible and inhuman. It initiates a discourse full of gaps and full of lights, filled with absences and overnourishing signs, without foresight or stability of intention, and thereby so opposed to the social function of language that merely to have recourse to a discontinuous speech is to open the door to all that stands above Nature.

For what does the rational economy of classical language mean, if not that Nature is a plenum, that it can be possessed, that it does not shy away or cover itself in shadows, but is in its entirety subjected to the toils of language? Classical language is always reducible to a persuasive continuum, it postulates the possibility of dialogue, it establishes a universe in which men are not alone, where words never have the terrible weight of things, where speech is always a meeting with the others. Classical language is a bringer of euphoria because it is immediately social. There is no genre, no written work of classicism which does not suppose a collective consumption, akin to speech; classical literary art is an object which circulates among several persons brought together on a class basis; it is a product conceived for oral transmission, for a consumption regulated by the contingencies of society: it is essentially a spoken language, in spite of its strict codification.

We have seen that on the contrary modern poetry destroyed relationships in language and reduced discourse to words as static things. This implies a reversal in our knowledge of Nature. The interrupted flow of the new poetic language initiates a discontinuous Nature, which is revealed only piecemeal. At the very moment when the withdrawal of functions obscures the relations existing in the world, the object in discourse assumes an exalted place: modern poetry is a poetry of the object. In it, Nature becomes a fragmented space, made of objects solitary and terrible, because the links between them are only potential. Nobody chooses for them a privileged meaning, or a particular use, or some service; nobody imposes a hierarchy on them, nobody reduces them to the manifestation of a mental behavior, or of an intention, of some evidence of tenderness, in short. The bursting upon us of the poetic word then institutes an absolute object; Nature becomes a succession of verticalities, of objects, suddenly standing erect, and filled with all their possibilities: one of these can be only a landmark in an unfulfilled, and thereby terrible, world. These unrelated objects—words adorned with all the violence of their irruption, the vibration of which, though wholly mechanical, strangely affects the next word, only to die out immediately—these poetic words exclude men: there is no humanism of modern poetry. This erect discourse is full of terror, that is to say, it relates man not to other men but to the most inhuman images in Nature: heaven, hell, holiness, childhood, madness, pure matter, etc.

At such a point, it is hardly possible to speak of a poetic mode of writing, for this is a language in which a violent drive toward autonomy destroys any ethical scope. The verbal gesture here aims at modifying Nature, it is the approach of a demiurge; it is not an attitude of the conscience but an act of coercion. Such, at least, is the language of those modern poets who carry their intention to the limit, and assume Poetry not as a spiritual exercise, a state of the soul or a placing of oneself in a situation, but as the splendor and freshness of a dream language. For such poets, it is as vain to speak about a mode of writing as of poetic feeling. Modern Poetry, in Char, for instance, is beyond this diffuse tone, this precious *aura*, which *are*, indeed, a mode of writing, usually termed poetic feeling. There is no objection to speaking of a poetic mode of writing concerning the classical writers and their epigones, or even concerning poetic prose in the manner of Gide's *Fruits of the Earth*, in which Poetry is in fact a certain linguistic ethos. In both cases, the mode of writing soaks up the style, and we can imagine that for people living in the seventeenth century, it was not easy to perceive an *immediate* difference between Racine and Pradon (and even less a difference of a poetic kind), just as it is not easy for a modern reader to pass judgment on those contemporary poets who use the same uniform and indecisive poetic mode of writing, because for them Poetry is a *climate* which means, essentially, a linguistic convention. But when the poetic language radically questions Nature by virtue of its very structure, without any resort to the content of the discourse and without falling back on some ideology, there is no mode of writing left, there are only styles, thanks to which man turns his back on society and confronts the world of objects without going through any of the forms of History or of social life.

1953

The World as Object

Hanging in the Dutch museums are works by a minor master who may be as deserving of literary renown as Vermeer. Saenredam painted neither faces nor objects, but chiefly vacant church interiors, reduced to the beige and innocuous unction of butterscotch ice cream. These churches, where there is nothing to be seen but expanses of wood and white-washed plaster, are irremediably unpeopled, and this negation goes much further than the destruction of idols. Never has nothingness been so confident. Saenredam's sugary, stubborn surfaces calmly reject the Italian overpopulation of statues, as well as the horror vacui professed by other Dutch painters. Saenredam is in effect a painter of the absurd; he has achieved a privative state of the subject, more insidious than the dislocations of our contemporaries. To paint so lovingly these meaningless surfaces, and to paint nothing else—that is already a "modern" aesthetic of silence.

Saenredam is a paradox: he articulates by antithesis the nature of classical Dutch painting, which has washed away religion only to replace it with man and his empire of things.

From *Critical Essays*, translated by Richard Howard (Evanston: North-western University Press, 1972).

Where once the Virgin presided over ranks of angels, man stands now, his feet upon the thousand objects of everyday life, triumphantly surrounded by his functions. Behold him, then, at the pinnacle of history, knowing no other fate than a gradual appropriation of matter. No limits to this humanization, and above all, no horizon: in the great Dutch seascapes (Cappelle's or Van de Venne's), the ships are crammed with people or cargo, the water is a ground you could walk on, the sea completely urbanized. A foundering vessel is always close to a shore covered with men and help; the human, here, is a virtue of numbers. As if the destiny of the Dutch landscape is to swarm with men, to be transformed from an elemental infinity to the plenitude of the registry office. This canal, this mill, these trees, these birds (Essaias van de Velde's) are linked by a crowded ferry; the overloaded boat connects the two shores and thus closes the movement of trees and water by the intention of a human movement, reducing these forces of Nature to the rank of objects and transforming the Creation into a facility. In the season most contrary to mankind, during one of those savage winters only history describes, Ruysdael still manages to put in a bridge, a house, a man walking down the road; the first warm spring shower is still a long way off, yet this man walking is actually the seed in the earth, for man himself is the seed, stubbornly pushing through this huge ocher sheet.

Here, then, men inscribe themselves upon space, immediately covering it with familiar gestures, memories, customs, and intentions. They establish themselves by means of a path, a mill, a frozen canal, and as soon as they can they arrange their objects in space as in a room; everything in them tends toward the *habitat* pure and simple: it is their heaven. There has been (eloquent) testimony to the domiciliary power of the Dutch canal boat; sturdy, securely decked, concave, it is as full as an egg and produces the egg's felicity: an absence of the void. Consider the Dutch still life: the object is never alone, and never privileged; it is merely there, among many others, painted between one function and another, participating in the disorder of the movements which have picked it up, put it down—in a word, *utilized*. There are objects wherever you look, on the tables, the walls, the floor: pots, pitchers over-turned, a clutter of baskets, a bunch of vegetables, a brace of game, milk pans, oyster shells, glasses, cradles. All this is man's space; in it he measures himself and determines his humanity, starting from the memory of his gestures: his *chronos* is covered by functions, there is no other authority in his life but the one he imprints upon the inert by shaping and manipulating it.

This universe of fabrication obviously excludes terror, as it excludes style. The concern of the Dutch painters is not to rid the object of its qualities in order to liberate its essence but, quite the contrary, to accumulate the secondary vibrations of appearance, for what must be incorporated into human space are layers of air, surfaces, and not forms or ideas. The only logical issue of such painting is to coat substance with a kind of glaze against which man may move without impairing the object's usefulness. Still-life painters like Van de Velde or Heda always render matter's most superficial quality: *sheen*. Oysters, lemon pulp, heavy goblets full of dark wine, long clay pipes, gleaming chestnuts, pottery, tarnished metal cups, three grape seeds—what can be the justification of such an assemblage if not to lubricate man's gaze amid his domain, to facili-tate his daily business among objects whose riddle is dissolved and which are no longer anything but easy surfaces?

An object's *use* can only help dissipate its essential form and emphasize instead its attributes. Other arts, other ages may have pursued, under the name of style, the essential core of things; here, nothing of the kind: each object is accom-panied by its adjectives, substance is buried under its myriad qualities, man never confronts the object, which remains dutifully subjugated to him by precisely what it is assigned to provide. What need have I of the lemon's principial form? What my quite empirical humanity needs is a lemon ready for use, half-peeled, half-sliced, half-lemon, half-juice, caught at the precious moment it exchanges the scandal of its perfect and useless ellipse for the first of its economic qualities, astringency. The object is always open, exposed, accompanied, until it has destroyed itself as closed substance, until it has cashed in all the functional virtues man can derive from stubborn matter. I regard the Dutch "kitchen scenes" (Buelkelaer's, for instance) less as a nation's indulgence of its own appetites (which would be more Belgian than Dutch; patricians like Ruyter and Tromp ate meat only once a week) than as a series of explanations concerning the *instrumentality* of foodstuffs: the units of nourishment are always destroyed as still lifes and restored as moments of a domestic *chronos*; whether it is the crisp greenness of cucumbers or the pallor of plucked fowls, everywhere the object offers man its *utilized* aspect, not its principial form. Here, in other words, is never a generic state of the object, but only circumstantial states.

Behold then a real transformation of the object, which no longer has an essence but takes refuge entirely within its attributes. A more complete subservience of things is unimaginable. The entire city of Amsterdam, indeed, seems to have been built with a view to this domestication: few substances here are not annexed to the empire of merchandise. Take the rubble in the corner of a vacant lot or near a railroad siding— what seems more indescribable: not an object, but an element! Yet in Amsterdam, consider this same rubble sifted and loaded onto a barge, led through the canals—you will see objects as clearly defined as cheeses, crates, vats, logs. Add to the vehicular movement of the water the vertical plane of the houses which retain, absorb, interpose, or restore the merchandise: that whole concert of pulleys, chutes, and docks effects a permanent mobilization of the most shapeless substances. Each house—narrow, flat, tilting forward as though to meet the merchandise halfway—suddenly opens at the top: here, pushing up into the sky, is nothing more than a kind of mystical mouth, the attic, as if each human habitat were merely the rising path of storage, hoarding, that great ancestral gesture of animals and children. As the city is built on water, there are no cellars, everything is taken up to the attic, raised there from outside. Thus objects interrupt every horizon, glide along the water and along the walls. It is objects which articulate space.

The object is by and large constituted by this mobility. Hence the defining power of all these Dutch canals. What we have, clearly, is a water-merchandise complex; it is water which makes the object, giving it all the nuances of a calm, planar mobility, collecting supplies, shifting them without perceptible transition from one exchange to another, making the entire city into a census of agile goods. Take a look at the canals of another minor master, Berckheyde, who has painted virtually nothing but this mild traffic of ownership: everything is, for the object, a means of procession; this bit of wharf is a cynosure of kegs, logs, tarpaulins; man has only to overturn or to hoist; space, obedient creature, does the rest—carries back and forth, selects, distributes, recovers, seems to have no other goal than to complete the projected movement of all these things, separated from matter by the sleek, firm film of *use*; here all objects are prepared for manipulation, all have the detachment and the density of Dutch cheeses: round, waxed, prehensible.

This separation is the extreme limit of the concrete, and I know only one French work which can claim to equal in its itemizing power that of the Dutch canals—our Civil Code. Consider the list of real estate and chattels: "domestic pigeons, wild rabbits, beehives, pond fish, wine presses, stills, ovens, manure and stable litter, wall hangings, mirrors, books and medals, linens, weapons, seeds, wines, hay," etc. Is this not exactly the universe of Dutch painting? Each represents the triumph of an entirely self-sufficient nominalism. Every definition and every manipulation of property produce an art of the catalogue, in other words, of the concrete itself, divided, countable, mobile. The Dutch scenes require a gradual and complete reading; we must begin at one edge and finish at the other, audit the painting like an accountant, not forgetting this corner, that margin, that background, in which is inscribed yet another perfectly rendered object adding its unit to this patient weighing of property or of merchandise.

When applied to social groups regarded by the period as inferior, this enumerative power constitutes certain men as objects. Van Ostade's peasants or Averkamp's skaters are entitled only to the existence of number, and the scenes grouping them must be read not as a repertory of fully human gestures, but rather as an anecdotic catalogue dividing and combining the various elements of a prehumanity; we must decipher the scene the way we read a puzzle. This is because Dutch painting obviously deals with two anthropologies, as distinctly separated as Linnaeus' zoological classes. It is no accident that the word "class" applies to both notions: there is the patrician class (*homo patricius*) and the peasant class (*homo paganicus*), and each encompasses human beings not only of the same social condition but also of the same morphology.

Van Ostade's peasants have abortive, shapeless faces; as if they were unfinished creatures, rough drafts of men, arrested at an earlier stage of human development. Even the children have neither age nor sex; they are identified only by their size. As the ape is separated from man, here the peasant is separated from the burgher precisely insofar as he is deprived of the ultimate characteristics of humanity, those of the *person*.

This subclass of men is never represented frontally, an attitude which presupposes at least a gaze: this privilege is reserved for the patrician or the cow, the Dutch totem animal and national provider. From the neck up, these peasants have only a blob which has not yet become a face, its lower part invariably slashed or blurred or somehow twisted askew; it is a shifting prehumanity which reels across space like so many objects endowed with an additional power of drunkenness or hilarity.

Turn now to the young patrician (Verspronck's, for example) frozen into the proposition of an idle god. He is an ultra-person, endowed with the extreme signs of humanity. Just as the peasant face falls short of creation, the patrician face achieves the ultimate degree of identity. This zoological class of rich Dutch burghers possesses, further, its characteristic features: chestnut hair, brown or plum-colored eyes, pinkish skin, prominent nose, soft red lips, and a play of fragile shadows round the salient points of the face. Virtually no portraits of women, except as regents of hospitals, dispensers of public funds, not private fun. Woman is assigned only an instrumental role, as an administrator of charity or a guardian of domestic economy. Man, and man alone, is human. Hence all Dutch painting—still lifes, seascapes, peasant scenes, regents—culminate in a purely masculine iconography whose obsessive expression is the guild portrait.

The guilds or *Doelen* are the subject of so many paintings that we cannot help suspecting the presence of a myth. The *Doelen* are rather like Italian Madonnas, Greek ephebes, Egyptian pharaohs, or German fugues—a classical theme which indicates to the artist the limits of nature. And just as all Madonnas, all ephebes, all pharaohs, and all fugues are somewhat alike, all guild faces are isomorphic. Here, once again, is proof that the face is a social sign, that there is a possible history of faces, and that the most direct product of nature is as subject to process and to signification as the most socialized institutions.

In the guild portraits, one thing is striking: the great size of the heads, the lighting, the excessive truth of the face. The face becomes a kind of hothouse flower, brought to perfection by careful forcing. All these faces are treated as units of one and the same horticultural species, combining generic resemblance and individual identity. There are huge fleshy blooms (Hals) or tawny nebulae (Rembrandt), but this universality has nothing to do with the glabrous neutrality of medieval portraits, which are entirely accessible, ready to receive the signs of the soul, and not those of the person: pain, joy, piety, and pity, a whole fleshless iconography of the passions. The similarity of faces in medieval art is of an ontological order, that of the *Doelen* portraits of a genetic one. A social class unequivocally defined by its economy (identity of commercial function, after all, justifies these guild paintings) is here presented in its anthropological aspect, and this aspect has nothing to do with the secondary characteristics of the physiognomy: it is not because of their seriousness or their confidence that these heads look alike, contrary to socialist-realist portraits, for example, which unify a representation of the workers, say, under a single sign of virility and tension (this is the method of a primitive art). Here the matrix of the human face is not of an ethical order, it is of a carnal order; it consists not of a community of intentions, but of an identity of blood and food; it is formed after a long sedimentation which has accumulated all the characteristics of a social particularity within a class: age, size, morphology, wrinkles, veins, the very order of biology separates the patrician caste from the functional substance (objects, peasants, landscapes) and imprisons it within its own authority.

Entirely identified by their social heredity, these Dutch faces are engaged in none of those visceral adventures which ravage the countenance and expose the body in its momentary destitution. What have they to do with the *chronos* of passion? Theirs is the *chronos* of biology; their flesh has no need, in order to exist, to anticipate or to endure events; it is blood which causes it to be and to command recognition; passion would be pointless, it would add nothing to existence. Consider the exception: Rembrandt's David does not weep, but half veils his head in a curtain; to close the eyes is to close the world, and in all Dutch painting no scene is more aberrant. This is because for once man is endowed with an adjectival quality; he slips from being to having, rejoins a humanity at grips with something else. If we could consider a painting out of the context of its technical or aesthetic rules, there would be no difference between a tearful fifteenth-century *Pietà* and some combative Lenin of contemporary Soviet imagery; for in either case, an attribute is provided, not an identity. This is precisely the converse of the little cosmos of Dutch art, where objects exist only by their qualities, whereas man, and man alone, possesses existence-in-itself. A substantive world of man, an adjectival world of things: such is the order of a creation dedicated to contentment.

What is it then which distinguishes these men at the pinnacle of their empire? It is the *numen*. The ancient *numen* was that simple gesture by which divinity signified its decisions, disposing of human destiny by a sort of infra-language consisting of pure demonstration. Omnipotence does not speak (perhaps because it does not think), it is content with gesture, even with a half gesture, a hint of a gesture, swiftly absorbed into the slothful serenity of the Divine. The modern prototype of the *numen* might be that circumspect tension, mixed with lassitude and confidence, by which Michelangelo's God draws away from Adam after having created him, and with a suspended gesture assigns him his imminent humanity. Each time the ruling class is represented, it must expose its *numen* or else the painting would be unintelligible. Consider the hagiography of the First Empire: Napoleon is a purely numinous figure, unreal by the very convention of his gesture. At first, this gesture still exists: the emperor is never represented idle; he points or signifies or acts. But there is nothing human about his gesture; it is not the gesture of the workman, *homo faber*, whose functional movement encompasses him in search of its own effect; it is a gesture immobilized in the least stable moment of its course; it is the idea of power, not its density, which is thus eternalized. The hand which rises slightly or gently comes to rest—the very suspension of movement—produces the phantasmagoria of a power alien to man. The gesture creates, it does not complete, and consequently its indication matters more than its course. Consider *The Battle of Eylau* (a painting to remove from its context, if ever there was one): what a difference in density between the excessive gestures of the ordinary mortals—shouting, supporting a wounded man, caracoling rhetorically—and the waxy impasto of the emperor-God, surrounded by motionless air, raising a hand huge with every signification at once, designating everything and nothing, creating with a terrible languor a future of unknown acts. This exemplary painting shows us just how the *numen* is constituted: it *signifies* infinite movement yet does not accomplish it, merely eternalizing the notion of power and not its substance in an embalmed gesture, a gesture arrested at the most fragile point of its fatigue, imposing on the man who contemplates and endures it the plenitude of an intelligible power.

Naturally, there is nothing warlike about the *numen* of these merchants, these Dutch burghers at banquets or grouped around a table to draw up their accounts, this class at once social and zoological. How, then, does it impose its unreality? By looking. It is the gaze which is the *numen* here, the gaze which disturbs, intimidates, and makes man the ultimate term of a problem. To be stared at by a portrait is always disconcerting. Nor is this a Dutch specialty. But here the gaze is collective; these men, even these lady regents virilized by age and function, all these patricians rest upon you the full weight of their smooth, bare faces. They are gathered together not to count their money—which they never bother with, despite the table, the ledger, the pile of gold—not to eat the food—despite its abundance—but to look at you, thereby signifying an existence and an authority beyond which you cannot go. Their gaze is their proof and it is yours. Consider Rembrandt's cloth merchants—one of them even stands up to get a better look at you. You become a matter of capital, you are an element of humanity doomed to participate in a *numen* issuing finally from man and not from God. There is no sadness and no cruelty in that gaze; it is a gaze without adjectives, it is only, completely, a gaze which neither judges you nor appeals to you; it posits you, implicates you; makes you exist. But this creative gesture is endless; you keep on being born, you are sustained, carried to the end of a movement which is one of infinite origin, source, and which appears in an eternal state of suspension. God and the emperor had the power of the hand, man has the gaze. All history reaches the grandeur of its own mystery in an endless look.

It is because the gaze of the *Doelen* institutes a final suspension of history, at the pinnacle of social happiness, that Dutch painting is not satiated, and that its class orientation culminates after all in something which also belongs to other men. What happens when men are, by their own means, content? What is left of man? The *Doelen* answer: a look is left. In this perfectly content patrician world, absolute master of matter and evidently rid of God, the gaze produces a strictly human interrogation and proposes an infinite postponement of history. There is, in these Dutch *Doelen*, the very contrary of a realistic art.

Consider Courbet's *Atelier*: it is a complete allegory. Shut up in a room, the artist is painting a landscape he does not see, turning his back to his (naked) model, who is watching him paint. In other words, the painter establishes himself in a space carefully emptied of any gaze but his own. Now, all art which has only two dimensions, that of the work and that of the spectator, can create only a platitude, since it is no more than the capture of a shopwindow spectacle by a painter-voyeur. Depth is born only at the moment the spectacle itself slowly turns its shadow toward man and begins to look at him.

1953

Baudelaire's Theater

WHAT is interesting about Baudelaire's plays[1] is not their dramatic content but their embryonic state: the critic's role is therefore not to dissect these sketches for the image of an achieved theater but, on the contrary, to determine in them the vocation of their failure. It would be futile—and probably cruel to Baudelaire's memory—to imagine the plays these germs might have produced; it is not so to seek out the reasons which kept Baudelaire in this state of imperfect creation, so far from the aesthetic of *Les Fleurs du mal*. How well Sartre has shown us that nonfulfillment itself is a choice, and that to have projected a dramatic *oeuvre* without writing it was for Baudelaire a significant form of his fate.

One notion is essential to the understanding of Baudelairean

From *Critical Essays*.

[1] We know of four projects: the first, *Ideolus* (or *Manoel*), is an unfinished drama in alexandrines written about 1843 (Baudelaire was twenty-two), in collaboration with Ernest Praron. The other three are scenarios: *La Fin de Don Juan* is little more than a plot outline; *Le Marquis du I*er *Houzards* is a kind of historical drama in which Baudelaire planned to study the case of an *émigré's* son, Wolfgang de Cadolles, torn between the ideas of his parents and his enthusiasm for the emperor. *L'Ivrogne*, the most Baudelairean of these scenarios, is the story of a crime: a drunk and lazy workman pushes his wife down a well he then fills with cobblestones; the play was to develop the situation indicated in a poem from *Les Fleurs du mal*, *Le Vin de l'assassin*.

theater: theatricality. What is theatricality? It is theater-minus-text, it is a density of signs and sensations built up on stage starting from the written argument; it is that ecumenical perception of sensuous artifice—gesture, tone, distance, substance, light—which submerges the text beneath the profusion of its external language. Of course theatricality must be present in the first written germ of a work, it is a datum of creation not of production. There is no great theater without a devouring theatricality—in Aeschylus, in Shakespeare, in Brecht, the written text is from the first carried along by the externality of bodies, of objects, of situations; the utterance immediately explodes into substances. One thing strikes us on the contrary in the three scenarios by Baudelaire (I set no store by *Ideolus*): these are purely narrative scenarios whose theatricality, even potentially, is very weak.

We must not let Baudelaire deceive us by such naïve indications as "very active, bustling production, great military pomp, settings of a poetic effect, fantastic statue, costumes of various nations," etc. This concern for externals, manifested intermittently, like a sudden remorse, affords no profound theatricality. Quite the contrary, it is the very generality of the Baudelairean impression which is alien to the theater: here, as elsewhere, Baudelaire is too intelligent; he substitutes concept for object, replaces the tavern of *L'Ivrogne* by the idea, the "atmosphere" of the tavern, offers the pure concept of military pomp instead of the materiality of flags or uniforms. Paradoxically, nothing attests better to impotence in the theater than this *total* character, somehow romantic, at least exotic, of vision. Each time Baudelaire refers to "production values," he sees them, naïvely, with a spectator's eye—in other words, fulfilled, static, ready-made, precooked and offering a seamless deception which has had time to do away with all traces of its own artifice. The "color of crime" necessary, for example, in the last act of *L'Ivrogne* is a critic's truth, not a dramatist's. In its initial movement, the production can be based only on the plurality and the literalness of objects. Baudelaire, on the other hand, conceives things in the theater only as accompanied by their dreamed-of doubles, endowed with a spirituality vaporous enough to unify them, to alienate them all the more. Now, nothing is more contrary to dramaturgy than the dream. The germs of true theater are always elementary movements of prehension or distancing: the surreality of theater objects is of a sensorial, not an oneiric order.

It is therefore not when Baudelaire speaks of production, of staging, that he is closest to a concrete theater. His authentic theatricality is the sentiment, indeed one might say the torment, of the actor's disturbing corporeality. In one scenario he proposes that Don Juan's son be played by a girl, in another that the hero be surrounded by lovely women each assigned a domestic function, and in a third that the drunkard's wife offer in her very body that appearance of modesty and fragility which call down rape and murder upon her. This is because for Baudelaire the actor's condition is a prostitution ("In a spectacle, in a dance, each takes his pleasure from all the participants"); his charm is therefore not experienced as an episodic and decorative character (contrary to the "bustling" staging, the movements of gypsies or the atmosphere of taverns), it is necessary to the theater as the manifestation of a primary category of the Baudelairean universe: artificiality.

The actor's body is artificial, but its duplicity is much more profound than that of the painted sets or the fake furniture of the stage; the grease paint, the imitation of gestures or intonation, the accessibility of an exposed body—all this is artificial but not factitious, and thereby a part of that delicate transcendence, of an exquisite, essential savor, by which Baudelaire has defined the power of the artificial paradise: the actor bears in himself the very overprecision of an excessive world, like that of hashish, where nothing is invented, but where everything exists in a multiplied intensity. This suggests that Baudelaire had an acute sense of the most secret and also the most disturbing theatricality, the kind which puts the actor at the center of the theatrical prodigy and constitutes the theater as the site of an ultra-incarnation, in which the body is double, at once a living body deriving from a trivial nature, and an emphatic, formal body, frozen by its function as an artificial object.

However, this powerful theatricality is merely vestigial in Baudelaire's projects for plays, whereas it flows powerfully through the rest of his work. It would seem that Baudelaire put his theater everywhere except, precisely, in his projects for plays. It is, moreover, a general fact of creation, this kind of marginal development of the elements of a genre—drama, novel, or poetry—within works which nominally are not made to receive them. For instance, France has put her historical drama everywhere in her literature except on stage. Baudelaire's theatricality is animated by the same power of evasion: wherever we do not expect it, it explodes; first and foremost in *Les Paradis artificiels*: here Baudelaire describes a sensory transmutation which is of the same nature as theatrical perception, since in both cases reality is assigned an emphatic accent, which is the stress of an ideality of things. Then in his poetry, at least wherever objects are united by the poet in a kind of radiant perception of matter, amassed, condensed as though on a stage, glowing with colors, lights, and cosmetics, touched here and there by the grace of the artificial; in every description of scenes, finally, for here the preference for a space deeper and stabilized by the painter's theocratic gesture is satisfied in the same manner as in the theater (conversely, "scenes" abound in the scenario of *Le Marquis du Ier Houzards*, which seems to come all of a piece out of Gros or Delacroix, just as *La Fin de Don Juan* or *L'Ivrogne* seem to come from a poetic rather than a strictly theatrical intention).

Thus Baudelaire's theatricality evades his theater in order to spread through the rest of his work. By a converse process, though one just as revealing, elements deriving from extra-dramatic orders abound in these scenarios, as if this theater were striving to destroy itself by a double movement of evasion and intoxication. As soon as it is conceived, the Baudelairean scenario is immediately steeped in novelistic categories: *La Fin de Don Juan*, at least the opening fragment we have of it, ends curiously with a pastiche of Stendhal; Don Juan speaks almost like Mosca: the few words he exchanges with his servant suggest the dialogue of the novel, in which the language of the characters, direct as it may be, retains that precious glaze, that chastened transparency we know Baudelaire applied to all the objects of his creation. Of course the text is no more than a sketch, and Baudelaire might have given his dialogue that absolute literality which is the fundamental status of language in the theater. But we are analyzing here the vocation of a failure and not the potentiality of a project: it is significant that in its nascent state, this ghost of a scenario should have the very tonality of a written literature, frozen by the page, without voice, without viscera.

Time and place, each time they are indicated, testify to the same horror of the theater, at least of the theater as we can imagine it in Baudelaire's day: act and scene are units which immediately hamper Baudelaire, which he repeatedly over-flows and whose regulation he always postpones: sometimes he feels that the act is too short, sometimes too long: in Act III of *Le Marquis du Ier Houzards* he inserts a flashback which even today only the cinema could manage; in *La Fin de Don Juan*, the scene gradually shifts from city to country, as in some abstract theater (*Faust*): in a general manner, even in its germ, this theater explodes, turns like an unstable chemical mixture, divides into "scenes" (in the pictorial sense of the term) or narratives. This is because, contrary to any true man of the theater, Baudelaire imagines a story entirely narrated, instead of starting from the stage; genetically, the theater is the subsequent creation of a fiction around an initial datum, which is always of a gestural order (liturgy in Aeschylus, actors' intrigues in Molière); Baudelaire evidently conceives the theater as a purely formal avatar, imposed after the fact upon a creative principle of a symbolic order (*Le Marquis du Ier Houzards*) or an existential one (*L'Ivrogne*). "I confess I have not given a thought to the staging," Baudelaire says at one point; impossible naïveté in any playwright, however minor.

Not that Baudelaire's scenarios are absolutely alien to an aesthetic of performance; but precisely insofar as they belong to a generally novelistic order, it is not theater but cinema which might best articulate them, for it is from the novel that cinema derives and not from the theater. The shifting locales, the flashbacks, the exoticism of the scenes, the temporal disproportion of the episodes, in short that torment of laying out the narration, to which Baudelaire's pre-theater testifies, might nourish a pure cinema. From this point of view, *Le Marquis du Ier Houzards* is a complete scenario: even the actors in this drama suggest the classical typology of cinema roles. This is because the actor, deriving from a novelistic character and not from a corporeal dream (as is still the case for Don Juan's son, played by a woman, or the drunkard's wife, object of sadism), has no need of the stage's dimension in order to exist: he belongs to a sentimental or social typology, not a morphological one: he is a pure narrative sign, as in the novel and as in the cinema.

What remains, then, which is strictly theatrical in Baudelaire's projects? Nothing, except precisely a pure recourse to the theater. It is as if the mere intention of someday writing plays had sufficed for Baudelaire and had exempted him from sustaining these projects with a strictly theatrical substance, suggested throughout his work but rejected in just those places where it might have been fulfilled. For to this theater which Baudelaire momentarily sought out, he eagerly lent the features most likely to eliminate it at once: a certain triviality, a certain puerility (surprising in relation to Baudelairean dandyism), deriving visibly from the supposed pleasures of the crowd, the "Odeonic" imagination of spectacular scenes (a battle, the emperor reviewing troops, a country dance hall, a gypsy camp, a complicated murder), a whole aesthetic of crude impressiveness, cut off from its dramatic motives or, one might say, a formalism of the theatrical act conceived in its effects most flattering to *petit bourgeois* sensibility.

With such a conception of theater, Baudelaire had to protect theatricality from the theater; fearing the sovereign artifice would be threatened by the collective character of the occasion, he hid it far from the stage, gave it refuge in his solitary literature, in his poems, his essays, his *Salons*; so that there is nothing left in this imaginary theater but the prostitution of the actor, the supposed pleasure of the public in the lies (and not in the artifice) of a grandiloquent production. This theater is trivial, but it is a triviality painful precisely insofar as it is pure conduct, mutilated as though deliberately of any poetic or dramatic depth, cut off from any development which might have justified it, crudely indicating that zone in which Baudelaire created himself from project to project, from failure to failure, until he built up that pure murder of literature, which we know since Mallarmé to be the torment and the justification of the modern writer.

It is therefore because the theater, abandoned by a theatricality which seeks refuge everywhere else, then fulfills to perfection a vulgar social nature, that Baudelaire chooses it briefly as the nominal site of an impulse and as the sign of what we would today call a commitment. By this pure gesture (pure because it transmits only his intention, and because this theater exists only as a project), Baudelaire rejoins, but this time on the level of creation, that sociability he pretended to postulate and to flee, according to the dialectic of a choice Sartre has so decisively analyzed. To bring a play to Holstein, the director of the Gaîté, was an action as reassuring as to flatter Sainte-Beuve, to canvas votes for the Academy, or to want the Legion of Honor.

And that is why these theatrical projects touch us so deeply: they belong in Baudelaire to that vast background of negativity against which rises finally the success of *Les Fleurs du mal* like an act which no longer owes anything to talent, that is, to literature. It took General Aupik, Ancelle, Théophile Gautier, Sainte-Beuve, the Academy, the ribbon of the Legion, and this pseudo-Odeonic theater, all these complacencies, accursed or abandoned moreover as soon as they were consented to, for Baudelaire's fulfilled work to be that responsible choice which made, in the end, his life into a great destiny. We would be ungrateful for *Les Fleurs du mal* if we failed to incorporate into its creator's history this agonizing Passion of vulgarity.

1954

The Face of Garbo

GARBO still belongs to that moment in cinema when capturing the human face still plunged audiences into the deepest ecstasy, when one literally lost oneself in a human image as one would in a philter, when the face represented a kind of absolute state of the flesh, which could be neither reached nor renounced. A few years earlier the face of Valentino was causing suicides; that of Garbo still partakes of the same rule of Courtly Love, where the flesh gives rise to mystical feelings of perdition.

It is indeed an admirable face-object. In *Queen Christina*, a film which has again been shown in Paris in the last few years, the makeup has the snowy thickness of a mask: it is not a painted face, but one set in plaster, protected by the surface of the color, not by its lineaments. Amid all this snow at once fragile and compact, the eyes alone, black like strange soft flesh, but not in the least expressive, are two faintly tremulous wounds. In spite of its extreme beauty, this face, not drawn but sculpted in something smooth and friable, that is, at once perfect and ephemeral, comes to resemble the flour-white

From *Mythologies*.

complexion of Charlie Chaplin, the dark vegetation of his eyes, his totem-like countenance.

Now the temptation of the absolute mask (the mask of antiquity, for instance) perhaps implies less the theme of the secret (as is the case with Italian half mask) than that of an archetype of the human face. Garbo offered to one's gaze a sort of Platonic Idea of the human creature, which explains why her face is almost sexually undefined, without however leaving one in doubt. It is true that this film (in which Queen Christina is by turns a woman and a young cavalier) lends itself to this lack of differentiation; but Garbo does not perform in it any feat of transvestism; she is always herself, and carries without pretense, under her crown or her wide-brimmed hats, the same snowy solitary face. The name given to her, *the Divine*, probably aimed to convey less a superlative state of beauty than the essence of her corporeal person, descended from a heaven where all things are formed and perfected in the clearest light. She herself knew this: how many actresses have consented to let the crowd see the ominous maturing of their beauty. Not she, however; the essence was not to be degraded, her face was not to have any reality except that of its perfection, which was intellectual even more than formal. The Essence became gradually obscured, progressively veiled with dark glasses, broad hats and exiles: but it never deteriorated.

And yet, in this deified face, something sharper than a mask is looming: a kind of voluntary and therefore human relation between the curve of the nostrils and the arch of the eyebrows; a rare, individual function relating two regions of the face. A mask is but a sum of lines; a face, on the contrary, is above all their thematic harmony. Garbo's face represents this fragile moment when the cinema is about to draw an existential from an essential beauty, when the archetype leans toward the fascination of mortal faces, when the clarity of the flesh as essence yields its place to a lyricism of Woman.

Viewed as a transition the face of Garbo reconciles two iconographic ages, it assures the passage from awe to charm. As is well known, we are today at the other pole of this evolution: the face of Audrey Hepburn, for instance, is individualized, not only because of its peculiar thematics (woman as child, woman as kitten), but also because of her person, of an almost unique specification of the face, which has nothing of the essence left in it, but is constituted by an infinite complexity of morphological functions. As a language, Garbo's singularity was of the order of the concept, that of Audrey Hepburn is of the order of the substance. The face of Garbo is an Idea, that of Hepburn, an Event.

1955

Striptease

STRIPTEASE—at least Parisian striptease—is based on a contradiction: Woman is desexualized at the very moment when she is stripped naked. We may therefore say that we are dealing in a sense with a spectacle based on fear, or rather on the pretense of fear, as if eroticism here went no further than a sort of delicious terror, whose ritual signs have only to be announced to evoke at once the idea of sex and its conjuration.

It is only the time taken in shedding clothes which makes voyeurs of the public; but here, as in any mystifying spectacle, the decor, the props, and the stereotypes intervene to contradict the initially provocative intention and eventually bury it in insignificance: evil is *advertised* the better to impede and exorcise it. French striptease seems to stem from what I have earlier called "Operation Margarine," a mystifying device which consists in inoculating the public with a touch of evil, the better to plunge it afterward into a permanently immune Moral Good: a few particles of eroticism, highlighted by the very situation on which the show is based, are in fact absorbed in a reassuring ritual which negates the flesh as surely as the

From *Mythologies*.

vaccine or the taboo circumscribe and control the illness or the crime.

There will therefore be in striptease a whole series of coverings placed upon the body of the woman in proportion as she pretends to strip it bare. Exoticism is the first of these barriers, for it is always of a petrified kind which transports the body into the world of legend or romance: a Chinese woman equipped with an opium pipe (the indispensable symbol of "Sininess"), an undulating vamp with a gigantic cigarette holder, a Venetian decor complete with gondola, a dress with panniers and a singer of serenades: all aim at establishing the woman *right from the start* as an object in disguise. The end of the striptease is then no longer to drag into the light a hidden depth, but to signify, through the shedding of an incongruous and artificial clothing, nakedness as a *natural* vesture of woman, which amounts in the end to regaining a perfectly chaste state of the flesh.

The classic props of the music hall, which are invariably rounded up here, constantly make the unveiled body more remote, and force it back into the all-pervading ease of a well-known rite: the furs, the fans, the gloves, the feathers, the fish-net stockings, in short, the whole spectrum of adornment, constantly makes the living body return to the category of luxurious objects which surround man with a magical decor. Covered with feathers or gloved, the woman identifies herself here as a stereotyped element of music hall, and to shed objects as ritualistic as these is no longer a part of a further, genuine undressing. Feathers, furs, and gloves go on pervading the woman with their magical virtue even once removed, and give her something like the enveloping memory of a luxurious shell, for it is a self-evident law that the whole of striptease is given in the very nature of the initial garment: if the latter is improbable, as in the case of the Chinese woman or the woman in furs, the nakedness which follows remains itself unreal, smooth, and enclosed like a beautiful slippery object, withdrawn by its very extravagance from human use: this is the underlying significance of the G-string covered with diamonds or sequins which is the very end of striptease. This ultimate triangle, by its pure and geometrical shape, by its hard and shiny material, bars the way to the sexual parts like a sword of purity, and definitively drives the woman back into a mineral world, the (precious) stone being here the irrefutable symbol of the absolute object, that which serves no purpose.

Contrary to the common prejudice, the dance which accompanies the striptease from beginning to end is in no way an erotic element. It is probably quite the reverse: the faintly rhythmical undulation in this case exorcises the fear of immobility. Not only does it give to the show the alibi of Art (the dances in strip shows are always "artistic"), but above all it constitutes the last barrier, and the most efficient of all: the dance, consisting of ritual gestures which have been seen a thousand times, acts on movements as a cosmetic, it hides nudity, and smothers the spectacle under a glaze of superfluous yet essential gestures, for the act of becoming bare is here relegated to the rank of parasitical operations carried out in an improbable background. Thus we see the professionals of striptease wrap themselves in the miraculous ease which constantly clothes them, makes them remote, gives them the icy indifference of skillful practitioners, haughtily taking refuge in the sureness of their technique: their science clothes them like a garment.

All this, this meticulous exorcism of sex, can be verified *a contrario* in the "popular contests" (*sic*) of amateur striptease: there, "beginners" undress in front of a few hundred spectators without resorting or resorting very clumsily to magic, which unquestionably restores to the spectacle its erotic power. Here we find at the beginning far fewer Chinese or Spanish women, no feathers or furs (sensible suits, ordinary coats), few disguises as a starting point—gauche steps, unsatisfactory dancing, girls constantly threatened by immobility, and above all by a "technical" awkwardness (the resistance of briefs, dress or bra) which gives to the gestures of unveiling an unexpected importance, denying the woman the alibi of art and the refuge of being an object, imprisoning her in a condition of weakness and timorousness.

And yet, at the Moulin Rouge, we see hints of another kind of exorcism, probably typically French, and one which in actual fact tends less to nullify eroticism than to tame it: the compère tries to give striptease a reassuring petit-bourgeois status. To start with, striptease is a *sport*: there is a Striptease Club, which organizes healthy contests whose winners come out crowned and rewarded with edifying prizes (a subscription to physical training lessons), a novel (which can only be Robbe-Grillet's *Voyeur*), or useful prizes (a pair of nylons, five thousand francs). Then, striptease is identified with a *career* (beginners, semi-professionals, professionals), that is, to the honorable practice of a specialization (strippers are skilled workers). One can even give them the magical alibi of work: *vocation*; one girl is, say, "*doing well*" or "*well on the way to fulfilling her promise*," or on the contrary "*taking her first steps*" on the arduous path of striptease. Finally and above all, the competitors are socially situated: one is a salesgirl, another a secretary (there are many secretaries in the Striptease Club). Striptease here is made to rejoin the world of the public, is made familiar and bourgeois, as if the French, unlike the American public (at least according to what one hears), following an irresistible tendency of their social status, could not conceive eroticism except as a household property, sanctioned by the alibi of weekly sport much more than by that of a magical spectacle: and this is how, in France, striptease is nationalized.

1955

The Lady of the Camellias

THEY still perform, in some part of the world or other, *The Lady of the Camellias* (it had in fact another run in Paris some time ago). This success must alert us to a mythology of Love which probably still exists, for the alienation of Marguerite Gautier in relation to the class of her masters is not fundamentally different from that of today's petit-bourgeois women in a world which is just as stratified.

Yet in fact, the central myth in *The Lady of the Camellias* is not Love, it is Recognition. Marguerite loves in order to achieve recognition, and this is why her passion (in the etymological, not the libidinal sense) has its source entirely in other people. Armand, on the other hand (who is the son of a District Collector of Taxes), gives an example of classical love: bourgeois, descended from essentialist culture, and one which will live on in Proust's analyses. This is a segregative love, that of the owner who carries off his prey; an internalized love, which acknowledges the existence of the world only intermittently and always with a feeling of frustration, as if the world were never anything but the threat of some theft (jealousy, quarrels, misunderstandings, worry, coolness, irritation,

From *Mythologies.*

89

etc.). Marguerite's Love is the perfect opposite of this. She was first touched to feel herself *recognized* by Armand, and passion, to her, was thereafter nothing but the permanent demand for this recognition; this is why the sacrifice which she grants M. Duval in renouncing Armand is by no means moral (in spite of the phraseology used), it is existential; it is only the logical consequence of the postulate of recognition, a superlative means (much better than love) of winning recognition from the world of the masters. And if Marguerite hides her sacrifice and gives it the mask of cynicism, this can only be at the moment when the argument really becomes Literature: the grateful and recognizing gaze of the bourgeois class is here delegated to the reader who in his turn *recognizes* Marguerite through the very mistake of her lover.

All this is to say that the misunderstandings which make the plot progress are not here of a psychological nature (even if the language in which they are expressed is abusively so): Armand and Marguerite do not belong socially to the same world and there can be no question between them of tragedy in the manner of Racine or subtle flirting in the manner of Marivaux. The conflict is exterior to them: we do not deal here with one passion divided against itself but with two passions of different natures, because they come from different situations in society. Armand's passion, which is bourgeois in type, and appropriative, is by definition a murder of the other; and that of Marguerite can only crown her effort to achieve recognition by a sacrifice which will in its turn constitute an indirect murder of Armand's passion. A simple social disparity, taken up and amplified by the opposition of two ideologies of love, cannot but produce here a hopeless entanglement, a hopelessness of which Marguerite's death (however cloying it is on the stage) is, so to speak, the algebraic symbol.

The difference between the two types of love stems of course from the difference of awareness in the two partners:

Armand lives in the essence of eternal love, Marguerite lives in the awareness of her alienation, she lives only through it: she knows herself to be, and in a sense *wills* herself to be a courtesan. And the behavior she adopts in order to adjust consists entirely in behavior meant to secure recognition: now she endorses her own legend exaggeratedly, and plunges into the whirlwind of the typical courtesan's life (like those homosexuals whose way of accepting their condition is to make it obvious), sometimes she makes one guess at a power to transcend her rank which aims to achieve recognition less for a "natural" virtue than for a devotion suited to her station, as if her sacrifice had the function, not of making manifest the murder of the courtesan she is, but on the contrary of flaunting a superlative courtesan, enhanced, without losing anything of her nature, with a bourgeois feeling of a high order.

Thus we begin to see better the mythological content of this love, which is the archetype of petit-bourgeois sentimentality. It is a very particular state of myth, defined by a semi-awareness, or to be more precise, a parasitic awareness. Marguerite *is aware* of her alienation, that is to say, she sees reality as an alienation. But she follows up this awareness by a purely servile behavior: either she plays the part which the masters expect from her, or she tries to reach a *value* which is in fact a part of this same world of the masters. In either case, Marguerite is never anything more than an alienated awareness: she sees that she suffers, but imagines no remedy which is not parasitic to her own suffering; she knows herself to be an object but cannot think of any destination for herself other than that of ornament in the museum of the masters. In spite of the grotesqueness of the plot, such a character does not lack a certain dramatic richness: true, it is neither tragic (the fate which weighs on Marguerite is social, not metaphysical), nor comic (Marguerite's behavior stems from her condition, not from her essence), nor as yet, of course, revolutionary (Marguerite brings no criticism to bear on her alienation). But at bottom she would need very little to achieve the status of the Brechtian character, which is an alienated object but a source of criticism. What puts this out of her reach—irremediably—is her positive side: Marguerite Gautier, "touching" because of her tuberculosis and her lofty speech, spreads to the whole of her public the contagion of her blindness: patently stupid, she would have opened their petit-bourgeois eyes. Magniloquent and noble, in one word, "serious," she only sends them to sleep.

1956

Myth Today

W<small>HAT</small> is a myth, today? I shall give at the outset a first, very simple answer, which is perfectly consistent with etymology: *myth is a type of speech.*[1]

MYTH IS A TYPE OF SPEECH

Of course, it is not *any* type: language needs special conditions in order to become myth: we shall see them in a minute. But what must be firmly established at the start is that myth is a system of communication, that it is a message. This allows one to perceive that myth cannot possibly be an object, a concept, or an idea; it is a mode of signification, a form. Later, we shall have to assign to this form historical limits, conditions of use, and reintroduce society into it: we must nevertheless first describe it as a form.

It can be seen that to purport to discriminate among mythical objects according to their substance would be entirely illusory: since myth is a type of speech, everything can be a myth provided it is conveyed by a discourse. Myth is not

From *Mythologies.*

[1] Innumerable other meanings of the word "myth" can be cited against this. But I have tried to define things, not words.

defined by the object of its message, but by the way in which it utters this message: there are formal limits to myth, there are no "substantial" ones. Everything, then, can be a myth? Yes, I believe this, for the universe is infinitely fertile in suggestions. Every object in the world can pass from a closed, silent existence to an oral state, open to appropriation by society, for there is no law, whether natural or not, which forbids talking about things. A tree is a tree. Yes, of course. But a tree as expressed by Minou Drouet is no longer quite a tree, it is a tree which is decorated, adapted to a certain type of consumption, laden with literary self-indulgence, revolt, images, in short with a type of social *usage* which is added to pure matter.

Naturally, everything is not expressed at the same time: some objects become the prey of mythical speech for a while, then they disappear, others take their place and attain the status of myth. Are there objects which are *inevitably* a source of suggestiveness, as Baudelaire suggested about Woman? Certainly not: one can conceive of very ancient myths, but there are no eternal ones; for it is human history which converts reality into speech, and it alone rules the life and the death of mythical language. Ancient or not, mythology can only have a historical foundation, for myth is a type of speech chosen by history: it cannot possibly evolve from the "nature" of things.

Speech of this kind is a message. It is therefore by no means confined to oral speech. It can consist of modes of writing or of representations; not only written discourse, but also photography, cinema, reporting, sport, shows, publicity, all these can serve as a support to mythical speech. Myth can be defined neither by its object nor by its material, for any material can arbitrarily be endowed with meaning: the arrow which is brought in order to signify a challenge is also a kind of speech. True, as far as perception is concerned, writing and pictures, for instance, do not call upon the same type of consciousness;

and even with pictures, one can use many kinds of reading: a diagram lends itself to signification more than a drawing, a copy more than an original, and a caricature more than a portrait. But this is the point: we are no longer dealing here with a theoretical mode of representation: we are dealing with *this* particular image, which is given for *this* particular signification. Mythical speech is made of a material which has *already* been worked on so as to make it suitable for communication: it is because all the materials of myth (whether pictorial or written) presuppose a signifying consciousness, that one can reason about them while discounting their substance. This substance is not unimportant: pictures, to be sure, are more imperative than writing, they impose meaning at one stroke, without analyzing or diluting it. But this is no longer a constitutive difference. Pictures become a kind of writing as soon as they are meaningful: like writing, they call for a *lexis*.

We shall therefore take *language, discourse, speech*, etc., to mean any significant unit or synthesis, whether verbal or visual: a photograph will be a kind of speech for us in the same way as a newspaper article; even objects will become speech, if they mean something. This generic way of conceiving language is in fact justified by the very history of writing: long before the invention of our alphabet, objects like the Inca *quipu*, or drawings, as in pictographs, have been accepted as speech. This does not mean that one must treat mythical speech like language; myth in fact belongs to the province of a general science, coextensive with linguistics, which is *semiology*.

MYTH AS A SEMIOLOGICAL SYSTEM

For mythology, since it is the study of a type of speech, is but one fragment of this vast science of signs which Saussure postulated some forty years ago under the name of *semiology*. Semiology has not yet come into being. But since Saussure himself, and sometimes independently of him, a whole section of contemporary research has constantly been referred to the problem of meaning: psychoanalysis, structuralism, eidetic psychology, some new types of literary criticism of which Bachelard has given the first examples, are no longer concerned with facts except inasmuch as they are endowed with significance. Now to postulate a signification is to have recourse to semiology. I do not mean that semiology could account for all these aspects of research equally well: they have different contents. But they have a common status: they are all sciences dealing with values. They are not content with meeting the facts: they define and explore them as tokens for something else.

Semiology is a science of forms, since it studies significations apart from their content. I should like to say one word about the necessity and the limits of such a formal science. The necessity is that which applies in the case of any exact language. Zhdanov made fun of Alexandrov the philosopher, who spoke of *"The spherical structure of our planet." "It was thought until now,"* Zhdanov said, *"that form alone could be spherical."* Zhdanov was right: one cannot speak about structures in terms of forms, and vice versa. It may well be that on the plane of "life," there is but a totality where structures and forms cannot be separated. But science has no use for the ineffable: it must speak about "life" if it wants to transform it. Against a certain quixotism of synthesis, quite platonic incidentally, all criticism must consent to the *ascesis*, to the artifice of analysis; and in analysis, it must match method and language. Less terrorized by the specter of "formalism," historical criticism might have been less sterile; it would have understood that the specific study of forms does not in any way contradict the necessary principles of totality and History. On the contrary: the more a system is specifically defined in its forms, the more amenable it is to historical criticism. To parody a well-known saying, I shall say that a little formalism turns one away from History, but that a lot brings one back to it. Is there a better example of total criticism than the description of saintliness, at once formal and historical, semiological and ideological, in Sartre's *Saint-Genet*? The danger, on the contrary, is to consider forms as ambiguous objects, half form and half substance, to endow form with a substance of form, as was done, for instance, by Zhdanovian realism. Semiology, once its limits are settled, is not a metaphysical trap: it is a science among others, necessary but not sufficient. The important thing is to see that the unity of an explanation cannot be based on the amputation of one or other of its approaches, but, as Engels said, on the dialectical coordination of the particular sciences it makes use of. This is the case with mythology: it is a part both of semiology inasmuch as it is a formal science, and of ideology inasmuch as it is a historical science: it studies ideas-in-form.[2]

Let me therefore restate that any semiology postulates a relation between two terms, a signifier and a signified. This relation concerns objects which belong to different categories, and this is why it is not one of equality but one of equivalence. We must here be on our guard, for despite common parlance which simply says that the signifier *expresses* the signified, we are dealing, in any semiological system, not with two, but with three different terms. For what we grasp is not at all one term after the other but the correlation which unites them: there are, therefore, the signifier, the signified, and the sign, which is the associative total of the first two terms. Take a bunch of roses: I use it to signify my passion. Do we have here, then,

---

[2] The development of publicity, of a national press, of radio, of illustrated news, not to speak of the survival of a myriad rites of communication which rule social appearances makes the development of a semiological science more urgent than ever. In a single day, how many really non-signifying fields do we cross? Very few, sometimes none. Here I am, before the sea; it is true that it bears no message. But on the beach, what material for semiology! Flags, slogans, signals, signboards, clothes, suntan even, which are so many messages to me.

only a signifier and a signified, the roses and my passion? Not even that: to put it accurately, there are here only "passioni-fied" roses. But on the plane of analysis, we do have three terms; for these roses weighted with passion perfectly and cor-rectly allow themselves to be decomposed into roses and pas-sion: the former and the latter existed before uniting and forming this third object, which is the sign. It is as true to say that on the plane of experience I cannot dissociate the roses from the message they carry, as to say that on the plane of analysis I cannot confuse the roses as signifier and the roses as sign: the signifier is empty, the sign is full, it is a meaning. Or take a black pebble: I can make it signify in several ways, it is a mere signifier; but if I weigh it with a definite signified (a death sentence, for instance, in an anonymous vote), it will become a sign. Naturally, there are between the signifier, the signified, and the sign, functional implications (such as that of the part to the whole) which are so close that to analyze them may seem futile; but we shall see in a moment that this distinc-tion has a capital importance for the study of myth as semio-logical schema.

Naturally these three terms are purely formal, and different contents can be given to them. Here are a few examples: for Saussure, who worked on a particular but methodologically exemplary semiological system—the language or *langue*—the signified is the concept, the signifier is the acoustic image (which is mental), and the relation between concept and image is the sign (the word, for instance), which is a concrete entity.[3] For Freud, as is well known, the human psyche is a stratification of tokens or representatives. One term (I refrain from giving it any precedence) is constituted by the manifest meaning of behavior, another, by its latent or real meaning (it is, for instance, the substratum of the dream); as for the third

[3] The notion of *word* is one of the most controversial in linguistics. I keep it here for the sake of simplicity.

term, it is here also a correlation of the first two: it is the dream itself in its totality, the parapraxis (a mistake in speech or behavior) or the neurosis, conceived as compromises, as economies effected thanks to the joining of a form (the first term) and an intentional function (the second term). We can see here how necessary it is to distinguish the sign from the signifier: a dream, to Freud, is no more its manifest datum than its latent content: it is the functional union of these two terms. In Sartrean criticism, finally (I shall keep to these three well-known examples), the signified is constituted by the original crisis in the subject (the separation from his mother for Baudelaire, the naming of the theft for Genet); Literature as discourse forms the signifier; and the relation between crisis and discourse defines the work, which is a signification. Of course, this tri-dimensional pattern, however constant in its form, is actualized in different ways: one cannot therefore say too often that semiology can have its unity only at the level of forms, not contents; its field is limited, it knows only one operation: reading, or deciphering.

In myth, we find again the tri-dimensional pattern which I have just described: the signifier, the signified, and the sign. But myth is a peculiar system, in that it is constructed from a semiological chain which existed before it: it *is a second-order semiological system*. That which is a sign (namely the associative total of a concept and an image) in the first system, becomes a mere signifier in the second. We must here recall that the materials of mythical speech (the language itself, photography, painting, posters, rituals, objects, etc.), however different at the start, are reduced to a pure signifying function as soon as they are caught by myth. Myth sees in them only the same raw material; their unity is that they all come down to the status of a mere language. Whether it deals with alphabetical or pictorial writing, myth wants to see in them only a sum of signs, a global sign, the final term of a first semiological chain. And it is precisely this final term which will become the first term of the greater system which it builds and of which it is only a part. Everything happens as if myth shifted the formal system of the first significations sideways. As this lateral shift is essential for the analysis of myth, I shall represent it in the following way, it being understood, of course, that the spatialization of the pattern is here only a metaphor:

Language	1. Signifier	2. Signified	
MYTH	3. Sign I SIGNIFIER		II SIGNIFIED
	III SIGN		

It can be seen that in myth there are two semiological systems, one of which is staggered in relation to the other: a linguistic system, the language (or the modes of representation which are assimilated to it), which I shall call the *language-object*, because it is the language which myth gets hold of in order to build its own system; and myth itself, which I shall call *metalanguage*, because it is a second language, *in which* one speaks about the first. When he reflects on a metalanguage, the semiologist no longer needs to ask himself questions about the composition of the language-object, he no longer has to take into account the details of the linguistic schema; he will only need to know its total term, or global sign, and only inasmuch as this term lends itself to myth. This is why the semiologist is entitled to treat in the same way writing and pictures: what he retains from them is the fact that they are both *signs*, that they both reach the threshold of myth endowed with the same signifying function, that they constitute, one just as much as the other, a language-object.

It is now time to give one or two examples of mythical speech. I shall borrow the first from an observation by

Valéry.[4] I am a pupil in the second form in a French *lycée*. I open my Latin grammar, and I read a sentence, borrowed from Aesop or Phaedrus: *quia ego nominor leo.* I stop and think. There is something ambiguous about this statement: on the one hand, the words in it do have a simple meaning: *because my name is lion.* And on the other hand, the sentence is evidently there in order to signify something else to me. Inasmuch as it is addressed to me, a pupil in the second form, it tells me clearly: I am a grammatical example meant to illustrate the rule about the agreement of the predicate. I am even forced to realize that the sentence in no way *signifies* its meaning to me, that it tries very little to tell me something about the lion and what sort of name he has; its true and fundamental signification is to impose itself on me as the presence of a certain agreement of the predicate. I conclude that I am faced with a particular, greater, semiological system, since it is co-extensive with the language: there is, indeed, a signifier, but this signifier is itself formed by a sum of signs, it is in itself a first semiological system (*my name is lion*). Thereafter, the formal pattern is correctly unfolded: there is a signified (*I am a grammatical example*) and there is a global signification, which is none other than the correlation of the signifier and the signified; for neither the naming of the lion nor the grammatical example is given separately.

And here is now another example: I am at the barber's, and a copy of *Paris-Match* is offered to me. On the cover, a young Negro in a French uniform is saluting, with his eyes uplifted, probably fixed on a fold of the tricolor. All this is the *meaning* of the picture. But, whether naïvely or not, I see very well what it signifies to me: that France is a great Empire, that all her sons, without any color discrimination, faithfully serve under her flag, and that there is no better answer to the de-

---

[4] *Tel Quel*, II.

tractors of an alleged colonialism than the zeal shown by this Negro in serving his so-called oppressors. I am therefore again faced with a greater semiological system: there is a signifier, itself already formed with a previous system (*a black soldier is giving the French salute*); there is a signified (it is here a purposeful mixture of Frenchness and militariness); finally, there is a presence of the signified through the signifier.

Before tackling the analysis of each term of the mythical system, one must agree on terminology. We now know that the signifier can be looked at, in myth, from two points of view: as the final term of the linguistic system, or as the first term of the mythical system. We therefore need two names. On the plane of language, that is, as the final term of the first system, I shall call the signifier: *meaning* (*my name is lion, a Negro is giving the French salute*); on the plane of myth, I shall call it: *form*. In the case of the signified, no ambiguity is possible: we shall retain the name *concept*. The third term is the correlation of the first two: in the linguistic system, it is the *sign*; but it is not possible to use this word again without ambiguity, since in myth (and this is the chief peculiarity of the latter), the signifier is already formed by the *signs* of the language. I shall call the third term of myth the *signification*. This word is here all the better justified since myth has in fact a double function: it points out and it notifies, it makes us understand something and it imposes it on us.

THE FORM AND THE CONCEPT

The signifier of myth presents itself in an ambiguous way: it is at the same time meaning and form, full on one side and empty on the other. As meaning, the signifier already postulates a reading, I grasp it through my eyes, it has a sensory reality (unlike the linguistic signifier, which is purely mental), there is a richness in it: the naming of the lion, the Negro's salute are credible wholes, they have at their disposal a suffi-

cient rationality. As a total of linguistic signs, the meaning of
the myth has its own value, it belongs to a history, that of the
lion or that of the Negro: in the meaning, a signification is
already built, and could very well be self-sufficient if myth did
not take hold of it and did not turn it suddenly into an empty,
parasitical form. The meaning is *already* complete, it postulates a kind of knowledge, a past, a memory, a comparative
order of facts, ideas, decisions.

When it becomes form, the meaning leaves its contingency
behind; it empties itself, it becomes impoverished, history
evaporates, only the letter remains. There is here a paradoxical permutation in the reading operations, an abnormal regres-
sion from meaning to form, from the linguistic sign to the
mythical signifier. If one encloses *quia ego nominor leo* in a
purely linguistic system, the clause finds again there a fullness,
a richness, a history: I am an animal, a lion, I live in a certain
country, I have just been hunting, they would have me share
my prey with a heifer, a cow and a goat; but being the stronger,
I award myself all the shares for various reasons, the last of
which is quite simply that *my name is lion.* But as the form of
the myth, the clause hardly retains anything of this long story.
The meaning contained a whole system of values: a history, a
geography, a morality, a zoology, a Literature. The form has
put all this richness at a distance: its newly acquired penury
calls for a signification to fill it. The story of the lion must
recede a great deal in order to make room for the grammatical
example, one must put the biography of the Negro in parentheses if one wants to free the picture, and prepare it to receive
its signified.

But the essential point in all this is that the form does not
suppress the meaning, it only impoverishes it, it puts it at a
distance, it holds it at one's disposal. One believes that the
meaning is going to die, but it is a death with reprieve; the
meaning loses its value, but keeps its life, from which the form

of the myth will draw its nourishment. The meaning will be for the form like an instantaneous reserve of history, a tamed richness, which it is possible to call and dismiss in a sort of rapid alternation: the form must constantly be able to be rooted again in the meaning and to get there what nature it needs for its nutriment; above all, it must be able to hide there. It is this constant game of hide-and-seek between the meaning and the form which defines myth. The form of myth is not a symbol: the Negro who salutes is not the symbol of the French Empire; he has too much presence, he appears as a rich, fully experienced, spontaneous, innocent, *indisputable* image. But at the same time this presence is tamed, put at a distance, made almost transparent; it recedes a little, it becomes the accomplice of a concept which comes to it fully armed, French imperiality: once made use of, it becomes artificial.

Let us now look at the signified: this history which drains out of the form will be wholly absorbed by the concept. As for the latter, it is determined, it is at once historical and intentional; it is the motivation which causes the myth to be uttered. Grammatical exemplarity, French imperiality, are the very drives behind the myth. The concept reconstitutes a chain of causes and effects, motives and intentions. Unlike the form, the concept is in no way abstract: it is filled with a situation. Through the concept, it is a whole new history which is implanted in the myth. Into the naming of the lion, first drained of its contingency, the grammatical example will attract my whole existence: Time, which caused me to be born at a certain period when Latin grammar is taught; History, which sets me apart, through a whole mechanism of social segregation, from the children who do not learn Latin; pedagogic tradition, which caused this example to be chosen from Aesop or Phaedrus; my own linguistic habits, which see the agreement of the predicate as a fact worthy of notice and illustration. The same goes for the Negro-giving-the-salute: as form, its meaning is shallow, isolated, impoverished; as the concept of French imperiality, here it is again tied to the totality of the world: to the general History of France, to its colonial adventures, to its present difficulties. Truth to tell, what is invested in the concept is less reality than a certain knowledge of reality; in passing from the meaning to the form, the image loses some knowledge: the better to receive the knowledge in the concept. In actual fact, the knowledge contained in a mythical concept is confused, made of yielding, shapeless associations. One must firmly stress this open character of the concept; it is not at all an abstract, purified essence; it is a formless, unstable, nebulous condensation, whose unity and coherence are above all due to its function.

In this sense, we can say that the fundamental character of the mythical concept is to be *appropriated*: grammatical exemplarity very precisely concerns a given form of pupils, French imperiality must appeal to such and such group of readers and not another. The concept closely corresponds to a function, it is defined as a tendency. This cannot fail to recall the signified in another semiological system, Freudianism. In Freud, the second term of the system is the latent meaning (the content) of the dream, of the parapraxis, of the neurosis. Now Freud does remark that the second-order meaning of behavior is its real meaning, that which is appropriate to a complete situation, including its deeper level; it is, just like the mythical concept, the very intention of behavior.

A signified can have several signifiers: this is indeed the case in linguistics and psychoanalysis. It is also the case in the mythical concept: it has at its disposal an unlimited mass of signifiers: I can find a thousand Latin sentences to actualize for me the agreement of the predicate, I can find a thousand images which signify to me French imperiality. This means that *quantitively*, the concept is much poorer than the signifier, it often does nothing but re-present itself. Poverty and richness are in reverse proportion in the form and the concept: to the qualitative poverty of the form, which is the repository of a rarefied meaning, there corresponds the richness of the concept which is open to the whole of History; and to the quantitative abundance of the forms there corresponds a small number of concepts. This repetition of the concept through different forms is precious to the mythologist, it allows him to decipher the myth: it is the insistence of a kind of behavior which reveals its intention. This confirms that there is no regular ratio between the volume of the signified and that of the signifier. In language, this ratio is proportionate, it hardly exceeds the word, or at least the concrete unit. In myth, on the contrary, the concept can spread over a very large expanse of signifier. For instance, a whole book may be the signifier of a single concept; and conversely, a minute form (a word, a gesture, even incidental, so long as it is noticed) can serve as signifier to a concept filled with a very rich history. Although unusual in language, this disproportion between signifier and signified is not specific to myth: in Freud, for instance, the parapraxis is a signifier whose thinness is out of proportion to the real meaning which it betrays.

As I said, there is no fixity in mythical concepts: they can come into being, alter, disintegrate, disappear completely. And it is precisely because they are historical that history can very easily suppress them. This instability forces the mythologist to use a terminology adapted to it, and about which I should now like to say a word, because it often is a cause for irony: I mean neologism. The concept is a constituting element of myth: if I want to decipher myths, I must somehow be able to name concepts. The dictionary supplies me with a few: Goodness, Kindness, Wholeness, Humaneness, etc. But by definition, since it is the dictionary which gives them to me, these particular concepts are not historical. Now what I need most often is ephemeral concepts, in connection with limited contingencies:

neologism is then inevitable. China is one thing, the idea which a French petit-bourgeois could have of it not so long ago is another: for this peculiar mixture of bells, rickshaws and opium dens, no other word possible but *Sininess*.[5] Unlovely? One should at least get some consolation from the fact that conceptual neologisms are never arbitrary: they are built according to a highly sensible proportional rule.

THE SIGNIFICATION

In semiology, the third term is nothing but the association of the first two, as we saw. It is the only one which is allowed to be seen in a full and satisfactory way, the only one which is consumed in actual fact. I have called it: the signification. We can see that the signification is the myth itself, just as the Saussurean sign is the word (or more accurately the concrete unit). But before listing the characters of the signification, one must reflect a little on the way in which it is prepared, that is, on the modes of correlation of the mythical concept and the mythical form.

First we must note that in myth, the first two terms are perfectly manifest (unlike what happens in other semiological systems): one of them is not "hidden" behind the other, they are both given *here* (and not one here and the other there). However paradoxical it may seem, *myth hides nothing*: its function is to distort, not to make disappear. There is no latency of the concept in relation to the form: there is no need of an unconscious in order to explain myth. Of course, one is dealing with two different types of manifestation: form has a literal, immediate presence; moreover, it is extended. This stems—this cannot be repeated too often—from the nature of the mythical signifier, which is already linguistic: since it is constituted by a meaning which is already outlined, it can

---

[5] Or perhaps *Sinity*? Just as if Latin/latinity = Basque/x, x = Basquity.

appear only through a given substance (whereas in language, the signifier remains mental). In the case of oral myth, this extension is linear (*for my name is lion*); in that of visual myth, it is multidimensional (in the center, the Negro's uniform, at the top, the blackness of his face, on the left, the military salute, etc.). The elements of the form therefore are related as to place and proximity: the mode of presence of the form is spatial. The concept, on the contrary, appears in global fashion, it is a kind of nebula, the condensation, more or less hazy, of a certain knowledge. Its elements are linked by associative relations: it is supported not by an extension but by a depth (although this metaphor is perhaps still too spatial): its mode of presence is memorial.

The relation which unites the concept of the myth to its meaning is essentially a relation of *deformation*. We find here again a certain formal analogy with a complex semiological system such as that of the various types of psychoanalysis. Just as for Freud the manifest meaning of behavior is distorted by its latent meaning, in myth the meaning is distorted by the concept. Of course, this distortion is possible only because the form of the myth is already constituted by a linguistic meaning. In a simple system like the language, the signified cannot distort anything at all because the signifier, being empty, arbitrary, offers no resistance to it. But here, everything is different: the signifier has, so to speak, two aspects: one full, which is the meaning (the history of the lion, of the Negro soldier), one empty, which is the form (*for my name is lion; Negro-French-soldier-saluting-the-tricolor*). What the concept distorts is of course what is full, the meaning: the lion and the Negro are deprived of their history, changed into gestures. What Latin exemplarity distorts is the naming of the lion, in all its contingency; and what French imperiality obscures is also a primary language, a factual discourse which was telling me about the salute of a Negro in uniform. But this distortion is not an obliteration: the lion and the Negro remain here, the concept needs them; they are half-amputated, they are deprived of memory, not of existence: they are at once stubborn, silently rooted there, and garrulous, a speech wholly at the service of the concept. The concept, literally, deforms, but does not abolish the meaning; a word can perfectly render this contradiction: it alienates it.

What must always be remembered is that myth is a double system; there occurs in it a sort of ubiquity: its point of departure is constituted by the arrival of a meaning. To keep a spatial metaphor, the approximative character of which I have already stressed, I shall say that the signification of the myth is constituted by a sort of constantly moving turnstile which presents alternately the meaning of the signifier and its form, a language-object and a metalanguage, a purely signifying and a purely imagining consciousness. This alternation is, so to speak, gathered up in the concept, which uses it like an ambiguous signifier, at once intellective and imaginary, arbitrary and natural.

I do not wish to prejudge the moral implications of such a mechanism, but I shall not exceed the limits of an objective analysis if I point out that the ubiquity of the signifier in myth exactly reproduces the physique of the *alibi* (which is, as one realizes, a spatial term): in the alibi too, there is a place which is full and one which is empty, linked by a relation of negative identity ("I am not where you think I am; I am where you think I am not"). But the ordinary alibi (for the police, for instance) has an end; reality stops the turnstile revolving at a certain point. Myth is a *value*, truth is no guarantee for it; nothing prevents it from being a perpetual alibi: it is enough that its signifier has two sides for it always to have an "elsewhere" at its disposal. The meaning is always there to *present*

the form; the form is always there to *outdistance* the meaning.
And there never is any contradiction, conflict, or split between
the meaning and the form: they are never at the same place. In
the same way, if I am in a car and I look at the scenery
through the window, I can at will focus on the scenery or on
the windowpane. At one moment I grasp the presence of the
glass and the distance of the landscape; at another, on the
contrary, the transparence of the glass and the depth of
the landscape; but the result of this alternation is constant: the
glass is at once present and empty to me, and the landscape
unreal and full. The same thing occurs in the mythical signifier: its form is empty but present, its meaning absent but full.
To wonder at this contradiction I must voluntarily interrupt
this turnstile of form and meaning, I must focus on each separately, and apply to myth a static method of deciphering, in
short, I must go against its own dynamics: to sum up, I must
pass from the state of reader to that of mythologist.

And it is again this duplicity of the signifier which determines the characters of the signification. We now know that
myth is a type of speech defined by its intention (*I am a
grammatical example*) much more than by its literal sense
(*my name is lion*); and that in spite of this, its intention is
somehow frozen, purified, eternalized, *made absent* by this
literal sense (*The French Empire? It's just a fact: look at this
good Negro who salutes like one of our own boys*). This constituent ambiguity of mythical speech has two consequences
for the signification, which henceforth appears both like a noti-
fication and like a statement of fact.

Myth has an imperative, buttonholing character: stemming
from a historical concept, directly springing from contingency
(a Latin class, a threatened Empire), it is *I* whom it has come
to seek. It is turned toward me, I am subjected to its intentional force, it summons me to receive its expansive ambiguity.
If, for instance, I take a walk in Spain, in the Basque coun-

try,[6] I may well notice in the houses an architectural unity, a common style, which leads me to acknowledge the Basque house as a definite ethnic product. However, I do not feel personally concerned, nor, so to speak, attacked by this unitary style: I see only too well that it was here before me, without me. It is a complex product which has its determinations at the level of a very wide history: it does not call out to me, it does not provoke me into naming it, except if I think of inserting it into a vast picture of rural habitat. But if I am in the Paris region and I catch a glimpse, at the end of the rue Gambetta or the rue Jean Jaurès, of a natty white chalet with red tiles, dark brown half timbering, an asymmetrical roof and a wattle-and-daub front, I feel as if I were personally receiving an imperious injunction to name this object a Basque chalet: or even better, to see it as the very essence of *basquity*. This is because the concept appears to me in all its appropriative nature: it comes and seeks me out in order to oblige me to acknowledge the body of intentions which have motivated it and arranged it there as the signal of an individual history, as a confidence and a complicity: it is a real call, which the owners of the chalet send out to me. And this call, in order to be more imperious, has agreed to all manner of impoverishments: all that justified the Basque house on the plane of technology—the barn, the outside stairs, the dovecote, etc.— has been dropped; there remains only a brief order, not to be disputed. And the adhomination is so frank that I feel this chalet has just been created on the spot, *for me*, like a magical object springing up in my present life without any trace of the history which has caused it.

For this interpellant speech is at the same time a frozen speech: at the moment of reaching me, it suspends itself, turns away and assumes the look of a generality: it stiffens, it makes

---

[6] I say "in Spain" because, in France, petit-bourgeois advancement has caused a whole "mythical" architecture of the Basque chalet to flourish.

itself look neutral and innocent. The appropriation of the concept is suddenly driven away once more by the literalness of
the meaning. This is a kind of *arrest*, in both the physical and
the legal sense of the term: French imperiality condemns the
saluting Negro to be nothing more than an instrumental signifier, the Negro suddenly hails me in the name of French imperiality; but at the same moment the Negro's salute thickens,
becomes vitrified, freezes into an eternal reference meant to
establish French imperiality. On the surface of language something has stopped moving: the use of the signification is here,
hiding behind the fact, and conferring on it a notifying look;
but at the same time, the fact paralyzes the intention, gives it
something like a malaise producing immobility: in order to
make it innocent, it freezes it. This is because myth is speech
stolen and restored. Only, speech which is restored is no
longer quite that which was stolen: when it was brought back,
it was not put exactly in its place. It is this brief act of larceny,
this moment taken for a surreptitious faking, which gives
mythical speech its benumbed look.

One last element of the signification remains to be examined: its motivation. We know that in a language, the sign is
arbitrary: nothing compels the acoustic image *tree* "naturally"
to mean the concept *tree*: the sign, here, is unmotivated. Yet
this arbitrariness has limits, which come from the associative
relations of the word: the language can produce a whole fragment of the sign by analogy with other signs (for instance one
says *aimable* in French, and not *amable*, by analogy with
aime). The mythical signification, on the other hand, is never
arbitrary; it is always in part motivated, and unavoidably contains some analogy. For Latin exemplarity to meet the naming
of the lion, there must be an analogy, which is the agreement
of the predicate; for French imperiality to get hold of the
saluting Negro, there must be identity between the Negro's
salute and that of the French soldier. Motivation is necessary

to the very duplicity of myth: myth plays on the analogy between meaning and form, there is no myth without motivated
form.[7] In order to grasp the power of motivation in myth, it is
enough to reflect for a moment on an extreme case. I have
here before me a collection of objects so lacking in order that I
can find no *meaning* in it; it would seem that here, deprived of
any previous meaning, the form could not root its analogy in
anything, and that myth is impossible. But what the form can
always give one to read is disorder itself: it can give a signification to the absurd, make the absurd itself a myth. This is
what happens when common sense mythifies surrealism, for
instance. Even the absence of motivation does not embarrass
myth; for this absence will itself be sufficiently objectified to
become legible: and finally, the absence of motivation will
become a second-order motivation, and myth will be re-estab-
lished.

Motivation is unavoidable. It is nonetheless very fragmentary. To start with, it is not "natural": it is history which
supplies its analogies to the form. Then, the analogy between
the meaning and the concept is never anything but partial: the
form drops many analogous features and keeps only a few:
it keeps the sloping roof, the visible beams in the Basque
chalet, it abandons the stairs, the barn, the weathered look,
etc. One must even go further: a *complete* image would exclude myth, or at least would compel it to seize only its very
completeness. This is just what happens in the case of bad
painting, which is wholly based on the myth of what is "filled

---

[7] From the point of view of ethics, what is disturbing in myth is precisely
that its form is motivated. For if there is a "health" of language, it is the
arbitrariness of the sign which is its grounding. What is sickening in myth
is its resort to a false nature, its superabundance of significant forms, as in
these objects which decorate their usefulness with a natural appearance. The
will to weigh the signification with the full guarantee of nature causes a kind
of nausea: myth is too rich, and what is in excess is precisely its motivation.
This nausea is like the one I feel before the arts which refuse to choose
between *physis* and *anti-physis*, using the first as an ideal and the second as
an economy. Ethically, there is a kind of baseness in hedging one's bets.

out" and "finished" (it is the opposite and symmetrical case of the myth of the absurd: here, the form mythifies an "absence," there, a surplus). But in general myth prefers to work with poor, incomplete images, where the meaning is already relieved of its fat, and ready for a signification, such as caricatures, pastiches, symbols, etc. Finally, the motivation is chosen among other possible ones: I can very well give to French imperiality many other signifiers beside a Negro's salute: a French general pins a decoration on a one-armed Senegalese, a nun hands a cup of tea to a bedridden Arab, a white schoolmaster teaches attentive pickaninnies: the press undertakes every day to demonstrate that the store of mythical signifiers is inexhaustible.

The nature of the mythical signification can in fact be well conveyed by one particular simile: it is neither more nor less arbitrary than an ideograph. Myth is a pure ideographic system, where the forms are still motivated by the concept which they represent while not yet, by a long way, covering the sum of its possibilities for representation. And just as, historically, ideographs have gradually left the concept and have become associated with the sound, thus growing less and less motivated, the worn-out state of a myth can be recognized by the arbitrariness of its signification: the whole of Molière is seen in a doctor's ruff.

READING AND DECIPHERING MYTH

How is a myth received? We must here once more come back to the duplicity of its signifier, which is at once meaning and form. It can produce three different types of reading by focusing on the one, or the other, or both at the same time.[8]

1. If I focus on an empty signifier, I let the concept fill the

---

[8] The freedom in choosing what one focuses on is a problem which does not belong to the province of semiology: it depends on the concrete situation of the subject.

form of the myth without ambiguity, and I find myself before a simple system, where the signification becomes literal again: the Negro who salutes is an *example* of French imperiality, he is a *symbol* for it. This type of focusing is, for instance, that of the producer of myths, of the journalist who starts with a concept and seeks a form for it.[9]

2. If I focus on a full signifier, in which I clearly distinguish the meaning and the form, and consequently the distortion which the one imposes on the other, I undo the signification of the myth, and I receive the latter as an imposture: the saluting Negro becomes the *alibi* of French imperiality. This type of focusing is that of the mythologist: he deciphers the myth, he understands a distortion.

3. Finally, if I focus on the mythical signifier as on an inextricable whole made of meaning and form, I receive an ambiguous signification: I respond to the constituting mechanism of myth, to its own dynamics, I become a reader of myths. The saluting Negro is no longer an example or a symbol, still less an alibi: he is the very *presence* of French imperiality.

The first two types of focusing are static, analytical; they destroy the myth, either by making its intention obvious, or by unmasking it: the former is cynical, the latter demystifying. The third type of focusing is dynamic, it consumes the myth according to the very ends built into its structure: the reader lives the myth as a story at once true and unreal.

If one wishes to connect a mythical schema to a general history, to explain how it corresponds to the interests of a definite society, in short, to pass from semiology to ideology, it is obviously at the level of the third type of focusing that one must place oneself: it is the reader of myths himself who must reveal their essential function. How does he receive this par-

---

[9] We receive the naming of the lion as a pure *example* of Latin grammar because we are, *as grownups*, in a creative position in relation to it. I shall come back later to the value of the context in this mythical schema.

ticular myth *today*? If he receives it in an innocent fashion, what is the point of proposing it to him? And if he reads it using his powers of reflection, like the mythologist, does it matter which alibi is presented? If the reader does not see French imperiality in the saluting Negro, it was not worth weighing the latter with it; and if he sees it, the myth is nothing more than a political proposition, honestly expressed. In one word, either the intention of the myth is too obscure to be efficacious, or it is too clear to be believed. In either case, where is the ambiguity?

This is but a false dilemma. Myth hides nothing and flaunts nothing: it distorts; myth is neither a lie nor a confession: it is an inflection. Placed before the dilemma which I mentioned a moment ago, myth finds a third way out. Threatened with disappearance if it yields to either of the first two types of focusing, it gets out of this tight spot thanks to a compromise —it *is* this compromise. Entrusted with "glossing over" an intentional concept, myth encounters nothing but betrayal in language, for language can only obliterate the concept if it hides it, or unmask it if it formulates it. The elaboration of a second-order semiological system will enable myth to escape this dilemma: driven to having either to unveil or to liquidate the concept, it will *naturalize* it.

We reach here the very principle of myth: it transforms history into Nature. We now understand why, *in the eyes of the myth consumer*, the intention, the adhomination of the concept can remain manifest without however appearing to have an interest in the matter: what causes mythical speech to be uttered is perfectly explicit, but it is immediately frozen into something natural; it is not read as a motive, but as a reason. If I read the Negro-saluting as symbol pure and simple of imperiality, I must renounce the reality of the picture, it discredits itself in my eyes when it becomes an instrument. Conversely, if I decipher the Negro's salute as an alibi of coloniality, I shatter the myth even more surely by the obviousness of its motivation. But for the myth reader, the outcome is quite different: everything happens as if the picture *naturally* conjured up the concept, as if the signifier *gave a foundation* to the signified: the myth exists from the precise moment when French imperiality achieves the natural state: myth is speech justified *in excess*.

Here is a new example which will help understand clearly how the myth reader is led to rationalize the signified by means of the signifier. We are in the month of July, I read a big headline in *France-Soir*: THE FALL IN PRICES: FIRST INDICATIONS. VEGETABLES: PRICE DROP BEGINS. Let us quickly sketch the semiological schema: the example being a sentence, the first system is purely linguistic. The signifier of the second system is composed here of a certain number of accidents, some lexical (the words: *first, begins, the* [fall]), some typographical (enormous headlines where the reader usually sees news of world importance). The signified or concept is what must be called by a barbarous but unavoidable neologism: *governmentality*, the Government presented by the national press as the Essence of efficacy. The signification of the myth follows clearly from this: fruit and vegetable prices are falling *because* the government has so decided. Now it so happens in this case (and this is on the whole fairly rare) that the newspaper itself has, two lines below, allowed one to see through the myth which it had just elaborated—whether this is due to self-assurance or honesty. It adds (in small type, it is true): "The fall in prices is helped by the return of seasonal abundance." This example is instructive for two reasons. Firstly it conspicuously shows that myth essentially aims at causing an immediate impression—it does not matter if one is later allowed to see through the myth, its action is assumed to be stronger than the rational explanations which may later belie it. This means that the reading of a myth is exhausted at one stroke. I cast a quick glance at my neighbor's *France-Soir*: I cull only a *meaning* there, but I read a true signification; I *receive* the presence of governmental action in the fall in fruit and vegetable prices. That is all, and that is enough. A more attentive reading of the myth will in no way increase its power or its ineffectiveness: a myth is at the same time imperfectible and unquestionable; time or knowledge will not make it better or worse.

Secondly, the naturalization of the concept, which I have just identified as the essential function of myth, is here exemplary. In a first (exclusively linguistic) system, causality would be, literally, natural: fruit and vegetable prices fall because they are in season. In the second (mythical) system, causality is artificial, false; but it creeps, so to speak, through the back door of Nature. This is why myth is experienced as innocent speech: not because its intentions are hidden—if they were hidden, they could not be efficacious—but because they are naturalized.

In fact, what allows the reader to consume myth innocently is that he does not see it as a semiological system but as an inductive one. Where there is only an equivalence, he sees a kind of causal process: the signifier and the signified have, in his eyes, a natural relationship. This confusion can be expressed otherwise: any semiological system is a system of values; now the myth consumer takes the signification for a system of facts: myth is read as a factual system, whereas it is but a semiological system.

MYTH AS STOLEN LANGUAGE

What is characteristic of myth? To transform a meaning into form. In other words, myth is always a language robbery. I rob the Negro who is saluting, the white and brown chalet, the seasonal fall in fruit prices, not to make them into examples or symbols, but to naturalize through them the Empire, my taste for Basque things, the Government. Are all primary languages a prey for myth? Is there no meaning which can resist this capture with which form threatens it? In fact, nothing can be safe from myth, myth can develop its second-order schema from any meaning and, as we saw, start from the very lack of meaning. But all languages do not resist equally well.

Articulated language, which is most often robbed by myth, offers little resistance. It contains in itself some mythical dispositions, the outline of a sign structure meant to manifest the intention which led to its being used: it is what could be called the *expressiveness* of language. The imperative or the subjunctive mode, for instance, are the form of a particular signified, different from the meaning: the signified is here my will or my request. This is why some linguists have defined the indicative, for instance, as a zero state or degree, compared to the subjunctive or the imperative. Now in a fully constituted myth, the meaning is never at zero degree, and this is why the concept can distort it, naturalize it. We must remember once again that the privation of meaning is in no way a zero degree: this is why myth can perfectly well get hold of it, give it for instance the signification of the absurd, of surrealism, etc. At bottom, it would only be the zero degree which could resist myth.

Language lends itself to myth in another way: it is very rare that it imposes at the outset a full meaning which it is impossible to distort. This comes from the abstractness of its concept: the concept of *tree* is vague, it lends itself to multiple contingencies. True, a language always has at its disposal a whole appropriating organization (*this* tree, *the* tree *which*, etc.). But there always remains, around the final meaning, a halo of virtualities where other possible meanings are floating: the meaning can almost always be *interpreted*. One could say that a language offers to myth an open-work meaning. Myth can easily insinuate itself into it, and swell there: it is a robbery by colonization (for instance: *the* fall in prices has started. But what fall? That due to the season or that due to the government? the signification becomes here a parasite of the article, in spite of the latter being definite).

When the meaning is too full for myth to be able to invade it, myth goes around it, and carries it away bodily. This is what happens to mathematical language. In itself, it cannot be distorted, it has taken all possible precautions against *interpretation*: no parasitical signification can worm itself into it. And this is why, precisely, myth takes it away en bloc; it takes a certain mathematical formula ($E = mc^2$), and makes of this unalterable meaning the pure signifier of mathematicity. We can see that what is here robbed by myth is something which resists, something pure. Myth can reach everything, corrupt everything, and even the very act of refusing oneself to it. So that the more the language-object resists at first, the greater its final prostitution; whoever here resists completely yields completely: Einstein on one side, *Paris-Match* on the other. One can give a temporal image of this conflict: mathematical language is a *finished* language, which derives its very perfection from this acceptance of death. Myth, on the contrary, is a language which does not want to die: it wrests from the meanings which give it its sustenance an insidious, degraded survival, it provokes in them an artificial reprieve in which it settles comfortably, it turns them into speaking corpses.

Here is another language which resists myth as much as it can: our poetic language. Contemporary poetry[10] is *a regressive semiological system*. Whereas myth aims at an ultra-signification, at the amplification of a first system, poetry, on the

---

[10] Classical poetry, on the contrary, would be, according to such norms, a strongly mythical system, since it imposes on the meaning one extra signified, which is *regularity*. The alexandrine, for instance, has value both as meaning of a discourse and as signifier of a new whole, which is its poetic signification. Success, when it occurs, comes from the degree of apparent fusion of the two systems. It can be seen that we deal in no way with a harmony between content and form, but with an *elegant* absorption of one form into another.

contrary, attempts to regain an infra-signification, a pre-semiological state of language; in short, it tries to transform the sign
back into meaning: its ideal, ultimately, would be to reach not
the meaning of words, but the meaning of things themselves.[11] This is why it clouds the language, increases as much
as it can the abstractness of the concept and the arbitrariness
of the sign and stretches to the limit the link between signifier
and signified. The open-work structure of the concept is here
maximally exploited: unlike what happens in prose, it is all the
potential of the signified that the poetic sign tries to actualize,
in the hope of at last reaching something like the transcendent
quality of the thing, its natural (not human) meaning. Hence
the essentialist ambitions of poetry, the conviction that it alone
catches *the thing in itself*, inasmuch, precisely, as it wants to
be an anti-language. All told, of all those who use speech,
poets are the least formalist, for they are the only ones who
believe that the meaning of the words is only a form, with
which they, being realists, cannot be content. This is why our
modern poetry always asserts itself as a murder of language, a
kind of spatial, tangible analogue of silence. Poetry occupies a
position which is the reverse of that of myth: myth is a semiological system which has the pretension of transcending itself
into a factual system; poetry is a semiological system which
has the pretension of contracting into an essential system.

But here again, as in the case of mathematical language, the
very resistance offered by poetry makes it an ideal prey for
myth: the apparent lack of order of signs, which is the poetic
facet of an essential order, is captured by myth, and transformed into an empty signifier, which will serve to *signify*

By *elegance* I mean the most economical use of the means employed. It is
because of an age-old abuse that critics confuse *meaning* and *content*. The
language is never anything but a system of forms, and the meaning is a
form.

[11] We are again dealing here with the *meaning*, in Sartre's use of the term,
as a natural quality of things, situated outside a semiological system (*Saint-
Genet*).

poetry. This explains the *improbable* character of modern poetry: by fiercely refusing myth, poetry surrenders to it bound hand and foot. Conversely, the *rules* in classical poetry constituted an accepted myth, the conspicuous arbitrariness of which amounted to perfection of a kind, since the equilibrium of a semiological system comes from the arbitrariness of its signs.

A voluntary acceptance of myth can in fact define the whole of our traditional Literature. According to our norms, this Literature is an undoubted mythical system: there is a meaning, that of the discourse; there is a signifier, which is this same discourse as form or writing; there is a signified, which is the concept of literature; there is a signification, which is the literary discourse. I began to discuss this problem in *Writing Degree Zero*, which was, all told, nothing but a mythology of literary language. There I defined writing as the signifier of the literary myth, that is, as a form which is already filled with meaning and which receives from the concept of Literature a new signification.[12] I suggested that history, in modifying the writer's consciousness, had provoked, a hundred years or so ago, a moral crisis of literary language: writing was revealed as signifier, Literature as signification; rejecting the false nature of traditional literary language, the writer violently shifted his position in the direction of an anti-nature of language. The subversion of writing was the radical act by which a number of writers have attempted to reject Literature as a mythical system. Every revolt of this kind has been a murder of Literature as signification: all have postulated the reduction of literary

---

[12] *Style*, at least as I defined it then, is not a form, it does not belong to the province of a semiological analysis of Literature. In fact, style is a substance constantly threatened with formalization. To start with, it can perfectly well become degraded into a mode of writing: there is a "Malraux-type" writing, and even in Malraux himself. Then, style can also become a particular language, that used by the writer *for himself and for himself alone*. Style then becomes a sort of solipsistic myth, the language which the writer speaks *to himself*. It is easy to understand that at such a degree of solidification, style calls for a deciphering. The works of J. P. Richard are an example of this necessary critique of styles.

discourse to a simple semiological system, or even, in the case of poetry, to a pre-semiological system. This is an immense task, which required radical types of behavior: it is well known that some went as far as the pure and simple scuttling of the discourse, silence—whether real or transposed—appearing as the only possible weapon against the major power of myth: its recurrence.

It thus appears that it is extremely difficult to vanquish myth from the inside: for the very effort one makes in order to escape its stranglehold becomes in its turn the prey of myth: myth can always, as a last resort, signify the resistance which is brought to bear against it. Truth to tell, the best weapon against myth is perhaps to mythify it in its turn, and to produce an *artificial myth*: and this reconstituted myth will in fact be a mythology. Since myth robs language of something, why not rob myth? All that is needed is to use it as the departure point for a third semiological chain, to take its signification as the first term of a second myth. Literature offers some great examples of such artificial mythologies. I shall only evoke here Flaubert's *Bouvard and Pécuchet*. It is what could be called an experimental myth, a second-order myth. Bouvard and his friend Pécuchet represent a certain kind of bourgeoisie (which is incidentally in conflict with other bourgeois strata): their discourse *already* constitutes a mythical type of speech; its language does have a meaning, but this meaning is the empty form of a conceptual signified, which here is a kind of technological unsatedness. The meeting of meaning and concept forms, in this first mythical system, a signification which is the rhetoric of Bouvard and Pécuchet. It is at this point (I am breaking the process into its components for the sake of analysis) that Flaubert intervenes: to this first mythical system, which already is a second semiological system, he superimposes a third chain, in which the first link is the signification, or final term, of the first myth. The rhetoric of Bouvard and Pécuchet becomes the form of the new system; the concept here is due to Flaubert himself, to Flaubert's gaze on the myth which Bouvard and Pécuchet had built for themselves: it consists of their natively ineffectual inclinations, their inability to feel satisfied, the panic succession of their apprenticeships, in short what I would very much like to call (but I see storm clouds on the horizon): bouvard-and-pécuchet-ity. As for the final signification, it is the book, it is *Bouvard and Pécuchet* for us. The power of the second myth is that it gives the first its basis as a naïveté which is looked at. Flaubert has undertaken a real archaeological restoration of a given mythical speech: he is the Viollet-le-Duc of a certain bourgeois ideology. But less naïve than Viollet-le-Duc, he has strewn his reconstitution with supplementary ornaments which demystify it. These ornaments (which are the form of the second myth) are subjunctive in kind: there is a semiological equivalence between the subjunctive restitution of the discourse of Bouvard and Pécuchet and their ineffectualness.[13]

Flaubert's great merit (and that of all artificial mythologies: there are remarkable ones in Sartre's work) is that he gave to the problem of realism a frankly semiological solution. True, it is a somewhat incomplete merit, for Flaubert's ideology, since the bourgeois was for him only an aesthetic eyesore, was not at all realistic. But at least he avoided the major sin in literary matters, which is to confuse ideological with semiological reality. As ideology, literary realism does not depend at all on the language spoken by the writer. Language is a form, it cannot possibly be either realistic or unrealistic. All it can do is either to be mythical or not, or perhaps, as in *Bouvard and Pécuchet*, countermythical. Now, unfortunately, there is no antipathy between realism and myth. It is well known how often our

[13] A subjunctive form because it is in the subjunctive mode that Latin expressed "indirect style or discourse," which is an admirable instrument for demystification.

"realistic" literature is mythical (if only as a crude myth of realism) and how our "literature of the unreal" has at least the merit of being only slightly so. The wise thing would of course be to define the writer's realism as an essentially ideological problem. This certainly does not mean that there is no responsibility of form toward reality. But this responsibility can be measured only in semiological terms. A form can be judged (since forms are on trial) only as signification, not as expression. The writer's language is not expected to *represent* reality, but to signify it. This should impose on critics the duty of using two rigorously distinct methods: one must deal with the writer's realism either as an ideological substance (Marxist themes in Brecht's work, for instance) or as a semiological value (the props, the actors, the music, the colors in Brechtian dramaturgy). The ideal of course would be to combine these two types of criticism; the mistake which is constantly made is to confuse them: ideology has its methods, and so has semiology.

THE BOURGEOISIE AS A JOINT-STOCK COMPANY

Myth lends itself to history in two ways: by its form, which is only relatively motivated; by its concept, the nature of which is historical. One can therefore imagine a diachronic study of myths, whether one submits them to a retrospection (which means founding an historical mythology) or whether one follows some of yesterday's myths down to their present forms (which means founding prospective history). If I keep here to a synchronic sketch of contemporary myths, it is for an objective reason: our society is the privileged field of mythical significations. We must now say why.

Whatever the accidents, the compromises, the concessions and the political adventures, whatever the technical, economic, or even social changes which history brings us, our society is still a bourgeois society. I am not forgetting that since 1789, in

France, several types of bourgeoisie have succeeded one another in power; but the same status—a certain regime of ownership, a certain order, a certain ideology—remains at a deeper level. Now a remarkable phenomenon occurs in the matter of naming this regime: as an economic fact, the bourgeoisie is *named* without any difficulty: capitalism is openly professed.[14] As a political fact, the bourgeoisie has some difficulty in acknowledging itself: there are no "bourgeois" parties in the Chamber. As an ideological fact, it completely disappears: the bourgeoisie has obliterated its name in passing from reality to representation, from economic man to mental man. It comes to an agreement with the facts, but does not compromise about values, it makes its status undergo a real *exnominating* operation: the bourgeoisie is defined as *the social class which does not want to be named*. "Bourgeois," "petit-bourgeois," "capitalism,"[15] "proletariat"[16] are the locus of an unceasing hemorrhage: meaning flows out of them until their very name becomes unnecessary.

This ex-nominating phenomenon is important; let us examine it a little more closely. Politically, the hemorrhage of the name "bourgeois" is effected through the idea of *nation*. This was once a progressive idea, which has served to get rid of the aristocracy; today, the bourgeoisie merges into the nation, even if it has, in order to do so, to exclude from it the elements which it decides are allogenous (the Communists). This planned syncretism allows the bourgeoisie to attract the numerical support of its temporary allies, all the intermediate, therefore "shapeless" classes. A long-continued use of the

---

[14] "The fate of capitalism is to make the worker wealthy," *Paris-Match* tells us.
[15] The word "capitalism" is taboo, not economically, but ideologically; it cannot possibly enter the vocabulary of bourgeois representations. Only in Farouk's Egypt could a prisoner be condemned by a tribunal for "anti-capitalist plotting" in so many words.
[16] The bourgeoisie never uses the word "Proletariat," which is supposed to be a left-wing myth, except when it is in its interest to imagine the Proletariat being led astray by the Communist Party.

word *nation* has failed to depoliticize it in depth; the political substratum is there, very near the surface, and some circumstances make it suddenly manifest. There are in the Chamber some "national" parties, and nominal syncretism here makes conspicuous what it had the ambition of hiding: an essential disparity. Thus the political vocabulary of the bourgeoisie already postulates that the universal exists: for it, politics is already a representation, a fragment of ideology.

Politically, in spite of the universalistic effort of its vocabulary, the bourgeoisie eventually strikes against a resisting core which is, by definition, the revolutionary party. But this party can constitute only a political richness: in a bourgeois culture, there is neither proletarian culture nor proletarian morality, there is no proletarian art; ideologically, all that is not bourgeois is obliged to *borrow* from the bourgeoisie. Bourgeois ideology can therefore spread over everything and in so doing lose its name without risk: no one here will throw this name of bourgeois back at it. It can without resistance subsume bourgeois theater, art, and humanity under their eternal analogues; in a word, it can ex-nominate itself without restraint when there is only one single human nature left: the defection from the name "bourgeois" is here complete.

True, there are revolts against bourgeois ideology. This is what one generally calls the avant-garde. But these revolts are socially limited, they remain open to salvage. First, because they come from a small section of the bourgeoisie itself, from a minority group of artists and intellectuals, without public other than the class which they contest, and who remain dependent on its money in order to express themselves. Then, these revolts always get their inspiration from a very strongly made distinction between the ethically and the politically bourgeois: what the avant-garde contests is the bourgeois in art or morals—the shopkeeper, the Philistine, as in the heyday of Romanticism; but as for political contestation, there is none.[17] What the avant-garde does not tolerate about the bourgeoisie is its language, not its status. This does not necessarily mean that it approves of this status; simply, it leaves it aside. Whatever the violence of the provocation, the nature it finally endorses is that of "derelict" man, not alienated man; and derelict man is still Eternal Man.[18]

This anonymity of the bourgeoisie becomes even more marked when one passes from bourgeois culture proper to its derived, vulgarized, and applied forms, to what one could call public philosophy, that which sustains everyday life, civil ceremonials, secular rites, in short, the unwritten norms of interrelationships in a bourgeois society. It is an illusion to reduce the dominant culture to its inventive core: there also is a bourgeois culture which consists of consumption alone. The whole of France is steeped in this anonymous ideology: our press, our films, our theater, our pulp literature, our rituals, our Justice, our diplomacy, our conversations, our remarks about the weather, a murder trial, a touching wedding, the cooking we dream of, the garments we wear, everything, in everyday life, is dependent on the representation which the bourgeoisie *has and makes us have* of the relations between man and the world. These "normalized" forms attract little attention, by the very fact of their extension, in which their origin is easily lost. They enjoy an intermediate position: being neither directly political nor directly ideological, they live peacefully between the action of the militants and the quarrels of the intellectuals; more or less abandoned by the former and the latter, they gravitate toward the enormous

[17] It is remarkable that the adversaries of the bourgeoisie on matters of ethics or aesthetics remain for the most part indifferent, or even attached, to its political determinations. Conversely, its political adversaries neglect to issue a basic condemnation of its representations: they often go so far as to share them. This diversity of attacks benefits the bourgeoisie, it allows it to camouflage its name. For the bourgeoisie should be understood only as synthesis of its determinations and its representations.

[18] There can be figures of derelict man which lack all order (Ionesco, for example). This does not affect in any way the security of the Essences.

mass of the undifferentiated, of the insignificant, in short, of Nature. Yet it is through its ethic that the bourgeoisie pervades France: practiced on a national scale, bourgeois norms are experienced as the evident laws of a natural order—the further the bourgeois class propagates its representations, the more naturalized they become. The fact of the bourgeoisie becomes absorbed into an amorphous universe, whose sole inhabitant is Eternal Man, who is neither proletarian nor bourgeois.

It is therefore by penetrating the intermediate classes that the bourgeois ideology can most surely lose its name. Petit-bourgeois norms are the residue of bourgeois culture, they are bourgeois truths which have become degraded, impoverished, commercialized, slightly archaic, or shall we say, out of date? The political alliance of the bourgeoisie and the petite bourgeoisie has for more than a century determined the history of France; it has rarely been broken, and each time only temporarily (1848, 1871, 1936). This alliance got closer as time passed, it gradually became a symbiosis; transient awakenings might happen, but the common ideology was never questioned again. The same "natural" varnish covers up all "national" representations: the big wedding of the bourgeoisie, which originates in a class ritual (the display and consumption of wealth), can bear no relation to the economic status of the lower middle class: but through the press, the news, and literature, it slowly becomes the very norm as dreamed, though not actually lived, of the petit-bourgeois couple. The bourgeoisie is constantly absorbing into its ideology a whole section of humanity which does not have its basic status and cannot live up to it except in imagination, that is, at the cost of an immobilization and an impoverishment of consciousness.[19] By spreading its representations over a whole catalogue of collective

---

[19] To induce a collective content for the imagination is always an inhuman undertaking, not only because dreaming essentializes life into destiny, but also because dreams are impoverished, and the alibi of an absence.

images for petit-bourgeois use, the bourgeoisie countenances the illusory lack of differentiation of the social classes: it is as from the moment when a typist earning twenty pounds a month *recognizes herself* in the big wedding of the bourgeoisie that bourgeois ex-nomination achieves its full effect.

The flight from the name "bourgeois" is not therefore an illusory, accidental, secondary, natural, or insignificant phenomenon: it is the bourgeois ideology itself, the process through which the bourgeoisie transforms the reality of the world into an image of the world, History into Nature. And this image has a remarkable feature: it is upside down.[20] The status of the bourgeoisie is particular, historical: man as represented by it is universal, eternal. The bourgeois class has precisely built its power on technical, scientific progress, on an unlimited transformation of nature: bourgeois ideology yields in return an unchangeable nature. The first bourgeois philosophers pervaded the world with significations, subjected all things to an idea of the rational, and decreed that they were meant for man: bourgeois ideology is of the scientist or the intuitive kind, it records facts or perceives values, but refuses explanations; the order of the world can be seen as sufficient or ineffable, it is never seen as significant. Finally, the basic idea of a perfectible mobile world produces the inverted image of an unchanging humanity, characterized by an indefinite repetition of its identity. In a word, in the contemporary bourgeois society, the passage from the real to the ideological is defined as that from an *anti-physis* to a *pseudo-physis*.

MYTH IS DEPOLITICIZED SPEECH

And this is where we come back to myth. Semiology has taught us that myth has the task of giving a historical intention

---

[20] "If men and their conditions appear throughout ideology inverted as in a camera obscura, this phenomenon follows from their historical vital process . . ." (Marx, *The German Ideology*).

a natural justification, and making contingency appear eternal. Now this process is exactly that of bourgeois ideology. If our society is objectively the privileged field of mythical significations, it is because formally myth is the most appropriate instrument for the ideological inversion which defines this society: at all the levels of human communication, myth operates the inversion of *anti-physis* into *pseudo-physis*.

What the world supplies to myth is a historical reality, defined, even if this goes back quite a while, by the way in which men have produced or used it; and what myth gives in return is a *natural* image of this reality. And just as bourgeois ideology is defined by the abandonment of the name "bourgeois," myth is constituted by the loss of the historical quality of things: in it, things lose the memory that they once were made. The world enters language as a dialectical relation between activities, between human actions; it comes out of myth as a harmonious display of essences. A conjuring trick has taken place; it has turned reality inside out, it has emptied it of history and has filled it with Nature, it has removed from things their human meaning so as to make them signify a human insignificance. The function of myth is to empty reality: it is, literally, a ceaseless flowing out, a hemorrhage, or perhaps an evaporation, in short, a perceptible absence.

It is now possible to complete the semiological definition of myth in a bourgeois society: *myth is depoliticized speech*. One must naturally understand *political* in its deeper meaning, as describing the whole of human relations in their real, social structure, in their power of making the world; one must above all give an active value to the prefix *de-*: here it represents an operational movement, it permanently embodies a defaulting. In the case of the soldier Negro, for instance, what is got rid of is certainly not French imperiality (on the contrary, since what must be actualized is its presence); it is the contingent, historical, in one word: *fabricated*, quality of colonialism.

Myth does not deny things, on the contrary, its function is to talk about them; simply, it purifies them, it makes them innocent, it gives them a natural and eternal justification, it gives them a clarity which is not that of an explanation but that of a statement of fact. If I *state the fact* of French imperiality without explaining it, I am very near to finding that it is natural and *goes without saying:* I am reassured. In passing from history to Nature, myth acts economically: it abolishes the complexity of human acts, it gives them the simplicity of essences, it does away with all dialectics, with any going back beyond what is immediately visible, it organizes a world which is without contradictions because it is without depth, a world wide open and wallowing in the evident, it establishes a blissful clarity: things appear to mean something by themselves.[21]

However, is myth always depoliticized speech? In other words, is reality always political? Is it enough to speak about a thing naturally for it to become mythical? One could answer with Marx that the most natural object contains a political trace, however faint and diluted, the more or less memorable presence of the human act which has produced, fitted up, used, subjected, or rejected it.[22] The language-object, which *"speaks things,"* can easily exhibit this trace; the metalanguage, which *speaks of things*, much less easily. Now myth always comes under the heading of metalanguage: the depoliticization which it carries out often supervenes against a background which is already naturalized, depoliticized by a general metalanguage which is trained to *celebrate* things, and no longer to *"act them."* It goes without saying that the force needed by myth to distort its object is much less in the case of a tree than in the case of a Sudanese: in the latter case, the political load is very near the surface, a large quantity of

---

[21] To the pleasure principle of Freudian man could be added the clarity principle of mythological humanity. All the ambiguity of myth is there: its clarity is euphoric.

[22] Cf. Marx and the example of the cherry tree (*The German Ideology*).

artificial nature is needed in order to disperse it; in the former case, it is remote, purified by a whole century-old layer of metalanguage. There are, therefore, strong myths and weak myths; in the former, the political quantum is immediate, the depoliticization is abrupt; in the latter, the political quality of the object has *faded* like a color, but the slightest thing can bring back its strength brutally: what is more *natural* than the sea? And what more "political" than the sea celebrated by the makers of the film *The Lost Continent*?

In fact, metalanguage constitutes a kind of preserve for myth. Men do not have with myth a relationship based on truth but on use: they depoliticize according to their needs. Some mythical objects are left dormant for a time; they are then no more than vague mythical schemata whose political load seems almost neutral. But this indicates only that their situation has brought this about, not that their structure is different. This is the case with our Latin-grammar example. We must note that here mythical speech works on a material which has long been transformed: the sentence by Aesop belongs to literature, it is at the very start mythified (therefore made innocent) by its being fiction. But it is enough to replace the initial term of the chain for an instant into its nature as language-object, to gauge the emptying of reality operated by myth: can one imagine the feelings of a *real* society of animals on finding itself transformed into a grammar example, into a predicative nature! In order to gauge the political load of an object and the mythical hollow which espouses it, one must never look at things from the point of view of the signification, but from that of the signifier, of the thing which has been robbed; and within the signifier, from the point of view of the language-object, that is, of the meaning. There is no doubt that if we consulted a *real* lion, he would maintain that the grammar example is a *strongly* depoliticized state, he would qualify as fully *political* the jurisprudence which leads him to claim a

prey because he is the strongest, unless we deal with a bourgeois lion who would not fail to mythify his strength by giving
it the form of a duty.

One can clearly see that in this case the political insignificance of the myth comes from its situation. Myth, as we know,
is a value: it is enough to modify its circumstances, the general
(and precarious) system in which it occurs, in order to regu-
late its scope with great accuracy. The field of the myth is in
this case reduced to the second form of a French *lycée*. But I
suppose that a child *enthralled* by the story of the lion, the
heifer, and the cow, and recovering through the life of the
imagination the actual reality of these animals, would appreciate with much less unconcern than we do the disappearance of
this lion changed into a predicate. In fact, we hold this myth to
be politically insignificant only because it is not meant for
us.

MYTH ON THE LEFT

If myth is depoliticized speech, there is at least one type of
speech which is the opposite of myth: that which *remains*
political. Here we must go back to the distinction between
language-object and metalanguage. If I am a woodcutter and I
am led to name the tree which I am felling, whatever the form
of my sentence, I "speak the tree," I do not speak about it.
This means that my language is operational, transitively linked
to its object; between the tree and myself, there is nothing but
my labor, that is to say, an action. This is a political language:
it represents Nature for me only inasmuch as I am going to
transform it, it is a language thanks to which I *"act the object"*; the tree is not an image for me, it is simply the meaning
of my action. But if I am not a woodcutter, I can no longer
"speak the tree," I can only speak *about* it, *on* it. My language
is no longer the instrument of an "acted-upon tree," it is the
"tree celebrated" which becomes the instrument of my lan-

guage. I no longer have anything more than an intransitive relationship with the tree; this tree is no longer the meaning of reality as a human action, it is an *image-at-one's-disposal*. Compared to the real language of the woodcutter, the language I create is a second-order language, a metalanguage in which I shall henceforth not "act the things" but "act their names," and which is to the primary language what the gesture is to the act. This second-order language is not entirely mythical, but it is the very locus where myth settles; for myth can work only on objects which have already received the mediation of a first language.

There is therefore one language which is not mythical, it is the language of man as a producer: wherever man speaks in order to transform reality and no longer to preserve it as an image, wherever he links his language to the making of things, metalanguage is referred to a language-object, and myth is impossible. This is why revolutionary language proper cannot be mythical. Revolution is defined as a cathartic act meant to reveal the political load of the world: it *makes* the world; and its language, all of it, is functionally absorbed in this making. It is because it generates speech which is *fully*, that is to say initially and finally, political, and not, like myth, speech which is initially political and finally natural, that Revolution excludes myth. Just as bourgeois ex-nomination characterizes at once bourgeois ideology and myth itself, revolutionary denomination identifies revolution and the absence of myth. The bourgeoisie hides the fact that it is the bourgeoisie and thereby produces myth; revolution announces itself openly as revolution and thereby abolishes myth.

I have been asked whether there are myths "on the left." Of course, inasmuch, precisely, as the left is not revolution. Left-wing myth supervenes precisely at the moment when revolution changes itself into "the left," that is, when it accepts to wear a mask, to hide its name, to generate an innocent metalanguage and to distort itself into "Nature." This revolutionary ex-nomination may or may not be tactical, this is no place to discuss it. At any rate, it is sooner or later experienced as a process contrary to revolution, and it is always more or less in relation to myth that revolutionary history defines its "deviations." There came a day, for instance, when it was socialism itself which defined the Stalin myth. Stalin, as a spoken object, has exhibited for years, in their pure state, the constituent characters of mythical speech: a meaning, which was the real Stalin, that of history; a signifier, which was the ritual invocation to Stalin, and the *inevitable* character of the "natural" epithets with which his name was surrounded; a signified, which was the intention to respect orthodoxy, discipline, and unity, *appropriated* by the Communist Parties to a definite situation; and a signification, which was a sanctified Stalin, whose historical determinants found themselves grounded in Nature, sublimated under the name of Genius, that is, something irrational and inexpressible: here, depoliticization is evident, it fully reveals the presence of a myth.[23]

Yes, myth exists on the left, but it does not at all have there the same qualities as bourgeois myth. *Left-wing myth is inessential*. To start with, the objects which it takes hold of are rare—only a few political notions—unless it has itself recourse to the whole repertoire of the bourgeois myths. Left-wing myth never reaches the immense field of human relationships, the very vast surface of "insignificant" ideology. Everyday life is inaccessible to it: in a bourgeois society, there are no "left-wing" myths concerning marriage, cooking, the home, the theater, the law, morality, etc. Then, it is an incidental myth, its use is not part of a strategy, as is the case with

---

[23] It is remarkable that Khrushchevism presented itself not as a political change, but essentially and only as a *linguistic conversion*. An incomplete conversion, incidentally, for Khrushchev devalued Stalin, but did not explain him —did not repoliticize him.

bourgeois myth, but only of a tactics, or, at the worst, of a deviation; if it occurs, it is as a myth suited to a convenience, not to a necessity.

Finally, and above all, this myth is, in essence, poverty-stricken. It does not know how to proliferate; being produced on order and for a temporally limited prospect, it is invented with difficulty. It lacks a major faculty, that of fabulizing. Whatever it does, there remains about it something stiff and literal, a suggestion of something done to order. As it is expressively put, it remains barren. In fact, what can be more meager than the Stalin myth? No inventiveness here, and only a clumsy appropriation: the signifier of the myth (this form whose infinite wealth in bourgeois myth we have just seen) is not varied in the least: it is reduced to a litany.

This imperfection, if that is the word for it, comes from the nature of the "left": whatever the imprecision of the term, the left always defines itself in relation to the oppressed, whether proletarian or colonized.[24] Now the speech of the oppressed can only be poor, monotonous, immediate: his destitution is the very yardstick of his language: he has only one, always the same, that of his actions; metalanguage is a luxury, he cannot yet have access to it. The speech of the oppressed is real, like that of the woodcutter; it is a transitive type of speech: it is quasi-unable to lie; lying is a richness, a lie presupposes property, truths, and forms to spare. This essential barrenness produces rare, threadbare myths: either transient, or clumsily indiscreet; by their very being, they label themselves as myths, and point to their masks. And this mask is hardly that of a pseudo-physis: for that type of physis is also a richness of a sort, the oppressed can only borrow it: he is unable to throw out the real meaning of things, to give them the luxury of an

---

[24] Today it is the colonized peoples who assume to the full the ethical and political condition described by Marx as being that of the proletariat.

empty form, open to the innocence of a false Nature. One can say that in a sense, left-wing myth is always an artificial myth, a reconstituted myth: hence its clumsiness.

MYTH ON THE RIGHT

Statistically, myth is on the right. There, it is essential; well-fed, sleek, expansive, garrulous, it invents itself ceaselessly. It takes hold of everything, all aspects of the law, of morality, of aesthetics, of diplomacy, of household equipment, of Literature, of entertainment. Its expansion has the very dimensions of bourgeois ex-nomination. The bourgeoisie wants to keep reality without keeping the appearances: it is therefore the very negativity of bourgeois appearance, infinite like every negativity, which solicits myth infinitely. The oppressed is nothing, he has only one language, that of his emancipation; the oppressor is everything, his language is rich, multiform, supple, with all the possible degrees of dignity at its disposal: he has an exclusive right to metalanguage. The oppressed *makes* the world, he has only an active, transitive (political) language; the oppressor conserves it, his language is plenary, intransitive, gestural, theatrical: it is Myth. The language of the former aims at transforming, of the latter at eternalizing.

Does this completeness of the myths of Order (this is the name the bourgeoisie gives to itself) include inner differences? Are there, for instance, bourgeois myths and petit-bourgeois myths? There cannot be any fundamental differences, for whatever the public which consumes it, myth always postulated the immobility of Nature. But there can be degrees of fulfillment or expansion: some myths ripen better in some social strata: for myth also, there are micro-climates.

The myth of Childhood-as-Poet, for instance, is an *advanced* bourgeois myth: it has hardly come out of inventive culture (Cocteau, for example) and is just reaching consumer culture (*L'Express*). Part of the bourgeoisie can still find it too obviously invented, not mythical enough to feel entitled to countenance it (a whole part of bourgeois criticism works only with duly mythical materials). It is a myth which is not yet well run in, it does not yet contain enough *Nature*: in order to make the Child-Poet part of a cosmogony, one must renounce the prodigy (Mozart, Rimbaud, etc.), and accept new norms, those of psychopedagogy, Freudianism, etc.: as a myth, it is still unripe.

Thus every myth can have its history and its geography; each is in fact the sign of the other: a myth ripens because it spreads. I have not been able to carry out any real study of the social geography of myths. But it is perfectly possible to draw what linguists would call the isoglosses of a myth, the lines which limit the social region where it is spoken. As this region is shifting, it would be better to speak of the waves of implantation of the myth. The Minou Drouet myth has thus had at least three waves of amplification: (1) *L'Express;* (2) *Paris-Match, Elle*; (3) *France-Soir*. Some myths hesitate: will they pass into tabloids, the home of the suburbanite of private means, the hairdresser's salon, the Métro? The social geography of myths will remain difficult to trace as long as we lack an analytical sociology of the press.[25] But we can say that its place already exists.

Since we cannot yet draw up the list of the dialectal forms of bourgeois myth, we can always sketch its rhetorical forms. One must understand here by *rhetoric* a set of fixed, regulated, insistent figures, according to which the varied forms of the mythical signifier arrange themselves. These figures are trans-

---

[25] The circulation of newspapers is an insufficient datum. Other information comes only by accident. *Paris-Match* has given—significantly, as publicity—the composition of its public in terms of standard of living (*Le Figaro*, July 12, 1955): out of each 100 readers living in town, 53 have a car, 49 a bathroom, etc., whereas the average standard of living in France is reckoned as follows: car, 22 percent; bathroom, 13 percent. That the purchasing power of the *Paris-Match* reader is high could have been predicted from the mythology of this publication.

parent inasmuch as they do not affect the plasticity of the signifier; but they are already sufficiently conceptualized to adapt to a historical representation of the world (just as classical rhetoric can account for a representation of the Aristotelian type). It is through their rhetoric that bourgeois myths outline the general prospect of this *pseudo-physis* which defines the dream of the contemporary bourgeois world. Here are its principal figures:

1. *The inoculation.* I have already given examples of this very general figure, which consists in admitting the accidental evil of a class-bound institution the better to conceal its principial evil. One immunizes the contents of the collective imagination by means of a small inoculation of acknowledged evil; one thus protects it against the risk of a generalized subversion. This *liberal* treatment would not have been possible only a hundred years ago. Then, the bourgeois Good did not compromise with anything, it was quite stiff. It has become much more supple since: the bourgeoisie no longer hesitates to acknowledge some localized subversions: the avant-garde, the irrational in childhood, etc. It now lives in a balanced economy: as in any sound joint-stock company, the smaller shares —in law but not in fact—compensate the big ones.

2. *The privation of History.* Myth deprives the object of which it speaks of all History.[27] In it, history evaporates. It is a kind of ideal servant: it prepares all things, brings them, lays them out, the master arrives, it silently disappears: all that is left for one to do is to enjoy this beautiful object without wondering where it comes from. Or even better: it can only come from eternity: since the beginning of time, it has been made for bourgeois man, the Spain of the *Blue Guide* has been made for the tourist, and "primitives" have prepared their

---

[26] Marx: ". . . we must pay attention to this history, since ideology boils down to either an erroneous conception of this history, *or to a complete abstraction from it*" (*The German Ideology*).

dances with a view to an exotic festivity. We can see all the disturbing things which this felicitous figure removes from sight: both determinism and freedom. Nothing is produced, nothing is chosen: all one has to do is to possess these new objects from which all soiling trace of origin or choice has been removed. This miraculous evaporation of history is another form of a concept common to most bourgeois myths: the irresponsibility of man.

3. *Identification.* The petit bourgeois is a man unable to imagine the Other.[27] If he comes face to face with him, he blinds himself, ignores and denies him, or else transforms him into himself. In the petit-bourgeois universe, all the experiences of confrontation are reverberating, any otherness is reduced to sameness. The spectacle and the tribunal, which are both places where the Other threatens to appear in full view, become mirrors. This is because the Other is a scandal which threatens his essence. Dominici cannot have access to social existence unless he is previously reduced to the state of a small simulacrum of the president of the Assizes or the Public Prosecutor: this is the price one must pay in order to condemn him justly, since Justice is a weighing operation and since scales can only weigh like against like. There are, in any petit-bourgeois consciousness, small simulacra of the hooligan, the parricide, the homosexual, etc., which periodically the judiciary extracts from its brain, puts in the dock, admonishes and condemns: one never tries anybody but analogues *who have gone astray*: it is a question of direction, not of Nature, for *that's how men are.* Sometimes—rarely—the Other is revealed as irreducible: not because of a sudden scruple, but because *common sense* rebels: a man does not have a white skin, but a black one, another drinks pear juice, not Pernod. How can one assimilate

[27] Marx: ". . . what makes them representative of the petit-bourgeois class, is that their minds, their consciousnesses do not extend beyond the limits which this class has set to its activities" (*The Eighteenth Brumaire*). And Gorky: "the petit bourgeois is the man who has preferred himself to all else."

the Negro, the Russian? There is here a figure for emergencies: exoticism. The Other becomes a pure object, a spectacle, a clown. Relegated to the confines of humanity, he no longer threatens the security of the home. This figure is chiefly petit-bourgeois. For, even if he is unable to experience the Other in himself, the bourgeois can at least imagine the place where he fits in: this is what is known as liberalism, which is a sort of intellectual equilibrium based on recognized places. The petit-bourgeois class is not liberal (it produces Fascism, whereas the bourgeoisie uses it): it follows the same route as the bourgeoisie, but lags behind.

4. *Tautology.* Yes, I know, it's an ugly word. But so is the thing. Tautology is this verbal device which consists in defining like by like (*"Drama is drama"*). We can view it as one of those types of magical behavior dealt with by Sartre in his *Outline of a Theory of the Emotions*: one takes refuge in tautology as one does in fear, or anger, or sadness, when one is at a loss for an explanation: the accidental failure of language is magically identified with what one decides is a natural resistance of the object. In tautology, there is a double murder: one kills rationality because it resists one; one kills language because it betrays one. Tautology is a faint at the right moment, a saving aphasia, it is a death, or perhaps a comedy, the indignant "representation" of the *rights* of reality over and above language. Since it is magical, it can of course only take refuge behind the argument of authority: thus do parents at the end of their tether reply to the child who keeps on asking for explanations: *"because that's how it is,"* or even better: *"just because, that's all"*—a magical act ashamed of itself, which verbally makes the gesture of rationality, but immediately abandons the latter, and believes itself to be even with causality because it has uttered the word which introduces it. Tautology testifies to a profound distrust of language, which is

rejected because it has failed. Now any refusal of language is a death. Tautology creates a dead, a motionless world.

5. *Neither-Norism.* By this I mean this mythological figure which consists in stating two opposites and balancing the one by the other so as to reject them both. (I want *neither* this *nor* that.) It is on the whole a bourgeois figure, for it relates to a modern form of liberalism. We find again here the figure of the scales: reality is first reduced to analogues; then it is weighed; finally, equality having been ascertained, it is got rid of. Here also there is magical behavior: both parties are dismissed because it is embarrassing to choose between them; one flees from an intolerable reality, reducing it to two opposites which balance each other only inasmuch as they are purely formal, relieved of all their specific weight. Neither-Norism can have degraded forms: in astrology, for example, ill luck is always followed by equal good luck; they are always predicted in a prudently compensatory perspective: a final equilibrium immobilizes values, life, destiny, etc.: one no longer needs to choose, but only to endorse.

6. *The quantification of quality.* This is a figure which is latent in all the preceding ones. By reducing any quality to quantity, myth economizes intelligence: it understands reality more cheaply. I have given several examples of this mechanism which bourgeois—and especially petit-bourgeois—mythology does not hesitate to apply to aesthetic realities which it deems on the other hand to partake of an immaterial essence. Bourgeois theater is a good example of this contradiction: on the one hand, theater is presented as an essence which cannot be reduced to any language and reveals itself only to the heart, to intuition. From this quality, it receives an irritable dignity (it is forbidden as a crime of "lese-essence" to speak about the theater *scientifically*: or rather, any intellectual way of viewing the theater is discredited as scientism or pedantic

language). On the other hand, bourgeois dramatic art rests on a pure quantification of effects: a whole circuit of computable appearances establishes a quantitative equality between the cost of a ticket and the tears of an actor or the luxuriousness of a set: what is currently meant by the "naturalness" of an actor, for instance, is above all a conspicuous quantity of effects.

7. *The statement of fact.* Myths tend toward proverbs. Bourgeois ideology invests in this figure interests which are bound to its very essence: universalism, the refusal of any explanation, an unalterable hierarchy of the world. But we must again distinguish the language-object from the metalanguage. Popular, ancestral proverbs still partake of an instrumental grasp of the world as object. A rural statement of fact, such as *"the weather is fine,"* keeps a real link with the usefulness of fine weather. It is an implicitly technological statement; the word, here, in spite of its general, abstract form, paves the way for actions, it inserts itself into a fabricating order: the farmer does not speak *about* the weather, he "acts it," he draws it into his labor. All our popular proverbs thus represent active speech which has gradually solidified into reflexive speech, but where reflection is curtailed, reduced to a statement of fact, and so to speak timid, prudent, and closely hugging experience. Popular proverbs foresee more than they assert, they remain the speech of a humanity which is making itself, not one which is. Bourgeois aphorisms, on the other hand, belong to metalanguage; they are a second-order language which bears on objects already prepared. Their classical form is the maxim. Here the statement is no longer directed toward a world to be made; it must overlay one which is already made, bury the traces of this production under a self-evident appearance of eternity: it is a counter-explanation, the decorous equivalent of a tautology, of this peremptory *because* which

parents in need of knowledge hang above the heads of their children. The foundation of the bourgeois statement of fact is *common sense*, that is, truth when it stops on the arbitrary order of him who speaks it.

I have listed these rhetorical figures without any special order, and there may well be many others: some can become worn out, others can come into being. But it is obvious that those given here, such as they are, fall into two great categories, which are like the Zodiacal Signs of the bourgeois universe: the Essences and the Scales. Bourgeois ideology continuously transforms the products of history into essential types. Just as the cuttlefish squirts its ink in order to protect itself, it cannot rest until it has obscured the ceaseless making of the world, fixated this world into an object which can be forever possessed, catalogued its riches, embalmed it, and injected into reality some purifying essence which will stop its transformation, its flight toward other forms of existence. And these riches, thus fixated and frozen, will at last become computable: bourgeois morality will essentially be a weighing operation, the essences will be placed in scales of which bourgeois man will remain the motionless beam. For the very end of myths is to immobilize the world: they must suggest and mimic a universal order which has fixated once and for all the hierarchy of possessions. Thus, every day and everywhere, man is stopped by myths, referred by them to this motionless prototype which lives in his place, stifles him in the manner of a huge internal parasite and assigns to his activity the narrow limits within which he is allowed to suffer without upsetting the world: bourgeois pseudo-physis is in the fullest sense a prohibition for man against inventing himself. Myths are nothing but this ceaseless, untiring solicitation, this insidious and inflexible demand that all men recognize themselves in this image, eternal yet bearing a date, which was built of them one day as if for all time. For the Nature, in which they are locked up under the pretext of being eternalized, is nothing but a Usage. And it is this Usage, however lofty, that they must take in hand and transform.

NECESSITY AND LIMITS OF MYTHOLOGY

I must, as a conclusion, say a few words about the mythologist himself. This term is rather grand and self-assured. Yet one can predict for the mythologist, if there ever is one, a few difficulties, in feeling if not in method. True, he will have no trouble in feeling justified: whatever its mistakes, mythology is certain to participate in the making of the world. Holding as a principle that man in a bourgeois society is at every turn plunged into a false Nature, it attempts to find again under the assumed innocence of the most unsophisticated relationships, the profound alienation which this innocence is meant to make one accept. The unveiling which it carries out is therefore a political act: founded on a responsible idea of language, mythology thereby postulates the freedom of the latter. It is certain that in this sense mythology *harmonizes* with the world, not as it is, but as it wants to create itself (Brecht had for this an efficiently ambiguous word: *Einverstandnis*, at once an understanding of reality and a complicity with it).

This harmony justifies the mythologist but does not fulfill him: his status still remains basically one of being excluded. Justified by the political dimension, the mythologist is still at a distance from it. His speech is a metalanguage, it "acts" nothing; at the most, it unveils—or does it? To whom? His task always remains ambiguous, hampered by its ethical origin. He can live revolutionary action only vicariously: hence the self-conscious character of his function, this something a little stiff and painstaking, muddled and excessively simplified which brands any intellectual behavior with an openly political foundation ("uncommitted" types of literature are infinitely more "elegant"; they are in their place in metalanguage).

Also, the mythologist cuts himself off from all the myth consumers, and this is no small matter. If this applied to a particular section of the collectivity, well and good.[28] But when a myth reaches the entire community, it is from the latter that the mythologist must become estranged if he wants to liberate the myth. Any myth with some degree of generality is in fact ambiguous, because it represents the very humanity of those who, having nothing, have borrowed it. To decipher the Tour de France or the "good French wine" is to cut oneself off from those who are entertained or warmed up by them. The mythologist is condemned to live in a theoretical sociality; for him, to be in society is, at best, to be truthful: his utmost sociality dwells in his utmost morality. His connection with the world is of the order of sarcasm.

One must even go further: in a sense, the mythologist is excluded from this history in the name of which he professes to act. The havoc which he wreaks in the language of the community is absolute for him, it fills his assignment to the brim: he must live this assignment without any hope of going back or any assumption of payment. It is forbidden for him to imagine what the world will concretely be like, when the immediate object of his criticism has disappeared. Utopia is an impossible luxury for him: he greatly doubts that tomorrow's truths will be the exact reverse of today's lies. History never ensures the triumph pure and simple of something over its opposite: it unveils, while making itself, unimaginable solutions, unforeseeable syntheses. The mythologist is not even in

---

[28] It is not only from the public that one becomes estranged; it is sometimes also from the very object of the myth. In order to demystify Poetic Childhood, for instance, I have had, so to speak, *to lack confidence* in Minou Drouet, the child. I have had to ignore, in her, under the enormous myth with which she is cumbered, something like a tender, open, possibility. It is never a good thing to speak *against* a little girl.

a Moses-like situation: he cannot see the Promised Land. For
him, tomorrow's positivity is entirely hidden by today's negativity. All the values of his undertaking appear to him as acts
of destruction: the latter accurately cover the former, nothing
protrudes. This subjective grasp of history in which the potent
seed of the future *is nothing but* the most profound apocalypse
of the present has been expressed by Saint-Just in a strange
saying: *"What constitutes the Republic is the total destruction
of what is opposed to it."* This must not, I think, be understood in the trivial sense of: "One has to clear the way before
reconstructing." The copula has an exhaustive meaning: there
is for some men a subjective dark night of history where the
future becomes an essence, the essential destruction of the
past.

One last exclusion threatens the mythologist: he constantly
runs the risk of causing the reality which he purports to protect, to disappear. Quite apart from all speech, the *D.S. 19* is a
technologically defined object: it is capable of a certain speed,
it meets the wind in a certain way, etc. And this type of reality
cannot be spoken of by the mythologist. The mechanic, the
engineer, even the user, *"speak* the object"; but the mythologist is condemned to metalanguage. This exclusion already has
a name: it is what is called ideologism. Zhdanovism has
roundly condemned it (without proving, incidentally, that it
was, *for the time being*, avoidable) in the early Lukács, in
Marr's linguistics, in works like those of Bénichou or Gold-
mann, opposing to it the reticence of a reality inaccessible to
ideology, such as that of language according to Stalin. It is
true that ideologism resolves the contradiction of alienated
reality by an amputation, not a synthesis (but as for Zhdanovism, it does not even resolve it): wine is objectively good,
and *at the same time*, the goodness of wine is a myth: here is
the aporia. The mythologist gets out of this as best he can: he
deals with the goodness of wine, not with the wine itself, just

as the historian deals with Pascal's ideology, not with the *Pensées* in themselves.[29]

It seems that this is a difficulty pertaining to our times: there is as yet only one possible choice, and this choice can bear only on two equally extreme methods: either to posit a reality which is entirely permeable to history, and ideologize; or, conversely, to posit a reality which is *ultimately* impenetrable, irreducible, and, in this case, poetize. In a word, I do not yet see a synthesis between ideology and poetry (by poetry I understand, in a very general way, the search for the inalienable meaning of things).

The fact that we cannot manage to achieve more than an unstable grasp of reality doubtless gives the measure of our present alienation: we constantly drift between the object and its demystification, powerless to render its wholeness. For if we penetrate the object, we liberate it but we destroy it; and if we acknowledge its full weight, we respect it, but we restore it to a state which is still mystified. It would seem that we are condemned for some time yet always to speak *excessively* about reality. This is probably because ideologism and its opposite are types of behavior which are still magical, terrorized, blinded, and fascinated by the split in the social world. And yet, this is what we must seek: a reconciliation between reality and men, between description and explanation, between object and knowledge.

1956

---

[29] Even here, in these mythologies, I have used trickery: finding it painful constantly to work on the evaporation of reality, I have started to make it excessively dense, and to discover in it a surprising compactness which I savored with delight, and I have given a few examples of "substantial psychoanalysis" about some mythical objects.

The Last Happy Writer

WHAT have we in common, today, with Voltaire? From a modern point of view, his philosophy is outmoded. It is possible to believe in the fixity of essences and in the chaos of history, but no longer in the same way as Voltaire. In any case, atheists no longer throw themselves at the feet of deists, who moreover no longer exist. Dialectics has killed off Manicheanism, and we rarely discuss the ways of Providence. As for Voltaire's enemies, they have disappeared, or been transformed: there are no more Jansenists, no Socinians, no Leibnizians; the Jesuits are no longer named Nonotte or Patouillet.

I was about to say: there is no longer an Inquisition. This is wrong, of course. What has disappeared is the theater of persecution, not persecution itself: the *auto-da-fé* has been subtilized into a police operation, the stake has become the concentration camp, discreetly ignored by its neighbors. In return for which, the figures have changed: in 1721 nine men and eleven women were burned at Grenada in the four ovens of the scaffold, and in 1723 nine men were burned at Madrid to celebrate the arrival of the French princess: they had doubt-

From *Critical Essays.*

less married their cousins or eaten meat on Friday. A horrible repression, whose absurdity sustains Voltaire's entire *oeuvre*. But between 1939 and 1945, six million human beings were killed, among others, because they were Jews—they, or their parents, or their grandparents.

We have not had a single pamphlet against that. But perhaps it is precisely because the figures have changed. Simplistic as it may appear, there is a proportion between the lightness of the Voltairean artillery and the sporadic artillery of religious crime in the eighteenth century: quantitatively limited, the stake became a principle, i.e., a target: a tremendous advantage for its opponent: such is the stuff of which triumphant writers are made. For the very enormity of racist crimes, their organization by the State, the ideological justifications with which they are masked—all this involves today's writer in much more than a pamphlet, demands a philosophy rather than an irony, an explanation rather than an astonishment. Since Voltaire, history has been imprisoned in a difficulty which lacerates any committed literature and which Voltaire never knew: *no freedom for the enemies of freedom*: no one can any longer give lessons in tolerance to anyone.

In short, what separates us from Voltaire is that he was a happy writer. Better than anyone else, he gave reason's combat a festive style. Everything is spectacle in his battles: the adversary's name—always ridiculous; the disputed doctrine— reduced to a proposition (Voltairean irony is invariably the exposure of a disproportion); the points scored, exploding in every direction until they seem to be a game, dispensing the onlooker from all respect and all pity; the very mobility of the combatant, here disguised under a thousand transparent pseudonyms, there making his European journeys a kind of feinting farce, a perpetual Scapinade. For the skirmishes between Voltaire and the world are not only a spectacle but a superlative spectacle, proclaiming themselves such in the fashion of those Punchinello shows Voltaire loved so much—he had a puppet theater of his own at Cirey.

Voltaire's first happiness was doubtless that of his times. Let there be no mistake: the times were very harsh, and Voltaire has everywhere described their horrors. Yet no period has helped a writer more, given him more assurance that he was fighting for a just and natural cause. The bourgeoisie, the class from which Voltaire came, already held most of its economic positions; a power in commerce and industry, in the ministries, in culture and the sciences, it knew that its triumph coincided with the nation's prosperity and the happiness of each citizen. On its side, potential power, certainty of method, and the still-pure heritage of taste; against it, all a dying world could display of corruption, stupidity, and ferocity. It was indeed a great happiness, a great peace to combat an enemy so uniformly condemnable. The tragic spirit is severe because it acknowledges, by obligation of Nature, its adversary's greatness: Voltaire had no tragic spirit: he had to measure himself against no living force, against no idea or individual that could induce him to reflect (except the past: Pascal, and the future: Rousseau; but he conjured them both away): Jesuits, Jansenists, or parliaments, these were great frozen bodies, drained of all intelligence and filled with no more than a ferocity intolerable to the heart and the mind. Authority, even in its bloodiest manifestations, was no more than a decor; merely subject such machinery to human eyes, and it would collapse. Voltaire had that sly and tender gaze (*Zaïre's very heart*, Mme de Genlis tells us, *was in his eyes*), whose destructive power lay in simply bearing life among those great blind masks which still ruled society.

It was, then, a singular happiness to have to do battle in a world where force and stupidity were continually on the same tack: a privileged situation for the mind. The writer was on history's side, all the happier in that he perceived history as a consummation, not as a transcendence which risked sweeping him along with it.

Voltaire's second happiness was precisely to forget history, at the very moment it was supporting him. In order to be happy, Voltaire suspended time; if he has a philosophy, it is that of immobility. We know what he thought: God created the world as a geometer, not as a father. Which means that He does not bother to accompany His creation and that, once regulated, the world no longer sustains relations with God. An original intelligence established a certain type of causality once and for all: there are no objects without ends, no effects without causes, and the relation between one and the other is immutable. Voltairean metaphysics is therefore never anything but an introduction to physics, and Providence a mechanics. For once God has left the world He created (like the clockmaker his clock), neither God nor man ever moves again. Of course good and evil exist; but we are to translate them as happiness and misery, not sin or innocence; for they are merely the elements of a universal causality; they have a necessity, but this necessity is mechanical, not moral: evil does not punish, good does not reward: they do not signify that God is, that He surveys all, but that He has been, that He has created.

If man should take it upon himself to turn from evil to good by a moral impulse, it is the universal order of causes and effects which he injures; he can produce, by this movement, only a farcical chaos (as Memnon does, the day he decides to be wise). Then what can man do with regard to good and evil? Not much: in this machinery which is the Creation, there is room only for a *game*, that is, the very slight amplitude the constructor allows his pieces in which to move. This game is reason. It is capricious—i.e., it attests to no direction of history: reason appears, disappears, with no other law than the very personal effort of certain minds: among the benefits of history (useful inventions, great works) there is a relation of contiguity, never of function. Voltaire's opposition to any intelligence of time is very intense. For Voltaire, there is no history in the modern sense of the word, nothing but chronologies. Voltaire wrote historical works expressly to say that he did not believe in history: the age of Louis XIV is not an organism, it is a cluster of chance meetings, here the dragonnades, there Racine. Nature itself, of course, is never historical: being essentially art, i.e., God's artifice, it cannot move or have moved: the mountains were not wrought by the earth and the waters, God created them once and for all for the use of His creatures, and the fossil fishes—whose discovery so excited the age—are only the prosaic leavings of picnicking pilgrims: there is no evolution.

The philosophy of time will be the contribution of the nineteenth century (and singularly of Germany). We might assume that the relativist lesson of the past is at least replaced in Voltaire, as in his entire age, by that of space. At first glance, this is what occurs: the eighteenth century is not only a great age of travel, the age in which modern capitalism, then preponderantly British, definitively organizes its world market from China to South America; it is above all the age when travel accedes to literature and engages a philosophy. We know the role of the Jesuits, by their *Edifying and Curious Letters*, in the birth of exoticism. From early in the century, these materials were transformed and soon produced a veritable typology of exotic man: we have the Egyptian Sage, the Mohammedan Arab, the Turk, the Chinese, the Siamese, and, most prestigious of all, the Persian. All these Orientals are philosophy teachers; but before saying which philosophy, we must note that just when Voltaire begins writing his Tales, which owe a great deal to Oriental folklore, the century has already elaborated a veritable rhetoric of exoticism, a kind of digest whose figures are so well formed and so well known that they can henceforth be utilized without troubling further over descriptions and astonishments; Voltaire will not fail to utilize them in this fashion, for he never troubled to be "original" (an entirely modern notion, moreover); for him, as indeed for any of his contemporaries, the Oriental is not the object, the term of a genuine consideration, but simply a cipher, a convenient sign of communication.

The result of this conceptualization is that the Voltairean journey has no density; the space Voltaire covers so obsessively (we do nothing but travel in his Tales) is not an explorer's space, it is a surveyor's space, and what Voltaire borrows from the allogeneous humanity of the Chinese and the Persian is a new limit, not a new substance; new habitations are attributed to the human essence, it flourishes from the Seine to the Ganges, and Voltaire's novels are less investigations than inspections of an owner whom we "orient" in no particular order because his estate never varies, and whom we interrupt by incessant stops during which we discuss not what we have seen but what we are. This explains why the Voltairean journey is neither realistic nor baroque (the picaresque vein of the century's first narratives has completely dried up); it is not even an operation of knowledge, but merely of affirmation; it is the element of a logic, the figure of an equation; these Oriental countries, which today have so heavy a weight, so pronounced an individuation in world politics, are for Voltaire so many forms, mobile signs without actual content, humanity at zero degrees (Centigrade), which one nimbly grasps in order to signify . . . oneself.

For such is the paradox of Voltairean travel: to manifest an immobility. There are of course other manners, other laws, other moralities than ours, and this is what the journey teaches; but this diversity belongs to the human essence and consequently finds its point of equilibrium very rapidly; it is enough to acknowledge it in order to be done with it: let man (that is, Occidental man) multiply himself a little, let the European philosopher be doubled by the Chinese Sage, the ingenious Huron, and universal man will be created. To aggrandize oneself in order to confirm, not in order to transform oneself—such is the meaning of the Voltairean voyage.

It was doubtless Voltaire's second happiness to be able to depend upon the world's immobility. The bourgeoisie was so close to power that it could already begin not to believe in history. It could also begin to reject any system, to suspect any organized philosophy, that is, to posit its own thinking, its own good sense as a Nature which any doctrine, any intellectual system would offend. This is what Voltaire did so brilliantly, and it was his third happiness: he ceaselessly dissociated intelligence and intellectuality, asserting that the world is an order if we do not try too much to order it, that it is a system if only we renounce systematizing it: this conduct of mind has had a great career subsequently: today we call it anti-intellectualism.

Notable is the fact that all of Voltaire's enemies could be named, that is, their being derived from their certainty: Jesuits, Jansenists, Socinians, Protestants, atheists, all enemies among themselves, but united under Voltaire's attack by their capacity to be defined by a word. Conversely, on the level of denominative systems, Voltaire escapes. Doctrinally, was he a deist? a Leibnizian? a rationalist? Each time, yes and no. He has no system except the hatred of system (and we know that there is nothing grimmer than this very system); today his enemies would be the doctrinaires of history, of science (*vide* his mockery of pure science in *The Man with Forty Ecus*), or of existence; Marxists, existentialists, leftist intellectuals— Voltaire would have hated them, covered them with incessant *lazzi*, as he did the Jesuits in his own day. By continuously setting intelligence against intellectuality, by using one to undermine the other, by reducing the conflicts of ideas to a kind of Manichean struggle between stupidity and intelligence, by identifying all system with stupidity and all freedom of mind with intelligence, Voltaire grounded liberalism on a contradiction. As system of the nonsystem, anti-intellectualism eludes and gains on both counts, perpetually ricocheting between bad faith and good conscience, between a pessimism of substance and a jig of form, between a proclaimed skepticism and a terrorist doubt.

The Voltairean festivity is constituted by this incessant alibi. Voltaire cudgels and dodges at the same time. The world is simple for a man who ends all his letters with the cordial salutation *Ecrasons l'infâme* (i.e., dogmatism). We know that this simplicity and this happiness were bought at the price of an ablation of history and of an immobilization of the world. Further, it is a happiness which excluded many, despite its dazzling victory over obscurantism. Thus, in accord with the legend, the anti-Voltaire is indeed Rousseau. By forcefully positing the idea of man's corruption by society, Rousseau set history moving again, established the principle of a permanent transcendence of history. But by doing so he bequeathed to literature a poisoned legacy. Henceforth, ceaselessly athirst and wounded by a responsibility he can never again completely honor or completely elude, the intellectual will be defined by his bad conscience: Voltaire was a happy writer, but doubtless the last.

1958

Buffet Finishes Off New York

Bernard buffet's New York will not unsettle many prejudices: it is a city of geometric heights, a petrified desert of grids and lattices, an inferno of greenish abstraction under a flat sky, a real Metropolis from which man is absent by his very accumulation; the implicit morality of our new Greuze is that we are distinctly happier in Belleville than in Manhattan. This is a folklore New York rather like Bizet's Spain or the Italy of the Théâtre Mogador: an exoticism which confirms the Frenchman in the excellence of his habitat.

According to Buffet, the architecture of this city is uniformly longiform and quadrangular. Here the grid reigns under its most ill-favored aspect: the contour, this black line which encloses everything, obviously intends to expel man from the city. By obsessively multiplying the window, by inlaying it with black, Buffet empties it, destroys it, makes the living edifice into a dead surface, as if number, unless it is swarming, must fatally establish an abstract order; Buffet geometrizes New York the better to depopulate it: everyone knows that abstraction is "sterile." Now, to my sense of it, one of the

From *The Eiffel Tower and Other Mythologies*, translated by Richard Howard (New York: Hill and Wang, 1979).

lessons of this marvelous city is that abstraction is alive, and it must paradoxically be a painter who denies us this truth. But no doubt only an "abstract" painter could do justice to New York, could understand that planes and lines, form and meaning are as intensely alive here as in one of Mondrian's compositions: here figuration cunningly serves to destroy: to paint is to deceive. Buffet has "figured" New York in order to get rid of it.

The same aggression is to be noted with regard to the city's great commonplace, the skyscraper. What is astonishing about the skyscraper is that it does not astonish. When we actually see one (but do we ever see one, actually?), the feeling it inspires is: *why not?* For Buffet, on the contrary, the skyscraper always seems to remain in an anthological state, and this is always what he presents, refining on the needle, that obsessive shape of his thin and angular style. As if his very canvas, in its material proportions, *makes* the skyscraper; for him the skyscraper is a Being, and a prejudged one. Of course Buffet is sometimes sensitive to the city's magnificent *breadth*, to the scope of its *base* (for New York is a splendidly *set* city, like all fabulous metropolises); hence he paints a veritable façade of structures, he sees New York full-face, which is a good way of freeing himself from it, or he suspends the great scroll of a bridge in his foreground; but even in these efforts at enlargement, height surreptitiously reappears: the panorama spreads out the skyscrapers only to profile them in a jerky succession, the bridge dominates them only to manifest their aggressive vigor in the distance. There is a mythic combat here between *the Base and the Summit*, as Char says; but instead of altitude being absorbed in the foreground mass (for New York is in fact a deep city, not a high one), Buffet bequeaths it his absurd solitude; he paints the skyscrapers as if they were empty cathedrals: he flattens the "landscape."

Buffet finishes off New York by depopulating the streets. I

am not saying that the truth of New York is a *swarm*, which is
a Neapolitan, a European notion. Urbanism itself, this checker-
board of nameless streets, is the price that has to be paid in
order that the streets be useful and no longer picturesque, in
order that men and objects circulate, adapt themselves to the
distances, rule effectively over this enormous urban nature:
the biggest city in the world (with Tokyo) is also the one we
possess in an afternoon, by the most exciting of operations,
since here *to possess* is *to understand*: New York exposes
itself to intellection, and our familiarity with it comes very
quickly. This is the purpose of these numbered streets, inflex-
ibly distributed according to regular distances: not to make
the city into a huge machine and man into an automaton, as
we are repeatedly and stupidly told by those for whom tor-
tuosity and dirt are the gauges of spirituality, but on the contrary to master the distances and orientations by the mind, to
put at one man's disposal the space of these twelve million,
this fabulous reservoir, this world emporium in which *all*
goods exist except the metaphysical variety. This is the purpose of New York's geometry: that each individual should be
poetically the owner of the capital of the world. It is not up,
toward the sky, that you must look in New York; it is down,
toward men and merchandise: by an admirable static paradox,
the skyscraper establishes the block, the block creates the
street, the street offers itself to man. Buffet of course proceeds
in the opposite direction: he empties the street, climbs up the
façades, grazes the surfaces, he rarefies: his New York is an
anti-city.

To paint New York from above, at the top, is to rely once
again on the first spiritualist myth, i.e., that geometry kills
man. In his way, Buffet follows in the wake of our venerable
moralists, for whom the refrigerator is antipathetic to the soul.
The intentional desolation of his New York—what can it
mean except that it is bad for man to live in groups, that num-

ber kills the spirit, that too many bathrooms are harmful to the spiritual health of a nation, that a world that is too "modern" is a sinister world, that we are bored when we are comfortable, in short, according to the most reactionary remark of human history, the alibi of all exploitations, that "money doesn't make happiness"? Myself, I can readily imagine that working in New York is a terrible thing, but it is not New York which is terrible, it is work. By making this city into a petrified, infantile necropolis looming up out of an "abstract" age (but not, alas! out of an abstract art), Buffet once again diverts history into metaphysics. Black looks at America always begin with the skyscrapers, and stick there. Yet what the Pilgrims unloaded from the *Mayflower* was not only empiricism, the spirit of enterprise, in short the seed which has doubtless produced the most stupendous city in the world, but also Puritanism and profit, money and metaphysics. What is good, Buffet discredits. And what is bad, he passes over in silence.

1959

Tacitus and
the Funerary Baroque

COUNTED, the murders in the *Annals* are few enough (some fifty for three principates); but read, their effect is apocalyptic: from element to mass, a new quality appears, the world is transformed.[1] Perhaps that is what the baroque is: a growing contradiction between unit and totality, an art in which extent is not additive but multiplicative, in short, the density of an acceleration: In Tacitus, from year to year, death *gels*, and the more divided the moments of this solidification become, the more inseparable their sum: generic Death is massive, not conceptual; the idea, here, is not the product of a reduction, but of a repetition. We know of course that terrorism is not a quantitative phenomenon; we know that during our Revolution the number of tortures was laughable; but we also know that for the next century, from Büchner to Jouve (I am thinking of his preface to selections from Danton), we have seen terrorism as a being, not a volume. A stoic during an enlightened despotism, a creature of the Flavians writing under Trajan the history of the Julio-Claudian tyranny,

From *Critical Essays*.

[1] "In the ninth year of the emperor's reign, Fortune suddenly deranged everything: Tiberius became a cruel tyrant, as well as an abettor of cruelty in others" (IV.1).

Tacitus is in the situation of a liberal living the atrocities of sans-culottism: for him the past is an hallucination, an obsessional theater, a scene even more than a lesson: death is a protocol.

And first of all, in order to destroy number starting from number, what must be paradoxically established is the unit. In Tacitus the great anonymous slaughters scarcely rank as facts, they are not values: such things are always slave massacres: collective death is not human, death begins only with the individual, in other words, with the patrician. Tacitean death always discloses a civil status; the victim holds office, he is a unit, *one*, enclosing his history, his character, his function, his name. Death itself is not algebraic: death is always a dying; it is almost never an effect; however rapidly evoked, death appears as a duration, a process to be relished; we can tell from certain vibrations of the sentence that each victim knew he was dying; Tacitus always gives this ultimate consciousness to the victims of torture, which is probably how he establishes these deaths in terrorism: because he cites man at the purest moment of his end; it is the contradiction between object and subject, between thing and consciousness, it is this final stoic suspense which makes dying a strictly human act: we kill like animals, we die like men: all the deaths in Tacitus are instants, both immobility and catastrophe, both silence and vision.

The act outshines its cause: there is no distinction between murder and suicide, it is the same dying, sometimes administered, sometimes prescribed: the presentation of death establishes death; whether the centurion delivers a blow or an order, it suffices that he appear, like an angel, for the irreversible to occur: the instant is there, the outcome accedes to the present. All these murders have scarcely any causes: delation is enough—a kind of death ray which works by remote control: crime is immediately absorbed into its magical denomination: once you are called guilty, by anyone, you are already doomed; innocence raises no problem, once you are branded. Moreover, it is because death is a raw fact, and not the element of a reason, that it is contagious: the wife follows her husband into suicide without being obliged to do so, relatives die in clusters as soon as one of them is condemned.[2] For those who fling themselves into it—like Gribouille, who leaps into the river to avoid the rain—death is life because it puts an end to the ambiguity of signs, it shifts us from the unnamed to the named. The act yields to its name: if the law forbids killing a virgin, then it suffices to rape her before strangling her: it is the name which is rigid, it is the name which is the order of the world. To accede to the security of the fatal name, the reprieved or pardoned person commits suicide. Not to die is not only an accident but a negative, almost a ridiculous state: it occurs only by inadvertence. Supreme reason of this absurd structure, Cocceius Nerva enumerates all his reasons for living (he is neither poor, nor ill, nor under suspicion), and despite the emperor's objurgations, he kills himself. And as a crowning confusion, the *Ratio*, eliminated at the moment of the irreparable, is restored *after the fact*: dead, the victim is paradoxically extracted from the funereal universe, introduced into a trial where death is not certain: Nero would have pardoned him, he says, if he had lived; or again, the victim is given a choice of demise; or yet again, the suicide's corpse is strangled so that his estate may be confiscated.

Since dying is a protocol, the victim is always shown in the decor of life: one dreaming on a promontory, another at table, another in his garden, another in his bath. Once death is presented, it is suspended a moment: we perform our toilet, we

---

[2] Vetus, his mother-in-law, and his daughter: "Then, in the same chamber, with the same weapon, they sundered their veins and hurried into a bath, covered each, as delicacy required, with a single garment . . ." (XVI.11).

visit our pyre, we recite verses, we add a codicil to our will: this is the complimentary interval of last words, the interval in which death utters itself. When the act occurs, it is always absorbed into an object: it is death's object which is there, death is *praxis, technē*, its mode is instrumental: dagger, sword, cudgel, noose, razor for opening veins, poisoned feather for tickling the throat, wadding chewed by the man dying of hunger, blankets for smothering, cliff from which the victim is thrown, ceiling which falls in (Agrippina), garbage cart in which escape is vain (Messalina)—death always employs the mild substance of life: wood, metal, cloth, innocent tools. In order to be destroyed, the body makes contact, exposes itself, seeks out the object's murderous function hidden under its instrumental surface: this world of terrorism is a world which has no need of the scaffold: it is the object which momentarily abandons its vocation, lends itself to death, supports it.

To die, in Tacitus, is to perceive life. Whence "the fashionable manner": to open the veins or have them opened, to make death liquid, in other words, to convert it to duration and purification: one sprinkles the gods and the bystanders with blood, death is a libation; it is suspended, procrastinated, and one exerts a capricious freedom over it at the very heart of its final fatality—like Petronius opening and closing his veins at will; like Paulina, Seneca's wife, rescued on Nero's orders and retaining for years, in the pallor of her drained face, the very sign of a communication with the void. For this world of dying signifies that death is both easy and resistant: it is ubiquitous and yet eludes; no one escapes it and yet it must be wrestled with, its means must be accumulated, hemlock added to bloodletting and the steam bath, the act ceaselessly retraced, like a drawing consisting of several lines whose final beauty derives both from the multiplication and the rectitude of the essential outline.

For perhaps that is what the baroque is: the torment of a finality in profusion. Tacitean death is an open system, subject at once to a structure and a contestation, to a repetition and a direction; it seems to proliferate on all sides and yet remains imprisoned in a great moral and existential intention. Here again, it is the vegetable image which substantiates the baroque: the deaths correspond, but their symmetry is false. Spread out in time, subject to a movement, like that of sprouts on the same stalk: the regularity is a delusion, life directs the funerary system, terrorism is not bookkeeping but vegetation: everything is reproduced and yet nothing is repeated; such is perhaps the meaning of this Tacitean universe, in which the brilliant description of the phoenix (VI.28) seems to construe death symbolically as the purest moment of life.

1959

PART TWO

from *On Racine*

1. THE STRUCTURE

THERE are three Mediterraneans in Racine: Classical, Hebrew, and Byzantine. But poetically, these three spaces form only a single complex of water, dust, and fire. The great tragic sites are arid lands, squeezed between the sea and the desert, shade and sun raised to the absolute state. One need merely visit Greece today to understand the violence of limitation, and how much Racinian tragedy, by its "constrained" nature, corresponds to these sites Racine had never seen: Thebes, Buthrotum, Troezen—these capitals of tragedy are villages. Troezen, where Phaedra dies, is a scorched knoll fortified by rubble. The sun produces a landscape that is pure, distinct, depopulated; life is without shade, which is simultaneously repose, secrecy, exchange, and flaw. Even outside the house, there is no real breath of air: there is the scrub, the desert, an unorganized space. The Racinian habitat knows only one dream of flight: the sea, the ships; in *Iphigénie*, a whole people remains imprisoned by the tragedy because the wind fails to rise.

On Racine, translated by Richard Howard (New York: Hill and Wang, 1964).

The Chamber

This geography sustains a special relation between the house and its exterior, between the Racinian palace and its hinterland. Although there is only one setting, according to the rules, one might say that there are three tragic sites. There is first of all the Chamber: vestige of the mythic cave, it is the invisible and dreadful place where Power lurks: Nero's throne room, Ahasuerus' palace, the Holy of Holies where the God of the Jews lives. This cavern has a frequent substitute: the King's exile, portentous because no one ever knows if the King is living or dead (Amurath, Mithridates, Theseus). The characters speak of this undefined site only with respect and terror, they scarcely dare enter it, they pass before it with anxiety. The Chamber is both the abode of Power and its essence, for Power is only a secret: its form exhausts its function, it kills by being invisible. In *Bajazet* it is the mutes and black Orcan who deal out death, extend by silence and darkness the terrible inertia of the hidden Power.[1]

The Chamber is contiguous to the second tragic site, which is the Antechamber, the eternal space of all subjections, since it is here that one *waits*. The Antechamber (the stage proper) is a medium of transmission; it partakes of both interior and exterior, of Power and Event, of the concealed and the exposed. Fixed between the world, a place of action, and the Chamber, a place of silence, the Antechamber is the site of language: it is here that tragic man, lost between the letter and

---

[1] The function of the throne room, the Royal Chamber, is well expressed in these lines from *Esther*:

Au fond de leur palais leur majesté terrible
Affecte à leurs sujets de se rendre invisible;
Et la mort est le prix de tout audacieux.
Qui sans être appelé se présente à leurs yeux. (I,3)

Their dread majesty elects to remain deep within their palace, invisible to their subjects; and death is the reward of any intruder who is seen there without being summoned.

the meaning of things, utters his reasons. The tragic stage is therefore not strictly secret;[2] it is rather a blind alley, the anxious passage from secrecy to effusion, from immediate fear to fear expressed. It is a trap suspected, which is why the posture the tragic character must adopt within it is always of an extreme mobility (in Greek tragedy, it is the chorus that waits, that moves in the circular space, or orchestra, in front of the palace).

Between the Chamber and the Antechamber stands a tragic object which menacingly expresses both contiguity and ex-change, the tangency of hunter and prey: the Door. Here one waits, here one trembles; to enter it is a temptation and a transgression: Agrippina stakes all her power at Nero's door. The Door has an active substitute, necessary when the Power wants to spy on the Antechamber or paralyze the character within it, and this is the Veil (*Britannicus, Esther, Athalie*). The Veil (or the Wall that has ears) is not an inert substance intended to conceal, it is an eyelid, symbol of the masked gaze, so that the Antechamber is a site-object encircled by a space-subject. The Racinian stage is thus a spectacle twice over: to the eyes of the Invisible and to the eyes of the spectator (the site that best expresses this tragic contradiction is the Seraglio of *Bajazet*).

The third tragic site is the Exterior. Between Antechamber and Exterior, there is no transition; they are joined as immediately as the Antechamber and the Chamber. This contiguity is expressed poetically by the "linear" nature of the tragic enclosure: the palace walls plunge down into the sea, the stairs lead to the ships ready to sail, the ramparts are a balcony above the battle itself, and if there are hidden passages, they no longer constitute part of the tragedy, they are already Flight. Thus the line that separates tragedy from its negation is

---

[2] On the enclosure of the Racinian site, see Bernard Dort, *Huis clos racinien*.

thin, almost abstract; what is involved is a *limit*, in the ritual sense of the word: the tragedy is simultaneously prison and protection against impurity, against all that is not itself.

The three exterior spaces: death, escape, event

The Exterior is in fact the site of non-tragedy; it contains three kinds of space: that of death, that of escape, that of the event. Physical death never belongs to tragic space: this is reputedly for reasons of propriety;[3] but what propriety rejects in carnal death is an element alien to tragedy, an "impurity," the density of a reality scandalous because it no longer proceeds from the order of language, which is the only tragic order: in tragedy one never dies because one is always talking. And conversely, for the hero, to leave the stage is to die, one way or another. Roxanne's *Go!*'s to Bajazet are death sentences, and this movement is the model of a whole series of exits in which it is enough for the executioner to dismiss or banish his prey to cause death, as if the mere contact with the outer air was enough to dissolve or blast: how many Racinian victims die because they are no longer protected by this tragic site which nonetheless, they said, made them suffer mortally (Britannicus, Bajazet, Hippolytus). The essential image of this exterior death, in which the victim slowly suffocates out of the tragic air, is the Berenician Orient, which interminably summons the heroes into non-tragedy. More generally, transplanted outside the tragic space, Racinian man *languishes* (*s'ennuie*): he experiences all real space as a succession of chains (Orestes, Antiochus, Hippolytus): here suffering is evidently a substitute for death: all behavior that suspends language causes life to stop.

The second exterior space is that of escape: but escape is never named except by the inferior caste of friends and ser-

---

[3] Atalide *kills herself* on stage but *expires* off. Nothing illustrates better the disjunction of gesture and reality.

vants; the confidants and minor figures (Acomat, Zares) constantly recommend escape to the hero on one of those countless ships that cruise in front of every Racinian tragedy, representing how immediate and how easy its negation is[4] (there is only one ship-prison in Racine, the one on which the captive Eriphyle falls in love with her ravisher). The Exterior, moreover, is a space ritually transmitted, that is, entrusted and assigned to all the non-tragic personnel, like a kind of reverse ghetto, since it is the amplitude of space that is taboo here, confinement that is a privilege: it is to and from the Exterior that this race of confidants, servants, messengers, matrons, and guards come and go, responsible for feeding tragedy with events: their entrances and exits are tasks, not signs or acts. In that infinite (and infinitely sterile) conclave which is every tragedy, they are the officious secretaries who preserve the hero from profane contact with reality, spare him what might be called the trivial kitchenry of *doing*, and transmit the event to him only when it is pared down, reduced to the state of pure cause. This is the third function of exterior space: to keep action in a kind of quarantine accessible only to a neutral population responsible for sifting events, extracting the tragic essence from each and bringing on stage only fragments of the external world, distilled as *news*, ennobled as *narratives* (battles, suicides, returns, murders, feasts, miracles). Confronting this exclusive order of language which is tragedy, action is impurity itself.

Moreover, nothing indicates better the physical disparity of the two kinds of space, internal and external, than a curious phenomenon of temporal distortion that Racine has described

---

[4] *Nos vaisseaux sont tout prêts et le vent nous appelle . . . (And.* III,1)
Our ships are ready and the wind favorable . . .
Des vaisseaux dans Ostie armés en diligence . . . (Bér. I,3)
Ships hastily armed in Ostia . . .
Déjà sur un vaisseau dans le port préparé . . . (Baj. III,2)
Already on a ship made ready in the harbor . . .

typically in *Bajazet*: between exterior time and confined time occurs the time the message takes, so that one is never certain the event reported is the same as the event produced. The external event is actually never *finite*, it does not complete its transformation into pure cause. Confined in the Antechamber, receiving from the world outside only the nourishment brought to him by the confidant, the hero lives in an irremediable uncertainty: he *misses* the event. There is always too much time, the time of space itself. This quite Einsteinian problem constitutes most of the tragic action.[5] In short, Racinian topography is convergent; everything leads to the tragic site, but everything is locked there. The tragic site is *stupefied,* caught between two fears, two hallucinations: that of extent and that of depth.

The horde

This, then, is a first definition of the tragic hero: he is a man confined, a man who cannot *get out* without dying; his limit is his privilege, captivity his distinction. Take away the servant class, paradoxically defined by its very freedom, and what is left in the tragic site? A caste glorious in proportion to its immobility. Where does it come from?

---

[5] *Mais, comme vous savez, malgré ma diligence,*
Un long chemin sépare et le camp et Byzance;
Mille obstacles divers m'ont même traversé,
Et je puis ignorer tout ce qui s'est passé. (*Baj.* I,1)

But, as you know, for all my haste, the road between the camp and Byzantium is a long one; a thousand different obstacles lay in my path, and I may know nothing of all that has occurred.

Ce combat doit, dit-on, fixer nos destinées;
Et même, si d'Osmin je compte les journées,
Le Ciel en a déjà réglé l'événement,
Et le Sultan triomphe ou fuit en ce moment. (*Baj.* I,2)

This battle is supposed to settle our fate; and even if I number Osmin's days, Heaven has already settled the outcome, and the Sultan triumphs or flees at this moment.

Darwin, Atkinson, and later Freud (in *Totem and Taboo*) have suggested that in the earliest period of our history, men lived in savage hordes. Each horde was subject to the most powerful male, who possessed women, children, and property without distinction. The sons were dispossessed of everything, for the father's strength prevented them from obtaining the sisters or mothers whom they coveted. If the sons happened to provoke the father's jealousy, they were pitilessly killed, castrated, or driven out. Hence, according to these authors, the sons ultimately banded together to kill the father and take his place. Once the father was out of the way, discord broke out among the sons; they quarreled bitterly over his inheritance, and it was only after a long period of fratricidal struggles that they managed to establish a rational alliance among themselves: each renounced his desire for his mother or sisters: the incest taboo was instituted.

Such a history, even if it is only a "romance," is the whole of Racine's theater. If we make one essential tragedy out of eleven, if we arrange in a kind of exemplary constellation this tribe of some fifty tragic characters who inhabit Racinian tragedy, we shall discover the figures and the actions of the primeval horde: the father, unconditional master of the sons' lives (Amurath, Mithridates, Agamemnon, Theseus, Mordecai, Jehoiada, even Agrippina); the women, simultaneously mothers, sisters, and mistresses, always coveted, rarely obtained (Andromache, Junia, Atalide, Monimia); the brothers, always enemies because they are quarreling over the inheritance of a father who is not quite dead and who returns to punish them (Eteocles and Polynices, Nero and Britannicus, Pharnaces and Xiphares); lastly, the son, mortally torn between terror of the father and the necessity of destroying him (Pyrrhus, Nero, Titus, Pharnaces, Athaliah). Incest, rivalry among the brothers, murder of the father, overthrow of the

sons—these are the fundamental actions of the Racinian theater.

We are not certain just what is being represented here. Is it,
as in Darwin's hypothesis, an extremely early folklore theme,
the virtually asocial state of humanity? Is it, as in Freud's
hypothesis, the primal history of the psyche, reproduced in the
childhood of every man? I merely observe that the Racinian
theater finds its coherence only on the level of this ancient
fable, situated far beyond history or the human psyche:[6] the
purity of the language, the grace of the alexandrines, the precision of the "psychology," the conformism of the metaphysics
are very slight protections; the archaic bedrock is there, close
at hand. This original action is not performed by *characters*, in
the modern sense of the word; Racine, with the age, called
them much more appositely *actors*; we are dealing, essentially,
with masks, with figures that differ from each other not according to their public status but according to their place in
the general configuration that keeps them confined; sometimes
it is their function that distinguishes them (father opposed to
son, for instance), sometimes it is their degree of emancipation with regard to the most regressive figure of their lineage
(Pyrrhus represents a more independent son than Nero, Pharnaces than Xiphares, Titus than Antiochus; Hermione represents a fidelity less supple than Andromache's). Thus the
Racinian discourse affords great masses of undifferentiated
language, as if, through different speeches, a single person
were expressing himself; in relation to such profound utterance, the extremely pure contour of the Racinian language
functions as a veritable command; here language is aphoristic,
not realistic; it is expressly intended for quotation.

---

[6] "Racine paints a man for us not as he is, but somewhat beneath and beside
himself, at the moment when the other members of his family, the doctor,
and the magistrates would in fact begin to be concerned, if it were not
just a play." (Charles Mauron, *L'Inconscient dans l'œuvre et la vie de
Racine*.)

The double Eros

The tragic unit is thus not the individual but the figure, or, better still, the function which defines that figure. In the primeval horde, human relations fall into two chief categories: the relation of lust and the relation of authority; it is these that recur obsessively in Racine.

The Racinian Eros is double. The first Eros is born between lovers who share a very early community of existence: they have been raised together, love each other (or one loves the other) from childhood (Britannicus and Junia, Antiochus and Berenice, Bajazet and Atalide); here love is generated by duration, a gradual maturation process; there is, then, a mediation between the two partners, a mediation of time, of the past, in short, of legality: it is the parents themselves who have established the legitimacy of this love. The beloved woman is a sister for whom lust is authorized and consequently appeased; such love might be called the sororal Eros; its future is tranquil, for it is thwarted only by what is outside itself; its success appears to derive from its very origin: because it has consented to start from a mediation, misfortune is not fatal to it.

The other Eros, on the contrary, is an immediate one; it is born abruptly; its generation admits of no latency, it appears in the manner of an absolute Event, which is usually expressed by a brutal *passé défini* (*je le vis, elle me plut,* etc.). This Eros-Event is the one that attaches Nero to Junia, Berenice to Titus, Roxanne to Bajazet, Eriphyle to Achilles, Phaedra to Hippolytus. The hero is seized by it, bound as in a rape, and this capture is always of a visual order (we shall return to this matter): to love is to see. This double Eros is incompatible, one cannot proceed from one to the other, from love-as-rape (which is always condemned) to love-as-duration (which is always coveted), and this impossibility constitutes one of the

fundamental forms of Racinian failure. Of course, the unsuccessful lover can always try to replace the immediate Eros
by a substitute; he can, for instance, enumerate the reasons to
which he is appealing;[7] he can try to introduce a mediation
into this relation, can appeal to causality; he can suppose that
merely by seeing him often enough, his beloved will come to
love him, that coexistence, the basis of sororal love, will ultimately produce that love. But these are, precisely, *reasons*—
that is, a language destined to mask an inevitable failure. The
sororal Eros is actually given as a utopia, far in the past or in
the future, whose institutional version will be marriage (so
important for Racine). The true Eros, the one that is *painted*,
in other words immobilized in the tragic tableau, is the immediate Eros. And precisely because this is a predatory Eros, it
supposes an entire physics, or strictly speaking an *optics* of the
image.

We know nothing of the age or the beauty of the Racinian
lovers. Periodically, critics debate whether Phaedra is very
young, if Nero is an adolescent, if Berenice is middle-aged, if
Mithridates is still attractive. We know of course the norms of
the period; we know that "one could declare one's love to a
girl of fourteen without her being rightly offended thereby,"
and that "a woman is ugly after she has lived thirty years."
But this matters little. Racinian beauty is abstract in that it is
always *named*: Racine says that Bajazet is lovable, that
Berenice has beautiful hands; the concept somehow gets rid of

---

[7] *Ouvrez les yeux, Seigneur, et songeons entre nous*
Par combien de raisons Bérénice est à vous. (*Bér.* III,2)

Open your eyes, my lord, and consider here the reasons why Berenice belongs
to you.

Quoi! Madame, les soins qu'il a pris pour vous plaire,
Ce que vous avez fait, ce que vous pouvez faire,
Ses périls, ses respects, et surtout vos appas,
Tout cela de son cœur ne vous répond-il pas? (*Baj.* I,3)

But, my lady, think of all he has done to please you, and all you have done,
all you can do still, his dangers, his respect, and most of all your own
beauty—does all this not answer for his heart?

the thing.[8] We might say that here beauty is a propriety, a class characteristic, not an anatomical disposition: no effort is made toward what might be called the body's *adjectivity*.

Yet the Racinian Eros (at least the immediate Eros, which will henceforth be our concern here) is never sublimated; emerging fully armed, entirely *finished*, from pure vision, it is immobilized in the perpetual fascination of the adverse body, it constantly reproduces the original scene that has formed it (Berenice, Phaedra, Eriphyle, Nero *relive* the birth of their love[9]); the recital these heroes make of it to their confidant is obviously not a matter of information but a veritable obsessive protocol. Moreover it is because love, in Racine, is a pure ordeal of fascination that it is so difficult to distinguish from hate; hate is openly physical, it is the acute sense of the other body. Like love, it is born from sight, feeds on it, and like love it produces a current of joy. Racine has given us the theory of this carnal hatred in his first play, *La Thébaïde*.[10]

What Racine expresses immediately, then, is alienation, not desire. This is evident if we examine Racinian sexuality, which is a sexuality of situation rather than of Nature. In Racine, sex itself is subject to the fundamental situation of the tragic figures among themselves, which is a relation of force. There

---

[8] *Cette fière princesse a percé son beau sein . . . (Théb.* V,5)
This proud princess has stabbed her lovely breast . . .
J'ai senti son beau corps tout froid entre mes bras . . . (V,5)
I felt his splendid body turn cold in my arms . . .
On sait qu'elle est charmante, et de si belles mains
Semblent vous demander l'empire des humains (Bér. II,2)
We know she is charming, and such beautiful hands seem to ask you for the throne
Bajazet est aimable; il vit que son salut . . . (Baj. I,2)
Bajazet is appealing; he saw that his survival . . .

[9] More generally, such narratives are not at all the dead wood of the tragedy; quite the contrary, they are the hallucinatory—that is, in a sense, the most profound—part.

[10] The theory of physical hatred is given in *La Thébaïde,* IV,1. The feudal system had sublimated the Eros of the adversaries by subjecting the duel to a knightly ritual. We find a trace of this sublimation in *Alexandre* (the conflict between Alexander and Porus); Alexander is chivalrous—but he is, precisely, outside the tragedy.

are no characters in the Racinian theater (which is why it is quite futile to argue about the individuality of the *dramatis personae*, to wonder whether Andromache is coquettish or Bajazet virile); there are only situations, in the almost formal sense of the word: everything derives its being from its place in the general constellation of strengths and weaknesses. The division of the Racinian world into strong and weak, into tyrants and captives, covers in a sense the division of the sexes: it is their situation in the relation of force that orchestrates some characters as virile and others as feminine, without concern for their biological sex. There are viriloid women (they need merely participate in Power: Axiane, Agrippina, Roxanne, Athaliah). There are feminoid men, not by character but by situation: Taxiles, whose cowardice is softness, accessibility to Alexander's strength; Bajazet, both captive and coveted, doomed by a strictly Racinian alternative to murder or to rape; Hippolytus, who is in Phaedra's power, desired by her and a virgin as well (Racine tried to "defeminize" Hippolytus by making him Aricia's lover, but without success, as the judgment of his contemporaries attests—the initial situation was too strong); lastly Britannicus, hated by Nero, is nonetheless in a certain erotic relation with him, for it is enough that hate coincide with Power for sex to be ambiguous; Nero delights in Britannicus' suffering as in that of a woman loved and tortured.[11] Here we find a first sketch of Racinian fatality: a simple relation, in origin purely circumstantial (captivity or tyranny), is converted into a biological datum; situation is converted into sex, chance into essence.

The constellations change little in Racinian tragedy, and sexuality is generally immobile. But if, by exception, the relation of force yields, if the tyranny weakens, sex itself tends to

[11] The erotic relation between Nero and Britannicus is explicit in Tacitus. As for Hippolytus, Racine has made him Aricia's lover to keep the public from taking him for an invert.

be modified, inverted. It is enough for Athaliah, the most virile of Racine's women, to become sensitive to Joash's "charm" and relax her power for her sexuality to be disturbed: once the constellation appears to be modified, a new division affects the character's being, a new sex appears, and Athaliah *becomes* a woman.[12] Inversely, those who are by condition outside any relation of force (that is, outside the tragedy) have no sex. Confidants, servants, advisers (Burrhus, for instance, is scornfully excluded from Eros by Nero[13]), never accede to sexual existence. And it is obviously in the most manifestly asexualized characters, matron (Oenone) or eunuch (Acomat), that the spirit most contrary to tragedy declares itself, the spirit of viability: only the absence of sex can authorize a definition of life not as a critical relation of forces, but as duration, and this duration as value. Sex is a tragic privilege insofar as it is the first attribute of the original conflict: it is not the sexes that create the conflict, it is the conflict that defines the sexes.

Disorder

Thus it is alienation that constitutes the Racinian Eros. As a consequence, the human body is not treated in plastic, but in magical terms. As we have seen, neither age nor beauty has any specificity here: the body is never given as an Apollonian object (for Racine, Apollonism is a canonical attribute of death, in which the body becomes a statue, that is, a glorified,

---

[12] *Ami, depuis deux jours, je ne la connais plus.*
Ce n'est plus cette reine éclairée, intrépide,
Elevée au-dessus de son sexe timide . . .
Elle flotte, elle hésite; en un mot, elle est femme. (*Ath.* III,3)

Friend, for the last two days I no longer recognize her. She is no longer that enlightened, fearless queen, raised above her timid sex. . . . She wavers, she hesitates; in a word, she is a woman.

[13] *Mais, croyez-moi, l'amour est une autre science,*
Burrhus; et je ferais quelque difficulté
D'abaisser jusque-là votre sévérité (*Brit.* III,1)

But love, believe me, is knowledge of another kind, Burrhus; and I should find it hard to reduce your severity to its level.

arranged past). The Racinian body is essentially disturbance, defection, disorder. Garments—which as we know extend the body in an equivocal way, both masking and flaunting it—are responsible for dramatizing the state of the body: they *weigh down* in transgression, they *come undone* in agitation; the implicit gesture, here, is *disrobing* (Phaedra, Berenice, Junia),[14] the simultaneous token of transgression and attraction, for in Racine carnal disorder is always a kind of blackmail, an attempt to compel pity (sometimes carried to the point of sadistic provocation).[15] This is the implicit function of all the physical disturbances so abundantly recorded by Racine: blushing, blanching, the abrupt succession of one and then the other, sighs, and finally tears, whose erotic power is so familiar. Here reality is always ambiguous, both expression and act, escape and blackmail: in short, the Racinian disorder is essentially a *sign*, that is, a signal and a commination.

The most spectacular agitation, that is, the one best suited to tragedy, is the kind that attacks Racinian man at his vital center, his language.[16] Suspension of speech, whose sexual nature has been suggested by certain authors, is very frequent in the Racinian hero; it perfectly expresses the sterility of the

---

[14] *Belle, sans ornements, dans le simple appareil*
D'une beauté qu'on vient d'arracher au sommeil. (*Brit.* II,2)
Lovely, unadorned, clad simply in her beauty torn from sleep.

Laissez-moi relever ces voiles détachés,
Et ces cheveux épars dont vos yeux sont cachés. (*Bér.* IV,2)
Let me bind these loosened veils, and smooth the hair that hides your eyes.

Que ces vains ornements, que ces voiles me pèsent! (*Phèd.* I,3)
How these vain adornments, how these veils weigh me down!

[15] *Laisse, laisse, Phénice, il verra son ouvrage* . . . (*Bér.* IV,2)
Leave me as I am, Phenice, he will see what he has done . . .

[16] Among others:
J'ai voulu lui parler, et ma voix s'est perdue . . . (*Brit.* II,2)
I tried to speak to her, and my voice failed . . .

Et dès le premier mot, ma langue embarrassée
Dans ma bouche vingt fois a demeuré glacée. (*Bér.* II,2)
And at the first word, my tongue froze in my mouth, however often I tried to speak.

Mes yeux ne voyaient plus, je ne pouvais parler . . . (*Phèd.* I,3)
My eyes went blind, I could not speak . . .

erotic relation, its immobility. To be able to break with
Berenice, Titus turns aphasiac, in one and the same movement
withdraws and apologizes. Here "I love you too much" and "I
don't love you enough" find, economically enough, a common
sign. To avoid speech is to avoid the relation of force, to avoid
tragedy: only the extreme heroes can attain this limit (Nero,
Titus, Phaedra), from which their tragic partner leads them
back as quickly as possible, *constraining* them in a sense to
recover a language (Agrippina, Berenice, Oenone). Muteness
has a gestural analogy: the swoon, or at least its noble version,
immobility. This is always a kind of bilingual act: as escape,
such paralysis tends to deny the tragic order; as blackmail, it
still participates in the relation of force. Each time a Racinian
hero resorts to bodily disorder, we have the indication of a
tragic bad faith: the hero *feints* with tragedy. All such behavior tends, in effect, to a frustration of tragic reality, being a
rejection (an ambiguous one, moreover, since to reject tragedy
may be to rediscover the world), a simulation of death, a
paradoxical, even a useful death, since one comes back to life.
Naturally, disorder is a privilege of the tragic hero, for he
alone is engaged in a relation of force. The confidants may
share the master's agitation—more often they attempt to calm
it—but they never employ the ritual language of disorder: a
handmaid does not faint. For example, the tragic hero cannot
sleep (except if he is a monster, like Nero, whose sleep is
wicked). Archas sleeps; Agamemnon lies awake, or better
still, indulging in a noble—because tormented—form of repose, he dreams.

In short, the Racinian Eros brings bodies into confrontation
only to destroy them. The sight of the adverse body disorders
language,[17] troubles it, whether by exaggerating it (in the

---

[17] Naturally, the fascination of the adverse body also occurs in situations of
hatred. Here is how Nero describes his relation to Agrippina:
Éloigné de ses yeux, j'ordonne, je menace . . .
Mais (je t'expose ici mon âme toute nue)

excessively rationalized harangues) or by silencing it. The Racinian hero never achieves *adequate* behavior toward the adverse body: real frequentation is always a failure. Then is there no moment when the Racinian Eros is happy? Yes, precisely when it is unreal. The adverse body confers happiness only when it is an image; the successful moments of Racinian Eros are always memories.

.   .   .

1960

Sitôt que mon malheur me ramène à sa vue,
Soit que je n'ose encor démentir le pouvoir
De ces yeux où j'ai lu si longtemps mon devoir . . .
Mais enfin mes efforts ne me servent de rien;
Mon génie étonné tremble, devant le sien. (Brit. II,2)

When she cannot see me, I threaten, command . . . But (I am showing you my heart laid bare) as soon as I am unlucky enough to be in her presence, I dare not dispute the power of those eyes that for so long defined my duty . . . All my efforts are futile: my awed spirit trembles before hers.

Authors and Writers

W<small>HO</small> speaks? Who writes? We still lack a sociology of language. What we know is that language is a power and that, from public body to social class, a group of men is sufficiently defined if it possesses, to various degrees, the national language. Now, for a very long time—probably for the entire classical capitalist period, i.e., from the sixteenth to the nineteenth century, in France—the uncontested owners of the language, and they alone, were authors; if we except preachers and jurists (enclosed moreover in functional languages), no one else spoke, and this "monopoly" of the language produced, paradoxically, a rigid order, an order less of producers than of production: it was not the literary profession which was structured (it has developed greatly in three hundred years, from the domestic poet to the businessman-writer), but the very substance of this literary discourse, subjected to rules of use, genre, and composition, more or less immutable from Marot to Verlaine, from Montaigne to Gide. Contrary to so-called primitive societies, in which there is witchcraft only through the agency of a witch doctor, as Mauss has shown, the literary institution transcended the literary functions, and

From *Critical Essays.*

185

within this institution, its essential raw material, language. Institutionally, the literature of France is its language, a half-linguistic, half-aesthetic system which has not lacked a mythic dimension as well, that of its clarity.

When, in France, did the author cease being the only one to speak? Doubtless at the time of the Revolution, when there first appear men who appropriate the authors' language for political ends. The institution remains in place: it is still a matter of that great French language, whose lexicon and euphony are respectfully preserved throughout the greatest paroxysm of French history; but the functions change, the personnel is increased for the next hundred years; the authors themselves, from Chateaubriand or Maistre to Hugo or Zola, help broaden the literary function, transform this institutionalized language of which they are still the acknowledged owners into the instrument of a new action; and alongside these authors in the strict sense of the word, a new group is constituted and develops, a new custodian of the public language. Intellectuals? The word has a complex resonance;[1] I prefer calling them here *writers*. And since the present may be that fragile moment in history where the two functions coexist, I should like to sketch a comparative typology of the author and the writer with reference to the substance they share: language.

The author performs a function, the writer an activity. Not that the author is a pure essence: he acts, but his action is immanent in its object, it is performed paradoxically on its own instrument: language; the author is the man who *labors*, who works up his utterance (even if he is inspired) and functionally absorbs himself in this labor, this work. His activity involves two kinds of norm: technical (of composition, genre, style) and artisanal (of patience, correctness, perfection). The

[1] Apparently the word *intellectual*, in the sense we give it today, was born at the time of the Dreyfus affair, obviously applied by the anti-Dreyfusards to the Dreyfusards.

paradox is that, the raw material becoming in a sense its own end, literature is at bottom a tautological activity, like that of those cybernetic machines constructed for themselves (Ashby's homeostat): the author is a man who radically absorbs the world's *why* in a *how to write*. And the miracle, so to speak, is that this narcissistic activity has always provoked an interrogation of the world: by enclosing himself in the *how to write*, the author ultimately discovers the open question par excellence: why the world? What is the meaning of things? In short, it is precisely when the author's work becomes its own end that it regains a mediating character: the author conceives of literature as an end, the world restores it to him as a means: and it is in this perpetual inconclusiveness that the author rediscovers the world, an alien world moreover, since literature represents it as a question—never, finally, as an answer.

Language is neither an instrument nor a vehicle: it is a structure, as we increasingly suspect; but the author is the only man, by definition, to lose his own structure and that of the world in the structure of language. Yet this language is an (infinitely) labored substance; it is a little like a superlanguage —reality is never anything but a pretext for it (for the author, *to write* is an intransitive verb); hence it can never explain the world, or at least, when it claims to explain the world, it does so only the better to conceal its ambiguity: once the explanation is fixed in a work, it immediately becomes an ambiguous product of the real, to which it is linked by perspective; in short, literature is always unrealistic, but its very unreality permits it to question the world—though these questions can never be direct: starting from a theocratic explanation of the world, Balzac finally does nothing but interrogate. Thus the author existentially forbids himself two kinds of language, whatever the intelligence or the sincerity of his enterprise: first, *doctrine*, since he converts despite himself, by his very project, every explanation into a spectacle: he is always an

inductor of ambiguity;[2] second, *evidence*, since he has consigned himself to language, the author cannot have a naïve
consciousness, cannot "work up" a protest without his message finally bearing much more on the working-up than on the
protest: by identifying himself with language, the author loses
all claim to truth, for language is precisely that structure
whose very goal (at least historically, since the Sophists), once
it is no longer rigorously transitive, is to neutralize the true
and the false.[3] But what he obviously gains is the power to
disturb the world, to afford it the dizzying spectacle of *praxis*
without sanction. This is why it is absurd to ask an author for
"commitment": a "committed" author claims simultaneous
participation in two structures, inevitably a source of deception. What we can ask of an author is that he be responsible;
again, let there be no mistake: whether or not an author is
responsible for his opinions is unimportant; whether or not an
author assumes, more or less intelligently, the ideological implications of his work is also secondary; an author's true
responsibility is to support literature as a failed commitment,
as a Mosaic glance at the Promised Land of the real (this is
Kafka's responsibility, for example).

Naturally, literature is not a grace, it is the body of the
projects and decisions which lead a man to fulfill himself (that
is, in a sense, to essentialize himself) in language alone: an
author is a man who wants to be an author. Naturally too,
society, which consumes the author, transforms project into
vocation, labor into talent, and technique into art: thus is born
the myth of fine writing: the author is a salaried priest, he is
the half-respectable, half-ridiculous guardian of the sanctuary

---

[2] An author can produce a system, but it will never be consumed as such.
[3] Structure of reality and structure of language: no better indication of the
difficulty of a coincidence between the two than the constant failure of
dialectic, once it becomes discourse: for language is not dialectic, it can
only say "we must be dialectical," but it cannot be so itself: language is
a representation without perspective, except precisely for the author's; but
the author dialecticizes himself, he does not dialecticize the world.

of the great French language, a kind of national treasure, a sacred merchandise, produced, taught, consumed, and exported in the context of a sublime economy of values. This sacralization of the author's struggle with form has great consequences, and not merely formal ones: it permits society—or Society—to distance the work's content when it risks becoming an embarrassment, to convert it into pure spectacle, to which it is entitled to apply a liberal (i.e., an indifferent) judgment, to neutralize the revolt of passion, the subversion of criticism (which forces the "committed" author into an incessant and impotent provocation)—in short, to recuperate the author: every author is eventually digested by the literary institution, unless he scuttles himself, i.e., unless he ceases to identify his being with that of language: this is why so few authors renounce writing, for that is literally to kill themselves, to die to the being they have chosen; and if there are such authors, their silence echoes like an inexplicable conversion (Rimbaud).[4]

The *writer*, on the other hand, is a "transitive" man, he posits a goal (to give evidence, to explain, to instruct), of which language is merely a means; for him language supports a *praxis,* it does not constitute one. Thus language is restored to the nature of an instrument of communication, a vehicle of "thought." Even if the writer pays some attention to style, this concern is never ontological. The writer performs no essential technical action upon language; he employs an utterance common to all writers, a *koinē* in which we can of course distinguish certain dialects (Marxist, for example, or Christian, or existentialist), but very rarely styles. For what defines the writer is the fact that his project of communication is *naïve*: he does not admit that his message is reflexive, that it

---

[4] These are the modern elements of the problem. We know that on the contrary Racine's contemporaries were not at all surprised when he suddenly stopped writing tragedies and became a royal functionary.

closes over itself, and that we can read in it, diacritically, anything else but what he means: what writer would tolerate a psychoanalysis of his language? He considers that his work resolves an ambiguity, institutes an irreversible explanation (even if he regards himself as a modest instructor); whereas for the author, as we have seen, it is just the other way around: he knows that his language, intransitive by choice and by labor, inaugurates an ambiguity, even if it appears to be peremptory, that it offers itself, paradoxically, as a monumental silence to be deciphered, that it can have no other motto but Jacques Rigaut's profound remark: *and even when I affirm, I am still questioning.*

The author participates in the priest's role, the writer in the clerk's; the author's language is an intransitive act (hence, in a sense, a gesture), the writer's an activity. The paradox is that society consumes a transitive language with many more reservations than an intransitive one: the writer's status, even today when writers abound, is much more problematic than the author's. This is primarily the consequence of a material circumstance: the author's language is a merchandise offered through traditional channels, it is the unique object of an institution created only for literature; the writer's language, on the contrary, can be produced and consumed only in the shadow of institutions which have, originally, an entirely different function than to focus on language: the university, scientific and scholarly research, politics, etc. Then, too, the writer's language is dependent in another way: because it is (or considers itself) no more than a simple vehicle, its nature as merchandise is transferred to the project of which it is the instrument: we are presumed to sell "thought" exclusive of any art; now the chief mythic attribute of "pure" thought (it would be better to say "unapplied" thought) is precisely that it is produced outside the channel of money: contrary to form (which costs a lot, as Valéry said), thought costs nothing, but it also does not sell itself, it gives itself—generously. This points up at least two new differences between author and writer. First, the writer's production always has a free but also a somewhat "insistent" character: the writer offers society what society does not always ask of him: situated on the margin of institutions and transactions, his language appears paradoxically more individual, at least in its motifs, than the author's language: *the writer's function is to say at once and on every occasion what he thinks*;[5] and this function suffices, he thinks, to justify him; whence the critical, urgent aspect of the writer's language: it always seems to indicate a conflict between thought's irrepressible character and the inertia of a society reluctant to consume a merchandise which no specific institution normalizes. Thus we see *a contrario*—and this is the second difference—that the social function of literary language (that of the author) is precisely *to transform thought* (or consciousness, or protest) *into merchandise*; society wages a kind of vital warfare to appropriate, to acclimatize, to institutionalize the risk of thought, and it is language, that model institution, which affords it the means to do so: the paradox here is that "provocative" *language* is readily accommodated by the literary institution: the scandals of language, from Rimbaud to Ionesco, are rapidly and perfectly integrated; whereas "provocative" *thought*, insofar as it is to be immediate (without mediation), can only exhaust itself in the no man's land of form: the scandal is never total.

I am describing here a contradiction which, in fact, is rarely pure: everyone today moves more or less openly between the two postulations, the author's and the writer's; it is doubtless the responsibility of history which has brought us into the

[5] This function of *immediate manifestation* is the very opposite of the author's: (1) the author hoards, he publishes at a rhythm which is not that of his consciousness; (2) he mediatizes what he thinks by a laborious and "regular" form; (3) he permits a free interrogation of his work, he is anything but dogmatic.

world too late to be complacent authors and too soon (?) to be heeded writers. Today, each member of the intelligentsia harbors both roles in himself, one or the other of which he "retracts" more or less well: authors occasionally have the impulses, the impatiences of writers; writers sometimes gain access to the theater of language. We want *to write something,* and at the same time *we write* (intransitively). In short, our age produces a bastard type: the author-writer. His function is inevitably paradoxical: he provokes and exorcises at the same time; formally, his language is free, screened from the institution of literary language, and yet, enclosed in this very freedom, it secretes its own rules in the form of a common style; having emerged from the club of men-of-letters, the author-writer finds another club, that of the intelligentsia. On the scale of society as a whole, this new group has a complementary function: the intellectual's style functions as the paradoxical sign of a non-language, it permits society to experience the dream of a communication without system (without institution): to write without "style," to communicate "pure thought" without such communication developing any parasitical message—that is the model which the author-writer creates for society. It is a model at once distant and necessary, with which society plays something of a cat-and-mouse game: it acknowledges the author-writer by buying his books (however few), recognizing their public character; and at the same time it keeps him at a distance, obliging him to support himself by means of the subsidiary institutions it controls (the university, for instance), constantly accusing him of intellectualism, i.e., in terms of myth, sterility (a reproach the author never incurs). In short, from an anthropological viewpoint, the author-writer is an excluded figure integrated by his very exclusion, a remote descendant of the accursed: his function in society as a whole is perhaps related to the one Lévi-Strauss attributes to the witch doctor: a function of complementarity, both witch doctor and intellectual in a sense stabilizing a disease which is necessary to the collective economy of health. And naturally it is not surprising that such a conflict (or such a contract, if you prefer) should be joined on the level of language; for language is this paradox: the institutionalization of subjectivity.

1960

The Photographic Message

T HE press photograph is a message. Considered overall this message is formed by a source of emission, a channel of transmission and a point of reception. The source of emission is the staff of the newspaper, the group of technicians certain of whom take the photo, some of whom choose, compose, and treat it, while others, finally, give it a title, a caption, and a commentary. The point of reception is the public which reads the paper. As for the channel of transmission, this is the newspaper itself, or, more precisely, a complex of concurrent messages with the photograph as center and surrounds constituted by the text, the title, the caption, the layout and, in a more abstract but no less "informative" way, by the very name of the paper (this name represents a knowledge that can heavily orientate the reading of the message strictly speaking: a photograph can change its meaning as it passes from the very conservative *L'Aurore* to the Communist *L'Humanité*). These observations are not without their importance for it can readily be seen that in the case of the press photograph the three traditional parts of the message do not call for the same

From *Image-Music-Text*, translated by Stephen Heath (New York: Hill and Wang, 1978).

method of investigation. The emission and the reception of the message both lie within the field of a sociology: it is a matter of studying human groups, of defining motives and attitudes, and of trying to link the behavior of these groups to the social totality of which they are a part. For the message itself, however, the method is inevitably different: whatever the origin and the destination of the message, the photograph is not simply a product or a channel but also an object endowed with a structural autonomy. Without in any way intending to divorce this object from its use, it is necessary to provide for a specific method prior to sociological analysis and which can only be the immanent analysis of the unique structure that a photograph constitutes.

Naturally, even from the perspective of a purely immanent analysis, the structure of the photograph is not an isolated structure; it is in communication with at least one other structure, namely the text—title, caption, or article—accompanying every press photograph. The totality of the information is thus carried by two different structures (one of which is linguistic). These two structures are cooperative but, since their units are heterogeneous, necessarily remain separate from one another: here (in the text) the substance of the message is made up of words; there (in the photograph) of lines, surfaces, shades. Moreover, the two structures of the message each occupy their own defined spaces, these being contiguous but not "homogenized," as they are for example in the rebus, which fuses words and images in a single line of reading. Hence, although a press photograph is never without a written commentary, the analysis must first of all bear on each separate structure; it is only when the study of each structure has been exhausted that it will be possible to understand the manner in which they complement one another. Of the two structures, one is already familiar, that of language (but not, it is true, that of the "literature" formed by the language use of the newspaper; an enormous amount of work is still to be done in this connection), while almost nothing is known about the other, that of the photograph. What follows will be limited to the definition of the initial difficulties in providing a structural analysis of the photographic message.

THE PHOTOGRAPHIC PARADOX

What is the content of the photographic message? What does the photograph transmit? By definition, the scene itself, the literal reality. From the object to its image there is of course a reduction—in proportion, perspective, color—but at no time is this reduction a *transformation* (in the mathematical sense of the term). In order to move from the reality to its photograph it is in no way necessary to divide up this reality into units and to constitute these units as signs, substantially different from the object they communicate; there is no necessity to set up a relay, that is to say a code, between the object and its image. Certainly the image is not the reality but at least it is its perfect *analogon* and it is exactly this analogical perfection which, to common sense, defines the photograph. Thus can be seen the special status of the photographic image: *it is a message without a code*; from which proposition an important corollary must immediately be drawn: the photographic message is a continuous message.

Are there other messages without a code? At first sight, yes: precisely the whole range of analogical reproductions of reality —drawings, paintings, cinema, theater. In fact, however, each of those messages develops in an immediate and obvious way a supplementary message, in addition to the analogical content itself (scene, object, landscape), which is what is commonly called the *style* of the reproduction; second meaning, whose signifier is a certain "treatment" of the image (result of the action of the creator) and whose signified, whether aesthetic or ideological, refers to a certain "culture" of the society receiving the message. In short, all these "imitative" arts comprise two messages: a *denoted* message, which is the *analogon* itself, and a *connoted* message, which is the manner in which the society to a certain extent communicates what it thinks of it. This duality of messages is evident in all reproductions other than photographic ones: there is no drawing, no matter how exact, whose very exactitude is not turned into a style (the style of "verism"); no filmed scene whose objectivity is not finally read as the very sign of objectivity. Here again, the study of these connoted messages has still to be carried out (in particular it has to be decided whether what is called a work of art can be reduced to a system of significations); one can only anticipate that for all these imitative arts—when common— the code of the connoted system is very likely constituted either by a universal symbolic order or by a period rhetoric, in short by a stock of stereotypes (schemes, colors, graphisms, gestures, expressions, arrangements of elements).

When we come to the photograph, however, we find in principle nothing of the kind, at any rate as regards the press photograph (which is never an "artistic" photograph). The photograph professing to be a mechanical analogue of reality, its first-order message in some sort completely fills its substance and leaves no place for the development of a second-order message. Of all the structures of information,[1] the photograph appears as the only one that is exclusively constituted and occupied by a "denoted" message, a message which totally exhausts its mode of existence. In front of a photograph, the feeling of "denotation," or, if one prefers, of analogical plenitude, is so great that the description of a photograph is literally

---

[1] It is a question, of course, of "cultural" or culturalized structures, not of operational structures. Mathematics, for example, constitutes a denoted structure without any connotation at all; should mass society seize on it, however, setting out for instance an algebraic formula in an article on Einstein, this originally purely mathematical message now takes on a very heavy connotation, since it *signifies* science.

impossible; *to describe* consists precisely in joining to the denoted message a relay or second-order message derived from a
code which is that of language and constituting in relation to
the photographic analogue, however much care one takes to be
exact, a connotation: to describe is thus not simply to be
imprecise or incomplete, it is to change structures, to signify
something different from what is shown.[2]

This purely "denotative" status of the photograph, the perfection and plenitude of its analogy, in short its "objectivity,"
has every chance of being mythical (these are the characteristics that common sense attributes to the photograph). In
actual fact, there is a strong probability (and this will be a
working hypothesis) that the photographic message too—at
least in the press—is connoted. Connotation is not necessarily
immediately graspable at the level of the message itself (it is,
one could say, at once invisible and active, clear and implicit)
but it can already be inferred from certain phenomena which
occur at the levels of the production and reception of the
message: on the one hand, the press photograph is an object
that has been worked on, chosen, composed, constructed,
treated according to professional, aesthetic, or ideological
norms which are so many factors of connotation; while on the
other, this same photograph is not only perceived, received, it
is *read*, connected more or less consciously by the public that
consumes it to a traditional stock of signs. Since every sign
supposes a code, it is this code (of connotation) that one
should try to establish. The photographic paradox can then be
seen as the co-existence of two messages, the one without a
code (the photographic analogue), the other with a code (the
"art," or the treatment, or the "writing," or the rhetoric, of the
photograph); structurally, the paradox is clearly not the collu-

---

[2] The description of a drawing is easier, involving, finally, the description of
a structure that is already connoted, fashioned with a *coded* signification in
view. It is for this reason perhaps that psychological texts use a great many
drawings and very few photographs.

sion of a denoted message and a connoted message (which is the—probably inevitable—status of all the forms of mass communication), it is that here the connoted (or coded) message develops on the basis of a message *without a code*. This structural paradox coincides with an ethical paradox: when one wants to be "neutral," "objective," one strives to copy reality meticulously, as though the analogical were a factor of resistance against the investment of values (such at least is the definition of aesthetic "realism"); how then can the photograph be at once "objective" and "invested," natural and cultural? It is through an understanding of the mode of imbrication of denoted and connoted messages that it may one day be possible to reply to that question. In order to undertake this work, however, it must be remembered that since the denoted message in the photograph is absolutely analogical, which is to say *continuous*, outside of any recourse to a code, there is no need to look for the signifying units of the first-order message; the connoted message on the contrary does comprise a plane of expression and a plane of content, thus necessitating a veritable decipherment. Such a decipherment would as yet be premature, for in order to isolate the signifying units and the signified themes (or values) one would have to carry out (perhaps using tests) directed readings, artificially varying certain elements of a photograph to see if the variations of forms led to variations in meaning. What can at least be done now is to forecast the main planes of analysis of photographic connotation.

CONNOTATION PROCEDURES

Connotation, the imposition of second meaning on the photographic message proper, is realized at the different levels of the production of the photograph (choice, technical treatment, framing, layout) and represents, finally, a coding of the photographic analogue. It is thus possible to separate out various connotation procedures, bearing in mind however that these procedures are in no way units of signification such as a subsequent analysis of a semantic kind may one day manage to define; they are not strictly speaking part of the photographic structure. The procedures in question are familiar and no more will be attempted here than to translate them into structural terms. To be fully exact, the first three (trick effects, pose, objects) should be distinguished from the last three (photogenia, aestheticism, syntax), since in the former the connotation is produced by a modification of the reality itself, of, that is, the denoted message (such preparation is obviously not peculiar to the photograph). If they are nevertheless included among the connotation procedures, it is because they too benefit from the prestige of the denotation: the photograph allows the photographer to *conceal elusively* the preparation to which he subjects the scene to be recorded. Yet the fact still remains that there is no certainty from the point of view of a subsequent structural analysis that it will be possible to take into account the material they provide.

1. *Trick effects.* A photograph given wide circulation in the American press in 1951 is reputed to have cost Senator Millard Tydings his seat; it showed the Senator in conversation with the Communist leader Earl Browder. In fact, the photograph had been faked, created by the artificial bringing together of the two faces. The methodological interest of trick effects is that they intervene without warning in the plane of denotation; they utilize the special credibility of the photograph—this, as was seen, being simply its exceptional power of denotation—in order to pass off as merely denoted a message which is in reality heavily connoted; in no other treatment does connotation assume so completely the "objective" mask of denotation. Naturally, signification is only possible to the extent that there is a stock of signs, the beginnings of a code. The signifier here is the conversational attitude of the two

figures and it will be noted that this attitude becomes a sign only for a certain society, only given certain values. What makes the speakers' attitude the sign of a reprehensible familiarity is the tetchy anti-Communism of the American electorate; which is to say that the code of connotation is neither artificial (as in a true language) nor natural, but historical.

2. *Pose.* Consider a press photograph of President Kennedy widely distributed at the time of the 1960 election: a half-length profile shot, eyes looking upward, hands joined together. Here it is the very pose of the subject which prepares the reading of the signifieds of connotation: youthfulness, spirituality, purity. The photograph clearly only signifies because of the existence of a store of stereotyped attitudes which form ready-made elements of signification (eyes raised heavenward, hands clasped). A "historical grammar" of iconographic connotation ought thus to look for its material in painting, theater, associations of ideas, stock metaphors, etc., that is to say, precisely in "culture." As has been said, pose is not a specifically photographic procedure, but it is difficult not to mention it insofar as it derives its effect from the analogical principle at the basis of the photograph. The message in the present instance is not "the pose" but "Kennedy praying": the reader receives as a simple denotation what is in actual fact a double structure—denoted-connoted.

3. *Objects.* Special importance must be accorded to what could be called the posing of objects, where the meaning comes from the objects photographed (either because these objects have, if the photographer had the time, been artificially arranged in front of the camera or because the person responsible for layout chooses a photograph of this or that object). The interest lies in the fact that the objects are accepted inducers of associations of ideas (bookcase = intellectual) or, in a more obscure way, are veritable symbols (the door of the gas chamber for Chessman's execution with its reference to the

funeral gates of ancient mythologies). Such objects constitute excellent elements of signification: on the one hand they are discontinuous and complete in themselves, a physical qualification for a sign, while on the other they refer to clear, familiar signifieds. They are thus the elements of a veritable lexicon, stable to a degree which allows them to be readily constituted into syntax. Here, for example, is a "composition" of objects: a window opening on to vineyards and tiled roofs; in front of the window a photograph album, a magnifying glass, a vase of flowers. Consequently, we are in the country, south of the Loire (vines and tiles), in a bourgeois house (flowers on the table) whose owner, advanced in years (the magnifying glass), is reliving his memories (the photograph album)—François Mauriac in Malagar (photo in *Paris-Match*). The connotation somehow "emerges" from all these signifying units which are nevertheless "captured" as though the scene were immediate and spontaneous, that is to say, without signification. The text renders the connotation explicit, developing the theme of Mauriac's ties with the land. Objects no longer perhaps possess a *power*, but they certainly possess meanings.

4. *Photogenia*. The theory of photogenia has already been developed (by Edgar Morin in *Le Cinéma ou l'homme imaginaire*) and this is not the place to take up again the subject of the general signification of that procedure; it will suffice to define photogenia in terms of informational structure. In photogenia the connoted message is the image itself, "embellished" (which is to say, in general sublimated) by techniques of lighting, exposure, and printing. An inventory needs to be made of these techniques, but only insofar as each of them has a corresponding signified of connotation sufficiently constant to allow its incorporation in a cultural lexicon of technical "effects" (as for instance the "blurring of movement" or "flowingness" launched by Dr. Steinert and his team to signify

space-time). Such an inventory would be an excellent opportunity for distinguishing aesthetic effects from signifying effects —unless perhaps it be recognized that in photography, contrary to the intentions of exhibition photographers, there is never *art* but always *meaning*; which precisely would at last provide an exact criterion for the opposition between good painting, even if strongly representational, and photography.

5. *Aestheticism.* For if one can talk of aestheticism in photography, it is seemingly in an ambiguous fashion: when photography turns painting, composition, or visual substance treated with deliberation in its very material "texture," it is either so as to signify itself as "art" (which was the case with the "pictorialism" of the beginning of the century) or to impose a generally more subtle and complex signified than would be possible with other connotation procedures. Thus Cartier-Bresson constructed Cardinal Pacelli's reception by the faithful of Lisieux like a painting by an early master. The resulting photograph, however, is in no way a painting: on the one hand, its display of aestheticism refers (damagingly) to the very idea of a painting (which is contrary to any true painting); while on the other, the composition signifies in a declared manner a certain ecstatic spirituality translated precisely in terms of an objective spectacle. One can see here the difference between photograph and painting: in a picture by a Primitive, "spirituality" is not a signified but, as it were, the very being of the image. Certainly there may be coded elements in some paintings, rhetorical figures, period symbols, but no signifying unit refers to spirituality, which is a mode of being and not the object of a structured message.

6. *Syntax.* We have already considered a discursive reading of object-signs within a single photograph. Naturally, several photographs can come together to form a sequence (this is commonly the case in illustrated magazines); the signifier of connotation is then no longer to be found at the level of any

one of the fragments of the sequence but at that—what the
linguists would call the suprasegmental level—of the concatenation. Consider for example four snaps of a presidential
shoot at Rambouillet: in each, the illustrious sportsman (Vincent Auriol) is pointing his rifle in some unlikely direction, to
the great peril of the keepers who run away or fling themselves
to the ground. The sequence (and the sequence alone) offers
an effect of comedy which emerges, according to a familiar
procedure, from the repetition and variation of the attitudes. It
can be noted in this connection that the single photograph,
contrary to the drawing, is very rarely (that is, only with much
difficulty) comic; the comic requires movement, which is to
say repetition (easy in film) or typification (possible in drawing), both these "connotations" being prohibited to the photograph.

TEXT AND IMAGE

Such are the main connotation procedures of the photographic image (once again, it is a question of techniques, not
of units). To these may invariably be added the text which
accompanies the press photograph. Three remarks should be
made in this context.

Firstly, the text constitutes a parasitic message designed to
connote the image, to "quicken" it with one or more second-
order signifieds. In other words, and this is an important historical reversal, the image no longer *illustrates* the words; it is
now the words which, structurally, are parasitic on the image.
The reversal is at a cost: in the traditional modes of illustration the image functioned as an episodic return to denotation
from a principal message (the text) which was experienced as
connoted since, precisely, it needed an illustration; in the relationship that now holds, it is not the image which comes to
elucidate or "realize" the text, but the latter which comes to
sublimate, patheticize, or rationalize the image. As however

this operation is carried out accessorily, the new informational totality appears to be chiefly founded on an objective (denoted) message in relation to which the text is only a kind of secondary vibration, almost without consequence. Formerly, the image illustrated the text (made it clearer); today, the text loads the image, burdening it with a culture, a moral, an imagination. Formerly, there was reduction from text to image; today, there is amplification from the one to the other. The connotation is now experienced only as the natural resonance of the fundamental denotation constituted by the photographic analogy and we are thus confronted with a typical process of naturalization of the cultural.

Secondly, the effect of connotation probably differs according to the way in which the text is presented. The closer the text to the image, the less it seems to connote it; caught as it were in the iconographic message, the verbal message seems to share in its objectivity, the connotation of language is "innocented" through the photograph's denotation. It is true that there is never a real incorporation since the substances of the two structures (graphic and iconic) are irreducible, but there are most likely degrees of amalgamation. The caption probably has a less obvious effect of connotation than the headline or accompanying article: headline and article are palpably separate from the image, the former by its emphasis, the latter by its distance; the first because it breaks, the other because it distances the content of the image. The caption, on the contrary, by its very disposition, by its average measure of reading, appears to duplicate the image, that is, to be included in its denotation.

It is impossible however (and this will be the final remark here concerning the text) that the words "duplicate" the image; in the movement from one structure to the other second signifieds are inevitably developed. What is the relationship of these signifieds of connotation to the image? To all appearances, it is one of making explicit, of providing a stress; the text most often simply amplifying a set of connotations already given in the photograph. Sometimes, however, the text produces (invents) an entirely new signified which is retroactively projected into the image, so much so as to appear denoted there. *"They were near to death, their faces prove it,"* reads the headline to a photograph showing Elizabeth and Philip leaving a plane—but at the moment of the photograph the two still knew nothing of the accident they had just escaped. Sometimes, too, the text can even contradict the image so as to produce a compensatory connotation. An analysis by Gerbner (*The Social Anatomy of the Romance Confession Cover Girl*) demonstrated that in certain romance magazines the verbal message of the headlines, gloomy and anguished, on the cover always accompanied the image of a radiant cover girl; here the two messages enter into a compromise, the connotation having a regulating function, preserving the irrational movement of projection-identification.

PHOTOGRAPHIC INSIGNIFICANCE

We saw that the code of connotation was in all likelihood neither "natural" nor "artificial" but historical, or, if it be preferred, "cultural." Its signs are gestures, attitudes, expressions, colors, or effects, endowed with certain meanings by virtue of the practice of a certain society: the link between signifier and signified remains, if not unmotivated, at least entirely historical. Hence it is wrong to say that modern man projects into reading photographs feelings and values which are characterial or "eternal" (infra- or trans-historical), unless it be firmly specified that *signification* is always developed by a given society and history. Signification, in short, is the dialectical movement which resolves the contradiction between cultural and natural man.

Thanks to its code of connotation the reading of the photograph is thus always historical; it depends on the reader's "knowledge" just as though it were a matter of a real language [*langue*], intelligible only if one has learned the signs. All things considered, the photographic "language" ["*langage*"] is not unlike certain ideographic languages which mix analogical and specifying units, the difference being that the ideogram is experienced as a sign whereas the photographic "copy" is taken as the pure and simple denotation of reality. To find this code of connotation would thus be to isolate, inventoriate, and structure all the "historical" elements of the photograph, all the parts of the photographic surface which derive their very discontinuity from a certain knowledge on the reader's part, or, if one prefers, from the reader's cultural situation.

This task will perhaps take us a very long way indeed. Nothing tells us that the photograph contains "neutral" parts, or at least it may be that complete insignificance in the photograph is quite exceptional. To resolve the problem, we would first of all need to elucidate fully the mechanisms of reading (in the physical, and no longer the semantic, sense of the term), of the perception of the photograph. But on this point we know very little. How do we read a photograph? What do we perceive? In what order, according to what progression? If, as is suggested by certain hypotheses of Bruner and Piaget, there is no perception without immediate categorization, then the photograph is verbalized in the very moment it is perceived; better, it is only perceived verbalized (if there is a delay in verbalization, there is disorder in perception, questioning, anguish for the subject, traumatism, following G. Cohen-Séat's hypothesis with regard to filmic perception). From this point of view, the image—grasped immediately by an inner metalanguage, language itself—in actual fact has no denoted state, is immersed for its very social existence in at least an initial layer of connotation, that of the categories of language. We know that every language takes up a position with regard to things, that it connotes reality, if only in dividing it up; the connotations of the photograph would thus coincide, *grosso modo*, with the overall connotative planes of language.

In addition to "perceptive" connotation, hypothetical but possible, one then encounters other, more particular, modes of connotation, and firstly a "cognitive" connotation whose signifiers are picked out, localized, in certain parts of the analogon. Faced with such and such a townscape, I *know* that this is a North African country because on the left I can see a sign in Arabic script, in the center a man wearing a gandoura, and so on. Here the reading closely depends on my culture, on my knowledge of the world, and it is probable that a good press photograph (and they are all good, being selected) makes ready play with the supposed knowledge of its readers, those prints being chosen which comprise the greatest possible quantity of information of this kind in such a way as to render the reading fully satisfying. If one photographs Agadir in ruins, it is better to have a few signs of "Arabness" at one's disposal, even though "Arabness" has nothing to do with the disaster itself; connotation drawn from knowledge is always a reassuring force—man likes signs and likes them clear.

Perceptive connotation, cognitive connotation; there remains the problem of ideological (in the very wide sense of the term) or ethical connotation, that which introduces reasons or values into the reading of the image. This is a strong connotation requiring a highly elaborated signifier of a readily syntactical order: conjunction of people (as was seen in the discussion of trick effects), development of attitudes, constellation of objects. A son has just been born to the Shah of Iran and in a photograph we have: royalty (cot worshipped by a crowd of servants gathering round), wealth (several nursemaids), hygiene (white coats, cot covered in Plexiglas), the nevertheless human condition of kings (the baby is crying)—

all the elements, that is, of the myth of princely birth as it is consumed today. In this instance the values are apolitical and their lexicon is abundant and clear. It is possible (but this is only a hypothesis) that political connotation is generally entrusted to the text, insofar as political choices are always, as it were, in bad faith: for a particular photograph I can give a right-wing reading or a left-wing reading (see in this connection an IFOP survey published by *Les Temps Modernes* in 1955). Denotation, or the appearance of denotation, is powerless to alter political opinions: no photograph has ever convinced or refuted anyone (but the photograph can "confirm") insofar as political consciousness is perhaps nonexistent outside the *logos*: politics is what allows *all* languages.

These few remarks sketch a kind of differential table of photographic connotations, showing, if nothing else, that connotation extends a long way. Is this to say that a pure denotation, a *this-side of language*, is impossible? If such a denotation exists, it is perhaps not at the level of what ordinary language calls the insignificant, the neutral, the objective, but, on the contrary, at the level of absolutely traumatic images. The trauma is a suspension of language, a blocking of meaning. Certainly situations which are normally traumatic can be seized in a process of photographic signification but then precisely they are indicated via a rhetorical code which distances, sublimates and pacifies them. Truly traumatic photographs are rare, for in photography the trauma is wholly dependent on the certainty that the scene "really" happened: *the photographer had to be there* (the mystical definition of denotation). Assuming this (which, in fact, is already a connotation), the traumatic photograph (fires, shipwrecks, catastrophes, violent deaths, all captured "from life as lived") is the photograph about which there is nothing to say; the shock photo is by structure insignificant: no value, no knowledge, at the limit no verbal categorization can have a hold on the process instituting the signification. One could imagine a kind of law: the more direct the trauma, the more difficult is connotation; or again, the "mythological" effect of a photograph is inversely proportional to its traumatic effect.

Why? Doubtless because photographic connotation, like every well-structured signification, is an institutional activity; in relation to society overall, its function is to integrate man, to reassure him. Every code is at once arbitrary and rational; recourse to a code is thus always an opportunity for man to prove himself, to test himself through a reason and a liberty. In this sense, the analysis of codes perhaps allows an easier and surer historical definition of a society than the analysis of its signifieds, for the latter can often appear as trans-historical, belonging more to an anthropological base than to a proper history. Hegel gave a better definition of the ancient Greeks by outlining the manner in which they made nature signify than by describing the totality of their "feelings and beliefs" on the subject. Similarly, we can perhaps do better than to take stock directly of the ideological contents of our age; by trying to reconstitute in its specific structure the code of connotation of a mode of communication as important as the press photograph we may hope to find, in their very subtlety, the forms our society uses to ensure its peace of mind and to grasp thereby the magnitude, the detours, and the underlying function of that activity. The prospect is the more appealing in that, as was said at the beginning, it develops with regard to the photograph in the form of a paradox—that which makes of an inert object a language and which transforms the unculture of a "mechanical" art into the most social of institutions.

1961

The Imagination of the Sign

Every sign includes or implies three relations. To start with, an interior relation which unites its signifier to its signified; then two exterior relations: a virtual one that unites the sign to a specific reservoir of other signs it may be drawn from in order to be inserted in discourse; and an actual one that unites the sign to other signs in the discourse preceding or succeeding it. The first type of relation appears clearly in what is commonly called a *symbol*; for instance, the Cross "symbolizes" Christianity, red "symbolizes" a prohibition to advance; we shall call this first relation, then, a *symbolic* relation, though we encounter it not only in symbols but also in signs (which are, roughly speaking, purely conventional symbols). The second type of relation implies the existence, for each sign, of a reservoir or organized "memory" of forms from which it is distinguished by the smallest difference necessary and sufficient to effect a change of meaning; in *lupum*, the element *-um* (which is a sign, and more precisely a morpheme) affords its meaning of "accusative case" only insofar as it is opposed to the (virtual) remainder of the declension (*-us, -i, -o,* etc.); red signifies prohibition only insofar as it is *systematically* opposed

From *Critical Essays.*

211

to green and yellow (of course, if there were no other color but red, red would still be opposed to the absence of color); this second type of relation is therefore that of the system, sometimes called paradigm; we shall therefore call it a *paradigmatic* relation. According to the third type of relation, the sign is no longer situated with regard to its (virtual) "brothers," but with regard to its (actual) "neighbors"; in *homo homini lupus, lupus* maintains certain connections with *homo* and with *homini*; in garment systems, the elements of an outfit are associated according to certain rules: to wear a sweater and a leather jacket is to create, between these two garments, a temporary but signifying association, analogous to the one uniting the words of a sentence; this level of association is the level of the syntagm, and we shall call the third relation the *syntagmatic relation*.

Now it seems that when we consider the signifying phenomenon (and this interest may proceed from very different horizons), we are obliged to focus on one of these three relations more than on the other two; sometimes we "see" the sign in its symbolic aspect, sometimes in its systematic aspect, sometimes in its syntagmatic aspect; this is occasionally the result of mere ignorance of the other relations: symbolism has long been blind to the formal relations of the sign; but even when the three relations have been defined (for example, in linguistics), each school tends to base its analysis on one of the sign's dimensions: one vision overflows the whole of the signifying phenomenon, so that we may speak, apparently, of different semiological consciousnesses (I refer, of course, to the consciousness of the analyst, not of the user, of the sign). Now, on the one hand, the choice of a dominant relation implies a certain ideology; and, on the other hand, one might say that each consciousness of the sign (symbolic, paradigmatic, and syntagmatic) corresponds to a certain moment of reflection, either individual or collective: structuralism, in particular, can

be defined historically as the passage from symbolic consciousness to paradigmatic consciousness: there is a history of
the sign, which is the history of its "consciousnesses."

The symbolic consciousness sees the sign in its profound,
one might almost say its geological, dimension, since for the
symbolic consciousness it is the tiered arrangement of signifier
and signified which constitutes the symbol; there is a consciousness of a kind of vertical relation between the Cross and
Christianity: Christianity is *under* the Cross, as a profound
mass of beliefs, values, practices, more or less disciplined on
the level of its form. The verticality of the relation involves
two consequences: on the one hand, the vertical relation tends
to seem solitary: the symbol seems to stand by itself in the
world, and even when we assert that it is abundant, it is abundant in the fashion of a "forest"—i.e., by an anarchic juxtaposition of profound relations which communicate, so to
speak, only by their roots (by what is signified); and on the
other hand, this vertical relation necessarily appears to be an
analogical relation: to some degree the form resembles the
content, as if it were actually produced by it, so that the symbolic consciousness may sometimes mask an unacknowledged
determinism: thus there is a massive privilege of resemblance
(even when we emphasize the inadequate character of the
sign). The symbolic consciousness has dominated the sociology of symbols and of course a share of psychoanalysis in its
early stages, though Freud himself acknowledged the inexplicable (nonanalogical) character of certain symbols; this moreover was the period when the very word *symbol* prevailed;
during all this time, the symbol possessed a mythic prestige,
the glamor of "richness": the symbol was rich, hence it could
not be reduced to a "simple sign" (today we may doubt the
sign's "simplicity"): its form was constantly exceeded by the
power and the movement of its content; indeed, for the sym-

bolic consciousness, the symbol is much less a (codified) form of communication than an (affective) instrument of participation. The word *symbol* has now gone a little stale; we readily replace it by *sign* or *signification*. This terminological shift expresses a certain crumbling of the symbolic consciousness, notably with regard to the analogical character of signifier and signified; nonetheless the symbolic consciousness remains typical, insofar as its analytical consideration is not interested in the formal relations of signs, for the symbolic consciousness is essentially the rejection of form; what interests it in the sign is the signified: the signifier is always a determined element.

Once the forms of two signs are compared, or at least perceived in a somewhat comparative manner, a certain paradigmatic consciousness appears; even on the level of the classical symbol, the least subtle of signs, if there is some occasion to perceive the variation of two symbolic forms, the other dimensions of the sign are immediately discovered; as in the case, for instance, of the opposition between *Red Cross* and *Red Crescent*: on the one hand, *Cross* and *Crescent* cease to entertain a "solitary" relation with what they respectively signify (Christianity and Islam), they are included in a stereotyped syntagm; and, on the other hand, they form between themselves an interplay of distinctive terms, each of which corresponds to a different signified: the paradigm is born. The paradigmatic consciousness therefore defines meaning not as the simple encounter of signifier and signified, but, according to Merleau-Ponty's splendid expression, as a veritable "modulation of co-existence"; it substitutes for the bilateral relation of the symbolic consciousness a quadrilateral or more precisely a homological relation. It is the paradigmatic consciousness which permitted Lévi-Strauss to reconceive the problem of totemism: whereas the symbolic consciousness vainly seeks the "dimensional," more or less analogical characters which unite a signifier (the totem) to a signified (the clan), the paradigmatic consciousness establishes a homology (as Lévi-Strauss calls it) between the relation of two totems and that of two clans. Naturally, by retaining in the signified only its demonstrative role (it designates the signifier and makes it possible to locate the terms of the opposition), the paradigmatic consciousness tends to empty it: but it does not thereby empty the signification. It is obviously the paradigmatic consciousness which has permitted (or expressed) the extraordinary development of phonology, a science of exemplary paradigms (*marked/nonmarked*): it is the paradigmatic consciousness which, through the work of Lévi-Strauss, defines the structuralist threshold.

The syntagmatic consciousness is a consciousness of the relations which unite signs on the level of discourse itself, i.e., essentially a consciousness of the constraints, tolerances, and liberties of the sign's associations. This consciousness has marked the linguistic endeavors of the Yale school and, outside linguistics, the investigations of the Russian formalist school, notably those of Propp in the domain of the Slavic folk tale (hence we may expect that it will eventually illuminate analysis of the major contemporary "narratives," from the *fait-divers* to the popular novel). But this is not the only orientation of the syntagmatic consciousness; of the three, it is certainly the syntagmatic consciousness which most readily renounces the signified: it is more a structural consciousness than a semantic one, which is why it comes closest to practice: it is the syntagmatic consciousness which best permits us to imagine operational groups, "dispatchings," complex classifications: the paradigmatic consciousness permits the fruitful return from decimalism to binarism; but it is the syntagmatic consciousness which actually permits us to conceive cybernetic "programs," just as it has permitted Propp and Lévi-Strauss to reconstruct the myth "series."

Perhaps we shall someday be able to return to the description of these semantic consciousnesses, attempt to link them to a history; perhaps we shall someday be able to create a semiology of the semiologists, a structural analysis of the structuralists. All we are endeavoring to say here is that there is probably a genuine imagination of the sign; the sign is not only the object of a particular knowledge, but also the object of a vision, analogous to the vision of the celestial spheres in Cicero's *Somnium Scipionis* or related to the molecular representations used by chemists; the semiologist *sees* the sign moving in the field of signification, he enumerates its valences, traces their configuration: the sign is, for him, a sensuous idea. Of the three (still fairly technical) consciousnesses discussed here, we must presume an extension toward much wider types of imagination, which we may find mobilized in many other objects than the sign.

The symbolic consciousness implies an imagination of depth; it experiences the world as the relation of a superficial form and a many-sided, massive, powerful *Abgrund*, and the image is reinforced by a very intense dynamics: the relation of form and content is ceaselessly renewed by time (history), the superstructure overwhelmed by the infrastructure, without our ever being able to grasp the structure itself. The paradigmatic consciousness, on the contrary, is a formal imagination; it *sees* the signifier linked, as if in profile, to several virtual signifiers which it is at once close to and distinct from: it no longer sees the sign in its depth, it sees it in its perspective; thus the dynamics attached to this vision is that of a summons: the sign is chosen from a finite organized reservoir, and this summons is the sovereign act of signification: imagination of the surveyor, the geometrician, the owner of the world who finds himself at his ease on his property, since man, in order to signify, has merely to choose from what is presented to him already prestructured either by his brain (in the binarist hypothesis), or by the material finitude of forms. The syntagmatic imagination no longer sees the sign in its perspective, it *foresees* it in its extension: its antecedent or consequent links, the bridges it extends to other signs; this is a "stemmatous" imagination of the chain or the network; hence the dynamics of the image here is that of an arrangement of mobile, substitutive parts, whose combination produces meaning, or more generally a new object; it is, then, a strictly fabricative or even *functional* imagination (the word is conveniently ambiguous, since it refers both to the notion of a variable relation and to that of a usage).

Such are (perhaps) the three imaginations of the sign. We may doubtless attach to each of them a certain number of different creations, in the most diverse realms, for nothing constructed in the world today escapes meaning. To remain in the realm of recent intellectual creation, among the works of the profound (symbolic) imagination, we may cite biographical or historical criticism, the sociology of "visions," the realist or introspective novel, and in a general way, the "expressive" arts or languages, postulating the signified as sovereign, extracted either from an interiority or from a history. The formal (or paradigmatic) imagination implies an acute attention to the *variation* of several recurrent elements; thus this type of imagination accommodates the dream and oneiric narratives, powerfully thematic works and those whose aesthetic implies the interplay of certain commutations (Robbe-Grillet's novels, for example). The functional (or syntagmatic) imagination nourishes, lastly, all those works whose fabrication, by arrangement of discontinuous and mobile elements, constitutes the spectacle itself: poetry, epic theater, serial music, and structural compositions, from Mondrian to Butor.

1962

The Plates of
the *Encyclopedia*

O<small>UR</small> literature has taken a long time to discover the object;
we must wait till Balzac for the novel to be the space not only
of pure human relations but also of substances and usages
called upon to play their part in the story of passions: could
Grandet have been a miser (literarily speaking) without his
candle ends, his lumps of sugar, and his gold crucifix? Long
before literature, the *Encyclopedia*, particularly in its plates,
practices what we might call a certain philosophy of the object, i.e., reflects on its being, produces at once an inventory
and a definition; technological purpose no doubt compelled the
description of objects; but by separating image from text, the
Encyclopedia committed itself to an autonomous iconography
of the object whose power we enjoy today, since we no longer
look at these illustrations with mere information in mind.

The plates of the *Encyclopedia* present the object, and this
presentation already adds to the illustration's didactic purpose
a more gratuitous justification, of an aesthetic or oneiric
order: the imagery of the *Encyclopedia* can best be compared

From *New Critical Essays*, translated by Richard Howard (New York:
Hill and Wang, 1980).

with one of those Great Expositions held the world over in the last century or so, and of which, in its period, the Encyclopedic illustration was a kind of ancestor: in both cases, we are concerned with a census and a spectacle: we consult the plates of the *Encyclopedia* as we would visit today's World's Fair in Brussels or New York. The objects presented are literally encyclopedic, i.e., they cover the entire sphere of substances shaped by man: clothes, vehicles, tools, weapons, instruments, furniture, all that man makes out of wood, metal, glass, or fiber is catalogued here, from the chisel to the statue, from the artificial flower to the ship. This Encyclopedic object is ordinarily apprehended by the image on three levels: anthological, since the object, isolated from any context, is presented *in itself*; anecdotic, when it is "naturalized" by its insertion into a large-scale *tableau vivant* (which is what we call a vignette); genetic, when the image offers us the trajectory from raw substance to finished object: genesis, essence, praxis, the object is thus accounted for in all its categories: sometimes it *is*, sometimes it is *made*, sometimes it even *makes*. Of these three states, assigned here and there to the object-as-image, one is certainly favored by the *Encyclopedia*: that of birth: it is good to be able to show how we can produce things from their very nonexistence and thus to credit man with an extraordinary power of creation: here is a countryside; the plenitude of Nature (meadows, hills, trees) constitutes a kind of human void from which we cannot see what will emerge; yet the image moves, objects are born, precursors of humanity: lines are drawn on the earth, stakes are pounded in, holes dug; a cross-section shows us, beneath a desert Nature, the powerful network of galleries and lodes: a mine is born. This is a kind of symbol: Encyclopedic man *mines* all Nature with human signs; in the Encyclopedic landscape, we are never alone; however strong the elements, there is always a fraternal *product* of man: the object is the world's human signature.

We know that a simple substance can make a whole story legible: Brecht has rediscovered the wretched essence of the Thirty Years' War by the radical treatment of fabrics, wicker, and wood. The Encyclopedic object emerges from general substances which are still those of the artisanal era. If we visit a World's Fair today, we perceive in all the objects exhibited two or three dominant substances, glass, metal, plastic no doubt; the substance of the Encyclopedic object is of a more vegetal age: it is wood which dominates in this great catalogue; it produces a world of objects easy on the eyes, already human by their substance, resistant but not brittle, constructible but not plastic. Nothing shows wood's humanizing power better than the *Encyclopedia*'s machines; in this world of technology (which is still artisanal, for the industrial is as yet unborn), the machine is obviously a capital object; now most of the *Encyclopedia*'s machines are made out of wood; they are enormous, highly complicated scaffoldings in which metal frequently supplies only notched wheels. The wood which constitutes them keeps them subservient to a certain notion of *play*: these machines are (for us) like big toys; contrary to modern images, man, always present in some corner of the machine, does not accompany it in a simple relation of surveillance; turning a crank, pressing a pedal, spinning a thread, he participates in the machine in a manner that is both active and delicate; the engraver represents him for the most part dressed neatly as a gentleman; this is not a worker but a little lord who plays on a kind of technological organ, all of whose gears and wheels are exposed; what is striking about the Encyclopedic machine is its absence of secrecy; in it there is no hidden place (spring or housing) which would magically conceal energy, as is the case with our modern machines (it is the myth of electricity to be a self-generated, hence enclosed, power); the energy here is essentially transmission, amplification of a simple human movement; the Encyclopedic machine is never anything but an enormous relay; man is at one term, the object at the other; between the two, an architectural milieu, consisting of beams, ropes, and gears, through which, like a light, human strength is simultaneously developed, refined, focused, and enlarged: hence, in the gauze-loom, a little man in a jacket, sitting at the keyboard of a huge wooden machine, produces an extremely fine web, as if he were playing music; elsewhere, in a completely bare room, containing only a maze of wood and tarred ropes, a young woman sitting on a bench turns a crank, while her other hand rests gently on her knee. a *simpler* idea of technology is inconceivable.

An almost naïve simplicity, a kind of Golden Legend of artisanry (for there is no trace of social distress): the *Encyclopedia* identifies the simple, the elementary, the essential, and the causal. Encyclopedic technology is simple because it is reduced to a two-term space: the causal trajectory which proceeds from substance to object; hence all the plates which involve some technological operation (of transformation) mobilize an aesthetic of bareness: huge, empty, well-lighted rooms, in which man cohabits alone with his work: a space without parasites, walls bare, tables cleared; the simple, here, is nothing but the vital; this is made explicit in the bakery; as a primary element, bread implies an austere site; on the other hand, pastry, belonging to the order of the superfluous, proliferates in instruments, operations, products, whose fussy ensemble constitutes a certain *baroque*. In a general way, the object's *production* sweeps the image toward an almost sacred simplicity; its *use*, on the other hand (represented at the moment of sale, in the shop), authorizes an embellishment of the vignette, abounding in instruments, accessories, and attitudes: austerity of creation, luxury of commerce, such is the double regime of the Encyclopedic object: the density of the image and its ornamental charge always signifies that we are shifting from production to consumption.

Of course, the object's pre-eminence in this world derives from an inventorying effort, but inventory is never a neutral idea; to catalogue is not merely to ascertain, as it appears at first glance, but also to appropriate. The *Encyclopedia* is a huge ledger of ownership; Bernard Groetheuysen has noted an opposition between the *orbis pictus* of the Renaissance, animated by the spirit of an adventurous knowledge, and the encyclopedism of the eighteenth century, based on a learning of appropriation. Formally (this is apparent in the plates), ownership depends on a certain dividing up of things: to appropriate is to fragment the world, to divide it into finite objects subject to man in proportion to their very discontinuity: for we cannot separate without finally naming and classifying, and at that moment, property is born. In mythic terms, possession of the world began not with Genesis but at the Flood, when man was obliged to name each kind of animal and to house it, i.e., to separate it from its next of species; the *Encyclopedia*, moreover, takes an essentially pragmatic view of Noah's ark; for it, the ark is not a ship—an object always more or less *oneiric*—but a long floating crate, a goods locker; the only problem it appears to offer the *Encyclopedia* is certainly not theological: it is the problem of its construction, or even, in more technical terms, as is only right, of its framing, and even more specifically, of its fenestration, since each of its windows corresponds to a typical pair of animals, thus divided, named, domesticated (docilely sticking their heads out the opening).

Encyclopedic nomenclature, whatever its technological esotericism on occasion, actually establishes a familiar possession. This is remarkable, for nothing logically obliges the object to be invariably friendly to man. The object, quite the contrary, is humanly a very ambiguous thing; we have noted that for a long time our literature did not acknowledge it; later (which is to say, on the whole, today), the object has been endowed with an unfortunate opacity; assimilated to an inhuman state of nature, its proliferation cannot be noted without a sentiment of apocalypse or of alienation: the modern object is either asphyxiation (Ionesco) or nausea (Sartre). The Encyclopedic object is on the contrary subjugated (we might say that it is precisely pure *object* in the etymological sense of the term), for a very simple and constant reason: it is on each occasion *signed* by man; the image is the privileged means of this human presence, for it permits discreetly locating a permanent man on the object's horizon; the plates of the *Encyclopedia* are always populated (they afford thereby a close relationship with another "progressive" or, to be more precise, bourgeois iconography: seventeenth-century Dutch painting); you can imagine the most naturally solitary, "savage" object; be sure that man will nonetheless appear in a corner of the image; he will be considering the object, or measuring it, or surveying it, using it at least as a spectacle; take the Giant's Causeway, that mass of terrifying basalt composed by Nature at Antrim, in Ireland; this inhuman landscape is, one might say, stuffed with humanity; gentlemen in tricornes, lovely ladies contemplate the horrible landscape, chatting familiarly; farther on, men are fishing, scientists are weighing the mineral substance: analyzed into functions (spectacle, fishing, science), the basalt is *reduced*, tamed, familiarized, because it is *divided*; what is striking in the entire *Encyclopedia* (and especially in its images) is that it proposes a *world without fear* (we shall see in a moment that the monstrous is not excluded, but in a category much more "surrealist" than terrifying). We can even specify more clearly what the man of the Encyclopedic image is reduced to—what is, in some sense, the very essence of his humanity: his hands. In many plates (and not the least beautiful), hands, severed from any body, flutter around the work (for their lightness is extreme); these hands are doubtless the symbol of an artisanal world (again we are concerned with traditional, virtually unmechanized trades, the steam engine is kept out of sight), as is seen by the importance of the tables (huge, flat, well lighted, often encircled by hands); but beyond artisanship, the hands are inevitably the inductive sign of the human essence: do we not see even today, in a less obvious fashion, that our advertising constantly returns to this mysterious motif, at once natural and supernatural, as if man could not get over having hands? It is not easy to be done with a civilization of the hand.

Hence in the immediate state of its representations, the *Encyclopedia* is constantly concerned to familiarize the world of objects (which is its primary substance) by adding to it the obsessive cipher of man. Yet beyond the letter of the image, this humanization implies an intellectual system of an extreme subtlety: the Encyclopedic image is human not only because man is represented in it but also because it constitutes a structure of *information*. This structure, though iconographic, is articulated in most instances like real language (the one which, in fact, we call *articulate*), whose two dimensions as revealed by structural linguistics it reproduces: we know, in fact, that all discourse involves signifying units and that these units are ordered according to two axes, one of substitution (paradigmatic), the other of contiguity (syntagmatic); each unit can thereby *vary* (potentially) with its parents, and *link* (in reality) with its neighbors. This is what happens, *grosso modo*, in an *Encyclopedia* plate. The majority of these plates are formed of two parts; in the lower part, the tool or the gesture (the object of the demonstration), isolated from any real context, is shown in its essence; it constitutes the informative unit, and this unit is generally *varied*: its aspects, elements, kinds are detailed; this part of the plate has the role of *declining* the object, of manifesting its paradigm; on the contrary, in the upper part or vignette, this same object (and its varieties) is apprehended in a lively scene (generally a scene of sale or manufacture, shop or workroom), linked to other objects within a real situation: here we rediscover the syntagmatic dimension of the message; and just as in oral discourse the system of the language, perceptible chiefly on the paradigmatic level, is somehow *hidden* behind the living stream of words, in the same way the Encyclopedic plate plays simultaneously on intellectual demonstration (by its objects) and on fictive life (by its scenes). Here is a trade plate (the pastrycook): down below, the ensemble of various instruments necessary to the profession; in this paradigmatic state, the instrument has no life: inert, frozen in its essence, it is merely a demonstrative schema, analogous to the quasi-academic form of a verbal or nominal paradigm; up above, on the contrary, the chopping board, the whisk (the pastrycooks were making *pâtés en croûte*), the sieve, the molds are arranged, linked together, "enacted" in a *tableau vivant*, exactly as the "cases" distinguished by grammar are ordinarily given without our thinking of them in real discourse, with this difference, that the Encyclopedic syntagm is of an extreme density of meaning; in informational language, we would say that the scene involves little "noise" (see, for instance, the workshop in which the chief operations of engraving are gathered together).

Most of the objects from the lower paradigm are therefore reassembled in the vignette under the heading of signs; whereas the figured nomenclature of the instruments, utensils, products, and gestures involves by definition no secrecy, the vignette, charged with a disseminated meaning, always presents itself a little like a riddle: we must decipher it, locate in it the informative units. The vignette has the riddle's actual density: *all* the information must turn up in the experienced scene (whence, upon scrutiny, a certain exploration of meaning); in the plate devoted to cotton, a certain number of accidents must necessarily refer to the exoticism of the vegetal realm: the palm, the stubble, the island, the Chinaman's shaved head, his long pipe (impractical, it would seem, for working with cotton but which evokes the image of opium), none of this information is innocent: the image is crammed with demonstrative significations; analogously, Demosthenes' lantern is admirable *because* two men are discussing it and pointing to it; it is an antiquity *because* it adjoins a ruin; it is situated in Greece *because* there is the sea, a boat; we contemplate its present state *because* a band of men are dancing in a ring nearby, performing something like the *bouzouki*. Of this kind of cryptographic vocation of the image, there is no better symbol than the two plates dedicated to the hemispheres; a sphere, enclosed by a fine network of lines, makes legible the outline of its continents; but these lines and these contours are only a light transparency behind which float, like a meaning *from behind*, the figures of the constellations (the Wagoner, the Dolphin, the Scales, the Dog).

However, the vignette, a condensate of meaning, also offers a resistance to meaning, and we might say that it is in this resistance, paradoxically, that the plate's language becomes a complete, an adult language. It is, as a matter of fact, apparent that for a reader of the period the scene itself often involves very little new information: who had not seen a pastrycook's shop, a tilled field, a river fishery? The vignette's function is therefore elsewhere: the syntagm (since it is with it that we are concerned) tells us here, once again, that language (and *a fortiori*, iconic language) is not pure intellectual communication: meaning is completed only when it is somehow naturalized in a complete action of man; for the *Encyclopedia*, too, there is a message only *in situation*, whereby we see how ambiguous, finally, the *Encyclopedia*'s didacticism is: very strong in the lower (paradigmatic) part of the plate, it is diluted at its syntagmatic level, to join (without actually being lost) what we must, in fact, call the fictive truth of any human action. At its demonstrative stage, the Encyclopedic plate constitutes a *radical language*, consisting of pure concepts, with neither word tools nor syntax; at the higher stage, this radical language becomes a human *langue*, it deliberately loses in intelligibility what it gains in experience.

The vignette does not have only an existential function, but also, one might say, an *epic* one; it is entrusted to represent the glorious term of a great trajectory, that of substance, transformed, sublimated by man, through a series of episodes and stations: this is symbolized perfectly by the cross-section of the mill, where we see the grain proceed from story to story to be resolved into flour. The demonstration becomes even stronger when it is deliberately artificial: through the weapon shop's open door, we see two men dueling out in the street: the scene is unlikely, though logical if one wants to show the ultimate term of the operation (subject of the plate), which is small-arms supply: there is a trajectory of the object which must be honored to the end. This trajectory is often paradoxical (whence the interest in showing the terms clearly); an enormous mass of wood and cordage produces a delicate flowered carpet: the finished object, so different from the apparatus which has given birth to it, is placed in view; the effect and the cause, juxtaposed, form a figure of meaning by contiguity (what is called metonymy): the framing of the loom finally *signifies* the carpet. The paradox reaches its (delicious) apogee when we can no longer perceive any relation of substance between the initial substance and the object arrived at: at the card-maker's, the playing cards are generated out of a

void, the hole in the cardboard; in the workshop of the arti-
ficial-flower maker, not only does nothing recall the flower, but
even the operations which lead to it are constantly antipathetic
to the idea of the flower: these are stampings, stencilings,
hammer taps, punch-outs: what relation between such shows
of strength and the anemone's fragile efflorescence? Precisely a
human relation, the relation of the omnipotent praxis of man,
which out of nothing can make everything.

Thus the *Encyclopedia* constantly testifies to a certain epic
of substance, but this epic is also in a sense that of the mind:
the trajectory of substance is nothing, for the Encyclopedist,
but the progress of reason: the image has a logical function *as
well*. Diderot says as much explicitly apropos of the machine
for making stockings, whose image will reproduce structure:
*"We may regard it as a single and unique reasoning of which
the work's fabrication is the conclusion; therefore there reigns
among its parts so great a dependence that were we to remove
even a single one, or to alter the form of those regarded as
least important, we should destroy the entire mechanism."*
Here we find prophetically formulated the very principle of
cybernetic ensembles; the plate, image of the machine, is indeed in its way a brain; we introduce substance into it and set
up the "program": the vignette (the syntagm) serves as a
conclusion. This logical character of the image has another
model, that of dialectics: the image analyzes, first enumerating
the scattered elements of the object or of the operation and
flinging them as on a table before the reader's eyes, then re-
composing them, even adding to them the density of the scene,
i.e., of life. The Encyclopedic mounting is based on reason: it
descends into analysis as deeply as is necessary in order to
"perceive the elements without confusion" (according to another phrase of Diderot's, precisely apropos of the drawings,
results of investigations on the spot made by draughtsmen in

the workshops): the image is a kind of rational synopsis: it illustrates not only the object or its trajectory but also the very mind which conceives it; this double movement corresponds to a double reading: if you read the plate from bottom to top, you obtain in a sense an experiential reading, you relive the object's epic trajectory, its flowering in the complex world of consumers; you proceed from Nature to sociality; but if you read the image from top to bottom, starting from the vignette, it is the progress of the analytic mind that you are reproducing; the world gives you the usual, the evident (the scene); with the Encyclopedist, you descend gradually to causes, to substances, to primary elements, you proceed from the experiential to the causal, you intellectualize the object. The privilege of the image—opposed in this to writing, which is linear —is to compel our reading to have no specific meaning: an image is always deprived of a logical vector (as certain modern experiences tend to prove); those of the *Encyclopedia* possess a precious circularity: we can read them starting from the experiential or, on the contrary, from the intelligible: the real world is not reduced, it is suspended between two great orders of reality, in truth, irreducible orders.

Such is the informative system of the Encyclopedic image. Yet the information does not end with what the image could say to the reader of its period: the modern reader also receives from this old image certain information which the Encyclopedist could not foresee: historical information, first of all: it is quite evident that the plates of the *Encyclopedia* are a mine of precious data as to the civilization of the eighteenth century (at least of its first half); oneiric information, if one may put it so, subsequently: the period object stirs in us certain strictly modern analogies; here is a phenomenon of connotation (connotation, a specific linguistic notion, is constituted by the development of a second meaning) which profoundly justifies the new edition of the old documents. Take, for example, the Lyons diligence; the *Encyclopedia* could aim at nothing but the objective—matte, one might say—reproduction of a certain means of transport; now it happens that this massive and closed trunk immediately wakens in us what we might call memories of the imagination: stories of bandits, kidnappings, ransoms, nocturnal transfers of mysterious prisoners, and, even closer to us, Westerns, the whole heroic and sinister myth of the mail coach is there, in this black object, innocently given, as a photograph of the period might have given it to us. There is a *depth* in the Encyclopedic image, the very depth of time which transforms the object into myth.

This leads to what we must call the Poetics of the Encyclopedic image, if we agree to define Poetics as the sphere of the infinite vibrations of meaning, at the center of which is placed the literal object. We can say that there is not one plate of the *Encyclopedia* which fails to vibrate well beyond its demonstrative intent. This singular vibration is above all an astonishment. Of course, the Encyclopedic image is always clear; but in a deeper region of ourselves, beyond the intellect, or at least in its profile, certain questions are born and exceed us. Consider the astonishing image of man reduced to his network of veins; here anatomical boldness unites with the great poetic and philosophic interrogation: *What is it?* What name to give it? How give a name? A thousand names rise up, dislodging each other: a tree, a bear, a monster, a hair shirt, a fabric, everything which overflows the human silhouette, distends it, draws it toward regions remote from itself, makes it overstep the divisions of Nature; yet, just as in the sketch of a master, the swarm of pencil strokes finally resolves into a pure and exact form, perfectly signifying, so here all the vibrations of meaning concur to impose upon us a certain idea of the object; in this initially human, then animal, then vegetal form we still recognize a kind of unique matter—vein, hair, or thread—and we accede to that great undifferentiated substance of which verbal or pictural poetry is the mode of knowledge: confronting the man of the *Encyclopedia* we must say *the fibrous*, as the ancient Greeks said *the moist* or *the warm* or *the round*: a certain essence of substance is here affirmed.

As a matter of fact, there cannot be anarchic poetry. The iconography of the *Encyclopedia* is poetic because its overflows of meaning always have a certain unity, suggest an ultimate meaning transcending all the *essays* of meaning. For example: the image of the womb is actually quite enigmatic; yet its metaphoric vibrations (as if it were a flayed ox, the interior of a body which dissolves and floats away) do not contradict the original traumatism attached to this object. There is a certain horror and a certain fascination common to some objects, which precisely establishes them in a homogeneous *class*, whose unity and identity is affirmed by Poetics. It is this profound order of metaphor which justifies—poetically—the recourse to a certain category of the *monstrous* (at least, according to the law of connotation, this is what we perceive in the presence of certain plates): anatomical monsters, as in the case of the enigmatic womb or that of the bust with the arms cut off, the breast opened, the face thrown back (meant to show the arteries of the thorax); surrealist monsters (those equestrian statues sheathed in wax and cords), huge and incomprehensible objects (halfway between the stocking and the wallet and which are neither one nor the other, in the stocking loom), subtler monsters (plates of poison with sharp, black crystals); all these transgressions of Nature make us understand that the poetic (for the monstrous can only be the poetic) is never established except by a displacement of the level of perception: it is one of the *Encyclopedia*'s great gifts to *vary* (in the musical sense of the term) the level on which one and the same object can be perceived, thereby liberating the very secrets of form: seen through the microscope, the flea becomes a horrible monster, caparisoned with plates of bronze, armed with steel spines, with the head of a wicked bird, and this monster achieves the strange sublimity of mythological dragons; elsewhere, and in another key, the snowflake, enlarged, becomes a complicated and harmonious flower. Is poetry not a certain power of *disproportion*, as Baudelaire saw so well, describing the effects of reduction and focusing that hashish induces?

Another exemplary category of the poetic (alongside the monstrous): a certain *immobility*. We always praise the movement of a drawing. Yet, by an inevitable paradox, the *image* of movement can only be arrested; in order to signify itself, movement must be immobilized at the extreme point of its course; it is this incredible, untenable repose that Baudelaire called the emphatic truth of gesture and that we find in demonstrative painting—that of Gros, for instance; to this suspended, oversignifying gesture we might give the name *numen*, for it is indeed the gesture of a god who silently creates man's fate, i.e., meaning. In the *Encyclopedia*, numinous gestures abound, for what man makes cannot be insignificant. In the chemical laboratory, for example, each character offers us *slightly* impossible actions, for in truth an action cannot be simultaneously effective and significant, a gesture cannot be altogether an action: the boy washing the pans, oddly, is not looking at what he is doing; his face, turned toward us, grants the operation he is performing a kind of demonstrative solitude; and if the two chemists are having a discussion, it is necessary that one of them raise a finger to signify by this emphatic gesture the learned character of the conversation. Similarly, in the drawing academy, the students are *caught* at the most improbable moment of their agitation. There is, in fact, a physical order in which Zeno's paradox is true, when the arrow flies and yet does not, flies by not flying, and this order is that of painting (here, of drawing).

As we see, Encyclopedic poetics are always defined as a certain unrealism. It is the *Encyclopedia*'s wager (in its plates) to be both a didactic work, based consequently on a severe demand for objectivity (for "reality"), and a poetic work in which the real is constantly overcome by *some other thing* (the *other* is the sign of all mysteries). By purely graphic means, which never resort to the noble alibi of *art*, Encyclopedic drawing explodes the exact world it takes as its subject. We may specify the meaning of this subversion which affects not only ideology (and in this the *Encyclopedia*'s plates singularly enlarge the dimensions of the enterprise) but also, in a much more serious manner, human rationality. In its very order (described here in the form of the syntagm and the paradigm, the vignette and the bottom of the page), the Encyclopedic plate accomplishes this *risk* of reason. The vignette, a realistic representation of a simple, familiar world (shops, workshops, landscapes) is linked to a certain tranquil evidence of the world: the vignette is calm, reassuring; what can be more deliciously domestic than the kitchen garden with its enclosing walls, its espaliers in the sun? What can be happier, more docile, than the fisherman at his line, the tailor sitting at his window, the feather vendors and the child talking to them? In this Encyclopedic heaven (the upper part of the plates), evil is infrequent; scarcely a trace of discomfort over the hard labors of the glassworkers, armed with pathetic tools, poorly protected against the terrible heat; and when Nature darkens, there always remains a man somewhere to reassure us: a fisherman with a torch beside the night sea, a scientist discoursing before the black basalts of Antrim, the surgeon's light hand resting on the body he is cutting open, figures of knowledge inserted into the heart of the storm (in the engraving of waterspouts). Yet as soon as we leave the vignette for the more analytic plates or images, the world's peaceful order gives way to a certain *violence*. All the forces of reason and unreason concur in this poetic disquiet; first of all metaphor itself makes an infinitely ambiguous object out of a simple, literal object: the sea urchin is *also* a sun, a monstrance: the named world is never certain, constantly fascinated by divined and inaccessible essences; and then, above all (and this is the final interrogation raised by these plates), the analytic mind itself, armed with triumphant reason, can only double the explained world by a new world *to be explained*, according to a process of infinite circularity which is that of the dictionary itself, wherein the world can be defined only by other words; by "entering" into details, by displacing the levels of perception, by revealing the hidden, by isolating the elements from their practical context, by giving objects an abstract essence, in short by "opening up" nature, the Encyclopedic image can only, at a certain moment, transcend Nature, attaining to a supernature: it is by dint of didacticism that a kind of wild surrealism is generated here (a phenomenon which we also find in an ambiguous mode in the disturbing encyclopedia Flaubert gives us in *Bouvard and Pécuchet*): do we want to show how equestrian statues are cast? We must wrap them in an extravagant apparatus of wax, tapes, and supports: what madness could attain to this *limit* (not to mention the violent demystification which reduces a warrior Louis XIV to this monstrous doll)? In a general way, the *Encyclopedia* is fascinated, at reason's instance, by the *wrong side* of things: it cross-sections, it amputates, it turns inside out, it tries to get behind Nature. Now any "wrong side" is disturbing: science and parascience are mixed, above all on the level of the image. The *Encyclopedia* constantly proceeds to an impious fragmentation of the world, but what it finds at the term of this fracture is not the fundamental state of pure causes; in most cases the image obliges it to recompose an object that is strictly *unreasonable*; once the first nature is dissolved, another nature appears, quite as formed as the first. In a word, the fracture of the world is impossible: a glance suffices—ours—for the world to be eternally complete.

1964

The Eiffel Tower

MAUPASSANT often lunched at the restaurant in the Tower, though he didn't care much for the food: *It's the only place in Paris,* he used to say, *where I don't have to see it.* And it's true that you must take endless precautions, in Paris, not to see the Eiffel Tower; whatever the season, through mist and cloud, on overcast days or in sunshine, in rain—wherever you are, whatever the landscape of roofs, domes, or branches separating you from it, *the Tower is there;* incorporated into daily life until you can no longer grant it any specific attribute, determined merely to persist, like a rock or the river, it is as literal as a phenomenon of Nature whose meaning can be questioned to infinity but whose existence is incontestable. There is virtually no Parisian glance it fails to *touch* at some time of day; at the moment I begin writing these lines about it, the Tower is there, in front of me, framed by my window; and at the very moment the January night blurs it, apparently trying to make it invisible, to deny its presence, two little lights come on, winking gently as they revolve at its very tip: all this night, too, it will be there, connecting me above Paris to each of my friends that I know are seeing it: with it we all comprise

From *The Eiffel Tower and Other Mythologies.*

a shifting figure of which it is the steady center: the Tower is friendly.

The Tower is also present to the entire world. First of all as a universal symbol of Paris, it is everywhere on the globe where Paris is to be stated as an image; from the Midwest to Australia, there is no journey to France which isn't made, somehow, in the Tower's name, no schoolbook, poster, or film about France which fails to propose it as the major sign of a people and of a place: it belongs to the universal language of travel. Further: beyond its strictly Parisian statement, it touches the most general human image-repertoire: its simple, primary shape confers upon it the vocation of an infinite cipher: in turn and according to the appeals of our imagination, the symbol of Paris, of modernity, of communication, of science or of the nineteenth century, rocket, stem, derrick, phallus, lightning rod or insect, confronting the great itineraries of our dreams, it is the inevitable sign; just as there is no Parisian glance which is not compelled to encounter it, there is no fantasy which fails, sooner or later, to acknowledge its form and to be nourished by it; pick up a pencil and let your hand, in other words your thoughts, wander, and it is often the Tower which will appear, reduced to that simple line whose sole mythic function is to join, as the poet says, *base and summit*, or again, *earth and heaven*.

This pure—virtually empty—sign—is ineluctable, *because it means everything*. In order to negate the Eiffel Tower (though the temptation to do so is rare, for this symbol offends nothing in us), you must, like Maupassant, get up on it and, so to speak, identify yourself with it. Like man himself, who is the only one not to know his own glance, the Tower is the only blind point of the total optical system of which it is the center and Paris the circumference. But in this movement which seems to limit it, the Tower acquires a new power: an object when we look at it, it becomes a lookout in its turn when we visit it, and now constitutes as an object, simultaneously extended and collected beneath it, that Paris which just now was looking at it. The Tower is an object which sees, a glance which is seen; it is a complete verb, both active and passive, in which no function, no *voice* (as we say in grammar, with a piquant ambiguity) is defective. This dialectic is not in the least banal, it makes the Tower a singular monument; for the world ordinarily produces either purely functional organisms (camera or eye) intended to see things but which then afford nothing to sight, what *sees* being mythically linked to what remains *hidden* (this is the theme of the voyeur), or else spectacles which themselves are blind and are left in the pure passivity of the visible. The Tower (and this is one of its mythic powers) transgresses this separation, this habitual divorce of *seeing* and *being seen*; it achieves a sovereign circulation between the two functions; it is a complete object which has, if one may say so, both sexes of sight. This radiant position in the order of perception gives it a prodigious propensity to meaning: the Tower attracts meaning, the way a lightning rod attracts thunderbolts; for all lovers of signification, it plays a glamorous part, that of a pure signifier, i.e., of a form in which men unceasingly put *meaning* (which they extract at will from their knowledge, their dreams, their history), without this meaning thereby ever being finite and fixed: who can say what the Tower will be for humanity tomorrow? But there can be no doubt it will always be something, and something of humanity itself. Glance, object, symbol, such is the infinite circuit of functions which permits it always to be something other and something much more than the Eiffel Tower.

In order to satisfy this great oneiric function, which makes it into a kind of total monument, the Tower must escape reason. The first condition of this victorious flight is that the Tower be an utterly *useless* monument. The Tower's inutility has always been obscurely felt to be a scandal, i.e., a truth, one that is precious and inadmissible. Even before it was built, it was blamed for being useless, which, it was believed at the time, was sufficient to condemn it; it was not in the spirit of a period commonly dedicated to rationality and to the empiricism of great bourgeois enterprises to endure the notion of a useless object (unless it was declaratively an *objet d'art*, which was also unthinkable in relation to the Tower); hence Gustave Eiffel, in his own defense of his project in reply to the Artists' Petition, scrupulously lists all the future uses of the Tower: they are all, as we might expect of an engineer, scientific uses: aerodynamic measurements, studies of the resistance of substances, physiology of the climber, radio-electric research, problems of telecommunication, meteorological observations, etc. These uses are doubtless incontestable, but they seem quite ridiculous alongside the overwhelming myth of the Tower, of the human meaning which it has assumed throughout the world. This is because here the utilitarian excuses, however ennobled they may be by the myth of Science, are nothing in comparison to the great imaginary function which enables men to be strictly human. Yet, as always, the gratuitous meaning of the work is never avowed directly: it is rationalized under the rubric of *use*: Eiffel saw his Tower in the form of a serious object, rational, useful; men return it to him in the form of a great baroque dream which quite naturally touches on the borders of the irrational.

This double movement is a profound one: architecture is always dream and function, expression of a utopia and instrument of a convenience. Even before the Tower's birth, the nineteenth century (especially in America and in England) had often dreamed of structures whose height would be astonishing, for the century was given to technological feats, and the conquest of the sky once again preyed upon humanity. In 1881, shortly before the Tower, a French architect had elaborated the project of a sun tower; now this project, quite mad technologically, since it relied on masonry and not on steel, also put itself under the warrant of a thoroughly empirical utility; on the one hand, a bonfire placed on top of the structure was to illuminate the darkness of every nook and cranny in Paris by a system of mirrors (a system that was undoubtedly a complex one!), and on the other, the last story of this sun tower (about 1,000 feet, like the Eiffel Tower) was to be reserved for a kind of sunroom, in which invalids would benefit from an air "as pure as in the mountains." And yet, here as in the case of the Tower, the naïve utilitarianism of the enterprise is not separate from the oneiric, infinitely powerful function which, actually, inspires its creation: use never does anything but shelter meaning. Hence we might speak, among men, of a true Babel complex: Babel was supposed to *serve* to communicate with God, and yet Babel is a dream which touches much greater depths than that of the theological project; and just as this great ascensional dream, released from its utilitarian prop, is finally what remains in the countless Babels represented by the painters, as if the function of art were to reveal the profound uselessness of objects, just so the Tower, almost immediately disengaged from the scientific considerations which had authorized its birth (it matters very little here that the Tower should be in fact useful), has arisen from a great human dream in which movable and infinite meanings are mingled: it has reconquered the basic uselessness which makes it live in men's imagination. At first, it was sought—so paradoxical is the notion of an empty monument—to make it into a "temple of Science"; but this is only a metaphor; as a matter of fact, the Tower is *nothing*, it achieves a kind of zero degree of the monument; it participates in no rite, in no cult, not even in Art; you cannot visit the Tower as a museum: there is nothing to see *inside* the Tower. This empty monument nevertheless receives each year twice as many visitors as the Louvre and considerably more than the largest movie house in Paris.

Then why do we visit the Eiffel Tower? No doubt in order to participate in a dream of which it is (and this is its originality) much more the crystallizer than the true object. The Tower is not a usual spectacle; to enter the Tower, to scale it, to run around its courses, is, in a manner both more elementary and more profound, to accede to a *view* and to explore the interior of an object (though an openwork one), to transform the touristic rite into an adventure of sight and of the intelligence. It is this double function I should like to speak of briefly, before passing in conclusion to the major symbolic function of the Tower, which is its final meaning.

The Tower looks at Paris. To visit the Tower is to get oneself up onto the balcony in order to perceive, comprehend, and savor a certain essence of Paris. And here again, the Tower is an original monument. Habitually, belvederes are outlooks upon Nature, whose elements—waters, valleys, forests—they assemble beneath them, so that the tourism of the "fine view" infallibly implies a naturist mythology. Whereas the Tower overlooks not Nature but the city; and yet, by its very position of a visited outlook, the Tower makes the city into a kind of Nature; it constitutes the swarming of men into a landscape, it adds to the frequently grim urban myth a romantic dimension, a harmony, a mitigation; by it, starting from it, the city joins up with the great natural themes which are offered to the curiosity of men: the ocean, the storm, the mountains, the snow, the rivers. To visit the Tower, then, is to enter into contact not with a historical Sacred, as is the case for the majority of monuments, but rather with a new Nature, that of human space: the Tower is not a trace, a souvenir, in short a culture; but rather an immediate consumption of a humanity made natural by that glance which transforms it into space.

One might say that for this reason the Tower materializes an imagination which has had its first expression in literature (it is frequently the function of the great books to achieve in advance what technology will merely put into execution). The nineteenth century, fifty years before the Tower, produced indeed two works in which the (perhaps very old) fantasy of a panoramic vision received the guarantee of a major poetic writing (*écriture*): these are, on the one hand, the chapter of *Notre-Dame de Paris* (*The Hunchback of Notre Dame*) devoted to a bird's-eye view of Paris, and on the other, Michelet's *Tableau chronologique*. Now, what is admirable in these two great inclusive visions, one of Paris, the other of France, is that Hugo and Michelet clearly understood that to the marvelous mitigation of altitude the panoramic vision added an incomparable power of *intellection*: the bird's-eye view, which each visitor to the Tower can assume in an instant for his own, gives us the world to *read* and not only to perceive; this is why it corresponds to a new sensibility of vision; in the past, to travel (we may recall certain—admirable, moreover—promenades of Rousseau) was to be thrust into the midst of sensation, to perceive only a kind of tidal wave of things; the bird's-eye view, on the contrary, represented by our romantic writers as if they had anticipated both the construction of the Tower and the birth of aviation, permits us to transcend sensation and to see things *in their structure*. Hence it is the advent of a new perception, of an intellectualist mode, which these literatures and these architectures of vision mark out (born in the same century and probably from the same history): Paris and France become under Hugo's pen and Michelet's (and under the glance of the Tower) intelligible objects, yet without—and this is what is new—losing anything of their materiality; a new category appears, that of concrete abstraction; this, moreover, is the meaning which we can give today to the word *structure*: a corpus of intelligent forms.

Like Monsieur Jourdain confronted with prose, every visitor to the Tower makes structuralism without knowing it (which does not keep prose and structure from existing all the same); in Paris spread out beneath him, he spontaneously distinguishes separate—because known—points—and yet does not stop linking them, perceiving them within a great functional space; in short, he separates and groups; Paris offers itself to him as an object virtually *prepared*, exposed to the intelligence, but which he must himself construct by a final activity of the mind: nothing less passive than the *overall view* the Tower gives to Paris. This activity of the mind, conveyed by the tourist's modest glance, has a name: decipherment.

What, in fact, is a panorama? An image we attempt to decipher, in which we try to recognize known sites, to identify landmarks. Take some view of Paris taken from the Eiffel Tower; here you make out the hill sloping down from Chaillot, there the Bois de Boulogne; but where is the Arc de Triomphe? You don't see it, and this absence compels you to inspect the panorama once again, to look for this point which is missing in your structure; your knowledge (the knowledge you may have of Parisian topography) struggles with your perception, and in a sense, that is what intelligence is: to *reconstitute*, to make memory and sensation cooperate so as to produce in your mind a simulacrum of Paris, of which the elements are in front of you, real, ancestral, but nonetheless disoriented by the total space in which they are given to you, for this space was unknown to you. Hence we approach the complex, dialectical nature of all panoramic vision; on the one hand, it is a euphoric vision, for it can slide slowly, lightly the entire length of a continuous image of Paris, and initially no "accident" manages to interrupt this great layer of mineral and vegetal strata, perceived in the distance in the bliss of altitude; but, on the other hand, this very continuity engages the mind in a certain struggle, it seeks to be deciphered, we must find *signs* within it, a familiarity proceeding from history and from myth; this is why a panorama can never be consumed as a work of art, the aesthetic interest of a painting ceasing once we try to *recognize* in it particular points derived from our knowledge; to say that there is a beauty to Paris stretched out at the feet of the Tower is doubtless to acknowledge this euphoria of aerial vision which recognizes nothing other than a nicely connected space; but it is also to mask the quite intellectual effort of the eye before an object which requires to be divided up, identified, reattached to memory; for the bliss of sensation (nothing happier than a lofty outlook) does not suffice to elude the questioning nature of the mind before any image.

This generally intellectual character of the panoramic vision is further attested by the following phenomenon, which Hugo and Michelet had moreover made into the mainspring of their bird's-eye views: to perceive Paris from above is infallibly to imagine a history; from the top of the Tower, the mind finds itself dreaming of the mutation of the landscape which it has before its eyes; through the astonishment of space, it plunges into the mystery of time, lets itself be affected by a kind of spontaneous anamnesis: it is duration itself which becomes panoramic. Let us put ourselves back (no difficult task) at the level of an average knowledge, an ordinary question put to the panorama of Paris; four great moments immediately leap out to our vision, i.e., to our consciousness. The first is that of prehistory; Paris was then covered by a layer of water, out of which barely emerged a few solid points; set on the Tower's first floor, the visitor would have had his nose level with the waves and would have seen only some scattered islets, the Etoile, the Pantheon, a wooded island which was Montmartre and two blue stakes in the distance, the towers of Notre-Dame, then to his left, bordering this huge lake, the slopes of Mont Valérien; and conversely, the traveler who chooses to put himself today on the heights of this eminence, in foggy weather, would see emerging the two upper stories of the Tower from a liquid base; this prehistoric relation of the Tower and the water has been, so to speak, symbolically maintained down to our own days, for the Tower is partly built on a thin arm of the Seine filled in (up to the rue de l'Université) and it still seems to rise from a gesture of the river whose bridges it guards. The second history which lies before the Tower's gaze is the Middle Ages; Cocteau once said that the Tower was the Notre-Dame of the Left Bank; though the cathedral of Paris is not the highest of the city's monuments (the Invalides, the Pantheon, Sacré-Coeur are higher), it forms with the Tower a pair, a symbolic couple, recognized, so to speak, by Tourist folklore, which readily reduces Paris to its Tower and its Cathedral: a symbol articulated on the opposition of the past (the Middle Ages always represent a dense time) and the present, of stone, old as the world, and metal, sign of modernity. The third moment that can be read from the Tower is that of a broad history, undifferentiated since it proceeds from the Monarchy to the Empire, from the Invalides to the Arc de Triomphe: this is strictly the History of France, as it is experienced by French schoolchildren, and of which many episodes, present in every schoolboy memory, touch Paris. Finally, the Tower surveys a fourth history of Paris, the one which is being made now; certain modern monuments (UNESCO, the Radio-Télévision building) are beginning to set signs of the future within its space; the Tower permits harmonizing these unaccommodated substances (glass, metal), these new forms, with the stones and domes of the past; Paris, in its duration, under the Tower's gaze, composes itself like an abstract canvas in which dark oblongs (derived from a very old past) are contiguous with the white rectangles of modern architecture.

Once these points of history and of space are established by
the eye, from the top of the Tower, the imagination continues
filling out the Parisian panorama, giving it its structure; but
what then intervenes are certain human functions; like the
devil Asmodeus, by rising above Paris, the visitor to the Tower
has the illusion of raising the enormous lid which covers the
private life of millions of human beings; the city then becomes
an intimacy whose functions, i.e., whose connections he deciphers; on the great polar axis, perpendicular to the horizontal curve of the river, three zones stacked one after the other,
as though along a prone body, three functions of human life:
at the top, at the foot of Montmartre, pleasure; at the center,
around the Opéra, materiality, business, commerce; toward
the bottom, at the foot of the Pantheon, knowledge, study;
then, to the right and left, enveloping this vital axis like two
protective muffs, two large zones of habitation, one residential,
the other blue-collar; still farther, two wooded strips, Boulogne and Vincennes. It has been observed that a kind of very
old law incites cities to develop toward the west, in the direction of the setting sun; it is on this side that the wealth of the
fine neighborhoods proceeds, the east remaining the site of
poverty; the Tower, by its very implantation, seems to follow
this movement discreetly; one might say that it accompanies
Paris in this westward shift, which our capital does not escape,
and that it even invites the city toward its pole of development,
to the south and to the west, where the sun is warmer, thereby
participating in that great mythic function which makes every
city into a living being: neither brain nor organ, situated a
little apart from its vital zones, the Tower is merely the witness, the gaze which discreetly fixes, with its slender signal, the
whole structure—geographical, historical, and social—of
Paris space. This deciphering of Paris, performed by the
Tower's gaze, is not only an act of the mind, it is also an
initiation. To climb the Tower in order to contemplate Paris

from it is the equivalent of that first journey, by which the young man from the provinces went up to Paris, in order to conquer the city. At the age of twelve, young Eiffel himself took the diligence from Dijon with his mother and discovered the "magic" of Paris. The city, a kind of superlative capital, summons up that movement of accession to a superior order of pleasures, of values, of arts and luxuries; it is a kind of precious world of which knowledge makes the man, marks an entrance into a true life of passions and responsibilities; it is this myth—no doubt a very old one—which the trip to the Tower still allows us to suggest; for the tourist who climbs the Tower, however mild he may be, Paris laid out before his eyes by an individual and deliberate act of contemplation is still something of the Paris confronted, defied, possessed by Rastignac. Hence, of all the sites visited by the foreigner or the provincial, the Tower is the first obligatory monument; it is a Gateway, it marks the transition to a knowledge: one must sacrifice to the Tower by a rite of inclusion from which, precisely, the Parisian alone can excuse himself: the Tower is indeed the site which allows one to be incorporated into a race, and when it regards Paris, it is the very essence of the capital it gathers up and proffers to the foreigner who has paid to it his initiational tribute.

From Paris contemplated, we must now work our way back toward the Tower itself: the Tower which will live its life as an object (before being mobilized as a symbol). Ordinarily, for the tourist, every object is first of all an *inside*, for there is no visit without the exploration of an enclosed space: to visit a church, a museum, a palace is first of all to shut oneself up, to "make the rounds" of an interior, a little in the manner of an owner: every exploration is an appropriation; this tour of the *inside* corresponds, moreover, to the question raised by the *outside*: the monument is a riddle, to enter it is to solve, to possess it; here we recognize in the tourist visit that initiational function we have just invoked apropos of the trip to the Tower; the cohort of visitors which is enclosed by a monument and processionally follows its internal meanders before coming back outside is quite like the neophyte who, in order to accede to the initiate's status, is obliged to traverse a dark and unfamiliar route within the initiatory edifice. In the religious protocol as in the tourist enterprise, being enclosed is therefore a function of the rite. Here, too, the Tower is a paradoxical object: one cannot be shut up within it since what defines the Tower is its longilineal form and its open structure: How can you be enclosed within emptiness, how can you visit a line? Yet incontestably the Tower is visited: we linger within it, before using it as an observatory. What is happening? What becomes of the great exploratory function of the *inside* when it is applied to this empty and depthless monument which might be said to consist entirely of an exterior substance?

In order to understand how the modern visitor adapts himself to the paradoxical monument which is offered to his imagination, we need merely observe what the Tower gives him, insofar as one sees in it an object and no longer a lookout. On this point, the Tower's provisions are of two kinds. The first is of a technical order; the Tower offers for consumption a certain number of performances, or, if one prefers, of paradoxes, and the visitor then becomes an engineer by proxy; these are, first of all, the four bases, and especially (for enormity does not astonish) the exaggeratedly oblique insertion of the metal pillars in the mineral mass; this obliquity is curious insofar as it gives birth to an upright form, whose very verticality absorbs its departure in slanting forms, and here there is a kind of agreeable challenge for the visitor; then come the elevators, quite surprising by their obliquity, for the ordinary imagination requires that what rises mechanically slide along a vertical axis; and for anyone who takes the stairs, there is the enlarged spectacle of all the details, plates, beams, bolts, which *make* the Tower, the surprise of seeing how this rectilinear form, which is consumed in every corner of Paris as a pure line, is composed of countless segments, interlinked, crossed, divergent: an operation of reducing an appearance (the straight line) to its contrary reality (a lacework of broken substances), a kind of demystification provided by simple enlargement of the level of perception, as in those photographs in which the curve of a face, by enlargement, appears to be formed of a thousand tiny squares variously illuminated. Thus the Tower-as-object furnishes its observer, provided he insinuates himself into it, a whole series of paradoxes, the delectable contraction of an appearance and of its contrary reality.

The Tower's second provision, as an object, is that, despite its technical singularity, it constitutes a familiar "little world"; from the ground level, a whole humble commerce accompanies its departure: vendors of postcards, souvenirs, knick-knacks, balloons, toys, sunglasses, herald a commercial life which we rediscover thoroughly installed on the first platform. Now any commerce has a space-taming function; selling, buying, exchanging—it is by these simple gestures that men truly dominate the wildest sites, the most sacred constructions. The myth of the moneylenders driven out of the Temple is actually an ambiguous one, for such commerce testifies to a kind of affectionate familiarity with regard to a monument whose singularity no longer intimidates, and it is by a Christian sentiment (hence to a certain degree a special one) that the spiritual excludes the familiar; in Antiquity, a great religious festival as well as a theatrical representation, a veritable sacred ceremony, in no way prevented the revelation of the most everyday gestures, such as eating or drinking: all pleasures proceeded simultaneously, not by some heedless permissiveness but because the ceremonial was never savage and certainly offered no contradiction to the quotidian. The Tower is

not a sacred monument, and no taboo can forbid a commonplace life to develop there, but there can be no question, nonetheless, of a trivial phenomenon here; the installation of a
restaurant on the Tower, for instance (food being the object of
the most symbolic of trades), is a phenomenon corresponding
to a whole meaning of leisure; man always seems disposed—if
no constraints appear to stand in his way—to seek out a kind
of counterpoint in his pleasures: this is what is called comfort.
The Eiffel Tower is a comfortable object, and moreover, it is
in this that it is an object either very old (analogous, for
instance, to the ancient Circus) or very modern (analogous to
certain American institutions such as the drive-in movie, in
which one can simultaneously enjoy the film, the car, the food,
and the freshness of the night air). Further, by affording its
visitor a whole polyphony of pleasures, from technological
wonder to haute cuisine, including the panorama, the Tower
ultimately reunites with the essential function of all major
human sites: autarchy; the Tower can live on itself: one can
dream there, eat there, observe there, understand there, marvel
there, shop there; as on an ocean liner (another mythic object
that sets children dreaming), one can feel oneself cut off from
the world and yet the owner of a world.

1964

Introduction to the
Structural Analysis of Narratives

THE narratives of the world are numberless. Narrative is first and foremost a prodigious variety of genres, themselves distributed amongst different substances—as though any material were fit to receive man's stories. Able to be carried by articulated language, spoken or written, fixed or moving images, gestures, and the ordered mixture of all these substances; narrative is present in myth, legend, fable, tale, novella, epic, history, tragedy, drama, comedy, mime, painting (think of Carpaccio's *Saint Ursula*), stained-glass windows, cinema, comics, news item, conversation. Moreover, under this almost infinite diversity of forms, narrative is present in every age, in every place, in every society; it begins with the very history of mankind and there nowhere is nor has been a people without narrative. All classes, all human groups, have their narratives, enjoyment of which is very often shared by men with different, even opposing,[1] cultural backgrounds. Caring nothing for the division between good and bad literature, narrative is interna-

From *Image-Music-Text*.

[1] It must be remembered that this is not the case with either poetry or the essay, both of which are dependent on the cultural level of their consumers.

tional, transhistorical, transcultural: it is simply there, like life itself.

Must we conclude from this universality that narrative is insignificant? Is it so general that we can have nothing to say about it except for the modest description of a few highly individualized varieties, something literary history occasionally undertakes? But then how are we to master even these varieties, how are we to justify our right to differentiate and identify them? How is novel to be set against novella, tale against myth, drama against tragedy (as has been done a thousand times) without reference to a common model? Such a model is implied by every proposition relating to the most individual, the most historical, of narrative forms. It is thus legitimate that, far from the abandoning of any idea of dealing with narrative on the grounds of its universality, there should have been (from Aristotle on) a periodic interest in narrative form and it is normal that the newly developing structuralism should make this form one of its first concerns—is not structuralism's constant aim to master the infinity of utterances [*paroles*] by describing the "language" ["*langue*"] of which they are the products and from which they can be generated. Faced with the infinity of narratives, the multiplicity of standpoints—historical, psychological, sociological, ethnological, aesthetic, etc.—from which they can be studied, the analyst finds himself in more or less the same situation as Saussure confronted by the heterogeneity of language [*langage*] and seeking to extract a principle of classification and a central focus for description from the apparent confusion of the individual messages. Keeping simply to modern times, the Russian formalists, Propp, and Lévi-Strauss have taught us to recognize the following dilemma: either a narrative is merely a rambling collection of events, in which case nothing can be said about it other than by referring back to the storyteller's (the author's) art, talent, or genius—all mythical forms of chance[2]—or else it shares with other narratives a common structure which is open to analysis, no matter how much patience its formulation requires. There is a world of difference between the most complex randomness and the most elementary combinatory scheme, and it is impossible to combine (to produce) a narrative without reference to an implicit system of units and rules.

Where then are we to look for the structures of narrative? Doubtless, in narratives themselves. *Each and every* narrative? Many commentators who accept the idea of a narrative structure are nevertheless unable to resign themselves to dissociating literary analysis from the example of the experimental sciences; nothing daunted, they ask that a purely inductive method be applied to narrative and that one start by studying all the narratives within a genre, a period, a society. This commonsense view is utopian. Linguistics itself, with only some three thousand languages to embrace, cannot manage such a program and has wisely turned deductive, a step which in fact marked its veritable constitution as a science and the beginning of its spectacular progress, it even succeeding in anticipating facts prior to their discovery.[3] So what of narrative analysis, faced as it is with millions of narratives? Of necessity, it is condemned to a deductive procedure, obliged first to devise a hypothetical model of description (what American linguists call a "theory") and then gradually to work down from this model toward the different narrative

---

[2] There does, of course, exist an "art" of the storyteller, which is the ability to generate narratives (messages) from the structure (the code). This art corresponds to the notion of *performance* in Chomsky and is far removed from the "genius" of the author, romantically conceived as some barely explicable personal secret.

[3] See the history of the Hittite *a*, postulated by Saussure and actually discovered fifty years later, as given in Emile Benveniste, *Problèmes de linguistique générale.*

species which at once conform to and depart from the model. It is only at the level of these conformities and departures that analysis will be able to come back to, but now equipped with a single descriptive tool, the plurality of narratives, to their historical, geographical and cultural diversity.[4]

Thus, in order to describe and classify the infinite number of narratives, a "Theory" (in this pragmatic sense) is needed and the immediate task is that of finding it, of starting to define it. Its development can be greatly facilitated if one begins from a model able to provide it with its initial terms and principles. In the current state of research, it seems reasonable[5] that the structural analysis of narrative be given linguistics itself as founding model.

I. THE LANGUAGE OF NARRATIVE

1. Beyond the sentence

As we know, linguistics stops at the sentence, the last unit which it considers to fall within its scope. If the sentence, being an order and not a series, cannot be reduced to the sum of the words which compose it and constitutes thereby a specific unit, a piece of discourse, on the contrary, is no more than the succession of the sentences composing it. From the

---

[4] Let us bear in mind the present conditions of linguistic description: ". . . linguistic 'structure' is always relative not just to the data or corpus but also to the grammatical theory describing the data," E. Bach, *An Introduction to Transformational Grammars*; "it has been recognized that language must be described as a formal structure, but that the description first of all necessitates specification of adequate procedures and criteria and that, finally, the reality of the object is inseparable from the method given for its description," Benveniste.

[5] But not imperative: see Claude Bremond, "La logique des possibles narratifs," *Communications* 8, 1966, which is more logical than linguistic. [Bremond's various studies in this field have now been collected in a volume entitled, precisely, *Logique du récit*; his work consists in the analysis of narrative according to the pattern of possible alternatives, each narrative moment—or function—giving rise to a set of different possible resolutions, the actualization of any one of which in turn produces a new set of alternatives.]

point of view of linguistics, there is nothing in discourse that is not to be found in the sentence: "The sentence," writes Martinet, "is the smallest segment that is perfectly and wholly representative of discourse."[6] Hence there can be no question of linguistics setting itself an object superior to the sentence, since beyond the sentence are only more sentences—having described the flower, the botanist is not to get involved in describing the bouquet.

And yet it is evident that discourse itself (as a set of sentences) is organized and that, through this organization, it can be seen as the message of another language, one operating at a higher level than the language of the linguists.[7] Discourse has its units, its rules, its "grammar": beyond the sentence, and though consisting solely of sentences, it must naturally form the object of a second linguistics. For a long time indeed, such a linguistics of discourse bore a glorious name, that of Rhetoric. As a result of a complex historical movement, however, in which Rhetoric went over to belles-lettres and the latter was divorced from the study of language, it has recently become necessary to take up the problem afresh. The new linguistics of discourse has still to be developed, but at least it is being postulated, and by the linguists themselves.[8] This last fact is not without significance, for, although constituting an autonomous object, discourse must be studied from the basis of linguistics. If a working hypothesis is needed for an analysis whose task is immense and whose materials infinite, then the most reasonable thing is to posit a homological relation between sentence and discourse insofar as it is likely that a similar formal organization orders all semiotic systems, whatever

[6] André Martinet, "Réflexions sur la phrase," in *Language and Society*.
[7] It goes without saying, as Jakobson has noted, that between the sentence and what lies beyond the sentence there are transitions; coordination, for instance, can work over the limit of the sentence.
[8] See especially: Benveniste, op. cit., Chapter 10; Z. S. Harris, "Discourse Analysis," *Language* 28, 1952; N. Ruwet, "Analyse structurale d'un poème français," *Linguistics* 3, 1964.

their substances and dimensions. A discourse is a long "sentence" (the units of which are not necessarily sentences), just as a sentence, allowing for certain specifications, is a short "discourse." This hypothesis accords well with a number of propositions put forward in contemporary anthropology. Jakobson and Lévi-Strauss have pointed out that mankind can be defined by the ability to create secondary—"self-multiplying"—systems (tools for the manufacture of other tools, double articulation of language, incest taboo permitting the fanning out of families) while the Soviet linguist Ianov supposes that artificial languages can only have been acquired after natural language: what is important for men is to have the use of several systems of meaning and natural language helps in the elaboration of artificial languages. It is therefore legitimate to posit a "secondary" relation between sentence and discourse—a relation which will be referred to as homological, in order to respect the purely formal nature of the correspondences.

The general language [*langue*] of narrative is one (and clearly only one) of the idioms apt for consideration by the linguistics of discourse[9] and it accordingly comes under the homological hypothesis. Structurally, narrative shares the characteristics of the sentence without ever being reducible to the simple sum of its sentences: a narrative is a long sentence, just as every constative sentence is in a way the rough outline of a short narrative. Although there provided with different signifiers (often extremely complex), one does find in narrative, expanded and transformed proportionately, the principal verbal categories: tenses, aspects, moods, persons. Moreover the "subjects" themselves, as opposed to the verbal predicates, readily yield to the sentence model; the actantial typology pro-

[9] One of the tasks of such a linguistics would be precisely that of establishing a typology of forms of discourse. Three broad types can be recognized provisionally: metonymic (narrative), metaphoric (lyric, poetry, sapiential discourse), enthymematic (intellectual discourse).

posed by A. J. Greimas[10] discovers in the multitude of narrative characters the elementary functions of grammatical analysis. Nor does the homology suggested here have merely a
heuristic value: it implies an identity between language and
literature (inasmuch as the latter can be seen as a sort of
privileged vehicle of narrative). It is hardly possible any
longer to conceive of literature as an art that abandons all
further relation with language the moment it has used it as an
instrument to express ideas, passion, or beauty: language
never ceases to accompany discourse, holding up to it the
mirror of its own structure—does not literature, particularly
today, make a language of the very conditions of language?[11]

2. Levels of meaning

From the outset, linguistics furnishes the structural analysis
of narrative with a concept which is decisive in that, making
explicit immediately what is essential in every system of meaning, namely its organization, it allows us both to show how a
narrative is not a simple sum of propositions and to classify
the enormous mass of elements which go to make up a narrative. This concept is that of *level of description*.[12]

A sentence can be described, linguistically, on several levels
(phonetic, phonological, grammatical, contextual) and these
levels are in a hierarchical relationship with one another, for,
while all have their own units and correlations (whence the
necessity for a separate description of each of them), no level

[10] See below III.1. Greimas's own account can be found in *Sémantique
structurale*.
[11] Remember Mallarmé's insight at the time when he was contemplating a
work of linguistics: "Language appeared to him the instrument of fiction: he
will follow the method of language (determine it). Language self-reflecting.
So fiction seems to him the very process of the human mind—it is this that
sets in play all method, and man is reduced to will." It will be recalled
that for Mallarmé "Fiction" and "Poetry" are taken synonymously.
[12] "Linguistic descriptions are not, so to speak, monovalent. A description is
not simply 'right' or 'wrong' in itself . . . it is better thought of as more
useful or less," M. A. K. Halliday, "General linguistics and its application
to language teaching," *Patterns of Language*.

on its own can produce meaning. A unit belonging to a particular level only takes on meaning if it can be integrated in a higher level; a phoneme, though perfectly describable, means nothing in itself: it participates in meaning only when integrated in a word, and the word itself must in turn be integrated in a sentence.[13] The theory of levels (as set out by Benveniste) gives two types of relations: distributional (if the relations are situated on the same level) and integrational (if they are grasped from one level to the next); consequently, distributional relations alone are not sufficient to account for meaning. In order to conduct a structural analysis, it is thus first of all necessary to distinguish several levels or instances of description and to place these instances within a hierarchical (integrationary) perspective.

The levels are operations.[14] It is therefore normal that, as it progresses, linguistics should tend to multiply them. Discourse analysis, however, is as yet only able to work on rudimentary levels. In its own way, rhetoric had assigned at least two planes of description to discourse: *dispositio* and *elocutio*.[15] Today, in his analysis of the structure of myth, Lévi-Strauss has already indicated that the constituent units of mythical discourse (mythemes) acquire meaning only because they are grouped in bundles and because these bundles themselves combine together.[16] As too, Tzvetan Todorov, reviving the distinction made by the Russian formalists, proposes working on two major levels, themselves subdivided: *story* (the argu-

---

[13] The levels of integration were postulated by the Prague School (vid. J. Vachek, *A Prague School Reader in Linguistics*, Bloomington 1964, p. 468) and have been adopted since by many linguists. It is Benveniste who, in my opinion, has given the most illuminating analysis in this respect; op. cit., Chapter 10.

[14] "In somewhat vague terms, a level may be considered as a system of symbols, rules, and so on, to be used for representing utterances," Bach, op. cit.

[15] The third part of rhetoric, *inventio*, did not concern language—it had to do with *res*, not with *verba*.

[16] *Structural Anthropology*.

ment), comprising a logic of actions and a "syntax" of characters, and *discourse*, comprising the tenses, aspects, and modes
of the narrative.[17] But however many levels are proposed and
whatever definition they are given, there can be no doubt that
narrative is a hierarchy of instances. To understand a narrative
is not merely to follow the unfolding of the story, it is also to
recognize its construction in "stories," to project the horizontal concatenations of the narrative "thread" onto an implicitly
vertical axis; to read (to listen to) a narrative is not merely to
move from one word to the next, it is also to move from one
level to the next. Perhaps I may be allowed to offer a kind of
apologue in this connection. In "The Purloined Letter," Poe
gives an acute analysis of the failure of the chief commissioner
of the Paris police, powerless to find the letter. His investigations, says Poe, were perfect *"within the sphere of his specialty"*;[18] he searched everywhere, saturated entirely the level of
the "police search," but in order to find the letter, protected by
its conspicuousness, it was necessary to shift to another level,
to substitute the concealer's principle of relevance for that of
the policeman. Similarly, the "search" carried out over a horizontal set of narrative relations may well be as thorough as
possible but must still, to be effective, also operate "verti-
cally": meaning is not "at the end" of the narrative, it runs
across it; just as conspicuous as the purloined letter, meaning
eludes all unilateral investigation.

A great deal of tentative effort is still required before it will
be possible to ascertain precisely the levels of narrative. Those
that are suggested in what follows constitute a provisional
profile whose merit remains almost exclusively didactic; they

---

[17] See T. Todorov "Les catégories du récit littéraire," *Communications* 8,
1966 [Todorov's work on narrative is now most easily accessible in two
books, *Littérature et signification; poétique de la prose.* For a short account
in English, see "Structural analysis of narrative," *Novel* I, 3, 1969.]
[18] [This in accordance with the Baudelaire version of the Poe story from
which Barthes quotes; Poe's original reads: "so far as his labors extended."]

enable us to locate and group together the different problems, and this without, I think, being at variance with the few analyses so far.[19] It is proposed to distinguish three levels of description in the narrative work: the level of *"functions"* (in the sense this word has in Propp and Bremond), the level of *"actions"* (in the sense this word has in Greimas when he talks of characters as actants) and the level of *"narration"* (which is roughly the level of "discourse" in Todorov). These three levels are bound together according to a mode of progressive integration: a function only has meaning insofar as it occupies a place in the general action of an actant, and this action in turn receives its final meaning from the fact that it is narrated, entrusted to a discourse which possesses its own code.

II. FUNCTIONS

1. The determination of the units

Any system being the combination of units of known classes, the first task is to divide up narrative and determine the segments of narrative discourse that can be distributed into a limited number of classes. In a word, we have to define the smallest narrative units.

Given the integrational perspective described above, the analysis cannot rest satisfied with a purely distributional definition of the units. From the start, meaning must be the criterion of the unit: it is the functional nature of certain segments of the story that makes them units—hence the name "functions" immediately attributed to these first units. Since the Russian formalists,[20] a unit has been taken as any segment of the story which can be seen as the term of a correla-

---

[19] I have been concerned in this introduction to impede research in progress as little as possible.

[20] See especially B. Tomachevski, "Thématique" (1925), in *Théorie de la littérature*, ed. T. Todorov. A little later, Propp in *Morphology of the Folktale* defined the function as "an act of a character, defined from the point of view of its significance for the course of the action."

tion. The essence of a function is, so to speak, the seed that it sows in the narrative, planting an element that will come to fruition later—either on the same level or elsewhere, on another level. If in *Un Cœur simple* Flaubert at one point tells the reader, seemingly without emphasis, that the daughters of the Sous-Préfet of Pont-l'Evêque owned a parrot, it is because this parrot is subsequently to have a great importance in Félicité's life; the statement of this detail (whatever its linguistic form) thus constitutes a function, or narrative unit.

Is everything in a narrative functional? Does everything, down to the slightest detail, have a meaning? Can narrative be divided up entirely into functional units? We shall see in a moment that there are several kinds of functions, there being several kinds of correlations, but this does not alter the fact that a narrative is never made up of anything other than functions: in differing degrees, everything in it signifies. This is not a matter of art (on the part of the narrator), but of structure; in the realm of discourse, what is noted is by definition notable. Even were a detail to appear irretrievably insignificant, resistant to all functionality, it would nonetheless end up with precisely the meaning of absurdity or uselessness: everything has a meaning, or nothing has. To put it another way, one could say that art is without noise (as that term is employed in information theory):[21] art is a system which is pure, no unit ever goes wasted,[22] however long, however loose, however tenuous may be the thread connecting it to one of the levels of the story.[23]

---

[21] This is what separates art from "life," the latter knowing only "fuzzy" or "blurred" communications. "Fuzziness" (that beyond which it is impossible to see) can exist in art, but it does so as coded element (in Watteau for example). Even then, such "fuzziness" is unknown to the written code: writing is inescapably distinct.

[22] At least in literature, where the freedom of notation (in consequence of the abstract nature of articulated language) leads to a much greater responsibility than in the "analogical" arts such as cinema.

[23] The functionality of a narrative unit is more or less immediate (and hence apparent) according to the level on which it operates: when the units are

From the linguistic point of view, the function is clearly a unit of content: it is "what it says" that makes of a statement a functional unit,[24] not the manner in which it is said. This constitutive signified may have a number of different signifiers, often very intricate. If I am told (in *Goldfinger*) that *Bond saw a man of about fifty*, the piece of information holds simultaneously two functions of unequal pressure: on the one hand, the character's age fits into a certain description of the man (the "usefulness" of which for the rest of the story is not nil, but diffuse, delayed); while on the other, the immediate signified of the statement is that Bond is unacquainted with his future interlocutor, the unit thus implying a very strong correlation (initiation of a threat and the need to establish the man's identity). In order to determine the initial narrative units, it is therefore vital never to lose sight of the functional nature of the segments under consideration and to recognize in advance that they will not necessarily coincide with the forms into which we traditionally cast the various parts of narrative discourse (actions, scenes, paragraphs, dialogues, interior monologues, etc.) still less with "psychological" divisions (modes of behavior, feelings, intentions, motivations, rationalizations of characters).

In the same way, since the "language" ["*langue*"] of narrative is not the language [*langue*] of articulated language [*langage articulé*]—though very often vehicled by it—narrative units will be substantially independent of linguistic units; they may indeed coincide with the latter, but occasionally, not systematically. Functions will be represented sometimes by units higher than the sentence (groups of sentences of varying

---

situated on the same level (as for instance in the case of suspense), the functionality is very clear; it is much less so when the function is saturated on the narrational level—a modern text, weakly signifying on the plane of the anecdote, only finds a full force of meaning on the plane of the writing. [24] "Syntactical units beyond the sentence are in fact units of content," A. J. Greimas, *Cours de sémantique structurale*, 1964. The exploration of the functional level is thus part of general semantics.

lengths, up to the work in its entirety) and sometimes by lower ones (syntagm, word, and even, within the word, certain literary elements only[25]). When we are told that—the telephone ringing during night duty at Secret Service headquarters— *Bond picked up one of the four receivers*, the moneme *four* in itself constitutes a functional unit, referring as it does to a concept necessary to the story (that of a highly developed bureaucratic technology). In fact, the narrative unit in this case is not the linguistic unit (the word) but only its connoted value (linguistically, the word /four/ never means "four"); which explains how certain functional units can be shorter than the sentence without ceasing to belong to the order of discourse: such units then extend not beyond the sentence, than which they remain materially shorter, but beyond the level of denotation, which, like the sentence, is the province of linguistics properly speaking.

2. Classes of units

The functional units must be distributed into a small number of classes. If these classes are to be determined without recourse to the substance of content (psychological substance for example), it is again necessary to consider the different levels of meaning: some units have as correlates units on the same level, while the saturation of others requires a change of levels; hence, straightaway, two major classes of functions, distributional and integrational. The former correspond to what Propp and subsequently Bremond (in particular) take as functions but they will be treated here in a much more detailed way than is the case in their work. The term *"functions"* will be reserved for these units (though the other units are also functional), the model of description for which has become

---

[25] "The word must not be treated as an indivisible element of literary art, like a brick in building. It can be broken down into much finer 'verbal elements.' " J. Tynianov, quoted T. Todorov in *Langages* 6, 1971.

classic since Tomachevski's analysis: the purchase of a revolver has for correlate the moment when it will be used (and
if not used, the notation is reversed into a sign of indecision,
etc.); picking up the telephone has for correlate the moment
when it will be put down; the intrusion of the parrot into
Félicité's home has for correlate the episode of the stuffing,
the worshipping of the parrot, etc. As for the latter, the integrational units, these comprise all the *"indices"* (in the very
broad sense of the word[26]), the unit now referring not to a
complementary and consequential act but to a more or less
diffuse concept which is nevertheless necessary to the meaning
of the story: psychological indices concerning the characters,
data regarding their identity, notations of "atmosphere," and
so on. The relation between the unit and its correlate is now
no longer distributional (often several indices refer to the
same signified and the order of their occurrence in the discourse is not necessarily pertinent) but integrational. In order
to understand what an indicial notation "is for," one must
move to a higher level (characters' actions or narration), for
only there is the indice clarified: the power of the administrative machine behind Bond, indexed by the number of telephones, has no bearing on the sequence of actions in which
Bond is involved by answering the call; it finds its meaning
only on the level of a general typology of the actants (Bond is
on the side of order). Indices, because of the, in some sort,
vertical nature of their relations, are truly semantic units: unlike "functions" (in the strict sense), they refer to a signified,
not to an "operation." The ratification of indices is "higher
up," sometimes even remaining virtual, outside any explicit
syntagm (the "character" of a narrative agent may very well
never be explicitly named while yet being constantly indexed),
is a paradigmatic ratification. That of functions, by contrast, is

[26] These designations, like those that follow, may all be provisional.

always "further on," is a syntagmatic ratification.[27] *Functions* and *indices* thus overlay another classic distinction: functions involve metonymic relata, indices metaphoric relata; the former correspond to a functionality of doing, the latter to a functionality of being.[28]

These two main classes of units, functions and indices, should already allow a certain classification of narratives. Some narratives are heavily functional (such as folk tales), while others on the contrary are heavily indicial (such as "psychological" novels); between these two poles lies a whole series of intermediary forms, dependent on history, society, genre. But we can go further. Within each of the two main classes it is immediately possible to determine two subclasses of narrative units. Returning to the class of functions, its units are not all of the same "importance": some constitute real hinge points of the narrative (or of a fragment of the narrative); others merely "fill in" the narrative space separating the hinge functions. Let us call the former *cardinal functions* (or *nuclei*) and the latter, having regard to their complementary nature, *catalyzers*. For a function to be cardinal, it is enough that the action to which it refers open (or continue, or close) an alternative that is of direct consequence for the subsequent development of the story, in short that it inaugurate or conclude an uncertainty. If, in a fragment of narrative, *the telephone rings*, it is equally possible to answer or not answer, two acts which will unfailingly carry the narrative along different paths. Between two cardinal functions however, it is always possible to set out subsidiary notations which cluster around one or other nucleus without modifying its alternative nature:

---

[27] Which does not mean that the syntagmatic setting out of functions may not *finally* hold paradigmatic relations between separate functions, as is recognized since Lévi-Strauss and Greimas.

[28] Functions cannot be reduced to actions (verbs), nor indices to qualities (adjectives), for there are actions that are indicial, being "signs" of a character, an atmosphere, etc.

the space separating *the telephone rang* from *Bond answered* can be saturated with a host of trivial incidents or descriptions —*Bond moved toward the desk, picked up one of the receivers, put down his cigarette*, etc. These catalyzers are still functional, insofar as they enter into correlation with a nucleus, but their functionality is attenuated, unilateral, parasitic; it is a question of a purely chronological functionality (what is described is what separates two moments of the story), whereas the tie between two cardinal functions is invested with a double functionality, at once chronological and logical. Catalyzers are only consecutive units, cardinal functions are both conseccutive and consequential. Everything suggests, indeed, that the mainspring of narrative is precisely the confusion of consecution and consequence, what comes *after* being read in narrative as what is *caused by*; in which case narrative would be a systematic application of the logical fallacy denounced by Scholasticism in the formula *post hoc, ergo propter hoc*—a good motto for Destiny, of which narrative all things considered is no more than the "language."

It is the structural framework of cardinal functions which accomplishes this "telescoping" of logic and temporality. At first sight, such functions may appear extremely insignificant; what defines them is not their spectacularity (importance, volume, unusualness or force of the narrated action), but, so to speak, the risk they entail: cardinal functions are the risky moments of a narrative. Between these points of alternative, these "dispatchers," the catalyzers lay out areas of safety, rests, luxuries. Luxuries which are not, however, useless: it must be stressed again that from the point of view of the story a catalyzer's functionality may be weak but not nil. Were a catalyzer purely redundant (in relation to its nucleus), it would nonetheless participate in the economy of the message; in fact, an apparently merely expletive notation always has a discursive function: it accelerates, delays, gives fresh impetus to the discourse, it summarizes, anticipates and sometimes even leads astray.[29] Since what is noted always appears as being notable, the catalyzer ceaselessly revives the semantic tension of the discourse, says ceaselessly that there has been, that there is going to be, meaning. Thus, in the final analysis, the catalyzer has a constant function which is, to use Jakobson's term, a phatic one:[30] it maintains the contact between narrator and addressee. A nucleus cannot be deleted without altering the story, but neither can a catalyst without altering the discourse.

As for the other main class of units, the indices, an integrational class, its units have in common that they can only be saturated (completed) on the level of characters or on the level of narration. They are thus part of a *parametrical* relation[31] whose second—implicit—term is continuous, extended over an episode, a character or the whole work. A distinction can be made, however, between *indices* proper, referring to the character of a narrative agent, a feeling, an atmosphere (for example suspicion) or a philosophy, and *informants*, serving to identify, to locate in time and space. To say that through the window of the office where Bond is on duty the moon can be seen half-hidden by thick billowing clouds, is to index a stormy summer night, this deduction in turn forming an index of atmosphere with reference to the heavy, anguish-laden climate of an action as yet unknown to the reader. Indices always have implicit signifieds. Informants, however, do not, at least on the level of the story: they are pure data with immediate signification. Indices involve an activity of de-

---

[29] Valéry spoke of "dilatory signs." The detective novel makes abundant use of such "confusing" units.

[30] [For the scheme of the six factors of verbal communication and their corresponding linguistic functions—emotive, conative, referential, phatic, metalinguistic, and poetic—see R. Jakobson, "Linguistics and Poetics" in *Style in Language*, ed. T. A. Sebeok.]

[31] N. Ruwet calls "parametrical" an element which remains constant for the whole duration of a piece of music (for instance, the tempo in a Bach allegro or the monodic character of a solo).

ciphering, the reader is to learn to know a character or an atmosphere; informants bring ready-made knowledge, their functionality, like that of catalyzers, is thus weak without being nil. Whatever its "flatness" in relation to the rest of the story, the informant (for example, the exact age of a character) always serves to authenticate the reality of the referent, to embed fiction in the real world. Informants are realist operators and as such possess an undeniable functionality not on the level of the story but on that of the discourse.[32]

Nuclei and catalyzers, indices and informants (again, the names are of little importance), these, it seems, are the initial classes into which the functional level units can be divided. This classification must be completed by two remarks. Firstly, a unit can at the same time belong to two different classes: to drink a whiskey (in an airport lounge) is an action which can act as a catalyzer to the (cardinal) notation of *waiting*, but it is also, and simultaneously, the indice of a certain atmosphere (modernity, relaxation, reminiscence, etc.). In other words, certain units can be mixed, giving a play of possibilities in the narrative economy. In the novel *Goldfinger*, Bond, having to search his adversary's bedroom, is given a master key by his associate: the notation is a pure (cardinal) function. In the film, this detail is altered and Bond laughingly takes a set of keys from a willing chambermaid: the notation is no longer simply functional but also indicial, referring to Bond's character (his easy charm and success with women). Secondly, it should be noted (this will be taken up again later) that the four classes just described can be distributed in a different way which is moreover closer to the linguistic model. Catalyzers,

[32] In "Frontières du récit," *Communications* 8, 1966 [reprinted in *Figures II*], Gérard Genette distinguishes two types of description: ornamental and significant. The second clearly relates to the level of the story; the first to that of the discourse, which explains why for a long time it formed a perfectly coded rhetorical "piece": *descriptio* or *ekphrasis*, a very highly valued exercise in neo-rhetoric.

indices, and informants have a common characteristic: in relation to nuclei, they are *expansions*. Nuclei (as will be seen in a moment) form finite sets grouping a small number of terms, are governed by a logic, are at once necessary and sufficient. Once the framework they provide is given, the other units fill it out according to a mode of proliferation in principle infinite. As we know, this is what happens in the case of the sentence, which is made up of simple propositions endlessly complicated with duplications, paddings, embeddings, and so on. So great an importance did Mallarmé attach to this type of structure that from it he constructed *Jamais un coup de dés*, a poem which with its "nodes" and "loops," its "nucleus words" and its "lace words," can well be regarded as the emblem of every narrative—of every language.

3. Functional syntax

How, according to what "grammar," are the different units strung together along the narrative syntagm? What are the rules of the functional combinatory system? Informants and indices can combine freely together: as for example in the portrait which readily juxtaposes data concerning civil status and traits of character. Catalyzers and nuclei are linked by a simple relation of implication: a catalyzer necessarily implies the existence of a cardinal function to which it can connect, but not vice versa. As for cardinal functions, they are bound together by a relation of solidarity: a function of this type calls for another function of the same type and reciprocally. It is this last relation which needs to be considered further for a moment—first, because it defines the very framework of the narrative (expansions can be deleted, nuclei cannot); second, because it is the main concern of those trying to work toward a structure of narrative.

It has already been pointed out that structurally narrative institutes a confusion between consecution and consequence, temporality and logic. This ambiguity forms the central problem of narrative syntax. Is there an atemporal logic lying behind the temporality of narrative? Researchers were still quite recently divided on this point. Propp, whose analytic study of the folk tale paved the way for the work going on today, is totally committed to the idea of the irreducibility of the chronological order: he sees time as reality and for this reason is convinced of the necessity for rooting the tale in temporality. Yet Aristotle himself, in his contrast between tragedy (defined by the unity of action) and historical narrative (defined by the plurality of actions and the unity of time), was already giving primacy to the logical over the chronological.[33] As do all contemporary researchers (Lévi-Strauss, Greimas, Bremond, Todorov), all of whom (while differing on other points) could subscribe to Lévi-Strauss's proposition that "the order of chronological succession is absorbed in an atemporal matrix structure."[34] Analysis today tends to "dechronologize" the narrative continuum and to "relogicize" it, to make it dependent on what Mallarmé called with regard to the French language *"the primitive thunderbolts of logic";* or rather, more exactly (such at least is our wish), the task is to succeed in giving a structural description of the chronological illusion—it is for narrative logic to account for narrative time. To put it another way, one could say that temporality is only a structural category of narrative (of discourse), just as in language [*langue*] temporality only exists in the form of a system; from the point of view of narrative, what we call time does not exist, or at least only exists functionally, as an element of a semiotic system. Time belongs not to discourse strictly speak-

---

[33] *Poetics.*
[34] Quoted by Claude Bremond, "Le message narratif," *Communications* 4, 1964 [Claude Lévi-Strauss, "La structure et la forme," *Cahiers de l'Institut de Science Economique Appliquée* 99, March 1960.]

ing but to the referent; both narrative and language know only a semiotic time, "true" time being a "realist," referential illusion, as Propp's commentary shows. It is as such that structural analysis must deal with it.[35]

What then is the logic which regulates the principal narrative functions? It is this that current work is actively trying to establish and that has so far been the major focus of debate. Three main directions of research can be seen. The first (Bremond) is more properly logical in approach: it aims to reconstitute the syntax of human behavior utilized in narrative, to retrace the course of the "choices" which inevitably face[36] the individual character at every point in the story and so to bring out what could be called an energetic logic,[37] since it grasps the characters at the moment when they choose to act. The second (Lévi-Strauss, Jakobson) is linguistic: its essential concern is to demonstrate paradigmatic oppositions in the functions, oppositions which, in accordance with the Jakobsonian definition of the "poetic,"[38] are "extended" along the line of the narrative (new developments in Greimas's work correct or complete the conception of the paradigmatic nature of functions).[39] The third (Todorov) is somewhat different in

[35] In his own way—as always perspicacious but left undeveloped—Valéry well expressed the status of narrative time: "The belief in time as agent and guiding thread is based on *the mechanism of memory and on that of combinatory discourse*," *Tel Quel* (my italics); the illusion is precisely produced by the discourse itself.

[36] This idea recalls Aristotle: *proairesis*, the rational choice of actions to be undertaken, is the foundation of *praxis*, the practical science which, contrary to *poiesis*, produces no object-work distinct from its agent. Using these terms, one can say that the analyst tries to reconstitute the praxis inherent in narrative.

[37] Such a logic, based on alternatives (*doing this or that*), has the merit of accounting for the process of dramatization for which narrative is usually the occasion.

[38] ["The poetic function projects the principle of equivalence of the axis of selection on to the axis of combination." Jakobson, "Linguistics and Poetics."]

[39] See A. J. Greimas, "Eléments pour une théorie de l'interprétation du récit mythique," *Communications* 8, 1966.

that it sets the analysis at the level of the "actions" (that is to say, of the characters), attempting to determine the rules by which narrative combines, varies, and transforms a certain number of basic predicates.

There is no question of choosing between these working hypotheses; they are not competitive but concurrent, and at present moreover are in the throes of elaboration. The only complement we will attempt to give them here concerns the dimensions of the analysis. Even leaving aside the indices, informants, and catalyzers, there still remains in a narrative (especially if it is a novel and no longer a tale) a very large number of cardinal functions and many of these cannot be mastered by the analyses just mentioned, which until now have worked on the major articulations of narrative. Provision needs to be made, however, for a description sufficiently close as to account for *all* the narrative units, for the smallest narrative segments. We must remember that cardinal functions cannot be determined by their "importance," only by the (doubly implicative) nature of their relations. A "telephone call," no matter how futile it may seem, on the one hand itself comprises some few cardinal functions (telephone ringing, picking up the receiver, speaking, putting down the receiver), while on the other, taken as a whole, it must be linkable—at the very least proceeding step by step—to the major articulations of the anecdote. The functional covering of the narrative necessitates an organization of relays the basic unit of which can only be a small group of functions, hereafter referred to (following Bremond) as a *sequence*.

A sequence is a logical succession of nuclei bound together by a relation of solidarity:[40] the sequence opens when one of its terms has no solidary antecedent and closes when another

---

[40] In the Hjelmslevian sense of double implication: two terms presuppose one another.

of its terms has no consequent. To take a deliberately trivial example, the different functions order a drink, obtain it, drink it, pay for it, constitute an obviously closed sequence, it being impossible to put anything before the order or after the payment without moving out of the homogeneous group *"Having a drink."* The sequence indeed is always nameable. Determining the major functions of the folk tale, Propp and subsequently Bremond have been led to name them (*Fraud, Betrayal, Struggle, Contract, Seduction*, etc.); the naming operation is equally inevitable in the case of trivial sequences, the "micro-sequences" which often form the finest grain of the narrative tissue. Are these namings solely the province of the analyst? In other words, are they purely metalinguistic? No doubt they are, dealing as they do with the code of narrative. Yet at the same time they can be imagined as forming part of an inner metalanguage for the reader (or listener) who can grasp every logical succession of actions as a nominal whole: to read is to name; to listen is not only to perceive a language, it is also to construct it. Sequence titles are similar enough to the *cover words* of translation machines which acceptably cover a wide variety of meanings and shades of meaning. The narrative language [*la langue du récit*] within us comprises from the start these essential headings: the closing logic which structures a sequence is inextricably linked to its name; any function which initiates a *seduction* prescribes from the moment it appears, in the name to which it gives rise, the entire process of seduction such as we have learned it from all the narratives which have fashioned in us the language of narrative.

However minimal its importance, a sequence, since it is made up of a small number of nuclei (that is to say, in fact, of "dispatchers"), always involves moments of risk and it is this which justifies analyzing it. It might seem futile to constitute

into a sequence the logical succession of trifling acts which go
to make up the offer of a cigarette (*offering, accepting, lighting, smoking*), but precisely, at every one of these points, an
alternative—and hence a freedom of meaning—is possible. Du
Pont, Bond's future partner, offers him a light from his lighter
but Bond refuses; the meaning of this bifurcation is that Bond
instinctively fears a booby-trapped gadget.[41] A sequence is
thus, one can say, a *threatened logical unit*, this being its
justification *a minimo*. It is also founded *a maximo*: enclosed
on its function, subsumed under a name, the sequence itself
constitutes a new unit, ready to function as a simple term in
another, more extensive sequence. Here, for example, is a
micro-sequence: *hand held out, hand shaken, hand released*.
This *Greeting* then becomes a simple function: on the one
hand, it assumes the role of an indice (flabbiness of Du Pont,
Bond's distaste); on the other, it forms globally a term in a
larger sequence, with the name *Meeting*, whose other terms
(*approach, halt, interpellation, sitting down*) can themselves
be micro-sequences. A whole network of subrogations structures the narrative in this way, from the smallest matrices to
the largest functions. What is in question here, of course, is a
hierarchy that remains within the functional level: it is only
when it has been possible to widen the narrative out step by
step, from Du Pont's cigarette to Bond's battle against Goldfinger, that functional analysis is over—the pyramid of functions then touches the next level (that of the Actions). There
is both a syntax within the sequences and a (subrogating)
syntax between the sequences together. The first episode of
Goldfinger thus takes on a "stemmatic" aspect:

[41] It is quite possible to identify even at this infinitesimal level an opposition
of paradigmatic types, if not between two terms, at least between two poles
of the sequence: the sequence *Offer of a cigarette* spreads out, by suspending
it, the paradigm *Danger/Safety* (demonstrated by Cheglov in his analysis of
the Sherlock Holmes cycle), *Suspicion/Protection, Aggressiveness/Friend-
liness.*

Hand held out Hand shaken Hand released   Etc.

Obviously this representation is analytical; the reader perceives a linear succession of terms. What needs to be noted, however, is that the terms from several sequences can easily be imbricated in one another: a sequence is not yet completed when already, cutting in, the first term of a new sequence may appear. Sequences move in counterpoint;[42] functionally, the structure of narrative is fugued: thus it is this that narrative at once "holds" and "pulls on." Within the single work, the imbrication of sequences can indeed only be allowed to come to a halt with a radical break if the sealed-off blocks which then compose it are in some sort recuperated at the higher level of the Actions (of the characters). *Goldfinger* is composed of three functionally independent episodes, their functional stemmas twice ceasing to intercommunicate: there is no sequential relation between the swimming-pool episode and the Fort Knox episode; but there remains an actantial relation, for the characters (and consequently the structure of their relations) are the same. One can recognize here the epic pattern (a "whole made of multiple fables"): the epic is a narrative broken at the functional level but unitary at the actantial level (something which can be verified in the *Odyssey* or in Brecht's plays). The level of functions (which provides the major part of the narrative syntagm) must thus be capped by a higher level from which, step by step, the first level units draw their meaning, the level of actions.

[42] This counterpoint was recognized by the Russian formalists, who outlined its typology; it is not without recalling the principal "intricate" structures of the sentence (see below V.1).

III. ACTIONS

1. Toward a structural status of characters

In Aristotelian poetics, the notion of character is secondary, entirely subsidiary to the notion of action: there may be actions without "characters," says Aristotle, but not characters without an action; a view taken over by classical theoreticians (Vossius). Later the character, who until then had been only a name, the agent of an action,[43] acquired a psychological consistency, became an individual, a "person," in short a fully constituted "being," even should he do nothing and of course even before acting.[44] Characters stopped being subordinate to the action, embodied immediately psychological essences; which essences could be drawn up into lists, as can be seen in its purest form in the list of "character parts" in bourgeois theater (the coquette, the noble father, etc.). From its very outset, structural analysis has shown the utmost reluctance to treat the character as an essence, even merely for purposes of classification; Tomachevski went so far as to deny the character any narrative importance, a point of view he subsequently modified. Without leaving characters out of the analysis altogether, Propp reduced them to a simple typology based not on psychology but on the unity of the actions assigned them by the narrative (*Donor of a magical agent, Helper, Villain,* etc.).

Since Propp, the character has constantly set the structural analysis of narrative the same problem. On the one hand, the characters (whatever one calls them—*dramatis personae* or *actants*) form a necessary plane of description, outside of which the slightest reported "actions" cease to be intelligible;

---

[43] It must not be forgotten that classical tragedy as yet knows only "actors," not "characters."

[44] The "character-person" reigns in the bourgeois novel; in *War and Peace*, Nikolai Rostov is from the start a good fellow, loyal, courageous, and passionate, Prince Andrei a disillusioned individual of noble birth, etc. What happens illustrates them, it does not form them.

so that it can be said that there is not a single narrative in the world without "characters,"[45] or at least without agents. Yet on the other hand, these—extremely numerous—"agents" can be neither described nor classified in terms of "persons"— whether the "person" be considered as a purely historical form, limited to certain genres (those most familiar to us it is true), in which case it is necessary to leave out of account the very large number of narratives (popular tales, modern texts) comprising agents but not persons, or whether the "person" is declared to be no more than a critical rationalization foisted by our age on pure narrative agents. Structural analysis, much concerned not to define characters in terms of psychological essences, has so far striven, using various hypotheses, to define a character not as a "being" but as a "participant." For Bremond, every character (even secondary) can be the agent of sequences, of actions which belong to him (*Fraud, Seduction*); when a single sequence involves two characters (as is usual), it comprises two perspectives, two names (what is *Fraud* for the one is *Gullibility* for the other); in short, every character (even secondary) is the hero of his own sequence. Todorov, analyzing a "psychological" novel (*Les Liaisons dangereuses*), starts not from the character-persons but from the three major relationships in which they can engage and which he calls base predicates (love, communication, help). The analysis brings these relationships under two sorts of rules: rules of *derivation*, when it is a question of accounting for other relationships, and rules of *action*, when it is a question of describing the transformation of the major relationships in the course of the story. There are many characters in

[45] If one section of contemporary literature has attacked the "character," it is not in order to destroy it (which is impossible) but to depersonalize it, which is quite different. A novel seemingly devoid of characters, such as *Drame* by Philippe Sollers, gets rid of the person to the benefit of language but nonetheless retains a fundamental play of actants confronting the very action of discourse. There is still a "subject" in this literature, but that "subject" is henceforth that of language.

Les Liaisons dangereuses but "what is said of them" (their predicates) can be classified. Finally, Greimas has proposed to describe and classify the characters of narrative not according to what they are but according to what they do (whence the name *actants*), inasmuch as they participate in three main semantic axes (also to be found in the sentence: subject, object, indirect object, adjunct) which are communication, desire (or quest), and ordeal.[46] Since this participation is ordered in couples, the infinite world of characters is, it too, bound by a paradigmatic structure (*Subject/Object, Donor/Receiver, Helper/Opponent*) which is projected along the narrative; and since an actant defines a class, it can be filled by different actors, mobilized according to rules of multiplication, substitution, or replacement.

These three conceptions have many points in common. The most important, it must be stressed again, is the definition of the character according to participation in a sphere of actions, these spheres being few in number, typical, and classifiable; which is why this second level of description, despite its being that of the characters, has here been called the level of Actions: the word *actions* is not to be understood in the sense of the trifling acts which form the tissue of the first level but in that of the major articulations of *praxis* (desire, communication, struggle).

2. The problem of the subject

The problems raised by a classification of the characters of narrative are not as yet satisfactorily resolved. Certainly there is ready agreement on the fact that the innumerable characters of narrative can be brought under rules of substitution and that, even within the one work, a single figure can absorb different characters.[47] Again, the actantial model proposed by

---

[46] *Sémantique structurale.*
[47] Psychoanalysis has widely accredited these operations of condensation.

Greimas (and adopted by Todorov in another perspective) seems to stand the test of a large number of narratives. Like any structural model, its value lies less in its canonic form (a matrix of six actants) than in the regulated transformations (replacements, confusions, duplications, substitutions) to which it lends itself, thus holding out the hope of an actantial typology of narratives.[48] A difficulty, however, is that when the matrix has a high classificational power (as is the case with Greimas's actants) it fails adequately to account for the multiplicity of participations as soon as these are analyzed in terms of perspectives and that when these perspectives are respected (as in Bremond's description) the system of characters remains too fragmented. The reduction proposed by Todorov avoids both pitfalls but has so far only been applied to one narrative. All this, it seems, can be quickly and harmoniously resolved. The real difficulty posed by the classification of characters is the place (and hence the existence) of the *subject* in any actantial matrix, whatever its formulation. *Who* is the subject (the hero) of a narrative? Is there—or not—a privileged class of actors? The novel has accustomed us to emphasize in one way or another—sometimes in a devious (negative) way—one character in particular. But such privileging is far from extending over the whole of narrative literature. Many narratives, for example, set two adversaries in conflict over some stake; the subject is then truly double, not reducible further by substitution. Indeed, this is even perhaps a common archaic form, as though narrative, after the fashion of certain languages, had also known a *dual* of persons. This

---

Mallarmé was saying already, writing of *Hamlet*: "Supernumeraries, necessarily! for in the ideal painting of the stage, everything moves according to a symbolic reciprocity of types amongst themselves or relatively to a single figure." *Crayonné au théâtre.*

[48] For example: narratives where object and subject are confounded in a single character, that is, narratives of the search for oneself, for one's own identity (*The Golden Ass*); narratives where the subject pursues successive objects (*Madame Bovary*), etc.

dual is all the more interesting in that it relates narrative to the structures of certain (very modern) games in which two equal opponents try to gain possession of an object put into circulation by a referee; a schema which recalls the actantial matrix proposed by Greimas, and there is nothing surprising in this if one is willing to allow that a game, being a language, depends on the same symbolic structure as is to be found in language and narrative: a game too is a sentence.[49] If therefore a privileged class of actors is retained (the subject of the quest, of the desire, of the action), it needs at least to be made more flexible by bringing that actant under the very categories of the grammatical (and not psychological) person. Once again, it will be necessary to look toward linguistics for the possibility of describing and classifying the personal (*je/tu*, first person/ second person) or apersonal (*il*, third person), singular, dual, or plural, instance of the action. It will—perhaps—be the grammatical categories of the person (accessible in our pronouns) which will provide the key to the actional level; but since these categories can only be defined in relation to the instance of discourse, not to that of reality,[50] characters, as units of the actional level, find their meaning (their intelligibility) only if integrated in the third level of description, here called the level of Narration (as opposed to Functions and Actions).

IV. NARRATION

1. Narrative communication

Just as there is within narrative a major function of exchange (set out between a donor and a beneficiary), so, homo-

---

[49] Umberto Eco's analysis of the James Bond cycle ("James Bond: une combinatoire narrative," *Communications* 8, 1966) refers more to game than to language.

[50] See the analysis of person given by Benveniste in *Problèmes de linguistique générale*.

logically, narrative as object is the point of a communication: there is a donor of the narrative and a receiver of the narrative. In linguistic communication, *je* and *tu* (*I* and *you*) are absolutely presupposed by one another; similarly, there can be no narrative without a narrator and a listener (or reader). Banal perhaps, but still little developed. Certainly the role of the sender has been abundantly enlarged upon (much study of the "author" of a novel, though without any consideration of whether he really is the "narrator"); when it comes to the reader, however, literary theory is much more modest. In fact, the problem is not to introspect the motives of the narrator or the effects the narration produces on the reader, it is to describe the code by which narrator and reader are signified throughout the narrative itself. At first sight, the signs of the narrator appear more evident and more numerous than those of the reader (a narrative more frequently says *I* than *you*); in actual fact, the latter are simply more oblique than the former. Thus, each time the narrator stops "representing" and reports details which he knows perfectly well but which are unknown to the reader, there occurs, by signifying failure, a sign of reading, for there would be no sense in the narrator giving himself a piece of information. *Leo was the owner of the joint*,[51] we are told in a first-person novel: a sign of the reader, close to what Jakobson calls the conative function of communication. Lacking an inventory however, we shall leave aside for the moment these signs of reception (though they are of equal importance) and say a few words concerning the signs of narration.[52]

Who is the donor of the narrative? So far, three conceptions

[51] *Double Bang à Bangkok* [secret agent thriller by Jean Bruce, 1959]. The sentence functions as a "wink" to the reader, as if he was being turned toward. By contrast, the statement *"So Leo had just left"* is a sign of the narrator, part of a process of reasoning conducted by a "person."
[52] In "Les catégories du récit littéraire" Todorov deals with the images of narrator and reader.

seem to have been formulated. The first holds that a narrative emanates from a person (in the fully psychological sense of the term). This person has a name, the author, in whom there is an endless exchange between the "personality" and the "art" of a perfectly identified individual who periodically takes up his pen to write a story: the narrative (notably the novel) then being simply the expression of an *I* external to it. The second conception regards the narrator as a sort of omniscient, apparently impersonal, consciousness that tells the story from a superior point of view, that of God:[53] the narrator is at once inside his characters (since he knows everything that goes on in them) and outside them (since he never identifies with any one more than another). The third and most recent conception (Henry James, Sartre) decrees that the narrator must limit his narrative to what the characters can observe or know, everything proceeding as if each of the characters in turn were the sender of the narrative. All three conceptions are equally difficult in that they seem to consider narrator and characters as real—"living"—people (the unfailing power of this literary myth is well known), as though a narrative were originally determined at its referential level (it is a matter of equally "realist" conceptions). Narrator and characters, however, at least from our perspective, are essentially "paper beings"; the (material) author of a narrative is in no way to be confused with the narrator of that narrative.[54] The signs of the narrator are immanent to the narrative and hence readily accessible to a semiological analysis; but in order to conclude that the author himself (whether declared, hidden or withdrawn) has "signs" at his disposal which he sprinkles through his work, it is necessary to assume the existence between this

---

[53] "When will someone write from the point of view of a *superior joke*, that is as God sees things from above?" Flaubert, *Letters*.

[54] A distinction all the more necessary, given the scale at which we are working, in that historically a large mass of narratives are without authors (oral narratives, folk tales, epics entrusted to bards, reciters, etc.).

"person" and his language of a straight descriptive relation which makes the author a full subject and the narrative the instrumental expression of that fullness. Structural analysis is unwilling to accept such an assumption: *who speaks* (in the narrative) is not *who writes* (in real life) and *who writes* is not *who* is.[55]

In fact, narration strictly speaking (the code of the narrator), like language, knows only two systems of signs: personal and apersonal. These two narrational systems do not necessarily present the linguistic marks attached to person (*I*) and non-person (*he*): there are narratives or at least narrative episodes, for example, which though written in the third person nevertheless have as their true instance the first person. How can we tell? It suffices to rewrite the narrative (or the passage) from *he* to *I*: so long as the rewriting entails no alteration of the discourse other than this change of the grammatical pronouns, we can be sure that we are dealing with a personal system. The whole of the beginning of *Goldfinger*, though written in the third person, is in fact "spoken" by James Bond. For the instance to change, rewriting must become impossible; thus the sentence "he saw a man in his fifties, still young-looking . . ." is perfectly personal despite the *he* ("I, James Bond, saw . . ."), but the narrative statement "the tinkling of the ice against the glass appeared to give Bond a sudden inspiration" cannot be personal on account of the verb "appeared," it (and not the *he*) becoming a sign of the apersonal. There is no doubt that the apersonal is the traditional mode of narrative, language having developed a whole tense system peculiar to narrative (based on the aorist[56]), designed to wipe out the present of the speaker. As Benveniste puts it: "In narrative, no one speaks." The personal instance

---

[55] J. Lacan: "Is the subject I speak of when I speak the same as the subject who speaks?"
[56] E. Benveniste, op. cit. [especially Chapter XIX].

(under more or less disguised forms) has, however, gradually invaded narrative, the narration being referred to the *hic et nunc* of the locutionary act (which is the definition of the personal system). Thus it is that today many narratives are to be found (and of the most common kinds) which mix together in extremely rapid succession, often within the limits of a single sentence, the personal and the apersonal; as for instance this sentence from *Goldfinger*:

His eyes,	*personal*
gray-blue,	*apersonal*
looked into those of Mr. Du Pont, who did	
not know what face to put on,	*personal*
for this look held a mixture of candor,	
irony, and self-deprecation.	*personal*

The mixing of the systems is clearly felt as a facility and this facility can go as far as trick effects. A detective novel by Agatha Christie (*The Sittaford Mystery*) only keeps the enigma going by cheating on the person of the narration: a character is described from within when he is already the murderer[57]—as if in a single person there were the consciousness of a witness, immanent to the discourse, and the consciousness of a murderer, immanent to the referent, with the dishonest tourniquet of the two systems alone producing the enigma. Hence it is understandable that at the other pole of literature the choice of a rigorous system should have been made a necessary condition of a work—without it always being easy fully to meet that condition.

Rigor of this kind—the aim of certain contemporary writers —is not necessarily an aesthetic imperative. What is called the psychological novel usually shows a mixture of the two sys-

---

[57] Personal mode: "It even seemed to Burnaby that nothing looked changed . . ." The device is still more blatant in *The Murder of Roger Ackroyd*, since there the murderer actually says *I*.

tems, successively mobilizing the signs of non-person and those of person; "psychology," that is, paradoxically, cannot accommodate itself to a pure system, for by bringing the whole narrative down to the sole instance of the discourse—or, if one prefers, to the locutionary act—it is the very content of the person which is threatened: the psychological person (of referential order) bears no relation to the linguistic person, the latter never defined by states of mind, intentions or traits of character but only by its (coded) place in discourse. It is this formal person that writers today are attempting to speak and such an attempt represents an important subversion (the public moreover has the impression that "novels" are no longer being written) for it aims to transpose narrative from the purely constative plane, which it has occupied until now, to the performative plane, whereby the meaning of an utterance is the very act by which it is uttered:[58] today, writing is not "telling" but saying that one is telling and assigning all the referent ("what one says") to this act of locution; which is why part of contemporary literature is no longer descriptive, but transitive, striving to accomplish so pure a present in its language that the whole of the discourse is identified with the act of its delivery, the whole *logos* being brought down—or extended—to a *lexis*.[59]

2. Narrative situation

The narrational level is thus occupied by the signs of narrativity, the set of operators which reintegrate functions and actions in the narrative communication articulated on its donor and its addressee. Some of these signs have already

---

[58] On the performative, see Todorov's "Les catégories du récit littéraire." The classic example of a performative is the statement *I declare war* which neither "constates" nor "describes" anything but exhausts its meaning in the act of its utterance (by contrast to the statement *the king declared war*, which constates, describes).

[59] For the opposition logos/lexis, see Genette, "Frontières du récit."

received study; we are familiar in oral literatures with certain codes of recitation (metrical formulas, conventional presentation protocols) and we know that here the "author" is not the person who invents the finest stories but the person who best masters the code which is practiced equally by his listeners: in such literatures the narrational level is so clearly defined, its rules so binding, that it is difficult to conceive of a "tale" devoid of the coded signs of narrative (*"once upon a time,"* etc.). In our written literatures, the "forms of discourse" (which are in fact signs of narrativity) were early identified: classification of the modes of authorial intervention (outlined by Plato and developed by Diomedes[60]), coding of the beginnings and endings of narratives, definition of the different styles of representation (*oratio directa, oratio indirecta* with its *inquit, oratio tecta*),[61] study of "points of view," and so on. All these elements form part of the narrational level, to which must obviously be added the writing as a whole, its role being not to "transmit" the narrative but to display it.

It is indeed precisely in a display of the narrative that the units of the lower levels find integration: the ultimate form of the narrative, as narrative, transcends its contents and its strictly narrative forms (functions and actions). This explains why the narrational code should be the final level attainable by our analysis, other than by going outside of the narrative object, other, that is, than by transgressing the rule of immanence on which the analysis is based. Narration can only receive its meaning from the world which makes use of it: beyond the narrational level begins the world, other systems (social, economic, ideological) whose terms are no longer simply narratives but elements of a different substance (historical facts,

---

[60] *Genus activum vel imitativum* (no intervention of the narrator in the discourse: as for example theater); *genus ennarativum* (the poet alone speaks: sententiae, didactic poems); *genus commune* (mixture of the two kinds: epic poems).

[61] H. Sorensen in *Language and Society.*

determinations, behaviors, etc.). Just as linguistics stops at the sentence, so narrative analysis stops at discourse—from there it is necessary to shift to another semiotics. Linguistics is acquainted with such boundaries which it has already postulated —if not explored—under the name of *situations*. Halliday defines the "situation" (in relation to a sentence) as "the associated non-linguistic factors,"[62] Prieto as "the set of facts known by the receiver at the moment of the semic act and independently of this act."[63] In the same way, one can say that every narrative is dependent on a "narrative situation," the set of protocols according to which the narrative is "consumed." In so-called archaic societies, the narrative situation is heavily coded;[64] nowadays, avant-garde literature alone still dreams of reading protocols—spectacular in the case of Mallarmé, who wanted the book to be recited in public according to a precise combinatory scheme, typographical in that of Butor, who tries to provide the book with its own specific signs. Generally, however, our society takes the greatest pains to conjure away the coding of the narrative situation: there is no counting the number of narrational devices which seek to naturalize the subsequent narrative by feigning to make it the outcome of some natural circumstance and thus, as it were, "disinaugurating" it: epistolary novels, supposedly rediscovered manuscripts, author who met the narrator, films which begin the story before the credits. The reluctance to declare its codes characterizes bourgeois society and the mass culture issuing from it: both demand signs which do not look like signs. Yet this is only, so to speak, a structural epiphenomenon: however familiar, however casual may today be the act of opening a novel or a newspaper or of turning on the television, nothing can prevent that humble act from installing in us,

---

[62] M. A. K. Halliday, op. cit.
[63] *Principes de noologie.*
[64] A tale, as Lucien Sebag stressed, can be told anywhere anytime, but not a mythical narrative.

all at once and in its entirety, the narrative code we are going to need. Hence the narrational level has an ambiguous role: contiguous to the narrative situation (and sometimes even including it), it gives on to the world in which the narrative is undone (consumed), while at the same time, capping the preceding levels, it closes the narrative, constitutes it definitively as utterance of a language [*langue*] which provides for and bears along its own metalanguage.

V. THE SYSTEM OF NARRATIVE

Language [*langue*] proper can be defined by the concurrence of two fundamental processes: articulation, or segmentation, which produces units (this being what Benveniste calls *form*), and integration, which gathers these units into units of a higher rank (this being *meaning*). This dual process can be found in the language of narrative [*la langue du récit*] which also has an articulation and an integration, a form and a meaning.

1. Distortion and expansion

The form of narrative is essentially characterized by two powers: that of distending its signs over the length of the story and that of inserting unforeseeable expansions into these distortions. The two powers appear to be points of freedom but the nature of narrative is precisely to include these "deviations" within its language.[65]

The distortion of signs exists in linguistic language [*langue*] and was studied by Bally with reference to French and German.[66] Dystaxia occurs when the signs (of a message) are no longer simply juxtaposed, when the (logical) linearity is disturbed (predicate before subject for example). A notable form

---

[65] Valéry: "Formally the novel is close to the dream; both can be defined by consideration of this curious property: *all their deviations form part of them.*"

[66] *Linguistique générale et linguistique française.*

of dystaxia is found when the parts of one sign are separated by other signs along the chain of the message (for instance, the negative *ne jamais* and the verb *a pardonné* in *elle ne nous a jamais pardonné*): the sign split into fractional parts, its signified is shared out among several signifiers, distant from one another and not comprehensible on their own. This, as was seen in connection with the functional level, is exactly what happens in narrative: the units of a sequence, although forming a whole at the level of that very sequence, may be separated from one another by the insertion of units from other sequences—as was said, the structure of the functional level is fugued.[67] According to Bally's terminology, which opposes synthetic languages where dystaxia is predominant (such as German) and analytic languages with a greater respect for logical linearity and monosemy (such as French), narrative would be a highly synthetic language, essentially founded on a syntax of embedding and enveloping: each part of the narrative radiates in several directions at once. When Bond orders a whiskey while waiting for his plane, the whiskey as indice has a polysemic value, is a kind of symbolic node grouping several signifieds (modernity, wealth, leisure); as a functional unit, however, the ordering of the whiskey has to run step by step through numerous relays (consumption, waiting, departure, etc.) in order to find its final meaning: the unit is "taken" by the whole narrative at the same time that the narrative only "holds" by the distortion and irradiation of its units.

This generalized distortion is what gives the language of narrative its special character. A purely logical phenomenon, since founded on an often distant relation and mobilizing a sort of confidence in intellective memory, it ceaselessly substi-

---

[67] Cf. Lévi-Strauss: "Relations pertaining to the same bundle may appear diachronically at remote intervals," *Structural Anthropology*. A. J. Greimas has emphasized the spacing out of functions.

tutes meaning for the straightforward copy of the events recounted. On meeting in "life," it is most unlikely that the
invitation to take a seat would not immediately be followed by
the act of sitting down; in narrative these two units, contiguous
from a mimetic point of view, may be separated by a long
series of insertions belonging to quite different functional
spheres. Thus is established a kind of *logical time* which has
very little connection with real time, the apparent pulverization of units always being firmly held in place by the logic that
binds together the nuclei of the sequence. "Suspense" is clearly
only a privileged—or "exacerbated"—form of distortion: on
the one hand, by keeping a sequence open (through emphatic
procedures of delay and renewal), it reinforces the contact
with the reader (the listener), has a manifestly phatic function; while on the other, it offers the threat of an uncompleted
sequence, of an open paradigm (if, as we believe, every sequence has two poles), that is to say, of a logical disturbance,
it being this disturbance which is consumed with anxiety and
pleasure (all the more so because it is always made right in the
end). "Suspense," therefore, is a game with structure, designed to endanger and glorify it, constituting a veritable
"thrilling" of intelligibility: by representing order (and no
longer series) in its fragility, "suspense" accomplishes the very
idea of language: what seems the most pathetic is also the
most intellectual—"suspense" grips you in the "mind," not in
the "guts."[68]

What can be separated can also be filled. Distended, the
functional nuclei furnish intercalating spaces which can be
packed out almost infinitely; the interstices can be filled in
with a very large number of catalyzers. Here, however, a new
typology comes in, for the freedom to catalyze can be regu-

---

[68] J. P. Faye, writing of Klossowski's *Baphomet*: "Rarely has fiction (or
narrative) so clearly revealed what it always is, necessarily: an experimentation
of thought on life." *Tel Quel* 22.

lated according both to the content of the functions (certain functions are more apt than others for catalyzing—as for example *Waiting*[69]) and to the substance of the narrative (writing contains possibilities of diaeresis—and so of catalyzing—far superior to those of film: a gesture related linguistically can be "cut up" much more easily than the same gesture visualized[70]). The catalystic power of narrative has for corollary its elliptic power. Firstly, a function (*he had a good meal*) can economize on all the potential catalyzers it covers over (the details of the meal)[71]; secondly, it is possible to reduce a sequence to its nuclei and a hierarchy of sequences to its higher terms without altering the meaning of the story: a narrative can be identified even if its total syntagm be reduced to its actants and its main functions as these result from the progressive upward integration of its functional units.[72] In other words, narrative lends itself to *summary* (what used to be called the *argument*). At first sight this is true of any discourse, but each discourse has its own kind of summary. A lyric poem, for example, is simply the vast metaphor of a single signified[73] and to summarize it is thus to give this signified, an operation so drastic that it eliminates the poem's identity (summarized, lyric poems come down to the signifieds *Love* and *Death*)—hence the conviction that poems cannot be

---

[69] Logically *Waiting* has only two nuclei: 1. the wait established 2. the wait rewarded or disappointed; the first, however, can be extensively catalyzed, occasionally even indefinitely (*Waiting for Godot*): yet another game—this time extreme—with structure.

[70] Valéry: "Proust divides up—and gives us the feeling of being able to divide up indefinitely—what other writers are in the habit of passing over."

[71] Here again, there are qualifications according to substance: literature has an unrivaled elliptic power—which cinema lacks.

[72] This reduction does not necessarily correspond to the division of the book into chapters; on the contrary, it seems that increasingly chapters have the role of introducing breaks, points of suspense (serial technique).

[73] N. Ruwet: "A poem can be understood as the outcome of a series of transformations applied to the proposition 'I love you.'" "Analyse structurale d'un poème français," *Linguistics* 3, 1964. Ruwet here refers precisely to the analysis of paranoiac delirium given by Freud in connection with President Schreber ("Psychoanalytic Notes on an Autobiographical Account of a Case of Paranoia").

summarized. By contrast, the summary of a narrative (if conducted according to structural criteria) preserves the individuality of the message; narrative, in other words, is *translatable* without fundamental damage. What is untranslatable is determined only at the last, narrational, level. The signifiers of narrativity, for instance, are not readily transferable from novel to film, the latter utilizing the personal mode of treatment only very exceptionally;[74] while the last layer of the narrational level, namely the writing, resists transference from one language to another (or transfers very badly). The translatability of narrative is a result of the structure of its language, so that it would be possible, proceeding in reverse, to determine this structure by identifying and classifying the (varyingly) translatable and untranslatable elements of a narrative. The existence (now) of different and concurrent semiotics (literature, cinema, comics, radio/television) would greatly facilitate this kind of analysis.

2. *Mimesis and meaning*

The second important process in the language of narrative is integration: what has been disjoined at a certain level (a sequence for example) is most often joined again at a higher level (a hierarchically important sequence, the global signified of a number of scattered indices, the action of a class of characters). The complexity of a narrative can be compared to that of an organization profile chart, capable of integrating backward and forward movements; or, more accurately, it is integration in various forms which compensates for the seemingly unmasterable complexity of units on a particular level. Integration guides the understanding of the discontinuous elements, simultaneously contiguous and heterogeneous (it is

[74] Once again, there is no relation between the grammatical "person" of the narrator and the "personality" (or subjectivity) that a film director puts into his way of presenting a story: the *camera-I* (continuously identified with the vision of a particular character) is exceptional in the history of cinema.

thus that they appear in the syntagm which knows only one dimension—that of succession). If, with Greimas, we call *isotopy* the unity of meaning (that, for instance, which impregnates a sign and its context), then we can say that integration is a factor of isotopy: each (integrational) level gives its isotopy to the units of the level below, prevents the meaning from "dangling"—inevitable if the staggering of levels were not perceived. Narrative integration, however, does not present itself in a serenely regular manner like some fine architectural style leading by symmetrical chicaneries from an infinite variety of simple elements to a few complex masses. Very often a single unit will have two correlates, one on one level (function of a sequence), the other on another (indice with reference to an actant). Narrative thus appears as a succession of tightly interlocking mediate and immediate elements; dystaxia determines a "horizontal" reading, while integration superimposes a "vertical" reading: there is a sort of structural "limping," an incessant play of potentials whose varying falls give the narrative its dynamism or energy: each unit is perceived at once in its surfacing and in its depth and it is thus that the narrative "works"; through the concourse of these two movements the structure ramifies, proliferates, uncovers itself—and recovers itself, pulls itself together: the new never fails in its regularity. There is, of course, a freedom of narrative (just as there is a freedom for every speaker with regard to his or her language), but this freedom is limited, literally *hemmed in*: between the powerful code of language [*langue*] and the powerful code of narrative a hollow is set up—the sentence. If one attempts to embrace the whole of a written narrative, one finds that it starts from the most highly coded (the phonematic, or even the merismatic, level), gradually relaxes until it reaches the sentence, the farthest point of combinatorial freedom, and then begins to tighten up again, moving progressively from small groups of sentences (micro-sequences), which are still very free, until it comes to the main actions, which form a strong and restricted code. The creativity of narrative (at least under its mythical appearance of "life") is thus situated *between two codes*, the linguistic and the translinguistic. That is why it can be said paradoxically that *art* (in the Romantic sense of the term) is a matter of statements of detail, whereas *imagination* is mastery of the code: "It will be found in fact," wrote Poe, "that the ingenious are always fanciful, and the *truly* imaginative never otherwise than analytic . . ."[75]

Claims concerning the "realism" of narrative are therefore to be discounted. When a telephone call comes through in the office where he is on duty, Bond, so the author tells us, reflects that "Communications with Hong Kong are as bad as they always were and just as difficult to obtain." Neither Bond's "reflection" nor the poor quality of the telephone call is the real piece of information; this contingency perhaps gives things more "life" but the true information, which will come to fruition later, is the localization of the telephone call, Hong Kong. In all narrative imitation remains contingent.[76] The function of narrative is not to "represent," it is to constitute a spectacle still very enigmatic for us but in any case not of a mimetic order. The "reality" of a sequence lies not in the "natural" succession of the actions composing it but in the logic there exposed, risked, and satisfied. Putting it another way, one could say that the origin of a sequence is not the observation of reality, but the need to vary and transcend the first *form* given man, namely repetition: a sequence is essentially a whole within which nothing is repeated. Logic has here an emancipatory value—and with it the entire narrative. It

---

[75] "The Murders in the Rue Morgue."

[76] G. Genette rightly reduces *mimesis* to passages of directly reported dialogue (cf. "Frontières du récit"); yet even dialogue always contains a function of intelligibility, not of mimesis.

may be that men ceaselessly reinject into narrative what they have known, what they have experienced; but if they do, at least it is in a form which has vanquished repetition and instituted the model of a process of becoming. Narrative does not show, does not imitate; the passion which may excite us in reading a novel is not that of a "vision" (in actual fact, we do not "see" anything). Rather, it is that of meaning, that of a higher order of relation which also has its emotions, its hopes, its dangers, its triumphs. "What takes place" in a narrative is from the referential (reality) point of view literally *nothing*;[77] "what happens" is language alone, the adventure of language, the unceasing celebration of its coming. Although we know scarcely more about the origins of narrative than we do about the origins of language, it can reasonably be suggested that narrative is contemporaneous with monologue, a creation seemingly posterior to that of dialogue. At all events, without wanting to strain the phylogenetic hypothesis, it may be significant that it is at the same moment (around the age of three) that the little human "invents" at once sentence, narrative, and the Oedipus.

1966

---

[77] Mallarmé: "A dramatic work displays the succession of exteriors of the act without any moment retaining reality and, in the end, anything happening." *Crayonné au théâtre.*

Flaubert and the Sentence

Long before Flaubert, writers had experienced—and expressed—the arduous labor of style, the exhaustion of incessant corrections, the sad necessity of endless hours committed to an infinitesimal output.[1] Yet in Flaubert, the dimension of this agony is altogether different; the labor of style is for him an unspeakable suffering (even if he speaks it quite often), an almost expiatory ordeal for which he acknowledges no compensation of a magical (i.e., aleatory) order, as the sentiment of inspiration might be for many writers: style, for Flaubert, is absolute suffering, infinite suffering, useless suffering. Writing is disproportionately slow (*"four pages this week," "five days for a page," "two days to reach the end of two lines"*); it requires an "irrevocable farewell to life," a pitiless sequestration; we may note in this regard that Flaubert's sequestration occurs uniquely for the sake of style, while Proust's, equally famous, has for its object a total recuperation of the work:

From *New Critical Essays*.

[1] Here are several examples from Antoine Albalat's book, *Le Travail du style, enseigné par les corrections manuscrites des grands écrivains* (1903): Pascal rewrote the 18th Provincial Letter thirteen times; Rousseau worked on *Émile* for three years; Buffon worked more than ten hours a day; Chateaubriand would spend twelve to fifteen hours at a time rewriting, erasing, etc.

Proust retires from the world because he has a great deal to say and because he is pressed by death, Flaubert because he has an infinite correction to perform; once sequestered, Proust adds endlessly (his famous *"paperolles"*), Flaubert subtracts, erases, constantly returns to zero, begins over again. Flaubertian sequestration has for its center (and its symbol) a piece of furniture which is not the desk but the divan: when the depths of agony are plumbed, Flaubert throws himself on his sofa[2]: this is his "marinade," an ambiguous situation, in fact, for the sign of failure is also the site of fantasy, whence the work will gradually resume, giving Flaubert a new substance which he can erase anew. Flaubert qualifies this Sisyphean circuit by a very strong word, *"Atrocious,"*[3] the sole recompense he receives for his life's sacrifice.[4]

Apparently, then, style engages the writer's entire existence, and for this reason it would be better to call it henceforth a *writing*: to write is to live (*"A book has always been for me,"* Flaubert says, *"a particular way of living"*), writing is the book's goal, not publication.[5] This precellence, attested—or purchased—by the very sacrifice of a life, somewhat modifies the traditional conceptions of "writing well," ordinarily given as the final garment (the ornament) of ideas or passions. First of all, according to Flaubert, the very opposition of form and content vanishes[6]: to write and to think are but one action, writing is a total being. Then comes, so to speak, the reversion

[2] "Sometimes when I feel empty, when expression is refractory, when after having scribbled many pages I discover I haven't made a single sentence, I fall on my couch and lie there stupefied in an inner marsh of ennui" (1852).

[3] "One achieves style only by atrocious labor, a fanatic and dedicated stubbornness" (1846).

[4] "I have spent my life depriving my heart of its most legitimate nourishment. I have led a laborious and austere existence. And now I can bear no more, I am at the end of my tether" (1875).

[5] ". . . I don't want to publish anything . . . I work with an absolute disinterestedness and without ulterior motive, without external preoccupation . . ." (1846).

[6] "For me, insofar as you have not separated form from content in a given sentence, I maintain that these are actually two words devoid of meaning" (1846).

of the merits of poetry over prose: poetry holds up to prose the mirror of its constraints, the image of a close-set, sure code: this model exerts an ambiguous fascination upon Flaubert, since prose must at once rejoin verse and exceed it, equal it, and absorb it. Finally, there is a special distribution of technical tasks required by the elaboration of a novel; classical rhetoric focused on the problems of *dispositio,* or order of the parts of discourse (which we must not confuse with *compositio,* or order of the internal elements of the sentence); Flaubert seems not to be interested in this; he does not neglect the tasks proper to narration,[7] but these tasks, evidently, have only a loose link with his essential project: to compose his work or any of its episodes is not "atrocious" but simply "wearisome."[8]

As an odyssey, Flaubertian writing (and how active a meaning we should like to give this word) thus confines itself to what we commonly call corrections of style. These corrections are not in any way rhetorical accidents; they affect the primary code, that of the language; they commit the writer to experiencing the structure of the language as a passion. Here we must prepare what we might call a linguistics (and not a stylistics) of corrections, somewhat symmetrical to what Henri Frei has called the grammar of mistakes.

The corrections writers make on their manuscripts may be readily classified according to the two axes of the paper on which they write; on the vertical axis are made the substitutions of words (these are the crossings out or "hesitations"); on the horizontal axis, the suppressions or additions of syntagms (these are the "recastings"). Now the axes of the paper

---

[7] See notably the account of the pages concerning various episodes of *Madame Bovary:* "I already have 260 pages which contain only preparations for action, more or less disguised expositions of characters (it is true that they are graduated), landscapes, places . . ."

[8] "I have a narration to compose; now the story is something which is very wearisome for me. I have to send my heroine to a ball" (1852).

are the very same thing as the axes of the language. The first corrections are substitutive, metaphorical; they tend to replace the sign initially inscribed by another sign chosen from a paradigm of affinitary and different elements; these corrections can then bear on the monemes (Hugo substituting *modest* for *charming* in "*Eden wakened, charming and nude*") or on the phonemes, when it is a matter of prohibiting certain assonances (which classical prose does not tolerate) or over-insistent homophonies held to be absurd (in French the sound of *Après cet essai fait: cétécéfé*). The secondary corrections (corresponding to the horizontal order of the page) are associative, metonymic; they affect the syntagmatic chain of the message, modifying its volume by diminution or enlargement according to two rhetorical models: ellipsis and catalysis.

In short, the writer possesses three main types of corrections: substitutive, diminutive, and augmentative: he can work by permutation, subtraction, or expansion. Now these three types have not altogether the same status, and moreover they have not had the same fortune. Substitution and ellipsis bear on limited groups. The paradigm is closed by the constraints of distribution (which oblige the writer, in principle, to permute only terms of the same class) and by those of meaning, which require him to exchange affinitary terms.[9] As we cannot replace a sign by just any other sign, we also cannot reduce a sentence indefinitely; the diminutive correction (ellipsis) eventually comes up against the irreducible cell of any sentence, the subject-predicate group (it will be understood that *in practical terms* the limits of ellipsis are often reached much sooner, by reason of various cultural constraints, such as eurhythmy, symmetry, etc.): ellipsis is limited by the structure of the language. This very structure permits us, on the contrary, to give

[9] We must not limit affinity to a purely analogical relation, and it would be wrong to suppose that writers permute only synonymous terms: a classical writer like Bossuet can substitute *laugh* for *weep*: the antonymous relation constitutes part of the affinity.

free rein, without limit, to augmentative corrections; on the one hand, the parts of speech can be indefinitely multiplied (if only by digression), and on the other (this is what particularly interests us here), the sentence may be indefinitely furnished with interpolations and expansions: the catalytic work is theoretically infinite; even if the structure of the sentence is actually governed and limited by literary models (in the manner of poetical meter) or by physical constraints (the limits of human memory, relative moreover, since classical literature admits the *period*, virtually unknown to ordinary speech), it remains nonetheless true that the writer, confronting the sentence, experiences the infinite freedom of speech, as it is inscribed within the very structure of language. Hence what is involved is a problem of freedom, and we must note that the three types of corrections of which we have just spoken have not had the same fortune; according to the classical ideal of style, the writer is required to rework his substitutions and his ellipses tirelessly, by virtue of the correlative myths of the "exact word" and of "concision," both guarantees of "clarity,"[10] while he is discouraged from any labor of expansion; in classical manuscripts, permutations and crossings out abound, but we find virtually no augmentative corrections except in Rousseau and above all in Stendhal, whose subversive attitude with regard to "fine style" is well known.

To return to Flaubert: the corrections he made on his manuscripts are doubtless varied, but if we abide by what he himself asserted and commented, the "atrocity" of style is concentrated in two points, which are the writer's two crosses. The first cross is the repetition of words; it is a matter of substitutive correction here, since it is the (phonic) form of the word

---

[10] It is a classical paradox—which in my opinion should be explored—that clarity should be given as the natural product of concision (see Mme Necker's remark, given in Brunot's *Histoire de la langue française*: "The shortest sentence is always preferable when it is also clear, *for it necessarily becomes more so*").

whose too-immediate return must be avoided, while retaining
the content; as we have said, the possibilities of correction are
limited here, which should lighten the writer's responsibility all
the more; yet here Flaubert manages to introduce the vertigo
of an infinite correction: the difficulty, for him, is not correction itself (actually limited), but discernment of the place
where it is necessary: certain repetitions appear, which had
not been noticed the day before, so that nothing can guarantee
that the next day new "mistakes" will not be discovered;[11]
thus, there develops an anxious insecurity, for it always seems
possible to *bear* new repetitions:[12] the text, even when it
has been meticulously worked over, is somehow *mined* with
risks of repetition: limited and consequently reassured in its
act, substitution again becomes free and consequently agonizing by the infinity of its possible emplacements: the paradigm
is of course closed, but since it functions with each significa-
tive unit, it is seized again by the infinity of the syntagm. The
second cross of Flaubertian writing is the transitions (or articulations) of the discourse.[13] As we might expect of a writer
who has continuously absorbed content in form—or more precisely contested this very antinomy—the linking of ideas is not
experienced directly as a logical constraint but must be defined
in terms of the signifier; what is to be obtained is fluidity, the
optimal rhythm of the course of speech, in a word *sequence*,
that *flumen orationis* already demanded by the classical
rhetoricians. Here Flaubert comes up against the problem of
syntagmatic corrections once more: the good syntagm is an

[11] Apropos of three pages of *Madame Bovary* (1853): "I will doubtless
discover in them a thousand repetitions of words which I'll have to get
rid of. At this moment, late as it is, I can see virtually none."
[12] This audition of a language within language (however erroneous) recalls
another audition quite as vertiginous: that which permitted Saussure to hear
a second, anagrammatic message in most verses of Greek, Latin, and Vedic
poetry.
[13] "What is atrociously difficult is the linking of ideas, so that they derive
naturally from each other" (1852). ". . . And then the transitions, the
sequence—what an entanglement!" (1853).

equilibrium between excessive forces of constriction and of dilatation; but whereas ellipsis is normally limited by the very structure of the sentential unit, Flaubert reintroduces an infinite freedom into it: once acquired, he turns it back and reorients it toward a new expansion: a matter of constantly "unscrewing" what is too tight: ellipsis now acquires the vertigo of expansion.[14]

For it is indeed a matter of vertigo: correction is infinite, it has no sure sanction. The corrective protocols are perfectly systematic—and in this they might be reassuring—but since their points of application are endless, no appeasement is possible:[15] they are groups at once structured and floating. Yet this vertigo does not have as its motif the infinity of discourse, the traditional field of rhetoric; it is linked to a linguistic object, known of course to rhetoric, at least from the moment when, with Dionysus of Halicarnassus and the anonymous author of *On the Sublime*, rhetoric had discovered "style," but to which Flaubert has given a technical and even metaphysical existence of an incomparable force, and which is *the sentence*.

For Flaubert, the sentence is at once a unit of style, a unit of work, and a unit of life; it attracts the essential quality of his confidences as his work as a writer.[16] If we rid the expression of any metaphorical resonance, we might say that Flau-

[14] "Each paragraph is good in itself, and there are pages I am certain are perfect. But just because of this, *it doesn't work*. It's a series of well-turned paragraphs which do not lead into each other. I'm going to have to unscrew them, loosen the joints" (1853).

[15] "I ended by leaving off the corrections; I had reached the point where I understood nothing—pressing too hard on a piece of work, it dazzles you; what seems to be wrong now in five minutes seems perfectly all right" (1853).

[16] "I'd rather die like a dog than rush my sentence through, before it's ripe" (1852).—"I only want to write three more pages . . . and find four or five sentences that I've been searching for, nearly a month now" (1853).—"My work is going very slowly; sometimes I suffer real tortures to write the simplest sentence" (1852).—"I can't stop myself, even swimming, I test my sentences, despite myself" (1876).—And especially this, which might serve as an epigraph for what has just been said about the sentence in Flaubert: "I'm going on again, then, with my dull and simple life, poor wretched thing, in which the sentences are adventures . . ." (1857).

bert has spent his life "making sentences"; the sentence is, so to speak, the work's double *reflection*, it is on the level of the fabrication of sentences that the writer has created the history of this work: the odyssey of the sentence and the novel of Flaubert's novels. Thus, the sentence becomes, in our literature, a new object: not only *de jure*, in Flaubert's numerous declarations in this regard, but *de facto*: a sentence by Flaubert is immediately identifiable, not by its "air," its "color," or some turn of phrase habitual to the writer—which we might say of any author—but because it always presents itself as a separate, finite object, which we might almost call transportable, though it never joins the aphoristic model, for its unit does not abide by the closure of its content, but by the evident project which has established it as an object: Flaubert's sentence is a *thing*.

As we have seen apropos of Flaubert's corrections, this thing has a history, and this history, issuing from the very structure of the language, is inscribed in every sentence by Flaubert. His drama (his confidences authorize us to use so novelistic a word) in confronting the sentence can be articulated as follows: the sentence is an object, in it a finitude fascinates, analogous to that finitude which governs the metrical maturation of verse; but at the same time, by the very mechanism of expansion, every sentence is unsaturable, there is no structural reason to stop it here rather than there. *Let us work in order to end the sentence* (in the fashion of a line of verse), Flaubert implicitly says at each moment of his labor, of his life, while contradictorily he is obliged to exclaim unceasingly (as he notes in 1853): *It's never finished.*[17] The Flaubertian sentence is the very trace of this contradiction, experienced intensely by the writer during the countless hours when he shuts himself up with it: it is like the gratuitous arrest

---

[17] "Ah! What discouragements sometimes, what a Sisyphean labor style is, and prose especially! *It's never finished!*" (1853).

of an infinite freedom, in it is inscribed a kind of metaphysical contradiction: because the sentence is free, the writer is condemned not to search for the *best* sentence, but to assume *every* sentence: no god, even the god of art, can establish it in its place.

As we know, this situation was not experienced in the same way during the entire classical period. Confronting the freedom of language, rhetoric had constructed a system of surveillance (promulgating since Aristotle the metrical rules of the "period" and determining the field of corrections, where the freedom is limited by the very nature of language, i.e., on the level of substitutions and ellipses), and this system granted the writer a slight freedom by limiting his choices. This rhetorical code—or secondary code, since it transforms the freedoms of language into constraints of expression—grows moribund by the middle of the nineteenth century; rhetoric withdraws and in a sense exposes the fundamental linguistic unit, the sentence. This new object—in which the writer's freedom is henceforth directly invested—Flaubert discovers with anguish. A writer appears a little later who will make the sentence into the site of a demonstration at once poetic and linguistic: Mallarmé's *Un coup de dés* is explicitly based on the infinite possibility of sentential expansion, whose freedom, so burdensome for Flaubert, becomes for Mallarmé the very meaning—a blank meaning—of *the book to come.* Henceforth the writer's brother and guide will no longer be the master of rhetoric but of linguistics, the one who reveals no longer figures of discourse but the fundamental categories of language.

1967

Lesson in Writing

THE puppets of Bunraku theater are from three to five feet in height. They are little men or women with movable limbs, hands, and mouth. Each puppet is worked by three men who remain in view, surrounding, supporting, and accompanying it. The principal operator controls the upper part of the doll and its right arm; his face is visible, smooth, clear, impassive, cold like "a white onion freshly washed."[1] The two assistants are clad in black, their faces hidden by a piece of cloth; the first, gloved but with thumb exposed, holds a large scissors mechanism with which he operates the doll's left arm and hand; the second, crawling along on his knees, supports the body, makes it walk. These men move about along a low trench which leaves them unconcealed. The scenery is behind them, as at the theater. To the side, there is a dais for the musicians and the narrators whose role is to *express* the text (a little as one presses out the juice of a fruit); this text is half-spoken, half-sung, and, punctuated with great plectrum strokes by the sami-

From *Image-Music-Text*.

1 Haiku by Basho:
*A white onion
freshly washed.
Feeling of cold.*

sen players, is at once measured and thrown off, given with violence and artifice. Sweating and motionless, the mouth-pieces sit behind little lecterns on which rests the writing they must vocalize, its vertical characters glimpsed from afar when they turn a page of their libretto; a triangle of stiff canvas fixed to their shoulders like a kite frames their faces, faces in throes to all the torments of the voice.

Antithesis is a privileged figure of our culture, doubtless because it corresponds well to our vision of good and evil and to that inveterate emblematism which has us turn every word into a watchword against its opposite (creativity versus intelligence, spontaneity versus reflection, truth versus appearance, etc.). Bunraku cares nothing for these contraries, for this antonymy that regulates our whole morality of discourse; concerned with a fundamental antilogy, that of the *animate/inanimate*, it disturbs it, dissipates it to the advantage of neither of the terms. With us, the marionette (Punch, for example) is there to hold up to the actor the mirror of his opposite, animating the inanimate but so as the better to reveal its degradation, the abjectness of its inertia; a caricature of "life," it affirms precisely thereby life's *moral* limits and serves to confine beauty, truth, and emotion in the living body of the actor—he who nevertheless makes of that body a lie. Bunraku on the other hand does not ape the actor, it rids us of him. How? Exactly by a certain reflection on the human body here conducted by inanimate matter with infinitely more rigor and excitement than by the animate body (endowed with a "soul"). The (naturalistic) Western actor is never beautiful, his body is intended as essentially physiological and not plastic; it is a collection of organs, a musculature of passions, whose every resource (voice, facial expressions, gestures) is subject to a kind of gymnastic drill. By a reversal that is specifically bourgeois, the actor's body, although built on a division of the essences of passion, then borrows from physiology the alibi of an organic unity, the unity of "life." In this way it is the actor who is a marionette and this despite the smooth flow of his acting, the model for which is not the caress but only the visceral "truth."

Thus, beneath a "living" and "natural" outward appearance, the Western actor maintains the division of his body and, consequently, the food of our fantasies. Voice, look, figure are in turn eroticized, like so many pieces of the body, like so many fetishes. The Western marionette too (as is evident in Punch) is a by-product of fantasy: as reduction, a grating reflection with an adherence to the human order ceaselessly recalled by a caricatural simulation, it lives not as a total body, totally vibrating, but as a rigid portion of the actor of whom it is an emanation; as automaton, it is again a fragment of movement, a start, a jolt, essence of discontinuity, fractured projection of bodily gestures; as doll finally, a reminiscence of the bit of material, of the genital swathe, it is indeed the phallic "little thing" (*das Kleine*), fallen from the body to become a fetish.

It may well be that the Japanese marionette retains something of this fantasy origin; the art of Bunraku, however, endows it with a different meaning. Bunraku does not aim at "animating" an inanimate object in such a way as to bring to life a piece of the body, a scrap of man, while preserving its vocation as "part"; it is not the simulation of the body that it is after, but, as it were, its concrete abstraction. Everything which we attribute to the total body and which is refused to our actors under pretense of a "living" organic unity is taken up and stated without any falsehood by the Bunraku puppet: fragility, discretion, sumptuousness, extraordinary nuance, abandonment of all triviality, melodic phrasing of gestures, in short those very qualities that the dreams of the old theology granted to the glorified body, namely impassiveness, clarity, agility, subtlety. This is what Bunraku accomplishes, this is how it converts the body fetish into a lovable body, this is how it refuses the antinomy of *animate/inanimate* and dismisses the concept hiding behind all *animation* of matter, that, quite simply, of "the soul."

Another opposition destroyed is that of *inner/outer*. Consider the Western theater of the last few centuries. Its function is essentially to reveal what is reputed to be secret ("feelings," "situations," "conflicts") while concealing the very artifice of the process of revelation (machinery, painting, makeup, sources of light). The Italian stage is the space of this deceit, everything there taking place in a room surreptitiously thrown open, surprised, spied on, and relished by a hidden spectator; a theological space, that of the moral failing: on the one side, under a light of which he pretends to be unaware, the actor, that is to say, gesture and speech; on the other, in the darkness, the public, that is to say, consciousness and conscience. Bunraku does not directly subvert the relation between stage and auditorium (any more than did Brecht), though Japanese theaters are infinitely less confined, less suffocating, less ponderous than ours. What it changes, more profoundly, is the driving link between character and actor which is always conceived by us as the expressive channel of an interiority. It has to be remembered that the agents of the spectacle in Bunraku are both visible and impassive. The men in black busy themselves around the doll but without any affectation of skill or discretion, without any promotional demagogy: silent, rapid, elegant, their actions are eminently transitive, operational, colored by that mixture of strength and subtlety that characterizes Japanese gestuality and that can be seen as the aesthetic envelope of efficacy. As for the master, it has already been said that his head is left uncovered, smooth and bare, without makeup, this conferring on him a *civic* (and not a theatrical) appearance; his face is offered to the spectator for reading, but what is so carefully and so preciously given to be

read is that there is nothing to be read—here we find that
exemption from meaning which does indeed illumine so many
works of the East and which we are scarcely able to comprehend, since for us to attack meaning is to conceal or oppose it,
never to absent it. With Bunraku, the sources of the theater
are exposed in their void. What is expelled from the stage is
hysteria, that is theater itself, and what is put in its place is the
action necessary for the production of the spectacle—work is
substituted for interiority.

It is thus futile to ask oneself as do certain Europeans
(Claudel among them) whether or not the spectator can forget
the presence of the manipulators. Bunraku practices neither
the dissimulation nor the emphatic disclosure of its various
mechanisms, hence ridding the animation of the actor of any
suggestion of the sacred and abolishing the metaphysical bond
that the West cannot stop itself from setting up between soul
and body, cause and effect, motor and machine, agent and
actor, Fate and man. God and creature:[2] if the manipulator is
not hidden, then why and how turn him into a God? In Bunraku, the puppet is held by no thread; without a thread, there
is no longer any metaphor, any Fate; puppet no longer aping
creature, man is no longer a puppet in the hands of the deity,
the *inner* no longer controls the *outer*.

Finally, a still more radical undertaking, Bunraku attacks
the writing of the spectacle. With us, such writing involves an
illusion of totality. "We find nothing more difficult," says
Brecht, "than to break with the habit of considering an artistic
production *as a whole*."[3] No doubt it is for this reason that
periodically, from the Greek *choréia* to the bourgeois opera,
we conceive of lyric art as the simultaneity of several modes of

---

[2] "Bunraku . . . is, quite simply, metaphysical theater . . . The puppet is
man. The manipulator is God. The assistants are the messengers of Fate."
J.-L. Barrault, "Le Bunraku," in *Cahiers Renaud-Barrault* 31, November 1960.
[3] Bertolt Brecht, "Alienation Effects in Chinese Acting," *Brecht on Theatre*—
with somewhat different wording.

expression (acted, sung, mimed) with a sole, indivisible, origin. This origin is the body and the required totality has for its model organic unity. Western spectacle is anthropomorphous:[4] gesture and speech (not to mention song) form but a single tissue, conglomerate and lubrificated like a unique muscle that sets expression going without ever dividing it: the unity of movement and voice produces *the one* who acts; in other words, it is in this unity that is constituted the person of the personage, that is, the actor. In Bunraku, however, no one is on stage, or, more precisely, no person has taken up position there. The (personal) corporal illusion disappears, not because the actors are made of wood and cloth (we saw that Bunraku designates on the contrary a certain *lovableness* of the human body) but because the codes of expression are detached from one another, pulled free from the sticky organicism in which they are held by Western theater.

In fact then, Bunraku practices three separate writings which are given for reading simultaneously in three areas of the spectacle: the marionette, the manipulator, the vociferator; the effected gesture, the effective gesture, the vocal gesture. The voice is what is really at stake in modernity, the voice as specific substance of language everywhere triumphantly pushed forward. Modern society (as has been repeated often enough) believes itself to be ushering in a civilization of the image, but what it actually establishes overall, and particularly in its leisure activities which are massively spoken, is a civilization of speech. In complete contrast, Bunraku has a *limited* conception of the voice; not suppressing it, it assigns it a clearly defined function that is essentially trivial. The narrator's voice gathers together extravagant declamation, tremulous quiver, shrill feminine tones, broken intonations, tears, paroxysms of anger and lamentation, supplication and aston-

---

[4] Aristotle: "The action . . . being one and whole like a living being," *Poetics* 1459a.

ishment, indecent pathos, the whole concoction of emotion openly prepared at the level of this visceral, inner body of which the larynx is the mediating muscle. Even then, such excess is only presented in terms of the very code of the excessive: the voice moves only through a few discontinuous signs of fury; expelled from a body that remains motionless, mounted in the triangle of the costume, linked to the book which guides it from the lectern, studded sharply by the slightly off-phased (and so non-pertinent) strokes of the samisen player, the vocal substance stays written, discontinued, obedient to an irony (if one accepts the word free from any sense of a caustic humor). Thus what the voice exteriorizes finally is not what it carries in it ("feelings") but itself, its own prostitution; while pretending to deliver over contents (anecdotes, passions), the signifier artfully does nothing but turn itself inside out, like a glove.

Hence the voice, without being eliminated (which would be a way of censuring it, that is, of indicating its importance), is set aside (theatrically, the narrators occupy a lateral dais). Bunraku gives the voice a counterbalance, or better, a countermarch, that of gesture. Gesture here is twofold: emotive gesture with the marionette (people cry at the suicide of the doll-lover); transitive action with the manipulators. In our theatrical art the actor pretends to engage in action but his actions are never anything but gestures: on stage, nothing but theater, and yet a theater that is ashamed. Bunraku (this is its definition) separates the act from the gesture: it exhibits the gesture, it allows the act to be seen; it exposes at once the art and the work, keeping for each its own particular writing. The voice (and there is then no risk in letting it run the gamut of its excesses) is folded into an immense volume of silence in which other traits, other writings, are inscribed with so much finesse. It is here that an extraordinary effect occurs: far from the voice and almost without mimicry, these silent writings—

the one transitive, the other gestural—produce an exaltation as special, perhaps, as the intellectual hyperaesthesia attributed to certain drugs. Speech being not purified (Bunraku knows no ascetic ambition) but, as it were, *massed* on the side, the tackily clinging substances of Western theater are dissolved: emotion no longer submerges everything in its flood but becomes matter for reading; the stereotypes disappear without however the spectacle falling into originality, the "stroke of genius." All of which has an evident kinship with the distancing effect recommended by Brecht, who was, as perhaps needs recalling, the first to understand and state the critical importance of Oriental theater. This distance, reputed by us to be impossible, useless or derisory and speedily abandoned, despite its being placed by Brecht very precisely at the center of revolutionary dramatic art (the latter doubtless explains the former), is what Bunraku shows—shows how it can function: by the discontinuity of codes, by the cæsura imposed in the different traits of the representation, so that the *copy* elaborated on the stage is not destroyed but shattered, scored, freed from the metonymical contagion of voice and gesture, soul and body, which entangles our actors.

A total spectacle, but divided, Bunraku evidently excludes improvisation, doubtless aware that the return to spontaneity is the return to all those stereotypes which go to make up our "inner depths." Here we have, as Brecht saw in connection with the Oriental actor whose lesson he wished to receive and propagate on this point too, the reign of the *quotation*,[5] the pinch of writing, the fragment of code, none of the promoters of the action being able to take responsibility in his own person for what he is never alone in writing. As in the modern

[5] "He limits himself from the start to simply quoting the character played. But with what art he does this! He only needs a minimum of illusion. What he has to show is worth seeing even for a man in his right mind." And elsewhere: "Once the idea of total transformation is given up, the actor speaks his part not as if he were improvising it himself but like a quotation."

text, the stressing of codes, references, discontinuous observations, anthological gestures, multiplies the written line, and this not by virtue of some metaphysical appeal but by the play of a combinatory set which opens in the entire space of the theater: what is started by the one is continued by the other, unendingly.

1968

PART THREE

The Third Meaning

RESEARCH NOTES ON SOME EISENSTEIN STILLS

Hₑᵣₑ is an image from *Ivan the Terrible* (I): two courtiers, two adjuvants, two supernumeraries (it matters little if I am unable to remember the details of the story exactly) are raining down gold over the young czar's head. I think it possible to distinguish three levels of meaning in this scene:

1) An informational level, which gathers together everything I can learn from the setting, the costumes, the characters, their relations, their insertion in an anecdote with which I am (even if vaguely) familiar. This level is that of communication. Were it necessary to find a mode of analysis for it, I should turn to the first semiotics (that of the "message"); this level, this semiotics, however, will be of no further concern here.

2) A symbolic level, which is the downpour of gold and which is itself stratified. There is the referential symbolism: the imperial ritual of baptism by gold. Then there is the diegetic symbolism: the theme of gold, of wealth, in *Ivan the Terrible* (supposing such a theme to exist), which makes a significant intervention in this scene. Then again there is the Eisensteinian symbolism—if by chance a critic should decide to demonstrate that the gold or the raining down or the curtain

From *Image-Music-Text*.

317

or the disfiguration can be seen as held in a network of displacements and substitutions peculiar to S. M. Eisenstein. Finally, there is a historical symbolism, if, in a manner even more widely embracing than the previous ones, it can be shown that the gold brings in a (theatrical) playing, a scenography of exchange, locatable both psychoanalytically and economically, that is to say semiologically. Taken in its entirety, this second level is that of *signification*. Its mode of analysis would be a semiotics more highly developed than the first, a second or neo-semiotics, open no longer to the science of the message but to the sciences of the symbol (psychoanalysis, economy, dramaturgy).

3) Is that all? No, for I am still held by the image. I read, I receive (and probably even first and foremost) a third meaning[1]—evident, erratic, obstinate. I do not know what its signified is, at least I am unable to give it a name, but I can see clearly the traits, the signifying accidents of which this—consequently incomplete—sign is composed: a certain compactness of the courtiers' make-up, thick and insistent for the one, smooth and distinguished for the other; the former's "stupid" nose, the latter's finely traced eyebrows, his lank blondness, his faded, pale complexion, the affected flatness of his hairstyle suggestive of a wig, the touching up with chalky foundation talc, with face powder. I am not sure if the reading of this third meaning is justified—if it can be generalized—but already it seems to me that its signifier (the traits to which I have tried to give words, if not to describe) possesses a theoretical individuality. On the one hand, it cannot be conflated with the

---

[1] In the classical paradigm of the five senses, the third sense is hearing (first in importance in the Middle Ages). This is a happy coincidence, since what is here in question is indeed *listening*: firstly, because the remarks by Eisenstein to which reference will be made are taken from a consideration of the coming of sound in film; second, because listening (no reference to the *phoné* alone) bears within it that metaphor best suited to the "textual": orchestration (SME's own word), counterpoint, stereophony.

I

II

III

IV

V

VI

VII

VIII

IX

X

XI

XII

XIII

XIV

XV

XVI

simple *existence* of the scene, it exceeds the copy of the referential motif, it compels an interrogative reading (interrogation bears precisely on the signifier not on the signified, on reading not on intellection: it is a "poetical" grasp); on the other, neither can it be conflated with the dramatic meaning of the episode: to say that these traits refer to a significant "attitude" of the courtiers, this one detached and bored, that one diligent (*"They are simply doing their job as courtiers"*), does not leave me fully satisfied; something in the two faces exceeds psychology, anecdote, function, exceeds meaning without, however, coming down to the obstinacy in presence shown by any human body. By contrast with the first two levels, communication and signification, this third level—even if the reading of it is still hazardous—is that of *signifiance*, a word which has the advantage of referring to the field of the signifier (and not of signification) and of linking up with, via the path opened by Julia Kristeva who proposed the term, a semiotics of the text.

My concern here lies not with communication but with signification and *signifiance*. I must therefore name as economically as possible the second and third meanings. The symbolic meaning (the shower of gold, the power of wealth, the imperial rite) forces itself upon me by a double determination: it is intentional (it is what the author wanted to say) and it is taken from a kind of common, general lexicon of symbols; it is a meaning which seeks me out, me, the recipient of the message, the subject of the reading, a meaning which starts with SME and which goes on *ahead of me;* evident certainly (so too is the other), but *closed* in its evidence, held in a complete system of destination. I propose to call this complete sign *the obvious meaning. Obvious* means *which comes ahead* and this is exactly the case with this meaning, which comes to seek me out. In theology, we are told, the obvious meaning is that "which presents itself quite naturally to the mind" and this again is the case here: the symbolics of the raining down of gold appears to me as forever having been endowed with a "natural" clarity. As for the other meaning, the third, the one "too many," the supplement that my intellection cannot succeed in absorbing, at once persistent and fleeting, smooth and elusive, I propose to call it *the obtuse meaning*. The word springs readily to mind and, miracle, when its etymology is unfolded, it already provides us with a theory of the supplementary meaning. *Obtusus* means *that which is blunted, rounded in form*. Are not the traits which I indicated (the make-up, the whiteness, the wig, etc.) just like the blunting of a meaning too clear, too violent? Do they not give the obvious signified a kind of difficulty prehensible roundness, cause my reading to slip? An obtuse angle is greater than a right angle: *an obtuse angle of 100°*, says the dictionary; the third meaning also seems to me greater than the pure, upright, secant, legal perpendicular of the narrative, it seems to open the field of meaning totally, that is infinitely. I even accept for the obtuse meaning the word's pejorative connotation: the obtuse meaning appears to extend outside culture, knowledge, information; analytically, it has something derisory about it: opening out into the infinity of language, it can come through as limited in the eyes of analytic reason; it belongs to the family of pun, buffoonery, useless expenditure. Indifferent to moral or aesthetic categories (the trivial, the futile, the false, the pastiche), it is on the side of the carnival. *Obtuse* is thus very suitable.

THE OBVIOUS MEANING

A few words with regard to the obvious meaning, even though it is not the object of this study. Here are two images in which it can be seen in its pure state. The four figures in II "sym-

bolize" three ages of life and the unanimity of mourning (Vakulinchuk's funeral). The clenched fist in IV, given in full
"detail," signifies indignation, anger mastered and channeled,
the determination of the struggle; metonymically joined to the
whole Potemkin story, it "symbolizes" the working class in all
its resolute strength, for, by a miracle of semantic intelligence,
this fist which is *seen wrong way up*, kept by its owner in a sort
of clandestinity (it is the hand which *first of all* hangs down
naturally along the trouser leg and which *then* closes, hardens,
thinks at once its future struggle, its patience and its prudence),
cannot be read as the fist of some hoodlum, of some fascist:
it is *immediately* a proletarian fist. Which shows that Eisenstein's "art" is not polysemous: it chooses the meaning, imposes it, hammers it home (if the signification is overrun by
the obtuse meaning, this is not to say that it is thereby denied
or blurred): the Eisensteinian meaning devastates ambiguity.
How? By the addition of an aesthetic value, emphasis. Eisenstein's "decorativism" has an economic function: it proffers
the truth. Look at III: in extremely classic fashion, grief comes
from the bowed heads, the expressions of suffering, the hand
over the mouth stifling a sob, but when once all this has been
said, very adequately, a decorative trait says it again: the
superimposition of the two hands aesthetically arranged in a
delicate, maternal, floral ascension toward the face bowing
down. Within the general detail (the two women), another detail is mirroringly inscribed; derived from a pictorial order as
a quotation of the gestures to be found in icons and *pietà*, it
does not distract but accentuates the meaning. This accentuation (characteristic of all realist art) has some connection with
the "truth" of *Potemkin*. Baudelaire spoke of *"the emphatic
truth of gesture in the important moments of life"*; here it is
the truth of the "important proletarian moment" which requires emphasis. The Eisensteinian aesthetic does not consti-

tute an independent level: it is part of the obvious meaning, and the obvious meaning is always, in Eisenstein, the revolution.

THE OBTUSE MEANING

I first had the conviction of the obtuse meaning with image V. A question forced itself upon me: what is it in this tearful old woman that poses for me the question of the signifier? I quickly convinced myself that, although perfect, it was neither the facial expression nor the gestural figuration of grief (the closed eyelids, the taut mouth, the hand clasped on the breast): all that belongs to the full signification, to the obvious meaning of the image, to Eisensteinian realism and decorativism. I felt that the penetrating trait—disturbing like a guest who obstinately sits on saying nothing when one has no use for him— must be situated somewhere in the region of the forehead: the coif, the headscarf holding in the hair, had something to do with it. In image VI, however, the obtuse meaning vanishes, leaving only a message of grief. It was then I understood that the scandal, supplement or drift imposed on this classic representation of grief came very precisely from a tenuous relationship: that of the low headscarf, the closed eyes and the convex mouth; or rather, to use the distinction made by SME himself between "the shadows of the cathedral" and "the enshadowed cathedral," from a relation between the "lowness" of the line of the headscarf, pulled down abnormally close to the eyebrows as in those disguises intended to create a facetious, simpleton look, the upward circumflex of the faded eyebrows, faint and old, the excessive curve of the eyelids, lowered but brought together as though squinting, and the bar of the half-opened mouth, corresponding to the bar of the headscarf and to that of the eyebrows, metaphorically speaking "like a fish out of water." All these traits (the funny headdress, the old woman, the squinting eyelids, the fish) have as their vague reference a somewhat low language, the language of a rather pitiful disguise. In connection with the noble grief of the obvious meaning, they form a dialogism so tenuous that there is no guarantee of its intentionality. The characteristic of this third meaning is indeed—at least in SME—to blur the limit separating expression from disguise, but also to allow that oscillation succinct demonstration—an elliptic emphasis, if one can put it like that, a complex and extremely artful disposition (for it involves a temporality of signification), perfectly described by Eisenstein himself when he jubilantly quotes the golden rule of the old Gillette: "*Just short of the cutting edge.*"

The obtuse meaning, then, has something to do with disguise. Look at Ivan's beard raised to obtuse meaning, in my opinion, in image VII; it declares its artifice but without in so doing abandoning the "good faith" of its referent (the historical figure of the czar): an actor disguised twice over (once as actor in the anecdote, once as actor in the dramaturgy) without one disguise destroying the other; a multi-layering of meanings which always lets the previous meaning continue, as in a geological formation, saying the opposite without giving up the contrary—a (two-term) dramatic dialectic that Brecht would have liked. The Eisensteinian "artifice" is at once falsification of itself—pastiche—and derisory fetish, since it shows its fissure and its suture: what can be seen in image VII is the join and thus the initial disjoin of the beard perpendicular to the chin. That the top of a head (the most "obtuse" part of the human person), that a single bun of hair (in image VIII) can be the *expression* of grief, that is what is derisory—for the expression, not for the grief. Hence no parody, no trace of burlesque; there is no aping of grief (the obvious meaning must remain revolutionary, the general mourning which accompanies Vakulinchuk's death has a historical meaning), and yet, "embodied" in the bun, it has a cut-off, a refusal of contamination; the populism of the woollen shawl (obvious meaning) stops at the bun; here begins the fetish—the hair—and a kind of *non-negating derision* of the expression. The whole of the obtuse meaning (its disruptive force) is staked on the excessive mass of the hair. Look at another bun (that of the woman in image IX): it contradicts the tiny raised fist, atrophies it without the reduction having the slightest symbolic (intellectual) value; prolonged by small curls, pulling the face in toward an ovine model, it gives the woman something *touching* (in the way that a certain generous foolishness can be) or *sensitive*—these antiquated words, mystified words if ever there were, with little that is revolutionary or political about them, must nevertheless be assumed. I believe that the obtuse meaning carries a certain *emotion*. Caught up in the disguise, such emotion is never sticky, it is an emotion which simply *designates* what one loves, what one wants to defend: an emotion value, an evaluation. Everyone will agree, I think, that SME's proletarian ethnography fragmented the length of Vakulinchuk's funeral, is constantly informed by something loving (using the word regardless of any specification as to age or sex). Maternal, cordial, virile, "sympathetic" without any recourse to stereotypes, the Eisensteinian people is essentially *lovable*. We savor, we love the two round-capped heads in image X, we enter into complicity, into an understanding with them. Doubtless beauty can work as an obtuse meaning; this is the case in image XI, where the extremely dense obvious meaning (Ivan's attitude, young Vladimir's half-wit foolishness) is anchored and/or set adrift by Basmanov's beauty. But the eroticism included in the obtuse meaning (or rather: the eroticism which this meaning picks up) is no respector of the aesthetic: Euphrosyne is ugly, "obtuse" (images XII and XIII), like the monk (image XIV), but this obtuseness exceeds the anecdote, becomes a blunting of meaning, its drifting. There is in the obtuse meaning an eroticism which includes the contrary of the beautiful, as also what falls outside such contrariety, its limit—inversion, unease, and perhaps sadism. Look at the flabby innocence of the "Children in the Fiery Furnace" (image XV), the schoolboyish ridicule of their mufflers dutifully tucked up to the chin, the curds-and-whey skin (of their eyes, of their mouths set in the skin) which Fellini seems to have remembered in the hermaphrodite of his *Satyricon*—the very same mentioned by Georges Bataille, notably in that text in *Documents* which situates for me one of the possible regions of obtuse meaning, "The Big Toe."[2]

Let us continue (if these examples will suffice to lead on to one or two more theoretical remarks). The obtuse meaning is not in the language-system (even that of symbols). Take away the obtuse meaning and communication and signification still remain, still circulate, still come through: without it, I can still state and read. No more, however, is it to be located in language use. It may be that there is a certain constant in Eisensteinian obtuse meaning, but in that case it is already a thematic language, an idiolect, this idiolect being provisional (simply decided by a critic writing a book on SME). Obtuse meanings are to be found not everywhere (the signifier is rare, a future figure) but *somewhere*: in other *authors* of films (perhaps), in a certain manner of reading "life" and so "reality" itself (the word is simply used here in opposition to the deliberately fictive). In image XVI from *Ordinary Fascism* (by Mikhail Romm), a documentary image, I can easily read an obvious meaning, that of fascism (aesthetics and symbolics of power, the theatrical hunt), but I can also read an obtuse meaning: the (again) disguised, blond silliness of the young quiver-bearer, the flabbiness of his hands and mouth (I cannot manage to describe, only to designate a location), Goering's thick nails, his trashy ring (this already on the brink of obvious meaning, like the treacly platitude of the imbecile smile of the

[2] [Georges Bataille, "Le gros orteil," *Documents*, Paris 1968, pp. 75–82.]

bespectacled man in the background—visibly an "arse-licker"). In other words, the obtuse meaning is not situated structurally, a semantologist would not agree as to its objective existence (but then what is an objective reading?); and if to me it is clear (to me), that is *still* perhaps (for the moment) by the same "aberration" which compelled the lone and unhappy Saussure to hear in ancient poetry the enigmatic voice of anagram, unoriginated and obsessive. Same uncertainty when it is a matter of *describing* the obtuse meaning (of giving an idea of where it is going, where it goes away). The obtuse meaning is a signifier without a signified, hence the difficulty in naming it. My reading remains suspended between the image and its description, between definition and approximation. If the obtuse meaning cannot be described, that is because, in contrast to the obvious meaning, it does not copy anything— how do you describe something that does not represent anything? The pictorial "rendering" of words is here impossible, with the consequence that if, in front of these images, we remain, you and I, at the level of articulated language—at the level, that is, of my own text—the obtuse meaning will not succeed in existing, in entering the critic's metalanguage. Which means that the obtuse meaning is outside (articulated) language while nevertheless within interlocution. For if you look at the images I am discussing, you can see this meaning, we can agree on it "over the shoulder" or "on the back" of articulated language. Thanks to the image (fixed, it is true; a factor which will be taken up later) or much rather thanks to what, in the image, is purely image (which is in fact very little), we do without language yet never cease to understand one another.

In short, what the obtuse meaning disturbs, sterilizes, is metalanguage (criticism). A number of reasons can be given for this. First and foremost, obtuse meaning is discontinuous, indifferent to the story and to the obvious meaning (as signification of the story). This dissociation has a de-naturing or at least a distancing effect with regard to the referent (to "reality" as nature, the realist instance). Eisenstein would probably have acknowledged this incongruity, this im-pertinence of the signifier, Eisenstein who tells us concerning sound and color: "Art begins the moment the creaking of a boot on the sound track occurs against a different visual shot and thus gives rise to corresponding associations. It is the same with color: color begins where it no longer corresponds to natural coloration . . ." Then, the signifier (the third meaning) is not filled out, it keeps a permanent state of *depletion* (a word from linguistics which designates empty, all-purpose verbs, as for example the French verb *faire*). We could also say on the contrary—and it would be just as correct—that this same signifier is not empty (cannot empty itself), that it maintains a state of perpetual erethism, desire not finding issue in that spasm of the signified which normally brings the subject voluptuously back into the peace of nominations. Finally, the obtuse meaning can be seen as an *accent*, the very form of an emergence, of a fold (a crease even) marking the heavy layer of informations and significations. If it could be described (a contradiction in terms), it would have exactly the nature of the Japanese *haiku*—anaphoric gesture without significant content, a sort of gash rased of meaning (of desire for meaning). Thus in image V:

> Mouth drawn, eyes shut squinting,
> Headscarf low over forehead,
> She weeps.

This accent—the simultaneously emphatic and elliptic character of which has already been mentioned—is not directed toward meaning (as in hysteria), does not theatricalize (Eisensteinian decorativism belongs to another level), does not even indicate an *elsewhere* of meaning (another content, added to the obvious meaning); it outplays meaning—subverts not the content but the whole practice of meaning. A new—rare—practice affirmed against a majority practice (that of signification), obtuse meaning appears necessarily as a luxury, an expenditure with no exchange. This luxury does not *yet* belong to today's politics but nevertheless *already* to tomorrow's.

Something has still to be said concerning the syntagmatic responsibility of the third meaning: what is its place in the movement of the anecdote, in the logico-temporal system without which, so it seems, it is impossible to communicate a narrative to the "mass" of readers and spectators? It is clear that the obtuse meaning is the epitome of a counter-narrative; disseminated, reversible, set to its own temporality, it inevitably determines (if one follows it) a quite different analytical segmentation to that in shots, sequences and syntagms (technical or narrative)—an extraordinary segmentation: counter-logical and yet "true." Imagine "following" not Euphrosyne's schemings, nor even the character (as diegetic entity or symbolic figure), nor even, again, the face of the Wicked Mother, but merely, in this face, this attitude, this black veil, the heavy, ugly flatness—you will then have a different time-scale, neither diegetic nor oneiric, a different film. A theme with neither variations nor development (the obvious meaning is fully thematic: there is a theme of the Funeral), the obtuse meaning can only come and go, appearing–disappearing. The play of presence/absence undermines the character, making of it a simple nub of facets; a disjunction expressed in another connection by SME himself: *"What is characteristic is that the different positions of one and the same czar . . . are given without link between one position and the next."*

Precisely. The *indifference* or freedom of position of the supplementary signifier in relation to the narrative allows us to situate with some exactitude the historical, political, theoretical task accomplished by Eisenstein. In his work, the story (the diegetic, anecdotal representation) is not destroyed—quite the contrary: what finer story than that of *Ivan* or *Potemkin*? This importance given to the narrative is necessary in order *to be understood* in a society which, unable to resolve the contradictions of history without a long political transaction, draws support (provisionally?) from mythical (narrative) solutions. The *contemporary* problem is not to destroy the narrative but to subvert it; today's task is to dissociate subversion from destruction. It seems to me that SME operates such a distinction: the presence of an obtuse, supplementary, third meaning—if only in a few images, but then as an imperishable signature, as a seal endorsing the whole of the work (and the whole of his work)—radically recasts the theoretical status of the anecdote: the story (the diegesis) is no longer just a strong system (the millennial system of narrative) but also and contradictorily a simple space, a field of permanences and permutations. It becomes that configuration, that stage, whose false limits multiply the signifier's permutational play, that vast trace which, by difference, compels what SME himself calls a *vertical* reading, that *false* order which permits the turning of the pure series, the aleatory combination (chance is crude, a signifier on the cheap) and the attainment of a structuration *which slips away from the inside*. It can thus be said that with SME we have to reverse the cliché according to which the more gratuitous a meaning, the more it will appear as a mere parasite of the story being narrated; on the contrary, it is this story which here finds itself in some sort parametric to the signifier for which it is now merely the field of displacement, the constitutive negativity, or, again, the fellow-traveler.

In other words, the third meaning structures the film *differently* without—at least in SME—subverting the story and for this reason, perhaps, it is at the level of the third meaning, and at that level alone, that the "filmic" finally emerges. The filmic is that in the film which cannot be described, the representation

which cannot be represented. The filmic begins only where
language and metalanguage end. Everything that can be *said*
about *Ivan* or *Potemkin* can be said of a written text (entitled
Ivan the Terrible or *Battleship Potemkin*) except this, the obtuse meaning; I can gloss everything in Euphrosyne, except the
obtuse quality of her face. The filmic, then, lies precisely here,
in that region where articulated language is no longer more
than approximative and where another language begins (whose
science, therefore, cannot be linguistics, soon discarded like a
booster rocket). The third meaning—theoretically locatable
but not describable—can now be seen as the *passage* from
language to *significance* and the founding act of the filmic
itself. Forced to develop in a civilization of the signified, it is
not surprising that (despite the incalculable number of films
in the world) the filmic should still be rare (a few flashes in
SME, perhaps elsewhere?), so much so that it could be said that
as yet the film does not exist (any more than does the text);
there is only "cinema," language, narrative, poetry, sometimes
extremely "modern," "translated" into "images" said to be
"animated." Nor is it surprising that the filmic can only be
located after having—analytically—gone across the "essential," the "depth" and the "complexity" of the cinematic work;
all those riches which are merely those of articulated language, with which we constitute the work and believe we exhaust it. The filmic is not the same as the film, is as far removed from the film as the novelistic is from the novel (I can
write in the novelistic without ever writing novels).

THE STILL

Which is why to a certain extent (the extent of our theoretical
fumblings) the filmic, very paradoxically, cannot be grasped
in the film "in situation," "in movement," "in its natural
state," but only in that major artefact, the still. For a long
time, I have been intrigued by the phenomenon of being in-

terested and even fascinated by photos from a film (outside a cinema, in the pages of *Cahiers du cinéma*) and of then losing everything of those photos (not just the captivation but the memory of the image) when once inside the viewing room— a change which can even result in a complete reversal of values. I at first ascribed this taste for stills to my lack of cinematic culture, to my resistance to film; I thought of myself as like those children who prefer the pictures to the text, or like those clients who, unable to attain the adult possession of objects (because too expensive), are content to derive pleasure from looking at a choice of samples or a department store catalogue. Such an explanation does no more than reproduce the common opinion with regard to stills which sees them as a remote subproduct of the film, a sample, a means of drawing in custom, a pornographic extract, and, technically, a reduction of the work by the immobilization of what is taken to be the sacred essence of cinema—the movement of the images.

If, however, the specific filmic (the filmic of the future) lies not in movement, but in an inarticulable third meaning that neither the simple photograph nor figurative painting can assume since they lack the diegetic horizon, the possibility of configuration mentioned earlier,[3] then the "movement" regarded as the essence of film is not animation, flux, mobility,

[3] There are other "arts" which combine still (or at least drawing) and story, diegesis—namely, the photo-novel and the comic strip. I am convinced that these "arts," born in the lower depths of high culture, possess theoretical qualifications and present a new signifier (related to the obtuse meaning). This is acknowledged as regards the comic strip but I myself experience this slight trauma of *significance* faced with certain photo-novels: *"their stupidity touches me"* (which could be a certain definition of obtuse meaning). There may thus be a future—or a very ancient past—truth in these derisory, vulgar, foolish, dialogical forms of consumer subculture. And there is an autonomous "art" (a "text"), that of the *pictogram* ("anecdotalized" images, obtuse meanings placed in a diegetic space); this art taking across historically and culturally heteroclite productions: ethnographic pictograms, stained-glass windows, Carpaccio's *Legend of Saint Ursula, images d'Epinal*, photo-novels, comic strips. The innovation represented by the still (in comparison with these other pictograms) would be that the filmic (which it constitutes) is *doubled* by another text, the film.

"life," copy, but simply the framework of a permutational un-folding and a theory of the still becomes necessary, a theory whose possible points of departure must be given briefly here in conclusion.

The still offers us the *inside* of the fragment. In this con-nection we would need to take up—displacing them—Eisen-stein's own formulations when envisaging the new possibilities of audio-visual montage: ". . . the basic center of gravity . . . is transferred to *inside* the fragment, into the elements included in the image itself. *And the center of gravity is no longer the element 'between shots'—the shock—but the element 'inside the shot'—the accentuation within the fragment . . .*" Of course, there is no audio-visual montage in the still, but SME's formula is general insofar as it establishes a right to the syn-tagmatic disjunction of images and calls for a *vertical* reading of the articulation. Moreover, the still is not a sample (an idea that supposes a sort of homogeneous, statistical nature of the film elements) but a quotation (we know how much importance presently accrues to this concept in the theory of the text): at once parodic and disseminatory. It is not a specimen chemically extracted from the substance of the film, but rather the trace of a superior *distribution* of traits of which the film as experienced in its animated flow would give no more than one text among others. The still, then, is the fragment of a second text *whose existence never exceeds the fragment*; film and still find them-selves in a palimpsest relationship without it being possible to say that one is *on top of* the other or that one is *extracted* from the other. Finally, the still throws off the constraint of filmic time; which constraint is extremely powerful, continuing to form an obstacle to what might be called the adult birth of film (born technically, occasionally even aesthetically, film has still to be born theoretically). For written texts, unless they are very conventional, totally committed to logico-temporal order, reading time is free; for film, this is not so, since the image cannot go faster or slower without losing its perceptual figure. The still, by instituting a reading that is at once instantaneous and vertical, scorns logical time (which is only an operational time); it teaches us how to dissociate the technical constraint from what is the specific filmic and which is the "indescribable" meaning. Perhaps it was the reading of *this other text* (here in stills) that SME called for when he said that a film is not simply to be seen and heard but to be scrutinized and listened to attentively. This seeing and this hearing are obviously not the postulation of some simple need to apply the mind (that would be banal, a pious wish) but rather a veritable mutation of reading and its object, text or film—which is a crucial problem of our time.

1970

Fourier

BEGINNINGS

I

ONE DAY I was invited to eat a couscous with rancid butter; the rancid butter was customary; in certain regions it is an integral part of the couscous code. However, be it prejudice, or unfamiliarity, or digestive intolerance, I don't like rancidity. What to do? Eat it, of course, so as not to offend my host, but gingerly, in order not to offend the conscience of my disgust (since for disgust *per se* one needs some stoicism). In this difficult meal, Fourier would have helped me. On the one hand, intellectually, he would have persuaded me of three things: the first is that the rancidness of couscous is in no way an idle, futile, or trivial question, and that debating it is no more futile than debating Transubstantiation;[1] the second is that by forcing me to lie about my likes (or dislikes), society is manifesting its *falseness*, i.e., not only its hypocrisy (which is banal) but also the vice of the social mechanism whose gearing is faulty; the third, that this same society cannot rest until it has guaranteed (how? Fourier has clearly explained it,

From *Sade/Fourier/Loyola*, translated by Richard Miller (New York: Hill and Wang, 1976).

[1] "First we will deal with the puerility of these battles over the superiority of sweet cream or little pies; we might reply that the debate will be no more ridiculous than our Religious Wars over Transubstantiation" (VII, 346).

but it must be admitted that it hasn't worked) the exercise of my manias, whether "bizarre" or "minor," like those of people who like old chickens, the eater of horrid things (like the astronomer Lalande, who liked to eat live spiders), the fanatics about butter, pears, bergamots, Ankles, or "Baby Dolls."[2] On the other hand, practically, Fourier would at once have put an end to my embarrassment (being torn between my good manners and my lack of taste for rancid things) by taking me from my meal (where, in addition, I was stuck for hours, a barely tolerable situation against which Fourier protested) and sending me to the Anti-Rancid group, where I would be allowed to eat fresh couscous as I liked without bothering anyone—which would not have kept me from preserving the best of relations with the Rancid group, whom I would henceforth consider as not at all "ethnic," foreign, strange, at for example a great couscous tournament, at which couscous would be the "theme," and where a jury of gastrosophers would decide on the superiority of rancid over fresh (I almost said: *normal*, but for Fourier, and this is his victory, there is no normality).[3]

---

[2] "Ankles" are men who like to scratch their mistress's ankle (VII, 335); the "Baby Doll" is a sixty-year-old man who, desirous of being treated like a spoiled child, wants the soubrette to punish him by "gently patting his patriarchal buttocks" (VII, 334).

[3] Fourier would, I am sure, have been enraptured at my friend Abd el Kebir's entry into the couscous tournament, in defense of the Rancid side, in a letter I received from him:

"I am not a Rancist either. I prefer couscous with pumpkin, and a light sprinkling of raisins—well blended, of course—and that produces: an insubordination of the expression.

"The apparent instability of the Moroccan peasant's culinary system proceeds, dear friend, from the fact that rancid butter is made in a strange underground hearth at the intersection of cosmic time and the time of consumption. Rancid butter is a kind of decomposed property, pleasing to interior monologue.

"Dug out in handfuls, rancid butter is worked in the following circular rite: a huge and magnificent ball of couscous is ejaculated into the throat to such an extent that the rancidity is neutralized. Fourier would call it a double-focus ellipse.

"This is why the peasant works to get rid of it: the parabole means a surplus, since the earth belongs to God. He inters the fresh butter, then extracts it when the time is ripe. However, the female is the one, the

II

Fourier likes compotes, fine weather, perfect melons, the
little spiced pastries known as *mirlitons,* and the company of
lesbians. Society and Nature hinder these tastes a bit: sugar is
(or was) expensive (more expensive than bread), the French
climate is insupportable except in May, September, and October, we know no sure method of detecting a melon's quality, in
Civilization little pastries bring on indigestion, lesbians are
proscribed and, blind for a long time as far as he himself was
concerned, Fourier did not know until very late in life that he
liked them. Thus the world must be remade for my pleasure:
my pleasure will be simultaneously the ends and the means: in
organizing it, in distributing it, I shall overwhelm it.

III

Everywhere we travel, on every occasion on which we feel
a desire, a longing, a lassitude, a vexation, it is possible to ask
Fourier, to wonder: What would he have said about it? What
would he make of this place, this adventure? Here am I one
evening in a southern Moroccan hotel: some hundred meters
outside the populous, tattered, dusty town, a park filled with
rare scents, a blue pool, flowers, quiet bungalows, hordes of
discreet servants. In Harmony, what would that give? First of
all, this: there would come to this place all who have this
strange liking, this low mania for dim lights in the woods,

---

squatter, always squatting down, who carries out the operation from above.
Slow and painstaking preparation, making my couscous taste rather androgy-
nous.

"Thus, I agree to act within its limits: the rancid is an imperative fantasy.
The pleasure is in eating with the group.

"Relating this manner of conserving butter underground to a traditional
practice of mental healing, the frenzied madman is buried for a day or two,
left almost naked, without food. When he is brought out, he is often reborn
or really dies. Between heaven and earth there are signs to be seen for those
who know.

"The high price put on couscous—a truly enigmatic material—obliges me to
sign off and to send you my friendly wishes."

candlelit dinners, a staff of native servants, night frogs, and a camel in a meadow beneath the window. Then this rectification: the Harmonians would scarcely have need of this place, luxurious owing to its temperature (spring in mid-winter), because, by acting on the atmosphere, by modifying the polar cap, this exotic climate could be transported to Jouy-en-Josas or Gif-sur-Yvette. Finally, this compromise: at certain times during the year, hordes of people, driven by a taste for travel and adventure, would descend upon the idyllic motel and there hold their councils of love and gastronomy (it would be just the place for our couscous investigations). From which, once again, it emerges: that Fourierist pleasure is the end of the tablecloth: pull the slightest futile incident, provided it concerns your happiness, and all the rest of the world will follow: its organization, its limits, its values; this sequence, this fatal induction which ties the most tenuous inflection of our desire to the broadest sociality, this unique space in which fantasy and the social combinative are trapped, this is very precisely *systematics* (but not, as we shall see, the system); with Fourier, impossible to relax without constructing a theory about it. And this: in Fourier's day none of the Fourierist system had been achieved, but today? Caravans, crowds, the collective search for fine climate, pleasure trips, exist: in a derisory and rather atrocious form, the organized tour, the planting of a vacation club (with its classed population, its planned pleasures) is there in some fairy-tale site; in the Fourierist utopia there is a twofold reality, realized as a farce by mass society: *tourism*—the just ransom of a fantasmatic system which has "forgotten" politics, whereas politics pays it back by "forgetting" no less systematically to "calculate" for our pleasure. It is in the grip of these two forgettings, whose confrontation determines total futility, insupportable emptiness, that we are still floundering.

THE CALCULATION OF PLEASURE

The motive behind all Fourierist construction (all combination) is not justice, equality, liberty, etc., it is pleasure. Fourierism is not a radical eudaemonism. Fourierist pleasure (*positive happiness*) is very easy to define: it is sensual pleasure: "amorous freedom, good food, insouciance, and the other delights that the Civilized do not even dream of coveting because philosophy has taught them to treat the desire for true pleasures as vice."[4] Fourierist sensuality is, above all, oral. Of course, the two major sources of pleasure are equally Love and Food, always in tandem; however, although Fourier pushes the claims of erotic freedom, he does not describe it sensually; whereas food is lovingly fantasized in detail (compotes, *mirlitons*, melons, pears, lemonades); and Fourier's speech itself is sensual, it progresses in effusiveness, enthusiasm, throngs of words, verbal gourmandise (neologism is an erotic act, which is why he never fails to arouse the censure of pedants).

This Fourierist pleasure is commodious, *it stands out*: easily isolated from the heteroclite hotchpotch of causes, effects, values, protocols, habits, alibis, it appears throughout in its sovereign purity: mania (the ankle scratcher, the filth eater, the "Baby Doll") is never captured save through the pleasure it procures for its partners, and this pleasure is never encumbered with other images (absurdities, inconveniences, difficulties); in short, there is no metonymy attached to it: pleasure is what it is, nothing more. The emblematic ceremony of this

[4] Let us briefly recall that in the Fourierist lexicon, *Civilization* has a precise (numbered) meaning: the word designates the 5th period of the 1st phase (Infancy of Mankind), which comes between the period of the federal patriarchate (the birth of large agriculture and manufacturing industry) and that of guaranteeism or demi-association (industry by association). Whence a broader meaning: in Fourier, *Civilization* is synonymous with wretched barbarism and designates the state of his own day (and ours); it contrasts with universal Harmony (2nd and 3rd phases of mankind). Fourier believed himself to be at the axis of Barbaric Civilization and Harmony.

isolation of essence would be a *museum orgy*: it consists of a simple exposition of the desirable, "a séance wherein notable lovers lay bare the most remarkable thing they have. A woman whose only beautiful feature is her bosom exposes only the bosom and is covered elsewhere . . ." (we refrain from commenting on the fetishist character of this framework, evident enough; his intention not analytical but merely ethical, Fourier would not deign to take fetishism into a symbolic, reductive system: that would be merely a mania *along with* others, and not inferior or superior to them).

Fourierist pleasure is free from evil: it does not include vexation, in the Sadean manner, but on the contrary dissipates it; his discourse is one of "general well-being": for example, in the war of love (game and theater), out of delicacy, in order not to disturb, no flags or leaders are captured. If, however, in Harmony, one chances to suffer, the entire society will attempt to divert you: have you had some failure in love, have you been turned down, the Bacchantes, Adventuresses, and other pleasure corporations will surround you and lead you off, instantly efface the harm that has befallen you (they exercise, Fourier says, philanthropy). But if someone has a mania to harass? Should they be allowed? The pleasure of harassing is due to a congestion; Harmony will decongest the passions, sadism will be reabsorbed: Dame Strogonoff had the unpleasant habit of harassing her beautiful slave by piercing her breast with pins; in fact, it was counterpassion: Dame Strogonoff was in love with her victim without knowing it: Harmony, by authorizing and favoring Sapphic loves, would have relieved her of her sadism. Yet a final threat: satiety: how to *sustain* pleasure? "How act so as to have a continually renewed appetite? Here lies the secret of Harmonian politics." This secret is twofold: on the one hand, change the race and, through the overall benefits of the societal diet (based on meats and fruits, with very little bread), form physiologically stronger men, fit for the renewal of pleasures, capable of digesting more quickly, of being hungry more frequently; and on the other hand, vary pleasures incessantly (never more than two hours at the same task), and from all these successive pleasures make one sole continual pleasure.

Here we have pleasure alone and triumphant, it reigns over all. Pleasure cannot be measured, it is not subject to quantification, its nature is the *overmuch* ("Our fault is not, as has been believed, to desire *overmuch*, but to desire *too little* . . ."); it is itself the measurement: "feeling" depends on pleasure: "The privation of the sensual need degrades feeling," and "full satisfaction in material things is the only way to elevate the feelings": counter-Freudianism: "feeling" is not the sublimating transformation of a lack, but on the contrary the panic effusion of an acme of satiety. Pleasure overcomes Death (pleasures will be sensual in the afterlife), it is the Federator, what operates the solidarity of the living and the dead (the happiness of the defunct will begin only with that of the living, they having in a way to *await* the others: no happy dead so long as on earth the living are not happy; a view of a generosity, a "charity" that no religious eschatology has dared). Pleasure is, lastly, the everlasting principle of social organization: whether, negatively, it induces a condemnation of all society, however progressive, that neglects it (such as Owen's experiment at New Lamarck, denounced as "too severe" because the societaries went barefoot), whether, positively, pleasures are made *affairs of State* (*pleasures* and not *leisure*: this is what separates—fortunately—the Fourierist Harmony from the modern State, where the pious organization of leisure time corresponds to a relentless censure of pleasure); pleasure results, in fact, from a *calculation*, an operation that for Fourier is the highest form of social organization and mastery; this calculation is the same as that of all societal theory, whose practice is to transform work into pleasure (and not to suspend work for the sake of leisure time): the barrier that separates work from pleasure in Civilization crumbles, there is a paradigmatic fall, philosophical conversion of the unpleasant into the attractive (taxes will be paid "as readily as the busy mother sees to those foul but attractive duties her infant demands"), and pleasure itself becomes an exchange value, since Harmony recognizes and honors, by the name of *Angelicate*, collective prostitution: it is in a way the monad of energy which in its thrust and scope ensures the advance of society.

Since pleasure is the Unique, to reveal pleasure is itself a unique duty: Fourier stands alone against everyone (especially against all the Philosophers, against all Libraries), he alone is right, and being right is the desirable thing: "Is it not to be desired that I alone am right, against everyone?" From the Unique derives the incendiary character of pleasure: it burns, shocks, frightens to speak of it: how many are the statements about the mortal shock brought on by the overabrupt revelation of pleasure! What precautions, what preparations of writing! Fourier experiences a kind of prophylactic obligation for dispassion (poorly observed, by the way: he imagines his "calculations" are boring and that reassures him, whereas they are delightful); whence an incessant restraint of the discourse: "fearing to allow you to glimpse the vastness of these pleasures, I have only dissertated on . . ." etc.: Fourier's discourse is never just propaedeutic, so blazing with splendor is its object, its center:[5] articulated on pleasure, the sectarian world is *dazzling*.

The area of Need is *Politics*, the area of Desire is what

[5] "If we could suddenly see this arranged Order, this work of God as it will be seen in its full functioning . . . it is not to be doubted that many of the Civilized would be struck dead by the violence of their ecstasy. The description [of the 8th Society] alone could inspire in many of them, the women in particular, an enthusiasm that would approach frenzy; it could render them indifferent to amusements, unsuited to the labors of Civilization" (I, 65).

Fourier calls *Domestics*. Fourier has chosen Domestics over Politics, he has constructed a domestic utopia (but can a utopia be otherwise? can a utopia ever be political? isn't politics: *every language less one*, that of Desire? In May 1968, there was a proposal to one of the groups that were spontaneously formed at the Sorbonne to study *Domestic Utopia*—they were obviously thinking of Fourier; to which the reply was made that the expression was too "studied," *ergo* "bourgeois"; politics is what forecloses desire, save to achieve it in the form of neurosis: political neurosis or, more exactly: the neurosis of politicizing).

MONEY CREATES HAPPINESS

In Harmony, not only is wealth redeemed, but it is also magnified, it participates in a play of felicitous metaphors, lending the Fourierist demonstrations either the ceremonial brio of jewels ("the diamond star in a radiant triangle," the decoration of amatory sainthood, i.e., widespread prostitution) or the modesty of the sou ("20 sous to Racine for his tragedy *Phèdre*": multiplied, true, by all the cantons that have chosen to honor the poet); the operations connected with money are themselves motifs in a delectable game: in the game of love, that of the redemption (repurchase) of captives. Money participates in the brilliance of pleasure ("The senses cannot have their full indirect scope without the intervention of money"): money is desirable, as in the best days of civilized corruption, beyond which it perpetuates itself by virtue of a splendid and "incorruptible" fantasy.

Curiously detached from commerce, from exchange, from the economy, Fourierist money is an analogic (poetic) metal, the sum of happiness. Its exaltation is obviously a countermeasure: it is because all (civilized) Philosophy has condemned money that Fourier, destroyer of Philosophy and critic of Civilization, rehabilitates it: *the love of wealth* being a pejorative *topos* (at the price of a constant hypocrisy: Seneca, the man who possessed 80 million sesterces, declared that one must instantly rid oneself of wealth), Fourier turns contempt into praise:[6] marriage, for example, is a ridiculous ceremony,[7] save "when a man marries a very rich woman; then there is occasion for rejoicing"; everything, where money is concerned, seems to be conceived in view of this counterdiscourse, frankly scandalous in relation to the literary constraints of the admonition: "Search out the tangible wealth, gold, silver, precious metals, jewels, and objects of luxury despised by philosophers."[8]

However, this fact of discourse is not rhetorical: it has that energy of language that in writing makes the discourse waver, it forms the basis for the major transgression against which *everyone*—Christians, Marxists, Freudians—for whom money continues to be an accursed matter, fetish, excrement, has spoken out: who would dare defend money? There is *no discourse* with which money can be compatible. Because it is completely solitary (Fourier does not find on this point among his colleagues, "literary agitators," any co-maniac), Fourierist transgression lays bare the most secret area of the Civilized conscience. Fourier exalted money because for him the image of happiness was properly furnished with the mode of life of

[6] "Whence a conclusion that may seem facetious but that will nonetheless be rigorously demonstrated; in the 18 societies of Combined Order, the most basic quality for the triumph of truth is the love of wealth" (I, 70). "Glory and science are truly desirable, of course, but quite insufficient when unaccompanied by fortune. Fame, trophies, and other illusions do not lead to happiness, which consists first of all in the possession of wealth . . ." (I, 14).

[7] "One must be born in Civilization to tolerate the sight of those indecent customs known as marriages, where one sees the simultaneous coincidence of magistrate and priest with the fools and drunks of the neighborhood" (I, 174).

[8] Since the coming of Harmony was imminent, Fourier counseled the Civilized to profit at once from the few goods of Civilization; this is the age-old theme (reversed, i.e., positive): Live to the full now, tomorrow is another day, it is futile to save, to keep, to transmit.

the wealthy: a shocking view today, in the eyes of the contestants themselves, who condemn all pleasure induced from
the bourgeois model. We know that metonymy (contagion) is
the purview of Error (of religion); Fourier's radical materialism stems from his constant, vigilant refusal of any metonymy.
For him, money is not a conductor of sickness but merely the
dry, pure element in a combinative to be reordered.

INVENTOR, NOT WRITER

To remake the world (including Nature), Fourier mobilized: an intolerance (for Civilization), a form (classification), a standard (pleasure), an imagination (the "scene"), a
discourse (his book). All of which pretty well defines the
action of the signifier—or the signifier in action. This action
continually makes visible on the page a glaring lack, that of
science and politics, that is, of the signified.[9] What Fourier
lacks (for that matter voluntarily) points in return to what we
ourselves lack when we reject Fourier: to be ironic about
Fourier is always—even from the scientific point of view—to
censure the signifier. Political and Domestic (the name of
Fourier's system),[10] science and utopia, Marxism and Fourierism, are like two nets whose meshes are of different sizes.
On the one hand, Fourier allows to pass through all the science that Marx collects and develops; from the political point
of view (and above all since Marxism has given an indelible
name to its shortcomings), Fourier is completely *off to one
side*, unrealistic and immoral. However, the other, facing, net

---

[9] ". . . seek the good only in operations having no relationship with the
administration or with the priesthood, that rest solely on industrial or
domestic measures and that are compatible with any government, without
having need of their intervention" (I, 5).
[10] ". . . to demonstrate the extreme facility of exiting from the civilized
labyrinth, without political upheaval, without scientific effort, but by a
purely domestic operation" (I, 126).

allows pleasure, which Fourier collects, to pass through.[11] Desire and Need pass through, as though the two nets were alternatively superimposed, playing at topping hands. However, the relationship of Desire and Need is not *complementary* (were they fitted one into the other, everything would be perfect), but *supplementary*: each is the *excess* of the other. The *excess*: what does not pass through. For example, seen from today (i.e., *after* Marx), politics is a necessary purge; Fourier is the child who avoids the purge, who vomits it up.

The vomiting of politics is what Fourier calls Invention. Fourierist invention ("For me, I am an inventor, and not an orator") addresses the absolutely new, that about which nothing has yet been said. The rule of invention is a rule of refusal: to doubt absolutely (more than did Descartes, who, Fourier thought, never made more than a partial and misplaced use of doubt), to be in opposition with everything being done, to treat only of what has not been treated, to stand apart from "literary agitators," Book People, to preach what Opinion holds to be *impossible*. It is in sum for this purely structural reason (*old/new*) and through a simple constraint of the discourse (to speak only where there has not yet been speech) that Fourier is silent about politics. Fourierist invention is a fact of writing, a deploying of the signifier. These words should be understood in the modern sense: Fourier repudiates *the writer*, i.e., the certified manager of good writing, of literature, he who guarantees decorative union and thus the fundamental separation of substance and form; in calling himself an inventor ("I am not a writer, but an inventor"), he places himself at the limit of meaning, what we today call Text. Perhaps, following Fourier, we should henceforth call *inventor*

---

[11] ". . . sophists deceive us about their incompetency in calculations of amatory or petty politics, and occupy us exclusively with ambitious or major politics . . ." (IV, 51).

(and not *writer* or *philosopher*) he who proposes new formulae and thereby invests, by fragments, *immensely and in detail*, the space of the signifier.

THE META-BOOK

The meta-book is the book that talks about the book. Fourier spends his time talking about his book in such a way that the work of Fourier that we read, indissolubly blending the two discourses, finally forms an autonomous book, in which form incessantly states form.

Fourier escorts his book a long way. For example, he imagines a dialogue between bookseller and client. Or elsewhere, knowing his book will be brought into court, he establishes a whole institutional system of defense (judge, jury, lawyers) and diffusion (the rich reader who wants to clear up some doubts for himself will call in the author to give lessons, as in sciences and the arts: "a kind of relationship without consequences, as with a merchant from whom one buys": after all, it is something like what a writer does today, going off on lecture tours to repeat words he has stated in writing).

As for the book itself, he posits rhetoric, i.e., the adaptation of types of discourse to types of readers: the *exposition* is addressed to the "Curious" (that is, to studious men); the *descriptions* (insights into the delights of private Destinies) are addressed to Voluptuaries or Sybarites; the *confirmation*, pointing up the blunders of the Civilized in thrall to the Spirit of Commerce, is addressed to the Critics. We can distinguish bits of *perspective* and bits of *theory* (I, 160); there will be *insights* (abstract), *summaries* (half-concrete), *elaborate dissertations* (bodies of doctrine). It follows that the book (a somewhat Mallarméan view) is not only pieced out, articulated (a banal structure), but, further, mobile, subject to a rule of *intermittent* actualization: the chapters will be inverted, the reading will be speeded up (expedited movement) or slowed down, according to the class of readers we want to reach; at its limit, the book is composed of nothing but jumps, full of holes like Fourier's manuscripts (especially *Le Nouveau Monde amoureux*), whose words are constantly missing, eaten by mice, and which therefore have the dimensions of an infinite cryptogram whose key will be given later.

This reminds us of reading in the Middle Ages, based on the work's legal discontinuity: not only was the ancient text (subject of medieval reading) *broken up* and its fragments then capable of being diversely combined, but, further, it was normal to conduct on any subject two independent and concurrent discourses, shamelessly put in a redundant relationship: Donatus's *ars minor* (abridged) and *ars major* (extended), the Modistes' *modi minores* and *modi majores*; this is the Fourierist opposition of insight-abridgment and dissertation. Yet the effect of this doubling up is twisted, paradoxical. We would expect that like any redundancy it would completely cover the subject, fill it out and end it (what can be added to a discourse that essentializes its purpose in résumé form and develops it in the form of an elaborate dissertation?). Now the contrary: the duplicity of the discourse produces an *interstice* through which the subject leaks away; Fourier spends his time in withholding the decisive utterance of his doctrine, concerning it he gives us only examples, seductions, "appetizers"; the message of his book is the announcement of a forthcoming message: *wait a little longer, I will tell you the essential very soon.* This method of writing could be called *counter-paralypse* (the paralypse is the rhetorical figure that consists in stating what one is not going to say and thus stating what one pretends not to say: *I shall not speak of . . .* followed by three pages). The paralypse implies the conviction that the indirect is a profitable mode of language; however, Fourier's countermarch, other than that it obviously translates the neurotic fear of failure (like that of a man afraid to jump—which Fourier,

transferring to the reader, utters as the mortal fear of pleasure), points out the vacuum of language: caught in the toils of
the meta-book, his book is *without subject*: its signified is
dilatory, incessantly withdrawn further away: only the signifier
remains, stretching out of sight, *in the book's future.*

THE OLD SHOE ABLAZE

Somewhere, Fourier speaks of "nocturnal furnishings."
What do I care that this expression is the trace of an earth-
shaking transport? I am carried away, dazzled, convinced by a
kind of *charm* in the expression, which is its delight. Fourier is
crammed full of these delights: no discourse was ever *happier*.
With Fourier, the expression derives its felicity (and ours)
from a kind of upheaval: it is excentric, displaced, it lives on
its own, outside its context (the context, the semanticists'
puzzler, has all the ingratitude of law: it reduces polysemy,
clips the wings of the signifier: doesn't all poetry consist in
liberating the word from its context? doesn't all philosophy
consist in putting it back?). I do not resist these pleasures,
they seem "true" to me: I have been "taken in" by the form.

Of what do these charms consist: of a counter-rhetoric, that
is, a way of contriving figures by introducing into their code a
"grain" (of sand, of madness). Let us here, once again (after
many centuries of rhetorical classification), distinguish tropes
(or simple metaboles) and figures (or ornaments that act
upon an entire syntagm). Fourier's metaphorical vein is the
path of truth; it supplies him with simple metaphors of a definitive precision ("from delivery vans we derive *fatigue dress*,
the gray cloak and trousers"), it clarifies meaning (monological function), but at the same time and contradictorily it clarifies *ad infinitum* (poetical function), not only because the
metaphor is drawn out, orchestrated ("Nocturnal furnishings
will be considerably assorted and composed of our vivid and
variously colored moons, next to which Phoebe will appear as

what she is, a pale ghost, a sepulchral lamp, a Swiss cheese. One would have to have as bad taste as the Civilized do to admire this pallid mummy"), but further and above all because the Fourierist syntagm simultaneously produces a sonorous pleasure and a logical vertigo. Fourier's enumerations (for his verbal "delirium," based on calculation, is basically enumerative) always contain a preposterous point, a twist, a wrinkle: ". . . the ostrich, the deer, the jerboa . . .": why the jerboa, unless for the sonorous flourish at the end, for the sound? "And what can Hell in its fury invent worse than the rattlesnake, the bug, the legion of insects and reptiles, the sea monsters, poisons, plague, rabies, leprosy, venereal disease, gout, and all the morbiferous virulences?": the bug and the sea monster? Rattlesnakes and venereal disease? This string of nonsense derives a final savor from the *morbiferous*, plump and brilliant, more alimentary than funereal, both sensual and ridiculous (Molièresque), that crowns it; for the enumerative *cumulus*, in Fourier, is as abrupt as the movement of the head of an animal, a bird, a child who has heard "something else": "There will remain only the useful strains, like the whiting, the herring, the mackerel, sole, tuna, tortoise, in short, all those that do not attack swimmers . . .": what charms us is not the content (after all, there is no question that these fish are beneficent), but a certain turn that makes the affirmation vibrate toward its opposite region: mischievously, through an irresistible metonymy seizing the words, a vague image becomes detached which, across the denegation, reveals the whiting and the mackerel in the process of attacking a swimmer . . . (a properly surrealist mechanism). Paradoxical, for it is always in the name of the "concrete" that Civilization claims to teach the "mad," it is always through the "concrete" that Fourier becomes absurd and charming at once: the "concrete" is constructed in a scene, the substance calls upon the practices metonymically attached to it; the coffee break refers to the whole of civilized bureaucracy: "Isn't it shocking to see thirty-year-old athletes crouched over desks and transporting a cup of coffee with their hairy arms, as though there weren't women and children to attend to the finicky functioning of offices and households?" This vivid representation provokes laughter because it is out of proportion with its signified; hypotypose usually serves to illustrate intense and noble passions (Racine: "Imagine, Céphise . . ."); in Fourier, it is demonstrative; a kind of anacoluthon intervenes between the domestic detail of the example and the scope of the utopian plan. This is the secret of these amusing syntagms frequent in Fourier (in Sade too) that join in a single sentence a very ambitious thought and a very futile object; starting from the notion of the culinary contests in Harmony ("thesis meals"), Fourier continues to concoct strange and delicious, ridiculous and decisive syntagms, in which the tiny pastries (which he so liked, *mirlitons*) are associated with highly abstract terms ("the 44 systems of tiny pastries," "the batches of tiny pastries anathemized by the council," "the tiny pastries adopted by the Council of Babylon," etc.). Very precisely, this is what we can now call *paragrammatics*: namely, the superimpression (in dual hearing) of two languages that are ordinarily foreclosed to each other, the braid formed by two classes of words whose traditional hierarchy is not annulled, balanced, but—what is more subversive—disoriented: Council and System lend their nobility to tiny pastries; tiny pastries lend their futility to Anathema, a sudden contagion *deranges* the institution of language.

The transgression Fourier commits goes even further. The frivolous object he promotes to demonstrative rank is very often a *base* object. This conversion is justified because Harmony recuperates what Civilization disdains and transforms it into a delightful good ("If the Vaucluse phalanstery harvests 50,000 melons or watermelons, almost 10,000 of them will be

set aside for its own consumption, 30,000 for exportation, and
10,000 will be of inferior grade and divided among horses,
cats, and for fertilizer": here we find that art of enumerative
cadence we have just mentioned: Fourierist enumeration is
always reverse conundrum: what is the difference between a
horse, a cat, and fertilizer? None, for the function of all three
is to reabsorb inferior-grade melons). Thus a poetics of rubbish is constructed, magnified by the societary economy (e.g.,
the old marinated chickens). Fourier knows this poetics well:
he knows the emblems of rubbish, the old shoe, the rag, the
sewer: an entire episode in *Le Nouveau Monde amoureux*
(VII, 362 *et seq.*) hymns the exploits of the new crusaders,
dealers in old shoes and boot cleaners, whose arrival at the
Euphrates crossing is greeted by a magnificent display of fire-
works "ending with an old shoe ablaze, beneath which is the
legend: Long live pious cobblers."

Naturally, Fourier was aware of the "ridiculousness" of his
demonstrative objects (of his rhetoric);[12] he was well aware
that the bourgeoisie is devoted to the hierarchical division of
languages, objects, and usages as strongly as it is to those of
class, that nothing is worse in their eyes than the crime of lèse-
language, and that one has only to join a noble (abstract)
word and a base (denoting a sensual or repulsive object) term
to be sure of loosing their zeal as proprietors (of "fine" language); he knew that people made fun of his faithful melons,
of the triumph of his leathery fowl, of the English debt paid off
in hens' eggs. Yet he assumed the incongruity of his demonstrations with a certain martyred air (the martyrdom of the
inventor). Thus to the paragrammaticism of his examples (in-

---

[12] "This respectable convoy of cobblers marches after them in pomp and
the finest boat is loaded with their baggage and this is the arm upon which
they learn to win the palms of true glory. Bah! glory in old shoes, our Civilized
will say; I was expecting this stupid response. And what fruit have they
gleaned from the trophies of St. Louis and Bonaparte who have led immense
armies vast distances only to have them drown in their trophies after having
ravaged the country and been execrated by it?" (VII, 364).

terweaving two exclusive languages, one noble, one outcast),
must be added a final, infinitely dizzier, ambiguity: that of
their utterance. Where is Fourier? in the invention of the example (old marinated chickens)? in the indignation he feels at
the laughter of others? In our reading, which simultaneously
encompasses the ridicule and his defense? The loss of the
subject in the writing has never been more complete (the subject becoming totally irreparable) than in these utterances
where the disconnection of the utterance occurs *ad infinitum*,
without a brake, on the model of the game of topping hands or
the game of "rock, scissors, paper": texts whose "ridiculousness" or "stupidity" is based on no certain utterance and over
which, consequently, the reader can never gain any advantage
(Fourier, Flaubert). "God," Fourier says, "displays a subtle
and judicious irony in creating certain products that are enigmatic in quality, like the melon, made for the innocent mystification of banquets ill suited to divine methods, without in any
way deceiving the gastronomes who cleave to the divine or
societary diet" [allusion to the difficulty that exists in choosing
a good melon, "such a perfidious fruit for the Civilized"]. "I
do not mean to say that God created the melon solely for the
sake of this jest, but it is part of that fruit's many uses. Irony is
never overlooked in the calculations of nature. . . . The melon
has among its properties that of *ironic harmony* . . ." (in short,
the melon is an element of a *writing*). What reader can hope
to *dominate* such an utterance—adopt it as a laughable or a
critical object, *dictate to it*, in a word?—in the name of *what
other language*?

HIEROGLYPHICS

Fourier wants to decipher the world in order to remake it
(for how remake it without deciphering it?).

Fourierist deciphering starts from the most difficult of situations, which is not so much the latency of signs as their con-

tent. There is a saying of Voltaire that Fourier refers to in this regard: "But what obscure night still enveileth nature?"; now, in this veil finally there is less the notion of mask than of a cloth. Once again, the task of the logothete, of the founder of language, is an endless cutting up of the text: the primary operation is to "grab" the cloth in order then to pull on it (to pull it off).

We must therefore in some measure make a distinction between deciphering and cutting up. Deciphering refers to a pregnant depth, to an area of relationships, to a distribution. In Fourier, deciphering is postulated, but in a completely minor way: it concerns the lies and pretenses of the Civilized classes: thus the "secret principles" of the bourgeois "who begins by debiting a hundred lies in his shop by virtue of the principles of free trade. Hence a bourgeois goes to hear Mass and returns to debit three to four hundred lies, to trick and steal from thirty or so buyers in line with the secret principle of businessmen: we are not working for glory, we want money" (VII, 246). Quite another thing, and of quite another order of importance, is cutting up—or systematization (putting to a system); this reading, an essential part of the Fourierist task, concerns all of Nature (societies, sentiments, forms, natural kingdoms) as it represents the total space of Harmony —Fourier's man being totally incorporated into the universe, including the stars; this is no longer a denunciatory, reductive reading (limited to the moral falsehoods of the bourgeoisie), but an exalting, integrating, restorative reading, extended to the plethora of universal forms.

Is the "real" the object of this second reading? We are accustomed to considering the "real" and the residue as identical: the "unreal," the fantasmatic, the ideological, the verbal, the proliferating, in short, the "marvelous," may conceal from us the "real," rational, infrastructural, schematic; from real to unreal there may be the (self-seeking) production of a screen

of arabesques, whereas from unreal to real there may be critical reduction, an alethic, scientific movement, as though the
real were at once more meager and more essential than the
superstructions with which we have covered it. Obviously,
Fourier is working on a conceptual material whose constitution denies this contrast and which is that of the *marvelous
real*. This marvelous real is contrasted with the marvelous
ideal of novels; it corresponds to what we might call, contrasting it directly with the novel, the novelesque. This marvelous
real very precisely is the signifier, or if one prefers, "reality,"
characterized, relative to the scientific real, by its fantasmatic
train. Now, the category under which this novelesque begins to
be read is the *hieroglyphic*, different from the symbol as the
signifier can be from the full, mystified sign.

The hieroglyph (the theory of which is set forth principally
in the *Théorie des Quatre Mouvements*, I, 31 *et seq.* and 286
et seq.) postulates a formal and arbitrary correspondence (it
depends on Fourier's free will: it is an idiolectal concept)
between the various realms of the universe, for example between forms (circle, ellipse, parabola, hyperbola), colors,
musical notes, passions (friendship, love, parental, ambition),
the races of animals, the stars, and the periods of societal
phylogenesis. The arbitrary obviously resides in the attribution: why is the ellipse the geometric hieroglyph for love? The
parabola for parenthood? Yet this arbitrary is just as relative
as is that of linguistic signs: we believe there to be an arbitrary
correspondence between the signifier /pear tree/ and the signified "pear tree," between some Melanesian tribe and its totem
(bear, god), because we spontaneously (i.e., by virtue of historical, ideological determinations) imagine the world in substitute, paradigmatic, analogical terms, and not in serial, associative, homological—in short, poetic—terms. Fourier has this
second imagination; for him, the basis of meaning is not substitution, equivalence, but the proportional series; just as the

signifier /pear tree/ or the signifier *bear* is *relatively* motivated
if taken in the series *pear tree–plum tree–apple tree* or in the
series *bear–dog–tiger*, so Fourierist hieroglyphics, detached
from any univocity, accede to language, i.e., to a system both
conventional and reasonable. The hieroglyphic, in fact, implies
a complete theory of meaning (whereas only too often, relying
on the presence of the dictionary, we reduce meaning to a
substitution): hieroglyphics, says Fourier, can be explained in
three ways: (1) *by contrast* (beehive/wasp's nest, elephant/
rhinoceros): this is the paradigm: the beehive is *marked* with
productivity, a characteristic absent in the wasp's nest; the elephant is marked with lengthy defenses, a trait reduced to a
short horn in the rhinoceros; (2) *by alliance* (the dog and the
sheep, the pig and the truffle, the donkey and the thistle): this
is the syntagm, metonymy: these elements usually go together;
(3) lastly, *by progression* (branches: giraffe, stag, buck, roe-
buck, reindeer, etc.): this, foreign to linguistic classification, is
the *series*, a kind of extended paradigm, consisting of differences and proximities, out of which Fourier creates the very
principle of societal organization, which basically consists in
putting in a phalanstery contrasting groups of individuals, each
group linked by an affinity: for example, the sectine of Flower-
lets, amateurs of small, varied flowers, contrasted to but coex-
isting with the Rosist sectine: it might be said that the series is
an actualized, syntagmatized paradigm, by virtue of the number of its terms, not only *livable* (whereas the semantic paradigm is subject to the law of rival, inexpiable opposites, which
cannot cohabit), but even *felicitous*. Progression (the series)
is undoubtedly what Fourier adds to meaning (as linguists
describe it for us), and consequently, what frustrates its arbitrary nature. Why, for example, in Association, is the giraffe
the hieroglyph for Truth (I, 286)? A farfetched notion and
assuredly unjustifiable if we try, desperately, to discover some
affinitive or even contrasting trait shared by Truth and this

huge mammiferous ungulant. The explanation is that the giraffe is caught up in a system of homologies: Association having the beaver as its practical hieroglyph (because of its associative and constructive abilities) and the peacock as its visual hieroglyph (because of the spread of its nuances), we need, across from but yet in the same series, that of animals, a properly unfunctional element, a kind of neuter, a zero degree of zoological symbolism: this is the giraffe, as useless as the Truth is in Civilization; whence a counter-giraffe (complex term of contrast): this is the Reindeer, from which we derive every imaginable service (in the societary order there will even be a new animal created, even more ecumenical than the Reindeer: the Anti-Giraffe).

So replaced in the history of the sign, the Fourierist construction posits the rights of a baroque semantics, i.e., open to the proliferation of the signifier, infinite and yet structured.

LIBERAL?

The combination of differences implies the respecting of the individuation of each term: there is no attempt to redress, to correct, to annul taste, whatever it may be (however "bizarre" it may be); quite the contrary, it is affirmed, it is emphasized, it is recognized, it is legalized, it is reinforced by associating everyone who wishes to indulge it: taste being thus incorporated, it is allowed to act in opposition to other tastes at once affinitive and different: a competitive game (of intrigue, but *coded*) is initiated between the amateurs of bergamot pears and the amateurs of butter pears: to the satisfaction of a simple taste (a liking for pears) is then added the exercise of other, formal, combinative passions: for example, *cabalistics*, or the passion for intrigues, and *butterfly*, if there are unstable Harmonians who take pleasure in switching from the bergamot pear to the butter pear.

From this semantic construction of the world it follows that, in Fourier's eyes, "association" is not a "humanist" principle: it is not a matter of bringing together everyone with the same mania ("co-maniacs") so that they can be comfortable together and can enchant each other by narcissistically gazing at one another; on the contrary, it is a matter of associating to combine, to contrast. The Fourierist coexistence of passions is not based on a liberal principle. There is no noble demand to "understand," to "admit" the passions of others (or to ignore them, indeed). The goal of Harmony is neither to further the conflict (by associating through similitude), nor to reduce it (by sublimating, sweetening, or normalizing the passions), nor yet to transcend it (by "understanding" the other person), but to exploit it for the greatest pleasure of all and without hindrance to anyone. How? By playing at it: by making a text of the conflictual.

PASSIONS

Passion (character, taste, mania) is the irreducible unity of the Fourierist combinative, the absolute grapheme of the utopian text. Passion is *natural* (nothing to be corrected about it, unless to produce a *contra-naturam*, which is what occurs in Civilization). Passion is *clean* (its being is pure, strong, shapely: only Civilized philosophy advises flaccid, apathetic passions, controls, and compromises). Passion is *happy* ("Happiness . . . consists in having many passions and ample means to satisfy them," I, 92).

Passion is not the idealized form of feeling, mania is not the monstrous form of passion. Mania (and even whim) is the very being of passion, the unit from which Attraction (attractive and attracting) is determined. Passion is neither deformable, nor transformable, nor reducible, nor measurable, nor substitutable: it is not a force, it is a number: there can be neither decomposition nor amalgamation of this happy, frank, natural monad, but only combination, up to the reunion of the *integral soul*, the trans-individual body of 1,620 characters.

THE TREE OF HAPPINESS

The passions (810 for each sex) spring, like the branches of a tree (the classifier's fetish tree) from three main trunks: *lustful-ness*, which includes the passions of feeling (one for each of the five senses), *group-ness* (four basic passions: honor, friendship, love, and family), and *serial-ness* (three distributive passions). The entire combinative stems from these twelve passions (whose pre-eminence is not moral, merely structural).

The first nine passions are derived from classical psychology, but the latter, formal, three are a Fourierist invention. The Dissident (or Cabalistic) is a reflective enthusiasm, a passion for intrigue, a calculating mania, an art of exploiting differences, rivalries, conflicts (here there is no difficulty in recognizing the paranoid texture); it is the delight of courtesans, women, and philosophers (intellectuals), which is why it can also be called the Speculative. The Composite (actually less well defined than its fellows) is the passion for excess, for (sensual or sublime) exaltation, for multiplication; it can be called the Romantic. The Variating (or Alternating or Butterfly) is a need for periodic variety (changing occupation or pleasure every two hours); we might say that it is the disposition of the subject who does not devote himself to the "good object" in a stable manner: a passion whose mythical prototype is Don Juan: individuals who constantly change occupation, manias, affections, desires, "cruisers" who are incorrigible, unfaithful, renegade, subject to "moods," etc.: a passion disdained in Civilization, but one Fourier places very high: the one that permits ranging through many passions at once, and like an agile hand on a multiple keyboard, creating a *harmoni-*

ous (appropriately put) vibration throughout the integral soul; an agent of universal transition, it animates that type of happiness that is attributed to Parisian sybarites, *the art of living well and fast, the variety and interconnection of pleasures,* rapidity of movement (we recall that for Fourier the mode of life of the possessing class is the very model of happiness).

These three passions are formal: included in the classification, they ensure its functioning ("mechanics"), or more precisely still: its game. If we compare the aggregate of the passions to a deck of cards or a chess set (as did Fourier), the three distributive passions are in sum the rules of this game; they state how to conciliate, balance, set in motion, and permit the transformation of the other passions, each of which would be nugatory in isolation, into a series of "brilliant and countless combinations." These rules of the game (these formal, distributive passions) are precisely the ones society rejects: they produce (the very sign of their excellence) "the characters accused of corruption, called libertines, profligates, etc.": as in Sade, it is syntax and syntax alone that produces the supreme immorality.

Thus the twelve radical passions (like the twelve notes in the scale). Naturally, there is a thirteenth (every good classifier knows he must have a supernumber in his chart and that he must make adjustments for the outcome of his system), which is the very trunk of the tree of passions: Unity-ness (or Harmonism). Unity-ness is the passion for unity, "the individual's tendency to reconcile his happiness with that of everything around him, and with every human type"; this supplementary passion produces the Originals, people who appear to be ill at ease in this world and who cannot accommodate themselves to the ways of Civilization; it is thus the passion of Fourier himself. Unity-ness is in no way a moral, recommendable passion (*love each other, unite with each other*), since the societal unit is a combinative, a structural game of differences; Unity-ness is in direct contrast to simplism, the vice of the Civilized spirit, "the use of the mind without the marvelous, or of the marvelous without the mind"; simplism "made Newton miss out on the discovery of the system of Nature and Bonaparte on the conquest of the world." Simplism (or totalitarianism, or monologism) would today be either the censure of Need or the censure of Desire; which, in Harmony (in Utopia), would be answered by the combined science of one and the other.

NUMBERS

Fourier's authority, the Reference, the Citation, the Science, the Anterior Discourse that enables him to speak and to have personal authority concerning the "carelessness of 25 learned centuries that failed to conceive of it," is *calculation* (as for us today it is formalization). This calculation need not be extensive or complicated: it is a *petty calculation*. Why petty? Because although important (the happiness of mankind depends upon it), this calculation is simple. Further, pettiness includes the notion of a certain affectionate complacence: Fourier's petty calculation is the simple lever that opens up the fantasmagory of adorable detail.

Everything occurs as though Fourier were searching for the very notion of detail, as though he had found it in a numeration or frantic subdivision of every object that came into his mind, as though this object instantly released in him a number or a classification: it is like a conditioned reflex that comes into play apropos a whole crazy total: "In Rome in the time of Varro there were 278 contradictory opinions concerning true happiness." A question of illicit liaisons (in Civilization)? They exist for Fourier only if he enumerates them: "During the twelve years of bachelorhood, man forms on the average 12 liaisons of illicit love, around 6 of fornication and 6 adulterous, etc." Everything is a pretext for numbering, from the age of the world (80,000 years) to the number of characters in it (1,620).

The Fourierist number is not rounded off, and in fact this is what gives it its insanity (a minor sociological problem: why does our society consider a decimal number "normal" and an intradecimal number "irrational"? At what point does normality occur?). This insanity is often justified by the even more insane reasons Fourier gives in denying the arbitrary constants in his accounts, or, which is even crazier still, displaces this arbitrary by justifying not the number given, but the standard for it: the height of societary man will be 84 thumbs or 7 feet; why? we will never know, but the unit of measurement is pompously justified: "I am not being arbitrary in indicating the foot of the King of Paris as a natural measurement; it has this property because it is equal to the 32nd part of the water level in suction pumps" (here we find that sudden twisting of the syntagm, the anacoluthon, the audacious metonymy that makes Fourier's "charm": in the space of a few words, we have suction pumps mingled with the height of societary man). The number exalts, it is an operator of glory, as is the triangular number of the Trinity in the Jesuit mode, not because it enlarges (which would destroy the fascination with detail), but because it demultiplies: "Consequently, if we divide by 810 the number of 36 million which the population of France has attained, we will find that in this Empire there exist 45,000 capable of equaling Homer, 45,000 capable of equaling Demosthenes, etc." Fourier is like a child (or an adult: the author of these lines, never having studied mathematics, has been very late in experiencing this feeling) discovering with enchantment the exorbitant power of combinatory analysis or geometrical progression. In the end, the number itself is not needed for this exaltation; one need only subdivide a class in order triumphantly to achieve this paradox: detail (literally: *minutia*) magnifies, like joy. It is a fury of expansion, of possession, and, in a word, of orgasm, by number, by classification: scarcely does an object appear than Fourier taxinomizes (we are tempted to say: sodomizes) it: is the husband unhappy in Civilized marriage? It is *immediately* for eight reasons (risk of unhappiness, expense, vigilance, monotony, sterility, widowhood, union, ignorance of his wife's infidelity). Does the word "harem" arise *currente calamo* into the sentence? *Immediately*, there are three classes of odalisks: honest women, petites bourgeoises, and courtesans. What happens to women over eighteen years of age in Harmony? nothing, save to be *classified: Wives* (themselves subdivided into *constant, doubtful*, and *unfaithful*), *Misses* or *Demi-dames* (they change protectors, but successively, having only one at a time), and *Galantes* (both further subdivided); for both terms in the series, two taxinomic embellishments: *Damsels* and *Independents*. Wealth? there are not only Rich and Poor, there are: the poor, those who scrape by, those who have just enough, the comfortable, and the rich. Of course, for anyone. with the contrary mania, tolerant neither of number nor of classification nor of system (numerous in Civilization, jealous of "spontaneity," of "life," of "imagination," etc.), the Fourierist Harmony would be hell itself: at thesis meals (contest meals), every course would have two labels, written in large letters, visible from afar and set on pivots, in both directions, "so that one can be read from across the table and the other the length of the table" (the present author has experienced a minor hell of this sort—but the system came from a French brain: in the American college where he took his meals, in order that the students might converse profitably while eating, and that they might benefit equally from the professor's lively discourse, each diner was supposed to advance one place at each meal, moving closer to the professorial sun, "in a clockwise direction," as the rule stated; there is little need to say that no "conversation" resulted from this astral movement).

Perhaps the *imagination of detail* is what specifically defines Utopia (opposed to political science); this would be logical, since detail is fantasmatic and thereby achieves the very pleasure of Desire. In Fourier, the number is rarely statistical (designed to assert averages, probabilities); it is, through the apparent finesse of its precision, essentially quantitative. Nuance, the game being stalked in this taxinomic hunting expedition, is a guarantee of pleasure (of fulfillment), since it determines a *just* combinative (knowing with whom to group ourselves in order to achieve complementarity with our own differences). Harmony must thus admit the operators of nuances, just as a tapestry workshop has specialists who are detailed to knot the threads. These nuance makers are: either operations (in Fourierist erotics, the "simple salute" is a preambular bacchanalia, a scrimmage enabling the partners to test each other before making a choice; during it, "trial caresses or reconnoiterings of the terrain" are practiced; this takes about eight minutes), or they are agents: there are: either "confessors" (these confessors do not hear any Fault: they "psychoanalyze" in order to elicit sympathies, often hidden by the subjects' appearance and ignorance: they are the decipherers of complementary nuances) or "dissolvents" (dissolvents, introjected into a group that has not yet found its just combinative, its "harmony," produce tremendous effects on it: they undo erroneous couplings by revealing to each his passions, they are transferers, mutators: thus lesbians and pederasts, who, thrown into the scrimmage, first accost the "champions of their own ilk," "recognize their own kind and sunder a good number of couples whom chance had united").

Nuance, the acme of number and of classification, has the *integral soul* as its total field, a human space defined by its amplitude, since it is the combinative dimension within which meaning is possible; no man is self-sufficient, no one his own integral soul: we need 810 characters of both sexes, or 1,620, to which are added the omnititles (the complex degree of contrasts) and the infinitesimal nuances of passion. The integral soul, a tapestry in which each nuance finds utterance, is the great sentence being sung by the universe: it is, in sum, the language of which each of us is but a word. The Language is immortal: "At the era of the planet's death, its great soul, and consequently ours, inherent in it, will pass on to another, new sphere, to a planet which will be implaned, concentrated, saturated . . ."

THE NECTARINE

In any classification of Fourier, there is always a portion that is reserved. This portion has various names: passage, composite, transition, neuter, triviality, ambiguity (we might call it: *supplement*); naturally, it has a number: it is the ⅛ of any collection. First, this ⅛ has a function, familiar to scientists: it is the legal margin of error. ("Calculations of attraction and Social Mobility are all subject to the ⅛ exception . . . it will always be understood.") Only, since in Fourier it is always a question of the *calculation of happiness*, error is at once ethical: when (abhorrent) Civilization "makes a mistake" (in its own system), it produces happiness: in Civilization, the ⅛ thus represents happy people. It is easy from this example to see that for Fourier the ⅛ portion does not derive from a liberal or statistical concession, from the vague recognition of a possible *deviation*, from a "human" failing in the system (to be taken philosophically); quite the contrary, it is a question of an important structural function, of a code constraint. Which one?

As a classifier (a taxinomist), what Fourier needs most are passages, special terms that permit making transitions (meshing) from one class to another,[13] the kind of lubricator the

---

[13] "Transitions are to passionate equilibrium what bolts and joints are to a framework."

combinatory apparatus must use so as not to creak; the reserved portion is thus that of Transitions or Neuters (the neuter is what comes *between* the mark and the non-mark, this sort of buffer, damper, whose role is to muffle, to soften, to fluidify the semantic *tick-tock*, that metronome-like noise the paradigmatic alternative obsessively produces: *yes/no, yes/no, yes/no*, etc.). The nectarine, which is one of these Transitions, damps the opposition of prune and peach, as the quince damps that of pear and apple: they belong to the ⅛ of fruits. This portion (⅛) is shocking because it is contradictory: it is the class in which everything that attempts to escape classification is swallowed up; however, this portion is also superior: the space of the Neuter, of the *supplement of classification*, it joins realms, passions, characters; the art of employing Transitions is the major art of Harmonian calculation: the neuter principle is controlled by mathematics, the pure language of the combinative, of the composed, the very badge of the *game*.

There are ambiguities in every series: the sensitive, the bat, the flying fish, the amphibians, the zoophytes, sapphism, pederasty, incest, Chinese society (half-barbaric, half-civilized, with harems and courts of law and etiquette), lime (fire and water), the nervous system (body and soul), twilights, coffee (ignominiously ignored for Mocha for 4,000 years, then suddenly the subject of a mercantile craze, passing from abjection to the highest rank), children (the third passionate sex, neither men nor women). Transition (mixed, Ambiguous, Neuter) is everything that is contrary duplicity, junction of extremes, and hence it takes as its emblematic form the ellipse, which has a double focus.

In Harmony, Transitions have a beneficent role; for example, they prevent monotony in love, despotism in politics: the distributive passions (composite, cabalistic, and butterfly) have a transitional role (they "mesh," ensure changes of "objects"); Fourier always reasoned contrariwise, what is beneficent in Harmony necessarily proceeds from what is discredited or rejected in Civilization: thus Transitions are "trivialities," ignored by civilized scholars as unworthy subjects: the bat, the albino, ugly ambiguous race, the taste for feathered fowl. The prime example of Trivial Transition is Death: transition ascending between Harmonian life and the happiness of the other life (sensual happiness), it "will shed all its odiousness when philosophy deigns to consent to study the transitions it proscribes as trivial." Everything rejected in Civilization, from pederasty to Death, has in Harmony a value that is eminent (but not pre-eminent: nothing dominates anything else, everything combines, meshes, alternates, revolves). This functional *justness* (this *justice*) is ensured by the ⅛ error. Thus, the *Neuter* is in opposition to the *Median*; the latter is a quantitative, not a structural, notion; it is the amount of the oppression to which the large number subjects the small number; caught in a statistical calculation, the intermediate swells up and engulfs the system (thus the *middle* class: the neuter, on the other hand, is a purely qualitative, structural notion; it is what *confuses* meaning, the norm, normality. To enjoy the *neuter* is perforce to be disgusted by the *average*.

SYSTEM/SYSTEMATICS

". . . that the real content of these systems is hardly to be found in their systematic form is best proved by the orthodox Fourierists . . . who, despite their orthodoxy, are the exact antipodes of Fourier: doctrinaire bourgeois."—MARX AND ENGELS, *German Ideology*

Fourier perhaps enables us to restate the following opposition (which we lately stated by distinguishing the novelistic from the novel, poetry from the poem, the essay from the dissertation, the writing from the style, production from the product, structuration from the structure[14]): the *system* is a

[14] *S/Z.*

body of doctrine within which the elements (principles, facts, consequences) develop logically, i.e., from the point of view of the discourse, rhetorically. The system being a closed (or monosemic) one, it is always theological, dogmatic; it is nourished by illusions: an illusion of transparency (the language employed to express it is purportedly purely instrumental, it is not a writing) and an illusion of reality (the goal of the system is to be *applied*, i.e., that it leave the language in order to found a reality that is incorrectly defined as the exteriority of language); it is a strictly paranoid insanity whose path of transmission is insistence, repetition, cathechism, orthodoxy. Fourier's work does not constitute a *system*; only when we have tried to "realize" this work (in phalansteries) has it become, retrospectively, a "system" doomed to instant fiasco; system, in the terminology of Marx and Engels, is the "systematic form," i.e., pure ideology, ideological reflection; *systematics* is the play of the system; it is language that is open, infinite, free from any referential illusion (pretension); its mode of appearance, its constituency, is not "development" but pulverization, dissemination (the gold dust of the signifier); it is a discourse without "object" (it only speaks of a thing obliquely, by approaching it indirectly: thus Civilization in Fourier) and without "subject" (in writing, the author does not allow himself to be involved in the imaginary subject, for he "performs" his enunciatory role in such a manner that we cannot decide whether it is serious or parody). It is a vast madness which does not end, but which permutates. In contrast to the system, monological, systematics is dialogical (it is the operation of ambiguities, it does not suffer contradictions); it is a writing, it has the latter's eternity (the perpetual permutation of meanings throughout History); systematics is not concerned with application (save as purist imagining, a theater of the discourse), but with transmission, (significant) circulation; further, it is transmittable only on condition it is *de-*

formed (by the reader); in the terminology of Marx and Engels, systematics would be the *real contents* (of Fourier). Here, we are not explaining Fourier's system (that portion of his systematics that plays with the system in an image-making way), we are talking solely about the several sites in his discourse that belong to systematics.

(Fourier puts the system to flight—cuts it adrift—by two operations: first, by incessantly delaying the definitive exposé until later: the doctrine is simultaneously highhanded and dilatory; next, by inscribing the system in the systematics, as dubious parody, shadow, game. For example, Fourier attacks the civilized [repressive] "system," he calls for an integral freedom [of tastes, passions, manias, whims]; thus, we would expect a spontaneistic philosophy, but we get quite the opposite: a wild system, whose very excess, whose fantastic tension, goes beyond system and attains systematics, i.e., writing: liberty is never the opposite of order, it is *order paragrammatized*: the writing must simultaneously mobilize an image and its opposite.)

THE PARTY

What is a "party"? (1) *a partitioning*, isolating one group from another, (2) an orgy, or *partouze*, as we say in French, wherein the participants are linked erotically, and (3) a hand, or *partie*, the regulated moment in a game, a collective diversion. In Sade, in Fourier, the party, the highest form of societary or Sadean happiness, has this threefold character: it is a worldly ceremony, an erotic practice, a social act.

Fourierist life is one immense party. At three-thirty in the morning on the summer solstice (little sleep is needed in Harmony), societary man is ready for the world: engaged in a succession of "roles" (each one being the naked affirmation of a passion) and subject to the combinative (meshing) rules of these roles: this very exactly is the definition of mundanity, which functions like a language: the mundane man is someone who spends his time *citing* (and *weaving* what he cites). The citations Fourier employs in blissfully describing the worldly life of societary man are drawn paradoxically (paragrammatically) from the repressive lexicons of the Civilized regime: the Church, State, Army, Stock Exchange, Salons, the penitentiary colony, and Scouting furnish the Fourierist party with its most felicitous images.[15]

All mundanity is dissociative: it is a matter of isolating oneself in order to retreat and to trace out the area within which the rules of the game can function. The Fourierist party has two traditional enclosures, that of time and that of place.

The topography of the phalanstery traces an original site which is broadly that of palaces, monasteries, manors, and great blocks of buildings in which are mingled an organization of the building and an organization of territory, so that (a very modern viewpoint) architecture and urbanism reciprocally withdraw in favor of an overall science of human space, the primary characteristic of which is no longer protection, but movement: the phalanstery is a retreat within which one moves (however, trips are taken outside the phalanstery: great mass excursions, ambulatory "parties"). Obviously, this space is functionalized, as shown in the following reconstruction (very approximate, since Fourierist discourse, like all writing, is irreducible).

The greatest concern of this organization is communication. Like the adolescent groups who live together during their summer vacations with constant pleasure and regretfully return home in the evenings, the societaries have only a tem-

---

[15] Innumerable locutions, such as: "Saints and Patrons beatified and canonized in the council of the Spheric Hierarchy." "Every pivotal sin is liable to a sevenfold reparation" (VII, 191)—true, that this reparation is hardly penitential, consisting as it does of making love seven times with seven different people. "The Official Journal of Gastronomic Transactions of the Army of the Euphrates" (VII, 378), etc.

porary place for undressing and sleeping, warmed only by a brazier. In contrast, Fourier describes with great predilection and insistence the covered, heated, ventilated galleries, sanded basements, and corridors raised on columns that connect the palaces or manors of neighboring Tribes. A private place is allowed solely for lovemaking, and even this is only so that the unions made during the bacchanalias, get-togethers, or meetings for the purpose of selecting a companion, can be consummated—or "sealed."

PEACEFUL PURSUITS

| Gardens | Meals
Study
Council | Winter
courtyard | Telegraph
Pigeons
Temple
Bell tower | Gardens |

Parade ground

| Noises:
Workshops
Forges
Children | Maneuvers | Caravansery
Balls
Visitors |

| Farming | Stables | Silos | Storerooms | Farming |

There are three stories, children on mezzanine

Corresponding to topographical delimitation is this apparatus for temporal enclosure called *timing*; since a passion (for investments, for objects) must be changed every two hours, the optimal time is a divided time (the function of *timing* is to demultiply duration, to superproduce time and thereby to augment life power: "The day will never be long enough for the intrigues and merry reunions produced by the new order": we might be listening to an adolescent who, on vacation, has discovered his "group"); for example, in the combined Order there are five meals (at 5 a.m., the matutinal or "eye opener," at 8 a.m., lunch, dinner at 1, snack at 6, and supper at 9), and two collations (at 10 and 4): reminiscent of the schedule in an old-fashioned sanatorium. Harmonian man—physiologically regenerated by a diet of happiness—sleeps only from 11 in the evening to 3:30 in the morning; he never makes love at night, a detestable Civilized habit.

Love (erotic happiness, including the sentimental *eros*) is the main business of the long Harmonian day: "In Harmony, where no one is poor and where everyone is acceptable for lovemaking until a very advanced age, everyone devotes a set part of the day to this passion and love thus becomes a principal business: it has its code, its tribunals [we already know that the penalties consist in new loves], its court, and its institutions." Like the Sadean *eros*, Fourier's is a classifier, a distributor: the population is divided into amorous classes. In Sade, there are storytellers, fuckers, etc.; in Fourier there are troops of Vestals, Youths and Favorites of both sexes, Genitors, etc. From Sade to Fourier, only the *ethos* of the discourse changes: here jubilant, there euphoric. For the erotic fantasy remains the same; it is that of *availability*: that every love demand *at once* find a subject-object to be *at its disposal*, either by constraint or by association; this is the province of the ideal orgy, or in French, *partouze*, a fantasmatic site, contra-civilized, where no one refuses himself to anyone, the purpose not being to multiply partners (not a quantitative problem!) but to abolish the wound of denial; the abundance of erotic material, precisely because it is a matter of Desire and not of Need, is not intended to constitute a "consumer society" of love, but, paradox, truly utopian scandal, to make Desire function in its contradiction, namely: to fulfill *perpetu-*

ally (*perpetually* meaning simultaneously *always* and *never* fulfilled; or: *never and always*: that depends on the degree of enthusiasm or bitterness in which the fantasy is concluded). This is the sense of the supreme amorous institution of Fourierist society: the Angelicate (another ecclesiastical citation): in Harmony, the Angelicate is this handsome couple who, through "philanthropy," properly give themselves to any man or woman desiring them (including the deformed). The Angelicate has an additional function, not philanthropic but mediatory: it *conducts* desire: as though, left on his own, every man were incapable of knowing whom to desire, as though he were blind, powerless to invest his desire, as though it were always up to others to show us *where the desirable is* (clearly not the principal function of so-called erotic representations in mass culture: conduction, not substitution); the Angelic couple is the apex of the amorous triangle: it is the vanishing point without which there can be no erotic *perspective*.[16]

The party, a ritual common in Sade and in Fourier, has as its "proof" a fact of the discourse which is to be found in both: the amorous practice cannot be uttered save in the form of a "scene," a "scenario," a "tableau vivant" (a strictly fantasmatic disposition): the Sadean "séances" which often even have a "setting": gardens, woods, colored veils, garlands of flowers, in Fourier the Cnidian novel. In fact, they are part of the very force of fantasy, of the destructive power it has over cultural models by using them *disrespectfully*, of "representing" the erotic scene in the most insipid colors and with the "proper" tone of petit-bourgeois art: Sade's most shocking

---

[16] Can a more Sadean classification be imagined than the following: the Angelicate is organized along three degrees of novitiate: (1) *cherubic* (the postulant must sacrifice an entire day to each member of the venerable choir); (2) *seraphic* (the sacrifice lasts several days and is offered to both sexes); (3) *sayidic* (the sacrifice is offered up to a chorus of patriarchs: probably even older!).

scenes, Fourier's pro-sapphic ravings, occur in a Folies-Bergère setting: a carnival-like conjunction of transgression and opera, the sober site of mad acts, where the *subject is swallowed up in its culture,* a decision that simultaneously sweeps away art and sex, denies transgression itself any gravity, prohibits its ritualization (by providing for widespread prostitution the stage setting of *The Pearl Fishers*), the headlong flight of the signified across the shifting of aesthetics or sex, which ordinary language tries to achieve in its fashion when it speaks (in French) of *ballets roses* and *ballets bleus* ("performances" by girls [pink] or boys [blue] "danced" before older men).

COMPOTES

An Eastern book says there is no better remedy for thirst than a little cold compote, well sweetened, followed by a few swallows of cool water. Fourier would have been doubly enchanted at this advice: first, because of the conjunction of solid and liquid (the exemplar of a Transition, a Mix, a Neuter, a Passage, a Twilight); next, because of its promotion of compotes to the status of a philosophical food (the *Compound*, not the Simple, slakes thirst, desire).

Harmony will be sweet. Why? For many reasons, constructed in superdetermination (the likely index of a fantasy). First because sugar is an *anti-bread*; since bread is a mystic object of Civilization, the symbol of labor and bitterness, the emblem of Need, Harmony will invert the use of bread and turn it into the colophon of Desire; bread will become a luxury food ("one of the most costly and most husbanded victuals"); in contrast, sugar will become wheat.[17] Next, because sugar, hereby promoted, mixed with fruit in a compote, will form the

---

[17] "Then Africa will cheaply furnish the commodities of its hot climate, cane sugar, which, pound for pound, will have the value of wheat, when it is cultivated by 70 million Africans and all the peoples of the Torrid Zone" (II, 14).

bread of Harmony, the basic nourishment of those who have become wealthy and happy.[18] In a way, all Harmony has grown out of Fourier's taste for compotes, as a man's desire can grow out of a child's dream (here the dream of Candyland, of lakes of jam, of chocolate mountains): the opus turns the far-off fantasy into sense: an entire construct with immense, subtle ramifications (the societary regime, the cosmogony of the new world) grows out of the etymological metaphor: the compote (*composita*) being a composite, a euphoric system of the Mixed is built up; for example: is a hyperglycemic diet dangerous to health? Fourier is quick to invent a countersugar, itself often highly sugared: "There will be no drawbacks to this abundance of sweets when we can counterbalance sugar's wormy influence with a great abundance of alcoholic wines for men, white wines for women and children, acid beverages like lemonade, tart cedar . . ." Or rather: on the carrousel of the signifier, no one can say *what comes first*, Fourier's taste (for sugar, the negation of anything conflictual? for mixed fruits? for cooked food transformed into a semi-liquid consistency?) or the exaltation of a pure form, the composite-compote, the combinative. The signifier (Fourier is in full accord) is a non-originated, non-determined material, a text.

THE WEATHER

Antique rhetoric, especially the medieval, included a special topic, the *impossibilia* (*adunata* in Greek); the *adunaton* was a common site, a *topos*, based on the notion of an *over-abundance*: two naturally opposite, enemy elements (vulture and dove) were presented as peacefully living together ("The fire burns within the ice / The sun grows dark / I see the moon

---

[18] "Then compotes made up of one-fourth sugar will be lavished on children, because an equal measure of it will be cheaper than bread . . . ; man's pivotal nourishment must not be bread, a simple victual derived from one zone, but sugared fruit, a composed victual allying the produce of two zones" (IV, 19).

about to fall / This tree moves from its place," wrote Théophile de Viau); the impossible image served to stigmatize a
hateful tense, a shocking *contra-naturam* ("We will have seen
everything!"). Once again, Fourier inverts the rhetorical site;
he uses the *adunaton* to celebrate the marvels of Harmony, the
conquest of Nature by contra-natural means; for example,
nothing is more incontestably "natural" (eternal) than the
brackishness of the sea, whose water is undrinkable; Fourier,
by the aromal action of the North Polar cap, turns it to lemonade (tart cedar): a positive *adunaton*.

Fourier's *adunata* are many. They can all be reduced to the
(very modern) conviction that man's farming modifies the
climate.[19] For Fourier, human "nature" is not deformable
(merely combinable), but "natural" nature is modifiable (the
reason being that Fourier's cosmogony is *aromal*, tied to the
notion of the sexual fluid, whereas his psychology is discontinuous, dedicated to arrangement, not to effluvium). This
topos of the *impossible* abides by the categories of antique
rhetoric:

I

Chronographies (temporal impossibilities). "We shall be
witness to a spectacle to be seen once on each globe: the
sudden passage from incoherence to social combination. . . .
During this metamorphosis, each year will equal a century of
existence," etc.

II

Topographies. Spatial impossibilities, very numerous, arise
from what we call geography: (1) *Climatology:* (a) Fourier
changes climates, makes the Pole into a new Andalusia and
moves the pleasant temperature of Naples and Provence to the

[19] ". . . the air is a field, subject as is the earth to industrious exploitation"
(III, 97).

coast of Siberia; (b) Fourier improves the seasons, hateful in civilized France (theme: *Spring has fled!*): "1822 had no winter, 1823 no spring at all. This confusion, which has gone on for ten years, is the result of an aromal lesion the planet is suffering because of the undue duration of chaos, civilized, barbarous and savage" (theme: *It's because of the Bomb*); (c) Fourier orders micro-climates: "The atmosphere and its protection are an integral part of our clothing. . . . In Civilization, no one ever dreamed of improving that part of the clothing we call atmosphere, with which we are perpetually in contact" (the theme of the phalanstery's corridors, heated and ventilated). (2) *Podology:* "[Crusaders of old shoes] . . . are carried off en masse to Jerusalem and brought out to cover over with good soil and plantations that Calvary where the Christians come to recite useless Our Father's; in three days, a fertile mountain has been created. Thus their religion consists in usefulness and agreeableness toward those countries to which our stupid piety brought only ravage and superstition." (3) *Physical Geography:* Fourier subjects the map of the world to a veritable plastic surgery: he moves continents, grafts climates, "lifts" South America (as we lift breasts), "lowers" Africa, pierces isthmuses (Suez and Panama), permutates cities (Stockholm is put in the place of Bordeaux, St. Petersburg of Turin), makes Constantinople the capital of the Harmonian world. (4) *Astronomy:* "Man is called upon to displace and replace the stars."

III

Prosographies: modifications of the human body: (a) *Stature:* "Mankind's height will increase 2 to 3 inches per generation, until it has attained the average of 84 inches or 7 feet for men." (b) *Age:* "Then the full span of life will be 144 years and vigor proportionate." (c) *Physiology:* "This multitude of meals is necessary for the ravenous appetite the New

Order will create. . . . Children raised in this way will acquire iron temperaments and will be subject to a renewal of appetite every 2 or 3 hours, due to the speedy digestion that will result from the delicacy of the food" (here again we touch on a Sadean theme: what in Fourier is the regulation of indigestion by digestion becomes inverted [or set right] in Sade, where indigestion rules the digestion—coprophagy requires good fecal matter). (d) *Sex:* "In order to confound the tyranny of men there must have existed for a century a third sex, male and female, stronger than man."

It is nugatory to stress the reasonable nature of these ravings, because certain of them are being implemented (acceleration of History, the modification of climate through agriculture or urbanization, the piercing of isthmuses, the transformations of soils, the conversion of desert sites into cultivated sites, the conquest of the heavenly bodies, the increase in longevity, the physical improvement of the race). The most insane (the most resistant) *adunaton* is not the one that upsets the laws of "Nature," but the one that upsets the laws of language. Neologisms are Fourier's *impossibilia*. It is easier to predict the subversion of "the weather" than to imagine, as does Fourier, a masculine form of a feminine word, *Fés* for *Fées:* the upheaval of a strange graphic configuration in which femininity has been sunk, there is the true *impossible:* the impossible garnered from sex and language: in "*matrones* (feminine) and *matrons* (masculine)," a new, monstrous, transgressor *object* has come to mankind.

1971

Writers, Intellectuals, Teachers

WHAT follows depends on the idea that there is a fundamental tie between teaching and speech. The idea is a very old one (did not the whole of our teaching spring from Rhetoric?) but it is possible today to consider it differently from yesterday: firstly, because there is a (political) crisis in teaching; secondly, because (Lacanian) psychoanalysis has shown the mechanism of the twists and turns of empty speech; lastly, because the opposition between speech and writing has become an obvious fact with effects that now need to be gradually drawn out.

Over against the teacher, who is on the side of speech, let us call a *writer* every operator of language on the side of writing; between the two, the intellectual, the person who prints and publishes his speech. Between the language of the teacher and that of the intellectual there is hardly any incompatibility (they often co-exist in a single individual); but the writer stands apart, separate. Writing begins at the point where speech becomes *impossible* (a word that can be understood in the sense it has when applied to a child).

From *Image-Music-Text*.

TWO CONSTRAINTS

Speech is irreversible: a word cannot be *retracted*, except precisely by saying that one retracts it. To cross out is here to add: if I want to erase what I have just said, I cannot do it without showing the eraser itself (I must say: *"or rather . . ."* *"I expressed myself badly . . ."*); paradoxically, it is ephemeral speech which is indelible, not monumental writing. All that one can do in the case of a spoken utterance is to tack on another utterance. The correcting and improving movement of speech is the wavering of a flow of words, a weave which wears itself out catching itself up, a chain of augmentative corrections which constitutes the favored abode of the unconscious part of our discourse (it is not by chance that psychoanalysis is linked to speech and not writing: dreams are spoken not written). The eponymous figure of the speaker is Penelope.

Nor is this all. We can only make ourselves understood (well or poorly) if we maintain a certain speed of delivery. We are like a cyclist or a film obliged to keep going so as to avoid falling or scratching. Silence and vacillation are equally forbidden: the articulatory speed binds each point of the sentence to what immediately follows or precedes (impossible to have the word "set off" toward distant and strange paradigms). Context is a structural given not of language but of speech and it is the very status of context to be reductive of meaning. The spoken word is "clear"; the banishment of polysemy (such banishment being the definition of "clarity") serves the Law— *all speech is on the side of the Law.*

Whoever prepares to speak (in a teaching situation) must realize the *mise en scène* imposed by the use of speech under the simple effect of a natural determination (stemming from the physical nature of articulatory breathing). This *mise en scène* develops as follows. Either the speaker chooses in all good faith a role of Authority, in which case it suffices to "speak well," in compliance with the Law present in every act of speech—without hesitation, at the right speed, clearly (which is what is demanded of good pedagogic speech: clarity, authority); the precise phrase is truly a sentence, a *sententia*, an act of penal speech. Or the speaker is bothered by all this Law that the act of speaking is going to introduce into what he wants to say, in which case, since it is impossible to alter the delivery (condemning one to "clarity") but possible to *excuse oneself* for speaking (for laying out the Law), he uses the irreversibility of speech in order to disturb its legality: correcting, adding, wavering, the speaker moves into the infinitude of language, superimposes on the simple message that everyone expects of him a new message that ruins the very idea of a message and, through the shifting reflection of the blemishes and excesses with which he accompanies the line of the discourse, asks us to believe with him that language is not to be reduced to communication. By all these operations, which come near the wavering movement of the Text, the imperfect orator hopes to render less disagreeable the role that makes every speaker a kind of policeman. Yet at the end of all this effort to "speak badly" another role is enforced, for the audience (nothing to do with the reader), caught in its own imaginary, receives these fumblings as so many signs of weakness and sends the speaker back the image of a master who is human, too human—*liberal*.

The choice is gloomy: conscientious functionary or free artist, the teacher escapes neither the theater of speech nor the Law played out on its stage: the Law appears *not in what is said but in the very fact of speech*. In order to subvert the Law (and not simply get around it), the teacher would have to undermine voice delivery, word speed, and rhythm to the point of *another* intelligibility. Or not speak at all; which, however, would be to rejoin other roles again—that of the great silent mind, mute with the weight of experience, or that of the militant who in the name of praxis dismisses all discourse as futile. Nothing to be done: language is always a matter of force, to speak is to exercise a will for power; in the realm of speech there is no innocence, no safety.

THE SUMMARY

Statutorily the discourse of the teacher is marked by the following characteristic: one can (one may) summarize it (a privilege it holds in common with the discourse of Members of Parliament). There is an exercise in our schools called *text reduction*,[1] a term which expresses nicely the ideology of the summary: on the one side the "thought," object of the message, element of knowledge, transitive or critical force; on the other the "style," ornament, province of luxury and leisure, and thus futility. To separate the thought from the style is in some sort to relieve the discourse of its sacerdotal robes, to secularize the message (hence the bourgeois conjuncture of the teacher and the Member of Parliament). "Form" is believed to be compressible and such compression is not judged essentially harmful—from a distance indeed, from our Western promontory, is the difference really so very great between the head of a living Jivaro and a shrunken Jivaro head?

It is difficult for a teacher to see the "notes" taken during his courses. He hardly wants to, either out of discretion (nothing more personal than "notes," despite the formal nature of the practice) or, more likely, from fear of contemplating himself in a reduced state, at once dead and substantial like a Jivaro treated by his fellows. No knowing whether what is taken (culled) from the flow of speech is scattered statements (formulae, sentences) or the gist of an argument, but in both cases what is lost is the supplement, the point of the advance

---

[1] [*"Réduction de texte,"* i.e., a form of précis.]

of the state of language. The summary is a disavowal of writing.

In contrasting consequence, the term "writer" (a term which here always refers to a practice, not to a social value) may be applied to any sender whose "message" (thereby immediately destroying its very nature as message) cannot be summarized, a condition the writer shares with the madman, the chatterbox, and the mathematician but which precisely writing (namely a certain practice of the signifier) has as its task to specify.

THE TEACHING RELATIONSHIP

How can the teacher be assimilated to the psychoanalyst? It is exactly the contrary which is the case: the teacher is the person analyzed.

Imagine that I am a teacher: I speak, endlessly, in front of and for someone who remains silent. I am the person who says *I* (the detours of *one*, *we*, or impersonal sentence make no difference), I am the person who, under cover of *setting out* a body of knowledge, *puts out* a discourse, *never knowing how that discourse is being received* and thus forever forbidden the reassurance of a definitive image—even if offensive—which would *constitute me*. In the *exposé*, more aptly named than we tend to think, it is not knowledge which is exposed, it is the subject (who exposes himself to all sorts of painful adventures). The mirror is empty, reflecting back to me no more than the falling away of my language as it gradually unrolls. Like the Marx Brothers disguised as Russian airmen (in *A Night at the Opera*—a work which I regard as allegorical of many a textual problem), I am, at the beginning of my exposé, rigged out with a large false beard which, drenched little by little with the flood of my own words (a substitute for the jug of water from which the *Mute*, Harpo, guzzles away on the Mayor of New York's rostrum), I then feel coming unstuck piecemeal in front of everybody. Scarcely have I made the audience smile with some "witty" remark, scarcely have I reassured it with some progressive stereotype, than I experience all the complacency of such provocations; I regret the hysterical drive, would like to retract it, preferring too late an austere to a "clever" discourse (but in that contrary case it is the "severity" of the discourse that would seem hysterical to me). Should some smile answer my remark or some gesture of assent my stereotype of intimidation, I immediately persuade myself that these manifestations of complicity come from imbeciles or flatterers (I am here describing an imaginary process). It is I who am after a response and who let myself go as far as to provoke it, yet it suffices that I receive a response for me to become distrustful. If I develop a discourse such that it coldly averts any response, I do not thereby feel myself to be any more in *true* (in the musical sense), for I must then glory in the solitude of my speech, furnish it with the alibi of missionary discourses (science, truth, etc.).

Thus, in accordance with psychoanalytic description (Lacan's, the perspicacity of which in this respect any speaker can confirm), when the teacher speaks to his audience, the Other is always there, *puncturing* his discourse. Were the discourse held tightly fastened by an impeccable intelligence, armed with scientific "rigor" or political radicality, it would nevertheless be punctured: it suffices that I speak, that my speech flow, for it to flow away. Naturally however, though every teacher occupies the position of a person in analysis, no student audience can claim the advantage of the opposite situation: firstly, because the psychoanalytic silence has nothing pre-eminent about it; secondly, because it happens that a subject, carried away, emerges and rushes to burn on speech, to join in the oratorical promiscuity (and should the subject remain obstinately silent, this is simply to give voice to the obstinacy of his muteness). Yet for the teacher, the student audience is still the exemplary Other in that it *has an air* of not speaking—and thus, from the bosom of its apparent flatness, speaks in you so much the louder: its implicit speech, which is mine, touches me all the more in that I am not encumbered by its discourse.

Such is the cross borne in every public act of speech. Whether the teacher speaks or whether the listener urges the right to speak, in both cases we go straight to the analytic couch: the teaching relationship is nothing more than the transference it institutes; "science," "method," "knowledge," "idea" come indirectly, are given *in addition*—they are *left-overs*.

THE CONTRACT

"Most of the time, the relations between humans suffer, often to the point of destruction, from the fact that the contract established in those relations is not respected. As soon as two human beings enter into reciprocal relationship, their contract, generally tacit, comes into force, regulating the form of their relations, etc."
—BRECHT

Although the demand expressed in the community space of a course is fundamentally intransitive, as is natural in any transferential situation, it is nonetheless overdetermined and shelters behind other, seemingly transitive, demands. These latter constitute the conditions of an implicit contract between the teacher and the taught, a contract which is "imaginary," no way in contradiction with the economic determination which impels the student to be in search of a career and the teacher to fulfill the terms of an employment.

Here pell-mell (in the order of the imaginary there is no founding motive) is what the teacher demands of those taught: (1) to acknowledge him in whatever "role" it may be—authority, benevolence, militancy, knowledge, etc. (any newcomer who cannot be placed as to the *image* he asks of you is immediately disturbing); (2) to act as relay, to extend him, to spread his style and ideas far afield; (3) to let himself be seduced, to assent to a loving relationship (granting all the sublimations, the distances, the checks consonant with the social reality and the presentiment of the futility of the relationship); (4) to allow him to honor the contract he has himself entered into with his employer, with society: the person taught is the necessary part of a (remunerated) practice, the object of a job, the matter of a production (even if difficult to define).

From his side, here pell-mell is what the person taught demands of the teacher: (1) to help him to a good professional training; (2) to fulfill the roles traditionally devolving to the teacher (scientific authority, transmission of a capital of knowledge, etc.); (3) to reveal the secrets of a technique (of research, for passing an examination); (4) under the banner of the secular saint Method, to be an instructor in ascesis, a *guru*; (5) to represent a "movement of ideas," a School, a Cause, to be its spokesman; (6) to admit him, the student, into the complicity of a special language; (7) for those possessed by the fantasy of the thesis (a timid practice of writing, at once disfigured and shielded by its institutional finality), to guarantee the reality of that fantasy; (8) to lend service—the teacher signs registration forms, testimonials, and so on.

This is simply a topic, a fund of choices which are not necessarily all actualized at the same time in a particular individual. It is at the level of the contractual totality, however, that is decided the *comfort* of the teaching relationship: the "good" teacher, the "good" student are those who accept philosophically the plurality of their determinations, perhaps because they know that the truth of a relationship of speech is *elsewhere*.

RESEARCH

What is a piece of "research"? To find out, we would need to have some idea of what a "result" is. What is it that one finds? What is it that one wants to find? *What is missing?* In what axiomatic field will the fact isolated, the meaning brought out, the statistical discovery be placed? No doubt it depends each time on the particular science approached, but from the moment a piece of research concerns the text (and the text extends very much further than the literary work) the research itself becomes text, production: to it, any "result" is literally *im-pertinent.* "Research" is then the name which prudently, under the constraint of certain social conditions, we give to the activity of writing: research here moves on the side of writing, is an adventure of the signifier, an excess of exchange—impossible to maintain the equation of a "result" *for* a "piece of research." Which is why the discourse to which a piece of research must be submitted (in teaching it) has as specialty, besides its parenetic function (*"Write!"*), to recall the research to its epistemological condition: whatever it searches for, it must not forget its nature as language—and it is this which renders finally inevitable an encounter with writing. In writing, the enunciation deludes the enounced by the effect of the language which produces it, a good enough definition of the productive, dissatisfied, progressive, critical element which is indeed ordinarily granted to "research." Such is the historical role of research: teach the scientist or scholar *that he speaks* (but if he knew it, he would *write*—and the whole idea of science, the whole of scientificity would be changed thereby).

THE DESTRUCTION OF STEREOTYPES

Someone writes to me that "a group of revolutionary students is preparing a destruction of the structuralist myth." I am captivated by the stereotypic consistency of the expression. The destruction of the myth begins from the very announcement of its putative agents with the finest of myths, the "group of revolutionary students"—quite as good as "war widows" or "old soldiers."

Usually the stereotype is a sad affair, since it is constituted by a necrosis of language, a prosthesis brought in to fill a hole in writing. Yet at the same time it cannot but occasion a huge burst of laughter: it takes itself seriously, believes itself to be closer to the truth because indifferent to its nature as language. It is at once corny and solemn.

Setting the stereotype at a distance is not a political task, for political language is itself made up of stereotypes, but a critical task, one, that is, which aims to call language into crisis. Such an activity allows one first and foremost to isolate the speck of ideology contained in every political discourse and to attack it like an acid capable of dissolving the greasiness of "natural" language (that is to say, of language which feigns ignorance of the fact of its nature as language). It is a way, too, of breaking with the mechanistic conception of language as mere response to stimuli of situation or action, a way of opposing the production of language to its simple and fallacious utilization. Then again, it jolts the discourse of the Other and constitutes a permanent operation of preanalysis. Lastly, the stereotype is at bottom a form of opportunism: one conforms to the reigning language, or rather to that in language which seems to *govern* (a situation, a right, a struggle, an institution, a movement, a science, a theory, etc.); to speak in stereotypes is to side with the power of language, an opportunism which must (today) be refused.

But is it not possible to "transcend" stereotypes instead of "destroying" them? The wish is unrealistic; operators of language have no other activity at their command than that of emptying what is full: language is not dialectical—it allows only a movement in two stages.

THE CHAIN OF DISCOURSES

It is because language is not dialectical (does not allow the third term other than as pure oratorical flourish, rhetorical assertion, pious hope) that discourse (discursivity) moves, in its historical impetus, by *clashes*. A new discourse can only emerge as the *paradox* which goes against (and often goes for) the surrounding or preceding *doxa*, can only see the day as difference, distinction, working loose *against* what sticks to it. For example, Chomskyan theory is constructed *against* Bloomfieldian behaviorism; linguistic behaviorism once liquidated by Chomsky, it is then *against* Chomskyan mentalism (or anthropologism) that a new semiotics is being developed, while Chomsky himself, in quest of allies, is forced to *jump* over his immediate predecessors and go back as far as the Port-Royal *Grammar*. But doubtless it is in one of the greatest thinkers of dialectics, Marx, that it would be the most interesting to verify the undialectical nature of language: Marx's discourse is almost entirely *paradoxical*, the *doxa* being now Proudhon, now someone else, and so on. This twofold movement of separation and renewal results not in a circle but, according to Vico's great and beautiful image, in a spiral and it is in this *drift* of circularity (of paradoxical form) that historical determinations are articulated. Hence it is always necessary to establish what *doxa* an author is opposing (this can sometimes be a very minority *doxa*, holding sway over a limited group). A teaching may equally be evaluated in terms of paradox, provided it is built on the following conviction: that a system calling for corrections, translations, openings, and negations is more useful than an unformulated absence of system—one may then avoid the immobility of prattle and connect to the historical chain of discourses, the progress (*progressus*) of discursivity.

METHOD

Some people talk avidly, demandingly of method; what they want in work is method, which can never be too rigorous or too formal for their taste. Method becomes a Law, but since that Law is devoid of any effect outside itself (nobody can say what a "result" is in "human sciences") it is infinitely disappointed; posing as a pure metalanguage, it partakes of the vanity of all metalanguage. The invariable fact is that a piece of work which ceaselessly proclaims its determination for method is ultimately sterile: everything has been put into the method, nothing is left for writing; the researcher repeatedly asserts that his text will be methodological but the text never comes. No surer way to kill a piece of research and send it to join the great waste of abandoned projects than Method.

The danger of Method (of a fixation with Method) is to be grasped by considering the two demands to which the work of research must reply. The first is a demand for responsibility: the work must increase lucidity, manage to reveal the implications of a procedure, the alibis of a language, in short must constitute a *critique* (remember once again that to *criticize* means *to call into crisis*). Here Method is inevitable, irreplaceable, not for its "results" but precisely—or on the contrary—because it realizes the highest degree of consciousness of a language *which is not forgetful of itself*. The second demand, however, is of a quite different order; it is that of writing, space of dispersion of desire, where Law is dismissed. *At a certain moment*, therefore, it is necessary to turn against Method, or at least to treat it without any founding privilege as one of the voices of plurality—as a *view*, a spectacle mounted in the text, the text which all in all is the only "true" result of any research.

QUESTIONS

To question is to want to know something. Yet in many intellectual debates the questions that follow the lecturer's talk are in no way the expression of a lack but the assertion of a plenitude. Under the cover of asking questions, I attack the speaker. *To question* then takes on its police sense: *to question* is to challenge, to interpellate. The person interpellated, however, must pretend to reply to the letter of the question, not to the manner in which it is posed. So a game is set up: although each person knows exactly what the intentions of the other really are, the game demands a reply to the content and not to the manner. If I am asked in a certain tone of voice *"What's the use of linguistics?"*, thereby signifying to me that it is of no use whatsoever, I must pretend to reply naïvely *"It helps to do this and that,"* and not, in accordance with the truth of the dialogue, "Why are you attacking me?" What I receive is the connotation; what I have to return is the denotation. In the space of speech, science and logic, knowledge and reasoning, questions and answers, propositions and objections are the masks of the dialectical relationship. Our intellectual debates are coded every bit as much as were the Scholastic disputations; we still have the stock roles (the "sociologistic," the "Goldmannian," the "Telquelian," etc.) but contrary to the *disputatio*, where such roles would have been ceremonial and have displayed the artifice of their function, our intellectual "intercourse" always gives itself "natural" airs: it claims to exchange only signifieds, not signifiers.

IN THE NAME OF WHAT?

I speak in the name of what? Of a function? A body of knowledge? An experience? What do I represent? A scientific capacity? An institution? A service? In fact, I speak only in the name of a language: I speak because I have written; writing is represented by its contrary, by speech. This distortion means that in writing *of* speech (on the subject of speech) I am condemned to the following aporia: denounce the imaginary of speech through the irreality of writing. Thus at this moment I am not describing any "authentic" experience, giving the picture of any "real" teaching, opening any "university" dossier. For writing can tell the truth on language but not the truth on the real (we are at present trying to find out what a real without language is).

THE STANDING POSITION

Can you imagine a more doubtful situation than that of talking for (or in front of) people who are standing up or who are visibly badly seated? What is being exchanged here? What is this discomfort the price of? What is my speech *worth*? How could the awkwardness of the hearer's position not lead to questions as to the validity of what is being heard? Is not the standing position eminently *critical*? And is it not thus, changing the scale, that political consciousness begins, in *un-ease*? Listening returns me the vanity of my own speech, its *price*, for, whether I like it or not, I am placed in a circuit of exchange; and listening is also the position of the person to whom I address myself.

FAMILIARITY

It sometimes happens, remnant of May '68, that a student speaks to a teacher in the familiar *tu* form, which gives us a strong, full sign, referring to the most psychological of signifieds: the will for militancy or mateyness—*muscle*. Since a morality of the sign is here imposed, it can be challenged in its turn and a subtler semantics preferred. Signs must be handled on a neutral ground and in French that ground is the polite *vous* form. The *tu* form can only break loose from the code in cases where it constitutes *a simplification of grammar* (as, for example, when talking to a foreigner with poor French). In such cases it is a matter of substituting a transitive practice for a symbolic attitude: instead of seeking to signify *just who* I think the other is (and so just who I think I am), I simply try to make myself clearly understood to him. But the strategy is also itself finally devious: the *tu* form is like all attitudes of flight; when a sign displeases me, when the meaning bothers me, I shift toward the operational, which becomes a censorship of the symbolic and thus the symbol of asymbolism. A great many political and scientific discourses are characterized by a shift of this kind (on which depends, notably, the whole of the linguistics of "communication").

AN ODOR OF SPEECH

As soon as one has finished speaking, there begins the dizzying turn of the image: one exalts or regrets what one has said, the way in which one said it, one *imagines oneself* (turns oneself over in image); speech is subject to remanence, it *smells*.

Writing has no smell: produced (having accomplished its process of production), it *falls*, not like a bellows deflating but like a meteorite disappearing; it will *travel* far from my body, yet without being something detached and narcissistically retained like speech; its disappearance holds no disappointment; it passes, traverses, and that's all. The time of speech exceeds the act of speech (only a jurist could have us believe that spoken words disappear, *verba volant*). Writing, however, has no past (if society obliges you to administer what you have written, you can only do it with the most profound boredom, the boredom of a false past). Which is why the discourse applied in commenting writing has a much less striking effect than that applied in commenting speech (though the stake is greater): I can *objectively* take account of the first for "I" am no longer there; the second, even if it is in praise, I can only try to get rid of, for it does no more than retighten the impasse of my imaginary.

(How is it then that this present text preoccupies me, that once completed, corrected, let go of, the text remains or returns in me as a state of doubt and, in a word, of fear? Is it not *written*, liberated by writing? I see that I cannot improve the piece, I have achieved the exact form of what I wanted to say; it is no longer a question of *style*. I conclude, therefore, that it is the very status of the piece which disturbs me; what plagues me in it is precisely that, dealing with speech, it cannot, *in writing itself*, fully liquidate speech. In order to write *of* speech (about speech) I am compelled to *refer* to illusions of experiences, memories, and feelings had by the subject I am when I speak, that I was when speaking: in such a writing the referential lingers on and it is that which smells to my own nostrils.)

OUR PLACE

Just as psychoanalysis, with the work of Lacan, is in the process of extending the Freudian topic into a topology of the subject (the unconscious is never there in *its* place), so likewise we need to substitute for the magisterial space of the past—which was fundamentally a religious space (the work delivered by the master from the pulpit above with the audience below, the flock, the sheep, the herd)—a less upright, less Euclidean space where no one, neither teacher nor students, would ever be *in his final place*. One would then be able to see that what must be made reversible are not social "roles" (is there any point in squabbling for "authority," for the "right" to speak?) but the regions of speech. Where is speech? In locution? In listening? In the *returns* of the one and the other? The problem is not to abolish the distinction in functions (*teacher/student*—after all, as Sade has taught us, order is one of the guarantees of pleasure) but to protect the instability and, as it were, the giddying whirl of the positions of speech. In the teaching space nobody should anywhere be in his place (I am comforted by this constant displacement: were I to *find my place*, I would not even go on pretending to teach, I would give up).

Yet is it not the case that the teacher has a fixed place, that of his *remuneration*, the place he occupies in the economy, in production? We come back to the same problem, our sole and continuing concern: the origin of a spoken discourse does not exhaust that discourse; once set off, it is beset by a thousand adventures, its origin becomes blurred, all its effects are not in its cause. It is this *excess* which here concerns us.

TWO TYPES OF CRITICISM

The mistakes that may be made in typing out a manuscript are so many meaningful incidents, incidents which by analogy help to shed light on the attitude it is necessary to adopt with regard to meaning when commenting a text.

Either the word produced by the mistake (if spoiled by a wrong letter) has no meaning, finds no textual contour, in which case the code is interrupted, creating an asemic word, a pure signifier; for example, instead of writing *officier* [officer] I write *offivier*, which is meaningless. Or the erroneous—mistyped—word, though not the word one intended to write, is a word identifiable in the lexicon, a word which means something: should I write *ride* [wrinkle] instead of *rude* [rude, rough], the new word exists in French and the sentence retains a meaning, even if eccentric. This is the choice (the voice?) of pun, anagram, semantic metathesis, spoonerism: there is a sliding *within the codes*—meaning remains but pluralized, cheated, without law of content, message, truth.

Each of these two types of mistake figures (or prefigures) a type of criticism. The first dismisses all meaning of the support text which is to lend itself only to a signifying efflorescence: its phonism alone is to be treated, but not interpreted; one associates, one does not decipher. Giving the reading *offivier* as opposed to *officier*, the mistake opens up for me the *right of association*—I am free to explode *offivier* toward *obvier* [obviate], *vivier* [fish stock], etc. It is not simply that the ear of this first criticism hears the cracklings of the phono pickup but rather that it desires to hear only them, making them into a new music. In the second type of criticism nothing is rejected by the "reading head"; it perceives both the meaning (the meanings) and its cracklings. The (historical) stake of these two types of criticism (I should like to be able to say that the field of the first is *signifiosis* and that of the second *signifiance*) is clearly different.

The first has in its favor the right of the signifier to spread out where it will (where it can?): what law, and what meaning, and with what basis, would restrain it? Once the philological (monological) law has been relaxed and the text eased open to plurality, why stop? Why refuse to push polysemy as far as asemy? In the name of what? Like any radical right, this one supposes a utopian vision of freedom: the law is lifted *all at once*, outside of any history, in defiance of any dialectic (hence the finally petit-bourgeois aspect of this style of demand). Yet the moment it evades all tactical reason while nevertheless remaining implanted in a specific (and alienated) intellectual society, the disorder of the signifier reverts into hysterical rambling: liberating reading from all meaning, it is ultimately *my* reading which I impose, for in *this* moment of History the economy of the subject is not yet transformed and the refusal of meaning (of meanings) falls back into subjectivity. At best, one can simply say that this radical criticism, defined by a foreclosure of the signified (and not by its slide), *anticipates* History, anticipates a new, unprecedented state in which the efflorescence of the signifier would not be at the cost of any idealist counterpart, of any closure of the person. To criticize, however, is to put into crisis, something which is not possible without evaluating the conditions of the crisis (its limits), without considering its historical moment. Thus the second type of criticism, that which applies itself to the division of meanings and the "trickery" of interpretation, appears (at least to me) more historically correct. In a society locked in the war of meanings and thereby under the compulsion of rules of communication which determine its effectiveness, the liquidation of the old criticism can only be carried forward *in* meaning (in the volume of meanings) and not outside it. In other words, it is necessary to practice a certain semantic enterism. Ideological criticism is today precisely condemned to operations of theft: the signified, exemption of which is the materialist task par excellence, is more easily "lifted" in the *illusion* of meaning than in its destruction.

TWO TYPES OF DISCOURSE

Let us distinguish two types of discourse:

Terrorist discourse is not necessarily bound up with the peremptory assertion (or the opportunist defense) of a faith, a truth, a certain justice; it can simply be the wish to accomplish the lucid adequation of the enunciation with the true violence of language, the inherent violence which stems from the fact that no utterance is able directly to express the truth and has no other mode at its disposal than the force of the word; thus an apparently terrorist discourse ceases to be so if, reading it, one follows the directions it itself provides, re-establishing in it the gap or dispersion, that is to say, the unconscious. Such a reading is not always easy: certain small-scale terrorisms which function above all by stereotypes themselves operate, like any discourse of good conscience, the foreclosure of the other scene; in short, these terrorisms *refuse writing* (they can be detected by something in them that remains rigid—the odor of seriousness given off by the commonplace).

Repressive discourse is not linked to declared violence but

to the Law. The Law here enters language as equilibrium: an equilibrium is postulated between what is forbidden and what is permitted, between commendable meaning and unworthy meaning, between the constraint of common sense and the probationary freedom of interpretations. Hence the taste shown by such discourse for motions of balance, verbal opposites, antitheses formulated and evaded, being *neither* for this *nor* for that (if, however, you do the double addition of the *neither* and *nors*, it will be seen that our *impartial, objective, human* speaker is *for* this, against *that*). Repressive discourse is the discourse of good conscience, liberal discourse.

THE AXIOMATIC FIELD

"All that is necessary," comments Brecht, "is to determine those interpretations of facts appearing within the proletariat engaged in the class struggle (national or international) which enable it to utilize the facts for its action. They must be synthesized in order to create an axiomatic field." Thus every fact possesses several meanings (a plurality of "interpretations") and among those meanings there is one which is proletarian (or at least which is of use to the proletariat in its struggle); by connecting the various proletarian meanings one constructs a revolutionary axiomatics. But who determines the meaning? According to Brecht, the proletariat itself (*"appearing within the proletariat"*). Such a view implies that class division has its inevitable counterpart in a division of meanings and class struggle its equally inevitable counterpart in a war of meanings: so long as there is class struggle (national or international), the division of the axiomatic field will be inexpiable.

The difficulty (despite Brecht's verbal assurance—*"All that is necessary"*) comes from the fact that a certain number of objects of discourse do not directly concern the proletariat (they find no interpretation within it) which cannot, however, remain indifferent to them, since they constitute, at least in advanced States which have wiped out both misery and folklore, the plenitude of the other discourse within which the very proletariat is compelled to live, nourish, and amuse itself. This discourse is that of culture (it is possible that in Marx's day the pressure of culture on the proletariat was weaker than it is now; in the absence of "mass communications," there was as yet no "mass culture"). How can you attribute a meaning for the struggle to something of no direct concern to you? How could the proletariat determine *within itself* an interpretation of Zola, Poussin, pop music, the Sunday sports paper, or the latest news item? To "interpret" all these cultural relays it needs *representatives*—those whom Brecht calls the "artists" or the "workers of the intellect" (a particularly malicious expression, at least in French, where the intellect is so nearly off the top of the head), those who have at their command the language of the indirect, the indirect as language; in a word, *oblates* who devote themselves to the proletarian interpretation of cultural facts.

Then begins, however, for these procurators of proletarian meaning, a real headache of a problem since their class situation is not that of the proletariat: they are not producers, a negative situation they share with (student) youth—an equally unproductive class with whom they usually form an alliance of language. It follows that the culture from which they have to disengage the proletarian meaning brings them back round to themselves and not to the proletariat. How is culture to be *evaluated*? According to its origin? Bourgeois. Its finality? Bourgeois again. According to dialectics? Although bourgeois, this does contain progressive elements; but what, *at the level of discourse*, distinguishes dialectics from compromise? And then again, with what instruments? Historicism, sociologism, positivism, formalism, psychoanalysis? Every one of them bourgeoisified. There are some who finally prefer to give up the problem, to dismiss all "culture"—a course which entails the destruction of all discourse.

In fact, even within an axiomatic field thought to be clarified by the class struggle, the tasks are various, occasionally contradictory, and, most importantly, established on different temporalities. The axiomatic field is made up of several specific axiomatics: cultural criticism proceeds *successively, diversely, and simultaneously* by opposing the Old with the New, historicism with sociologism, formalism with economism, psychoanalysis with logico-positivism, and then again, *by a further turn*, empirical sociology with monumental history, the New with the strange (the foreign), historicism with formalism, scientism with psychoanalysis, and so on. Applied to culture, critical discourse can only be a silk shot through with tactics, a tissue of elements now past, now circumstantial (linked to contingencies of fashion), now finally and frankly utopian. To the tactical necessities of the war of meanings is added the strategic conception of the new conditions which will be given the signifier when that war comes to an end. Cultural criticism, that is, must be *impatient*, it cannot be carried on without desire. Hence all the discourses of Marxism are present in its writing: the apologetic (glorify revolutionary science), the apocalyptic (destroy bourgeois culture), and the eschatological (desire and call for the undivision of meaning, concomitant on class undivision).

OUR UNCONSCIOUS

The problem posed is this: how can the two great *epistemes* of modernity, namely the materialist and the Freudian dialectics, be made to intersect, to unite in the production of a new human relation (it is not to be excluded that a third term may be hidden in the interdiction of the first two)? That is to say: how can we aid the interaction of these two desires—to change the economy of the relations of production and to change the economy of the subject? (For the moment psychoanalysis appears to be the force best fitted for the second of the tasks but other topics can be imagined, those of the East, for example.)

The path of this comprehensive work lies through the following question: what is the relation between class determination and the unconscious? By what displacement does this determination slip in between subjects? Certainly not by "psychology" (as though there were mental contents— bourgeois/proletarian/intellectual/etc.) but quite obviously by language, by discourse: the Other—who speaks, who is all speech—is social. On the one hand, the proletariat may well be *separated* but it is still bourgeois language, in its degraded petit-bourgeois form, which speaks unconsciously in the proletariat's cultural discourse; on the other, the proletariat may well be mute but it still speaks in the discourse of the intellectual, not as canonical founding voice but as unconscious. It suffices in this respect to see how it *knocks* on all our discourses (explicit reference by the intellectual to the proletariat in no way prevents the latter from occupying the place of the unconscious in our discourse). Only the bourgeois discourse of the bourgeoisie is tautological: the unconscious of bourgeois discourse is indeed the Other, but that Other is another bourgeois discourse.

WRITING AS VALUE

Evaluation precedes criticism. There is no putting into crisis without evaluation. Our value is writing, an obstinate reference which, apart from the fact that it must often irritate, seems in the eyes of some to involve a risk—that of developing a certain *mystique*. The reproach has its malice, for it reverses point by point the importance we attach to writing, regarded, in this tiny intellectual region of our Western world, as *the materialist field par excellence*. Though issuing from

Marxism and psychoanalysis, the theory of writing tries to displace—without breaking with—that place of origin: on the one hand, it rejects the temptation of the signified, that is the deafness to language, to the excessive return of its effects; on the other, it is opposed to speech in that it is not transferential and outplays—admittedly partially, in extremely narrow, particularist social limits even—the traps of "dialogue." There is in writing the beginnings of a mass gesture: against all discourses (modes of speech, instrumental writings, rituals, protocols, social symbolics), writing alone today, even if still in the form of luxury, makes of language something *atopical*, without place. It is this dispersion, this unsituation, which is materialist.

PEACEABLE SPEECH

One of the things that can be expected from a regular meeting together of speakers is quite simply *goodwill*, that the meeting figure a space of discourse divested of all sense of aggressiveness.

Such a divestiture arouses resistances. The first is of a cultural nature: the refusal of violence is commonly seen as a humanist lie, courtesy (minor mode of that refusal) as a class value and openness as a mystification related to the liberal idea of dialogue. The second resistance is of an imaginary order: many people want a conflictual discourse from motives of psychic liberation; the removal of confrontation is said to have something frustrating about it. The third resistance is of a political order: polemic is an essential arm in the struggle, any space of discourse must be splintered in order that its contradictions may emerge—it must be kept under scrutiny.

What is preserved in these three resistances, however, is ultimately the unity of the neurotic subject, which *comes together* in the forms of conflict. Yet we know that violence is always there (in language) and it is precisely this that can lead us to decide to bracket out its signs and thus to dispense with a rhetoric; violence must not be absorbed by the code of violence.

The first advantage of this would be to suspend or at least to delay the roles of speech—so that listening, speaking, replying, I never be the actor of a judgment, a subjection, an intimidation, the advocate of a Cause. No doubt peaceable speech will finally secrete its own role, since, whatever I say, the other continues to read me as an image; but in the time put into eluding such a role, in the work of language accomplished by the community week after week toward the abolition from its discourse of all stichomythia, a certain dispropriation of speech (from then on close to writing) may be attained—or again, *a certain generalization of the subject.*

Perhaps this is what is found in certain experiences with drugs (in the experience of certain drugs). Though not smoking oneself (if only because of bronchial inability to inhale the smoke), it is impossible to remain insensible to the general goodwill that pervades certain places abroad where cannabis is smoked. The movements, the (few) words spoken, the whole relationship of the bodies (a relationship nevertheless immobile and distant), everything is relaxed, disarmed (hence totally unlike drunkenness, the legal form of violence in the West); the space seems to be the product of a subtle ascesis (one can sometimes read in it a certain *irony*). A meeting for speech should, I think, aim at this *suspension* (no matter of what—the desire is for a form), try to rejoin an *art of living*, the greatest of all the arts according to Brecht (such a view is more dialectical than it appears, in that it compels the distinction and evaluation of the customs of violence). In short, within the very limits of the teaching space as given, the need is to work at patiently tracing out a pure form, that of a *floating* (the very form of the signifier); a floating which would not destroy anything but would be content simply to disorientate the Law. The necessities of promotion, professional obligations (which nothing then prevents from being scrupulously fulfilled), imperatives of knowledge, prestige of method, ideological criticism—everything is there, but *floating*.

1971

from *The Pleasure of the Text*

I AM offered a text. This text bores me. It might be said to *prattle*. The prattle of the text is merely that foam of language which forms by the effect of a simple need of writing. Here we are not dealing with perversion but with demand. The writer of this text employs an unweaned language: imperative, automatic, unaffectionate, a minor disaster of static (those milky phonemes which the remarkable Jesuit, van Ginnekin, posited between writing and language): these are the motions of ungratified sucking, of an undifferentiated orality, intersecting the orality which produces the pleasures of gastrosophy and of language. You address yourself to me so that I may read you, but I am nothing to you except this address; in your eyes, I am the substitute for nothing, for no figure (hardly that of the mother); for you I am neither a body nor even an object (and I couldn't care less: I am not the one whose soul demands recognition), but merely a field, a vessel for expansion. It can be said that after all you have written this text quite apart

The Pleasure of the Text, translated by Richard Miller (New York: Hill and Wang, 1975).

from bliss; and this prattling text is then a frigid text, as any demand is frigid until desire, until neurosis forms in it.

Neurosis is a makeshift: not with regard to "health" but with regard to the "impossible" Bataille speaks of ("Neurosis is the fearful apprehension of an ultimate impossible," etc.); but this makeshift is the only one that allows for writing (and reading). So we arrive at this paradox: the texts, like those by Bataille—or by others—which are written against neurosis, from the center of madness, contain within themselves, *if they want to be read*, that bit of neurosis necessary to the seduction of their readers: these terrible texts are *all the same* flirtatious texts.

Thus every writer's motto reads: *mad I cannot be, sane I do not deign to be, neurotic I am.*

The text you write must prove to me *that it desires me*. This proof exists: it is writing. Writing is: the science of the various blisses of language, its Kama Sutra (this science has but one treatise: writing itself).

Sade: the pleasure of reading him clearly proceeds from certain breaks (or certain collisions): antipathetic codes (the noble and the trivial, for example) come into contact; pompous and ridiculous neologisms are created; pornographic messages are embodied in sentences so pure they might be used as grammatical models. As textual theory has it: the language is redistributed. Now, *such redistribution is always achieved by cutting*. Two edges are created: an obedient, conformist, plagiarizing edge (the language is to be copied in its canonical state, as it has been established by schooling, good

usage, literature, culture), and *another edge,* mobile, blank
(ready to assume any contours), which is never anything but
the site of its effect: the place where the death of language is
glimpsed. These two edges, *the compromise they bring about,*
are necessary. Neither culture nor its destruction is erotic; it is
the seam between them, the fault, the flaw, which becomes so.
The pleasure of the text is like that untenable, impossible,
purely *novelistic* instant so relished by Sade's libertine when he
manages to be hanged and then to cut the rope at the very
moment of his orgasm, his bliss.

Whence, perhaps, a means of evaluating the works of our
modernity: their value would proceed from their duplicity. By
which it must be understood that they always have two edges.
The subversive edge may seem privileged because it is the edge
of violence; but it is not violence which affects pleasure, nor is
it destruction which interests it; what pleasure wants is the site
of a loss, the seam, the cut, the deflation, the *dissolve* which
seizes the subject in the midst of bliss. Culture thus recurs as
an edge: in no matter what form.

· · ·

The stereotype is the word repeated without any magic, any
enthusiasm, as though it were natural, as though by some
miracle this recurring word were adequate on each occasion
for different reasons, as though to imitate could no longer be
sensed as an imitation: an unconstrained word that claims
consistency and is unaware of its own insistence. Nietzsche has
observed that "truth" is only the solidification of old metaphors. So in this regard the stereotype is the present path of
"truth," the palpable feature which shifts the invented ornament to the canonical, constraining form of the signified. (It
would be good to imagine a new linguistic science that would
no longer study the origin of words, or etymology, or even

their diffusion, or lexicology, but the progress of their solidification, their densification throughout historical discourse; this science would doubtless be subversive, manifesting much more than the historical origin of truth: its rhetorical, *languaging* nature.)

The distrust of the stereotype (linked to the bliss of the new word or the untenable discourse) is a principle of absolute instability which respects nothing (no content, no choice). Nausea occurs whenever the liaison of two important words *follows of itself*. And when something follows of itself, I abandon it: that is bliss. A futile annoyance? In Poe's story, M. Valdemar, hypnotized and moribund, is kept alive in a cataleptic state by the repetition of the questions put to him ("Are you asleep, M. Valdemar?"); however, this survival is untenable: the false death, the atrocious death, is what has no end, the interminable. ("For God's sake!—quick!—put me to sleep —or, quick—waken me!—quick!—I say to you that I am dead!") The stereotype is this nauseating impossibility of dying.

In the intellectual field, political choice is a suspension of language—thus a bliss. Yet language resumes, in its consistent stable form (the political stereotype). Which language must then be swallowed, without nausea.

Another bliss (other edges): it consists in de-politicizing what is apparently political, and in politicizing what apparently is not. —Come now, surely one politicizes what *must* be politicized, and that's all.

Nihilism: "superior goals depreciate." This is an unstable, jeopardized moment, for other superior values tend, immediately and before the former are destroyed, to prevail; dialectics only links successive positivities; whence the suffocation at the very heart of anarchism. How *install* the deficiency of any superior value? Irony? It always proceeds from a *sure* site. Violence? Violence too is a superior value, and among the best coded. Bliss? Yes, if it is not spoken, doctrinal. The most consistent nihilism is perhaps *masked*: in some way *interior* to institutions, to conformist discourse, to apparent finalities.

. . .

Why do some people, including myself, enjoy in certain novels, biographies, and historical works the representation of the "daily life" of an epoch, of a character? Why this curiosity about petty details: schedules, habits, meals, lodging, clothing, etc.? Is it the hallucinatory relish of "reality" (the very materiality of "*that once existed*")? And is it not the fantasy itself which invokes the "detail," the tiny private scene, in which I can easily take my place? Are there, in short, "minor hysterics" (these very readers) who receive bliss from a singular theater: not one of grandeur but one of mediocrity (might there not be dreams, fantasies of mediocrity)?

Thus, impossible to imagine a more tenuous, a more insignificant notation than that of "today's weather" (or yesterday's); and yet, the other day, reading, trying to read Amiel, irritation that the well-meaning editor (another person foreclosing pleasure) had seen fit to omit from this Journal the everyday details, what the weather was like on the shores of Lake Geneva, and retain only insipid moral musing: yet it is this weather that has not aged, not Amiel's philosophy.

Art seems compromised, historically, socially. Whence the effort on the part of the artist himself to destroy it.

I see this effort taking three forms. The artist can shift to another signifier: if he is a writer, he becomes a filmmaker, a painter, or, contrariwise, if he is a painter, a filmmaker, he works up interminable critiques of the cinema, painting, deliberately reduces the art to his criticism. He can also "dismiss" writing and become a scientist, a scholar, an intellectual theorist, no longer speaking except from a moral site cleansed of any linguistic sensuality. Finally, he can purely and simply scuttle himself, stop writing, change trades, change desires.

Unfortunately, this destruction is always inadequate; either it occurs outside the art, but thereby becomes impertinent, or else it consents to remain within the practice of the art, but quickly exposes itself to recuperation (the avant-garde is that restive language which is going to be recuperated). The awkwardness of this alternative is the consequence of the fact that destruction of discourse is not a dialectic term *but a semantic term*: it docilely takes its place within the great semiological "versus" myth (*white* versus *black*); whence the destruction of art is doomed to only *paradoxical* formulae (those which proceed literally against the *doxa*): both sides of the paradigm are glued together in an ultimately complicitous fashion: there is a structural agreement between the contesting and the contested forms.

(By *subtle subversion* I mean, on the contrary, what is not directly concerned with destruction, evades the paradigm, and seeks some *other* term: a third term, which is not, however, a synthesizing term but an eccentric, extraordinary term. An example? Perhaps Bataille, who eludes the idealist term by an *unexpected* materialism in which we find vice, devotion, play, impossible eroticism, etc.; thus Bataille does not counter modesty with sexual freedom but . . . with *laughter*.)

The text of pleasure is not necessarily the text that recounts pleasures; the text of bliss is never the text that recounts the kind of bliss afforded literally by an ejaculation. The pleasure of representation is not attached to its object: pornography is not *sure*. In zoological terms, one could say that the site of textual pleasure is not the relation of mimic and model (imitative relation) but solely that of dupe and mimic (relation of desire, of production).

We must, however, distinguish between *figuration* and *representation*.

Figuration is the way in which the erotic body appears (to whatever degree and in whatever form that may be) in the profile of the text. For example: the author may appear in his text (Genet, Proust), but not in the guise of direct biography (which would exceed the body, give a meaning to life, forge a destiny). Or again: one can feel desire for a character in a novel (in fleeting impulses). Or finally: the text itself, a diagrammatic and not an imitative structure, can reveal itself in the form of a body, split into fetish objects, into erotic sites. All these movements attest to a *figure* of the text, necessary to the bliss of reading. Similarly, and even more than the text, the film will *always* be figurative (which is why films are still worth making)—even if it represents nothing.

Representation, on the other hand, is *embarrassed figuration*, encumbered with other meanings than that of desire: a space of alibis (reality, morality, likelihood, readability, truth, etc.). Here is a text of pure representation: Barbey d'Aurevilly writes on Memling's Virgin: "She stands upright, very perpendicularly posed. Pure beings are upright. By posture and by movement, we know the chaste woman; wantons droop, languish and lean, always about to fall." Note in passing that the representative undertaking has managed to engender an art (the classical novel) as well as a "science" (graphology, for example, which deduces from the attenuation of a single letter the listlessness of the writer), and that it is consequently fair, without any sophistry, to call it immediately ideological (by the historical extent of its signification). Of course, it very often happens that representation takes desire itself as an object of imitation; but then, such desire never leaves the frame, the picture; it circulates among the characters; if it has a recipient, that recipient remains interior to the fiction (consequently, we can say that any semiotics that keeps desire within the configuration of those upon whom it acts, however new it may be, is a semiotics of representation. That is what representation is: when nothing emerges, when nothing leaps out of the frame: of the picture, the book, the screen).

No sooner has a word been said, somewhere, about the pleasure of the text, than two policemen are ready to jump on you: the political policeman and the psychoanalytical policeman: futility and/or guilt, pleasure is either idle or vain, a class notion or an illusion.

An old, a very old tradition: hedonism has been repressed by nearly every philosophy; we find it defended only by marginal figures, Sade, Fourier; for Nietzsche, hedonism is a pessimism. Pleasure is continually disappointed, reduced, deflated, in favor of strong, noble values: Truth, Death, Progress, Struggle, Joy, etc. Its victorious rival is Desire: we are always being told about Desire, never about Pleasure; Desire has an epistemic dignity, Pleasure does not. It seems that (our) society refuses (and ends up by ignoring) bliss to such a point that it can produce only epistemologies of the law (and of its contestation), never of its absence, or better still: of its nullity. Odd, this philosophical permanence of Desire (insofar as it is never satisfied): doesn't the word itself denote a "class notion"? (A rather crude presumption of proof, and yet noteworthy: the "populace" does not know Desire—only pleasures.)

So-called erotic books (one must add: of recent vintage, in order to except Sade and a few others) *represent* not so much the erotic scene as the expectation of it, the preparation for it, its ascent; that is what makes them "exciting"; and when the scene occurs, naturally there is disappointment, deflation. In other words, these are books of Desire, not of Pleasure. Or, more mischievously, they represent Pleasure *as seen by psychoanalysis*. A like meaning says, in both instances, that *the whole thing is very disappointing*.

(The monument of psychoanalysis must be traversed—not bypassed—like the fine thoroughfares of a very large city, across which we can play, dream, etc.: a fiction.)

There is supposed to be a mystique of the Text. —On the contrary, the whole effort consists in materializing the pleasure of the text, in making the text *an object of pleasure like the others*. That is: either relate the text to the "pleasures" of life (a dish, a garden, an encounter, a voice, a moment, etc.) and to it join the personal catalogue of our sensualities, or force the text to breach bliss, that immense subjective loss, thereby identifying this text with the purest moments of perversion, with its clandestine sites. The important thing is to equalize the field of pleasure, to abolish the false opposition of practical life and contemplative life. The pleasure of the text is just that: claim lodged against the separation of the text; for what the text says, through the particularity of its name, is the ubiquity of pleasure, the atopia of bliss.

Notion of a book (of a text) in which is braided, woven, in the most personal way, the relation of every kind of bliss: those of "life" and those of the text, in which reading and the risks of real life are subject to the same anamnesis.

Imagine an aesthetic (if the word has not become too depreciated) based entirely (completely, radically, in every sense of the word) on the *pleasure of the consumer*, whoever he may be, to whatever class, whatever group he may belong, without respect to cultures or languages: the consequences would be huge, perhaps even harrowing (Brecht has sketched such an aesthetic of pleasure; of all his proposals, this is the one most frequently forgotten).

. . .

In antiquity, rhetoric included a section which is forgotten, censored by classical commentators: the *actio*, a group of formulae designed to allow for the corporeal exteriorization of discourse: it dealt with a theater of expression, the actor-orator "expressing" his indignation, his compassion, etc. *Writing aloud* is not expressive; it leaves expression to the pheno-text, to the regular code of communication; it belongs to the geno-text, to significance; it is carried not by dramatic inflections, subtle stresses, sympathetic accents, but by the *grain* of the voice, which is an erotic mixture of timbre and language, and can therefore also be, along with diction, the substance of an art: the art of guiding one's body (whence its importance in Far Eastern theaters). Due allowance being made for the sounds of the language, *writing aloud* is not phonological but phonetic; its aim is not the clarity of messages, the theater of emotions; what it searches for (in a perspective of bliss) are the pulsional incidents, the language lined with flesh, a text where we can hear the grain of the throat, the patina of consonants, the voluptuousness of vowels, a whole carnal stereophony: the articulation of the body, of the tongue, not that of meaning, of language. A certain art of singing can give an idea of this vocal writing; but since melody is dead, we may find it more easily today at the cinema. In fact, it suffices that the cinema capture the sound of speech *close up* (this is, in fact, the generalized definition of the "grain" of writing) and make us hear in their materiality, their sensuality, the breath, the gutturals, the fleshiness of the lips, a whole presence of the

human muzzle (that the voice, that writing, be as fresh, supple, lubricated, delicately granular and vibrant as an animal's
muzzle), to succeed in shifting the signified a great distance
and in throwing, so to speak, the anonymous body of the actor
into my ear: it granulates, it crackles, it caresses, it grates, it
cuts, it comes: that is bliss.

1973

from *Roland Barthes by Roland Barthes*

Actif/réactif — Active/reactive

In what he writes, there are two texts. Text I is reactive, moved by indignations, fears, unspoken rejoinders, minor paranoias, defenses, scenes. Text II is active, moved by pleasure. But as it is written, corrected, accommodated to the fiction of Style, Text I becomes active too, whereupon it loses its reactive skin, which subsists only in patches (mere parentheses).

. . .

La baladeuse — The caboose

There used to be a white streetcar that ran between Bayonne and Biarritz; in the summer, an open car was attached to it: the caboose. Everyone wanted to ride in that car: through a rather empty countryside, one enjoyed the view, the movement, the fresh air, all at the same time. Today neither the streetcar nor the caboose exists, and the trip from Biarritz is anything but a pleasure. This is not to apply a mythic embel-

Roland Barthes by Roland Barthes, translated by Richard Howard (New York: Hill and Wang, 1977).

lishment to the past, or to express regrets for a lost youth by
pretending to regret a streetcar. This is to say that the art of
living has no history: it does not evolve: the pleasure which
vanishes vanishes for good, there is no substitute for it. Other
pleasures come, which replace nothing. *No progress in pleasures*, nothing but mutations.

. . .

Et si je n'avais pas lu . . . — And if I hadn't read . . .

And if I hadn't read Hegel, or *La Princesse de Clèves,* or
Lévi-Strauss on *Les Chats,* or *l'Anti-Œdipe?* —The book
which I haven't read and which is frequently *told to me* even
before I have time to read it (which is perhaps the reason I
don't read it): this book exists to the same degree as the
other: it has its intelligibility, its memorability, its mode of
action. Have we not enough freedom to receive a text *without
the letter?*

(Repression: not to have read Hegel would be an exorbitant defect for a philosophy teacher, for a Marxist intellectual,
for a Bataille specialist. But for me? Where do my reading
duties begin?)

The person who makes a practice of writing agrees cheerfully enough to diminish or to divert the acuity, the responsibility of his ideas (one must risk this in the tone one usually
employs in saying: *What does it matter to me? don't I have
the essentials?*): in writing there would be the pleasure of a
certain inertia, a certain mental *facility*: as if I were more indifferent to my own stupidity when I write than when I speak
(how often professors are more intelligent than writers).

. . .

Qu'est-ce que l'influence? — What is influence?

It is clear in the *Critical Essays* how the subject of the writing "evolves" (shifting from an ethic of commitment to an ethic of the signifier): he evolves according to the authors he treats, in order. The inducing object, however, is not the author I am talking about but rather *what he leads me to say about him*: I influence myself *with his permission*: what I say about him forces me to think as much about myself (or not to think as much), etc.

Hence there must be a distinction between the authors about whom one writes, and whose influence is neither external nor anterior to what one says about them, and (a more classical conception) the authors whom one reads; but what comes to me from the latter group? A kind of music, a pensive sonority, a more or less dense play of anagrams. (I had my head full of Nietzsche, whom I had just been reading; but what I wanted, what I was trying to collect, was a song of sentence-ideas: the influence was purely prosodic.)

       .   .   .

J'aime, je n'aime pas — I like, I don't like

I like: salad, cinnamon, cheese, pimento, marzipan, the smell of new-cut hay (why doesn't someone with a "nose" make such a perfume), roses, peonies, lavender, champagne, loosely held political convictions, Glenn Gould, too-cold beer, flat pillows, toast, Havana cigars, Handel, slow walks, pears, white peaches, cherries, colors, watches, all kinds of writing pens, desserts, unrefined salt, realistic novels, the piano, coffee, Pollock, Twombly, all romantic music, Sartre, Brecht, Verne, Fourier, Eisenstein, trains, Médoc wine, having change, *Bouvard and Pécuchet*, walking in sandals on the lanes of southwest France, the bend of the Adour seen from Doctor L.'s house, the Marx Brothers, the mountains at seven in the morning leaving Salamanca, etc.

I don't like: white Pomeranians, women in slacks, geraniums, strawberries, the harpsichord, Miró, tautologies, animated cartoons, Arthur Rubinstein, villas, the afternoon, Satie, Bartók, Vivaldi, telephoning, children's choruses, Chopin's concertos, Burgundian branles and Renaissance dances, the organ, Marc-Antoine Charpentier, his trumpets and kettledrums, the politico-sexual, scenes, initiatives, fidelity, spontaneity, evenings with people I don't know, etc.

I like, I don't like: this is of no importance to anyone; this, apparently, has no meaning. And yet all this means: *my body is not the same as yours.* Hence, in this anarchic foam of tastes and distastes, a kind of listless blur, gradually appears the figure of a bodily enigma, requiring complicity or irritation. Here begins the intimidation of the body, which obliges others to endure me *liberally*, to remain silent and polite confronted by pleasures or rejections which they do not share.

(A fly bothers me, I kill it: you kill what bothers you. If I had not killed the fly, it would have been *out of pure liberalism*: I am liberal in order not to be a killer.)

. . .

De l'écriture à l'oeuvre — From writing to the work

Snare of infatuation: to suggest that he is willing to consider what he writes as a work, an *"oeuvre"*—to move from the contingency of writings to the transcendence of a unitary, sacred product. The word *"oeuvre"* is already a part of the image-repertoire.

The contradiction is one between writing and the work (as for the Text, that is a magnanimous word: it shows no partiality to this difference). I delight continuously, endlessly, in writing as in a perpetual production, in an unconditional dispersion, in an energy of seduction which no legal defense of the subject I fling upon the page can any longer halt. But in our mercantile society, one must end up with a work, an "*oeuvre*": one must construct, i.e., *complete*, a piece of merchandise. While I write, the writing is thereby at every moment flattened out, banalized, made guilty by the work to which it must eventually contribute. How to write, given all the snares set by the collective image of the work? —Why, *blindly*. At every moment of the effort, lost, bewildered, and driven, I can only repeat to myself the words which end Sartre's *No Exit*: Let's go on.

Writing is that *play* by which I turn around as well as I can in a narrow place: I am wedged in, I struggle between the hysteria necessary to write and the image-repertoire, which oversees, controls, purifies, banalizes, codifies, corrects, imposes the focus (and the vision) of a social communication. On the one hand I want to be desired and on the other not to be desired: hysterical and obsessional at one and the same time.

And yet: the closer I come to the work, the deeper I descend into writing; I approach its unendurable depth; a desert is revealed; there occurs—fatal, lacerating—a kind of *loss of sympathy*: I no longer feel myself to be *sympathetic* (to others, to myself). It is at this point of contact between the writing and the work that the hard truth appears to me: *I am no longer a child*. Or else, is it the *ascesis* of pleasure which I am discovering?

. . .

Projets de livres — Projected books

(These ideas are from different periods): *Journal of Desire* (Desire's daily entries, in the field of reality). *The Sentence* (ideology and erotics of the Sentence). *Our France* (new mythologies of today's France; or rather: am I happy/unhappy to be French?). *The Amateur* (record what happens to me when I paint). *Linguistics of Intimidation* (of Value, of the war of meanings). *A Thousand Fantasies* (to write one's fantasies, not one's dreams). *Ethology of the Intellectuals* (quite as important as the behavior of ants). *The Discourse of Homosexuality* (or: the discourses of homosexuality, or again: the discourse of homosexualities). An *Encyclopedia of Food* (dietetics, history, economy, geography, and above all, *symbolics*). A *Life of Illustrious Men* (read a lot of biographies and collect certain features, biographemes, as was done for Sade and Fourier). A *Compilation of Visual Stereotypes* ("Saw a North African in dark clothes, *Le Monde* under his arm, paying court to a blond girl sitting in a café"). *The Book/Life* (take some classic book and relate everything in life to it for a year). *Incidents* (mini-texts, one-liners, haiku, notations, puns, everything that falls, like a leaf), etc.

. . .

La seiche et son encre — The cuttlefish and its ink

I am writing this day after day; it takes, it sets: the cuttlefish produces its ink: I tie up my image-system (in order to protect myself and at the same time to offer myself).

How will I know that the book is finished? In other words, as always, it is a matter of elaborating a language. Now, in every language the signs return, and by dint of returning they end by saturating the lexicon—the work. Having uttered the substance of these fragments for some months, what happens to me subsequently is arranged quite spontaneously (without forcing) under the utterances that have already been made: the structure is gradually woven, and in creating itself, it increasingly magnetizes: thus it constructs for itself, without any plan on my part, a repertoire which is both finite and perpetual, like that of language. At a certain moment, no further transformation is possible but the one which occurred to the ship *Argo*: I could keep the book a very long time, by gradually changing each of its fragments.

Projet d'un livre sur la sexualité
— A projected book on sexuality

A young couple comes into my compartment and sits down; the woman is blond, made up; she is wearing big dark glasses, reads *Paris-Match*; she has a ring on each finger, and each nail on both hands is painted a different color from its two neighbors; the nail of the middle finger, a shorter nail painted a deep carmine, broadly designates the finger of masturbation. From this—from the *enchantment* this couple casts upon me, so that I cannot take my eyes off them—comes the idea of a book (or of a film) in which there would be, in this way, nothing but secondary sex characteristics (nothing pornographic); in it one would grasp (would try to grasp) the sexual "personality" of each body, which is neither its beauty nor even its "sexiness" but the way in which each sexuality immediately lets itself be read; for the young blonde with the harlequin nails and her young husband with his tight pants and warm eyes were wearing their couple-sexuality like the legion-of-honor ribbon in a buttonhole (*sexuality* and *respectability* relating to the same kind of display), and this *legible* sexuality (as Michelet would certainly have read it) filled the compartment, by an irresistible metonymy, much more certainly than any series of coquetries.

Le sexy — Sexiness

Different from secondary sexuality, the sexiness of a body (which is not its beauty) inheres in the fact that it is possible to discern (to fantasize) in it the erotic practice to which one subjects it in thought (I conceive of this particular practice, specifically, and of no other). Similarly, distinguished within the text, one might say that there are *sexy sentences*: disturbing by their very isolation, as if they possessed the promise which is made to us, the readers, by a linguistic practice, as if we were to seek them out by virtue of a pleasure *which knows what it wants*.

. . .

Plus tard — Later

He has a certain foible of providing "introductions," "sketches," "elements," postponing the "real" book till later. This foible has a rhetorical name: *prolepsis* (well discussed by Genette).

Here are some of these projected books: a History of Writing, a History of Rhetoric, a History of Etymology, a new Stylistics, an Aesthetics of textual pleasure, a new linguistic science, a Linguistics of Value, an inventory of the languages of love, a fiction based on the notion of an urban Robinson Crusoe, a summa on the *petite bourgeoisie*, a book on France entitled—in the manner of Michelet—*Our France*, etc.

These projects, generally heralding a summative, excessive book, parodic of the great monument of knowledge, can only be simple acts of discourse (prolepses indeed); they belong to the category of the dilatory. But the dilatory, denial of reality (of the realizable), is no less alive for all that: these projects live, they are never abandoned; suspended, they can return to life at any moment; or at least, like the persistent trace of an obsession, they fulfill themselves, partially, indirectly, *as gestures*, through themes, fragments, articles: the History of Writing (postulated in 1953) engenders twenty years later the idea of a seminar on a history of French discourse; the Linguistics of Value, however remotely, orients this very book. *The mountain gives birth to a mouse?* This disdainful proverb must be reversed in a positive sense: the mountain is not any too much to make a mouse.

Fourier never describes his books as anything but the heralds of the perfect Book, which he will publish later (perfectly clear, perfectly persuasive, perfectly complex). The Annunciation of the Book (the *Prospectus*) is one of those dilatory maneuvers which control our internal utopia. I imagine, I fantasize, I embellish, and I polish the great book of which I am incapable: it is a book of learning and of writing, at once a perfect system and the mockery of all systems, a summa of intelligence and of pleasure, a vengeful and tender book, corrosive and pacific, etc. (here, a foam of adjectives, an explosion of the image-repertoire); in short, it has all the qualities of a hero in a novel: it is the one coming (the *adventure*), and I herald this book that makes me my own John the Baptist, I prophesy, I announce . . .

If he often foresees books to write (which he does not write), it is because he postpones until later what bores him. Or rather, he wants to write *right away* what it pleases him to write, and not something else. In Michelet, what makes him want to rewrite are those carnal themes, the coffee, the blood, the sisal, the wheat, etc.; thus one will construct a thematic criticism for oneself, but in order not to risk it theoretically against another school—historical, biographical, etc.—for the fantasy is too egoistic to be polemical, one declares that one is concerned with no more than a *precriticism*, and that the "real" criticism (which is that of other people) will come later.

Being incessantly short of time (or you imagine yourself to be), caught up in deadlines and delays, you persist in supposing that you are going to get out of it by putting what you have to do in order. You make programs, draw up plans, calendars, new deadlines. On your desk and in your files, how many lists of articles, books, seminars, courses to teach, telephone calls to make. As a matter of fact, you never consult these little slips of paper, given the fact that an anguished conscience has provided you with an excellent memory of all your obligations. But it is irrepressible: you extend the time you lack by the very registration of that lack. Let us call this *program compulsion* (whose hypomaniacal character one readily divines); states and collectivities, apparently, are not exempt from it: how much time wasted in *drawing up programs*? And since I anticipate writing an article on it, the very notion of program itself becomes a part of my program compulsion.

Now let us reverse all this: these dilatory maneuvers, these endlessly receding projects may be writing itself. First of all, the work is never anything but the metabook (the temporary commentary) of a work to come which, *not being written*, becomes this work itself: Proust, Fourier never wrote anything but such a "Prospectus." Afterward, the work is never monumental: it is a *proposition* which each will come to saturate as he likes, as he can: I bestow upon you a certain semantic substance to run through, like a ferret. Finally, the work is a (theatrical) *rehearsal*, and this rehearsal, as in one of Rivette's films, is verbose, infinite, interlaced with commentaries, excursuses, shot through with other matters. In a word, the work is a tangle; its being is the *degree*, the step: a staircase that never stops.

. . .

1975

from *A Lover's Discourse*

IN PRAISE OF TEARS

pleurer / crying

The amorous subject has a particular propensity to cry: the functioning and appearance of tears in this subject.

1. The slightest amorous emotion, whether of happiness or of disappointment, brings Werther to tears. *Werther* Werther weeps often, very often, and in floods. Is it the lover in Werther who weeps, or is it the romantic?

It is perhaps a disposition proper to the amorous type, this propensity to dissolve in tears? Subjected to the Image-repertoire, he flouts the censure which today forbids the adult tears and by which a man means to protest his virility (Piaf's satisfaction and maternal tenderness: *"Mais vous pleurez, Milord!"*). By releasing his tears without constraint, he follows the orders of the amorous body, which is a body in liquid expansion, a bathed body: to weep

A Lover's Discourse, translated by Richard Howard (New York: Hill and Wang, 1978).

together, to flow together: delicious tears finish off the reading of Klopstock which Charlotte and Werther perform together. Where does the lover obtain the right to cry, if not in a reversal of values, of which the body is the first target? He accepts rediscovering the *infant body*.

Schubert

Further, here, the amorous body is doubled by a historical one. Who will write the history of tears? In which societies, in which periods, have we wept? Since when is it that men (and not women) no longer cry? Why was "sensibility," at a certain moment, transformed into "sentimentality"? The images of virility are shifting; the Greeks as well as our audiences of the seventeenth century cried a great deal at the theater. St. Louis, according to Michelet, suffered at not having received the gift of tears; on the one occasion that he felt tears running gently down his face,

Michelet

"They seemed to him delectable and comforting, not only to the heart but to the tongue." (Similarly: in 1199, a young monk set out for a Cistercian abbey in Brabant in order to obtain, by the tears of its inmates, the gift of tears.)

(A Nietzschean problem: How do History and Type combine? Is it not up to the type to formulate—to form—what is out of time, ahistorical? In the lover's very tears, our society represses its own timelessness, thereby turning the weeping lover into a lost object whose repression is necessary to its "health." In Rohmer's film *The Marquise of O*, the lovers weep and the audience giggles.)

2.   Perhaps "weeping" is too crude; perhaps we must not refer all tears to one and the same signification; per-

SCHUBERT: *"Lob der Tränen"* (In Praise of Tears), poem by A. W. Schlegel.

haps within the same lover there are several subjects who engage in neighboring but different modes of "weeping." Which is that "I" who has "tears in my eyes"? Which is that other self who, on a certain day, was "on the verge of tears"? Who am I who pours out "all the tears in my body"? or who sheds, upon waking, "a torrent of tears"? If I have so many ways of crying, it may be because, when I cry, I always address myself to someone, and because the recipient of my tears is not always the same: I adapt my ways of weeping to the kind of blackmail which, by my tears, I mean to exercise around me.

3.   By weeping, I want to impress someone, to bring pressure to bear upon someone ("Look what you have done to me"). It can be—as is commonly the case—the other whom one thus constrains to assume his commiseration or his insensibility quite openly; but it can also be oneself: I make myself cry, in order to prove to myself that my grief is not an illusion: tears are signs, not expressions. By my tears, I tell a story, I produce a myth of grief, and henceforth I adjust myself to it: I can live with it, because, by weeping, I give myself an emphatic interlocutor who receives the "truest" of messages, that of my body, not that of my speech: "Words, what are they? One tear will say more than all of them."

Schubert

GOSSIP

potin / gossip

Pain suffered by the amorous subject when he finds that the loved being is the subject of "gossip" and hears that being discussed promiscuously.

SCHUBERT: *"Lob der Tränen."*

1.   On the road from Phalerum, a bored traveler catches sight of another man walking ahead of him, catches up and asks him to tell about the banquet given by Agathon. Such is the genesis of the theory of love: an accident, boredom, a desire to talk, or, if you will, a gossip lasting a little over a mile. Aristodemus has been to the famous banquet; he has described it to Apollodorus, who, on the road from Phalerum, tells the story of Glaucon (a man, it is said, without any philosophic culture) and thereby, by the book's mediation, tells it to us, who are still discussing it. The *Symposium* is therefore not only a "conversation" (we are discussing a question) but also a gossip (we are speaking together about others).

Symposium

This work derives, then, from two different linguistic series, generally repressed—since official linguistics concerns itself only with the message. The first series would postulate that no question (*quaestio*) can be put without the texture of an interlocution; to speak of love, the guests not only speak together, *from image to image, from place to place* (in the *Symposium*, the arrangement of the couches has a great importance), but further imply in this general discourse the amorous links which bind them (or which they imagine bind the others): such would be the linguistics of "conversation." The second series would say that to speak is always to say something about someone; in speaking about the banquet, about Love, it is about Socrates, about Alcibiades, and about their friends that Glaucon and Apollodorus are talking: the "subject" comes to light by gossip. An active philology (that of the forces of language) would therefore include two necessary

Symposium

SYMPOSIUM: Beginning.
SYMPOSIUM: Agathon: "Come here, O Socrates, take the couch next to mine, so that I might benefit by the wise thoughts that have struck you out there on the porch." And Alcibiades's entrance.

linguistic series: that of interlocution (speaking to another) and that of delocution (speaking about someone).

2.   Werther has not yet made Charlotte's acquaintance; but in the carriage taking him to the ball (which is to pass Charlotte on the way), a friend—the voice of Gossip—discusses for Werther's benefit the woman whose image will in a few seconds so delight him: she is already engaged, he must not fall in love with her, etc. Thus gossip summarizes and heralds the story to come. Gossip is the voice of truth (Werther will fall in love with an object belonging to another), and this voice is magical: the friend is a wicked fairy who, under cover of admonishment, predicts and enforces.

When the friend speaks, her discourse is insensitive (a fairy has no pity): the gossip is light, cold, it thereby assumes the status of a kind of objectivity; its voice, in short, seems to double the voice of knowledge (*scientia*). These two voices are reductive. When knowledge, when science speaks, I sometimes come to the point of hearing its discourse as the sound of a gossip which describes and disparages lightly, coldly, and objectively what I love: which speaks of what I love *according to truth*.

3.   Gossip reduces the other to *he/she*, and this reduction is intolerable to me. For me the other is neither *he* nor *she*; the other has only a name of his own, and her own name. The third-person pronoun is a wicked pronoun: it is the pronoun of the non-person, it absents, it annuls. When I realize that common discourse takes possession of my other and restores that other to me in the bloodless form of a universal substitute, applied to all the things which are not here, it is as if I saw my other dead,

reduced, shelved in an urn upon the wall of the great mausoleum of language. For me, the other cannot be a *referent*: you are never anything but you, I do not want the Other to speak of you.

WHY?

pourquoi / why

Even as he obsessively asks himself why he is not loved, the amorous subject lives in the belief that the loved object does love him but does not tell him so.

1.   There exists a "higher value" for me: my love. I never say to myself: "What's the use?" I am not nihilistic. I do not ask myself the question of ends. Never a "why" in my monotonous discourse, except for one, always the same: *But why is it that you don't love me?* How can one not love this *me* whom love renders perfect (who gives so much, who confers happiness, etc.)? A question whose insistence survives the amorous episode: "Why didn't you love me?"; or again: *O sprich, mein herzallerliebstes Lieb, warum verliessest du mich?*—O tell, love of my heart, why have you abandoned me?

Nietzsche

Heine

2.   Soon (or simultaneously) the question is no longer "Why don't you love me?" but "Why do you only love me *a little*?" How do you manage to love *a little*? What does that mean, loving "a little"? I live under the regime of *too much* or *not enough*; greedy for coincidence as I am, everything which is not total seems parsimonious; what I

NIETZSCHE: "What does nihilism signify? *That the higher values are losing their value.* The ends are lacking, there is no answer to this question 'What's the use?' "
HEINE: *"Lyrisches Intermezzo."*

want is to occupy a site *from which quantities are no longer perceived,* and from which all accounts are banished.

Or again—for I am a nominalist: Why don't you *tell me* that you love me?

3. The truth of the matter is that—by an exorbitant

Freud   paradox—I never stop believing that I am loved. I hallucinate what I desire. Each wound proceeds less from a doubt than from a betrayal: for only the one who loves can betray, only the one who believes himself loved can be jealous: that the other, episodically, should fail in his being, which is to love me—that is the origin of all my woes. A delirium, however, does not exist unless one wakens from it (there are only retrospective deliriums): one day, I realize what has happened to me: I thought I was suffering from not being loved, and yet it is because I thought I was loved that I was suffering; I lived in the complication of supposing myself simultaneously loved and abandoned. Anyone hearing my intimate language would have had to exclaim, as of a difficult child: *But after all, what does he want?*

(*I love you* becomes *you love me.* One day, X receives some orchids, anonymously: he immediately hallucinates their source: they could only come from the person who loves him; and the person who loves him could only be the person he loves. It is only after a long period of investigation that he manages to dissociate the two inferences: the person who loves him is not necessarily the person he loves.)

FREUD: "We must take into account the fact that the hallucinatory psychosis of desire not only . . . brings concealed or repressed desires to consciousness but, further, represents them in all good faith as realized."

RAVISHMENT

ravissement / ravishment

The supposedly initial episode (though it may be reconstructed after the fact) during which the amorous subject is "ravished" (captured and enchanted) by the image of the loved object (popular name: *love at first sight*; scholarly name: enamoration). Imagining himself dead, the amorous subject sees the loved being's life continue as if nothing had happened.

1.   Language (vocabulary) has long since posited the equivalence of love and war: in both cases, it is a matter of *conquering, ravishing, capturing,* etc. Each time a sub-

Djedidi

ject "falls" in love, he revives a fragment of the archaic time when men were supposed to carry off women (in order to ensure exogamy): every lover who falls in love at first sight has something of a Sabine Woman (or of some other celebrated victim of ravishment).

However, there is an odd turnabout here: in the ancient myth, the ravisher is active, he wants to seize his prey, he is the subject of the rape (of which the object is a Woman, as we know, invariably passive); in the modern myth (that of love-as-passion), the contrary is the case: the ravisher wants nothing, does nothing; he is motionless (as any image), and it is the ravished object who is the real subject of the rape; the *object* of capture becomes the *subject* of love; and the *subject* of the conquest moves into the class of loved *object*. (There nonetheless remains a public vestige of the archaic model: the lover—the one who has been ravished—is always implicitly feminized.)

DJEDIDI, *La Poésie amoureuse des Arabes*: in Arabic, for instance, *fitna* refers to both material (or ideological) warfare and the enterprise of sexual seduction.

This singular reversal may perhaps proceed from the fact that for us the "subject" (since Christianity) is *the one who suffers*: where there is a wound, there is a subject:

Parsifal *die Wunde! die Wunde!* says Parsifal, thereby becoming "himself"; and the deeper the wound, at the body's center (at the "heart"), the more the subject becomes a subject: for the subject is *intimacy* ("The wound . . . is of a frightful intimacy"). Such is love's wound: a radical chasm (at the "roots" of being), which cannot be closed, and out of

Ruysbroeck which the subject drains, constituting himself as a subject in this very draining. It would suffice to imagine our Sabine Woman wounded to make her into the *subject* of a love story.

2.   Love at first sight is a hypnosis: I am fascinated by an image: at first shaken, electrified, stunned, "paralyzed" as Menon was by Socrates, the model of loved objects, of captivating images, or again converted by an apparition, nothing distinguishing the path of enamoration from the Road to Damascus; subsequently ensnared, held fast, immobilized, nose stuck to the image (the mirror). In that moment when the other's image comes to ravish me for the first time, I am nothing more than the Jesuit Athanasius

Athanasius   Kirchner's wonderful Hen: feet tied, the hen went to sleep
Kirchner   with her eyes fixed on the chalk line, which was traced not far from her beak; when she was untied, she remained motionless, fascinated, "submitting to her vanquisher," as the Jesuit says (1646); yet, to waken her from her enchantment, to break off the violence of her Image-repertoire (*vehemens animalis imaginatio*), it was enough to

RUYSBROECK: "The marrow of the bones wherein the roots of life reside is the center of the wound . . . The gaping thing which is deep within man does not readily close."
ATHANASIUS KIRCHNER: *Experimentum mirabile de imaginatione gallinae.*

tap her on the wing; she shook herself and began pecking in the dust again.

Freud

Werther

3.   The hypnotic episode, it is said, is ordinarily preceded by a twilight state: the subject is in a sense empty, available, offered unwittingly to the rape which will surprise him. In the same way Werther describes at some length the trivial life he leads at Wahlheim before meeting Charlotte: no mundanity, no leisure, only reading Homer, a kind of blank and prosaic daily round, lulling him (he has nothing but pease porridge). This "wondrous serenity" is merely a waiting—a desire: I never fall in love unless I have wanted to; the emptiness I produce in myself (and on which, like Werther, quite innocently, I pride myself) is nothing but that interval, longer or shorter, when I glance around me, without seeming to, looking for *who to love*. Of course love requires a release switch, just as in the case of animal rape; the bait is occasional, but the structure is profound, regular, just as the mating season is seasonal. Yet the myth of "love at first sight" is so powerful (something that falls over me, without my expecting it, without my wanting it, without my taking the least part in it) that we are astonished if we hear of someone's *deciding* to fall in love: for example, Amadour see-

Heptameron

ing Florida at the court of the Viceroy of Catalonia: "After having gazed at her a long while, *he determined upon loving her*": *se délibéra*. Indeed, shall I deliberate if I must go mad (is love, then, that madness *I want*?)?

4.   In the animal world, the release switch of the sexual mechanism is not a specific individual but only a form, a bright-colored fetish (which is how the Image-repertoire starts up). In the fascinating image, what impresses me (like a sensitized paper) is not the accumulation of its

details but this or that inflection. What suddenly manages to touch me (ravish me) in the other is the voice, the line of the shoulders, the slenderness of the silhouette, the warmth of the hand, the curve of a smile, etc. Whereupon, what does the aesthetic of the image matter? Something accommodates itself exactly to my desire (about which I know nothing); I shall therefore make no concessions to style. Sometimes it is the other's conformity to a great cultural model which enthralls me (I imagine I see the other painted by an artist of the past); sometimes, on the contrary, it is a certain insolence of the apparition which will open the wound: I can fall in love with a slightly vulgar attitude (assumed out of provocation): there are subtle, evanescent trivialities which swiftly pass over the other's body: a brief (but excessive) way of parting the fingers, of spreading the legs, of moving the fleshy part of the lips in eating, of going about some very prosaic occupation, of making one's body utterly idiotic for an instant, to keep oneself in countenance (what is fascinating about the other's "triviality" is just this, perhaps: that for a very brief interval I surprise in the other, detached from the rest of his person, something like a gesture of prostitution). The feature which touches me refers to a fragment of behavior, to the fugitive moment of an attitude, a posture, in short to a *scheme* (σχῆμα, *schema*, is the body in movement, in situation, in life).

Flaubert

etymology

5.   Stepping out of the carriage, Werther sees Charlotte for the first time (and falls in love with her), framed by the door of her house (cutting bread-and-butter for the

FLAUBERT: "And it seems that you are here, when I read love stories in books. —Everything that is taxed with being exaggerated, you have made me feel, Frédéric said. I understand how Werther could behave that way about Charlotte's bread-and-butter" (*Sentimental Education*).
ETYMOLOGY: *Trivialis*: to be found at every crossroads (*trivium*).

children: a famous scene, often discussed): the first thing
we love is *a scene.* For love at first sight requires the very
sign of its suddenness (what makes me irresponsible, subject to fatality, swept away, ravished): and of all the arrangements of objects, it is the scene which seems to be
seen best for the first time: a curtain parts: what had not
yet ever been seen is discovered in its entirety, and then
devoured by the eyes: what is immediate stands for what
is fulfilled: I am initiated: the scene *consecrates* the object
I am going to love.

Lacan

Anything is likely to ravish me which can reach me
through a ring, a rip, a rent: "The first time I saw X
through a car window: the window shifted, like a lens
searching out *who to love* in the crowd; and then—
immobilized by some *accuracy* of my desire?—I focused
on that apparition whom I was henceforth to follow for
months; but the other, as if he sought to resist this fresco
in which he was lost as a subject, whenever he was subsequently to appear in my field of vision (walking into the
café where I was waiting for him, for example) did so
with every precaution, *a minimo,* impregnating his body
with discretion and a kind of indifference, delaying his
recognition of me, etc.: in short, trying to keep himself out
of the picture."

Is the scene always visual? It can be aural, the frame can
be linguistic: I can fall in love with *a sentence spoken to
me*: and not only because it says something which manages to touch my desire, but because of its syntactical turn
(framing), which will inhabit me *like a memory.*

6.   When Werther "discovers" Charlotte (when the
curtain parts and the scene appears), Charlotte is cutting

LACAN: *Le Séminaire,* I.

bread-and-butter. What Hanold falls in love with is a woman walking (*Gradiva*: the one who comes toward him), and furthermore glimpsed within the frame of a bas-relief. What fascinates, what ravishes me is the image of a body *in situation*. What excites me is an outline in action, *which pays no attention to me*: Grusha, the young servant, makes a powerful impression on the Wolf-man: she is on her knees, scrubbing the floor. For the posture of action, of labor, guarantees, in a way, *the innocence of the image*: the more the other grants me signs of his occupation, of his indifference, of my absence, the surer I am of surprising him, as if, in order to fall in love, I had to perform the ancestral formality of rape, i.e., surprise (I surprise the other and thereby he surprises me: I did not expect to surprise him).

Freud

7.   There is a deception in amorous time (this deception is called: the love story). I believe (along with everyone else) that the amorous phenomenon is an "episode" endowed with a beginning (love at first sight) and an end (suicide, abandonment, disaffection, withdrawal, monastery, travel, etc.). Yet the initial scene during which I was ravished is merely reconstituted: it is *after the fact*. I reconstruct a traumatic image which I experience in the present but which I conjugate (which I speak) in the past:

Racine

Je le vis, je rougis, je pâlis à sa vue.
Un trouble s'éleva dans mon âme éperdue.
I saw him, blushed, turned pale when our eyes met.
Confusion seized my bewildered soul.

FREUD: *The Wolf-man.*
RACINE: *Phèdre.*

Love at first sight is always spoken in the past tense: it might be called an *anterior immediacy*. The image is perfectly adapted to this temporal deception: distinct, abrupt, framed, it is already (again, always) a memory (the nature of the photograph is not to represent but to memorialize): when I "review" the scene of the rape, I retrospectively create a stroke of luck: this scene has all the magnificence of an accident: I cannot get over having had this good fortune: to meet what matches my desire; or to have taken this huge risk: instantly to submit to an unknown image (and the entire reconstructed scene functions like the sumptuous montage of an ignorance).

J.-L.B.

REGRETTED?

regretté / regretted

Imagining himself dead, the amorous subject sees the loved being's life continue as if nothing had happened.

1.   Werther overhears Lotte and one of her friends gossiping; they are talking quite indifferently about a dying man: "And yet . . . if you were to die, if you vanished out of their lives? . . . Would your friends even notice? How deeply would they feel the loss? How long would your disappearance affect their destiny? . . ."

Werther

Not that I imagine myself dying without leaving regrets behind: the obituary is determined: rather that through the mourning itself, which I do not deny, I *see* the lives of others continuing, without change; I see them persevering in their occupations, their pastimes, their problems, frequenting the same places, the same friends; nothing would

J.-L.B.: Conversation.

change in the train of their existence. Out of love, the delirious assumption of Dependence (I have an *absolute* need of the other), is generated, quite cruelly, the adverse position: no one has any real need of me.

J.-L.B.

(Only the Mother can regret: to be depressed, it is said, is to resemble the Mother as I imagine her regretting me eternally: a dead, motionless image out of the *nekuia*; but the others are not the Mother: for them, mourning; for me, depression.)

2.   What increases Werther's panic is that the dying man (in whom he projects himself) is being *gossiped* about: Charlotte and her friends are "silly women" speaking frivolously about death. I envision myself nibbled up by others' words, dissolved in the ether of Gossip. And the Gossip will continue without my constituting any further part of it, no longer its object: a linguistic energy, trivial and tireless, will triumph over my very memory.

"HOW BLUE THE SKY WAS"

rencontre / encounter

The figure refers to the happy interval immediately following the first ravishment, before the difficulties of the amorous relationship begin.

1.   Though the lover's discourse is no more than a dust of figures stirring according to an unpredictable order, like a fly buzzing in a room, I can assign to love, at least retrospectively, according to my Image-repertoire, a settled course: it is by means of this *historical* hallucination

J.-L.B.: Conversation.

that I sometimes make love into a romance, an adventure. This would appear to assume three stages (or three acts): first comes the instantaneous capture (I am ravished by an image); then a series of encounters (dates, telephone calls, letters, brief trips), during which I ecstatically "explore" the perfection of the loved being, i.e., the unhoped-for correspondence between an object and my desire: this is the sweetness of the beginning, the interval proper to the idyll. This happy period acquires its identity (its limits) from its opposition (at least in memory) to the "sequel": the "sequel" is the long train of sufferings, wounds, anxieties, distresses, resentments, despairs, embarrassments, and deceptions to which I fall prey, ceaselessly living under the threat of a downfall which would envelop at once the other, myself, and the glamorous encounter that first revealed us to each other.

Ronsard

2.   Some lovers do not commit suicide: it is possible for me to emerge from that "tunnel" which follows the amorous encounter. I see daylight again, either because I manage to grant unhappy love a dialectical outcome (retaining the love but getting rid of the hypnosis) or because I abandon that love altogether and set out again, trying to reiterate, with others, the encounter whose dazzlement remains with me: for it is of the order of the "first pleasure" and I cannot rest until it recurs: I affirm the affirmation, I begin again, without repeating.

(The encounter is radiant; later on, in memory, the subject will telescope into one the three moments of the

RONSARD: *"Quand je fus pris au doux commencement*
D'une douceur si doucettement douce . . ."
When I was caught up in the sweet beginning
Of a sweetness so deliciously sweet . . . (*"Doux fut le trait"*)

amorous trajectory; he will speak of "love's dazzling tunnel.")

3.   In the encounter, I marvel that I have found some-one who, by successive touches, each one successful, un-failing, completes the painting of my hallucination; I am like a gambler whose luck cannot fail, so that his hand unfailingly lands on the little piece which immediately completes the puzzle of his desire. This is a gradual dis-covery (and a kind of verification) of affinities, complici-ties, and intimacies which I shall (I imagine) eternally sustain with the other, who is thereby becoming "my other": I am totally given over to this discovery (I trem-ble within it), to the point where any intense curiosity for someone encountered is more or less equivalent to love (it is certainly love which the young Moraïte feels for the traveler Chateaubriand, greedily watching his slightest ges-ture and following him until his departure). At every mo-ment of the encounter, I discover in the other another myself: *You like this? So do I! You don't like that? Nei-ther do I!* When Buvard and Pécuchet meet for the first time, they marvel over the catalogue of their shared tastes: the scene, beyond all doubt, is a love scene. The Encounter casts upon the (already ravished) amorous subject the dazzlement of a supernatural stroke of luck: love belongs to the (Dionysiac) order of the Cast of the dice.

Chateau-
briand

Buvard and
Pécuchet

(Neither knows the other yet. Hence they must tell each other: "This is what I am." This is narrative bliss, the kind which both fulfills and delays knowledge, in a word,

R.H.

CHATEAUBRIAND: *Travels in Egypt, Palestine, Greece and Barbary.*
R.H.: Conversation.

restarts it. In the amorous encounter, I keep rebounding—
I am *light*.)

REVERBERATION

retentissement / reverberation

Fundamental mode of amorous subjectivity: a word, an image
reverberates painfully in the subject's affective consciousness.

1.   What echoes in me is what I learned with my body:
something sharp and tenuous suddenly wakens this body,
which, meanwhile, had languished in the rational knowledge of a general situation: the word, the image, the
thought function like a whiplash. My inward body begins
vibrating as though shaken by trumpets answering each
other, drowning each other out: the incitation leaves its
trace, the trace widens and everything is (more or less
rapidly) ravaged. In the lover's Image-repertoire, nothing
distinguishes the most trivial provocation from an authentically consequent phenomenon; time is jerked forward (catastrophic predictions flood to my mind) and
back (I remember certain "precedents" with terror):
starting from a negligible trifle, a whole discourse of memory and death rises up and sweeps me away: this is the
kingdom of memory, weapon of reverberation—of what
Nietzsche called *ressentiment*.

(Reverberation comes from Diderot's "unforeseen incident which . . . suddenly alters the state of the characters": it is a *coup de théâtre*, the "favorable moment" of a
painting: pathetic scene of the ravaged, prostrated subject.)

2. The space of reverberation is the body—that imaginary body, so "coherent" (coalescent) that I can experience it only in the form of a generalized pang. This pang (analogous to a blush which reddens the face, with shame or emotion) is a sudden panic. In the usual kind of panic—the stage fright which precedes some sort of performance—I see myself in the future in a condition of failure, imposture, scandal. In amorous panic, I am afraid of my own destruction, which I suddenly glimpse, inevitable, clearly formed, in the flash of a word, an image.

Diderot

3. When his sentences ran dry, Flaubert flung himself on his divan: he called this his "marinade." If the thing reverberates too powerfully, it makes such a din in my body that I must halt any occupation; I stretch out on my bed and give in without a struggle to the "inner storm"; contrary to the Zen monk who empties himself of his images, I let myself be filled by them, I indulge their bitterness to the full. Depression has its own—encoded—*gestus*, then, and doubtless that is what limits it; for it suffices that at a given moment I can substitute another (even blank) gesture for this one (getting up, going to my desk, without necessarily working there, right away), to make the reverberation die down, giving way to no more than *ennui*. The bed (by day) is the site of the Image-repertoire; the desk is once again, and whatever one does there, reality.

Ruysbroeck

4. X tells me about a disagreeable rumor which concerns me. This incident reverberates within me in two ways: on the one hand, I receive the object of the message at point-blank range, outraged by its imposture, eager to

DIDEROT: "The word is not the thing, but a flash in whose light we perceive the thing."

deny it, etc.; on the other hand, I am perfectly conscious of the little impulse of aggression which has impelled X—without his being exactly aware of it himself—to pass on this wounding intelligence. Traditional linguistics would analyze only the message: conversely, active Philology would try especially to interpret, to evaluate the (here, reactive) force which directs (or attracts) it. Now, what is it that I do? I conjugate the two linguistic series, amplify them by each other: I establish myself, however painfully, in the very substance of the message (i.e., the content of the rumor), while I bitterly and mistrustfully scrutinize the force which warrants it: I lose on both counts, wounded on all sides. This is reverberation: the zealous practice of a perfect reception: contrary to the analyst (and with reason), far from "floating" while the other speaks, I listen *completely*, in a state of total consciousness: I cannot keep from hearing everything, and it is the purity of this reception which is painful to me: who can tolerate without pain a meaning that is complex and yet purified of any "noise" or interference? Reverberation makes reception into an intelligible din, and the lover into a monstrous receiver, reduced to an enormous auditive organ—as if listening itself were to become a state of utterance: in me, it is the ear which speaks.

AUBADE

réveil / waking

Various modes by which the amorous subject finds upon waking that he is once again besieged by the anxieties of his passion.

Werther   1.   Werther speaks of his exhaustion ("Let me suffer to the end: for all my exhaustion, I still have strength enough for that"). Amorous anxiety involves an expenditure which tires the body as harshly as any physical labor. "I suffered so much," someone said, "I struggled so hard all day with the image of the loved being, that I always slept very well at night." And Werther, shortly before committing suicide, goes to bed and sleeps very soundly.

S.S.

Werther

2.   Modes of waking: sad, wracked (with tenderness), affectless, innocent, panic-stricken (Octave comes to, after fainting: "All of a sudden his miseries were clear in his mind: one does not die of pain, or he was a dead man at that moment").

Stendhal

MAKING SCENES

scène / scene

The figure comprehends every "scene" (in the household sense of the term) as an exchange of reciprocal contestations.

1.   When two subjects argue according to a set exchange of remarks and with a view to having the "last word," these two subjects are *already* married: for them the scene is an exercise of a right, the practice of a language of which they are co-owners; *each one in his turn,* says the scene, which means: *never you without me,* and reciprocally. This is the meaning of what is euphemistically called *dialogue:* not to listen to each other, but to submit in common to an egalitarian principle of the distribution of language goods. The partners know that the confrontation in which they are engaged, and which will not separate them, is as inconsequential as a perverse

S.S.: Reported by S.S.
STENDHAL: *Armance.*

form of pleasure (the scene is a way of taking pleasure without the risk of having children).

Nietzsche

With the first scene, language begins its long career as an agitated, useless thing. It is dialogue (the joust of two actors) which corrupted Tragedy, even before Socrates appeared on the scene. Monologue is thereby pushed back to the very limits of humanity: in archaic tragedy, in certain forms of schizophrenia, in amorous soliloquy (at least

Jakobson

as long as I "keep" my delirium and do not yield to the desire to draw the other into a set contestation of language). It is as if the proto-actor, the madman, and the lover refused to posit themselves as hero of speech and to submit to adult language, the social language to which they are prompted by the wicked *Eris*: the language of universal neurosis.

Werther

2.   *Werther* is pure discourse of the amorous subject: the (idyllic, anguished) monologue is broken only once, at the end, just before the suicide: Werther pays a visit to Charlotte, who asks him not to come and see her again before Christmas Day, thereby signifying to him that he must visit less frequently and that henceforth his passion will no longer be "received": there follows a scene. The scene starts with a disagreement: Charlotte is embarrassed, Werther is excited, and Charlotte's embarrassment excites Werther all the more: thus the scene has only one subject, divided by a differential of energy (the scene is *electric*). So that this disequilibrium can *catch* (like a motor), so that the scene can get into its proper gear,

NIETZSCHE: "There already had existed something analogous in the exchange of remarks between the hero and the choryphaeus, but since the one was subordinate to the other, dialectical *combat* was impossible. But once two principal characters stood face to face, there was born, conforming to a profoundly Hellenic instinct, the battle of words and of arguments: amorous dialogue [what we mean by *the scene*] was unknown to Greek tragedy."

there must be a bait or decoy which each of the two partners tries to draw into his own camp; this bait is usually a fact (which one affirms and the other denies) or a decision (which one imposes and the other rejects: in *Werther*, to visit less frequently). Agreement is logically impossible insofar as what is being argued is not the fact or the decision, i.e., something which is outside language, but only precedes it: the scene has no object or at least very soon loses its object: it is that language whose object is lost. It is characteristic of the individual remarks in a scene to have no demonstrative, persuasive end, but only an origin, and this origin is never anything but immediate: in the scene, I cling to what has just been said. The (divided and yet mutual) subject of the scene is uttered in distichs: this is stichomythia, the archaic model of all the scenes in the world (when we are in a "state of scene," we speak in "rows" of words). Yet, whatever the regularity of this mechanism, the initial differential must be discoverable in each distich: thus Charlotte always turns her argument toward general propositions ("It's because it is impossible that you desire me at all"), and Werther always brings his argument back to contingence, god of amorous injury ("Your decision must have been made by Albert"). Each argument (each verse of the distich) is chosen so that it will be symmetrical and, so to speak, equal to its brother, and yet augmented with an additional protest; in short, with a *higher bid*. This bid is never anything but Narcissus' cry: *Me! And me! What about me!*

etymology

3.   The scene is like the Sentence: structurally, there is no obligation for it to stop; no internal constraint exhausts it, because, as in the Sentence, once the core is given (the

ETYMOLOGY: στίχος (*stichos*): row, file.

fact, the decision), the expansions are infinitely renewable. Only some circumstance external to its structure can interrupt the scene: the exhaustion of the two partners (that of only one would not suffice), the arrival of a third party (in *Werther*, it is Albert), or else the sudden substitution of desire for aggression. Unless these accidents are employed, no partner has the power to check a scene. What means might I have? Silence? It would merely quicken the *will to have* the scene; I am therefore obliged to answer in order to soothe, to erase. Reasoning? None is of such pure metal as to leave the other partner without something to say. Analysis of the scene itself? To shift from the scene to the metascene merely means opening another scene. Flight? This is the sign of a defection already achieved: the couple is *already* undone: like love, the scene is always reciprocal. Hence, the scene is interminable, like language itself: it is language itself, taken in its infinity, that "perpetual adoration" which brings matters about in such a way that since man has existed, *he has not stopped talking.*

(The good thing about X was that he never exploited the sentence that was given to him; by a kind of rare *askesis, he did not take advantage of language.*)

4.   No scene has a meaning, no scene moves toward an enlightenment or a transformation. The scene is neither practical nor dialectical; it is a luxury—and idle: As inconsequential as a perverse orgasm: it does not leave a mark, it does not sully. Paradox: in Sade, violence, too, does not leave a mark; the body is instantaneously restored—for new expenditures: endlessly lacerated, tainted, crushed, Justine is always fresh, whole, rested; the same is true of the scene's partners: they are reborn from the past scene

Sade

as if nothing had occurred. By the very insignificance of its
tumult, the scene recalls the Roman style of vomiting: I
tickle my uvula (I rouse myself to contestation), I vomit
(a flood of wounding arguments), and then, quite calmly,
I begin eating again.

5.   Insignificant as it is, the scene nonetheless struggles
against insignificance. Each partner of a scene dreams of
having the *last word*. To speak last, "to conclude," is to
assign a destiny to everything that has been said, is to
master, to possess, to absolve, to bludgeon meaning; in the
space of speech, the one who comes last occupies a sovereign position, held, according to an established privilege,
by professors, presidents, judges, confessors: every language combat (the *machia* of the Sophists, the *disputatio*
of the Scholastics) seeks to gain possession of this position; by the last word, I will disorganize, "liquidate" the
adversary, inflicting upon him a (narcissistically) mortal
wound, cornering him in silence, castrating him of all
speech. The scene passes with a view to this triumph:
there is no question whatever that each remark should
contribute to the victory of a truth, gradually constructing
this truth, but only that the *last* remark be the right one: it
is the last throw of the dice which counts. The scene bears
no resemblance to a chess game, but rather to a game of
hunt-the-slipper: yet here the game is inverted, for the
victory goes to the one who manages to keep the slipper in
his hand at the very moment the game stops: the slipper
changes hands throughout the scene, and the victory goes
to the player who captures that little creature whose possession assures omnipotence: the last word.

     In *Werther*, the scene is crowned with a blackmail:
Werther   "Grant me only a little peace and everything will be settled," Werther says to Charlotte in a plaintive yet threat-

ening tone: which is to say: "You will soon be rid of me":
a proposition marked with a certain voluptuous quality,
for it is in fact hallucinated as a *last word*. In order that
the subject of the scene be furnished with a truly peremptory last word, it requires no less than suicide: by the
announcement of suicide, Werther immediately becomes
the stronger of the two: whereby we see once again that
only death can interrupt the Sentence, the Scene.

What is a hero? The one who has the last word. Can we
think of a hero who does not speak before dying? To
renounce the last word (to refuse to have a scene) derives, then, from an anti-heroic morality: that of Abraham: to the end of the sacrifice demanded of him, he does
not speak. Or else, as a more subversive because less theatrical riposte (silence is always sufficient theater), the
last word may be replaced by an incongruous pirouette:
this is what the Zen master did who, for his only answer to
the solemn question "What is Buddha?," took off his san-
dal, put it on his head, and walked away: impeccable
dissolution of the last word, mastery of non-mastery.

Kierkegaard

"NO CLERGYMAN ATTENDED"

seul / alone

The figure refers, not to what the human solitude of the amorous
subject may be, but to his "philosophical" solitude, love-as-passion
being accounted for today by no major system of thought (of
discourse).

1.   What do we call that subject who persists in an
"error" against and counter to everyone, as if he had before himself all eternity in which to be "mistaken"? We

KIERKEGAARD: *Fear and Trembling.*

call him a *relapse*. Whether it be from one lover to the next or within one and the same love, I keep "falling back" into an interior doctrine which no one shares with me. When Werther's body is taken by night to a corner of the cemetery, near two lindens (the tree whose simple odor is that of memory and sleep), "no clergyman attended" (the novel's last sentence). Religion condemns in Werther not only the suicide but also, perhaps, the lover, the utopian, the class heretic, the man who is "ligatured" to no one but himself.

Werther

etymology

2.   In the *Symposium*, Eryximachus notes with some irony that he has read somewhere a panegyric of salt, but nothing on Eros, and it is because Eros is censured as a subject of conversation that the little society of the *Symposium* decides to make this the subject of its round table: rather like today's intellectuals reluctantly agreeing to discuss, precisely, Love and not politics, (amorous) Desire and not (social) Need. The eccentricity of the conversation derives from the fact that this conversation is systematic: what the guests try to produce are not proved remarks, accounts of experiences, but a doctrine: for each of them, Eros is a system. Today, however, there is no system of love: and the several systems which surround the contemporary lover offer him no room (except for an extremely devaluated place): turn as he will toward one or another of the received languages, none answers him, except in order to turn him away from what he loves. Christian discourse, if it still exists, exhorts him to repress and to sublimate. Psychoanalytical discourse (which, at least, describes his state) commits him to give up his Image-repertoire as lost. As for Marxist discourse, it has

Symposium

ETYMOLOGY: *Religare*, to tie together, to ligature.

nothing to say. If it should occur to me to knock at these doors in order to gain recognition *somewhere* (wherever it might be) for my "madness" (my "truth"), these doors close one after the other; and when they are all shut, there rises around me a wall of language which oppresses and repulses me—unless I *repent* and agree to "get rid of X."

("I have had that nightmare about a loved person who was sick in the street and begged the passers-by for help; but everyone refused him harshly, despite my own hysterical attempts to obtain medicine; the anguish of this loved person then became hysterical, for which I reproached him. I understood a little later that his person was myself —of course; who else is there to dream about?: I was appealing to all the passing languages (systems), rejected by them and pleading with all my might, *indecently*, for a philosophy which might 'understand' me—might 'shelter' me.")

3.   The lover's solitude is not a solitude of person (love confides, speaks, tells itself), it is a solitude of system: I am alone in making a system out of it (perhaps because I am ceaselessly flung back on the solipsism of my discourse). A difficult paradox: I can be understood by everyone (love comes from books, its dialect is a common one), but I can be heard (received "prophetically") only by subjects who have *exactly and right now* the same language I have. Lovers, Alcibiades says, are like those a viper has bitten: "They are unwilling, it is said, to speak

Symposium of their misfortune to anyone except those who have been victims of it as well, as being the only ones in a position to conceive and to excuse all they have dared to say and do in the throes of their pain": paltry troupe of "Starved souls," the Suicides for love (how many times will not one

Ruysbroeck and the same lover commit suicide?), to whom no great language (save, fragmentarily, that of the passé Novel) lends its voice.

4.　　　Like the early mystic, scarcely tolerated by the ecclesiastical society in which he lived, as an amorous subject I neither confront nor contest: quite simply, I have no dialogue: with the instruments of power, of thought, of knowledge, of action, etc.; I am not necessarily "depoliticized": my deviation consists in not being "excited." In return, society subjects me to a strange, public repression: no censure, no prohibition: I am merely suspended *a humanis*, far from human things, by a tacit decree of insignificance: I belong to no repertoire, participate in no asylum.

5.　　　Why I am alone:

> *"Every man has his wealth,*
> *I alone appear impoverished.*
Tao > *My mind is that of an ignorant man*
> *because it is very slow.*
> *Every man is clear-sighted,*
> *I alone am in darkness.*
> *Every man has a sharp wit,*
> *I alone have a clouded mind*
> *Which floats with the sea, blows with the wind.*
> *Every man has his goal,*
> *I alone have the dull mind of a peasant.*
> *I alone am different from other men,*
> *For I seek to suckle at my Mother's breast."*

TAO: *Tao Te Ching.*

THE UNCERTAINTY OF SIGNS

signes / signs

Whether he seeks to prove his love, or to discover if the other loves him, the amorous subject has no system of sure signs at his disposal.

Balzac

1. I look for signs, but of what? What is the object of my reading? Is it: am I loved (am I loved no longer, am I still loved)? Is it my future that I am trying to read, deciphering in what is inscribed the announcement of what will happen to me, according to a method which combines paleography and manticism? Isn't it rather, all things considered, that I remain suspended on this question, whose answer I tirelessly seek in the other's face: *What am I worth?*

Stendhal

2. The power of the Image-repertoire is immediate: I do not look for the image, it comes to me, all of a sudden. It is afterward that I return to it and begin making the good sign alternate, interminably, with the bad one: "What do these abrupt words mean: you have all my respect? Was anything ever colder? Is this a complete return to the old intimacy? Or a polite way to cut short a disagreeable explanation?" Like Stendhal's Octave, I never know what is *normal*; lacking (as I well know) all reason, I would prefer, in order to decide on an interpretation, to trust myself to common sense; but common sense affords me no more than contradictory evidence: "After

BALZAC: "She was learned and she knew that the amorous character has its signs in what are taken for trifles. A knowledgeable woman can read her future in a simple gesture, as Cuvier could say, seeing the fragment of a paw: this belongs to an animal of such-and-such a size," etc. (*The Secrets of the Princess of Cadignan*).
STENDHAL: *Armance.*

all, it's not really normal to go out in the middle of the night and to come home four hours later!" "After all, it's only normal to go out and take a walk when you can't sleep," etc. A man who wants the truth is never answered save in strong, highly colored images, which nonetheless turn ambiguous, indecisive, once he tries to transform them into signs: as in any manticism, the consulting lover must make his own truth.

3.   Freud to his fiancée: "The only thing that makes me suffer is being in a situation where it is impossible for me to prove my love to you." And Gide: "Everything in her behavior seemed to say: Since he no longer loves me, nothing matters to me. Now, I still loved her, and in fact I had never loved her so much; but it was no longer possible for me to prove it to her. That was much the worst thing of all."

Signs are not proof, since anyone can produce false or ambiguous signs. Hence one falls back, paradoxically, on the omnipotence of language: since nothing assures language, I will regard it as the sole and final assurance: *I shall no longer believe in interpretation.* I shall receive every word from my other as a sign of truth; and when I speak, I shall not doubt that he, too, receives what I say as the truth. Whence the importance of *declarations*; I want to keep wresting from the other the formula of his feeling, and I keep telling him, on my side, that I love him: nothing is left to suggestion, to divination: for a thing to be known, it must be spoken; but also, once it is spoken, even very provisionally, it is true.

.   .   .

1977

FREUD: *Letters.*
GIDE: *Journal,* 1939.

Inaugural Lecture, Collège de France

I SHOULD probably begin with a consideration of the reasons which have led the Collège de France to receive a fellow of doubtful nature, whose every attribute is somehow challenged by its opposite. For though my career has been academic, I am without the usual qualifications for entrance into that career. And though it is true that I long wished to inscribe my work within the field of science—literary, lexicological, and sociological—I must admit that I have produced only essays, an ambiguous genre in which analysis vies with writing. And though it is also true that very early on I associated my investigations with the birth and development of semiotics, it is true as well that I have scarcely any claim as its representative, so inclined was I to shift its definition (almost as soon as I found it to be formed) and to draw upon the eccentric forces of modernism, located closer to the journal *Tel Quel* than to many other periodicals which testify to the vigor of semiological inquiry.

Lecture in inauguration of the Chair of Literary Semiology, Collège de France, to which Barthes was elected. The lecture was delivered on January 7, 1977, and published as *Leçon* (Paris: Editions du Seuil) in 1978. Translated by Richard Howard.

It is then a patently impure fellow whom you receive in an establishment where science, scholarship, rigor, and disciplined invention reign. In the interests of discretion, then, and out of a personal inclination to escape intellectual difficulty through the interrogation of my own pleasure, I shall turn from the reasons which have induced the Collège de France to welcome me—for they are uncertain, in my view—and address those which make my entry here more joyful than honorific; for an honor can be undeserved—joy never is. It is my joy to encounter in this place the memory or presence of authors dear to me and who teach or have taught at the Collège de France. First, of course, comes Michelet, through whom, at the start of my intellectual life, I discovered the sovereign place of History in the study of man, and the power of writing, once scholarship accepts that commitment. Then, closer to us, Jean Baruzi and Paul Valéry, whose lectures I attended as an adolescent in this very hall. Then, closer still, Maurice Merleau-Ponty and Emile Benveniste. As for the present, allow me to exempt from the discretion and silence incumbent upon friendship the affection, intellectual solidarity, and gratitude which bind me to Michel Foucault, for it is he who kindly undertook to present this chair and its occupant to the Assembly of Professors.

Another kind of joy, more sober because more responsible, is mine today as well: that of entry into a place that we can strictly term *outside the bounds of power*. For if I may, in turn, interpret the Collège, I shall say that it is, as institutions go, one of History's last stratagems. Honor is usually a diminution of power; here it is a subtraction, power's untouched portion. A professor's sole activity here is research: to speak—I shall even say to dream his research aloud—not to judge, to give preference, to promote, to submit to controlled scholarship. This is an enormous, almost an unjust, privilege at a time when the teaching of letters is strained to the point of

exhaustion between the pressures of technocracy's demands
and of revolutionary desire, the desire of its students. To teach
or even to speak outside the limits of institutional sanction is
certainly not to be rightfully and totally uncorrupted by power;
power (the *libido dominandi*) is there, hidden in any discourse, even when uttered in a place outside the bounds of
power. Therefore, the freer such teaching, the further we must
inquire into the conditions and processes by which discourse
can be disengaged from all will-to-possess. This inquiry constitutes, in my view, the ultimate project of the instruction inaugurated today.

Indeed, it is power with which we shall be concerned, indirectly but persistently. Our modern "innocence" speaks of
power as if it were a single thing: on one side those who have
it, on the other those who do not. We have believed that power
was an exemplarily political object; we believe now that power
is also an ideological object, that it creeps in where we do not
recognize it at first, into institutions, into teaching, but still
that it is always one thing. And yet, what if power were plural,
like demons? "My name is Legion," it could say; everywhere,
on all sides, leaders, massive or minute organizations, pressure
groups or oppression groups, everywhere "authorized" voices
which authorize themselves to utter the discourse of all power:
the discourse of arrogance. We discover then that power is
present in the most delicate mechanisms of social exchange:
not only in the State, in classes, in groups, but even in fashion,
public opinion, entertainment, sports, news, family and private
relations, and even in the liberating impulses which attempt to
counteract it. I call the discourse of power any discourse
which engenders blame, hence guilt, in its recipient. Some expect of us as intellectuals that we take action on every occasion against Power, but our true battle is elsewhere, it is
against *powers* in the plural, and this is no easy combat. For if

it is plural in social space, power is, symmetrically, perpetual in historical time. Exhausted, defeated here, it reappears there; it never disappears. Make a revolution to destroy it, power will immediately revive and flourish again in the new state of affairs. The reason for this endurance and this ubiquity is that power is the parasite of a trans-social organism, linked to the whole of man's history and not only to his political, historical history. This object in which power is inscribed, for all of human eternity, is language, or to be more precise, its necessary expression: the language we speak and write.

Language is legislation, speech is its code. We do not see the power which is in speech because we forget that all speech is a classification, and that all classifications are oppressive: *ordo* means both distribution and commination. Jakobson has shown that a speech-system is defined less by what it permits us to say than by what it compels us to say. In French (I shall take obvious examples) I am obliged to posit myself first as subject before stating the action which will henceforth be no more than my attribute: what I do is merely the consequence and consecution of what I am. In the same way, I must always choose between masculine and feminine, for the neuter and the dual are forbidden me. Further, I must indicate my relation to the other person by resorting to either *tu* or *vous*; social or affective suspension is denied me. Thus, by its very structure my language implies an inevitable relation of alienation. To speak, and, with even greater reason, to utter a discourse is not, as is too often repeated, to communicate; it is to subjugate: the whole language is a generalized *rection*.

I am going to quote a remark of Renan's. "French, ladies and gentlemen," he once said in a lecture, "will never be the language of the absurd; nor will it ever be a reactionary language. I cannot imagine a serious reaction having French as its organ." Well, Renan was, in his way, perspicacious. He realized that language is not exhausted by the message engendered by it. He saw that language can survive this message and make understood within it, with a frequently terrible resonance, something other than what it says, superimposing on the subject's conscious, reasonable voice the dominating, stubborn, implacable voice of structure, i.e., of the species insofar as that species speaks. Renan's error was historical, not structural; he supposed that French—formed, as he believed, by reason—compelled the expression of a political reason which, to him, could only be democratic. But language—the performance of a language system—is neither reactionary nor progressive; it is quite simply fascist; for fascism does not prevent speech, it compels speech.

Once uttered, even in the subject's deepest privacy, speech enters the service of power. In speech, inevitably, two categories appear: the authority of assertion, the gregariousness of repetition. On the one hand, speech is immediately assertive: negation, doubt, possibility, the suspension of judgment require special mechanisms which are themselves caught up in a play of linguistic masks; what linguists call modality is only the supplement of speech by which I try, as through petition, to sway its implacable power of verification. On the other hand, the signs composing speech exist only insofar as they are recognized, i.e., insofar as they are repeated. The sign is a follower, gregarious; in each sign sleeps that monster: a stereotype. I can speak only by picking up what *loiters* around in speech. Once I speak, these two categories unite in me; I am both master and slave. I am not content to repeat what has been said, to settle comfortably in the servitude of signs: I speak, I affirm, I assert *tellingly* what I repeat.

In speech, then, servility and power are inescapably intermingled. If we call freedom not only the capacity to escape power but also and especially the capacity to subjugate no one, then freedom can exist only outside language. Unfortunately, human language has no exterior: there is no exit. We can get out of it only at the price of the impossible: by mystical singularity, as described by Kierkegaard when he defines Abraham's sacrifice as an action unparalleled, void of speech, even interior speech, performed against the generality, the gregariousness, the morality of language; or again by the Nietzschean "yes to life," which is a kind of exultant shock administered to the servility of speech, to what Deleuze calls its reactive guise. But for us, who are neither knights of faith nor supermen, the only remaining alternative is, if I may say so, to cheat with speech, to cheat speech. This salutary trickery, this evasion, this grand imposture which allows us to understand speech *outside the bounds of power*, in the splendor of a permanent revolution of language, I for one call *literature*.

I mean by *literature* neither a body nor a series of works, nor even a branch of commerce or of teaching, but the complex graph of the traces of a practice, the practice of writing. Hence, it is essentially the text with which I am concerned— the fabric of signifiers which constitute the work. For the text is the very outcropping of speech, and it is within speech that speech must be fought, led astray—not by the message of which it is the instrument, but by the play of words of which it is the theater. Thus I can say without differentiation: literature, writing, or text. The forces of freedom which are in literature depend not on the writer's civil person, nor on his political commitment—for he is, after all, only a man among others—nor do they even depend on the doctrinal content of his work, but rather on the labor of displacement he brings to bear upon the language. Seen in this light, Céline is quite as important as Hugo, and Chateaubriand as important as Zola. By this I am trying to address a responsibility of form; but this responsibility cannot be evaluated in ideological terms—which is why the sciences of ideology have always had so little hold over it. Of these forces of literature, I wish to indicate three, which I shall discuss in terms of three Greek concepts: *Mathesis, Mimesis, Semiosis.*

Literature accommodates many kinds of knowledge. In a novel like *Robinson Crusoe* there is a historical knowledge, a geographical, a social (colonial), a technological, a botanical, an anthropological knowledge (Robinson proceeds from Nature to culture). If, by some unimaginable excess of socialism or barbarism, all but one of our disciplines were to be expelled from our educational system, it is the discipline of literature which would have to be saved, for all knowledge, all the sciences are present in the literary monument. Whereby we can say that literature, whatever the school in whose name it declares itself, is absolutely, categorically *realist*: it is reality, i.e., the very spark of the real. Yet literature, in this truly encyclopedic respect, displaces the various kinds of knowledge, does not fix or fetishize any of them; it gives them an indirect place, and this indirection is precious. On the one hand, it allows for the designation of possible areas of knowledge—unsuspected, unfulfilled. Literature works in the interstices of science. It is always behind or ahead of science, like the Bolognese stone which gives off by night what it has stored up by day, and by this indirect glow illuminates the new day which dawns. Science is crude, life is subtle, and it is for the correction of this disparity that literature matters to us. The knowledge it marshals is, on the other hand, never complete or final. Literature does not say that it knows something, but that it knows *of* something, or better, that it knows *about* something—that it knows about men. What it knows about men is what we might call the great *mess* of language, upon which men work and which works upon them. Literature can reproduce the diversity of sociolects, or, starting from this diversity, and suffering its laceration, literature may imagine and seek to elaborate a limit-language which would be its zero degree. Because it *stages* language instead of simply using it, literature feeds knowledge into the machinery of infinite reflexivity. Through writing, knowledge ceaselessly reflects on knowledge, in terms of a discourse which is no longer epistemological, but dramatic.

It is good form, today, to contest the opposition of sciences and letters, insofar as the number of relations, whether of model or method, uniting these two regions and often erasing their frontier is increasing, and it is possible that this opposition will appear one day to be a historical myth. But from the point of view of language, which is ours here, this opposition is pertinent; moreover it does not necessarily set up the opposition between the real and the fantastic, the objective and the subjective, the True and the Beautiful, but only different loci of speech. According to scientific discourse—or a certain discourse of science—knowledge is statement; in writing, it is an act of stating. The statement, the usual object of linguistics, is given as the product of the subject's absence. The act of stating, by exposing the subject's place and energy, even his deficiency (which is not his absence), focuses on the very reality of language, acknowledging that language is an immense halo of implications, of effects, of echoes, of turns, returns, and degrees. It assumes the burden of making understood a subject both insistent and ineffable, unknown and yet recognized by a disturbing familiarity. Words are no longer conceived illusively as simple instruments; they are cast as projections, explosions, vibrations, devices, flavors. Writing makes knowledge festive.

The paradigm I am proposing here does not follow the functional division: it is not aimed at putting scientists and researchers on one side, writers and essayists on the other. On the contrary, it suggests that writing is to be found wherever words have flavor (the French words for *flavor* and *knowledge* have the same Latin root). Curnonski used to say that in cooking "things should have the taste of what they are."

Where knowledge is concerned, things must, if they are to become what they are, what they have been, have that ingredient, the salt of words. It is this taste of words which makes knowledge profound, fecund. I know for instance that Michelet proposes much that is denied by historical scholarship. Nonetheless Michelet founded something on the order of an ethnology of France, and each time a historian displaces historical knowledge, in the broadest sense of the term and whatever its object, we find, quite simply, writing.

Literature's second force is its force as representation. From ancient times to the efforts of our avant-garde, literature has been concerned to represent something. What? I will put it crudely: the real. The real is not representable, and it is because men ceaselessly try to represent it by words that there is a history of literature. That the real is not representable, but only demonstrable, can be said in several ways: either we can define it, with Lacan, as the *impossible*, that which is unattainable and escapes discourse, or in topological terms we observe that a pluri-dimensional order (the real) cannot be made to coincide with a unidimensional order (language). Now, it is precisely this topological impossibility that literature rejects and to which it never submits. Though there is no parallelism between language and the real, men will not take sides, and it is this refusal, perhaps as old as language itself, which produces, in an incessant commotion, literature. We can imagine a history of literature, or better, say, of productions of language, which would be the history of certain (often aberrant) verbal *expedients* men have used to reduce, tame, deny, or, on the contrary, to assume what is *always* a delirium, i.e., the fundamental inadequation of language and the real. I said a moment ago, apropos of knowledge, that literature is categorically realist, in that it never has anything but the real as its object of desire; and I shall say now, without contradicting myself—

because I am here using the word in its familiar acceptation—
that literature is quite as stubbornly unrealistic; it considers
sane its desire for the impossible.

This function—perhaps perverse, therefore fitting—has a
name: it is the utopian function. Here we come back to History. For it is in the second half of the nineteenth century, one
of the grimmest periods of calamitous capitalism, that literature finds its exact figure, at least for us Frenchmen, in Mallarmé. Modernity—our modernity, which begins at this period
—can be defined by this new phenomenon: that *utopias of
language* are conceived in it. No "history of literature" (if
such is still to be written) could be legitimate which would be
content, as in the past, to link the various schools together
without indicating the gap which here reveals a new prophetic
function, that of writing. "To change language," that Mallarméan expression, is a concomitant of "To change the
world," that Marxian one. There is a *political* reception of
Mallarmé, of those who have followed him and follow him
still.

From this there follows a certain ethic of literary language,
which must be affirmed, because it is contested. We often
reproach the writer, the intellectual, for not writing "everyone's" language. But it is good that men, within the same
language—for us, French—should have several kinds of
speech. If I were a legislator (an aberrant supposition for
someone who, etymologically speaking, is an "an-archist"),
far from imposing a unification of French, whether bourgeois
or popular, I would instead encourage the simultaneous ap-
prenticeship to several French forms of speech, of various
function, promoted to equality. Dante seriously debates which
language he will use to write the *Convivio*: Latin or Tuscan?
Nor is it for political or polemical reasons that he chooses the
vulgar tongue: it is by considering the appropriateness of ei-

ther language to his subject. The two forms of speech—as for us, classical French and modern French, written French and spoken French—thus form a reservoir from which he is free to draw, *according to the truth of desire*. This freedom is a luxury which every society should afford its citizens: as many languages as there are desires—a utopian proposition in that no society is yet ready to admit the plurality of desire. That a language, whatever it be, not repress another; that the subject may know without remorse, without repression, the bliss of having at his disposal two kinds of language; that he may speak this or that, according to his perversions, not according to the Law.

Utopia, of course, does not save us from power. The utopia of language is salvaged as the language of utopia—a genre like the rest. We can say that no writer who began in a rather lonely struggle against the power of language could or can avoid being coopted by it, either in the posthumous form of an inscription within official culture, or in the present form of a mode which imposes its image and forces him to conform to expectation. No way out for this author than to shift ground— or to persist—or both at once.

To persist means to affirm the Irreducible of literature, that which resists and survives the typified discourses, the philosophies, sciences, psychologies which surround it, to act as if literature were incomparable and immortal. A writer—by which I mean not the possessor of a function or the servant of an art, but the subject of a praxis—must have the persistence of the watcher who stands at the crossroads of all other discourses, in a position that is *trivial* in relation to purity of doctrine (*trivialis* is the etymological attribute of the prostitute who waits at the intersection of three roads). To persist means, in short, to maintain, over and against everything, the force of drift and of expectation. And it is precisely because it

persists that writing is led to shift ground. For power seizes
upon the pleasure of writing as it seizes upon all pleasure, to
manipulate it and to make of it a product that is gregarious,
nonperverse, in the same way that it seizes upon the genetic
product of love's pleasure, to turn it into soldiers and fighters
to its own advantage. *To shift ground*, then, can mean: to go
where you are not expected, or, more radically, to *abjure* what
you have written (but not necessarily what you have thought),
when gregarious power uses and subjugates it. Pasolini was
thus led to "abjure" (as he said) his "trilogy of life" films
because he realized that power was making use of them—yet
without regretting the fact that he made them in the first place.
"I believe," he said in a text published posthumously, "that
before action we must never in any case fear annexation by
power and its culture. We must behave as if this dangerous
eventuality did not exist. . . . But I also believe that *afterward*
we must be able to realize how much we may have been used
by power. And then, if our sincerity or our necessity has been
controlled or manipulated, I believe we must have the courage
to abjure."

To persist and, at the same time, to shift ground relates, in
short, to a kind of acting. We must therefore not be surprised
if on the impossible horizon of linguistic anarchy—at that
point where language attempts to escape its own power, its
own servility—we find something which relates to theater. To
designate the impossible in language, I have cited two authors:
Kierkegaard and Nietzsche. Yet both have written. It was in
each instance, however, in a reversal of identity, as a performance, as a frenzied gambling of proper names—one by incessant recourse to pseudonymity, the other by proceeding, at the
end of his writing life, as Klossowski has shown, to the limits
of the histrionic. We might say that literature's third force, its
strictly semiotic force, is to *act* signs rather than to destroy
them—to feed them into a machinery of language whose

safety catches and emergency brakes have exploded; in short, to institute, at the very heart of servile language, a veritable heteronymy of things.

Which brings us to semiology.

First of all we must repeat that the sciences (at least those in which I have done any reading at all) are not eternal; they are values which rise and fall on an Exchange—the Exchange of History. In this regard, it suffices to recall the exchange fate of Theology, now a diminished area of discourse, yet once so sovereign a science as to be placed outside and above the Septenium. The fragility of the so-called human sciences derives perhaps from this: that they are *unforeseeing* sciences (whence the disappointments and the taxonomic discomfort of Economics)—which immediately alters the notion of science. Even the science of desire, psychoanalysis, must die one of these days, though we all owe it a great deal, as we owe a great deal to Theology: for desire is stronger than its interpretation.

Semiology, which we can canonically define as the science of signs, of all signs, has emerged from linguistics through its operational concepts. But linguistics itself, somewhat like economics (and the comparison is perhaps not insignificant), is, I believe, in the process of splitting apart. On the one hand, linguistics tends toward the formal pole, and, like econometrics, it is thereby becoming more formalized; on the other hand, linguistics is assimilating contents that are more and more numerous and remote from its original field. Just as the object of economics today is everywhere, in the political, the social, the cultural, so the object of linguistics is limitless. Speech, according to an intuition of Benveniste's, is the social itself. In short, either due to excessive ascesis or excessive hunger, whether famished or replete, linguistics is deconstructing itself. It is this deconstruction of linguistics that I, for my part, call *semiology*.

You may have noticed that in the course of my presentation
I have surreptitiously shifted from language to discourse, in
order to return, sometimes without warning, from discourse to
language, as if I were dealing with the same object. I believe,
indeed, that today, within the pertinence chosen here, language
and discourse are undivided, for they move along the same
axis of power. Yet initially this originally Saussurian distinction
(the pairing was *Langue/Parole*) was very useful; it gave
semiology the courage to begin. By this opposition, I could
reduce discourse, miniaturize it into a grammatical example,
and thereby hope to hold all human communication under my
net, like Wotan and Loge securing Alberich transformed into a
tiny toad. But the example is not "the thing itself," and the
matter of language cannot be held or contained in the limits of
the sentence. It is not only the phonemes, the words, and the
syntactical articulations which are subject to a system of controlled freedom, since we cannot combine them arbitrarily; it
is the whole stratum of discourse which is fixed by a network
of rules, constraints, oppressions, repressions, massive and
blurred at the rhetorical level, subtle and acute at the grammatical level. Language flows out into discourse; discourse
flows back into language; they persist one above the other like
children topping each other's fists on a baseball bat. The distinction between language and discourse no longer appears
except as a transitory operation—something, in short, to "abjure." There has come a time when, as though stricken with a
gradually increasing deafness, I hear nothing but a single
sound, that of language and discourse mixed. And linguistics
now seems to me to be working on an enormous imposture, on
an object it makes improperly clean and pure by wiping its
fingers on the skein of discourse, like Trimalchio on his slaves'
hair. Semiology would consequently be that labor which collects the impurity of language, the waste of linguistics, the
immediate corruption of the message: nothing less than the

desires, the fears, the appearances, the intimidations, the advances, the blandishments, the protests, the excuses, the aggressions, the various kinds of music out of which active language is made.

I know how personal such a definition is. I know whereof it compels my silence: in one sense, and quite paradoxically, all of semiology, the semiology which is being studied and already acknowledged as the positive science of signs, which is developing in periodicals, associations, universities, and study centers. Nevertheless, it seems to me that the intention behind the establishment of a chair at the Collège de France is not so much the consecration of a discipline as the allowing for the continuance of a certain individual labor, the adventure of a certain subject. Now, semiology, so far as I am concerned, started from a strictly emotional impulse. It seemed to me (around 1954) that a science of signs might stimulate social criticism, and that Sartre, Brecht, and Saussure could concur in this project. It was a question, in short, of understanding (or of describing) how a society produces stereotypes, i.e., triumphs of artifice, which it then consumes as innate meanings, i.e., triumphs of Nature. Semiology (my semiology, at least) is generated by an intolerance of this mixture of bad faith and good conscience which characterizes the general morality, and which Brecht, in his attack upon it, called the Great Habit. *Language worked on by power:* that was the object of this first semiology.

Semiology then shifted ground, took on a different coloration, while retaining the same political object—for there is no other. This shift occurred because the intellectual community has changed, if only through the break of May '68. On the one hand, contemporary studies have modified and are modifying the critical image of the social subject and of the speaking subject. On the other hand, it has appeared that, insofar as the machinery of contestation was multiplying, power itself, as a

discursive category, was dividing, spreading like a liquid leaking everywhere, each opposition group becoming in its turn
and in its way a pressure group and intoning in its own name
the very discourse of power, the universal discourse. Political
bodies were seized with a kind of moral excitement, and even
when claims were being made for pleasure, the tone was
threatening. Thus we have seen most proposed liberations,
those of society, of culture, of art, of sexuality, articulated in
the forms of the discourse of power. We took credit for restoring what had been crushed, without seeing what else we
crushed in the process.

   If the semiology I am speaking of then returned to the Text,
it is because, in this concert of minor dominations, the Text
itself appeared as the very index of *nonpower*. The Text contains in itself the strength to elude gregarious speech (the
speech which incorporates), even when that speech seeks to
reconstitute itself in the Text. The Text always postpones—
and it is this movement of *mirage* I have attempted to describe
and to justify just now in speaking of literature. The Text
procrastinates elsewhere, toward an unclassified, atopic site, so
to speak, far from the topoi of politicized culture, "that obligation to form concepts, species, forms, ends, laws . . . that
world of identical cases," of which Nietzsche speaks. Gently,
transitorily, the text raises that cope of generality, of morality,
of in-difference (let us clearly separate this prefix from the
root), which weighs on our collective discourse. Literature
and semiology thereby combine to correct each other. On one
side, the incessant return to the text, ancient or modern, the
regular plunge into the most complex of signifying practices,
i.e., writing (since writing operates with ready-made signs),
forces semiology to work on differences, and keeps it from
dogmatizing, from "taking"—from taking itself for the universal discourse which it is not. And on the other side, semiotic
scrutiny, focused on the text, forces us to reject the myth

usually resorted to in order that literature may be saved from the gregarious speech surrounding and besetting it—from the myth of pure creativity. The sign must be thought—or re-thought—the better to be deceived.

The semiology I speak of is both *negative* and *active*. Someone bedeviled throughout life, for better and for worse, by language, can only be fascinated by the forms of its void—as against its emptiness. The semiology proposed here is there-fore negative—or better still, however heavy the term, *apophatic*—not in that it repudiates the sign, but in that it denies that it is possible to attribute to the sign traits that are positive, fixed, ahistoric, acorporeal, in short: scientific. This apophatic quality involves at least two consequences which directly concern the teaching of semiology.

The first is that semiology cannot itself be a metalanguage, though at its origin it was entirely so predisposed, since it is a language about languages. It is precisely in reflecting on the sign that semiology discovers that every relation of exteriority of one language to another is, *in the long run*, untenable. Time erodes my power of distance, mortifies it, turns this distance into sclerosis. I cannot function *outside* language, treating it as a target, and *within* language, treating it as a weapon. If it is true that the subject of science is that very subject which is not shown, and that it is ultimately this retention of the spectacle that we call "metalanguage," then what I am led to assume, in speaking of signs with signs, is the very spectacle of this bi-zarre coincidence, of that strange squint which relates me to the Chinese shadow-casters when they show both their hands and the rabbit, the duck, and the wolf whose silhouettes they simulate. And to those who take advantage of this condition to deny that active semiology, the semiology which writes, has anything to do with science, we must reply that it is by an epistemological abuse, *which in fact is beginning to crumble*, that we identify metalanguage and science, as if one were the necessary condition of the other, whereas it is only its historical, hence challengeable, sign. It may be time to distinguish the metalinguistic, which is a label like any other, from the scientific, whose criteria are elsewhere (perhaps, let it be said in passing, what is strictly scientific is the destruction of the science which precedes).

Semiology has a relation to science, but it is not a discipline (this is the second consequence of its apophatic quality). What relation? An ancillary relation: it can help certain sciences, can be their fellow traveler for a while, offering an operational protocol starting from which each science must specify the difference of its corpus. Thus, the best-developed part of semiology, the analysis of narrative, can be useful for History, ethnology, textual criticism, exegesis, and iconology (every image is, in a way, a narrative). In other words, semiology is not a grid; it does not permit a direct apprehension of the real through the imposition of a general transparency which would render it intelligible. It seeks instead to elicit the real, in places and by moments, and it says that these efforts to elicit the real are possible without a grid. It is in fact precisely when semiology comes to be a grid that it elicits nothing at all. We can therefore say that semiology has no substitutive role with regard to any discipline. It is my hope that semiology will replace no other inquiry here, but will, on the contrary, help all the rest, that its chair will be a kind of wheelchair, the wild card of contemporary knowledge, as the sign itself is the wild card of all discourse.

This negative semiology is an active semiology: it functions outside death. I mean by this that it does not rest on a "semiophysis," an inert naturalness of the sign, and that it is also not a "semioclasty," a destruction of the sign. Rather, to continue the Greek paradigm, it is a *semiotropy*; turned toward the sign, this semiology is captivated by and receives the sign, treats and, if need be, imitates it as an imaginary spectacle. The semiologist is, in short, an artist (the word as I use it here neither glorifies nor disdains; it refers only to a typology). He plays with signs as with a conscious decoy, whose fascination he savors and wants to make others savor and understand. The sign—at least the sign he sees—is always immediate, subject to the kind of evidence that leaps to the eyes, like a trigger of the imagination, which is why this semiology (need I specify once more: the semiology of the speaker) is not a hermeneutics: it paints more than it digs, *via di porre* rather than *via de levare*. Its objects of predilection are texts of the Image-making process: narratives, images, portraits, expressions, idiolects, passions, structures which play simultaneously with an appearance of verisimilitude and with an uncertainty of truth. I should like to call "semiology" the course of operations during which it is possible—even called for—to play with the sign as with a painted veil, or again, with a fiction.

This pleasure of the imaginary sign is conceivable now due to certain recent mutations, which affect culture more than society itself: the use we can make of the forces of literature I have mentioned is modified by a new situation. On one hand and first of all, the myth of the great French writer, the sacred depositary of all higher values, has crumbled since the Liberation; it has dwindled and died gradually with each of the last survivors of the *entre-deux-guerres*; a new *type* has appeared, and we no longer know—or do not yet know—what to call him: writer? intellectual? scribe? In any case, literary mastery is vanishing; the writer is no longer center stage. On the other hand and subsequently, May '68 has revealed the crisis in our teaching. The old values are no longer transmitted, no longer circulate, no longer impress; literature is desacralized, institutions are impotent to defend and impose it as the implicit model of the human. It is not, if you like, that literature is destroyed; rather *it is no longer protected*, so that this is the moment to deal with it. Literary semiology is, as it were, that journey which lands us in a country free by default; angels and dragons are no longer there to defend it. Our gaze can fall, not without perversity, upon certain old and lovely things, whose signified is abstract, out of date. It is a moment at once decadent and prophetic, a moment of gentle apocalypse, a historical moment of the greatest possible pleasure.

If then, in this teaching which, given its very location, expects no sanction other than the loyalty of its auditors, if method intervenes as a systematic procedure, it cannot be a heuristic method meant to result in decoding. Method can bear only upon language itself, insofar as it struggles to baffle any discourse *which takes*, which is why we can justly claim that method, too, is a Fiction—a proposition already advanced by Mallarmé when he thought of preparing a thesis in linguistics: "All method is a fiction. Language has appeared as the instrument of fiction; it will follow the method of language, language reflecting upon itself." What I hope to be able to renew, each of the years it is given me to teach here, is the manner of presentation of the course or seminar, in short, of "presenting" a discourse without imposing it: that would be the methodological stake, the *quaestio*, the point to be debated. For what can be oppressive in our teaching is not, finally, the knowledge or the culture it conveys, but the discursive forms through which we propose them. Since, as I have tried to suggest, this teaching has as its object discourse taken in the inevitability of power, method can really bear only on the means of loosening, baffling, or at the very least, of lightening this power. And I am increasingly convinced, both in writing and in teaching, that the fundamental operation of this loosening method is, if one writes, fragmentation, and, if one teaches, digression, or, to put it in a preciously ambiguous word, *excursion*. I should therefore like the speaking and the listening that will be interwoven here to resemble the comings and goings of a child playing beside his mother, leaving her, returning to bring her a pebble, a piece of string, and thereby tracing around a calm center a whole locus of play within which the pebble, the string come to matter less than the enthusiastic giving of them.

When the child behaves in this way, he in fact describes the comings and goings of desire, which he endlessly presents and represents. I sincerely believe that at the origin of teaching such as this we must always locate a fantasy, which can vary from year to year. This, I know, may seem provocative: how, in the context of an institution, however free it may be, dare we speak of a phantasmic teaching? Yet if we consider for a moment the surest of human sciences, if we consider History, how can we help acknowledging that it has a continuous relation with fantasy? This is what Michelet understood: History is ultimately the history of the phantasmic site par excellence, that of the human body. It was by starting from this fantasy, linked for him with the lyric resurrection of past bodies, that Michelet could make History into an enormous anthropology. Science can thus be born of fantasy. It is to a fantasy, spoken or unspoken, that the professor must annually return, at the moment of determining the direction of his journey. He thereby turns from the place where he is expected, the place of the Father, who is always dead, as we know. For only the son has fantasies; only the son is alive.

The other day, I reread Thomas Mann's novel *The Magic Mountain*. This book deals with a disease I know well, tuberculosis. By my reading, I held in consciousness three moments of this disease: the moment of the story, which takes place before World War I; the moment of my own disease, around 1942; and the present moment, when this disease, vanquished by chemotherapy, has no longer the same aspect it once had. Now, the tuberculosis I experienced is, down to virtually the last detail, the tuberculosis of *The Magic Mountain*. The two moments were united, equally remote from my own present. I then realized with stupefaction (only the obvious can stupefy) that *my own body was historical*. In a sense, my body is the contemporary of Hans Castorp, the novel's hero; my body, still unborn, was already twenty years old in 1907, the year when Hans entered and took up residence in "the country up there." My body is much older than I, as if we always kept the age of the social fears with which life has accidentally given us contact. Therefore, if I want to live, I must forget that my own body is historical. I must fling myself into the illusion that I am contemporary with the young bodies present before me, and not with my own body, my past body. In short, I must be periodically reborn. I must make myself younger than I am. At fifty-one, Michelet began his *vita nuova*, a new work, a new love. Older than he (you will understand that this parallel is out of fondness), I too am entering a *vita nuova*, marked today by this new place, this new hospitality. I undertake therefore to let myself be borne on by the force of any living life, forgetfulness. There is an age at which we teach what we know. Then comes another age at which we teach what we do not know; this is called *research*. Now perhaps comes the age of another experience: that of *unlearning*, of yielding to the unforeseeable change which forgetting imposes on the sedimentation of the knowledges, cultures, and beliefs we have traversed. This experience has, I believe, an illustrious and outdated name, which I now simply venture to appropriate at the very crossroads of its etymology: *Sapientia*: no power, a little knowledge, a little wisdom, and as much flavor as possible.

1977

Deliberation

I'VE never kept a journal—or rather I've never known if I should keep one. Sometimes I begin, and then, right away, I leave off—and yet, later on, I begin again. The impulse is faint, intermittent, without seriousness and of no doctrinal standing whatever. I guess I could diagnose this *diary disease*: an insoluble doubt as to the value of what one writes in it.

Such doubt is insidious: it functions by a kind of delayed action. Initially, when I write the (daily) entry, I experience a certain pleasure: this is simple, this is easy. Don't worry about finding *something to say*: the raw material is right here, right now; a kind of surface mine; all I have to do is bend over—I don't need to transform anything: the crude ore has its own value, etc. Then comes the second phase, very soon after the first (for instance, if I reread today what I wrote yesterday), and it makes a bad impression: the text doesn't hold up, like some sort of delicate foodstuff which "turns," spoils, becomes unappetizing from one day to the next; I note with discouragement the artifice of "sincerity," the artistic mediocrity of the "spontaneous"; worse still: I am disgusted and irritated to find a "pose" I certainly hadn't intended: in a journal situation,

"Délibération" was published in *Tel Quel*, No. 82, Winter 1979. Translated by Richard Howard.

and precisely because it doesn't "work"—doesn't get transformed by the action of work—*I* is a *poseur*: a matter of
effect, not of intention, the whole difficulty of literature is here.
Very soon, continuing my reperusal, I get tired of these verb-
less sentences ("Sleepless night. And the third in a row," etc.)
or sentences whose verb is carelessly condensed ("Passed two
girls in the Place St-S.")—and try as I will to re-establish the
propriety of a complete form ("I passed . . ." "I spent a
sleepless night"), the matrix of any journal, i.e., the reduction
of the verb, persists in my ear and exasperates me like a
refrain. In a third phase, if I reread my journal pages several
months, several years after having written them, though my
doubt hasn't dissipated, I experience a certain pleasure in rediscovering, thanks to these lines, the events they relate, and
even more, the inflections (of light, of atmosphere, of mood)
they bring back. In short, at this point no literary interest
(save for problems of formulation, i.e., of phrasing), but a
kind of narcissistic attachment (faintly narcissistic—let's not
exaggerate) to *my* doings (whose recall is inevitably ambiguous, since to remember is also to acknowledge and to lose
once again what will not recur). But still, does this final indulgence, achieved after having traversed a phase of rejection,
justify (systematically) keeping a journal? Is it *worth the
trouble*?

   I am not attempting any kind of analysis of the "Journal"
genre (there are books on the subject), but only a personal
deliberation, intended to afford a practical decision: should I
keep a journal *with a view to publication*? Can I make the
journal into a "work"? Hence I refer only to the functions
which immediately come to mind. For instance, Kafka kept a
diary in order to "extirpate his anxiety," if you prefer, "to find
salvation." This motive would not be a natural one for me, or
at least not a constant one. Nor would the aims traditionally

attributed to the intimate Journal; they no longer seem pertinent to me. They are all connected to the advantages and the prestige of "sincerity" (to express yourself, to explain yourself, to judge yourself); but psychoanalysis, the Sartrean critique of bad faith, and the Marxist critique of ideologies have made "confession" a futility: sincerity is merely a second-degree Image-repertoire. No, the Journal's justification (as a work) can only be *literary* in the absolute, even if nostalgic, sense of the word. I discern here four motives.

The first is to present a text tinged with an individuality of writing, with a "style" (as we used to say), with an idiolect proper to the author (as we said more recently); let us call this motive: poetic. The second is to scatter like dust, from day to day, the traces of a period, mixing all dimensions and proportions, from important information to details of behavior: don't I take great pleasure in reading Tolstoy's journal to discover the life of a Russian nobleman in the nineteenth century? Let us call this motive: historical. The third is to constitute the author as an object of desire: if an author interests me, I may want to know the intimacy, the *small change* of his time, his tastes, his moods, his scruples; I may even go so far as to prefer his person to his work, eagerly snatching up his Journal and neglecting his books. Hence I can attempt—making myself the author of the pleasure others have been able to afford me—I can attempt in my turn to seduce, by that swivel which shifts from writer to person, and vice versa; or, more seriously, I can attempt to prove that "I am worth more than what I write" (in my books): the writing in my Journal then appears as a *plus power* (Nietzsche: *Plus von Macht*), which it is supposed will compensate the inadequacies of public writing; let us call this motive: utopian, since it is true that we are never done with the Image-repertoire. The fourth motive is to constitute the Journal as a workshop of sentences: not of "fine phrases," but of correct ones, exact language: constantly to refine the exactitude of the speech-act (and not of the speech), according to an enthusiasm and an application, a fidelity of intention which greatly resembles passion: "Yea, my reins shall rejoice, when thy lips speak right things" (Proverbs 23, xvi). Let us call this motive: amorous (perhaps even: idolatrous—I idolize the Sentence).

For all my sorry impressions, then, the desire to keep a Journal is conceivable. I can admit that it is possible, in the actual context of the Journal, to shift from what at first seemed to me improper in literature to a form which in fact rallies its qualities: the individuation, the scent, the seduction, the fetishism of language. In recent years, I have made three attempts; the first and most serious one—because it occurred during my mother's last illness—is the longest, perhaps because it corresponded in some degree to the Kafkaesque goal of extirpating anxiety by writing; each of the other two concerned only one day: they are more experimental, though I can't reread them without a certain nostalgia for the day that has passed (I give only one of these, the second one involving others besides myself).

I

U——, July 13, 1977

Madame ***, the new cleaning woman, has a diabetic grandson she takes care of, we are told, with devotion and expertise. Her view of this disease is confused: on the one hand, she does not admit that diabetes is hereditary (which would be a sign of inferior stock), and on the other, she insists that it is fatal, absolving any responsibility of origin. She posits disease as a social image, and this image is beset with pitfalls. The Mark certainly appears as a source of pride and of pain: what is was for Jacob-Israel, dislocated, disconnected by the Angel: delight and shame of being re-marked.

Depression, fear, anxiety: I see the death of a loved one, I panic, etc. Such an imagination is the very opposite of faith. For constantly to imagine the inevitability of disaster is constantly to accept it: to utter it is to assert it (again the fascism of language). By imagining death, I discourage the miracle. In Ordet *the madman did not speak, refused the garrulous and peremptory language of inwardness. Then what is this incapacity for faith? Perhaps a very human love? Love, then, excludes faith? And vice versa?*

Gide's old age and death (which I read about in Mme van Rysselberghe's Cahiers de la petite dame*) were surrounded by witnesses. But I do not know what has become of these witnesses: no doubt, in most cases, dead in their turn: there is a time when the witnesses themselves die without witnesses. Thus History consists of tiny explosions of life, of deaths without relays. Our human impotence with regard to transition, to any science of degrees. Conversely, we can attribute to the classical God the capacity to see an infinity of degrees: "God" as the absolute Exponential.*

(Death, real death, is when the witness himself dies. Chateaubriand says of his grandmother and his great-aunt: "I may be the only man in the world who knows that such persons have existed": yes, but since he has written this, and written it well, we know it too, insofar, at least, as we still read Chateaubriand.)

July 14, 1977

A little boy—nervous, excited, like any number of French kids, who so quickly pretend to be grown up, is dressed up as a musical-comedy grenadier (red and white); doubtless he will precede the band.

Why is Worry harder to bear here than in Paris? —This Village is a world so natural, so exempt from any extrava-

gance, that the impulses of sensibility seem entirely out of place. I am excessive, hence excluded.

It seems to me I learn more about France during a walk through the village than in whole weeks in Paris. Perhaps an illusion? The realist *illusion? The rural, village, provincial world constitutes the traditional raw material of realism. To be a writer meant, in the nineteenth century, to write from Paris about the provinces. The distance makes everything signify. In Paris, in the street, I am bombarded with information—not with signification.*

July 15, 1977

At five in the afternoon, how calm the house is, here in the country. Flies. My legs ache a little, the way they did when I was a child and had what was called growing pains—or when I was getting the grippe. Everything is still, peaceful, asleep. And as always, the sharp awareness, the vivacity of my own "seediness" (a contradiction in terms).

X visits: in the next room, he talks endlessly. I do not dare close the door. What disturbs me is not the noise but the banality of the conversation (if at least he talked in some language unknown to me, and a musical one!). I am always amazed, even flabbergasted by the resistance of others: for me, the Other is the Indefatigable. Energy—and especially verbal energy—stupefies me: this is perhaps the only time (aside from violence) when I believe in madness.

July 16, 1977

Again, after overcast days, a fine morning: luster and subtlety of the atmosphere: a cool, luminous silk. This blank moment (no meaning) produces the plenitude of an evidence: that it is worthwhile being alive. The morning errands (to the grocer, the baker, while the village is still almost deserted) are something I wouldn't miss for anything in the world.

Mother feeling better today. She is sitting in the garden, wearing a big straw hat. As soon as she feels a little better, she is drawn by the house, filled with the desire to participate; she puts things away, turns off the furnace during the day (which I never do).

This afternoon, a sunny, windy day, the sun already setting, I burned garbage at the bottom of the garden. A complete course of physics to follow; armed with a long bamboo pole, I stir the heaps of paper, which slowly burn up; it takes patience —who would have guessed how long paper can resist the fire? On the other hand, the emerald-green plastic bag (the garbage bag itself) burns very fast, leaving no trace: *it literally vanishes. This phenomenon might serve, on many an occasion, as a metaphor.*

Incredible incidents (read in the Sud-Ouest *or heard on the radio? I don't remember): in Egypt, it has been decided to execute those Moslems who convert to another religion. In the U.S.S.R., a French agent was expelled because she gave a present of underwear to a Soviet friend. Compile a* contemporary *dictionary of intolerance (literature, in this case Voltaire, cannot be abandoned, so long as the evils subsist to which it bears witness).*

July 17, 1977

As if Sunday morning intensifies the good weather. Two heteroclite intensities reinforce each other.

I never mind doing the cooking. I like the operations *involved. I take pleasure in observing the changing forms of the food as they occur (colorations, thickenings, contractions, crystallizations, polarizations, etc.). There is something a little perverse about this observation. On the other hand, what I can't do, and what I always do badly, are proportions and schedules: I put in too much oil, afraid everything will burn; I leave things too long on the fire, afraid they won't be cooked through. In short, I'm afraid* because I don't know *(how much, how long). Whence the security of a code (a kind of guaranteed knowledge): I'd rather cook rice than potatoes because I know it takes seventeen minutes. This figure delights me, insofar as it's precise (to the point of being preposterous); a round number would seem contrived, and just to be certain, I'd add to it.*

July 18, 1977

Mother's birthday. All I can offer her is a rosebud from the garden; at least it's the only one, and the first one since we're here. Tonight, M. is coming for dinner and will cook the dinner itself: soup and a pimento omelette; she brings champagne and almond cookies from Peyrehorade. Mme L. has sent flowers from her garden, delivered by one of her daughters.

Moods, *in the strong, Schumannian sense: a broken series of contradictory impulses: waves of anxiety, imaginations of the worst, and unseasonable euphorias. This morning, at the core of Worry, a crystal of happiness: the weather (very fine, very light and dry), the music (Haydn), coffee, a cigar, a good pen, the household noises (the human subject as caprice: such discontinuity alarms, exhausts).*

July 19, 1977

Early in the morning, coming back with the milk, I stop in the church to have a look around. It has been remodeled according to the prescribed New Look: now it resembles nothing so much as a Protestant establishment (only the wooden galleries indicate a Basque tradition); no image, the altar has become a simple table, no candle of course. Too bad, isn't it?

Around six in the evening, I doze on my bed. The window is wide open, the gray day has lifted now. I experience a certain floating euphoria: everything is liquid, aerated, drinkable *(I drink the air, the moment, the garden). And since I happen to be reading Suzuki, it seems to me that I am quite close to the state that Zen calls* sabi; *or again (since I am also reading Blanchot), to the "fluid heaviness" he speaks of apropos of Proust.*

July 21, 1977

Some bacon, onions, thyme, etc.: simmering, the smell is wonderful. Now this fragrance is not that of food as it will be served at table. There is an odor of what is eaten and an odor of what is prepared (observation for the "Science of Motley," or "diaphorology").

July 22, 1977

For some years, a unique project, apparently: to explore my own stupidity, or better still: to utter *it, to make it the object of my books. In this way I have already* uttered *my "egoist" stupidity and my "lover's" stupidity. There remains a third kind, which I shall someday have to get on paper: political stupidity. What I think of events politically (and I never fail to think something), from day to day, is stupid. It is a stupidity which I should now* utter *in the third book of this little trilogy: a kind of* Political Diary. *It would take enormous courage, but maybe this would exorcise that mixture of boredom, fear, and indignation which the Politician (or rather Politics) constitutes for me.*

"I" is harder to write than to read.

Last night, at Casino, *the Anglet supermarket, with E.M., we were fascinated by this Babylonian Temple of Merchandise. It is really the Golden Calf: piles of (cheap) "wealth," gathering of the species (classified by types), Noah's ark of things (Swedish clogs to eggplants), predatory stacking of carts. We are suddenly convinced that people will buy anything (as I do myself): each cart, while parked in front of the cash register, is the shameless chariot of manias, impulses, perversions, and cravings: obvious, confronting a cart proudly passing before us, that there was no need to buy the cellophane-wrapped pizza ensconced there.*

I'd like to read (if such a thing exists) a History of Stores. What happened before Zola and Le Bonheur des dames?

August 5, 1977

Continuing War and Peace, *I have a violent emotion, reading the death of old Prince Bolkonsky, his last words of tenderness to his daughter ("My darling, my friend"), the Princess's scruples about not disturbing him the night before, whereas he was calling her; Marie's feeling of guilt because for a moment she wanted her father to die, anticipating that she would thereby gain her freedom. And all this, so much tenderness, so much poignance, in the midst of the crudest scuffles, the arrival of the French, the necessity of leaving, etc.*

Literature has an effect of truth much more violent for me than that of religion. By which I mean, quite simply, that literature is like religion. And yet, in this week's Quinzaine, *Lacassin declares peremptorily: "Literature no longer exists except in textbooks." Whereby I am dismissed, in the name of . . . comic strips.*

August 13, 1977

This morning, around eight, the weather was splendid. I had an impulse to try M.'s bicycle, to go to the baker's. I haven't ridden a bike since I was a kid. My body found this operation very odd, difficult, and I was afraid (of getting on, of getting off). I told all this to the baker—and as I left the shop, trying to get back on my bike, of course I fell off. Now by instinct I let myself fall excessively, legs in the air, in the silliest posture imaginable. And then I understood that it was this silliness which saved me (from hurting myself too much): I accompanied my fall and thereby turned myself into a spectacle, I made myself ridiculous; but thereby, too, I diminished its effect.

All of a sudden, it has become a matter of indifference to me whether or not I am modern.

(. . . And like a blind man whose finger gropes along the text of life and here and there recognizes "what has already been said.")

II

Paris, April 25, 1979

Futile Evening:

Yesterday, around seven in the evening, under a cold rain in a bad spring, I ran to catch the No. 58 bus. Oddly, there were only old people on the bus. One couple was talking very loudly about some History of the War (which? you can't tell anymore): "No distance, no perspective," the man was saying admiringly, "only details." I got off at the Pont Neuf. Since I was early, I lingered a little along the Quai de la Mégisserie. Workmen in blue smocks (I could smell how badly paid they were) were brutally stacking big cages on dollies where ducks and pigeons (all fowls are so stupid) were fluttering in hysterics, sliding in heaps from one side to the other. The shops were closing. Through the door, I saw two puppies: one was teasing the other, which kept rebuffing him in a very human manner. Once again, I had a longing to have a dog: I might have bought this one (a sort of fox terrier), which was irritated and showed it in a way that was indifferent and yet not haughty. There were also plants and pots of kitchen herbs for sale. I envisioned myself (both longingly and with horror) stocking up on the lot before going back to U., where I would be living for good, coming to Paris only for "business" and shopping. Then I walked down the deserted and sinister rue des Boudonnais. A driver asked me where the BHV was: oddly enough, he seemed to know only the abbreviation, and had no idea where or even what the Hôtel de Ville was. At the (crumbling) Galerie de l'Impasse, I was disappointed: not by D.B.'s photographs (of windows and blue curtains, taken with a Polaroid camera), but by the chilly atmosphere of the opening: W. wasn't there (probably still in America), nor R. (I was forgetting: they've quarreled). D.S., beautiful and daunting, said to me: "Lovely, aren't they?" "Yes, very lovely" (but it's thin, there's not enough here, I added under my breath). All of which was pathetic enough. And since, as I've grown older, I have more and more courage to do what I like, after a second quick tour of the room (staring any longer wouldn't have done more for me), I took French leave and indulged in a futile spree, from bus to bus and movie house to movie house. I was frozen, I was afraid of having caught bronchitis (this happened to me several times). Finally, I warmed up a little at the Flore, ordering some eggs and a glass of Bordeaux, though this was a very bad day: an insipid and arrogant audience: no face to be interested in or about which to fantasize, or at least to speculate. The evening's pathetic failure has impelled me to begin, at last, the reformation of my life which I have had in mind so long. Of which this first note is the trace.

(On rereading: this bit gave me a distinct pleasure, so vividly did it revive the sensations of that evening; but curiously,

in reading it over, what I remembered best was what was not
written, *the interstices of notation: for instance, the gray of
the rue de Rivoli while I was waiting for the bus; no use trying
to describe it now, anyway, or I'll lose it again instead of some
other silenced sensation, and so on, as if resurrection always
occurred* alongside *the thing expressed: role of the Phantom,
of the Shadow.)*

However often I reread these two fragments, nothing tells
me they are publishable; nothing tells me, on the other hand,
that they are not. Which raises a problem that is beyond me—
the problem of "publishability"; not: "is it good or is it bad?"
(a form every author gives to his question), but "is it publishable or not?" This is not only a publisher's question. The
doubt has shifted, slides from the text's quality to its image. I
raise for myself the question of the text from the Other's point
of view; the Other is not the public, here, or any particular
public (this is the publisher's question); the Other, caught up in
a dual and somehow personal relation, is *anyone who will read
me.* In short, I imagine that my Journal pages are put in front
of "whom I am looking at," or under the silence of "whom I
am speaking to." —Is this not the situation of any text? —No.
The text is anonymous, or at least produced by a kind of *nom
de guerre,* that of the author. This is not at all true of the
Journal (even if its "I" is a false name): the Journal is a
"discourse" (a kind of *written word* according to a special
code), not a text. The question I raise for myself: *"Should I
keep a journal?"* is immediately supplied, in my mind, with a
nasty answer: *"Who cares?",* or, more psychoanalytically:
"It's your problem."

All I have left to do is analyze the reasons for my doubt.
Why do I suspect, *from the point of view of the Image,* Journal writing? I believe it is because this writing is stricken, in my

eyes, as though with an insidious disease, with negative characteristics—deceptive and disappointing, as I shall try to say.

The Journal corresponds to no *mission*. Nor is this word laughable. The works of literature, from Dante to Mallarmé, Proust, and Sartre, have always had, for those who wrote them, a kind of social, theological, mythic, aesthetic, moral end. The book, "architectural and premeditated," is supposed to reproduce an order of the world, it always implies, I believe, a monist philosophy. The Journal cannot achieve the status of the Book (of the Work); it is only an Album, to adopt Mallarmé's distinction (it is Gide's life which is a "work," not his Journal). The Album is a collection of leaflets not only interchangeable (even this would be nothing), but above all *infinitely suppressible*: rereading my Journal, I can cross out one entry after the next, to the complete annihilation of the Album, with the excuse that "I don't like this one": this is the method of Groucho and Chico Marx, reading aloud and tearing up each clause of the contract which is meant to bind them. —But can't the Journal, in fact, be considered and practiced as that form which essentially expresses the inessential of the world, the world as inessential? —For that, the Journal's subject would have to be the world, and not me; otherwise, what is uttered is a kind of egotism which constitutes a screen between the world and the writing; whatever I do, I become consistent, confronting the world which is not. How to keep a Journal without egotism? That is precisely the question which keeps me from writing one (for I have had just about enough egotism).

Inessential, the Journal is unnecessary as well. I cannot invest in a Journal as I would in a unique and monumental work which would be dictated to me by an incontrovertible desire. The regular writing of the Journal, a function as daily as any other physiological one, no doubt implies a pleasure, a comfort, but not a passion. It is a minor mania of writing, whose necessity vanishes in the trajectory which leads from the entry produced to the entry reread: "I haven't found that what I've written so far is particularly valuable, nor that it obviously deserves to be thrown away" (Kafka). Like any subject of perversion (I am told), subjected to the "yes, but," I know that my text is futile, but at the same time (by the same impulse) I cannot wrest myself from the belief that it exists.

Inessential, uncertain, the Journal is also inauthentic. I don't mean by this that someone who expresses himself in one is not sincere. I mean that its very form can only be borrowed from an antecedent and motionless Form (that, precisely, of the intimate Journal), which cannot be subverted. Writing my Journal, I am, by status, doomed to simulation. A double simulation, in fact: for every emotion being a copy of the same emotion one has read somewhere, to report a mood in the coded language of the Collection of Moods is to copy a copy: even if the text was "original," it would already be a copy; all the more so, if it is familiar, worn, threadbare: "The writer, by his pains, those dragons he has fondled, or by a certain vivacity, must set himself up, in the text, as a witty histrion" (Mallarmé). What a paradox! By choosing the most "direct," the most "spontaneous" form of writing, I find myself to be the clumsiest of ham actors. (And why not? Are there not "historic" moments when one must be a ham actor? By practicing to the bitter end an antiquated form of writing, do I not say that I love literature, that I love it in a harrowing fashion, at the very moment when it is dying? I love it, therefore I imitate it—but precisely: not without complexes.)

All of which says more or less the same thing: that the worst torment, when I try to keep a Journal, is the instability of my judgment. Instability? Rather its inexorably descending curve. In the Journal, Kafka pointed out, the absence of a notation's value is always recognized too late. How to transform what is written at white heat (and take pride in the fact) into a nice cold dish? It is this waste, this dwindling which constitutes the Journal's uneasiness. Again Mallarmé (who moreover did not keep one): "Or other verbiage become just that, provided it is exposed, persuasive, pensive and true when one confides it in a whisper": as in that fairy tale, under the effect of a curse and an evil power, the flowers that fall from my mouth are changed into toads. "When I say something, this thing immediately and definitively loses its importance. When I write it here, it also loses it, but sometimes gains another importance" (Kafka). The difficulty proper to the Journal is that this secondary importance, liberated by writing, is not certain: it is not certain that the Journal recuperates the word and gives it the resistance of a new metal. Of course writing is indeed that strange activity (over which, hitherto, psychoanalysis has had little hold, understanding it with difficulty), which miraculously arrests the hemorrhaging of the Image-repertoire, of which speech is the powerful and pathetic stream. But precisely: however "well written," is the Journal "writing"? It struggles, swells, and stiffens: am I as big as the text? Never! you aren't even close. Whence the depressive effect: acceptable when I write, disappointing when I re-read.

At bottom, all these failures and weaknesses designate quite clearly a certain defect of the subject. This defect is existential. What the Journal posits is not the tragic question, the Madman's question: "Who am I?", but the comic question, the Bewildered Man's question: "Am I?" A comic—a comedian, that's what the Journal keeper is.

In other words, I never get away from myself. And if I never get away from myself, if I cannot manage to determine what the Journal is "worth," it is because its literary status slips through my fingers: on the one hand, I experience it, through its facility and its desuetude, as being nothing more

than the Text's limbo, its unconstituted, unevolved, and immature form; but on the other hand, it is all the same a true scrap
of that Text, for it includes its essential torment. This torment,
I believe, consists in this: that literature is *without proofs*. By
which it must be understood that it cannot prove, not only
what it says, but even *that* it is worth the trouble of saying it.
This harsh condition (Play and Despair, Kafka says) achieves
its very paroxysm in the Journal. But also, at this point, everything turns around, for out of its impotence to prove, which
excludes it from the serene heaven of Logic, the Text draws a
flexibility which is in a sense its essence, which it possesses as
something all its own. Kafka—whose Journal is perhaps the
only one that can be read without irritation—expresses this
double postulation of literature to perfection: Accuracy and
Inanity: ". . . I was considering the hopes I had formed for
life. The one which appeared the most important or the most
affecting was the desire to acquire a way of seeing life (and,
what was related, of being able, by writing, to convince others) in which life would keep its heavy movement of rise and
fall, but would at the same time be recognized, and with a no
less admirable clarity, as a nothing, a dream, a drifting state."
Yes, that is just what the ideal Journal is: at once a rhythm
(rise and fall, elasticity) and a trap (I cannot join my image):
a writing, in short, which tells the truth of the trap and guarantees this truth by the most formal of operations, rhythm. On
which we must doubtless conclude that I can rescue the Journal on the one condition that I labor it *to death*, to the end of
an extreme exhaustion, like a *virtually* impossible Text: a
labor at whose end it is indeed possible that the Journal thus
kept no longer resembles a Journal at all.

1979

MORE PRAISE FOR

The Secret Parts of Fortune

"Few journalists inspire the kind of cult following that Rosenbaum has."

—Scott McLemee, *Newsday*

"Memorable essays . . . immensely learned and funny."

—Maureen Corrigan, NPR's "Fresh Air"

"He might have a serious rival if Tom Wolfe were still a frequent writer of nonfiction, but even then Rosenbaum would probably be my favorite."

—Timothy Noah, *Washington Monthly*

"A natural-born contrarian, Ron Rosenbaum is a journalistic Sherlock Holmes out to jimmy the lock on the American soul."

—Albert Mobilio, *e-Company Now*

"A fascinating, funny, and disturbing study of cultural riddles."

—Sherry Simpson, *San Francisco Chronicle*

"One of the 10 best books of the year."

—Walter Kirn, *GQ*

"One of the best nonfiction books of the year."

—Amazon.com

"Ron Rosenbaum's account of current Dead Sea Scroll controversies is a worthy successor to Edmund Wilson's reportage."

—Geza Vermes, professor, Oxford University

"I plan on hanging Ron Rosenbaum's 'marriage proposal' [column] in a prominent place. Should my husband begin to take me for granted, he will be reminded that I am not without options."

—Rosanne Cash

"Ron Rosenbaum is one of the few distinctive voices of modern American literary journalism."

—Thomas Powers

"Ron Rosenbaum is among the most thoughtful and insightful interpreters of our fractured fin-de-siècle society. He pursues the elusive and the complicated with great clarity."

—Robert Stone

"You made me look like a f———g lunatic."

—Oliver Stone

THE SECRET PARTS
OF FORTUNE

The

SECRET PARTS

OF FORTUNE

THREE DECADES OF

INTENSE INVESTIGATIONS

AND EDGY ENTHUSIASMS

RON ROSENBAUM

Perennial

An Imprint of HarperCollins*Publishers*

Original publication data about the essays in this work can be found in the "Sources" section, beginning on p. 761.

A hardcover edition of this book was published in 2000 by Random House, Inc. It is here reprinted by arrangement with Random House, Inc.

HarperCollins books may be purchased for educational, business, or sales promotional use. For information please write: Special Markets Department, HarperCollins Publishers Inc., 10 East 53rd Street, New York, NY 10022.

First Perennial edition published 2001.

Designed by Victoria Wong

The Library of Congress has catalogued the hardcover edition as follows:

Rosenbaum, Ron.
    The secret parts of fortune : three decades of intense investigations and edgy enthusiasms / Ron Rosenbaum.
      p.   cm.
    Includes index.
    ISBN 0-375-50338-2
    1. United States—Civilization—1970– 2. Popular culture—United States—History—20th century. 3. United States—Social life and customs—1971– 4. United States—Intellectual life—20th century. I. Title.
E169.12.R643 2000
973.92—dc21   99-089067

ISBN 0-06-093446-8 (pbk.)

01 02 03 04 05 ❖/RRD 10 9 8 7 6 5 4 3 2 1

For my sister, Ruth Rosenbaum,
a far far better person than I,
who has been a lifelong source of strength,
inspiration, and laughter.

Foreword

ERROL MORRIS

Ron Rosenbaum is one of the great masters of the metaphysical detective story, a nonfiction writer in the spirit of Borges, Nabokov, and Poe. Like Poe, he can take a tabloid story (the death of identical twin gynecologists, a motel suicide, a suicide doctor) and turn it into profound and nightmarish art. And like Dupin, Poe's alter ego, he is a supreme investigator. Yet he goes Dupin one better. Poe, after all, had to disguise himself as an all-knowing detective. In his investigation of historical enigmas, Ron lays his cards on the table—his doubts about the evidence, even his doubts about himself. He appears in his own stories often perplexed, sometimes bemused, occasionally even tortured by his own investigations.

I have been reading Ron's stories for many years, but it wasn't until I saw his pieces assembled that a grand scheme, a master plan became evident. This is a collection in which the many parts are great, and the sum of the parts even greater. Here is a vision, an entire cosmology, or, if you prefer, an anti-cosmology. Because the central feature of Ron's grand scheme, his master plan, is to squelch grand schemes and master plans, to defeat our natural human tendency to retreat into easy answers and bogus explanations. Many of these stories are skeptical examinations of our great need to create grand taxonomies, systems of classification that pretend to comprehensiveness. (Take Elisabeth Kübler-Ross, whose effort to provide a definitive chronology of death results in a bizarre evasion of it.) There is something immensely appealing about watching someone in combat with the world, wrestling with our attempts to understand the world, trying to talk the world into making sense of itself.

Ron provides a clue to his attitude in his metaphor of the lost safe-deposit box, a metaphor for truth that exists but that may be beyond our grasp. These are not essays about the impossibility of knowledge, they're skeptical *and* hopeful. Borges cites a line from Chesterton: There is nothing more terrifying than a labyrinth without a center. Ron's labyrinth is a labyrinth of theories, evidence, interpretations, and misconceptions—but it has a center, if not some ultimate truth then a sliver of it, a standpoint from which one can at least decide what the untruths are.

And so the reader should look for at least three Rons in these essays.

- Ron, the connoisseur of irrationality and insanity, who savors the astonishing varieties of error for, as he calls it, that "frisson of strangeness" they offer. It is the Ron who manages to evoke that lost-in-the-funhouse feeling, of being odd man out on the psycho ward that is the world.
- Ron, the detective in search of the "lost safe-deposit box," *his* search for the overlooked connection in the morass of possibilities that might provide an important clue as to what *really* happened, who we really are. (This is the Ron who identifies with those like Alan Bullock who are still wrestling with such knotty subjects as the enigma of evil and the vexing question, Do we know, can we be sure of, anything at all?)
- Ron, the moralist, the guy who makes it absolutely clear that he has standards: that some things won't wash and he won't be toyed with. That we don't live in a world where everything goes, everything is acceptable, all options have equal weight—no, no, no. There is a scale of value that has to be applied. This has produced some of his most powerful and also extremely funny (and by funny, I mean often laugh-out-loud funny) work, something deeper than conventional journalism, an attempt to probe the madness behind the world. His subjects are ostensibly nonfiction, but his real subject is the fictions we project on the world and ourselves.

And yet he is no glib postmodernist. There is no hint of the claim that we should give up on truth and reality altogether, that we can't possibly hope to know anything about the world when our ability to judge, to perceive, to reason, are hopelessly colored by self-interest, wishful thinking, and self-deception. His work is a powerful attempt to find a way around this dilemma. It's an attempt to *recover* the world by compulsively examining and reexamining our misconceptions of it.

I remember reading one of his Hitler essays and realizing, Oh my God, he's doing something extraordinary. He's up to something new and unique, chronicling the way people's interpretations of themselves (and others) shape and distort what they project onto history. This is not to say that history itself is subjective but to recognize the way it's often *driven* by subjectivity.

And so, for Ron truth exists and *must* be sought after, even if it sometimes can't be known with certainty. There's a terrific moment in "Oswald's Ghost." It illustrates Ron's belief that you can get so lost in a labyrinth of detail you not only lose the forest for the trees, you lose the trees as well. It's when the Kierkegaard scholar–turned–private eye talks about the unreliability of evidence, the fact that some piece of the puzzle may forever be missing. Yet we continue to search for those elusive certainties knowing that the only place to start is *us*—the whole mess: the evasions, the confusions, the misconceptions. Ron has made the point better than anybody else I can think of: The proper route to an understanding of the world is an examination of our errors about it.

The great Rosenbaum line, the epigram I love more than any other, the one that repeats itself in my mind again and again, is the one about the underlying mechanism of illusion and belief in the world of unorthodox cancer cures. He's speculating about the way false hope derived from bad science nonetheless seems to work miracles for many of these people. He's worried that by exposing this mechanism, he's done something terribly wrong. He's given away the game. He's deprived them of the one thing that could provide a cure: hope. And then he decides he can't really kill it because, after all is said and done, "*False* hope springs eternal."

Here is Ron in a nutshell. It is his version of Pandora's box: Is the hope at the bottom of the box a good thing or a bad thing? It is that admixture of principled hopefulness and intense skepticism that characterizes what he does.

Quite simply, I love Ron's work. I believe it will last. I want *everybody* to read it.

—Cambridge, Massachusetts
January 2000

Errol Morris's nonfiction films include *The Thin Blue Line; A Brief History of Time; Gates of Heaven; Fast, Cheap & Out of Control;* and *Mr. Death: The Rise and Fall of Fred A. Leuchter, Jr.* Before becoming a filmmaker, he was a doctoral student of philosophy at Berkeley and a private investigator in New York.

Contents

Two Singers

Some Personal Matters

Hitler, Singer, Pharaoh, and Shakespearean Romance

Introduction: Ancient Mariners and Airport Motels

The Dream of the Great Decipherment

"It is the glory of God to conceal a thing . . ."
—*Proverbs 25:2*

I'm not sure what to believe about God, but I do sort of like the notion of a God who takes delicious pleasure—who *glories*—in hiding things from us. The proverb (which was singled out for imitation by Francis Bacon) goes on to add, "and it is the honor of kings to search out a matter."

I don't know about the honor of kings, but the proverb does say something about the seductiveness of the hidden: the primal, almost theological, root of the hide-and-seek impulse in human beings. Whether its source is in the longing to find the hidden face—or at least the latent fingerprints—of God, or in something more secular, even sexual, there is this persistent, ineradicable conviction that the ultimate truths, the truths behind appearances, the keys to unlock the tormenting mysteries of existence, are always hidden, just beyond our grasp, or inscribed in indecipherable code.

It ain't necessarily so, of course. It may just be consoling to believe that what is hidden could explain and perhaps diminish the terror of that which is all too apparent. Whether or not it is the glory (or the mischief) of God to hide a thing, the glory of man is to fantasize about the hidden. The search for the hidden hand, the hidden springs, the hidden handshake behind history attracts a certain kind of glory seeker, Ancient Mariner, mad scholar, Wandering Jew. And some who are all of the above.

He still haunts me, his shambling figure, the crumpled sheaf of sheet music clutched to his chest, the visionary gleam in his eyes. My first Ancient Mariner. Looking back now, I can see a way in which his figure, his story, a story I tried and failed to write, is the figure in the carpet for many of the stories I later did.

I came across him, or rather he tracked me down, not long after I published a story—it was only my second byline in a magazine—that convinced him I might be the one to tell *his* story, his great decipherment disclosure. The story that persuaded him of my special receptivity was entitled "Secrets of the Little Blue Box." It was a story that took me into the world of a small cabal of blind electronics geniuses who called themselves "phone phreaks"—proto-hackers who had deciphered the musical tones the phone company used to run its electronic switching systems (a tone of 1,100 cycles per second combined with one of 700 cps would produce the signal for the digit 2, for instance). The cps numbers had been disclosed in obscure Bell Labs technical journals that were soon either stolen or removed from tech-school library shelves—but not before the secret to the codes was out and it was too late.

It was a coup that allowed the phone phreaks to hack into the phone company's long-distance lines and make free calls all over the world with their tone-generating "blue boxes." More important, it allowed them to set up their own secret web of conference lines, a primitive internet of blind tech wizards and their sighted acolytes that was the matrix from which hacker culture and such legendary cyber-outlaws as "Captain Crunch" as well as cyber-entrepreneurs such as Steve Jobs and Steve Wozniak emerged.*

Anyway, the haunted-looking figure clutching the sheaves of sheet music who tracked me down after the phone-phreaks piece came out told me he had something momentous to communicate. It, too, was a decipherment of truths encoded in musical tones, but one with far more profound implications than mere telecommunication, he said.

His name I recall as "Norman Bloom," perhaps because his corpulent fig-

---

*Jobs has said that the Apple partnership began when he and Wozniak read my "blue box" story and tried to manufacture the illicit devices in their parents' garages. Captain Crunch, I understand, has long since put his genius to lawful ends, but his legend lives on.

ure, jowly face, and raccoon eyes made him look more than a little like a long-lost brother of Harold Bloom, whose course in the Romantic poets at Yale—or as Bloom liked to call them, "the Visionary Company"—had attuned me to the Ancient Mariners of the world, the ones who, as Coleridge's did, "Stoppeth one of three" to download their unbearable visionary tales. More often than not, the one in three they stoppeth turneth out to be me.

Norman Bloom's albatross, that thick sheaf of sheet music he carried clutched to his chest, looked much like an illuminated manuscript. It was, I recall, the complete notation for Bach's *Goldberg Variations,* but entwined around the staves and clefs were intricate wreaths of spidery lines: handwritten annotations and algebraic formulae that seemed to bloom and flicker around the musical notes.

It looked like an illuminated manuscript produced by a mad vision-intoxicated monk, an ecstatic Kabbalist. What it illuminated, Norman Bloom told me, what his annotations and algebraic formulae revealed was that, embedded, encrypted in the musical notations of the *Goldberg Variations* were messages from God transmitted through the medium of Bach.

I can't recall now, over the distance of years, whether Norman Bloom believed Bach was *aware* of the messages he was transmitting or merely the unconscious medium of transmission. Nor was it clear why, after three centuries, the disclosure had been vouchsafed to one Wandering Jew in Greenwich Village. But I recall Norman Bloom telling me he had been both a mathematical and musical prodigy, and his combined talents had enabled him to decode the disclosure and appreciate both the breathtaking beauty of the web of divine intelligibility woven so skillfully into mathematical relationships between the musical notes—and the urgency of its message, which I recall had something to do with the apocalyptic prophecies of the Book of Revelations, that curse of so many overamped intellects.

I listened patiently to Norman Bloom for several hours on several occasions in several Village coffee shops, not in the belief that there was a "Bible code" embedded in the music of Bach, but rather out of a fascination with his peculiar *confidence,* the confidence of someone who felt he had cracked the code of Creation, deciphered the secret pattern beneath the surface of appearances. Someone with the transcendent certainty he had Figured It All Out.

It was a phenomenon I'd read about, not just the conviction of blood-simple Flannery O'Connor street preachers, but just as often the last great affliction of noble minds. John Maynard Keynes reminds us in his study of Isaac Newton's unpublished papers that those who worship Newton as the founder of modern mathematics, of the Enlightenment itself, have always been uncomfortable with the project Newton thought was his *real* contribution to human knowledge, one he thought far more important than his disclosure of the secrets of gravity and the laws of motion: his "discovery" of a secret mathematical code in the Book of Revelations that Newton labored much of the latter part of his life to decipher.*

I never wrote the story Norman Bloom wanted me to write. I never wrote any story at all. I was skeptical of his claims, but I lacked the requisite musical and mathematic expertise to dispute them authoritatively. I suppose I could have written a story about Norman Bloom as a Village character, an homage to Joseph Mitchell and "Joe Gould's Secret" (the story of another Village character who had it All Figured Out), but I didn't have the heart to hurt his feelings. I was touched in a way by his dignity and his doggedness and his trust in me. But if I didn't write the story, in a way it inscribed itself on *me,* stayed with me: that image of the Wandering Jew, his disclosure, his decipherings . . . that serenity, that sense of intimacy with hidden secrets. I kept finding myself in stories and situations that brought this figure in the carpet back to life.

I thought of Norman Bloom, for instance, on a remarkable evening in Jerusalem in the courtyard garden of the American Colony Hotel when I was the recipient of an extraordinary disclosure from a pillar of the elite Dead Sea Scroll–scholar establishment, the head of Princeton Theological Seminary's Dead Sea Scrolls publishing project. A man of great learning, great dignity, and accomplishment who, nonetheless, after a couple of White Russians prepared in the manner of Ibrahim, his favorite bartender, let down his hair sufficiently to confide his continuing wonderment at what he characterized as "The Curse of the Scrolls."

Perhaps it was the storybook setting, the American Colony Hotel having long been a haunt of adventurers, mystics, and romantics; T. E. Lawrence, Graham Greene, and Glubb Pasha had passed through its arabesqued portals. Whatever the cause of his candor, he proceeded to spin tale after tale of how this or that brilliant scholar, this or that overpowering intellect, this or that fearsomely learned linguist or theologian had come to grief, misfortune, tragedy, self-destruction in the obsessive pursuit of the elusive truth about the

---

*Curiously, Isaac Newton himself believed that, as one biographer put it, "the model Pythagoras had developed for musical scales and the harmony of certain notes was in fact a metaphor or model for the universe." Recently a Columbia University physicist, Dr. Brian Greene, suggested that intimations of the inner secrets of quantum phenomena may be found in the harmonics of Bach. And I'm told that in the latter part of his life the pianist Glenn Gould was convinced he'd decrypted coded messages of some sort in, yes, Bach's *Goldberg Variations.* At any moment I expect Norman Bloom to reemerge with a best-seller, *The Bach Code.* Although he seems to have been preempted by Norman Podhoretz, who published, in the December 1999 issue of the British magazine *Prospect,* an essay entitled "Was Bach Jewish?" in which he argued that "encapsulated in the music of Bach" may be "the most convincing demonstration" of the hidden mysteries of Jewish law and faith.

Scrolls—in the attempt to decode the fragmented allegories inscribed upon those maddeningly enigmatic two-thousand-year-old documents that a Bedouin shepherd had found in a cave in the cliffs where Judaean desert meets the Dead Sea.

I had just come in that afternoon from an expedition to the Judaean desert that took me into the bat-infested caves that honeycomb those cliffs, the caves where the Scroll writers, a sect of ascetic interpreters and prophesiers, had hidden their prophetic allegories when (most likely) the Romans had sacked their monastic desert abode sometime in the century before or after the birth of Christ.

It was an expedition that I'd unwisely extended by clambering up to the top of the cliffs and wandering into the stony sterility and the brutal, baking June heat of the Judaean desert floor—110 and climbing. It was a destabilizing vista, all red rock, blazing heat-shimmer, and dust, one that helped explain why this barren landscape had often been haunted by Visions and Voices.

The Dead Sea Scroll writers had visions here, too: They thought they'd broken the code in the Bible, the one that encrypted the date and time of the apocalypse in the Book of Daniel. They thought they'd found the secret of the Evil Ones on earth, the Fallen Angels in the apocryphal Book of Enoch. Some scholars argue that these are the Jews who gave birth to Christianity. But the attempt to decipher the cryptonyms and allegories and identities of the Scroll writers was itself further complicated by the fact that certain of the Scrolls existed only in a vast array of tatters, the remnants they'd been torn into by the Bedouins who at first used them for scrap. For a half century since the 1947 discovery, some of the most brilliant, erudite, and linguistically and theologically sophisticated minds on the planet had been devoting themselves to solving this maddening jigsaw puzzle and then decrypting the result—or trying to use the decryption to solve the jigsaw puzzle.

The results were often destabilizing: There had been sudden conversions in which Christians became Jews; Jews, Christians; atheists, believers; believers, atheists. There had been self-destruction through drink, obsession, madness. There had been personal suicide—with a pistol in a Cairo hotel room. There had been professional suicide with loony anti-Semitic remarks in one case and with the dogmatic assertion that Christianity had originated as a psychedelic-mushroom cult in another.

At one point or another, the attempt to find the fingerprints of God in torn inscriptions on tattered scraps of ancient exegesis had suddenly given birth to blazing visions in the minds of those brilliant biblical savants: an intimation of a secret pattern in the jigsaw puzzle not previously vouchsafed to others. A figure unscrolled itself in the carpet, they became possessed by the idea they'd uncovered a disclosure from God, about God, about Jesus, even about the Holocaust. (One scholar believed "The Wicked Priest" in the scroll texts was the ur-Source of the anti-Semitism that ultimately engendered Adolf Hitler.) And it drove them like the furies beyond the bounds of reason. The Curse of the Scroll scholars had turned them into Ancient Mariners.

Still, despite their unfortunate fate—or because of it—I felt myself drawn to Scroll-scholar types, to those who risked disintegration, destabilization, in the single-minded, even self-destructive devotion to the decipherment of such enigmas. There's something thrilling about the passion, even the madness of scholars when ultimate truths are at stake. It was what drew me to Hitler scholars and theorists. Even when I disagreed, I admired their willingness to stare inexplicable horror—and the horror of inexplicability—in the face in the quest for its origins. There are more comfortable ways to spend one's life. There may be some Norman Bloom in such scholars, but there is a tragic dimension: They are Ahabs as well.

But not all such quests must necessarily be so grim. There is some primal pleasure in the process of decipherment, in decoding and disclosing the secret parts of things. The primal pleasure of exegesis that draws Talmudists to seek to tease out the spirit beneath the letter of the Holy Book, that draws journalists to seek to tease out the subtexts in the stories in the Book of Life, that draws Shakespeare scholars to try to grasp the elusive ghost of Shakespeare's intentions in the often-corrupt texts he left behind.

As I write these words in fact, I've been spending considerable time with Shakespearean scholars and textual editors and getting from them some sense of the pleasures of a life devoted to decrypting Shakespearean enigmas. Over lunch in London, one of them, Eric Sams—a brilliant, cantankerous, and controversial "independent scholar," a specialist in German musicology whose Shakespearean conjectures, published in the *TLS* and elsewhere, have won the respect if not the agreement of many mainstream academics—was telling me about the origin of his passion for Shakespeare studies, for retrieving even from the corrupt "Bad Quartos" some intimation of what was and what wasn't the true product of the Bard. Sams had been a cryptanalyst during World War II, he told me; he'd been detailed to the legendary Bletchley Park code-breaking station, the home of the famous Enigma Machine, the decoding engine that had enabled the Brits to crack the top-secret ciphers of Hitler's high command throughout the war—and may have been responsible, as much as any single weapon or general, for winning the war.

Sams himself had been assigned the task of attempting to crack the even more formidable Japanese cipher known as MAGIC. And he wasn't the only one, he told me: Some of the foremost Shakespearean textual scholars of the century, the elite group of initiates who'd devoted their lives to deciphering the enigma of Shakespeare's MAGIC, had been trained as cryptanalysts during the war.*

I thought—still think—this is a wonderful detail, and I loved the fierce joy with which Sams and his fellow Shakespeareans delve into the dramas behind the textual variants, the subtextual dramas of errant compositors, "foul papers," "fair copies," incidentals, and accidentals, the analysis of all of which *might,* after scrupulous study, yield up the decipherment of one Shakespearean variant that betrayed the author's own revising hand—rather than a compositor's wandering eye.

There's a line from *Hamlet* that I found myself thinking about as I was rereading and selecting stories for this collection. A line that captures something about a certain kind of obsessive to be found herein and the special kind of enigmas they obsess over. A line that conjures up the special state of mind of the Ancient Mariner, the mad scholar, the Mystery Tramp radiant in rags with the ecstatic conviction that he or she has been initiated into the secret speech, the esoteric language, the secret springs of things.

It's a line found in the second act of *Hamlet,* when the prince's former schoolmates, Rosencrantz and Guildenstern, show up at Elsinore and greet him with a pretense of jovial camaraderie designed to camouflage their secret mission to spy on him for the king. Hamlet asks them how they're doing.

"As the indifferent children of the earth," Rosencrantz replies.

"On Fortune's cap, we are not the very button," Guildenstern avers.

"Nor the soles of her shoe?" Hamlet hopes.

"Neither," says Guildenstern.

"Then you live about her waist, or in the middle of her favors?" Hamlet asks.

"Faith, her privates, we," puns Guildenstern, making the sexual allusion more explicit.

"In the secret parts of Fortune?" Hamlet responds.

The secret parts of Fortune: It seemed to me, the more closely I read the exchange, that there is more resonance to the phrase than a mere third iteration of the same sexual pun. It seems that Hamlet—almost as he says it—discovers a deeper dimension to "the secret parts of Fortune." "In the secret parts of Fortune?" is a question, recall, one that almost reads as a meditative aside, a question he seems to ask of himself, a momentary six-word soliloquy before Hamlet returns to the railleries with his two-faced friends by denouncing Fortune as a "strumpet." "In the secret parts of Fortune?": The metaphor moves

---

*I wouldn't, by the way, want anyone to confuse these textual scholars with the sad delusives who claim to have found a cipher in the secret parts of Shakespeare that "proves" the Bard was really Francis Bacon.

from the physical to the metaphysical, from the private parts of the personified goddess, Fortune, to that which the "secret parts" alludes to on another level: the secret workings of Fate, the hidden hand or the hidden plan behind history and human destiny. It suggests the secret *arts* of Fortune, the weaving and un-weaving of destinies by will or witchcraft, the magic in the web. And it sug-gests the secret parts Fortune *plays,* the guises and disguises her actors on earth assume. Fortune as playwright: the plots she designs as the secret dramatist of our lives. Plots and designs whose decipherment is the grail of so many of the seekers herein. A grail whose possession promises that Fortune, Fate, the "divinity that shapes our ends," will no longer seem so terrifyingly cruel and arbitrary; promises that once we have been initiated into Fortune's secret parts, the inexplicable and the tragic will at least somehow make *sense*.

That's what you hear in the tone of the Ancient Mariners, the almost leering insinuation of intimacy with the secret parts of Fortune that only an initiate can have. An initiate who sees beneath the surface appearances of chance and accident to the level where Everything Makes Sense. It's probably no accident that Coleridge has his Ancient Mariner haunt the fringes of a wedding feast, that he lures a wedding guest from the public celebration of one kind of Eros to the private incantatory confidences of another kind of desire: the desperate desire to possess the secret parts of ultimate enigmas. And it's probably no ac-cident that the authors of the King James Bible (perhaps including Shake-speare himself), in choosing a euphemism for embodied Eros, selected the verb *to know.* Adam and Eve *knew* each other: They had carnal *knowledge.* The search for the secret parts of Fortune is, however intellectualized, still somehow carnal, no less a matter of Desire.

A higher desire, perhaps, but one that can burn as hot as hell. One that can take unusual forms. In W. H. Sheldon, for instance, the eccentric eugenics vi-sionary who was the shadowy figure behind "The Great Ivy League Nude Posture Photo Scandal," it was the conviction that the secret springs of human character and fate could be reduced to and divined from the three-digit num-ber that expressed the body's "somatotype." Even more remarkable was the fact that he was able to talk scores of America's elite colleges into letting him take pictures of tens of thousands of naked eighteen-year-old freshmen in the name of a pseudoscience with a master-race hidden agenda.

In the case of Elisabeth Kübler-Ross and some of her closest followers, it took the form of a belief that all that was hidden about death could be reduced to numbers, numbered stages—a delusion that inexorably led some of them to the desire to go to bed with the dead.

It's there in the persistent conviction of certain Hitler explainers who be-lieve the hidden source of Hitler's anti-Semitism must have been some oc-cluded encounter with a Jew, an occult magus, or even the teeth of a billy goat (the apocryphal source of a secret Hitler wound). It's there in the persistence of esoteric and occult "ancient wisdom," "secret knowledge" imagery in contemporary American Get-Rich-Quick literature, which promises to unlock the secret path to fortunes. It's there in the desire of conspiracy theorists to believe that the numinous Hand of Fate can be given a local habitation and a name, a name such as Skull and Bones.*

It's there in the quest for the esoteric alchemy of the cancer cell by "unorthodox" healers; it's there in the quixotic effort to find the oxymoronic grail of "authentic" canned laughter by a descendant of America's least funny philosopher, Ralph Waldo Emerson. It's there in an intellect as subtle and skeptical as that of the great Murray Kempton, who disclosed to me his quest as a writer in a line from the seventeenth-century historian Clarendon about the longing to find the hidden "finger of God" in the affairs of men.

What's behind the recurrent dream of decipherment? I thought there might be a clue in a spooky moment during my odyssey into the realm of the below-the-border "unorthodox" cancer cure clinics in Tijuana and Ensenada. A clue disclosed in a monologue delivered by a "metabolic technician" at one of the most deluxe and lucrative—and somewhat menacing—clinics. Perched on a cliff overlooking the Pacific at Ensenada, the place reminded me of one of those sinister rehab joints run by disbarred medics in Raymond Chandler's *The Long Goodbye*.

In the course of describing the appallingly indiscriminate variety of treatments available—from fetal sheep–cell injections to coffee enemas—the metabolic technician began spinning a tale about one of the martyrs of the "unorthodox" cancer cure movements of the thirties, a certain Dr. Koch, who was allegedly driven to his death by the persecutions of the medical establishment. In despair, just before his death, he supposedly locked the chemical formula for his cure in a safe-deposit box somewhere in Detroit. A hiding place, the metabolic technician told us, he was trying to retrace even now—although he feared that Dr. Koch's secret elixir, the Philosopher's Stone of cancer cures, might be lost forever. Because even if he tracked down the safe-deposit box through the tangle of trusts that controlled it, the cure might still be beyond retrieval. You see, he told us, the martyred healer had encoded it in some matrix of numbers whose decryption might now be impossible.

Years later, I was surprised to come across a couple of instances of uncannily similar lost-safe-deposit-box legends in tracking down some loose ends

---

*In case anyone wonders about the image on the jacket of this book, it is yours truly hurrying away from the padlocked door to the legendary "Tomb" of the Skull and Bones secret society on the Yale campus in New Haven. (The skull, I should note, does not—as far as I know—belong to any of the members.)

of persistent Hitler apocrypha.* I'd argued, in the introduction to *Explaining Hitler,* that the belief in a lost encoded explanation in some safe-deposit box or other is an expression of a desperate kind of epistemological *optimism.* The belief that the most troubling mysteries (the malignancy of the cancer cell, the malignancy of Hitler's mind) are ultimately explicable—even if the explanation is locked away, inaccessible—seems somehow more consoling than a vision of utter inexplicability.

It's akin to the longing for, the desperate belief in, Hidden Variables within the atomic nucleus (the secret parts of particles?) that made Albert Einstein, till the day he died, a dissenter from the chilling vision of randomness and uncertainty implicit in quantum theory.

Kim Philby, Danny Casolaro, and the Octopus of Paranoia

Of course, there's a danger in believing everything is part of a Hidden Plan, that there are no accidents: the danger of finding too *much* intelligibility encoded in the incidentals and accidentals of life, the danger that goes by the name paranoia. The overconfident belief that one is on intimate speaking terms with the secret parts of Fortune.

There are two emblematic figures of paranoia in these pages: Kim Philby, perhaps its most clever progenitor, and Danny Casolaro, perhaps its most representative victim—if you don't count as victim James Jesus Angleton. (Angleton was the CIA counterintelligence guru Philby drove to paranoid self-destruction.) But I didn't know James Angleton—well, I did have one cryptic phone conversation with the legendary master spy before he died, one in which we spoke allusively about our mutual fondness for the literary criticism of William Empson, author of *Seven Types of Ambiguity* (an appreciation of ambiguity—the enemy of paranoia—which Angleton crucially abandoned or perverted in his mad pursuit of a Philbian mole).

But I did know Danny Casolaro, and sometimes when I envision him lying dead in a blood-streaked bathtub staring up at the concrete ceiling of a cheap motel room in West Virginia, I find myself thinking: *There but for fortune.* . . .

He'd been waiting, Danny told everybody, for the Final Revelation, the final proofs, decipherments, and disclosures of the conspiracy to end all conspiracies, the one he claimed to have discovered, the one he called "The Octopus." The one Danny, in effect, strangled himself with. My phone number

---

*And, come to think of it, the image can be found in a number of other stories in this collection: It's there in the enigma of the history hidden in Ben Hecht's suitcase; it's there in the lost trunk of Charles Portis's fictive success guru, Dix; it's there in the fantasies projected upon the interior of Skull and Bones, the interior of the "little blue box," and the contents of Mary Meyer's lost diary. And the secret parts of the Jordanian prostitutes in the exotic Scroll-smuggling fantasy of John Strugnell.

was found in his appointment book at the death scene; apparently, he wanted to tell me what he'd told a number of others he'd reached in the days before his death: that he'd cracked the code at last, he'd broken open the safe that held the secret parts of Fortune.

When Danny started calling me in 1990, I hadn't heard from him in more than a decade. I'd first run into him during the latter stages of the Watergate affair, when I was researching a story for *The New Republic* on heretical Watergate theories. A number of conspiracy theorists on the right had cited Danny's research (on the "Democrat trap" conspiracy theory: that the Nixon team was set up to be busted at the Watergate), although he didn't seem to have gotten it into print anywhere under his own byline. But I was intrigued by his Gatsbyesque aura and his sideline of raising Arabian thoroughbreds in Virginia horse country—he was not the usual ink-stained investigative reporter.

After a checkered career in and out of print, Danny had ended up as the publisher/writer of a computer-industry newsletter when he'd suddenly been seized by the investigative impulse again. Driven by a relatively obscure eddy in the whirlpool of conspiracy theories surrounding the alleged October Surprise scandal, he went from obsessed with it to possessed by it. Possessed by conspiracy-theory fever—and led on by some sinister fantasists and enablers in conspiracy-theory culture—Danny became convinced he was on the trail of the ultimate conspiracy, the key to all mysteries (a grandiose analogue of Casaubon's "Key to all Mythologies" in *Middlemarch*), the key that would disclose the links among all the spectacular and disturbing intelligence-world scandals and mysteries from the Bay of Pigs to Dallas, from Watergate and Iran-contra to the Mole War and the October Surprise. All of them—the secret parts of America's misfortunes—Danny believed, could be explained by a single configuration, one many-tentacled figure in the carpet, a secret Skull and Bones of intelligence-world conspirators that Danny melodramatically dubbed "The Octopus."

The problem was that the proof always seemed to be just beyond his reach. He was sure he was onto something big, but the corroboration fell short of convincing the mainstream media he hoped to get validation from. When he made those phone calls before his death—in the days before he was found in the motel bathtub with his wrists slashed by a razor blade—he let it be known that he was heading to West Virginia to rendezvous with a source who was at last going to give him the corroboration, the missing links he'd been looking for.

After his bloody corpse was found, there were many ready to believe that he had been silenced by The Octopus, whose assassins tried to make it look like suicide. Many believed he was silenced because he knew too much, was getting too close, getting in too deep. If he turned up dead, he'd told friends, don't believe it was suicide. But after months of investigation, I came to believe that Danny's death might have been a Gatsbyesque final gesture—a suicide he stage-managed to *look* like murder—to give his death (and thus his life) an ex post facto grandeur. Make *it* the corroboration for a conspiracy, the corroboration he couldn't find in life. I came to believe, in other words, that Danny was not the victim of a conspiracy but rather of conspiracy *theory*—strangled by his own octopus.

When I say "there but for fortune," I'm speaking of the way I was myself tempted early on by the lure of certain conspiracy-theory visions. It grew out of skepticism over the inadequacy of the official stories and a contrarian disposition—a predisposition to distrust the all-too-smug defenders of the consensus wisdom. All of which is useful, I think, for any investigator; investigative reporting is a kind of controlled flirtation with paranoia, in which hypotheses of hidden coherence have to be tested against the visible evidence. But there is a border one can cross: from challenging certainty with uncertainty to replacing one unfounded certainty with another unfounded certainty.

One sign that one has crossed that border is the adoption of a certain tone, a tone of all-knowingness, of the initiate into the secret parts of fortune condescending to a naive outsider, one who doesn't know the secret rhetorical handshake. The last few times I spoke to Danny Casolaro, I could hear the way that tone had crept into his voice. It was a tone I'd heard from Norman Bloom, a tone I'd heard from "unorthodox" cancer cure savants, from Scroll scholars, spies, and assassination buffs. It's not that I think there are no such things as conspiracies. History, in fact, is full of them: Julius Caesar and Abraham Lincoln died because of them. JFK, I've come to believe, after a long, wrenching turnaround, probably did not.* One judges each case on the merits and specifics, however, not on an abstract prejudice for or against conspiracies. My resistance to the seductions of certainty Danny fell prey to may have more to do with the great subverter of conspiracy-theory certainty: ambiguity. I was saved by *Seven Types of Ambiguity.* I was saved by close reading.

Saved, really, by a couple of books that initiated me early on into the appreciation of ambiguity, into the double meanings and doubt that riddle the evidence and subvert the kind of confidence about origins and causes that characterizes grandiose theorists.

I don't claim any special virtue for this. It was more a matter of luck that at an impressionable age instead of coming under the spell of Freud or Marx, say, I was handed Brooks and Warren. A gifted high-school teacher who knew I loved Robert Penn Warren's *All the King's Men* (still one of the great evoca-

---

*The remaining, not inconsiderable JFK mystery, I believe, is not whether Oswald fired a shot but why: Who *was* Oswald?

tions of the tragic ambiguity of political ambition) introduced me to *Understanding Poetry,* the anthology put together by Robert Penn Warren and Cleanth Brooks, the sophisticated teaching tool of what I later learned was known as the New Criticism. It wasn't very new by the time I got to Yale; Warren was still teaching there, but the New Critics, those who emphasized "close reading," were being supplanted by the postmodern theorists who claimed that close reading concealed a hidden ideological agenda (or perhaps that it didn't share *their* ideological agenda).

But to me, Brooks and Warren, close reading, Empsonian ambiguity, was more than a way of looking at poetry, a way of unlocking the secret parts of great literature. It was also, later, to become my chief asset as an investigative reporter, my substitute for formal journalism-school training. I came to find that the attentiveness to ambiguity one develops in a close reading of seventeenth-century metaphysical poetry (my concentration in college) could be applied to the kinds of texts one came across as a journalist: trial transcripts, autopsy reports, congressional-hearing records, Mob wiretap pickups, and the like.

And the transcripts of face-to-face interviews: I'm always too on edge in the course of doing an interview, too busy worrying about my next question, too worried about whether the tape is running, to really *hear* the interview, to really listen to what's going on, to take note of what the verbal tics, recurrent phrases, rhetorical devices, and slips of the tongue sometimes reveal. I'm always amazed to discover, on reading the transcript of an interview over for a third time, how much more emerges in some slip or tic, the shadow of some submerged truth that belies the surface intention of the words.

My other lucky break was a chance encounter in a high-school library with Murray Kempton's remarkable memoir, *Part of Our Time,** which is important in many ways, but for me it was an introduction to the close reading of history and politics, to reading for irony and paradox, courage and weakness, not just who's right or wrong on the issues. Kempton was the master of "negative capability," Keats's phrase for the ability to hold in the mind conflicting, even contradictory, perceptions about a phenomenon without reducing it to singularity. To *relish* the contradictions rather than collapse them.

Close reading doesn't always solve mysteries, but it can sometimes *unsolve* them, which is often a healthy thing when the longing for "closure" results in a kind of premature certainty. Perhaps my favorite close-reading moment herein is the one in which it helped to convince a killer in Florida's Death Row prison, one Ottis Toole, to "unsolve" a string of murders by retracting the phony confessions he'd made to help his "runnin' buddy" Henry Lee Lucas perpetuate his grandiose serial-killer hoax.

---

*Now at last back in print in a Modern Library edition.

I'm convinced it was an act of close reading—the ironic inflection I read into Toole's words when I read back to him the published transcript of his lurid confession to killing and cannibalism—that caused him to cop to the fraud. Underneath the arson-murderer that he was, lurked a sensitive *reader* who knew the *false tone* subverted the overt content of his confessions, gave away the lie. "That whole fucking book is lies," he finally conceded. It was the closest thing to a Perry Mason moment in my reporting career, and I owe it to Brooks and Warren.

A word here about "literary journalism," a phrase that has been applied to a wide array of narrative nonfiction (the plainer term I prefer) and essays, including some of mine. It's a somewhat unfortunate term, as much a curse as a compliment because it suggests highfalutin literary flourishes or highbrow slumming. It can offend hardworking reporters by suggesting they lack literary touches or provoke literary folk who feel no journalism (defined as anything that requires venturing outside the study and talking to strangers) can approach the cloud-wreathed peaks of the true literary sensibility.

I have mixed feelings about it. Perhaps the best compressed way to describe it is "journalism that asks the questions literature asks." In my work anyway, it has meant an increasing preoccupation with the questions of theodicy, the subdiscipline of theology devoted to the problems of reconciling the persistence of evil and injustice with the belief in an all-powerful God or an intelligible moral order. Questions of theodicy are at the heart of the obsession of the original Dead Sea Scroll writers, who drove themselves to explicatory frenzies trying to decode or divine an explanation in the prophetic books for the way they felt God had hidden His face from His most faithful. Those same questions are there in the debate among post-Holocaust theologians and philosophers attempting to explain Hitler—and they are there, haunting the survivors, in Isaac Bashevis Singer's *Shadows on the Hudson*.

A kind of displaced theodicy lurks privily, I'd suggest, in the obsession with J. D. Salinger's silence: How dare a writer, a creator, someone we've endowed with the power to give us Answers, hide his face from us? It's there in Murray Kempton's citation from Clarendon about finding the hidden finger of God in the affairs of men. It's something I was surprised to find surfacing in my work as early as my inquiry into the curious ministry of Reverend Willard Fuller, dental faith healer, who claimed that, with his intercession, God turns decaying teeth to gold. I don't know if I, or anyone, can ever satisfactorily answer the mysteries of theodicy other than the fictive solution I refer to at the close of the dental-faith-healer story:

Just what is God doing filling teeth in a HoJo's banquet room when there are bellies to fill in Bangladesh? I think He owes us an explanation. The only one I can think of is the one offered in Stanley Elkin's remarkable novel of life in Hell, *The Living End.* At the end of *The Living End,* Elkin's tormented hero finally gets to confront God and ask Him to explain His behavior; why He lets people suffer, why history seems so madly unjust, why human life is so weird. *"Because,"* Elkin's God answers, *"it makes a better story."*

But literary journalism can also mean applying a kind of journalistic inquisitiveness to literary questions. To see works of literature offering mysteries to investigate that are as recalcitrant and resonant as the mysteries of the human heart. Looking back over my *New York Observer* columns, I was struck by how many involved unresolved literary enigmas, and how many of those I returned to over and over again, however resistant they were to final resolution. I've devoted no less than four columns to the identity of the unreliable narrator in Nabokov's *Pale Fire,* his novel in the form of a mad scholar's footnotes. Three to the alleged Shakespeare "Funeral Elegy" question (was the long-ignored sententious six-hundred-line poem by "W.S." a late work of Shakespeare?). I devoted three to the mysterious physics and metaphysics of love in *De rerum natura,* the epic poem on the nature of the universe by the Roman visionary Lucretius. Three to Jorge Luis Borges's curious recurrent attempt to refute the existence of Time.

Asking these sorts of questions—looking for the secret subtexts of genius, I guess—can, I believe, often tell us just as many important and unfamiliar things about the human project as the investigation of more conventional targets does. The revelation that a politician is corrupt shouldn't surprise us anymore or cause us to revise our estimation of human nature. Nor should it surprise us to learn, in well-wrought narratives of extreme survival, Everest tragedies, and maritime disasters, that nature is cruel and treacherous. But it seems to me there are Everests of human nature, peaks of creation, works whose contours have yet to be fully mapped, that can tell us something new about the extreme reaches of the imagination we hadn't imagined before. I feel that way trying to map out the *terra incognita* to be found in Nabokov and Shakespeare: This is not just literature, this is news! Certainly as revelatory as anything likely to be found in the footnotes to the Warren Report.

Still, I've always been a student of footnotes. Footnotes in more than the strict sense of appendages to a text signaled by asterisks, daggers, or superscript numerals. I also mean footnotes in the sense of small, discrete, often overlooked details, apparent appendages of the main body not just of a book but of some extratextual phenomenon as well. Often they manifest themselves as "conspicuous irrelevancies," as the New Critics called them, in the sense that they only seem at first to be irrelevant but turn out to reflect unexpected truths about the whole. Footnotes in the larger sense can be the universe in a grain of sand, the trapdoor to Wonderland, the secret parts that often turn out to be the secret heart of the matter.*

I think my favorite footnote moment in these stories may be "The War of Kissinger's Footnote," chronicled in "The Subterranean World of the Bomb." It's an illustration of what the war-gamers called "the esoteric strategy," the way the grand—and potentially apocalyptic—game of nuclear feint and bluff was played in that remarkable and not necessarily unrepeatable era, when world-destroying thermonuclear arsenals were targeted on each other. It was a moment when a single potentially explosive footnote, one that first was appended, then withdrawn, and then restored to the printed text of a Henry Kissinger speech threatened to put hundreds of thousands of megatons of nuclear-tipped missiles on "hair trigger launch status."

What drew me first into the deliciously convoluted Angleton-Philby Mole War was a provocative footnote in Thomas Powers's biography of CIA chief Richard Helms *(The Man Who Kept the Secrets)*. It was a footnote that explicated another footnote in another Mole War chronicle, one that suggested the CIA's James Angleton was playing a "deep game"—that *he* was running Philby, that he, Angleton, was the real puppet master of the Ultimate Mole. What *was* the real "deep game" going on? Was the "deep game" footnote part of a deeper game, as Powers speculated: an Angleton-planted "black valentine" designed to cause paranoia about Philby in the mind of his KGB bosses? It's extremely convoluted, yes, and it could be taken as an indication that they're all, the Mole War obsessives, quite mad. But in this case, I think a close reading of the footnote-on-the-footnote** was justified; it dramatically embodied the "wilderness of mirrors" Angleton's Philby paranoia had created. A wilderness with real consequences for the secret history of our time and how we interpret it.

Edgy Enthusiasms

Sometimes I think that I write and report only as a way of giving myself a rationale to read—or to keep reading alone from consuming me entirely. One of

---

*Footnote on footnotes: It's probably no accident some of my favorite fiction *(Pale Fire)* and my favorite nonfiction *(The Anatomy of Melancholy;* "Shipping Out," David Foster Wallace's brilliant exegesis of his "five-star luxury cruise" experience) is footnote riddled. It's probably no accident that a defining image of Adolf Hitler, "the laughing Hitler," emerged in my examination of a remarkable page-long footnote on Hitler's "slips" in Lucy S. Dawidowicz's valuable work *The War Against the Jews.* (By the way, I have added a number of updating and explicating footnotes, indicated with asterisks, to the pieces herein.)

**Footnote on the "footnote-on-the-footnote" (sorry, can't resist): As late as 1994 in London, certain aging spies from MI6 were still trying to convince me that it was all a deep game: that Philby was not a double but an *unwitting* triple agent, working for them. False hope springs eternal.

the things I love about my *New York Observer* column has been that it affords me a return to the pure pleasures of close reading—not just of literature but of texts tossed up by the culture, such as the Zagat guide, or the Lucent "Big O" logo.

I'd like to mention the circumstances that gave rise to many of these essays, the "Edgy Enthusiast" column in the *Observer.* It began when I declined an offer from Peter Kaplan and his then deputy, Eric Etheridge, to become one of the *Observer*'s "diarist" columnists. I didn't want to write about myself in isolation, but I did have another idea for a different kind of column: all praise all the time. I had this idea that it might be healthy, immersed as I had been for nearly a decade in the dark side of human nature (working on the Hitler book), to devote myself to writing about things I thought were beautiful, brilliant, redemptive—books, films, music, whatever. But *only* praise. The perfect place to finally live up to both my grandmothers' advice: If you don't have anything nice to say, don't say anything at all.

All praise all the time and *no peg*! That was my other understanding with the *Observer.* The peg—for those blessedly unfamiliar with this innocent-looking but insidious little magazine-jargon word—is shorthand for the topical rationale for assigning or running a piece. Most often, lately anyway, shorthand for what about-to-be-released movie does this story tie into, and can we get the piece before the movie's release date because we won't care about it afterward.

The peg is, I believe, the bane, the self-destruction of magazine journalism. I'm not against topicality per se; I've done pieces that have pegs. I'm just against the doctrine that insists on *only* the topical and defines topical in the most obvious way—the way most attached to the timetables of the publicity-industrial complex. I prefer things that become topical because some obsessed writer cares about it enough to compel attention to it.

So that's what I proposed to Kaplan and Etheridge, and I'll always be grateful for their support for what certainly looked at first like an unusual, even unpromising experiment. In my earliest weekly columns I produced only about five hundred words divided up into brief, numbered encomiums. And in the beginning I made them defiantly obscure, beyond the reach of any *possible* peg, preferring on principle books that were out of print (such as *The Anatomy of Melancholy,* one of my favorite idiosyncratic masterpieces;* still, a

---

*Now back in print, albeit in an extremely expensive four-volume Oxford University Press scholarly edition, although my deeply erudite friend Jesse Sheidlower, now with the *Oxford English Dictionary,* tells me that an affordable photo-reprint of the 1836 edition (reprinted from the revised 1651 folio, he insists I add) is sometimes available from Thornton's Bookstore in Oxford (ISBN 085-455-0224). No home should be without it!

thousand-page seventeenth-century treatise on the definition and cure of melancholy as found in thousands of forgotten writers of antiquity was gratifyingly peg-challenged).

What I found most gratifying, though, was the response of the *Observer* readership: The absence of a peg didn't seem to trouble them; in fact, there seemed to be an appetite for reading about works that hadn't been published just that week or even that millennium. When I wrote about Lucretius's first-century B.C. creation poem, say, or Wilkie Collins's *Armadale* (a lesser known nine-hundred-page novel by Dickens's dark doppelgänger, the author of *The Woman in White*), or my theory of Austen archetypes (how you could classify readers' personality types on the basis of what they named as their favorite Jane Austen novel),* I got thoughtful letters from readers who really seemed to care about these questions. I felt I'd found a secret society of readers who shared the belief that certain writers and certain works are their own ever-valid pegs.

It meant a lot to me to be able to champion writers I thought had not been given their due and, in the case of Charles Portis, for instance (whose works I praised first in the *Observer* and then in the *Esquire* column reprinted here), to succeed in convincing a smart publisher to bring his best work back into print.

There did come a time when something other than praise began to intrude itself into the enthusiasm. In one sense it had always been there: Often, my way of praising some work I admired entailed irritable preliminary remarks about those who failed to see the light. In order to praise Dickens, for instance, I felt the need to rail with mock bitterness against anti-Dickens snobbery among what I called "half-bright intellectuals." (In fact, I'd initially wanted to call the column "The Irritable Enthusiast," and I still want to make clear that the "Edgy" in "Edgy Enthusiast" is *not* used in the fashionable recent sense of "cutting edge"—although I think Lucretius, who wrote two millennia ago about the double-edged nature of love in the person of the goddess Venus, *deserves* cutting-edge status far more than Mars-Venus promoter John Gray, say.)** I mean edgy in the sense of ill at ease.

Still, I was managing my edginess within the framework of enthusiasm for more than two years; the turning point came when I happened upon a published excerpt from Bill Gates's first book, one that contained Gates's titanically clueless description of his high-tech dream house—a childish vision of a nightmarish virtual prison—a house that was greeted with gee-whiz wonder

---

*Emma the choice of witty control freaks; *Mansfield Park* the choice of kinky or repressed sensualists; *Pride and Prejudice* often an indicator of conventionality; *Persuasion* the choice of hopeless romantics like myself who know that the original unhappy ending is the more authentic one.

**I haven't reprinted my attack on Mr. Mars-and-Venus, but I wanted to mention it in a footnote mainly because I'm fond of the tag line: "Go Back to Uranus, John Gray."

by much of the media. It was enough to break through the enthusiasm barrier, and it was one step from there to moments of pure edginess, occasional anger.

You won't find all of those here for a number of reasons: By now, everyone loathes Starbucks' Orwellian New Age Culture.* (I consider the fact that the *Austin Powers* sequel made Starbucks the official headquarters of the very evil "Dr. Evil" sufficient vindication for my long-running battle with the smug Seattle chain.) And by now, many have come to agree with me about how wildly overhyped *Seinfeld* was. And I guess it makes me too sad to recapitulate my quixotic campaign to save the late, lamented Books & Co., the bookstore as work of art, the one that the Philistines of the Whitney Museum of American Art strangled in order to speculate in real estate.**

And I suppose my celebration of the Barneys bankruptcy as "The Death of Fabulousness" (which blamed the "Four Designers of the Apocalypse" for threatening to restore communist rule in Russia by provoking populist outrage against a gangster plutocracy, thus setting the stage for nuclear annihilation) was, if true metaphorically, a bit overstated.

There's only one shamelessly angry piece here, one that I don't feel any need to apologize for, because I'm still just as angry as when I wrote it: the one on Charlie Chaplin and Roberto Benigni. I have also included a few shamelessly personal pieces, memoirs, and pleas—most notably my admittedly hyperbolic cats and dogs argument ("Stumpy versus Lucille: The Great Pet Debate") and my "(Modest) Proposal to Rosanne Cash."

I worry that some may miss the humor or the tongue-in-cheek hyperbole of some of these pieces. When I dedicated one of my books to my father, a lovely guy with a wonderful sense of humor, I used as a tribute to him the line from Rafael Sabatini's picaresque thriller *Scaramouche:* "He was born with the gift of laughter and the sense that the world was mad." My father bequeathed me a spirit of mischief, let's call it, but some people seem to find something amiss in it. Recently, at the close of an interview about *Explaining Hitler,* a very serious-minded radio talk-show host asked me, as if he were framing an indictment: "How do you reconcile writing about these subjects [Hitler and the Holocaust], and then in the *Observer* you write a marriage proposal to Rosanne Cash?" What I replied was that, like many people, I had a serious side and a less serious, even playful side. I don't see the problem.

---

*Although I believe no other writer can claim the distinction of having been actually *banned* from a Starbucks.

**I should add that a couple of my quixotic crusades were more successful: I helped keep the brilliant movie-satire show *Mystery Science Theater 3000* on the air for a couple of years more after a threat of cancellation. And I convinced the new owners of the Chrysler Building to keep their beautiful spire lights lit all night long instead of shutting them off at 2 A.M. So if you're out late some night in Manhattan, please gaze upon them and think of me.

. . .

This book is organized by decades, but I'm not sure if it should be read chronologically. I hope readers will skip around. And I'm not sure the decade changes are as pronounced as one that has been taking place irrespective of decade lines: an increasing willingness to write more explicitly about ideas. I shied away from explicit discussion of ideas in many of my early stories because it seemed to me so much writing about ideas was windy, abstract, agenda-bound special pleading. I wanted to tell *stories*. And I was influenced by a belief that narrative alone, if you shaped and toned it right, could evoke or disclose the ideas implicit in one's thinking about the story one was telling. There are problems with that.* I recall once returning from a magazine assignment to cover a Super Bowl in Houston and filing a first draft that virtually ignored the game and consisted, its whole central section anyway, of a long and detailed third-person account of a convention going on at the Astrodome the week before the Super Bowl. A convention, an exposition of artificial cattle-insemination technology manufacturers, featuring fearsome-looking liquid nitrogen–cooled semen canisters and . . . well, I don't want to go into some of the receptor apparatus here (the secret parts of cattle fortunes). Although I did at great length in this draft until my editor (Jon Larsen at *New Times*) asked, "Um, Ron, do we need the bull semen–extraction section?"

"But don't you *understand*," I protested, "it's a way of talking about the way the Super Bowl is marketing masculinity."

"Well, if that's true," he said (very sagely, I now realize), "couldn't you just come out and say that somehow?"

I don't know. I think it's important that journalists investigate ideas as thoroughly as they do politics and crime (ideas often engender political crimes).** Nonetheless, I still prefer to write about ideas as they emerge from the labyrinth of particulars, as they emerge from *stories*. I still need a nudge now and then to make the implicit explicit. For instance, I'm grateful to Jack Rosenthal (at *The New York Times Magazine*) for encouraging me to make explicit what I thought the whole nude-posture-photo scandal said about our in-

---

*One problem is that the seeming omniscience of seamless third-person narrative can often sweep under the rug of its self-assurance the doubts, conflicts, and contradictions in the evidence; can subtly conceal its point of view and manipulate the reader's without obviously seeming to. While the often more awkward first-person interpolation at least lets the reader in on the narrator's questions and more candidly communicates his point of view.

**Another way of saying this is that ideas are too important to be left to intellectuals alone. The watchword of post-Watergate investigative journalism, "follow the money," while still invaluable, needs to be supplemented these days by "follow the ideas." The investigation of political corruption needs to be accompanied by closer scrutiny of the more subtle forms of intellectual and ideological corruption; hidden agendas are just as important to expose as hidden bank accounts. An example: the smart, skeptical investigation of ideas one can find in *Lingua Franca*.

fatuation with science and the desperate longing to reduce the mystery of human behavior to a number.

*Un*solving mysteries often does the opposite: multiplies and deepens uncertainties rather than reduces them to a number. (I'd once thought of calling this book—as an homage to my beloved *Anatomy of Melancholy*—"The Anatomy of Uncertainty." Okay, as a title it's not *Gone with the Wind,* but still. . . .) Nonetheless, there are pleasures and rewards to deepening rather than resolving enigmas. Take Nabokov's butterfly studies, his exquisitely attentive, lifelong close reading of the minute variations in butterfly wing markings and the differential morphology of *lepidoptera* genitalia (the secret parts of butterflies).

What was he really looking for? I found myself poring over a remarkable object, the handmade, one-of-a-kind book Nabokov had constructed by binding together his scientific papers on butterflies and illustrating them with his pastel pencil drawings of his favorite specimens. It was a gift to his beloved wife, Véra, that turned up in the archive of their personal library after her death.

I loved that book, loved the way it showed the hand of its creator, loved the way in which it was Nabokov's attempt to read the palm of a rival Creator: Nabokov trying to decrypt the secret language of biological creation inscribed in the markings on butterfly wings, the grammar of beauty, sex, and identity disclosed in the shifting shapes and patterns. He was reading the butterfly wings like a Scroll!

In a way, Nabokov was looking for something similar to what Norman Bloom was looking for in Bach. But for Nabokov, decoding the esoteric language didn't end the mystery, it deepened his sense of awe at what remained hidden: the nature of the Design or the Designer behind the decrypts.

The Airport Motels of Literature

I hope this doesn't sound unforgivably sentimental but what I kept thinking about as I was rereading some of these stories were the parts left out, the parts left unwritten, the parts having to do with the journeys between stations. Not crucial facts so much as the experience of spending months, sometimes years wandering all over the map, often at a loss—on many levels—trying to figure them out. All the detours, the doublings back, the apparently useless digressions and dead ends, the long drives listening to the late-night clear-channel stations pour into the dashboard radio. Maybe because they mirror the mental journey, the meandering path of the train of thought as it chugs all over the landscape.

I'm writing this now, this section, at an airport motel, the Little Rock Airport Holiday Inn, where the view of the rain-swept runways out my window is partly obscured by the neon *o* in *Holiday.* I'm writing this at the end of a long, digressive road trip through the Deep South. One that began in an airport Holiday Inn in Birmingham, Alabama, took me south and west to Tuscaloosa (home of the Dreamland Barbecue Shack), where I interviewed a Shakespeare scholar at the University of Alabama, then north to Oxford, Mississippi, a town I came to love when I covered the semi-ridiculous Elvis scholars' conference there. Then up to Memphis and west across the Mississippi Delta to Little Rock, where I was hoping to meet up with the reclusive author Charles Portis, who had refused me an interview but had agreed to meet me at a Waffle House for breakfast.

In any case, in the course of this drive, I was thinking of all the other long drives that were left out of the stories herein and the ways in which they often supply the missing or hidden pieces of the jigsaw puzzles—or the perspective to see the pictures emerging. All the motels I holed up in while waiting around for someone to show up, or agree to talk to me. Some extremely sad motels as well. The Holiday Inn at Huntsville, Texas, perhaps the saddest, least appropriately named Holiday Inn of them all, the one where the relatives of Death Row convicts and their victims come to wait out the hours before an execution date. The Travelodge in Gila Bend, Arizona, where I found, in the room of suicidal Gatsby-wannabe David Whiting, the Gideon Bible in which he'd inscribed the last hopeless traces of his devotion to his Daisy. The bleak motel room where another writer, Danny Casolaro, inscribed his last lines on his wrists, in blood.

Writing these concluding words in an airport Holiday Inn, I feel like I've come full circle in a way. When I first started out as a reporter, I came to love Holiday Inns, in part for their predictability as an observation base in unfamiliar territory at a time when just about everywhere was unfamiliar territory for me. But this place, where I'm drafting this coda, it's more than just a Holiday Inn; it's an *airport* Holiday Inn, and there's an especially intensified sense of transience—and urgency—about airport motels. The sense you get over the years from arguments and assignations overheard in elevators and through thin plaster and drywall, from the stories told by the Ancient Mariners who buttonhole you in airport-motel bars while they wait out the weather that canceled their flights. A sense of risk and flight, of people running away or running toward some life-changing fate. Airport motels, Charles Portis told me at our breakfast at the Waffle House, are the spiritual successors to the railway-terminal hotels in medium-size cities. Those temples of transience that often used to be somewhat unfortunately but often accurately named the Terminal Hotel. Although airport motels more often conjure up eros rather than death. One scholar coined the phrase *the erotics of transience* about the motel-punctuated driving experience.

I'm not alone in feeling this way about motels, I think. (Nabokov was there first, of course.) I always loved that passage in the introduction to *Slouching Towards Bethlehem,* in which Joan Didion talks about her handicaps as a journalist. How "I do not like to make telephone calls and would not like to count the mornings I have sat on some Best Western motel bed somewhere and tried to force myself to put through the call to the assistant district attorney." She doesn't want to count the mornings, but I have a feeling she recalls them not without a certain fondness.

I liked her candor about her shyness as well because one reason I took to journalism was that it helped me get over an almost congenital shyness that had something to do with my bright red hair and the unwanted attention it brought me. Getting out and doing stories, trying to answer questions, to solve mysteries, were my excuses to "force myself to put through the call," to rouse myself from reading and make contact with a realm outside myself. To talk to strangers.

So I'd like to end this on a note of gratitude. Gratitude to the strangers who did agree to talk to me when I finally put through that call. Gratitude to all the waitresses and motel clerks who didn't treat me with the suspicion I probably deserved as I hung around some desolate locale, apparently up to no good. Gratitude to all the people on all the magazines who helped shepherd these stories into print. And gratitude also to the magazine story itself as a form, and to the readers who have supported it.

It's a form whose death is always being announced prematurely. (Robert Sam Anson used to pityingly call me "The Last Magazine Writer.") And perhaps it *may* be dying out, it may be that soon there will be nothing but celebrity profiles in magazines. But for a person like me with no aptitude for any more legitimate profession, it has been a blessing that some people, some editors and readers, still want stories and speculative essays.

I've always felt that magazine stories suffer unduly from the transience of their binding media. I guess you could say magazine stories are the airport motels of literature, rarely given the respect the more palatially constructed grand hotels in hardcover get, however empty of life some of their grand interiors might be. In fact, I'd suggest that at least as many urgent and life-changing moments take place under the covers, between the sheets of airport motels, and between the covers, on the sheets of magazine pages, than in the somber somnolence of the Plazas and the Four Seasons of life and literature.

So I'm grateful to the airport motels of life and literature. And to the Ancient Mariners who more often than not set me off on these odysseys, which, if rarely dangerous, were certainly threatening to the hope of a secure and well-ordered existence. And I hope you'll forgive me for this one final disclosure: just how much a pleasure it's been to do this rather than try to hold down a real job. It's sometimes been lonely, there's been debt and doubt. But I wouldn't have missed it for the world.

—Little Rock
New York City
January 2000

THE
SEVENTIES

Dream Dancing

In Which We Enter the Realm of Richard Roffman
and His Unknown Famous People

The first time I met Richard H. Roffman he was still representing Big Ed Carmel. You might remember Big Ed, the nearly nine-foot-tall "gentle Jewish giant from the Bronx," from the celebrated Diane Arbus photograph of the big guy with his pint-size parents in their living room up on the Grand Concourse.

Back then, p.r. man Roffman was trying to promote interest in a film career for Big Ed, an effort that never got very far, no doubt due to the shortage of really good parts for nine-foot-tall men.

But it was not long before I discovered that Richard H. Roffman is a giant in his own right—a towering figure in a strange subculture of showbiz dreamers, would-be celebrities, and stand-ins for stars that Roffman runs out of his living room on West End Avenue.

Roffman is more than a p.r. man—he's the ringmaster of a self-contained, self-fulfilling world that offers the complete "celebrity treatment" to a client: gala openings at restaurants represented by Roffman's p.r. business, radio and cable-TV talent showcases on Roffman-purchased airtime, guest shots on Roffman-hosted talk shows, conspicuous mention in "Roffman News Service" releases and appearance in celebrity-type "overheard while dining at . . ." anecdotes sent out by Roffman to show-business and gossip columnists (who cares if the items never run?—the fact that you have a press agent sending items about you to real columnists is halfway to real celebrity-hood right there). All of this is accompanied by accolades from a cult composed of fellow Roffman-client "celebrities" who treat one another as if they were all real celebrities and nourish one another's cherished mutual illusions.

The success of the Roffman apparatus is all the more extraordinary when you consider that the clients involved do not exactly have the stellar magnitude of the celebs who employ John Springer, Bobby Zarem, and other established p.r. hotshots.

There is Monde, "Genie of the Accordion" and inventor of "the celebrity handshake glove." There is Yoga-donis, "the singing psychic." There's Tino Valenti, invariably identified as "the society troubadour"; someone known as "Count Gregory"; Dr. Joseph Yellis, "podiatrist-humorist." Several other clients of hyphenated accomplishments include a "songwriter-furrier," a "singer-artist-civic leader from Guyana," and Dr. Murray C. Kaye, described as "civic leader and retail beauty-world industrialist-owner of Murray Kaye Way beauty salon and frequently a guest on radio and TV shows . . . to discuss current problems."

The most recent Roffman client roster includes these other current favorites, along with the inimitable Roffmanesque descriptions of their talents:

—"Ugly George Urban, video cameraman heavy on adult material—wears silver suit."
—"Jos Gabriele, equinologist expert on horse racing, former wrestler investment counsellor."
—"Nat Lehrfeld, furrier who does sculpture out of seashells."
—"Princess Audrey Kargere, colorologist."
—"Harold Blum, cookie wholesaler."
—"Gregg Peters, an Elvis Presley soundalike lookalike."
—"Andrew Clay, young singer, a comedian, a John Travolta lookalike, soundalike, actalike."

In Roffman News Service press releases, the chance remarks of Roffman luminaries are accorded all the attention and awe given an Andy or Liza by Suzy and Liz. Consider some of the following items culled from Roffman releases over the years:

Six vegetarian dachshunds are available for placement by noted singing psychic Adonaiasis. At a press conference held at the Lotos Eaters Chinese Restaurant, Adonaiasis, a tall, handsome, blond young man of muscular physique said:

"I sadly must give up these wonderful dogs, for I am getting so very busy with my consultation and personal advisory services and can only find time to give personal attention to a very few loved ones of the canine world. . . ."

The Whirling Dervish Society presented an award to Tino Valenti, the Society Troubadour, Raconteur, Character actor, Artist, Fashion Designer, Singer, Guitarist, Bicyclist, Lecturer, Producer, Director for being the Busiest Man of Quality Around.

Vance Packard, the songwriter of many hit tunes (not the author of best-selling books, yes there are two gentlemen with that same name), disclosed while dining at the Adam's Rib restaurant that he is planning to open a unique beauty salon in the early part of the year.

Mikulas Grosz, a sightless violinist with a "genius" mind for discussions of all the problems of the day, even though they do not relate to music or the questions of the blind, will become a regular panelist on the Richard H. Roffman and His Friends Show, which is taped at the 86th Street Hofbrau House restaurant. This is one of the first times a sightless personality has been a regular participant in a talk show, according to informal research.

Richard H. Roffman, well-known newspaper man, publicist attorney, and theatrical producer, has been on the air continuously since 1935 and is celebrating his thirty-fifth continuous year of radio broadcasting in this city. At a reception held at the 86th Street Hofbrau House he was honored by the Greater New York Citizens Society for distinguished service in the communications world. Presented with a citation by Dr. Murray C. Kaye, civic leader and retail beauty world industrialist, Roffman declared . . .

After reading these curious releases for a year or so, I began asking reporters around town whether they'd heard of this Roffman guy. A mystified look would cloud their expressions. What *is* the story on that guy? they'd ask. Is he for real, or is it some kind of concept art? Have you *seen* those releases?

I decided to get a glimpse of Roffman's world firsthand. And so, one warm spring evening some time ago, I attended one of the many award ceremonies that crowd the Roffman social calendar. This particular one took place in a big banquet room in the back of a now defunct place called Phil Gluckstern's Fancy Kosher Dairy Restaurant in the theater district.

As I walked in, the first of many "entertainers"—I can't recall if it was the songwriter-furrier or the podiatrist-humorist—was giving the first of many tributes to "the wonderful Mr. Dick Roffman," following which the entertainer would sing a song or tell some jokes, the audience would applaud or laugh vociferously, and Mr. Dick Roffman would then introduce the next "award-winning" performer with effusive praise. Mr. Dick Roffman is a big, jolly giant of a fellow with a gleaming bald dome and an unflagging geniality that gave an air of dignity to the relentlessly amateurish proceedings.

The "celebrities" all seemed deadly serious about themselves. Roffman's attitude was harder to figure out. Was he deluding these people or was he fulfilling their fantasies in a harmless, satisfying way? Was Roffman a benign Walter Mitty or a conniving charmer cynically toying with the dreams his clients entrusted to him?

I needed a closer look at the Roffman operation. I spent hours during the day watching him weave his web of contacts and connections; I followed him on his nightly rounds along the freebie, due-bill, and press-review-party circuit; and, finally, I spent a strange night at a Roffman-inspired Tribute to Richard H. Roffman, where I learned the secret of "Dream Dancing."

Dick Roffman begins his day by turning on his TV set and watching with almost religious veneration *The Joe Franklin Show*. Joe is an idol to Roffman, who often boasts of the time he was actually asked to fill in for Joe at some promotional dinner at Luchow's. Besides, the show is a good source of potential clients and may be a big-break guest shot for a current client.

With Joe's show over, Roffman turns on his two phone lines, and the calls start pouring in. Roffman spends the next six hours taking calls, making connections, setting up deals. It goes something like this.

Ring. "Yes, this is Richard H. Roffman. Yes, I *had* called earlier. To say I was representing a gentleman named George Friedensohn, an international monetary expert who is desirous of talking about the impending collapse of the Western world. He is available for a limited number of talk shows—what station is this again?"

Ring. "Hold one moment, please, that's my other phone. Hello, who is this? Mrs. Marvell? You're looking for a man who owns a stone quarry. Hold on, please. Hello again. Yes, Mr. Friedensohn is available for a limited number of talk shows. There's a real catastrophe approaching. Please get back to me. Hello again, Mrs. Marvell. Now, what's the point you're making about a stone quarry? There's a natural stone with a pink-and-white stripe? Yes, what is it you want me—for a lighthouse? Oh, for ranch houses? Okay. A man named Sam Shapiro at 60 East Forty-second is in the mortgage-finance business and works with a lot of builders; he might be a good contact for that."

Ring. "Hello, dear. Hold on, Mrs. Marvell. You have a portrait of Shakespeare done by who? . . . I see, I see. So what is it you need? You need an art dealer, a fine-art dealer. Well, let me think about it—call me tomorrow morning. Hello again, Mrs. Marvell. Yes, *Sam Shapiro*. What's that? You need a lawyer to handle your extra money? I could handle your extra money. Oh, I see. You *owe* somebody money. Try a very fine lawyer named Milton Notarius— he's also in 60 East Forty-second. N-O-T-A-R-I-U-S. Easy to remember. He happens to be a good friend of mine, and I'm sure he can guide you properly."

Roffman puts the phone down. "I get all kinds of calls after being in show business forty years. Now this Mrs. Marvell, somehow she's come into some pink marble, or maybe it is somebody's given her the right to sell this pink marble for them if she can find a buyer. She's an older woman who never gives up, despite the fact that she's half-blind—she has an indomitable spirit. She's always working on deals. She's always trying to make money and bring people together. She loves to be the catalyst."

A description that fits Roffman himself, and so, since the phone is temporarily silent, I ask him how he actually makes a living.

"Well, I don't have any fixed fees. I always say to people if anything happens, remember me if you can, because I feel that if you tie people up to things you get to a point where they may rely on you and maybe you can't help them solve their problems. Then you're *misleading* them. I try to avoid that."

Ring. "Hello. Yes. Yeah. Oh yes. You talked to me about something at a yeshiva at Brooklyn Saturday night. Wait, I want to get all the information because one of my chief associates is going to cover it personally."

Ring. "Hold on, Bernice. Great. I've got on the phone the chief representative of an Israeli magician. [Picks up other phone.] What do you call it again? He's a what? Ah hah. [Back to second phone.] He's known as 'The Wizard of Ouz.' [Back to first phone.] Do you spell Ouz O-U-Z? Yes? And is it like Hebrew humor? I see a general English magic show for Jewish audiences. Just one second. I'll take all the information because my associate is on the other phone. [Back to other phone.] Bernice, this guy might be great on your cable-TV show. 'The Wizard of Ouz.' "

He seems ready to put the two phones together to make the connection. Decides against it, gives the Wizard's number to Bernice, and returns to the Wizard's manager.

When the phone is silent again, Roffman begins filling me in on his forty years of wheeling and dealing and how he got to be the "Best Kept Secret in New York," as he likes to call himself, this hub, catalyst, social director for such a strange assortment of people.

His father, "the distinguished orchestra leader and composer" (as Roffman releases invariably describe the late Maurice Roffman), raised young Richard in the theatrical society of the early-twentieth-century Upper West Side. (Roffman doesn't look it, but he's in his sixties already.) Although the distinguished leader and composer never achieved stellar renown ("His most well-known composition was something you may never have heard of called 'Hula Formal' that he was personally commissioned to do by Arthur Murray to promote his hula lessons, I think"), nonetheless the late distinguished etc. was someone who was invariably *recognized* as something of a celebrity in the neighborhood.

"As a child the greatest thrill of my life was to walk with my father on Broadway and have people recognize him," Roffman recalls.

In fact, Roffman reveals he was something of a celebrity himself back then: "I was an actor as a child in a number of early Vitagraph movies and one or two *Our Gang* comedies."

Now he has his own gang of sorts and . . . *ring* . . . one of them is on the phone now.

It's Tino Valenti, invariably described by Roffman as a "society trouba-dour" although he is vague as to what that means.

"Yes, Tino. Are you feeling better? A package? Sure I'll bring it over. It's not a large package. Good, I'll bring it over. No, not much going on tonight. There's that restaurant opening and then the party at the Yugoslav mission, but that's about it. Fine, Tino, see you later."

Tino, Roffman tells me, is a show-business friend of long standing. "He was Rudolph Valentino's stand-in back in the thirties."

"His stand-in?" I ask. "You mean his understudy or stunt man?"

"Not exactly," says Roffman. "Tino didn't really *look* like Valentino, but he didn't have to. They just needed someone to stand in his place so they could set up the scene while Rudy was getting ready to come out of his dressing room."

"Did Tino give himself that name because of Valentino?"

"Well, it was a very important influence on his career, which needless to say was not as fabulous as Rudy's, but Tino has many friends and admirers, and he's truly what we like to call a multitalent, singer-guitarist-entertainer-raconteur-all-around troubadour, as I like to say."

Roffman returns to the Richard Roffman saga.

There were sensational celebrity-chasing exploits as a young reporter for Hearst's *Journal American* in the early thirties, and finally his first venture into what was to be forty-five consecutive years of broadcasting. His first radio show had the hauntingly evocative title *Real Stories from Real Life.*

"It was a big show; there were many, many famous people who were on it. Many well-known actors and actresses got their start with me on that show."

Who, for example? I asked.

"Well, I'd have to search my files to find a name, but it's true that *at least* six men and six women whose names became well known in film and theater, although not so much in television, started out in radio and were busy from this show."

Famous as *Real Stories from Real Life* may have made some of its actors, it wasn't exactly a gold mine for Roffman himself, and he pursued, in the mean-time, some enterprising ventures with some very curious gadgets, inventions, and sales promotions.

His biggest success, he says, was promotion for an invention he describes as "a pressure cooker that was unexplodable." Unfortunately, the next venture was either way ahead, or way behind, the times.

"We called it 'Re Nu Cell.' It was a plastic machine with gadgets such that you attach a glass cup to the skin and there's alternate suction and pressure that's supposed to be beneficial. It was based on ancient truths or something like that."

Roffman concedes, "This thing was never as successful as the Diner's Club or apple pie," but he does note proudly that "we never had trouble with the medical authorities."

There was a brief stint as p.r. man for the Stork Club in the mid-forties after he left the *Journal American*. There was a job as promotion editor of *Modern Knitting* ("We got Klavan and Finch to knit on the air—it was a radio first"). His radio interviews provided him with clients and a way of giving clients their first big-time exposure on the air, even if most of Roffman's shows had to be bought with his own money. Many of them, realistically, couldn't hope for much more. He began to develop a whole social life centered on his clients.

I asked Roffman how he managed to attract such a curious range of people.

"Well, for one thing, I'm listed in the Yellow Pages as a publicist. I'm listed in two different ways, actually. I'm listed under 'Public Relations' and also under 'Publicity,' and I also list in one of the ads the kinds of accounts in which I specialize."

Another secret of his success, Roffman confides, is that he makes sure he gets himself listed with every U.S. consulate around the world as a New York City p.r. man specializing in show business and inventions, so that foreigners seeking to come to the land of opportunity to market themselves or their products will be more likely to call him up. This explains the number of exotically based people Roffman represents. A Sephardic Jew from Bombay, a Finnish woodworker, a Yugoslav baker, etc., etc. Why does Roffman content himself with this sort of clientele? "I could have gone in for the big celebrities," he says. "I could have gone for the big clients. But I'm content to be the Woolworth of the publicity business rather than the Tiffany."

By four in the afternoon, after nearly a hundred calls, Roffman declares he will take no more. It is time to make his rounds. His rounds, from the sampling I did following him, seem to consist of generous helpings from the freebie–due bill circuit, created by other p.r. enterprises. He's on the press lists for every promotion party, art opening, and p.r. event imaginable, in addition to representing a seemingly endless array of uptown Chinese restaurants and other eating places that issue "due bills," or meals in exchange for service or promotional work. That afternoon we attended a promotional cocktail party at Adam's Apple, a frequent beneficiary of "heard at" items in the Roffman News Service releases, then an opening party at an East Side Jamaican restaurant with a hearty dinner, gratis.

Capping off this particular evening was a reception at the Yugoslav mission on upper Fifth Avenue. I never found out for whom or what the reception was, nor why Roffman was invited, although he does seem to have a number of Yugoslav clients, including a guy who wants to market a line of Balkan frozen foods.

The reception is quite elaborate and formal. Not much English is spoken, but there is definitely much strong slivovitz making itself felt as formally dressed waiters press glass after glass into visitors' hands. I meet a man named Wambly Bald, who says he's known Roffman since their tabloid-reporter days. I express my continued mystification as to the nature, extent, and reality of the Roffman world.

"You have to understand his secret," Wambly Bald tells me.

"His secret?"

"Don't listen to anything he tells you," says Roffman, looming up out of the reception throng and then passing on to greet a Balkan buddy.

"You have to understand his secret," Wambly Bald repeats. "He's the Pied Piper."

"The Pied Piper?"

"The Pied Piper of New York. That explains why they all follow him and live their lives around him. He's the Pied Piper."

Not entirely satisfied with that explanation, I looked forward to the upcoming Roffman Birthday Tribute for a chance to meet with these allegedly spellbound grown-up children who make up the Roffman world. The Birthday Tribute was being thrown by the Friends of Richard H. Roffman in association with several civic groups that were headed by Murray C. Kaye and other Roffman associates. It's not clear whether Roffman throws these tributes for himself or they're thrown for him, but in typical Roffman fashion both tributee and tributors benefit, since the Friends of Richard H. Roffman get to perform their songs, dances, and comedy acts before an appreciative audience they might not command at some more neutral booking.

In any case, this tribute was to be held in the basement banquet room of the Factoria, a short-lived pasta palace on East Fifty-eighth Street.

The party was going strong when I arrived that night. Before I could make my way through the crowd, a small, determined-looking man with iron-gray hair approached me, handed me a mimeographed leaflet, and warned me about "the Atlanteans" at the party.

"They look like ordinary people but they're spies from Atlantis. They have ways of recognizing each other and communicating that we don't know."

"How do you know I'm not one?" I asked.

"You might be. I might be. You can't tell. Read this."

He pointed to his leaflet. An open letter to the U.N. General Assembly. He demanded the right to present evidence that the original astronauts who had landed on the moon had been kidnapped and replaced by lookalike aliens who were actually Atlantean spies.

And, indeed, Roffman's world of make-believe and lookalike celebrity was not unlike a secret Atlantean subculture beneath the surface of New York life. The Roffmanites all had their common signs and mutual recognitions. A submerged kingdom of their own.

The very next person I came across at the tribute enforced this sense of an invisible realm.

It was a Cowboy Jack Willis, the ex-prizefighter-poet and lecturer on health and nutrition. I had run into Cowboy Jack once before—at a "Gala Bon Voyage Party for Joe Franklin's Cruise Down Memory Lane" on a Greek liner about to depart down said lane via Joe's clips of Silent Era Stars. Cowboy Jack wasn't going on the cruise. He and some other Roffmanites were circulating like Atlanteans among the revelers. I asked Jack what he was doing at the Birthday Tribute, and discovered he was a longtime Roffmanite and a true fan of the gentle giant of West End Avenue. In fact, Jack had come to the Birthday Tribute with a freshly minted poem, an ode to Richard Roffman he planned to read to climax the night's festivities.

Cowboy Jack began to give me a full-voiced preview of the ode. " 'Hail to thee, Sir Richard Roffman,' it begins," he confided. "I compare him to King Arthur and his Knights of the Round Table. I see him as a reincarnation of one of King Arthur's knights." The poem ended with the imagery intact: "Happy Birthday, Sir Richard the Roffman / May your heart never shed any tears."

One after another, the Roffmanites I met at this tribute expressed their gratitude to their cult leader for helping them "make it." They'd always dreamed of being in show business, they'd say, and "Dick Roffman made my dreams come true."

Some Roffmanites I met at the tribute:

There was George Friedensohn, "the international monetary expert prepared to predict the impending collapse of the Western world on talk shows." Friedensohn, appropriately, turned out to be an intense, brooding fellow much given to scowling when his prophecies were not taken seriously enough. He flew into a raging tirade about my insensitivity to impending monetary doom when I ventured to ask him how much he charged for his "private consultations" on pre-apocalyptic investment strategies. When he calmed down, he did tell me he was pleased with Roffman's p.r. work for him. "His was by far the lowest bid," the canny monetary expert confided, "and he has succeeded in getting me on some real talk shows."

Then there was Eddie Rane, tirelessly promoted in Roffman releases as "the new Russ Columbo voice." I confessed to Eddie I wasn't familiar with the original Mr. Columbo. "He was said to have the most perfect voice of all back in the thirties," Eddie told me. "If he had stayed around, Crosby wouldn't have been Crosby; *he* would have been Crosby. But he died at age twenty-four. People say I look and sound just like him." Eddie looks like he's safely past the fateful age at which the original expired. But he carries on and pronounces himself pleased at the "bookings" he gets at Roffman-related activities.

There was a woman who, with surprising reticence, would describe herself only as "someone who's been in show business a long time and who has known Roffman 'from the beginning.' "

"What do I think of him? I think he's a jerk, that's what," she said.

A jerk?

"For being too nice to people. He's too good to too many people. They take advantage of him. He doesn't know how to take care of himself. He could have had the biggest clients if he wanted. From when he started out. But he likes these people even if he never makes a dime off them."

There was a final conversation I had that night, after the tributes to Roffman were read, sung, declaimed, and the performers performed to one another's applause. As I was leaving, I ran into a Roffman connection who described himself as a "big booker of 'socials' " for specialized singles groups (one hundred doctor and dentist widowers to meet one hundred widows who have money to invest in plays, etc.). Roffman, it seems, has an extensive match-making practice of this sort, with all his contacts, plus restaurants willing to host socials and clients to entertain. The "socials" organizer was telling me about the "musico-chemico-emotional" science of making these socials genuinely sociable. "Background music is the key," he declared. "You've got to have the right ground fertilized for romance." He'd been experimenting for years with types of various background music for the get-acquainted stage of the socials, and he was convinced that there was one tape more than any other which made magic between people.

"What was it?" I asked.

"*Dream Dancing,*" he said.

"*Dream Dancing*?"

"Yes. By Ray Anthony and his orchestra. Don't ask me why, but with *Dream Dancing,* if you've got a decent list-maker to start out with, you can't miss."

Dream Dancing. Roffman's clients are, most of them, Dream Dancers of one sort or another, Roffman himself the composer and choreographer of the background music, the Ray Anthony of their celebrity waltz.

Secrets of the Little Blue Box

In Which We Explore the Web of the Original Hackers

There is an underground telephone network in this country. Al Gilbertson[1] discovered it the day after his arrest for manufacturing illegal "blue boxes." A crime he is not exactly repentant about. I am sitting in the living room of the creator of the blue box. Gilbertson is holding one of his shiny black-and-silver* blue boxes comfortably in the palm of his hand, pointing out the thirteen little red push buttons sticking up from the console. He is dancing his fingers over the buttons, tapping out discordant beeping electronic jingles. He is trying to explain to me how his little blue box does nothing less than place the entire telephone system of the world, satellites, cables, and all, at the service of the blue-box operator, free of charge.

"Essentially it gives you the power of a super operator. You seize a tandem with this top button," he presses the top button with his index finger and the blue box emits a high-pitched *cheep*, "and like that"—*cheep* goes the blue box again—"you control the phone company's long-distance switching systems

[1]His real name has been changed.

Blue box is a hacker term of art rather than a color description.

from your cute little Princess phone or any old pay phone. And you've got anonymity. An operator has to operate from a definite location: The phone company knows where she is and what she's doing. But with your beeper box, once you hop onto a trunk, say from a Holiday Inn 800 number, they don't know where you are, or where you're coming from, they don't know how you slipped into their lines and popped up in that 800 number. They don't even know anything illegal is going on. And you can obscure your origins through as many levels as you like. You can call next door by way of White Plains, then over to Liverpool by cable, and then back here by satellite. You can call yourself from one pay phone all the way around the world to a pay phone next to you. And you get your dime back, too."

"And they can't trace the calls? They can't charge you?"

"Not if you do it the right way. But you'll find that the free-call thing isn't really as exciting at first as the feeling of power you get from having one of these babies in your hand. I've watched people when they first get hold of one of these things and start using it, and discover they can make connections, set up crisscross and zigzag switching patterns back and forth across the world. They hardly talk to the people they finally reach. They say hello and start thinking of what kind of call to make next. They go a little crazy." He looks down at the neat little package in his palm. His fingers are still dancing, tapping out beeper patterns.

"I think it's something to do with how small my models are. There are lots of blue boxes around, but mine are the smallest and most sophisticated electronically. I wish I could show you the prototype we made for our big syndicate order."

He sighs. "We had this order for a thousand beeper boxes from a syndicate front man in Las Vegas. They use them to place bets coast to coast, keep lines open for hours, all of which can get expensive if you have to pay. The deal was a thousand blue boxes for $300 apiece. Before then we retailed them for $1,500 apiece, but $300,000 in one lump was hard to turn down. We had a manufacturing deal worked out in the Philippines. Everything ready to go. Anyway, the model I had ready for limited mass production was small enough to fit inside a flip-top Marlboro box. It had flush touch panels for a keyboard, rather than these unsightly buttons sticking out. Looked just like a tiny portable radio. In fact, I had designed it with a tiny transistor receiver to get one AM channel so in case the law became suspicious the owner could switch on the radio part, start snapping his fingers, and no one could tell anything illegal was going on. I thought of everything for this model—I had it lined with a band of thermite which could be ignited by radio signal from a tiny button transmitter on your belt, so it could be burned to ashes instantly in case of a bust. It was beautiful. A beautiful little machine. You should have seen the faces on these syndicate guys when they came back after trying it out. They'd hold it in their palm like they never wanted to let it go, and they'd say, 'I can't believe it. I can't believe it.' *You* probably won't believe it until you try it."

You Can Call Long Distance for Less Than You Think

"You see, a few years ago the phone company made one big mistake," Gilbertson explains two days later in his apartment. "They were careless enough to let some technical journal publish the actual frequencies used to create all their multifrequency tones. Just a theoretical article some Bell Telephone Laboratories engineer was doing about switching theory, and he listed the tones in passing. At ———— [a well-known technical school] I had been fooling around with phones for several years before I came across a copy of the journal in the engineering library. I ran back to the lab and it took maybe twelve hours from the time I saw that article to put together the first working blue box. It was bigger and clumsier than this little baby, but it worked."

It's all there on public record in that technical journal written mainly by Bell Lab people for other telephone engineers. Or at least it *was* public. "Just try and get a copy of that issue at some engineering-school library now. Bell has had them all red-tagged and withdrawn from circulation," Gilbertson tells me.

"But it's too late. It's all public now. And once they became public the technology needed to create your own beeper device is within the range of any twelve-year-old kid, any twelve-year-old *blind* kid, as a matter of fact. And he can do it in *less* than the twelve hours it took us. Blind kids do it all the time. They can't build anything as precise and compact as my beeper box, but theirs can do anything mine can do."

"How?"

"Okay. About twenty years ago AT&T made a multibillion-dollar decision to operate its entire long-distance switching system on twelve electronically generated combinations of six master tones. Those are the tones you sometimes hear in the background after you've dialed a long-distance number. They decided to use some very simple tones—the tone for each number is just two fixed single-frequency tones played simultaneously to create a certain beat frequency. Like 1,300 cycles per second and 900 cycles per second played together give you the tone for digit 5. Now, what some of these phone phreaks have done is get themselves access to an electric organ. Any cheap family home-entertainment organ. Since the frequencies are public knowledge now—one blind phone phreak has even had them recorded in one of those talking books for the blind—they just have to find the musical notes on the organ which correspond to the phone tones. Then they tape them. For instance, to get Ma Bell's tone for the number 1, you press down organ keys F^5

and A^5 [900 and 700 cycles per second] at the same time. To produce the tone for 2 it's F^5 and C^6 [1100 and 700 cps]. The phone phreaks circulate the whole list of notes so there's no trial and error anymore."

He shows me a list of the rest of the phone numbers and the two electric organ keys that produce them.

"Actually, you have to record these notes at 3¾ inches-per-second tape speed and double it to 7½ inches-per-second when you play them back, to get the proper tones," he adds.

"So once you have all the tones recorded, how do you plug them into the phone system?"

"Well, they take their organ and their cassette recorder, and start banging out entire phone numbers in tones on the organ, including country codes, routing instructions, 'KP' and 'Start' tones. Or, if they don't have an organ, someone in the phone-phreak network sends them a cassette with all the tones recorded, with a voice saying 'Number 1,' then you have the tone, 'Number 2,' then the tone, and so on. So with two cassette recorders they can put together a series of phone numbers by switching back and forth from number to number. Any idiot in the country with a cheap cassette recorder can make all the free calls he wants."

"You mean you just hold the cassette recorder up to the mouthpiece and switch in a series of beeps you've recorded? The phone thinks that anything that makes these tones must be its own equipment?"

"Right. As long as you get the frequency within thirty cycles per second of the phone company's tones, the phone equipment thinks it hears its own voice talking to it. The original granddaddy phone phreak was this blind kid with perfect pitch, Joe Engressia, who used to whistle into the phone. An operator could tell the difference between his whistle and the phone company's electronic tone generator, but the phone company's switching circuit can't tell them apart. The bigger the phone company gets and the further away from human operators it gets, the more vulnerable it becomes to all *sorts* of phone phreaking."

"What about the recent series of blue-box arrests all across the country— New York, Cleveland, and so on?" I asked. "How were they caught so easily?"

"From what I can tell, they made one big mistake: They were seizing trunks using an area code plus 555-1212 instead of an 800 number. Using 555 is easy to detect because when you send multifrequency beep tones off 555 you get a charge for it on your tape and the accounting computer knows there's something wrong when it tries to bill you for a two-hour call to Akron, Ohio, information, and it drops a trouble card which goes right into the hands of the security agent if they're looking for blue-box users.

"Whoever sold those guys their blue boxes didn't tell them how to use them properly, which is fairly irresponsible. And they were fairly stupid to use them at home all the time.

"But what those arrests really mean is that an awful lot of blue boxes are flooding into the country and that people are finding them so easy to make that they know how to make them before they know how to use them. Ma Bell is in trouble."

And if a blue-box operator or a cassette-recorder phone phreak sticks to pay phones and 800 numbers, the phone company can't stop them?

"Not unless they change their entire nationwide long-lines technology, which will take them a few billion dollars and twenty years. Right now they can't do a thing. They're screwed."

Captain Crunch Demonstrates His Famous Unit

Al Gilbertson discovered the underground telephone network the very day news of his own arrest hit the papers. That evening his phone began ringing. Phone phreaks from Seattle, from Florida, from New York, from San Jose, and from Los Angeles began calling him and telling him about the phone-phreak network. He'd get a call from a phone phreak who'd say nothing but, "Hang up and call this number."

When he dialed the number he'd find himself tied into a conference of a dozen phone phreaks arranged through a quirky switching station in British Columbia. They identified themselves as phone phreaks, they demonstrated their homemade blue boxes, which they called "M-F-ers" (for "multifrequency," among other things), for him, they talked shop about phone-phreak devices. They let him in on their secrets on the theory that if the phone company was after him he must be trustworthy. And, Gilbertson recalls, they stunned him with their technical sophistication.

I ask him how to get in touch with the phone-phreak network. He digs around through a file of old schematics and comes up with about a dozen numbers in three widely separated area codes.

"Those are the centers," he tells me. Alongside some of the numbers he writes in first names or nicknames: names like Captain Crunch, Dr. No, Frank Carson (also a code word for free call), Marty Freeman (code word for M-F device), Peter Perpendicular Pimple, Alefnull, and The Cheshire Cat. He makes checks alongside the names of those among these top twelve who are blind. There are five checks.

I ask him who this Captain Crunch person is.

"Oh. The Captain. He's probably the most legendary phone phreak. He calls himself Captain Crunch after the notorious Cap'n Crunch 2,600 whistle." (Several years ago, Gilbertson explains, the makers of Cap'n Crunch breakfast cereal offered a toy-whistle prize in every box as a treat for the Cap'n Crunch set. Somehow a phone phreak discovered that the toy whistle just happened to produce a perfect 2,600-cycle tone, the key entry tone that allowed phone phreaks to hack into the system. When the man who calls himself Captain Crunch was transferred overseas to England with his Air Force unit, he would receive scores of calls from his friends and "mute" them—make them free of charge to them—by blowing his Cap'n Crunch whistle into his end.)

"Captain Crunch is one of the older phone phreaks," Gilbertson tells me. "He's an engineer who once got in a little trouble for fooling around with the phone, but he can't stop. Well, this guy drives across country in a Volkswagen van with an entire switchboard and a computerized super-sophisticated M-F-er in the back. He'll pull up to a phone booth on a lonely highway somewhere, snake a cable out of his bus, hook it onto the phone and sit for hours, days sometimes, sending calls zipping back and forth across the country, all over the world. . . ."

Back at my motel, I dialed the number he gave me for "Captain Crunch" and asked for G———— T————, the name he uses when he's not dashing into a phone booth beeping out M-F tones faster than a speeding bullet, and zipping phantomlike through the phone company's long-distance lines.

When the Captain answered the phone and I told him I was preparing a story for *Esquire* about phone phreaks, he became very indignant.

"I don't do that. I don't do that anymore at all. And if I do it, I do it for one reason and one reason only. I'm learning about a system. The phone company is a System. A computer is a System. Do you understand? If I do what I do, it is only to explore a System. Computers. Systems. That's my bag. The phone company is nothing but a computer."

A tone of tightly restrained excitement enters the Captain's voice when he starts talking about Systems. He begins to pronounce each syllable with the hushed deliberation of an obscene caller.

"Ma Bell is a system I want to explore. It's a beautiful system, you know, but Ma Bell screwed up. It's terrible because Ma Bell is such a beautiful system, but she screwed up. I learned how she screwed up from a couple of blind kids who wanted me to build a device. A certain device. They said it could make free calls. I wasn't interested in free calls. But when these blind kids told me I could make calls into a computer, my eyes lit up.* I wanted to learn about computers. I wanted to learn about Ma Bell's computers. So I built the little device. Only I built it wrong and Ma Bell found out. Ma Bell can detect things

---

*Right here we witness the dawn of the hacker era as a gleam in Captain Crunch's eye.

like that. Ma Bell knows. So I'm strictly out of it now. I didn't do it. Except for learning purposes." He pauses. "So you want to write an article. Are you paying for this call? Hang up and call this number."

He gives me a number in an area code a thousand miles north of his own. I dial the number.

"Hello again. This is Captain Crunch. You are speaking to me on a toll-free loop-around in Portland, Oregon. Do you know what a toll-free loop-around is? I'll tell you."

He explains to me that almost every exchange in the country has open test numbers which allow other exchanges to test their connections with it. Most of these numbers occur in consecutive pairs, such as (302) 956-0041 and 956-0042. Well, certain phone phreaks discovered that if two people from anywhere in the country dial those two consecutive numbers they can talk together just as if one had called the other's number, with no charge to either of them, of course.

"Your voice is looping around in a 4A switching machine up there in Canada, zipping back down to me," the Captain tells me. "My voice is looping around up there and back down to you. And it can't ever cost anyone money. The phone phreaks and I have compiled a list of many, many of these numbers. You would be surprised if you saw the list. I could show it to you. But I won't. I'm out of that now. I'm not out to screw Ma Bell. I know better. If I do anything it's for the pure knowledge of the System. You can learn to do fantastic things. Have you ever heard eight tandems stacked up? Do you know the sound of tandems stacking and unstacking? Give me your phone number. Okay. Hang up now and wait a minute."

Slightly less than a minute later the phone rings and the Captain is on the line, his voice sounding far more excited, almost aroused.

"I wanted to show you what it's like to stack up tandems. To stack up tandems."* (Whenever the Captain says "stack up" it sounds as if he is licking his lips.)

"How do you like the connection you're on now?" the Captain asks me. "It's a *raw* tandem. A *raw* tandem. Ain't nothin' up to it but a tandem. Now I'm going to show you what it's like to stack up. Blow off. Land in a faraway place. To stack *that* tandem up, whip back and forth across the country a few times, then shoot on up to Moscow.

"Listen," Captain Crunch continues. "Listen. I've got a line tie on my switchboard here, and I'm gonna let you hear me stack and unstack tandems. Listen to this. I'm gonna blow your mind."

First I hear a super rapid-fire pulsing of the flutelike phone tones, then a

---

*Tandems are the two-way relays of the phone company's internal switching system.

pause, then another popping burst of tones, then another, then another. Each burst is followed by a *beep-kachink* sound.

"We have now stacked up four tandems," said Captain Crunch, sounding somewhat remote. "That's four tandems stacked up. Do you know what that means? That means I'm whipping back and forth, back and forth twice, across the country, before coming to you. I've been known to stack up twenty tandems at a time. Now, just like I said, I'm going to shoot up to Moscow."

There is a new, longer series of beeper pulses over the line, a brief silence, then a ring.

"Hello," answers a far-off voice.

"Hello. Is this the American Embassy Moscow?"

"Yes, sir. Who is this calling?" says the voice.

"Yes. This is test board here in New York. We're calling to check out the circuits, see what kind of lines you've got. Everything okay there in Moscow?"

"Okay?"

"Well, yes, how are things there?"

"Oh. Well, everything okay, I guess."

"Okay. Thank you." They hang up, leaving a confused series of *beep-kachink* sounds hanging in mid-ether in the wake of the call before dissolving away.

The Captain is pleased. "You believe me now, don't you? Do you know what I'd like to do? I'd like to call up your editor at *Esquire* and show him *just* what it sounds like to stack and unstack tandems. I'll give him a show that will *blow his mind*. What's his number?"

I ask the Captain what kind of device he was using to accomplish all his feats. The Captain is pleased at the question.

"You could tell it was special, couldn't you? Ten pulses per second. That's faster than the phone company's equipment. Believe me, this unit is *the* most famous unit in the country. There is no other unit like it. Believe me."

"Yes, I've heard about it. Some other phone phreaks have told me about it."

"They have been referring to my, ahem, unit? What is it they said? Just out of curiosity, did they tell you it was a highly sophisticated computer-operated unit, with acoustical coupling for receiving outputs and a switchboard with multiple-line capability? Did they tell you that the frequency tolerance is guaranteed to be not more than .05 percent? The amplitude tolerance less than .01 decibel? Those pulses you heard were perfect. They just come faster than the phone company. Those were high-precision op-amps. Op-amps are instrumentation amplifiers designed for ultrastable amplification, super-low distortion, and accurate frequency response. Did they tell you it can operate in temperatures from minus 55 degrees centigrade to plus 125 degrees centigrade?"

I admit that they did not tell me all that.

"I built it myself," the Captain goes on. "If you were to go out and *buy* the components from an industrial wholesaler it would cost you at least $1,500. I once worked for a semiconductor company and all this didn't cost me a cent. Do you know what I mean? Did they tell you about how I put a call completely around the world? I'll tell you how I did it. I M-F-ed Tokyo inward, who connected me to India, India connected me to Greece, Greece connected me to Pretoria, South Africa, South Africa connected me to South America, I went from South America to London, I had a London operator connect me to a New York operator, I had New York connect me to a California operator, who rang the phone next to me. Needless to say I had to shout to hear myself. But the echo was far out. Fantastic. Delayed. It was delayed twenty seconds, but I could hear myself talk to myself."

"You mean you were speaking into the mouthpiece of one phone sending your voice around the world into your ear through a phone on the other side of your head?" I asked the Captain. I had a vision of something vaguely auto-erotic going on, in a complex electronic way.

"That's right," said the Captain. "I've also sent my voice around the world one way, going east on one phone, and going west on the other, going through cable one way, satellite the other, coming back together at the same time, ringing the two phones simultaneously and picking them up and whipping my voice both ways around the world and back to me. Wow. That was a mind blower."

"You mean you sit there with both phones on your ear and talk to yourself around the world," I said incredulously.

"Yeah. Um-hum. That's what I do. I connect the phones together and sit there and talk."

"What do you say? What do you say to yourself when you're connected?"

"Oh, you know. Hello test one two three," he says in a low-pitched voice.

"Hello test one two three," he replies to himself in a high-pitched voice.

"Hello test one two three," he repeats again, low-pitched.

"Hello test one two three," he replies, high-pitched.

"I sometimes do this: *Hello* hello *hello* hello, *hello,* hello," he trails off, and breaks into laughter.

Why Captain Crunch Hardly Ever Taps Phones Anymore

Using internal phone-company codes, phone phreaks have learned a simple method for tapping phones. Phone-company operators have in front of them a board that holds verification jacks. It allows them to plug into conversations in case of emergency, to listen in to a line to determine if the line is busy or the circuits are busy. Phone phreaks have learned to beep out the codes which lead them to a verification operator, tell the verification operator they are switchmen from some other area code testing out verification trunks. Once the operator hooks them into the verification trunk, they disappear into the board for all practical purposes, slip unnoticed into any one of the 10,000 to 100,000 numbers in that central office without the verification operator knowing what they're doing, and of course without the two parties to the connection knowing there is a phantom listener present on their line.

Toward the end of my hour-long first conversation with him, I asked the Captain if he ever tapped phones.

"Oh no. I don't do that. I don't think it's right," he told me firmly. "I have the power to do it but I don't. . . . Well, one time, just one time, I have to admit that I did. There was this girl Linda, and I wanted to find out . . . you know. I tried to call her up for a date. I had a date with her the last weekend and I thought she liked me. I called her up, man, and her line was busy, and I kept calling and it was still busy. Well, I had just learned about this system of jumping into lines and I said to myself, 'Hmmm. Why not just see if it works. It'll surprise her if all of a sudden I should pop up on her line. It'll impress her, if anything.' So I went ahead and did it. I M-F-ed into the line. My M-F-er is powerful enough when patched directly into the mouthpiece to trigger a verification trunk without using an operator the way the other phone phreaks have to.

"I slipped into the line and there she was talking to another boyfriend. Making sweet talk to him. I didn't make a sound because I was so disgusted. So I waited there for her to hang up, listening to her making sweet talk to another guy. You know. So as soon as she hung up I instantly M-F-ed her up and all I said was, 'Linda, we're through.' And I hung up. And it blew her head off. She couldn't figure out what the hell had happened.

"But that was the only time. I did it thinking I would surprise her, impress her. Those were all my intentions were, and well, it really kind of hurt me pretty badly, and . . . and ever since then I don't go into verification trunks."

Moments later my first conversation with the Captain comes to a close.

"Listen," he says, his spirits somewhat cheered, "listen. What you are going to hear when I hang up is the sound of tandems unstacking. Layer after layer of tandems unstacking until there's nothing left of the stack, until it melts away into nothing. *Cheep, cheep, cheep, cheep,*" he concludes, his voice descending to a whisper with each cheep.

He hangs up. The phone suddenly goes into four spasms: *kachink cheep. Kachink cheep kachink cheep kachink cheep,* and the complex connection has wiped itself out like the Cheshire cat's smile.

The M-F Boogie Blues

The next number I choose from the select list of phone-phreak illuminati prepared for me by the blue-box inventor is a Memphis number. It is the number of Joe Engressia, the first and still perhaps the most accomplished blind phone phreak.

Three years ago Engressia was a nine-day wonder in newspapers and magazines all over America because he had been discovered whistling free long-distance connections for fellow students at the University of South Florida. Engressia was born with perfect pitch; he could whistle phone tones better than the phone-company equipment.

Engressia might have gone on whistling in the dark for a few friends for the rest of his life if the phone company hadn't decided to expose him. He was warned, disciplined by the college, and the whole case became public. In the months following media reports of his talent, Engressia began receiving strange calls. There were calls from a group of kids in Los Angeles who could do some very strange things with the quirky General Telephone and Electronics circuitry in L.A. suburbs. There were calls from a group of mostly blind kids in ———, California, who had been doing some interesting experiments with Cap'n Crunch whistles and test loops. There was a group in Seattle, a group in Cambridge, Massachusetts, a few from New York, a few scattered across the country. Some of them had already equipped themselves with cassette and electronic M-F devices. For some of these groups, it was the first time they knew of the others.

The exposure of Engressia was the catalyst that linked the separate phone-phreak centers together. They all called Engressia. They talked to him about what he was doing and what they were doing. And then he told them—the scattered regional centers and lonely independent phone phreakers—about each other, gave them each other's numbers to call, and within a year the scattered phone-phreak centers had grown into a nationwide underground.

Joe Engressia is only twenty-two years old now, but along the phone-phreak network he is "the old man," accorded by phone phreaks something of the reverence the phone company bestows on Alexander Graham Bell. He seldom needs to make calls anymore. The phone phreaks all call him and let him know what new tricks, new codes, new techniques they have learned. Every night he sits like a sightless spider in his little apartment receiving messages from every tendril of his web. It is almost a point of pride with Joe that *they* call *him*.

But when I reached him in his Memphis apartment that night, Joe Engressia was lonely, jumpy, and upset.

"God, I'm glad somebody called. I don't know why tonight of all nights I don't get any calls. This guy around here got drunk again tonight and propositioned me again. I keep telling him we'll never see eye to eye on this subject, if you know what I mean. I try to make light of it, you know, but he doesn't get it. I can hear him out there getting drunker and I don't know what he'll do next. It's just that I'm really all alone here. I just moved to Memphis, it's the first time I'm living out on my own, and I'd hate for it to all collapse now. But I won't go to bed with him. I'm just not very interested in sex and even if I can't see him I *know* he's ugly.

"Did you hear that? That's him banging a bottle against the wall outside. He's nice. Well, forget about it. You're doing a story on phone phreaks? Listen to this. It's the 'MF boogie' blues."

Sure enough, a jumpy version of "Muskrat Ramble" boogies its way over the line, each note one of those long-distance phone tones. The music stops. A huge roaring voice blasts the phone off my ear: "AND THE QUESTION IS," roars the voice, "CAN A BLIND PERSON HOOK UP AN AMPLIFIER ON HIS OWN?"

The roar ceases. A high-pitched operator-type voice replaces it. "This is Southern Braille Tel. & Tel. Have tone, will phone."

This is succeeded by a quick series of M-F tones, a swift *kachink* and a deep reassuring voice: "If *you* need home care, call the visiting-nurses association. First National time in Honolulu is four thirty-two P.M."

Joe back in his Joe voice again: "Are we seeing eye to eye? '*Si, si,*' said the blind Mexican. Ahem. Yes. Would you like to know the weather in Tokyo?"

This swift manic sequence of phone-phreak vaudeville stunts and blind-boy jokes manages to keep Joe's mind off his tormentor only as long as it lasts.

"The reason I'm in Memphis, the reason I have to depend on that guy, is that this is the first time I've been able to live on my own and make phone trips on my own. I've been banned from all central offices around home in Florida, they knew me too well, and at the university some of my fellow scholars were always harassing me because I was on the dorm pay phone all the time and making fun of me because of my fat ass, which of course I do have, it's my physical fatness program, but I don't like to hear it every day, and if I can't phone trip and I can't phone phreak, I can't imagine what I'd do, I've been devoting three quarters of my life to it.

"I moved to Memphis because I wanted to be on my own as well as because it has a Number 5 crossbar switching system and some interesting little independent phone-company districts nearby and so far they don't seem to know who I am so I can go on phone tripping, and for me phone tripping is just as important as phone phreaking."

Phone tripping, Joe explains, begins with calling up a central-office switch room. He tells the switchman in a polite earnest voice that he's a blind college student interested in telephones, and could he perhaps have a guided tour of the switching station? Each step of the tour Joe likes to touch and feel relays, caress switching circuits, switchboards, crossbar arrangements.

So when Joe Engressia phone phreaks he *feels* his way through the circuitry of the country. In this electronic garden of forking paths, he feels switches shift, relays shunt, crossbars swivel, tandems engage and disengage even as he hears—with perfect pitch—his M-F pulses make the entire Bell system dance to his tune.

Just one month ago Joe took all his savings out of his bank and left home, over the emotional protests of his mother. "I ran away from home almost," he likes to say. Joe found a small apartment house on Union Avenue and began making phone trips. He'd take a bus a hundred miles south into Mississippi to "see" some old-fashioned Bell equipment still in use in several states, which had been puzzling him. He'd take a bus three hundred miles to Charlotte, North Carolina, to get a feel for some brand-new experimental equipment. He hired a taxi to drive him twelve miles to a suburb to tour the office of a small phone company with some interesting idiosyncrasies in its routing system. He was having the time of his life, he said, the most freedom and pleasure he had known.

In that month he had done very little long-distance phone phreaking from his own phone. He had begun to apply for a job with the phone company, he told me, and he wanted to stay away from anything illegal.

"Any kind of job will do, anything as menial as the most lowly operator. That's probably all they'd give me because I'm blind. Even though I probably knew more than most switchmen. But that's okay. I *want* to work for Ma Bell. I don't hate Ma Bell the way Gilbertson and some phone phreaks do. I don't want to screw Ma Bell. With me it's the pleasure of pure knowledge. There's something beautiful about the system when you know it intimately the way I do. But I don't know how much they know about me here. I have a very intuitive feel for the condition of the line I'm on, and I think they're monitoring me off and on lately, but I haven't been doing much illegal. I *have* to make a few calls to switchmen once in a while which aren't strictly legal, and once I took an acid trip and was having these auditory hallucinations as if I were trapped and these planes were dive-bombing me, and all of a sudden I *had* to phone phreak out of there. For some reason I had to call Kansas City, but that's all."

A Warning Is Delivered

At this point—one o'clock in my time zone—a loud knock on my motel-room door interrupts our conversation. Outside the door I find a uniformed security guard who informs me that there has been an "emergency phone call" for me while I have been on the line and that the front desk has sent him up to let me know.

Two seconds after I say good-bye to Joe and hang up, the phone rings.

"Who were you talking to?" the agitated voice demands. The voice belongs to Captain Crunch. "I called because I decided to warn you of something. I decided to warn you to be careful. I don't want this information you get to get to the radical underground. I don't want it to get into the wrong hands. What would you say if I told you it's possible for three phone phreaks to saturate the phone system of the nation? Saturate it. Busy it out. All of it. I know how to do this. I'm not gonna tell. A friend of mine has already saturated the trunks between Seattle and New York. He did it with a computerized M-F-er hitched into a special Manitoba exchange. But there are other, easier ways to do it."

Just three people? I ask. How is that possible?

"Have you ever heard of the long-lines guard frequency? Do you know about stacking tandems with 17 and 2,600? Well, I'd advise you to find out about it. I'm not gonna tell you. But whatever you do, don't let this get into the hands of the radical underground."

(Later Gilbertson the inventor confessed that while he had always been skeptical about the Captain's claim of the sabotage potential of trunk-tying phone phreaks, he had recently heard certain demonstrations which convinced him the Captain was not speaking idly. "I think it might take more than three people, depending on how many machines like Captain Crunch's were available. But even though the Captain *sounds* a little weird, he generally turns out to know what he's talking about.")

"You know," Captain Crunch continues in his admonitory tone, "you know the younger phone phreaks call Moscow all the time. Suppose everybody were to call Moscow. I'm no right-winger. But I value my life. I don't want the Commies coming over and dropping a bomb on my head. That's why I say you've got to be careful about who gets this information."

The Captain suddenly shifts into a diatribe against those phone phreaks who don't like the phone company.

"They don't understand, but Ma Bell knows everything they do. Ma Bell knows. Listen, is this line hot? I just heard someone tap in. I'm not paranoid, but I can detect things like that. Well, even if it is, they know that I know that they know that I have a bulk eraser. I'm very clean." The Captain pauses, evidently torn between wanting to prove to the phone-company monitors that he does nothing illegal, and the desire to impress Ma Bell with his prowess. "Ma Bell knows the things I can do," he continues. "Ma Bell knows how good I am. And I am *quite* good. I can detect reversals, tandem switching, everything that goes on on a line. I have relative pitch now. Do you know what that *means*? My ears are a $20,000 piece of equipment. With my ears I can detect things they can't hear with their equipment. I've had employment problems. I've lost jobs. But I want to show Ma Bell how good I am. I don't want to screw her, I want to work for her. I want to do good for her. I want to help her get rid of her flaws and become perfect. That's my number-one goal in life now." The Captain concludes his warnings and tells me he has to be going. "I've got a little action lined up for tonight," he explains, and hangs up.

Before I hang up for the night, I call Joe Engressia back. He reports that his tormentor has finally gone to sleep—"He's not *blind* drunk, that's the way I get, ahem, yes; but you might say he's in a drunken stupor." I make a date to visit Joe in Memphis in two days.

A Phone-Phreak Cell Takes Care of Business

The next morning I attend a gathering of four phone phreaks in ———— (a California suburb). The gathering takes place in a comfortable split-level home in an upper-middle-class subdivision. Heaped on the kitchen table are the portable cassette recorders, M-F cassettes, phone patches, and line ties of the four phone phreaks present. On the kitchen counter next to the telephone is a shoe-box-size blue box with thirteen large toggle switches for the tones. The parents of the host phone phreak, Ralph, who is blind, stay in the living room with their sighted children. They are not sure exactly what Ralph and his friends do with the phone or if it's strictly legal, but he is blind and they are pleased he has a hobby that keeps him busy.

The group has been working at reestablishing the historic "2111" conference, reopening some toll-free loops, and trying to discover the dimensions of what seem to be new initiatives against phone phreaks by phone-company security agents.

It is not long before I get a chance to see, to hear, Randy at work. Randy is known among the phone phreaks as perhaps the finest con man in the game. Randy is blind. He is pale, soft, and pear-shaped, he wears baggy pants and a wrinkly nylon white sport shirt, pushes his head forward from hunched shoulders somewhat like a turtle inching out of its shell. His eyes wander, crossing and recrossing, and his forehead is somewhat pimply. He is only sixteen years old.

But when Randy starts speaking into a telephone mouthpiece, his voice becomes so stunningly authoritative it is necessary to look again to convince yourself it comes from chubby adolescent Randy. Imagine the voice of a crack oil-rig foreman, a tough, sharp, weather-beaten Marlboro man of forty. Imagine the voice of a brilliant performance-fund gunslinger explaining how he beats the Dow by 30 percent. Then imagine a voice that could make those two sound like Stepin Fetchit. That is sixteen-year-old Randy's voice.

He is speaking to a switchman in Detroit. The phone company in Detroit had closed up two toll-free loop pairs for no apparent reason, although heavy use by phone phreaks all over the country may have been detected. Randy is telling the switchman how to open up the loop and make it free again:

"How are you, buddy. Yeah, I'm on the board out here in Tulsa, Oklahoma, and we've been trying to run some tests on your loop-arounds, and we find 'em busied out on both sides. . . . Yeah, we've been getting a 'BY' on them, what d'ya say, can you drop cards on 'em? Do you have 08 on your number group? Oh that's okay, we've had this trouble before, we may have to go after the circuit. Here, lemme give 'em to you: your frame is 05, vertical group 03, horizontal 5, vertical file 3. Yeah, we'll hang on here. . . . Okay, found it? Good. Right, yeah, we'd like to clear that busy out. Right. Now pull your key from NOR over to LCT. Yeah. I don't know why that happened, but we've been having trouble with that one. Okay. Thanks a lot, fella. Be seein' ya."

Randy hangs up, reports that the switchman was a little inexperienced with the loop-around circuits on the miscellaneous trunk frame, but that the loop has been returned to its free-call status.

Delighted, phone-phreak Ed returns the pair of numbers to the active-status column in his directory. Ed is a superb and painstaking researcher. With almost Talmudic thoroughness he will trace tendrils of hints through soft-wired mazes of intervening phone-company circuitry back through complex linkages of switching relays to find the location and identity of just one toll-free loop. He spends hours and hours, every day, doing this sort of thing. He has compiled a directory of eight hundred "Band-six in-WATS numbers" located in over forty states. Band-six in-WATS numbers are the big 800 numbers—the ones that can be dialed into free from anywhere in the country.

Ed the researcher, a nineteen-year-old engineering student, is also a superb technician. He put together his own working blue box from scratch at age seventeen. (He is sighted.) This evening, after distributing the latest issue of his in-WATS directory (which has been typed into Braille for the blind phone phreaks), he announces he has made a major new breakthrough:

"I finally tested it and it works, perfectly. I've got this switching matrix which converts any touch-tone phone into an M-F-er."

The tones you hear in touch-tone phones are *not* the M-F tones that operate the long-distance switching system. Phone phreaks believe AT&T had deliberately equipped touch tones with a different set of frequencies to avoid putting the six master M-F tones in the hands of every touch-tone owner. Ed's complex switching matrix puts the six master tones, in effect puts a blue box, in the hands of every touch-tone owner.

Ed shows me pages of schematics, specifications, and parts lists. "It's not easy to build, but everything here is in the Heathkit catalog."

Ed asks Ralph what progress he has made in his attempts to reestablish a long-term open conference line for phone phreaks. The last big conference— the historic "2111" conference—had been arranged through an unused Telex test-board trunk somewhere in the innards of a 4A switching machine in Vancouver, Canada. For months, phone phreaks could M-F their way into Vancouver, beep out 604 (the Vancouver code) and then beep out 2111 (the internal phone-company code for Telex testing), and find themselves at any time, day or night, on an open wire talking with an array of phone phreaks from coast to coast, operators from Bermuda, Tokyo, and London who are phone-phreak sympathizers, and miscellaneous guests and technical experts. The conference was a massive exchange of information. Phone phreaks picked one another's brains clean, then developed new ways to pick the phone company's brains clean. Ralph gave "MF boogie" concerts with his home-entertainment-type electric organ, Captain Crunch demonstrated his round-the-world prowess with his notorious computerized unit and dropped leering hints of the "action" he was getting with his girlfriends. (The Captain lives out or pretends to live out several kinds of fantasies to the gossipy delight of the blind phone phreaks who urge him on to further triumphs on behalf of all of them.) The somewhat rowdy Northwest phone-phreak crowd let their bitter internal feud spill over into the peaceable conference line, escalating shortly into guerrilla warfare; Carl, the East Coast international phone relations expert, demonstrated newly opened direct M-F routes to central offices on the island of Bahrain in the Persian Gulf, introduced a new phone-phreak friend of his in Pretoria, and explained the technical operation of the new Oakland-to-Vietnam linkages. (Many phone phreaks pick up spending money by M-F-ing calls from relatives to Vietnam GI's, charging $5 for a whole hour of trans-Pacific conversation.)

Day and night the conference line was never dead. Blind phone phreaks all over the country, lonely and isolated in homes filled with active sighted brothers and sisters, or trapped with slow and unimaginative blind kids in strait-jacket schools for the blind, knew that no matter how late it got they could dial up the conference and find instant electronic communion with two or three other blind kids awake over on the other side of America. Talking together on a phone hookup, the blind phone phreaks say, is not much different from being there together. Physically, *there* was nothing more than a two-inch-square wafer of titanium inside a vast machine on Vancouver Island. For the blind kids, *there* meant an exhilarating feeling of being *in touch,* through a kind of skill and magic which was peculiarly their own.

Last April 1, however, the long Vancouver Conference was shut off. The phone phreaks knew it was coming. Vancouver was in the process of converting from a step-by-step system to a 4A machine, and the 2111 Telex circuit was to be wiped out in the process. The phone phreaks learned the actual day on which the conference would be erased about a week ahead of time over the phone company's internal-news-and-shop-talk recording.

For the next frantic seven days every phone phreak in America was on and off the 2111 conference twenty-four hours a day. Phone phreaks who were just learning the game or didn't have M-F capability were boosted up to the conference by more experienced phreaks so they could get a glimpse of what it was like before it disappeared. Top phone phreaks searched distant area codes for new conference possibilities without success. Finally in the early morning of April 1, the end came.

"I could feel it coming a couple hours before midnight," Ralph remembers. "You could feel something going on in the lines. Some static began showing up, then some whistling wheezing sound. Then there were breaks. Some people got cut off and called right back in, but after a while some people were finding they were cut off and couldn't get back in at all. It was terrible. I lost it about one A.M., but managed to slip in again and stay on until the thing died . . . I think it was about four in the morning. There were four of us still hanging on when the conference disappeared into nowhere for good. We all tried to M-F up to it again, of course, but we got silent termination. There was nothing there."

The Legendary Mark Bernay Turns Out to Be "The Midnight Skulker"

Mark Bernay. I had come across that name before. It was on Gilbertson's select list of phone phreaks. The California phone phreaks had spoken of a mysterious Mark Bernay as perhaps the first and oldest phone phreak on the West Coast. And in fact almost every phone phreak in the West can trace his origins either directly to Mark Bernay or to a disciple of Mark Bernay.

It seems that five years ago this Mark Bernay (a pseudonym he chose for himself) began traveling up and down the West Coast pasting tiny stickers in phone booths all along his way. The stickers read something like "Want to hear an interesting tape recording? Call these numbers." The numbers that followed were toll-free loop-around pairs. When one of the curious called one of the numbers he would hear a tape recording prehooked into the loop by Bernay that explained the use of loop-around pairs, gave the numbers of several more, and ended by telling the caller, "At six o'clock tonight this recording will stop and you and your friends can try it out. Have fun."

"I was disappointed by the response at first," Bernay told me, when I finally reached him at one of his many numbers and he had dispensed with the usual "I never do anything illegal" formalities with which experienced phone phreaks open most conversations. "I went all over the coast with these stickers not only on pay phones, but I'd throw them in front of high schools in the middle of the night, I'd leave them unobtrusively in candy stores, scatter them on main streets of small towns. At first hardly anyone bothered to try it out. I would listen in for hours and hours after six o'clock and no one came on. I couldn't figure out why people wouldn't be interested. Finally these two girls in Oregon tried it out and told all their friends and suddenly it began to spread."

Before his Johnny Appleseed trip Bernay had already gathered a sizable group of early pre–blue box phone phreaks together on loop-arounds in Los Angeles. Bernay does not claim credit for the original discovery of the loop-around numbers. He attributes the discovery to an eighteen-year-old reform-school kid in Long Beach whose name he forgets and who, he says, "just disappeared one day." When Bernay himself discovered loop-arounds independently, from clues in his readings in old issues of the *Automatic Electric Technical Journal,* he found dozens of the reform-school kid's friends already using them. However, it was one of Bernay's disciples in Seattle who introduced phone phreaking to blind kids. The Seattle kid who learned about loops through Bernay's recording told a blind friend, the blind kid taught the secret to his friends at a winter camp for blind kids in Los Angeles. When the camp session was over these kids took the secret back to towns all over the West. This is how the original blind kids became phone phreaks. For them, for most phone phreaks in general, it was the discovery of the possibilities of loop-arounds which led them on to far more serious and sophisticated phone-phreak methods, and which gave them a medium for sharing their discoveries.

A year later a blind kid who moved back east brought the technique to a blind kids' summer camp in Vermont, which spread it along the East Coast. All from a Mark Bernay sticker.

Bernay, who is nearly thirty years old now, got his start when he was fifteen and his family moved into an L.A. suburb serviced by General Telephone and Electronics equipment. He became fascinated with the differences between Bell and GT&E equipment. He learned he could make interesting things happen by carefully timed clicks with the disengage button. He learned to interpret subtle differences in the array of clicks, whirrs, and *kachinks* he could hear on his lines. He learned he could shift himself around the switching relays of the L.A. area code in a not-too-predictable fashion by interspersing his own hook-switch clicks with the clicks within the line. Independent phone companies—there are nineteen hundred of them still left, most of them tiny island principalities in Ma Bell's vast empire—have always been favorites with phone phreaks, first as learning tools, then as Archimedes platforms from which to manipulate the huge Bell system. A phone phreak in Bell territory will often M-F himself into an independent's switching system, with switching idiosyncrasies that can give him marvelous leverage over the Bell System.

"I have a real affection for Automatic Electric equipment," Bernay told me. "There are a lot of things you can play with. Things break down in interesting ways."

Shortly after Bernay graduated from college (with a double major in chemistry and philosophy), he graduated from phreaking around with GT&E to the Bell System itself, and made his legendary sticker-pasting journey north along the coast, settling finally in Northwest Pacific Bell territory. He discovered that if Bell does not break down as interestingly as GT&E, it nevertheless offers a lot of "things to play with."

Bernay learned to play with blue boxes. He established his own personal switchboard and phone-phreak research laboratory complex. He continued his phone-phreak evangelism with ongoing sticker campaigns. He set up two recording numbers, one with instructions for beginning phone phreaks, the other with latest news and technical developments (along with some advanced instruction) gathered from sources all over the country.

These days, Bernay told me, he has gone beyond phone phreaking itself. "Lately I've been enjoying playing with computers more than playing with phones. My personal thing in computers is just like with phones, I guess—the kick is in finding out how to beat the system, how to get *at* things I'm not supposed to know about, how to *do* things with the system that I'm not supposed to be able to do."

As a matter of fact, Bernay told me, he had just been fired from his computer-programming job for doing things he was not supposed to be able to do. He had been working with a huge time-sharing computer owned by a large corporation but shared by many others. Access to the computer was limited to those programmers and corporations that had been assigned certain passwords. And each password restricted its user to access to only the one section of the computer cordoned off from its own information storager. The password system prevented companies and individuals from stealing each other's information.

"I figured out how to write a program that would let me read everyone else's password," Bernay reports. "I began playing around with passwords. I began letting the people who used the computer know, in subtle ways, that I knew their passwords. I began dropping notes to the computer supervisors with hints that I knew what I know. I signed them 'The Midnight Skulker.' I kept getting cleverer and cleverer with my messages and devising ways of showing them what I could do. I'm sure they couldn't imagine I could do the things I was showing them. But they never responded to me. Every once in a while they'd change the passwords, but I found out how to discover what the new ones were, and let them know. But they never responded directly to The Midnight Skulker. I even finally designed a program which they could use to prevent my program from finding out what it did. In effect I told them how to wipe me out, The Midnight Skulker. It was a very clever program. I started leaving clues about myself. I wanted them to try and use it, and then try to come up with something to get around that and reappear again. But they wouldn't play. I wanted to get caught. I mean, I didn't want to get caught personally, but I wanted them to notice me and admit that they noticed me. I wanted them to attempt to respond, maybe in some interesting way."

Finally the computer managers became concerned enough about the threat of information-stealing to respond. However, instead of using The Midnight Skulker's own elegant self-destruct program, they called in their security personnel, interrogated everyone, found an informer to identify Bernay as The Midnight Skulker, and fired him.

"At first the security people advised the company to hire me full time to search out other flaws and discover other computer freaks. I might have liked that. But I probably would have turned into a double double agent rather than the double agent they wanted. I might have resurrected The Midnight Skulker and tried to catch myself. Who knows? Anyway, the higher-ups turned the whole idea down."

You Can Tap the FBI's Crime-Control Computer in the Comfort of Your Own Home, Perhaps

Computer freaking may be the wave of the future.* It suits the phone-phreak sensibility perfectly. Gilbertson, the blue-box inventor and a lifelong phone phreak, has also gone on from phone phreaking to computer freaking. Before he got into the blue-box business Gilbertson, who is a highly skilled programmer, devised programs for international currency arbitrage.

But he began playing with computers in earnest when he learned he could use his blue box in tandem with the computer terminal installed in his apartment by the instrumentation firm he worked for. The printout terminal and keyboard were equipped with acoustical coupling, so that by coupling his little ivory Princess phone to the terminal and then coupling his blue box on that, he could M-F his way into other computers with complete anonymity, and without charge; program and reprogram them at will; feed them false or misleading information; tap and steal from them. He explained to me that he taps computers by busying out all the lines, then going into a verification trunk, listening in to the passwords and instructions one of the time sharers uses, and then M-F-ing in and imitating them. He believes it would not be impossible to creep into the FBI's crime-control computer through a local police computer terminal and phreak around with the FBI's memory banks. He claims he has succeeded in reprogramming a certain huge institutional computer in such a way that it has cordoned off an entire section of its circuitry for his personal use, and at the same time conceals the arrangement from anyone else's notice. I have been unable to verify this claim.

Like Captain Crunch, like Alexander Graham Bell (pseudonym of a disgruntled-looking East Coast engineer who claims to have invented the

*Okay, am I a prophet or what? This was 1971.

"black box" and now sells black and blue boxes to gamblers and radical heavies), like most phone phreaks, Gilbertson began his career trying to rip off pay phones as a teenager. Figure them out, then rip them off. Getting his dime back from the pay phone is the phone phreak's first thrilling rite of passage. After learning the usual eighteen different ways of getting his dime back, Gilbertson learned how to make master keys to coin-phone cash boxes and get everyone else's dimes back. He stole some phone-company equipment and put together his own home switchboard with it. He learned to make a simple "bread-box" device, of the kind used by bookies in the thirties (bookie gives a number to his betting clients; the phone with that number is installed in some widow lady's apartment, but is rigged to ring in the bookie's shop across town; cops trace big betting number and find nothing but the widow).

Not long after that afternoon in 1968 when, deep in the stacks of an engineering library, he came across a technical journal with the phone tone frequencies and rushed off to make his first blue box, Gilbertson abandoned a very promising career in physical chemistry and began selling blue boxes for $1,500 apiece.

"I had to leave physical chemistry. I just ran out of interesting things to learn," he told me one evening. We had been talking in the apartment of the man who served as the link between Gilbertson and the syndicate in arranging the big $300,000 blue-box deal, which fell through because of legal trouble. There has been some smoking.

"No more interesting things to learn," he continues. "Physical chemistry turns out to be a sick subject when you take it to its highest level. I don't know. I don't think I could explain to you how it's sick. You have to be there. But you get, I don't know, a false feeling of omnipotence. I suppose it's like phone phreaking that way. This huge thing is there. This whole system. And there are holes in it and you slip into them like Alice and you're pretending you're doing something you're actually not, or at least it's no longer *you* that's doing what you were doing. It's all Lewis Carroll. Physical chemistry and phone phreaking. That's why you have these phone-phreak pseudonyms like The Cheshire Cat, The Red King, and The Snark. But there's something about phone phreaking that you don't find in physical chemistry." He looks up at me:

"Did you ever steal anything?"

Well yes, I—

"Then you know! You know the rush you get. It's not just knowledge, like physical chemistry. It's forbidden knowledge. You know. You can learn about anything under the sun and be bored to death with it. But the idea that it's illegal. Look, you can be small and mobile and smart and you're ripping off somebody large and powerful and very dangerous."

People like Gilbertson and Alexander Graham Bell are always talking about ripping off the phone company and screwing Ma Bell. But if they were shown a single button and told that by pushing it they could turn the entire circuitry of AT&T into molten puddles, they probably wouldn't push it. The disgruntled-inventor phone phreak needs the phone system the way the lapsed Catholic needs the Church, the way Satan needs a God, the way The Midnight Skulker needed, more than anything else, response.

Later that evening Gilbertson finished telling me how delighted he was at the flood of blue boxes spreading throughout the country, how delighted he was to know that "this time they're really screwed." He suddenly shifted gears.

"Of course, I do have this love/hate thing about Ma Bell. In a way I almost *like* the phone company. I guess I'd be very sad if they were to go away or if their services were to disintegrate. In a way it's just that after having been so good they turn out to have these things wrong with them. It's those flaws that allow me to get in and mess with them, but I don't know. There's something about it that gets to you and makes you want to *get to it,* you know."

I ask him what happens when he runs out of interesting, forbidden things to learn about the phone system.

"I don't know, maybe I'd go to work for them for a while."

"In security even?"

"I'd do it, sure. I'd just as soon play—I'd just as soon work on either side."

Even figuring out how to trap phone phreaks? I said, recalling Mark Bernay's game.

"Yes, that might be interesting. Yes, I could figure out how to outwit the phone phreaks. Of course if I got too good at it, it might become boring again. Then I'd have to hope the phone phreaks got much better and outsmarted me for a while. That would move the quality of the game up one level. I might even have to help them out, you know, 'Well kids, I wouldn't want this to get around but did you ever think of—?' I could keep it going at higher and higher levels forever."

The dealer speaks up for the first time. He has been staring at the soft blinking patterns of lights and colors on the translucent tiled wall facing him. Actually there are no patterns: The color and illumination of every tile is determined by a computerized random-number generator designed by Gilbertson which ensures that there can be no meaning to any sequence of events in the tiles.

"Those are nice games you're talking about," says the dealer to his friend. "But I wouldn't mind seeing them screwed. A telephone isn't private anymore. You can't say anything you really want to say on a telephone or you have to go through that paranoid bullshit. 'Is it cool to talk on the phone?' I mean, even if it is cool, if you have to ask 'Is it cool?' then it isn't cool. You know. Like those blind kids, people are going to start putting together their own private telephone companies if they want to really talk. And you know what else. You don't hear silences on the phone anymore. They've got this time-sharing thing on long-distance lines where you make a pause and they snip out that piece of time and use it to carry part of somebody else's conversation. Instead of a pause, where somebody's maybe breathing or sighing, you get this blank hole and you only start hearing again when someone says a word and even the beginning of the word is clipped off.* Silences don't count—you're paying for them, but they take them away from you. It's not cool to talk [i.e., if you're paranoid about being tapped], and you can't hear someone when they don't talk. What the hell good is the phone? I wouldn't mind seeing them totally screwed."

The Big Memphis Bust

Joe Engressia never wanted to screw Ma Bell. His dream had always been to work for her.

The day I visited Joe in his small apartment on Union Avenue in Memphis, he was upset about another setback in his application for a telephone job.

"They're stalling on it. I got a letter today telling me they'd have to postpone the interview I requested again. My landlord read it for me. They gave me some runaround about wanting papers on my rehabilitation status but I think there's something else going on."

When I switched on the forty-watt bulb in Joe's room—he sometimes forgets when he has guests—it looked as if there was enough telephone hardware to start a small phone company of his own.

There is one phone on top of his desk, one phone sitting in an open drawer beneath the desktop. Next to the desk-top phone is a cigar-box-size M-F device with big toggle switches, and next to that is some kind of switching and coupling device with jacks and alligator plugs hanging loose. Next to that is a Braille typewriter. On the floor next to the desk, lying upside down like a dead tortoise, is the half-gutted body of an old black standard phone. Across the room on a torn and dusty couch are two more phones, one of them a touch-tone model; two tape recorders; a heap of phone patches and cassettes; and a life-size toy telephone.

Our conversation is interrupted every ten minutes by phone phreaks from all over the country ringing Joe on just about every piece of equipment but the toy phone and the Braille typewriter. One fourteen-year-old blind kid from

---

The New York Times recently (late 1999) reported that radio stations are now snipping pauses and silences out of talk-radio shows, the better to squeeze in more ads.

Connecticut calls up and tells Joe he's got a girlfriend. He wants to talk to Joe about girlfriends. Joe says they'll talk later in the evening when they can be alone on the line. Joe draws a deep breath, whistles him off the air with an ear-splitting 2,600-cycle whistle. Joe is pleased to get the calls but he looks worried and preoccupied this evening, his brow constantly furrowed over his dark, wandering eyes. In addition to the phone-company stall, he has just learned that his apartment house is due to be demolished in sixty days for urban renewal. For all its shabbiness, the Union Avenue apartment has been Joe's first home of his own, and he's worried that he may not find another before this one is demolished.

But what really bothers Joe is that switchmen haven't been listening to him. "I've been doing some checking on 800 numbers lately, and I've discovered that certain 800 numbers in New Hampshire couldn't be reached from Missouri and Kansas. Now it may sound like a small thing, but I don't like to see sloppy work; it makes me feel bad about the lines. So I've been calling up switching offices and reporting it, but they haven't corrected it. I called them up for the third time today and instead of checking they just got mad. Well, that gets me mad. I mean, I do try to help them. There's something about them I can't understand—you want to help them and they just try to say you're defrauding them."

It is Sunday evening and Joe invites me to join him for dinner at a Holiday Inn. Frequently on Sunday evening Joe takes some of his welfare money, calls a cab, and treats himself to a steak dinner at one of Memphis's thirteen Holiday Inns. Memphis is the headquarters of Holiday Inn. Holiday Inns have been a favorite for Joe ever since he made his first solo phone trip to a Bell switching office in Jacksonville, Florida, and stayed in the Holiday Inn there. He likes to stay at Holiday Inns, he explains, because they represent freedom to him and because the rooms are arranged the same all over the country so he knows that any Holiday Inn room is familiar territory to him. Just like any telephone.

Over steaks in the Pinnacle Restaurant of the Holiday Inn Medical Center on Madison Avenue in Memphis, Joe tells me the highlights of his life as a phone phreak.

At age seven, Joe learned his first phone trick. A mean baby-sitter, tired of listening to little Joe play with the phone as he always did, constantly, put a lock on the phone dial. "I got so mad. When there's a phone sitting there and I can't use it . . . so I started getting mad and banging the receiver up and down. I noticed I banged it once and it dialed one. Well, then I tried banging it twice. . . ." In a few minutes Joe learned how to dial by pressing the hook switch at the right time. "I was so excited I remember going 'whoo whoo' and beat a box down on the floor."

At age eight Joe learned about whistling. "I was listening to some intercept nonworking-number recording in L.A.—I was calling L.A. as far back as that, but I'd mainly dial nonworking numbers because there was no charge, and I'd listen to these recordings all day. Well, I was whistling 'cause listening to these recordings can be boring after a while even if they are from L.A., and all of a sudden, in the middle of whistling, the recording clicked off. I fiddled around whistling some more, and the same thing happened. So I called up the switch room and said, 'I'm Joe. I'm eight years old and I want to know why when I whistle this tune the line clicks off.' He tried to explain it to me, but it was a little too technical at the time. I went on learning. That was a thing nobody was going to stop me from doing. The phones were my life, and I was going to pay any price to keep on learning. I knew I could go to jail. But I had to do what I had to do to keep on learning."

The phone is ringing when we walk back into Joe's apartment on Union Avenue. It is Captain Crunch. The Captain has been following me around by phone, calling up everywhere I go with additional bits of advice and explanation for me and whatever phone phreak I happen to be visiting. This time the Captain reports he is calling from what he describes as "my hideaway high up in the Sierra Nevada." He pulses out lusty salvos of M-F tones and tells Joe he is about to "go out and get a little action tonight. Do some phreaking of another kind, if you know what I mean." Joe chuckles.

The Captain then tells me to make sure I understand that what he told me about tying up the nation's phone lines was true, but that he and the phone phreaks *he* knew never used the technique for sabotage. They only learned the technique to help the phone company.

"We do a lot of troubleshooting for them. Like this New Hampshire/Missouri WATS-line flaw I've been screaming about. We help them more than they know."

After we say good-bye to the Captain and Joe whistles him off the line, Joe tells me about a disturbing dream he had the night before: "I had been caught and they were taking me to a prison. It was a long trip. They were taking me to a prison a long long way away. And we stopped at a Holiday Inn and it was my last night ever at a Holiday Inn, and it was my last night ever using the phone and I was crying and crying, and the lady at the Holiday Inn said, 'Gosh, honey, you should never be sad at a Holiday Inn. You should always be happy here. Especially since it's your last night.' And that just made it worse and I was sobbing so much I couldn't stand it."

Two weeks after I left Joe Engressia's apartment, phone-company security agents and Memphis police broke into it. Armed with a warrant, which they left pinned to a wall, they confiscated every piece of equipment in the room, including his toy telephone. Joe was placed under arrest and taken to the city jail, where he was forced to spend the night since he had no money and knew no one in Memphis to call.

It is not clear who told Joe what that night, but someone told him that the phone company had an open-and-shut case against him because of revelations of illegal activity he had made to a phone-company undercover agent.

By morning Joe had become convinced that the reporter from *Esquire,* with whom he had spoken two weeks ago, was the undercover agent. He probably had ugly thoughts about someone he couldn't see gaining his confidence, listening to him talk about his personal obsessions and dreams, while planning all the while to lock him up.

"I really thought he was a reporter," Engressia told the *Memphis Press-Scimitar.* "I told him everything. . . ." Feeling betrayed, Joe proceeded to confess everything to the press and police.

As it turns out, the phone company *did* use an undercover agent to trap Joe, although it was not the *Esquire* reporter.

Ironically, security agents were alerted and began to compile a case against Joe because of one of his acts of love for the system: Joe had called an internal service department to report that he had located a group of defective long-distance trunks, and to complain again about the New Hampshire/Missouri WATS problem. Joe always liked Ma Bell's lines to be clean and responsive. A suspicious switchman reported Joe to the security agents who discovered that Joe had never had a long-distance call charged to his name.

Then the security agents learned that Joe was planning one of his phone trips to a local switching office. The security people planted one of their agents in the switching office. He posed as a student switchman and followed Joe around on a tour. He was extremely friendly and helpful to Joe, leading him around the office by the arm. When the tour was over he offered Joe a ride back to his apartment house. On the way he asked Joe—one tech man to another—about "those blue boxes" he'd heard about. Joe talked about them freely, talked about his blue box freely, and about all the other things he could do with the phones.

The next day the phone-company security agents slapped a monitoring tap on Joe's line, which eventually picked up an illegal call. Then they applied for the search warrant and broke in.

In court Joe pleaded not guilty to possession of a blue box and theft of service. A sympathetic judge reduced the charges to malicious mischief and found him guilty on that count, sentenced him to two thirty-day sentences to be served concurrently, and then suspended the sentence on condition that Joe promise never to play with phones again. Joe promised, but the phone company refused to restore his service. For two weeks after the trial Joe could not be reached except through the pay phone at his apartment house, and the landlord screened all calls for him.

Phone phreak Carl managed to get through to Joe after the trial, and reported that Joe sounded crushed by the whole affair.

"What I'm worried about," Carl told me, "is that Joe means it this time. The promise. That he'll never phone phreak again. That's what he told me, that he's given up phone phreaking for good. I mean his entire life. He says he knows they're going to be watching so closely for the rest of his life he'll never be able to make a move without going straight to jail. He sounded very broken up by the whole experience of being in jail. It was awful to hear him talk that way. I don't know. I hope maybe he had to sound that way. Over the phone, you know."

He reports that the entire phone-phreak underground is up in arms over the phone company's treatment of Joe. "All the while Joe had his hopes pinned on his application for a phone-company job, they were stringing him along, getting ready to bust him. That gets me mad. Joe spent most of his time helping them out. The bastards. They think they can use him as an example. All of a sudden they're harassing us on the coast. Agents are jumping up on our lines. They just busted ————'s mute yesterday and ripped out his lines. But no matter what Joe does, I don't think we're going to take this lying down."

Two weeks later my phone rings and about eight phone phreaks in succession say hello from about eight different places in the country, among them Carl, Ed, and Captain Crunch. A nationwide phone-phreak conference line has been reestablished through a switching machine in ————, with the cooperation of a disgruntled switchman.

"We have a special guest with us today," Carl tells me.

The next voice I hear is Joe's. He reports happily that he has just moved to a place called Millington, Tennessee, fifteen miles outside of Memphis, where he has been hired as a telephone-set repairman by a small independent phone company. Someday he hopes to be an equipment troubleshooter.

"It's the kind of job I dreamed about. They found out about me from the publicity surrounding the trial. Maybe Ma Bell did me a favor busting me. I'll have telephones in my hands all day long."

Postscript to "Secrets of the Little Blue Box"

This story has had the most curious sort of ongoing repercussions. A recent biography of Steve Jobs, cofounder of Apple Computer with Steve Wozniak, describes how the Jobs-Wozniak partnership was first forged when, as California teenagers, they read "Secrets of the Little Blue Box" in *Esquire,* sought out the missing tone codes (which I'd deliberately left out of my story) in technical journals and tried manufacturing little blue boxes in Jobs's garage. (Jobs later confirmed this to me in person.)

Then there's "Captain Crunch," already a living legend when I first wrote about him, now a kind of mythic founder figure of computer hacker culture, which grew out of the outlaw-technology mystique of phone phreaks. Crunch's trajectory is emblematic of the divided nature of hacker consciousness. This onetime subversive techno-outlaw went legit—indeed, became establishment; he's still spoken of with awe, but these days it's as one of the patriarchs of the personal computer software revolution, having put his genius to work in programming the breakthroughs that made the p.c. user-friendly to the masses.

The other side of hacker-phreak consciousness—the outlaw, rebel romantic, sometimes Dark Side of the Force—can be found embodied in the visionary sensibility of cyber punk fiction (like William Gibson's *Neuromancer*) and the more diabolical of the computer virus creators (like the nihilist hackers who designed the AIDS-data-destroying computer virus of late 1989). Phone phreaks have become plot devices in innumerable films ever since *War-Games.*

But to me the real heroes of the story are still the blind phone phreaks like Joe Engressia who created their etheric outlaw network not for dazzle or for fraud, but for the kind of extrasensory communion they achieved up on a tandem. In the spring of 1999, three blind Arab brothers pleaded guilty in an Israeli court to tapping into high-security Israeli army telephone switchboards using Braille keyboards. "Once we were in we listened to the different clicks and tones," Munther Badir said, "and made connections by imitating them." Mostly they used their skill to order free TV sets from Israel's home-shopping network. Still they are evidence that the spirit of Joe Engressia lives.

Inside the Canned Laughter War

In Which We Investigate the Concept of "Authentic" Canned Laughter

It's been an uphill struggle for Ralph Waldo Emerson III and his canned laughter machine. Since 1970, Ralph's been trying to convince TV producers that the super-sophisticated laugh machine he designed can lay down laugh tracks light years ahead of the leading laugh maker in the business.

For as long as anyone can remember, the laugh-canning industry has been dominated by that one man, the legendary and secretive Charlie Douglass, "King of Canned Laughter," and Charlie's patented laugh machine.

"Charlie's got into a position in this business where he can do no wrong," Ralph grumbles. "It's become an automatic thing: You want laughs you go to Charlie, he's got the golden ears, they all say."

Ralph thinks the "golden ears" mystique has deafened TV people to the declining quality of most of the canned laughter you hear these days. "What they don't realize is what you get when you get Charlie to do your laughs are Charlie laughs . . . you get that universal Charlie Douglass sound. And it's sad because some of his material is very old. Very tired."

But Ralph Waldo Emerson III—a direct descendant, he says, of Emerson the New England poet and philosopher—has more than mere technological gripes about Charlie's laughs. He has *philosophical* objections.

That universal Charlie Douglass sound creates a profound "detachment" between the TV viewer and the ghostly host of canned laughers, Ralph says. "You get the feeling that here's the performer and here's this black box making laughs. There's no feeling of *oneness* with the audience," Ralph complains.

Ralph and I are chatting in an ABC-TV sound-studio control room, and Ralph is preparing to demonstrate for me his machine—the one he believes can bring oneness back to canned laughter.

"You are looking at the most sophisticated, most versatile machine of the bunch," Ralph tells me as he unbolts the waist-high blue-and-chromium-cased laugh box. He selects some cassette cartridges of laugh loops from his carefully coded laugh library, loads them into slots in the laugh machine and plugs the machine into his Rapid Cue master control console.

"I've got eighteen grades of laughter here," he says, turning to the console, which is covered with red, white, and yellow rows of square buttons.

"Listen—this is a number one." He touches a red button and someone starts chuckling. A few more people break into pleasantly indulgent after-dinner laughs that mingle with sporadic throaty chortles and incipient giggles. A muted, curiously comforting and intimate sound fills the nearly empty studio.

"That's your basic chuckle track," Ralph says. "Now I'm gonna bring in some more people, give it some more body. Here's a number nine." He touches another red button, then reaches over to the right-hand side of the console and slides a few arrow-shaped fader knobs up and down in their slots.

"Here now you've got the body of the audience going and what you can do with the faders is bring up some chuckles or accents or whistles and cheers, and down here you've got your giggle track and you can trail off into that, and this one here, this number nine on the white row, is the most powerful—I call it my 'pants dropper.' "

After the screaming gasps of the pants dropper die out, Ralph fades down to a mixture of giggles and exhausted whimpers on one of his taper-off loops, then builds back up to a rhythmic full-bodied roar, comes down to chuckles again and lets me take over the controls.

To put his laughs on the soundtrack of an actual show, Ralph just hooks the speaker of his laugh machine into the tape of the show, sits at his console watching the show on a monitor, and plays his laughs and applause directly onto one of the eight tracks of the show's master tape. "Without being arrogant," Ralph confides, "I think I know what's funny and what isn't, but more important, I know what's *supposed* to be funny."

There's no show on the monitor this morning, just an empty studio and the two of us pushing buttons and making wave after wave of phantom studio audiences crack up. And the strange thing is that it's pretty funny all by itself, this straight dose of unadulterated canned laughter. No silly jokes to get in the way. Very infectious stuff. I couldn't help myself, I broke up and began laughing along with the machine.

Ralph smiles proudly. "I can take anyone and sit 'em down here and in a minute I can have them laughing. I could prove to the biggest doubter that he's not standing on solid ground because if you're sitting here laughing at this stupid machine. . . ."

It was five years ago that ABC executives urged Ralph to take on the Titan of Titters. A daring project. Charlie Douglass may not have invented canned laughter itself, but he patented the machine that has made laugh tracks a household sound in America. Charlie and his laugh machines still produce most of the "sweetened" laughter and applause you will hear on prime time tonight. That's right, "sweetened." The people who produce shows like *The Mary Tyler Moore Show, Cher, M*A*S*H,* etc., don't like to say they use "canned laughter." They prefer to say that they augment their studio-audience sound with "electronic sweetening," which usually means laughs from Charlie Douglass's laugh machine. Even those shows that boast of being "recorded live" before a "live studio audience" still use a bit of prerecorded sweetening here and there to help out "lines that get a laugh in the dress rehearsal, say, but for some reason don't in the final taping," as one sitcom producer explained to me. "It's not a cheat using it that way. Well, it's only *half* a cheat." And sweeteners are slipping into some of the most traditional live shows on TV. Two network people, both of whom refused to be identified for fear of losing their jobs, told me that the Rose Bowl Parade often uses sweetening to create that "smattering of applause" effect as each floral float goes by, and that ever since a well-known comedian bombed with his monologue on an Oscar broadcast, the Academy Awards show has standby sweetening on tap for laughter and applause.

It all started around the time of *My Little Margie* in 1954. Or maybe it was 1955 with *Our Miss Brooks.* You hear different stories. But sometime in the mid-fifties, Charlie Douglass, a CBS radio-and-TV sound man, left the network and took a laugh-track machine to Desilu studios. Desilu was just beginning to turn out the first of the filmed non-audience comedies that would soon take over the airwaves. With his machine, Charlie was able to transform himself into a one-man studio audience for hire, the kind of audience that would laugh at just about anything.

From the outset, Charlie surrounded his laugh-making business with an aura of mystery and an apparent obsession with secrecy. He put padlocks on the laugh machine, refused all requests for interviews, discouraged publicity. It was rumored that his early contracts pledged him to a vow of silence to protect the identities of certain comedian and celebrity clients who swore publicly they never used a laugh machine. Rival laugh men suggest that all the secrecy is just a clever merchandising gimmick to make Charlie's laugh-making technology seem more complex and mysterious than it is. They're convinced that the padlocks conceal nothing more than repeating loops of pre-recorded laughs activated by the keyboard on the outside of the laugh box.

About those first Desilu laugh tracks, the ones that established that unmistakable "canned" sound: Who *are* those people and why are they laughing in that peculiar way? I've heard it suggested that some of the laughs on Charlie's classic early laugh tracks were taken from tapes of old Burns and Allen radio shows—the cruel corollary being that, by now, half the people you hear yukking it up on any given rerun of *The Gale Storm Show* are dead.

But several rival laugh men had a more interesting explanation.

"The way I heard it," one of them told me, "they'd get an audience in a preview theater, put cans on their head, put an *I Love Lucy* show on the screen and let Charlie mike the house."

"Put what on their heads?"

"Cans—earphone headsets. They run the audio into the headsets so that when you mike the house for laughs you don't get the audio from the show mixed in with your laughs. You get very clean laughs that way; that's what Charlie was known for from the beginning—he always had really clean stuff."

Picture yourself in one of those early preview theater audiences. There's a blown-up kinescope of *I Love Lucy* on the screen, and you are surrounded by strangers with headsets on and wires coming out of their ears. Enough to make you laugh all by itself. But will it be your normal laugh or will it be a little nervous, a bit hollow? And when you *do* laugh you might as well be laughing alone in a cave, because your padded earphones isolate you from the sound of the laughter of the can-heads around you. None of that mutual jollying, none of the infectious crosscurrents you find in any ordinary audience. That special "canned" resonance, perhaps even the phrase "canned laughter," may be traced to these very cans.

But any chronicle of canned laughter, however brief, cannot fail to cite the daring conceptual breakthrough made manifest by such shows as *The Real McCoys* back in the mid-fifties, the breakthrough that made possible the canned laughter takeover of the airwaves.

Grandpa McCoy goes out into the pasture to milk a cow. Real pasture, real cow. Something funny happens, like maybe the cow steps on Grandpa's hat. Suddenly there's a big roar of laughter from out of nowhere—well, from out of Charlie's laugh machine. Now, nobody watching *The Real McCoys* on his home screen is expected to believe that the laughter he hears is the real McCoy—that there's a real audience out there squatting in the cow pasture and yukking it up. All pretense to realism in canned laughter was abandoned. People who could accept the idea of an ethereal laugh materializing in a cow pasture could get used to the idea of a laugh materializing anywhere, even after the lines of a show like *My Mother, the Car.* Canned laughter became pure sound, Mirth Muzak. Before long, any new sitcom pilot that wanted a chance with the network biggies had to come to the screening room equipped with a lush Charlie Douglass laugh arrangement if it expected to be taken seriously.*

Ralph Waldo Emerson III was by no means the first to challenge the King of Canned Laughs. There was the NBC hippo-roar machine, for instance.

Back in 1957, NBC put together a team of their best sound-effects men and told them to come up with a laugh machine for the network's own use. The intensive search ultimately led ace NBC sound man Austin Beck to Disneyland to check out a machine called the MacKenzie Repeater. Disneyland technicians had installed the Repeater inside certain simulated wild animals—the half-submerged hippo in the jungle river of Adventureland, for instance—in order to get them to roar on cue.

While NBC electronics technicians worked feverishly to adapt the hippo roar to the roars of canned laughter, veteran NBC sound man Monty Fraser (he's known in broadcasting as the man who produced the sound of Fibber McGee's closet)** compiled a basic laugh library of audience laughs from the old George Gobel show. The NBC laugh-machine team even came up with an added device especially to please Milton Berle: a flickering neon bulb placed on top of the camera, wired to the newly adapted MacKenzie laugh machine; the bulb flickered as long as the machine laughed and Berle could know exactly how long his canned laugh lasted, so that he wouldn't step on it with the opening line of his next joke. But despite all its efforts and many improvements, NBC never has been able to lure a substantial number of clients away from Charlie Douglass with its hippo-roar machine, a fact that continues to pique some NBC laugh men.

"It's kind of a clique thing," one of the NBC laugh men tells me. Billy was part of the original NBC laugh team and he still does laughs for the network. "A clique in the sense that all the old comedians, like Burns and Hope, they stick together and they stick with Charlie. He's kind of like the Cadillac of the business. He's got the name; it doesn't matter if his material sounds older."

Ralph Waldo Emerson III is about to play a very special reel of tape for me. Ralph has just removed the reel from a padlocked file drawer in his laugh laboratory, and he's threading it into the lab's big Ampex 440 playback machine.

---

*Testimony to the fact that this still remains a rule of the game on network TV can be found in a 1999 *New Yorker* piece (by Tad Friend) about the losing struggle of Aaron Sorkin, filmmaker and series creator, to keep his network from imposing a laugh track on his "realistic" sitcom *Sports Center.*

**An ancient radio gag about an overstuffed closet collapsing tumultuously when opened.

What's on this special reel? Not Ralph's own laughs. In the past few hours he's played enough of them to convince me of their quality. In the past few hours he's also revealed the three main sources of canned laughs for the entire ABC network (two obscure and canceled situation comedies—*A Touch of Grace* and *Thicker Than Water*—and *The Jonathan Winters Show*). He's confided to me the philosophical principle that guides his sweetening style ("What I do is give you the live-sounding laugh that *would have been there* had the show been done before a live audience. Nothing phony about that"), a kind of ex post facto existentialism.

He's told me how he's confronted and resolved the moral qualms he feels about making his living from canned laughter. "Somebody's got to do it," he told me grimly. "Like I said to my wife before I went into it. This is the one chance I'll have in my life to take something I really hate and take it away from caricature and turn it into an art form."

And he's told me about the hard times, when they laughed when he sat down at his laugh machine. "When I first started I had to audition. I'd play my laughs and people would say, 'What's that?'—they were so used to Charlie they'd lost contact with what real laughs are. I had to really come on strong, I had to be ten times better than anything else available."

And he's tried—not entirely successfully—to convince me that he's not really preoccupied with Charlie and couldn't care less about the mystique surrounding Charlie's laughs.

"That there's a mystique at all is the amazing thing to me. What's the mystery? It's shit. What am I worrying about it for? The stuff I've got is much better. But there is no animosity between Charlie and myself. It's more like I'm Avis and he's Hertz."

But despite all this talk, the tape Ralph is about to play is going to be the real clincher. Ralph was able to make this one-of-a-kind tape as a result of an unprecedented head-to-head sweetening contest with Charlie Douglass himself. The occasion was the production of an ABC Julie Andrews special. Union rules forbid independent laugh contractors like Charlie from working on network property. But several Charlie loyalists among the guest stars insisted on taking the show off the network lot to have their own segments sweetened by Charlie himself. "There was a big flap over who was gonna sweeten the show, me or Charlie. Incredible battles," Ralph recalls.

When a truce between the rival laugh men was finally negotiated, Charlie was awarded the sweetening of two thirds of the show, Ralph one third. Toward the end of the somewhat bitter sweetening contest that ensued, Ralph decided to isolate and thoroughly study his opponent's legendary laughs. He took a master tape of Charlie's two thirds of the show, isolated the sweetening track, and made a high-quality recording of Charlie's laughs in action.

"That's what's on this reel," Ralph says as he switches it on. "Pure Charlie tracks. I wanted to study them, see if I could figure out what the secret is, what it is about Charlie's stuff. Listen, you can hear for yourself."

A familiar-sounding wave of applause washes over the laugh lab. More applause. Ralph works the fast forward. Some laughs now.

Ralph proceeds to take me on a guided tour of these Charlie tracks, clinically analyzing all the weaknesses he believes he's discovered. He even has an unkind word to say for the silences between the laughs: "If you listen carefully you can hear those awful mechanical things going on inside the machine."

Then Ralph takes off the Charlie reel and threads in a reel with his third of that memorable Julie Andrews showdown.

"Listen to this and tell me you don't hear the difference," Ralph tells me.

I listen and I hear the difference and all at once I understand why Ralph has been having trouble breaking Charlie's monopoly. Ralph's laughs do seem to have a greater clarity, more natural-sounding beginnings, more naturally tapered "tails," as he calls them. And some of the Charlie laughs he played for me do tend to roar on and roar off in a homogeneous blur, and they do tend to taper off into some very familiar and repetitive-sounding hollow chuckles, and Charlie's applause can sound more like the roar of the ocean in a conch shell than an audience. But there's something warm and familiar and comforting about these Charlie tracks. They don't sound like real laughter, but they do sound like real *canned* laughter, the kind we're conditioned to accept, not as audience response but as soothing background noise. After Charlie's comforting confections, Ralph's naturalistic attempts to imitate a "live," "real" audience sound jarring and unnatural.

Ralph complains that "Charlie's sound has been around so long people don't know what real laughter sounds like anymore; they don't like it when they hear it." For the TV world it's a case of he who laughs first laughs best, and Charlie laughed first.

But Ralph did come away from that canned laughter contest with one consoling, if ironic, triumph.

Ralph switches off the tape and smiles. "You want to know what happened at the end of that Julie Andrews sweetening? One of the producers who wasn't really in touch with who was sweetening what ran in here one day and he's listening to a segment of the show—a comedy sketch by Alice Ghostley—that I had done the laughs for. Well, this guy listens to it and announces to everyone, 'Those are great laughs; that's what makes Charlie Douglass great.' You shoulda seen him when I told him who did those laughs." Ralph chuckles at the memory. It has the unsweetened sound of a last laugh.

. . .

And what of the legendary Charlie Douglass? He was somewhere in Germany the first time I tried to contact him. Someone had unloaded a batch of early Dean Martin–Jerry Lewis comedy-hour shows on a German TV station. The German station had Charlie flown to Munich to dub some of his laughs onto the sound track so that they would follow the new dubbed-in-German Jerry Lewis punch lines.

Charlie's secretary assured me that even if he were around the corner from me in Hollywood he might as well be in Munich because he never, never talked to reporters about his business. I begged her to get Charlie to call me after he returned from the Munich sweetening, just so I could hear the sound of his voice.

A week later I received a phone call. The voice on the line identified himself as Charlie Douglass and told me politely that he had never varied from his no-talk rule and wouldn't make an exception for me.

I tried to counter by telling him that other laugh men were talking openly about their work. Why did he persist in being so secretive?

"I think they're foolish to open up anything like this," Charlie told me. "You might have the best intentions, but there are many others who would jump on us. They'd crucify us. Then the government would get ahold of it and you'd never know what was happening."

"What would the government want with sweeteners?"

"You never know. I just think for everybody's welfare it would be better if nobody talked, and I'm not going to."

As a last resort I asked the voice on the phone if I could just meet with him in the flesh, to verify that the elusive Charlie Douglass himself was real and not canned.

"I'm sure there are lots of people who will verify I'm real," Charlie said. But he wouldn't say who.

Postscript to "Inside the Canned Laughter War"

The belief in the concept of "authentic canned laughter" persists. The new sophisticated rationale was explained to me recently by an industry insider.

Shows that like to boast they are done "in front of a live studio audience"—which suggest that the laughs you hear are the laughs they got—rationalize it this way: Shows done in front of live audiences often require several takes, including dress rehearsals. Sometimes a line that gets a laugh in one take doesn't get it in a final run-through that works better for other lines. So what's the harm in adding a laugh to the line that really earned it at least once before? From there it's one step to punching up another laugh to "even things out" and one more step to sweetening a line that really *should* have gotten a laugh if the audience wasn't so worn out from all the takes. False laughter springs eternal.

The Subterranean World of the Bomb

In Which We Seek the Secrets of SIOP and the Parameters of "Nuke-Porn"

Did anyone ever tell you about the last letter of Our Lady of Fatima? It's more than a dozen years since the night it was revealed to me, but I remember the circumstances exactly. I was in an all-night place called the Peter Pan Diner with a high-school buddy of mine. It was 1964, I was seventeen, and we had been arguing for hours, as we often would, about such matters as the nature of Time before the creation of the universe and the mystery of the afterlife, when this guy hit me with the Fatima prophecy. He said he'd heard it from some seminarians who said they'd heard it from people in the church hierarchy, who said it was a hush-hush matter of intense concern to the Vatican, and to His Holiness himself.

Back in 1913, the way he told it, a holy apparition appeared to three Portuguese children near the shrine to the Virgin at Fatima. The heavenly messenger handed the kids three sealed letters for transmittal to the pope. Eyes only.*

The first letter—marked for immediate unsealing—astonished Pope Pius X

---

*Needless to say, his version bears only a proximate relation to the actual legend.

with a graphic description of a horrifying world war, this just months before the guns of August opened fire. The second letter, said to be marked "Do not open for twenty-five years," shocked Pius XI in 1938 with its vision of an even more terrible tragedy about to engulf civilization.

And then just last year—and here my friend's voice dropped, presumably to avoid frightening the people drinking coffee at the next table—just last year, he said, that wonderful man, the late Pope John, unsealed the third and last letter.

The last letter. The chill I felt creeping over me could not be ascribed to the Peter Pan Diner's creaky air conditioner.

"What was in it?" I asked.

"Nobody knows," my friend said.

"What do you mean, nobody knows? They knew about the other ones."

"Yes," said my friend. "But this one is different. They say that when the Holy Father opened it and read what was inside he fainted on the spot. And that he never recovered. And that Pope Paul ordered the letter to be resealed and never opened again. Want to know why? Because the letter tells the exact date of when a total nuclear war that will destroy the entire human race will break out and the Pope can't let it out because of the mass suicides and immorality if people were to learn exactly when they were going to die."

On January 13, 1975, *The New York Times* published a brief dispatch headed AIR FORCE PANEL RECOMMENDS DISCHARGE OF MAJOR WHO CHALLENGED "FAIL-SAFE" SYSTEM.

"What Major Hering has done," according to the lawyer for the ICBM launch officer, "is to ask what safeguards are in existence at the highest level of government to protect against an unlawful launch order . . . what checks and balances there are to assure that a launch order could not be affected by the president gone berserk or by some foreign penetration of the command system."

The major was not a hysterical peacenik. A combat veteran of Vietnam, he insisted he would have no moral scruples about killing 10 million or so people with his fleet of missiles. He just wanted to make sure that when he got the launch order it wasn't coming from an impostor or a madman.

Sorry, major, the Air Force replied, a missile crewman like you at the bottom of the chain of command has no "need to know" the answer to that question. In fact, you have no business asking it. When the *Times* story appeared, the Air Force already was on its way to hustling the major into suspension and early retirement.

Interesting, I thought to myself back in '75 as I tore out the story. But so many years after *Dr. Strangelove* and *Fail-safe,* how was it possible that this question did not have a satisfying, reassuring answer, even if the Air Force did not want to disclose it to this troublesome major? And so I filed the clipping away in the semi-oblivion of my "possible stories" file.

Two years later I was prowling the corridors of the Pentagon with that now-tattered clipping and a need to know. I was trying to find someone who could give me a satisfactory, reassuring answer to Major Hering's question. I wasn't getting any answers. What I was getting, I realized, right there in the Pentagon, was an onset of Armageddon fever unlike any since that night in the Peter Pan Diner when I heard about the Fatima prophecy.

I think it had something to do with seeing the man with the black briefcase face-to-face. It happened in a parking lot in Deerfield Beach, Florida, in January 1976. I was traveling with and reporting on President Ford's presidential primary campaign. The man with the black briefcase was traveling with President Ford, ready in case the president had to interrupt his Florida primary campaign to wage a nuclear war.

You know about the black briefcase, don't you? Inside are the Emergency War Order (EWO) authentification codes, which are changed frequently and are supposed to ensure that only the president, their possessor, can authorize a thermonuclear missile or bomber launch. When then-President Richard Nixon boasted to a group of congressmen shortly after the "Saturday Night Massacre"* that "I could go into the next room, make a telephone call, and in twenty-five minutes seventy million people will be dead," he left out one detail: He would have to take the black briefcase into the room with him.

That day in Deerfield Beach, Commander in Chief Ford was making his way through throngs of suntanned senior citizens and pale Secret Service men out onto a fishing pier to pose with a prize marlin. Passing up a glimpse of the big fish, I was ambling back across a parking lot toward the press bus when suddenly I came upon the man with the black briefcase.

Somehow he seemed to have become separated from the presidential party in the procession toward the pier, and now he stood fully and formally uniformed in the midst of baggy Bermuda shorts and tropical shirts. Peering about, looking for his lost Commander in Chief, the nuclear-briefcase man looked cut off, detached, uncertain how to respond. And in a different sense so was I. I felt a peculiar sense of dislocation staring at that briefcase. (In case you're interested it's a very slim and elegant one: supple black pebble-grained leather with a flap of soft leather fastened by four silver snaps.)

If you wanted to get technical you could say that if the word of a surprise attack on the way reached the president while he was posing with the prize fish, the fact that the man with the black briefcase was here with me and not

*The dramatic October 1973 firing of Watergate Special Prosecutor Archibald Cox.

out on the pier might delay our potential for nuclear retaliation by several, perhaps crucial, seconds. On the other hand some half-a-billion citizens on the other side of the world might enjoy two or three more breaths before their lives were snuffed out by missiles sent by the black-briefcase code. Silly to make these calculations, but what is the proper response to the intimate presence of a key element of the doomsday trigger system? Scream bloody murder? Or should one take, as I did at the time, a detached, aesthetic approach to the tableau—relish the piquant frisson of irony at that artifact of instant apocalyptic death standing like a scarecrow amidst the sun-ripening age of the retirees?

Last year when I came upon the Major Hering clipping and read it again, that unsettling vision of the man with the black briefcase came to mind. And my response was different. This time *I* felt possessed by a "need to know," a compulsion that eventually led to a 4,000-mile tour of the nuclear trigger system, a pilgrimage that led me down into the Underground Command Post of the Strategic Air Command, up into B-52 bomb bays, down into missile silos, and deep into the heart of the hollowed-out mountain that houses our missile-attack warning screens.

My first stop was Washington, D.C., where, in the course of doing some preliminary research, I came upon a very unsettling document that has kept me up for many nights since. Entitled "First Use of Nuclear Weapons: Preserving Responsible Command and Control," it is the transcript of a little-noticed set of congressional hearings held in March 1976. The transcripts represent a concerted effort by the International Security Subcommittee of the House Committee on International Affairs to get the answers to Major Hering's question (indeed, it seems the Hering controversy in part provoked the hearings) and to questions about the curious behavior of then–Defense Secretary James Schlesinger in the last days of the Nixon presidency.

As the impeachment process wore on and reports circulated about the president's potentially unstable temperament at the time, Schlesinger took an extraordinary action: He sent out orders to the various communications centers in the nuclear chain of command to report back to him, Schlesinger, any "unusual" orders from the president. The implication was that Schlesinger wanted to know about and perhaps veto a potentially deranged Nixon whim to nuke Vladivostok or the House Judiciary Committee.

The brief flare-up over the Schlesinger order illuminated little more than the extent of consensus ignorance on just how we actually will do it when we do it. Like the facts of life to a bemused child, the facts of nuclear death, before it comes, are more like vague notions than actual clinical details.

We know there is no button wired into the Great Seal in the Oval Office. But that one phone call, the one that kills the seventy million—just where does it go? Who answers? Will the people who answer be loyal to the president or to the secretary of defense if the president's mental condition is suspect? If the secretary of defense could veto a launch by a mad president, could a secretary of defense *initiate* a launch if he felt the president was playing Hamlet and was mad *not* to launch?

The Command and Control hearings document reprints in its appendix a disturbing analysis of these questions by a professor of government at Cornell named Quester. Among other observations, Professor Quester suggests that it is the very precautions taken to thwart a madman general like *Strangelove*'s Jack D. Ripper that have left us at the mercy of a madman president. Making sure that no one *below* the president can launch a nuclear war means giving to the president alone more unchecked power to do it himself on a whim and a single phone call. But the more power placed in the president's hands alone, the more vulnerable the entire U.S. nuclear arsenal is to being disarmed by simply knocking off the president. There must be some provision for a retaliatory threat to be credible in the event a "suitcase bomb," for instance, results in the death of the president, vice president, and most of the cabinet, and no one can remember whether it's the secretary of agriculture or commerce who is constitutionally mandated to decide whether we bomb Russia or China or both.

If such contingency plans—for physical rather than constitutional launch orders—exist, as Quester believes, then in effect we are almost back where we started. Because "Plan R," the linchpin of General Jack D. Ripper's surprise nuke attack plan in *Strangelove,* was just that sort of contingency plan—devised to ensure that our bombers would attack their targets even if the U.S. command authority were vaporized in a surprise attack.

Professor Quester's analysis opens up a dismaying number of disturbing paradoxes in "Command and Control" theory as well as practice. More disturbing than any one of these questions is the fact that these problems haven't been solved to everyone's satisfaction by this time. I felt a sinking feeling reading Quester and the other documentary analyses attached to the hearings: Oh God, did I really have to worry about this? Weren't people scared enough that it had been taken care of completely by now?

I went through the hearing testimony without much consolation. Some admirals and generals complained to the subcommittee that the new failsafe systems were too stringent—that, in fact, they were worried that they might not be able to launch their nukes when the time came because of all the red tape the bureaucrats had put between them and their missiles. But when the committee tried to get the answers to questions such as those raised by Quester about the actual control of nuclear weapons at the top of the chain of command and the mechanics of the transfer of constitutional succession, they were told either that such information was classified and they had no "need to know," or that "no one was sure" what would obtain.

So I took my underlined and annotated copy of the Command and Control hearings transcript over to the Pentagon. Most questions were referred to the Strategic Air Command headquarters in Omaha, Nebraska, and that's when SAC gave me the big invitation.

Would I like, the SAC people asked, to visit the Underground Command Post buried beneath the Nebraska prairie? Would I like a tour through a Looking Glass Plane—one of the curiously named "airborne command posts" that would take over the launching of missiles if the SAC Underground Command Post suffered a direct five-megaton hit? Would I like to go to a missile base in North Dakota and descend into an operational launch capsule and crawl into a B-52 bomb bay? Would I like to enter the hollowed-out mountain in Colorado that housed the headquarters of the North American Air Defense Command, the supersensitive safety catch on the nuclear trigger?

Thermonuclear Porn Revisited

The nearest motel to the SAC Command Post is a Ramada Inn in a place called Bellevue, Nebraska. I stayed up late the night before my descent into the underground war room rereading *Fail-safe,* spellbound once again by the scenes in the war room—half the book takes place there—the very underground war room to which I was to descend the next morning. Rereading *Fail-safe* was one of the final assignments in the task of preparation I'd given myself in the month between my visit to the Pentagon and my actual departure for triggerworld. The overall task had been to recapitulate the onset of the thermonuclear fever I suffered as an adolescent by rereading, in the order I'd originally devoured them, all the classics of a genre I've come to call thermonuclear pornography. Back when I was a kid I'd read it all.

I'd started with the soft-core stuff: the tear-jerking, postattack tristesse of the slowly expiring Australian survivors in *On the Beach,* spiced as it was with a memorable seduction ploy in which a doom-maddened woman goes so far as to unfasten her bikini top on a first date, a hint of the unleashed inhibitions the end of the world could engender. This only aroused my appetite for the more explicit stuff: such nuclear foreplay novels as *Red Alert* and *Fail-safe,* with their mounting urgencies as the stiffening finger on the atomic button brought the trembling world to the brink of "going all the way," to use a metaphor from another adolescent preoccupation whose urgencies may indeed have fueled this one. To a bored and repressed high-school student, nuclear war novels were not about skin-searing blast-burns but were dramas of inhibition and release. In that sense the foreplay genre was somehow unsatisfying, ending, as most of them did, with some chastening and guilty retreats and vows of eternal nuclear chastity forevermore. Fruitlessly, I scoured the subgenres of post–World War III science fiction (mutants stalk humans in the rubble; wise aliens sift through ruins for clues to the extinction of life on Planet III) for at least a retrospective fantasy of what the actual outbreak of Armageddon would be like, but all they delivered were teasing references of the sort Woody Allen parodied in *Sleeper* ("We believe that the individual responsible for touching off the thermonuclear catastrophe was a man named Albert Shanker but . . .").

It was not until I began reading the truly hard-core stuff—the strategists— that I found some measure of voyeuristic satisfaction. Reading Herman Kahn's *On Escalation* was like coming upon an illustrated marriage manual after trying to figure out sex from Doris Day movies. I followed the exquisitely fine gradations on the forty-four-step escalation ladder erected by Herman Kahn, with its provocatively titled rungs like No. 4, "Hardening of Position"; No. 11, "Super Ready Status"; No. 37, "Provocative Counter Measures"; all the way up to the ultimate and total release of No. 44, "Spasm War."

That night in Bellevue I felt a renewed rush of that thermonuclear prurience when I reread the first big war-room scene in *Fail-safe.*

Do you remember the war-room scenes in *Fail-safe?* Do you remember *Fail-safe?* That was the trembling-on-the-brink novel that wasn't funny like *Strangelove.* Or witty. But powerful. In *Fail-safe,* a condenser burnout in a war-room machine fails to send a "recall message" to a nuclear-armed B-52 as it approaches its "failsafe point," and the bomber heads toward target Moscow as men in the White House and the SAC war room try to defuse the fateful, final explosion.[1]

Back to the war-room scenes in *Fail-safe.* Here's something you might *not* remember about those scenes, something I recalled only on rereading the novel. When the big crisis occurs, the war room is sealed off and two civilian

---

[1] *Fail-safe* and *Dr. Strangelove* are based on mistaken premises, as Sidney Hook pointed out in his contemporaneous polemic *The Fail-safe Fallacy.* The Air Force never had a policy of ordering planes to strike their targets unless recalled at a certain point. Bombers would fly to designated points outside Soviet airspace during alerts, but the policy, now known as "positive control" rather than the tainted "failsafe," required that a bomber turn around and head back unless it received a direct voice-communication order to strike. A mechanical failure might cause a plane to turn back by mistake but not to head for Moscow. Unfortunately, Hook falls victim to a fallacy of his own in *The Fail-safe Fallacy,* assuming that by discrediting a key assumption in a speculative novel he has somehow discredited the notion that we have *any* reason to fear a nuclear war caused by mechanical failure. In fact, warnings of possible surprise attacks have been triggered on NORAD radar screens by flights of Canada geese and the reflection of the moon under peculiar atmospheric conditions. Under certain contemplated alert postures—the hair-trigger, or launch-on-warning, stance, for instance—such mechanical errors could be enough to launch our entire arsenal mistakenly.

visitors touring the place, just as I will be, are trapped inside as the greatest drama in history unfolds before them.

Before falling asleep that night in my Ramada Inn room, I must admit I entertained myself with some old-fashioned nuke-porn fantasies. After all, the SALT talks had broken down, détente was crumbling into recriminations about human rights. Jimmy Carter was flying around in his nuclear emergency command plane and running nuclear-alert escape drills at the White House. Did he know something we didn't? Alarmist articles with ominous titles such as "Why the Soviet Union Thinks It Can Fight and Win a Nuclear War" were appearing in sober journals. A Soviet surprise attack could happen at any time, warned Professor Richard Pipes in *Commentary*. What if it were to happen tomorrow? I fantasized. What if, as in *Fail-safe,* I was to find myself trapped on the Command Balcony when the real thing began and the footprints of incoming missiles began stalking across the big war-room screens?

"What an exciting prospect"—that memorable phrase of John Dean's on the White House tapes leaped to mind. I wouldn't mind it one bit; I realized that in some small way I might be hoping for it. That I could entertain such shameful speculation indicates not only that nuclear annihilation appeals to infantile fantasies of grandiosity but also that it is almost impossible to take the idea of nuclear annihilation to heart, so that it can be felt the way other deaths are feared and felt. What sane human could be excited at the prospect of his friends and loved ones dying on the morrow? Yet there is something in the totality of the way we think of nuclear death that not only insulates but appeals. I think it has to do with some early extreme ways of phrasing and thinking about it.

When early strategists began to talk about the totality of nuclear war, they used phrases like "the death of consciousness" on the planet. Henry Kissinger used the only slightly more modest phrase "an end to history." Without consciousness not only is there no history, there is no sorrow, no pain, no remorse. No one is missing or missed. There is nothing to feel bad about because nothing exists to feel. A death so total becomes almost communal. The holocaust of the European Jews left behind millions to feel horror, bitterness, and loss. When people began applying the word *holocaust* to nuclear war they meant a holocaust with no survivors, or one in which, to use the well-known phrase, "the survivors would envy the dead." Even now, when a much-disputed scientific report on "nuclear winter" argues the probability for long-term post-holocaust survival, at least in the southern hemisphere, one does not, if one is an American, think of surviving a total nuclear war. One thinks of dying in a flash before there's time to feel the pain. Could that be the attraction, if that word may be used, of nuclear war? Is there some Keatsian element "half in love with easeful death" in our fantasies of the end?

Back in 1957 Norman Mailer wrote in *The White Negro* that the absolute-ness of the idea of nuclear annihilation will liberate the psychopath within us, and indeed, Charles Manson wrote of the welcome cleansing prospect of atomic war. In a curiously similar passage in a letter home from Korea, David ("Son of Sam") Berkowitz wrote of his desire for release from atomic fear.

Such theories perhaps account for the perverse fantasy "attractions" of Armageddon, but how to account for the desensitization to the reality? As the demons of nuke-porn fantasies gathered about me in my Bellevue room that night I began to wonder if the very structure of the nuke-porn genre I'd been rereading that had been so stimulating in my adolescence—that thrilling sense of the imminence of release it created—might contribute to the problem of response I felt as an adult. The cumulative effect of pornography, particularly on a virginal sensibility, is to arouse expectations of intensity that reality some-times fails to deliver. Back in junior high and high school, saturation with nuke porn led me to a preoccupation with the dates and deadlines, with that familiar adolescent question, "When will it finally happen?"

Of course there was always an erotic component to the original thermonu-clear fever. According to one study of the premillennial fevers that have swept religious communities (from the early Christians, who castrated themselves to avoid the heightened temptation to sin in the little time remaining before the Second Coming, to the wave of ark-building that swept the Rhine when a noted sixteenth-century astrologer predicted a Second Flood), in almost every instance the terror at the prospect of the end of the world was mingled with "fierce joy, sexual orgies, and a kind of strange receptivity."

Back in October 1962, during the Cuban Missile Crisis, when it seemed at last it *would* happen, it was with thrilled anticipation and fevered fantasies that my (male) high-school cronies and I regarded the Soviet ships approach-ing the imaginary blockade line in the Atlantic Ocean, breach of which could shortly trigger all-out war. The chief fantasy engendered in the giddiness of the lunchrooms and locker rooms was this: As soon as the Absolute Final Warning came over the p.a. we'd steal a car and approach one of the girls at the other lunch table with the following proposition: The bombs are gonna fall in twenty-four hours. You don't want to die a virgin, do you?

But the October crisis passed and we were all still virgins. There still re-mained homework to do before graduation. The famous *Bulletin of the Atomic Scientists* doomsday clock has hovered close to the witching hour for three decades and we still haven't heard the chimes of midnight. The Fatima prophecy still had power to chill me when I heard it in 1964—after all, hadn't C. P. Snow declared in 1960 that nuclear war was a "mathematical certainty" by the end of the decade? But by 1970, when the C. P. Snow deadline passed, I'd forgotten there was something special to celebrate.

It's not that these people were false prophets—indeed, at worst they may have been merely premature, at best they may have issued self-*un*fulfilling prophecies; by arousing enough concern they helped prevent or postpone that which they predicted. But whatever processes of internalizing, eroticizing, or numbing were responsible, there is no question that the seventies have been a decade almost totally desensitized to the continued imminence of doom that caused hysteria fifteen years ago.

What happened to the superheated apocalyptic fever that pervaded the national consciousness from the mid-fifties to the early sixties? The bombs are still there, and the Threat, but when was the last time you had an opinion on the morality of massive retaliation? Can you even recall having an opinion on the gun-in-the-fallout-shelter question? Ban-the-bomb marches? The better-Red-than-dead debate? Does anyone live his life as if the End were really twenty-five minutes away? Why did we say Good-bye to All That? Or did we?

In his study of Sabbatai Sevi, the fabulous false messiah of seventeenth-century Palestine, scholar Gershom Scholem distinguishes between two strains of eschatological (end of the world) sensibilities: the apocalyptic and the mystical. In the apocalyptic mode, the various revelations of cataclysmic messianic advents and, to shift to a Christian example, the visions of the titanic last battle at Armageddon are taken to represent actual physical upheavals, literal military battles that will be waged on the surface of the earth. In the mystical mode, on the other hand, these climactic wars between the forces of God and His Adversary, and similar upheavals described in sacred books, are said to be waged *internally*—within the mystical body *(corpus mysteriosum)* of the believer—for possession not of the world, but of the soul.

After reading the literature of nuclear annihilation it seems clear to me that what happened in the mid-sixties was an internalization of the apocalyptic fevers and their transformation into mystical symptoms.

When the test-ban treaty drove the visible mushroom clouds underground in 1963, it was not long before there sprang up among post-Hiroshima progeny the impulse to ingest magic mushrooms and their psychedelic cognates. The experience of "blowing the mind" from within was an eroticized replication of the no-longer-visible explosion. The once-feared death of consciousness on earth threatened by nuclear annihilation was replaced by the desire for the annihilation of the ego. It's possible that the concept of "bad vibes" can be seen as a cognate of invisible radiation. A generation that grew up with the fear of the ineradicable contamination of its mother's milk by fallout has developed a mystical obsession with the purity of all it ingests, and it can be argued that Jack D. Ripper, the nuke-mad commander in *Strangelove,* obsessed with the purity of his "precious bodily fluids," is the spiritual godfather of the health-food movement. The guru who offers a short circuit to "the clear light" is particularly seductive to a generation that expected to be short-circuited to heaven by the "light brighter than a thousand suns."

That short-circuiting of time had long-term characterological effects that are only now being revealed: a belief that one would never live to be a grown-up discouraged any patience for the acceptance of the need to grow up. Indeed, like Peter Pan (not the diner), the bomb allowed the transformation of the present into a never-never land in which no gratification need be postponed and one could celebrate here what Tom Wolfe aptly called the "happiness explosion" instead of the unhappy one we once feared.

In a similar way the antiwar movement, which grew in part out of the ban-the-bomb fervor, found part of itself seduced into a mystical fascination with making bombs. One of the women survivors of the Weather Underground townhouse–bomb-factory explosion wrote a poem called "How It Feels to Be Inside an Explosion"—perhaps the ultimate internalization.

The persistence of the explosive word *blow* in the slang of the late sixties and early seventies may in itself be a residue of the internalization of the apocalyptic. Why else do we describe ourselves as feeling blown away, and getting blown over, blown out, getting the mind blown, getting blown (sexually). And is it an accident that the moving epitaph Ken Kesey spoke for the climactic failure of his attempt at a mystical group-mind fusion that failed to transcend fission was, as Tom Wolfe records it, "We blew it."

As morning approached, I was relieved that at last I would be able to stop fantasizing about the nuclear trigger. I was going to put my finger on it.

Alone with the Sanest Men in America

They call it the "Command Balcony" of the war room, and it was to be, after two preparatory briefings, my first vision of triggerland. The Command Balcony—I loved the lofty theatricality of the name—was where the president's phone call would be answered when he decided the time had come to unleash the missiles.

Uneasy is the descent into the war room. One is led down steel corridors where hard-nosed security-detachment men wearing blue berets and conspicuously displayed pearl-handled pistols guard the blastproof doors which are marked NO LONE ZONE. The doors, my guide reassures me, are also gas- and radiation-proof and able to withstand a direct hit with a five-megaton warhead. This is not totally reassuring. In order to take my mission to the command post with proper seriousness, I had absorbed a full-scale "Briefing on Soviet Strategic Capabilities," which emphasized the growing threat from larger Soviet missiles able to deliver a "throw-weight" up to twenty megatons with increasing accuracy. But no matter. Provisions have been made against the sudden vaporization of these underground premises. The instant the circuits begin to melt, all command-post functions will instantly revert to the "Looking Glass Plane." This curious code name is given to the airborne command post, one of a rotating fleet of planes that have been circling the Midwest since February 1961 ready to take over the running of the war from above the blasts.

At first I thought the code name "Looking Glass" must refer to the post-attack function—reflecting messages back and forth to surviving authorities at various points on the ground, or perhaps to the mirror-bright aluminum bottom half of the plane designed to deflect the glare of the nuclear blasts from the battle below. I couldn't believe the Air Force would deliberately allude to that dark Carrollian fantasy of hallucinatory chess. But when I asked my guide, an Air Force major, about the origin of "Looking Glass" he told me, "Sir, I can't say for sure but I assume they had that Lewis Carroll book in mind." Later that day I would be taken through an actual Looking Glass Plane on standby for an eight-hour shift aloft. But that morning when I went through the blastproof doors and out onto the Command Balcony marked the moment I was truly through the looking glass—although, as I would soon find out, not the side I thought.

The Command Balcony is a glassed-in mezzanine of the small two-story theater that is the war room of the Strategic Air Command. In the orchestra pit below, the "battle staff" works away at computer terminals and radar displays complete with all the glowing dials you see in melodramatic movies. Looming over all, of course, is the fourth wall of the theater—the "big board." Its six two-story-high panels dominate the view from the Command Balcony. Above the open panel closest to me the alert-status indicator reads 1 on a scale of 5. During the October War of 1973 it read 3; a whirling red light flashed above the big board and a message flashed on ordering the battle staff to cease all unnecessary tasks and stand by for orders.

This morning as I walked in the big board was blanked out. For security purposes, I was told. It was not until some moments later that I was to look up and see that fateful sign on the big board. First I wanted to sit in the command swivel chair. There it was ahead of me, a big black swivel chair in the central well of the Command Balcony. The chair is reserved, in time of nuclear war, for the commander in chief of the Strategic Air Command, or CINCSAC, as he's known on the Command Balcony. It's from this chair that CINCSAC will gaze at the big board and make his moves in the decisive first minutes of nuclear war. On a panel in front of the CINCSAC swivel chair are the red phone and the gold phone. The president and the Joint Chiefs call in the orders on the gold phone. CINCSAC executes them on the red phone.

"The president can make you a general," observed onetime CINCSAC

General Curtis LeMay, who sat in this chair for many years, "but only communications can make you a commander."

I seated myself in the swivel chair. I picked up the gold phone. I picked up the red phone. The battle staff was humming away beneath me. And for a moment, sitting there in the CINCSAC swivel chair, indulging myself in the seductive grandiosity of this position in the last synapse between command and execution of that awesome final order, for a moment I felt like a commander.

I also felt like a child, let loose with the war toy I'd always wanted.

But suddenly, when I looked up from my command-chair reverie to the big board, I felt foolish. A three-line message had flashed onto the big board. Could this be It? Not quite. When I read it I cringed. All my fantasies fled in embarrassment. This is what the message said:

> WELCOME MR. RON ROSENBAUM
> FROM HARPER [*sic*] MAGAZINE
> TO COMMAND BALCONY SAC HEADQUARTERS

Then an Air Force photographer stepped forward to take my picture in the command chair as a memento, and then a whole dog-and-pony show of a briefing began, featuring a call on the red phone from the Looking Glass Plane airborne with a preprogrammed "Greetings from the captain and crew to Mr. Rosenbaum, distinguished visitor to SAC's command post."

I could go on. It was in many ways a fascinating briefing but from the moment I saw that first WELCOME sign on the big board I had the sinking feeling they had turned this place, this focal point of nuke-porn fantasies, into a tourist trap. It might as well have been Disneyworld or some bankrupt and bogus "astronaut-land" in some bypassed south Florida subdivision for all the magic that remained. Suddenly all that had seemed forbidden, awesome about the stage upon which civilization's final drama may be played appeared like cheap stage tricks. Even the dimmed lights, "the pools of darkness" that in *Fail-safe* "gave the sense of immensity of almost limitless reach," were dimmed only for the duration of my stay on the Command Balcony. They were dimmed to make a slide show, complete with flashlight pointer, more visible as it was projected on the screen. I felt cheated, teased with the illusion of command, then brought down to earth feeling like a cranky, disappointed tourist. A thermonuclear crisis would just not seem at home here on the Command Balcony any more than on a high-school auditorium stage.

And that perhaps was the point. The Strategic Air Command is proud of its command-and-control system, does not think of it as an exotic, thrilling Strangelovian mechanism. It's *just* a mechanism, a sophisticated one, but a neutral mechanism they administer, certainly not an evil one—it hasn't done any evil, it hasn't really done anything except be there so long it's become routine.

That moment on the Command Balcony, I later realized, was the point at which I passed through to the other side, a Looking Glass of sorts. I was the one who had been living in a fever of Carrollian nightmares. The world I'd stepped into was relentlessly sane, its people very well adjusted. The paradoxical metaphysic of deterrence theory had become part of their ground of being. No one gave it a second thought, seldom a first. They spent little time in reflection of any kind, much less a Looking Glass sensibility. They were not there to shoot missiles and kill people. They were there *to act as if they would* shoot missiles and kill people because by so doing they'd never have to actually do it. They were content that their role was ceaselessly to rehearse, never perform that one final act.

They could have fooled me. I was fascinated by the aplomb of the missile crewmen I met. These are the guys who will actually pull the trigger for us. Of course they don't pull a trigger, they twist a key. Each two-man crew of "launch control officers" must twist their respective keys simultaneously to generate a "launch vote" from their capsule, and the two-man "launch vote" of another capsule is required before the four twisted keys can together send from ten to fifty Minutemen with MIRVed warheads irrevocably on their way to their targets.

These men will not be voting alone, of course. When we pay our income taxes we are casting our absentee ballot in favor of a launch vote, and, should the time ever come, in favor of the mass murder of tens of millions of innocents.* Morally, metaphorically, our finger is on the trigger too. But theirs are on it physically day in and day out for years.

I tried to get them to talk about it. Up at Minot AFB the Fifty-fifth Missile Wing helicoptered me out to an operational Minuteman-missile launch capsule nestled in the midst of vast fields of winter wheat. Fifty feet below the topsoil in the capsule I tried to edge into larger subjects—does it make a difference being able to know your target?—but there seemed to be nervousness on both sides, perhaps because of the presence of a senior officer and a tape recorder. Fortunately, at the last minute I was able to arrange, as the final unofficial stop in my tour of the nuclear fortifications, a different kind of meeting with missile crewmen.

Let me tell you about that last stop. Because it was there that I finally got

---

*The doctrine of massive retaliation, under the theory of "Mutually Assured Destruction" mandated retaliatory nuclear destruction of whole cities, Hiroshima style, rather than military targets since a retaliatory strike presumed an enemy had already emptied its missile silos on us in a first strike.

the feel of those brass launch keys—I actually got to twist them and get the feel of launching a nuke—and it was there that I first discussed such issues as nuclear surrender and the Judo—yes, Judo—Christian ethic, and it was there that I first learned the secret of the spoon and the string.

I can't tell you exactly where it was—I agreed to keep the name of the base and the names of the missile men I spoke to out of the story. But I can tell you it was a Minuteman base and the men I spoke to were all launch-control officers. And these are no ordinary missile crewmen. Even among the highly skilled Minutemen men these are the crème de la crème I'm visiting with this Saturday morning. These six guys in their blue Air Force fatigues and brightly colored ascots are a special crack crew of missile men culled from capsules all over the base into a kind of all-star team. This morning they are practicing in a launch-capsule "problem simulator" for the upcoming "Olympic Arena" missile-crew competition out at Vandenberg AFB, where they will represent the honor of their base in a kind of World Series of missile-base teams.

You see, the Air Force goes to some length to imbue the men in its missile squadrons with a military esprit—a task rendered difficult by the sedentary and clerical nature of military-capsule duty. Missile men never need learn to fly a plane and most don't. The romantic flyboy spirit is something of a handicap for men condemned to spend twenty-four hours in a twenty-by-nine-by-ten-foot capsule. There's no need to develop that special brand of nerve and confidence Tom Wolfe, in his study of astronauts, called "the right stuff." The right stuff for a missile crewman is a disposition far more phlegmatic and stolid. So the typical missile crewman of the sample I met was often a pudgy bespectacled graduate of a Southern technical school with a low-key, good-ol'-boy sense of humor who volunteered for missile duty because the Air Force would pay for the accounting degree he could earn in his spare time in the launch capsule. The Air Force is still run by flyboys who tend to treat the missile crewmen as junior partners. Still, the Air Force tries to incorporate the missile men into its traditional gung-ho spirit. It gives them all dashing ascots to wear, as if they were units of some Australian Ranger battalion trained to kill men with their bare hands, when all they actually are expected to do with their bare hands is twist a key. (One almost suspects some deadpan tongue-in-cheek flyboy parody in the ascot touch.) And there are all sorts of patches and merit badges for the annual Olympic Arena competition, which is strenuously promoted and prepped for all year round.

This morning these missile men have been practicing for Olympic Arena in a special glass-walled launch-control capsule simulator that replicates the conditions of the big missile Olympic games. These are not as dramatic as they might sound—no jousting between Titans and Minutemen, no target shooting, no actual launchings at all, in fact. Instead the competition consists of "problems" computer-fed into the capsule simulators, and the crews go through the checklists in their capsule operations manuals to solve the problems. Problems thrown at them can be anything from retargeting half their missiles from Leningrad to Moscow to putting out a fire in the capsule trash bin. For every possible problem it seems there is a checklist to follow, and the activity I watch in the capsule consists mainly of finding the right checklist in the right briefing book and following the instructions. Victory goes to those who follow their checklists most attentively. More like a CPA competition than an Arthurian tournament.

During a break in the problem solving I am invited into the capsule simulator to look around. It is exactly like the working missile capsule I had been permitted access to a few days ago in every respect but one: the keys. In the working missile capsule the keys are locked securely in a fire engine–red box that is to be opened only in time of high-level nuclear alert. But as soon as I walked into the simulator that morning I caught sight of the now-familiar bright red box with its little red door wide open. And then I saw the keys. They gleamed brassily, each of them inserted into their slots in the two launch consoles, just as they will be in the last seconds before launch. Apparently the keys had been left there from a launch-procedure problem. I looked at the key closest to me. It had a round brass head and looked like an old-fashioned apartment key. It was stuck into a slot with three positions marked upon it: SET on top, and LAUNCH to the right. This particular key was turned to OFF at the left.

I asked one of the crewmen if I could get a feel of what it would be like to turn the key.

"Sure," he said. "Only that one there, the deputy commander's, the spring-lock mechanism is a little worn out. Come over here and try the commander's key." First I tried the deputy's key all the way to the right from OFF to LAUNCH. Almost no resistance whatsoever. Very little tension.

"Come over and try the other one," one of the crewmen suggested. "That'll give you the real feel of a launch."

To launch a missile, both launch-control officers in the capsule must twist their respective keys to the right within two seconds of each other and hold them there for a full two seconds. The key slots are separated by twelve feet so no one man can either reach over or run over from one key to another and single-handedly send in a "launch vote." Even if this were to happen, a two-key-twist, two-man "launch vote" from a second capsule in the squadron is still required to send any one missile off.

I sat down in the commander's chair—it's not unlike an economy-class airline seat, complete with seat belt. I turned the key to LAUNCH. This time it took some healthy thumb pressure to make the twist, and some forearm muscular tension to hold it in LAUNCH. Not a teeth-clenching muscular contraction—the closest thing I can compare it to is the feeling you get from twisting the key in one of the storage lockers at Grand Central Terminal. Nothing special, but the spring-lock resistance to the launch twist is enough to require a sustained effort of will from the person doing the twisting. For two seconds that person and at least three other people must consciously believe they are doing the right thing killing that many millions of people. Two seconds is perhaps time for reflection, even doubt.

Later, outside the simulator, I asked the missile crewmen if they'd ever imagined themselves having a doubt about their grip on the keys when the time came for that final twist of the wrist. What made them so sure they'd actually be able to do it, or did they just not think of the consequences?

"No," one of the crewman said. "During training out at Vandenberg they'd show the whole class films of the effects of nuclear blasts, Hiroshima and all that, just so we wouldn't have any mistake as to what we're getting into. It's true that they ask you if you will carry out a properly authenticated launch order, and they check your psychological reaction, and the checking doesn't stop there. We're constantly required to check each other for some signs of unusual behavior. But you have to understand that when the launch order comes it won't come as a sudden new trauma. We get practice alerts and retargeting procedures all the time, and the launch will just be a few more items on a procedural checklist we've gone through thousands of times."

By this time we'd adjourned to a small, concrete-floored room containing vending machines for Coke and candy and a few scratched metal folding chairs. Being in a room with the sanest men in America can be disconcerting. And these men were—officially—extremely sane. That constant psychological checking of each other they spoke about is part of the Air Force's Human Reliability Program, which is supposed to be a kind of mental early-warning system to catch people with access to nuclear warheads who are going insane, before their madness turns violent or, worse, cunning.

Of course the Air Force definition of sanity might seem a bit narrow to some, involving as it does the willingness to take direct part in the killing of, say, 10 million people by twisting a key when the proper order is given, while insanity means trying to kill them without proper orders or refusing to kill them despite orders. Nonetheless it is fascinating to read through Air Force Regulation 35-99, Chapter 7, "Psychiatric Considerations of Human Reliability," which is the missile-base commander's guide to early detection of "Concealed Mental Disorders." Regulation 35-99 divides these hidden threats into four categories: "The Suspicious," "The Impulsive," "The Depressed," and "Those with Disturbances of Consciousness." Regulation 35-99 then details "the early signs in observable behavior that strongly suggest the possibility of present or emerging mental disorder" in each category.

Now the trickiest category, according to Regulation 35-99, is "The Suspicious" (don't ask me what school of psychopathology this taxonomy comes from), which enumerates thirteen "clues to paranoid traits." Tricky, because as the Air Force points out, "the following clues are sometimes seen in normal everyday behavior." Indeed, it is difficult to read the description of the thirteen clues without thinking of the "normal everyday behavior" of nuclear powers.

There is, for instance: "a. Arrogance—wherein the individual assumes or presumes the possession of superior, unique, or bizarre abilities, ideas, or theories."

Now, one would think that a man able to participate in the launch of up to thirty separate nuclear warheads and help extinguish human civilization with a twist of his key would be a bull-goose loony not to "presume the possession of superior, unique, or bizarre abilities." The implication here is that sanity in a launch means *not* thinking about this reality, sanity means the kind of studied insanity or fugue state that ignores one's true relation to the world. Then there is: "b. Lack of humor—especially the inability to laugh at oneself, one's mistakes or weaknesses." Now that is pretty funny. When you think about all the occasions for merriment there must be down there at the controls of an ICBM launch capsule, it's hard to believe anyone would be crazy enough not to see the humor in it all. It's good to know that Regulation 35-99 will keep an eye out to yank the occasional gloomy gus right out of there, so we can be assured that when we go we'll die laughing.

Now clue "l."—"legal or quasilegal controversy about pay, time, accidents, unsatisfactory purchases, or matter of authority"—is an interesting one for a couple of reasons. This "paranoid trait," according to the regulation, "is often seen in conjunction with 'letters to the editor,' 'to the president of the company,' or 'to senior commanders.' " One can immediately see the appeal of this definition to the senior commanders who administer the regulation. But it raises interesting questions. One does not want the launch capsules filled with teeth-gnashing irritable cranks, yet the presumption of irrationality that attaches to any question about "matters of authority" assumes that all authority is rational, an assumption that was implicitly challenged by Secretary of Defense Schlesinger when he tried to ensure that if President Nixon went batty and decided to launch a few nukes during the impeachment crisis, someone *would* question his authority.

But for the moment let us leave Regulation 35-99 behind with a parting glance at the Air Force's official characterization of the Mad Bomber. He comes under subsection 7-14, which cites "Some Specific Cases of the Paranoid Schizophrenic" for the missile-base commander to have in mind when he's checking out his men. The only other "specific case" mentioned in this subsection is an unnamed "would-be assassin of President Roosevelt [who] came to Washington to shoot the President and thus to draw public attention to the buzzing sensation in his head."

"To the Mad Bomber of New York," according to the regulation, "the need for revenge seemed paramount, dating back to an ancient grudge against a public utility company."

And yet isn't our nuclear retaliatory policy based on our belief in revenge— that any strike against us must be avenged with nuclear warheads even if it means destroying the rest of human society? Just as planting bombs in public places did not restore the Mad Bomber his pension rights (apparently the source of his grudge against Con Ed), neither would a retaliatory nuclear strike restore the lives or freedom lost from the strike we suffered first. Could this analysis of the Mad Bomber have been a sly comment on the sanity of the nuclear balance of terror slipped into the Air Force insanity definitions by some military shrink with a sense of irony?

In any case let us return to that vending-machine room off the launch-capsule simulator, where a discussion ensues with the sanest men in America, which gets into the basic question of revenge by way of Las Vegas and leads us to the secret of the spoon and string.

I don't want you to get the wrong idea about these missile crewmen. I soon discovered that the Human Reliability Program in practice does not necessarily eliminate all but docile automatons. These missile men have lively responsive intelligences and very upbeat personalities. And despite their devotion to pure professionalism, even they are not entirely unconscious of the ironies of their particular profession. They, too, occasionally get that sense of dislocation at the awesomeness of their position and the ordinariness of their life. I got that sense from listening to one of the crewmen tell me a story about a curiously dislocating encounter he had in a Las Vegas hotel.

He'd accumulated some leave time from the long hours of vigils he had spent down in his launch-control capsule, and he'd decided to spend it in the gambling palaces of Vegas.

"I went alone and one night I wanted to get into one of the big floor shows they have," he told me. "Well, when I asked for a ringside table they told me that as I was by myself, would I mind sharing with another couple. I say okay and these two people introduce themselves. The guy says they're from North Carolina where he's a dentist. Then he asks me what I do."

Introductions can sometimes be awkward for a Minuteman launch-control officer. A stranger will casually ask him his line of work and if he just comes out and says "I'm a Minuteman-missile launch-control officer," well, it's not as if everyone will stare into his eyes for signs of incipient missile-shooting madness, but there is, sometimes, a feeling of wary scrutiny. People don't know exactly how to respond to the unprepossessing presence of a man who is the most powerful and deadly warrior in human history.

"But not this dentist." He displayed none of the usual fears about Strangeloves in disguise, no suppressed whiff of awe at the personified presence of the end of the world.

"Hell no," the missile crewman was telling me. "The only thing this guy was worrying about was whether the thing would actually take off when it came time for wartime launch. He kept saying, 'I just want that bird to fly when the time comes.' He kept saying, 'I want that bird to fly.' "

The crewman shook his head. "It was funny because when the bird flies that means he and his family are probably vaporized. I couldn't figure it. It used to be people you'd run into would worry we'd go off half-cocked and start a war. Now this guy was all excited like he couldn't wait to see it."

"Fact is," said another missile crewman, "most of us have never even launched even a test down at the Vandenberg range. And nothing's ever been test-launched from an operational silo. Once they had a program that was going to let us launch from one of our silos. No warhead of course. From here into the Pacific. But some Indian tribe objected to missiles flying over their sacred burial ground or something and they canceled it. I can maybe see what that dentist was getting at. You sit down there and you know you've got launch capability and you know when you and your buddy turn the keys she'll fly all right but you sure would feel more comfortable if you had it happen once. I tell you I've spent a year and a half underground and I'm halfway to my M.S., but for all those hours down there, when I get out I sure would like to be able to say 'I launched a missile.' "

Again I asked these sanest of all men how they could be sure they'd be able to launch when they knew it was for real.

"One thing you have to remember," one of the crewmen told me, "is that when I get an authenticated launch order I have to figure my wife and kids'd be dead already up above. The base is ground zero. Why shouldn't I launch? The only thing I'd have to look forward to if I ever got up to the surface would be romping around with huge mutant bunny rabbits." We all laughed. It seemed funny at the time.

"Okay, then, put it this way," I said. "If you assume that when you get the launch order everyone on our side has been devastated by a Soviet first strike, is there any purpose served by destroying what's left of humanity by retaliating purely for revenge?"

"What it all comes down to," said one of the older crewmen, "is the Judo-Christian ethic."

"You mean Judeo-Christian," one of the others murmured.

"Right, like I said, the *Judo*-Christian ethic teaches that you never strike first but if someone hits you, you can strike back."

"Wait a minute," I said. "Isn't it Christian to forgive, turn the other cheek, rather than seek revenge? Say you're Jimmy Carter, a serious Christian, and you're president when the whole deterrence thing fails and for some reason the Soviets are tempted to strike or preempt our strike. You see those missiles coming in on the radar screen and know mass murder is about to happen to your people and nothing you can do will stop it. Is there any point in committing another act of mass murder?"

"You think he should surrender?" one of the crewmen asked me.

"I don't know," I said, taken aback by the abruptness of his question.

"That's the thing, you know," another crewman said. "Once you start thinking about all that your head starts going in circles. You got to change the subject. There's a point where you gotta stop asking questions and go to work. You've just got to have faith that you're doing the right thing. It all comes down to professionalism. We know our presence here helps deter war and . . ."

"Course we thought about the problem if we get a launch order if one of us in a capsule crew suddenly turns peacenik at the last minute," one of the crewmen interrupted to say. "And we came up with a solution. We figured out that the whole two-key thing is really bullshit when you get down to it because we figured out how to get a launch with just one man and a spoon and a string."

"Spoon and a string?"

"Well," the crewman continued, "what you do is rig up a thing where you tie a string to one end of a spoon and tie the other end to the guy's key. Then you can sit in your chair and twist your key with one hand while you yank on the spoon with the other hand to twist the other key over." Now, this guy was talking about using some old-fashioned ingenuity to carry out an authorized "execution order." It could of course be used in the service of an unauthorized launch conspiracy. Since launching an ICBM still requires a launch vote from two separate launch-control capsules, it would require two men in cahoots with two spoons and two strings—and probably two pistols—to carry out such an unlikely caper; however, since the two-key system is at the heart of the credibility of the entire command-and-control system, someone in the Air Force just might want to get out a spoon and string, go down into a capsule, and see whether someone might have overlooked a little safeguard.

Nevertheless, I actually found myself more reassured by the missile crewmen's willingness to tell me about the spoon-and-string trick than I was frightened by its possible application. The kind of person who'd cheerfully volunteer the spoon-and-string story is not the kind of person who'd be likely to conspire to use it to try to provoke World War III.

In fact, I was quite impressed with the robust psychological health of the missile crewmen. If they didn't engage in rigorous analysis of the moral consequences of their triggerman role, none of them seemed at all the type to want to conspire to start a nuclear war. They put in a lot of idle hours down in the capsule studying for accounting and law degrees, and a nuclear war would seriously disrupt their professional prospects when they got out. Meeting the missile men was the most reassuring part of my trip.

. . .

Major Hering, you'll recall, was likewise not the least concerned with the mental health of his fellow crewmen. He was worried about the upper links in the chain of command. And unhappily, as one studies those upper reaches more closely, the chain of command seems less like a chain than a concatenation of spoons and strings.

How will Vice President Mondale, off in Hawaii when a suitcase bomb blows up the White House, wage nuclear war from Waikiki with no black-briefcase man at his side? And don't think President Carter, notified of what looks on the radar screens like a surprise attack, will be able to dip into Russian literature (as Henry Fonda does in *Fail-safe*) to help him decide whether to retaliate against Moscow and Leningrad, or Leningrad and Kiev. If, in fact, the Joint Chiefs do decide to consult the Constitutional Commander in Chief on the nature of a retaliatory response (faced with a "use it or lose it" situation military commanders tend to shoot first and consult the Supreme Court later; the Joint Chiefs have no need of the president to launch the missiles physically if they feel he's wavering when the time has come to strike back), what they will present to the president will be a series of preprogrammed attack options generated by our chief nuclear war-gaming computer, the SIOP machine.

SIOP, I should explain, stands for "Single Integrated Operating Plan." It is *the* basic nuclear war plan for all U.S. forces and details exactly which missiles and which bombers will blow up which targets in case of nuclear attack. The SIOP machine is a vast computer complex in a subbasement of the Underground Command Post that generates the Emergency War Orders for transmittal to each element of the SIOP attack. In addition, the SIOP machine is constantly war-gaming its own war plan against its own estimate of the Russian war plan, which SIOP calls RISOP, and updating itself after it counts the computerized death score.

What this means in practice is that the key decisions about how we will respond *in every conceivable nuclear crisis* have already been programmed by the SIOP machine. Most of us may not think of nuclear war at all these days. The SIOP machine thinks about nuclear war for us twenty-four hours a day. The SIOP will run our nuclear war for us.

In fact, the only moment in my entire sentimental journey I felt genuinely "in touch" with nuclear war was the time I felt the SIOP machine. I don't think it's on the regular tourist trail in triggerworld, but I made a special request to see the SIOP machine after reading so much about its awesome capabilities. Even in sophisticated strategic literature the SIOP is spoken of with reverential, almost Delphic, awe, and its pronouncements are surrounded with Delphic mystery. No one even knows how many targets are on the SIOP hit list.

One scholarly study of recent nuclear targeting strategy devoted a long footnote to examining whether a fragmentary declassified report which declared that there were 25,000 targets in the SIOP really might have been a misprint, perhaps deliberate, for 2,500 targets.

The secrets inside the SIOP machine, our actual war plans, are perhaps the most secret secrets in America. According to a two-part report by Seymour Hersh in *The New York Times* (December 1973), a story whose full implications were lost in the Watergate deluge, the Nixon administration's hysterical and ultimately self-destructive reaction to the Daniel Ellsberg affair may have been triggered not by his release of the Pentagon Papers but by the possibility—explored secretly in the highest councils of the Nixon White House—that Ellsberg might also release some of the sacred SIOP secrets. In 1961, in the days when he was an eager young Rand Corporation analyst, a fledgling Strangelove who had already made a highly respected debut with a pamphlet on the "Art of Nuclear Blackmail," Ellsberg had been summoned by the Pentagon to review the existing system for the command and control of the nuclear-weapons trigger. As part of that work Ellsberg was permitted to review the SIOP and the Joint Strategic Target List. In a recent talk on "the nature of modern evil" at the *Catholic Worker*,* Ellsberg, now repentant, described his first look at the primitive SIOP. It shocked him, he said, to learn we had only one nuclear war targeting plan: hit 400 targets in Russia and China. Estimated casualties: 325 million. Whether Ellsberg went on to help redesign the SIOP he would not say, and whether he had any significant knowledge of the SIOP secrets as it evolved into a sophisticated computerized targeting system Ellsberg would not say. But according to Hersh's unnamed source (who sounds like Nixon aide John Ehrlichman), the very possibility that Ellsberg would reveal sacred SIOP secrets the way he revealed the Pentagon Papers—the possibility that he would thereby show the Russians our hand in the bluffing game that is deterrence strategy—was enough to drive Nixon and Kissinger up the wall. According to this theory all the seamy things done to Ellsberg and the Watergate cover-up that was necessary to cover *them* up can be traced to fear for the sanctity of the SIOP.

Well, you might say, doesn't everyone know what we'll do when attacked? What difference does it make which missiles go where when they all go *boom* and make everyone dead? It makes a difference to the strategists. For them the game of deterrence, the delicate balance of terror, is not a stalemate but an ongoing poker game in which the dynamics of bluff, ambiguity, and esoteric as opposed to declaratory policies are constantly shifting. As Bernard Brodie, the

*The Lower East Side paper published by the disciples of Dorothy Day, the nonviolent antiwar activist.

elegant grand master of civilian nuclear strategists, notes, "Good military planning should distinguish between what the president says he'll do and what he's likely to do." Kissinger, an unreconstructed Machiavellian among strategists, called the latter—our real plans as opposed to what we say we'll do—the esoteric strategy.

Inside the SIOP machine are not only the secret war plans of our esoteric strategy but, in addition, a wide array of targeting options based on computerized war-gaming of possible Soviet responses to our responses to their responses. One missile crewman I spoke to, overwhelmed by the majesty and complexity of the SIOP, burst into a veritable ode to its chivalric, jousting-like possibilities. "Just think," he said, "we're engaged in a test of wills with the Soviets somewhere and they push us too hard and push comes to shove, we don't have to choose between incinerating the planet and giving up. With the new SIOP options we can pinpoint a shot across the Kamchatka Peninsula and if they don't start listening to reason just walk those Nudets [Air Force word for nuclear detonation] across Siberia till they start to feel the heat in Moscow. Course they'll probably start on the Gulf of Mexico with theirs, walk 'em across to Houston, and start to head north, but we'll have our response to that all programmed in the SIOP. You know something else? I understand that before Carter took office he was given a detailed SIOP briefing and the guy was so shaken by it, that's why he suddenly comes out and says we got to abolish all nuclear weapons. The SIOP was too much for him. He just couldn't handle it."

So what actually goes on within the SIOP machine? Many nuclear wars: "practice" wars between SIOP and RISOP. After each battle a computer program counts the dead, estimates the damages, and looks for a way to improve the score in our favor in the next nuclear war. The predictive value of the nuclear wars waged within the SIOP machine is handicapped since it has to match itself against its own estimate of RISOP, which, like SIOP, consists of preplanned reactions that can be changed or rejected by national leaders in the heat of crisis. So the wars within SIOP can become a tenuous solipsistic affair, like a computer playing chess with itself. Still it is awesome being in a room in which the world has ended in so many possible ways, perhaps even the precise way it will.

Toward the end of my tour of the SIOP machine I asked the colonel guiding me through the warrens of computers in the SIOP subbasement if I could touch the machine. He looked at the captain accompanying me and shrugged. Not far from me was a first-generation computer element of the SIOP machine. On top of its stacked magnetic tapes was a red "Top Secret" sign, but there was nothing secret for me to see. Only to feel. So I put my hand on its gray alloyed surface and felt in my palm the residual hum and tremor of the thousands of nuclear wars waged by SIOP and RISOP, those ceaselessly clashing computer programs, locked like Gog and Magog in endless Armageddons within its ghostly circuitry.

That was the closest I came to the answers. The answers to Major Hering's question. To my questions about the nitty-gritty details of our actual as opposed to our declared or bluffed targeting strategy. All the answers but one. What happens if we lose?

It was at the very end of my tour of the SIOP machine that I happened to ask an innocuous question that led me down the road into the swamp of "surrender studies."

"In all these wars between SIOP and RISOP," I asked the colonel in charge of the SIOP room, "do we always win?"

The colonel seemed taken aback. He said something about "programming optimum outcomes" or something like that.

"Well, does SIOP ever admit defeat to RISOP or surrender to it?"

"I should hope not," he said.

I had heard whispers about forbidden "surrender studies" when I was down in Washington, whispers about people who have been hounded out of government for daring to suggest that, despite our endless contingency planning and war-gaming, we wouldn't know how to surrender if forced to because we're not permitted to consider the possibility of a loss. It sounded silly, and until that brief exchange in the SIOP room I'd assumed—as I had when I first read of Major Hering's question—that someone somewhere had the answers. But now I was told that even the SIOP machine was not programmed to consider surrender. And so when I returned from my pilgrimage I decided to track down these surrender studies I'd heard about.

What I discovered was that in the entire exotic garden of nuclear-war-fighting strategy theory, surrender is the one forbidden fruit. A subject more unthinkable than The Unthinkable itself. In fact, thinking about it has actually been declared illegal in some cases.

Indeed, the short, sad history of surrender studies in the nuclear age reveals that the few intrepid theoreticians who have ventured into that terra incognita have come back scarred by the charge that just talking about it can cause it. Back in 1958 a Rand Corporation analyst by the name of Paul Kecskemeti published a modest scholarly monograph entitled *Strategic Surrender*. Beginning with the premise that surrender, like war, is an extension of politics by other means, Kecskemeti explored the various strategies of twentieth-century surrenders—what each party to a surrender was able to win and lose (yes, a loser can "win" a surrender by getting more concessions than his actual strength should command). High marks go to the Vichy French and Germans for their eminently professional disposition of the surrender of France in 1940, he says; a pathetic failing grade to the Americans and Italians who botched the surrender of Italy in 1943. Though his is largely a historical study Kecskemeti did append to the work a section on "Surrender in Future Strategy," with a subsection on "Surrender in Nuclear War"—the latter slightly more than one page long. That was enough. When his book appeared, the great Red-or-dead debate still raged across the land and Kecskemeti had been gracious enough in his preface to acknowledge that "this study was prepared as part of the research program undertaken for the United States Air Force by the Rand Corporation." Swift and massive retaliation fell upon the book. You could call it overkill. There were outcries from the warlords of Congress that taxpayer money was being used to pave the way for capitulation to the Soviets. President Eisenhower was described as upset and horrified as he demanded an immediate explanation from the Pentagon. "I've never seen Ike more mad," said one aide. Everything at the Pentagon stopped for two hours while they tried to get to the bottom of the surrender-study flap. *The New York Times* reported a "tumultuous session" of Congress, and "the most heated debate of the year" brought forth near unanimous passage of one of the strangest resolutions ever to issue from that body. This one, attached as a rider to an appropriations bill and passed in August 1958, specifically forbade the use of any federal funds to finance the study of surrender.

On the inside cover of the library-battered copy of *Strategic Surrender* I have in my hands, some outraged reader has scrawled: "Americans would rather die on their feet than live on their knees." It's an attitude that has made even the boldest nuclear strategists a bit gun-shy about discussing surrender. In what seems like a characteristically black-humored recognition of the delicacy of using the forbidden word, the index to the second edition of Henry Kissinger's early study of *Nuclear Weapons and Foreign Policy* contains the following laconic citation: "Unconditional Surrender. *See* Victory, Total."

Even the fearless Herman Kahn, forever urging us to call a spade a spade and a grave a grave in matters of nuclear war, prefers to discuss "responses to postattack blackmail" rather than "surrender negotiations." In his treatise *On Thermonuclear War,* Kahn grumbles that "the investigation of the feasibility of various [postattack] blackmail tactics is not only a difficult technical question, but seems contrary to public policy as set forth in recent legislation forbidding use of federal funds for the study of 'surrender.' " But the master strategist is something less than his usual crusading self when he quits the subject with the terse comment that "such research is important." When he publishes research on surrender problems, Kahn talks of "conflict termination." He talks of "crisis resolution," and, most ingenious of all, "de-escalation." None, not even he, dares call it surrender.

Officially, anyway. Inconclusive inquiries to the Defense Department failed to turn up any indication that the surrender-study ban had ever been repealed, although no one there seemed to know of its existence or was prepared to believe its existence, even after I read them several front-page *New York Times* stories on the controversy.

Kecskemeti remembers. I spoke to him last summer, almost two decades after the big fuss, and it sounded to me as if in his scholarly way he was still steamed up about what happened to his book. He blamed it on "a stupid article in the *St. Louis Post,*" leaked, he said, by Missouri Senator Symington, the former secretary of the Air Force, who was preparing to run for president on a Strengthen-America's-Defenses platform.

Kecskemeti described the Senate debate on surrender. "Sensational, demagogic—and silly," he says. "My book was totally misunderstood. The question is whether great powers are able to end a war short of total annihilation. If this is to be done it must be thought about ahead of time."

The Seductions of Strategy

My pursuit of what might seem like the arcana of surrender studies led me next to a question, another one of those Carrollian rabbit holes in the landscape of nuclear strategy, that is even more fundamental and immediate: Will we respond to a Soviet nuclear attack at all? Is it possible in some circumstances, despite our declarations, that we just won't retaliate?

I first came upon this notion in an elegant analysis of "War Termination" by Fred Ikle, the hawkish former head of the Arms Control and Disarmament Agency. (Ikle took over after the doves there were purged in exchange for Henry Jackson's support of the original SALT agreement.) In the conclusion of his analysis Ikle argues that deterrence—the threat of nuclear retaliation if we are attacked—commits us to a morally abhorrent, genocidal, retaliatory vengeance if the threat fails and we *are* attacked. The logical implication is that in the aftermath of a Soviet surprise attack, we might surrender without firing a shot.

Turn the other cheek and give in.

No less a person than Richard Nixon acknowledged the possible wisdom of such a course of action. Consider the situation I'd be in, Nixon said, "if the Soviet Union, in a surprise attack, were able to destroy all of America's fixed land-based missile force and would confront the U.S. with a choice of doing nothing or launching air- and sea-based nuclear forces only to see the U.S.S.R. inflict even more damage upon us in return." The implication is that Nixon would have surrendered in such circumstances.

I used to have long arguments on this point back in high school. What good would pure vengeance do you if you're dead, I'd ask. Ridiculous, my friends would say: If *they* knew someone like you was running things and bluffing they'd be more likely to attack. So don't tell them, I'd say, make them think we will strike back but if it does happen, don't. What is to be gained by killing off the rest of the human race?

I had long dismissed this as a naive adolescent hobbyhorse of mine until I tried the question out on the missile crewmen that morning and found it provoked an interesting discussion about the Judeo-Christian ethic. I was even more surprised to find, when I plunged back into the literature of nuclear strategy upon return from my tour, that "Deterrence as a Great Big Bluff" is discussed by some of the most sophisticated nuclear strategists as a very real possibility.

The most rational deterrence policy, writes Bernard Brodie, perhaps the most authoritative and rational of the first generation of strategists, involves convincing an enemy that we are utterly inflexible, vindictive, and even irrationally committed to retaliation against a potential attack, no matter what.

But, argues Brodie, that most rational deterrence policy "involves commitment to a strategy of response which, if we ever had to execute it, might then look foolish." In other words, a rational person may decide it's foolish to retaliate. "It remains questionable," Fred Ikle tells us, "whether the execution of a retaliatory strike can serve the national interests once it has failed as a threat." And there it is again, in the most graphic terms possible, in, of all places, *Strategic Review,* one of the most militantly—albeit scholarly—hawkish nuclear-strategy journals. In the February 1976 issue of *Strategic Review* military strategy writer R. J. Rummel asks, "If deterrence fails would a president push the button? Of course not."

What does this mean? Is Jimmy Carter, who pledged never to lie to the American people, bluffing us along with the Russians? Is that part of the esoteric strategy? Has he secretly decided he won't push the button in that situation? Do the Joint Chiefs know? Would they let him get away with it? Do we want him to tell us, and thus the Russians, making an attack at least marginally more likely?

As you can see, once you get into the Looking Glass world of esoteric strategy, answers become elusive as the questions develop elaborate mirror images: What do we think they think we think they think about what we plan to do? Nuclear war is waged these days not with missiles but with conceptions of missile strategies, with manipulations of perceptions and metaphysical flanking maneuvers. Mental nuclear war (after Blake's "Milton": "I shall not cease from mental fight . . .") goes on all the time, often in obscure and veiled forms.

Consider the esoteric implications behind the appearance and disappearance of a single footnote from the prepared text of a speech Henry Kissinger delivered to the Commonwealth Club of San Francisco on February 3, 1976. Appended to his otherwise unremarkable address on "The Permanent Challenge of Peace: U.S. Policy Toward the Soviet Union" was an eight-line footnote—appended, that is, to some printed versions of the speech and not to others. The official version delivered to the Soviet embassy by the State Department did have the footnote, and there was a message for the Soviets in that footnote, a veiled threat of great consequence between these lines:

> To be sure, there exist scenarios in planning papers which seek to demonstrate how one side could use its strategic forces and how in some presumed circumstance it would prevail. But these confuse what a technician can calculate with what a responsible statesman can decide. They are invariably based on assumptions such as that one side would permit its missile silos to be destroyed without launching its missiles before they are actually hit—on which no aggressor could rely where forces such as those possessed by either the U.S. or the U.S.S.R. now and in the years ahead are involved.

Now the real subject of this footnote is a declared U.S. nuclear strategy known as the "ride out" doctrine. Under it, we have committed ourselves not to respond immediately to a Soviet missile attack we see developing on our radar screens. Instead, incredible as it may sound at first, we are pledged to just sit back and track the incoming missiles, presumably aimed at our missile silos, watch as they blast holes in the Great Plains, ride out the attack, count up the number of missiles we still have left in working order, and *then,* and only then, strike back.

There are several strategic considerations behind what sounds like very odd behavior. First, we have confidence that our silos, for now at least, are sufficiently "hardened" so that the Soviets could not confidently expect to knock enough of them out to cripple our ability to retaliate. Second, confidence in our ability to ride out an initial attack allows us the luxury of not having to fire off our missiles merely on the basis of a radar warning that our silos are under attack; which means that we are less likely to be put in the "use it or lose it" dilemma, as the strategists call it, and precipitously launch our missile force on the basis of perhaps mistaken warnings or small accidental Soviet launches. Finally, declaring that we'll keep our missiles in their silos during a first strike against us almost compels the Soviets to target on them rather than on our large cities. They are bait of a sort.

Between the lines of that footnote there was an explicit message for Soviet nuclear strategists: a warning to them that if they attempted to develop a silo-busting missile capability—warheads accurate and powerful enough to destroy our Minutemen *inside* their hardened silos—they'd be making a big mistake and wasting billions of dollars. Because if they did develop that capacity we could simply renounce our "ride out" policy and shift to a "launch on warning" stance. This would make them look silly because under that posture, at the first sign of attack our missiles would let fly and the billions of dollars the Soviets had spent on a silo-busting capacity would be wasted busting empty silos.

Of course there are grave dangers to a launch-on-warning policy. Critics call it a "hair trigger" posture. And indeed if the Soviets thought we had shifted to it, they would, in the event of an accidental launch on their part, feel compelled to launch the rest of their arsenal because they'd know our hair trigger would be sending ours their way before we'd have time to verify whether it was an accident.

When the footnote set off a controversy over a possible U.S. "hair trigger" stance, and the footnote was dropped and then restored again, the State Department blandly denied there had been any change in U.S. policy. And officially there had not been. But Kissinger was playing what his former aide, Morton Halperin, calls the game of "the clever briefer." The footnote was designed to frustrate the ambitions of a hypothetical wily Kremlin advocate making a brief for a silo-busting capacity. "You want us to spend billions for this," a Soviet leader would reply to "the clever briefer." "But Kissinger has declared they will go to launch-on-warning if we do it and we will have gained nothing for our billions. What do you say to that?"

There is no good answer. Even though the footnote was deleted and the veiled warning shrouded in ambiguity, raising the possibility should be enough to defeat the arguments of "the clever briefer." That doesn't mean that the feint worked, that we won the War of Kissinger's Footnote. Indeed some military critics argue that Kissinger's subtle Machiavellianism was no match for the Soviets' mushrooming megatonnage. But that, in any event, gives you an idea how the game is played.

By this time, several months after my return from the nuclear shrines, several months of immersion in the literature of nuclear strategy, pursuing the paradoxes of esoteric and declaratory strategy ostensibly to write about the state of the art, I realized something was happening to me. I was becoming obsessed by the art, hooked again as I was as an adolescent by the piquant intellectual seductiveness of nuclear strategy. Finally, last August, I felt compelled to make a second pilgrimage. I was looking for some way to escape from the accumulation of nuclear esoterica I had submerged myself in and all of which seemed to be insulating me further from rather than bringing me more "in touch" with nuclear war, whatever that meant—I was sure I would know it if I felt it.

So I flew up to Boston on Hiroshima Day 1977. A small item in Boston's *Real Paper* had attracted my attention: Someone was actually going to hold an old-fashioned ban-the-bomb-type demonstration up there to commemorate the victims of the Hiroshima and Nagasaki bombings. I'm not talking about one of those anti–nuclear-power demonstrations. These have become very fashionable of late after the organizational success of the Clamshell Alliance's mass civil disobedience on the site of the proposed Seabrook nuclear reactor. There's no shortage of anti–nuclear-power demonstrations.

But a demonstration against nuclear weapons. How odd. As a sometime chronicler of the antiwar demonstrations of the late sixties and early seventies I knew that the only people who still did that were the small and aging band of the pacifist faithful, the War Resisters League, and other, smaller, old-fashioned peace groups; and I couldn't recall the last time I'd heard of them doing anything. This demonstration, part of a series of Hiroshima Day actions, seemed to have been engendered by many of the old peace-movement people hoping to rebuild the kind of mass movement that had disappeared after the test-ban treaty was approved. Apparently this was causing some ruffled feathers among the anti–nuclear-power partisans. According to a friend of mine in Boston, the Clamshell Alliance had refused to give its support to the Hiroshima Day demonstration because "some of them think it's just these old peace-movement people trying to take advantage of the energy the Clamshell people have established. The Clamshell people believe it's important to organize a base in the community rather than just to demonstrate." This snooty attitude confirmed a theory I'd had that the anti–nuclear-power movement was a way for activists to sublimate their feelings of impotence in the face of the massive nuclear-weapons establishment. You can prevent a reactor from being built, you can even shut it down if it's unsafe, but the nuclear warheads are already there, they are extremely unsafe, but no one believes they'll ever go away.

I remember how far gone into the swamp of strategic thinking I was by the time I arrived at Faneuil Hall for the opening speeches of the Hiroshima-Nagasaki ban-the-bomb demo-commemoration. I can remember because my first few pages of notes on that event are devoted to a four-line joke I found written on a wall of the men's room at Faneuil Hall and an analysis of the way that particular joke illuminated the dilemma of "just-war" theologians who employ the principle of "double effect" (developed in the thirteenth century to justify the use of the catapult as a siege weapon) to justify the "unintentional" slaughter of innocents contemplated by certain nuclear retaliatory strategies.

The joke on the men's-room wall was unusual only in that it was not really dirty, just mildly "sick."

"How did you get that flat tire?" it began.

"I ran over a milk bottle."

"Didn't you see it?"

"No, the damn kid was carrying it under his coat."

Get it? Now let me explain what this has to do with nuclear war. The late fifties and early sixties were full of heady debate for theologians with almost everyone wrestling with the problem of whether conduct of thermonuclear war could, or should, be guided by the same moral principles that were used to define a "just war" or whether thermonuclear war must be considered beyond the bounds of anything justifiable under any circumstances. Even thornier was the question of whether possession of nuclear weapons for deterrent purposes without use, but with the threat of potential use, could be moral if use was immoral. And were some kinds of use, some kinds of threatened use, better than other kinds of threats? No one wrestled more heroically with these problems than Protestant theologian Paul Ramsey. No one tried more strenuously to demonstrate that the application of complex Judeo-Christian moral principles to the most esoteric elements of nuclear strategy was a possible, indeed important, enterprise. Differing with Christian pacifists and "international realists," both of which schools insisted that no moral distinctions could apply to such an essentially immoral or amoral (respectively) enterprise, Ramsey plunged into the thicket of targeting strategy. For my money his finest or most ridiculous hour is his attempt to synthesize an acceptably Christian deterrent posture: He calls for a declared policy of massive countercity retaliation that will really be a bluff.

Here the milk-bottle joke is instructive. According to Ramsey's just-war reasoning (and assuming the milk bottle is some deadly weapon), it is okay to run over the boy as long as you *intend* to run over only the milk bottle. Or to apply it now to nuclear targeting, it is okay to respond to a nuclear strike by hitting an enemy's military targets (counterforce targeting) and killing tens of millions of people who happen to live within radiation range—it is okay so long as you *intend* to knock out only the military installations and the killing of innocent civilians is "unintentional" collateral damage resulting from the "double effect" of an ICBM on both combatant and noncombatant elements of the population.

This rationalization was developed to justify the use of the catapult as a siege weapon since it was impossible to see over the besieged walls to make sure the catapulted projectile hit only the combatants within a city. Ramsey also endorses a modified "bluff of deterrence" position: He believes that an *efficacious* deterrent threat requires that we declare we will wreak retaliation on cities, but that when the moment for retaliation comes we should adhere to counterforce military targeting or none at all. Ramsey's efforts are a heroic act of rational apologetics, but one can't help but wonder if they don't serve to legitimize all forms of nuclear response since only a few scholastic quibbles seem to separate the sanctified from the unsanctified bomb blast.

I have been staring at blast wounds and radiation burns on and off for two days. The organizers of the three-day demonstration had assembled every major Hiroshima documentary film and they were running them over and over in various church basements around Boston. In addition, there was a round-the-clock three-day standing vigil in memory of the victims of Hiroshima and Nagasaki. At first, rather than standing in public I preferred to sit in anonymity and watch the wound films. I felt that after all the intellectualizing over the metaphysics of deterrence theory I might have lost a sense of compassion and that a good dose of Hiroshima horrors might bring me back to my humanity.

I was wrong. Too many pictures of wounds end up blurring the distinctions between the agony left behind by *any* war and the potential for utter annihilation to be feared from the next one. After all, the missile crewmen told me they had been shown graphic films of Hiroshima before being asked if they'd be willing to twist those keys. And still they'd said yes.

At last, driven by shame, perhaps at my lack of response to the wound watch, I headed for the plaza outside Faneuil Hall, where I resolved to spend the hours until dawn standing silently in the memorial vigil for victims of Hiroshima and Nagasaki. The vigil—a semicircle of people standing still around a mushroom-shaped memorial—had been going on round the clock since the anniversary hour of the Hiroshima bombing, and would continue until eleven the next morning, the time the bomb hit Nagasaki. I had actually resolved to stay up all night in the vigil on each of the previous two nights, but it was raining one night and there were some friends to see the second night and I never quite made it out onto the plaza. But this time I was determined to make it nonstop through to the dawn, hoping to do some quiet thinking about the whole matter. Instead of running around looking for another esoteric document, another trigger icon to touch, another fantasy to explore, I needed to stand still and think for a while.

The sociable sounds of a late-night singles-bar complex and the aromas of an all-night flower market wafted over to that part of the plaza where memories of mass death were being memorialized in defiance of the summer merriment. The semicircle around the mushroom-cloud memorial was manned mainly by members of the old peace-movement crowd sprinkled with some young Boston Brahmin pacifist types. On a nearby bench, apparently keeping an intermittent vigil on the vigil, were two shopping-bag ladies. They spent most of their time endeavoring to fix the mechanism of a rusty, skeletal umbrella someone must have discarded many rains ago. There was a rambling discussion in some obscure mode of communication in which I could make out references to cancer of the thyroid, which one or both of them thought she was getting. About two or three A.M., a wino tried to challenge the silent vigilants to argument on nuclear strategy but he tired of the lack of response. The singles bar closed up and until dawn there was little but silence to disturb the thinking I wanted to do.

For the first three hours I tried my best to think about the victims of Hiroshima and Nagasaki, but I was thinking mainly about my feet. Should I shift my weight from the right to the left and back again, or divide it between the soles of both? Which strategy was more likely to get me through the morning with the least discomfort? (Ever since high-school days working in a supermarket job I've had trouble standing up for prolonged periods. I have high arches, you see, and . . .)

God, how inhumane, you must be thinking to yourself. This guy is at a memorial for 180,000 people blasted and burned and he's talking about his high arches. In my defense I would say I was aware of the absurdity of it—the emblematic absurdity, at least. By spending an inordinate amount of time thinking about my physical stance I was avoiding what I felt was my duty in this story, in life, to find a comfortable stance, *the* correct strategic stance, or at least a moral position, on the subtleties and the stark crudities of nuclear war.

As I shifted about for a stance I recalled my final phone conversation with Major Hering. It had taken me some time to track him down. He's an ex-major now and he and his family have had to shift location more than once as he looks for the right position, readjusts to the civilian job market. In the meantime he'd been doing some long-haul trucking in order to make ends meet.

At first the Air Force had tried to disqualify him for missile-crewman service under the provisions of the human-reliability regulation: Because he wanted to be reassured a launch he executed was constitutional, he was, they tried to say, unreliable. When that failed, the Air Force removed him from missile-crewman service and tried to transfer him to other duties. The major appealed that decision all the way up to the Secretary of the Air Force, lost, and then took an early retirement. He really had *wanted* to be a missile crewman and he fought his appeal fiercely with copious research into command-and-control problems to support his thesis. He told me he had a number of filing cabinets filled with documents that supported his position and revealed new unanswered questions, and he felt I should read through the files and the transcript of his hearings and appeals before I spoke to him. "It'll take you about a week or more of reading," the ex-major told me. I'd have to wait until after his next truck run, and after his new job was resolved. Then he'd be prepared to get back into it with me. "This whole thing has taken a lot out of me, as you can imagine, so I'd want to know you're serious before getting back into it all again," he said. The next time I called his number he'd moved to another city and I decided to pass up the filing cabinets.

I had a feeling that Major Hering's question had cost him a lot, cost him a comfortable couple of years down in the cozy launch-control capsules, years in which as it turned out he never would have had to face the constitutional command question his stringent conscience compelled him to ask. Cost him a promising military career and a couple of years of his life trying to extract from fragmentary unclassified sources what were the contingency plans for constitutional succession problems at the top of the chain of command and control. Finding himself alone among all missile crewmen in thinking independently on such questions must have been a burden.

Should We Call Our Own Bluff?

Kecskemeti, Ramsey, all those who try to think about nuclear war as more than the three-dimensional chess of the strategists suffer for their efforts.

There are two kinds of "unthinkables" in the thinking on this subject. There is the fashionable "unthinkable" of Kahn and company (how many million casualties are "acceptable" in a nuclear war: twenty? forty?), which in fact was never unthinkable at all to the Defense Department and defense contractors who funded this self-proclaimed daring intellectual adventure. And then there are unfashionable unthinkable questions. Major Hering's question. Unilateral disarmament. Remember that? While Herman Kahn's unthinkables have bankrolled him into a comfortable existence giving posh seminars on the shape of centuries to come, a man like David McReynolds, the War Resisters League organizer who helped lead the big ban-the-bomb demonstrations in the sixties, sits in a drafty old room near the Bowery and speaks to an audience of five. He's raising again the question of unilateral disarmament at an anarchist-sponsored "Freespace University." In addition to the moderator and me, there are two men off the Bowery with shopping bags who seem mainly interested in getting out of the rain. There's an unreconstructed Stalinist who keeps changing the subject to a long-winded defense of the legitimacy of Soviet intervention in Czechoslovakia (counterrevolutionary provocation, he says) and an ex-Marine who begins all his questions with long quotations from Marcus Aurelius.

Despite it all, McReynolds delivers a brilliant polemical analysis of deterrence theory, in which he argues that unilateral disarmament is the only moral alternative to the mass murder for vengeance our declared retaliatory policy calls for. Despite Air Force Regulation 35-99, McReynolds may be the sanest man in America on this subject, yet he has me and a Marcus Aurelius freak to listen to him, if you don't count the shopping-bag men.

Speaking of shopping-bag people, it's getting close to dawn now at this vigil we've drifted away from. I've drifted into a trance after settling into a more or less comfortable stance, but the shopping-bag women bring me out of it with a vociferous discussion of the skeletal umbrella and more talk of thyroid cancer. I recall a groggy illumination at this point: Here, before me, was a perfect emblem of what I'd been trying to think about. The shopping-bag ladies were not unlike sophisticated nuclear strategists, arguing in their peculiar language over the operation of that rickety contraption of an umbrella which, like the contrivance of deterrence theory, provides only symbolic protection for the two powers who seek shelter beneath its empty framework. It also struck me that these women had been talking about cancer of the thyroid as they watched the vigil. An increased incidence of thyroid cancer was a much-feared consequence of strontium 90 in the fallout-scare days of the late fifties and early sixties. They were still *thinking* about it, these two women. Maybe, unlike the rest of us, they never stopped thinking about it. Maybe that's what drove them to the streets and shopping bags. Maybe they were among the unfortunate few who have not been afflicted by that mass repression we've used to submerge nuclear arousal in our consciousness. Who else do you know who talks about it?

Well, I figured it all out after dawn. My stance.

The illumination I finally received that morning came in the notion of a simple modest proposal. Open up the SIOP. The most frustrating barrier to intelligent thinking about the strategic and moral consequences of our nuclear policy is our continued preoccupation with esoteric strategy—with bluff, ambiguity, and mirror-image metaphysics.

Every targeting strategy, every targeting option the SIOP machine presents to the National Command Authority, represents a profound moral choice. An eye for an eye. Or two eyes. Two cities or one. Total vindictive retribution. Symbolic response or none at all. It's impossible to calculate the moral consequences we as individuals bear for such choices made in our name if the actual content of the choice is hidden behind the sleight of hand of esoteric strategy.

Should we resign ourselves and allow the SIOP machine and its think-tank tenders to make perhaps the most important decisions ever made, to churn out "optimum outcomes" according to definitions of "optimum" values that remain hermetically sealed in its program? We have no way to engage the machine or those who program it in debate over those values or the options they generate. If we were to move toward an openly determined SIOP, we would have to reveal our bluffs, lay our cards on the table. Games of bluff are inevitably incompatible with democratic decision making since an electorate can't vote to bluff by policy without, of course, betraying any possible success to an adversary.

Well, let them know. Let us know. Let us no longer be insulated from the master target list, from the master targeting strategy, from the moral options.

We are all missile crewmen—all of us who pay taxes pay for the twin brass keys, even if we won't twist them ourselves when the time comes. But in one way or another we all have our finger on the trigger, and it's about time we knew where we're aiming, who's really giving the orders to fire, and whether we ought to obey.

Postscript to "The Subterranean World of the Bomb"

One might have thought that the collapse of the Soviet Union would have made moot many of the difficult arguments over the theory, the ethics, the theology of the nuclear-targeting strategies explored in "The Subterranean World of the Bomb." But I was surprised to see a candid admission of second thoughts—of retrospective torment and uncertainty—over the ethics of Mutually Assured Destruction by none other than Peregrine Worsthorne, who in the eighties was one of the most vocal supporters of the Reagan–Thatcher better-dead-than-Red nuclear war–fighting stance. In a remarkable 1996 essay in *The Spectator* (U.K.), Mr. Worsthorne conceded that there was a theological dimension to these questions; he admitted theological doubt about a strategy that could have exterminated all humanity, the innocent and the guilty alike.

What troubled Worsthorne was the unspoken implication of the mutual bluffing game at the heart of the Mutually Assured Destruction doctrine. It was a doctrine that may well have succeeded in preventing nuclear war, and in preventing major conventional wars as well. But it was a doctrine founded upon a pledge to commit unprecedented acts of mass murder to bolster its credibility—massive retaliation with planet-killing quantities of strategic nuclear strikes in response to any Soviet use of tactical nuclear weapons in Central Europe, for instance. Worsthorne wondered aloud in *The Spectator* whether that pledge (which he assured readers from personal knowledge of Reagan and Thatcher and the men with their fingers on the nuclear triggers in the eighties was *not* a metaphysical bluff but a serious, iron-willed determination) was fundamentally immoral. The doctrine succeeded, it helped defeat an Evil Empire, he knows that, but he can't help feeling uneasy about the kind of threat that secured that success. A success that seems precarious and lucky

when the slightest slip might have implicated its principals in vaster slaughters of the innocent than either Hitler or Stalin had perpetrated in their two benighted lifetimes, however "well-intentioned" the doctrine behind nuclear slaughter might have been.

The question cannot be answered in retrospect, but that the question should still be asked, by a proponent of the doctrine, suggests to me that the questions I raised in "The Subterranean World of the Bomb" were not idle ones—although the practical questions I raised, such as the fate of "surrender studies" and the revelation of a spoon-and-string flaw in the launch-control system, may have had more lasting consequences.

Of a Fire at the Billy Rose

In Which Peter Brook's *Dream* (Literally) Ignites on Stage

Fire broke out backstage at the Billy Rose Theatre at about ten P.M. Saturday, January 23, at just that moment in *A Midsummer Night's Dream* when the time schemes of the people of the play and of the people in the audience begin to approach erotic synchronicity.

The fire broke out at the beginning of the play's final scene, after the three Athenian couples, who have just wed but have not yet consummated their marriages, enter and seat themselves on cushions to become, themselves, an audience for one final diversion before retiring to bridal chambers in the palace.

> *Come what masques what dances shall we have*
> *To wear away this long age of three hours*
> *Between our after supper and bedtime*
> *What revels are in hand? Is there no play*
> *To ease the anguish of a torturing hour?*

Theseus demands.

It's nice to assume, heuristically, that *A Midsummer Night's Dream* was an epithalamium first written for an audience of perhaps three high-born Elizabethan newlyweds and first performed on the evening of their wedding day shortly before their first bedtime together. Then this primal, most fortunate of all audiences for the *Dream* will have been watching the play for almost three hours when the final scene begins. The remaining thirty minutes of those three hours the Elizabethan newlyweds spend watching Shakespeare's play fuse with the thirty-minute "long age of three hours" the Athenians on stage spend watching Peter Quince's *Pyramus and Thisbe* play. Both audiences of newlyweds pass the waning of that last pale crescent of a play locked together in the same erotic time scheme. For the couples in both audiences, Elizabethan and Athenian, the completion of the final act of Peter Quince's play will signal the beginning of a first act of their own.

So there is, unfortunately, always a subtle sense of loss to be expected watching this last act of *A Midsummer Night's Dream,* if the performance you watch is not an epithalamium for you, if your bedchamber is not another room of the palace. At that first performance the play was offered in the tentative spirit of a wedding gift—I know it's not much but it's the best I can do—and offered in turn the excitement of revealing how good it was to its own players for the first time. Since then in most performances the tentativeness of a first night, of a gift, has been lost; players and audience know almost too well how perfectly even Peter Quince's imperfect play works.

By feeling these losses, by feeling a detachment from a most favored, primal audience, you are, as a kind of compensation, able to see the play through one more delicate proscenium of focal distance—there is a new aesthetic delight in seeing how nicely and intricately the play works when considered as a formal epithalamium. The last act becomes less an erotic piece of time and more a finely jeweled timepiece.

Peter Brook has the Athenian newlyweds enter for this final scene carrying candles and sparklers that flare and flicker, amorously consuming themselves as the couples languish on their cushions awaiting the play.

"Call Philostrate," says Theseus on stage.

"Fire," says a man in the audience.

The word is spoken tentatively—it is less a cry than a rather startled observation. In fact before his voice rises very high, the last phoneme of "Fire" is muffled in a kind of shocked silence, almost sucked back in with the sudden breath everyone has taken—as if recognizing how indecent it was to cry "Fire" in a crowded theater even if the theater *is* on fire. One wonders how Justice Holmes would have handled himself in a case of this sort.

"Say what abridgment have you for this evening?" Theseus demands grandly of Philostrate, master of the revels.

"*Fire!*" insists another voice from the audience. No reservation this time: The man's voice cracks with panic in the middle of the word.

A big clump of a dozen people down in the right front of the orchestra suddenly rise to their feet, and cries of "Fire" rise around them until, like Hercules's Spartan hounds earlier in the play, they "seemed all one mutual cry."

As people up front rise and push toward the aisle they point, some of them, up, high up, toward the rear of stage right, where the rest of us see for the first time thick pale-gray smoke rising above the tall flats.

Back in row M the smoke doesn't seem particularly threatening yet, perhaps just a theatrical effect. In fact so deeply are we into play-watching by that time that the smoke makes for more pleasant watching rather than alarm, as clouds of it, barred with the glow of spotlights, drift up through the shadowy spaces above and behind the gleaming white playing area.

Theseus, giving no hint he has noticed the uprising in the audience in front of him or the smoke rising behind him, continues to demand copiously of Philostrate:

> *What masque? What music?*
> *How shall we beguile*
> *The lazy time if not with some delight?*

The smoke thickens and rolls up more rapidly. By now the entire population of the orchestra seats up front is rising up and bundling itself into the aisles. A few of the first refugees battling up the aisle pass the stoics in row M, looking slightly guilty about their agitation and haste, composing their faces as if to say, "Of course, it's not the *fire,* but we *do* have another engagement and we just must be off."

Just as the first push for the exits begins to break into a full rush, an amazing Voice floats up above the confusion in the orchestra and stops everyone dead in their tracks. The voice, a woman's, a grande dame's, just radiates, blankets the place in fact, with her presence and authority, a fusion perhaps of Bella Abzug and Florence Nightingale.

"Everyone. Sit. Down," the voice commands. Hands outstretched grandly she motions them all to be seated.

"Sit. Down. Don't. Run. Just. Sit. Down."

People standing in front of their seats, poised for flight a moment ago, begin shuffling around as if to show her they are looking around for their seats. My companion informs me that we have just heard the voice of *the* cosmic Girl Scout Leader.

Back in row M no one wants to get up anyway. We sit rapt in a sweet reluctance to stir awake from a particularly delightful dream. Many of those up front, closer to the fire, take their seats now, reassured perhaps that this fire business may still turn out to be some big special effect Peter Brook has dreamed up, some trendy bit of audience participation, no doubt.

Theseus and Philostrate meanwhile have been continuing their dialogue, under heavy fire. Some of the other players on stage, who see the smoke, seem to be having difficulty maintaining their air of nuptial jollity. And Theseus does seem to rush his next line as if to hurry the laugh it guarantees and bring the audience back to the comedy at hand that much sooner:

> *"The battle with the Centaurs, to be sung*
> *By an Athenian eunuch to the harp."*
> *We'll none of that.*

He gets a very good laugh, but in midair the laugh turns itself into a gasp as flames break into sight for the first time and things appear really out of hand.

All over the theater people are panicking and choking the aisles. Even back in contemplative row M the flames look bad. There is an icy adrenaline rush, and since this is my first theater fire I flash on fantasies of the Cocoanut Grove and fighting to the death for exits.

Theseus is finally forced to stop pretending that nothing unusual is going on. Breaking off just about as he is saying " 'The riot of the tipsy Baccha- nals,' " and barely glancing over his shoulder to take in the fire, he steps toward us and tells us, "Don't panic. Just stay where you are. There's no need to panic."

Everyone continues to panic.

Just then Philostrate—he is John Kane, who is also Puck—steps forward to the edge of the stage. Dressed in a ballooning black silk jumpsuit and a tall tasseled fez, he leans forward in just that attitude Puck has assumed earlier in the play when he is about to offer a delicious aside, a puckish confidence, a confidential wink. "Now everyone, please stay where you are. *I'm* going to go backstage and *I'm* going to see just what's going on." He turns as if to go, then, as if anticipating our thoughts, turns back to us again, raises a cautioning finger, and reassures us, "I'll be right back. Don't go away." He disappears be- hind stage. A breathtaking performance. It is London in the blitz. Mr. Chips. There'll always be an England. Her Majesty expects . . .

It was also quite like Puck: A little mishap like this is nothing Robin can't make amends for ere long, hasn't he just finished making amends for "this night's accidents"—even the ones he's caused—in the nightmarish woods?

And ten seconds later he is back to give us this reassuring news: *"Just* as I thought. Nothing to worry about. The sprinkler system's already turned on and working at it. They're all hard at work at it back there. All is well."

A great cheer arises for the plucky sprinkler system, for all of them back there so hard at work at it, and for Puck. Never have so many . . .

With a barely raised eyebrow and a deferential flourish Puck steps gracefully back into Philostrate's place and leans over to Theseus, asking mildly, "You were saying, my lord . . . ?"

Just like that. Just like that he has upstaged the fire and has us watching the play again. Smoke and now steam (the work of the sprinkler system, no doubt) still pile up over the flats, but the audience is shuffling back to their seats. Just like that he has slipped us all back into the fabric of the play and knit the loose ends together. Who was that masqued man?

Taking his cue from Puck/Philostrate, Theseus takes up the play again. He takes it up again, not where he left off but back at the very line that was interrupted by the first cry of "Fire." Perhaps also as a kind of tribute he begins again by summoning up Philostrate/Puck:

> *Is there no play*
> *To ease the anguish of a torturing hour?*
> *Call Philostrate.*

Philostrate steps forward with rather elaborate humility and gets another delighted cheer.

"Here, *mighty Theseus,*" he enunciates carefully through a widening puckish grin. It's hard to explain how perfectly funny this line was at that particular time. It will never work so well again. It had something to do with the way Philostrate rolled his eyes from mighty Theseus out to us in the audience. Puck treated us to just that same fallen-angel look when Oberon accused him of responsibility for the tangled strife of accidents and lovers in the woods, and Puck could barely conceal his delight at how amusingly things turned out.

"Say what abridgment you have for this evening," Theseus demands of Philostrate, lingering ruefully over "abridgment," and grinning warily at Philostrate/Puck as if implying his complicity in the late unexpected abridgment.

Philostrate is grinning so puckishly at the way things have turned out, he seems half-ready to take credit for staging the fire. The drama of the fire has quickened fresh delights in every line of this second-time-around dialogue, and both players and audience are reveling together in the new pleasures.

Theseus and Philostrate turn their dialogue into an elegant comedy within the Comedy. Each perfect exchange and re-exchange of glances between a mock-heroic Philostrate/Puck and a seemingly bewildered Theseus/Oberon offered new images of the paradox of the Player—responsible for everything and for nothing on stage; at times self-effacing in his humility as mere player, at times overreaching in his pretension to be play maker; shadow and moonlight; Bottom the Weaver and Puck the mender, contraries waxing and waning together within one circumference.

The fire has been forgotten, but steam and flakes of black ash are now drifting up from backstage and showering down from the rafters on players and audience, setting them coughing and wiping their eyes.

Theseus, beleaguered again, this time just a few lines after he has passed his earlier forced stopping place, fortunately has a lovely coincidence of a line to deliver in the middle of the steam and soot shower:

> *That is hot ice and wondrous strange snow.*
> *How shall we find the concord of this discord?*

"A play there is my lord," replies Philostrate, describing the paradoxical play about to be presented by Peter Quince,

> *Which when I saw rehearsed, I must confess,*
> *Made mine eyes water; but more merry tears*
> *The passion of loud laughter never shed.*

Things are beginning to turn out almost too cleverly now. Since the fire, the lines of the play have been proving so resilient and responsive they seem to be able to comment upon their own interruption from without and even on the audience's reaction to it all. The play seems to be able to find the concord of its sudden discord in its own lines. The best comedies can laugh at themselves in more ways than one.

The fire produced no other self-fulfilling prophecies as explicit as those, but there was nothing in the remainder of the play, no line, no performance, that was not touched and illuminated by it. The fire revealed how much *A Midsummer Night's Dream* is a play about the vulnerability of play making to accident and collapse, about the dependence of the play maker upon an imagination more comprehensive than his own—the audience's, for instance—to save him from himself, to make amends for his offenses, and transform his foolish near-tragedies into comedies.

By revealing play maker and players to be so vulnerable to mishap, by picturing himself as a hapless Peter Quince (or perhaps as Bottom, would-be player of all roles), Shakespeare offers his audience the chance to exercise compassion and forgiveness for some "palpable gross" failures and to rise thereby above themselves to a godlike dignity. The playwright offers to look foolish, to seem to make an ass of himself, to fail so that we may better succeed at forgiving. As Theseus does in those lovely lines defending Peter Quince and his players: "The best in this kind are but shadows."

The only trouble with Peter Quince's play is that it fails almost too cleverly and too profoundly and almost succeeds in comprehending the larger play surrounding it.

But the fire broke up the jewellike precision of carefully staged mishaps and amends, and offered the players and audience a chance to discover each other by surprise outside the carefully artificed images of themselves within the play, and to re-enter the artifice with renewed delight. The fire returned to the play the tentativeness and excitement of a genuine epithalamium. A new, more immediate, no less erotic synchronicity of mood, special to that night's performance and that night's audience, could be felt in the theater, palpable in its sweetness.

As the theater emptied out a half hour later and we began to drift away, fire sirens suddenly blasted through the air. Two huge hook and ladder trucks, sirens in mutual cry, swung over to Forty-first Street from Broadway and slammed on their brakes in front of the theater. Firemen jumped down, grabbed axes, unrolled hoses, and rushed into the theater. No one minded their appearing thirty minutes too late, and no one objected to their taking the fire so literally. Things had worked out so nicely in the past thirty minutes that we needed some assurance that "this night's accident" had been a real fire, neither staged nor dreamed.

Postscript to "Of a Fire at the Billy Rose"

The events herein took place in January 1971, four months after I'd first seen Peter Brook's Royal Shakespeare Company production of *A Midsummer Night's Dream* at Stratford-on-Avon. That first time changed my life in the sense that it made me into a lifelong student/devotee of Shakespeare, someone forever seeking, rarely finding, a theater experience as electrifying as that. I'm not alone in describing the production as life changing. Both Trevor Nunn and Nicholas Hytner, who succeeded Brook as acclaimed RSC directors, told me that it changed their lives and, according to Hytner, those of his whole generation of Shakespearean actors and directors. The Brook *Dream* is often misunderstood or mischaracterized for its outward shows, the trapezes, jugglers, et cetera, when what made it so extraordinary was not what was new but what was radically *old*—a command of the language by the actors so complete that the words seemed to spring from them with the same fresh-minted clarity one imagines they had when the play was first performed.

Alas, I'd only been writing for a little more than a year when I witnessed this, and my own command of the language doesn't do justice to this incandescent moment when the *Dream* ignited, something almost beyond words anyway. Still, I think it merits preserving as the only first-person account of a remarkable moment in a historic production. And witnessing it may explain the difficulty I have appreciating, even tolerating, so much contemporary theater, a difficulty I describe later on in "My Theater Problem—and Ours."

Dead Ringers

In Which We Attempt to Disentangle the Strange Lives and
Deaths of the Marcus Brothers, Twin Gynecologists*

It was the striped shorts that caused the mixup at the morgue. When the cops
and the maintenance man broke into apartment 10H, slogged their way
through the debris covering the living-room floor and found the bodies in the
bedroom, they found themselves with an identity problem as well. The maintenance man was certain the bodies in question were gynecologist Cyril Marcus—the tenant of 10H—and his twin brother, gynecologist Stewart Marcus,
but he wasn't certain which body belonged to which twin.

Visibility was not favorable to making any kind of identification. The warm
moist July air that rushed into the apartment with the cops hit the bone-dry
chill within, precipitating a mist that rolled across the living-room floor into
the bedroom, picking up fumes from rotting chicken salad sandwiches and
human excrement on the way, fogging up the death scene with its sickly vapors.

Not the sort of atmosphere to encourage leisurely speculation about the
identity of twins, not that they looked at all identical in death. One twin lay

*Coauthor: Susan Edmiston.

facedown across the head of one of the twin beds, the other faceup on the floor at the foot of the other twin bed. The face of the face-up twin retained the frozen clarity of recent death. The other twin had no face. Dead longer, his features had been blotted out by decomposition. The face-up twin on the floor wore nothing but a pair of long black socks bunched down around his ankles and a flimsy shroud of paper toweling he had apparently pulled across his body in the moments before death. The face-down twin had only a black sock dangling from his left foot and a pair of blue striped shorts on his body.

The maintenance man thought those striped shorts might be a clue; he thought he had seen them once before. Some time ago he had been doing some minor repair work in this apartment and he recalled Dr. Cyril Marcus walking around in shorts much like the ones on the body facedown on the bed.

That's what he told the cops, and that's what the cops told the man from the morgue wagon who arrived later to bundle up the bodies and take them away for autopsy. The man from the morgue wagon wrote CYRIL MARCUS on the red ID tags he attached to the toe and wrist of the twin on the bed and STEWART MARCUS on the tags he put on the other.

It was the other way round. Stewart had either been wearing his brother Cyril's striped shorts when he died or a similarly striped pair of his own. In any case, when the two bodies were finally wheeled into the basement receiving room of the morgue, the clerk there assigned the body tagged CYRIL to body locker No. 109 and the one tagged STEWART to locker No. 33.

That night at the morgue, when the ex-wife of Cyril Marcus could not identify the faceless body from locker No. 109—the one tagged CYRIL—the medical examiners suspected a mixup. They summoned a forensic odontologist, a specialist in making identifications from dental charts, to examine X rays of the twins' teeth. When he finally declared that CYRIL was Stewart and STEWART was Cyril, someone went back and corrected the body-locker registration cards, switching the numbers rather than the names.

By this time it was too late. The story had hit the papers on Thursday, July 17. The New York *Daily News* gave it the full front-page-headline treatment reserved for spectacular deaths in luxury buildings: FIND TWIN DOCS DEAD IN POSH PAD. The *Times,* more reticent at first, subsequently moved the twins story up to the front page when the issue of the regulatory practices of the medical profession grew out of the deaths. Most of the original stories had one thing in common: Dependent as the reporters were on police and morgue sources, they had Cyril on the bed in shorts and Stewart on the floor in socks. In death as in life, the Marcus twins had left confusion over identity in their wake. Confusion and mystery: In the waning weeks of that summer, it seemed that every citizen of New York City who had ever been to a gynecologist, every person who had ever known a twin or twins, and many who had done neither, had a theory or two about the Marcus twins and how they died.

．．．

They called themselves infertility specialists, but in the eyes of many of their grateful patients they were nothing less than fertility gods. The God of Genesis, one recalls, was a busy gynecologist and fertility specialist. The wives of Abraham, of Isaac, and of Jacob all suffered from barrenness until God intervened and caused them to conceive. Bringing fertility out of barrenness is, in fact, a distinguishing metaphor of the Old Testament: The fertility of the promised land is only for those who obey the commandments delivered in the barren desert. In almost all cultures, anyone who has the touch, the divine inspiration, or whatever it takes to induce conception, is regarded as a holy man. The Marcus brothers were secularized heirs of this tradition, pioneers in the use of a whole repertoire of medical techniques—hormones, surgery, fertility drugs—to accomplish the magic that shamans had performed in the past.

"They were like gods," said one woman who had gone to several gynecologists and endured years of hopelessness before treatment by the Marcus brothers helped her conceive and give birth to her first child. "They were miracle workers," said another woman. "It was like magic," said a third.

Women from all over the East made pilgrimages to the Marcuses' office and to the Gynecological Infertility Clinic they presided over at New York Hospital. Women who had been to gynecologist after gynecologist, taken test after test, drug after drug and had yet to conceive. Women who were approaching or passing forty and desperately wanted a child before it was too late. Women who were able to conceive, but who had suffered miscarriage after miscarriage, hoping to deliver just one healthy child. "A lot of the women in that office were last-chance Charlies," said one patient, who eventually gave birth to two healthy children under the supervision of the Marcus brothers.

There are, in fact, hundreds of healthy children all over the country who wouldn't exist today had it not been for the Marcus brothers—children named Stewart and Cyril, even Marc, by grateful parents. Some women are so grateful they speak as if, in some ghostly way, the twins had actually fathered their children. "I had my first baby by Cyril," they'll say, or, "Stewart finally got me pregnant. He did everything but plant the seed."

The homicide cops ruled out murder almost immediately. The door to the death-scene apartment was double-locked from the inside, which meant either that one of the dead twins within murdered the other and took his own life, or—more likely, since there were no signs of violence on either body—both took their own lives in one way or another.

At first the way seemed obvious. The man from the morgue found a number of yellow Nembutal (a common barbiturate sleeping pill) capsules scattered on the floor around the bodies. The homicide cops found a number of empty vials labeled Demerol throughout the sea of rubbish elsewhere in the apartment. The maintenance man discovered dozens more empty Nembutal bottles in a kitchen cabinet.

Then an odd development. The toxicologist in the medical examiner's office reported that *no* Demerol and *no* barbiturates had been found in either body. The findings seemed to rule out suicide by any well-known drug.

"I don't mind telling you we have a major medical mystery on our hands," said acting Chief Medical Examiner Dominick DiMaio. "We've exhausted all the regular possibilities and now we're going for rare things—exotic is the word, I guess."

One week later, when all tests for exotic killer drugs turned out negative, too, the medical examiner's office proposed an exotic theory instead: The twins didn't die from drugs, they died from lack of drugs; they were both chronic barbiturate addicts who died from the convulsions and seizures accompanying "acute pentobarbital withdrawal." This explanation didn't satisfy many people. It assumed the twins went into simultaneous comas from heavy barbiturate *use;* stayed in the comas long enough to metabolize all the barbiturates in their systems; emerged from the comas to go immediately into seizures so simultaneous and incapacitating that neither could make use of the anticonvulsants also found at the death scene. It also assumed neither twin could call for help or help the other. The theory apparently didn't even satisfy the medical examiner himself. He quietly sent Marcus-twin tissue samples out to another lab for further analysis.

Meanwhile, an even more exotic possibility—the bleeding hemorrhoid theory—came from an unlikely source: Dr. Hugh Luckey, the president of New York Hospital–Cornell Medical Center, where the two doctors had practiced for fourteen years. Dr. Luckey and his hospital—one of the oldest (1771) and most highly respected in the country—were under considerable pressure at the time. Questions had been raised by the Marcus brothers' bizarre death about New York Hospital's procedures to protect patients. A *New York Times* story strongly suggested that the twins had been drug abusers for years and cited a report that one of them—apparently under the influence—had staggered into a hospital operating room and ripped an anesthetic mask off a patient's face. (The hospital denied it ever happened.) A *Times* editorial attacked the hospital for "stonewalling" inquiries about the Marcuses' role at the hospital; a Queens congressman called the Marcus affair "a medical Watergate" and called for a cutoff of federal funds to the hospital until all questions were answered.

So it is understandable that Dr. Luckey and hospital officials might want to cast doubt on barbiturate-related theories of the twin doctors' deaths.

"Just because there were barbiturate bottles doesn't mean they died of barbiturate withdrawal," Dr. Luckey said. "I will tell you something: Any smart physician could dispose of himself by a mechanism which could never be discovered by anyone, including his insurance companies. . . . No relationship to the Marcus brothers, I have no evidence, but I know the way I'd do it if I were going to."

How would Dr. Luckey do it?

"By injecting something in places where you'd never find it [the injection mark]. Like in a hemorrhoid. A hemorrhoid bleeds, you know. . . ."

Dr. Luckey and fellow hospital executives seemed to relish the mystery surrounding the Marcus brothers' decline and death. Toward the close of a lengthy interview during which Dr. Luckey claimed he had not the slightest clue to the mysterious malady that destroyed the twins' brilliant careers, Dr. Luckey and hospital administrator Dr. Mel Platt engaged in a curious dialogue, apparently to discourage further inquiry, reproduced here, verbatim:

PLATT: If I could figure it out I'd write the greatest novel of all times, because this is an enigma that's going to be with us for a long time.
LUCKEY: And I'd buy the movie rights. You're damn right. I can tell you this: You're not gonna find out.
PLATT: You're not gonna find out.
LUCKEY: You're not gonna find out.
PLATT: I wish I could find out.
LUCKEY: That's the honest-to-God truth. You're not gonna find out.

The homicide cops found something out. They were able to piece together the bare outline of the sequence of the deaths, enough to uncover the most perplexing question of all. The smell of a decomposing body, a smell the maintenance man swore he could not mistake after combat service in World War II, was detectable as early as Monday, July 14. Yet on Tuesday, July 15, two separate doormen saw a man they identified as Cyril Marcus stagger out of the apartment building, disappear and return, weaving and stumbling, to another entrance, where a relief doorman accompanied him up the elevator to the tenth floor. He declined any assistance entering the apartment and shortly thereafter told his answering service he wanted no further calls.

What was Cyril doing when Stewart died? Why did he stay with the body at first, then leave it? But most of all, *why did he go back*?

Dr. Alan Guttmacher might be able to suggest an answer to that last question—if he were alive. Twenty years ago, Guttmacher, himself a twin, an expert on twins, and a gynecologist, too, intervened forcefully in the lives of the Marcus twins: He succeeded in splitting them apart for the first and last times of their lives.

Dr. Guttmacher had strong views about twins. He called them monsters.

That's the quasi-medical term—descended from an eighteenth-century mid-wife's manual—for twins who are physically conjoined at birth, a phenomenon we now call Siamese twins.

"All separate identical twins may be regarded as monsters who have successfully escaped the various stages of monstrosity," Dr. Guttmacher wrote. Monsters lucky enough to escape physical conjoinment must constantly be on guard against slipping back into some sort of monsterhood through *psychic* conjoinment. Because of the constant peril of mutually confused identities, Guttmacher comes close to calling physically conjoined monsters *healthier* than most ordinary identical twins. "No Siamese twins have ever been known to succumb to dementia," he points out. "Nor have any sought to end the lives they are doomed to live together."

They were born on June 2, 1930, Stewart leading the way, Cyril following two minutes behind, a pattern of dominance that continued into their childhood and adolescence—Stewart the natural leader, outgoing, effervescent; Cyril more withdrawn and quiet, unlike his brother, a left-hander, but otherwise apparently content to serve as his brother's right-hand man.

When the two of them ran for class office at Bayonne, New Jersey, High School, it was Stewart who ran for president, Cyril for treasurer. (Both lost.) Both were selected for the National Honor Society, but it was Stewart who won the B'nai B'rith essay contest. Both were considered extremely bright, but it was Stewart who became valedictorian, Cyril who settled for salutatorian. Both got the usual laudatory yearbook captions, but it was Stewart who was described as the twin "bound to win." Both went to the senior prom, but it was Stewart and his date, not Cyril and his, who got their pictures published in the school paper.

They shared the same group of bright, highly competitive friends, but went everywhere together. Although a story about them in the Bayonne High School paper notes that "they wouldn't be seen in each other's clothes," they both wore the same *kind* of clothes and, in fact, seem to have developed a practice of wearing matching outfits of different shades—Stewart light, Cyril dark.

"The Marcus brothers look shrewd in their corduroy jackets, Stewart in tan and Cyril in dark brown," said a report on high-school fashions in the school paper. In many of their yearbook photos Stewart wears a light double-breasted suit, Cyril a dark one. And in a group picture of six sets of twins accompanying a school-paper story entitled DOUBLE TROUBLE AT BAYONNE HIGH, Stewart wears white, Cyril black.

In this double-trouble story there's a provocative statement about the Marcuses' childhood: "If one of them got into mischief both were spanked by their mother to be sure that the right one was punished."

This is exactly the sort of thing that Guttmacher had in mind when he wrote that identical twins reared together can't develop the sense of "my." Making each suffer for the acts of the other makes the difficulties twins have developing separate identities even more severe. One psychoanalytic theorist holds that "the confusion this creates may make them feel that nothing is personal and unique about them . . . misunderstood, lonely, angry . . . there is only one person for whom they are unique: That is their own twin."

Eight years after high school, the Marcus twins were confronted by Dr. Guttmacher. Stewart and Cyril were both first-year residents at New York's Mount Sinai Hospital, where Dr. Guttmacher was chairman of the gynecology department. Their careers since high school, Guttmacher could see from their résumés, were nearly identical. Same college (Syracuse). Same fraternity. Same academic honors. Same medical school (also Syracuse). Shared the same cadaver in first-year anatomy class. Same medical honoraries. Same internship program at Mount Sinai. Same residency program in gynecology at Mount Sinai. Twenty-six years together, and they were expecting to spend at least three more years together at Sinai.

To Guttmacher, steeped in twins research, it must have looked as if Stewart and Cyril were heedless of how they were imperiling the psychic separation that distinguished them from—Guttmacher's word—monsters. Already the all-too-easy insularity and self-sufficiency of their twinship seemed to be causing them difficulties getting along with outsiders. "They were arrogant, resentful of criticism, disobedient of orders . . . there were tremendous conflicts with the other residents," recalls Dr. Joseph Rovinsky, former chief resident in gynecology at Sinai.

Dr. Guttmacher decided to try to sever the conjoinment he saw crippling their individual development. He declared that he would prevent them from continuing their residencies together at Sinai or anywhere else. "He absolutely refused to recommend them to the same hospital. He absolutely insisted that they apply to separate programs," Rovinsky recalls. Not only that, he arranged it so that there would be a whole continent separating them: Stewart was exiled to a program at Stanford's University Hospital, while Cyril was transferred to New York's Joint Diseases Hospital.

The traumatic three-thousand-mile separation seems to have lasted but a year. Stewart's superior at Stanford, Dr. Charles McLennan, is certain Stewart left Stanford to continue his residency somewhere else, "in some sort of orthopedic hospital," he thinks. Oddly, Stewart's curriculum vitae omits any mention of where he spent this missing year. Could it be that—as in classic tales of star-crossed lovers—he slipped away from Stanford and made his way back to Cyril's side at the orthopedically oriented Joint Diseases Hospital?

The year after that found Stewart back at Stanford again. Could Dr. Guttmacher have discovered a reunion at Joint Diseases and ordered Stewart back to Stanford? No one has been able to say what Stewart was doing that missing year; and Dr. Guttmacher died one year before the Marcus twins.

Whatever the case, the second separation proved to be the longest time they would ever be apart. Cyril, it appears, reacted more strongly to being alone. After two years away from Stewart he got married. After a third year he fathered a child and accepted a position at New York Hospital. But by the end of that third year Cyril had arranged it so that he and Stewart would be back together again: He had found a sympathetic patron in the head of the department of obstetrics and gynecology at New York Hospital, someone who had none of Dr. Guttmacher's reservations about twin togetherness and who agreed to bring Stewart back to Cyril's side again.

This reunion signaled the beginning of another kind of marriage for the twins. They seem to have consented to wed their individual career ambitions into a single two-headed unit. As in most career-oriented marriages, one partner ended up making the sacrifices and doing the day-to-day drudgery to permit the other to work for the greater glory of them both. In this one, Stewart did the glamorous laboratory research, getting foundation grants, delivering papers at academic medical conferences all over the world, while Cyril stayed "home" and did most of the messy clinical housework, doggedly building up a big income-earning private practice for both of them.

"In order for Stewart to conduct his laboratory work, Cyril did more than his share in the office; he sacrificed some of his own ambitions to work in the lab," recalls Dr. Fritz Fuchs, who became chairman of the department of obstetrics and gynecology at New York Hospital in 1965.

Despite the unfair division of labor—particularly the obstetric labor that had to be attended to at all hours of the night—the twins' career marriage was a fertile one at first. Cyril's clinical experience stimulated Stewart's research and Stewart's research gave birth to new ideas for treatment of infertility in the private practice Cyril presided over.

They delivered a number of scientific papers under both their names. They conceived and edited a large collection of contemporary research in their field that was published in 1967 as *Advances in Obstetrics and Gynecology,* a book that gave them a national reputation as scholars and practitioners. New York Hospital put them in charge of its infertility clinic.

Meanwhile, their private practice began attracting well-born and well-known women, the wives of celebrities. The twins delighted in the limousines that would pull up to their office; they liked to let certain patients know that they could discriminate between the styles of Mainbocher and Norell. They didn't like to let certain people know they grew up in Bayonne; Stewart told one they were from Short Hills. In one sense they were doted upon as a doubly interesting version of a peculiarly New York institution—the fashionable Park Avenue gynecologist. In a more special sense, through their infertility work, they were becoming objects of awe, even worship, of patients who benefited from their green thumb for babies. If they recalled Dr. Guttmacher's warnings about the consequences of failure of twins to separate, it would only have been to laugh at how wrong he was.

Sometime after 1967, signs of strain began to show up in both Cyril's marriages. That year Stewart accepted an offer of a full-time associate professorship at New York Hospital–Cornell Medical Center. Cyril was not given one. Accepting the offer meant that Stewart had to give up private practice outside the hospital. It was an important step toward his ultimate goal of becoming department chairman at a teaching hospital. But when he accepted, the entire weight of the private practice suddenly fell upon Cyril. It came at a bad time. Cyril's wife had just given birth to their second child, but Cyril now had even less time for his family. He had to abandon entirely his own limited research efforts, work more hours than ever at the painstaking infertility work at his office, and lose more sleep than ever from the emergency obstetric calls at night. According to one nurse who worked for him back then, he began taking amphetamines.

Stewart, on the other hand, was enjoying more freedom than ever. He never married. He told people who asked that he never would and wasn't "missing anything" by not having a wife and children as did his twin. He no longer had to spend time with the anxious, despairing, barren women Cyril had to face. He continued to travel to gynecological conferences all over the world, while Cyril's wife complained that Cyril couldn't get time off from his practice to take her anywhere. And, according to friends, she found Cyril too much of a perfectionist (not so surprising a flaw to turn up in one who had spent his entire life up until his marriage in the shadow of a brother-partner who was always a shade more perfect than he).

In late 1969, Cyril's wife asked for a divorce. People who knew him described Cyril as shattered, painfully depressed. In April 1970, he moved out of their East End Avenue home and into apartment 10H at 1163 York Avenue, alone for the first time since Dr. Guttmacher had separated him from Stewart. He got himself a dog for a companion, hoping that the presence of the pet would encourage his children to visit him more often. But neighbors in the building complained about the dog's barking and forced Cyril to get rid of it. Lacking close friends, he took to confessing his unhappiness to puzzled patients in his private practice, occasionally calling them at home late at night from places like Danny's Hide-A-Way and P. J. Clarke's to ramble on about such obsessions as French restaurants and Catherine Deneuve. He started taking sedatives.

Then one morning, in the summer of 1972, Stewart got a phone call from a man who identified himself as Bill Terrell, the handyman at Cyril's apartment complex.

"I think we have a problem here," Terrell said. "I'm pretty sure your brother's in trouble; I'm inclined to think he's unconscious."

" 'Just a minute,' " Terrell recalls Stewart replying. Terrell heard the sound of the phone receiver on Stewart's end being set down. He waited a moment. He waited a minute and a half.

"Then I said, 'Hey, Doctor, you know I'm talking to you.' Then he said, 'You're right,' and I said, 'I'm right about what?' And he said, 'You're right something's wrong.' "

It took Terrell a while, he recalls, to break through the strange passivity that settled over Stewart and to convince him to hurry over to Cyril's building. When they broke through the door, they found Cyril fully dressed, motionless on the floor of the foyer of apartment 10H, looking as if he had lost consciousness while crawling toward the house phone in the hall.

"He's dead," said Stewart, without approaching the body.

"I got down close to him," Terrell recalls, "and I said, 'He's not dead, but he's just about gone.' "

"Give him mouth-to-mouth resuscitation," Stewart said.

"I said, 'You're the doctor, you do it,' " Terrell recalls. "He was kind of dumbfounded. Still standing there."

Fortunately, at this point, according to Terrell, some other doctors in the building arrived and gave Cyril mouth-to-mouth resuscitation. "I'm positive it wasn't the brother who did it," Terrell says.

It didn't appear to be a suicide attempt. Cyril was fully dressed and apparently ready to leave the apartment when he collapsed, and he seemed to be trying to call for help when he lost consciousness.

What happened to Cyril? Hospital treatment records remain confidential. However, there are two phone calls that suggest an answer. An anonymous call came to the medical examiner's office not long after the Marcus brothers' death hit the papers last July. The caller suggested that the medical examiner look into the possibility that Cyril suffered a stroke back in 1972 and was hospitalized in a coma. The anonymous caller's information seemed to fit in with the substance of a revealing telephone conversation Stewart had had with a friend, just one day after Cyril's mysterious collapse.

It was nip and tuck with Cyril's life, Stewart told the friend. He was not sure exactly what happened, Stewart said, but he was terribly concerned about brain damage Cyril might have suffered from cerebral anoxia—lack of oxygen for brain cells—while he was unconscious.

The friend, who also knew Cyril, couldn't be sure himself whether Stewart's brain-damage fears were justified. After the collapse, the friend said, "Cyril was functioning, but as time went on, in other matters, in the course of a telephone conversation, he'd repeat himself. Something had happened to alter his functioning in some way. It was just not the same old Cyril."

The friend is convinced that Cyril's collapse, Stewart's fear of brain damage to his brother, and the crippling conjoinment that grew out of the aftermath led inevitably to their mutual decline.

"It was all down down down after that. . . . The more Cyril deteriorated, the more Stewart involved himself in trying to bail him out and maintain a good front. Maybe Stewart was hoping that by not letting down the front, things would work out. He would always reassure me, Cyril's fine, he's fine. Maybe it was wishful thinking, like trying to save a drowning man who pulls his rescuer down with him."

Physically, they drew closer in the months that followed Cyril's collapse. Stewart quit a recently assumed post as chief of obstetrics and gynecology at Nassau County Medical Center and moved back into New York City full-time to an apartment just three blocks away from Cyril's. Stewart had taken the Nassau County post with the expectation that with it would come the chance to head the ob-gyn department at an important new teaching hospital being built at Stony Brook, Long Island. When that promise was not fulfilled, he quit to return to commit himself to preserving Cyril. The last separation was over.

In the fall of 1972, they signed on as surgeons in a big abortion clinic. The shift from the promotion of conception to abortion may have had something to do with money. Abortions are quick and simple to perform, and for the amount of time they take, the fees are very high. An infertility case can take many months of painstaking tests, office visits, exploratory procedures, and often complex and delicate operations. Cyril had alimony to worry about. Stewart had Cyril to worry about. But the shift from top-rank infertility research to hack abortion work must have been devastating to Stewart's self-esteem. In November 1972, Stewart's altered behavior so antagonized his publisher that the proposed second volume of the brothers' book had to be canceled. He alienated the top-name contributors to the volume by failing to return their manuscripts. His research career began to disintegrate.

Why did he do it? Why did Stewart allow his career to slide down the drain to prop up Cyril? Is it possible he blamed himself for the anoxia he thought Cyril might have suffered? Brain-cell death is a question of seconds, and Stewart had hesitated twice while his brother lay unconscious—once on the phone and once in front of Cyril's body, when he refused to give his brother the resuscitation needed to save his life. Could Stewart also have blamed himself for the sacrifices his twin had made for his research career, sacrifices that may have contributed to the breakup of Cyril's marriage, and could Stewart have decided on some level to sacrifice that career in return?

Or was it no sacrifice at all? Some theories of twinship say that behind the apparent closeness of twins is "an intense rivalry situation . . . hostile death wishes which in turn demand repression that again brings the twins together."

Such a theory suggests the possibility that Stewart hesitated that morning because, at some level, he wanted Cyril to die.

The pressures of the aftermath of Cyril's collapse began to affect their private practice. Patients began to report instances of bizarre, even terrifying, behavior. There were the mutual impersonations, for instance. One twin would leave his patient in the middle of an examination and the other would return to the stirrups to complete the job. Once Stewart confided to a patient whom he had failed to fool with a Cyril impersonation that the two of them had played the impersonation game with fourteen patients so far that day and that they'd been able to fool nine of them. "Our mother has trouble telling us apart," he said.

There are indications that after Cyril's collapse, Stewart began impersonating his brother in earnest. Some patients recall leaving messages for Cyril and getting a return call from someone who may have been Stewart. Then another call from the real Cyril, who seemed unaware of his brother's impersonation.

And one patient reported that she called Cyril for advice and heard him reply to her questions in a slurred halting voice, frequently pausing to wait for answers from a voice in the background. She was certain it was Stewart telling Cyril what to say.

Then there were the temper tantrums, occasionally violent. One patient, who had been hospitalized toward the end of her ninth month of pregnancy, recalls complaining to Cyril that her intravenous needle gave her pain. "He picked up that bottle of intravenous fluid and he slammed it down on the tray." When another patient disobeyed Cyril's orders and got out of bed, subsequently suffering a miscarriage, he berated her almost vengefully. They flew into rages when their medical commandments were violated or even questioned; they were jealous ("Thou shalt have no gynecologists before us" was one commandment); they demanded unquestioning faith and obedience.

As their office became less crowded they began to spend more of their idle time engaged in long rambling discourses with certain patients. Cyril startled one with a detailed story about a woman he claimed to have treated for certain after-effects of intercourse with a large dog.

Even with all this odd behavior, it was a seemingly innocuous insurance-form phobia that did more than anything to hasten the twins' downfall. The Marcuses had a powerful aversion to filling out insurance forms for their patients and would go to bizarre lengths to avoid doing so.

As far back as 1965, one patient reported, she had had to go through months and months of calling, pleading, and personal visits to get them to sign one simple form. Over the years the twins seemed to have developed an elaborate hierarchy of defenses against signing forms they did not want to sign. They'd refuse to respond to phone requests. They'd refuse to receive requests sent by registered mail; they'd tell patients who came to the office to get their forms signed that they'd already sent them out by mail; when the forms never arrived by mail they'd claim the post office lost them or their mailbox must have caught fire. When the tormented women turned the problem over to their husbands, the twins would make them jump through the same hoops all over again.

Toward the end, they began with increasing frequency to make use of an even more ingenious scheme to avoid forms: They refused to send bills. In many cases they seemed to prefer forgoing a fee to filling out the forms that went with it. This was no real advantage to the patients: Many were billed by the hospital as well, and insurance companies required the doctors to bill them or fill out forms before reimbursement was issued.

It was an ingenious device, this no-bill method of avoiding forms, and they might have gotten away with it had it not been for Mrs. Evelyn Chait, a housewife in New Jersey and an early victim of the form phobia. Starting in 1971, she waged a four-year campaign to get her forms filled out. She wrote letter after letter, suffered through excuse after excuse, sent her husband on countless missions. She took her case to outside agencies, amassing a foot-high file of correspondence on the byzantine twists and dodges Cyril employed to avoid her forms. She stalked him through one ineffectual bureaucracy after another. At last, late in 1974, she found an agency that was willing to take some action. The New York State Department of Professional Conduct assigned an investigator of medical scandals to the case. He set in motion a process that would result in a formal presentation of charges against Cyril and Stewart Marcus by a panel of doctors.

Sometime in April 1974, Cyril Marcus took a headlong fall. He would take a number of falls in the year to come—the autopsy doctors found a number of old abrasions on his knees characteristic, they said, of chronic alcohol or drug users. This fall was the most unfortunate. It came outside an operating room in New York Hospital, where he was scheduled to perform an operation. He staggered and collapsed in a way that suggested he was under the influence of drugs.

They wheeled Cyril, sweating and pale, to the emergency room, where a staff doctor treated him and hospitalized him. An agitated Stewart appeared on the scene. Dr. Fuchs, who was present, asked Cyril to take a medical leave of absence and suggested that it would be a good idea if Stewart, too, took a vacation since he was so concerned about his brother and looked tired himself.

The following August, when the twins were permitted to return to the hospital, they had the feeling people were watching them and talking about them.

They were right. Hospital administrator Luckey had ordered the twins placed under "extremely close one-to-one surveillance" every moment they were near a patient. "We have great agents in this hospital," Dr. Luckey would later boast. "This place would make the CIA green with envy. Everything gets back to us."

The twins began to withdraw from this scrutiny, admitting only eighteen patients in the eleven months between their return in August and their deaths in July. They retreated to the relative privacy of their private practice. There, things began to grow stranger by the month. The nurse who began working there toward the end of 1974 found it hard to believe some of the things that were happening in that office.

In the spring of 1975, the nurse confided to a patient what it had been like. When they first came back from their leave of absence, she said, the twins had "tried to straighten up and get better, but it didn't last long." They were taking amphetamines in the office, she said; they would become irrationally angry and blow up at some patients. Their form–filling out phobia continued. The twins asked her to fend off frustrated form seekers for them, creating one situation so explosive she began to fear for her life: An enraged husband who had been fighting his way for months through evasions and postponements seeking to get his wife's records transferred to another doctor finally burst into Cyril Marcus's inner office. In the argument that ensued, someone drew a gun.

Then there was the spontaneous-abortion incident. Late that spring, one of Cyril's patients checked herself into New York Hospital in the midst of a spontaneous abortion. The woman and her husband (a doctor) raised questions about whether Cyril's failure to follow through on certain progesterone tests had been a factor in the miscarriage. When Cyril arrived at the hospital, according to the nurse's story, the patient "was lying there bleeding, and Cyril came in—he was really out of it—and he looked at her and said, 'Do you want to go home now?' She obviously needed some attention, and what happened was a couple of the doctors sent him away and took over and took care of her."

The nurse said that things had been getting worse that spring; the practice was deteriorating, the office rent in arrears, the air conditioner unrepaired. The twins frequently called, telling her in slurred voices that they would be unable to come in for the day's appointments. Cyril in particular, she said, had been losing weight and acting more and more strangely. The nurse was convinced that everyone at the hospital was talking about the twins and their odd behavior—that, in fact, the constant gossip about them was one factor contributing to their drug taking—but that no one at the hospital would do anything about the situation in their private practice. The nurse said she had been to see Chairman Fuchs twice about the situation, that she told him she wanted to leave but that Fuchs had said, "Why don't you stay with them so you can at least help out the patients?"

Meanwhile, the investigator for the state's Department of Professional

Conduct was beginning to close in on the twins. Pursuing the complaints of Mrs. Chait, the investigator found himself getting the same runaround the patients and their husbands were complaining of. The twins wouldn't come to the phone when they *were* in; twice when they finally came to the phone they hung up on him. Finally the investigator threatened to slap Cyril with a subpoena if he failed to make an appearance to explain himself. On the appointed day in October 1974, someone who identified himself as Cyril Marcus showed up in the investigator's office.

"He was very cordial, he was very polite, and he was obviously not Cyril," the investigator recalled. "Cyril was a damaged individual, and in tight situations Stewart took over from Cyril," a colleague explained.

By June, the investigator had eleven more unresolved allegations against the twins; this time he hit them both with subpoenas for appearances on the same day. Neither showed up. Belatedly the twins called and asked for an adjournment. Then another. On June 27, 1975, the director of the agency authorized presentation of charges against them to a special panel of five doctors. The panel voted unanimously to charge the twins with "unprofessional conduct" and ordered them to appear for a trial.

By this time Stewart must have known that the secrets of Cyril's behavior were slipping out. In June he received a disturbing call from Dr. Roger Steinhardt, chairman of the New York County Medical Society Board of Censors. The board, too, had been investigating increasing complaints about the twins' failure to fill out forms and had finally produced—after the usual months of postponements—an appearance at the board's office by one of the twins, who identified himself as Cyril. "All of us sensed something strange . . . awry" about the appearance of this twin, Steinhardt recalls. They found him "affable and easygoing," which does not sound like the emaciated and sickly Cyril. Acting on an informal basis, after getting a hint of Cyril's condition since his 1972 collapse, Dr. Steinhardt called Stewart and asked him if his twin was ill or emotionally disturbed or if perhaps he had suffered a "cerebral accident." Stewart denied everything, but Steinhardt's tactfully phrased inquiry must have tipped Stewart off that his front for Cyril was crumbling. (Nor was Steinhardt completely satisfied with Stewart's denial: He contacted the twins' department chairman at New York Hospital and set up an appointment to discuss the situation. But Dr. Steinhardt's secretary got his calendar confused; Steinhardt failed to show up for the meeting, and before it could be rescheduled the twins were dead.)

The twins didn't know about the panel's investigation of them, they didn't know about the planned Steinhardt-Fuchs rendezvous, but in late May 1975, department head Fuchs ordered them to appear at the hospital and told them something even more devastating.

"I called them into my office," Fuchs recalls, "and said, 'Look, there is someone on the hospital staff who thinks that you might have a drug problem.' I asked them if there were anything I could do to help them get treatment and offered to let them take a medical leave of absence."

The twins denied the drug allegation, but Fuchs's offer of a leave was more like an ultimatum. He gave them three choices: They could accept a medical leave for treatment; they could voluntarily resign; or they could do nothing and Fuchs would be forced to recommend to the hospital's medical board that they be dropped.

The twins protested that Fuchs had given them unacceptable choices— they'd lose their livelihood if they had to take a medical leave, they'd lose their livelihood if they had to resign their hospital privileges, and they'd lose their reputation either way because leaving would confirm everyone's worst suspicions about them. Unmoved, Fuchs gave them two weeks to decide.

In the difficult days that followed the ultimatum they began to withdraw even further from their practice, sometimes failing to show up at all. One of the last patients to see one of the twins in their office describes a sad and revealing encounter with Cyril. It happened sometime close to their forty-fifth birthday, June 2, 1975. She found herself alone in the office with Cyril. "There was no one else there in the two hours I spent with him. It was a little peculiar," she recalls. "He looked thinner and he looked sick, I would say, physically, and he seemed lonely. He was very upset about Ozzie Nelson's death."

The woman asked Cyril what troubled him so much about Ozzie's death. "Well," Cyril said, "it's just a shame. The good, like Ozzie Nelson, die and then people like Nixon and Mayor Beame are still around."

Cyril then shifted this cheerful conversation from Ozzie (could he perhaps have been thinking about where Ozzie's death left Harriet, the other half of that inseparable couple?) to twins, cancer, and death.

"He got into this cancer business," the woman recalls, "and he said, 'Do you know who dies of the same thing?' and I said, 'What?' and he said, 'Twins.' He said identical twins often come down with the same thing, cancer or whatever, and die together or close. Identical twins, or even fraternal twins, are very joined emotionally and whatever, and he said, 'Of course my brother and I are not identical.' " Nor were Ozzie and Harriet.[1]

---

[1]Almost everyone who knew the twins assumed they were identicals, and until the Ozzie Nelson conversation there is only one indication on record to suggest otherwise. Thirty years earlier the "double trouble" story in their high-school paper described the Marcus brothers as "fraternal twins who happen to look very much alike." The possibility must be allowed that the Marcuses were fraternal twins who relished being mistaken for identicals, perhaps even *posed* as identicals because of the special awe identicals evoke. Certainly by the time they reached Dr. Guttmacher their lives had been lived as identicals, and by the time of Ozzie Nelson's death, they may have wondered whether it was too late to escape the common fate so often suffered by identicals.

. . .

Stewart Marcus had a cancer theory. It didn't involve twins, but it did involve paired organs. Back in 1960, when Stewart was a promising young research gynecologist, he researched and wrote—with the aid of Cyril—a paper on the gynecological implications of "the theory of multicentric origin" of cancers. The paper warned gynecologists to be alert to the fact that when any one organ develops a carcinoma, its paired organ—or any other organ composed of tissue "with the same embryological origin"—is likely to have a latent precancerous fertility and may suddenly give birth to a similar malignancy.

The story of the final siege is Stewart's story.

June 12 was the day the twins were supposed to reply to Dr. Fuchs's ultimatum. Fuchs heard nothing from them all day. Finally he called them, reached Stewart, and asked if they had decided to take a leave, resign, or allow themselves to be dropped from the hospital staff. Stewart told Fuchs they still hadn't been able to make up their minds, asked for more time, and promised to call Fuchs with the decision on June 16. He didn't. Fuchs called him again, and again Stewart told him the twins hadn't been able to make up their minds. "Well, now it is out of my hands," Fuchs told him, and proceeded to write the hospital medical board recommending against rehiring the twins.

Still Stewart could have saved himself. Fuchs's recommendation was not final and both twins were entitled to contest it before the medical board. Stewart might have won. "If they had fought it, we might have had a tough time making it stand, especially on Stewart," one member of the medical board conceded. "Hell, Stewart hadn't done much more than miss some clinic appointments."

Sergeant Breen of the Fourth Homicide Squad paid a visit to Stewart's Sixtyfifth Street apartment after taking an inventory of the death-scene mess at Cyril's place. According to Sergeant Breen, the scene at Stewart's place was "a repeat" of the one at Cyril's: the same pills, the same piles of newspapers and unopened mail, the same half-eaten food scattered about. According to the doorman in his building, in the past year Stewart had had no visitors to his apartment other than his brother Cyril, and for a full year Stewart had forbidden anyone from the building to enter his apartment at any time. In addition, the doorman said that for about a month before Stewart's death he hadn't seen him at all.

What all this suggests is that in their last year the prophecy implicit in Stewart's cancer paper and in Cyril's Ozzie Nelson story was coming true: The emotional malignancy that had seized upon Cyril some time ago had begun to take possession of what remained of Stewart's private life. For a year he saw no one but a sick mirror image of himself. Until that last month the twins had, at least, locked up their paired afflictions in separate secret compartments. But

Stewart's decision not to fight for his job, to make Cyril's losses his losses, made any further separation superfluous, and in mid-June Stewart moved out of his apartment and into a final folie à deux at Cyril's place.

The piles of papers began to accumulate as far back as April: Found beneath Cyril's dead body was a full-page ad from an April 7 issue of the *Times,* appealing for aid for Saigon war orphans. Appointments had been neglected for long before that. Taped on Cyril's bathroom mirror were an "Important Notice" from the IRS dated November 1973, and a reminder about an appointment with a neurologist who had been dead since the fall of 1974.

But even amid the final chaos they created, there were clues that in the last month the twins made pathetic efforts to maintain a life outside the double-locked doors of apartment 10H. It was possible to glimpse amongst the debris the implements of cleanliness and grooming that had always produced the "immaculate" and "meticulous" impression the Marcus brothers invariably made on others. Even at the very end, when everyone noticed Cyril losing weight and Stewart growing pale, their suits were freshly creased and their faces closely shaved.

At the time of their death, the bathtub and bathroom sink in 10H were encrusted with spilled instant-coffee powder, but resting on top of these stains was a spray can of Right Guard deodorant, a can of shaving cream, a squeeze bottle of Q.T. quick-tanning lotion, razors, even nail clippers. These all suggest a continuing effort up until the end to save face—the Q.T., in fact, may have been used to cover the pallor that had begun to attract attention to their faces.

Even the state of dress—or undress—in which the dead twins were found may reflect the undying efforts of one segment of their psyches to preserve some last bit of fastidiousness in the face of the filth about to engulf them. The relative nakedness in which the twins were found has inspired some prurient speculation about their activities together, but there's a less lurid explanation for it: The only way to keep clothes clean from contamination and presentable for wearing outside that apartment would be to avoid wearing them at all inside. And wearing over-the-calf socks can be seen as a last-ditch survival of that part of their psyches that would not allow itself to be tainted by stepping in the debris tolerated by whatever disorder possessed the rest of their personalities.

They may have made one last effort to clean themselves up in a more fundamental way. Among the barbiturates on the floor, police also found an emptied prescription bottle of Dilantin, an anticonvulsant drug sometimes used to treat the seizures characteristic of narcotic withdrawal. It's possible that Stewart tried to get Cyril to kick the barbiturate habit with the help of Dilantin or that they were both preparing one last attempt to salvage their medical careers—Cyril called at least one colleague that summer to ask about the possibility of a job in another city. If there was an attempt, it failed: Dates on prescription bottles indicate that they went back to buying barbiturates not long after they brought the Dilantin home.

On July 10, 1975, the New York Hospital medical board met to consider the cases of Cyril and Stewart Marcus. Neither twin appeared to defend himself. The decision of the board to drop them from the staff became final. Considering the pending state agency indictment, for all practical purposes they were through as doctors. The twins had finally been driven, by circumstances of their own creation, back into the kind of isolation and conjoinment they had not shared since childhood, indeed since the womb.

The remnants of their last days together suggest that in some respects the twins lived out a kind of nightmarish children's party. There were dozens of bottles of sweet soda pop all over the place—wild cherry, strawberry, vanilla cream, Rooti root beer, Coca-Cola. There were cookies, cakes, and ice cream, too. And they never had to clean up.

As he had with their delivery into the world, Stewart led the way in delivering them out of it. Sometime between July 10 and July 14, he took an overdose of barbiturates and died. That's the final official theory of the medical examiner about Stewart's death. (Samples of Stewart's tissue sent to an outside toxicologist revealed that the original toxicological report had been in error.) The official report does not say whether it was an accidental overdose or a deliberate suicide. It just states "Circumstances Undisclosed."

Clues at the death scene point a different way. Found on the floor beneath the sock dangling from Stewart's left foot was a metal box with the words "wills/insurance" on it. The presence of the opened box suggests there may have been a realistic discussion of the consequences of accidental and intentional death for heirs and beneficiaries. Stewart died without a will and his possessions reverted to his parents, but Cyril seems to have made provision for his two daughters. Circumstances suggest a complex, harrowing chronology. It goes like this: On July 10, the twins pass up their last chance to save their hospital careers and decide to take a final leave of absence together. They take large doses of Nembutal together and go into a barbiturate coma. Stewart dies. Cyril doesn't. Perhaps because of a higher tolerance, his dose is not fatal and he awakens hours, even days, later to find himself alone with the dead body of his brother.

If we think of the story of these twins as a kind of love story, it's possible to imagine Cyril waking up and experiencing something akin to the desolation of Juliet when she wakes from her drugged sleep in the crypt of the Capulets. She finds her lover dead beside her and herself alone in a "nest of death, contagion and unnatural sleep."

On Tuesday, July 14, Cyril lurches one last time out of the twins' final nesting place. He stumbles as he is about to cross the threshold to the outside world. The doorman who offers to assist Cyril thinks he "looks like death." Out on the sidewalk Cyril looks at life without Stewart. The first thing he will have to do, he knows, is explain things. It's not hard to explain why he returned so soon to that crypt in 10H. Only in those two minutes he languished in the womb after his brother's departure could Cyril have been more alone.

He double-locked the door behind him. He pushed an armchair up against it as a further barricade. He took off the clothes he had worn for his last venture outside. He may well have clothed Stewart's body in a pair of his own striped shorts. He put a sheet of paper in his typewriter and typed his ex-wife's address on it. He left the rest blank.

The only thing we know for sure about the way Cyril died is that he didn't take the easy way out. He didn't take pills. He may well have paced the apartment keeping watch over his brother's body. For the first time in his life, he was truly his older brother's keeper.

How he finally died is still a mystery: The medical examiner has no positive proof, he offers only "diagnosis by exclusion": circumstantial evidence that indicates Cyril was a barbiturate addict, there were no barbiturates—even after three series of tests and retests—found in Cyril's body, therefore Cyril must have died from barbiturate withdrawal. But the medical examiners concede that Cyril's body showed no signs of the bruises, mouth and tongue bites, or brain hemorrhages that characterize the fatal convulsions of narcotic withdrawal. One source in the medical examiner's office suggests that inanition—exhaustion from lack of nourishment—and a failure of the will to live may have contributed. And the literature of twins is filled with cases in which one member of a pair of identical or conjoined twins sickens and dies and the other, though perfectly healthy, slips into death for no good reason but reunion.

Dr. Guttmacher, the twin who first tried to separate the Marcuses, describes the touching death of Barnum's original Siamese twins, Chang and Eng: When Eng was awakened and told that Chang had died, Eng sighed and said in a resigned fashion, "Then I am going also." And he did, although there was nothing physically wrong with him.

But perhaps the best clue to the nature of their love and their death could be found right in the middle of the littered living-room floor of the death scene. Facedown on top of a pile of papers, barely visible in one of the autopsy photos in the medical examiner's file, was a paperback novel by Iris Murdoch, opened as if someone were holding the place. It was the only novel visible in the apartment, in fact it was the only book removed from the shelves, which mainly contained scientific literature. The Marcus twins were not known among their colleagues as big novel readers, and the prose of Iris Murdoch does not seem like their cup of tea in any case. It is reasonable to assume that whichever twin was reading that particular book in the last days of his life had chosen it for some good reason.

It's a novel about two brothers, one of them part of a heterosexual couple, one of them part of a homosexual couple. The other central figure is a malignant scientist who makes a bet that he can separate both pairs. He succeeds and fails. The heterosexual couple splits and the heterosexual brother kills himself. The homosexual couple survives. Looking at the story of the Marcus brothers in its kindest light, as the story of twins for whom separation was always a fate worse than death, the title of that novel might serve as an epitaph. It was *A Fairly Honorable Defeat*.

Troy Donahue Was Always Just Like He Is

In Which We Learn the Truth about Hitler and the Beautiful People

Why interview Troy Donahue anyway?

"Believe me, you won't believe Troy when you see him," the press agent tells me. "He's a bearded hippie! And believe me, *he is fantastic in this picture.* He plays Charles Manson! Actually we can't call him Charles Manson because of the legal thing, but it's the Charles Manson story. Troy is this sex- and drug-crazed Jesus-type cult leader of a hippie commune who kills a pregnant actress and her Hollywood friends. You see the parallel? This is going to be a very big picture. I have a feeling this is going to be bigger than *Love Story.*"

And if that's not enough, the press agent offers another enticement. "Listen, we'll take you to lunch with Troy at the Top of the Sixes. You'll like the Top of the Sixes. They have steaks and seafood. Do you like steak?" The press agent sets a date for the Top of the Sixes and promises to send me Troy's "bio." He tells me I will recognize him, the agent, "because I wear wild shirts and wide ties. But I guarantee you won't recognize Troy."

From the "Biography of Troy Donahue" received special delivery the next day:

Troy Donahue returns to the screen as Moon, the passion-possessed leader of a vengeful hippie cult . . . in this poignant, moving drama which is inspired by the awesome series of events surrounding the Sharon Tate murder case and other related wanton killings of this decade.

Enclosed with the bio is a newspaper story headlined TROY DONAHUE NOW BEARDED HIPPIE. The story features before and after photos of Troy, showing him as sunny angelic Sandy Winfield II of Warner Bros.' *Surfside 6* and then as sullen, demonic Moon. A note from the press agent attached to the story states: "This Associated Press story on the 'new' Troy Donahue appeared not only in the Sunday New Jersey Bergen *Record* but in countless other major Sunday newspapers in the nation."

Troy is dressed in white. White sneakers, white Levi's, white T-shirt, white Levi jacket. A silver crucifix and some other trinkets hang from a chain around his neck. Troy is a large man and his white clothes look a little too small for him, as if he doesn't want to admit he has put on weight. He looks like those one-time slim and healthy California surfers who grow older, grow paunchy, and turn into bikers. There are gray hairs scattered through Troy's blond beard, and tiny red crinkles of visible veins on his cheeks. Troy is thirty-five.

I'll never forget Troy's first words to me, when he stepped over his motorcycle helmet to greet me at his table at the Top of the Sixes. This is a literal transcription: "Hey brother. Dig the scene. Dig the scene. Wow man. Dig the scene."

If I had any doubts left that Troy was in fact a bearded hippie, he set them at rest when he twisted the conventional handshake I had offered into an interesting version of the Movement "power" grip, and concluded the greeting by saying, "Yeah. Dig the scene." Just us hippies together.

Well, there were two others waiting at Troy's table in addition to us hippies. There was the press agent, in a wild shirt and a wide tie, and Bob Roberts, the producer of *Sweet Savior,* Troy's Charles Manson movie.

"Don't sit next to them," Troy told me. "Sit over here next to me so we can really rap."

When I am seated and turn to Troy, I find we are looking into each other's eyes. The heavy gaze continues in silence until Troy breaks it off, and nods slowly. "Yeah. Right," he says with finality.

We begin to talk about Charles Manson. "I knew the dude," Troy tells me. "I used to play volleyball with him on the beach at L.A. years ago. He had short hair back then, but even then he was very big with the chicks."

"What was his secret?" I asked.

"It was his cock," says Troy.

"His cock?"

"His cock."

Before I could ask Troy for more details the press agent interrupts: "Of course the film is not completely about Charles Manson. We have Troy there at the scene to commit the murder himself while Manson didn't do it himself. We rented a whole mansion in Teaneck, New Jersey, for the murder scene. The script was written by a Pulitzer Prize winner, although under a pseudonym. Troy's performance is going to shock people. I think it's an Oscar performance although the Academy would never have the guts to give it to him."

Troy talks about his role: "It was a bad scene, man," says Troy to me. "It was real. You know, but it was dirty. I felt dirty, man, evil. But it had to be done. But it's real. Death is real. Wow. Down there just a few blocks away they killed, what's his name, Joe Columbo.* That's heavy. It's funny. Sitting here and talking when it's so real out there. Last night I'm with this black girl in a bar. Beautiful girl, and I'm sitting next to her just wanting to get my cock into her, and she turns to me and says, 'You know the guy who killed Columbo is black. You know what that means.' That's heavy, man. That's real."

"I would make a prediction right now," producer Bob Roberts declares in the silence that follows. "I would predict there would be more murders. This Manson thing will be just the beginning. This movie is not about an isolated incident, it's about what's to come. And there *will* be more murders."

The press agent looks over at me nervously, then back at the producer: "Bob, maybe you shouldn't predict murders. Maybe you should change that to tragedies." He turns to me. "Say that Bob feels that this is a movie about a tragedy which may not, let's see, which may not be the last of its kind."

"But I think there will be *murders* too," says Bob a little disconsolately. "I'm willing to be quoted as predicting murders."

"I just don't think it's a good idea," says the press agent.

"Shut up! You don't know anything," Troy tells the press agent.

"That's nice," the press agent says with some dignity. There is an embarrassed silence at the table.

"Oh hey man, I'm just kidding. Here." Troy reaches for the press agent's hand, takes it into a firm "power" grip, looks him in the eye. "Brothers. Right?" The press agent nods dubiously.

Troy gets back on the subject of Charles Manson and begins explaining how Manson either was or wasn't just like Hitler. "So I said to David Frost, I said, 'Did Hitler do it? I mean did he? He didn't. Man, Hitler didn't do it. You know what I mean?' And Frost looks at me and says, 'He didn't do it?' And I said, 'No man, he didn't do it, did he?' It blew Frost's mind. All he could say was, 'He *didn't* do it?' "

---

*A mafia chieftain killed by a black hitman working for a rival family.

Troy looks at me. "But the thing is he really *did* do it. Can you dig it? He *did* do it."

"Do what?" I asked.*

"I think it's more than Hitler," said the producer before Troy can respond. "It's not just Hitler. It's the beautiful people."

"Right on," says Troy softly.

"The beautiful people," repeats the producer. "I don't want people to get the idea this is an antihippie movie, because it really portrays the degeneracy and depravity of the beautiful people as well as the hippies. That whole Holly-wood scene."

"That's right, man," says Troy. "I know that scene. I've been there. It's these people, man. It's a thrill to cruise the Strip and pick up some groovy-looking hippies and take them home and play with them. Play with them. You know what I mean. Games, dig it. People playing with people. That's what they were all into. I was there when it happened."

"You were *there*?"

"I wasn't there in person, but I was *there*. You dig it. I was there. We were all there."**

"I'll tell you one thing," says the press agent, breaking in on Troy's reverie. "This movie is going to polarize. I mean that. It's going to polarize this coun-try. That's why it's going to be so big. I would not be surprised if it isn't big-ger than *Love Story* and one reason will be because of this polarization."

Troy is still there. "I was there. You were there. We were all there," he tells us. "I was sitting just a few yards down in the canyon when it happened. I could feel it happen. It was like a warning."

I asked Troy if it was hard on him personally trying to play Charles Manson on screen. "No, man. I'm just an actor."

"Wait till you see his performance. It's an Oscar winner," said the press agent.

But how had he been able to get into the Manson part? Had he done acid? "I took acid, man. I took acid and I met the Man. I met the *Man*. And the Man said cool it."

"Cool it?"

"Cool it. That's what he said. I was with these doctors, and . . . now you know some people take two-hundred-fifty, three-hundred-fifty mikes and play around and think they did acid. But I did acid. I was with these doctors in

---

*I've long pondered Troy's Hitler theory, and even after spending more than ten years researching a book on Hitler theories its cryptic wisdom still eludes me, but I *think* what he's saying is a variation on the idea that "Hitler didn't do it, we *all* did it"—i.e., all humanity is responsible for Hitler's crimes. But I could be only scratching the surface.

**See, this kind of fits in with the we-were-all-Hitler concept.

Miami and I was standing by this metal railing watching the ocean and all of a sudden there was a thunderstorm, man, like the end of the world. And lightning, man. So I'm holding on and this lightning hits the railing, comes right along to me and right through me. I should have been fried, man. Then I knew. Cool it. That's what the Man was saying. Cool it."

"Troy's still big with the women, though," the producer interjects. "I don't know how he does it. Have you got that set up with the girl in the hotel, Troy, this afternoon? You do, don't you? I don't know how he keeps going."

Troy points to his crotch and grins. "The day I stop going here is the day I stop going. Going to see [a black singer] tonight. Wow."

The press agent takes out some glossy pictures. There is Troy in shoulder-length hair, parted blond beard, and black leather jacket leaning familiarly on the shoulder of a stout pregnant woman.

"She plays the Sharon Tate type," the press agent explains. "And the amazing thing is she was really pregnant during the shooting. Isn't that something?"

He takes out another glossy and there's Troy in a shot from one of his Warner Bros. Connie Stevens movies, a blond wave in his neatly parted hair, wearing a neat sweater and sport-shirt. "And here's Troy before. You could use these as before and after pictures."

"Yeah, but that's bullshit," says Troy. "That 'before and after' thing is bullshit. I was always the way I am now. See that picture of me with my hands in my pockets, looking so clean-cut? You know what I've got in my pocket? You know what?"

I shake my head no.

Troy gives me a sly look, puts two fingers up to his mouth, and takes an imaginary drag on an imaginary joint. "You know what I'm talking about now? That's right," he says with satisfaction.

Our conversation is interrupted by three elderly ladies who have come over from a nearby table to ask for Troy's autograph.

"I can't believe it. The women still recognize him everywhere," the press agent says.

Troy flirts graciously with the ladies who say they want the autographs for their nieces and granddaughters. When they leave to return to their table, Troy turns to me. "Crazy. Aren't they great. Wow. Look at those heavy legs." He smacks his lips. "Wouldn't you like to mow their lawns?"

"Troy, you have a two-thirty appointment at that hotel, don't you? I don't believe this guy and his women."

Troy wants to finish explaining how there was never any before and after. "I was always like this, man. All I want in life is maybe three drinks and like half a joint"—he takes another drag from his imaginary joint—"and then I hop on my bike and I'm off. That's the real Troy Donahue, you know. It's because I'm spontaneous. Spontaneous, man. I'm so spontaneous I could cry. Sometimes I go to movies and just cry. Listen, have you got any more questions? Anything else you want to know?"

"What about that crucifix you're wearing around your neck?" I ask him. "How much does it mean to you?"

"Listen man, I'm not into any cults or anything. I don't believe in cults. Look, it's not just the crucifix. That's for my Man, but I've also got this Hebrew letter here, it's a Hebrew symbol. I don't know what it stands for but it's good to have. Then I've got this little Buddha figure here and, dig this, he's got one ear missing, which is very heavy. You know what that means, don't you? Then this thing here, this is just a piece of junk to remind me of the junk in the world."

Troy gets up to leave. He picks up his motorcycle helmet and takes out of it a shiny white package which had been stuffed inside. "You want to see junk. Look at this. Somebody up at the Warner Bros. promo office laid this on me."

He hands me a package which turns out to be a white T-shirt with three bright red roses emblazoned on the front. Superimposed over the roses in large jolly letters is the word "JUNK." Below that are the words "Dusty and Sweets McGee," the title of Warner Bros.' newly released junkie movie.

"You can have that if you want," Troy tells me.

I thank Troy but decline.

"Well, I'm off on my cycle now, man. Wish I had one of these"—he takes a final drag on his imaginary joint. "Listen, are you really gonna write this up? You really are. Wow. You know if you do, you know that before and after shit—it's been done before, man. It's not me. I was always just like I am, man."

"Troy is a fantastic guy, isn't he?" says the press agent after Troy leaves.

"Troy is a fantastic guy to work with," says the producer. "I was amazed. He was on time for everything; he's signed for two more pictures with me. In the next one he's playing a Weatherman leader in a picture called *The Weathermen.* Then in '72 there's another big one called *The Lucifer Cell.* It's about a Chinese Communist invasion of the U.S. that succeeds. Troy is an underground resistance fighter."

"The whole thing's going to be very big. This picture. Listen," says the press agent, "one thing you might want to mention in your story is that the company that's distributing this picture is a publicly owned company. It's traded over the counter. That's kind of interesting, you know, you might want to work that into the story when you mention that Trans-World Attractions Corporation is producing and distributing Troy's movie. You know. That it's publicly owned. Something like that. I'll tell you it's only selling for maybe a buck a share now, right, Bob? But when this picture is released. . . . Of course it wouldn't be ethical for me to tell you to buy. . . ."

"But I could tell him, couldn't I?" chuckled the producer.

A young sweet-faced girl wearing a black robe and a large silver crucifix stops me on the sidewalk outside 666 Fifth Avenue (see Revelations 13:18 about that). In a spacey voice the girl asks if I would like to help the work of a group called the Process, the Church of the Final Judgment.* The girl hands me a slip of paper on which the address of the Church of the Final Judgment has been typed. The slip is decorated with the head of Jesus and the horned head of the devil. The girl explains: "We believe each of us has both Christ *and* Satan within us. We believe that we must acknowledge that Satan is in us. Then we can begin to love Satan the way Christ loves, and Satan will be transformed."

The girl, who says she is an acolyte of the Church of the Final Judgment, points to a passage in a booklet explaining "the Process": "Through Love Christ and Satan have destroyed their enmity and have come together for the End; Christ to Judge, Satan to Execute the Judgment." The explanation of the Process continues later with an interesting universal law: "Anything we give, whether positive or negative, will be returned to us in full measure."

I accept the pamphlet from the girl and buy a more detailed book about the Process from her. As she is digging around in her tote bag for change, I notice a familiar shiny white package sticking out. I ask her about it. "Oh, some guy came along a little while ago and gave it to me. I didn't really want it, but he didn't stop to ask whether I did or not."

The girl takes it out. It is Troy's "Junk" T-shirt. She is young enough and sweet-looking enough to have been one of the girls in my junior high school who mooned over Troy a decade ago.

"Did you know that was Troy Donahue who gave it to you?" I asked.

"I don't know. It was just this tall guy with a bike helmet who looked like he was in a hurry. Who is Troy Donahue? Look, would you like it? I really have no need for it."

I have the "Junk" T-shirt now.

---

*Some writers would later try to connect the Process to the Manson cult, and serial killer David Berkowitz would later make the dubious uncorroborated claim that the Process was behind the "Son of Sam" killings.

A Killing in Camelot

In Which We Seek to Solve the "Unsolved" Murder
of Mary Meyer*

The paint was still damp on Mary Meyer's final canvas when she left her studio for a walk. It was a circular canvas. In her recent work she had been exploring the effects of swaying velvety semicircles of color across unprimed circles of canvas.

She pointed an electric fan at the undried painting. It was a chilly fall day; she put on gloves, pulled on a sweater and a sweatshirt over her blouse, and covered those three layers with a heavy blue cable-knit angora, complete with hood.

From the outside, the studio looked like the garage it had once been. It was one among a row of garages along an alleyway behind the backs of two rows of brick townhouses fronting on N and O streets in Georgetown. Since her divorce, she had spent three or four days a week working in her studio, a few steps away from some of her closest friends, whose homes abutted that alley. Her sister, Tony, and Tony's husband, Ben Bradlee, lived on one end; Mr. and Mrs. John Kennedy lived on the other end until they moved to the White

*Coauthor: Phillip Nobile.

House. Occasionally, Mary Meyer would take walks with Jackie along the towpath paralleling the old Chesapeake and Ohio barge canal.

That was where she was heading now, in fact: out the alley, left on Thirty-fourth Street, down to the footbridge that leads across the canal and onto the towpath between the canal and the wooded embankment that descends to the Potomac.

She reached the towpath about noon that day, Monday, October 12, 1964. John F. Kennedy had been dead almost a year. It was two days away from Mary Meyer's forty-fourth birthday.

Air Force Lieutenant William Mitchell left the Pentagon Athletic Center on the Virginia side of the Potomac about noon, crossed over the Key Bridge, exited down the steps to the towpath and began his regular run two miles west to a fishing spot on the river called Fletcher's Landing and back again. He passed three people on his way west—a middle-aged couple and a young white man in Bermuda shorts.

He passed two more people on his way back east to Key Bridge. First there was the woman in a blue hooded sweater. He met her just as she was crossing the wooden footbridge a mile from Key Bridge. He came to a full stop in front of the bridge and allowed her to cross it alone to avoid jostling her in midpassage. Picking up speed again, 200 yards farther east, the lieutenant came upon a black man walking in the same direction as the woman. The man seemed to the lieutenant to be about his size, wearing a light-colored windbreaker, dark slacks and a peaked golf hat. The man's face didn't leave much of an impression on the lieutenant.

Henry Wiggins had just raised the hood of the gray Rambler when he heard the screams. Wiggins had been pumping gas at the M Street Esso station when he got a call to take his truck over to Canal Road, where a Rambler with a dead battery was stalled on a shoulder across from the canal.

The screams were coming from the vicinity of the canal. It was a woman. "Someone help me, someone help me," she cried. Then there was a gunshot. Wiggins ran across the road to the stone wall above the canal. A second gunshot. When he looked over the wall, Wiggins saw a black man in a light jacket, dark slacks, and a dark cap standing over the body of a white woman in a blue sweater. Wiggins saw the man place a dark object in the pocket of his windbreaker, then watched him disappear down the far side of the towpath into the wooded incline dropping down to the edge of the Potomac.

James Angleton was angry at his wife, Cicely. Here he was in the middle of a big conference at CIA headquarters—Angleton was then chief of counterintelligence for the CIA—and his wife was interrupting the meeting with a silly fantasy. According to a radio bulletin, an unidentified woman had been slain on the towpath that afternoon, and Cicely was sure the victim was their old friend Mary Meyer. She had often warned Mary not to go there alone.

Angleton dismissed his wife's anxiety. That evening they had planned to drive Mary Meyer to a poetry reading and he saw no reason to change anything.

When they arrived at Mary's home that night, her car was in the driveway, yet the lights were out inside. A sign hanging on her door said "Free Kittens—Ring Bell or Call." No one answered the bell. At his wife's insistence, Angleton checked Mary's answering service. They told him Mary had been murdered. The Angletons hurried to the Bradlees' home, where they helped make funeral arrangements. Later that night, Angleton returned and rescued three kittens from the empty house.

Soon the CIA chief would learn he had a mission of great delicacy to perform. An intimate of Mary Meyer's had charged him with recovering and disposing of her secret diary, a diary that contained references to a very special affair.

The manhunt began less than five minutes after the murder. When Henry Wiggins phoned the D.C. police from the nearby Esso station, the dispatcher sent squad cars full of men from all over the precinct racing to seal off the five well-marked exits from the towpath across the canal to the streets of Georgetown. With the exits sealed off soon enough, police figured they'd trapped the murderer on the hilly wooded strip of bank between the canal and the river (which was chilly and too wide at that point to afford an escape).

Officer Warner was heading east through the underbrush along the roadbed of the old C & O tracks. He emerged from a detour into a shadowy spillway to find standing, in the middle of the tracks, a short wiry black man, dripping wet and covered with grass and twigs. Water ran out of the wallet the man offered as identification. He said his name was Raymond Crump, Jr. He had been fishing around the bend, he told the officer, had fallen asleep on the riverbank, and woke up only when he found himself sliding down the bank into the water.

Officer Warner asked Raymond Crump, Jr., to show him exactly where "around the bend" he had been fishing. Raymond Crump started to lead him west along the shore. They didn't get far.

When he arrived at the body with the medical examiner and eyewitness Wiggins in tow, Detective Bernard Crooke was struck immediately by how beautiful the murdered woman was. "I've seen a lot of dead women," Detective

Crooke says, "but none who looked beautiful when dead. She even looked beautiful with a bullet in her head."

Crooke didn't have much time to reflect upon this. A few minutes after he arrived, as he was still trying and failing to find some identification on the body, a cry went up from Henry Wiggins, who was peering down the bank that descended from the towpath to the C & O roadbed and then down to the river. Wiggins was pointing at two figures on the roadbed below. One was Officer Warner; the other was Raymond Crump, Jr. "That's him," shouted Wiggins, pointing at Crump.

Five minutes later, a handcuffed Crump was brought before Crooke. "Why is your fly open?" Crooke asked Crump.

"You did it," Crump said. Crooke didn't like that. He didn't like the fishing alibi Crump told him, but Crump stuck to his story. As he was led past Mary Meyer's body toward a squad car to be booked, Crump looked down at the blue angora–clad body.

"You think I did that?" he asked.

Crooke thought he did it. Then came what was for Crooke the clincher. He was interrogating Crump back at the stationhouse when one of the men who had been searching the shoreline for the still missing murder weapon brought back to Crooke something he had found in the Potomac—a light-colored windbreaker jacket with a half-empty pack of Pall Malls in one of the pockets. Crooke told Crump to try it on. According to Crooke, it fit Crump perfectly.

"It looks like you got a stacked deck," Crooke recalls Crump telling him. Then Crump began to cry. Crooke says he patted him on the back, but the sobs only increased.

Ms. Dovey Roundtree is a black woman, an ordained minister of the African Methodist Episcopal Church and one of the best homicide lawyers in Washington. She claims an acquittal rate of 80 percent for clients accused of murder. In addition to an impressive legal intellect and an aggressive courtroom style, she brings to the task of winning over a jury some of the righteous fervor and persuasive eloquence of the pulpit.

One day in December 1964 a black woman, a churchgoing A.M.E. Christian, came to Ms. Roundtree's law offices and asked for her help. Her son, Raymond Crump, Jr., stood accused of first-degree murder and couldn't make bail. Her son was innocent, the mother told Ms. Roundtree. She knew in her heart he was a meek, gentle boy. He had had some hard times—a bad accident a year ago, troubles with his wife, some problems with drinking and work— but he was not a murderer. Roundtree took the case. She started her own private investigation: She was determined to find out who this woman Mary Meyer was, and who her friends were.

.   .   .

It was a wedding of special grace and promise. When Mary Eno Pinchot and Cord Meyer, Jr., married in the bride's Park Avenue home in the spring of 1945, life seemed rather splendid. They were both monied, talented, and justly full of expectation. She was the most beautiful girl in Vassar's class of '42. He graduated Yale Phi Beta Kappa, summa cum laude, and won the Alpheus Henry Snow Award as "the senior adjudged by the faculty to have done the most for Yale by inspiring his classmates."

Mary came from one of America's prominent political families—the Pinchots of Pennsylvania. Her uncle Gifford Pinchot, a two-term governor of his home state in the twenties and thirties as well as a noted forester, was often mentioned as a dark horse for the Republican presidential nomination. Her father, Amos Pinchot, a radical lawyer, helped organize the breakaway Bull Moose Party for Teddy Roosevelt in 1912. He later became a pacifist and an America First critic of FDR's internationalism. Our declaration of war against the Axis drove him to attempt suicide. The Pinchot fortune, based on the lucrative dry goods business of Mary's paternal grandfather, James, and augmented by the large inheritance of his wife, Mary Eno, reached into the millions.

Cord's bloodlines were less illustrious but similarly marked by wealth and politics. His great-grandfather grew rich in sugar and his grandfather, a state chairman of the New York Democratic Party, in Long Island real estate. Cord Meyer, Sr., served as a diplomat in Cuba, Italy, and Sweden before retiring from government service when he fathered a second set of twin sons in the twenties.

At the time of the marriage, Cord was serving as a military aide to Commander Harold E. Stassen, then a U.S. delegate at the drafting of the United Nation's Charter in San Francisco. He had lost an eye to a Japanese grenade on Guam and published "Waves of Darkness," a moving, often anthologized short story of the disillusions of war, in the December 1945 *Atlantic*. In 1947 the Junior Chamber of Commerce named him one of the ten outstanding young men in the United States. As spokesman for the liberal United World Federalists, he crusaded across the country for the idea of world government. After listening to one of Cord's speeches, Merle Miller noted in his journal: "If Cord goes into politics he'll probably not only be president of the United States; he may be the first president of the parliament of man. And if he does become a writer, he's sure to win the Nobel Prize."

Cord did not fulfill Miller's prophecy. At the urging of Allen Dulles, he joined the Central Intelligence Agency in 1951 and developed into a determined anti-Communist operative, eventually rising to the post of assistant deputy director of plans, better known as the dirty tricks department.

By 1956, after eleven years of marriage, Mary, then thirty-six, could no longer tolerate living with Cord and the CIA, a business she hated. She divorced him and moved across the Potomac from McLean, Virginia, where RFK was her next-door neighbor and friend, to a Georgetown townhouse around the corner from her sister, Mrs. Benjamin Bradlee, and their mutual good friend Senator John Kennedy.

It was Mary, not Cord, who eventually attained the White House. The grace and promise of their wedding was twisted in unforeseen fashion. While he sulked in the CIA, even briefing JFK on occasion, she became the secret Lady Ottoline of Camelot.

Jack and Mary first met at Vassar. Kennedy (Harvard '40) dated several members of Mary's class, including her chum Dorothy Burns. "Everybody knew everybody then," says Scottie Fitzgerald Smith, F. Scott Fitzgerald's daughter and Mary's classmate. The women closest to Mary on campus refused to reminisce about her. But interviews with acquaintances indicate that she did not particularly distinguish herself at Vassar. Selection for the daisy chain, a wreath of daisies borne at graduation by the comeliest and most personable sophomores, seems her only honor. "Mary wasn't very gregarious," Scottie Smith remarks. "She didn't mingle about. She was an independent soul. I always thought of her as a fawn running through the forest."

A short story entitled "Futility" in the April 1941 *Vassar Review and Little Magazine,* the single extant sample of her campus writing, suggests a free and wildly imaginative spirit. A young lady, bored with the "chicly cadaverous" women who are "being too killing about Noël Coward's love life" at a Park Avenue cocktail party, runs off to a hospital for a strange operation. She wants to have the ends of her optical nerves attached to the hearing part of the brain and the auditory ends to the seeing part so that everything she sees she hears and vice versa. The surgery was a success. The young lady returned to the apartment now empty of partygoers and lay down on the hostess's sofa. Mary concluded the fantasy: "The lighted aquarium, like a window to a green outdoors, shone above the mantle in the dark room. The copper fish undulated aimlessly among the other weeds, and as she watched them, she heard the far-off buzz of men's and women's voices chattering in the room, the sound of glass clinking against ice, Beatrice's voice rising and falling. The low murmur hummed on and on, and Ruth fell asleep. And because her eyes were closed, she heard nothing to disturb her, and slept forever on the chartreuse couch."

After Vassar, Mary went to work for the United Press in New York City, and there fell in love with Bob Schwartz, a home-front staffer for the GI newspaper *Yank.* For the sake of Mary's mother, they maintained separate quarters, but their intense three-year involvement was public knowledge. The Pinchots accepted the relationship. The couple traveled together and passed many weekends at the several-thousand-acre Pinchot estate in the Poconos. Now an entrepreneur in Tarrytown, New York, Schwartz would say only that he was Mary's first love and that he had ended it in 1944, before Cord returned from the Pacific. "Mary was unbelievable to behold," Schwartz avowed. "She was uncompromising about her view of the world and had great strength about it."

Although Mary considered medical school, she took her thirty-dollar-a-week feature-writing job at U.P. seriously. In 1944 she freelanced three well-turned pieces on "meteorbiology," venereal disease, and college sex courses for *Mademoiselle.* Criticizing squeamish public attitudes toward the wartime epidemic of syphilis and gonorrhea, she wrote, "Though the spirochete is better barred from the body, there's no reason to ban awareness of it from the mind." In "Credits for Love," she endorsed sex education "as a means to a happier and less hazardous private life."

Scottie Fitzgerald Smith was at *Time* during this same period and saw a lot of Mary. They lunched and partied together. Scottie recalls that Mary enjoyed skinny-dipping *ensemble* in the bubbling "champagne pond" under the idyllic waterfall on the Pocono property. "She was unconventional and broke the rules of our generation. But her unconventionality was quiet and disciplined. She was never a showoff." Asked to describe Mary's appeal to men, her old friend remarked, "Mary had perfectly lovely skin and coloring. She always looked like she had just taken a bath. A man once told me that she reminded him of a cat walking on a roof in the moonlight. She had such tremendous poise. Whether she was merely shy or just controlled, I don't know. She was very cool physically and psychologically, a liberated woman long before it was fashionable."

Mary's first son, named Quentin after Cord's twin, who had died on Okinawa, was born in 1946. She thereupon combined motherhood and manuscript reading at *Atlantic Monthly* while Cord studied at Harvard. Soon she retired from her literary career to assist her husband's world government efforts and bear two more sons, Michael and Mark. After the divorce was all but decided in 1956, Michael was killed by a car in McLean. This tragedy affected both parents deeply, but it did not bring them back together; it could not salvage the marriage. "She respected Cord but wanted to make it on her own as a painter," explains a Washington intimate. "Why should she have to go to dinners with the director of the CIA when she'd rather be in her studio?"

After the separation, Mary fell under the influence of Kenneth Noland, a painter who was one of the founders of what became known as the "Washington Color School." Inspired by Helen Frankenthaler's revolt against the "too painterly" qualities of Abstract Expressionism, Noland and the late Morris Louis, both residents of Washington in the fifties, began experimenting with new techniques of applying paint to canvas. They made color, rather than structure or subject, their primary concern. They and their disciples tended to concentrate on a single format. Louis worked with the bleeding edge, Noland on targets, and Gene Davis in stripes. This small community significantly affected the history of American art and made some of its members famous and wealthy.

Mary chose to paint in *tondo;* that is, on rounded canvases. Like her lover, Noland, four years her junior, she focused on circular swaths of color. Her painting *Blue Sky* hangs in the Manhattan apartment of poet Barbara Higgins, a friend from the early sixties. *Blue Sky,* a very early work, is a six-foot-by-five-and-a-half-foot rectangle, but large semicircular bands of green, blue, and orange color resting above and below two hard-edged horizontal lines show evidence of her later direction. "When Mary started painting large pictures, she began freeing herself," Mrs. Higgins says. "She felt she was making a breakthrough and was happier than I'd ever seen her."

Mary's long friendship with John F. Kennedy continued throughout their respective marriages. She regularly attended Kennedy White House soirées in the company of her sister, Tony, and Ben Bradlee. We now know that a sexual relationship began in January 1962. In September 1963, Mary and Tony Bradlee flew with JFK in the presidential helicopter to the Pinchot estate in Milford, Pennsylvania, where JFK officially accepted on behalf of the government the donation of a mansion and some land.

"That in itself was probably not enough to command the president's presence," writes Ben Bradlee in *Conversations with Kennedy,* "but a chance to see where his friends the Pinchot girls had grown up, and especially a chance to see their mother, was apparently irresistible. . . ."

A few weeks later, in the awful month of November 1963, Mary Meyer's first show opened at Washington's Jefferson Place Gallery. The reviews were quite good, recalls Nesta Dorrance, then director of the now-defunct gallery. She feels it was too soon for Mary's potential as an artist to be judged.

The friends of Mary Meyer choose words like "warmth . . . vibrance . . . loyalty . . . mystery and strength" to describe her.

"Mary had a half-sister, Rosamond, a Broadway actress who committed suicide in 1938," one friend remarked. "Rosamond used to go down to the Pinchot stables at midnight, saddle a horse, and gallop at full speed across the estate. Mary was awed by her, she thought it was poetic. That was the feeling we all had for Mary."

On the Saturday following Mary Meyer's murder, five people gathered at her Georgetown home and tore it apart searching for the secret diary. Sometime before she died, Mary had entrusted to her friends James and Ann Truitt the fact of her affair with JFK and the existence of a diary recounting some of her evenings with the president. Truitt was then a vice president of *The Washington Post;* his wife, Ann, was a sculptor and confidante of Mary. Before they departed for Tokyo in 1963, where Truitt was to become *Newsweek* bureau chief, Mary discussed the disposition of her diary in the event of her death. She asked them to preserve it, and to show it to her son Quentin when he reached the age of twenty-one.

The Truitts were still in Tokyo when they received word of the towpath murder, and the responsibility for the diary was communicated to their mutual friend James Angleton, through still uncertain channels.

Mary Meyer was accustomed to leaving her diary in the bookcase in her bedroom where, incidentally, she kept clippings of the JFK assassination. The diary was not there after her death.

Angleton therefore brought some of the specialized tools of his black-bag trade—white gloves, drills, etc.—to the task of combing the house. Also there to aid in the search were other members of Mary Meyer's circle: Tony Bradlee; Cord Meyer; a former college roommate, Ann Chamberlain; and Angleton's wife, Cicely.

They tapped walls, looked in the fireplace, and turned over bricks in the garden, finding nothing and exhausting themselves in the process. Cord lit a smoky fire, Angleton pitched in washing dishes, and the whiskey flowed. One frustrated seeker went out into the garden and yelled up to the sky, "Mary, where's your damned diary?"

It wasn't in the house at all. Tony located it in Mary's studio later, along with the canvases she was readying for what would have been her second gallery show. The diary was in a locked steel box filled with hundreds of letters.

Neither the police nor the prosecutor was aware of the existence of a diary when Raymond Crump went on trial for the murder of Mary Meyer on July 19, 1965.

"This is a classic textbook case of circumstantial evidence," Prosecutor Albert Hantman told the jury.

Prosecutor Hantman was missing certain direct links in what seemed on the surface an airtight case. He didn't have the murder weapon. He'd had the riverbank searched, he'd had scuba divers rake through the muck at the bottom of the Potomac. No gun. And his eyewitness, Henry Wiggins, would only testify to a "glance" at the man he saw standing over Mary Meyer's body. Hantman's case had many strengths despite this. Crump's fishing alibi sounded implausible in many ways. He claimed he'd lost his fishing pole and "chicken hair" bait in his fall into the Potomac. But a nosy neighbor had observed him leaving home that morning carrying no fishing tackle at all and wearing a dark plaid cap and a light-colored windbreaker that matched those worn by the assailant.

Hantman decided the only way to prove that Mary Meyer's murderer and Raymond Crump were one and the same man was to reconstruct in detail the movements of each before, during, and after the murder, and to prove that no one but Raymond Crump was present on or about the towpath when Mary Meyer died.

Hantman even went so far as to try to introduce a large tree branch into court as evidence. Hantman justified this unusual request by claiming that the position of the bloodstains on the tree—and he waved about in open court a vial of Mary Meyer's blood scraped from the tree—would support his reconstruction of Mary Meyer's death struggle.

The murderer first tried to drag Mary Meyer down into the bushes on the bank behind the towpath, the prosecutor told the jury, hinting strongly at a sexual motive for the initial assault. Then, Hantman said, "she grabbed the tree . . . holding on for her life. She didn't want to lose sight of the people; and he was attempting to pull her down behind the canal. She struggled and fought. His jacket was torn. Her slacks were torn. His finger was cut. She had abrasions and contusions on various parts of her body. He shot her once and she resisted. She broke away from him. She ran across the towpath. She fell. She was alive and he had to shoot her again so she couldn't identify him."

By trying to prove everything so precisely from circumstantial evidence, Hantman left Roundtree several opportunities to challenge successfully any absolute interpretation of such elements as the bloodstains and hair fiber analysis. She forced a National Park Service mapmaker to concede that there were other possible exits from the riverbank area that had not been sealed off by the police. In the end she rested her case without calling a single witness. Instead, she presented a powerful final summation that came down hard on Air Force Lieutenant Mitchell's description of the man following Mary Meyer on the towpath as "about my size." William Mitchell's size was five-foot-eight, 145 pounds. Roundtree told the jury: "Look at this little man, Ray Crump. He is your Exhibit A." Crump, she said, was only five-foot-three. She reminded the jury that "only the official exits had been sealed" and raised the specter of "a phantom" killer who escaped the manhunt by way of an unmarked exit.

Dramatic as Roundtree's summation was, Prosecutor Hantman pushed the pitch of the drama almost over the edge into farce in his rebuttal argument. He decided to take on directly Roundtree's Exhibit A—Ray Crump's short stature as compared to the five-foot-eight height of the man William Mitchell had observed following Mary Meyer. Hantman played his trump: the elevator shoe demonstration. "The defendant," Hantman said, "was five-foot-five-and-a-half when he was taken to identification."

Then Hantman dramatically placed government Exhibit 17 on the lectern in full view of the jury. Government Exhibit 17 was a pair of Ray Crump's shoes—the pair he was wearing when he was arrested.

"Look at the heels of these shoes," Hantman cried. "They are practically Adler-heel shoes. There are at least . . . two inches of heel on that pair of shoes. . . . This is what gave Lieutenant Mitchell the appearance that this defendant was his size."

The case went to the jury on July 29, 1965. After five hours of deliberation the jury foreman sent to the judge for answers to the following questions: "Was Ray Crump right-handed or left-handed? Did the police ever permit Crump to show them where he claimed to be fishing and from where he fell?"

The judge told the jury they would have to depend upon their own recollection for the answers to those questions. The jury deliberated for a few more hours, then sent a second note to the judge informing him they were deadlocked eight to four. They did not say which way. The judge instructed them they were not "hopelessly" deadlocked and ordered them to return to their deliberations. At 11:35 A.M. on July 30, after a total of eleven hours, they sent word they had finally reached a verdict. They found Raymond Crump not guilty.

The acquittal left the murder of Mary Meyer officially unsolved. But Washington police never reopened the investigation. They closed the towpath murder file after the trial. "Without a full confession and witnessing it myself," remarks Inspector Bernard Crooke, "there's no question in my mind that Ray Crump shot Mary Meyer." Like the detective in the film *Laura,* Crooke became somewhat captivated by the victim. He leafed through several old homicide notebooks stored in his current office at Third District Headquarters on V Street to refresh his recollection of the case. Homicide detectives interviewed at least one hundred friends of Mary Meyer. Apparently, nothing untoward turned up; any prior association with Crump was ruled out after a check of her personal belongings. Crooke recalls going through her deep, narrow townhouse and being amused by the contrast of the exquisite antique furnishings and the starkly functional bathroom with a sunken tub. Crooke was also struck by the formal written invitation to a simple date with a gentleman that he found on her desk. "We learned that she was seeing several men," he says, "and when you look twenty-five and you're free . . . She would have quickened the pulse of many men."

Crooke discovered a diary-type calendar in Mary Meyer's home, but not any larger diary. "I'd have been very upset at the time if I knew the deceased's diary had been destroyed."

Dovey Roundtree believes Mary Meyer's murderer is still at large, although she has no particular person in mind. In her pretrial investigation,

Roundtree pursued the ghost of Mary Meyer in the hope of locating another suspect or a suggestion of one. If her client was innocent, as she truly believed, then somebody else, perhaps a boyfriend, committed the act. Although she despised making sexual innuendos about dead women in court, she was prepared to raise the matter. "She had a lot of different men," Roundtree comments in her law office at Roundtree, Knox, Hunter and Pendarvis. "Some were younger. For a woman her age, you'd think she'd just have one person. I thought it was unusual even though she was an artist. I was looking for motivation. I narrowed it down to people who knew her and her habits, who may have argued with her and had a confrontation. I thought we were getting close to something sexual or some other reason which I didn't understand myself. But after the prosecution introduced a mountain of evidence, I decided to keep my case as simple as possible. Hantman was a most frustrated man. He wanted Ray Crump on the witness stand and would have destroyed him. Ray had goofed off from work and took a six-pack of beer fishing to get away from his bitchin' wife. They wanted to massacre and burn this boy. If I failed, he would die."

Roundtree recalls a number of anonymous phone calls in the course of the case, directing her to secret meetings. Wary of a trap, she stayed away.

The trial proceedings seemed rushed to her. She learned that Mary Meyer had a high White House clearance and that her diary was burned before the trial. "I thought the government had something to do with the whole case," she says. Her client, Ray Crump, left Washington after the trial. He thinks he was framed the first time, she says, and lives in fear that someone will come after him again.

Fourteen years after the murder, the *National Enquirer* disinterred the untold story of Mary Meyer in its issue dated March 2, 1976. The bold front-page headline read JFK TWO YEAR WHITE HOUSE ROMANCE . . . SOCIALITE THEN MURDERED AND DIARY BURNED BY CIA. The tabloid's eager source was James Truitt. According to Truitt, whose quotes take up almost the entire text, JFK first asked her to go to bed with him in the White House in December 1961. A current involvement with an artist caused her to reject his proposal. But beginning in January she kept regular sexual rendezvous with the president until his assassination. "She said she had to tell someone what was happening," Truitt informed the *Enquirer.* "So she confided in me and my former wife, Ann."

If Truitt's revelations are to be believed, Mary loved JFK but realized their liaison would be limited to brief encounters even though, as she told Truitt, he felt "no affection of a lasting kind" for his wife. Their arrangement apparently had its comic moments. Truitt's notes record an episode in July of 1962 during which Mary turned on JFK with two joints of marijuana. He laughed as he mentioned an imminent White House conference on narcotics. "This isn't like cocaine," he reputedly said. "I'll get you some of that."

Furthermore, the *Enquirer* disclosed that Mary's personal diary, containing references to JFK and several love letters from him, was discovered by her sister, Tony Bradlee, in her garage studio and surrendered to James Angleton of the CIA, who had aided in the search.

The *Enquirer* account raised the question of an official CIA connection to the death. The tabloid called the murder "unsolved" and suggestively characterized the official view of the case as "a lone gunman" theory. Immediately after the acquittal of Ray Crump there was talk in Georgetown circles of the possibility of conspiracy in Mary Meyer's death—one person close to the case heard speculation about "KGB sacrificial murders." And Patrick Anderson's subsequent novel, *The President's Mistress,* postulates a Georgetown paramour of a Kennedyesque president murdered by an overzealous aide in a struggle over a memoir of the White House affair. But no evidence to support such talk has ever been uncovered, and no one has ever pointed to a better suspect than Ray Crump. Even if someone other than Ray Crump did kill Mary Meyer—another black man in a light windbreaker, dark slacks and golf cap—in the absence of evidence to the contrary from any source, the violence done to her on the towpath that day is more likely to have been random rather than conspiratorial. None of the many friends of Mary Meyer has suggested any other motive.

The real questions left unanswered in the wake of the *Enquirer* revelation circle around Mary Meyer's diary: What was in it, who read it, what became of it, what if anything did it reveal about the nature of her relationship with JFK, and why did the people involved in the search for the diary behave so strangely when its existence became public after fourteen years of silence?

The close circle of friends that linked Mary Meyer and JFK had gathered at her home in the wake of her murder to search for the diary in order to fulfill one of her final requests. Some of them had even, several years later, attended a séance in Upper Marlboro, Maryland, at which some attempt was made to establish "contact" with her departed spirit. And for fourteen years all of them had kept the story not only out of the public press but for the most part out of the mainstream of subterranean Washington gossip. For years before Judith Exner or any of the women with whom JFK consorted became household names in the mass media, the names of many of them were quite familiar to the Georgetown Camelot set.

But the Mary Meyer revelation shocked even some veteran observers of that scene. "It was a bombshell," said one, "not because it *happened* but because nobody I know ever heard a whisper."

After the secret legacy shared by the circle of friends became tabloid headlines in 1976, all the resentments, hatreds, bitterness, and infighting that had been building among the members of the circle since the deaths of the secret lovers suddenly broke out into the open. Without that shared secret they appeared to have nothing to unite them. James Truitt betrayed his confidence to get Ben Bradlee, Bradlee's newspaper questioned Truitt's mental health, Bradlee accused Angleton of a lock-pick "break-in" at Mary Meyer's studio, Angleton called Bradlee a liar, Tony Bradlee, now divorced from Ben, contradicted her husband's version of some of the key events.

The aftermath is a tale of disappointed expectations, revenge, and disloyalty, as sad and pathetic in its way as the death of Mary Meyer and the destruction of other illusions of Camelot.

James Truitt strongly resents Ben Bradlee. The fact that he would trample the memory of his beloved friend Mary to embarrass Bradlee is one measure of his animus. In happier days, Truitt held a position of some importance at *The Washington Post.* He was the right-hand man of its publisher, Philip Graham. After Graham shot himself in the summer of 1963, Truitt wound up in the Tokyo bureau of *Newsweek,* another *Post* company. Bradlee, transferred to the *Post* from *Newsweek*'s Washington bureau in 1965, brought Truitt back to Washington, where he worked on the paper's new "Style" section. Unfortunately, he did not perform especially well and had a nervous breakdown in 1969. Truitt believes that Bradlee conspired to have him fired and that the *Post* did not keep certain promises to him after Graham's suicide. Truitt told *Enquirer* researcher Bernie Ward that he exposed the Mary Meyer affair with JFK in order to show up Bradlee. "Here is this great crusading Watergate editor who claimed to tell everything in his Kennedy book," Ward quotes Truitt as saying, "but really told nothing."

If the executive editor of the *Post* covered up for JFK, his paper did not extend the same courtesy to Truitt. The *Post* gave front-page attention to Truitt's crack-up in its February 23 story on the Mary Meyer revelations. After reporting the *Enquirer*'s assertions in detail, including confirmation of the upcoming narcotics conference that JFK supposedly referred to while stoned in the White House, *Post* staffer Don Oberdorfer cited a doctor's certification contained in court records that Truitt had suffered from a mental illness "such as to impair his judgment and cause him to be irresponsible." An anonymous Washington attorney added that Truitt had threatened Bradlee and others in recent years with exposure of the "alleged scandals." Thus the *Post,* while giving admirable play to an extremely touchy subject, created the hard impression that Truitt was an unreliable source—even though most believe Bradlee knew that Truitt was essentially truthful about Mary Meyer and JFK.

The motives behind the Angleton-Bradlee clash are less clear. They also had been friends. But as far back as 1965 Bradlee seems to have hurt Angleton in the *Post*. According to one source, in 1968 Bradlee took the initiative to write an unsigned *Post* story on a book by Kim Philby (Britain's counterintelligence chief in the pay of the KGB), a story that purposely ignored all favorable references to Angleton while quoting the unfavorable mentions. When Angleton asked him why he treated a friend like that, Bradlee is said to have denied authorship.

Their feud burst forth again over the matter of Mary Meyer. A *Post* reporter close to Bradlee recalls that Bradlee informed him long ago that he, Bradlee, had caught Angleton breaking into Mary's studio in quest of the hot document. "Ben was surprised to see him there with his lock pick," he says. *Post* columnist Nicholas Von Hoffman cited the same hearsay in *The New York Review of Books* (June 10, 1976), where he observed that the residence of a presidential paramour "was broken into by a CIA agent and her diary burned." During Seymour Hersh's attempt to pin down his CIA domestic surveillance scoop, a man from the *Times* called Angleton and accused him of the studio break-in.

Ben Bradlee, who seems to have been telling the Angleton lock-pick tale around town for some time, stood by its accuracy. "Angleton was trying to get in," he affirmed in a phone interview, "but ultimately he was invited in." But Bradlee, while he could not account for Angleton's lock-picking zeal, quickly disavows any CIA angle. "If there was anything there," Bradlee said regarding the agency's shadow over the case, "I would have done it [written the story] myself."

Angleton angrily denies the break-in charge. "It is a total lie," Angleton told us. "I was never at the studio."

One source, who tends to take Angleton's side in the Angleton-Bradlee dispute, also accuses Bradlee of disloyalty to Mary Meyer. According to the source, Bradlee considered exposing her affair with JFK himself in *Conversations with Kennedy,* until others pressured him against it.

In fact, Bradlee did allude to JFK's fascination with Mary Meyer in the following passage:

> The conversation ended, as those conversations often ended, with his views on some of the women present—the overall appeal of the daughter of Prince Paul of Yugoslavia and Mary Meyer. "Mary would be rough to live with," Kennedy noted, not for the first time. And I agreed, not for the first time.

What did JFK mean? "I don't know," Bradlee told us. What sort of woman was Mary? "She was marvelous," he said. (The Bradlee-Kennedy exchange on Mary Meyer took place in February of 1962—just a month after the affair was inaugurated in Truitt's chronology.)

Also, according to the same source allied to Angleton, Mary Meyer herself was not on speaking terms with Bradlee for the last six months of her life because she felt he had given away a confidence of hers in *Newsweek*. Bradlee continues to deny that he was aware of the JFK–Mary Meyer affair before the *Enquirer* story—even though, as he admitted to us, he read through the diary in 1964.

"Were you surprised to learn of the liaison?" we asked Bradlee.

"Of course I was surprised," he said. "I was amazed."

The whole story of the life, death, and resurrection of Mary Meyer is immensely complex and is not complete here. Many friends and relatives understandably drew back from the public controversy. Many refused all comment, others misled and misspoke. However, from unpublished materials and interviews with intimate sources, we have found certain things that can be said about the contents of the diary and the letters and the nature of the affair itself.

James Angleton read those letters. He also read the diary. He cataloged the letters. He took notes on some of them. He offered certain people the opportunity to repossess letters they had written to Mary Meyer.

In a letter Angleton wrote to Truitt after the diary search, he said two other persons whom Angleton identified only as "M" and "F" had read the diary. "M" and "F" told Angleton they wanted to preserve certain edited parts. One other person was permitted to see the diary: Mary Meyer's older son, Quentin, then eighteen, read deeply in the private papers and subsequently wrote his brother, Mark, about the contents.

In an unpublished draft of the *Enquirer* story, Mary's sister, Tony, reveals far more about Mary, JFK, and the diary.

"Mary and JFK did have a close relationship. You obviously know that much and that's true," she told the *Enquirer,* according to this draft. She continued:

> I didn't know anything at all about it at the time. What I understand of it afterwards, it was a fling, another of Jack's flings. If Mary had any relationship of the kind she went into it with her eyes open.
>
> We did find it [the diary] in the studio. I don't remember where. It may have been in a filing cabinet. I was the one who found it. We were going through her belongings and there it was. Yes, it's true we were looking for it. None of us read it. We were all honor bound not to. [Here Truitt wrote "no" in the margin.] The diary was a slim volume. All I remember is that it was like a sketchbook with a nice paisley-colored cover on it. It was kind of a loose leaf book, nothing like Ben's book he was taking things down in, just a woman's notes about what she had been doing. I swear I don't remember what was in it, I went through it so quickly. And I remember there were some JFK's in it. There were some references to him. It was a dreadful time but as I remember it had pencil marks. It was

very cryptic and difficult to understand. Not much there but some reference to JFK. I felt it was something we shouldn't look at. There were some references to him. But the diary was destroyed. I'll tell you that much is true.

When James Angleton read the diary, he thought that although Mary Meyer's prose was informal, the implications in the entries were transparent. Angleton decided that in the wrong hands the diary might be troublesome to the children and others. (Angleton had a fatherly relationship to Mary Meyer's sons, and later, when Cord Meyer left for London to assume his present post as CIA station chief, Angleton became trustee for the children.)

"I burned them," Angleton later wrote Truitt. Yet Angleton also wrote Truitt that he had informed certain members of Mary Meyer's family that the papers still reposed somewhere at the Pinchot estate in Milford.

Does the diary still exist? Unless it shows up again somehow, only those familiar with its contents can help us form a judgment about the real nature of the twenty-month relationship between Mary Meyer and John F. Kennedy.

One person who is in a unique position to comment authoritatively on that relationship, and who has never before spoken to the press about it, agreed to entertain a limited number of questions about the affair:

"How could a woman so admired for her integrity as Mary Meyer traduce her friendship with Jackie Kennedy?"

"They weren't friends," he said curtly.

"Did JFK actually *love* Mary Meyer?"

"I think so."

"Then why would he carry on an affair simultaneously with Judy Exner?"

"My friend, there's a difference between sex and love."

"But why Mary Meyer over all other women?"

"He was an unusual man. He wanted the best."

Postscript to "A Killing in Camelot"

In the years since this story appeared, the mystique surrounding what might have been revealed in the missing diary of Mary Meyer has assumed mythic proportions in conspiracy-theory literature.

One night in the Hollywood Hills, well into the late eighties, a well-known West Coast figure handed me a long missive from a private conspiracy-theory investigator who claimed that the murder of Mary Meyer was the key to just about Everything—all the scandals and tragedies of the post-Dallas world. In essence, it went something like this: Mary Meyer was murdered because of what she knew about the CIA plot to kill JFK; James Angleton seized her diary because it revealed the truth about the assassination; later on, Angleton, as Deep Throat, exposed Watergate to *The Washington Post* to depose Nixon, because Nixon planned to expose the truth about the CIA's role in JFK's death—which was *really* what was erased from the eighteen-minute gap on the Watergate tape. I think I might have left something out—the murder of John Lennon might also figure in—but you get the picture. Mary Meyer's missing diary, like the eighteen-minute erasure, has become a black hole into which all the secret truths of our time have disappeared.

This entire Ultimate Conspiracy Theory fantasy seemed to be founded upon the "fact" that Mary Meyer's murder was "officially unsolved," the only suspect acquitted by a jury. Although according to the L.A. figure who showed me the Letter That Explained It All, there was one further fact that made it look like the cover-up was still going on: the missing transcript.

He'd hired a private eye, my L.A. friend explained. He'd been intrigued enough by the unsolved status of Mary Meyer's death to put a gumshoe on the case. This was more than abstract historical curiosity. He felt he owed it to Mary Meyer. He'd known her briefly—intensely but platonically, he said—and clearly worshiped her. Spoke of her exquisite beauty and intellect, saw her as a clandestine crusader for peace in the hawkish upper echelons of Camelot—on a mission, in her White House trysts, to turn JFK's head toward peace.

But the private eye my friend hired hadn't gotten very far before he reached a dead end. The transcript of the murder trial of the man accused of shooting Mary Meyer had disappeared from the D.C. courthouse archives, he said. The obvious conclusion was that it had been removed because it contained a clue to the conspiracy.

Not quite. I'd read the transcript when it was still there in the D.C. court clerk's office—read it with great avidity and attentiveness, read it hoping to find some clue, some evidence of conspiracy, some flaw in the prosecution's lone-gunman theory. It certainly would have made a bigger story if there'd been a hole in the case that pointed to a more sinister explanation of the prosecution's theory of a random assault by a stranger.

That night when I told the L.A. guy that I'd actually read what he'd thought of as The Missing Transcript, I had the strange sensation of being implored: *You're the only one in the world who can tell us.* What did the "missing" transcript reveal? Was there a conspiracy?

What I told him was, in essence: no. That having not only read the transcript but having reinvestigated the whole case, interviewed most of the principals, I'd come to believe in the lone-gunman theory of this case. That the fatal shot *was* fired in the midst of a random assault by a stranger. That the prosecution may *perhaps* have indicted the wrong lone gunman on the basis of imperfect eyewitness testimony. But that no evidence was ever adduced that gives the slightest hint there was a conspiracy behind Mary Meyer's murder—or that her death had any relation to her secret liaison with JFK.

Indeed, the only real conspiracy was the one that took shape after her death, the one in which her high-placed friends conspired in a well-meaning attempt to preserve the secrecy of the affair with JFK described in her diary.

A recent careful reinvestigation of the murder charge (in Nina Burleigh's 1998 biography of Mary Meyer, *A Very Private Woman*) turned up nothing to dispute the lone-gunman theory of the case. Burleigh does, however, reopen the question of the final fate of the much sought-after diary. Angleton claimed to have burned it. But in a 1995 letter to *The New York Times Book Review,* two of Mary Meyer's closest friends said that while Angleton initially took possession of the diary, he later returned it to them, at which point *they* burned it. Ms. Burleigh raises the possibility that Angleton had it photocopied and kept that copy for himself before giving it over to be consigned to the flames.

Chariots of the Insurance Salesmen

In Which We Track the Occult Masters of
Get-Rich-Quick Literature

The secret of "Sex Transmutation." Psychic energy from the mystic council of Cosmic Guardians. "Internal bathing." The Five Clay Tablets inscribed with the wisdom of Dabasir, the camel trader of Babylon. Master Mind communion with the Infinite Intelligence.

What is all this gibberish? A catalog of demented counterculture catchphrases? Some parody of hippy-dippy Von Däniken lore?

Far from it. These are just a sampling of the weird doctrines and occult rituals that spellbind the millions of mainstream, conventional Middle Americans who are part of the strange subculture of success-secret seekers and get-rich-quick dreamers.

You've seen the ads for the swamis of this subculture skulking in the back pages of magazines amid come-ons for sensual black satin sheets and the mystic secrets of the Rosicrucians. "Secrets of the Money Masters Revealed," the ads say. "I earned $35,000 in one day at home in bed with the flu," they proclaim. "Who else wants to get in on this Bonanza of Fast Capital Buildup?" they ask.

Perhaps you've been curious about these ads, even tempted to send away for one of the offers. Just for laughs, of course. But you're slightly embarrassed about what the postman might think if your copy of *The Money-Master's Manual* doesn't arrive in a plain brown wrapper. And besides, as a sophisticated New Yorker it's hard for you to imagine there could be anything to these success schemes. You feel confident that Felix Rohatyn didn't get his start by clipping one of these coupons. Certainly such appeals are unfashionable now in an age that believes in the subtleties of the corporate game player. The rhetoric of these get-rich-quick ads seems a throwback to the cruder entrepreneurial frenzies of an earlier America. And yet . . .

Just this spring,* the Yale alumni magazine devoted an entire special issue to the crisis of contemporary capitalism. The concerned contributors bemoaned the loss of faith in the entrepreneurial ideal that had once been at the heart of the American system.

If only the distinguished contributors to the symposium on capitalism had—as I have—sent away for *The Money-Master's Manual,* with its amazing Plan 360 A. If only they'd carefully read through *The Millionaire Book of Successful Little Businesses,* with its advice on how to cash in on selling elephant garlic and bronzed baby booties. If only they'd met Joe Karbo, author of *The Lazy Man's Way to Riches,* and taken a ride in his Rolls-Royce. If only they'd read *Roman Reports,* a strange and wonderful digest of each and every one of the nearly three hundred get-rich-quick-scheme offers being peddled in print; if only they'd read the "Towers Club" newsletter, a kind of lonely-hearts pen-pal club for impassioned success-secret seekers, they might have a different perspective on the vigor of the capitalist dream.

I have and I do. For some years, I've been sending away for this stuff. I've got cartons full of it. I've made a pilgrimage to the Pacific Ocean villa where Joe Karbo, the guru of *The Lazy Man's Way to Riches,* took me for a drive in his Rolls-Royce to prove he was Genuinely Rich. I've studied the whole literature of the subculture, the sacred and esoteric texts that date back to the Golden Age of Get Rich in the 1920s, to ancient Babylon, biblical Bethlehem, and perhaps even to insurance salesmen from another galaxy. My name is now on all the mailing lists. I get letters from Taiwan offering to set me up in the jewelry business, ads for books like *Health Secrets from the Orient* and *The Miracle of Universal Psychic Power: How to Pyramid Your Way to Prosperity.*

What I've discovered is that, just as the old Roman mystery cults continued to flourish for centuries after the Emperor Constantine made Christianity the state religion of Rome, so too does fervent faith in capitalism survive the official reign of American state bureaucratism. Only now, capitalist individualism has become a mystery cult. The essential element in almost every success-

*1979.

secret program I've studied is capitalist voodoo—the use of mystical, occult techniques, "long-lost secrets of the ancients," and such: the conversion of the whole repertoire of spiritual techniques of the East to help accumulate the cash of the West.

The origins of this Gnostic mystical capitalism can be traced back beyond Emersonian transcendentalism; its consequences are as contemporary as Werner Erhard's est and Jimmy Carter's smile. Let me take you on a guided tour.

The Hill Theory of Sex Transmutation

No author in the inspirational-greed book business is more universally revered—even by competitors—than the late Napoleon Hill, author of the single most influential success-secret book, *Think and Grow Rich*. Among the millions of enthusiastic readers influenced by Hill's book was a young insurance salesman named Jack Rosenberg, who later thought he ought to change his name to Werner Erhard and grew rich with his own amalgam of East and West called "est." If the young Werner has followed his guru Hill faithfully, no small part of the success of est must be attributed to Napoleon Hill's secret of sex transmutation. Napoleon Hill is the D. H. Lawrence of success theorists, fusing elements of Western sexual hydraulics with what seems like the Tantric influences from the East.

"Sex Transmutation" is not some bizarre new Danish operation; it's a scientific principle Hill claims he discovered in the course of twenty years of research into the sex lives and careers "of over 25,000 people." The fruits of this stimulating research have been codified by Hill into several general and specific theories of sex, beginning with the "three constructive potentialities" of sex.

The third purpose of sex, says Hill, is its use of sexual desire as "a driving force" which, "when harnessed and transmuted . . . is capable of lifting men into that higher sphere of thought which enables them to master the sources of worry and petty annoyance which beset their pathway on the lower plane."

Untransmuted desire can be dangerous, Hill warns: "A sex-mad man is not essentially different from a dope-mad man." But desire diverted from carnal coupling and *harnessed* to such things on the Higher Plane as selling insurance can be the secret of making big bucks fast: "Master salesmen attain the status of mastery in selling because they . . . *transmute* the energy of sex into sales enthusiasm! . . . The salesman who knows how to take his mind off the subject of sex, and direct it in sales effort with as much enthusiasm and determination as he would apply to its original purpose, has acquired the art of sex transmutation."

Hill is not too explicit on how a salesman sets out to transmute the lust in his heart to the sales-producing smile on his face. Instead, he returns to his twenty years' research and offers us the names of the thirteen greatest sex transmuters in history. Each of them, says Hill, "was known to have been of a highly sexed nature. The genius which was theirs undoubtedly found its source of power in transmuted sex energy."

Here they are, Hill's hit parade of heavy sex transmuters: George Washington, William Shakespeare, Abe Lincoln, Ralph Waldo Emerson, Robert Burns, Thomas Jefferson, Elbert Hubbard, Elbert H. Gary, Woodrow Wilson, John H. Patterson, Andrew Jackson, Enrico Caruso, and Napoleon.

Now the question that leaps to mind is what exactly did Shakespeare, Lincoln, and Elbert H. Gary *do* (or not do) to achieve their superb transmutations?

There are hints. Hill talks of damming a river in one place so that it will flow into another channel. In this new channel the transmuted desire will " 'step up' the mind," get it " 'keyed up' to high rates of vibrations." In his chapter on sex transmutation, Hill goes on at length to explain how the "highly sexed" transmutee/salesman can use his "keyed up" animal magnetism to mesmerize the prospective customer into opening up his wallet. The legendary horniness of the traveling salesman may have less to do with the charms of farmers' daughters than with the state of his sex transmutation. The sale, of course, is an attempted seduction, the last refuge of the erotic tension of courtship in America, the patter of the seller the most impassioned love poetry we have.

Reading success-secret literature, it's impossible not to recall the nineteenth-century English pornography Steven Marcus analyzed in *The Other Victorians,* a study of the underside of the official sexual ethic of that time. Marcus points out that throughout that literature transactions of sex are frequently spoken of in metaphors of commerce: Ejaculations are "spendings," for instance. But in the literature of the success-secret gurus—the underside of the official American success ethic—the opposite happens, and the transactions of commerce become sexualized. In the "pornotopia" of the "other Victorians" everything in the world is aroused and ready to "spend," while in the blissful vision of success-secret literature—"Greedonia," let's call it—the world of sexuality exists to "spend" wealth into your hands, breed it in your pockets, if you know the secret of sex transmutation.

A Visit with a "Genuinely Rich" Success Guru

We could continue to explore some of the weirdnesses of Napoleon Hill's world. I could tell you about his belief in the necessity of enemas (or "internal bathing" to avoid "autointoxication," as he phrases it) to any good success program, but it's time to move on and pay a visit to one of the up-and-coming new breed of success gurus following in Hill's wake—Joe Karbo, author of *The Lazy Man's Way to Riches.*

It was Joe Karbo's ad that first lured me into the world of success-secret gurus. Not the ad itself but the place in which it appeared: *Commentary.* If you're familiar with that distinguished intellectual journal, you'll be aware that full-page ads tend to reflect its erudite content—offerings of eighteen-volume library editions of Spinoza and the like. But there, in the midst of those distinguished pages, was a full-page hard-sell blast entitled "The Lazy Man's Way to Riches," with Joe boasting proudly in the accompanying copy that "I have two boats and a Cadillac . . . I live in a home that's worth $100,000. . . . I'll show you how I did it—the Lazy Man's Way—a secret I've shared with just a few friends 'til now."

Not long afterward I arranged to visit Joe at his split-level oceanfront office in Huntington Beach, California, not far from the $100,000 house. Joe had recently traded up from his Cadillac to a new Rolls-Royce, he told me right off. Did I want to go for a ride?

Joe's a husky, genial guy around fifty, with the deep, well-modulated voice of a professional pitchman. Joe was, in fact, one of the pioneering pitchmen of late-night TV in L.A. During the late forties and early fifties, when there was no official limit on the length of nighttime commercials, Joe would come on and do those endless epic pitches for freezer plans, used cars, vegetable choppers, and the like, pioneering the orotund style of relentless harangue that was responsible for getting an official time limit placed on commercials.

"I pioneered a new type of selling," Joe tells me. "Being honest is what it was—sell yourself is what I mean, be a salable product yourself and you can sell anything," he explains. "I made and blew several small fortunes back then," Joe says. "Then I hit bottom." New ownership dumped Joe from his all-night-pitch post; he found himself broke and heavily in debt.

It was then, Joe says, he made the momentous discoveries that went into Dyna/Psyc, the motivational system that was the heart of the Lazy Man's Way. He took a Dale Carnegie course, read Napoleon Hill's *Think and Grow Rich,* works by W. Clement Stone, and others. He put them all together with some mystical techniques from the East. Then he went into mail order. He sold such items as tinted driving glasses and helped re-create his fortune. Then he sold his system for making money and really began to rake in the cash.

It was lunchtime and Joe volunteered to drive us in his new Rolls over to his nearby yacht club. The forest-green cruise-ship-size Rolls is more than a vehicle for Joe. It's a symbol of his legitimacy, like the notarized statements from his accountant and banker testifying to the $100,000 price tag on his house that Joe reprints in his full-page ads. Many of the people who run these get-rich-quick ads, Joe grumbles to me, *are not actually rich.*

By following his system, Joe says, anyone who really wants a Rolls can have it. All you need to do is make it part of your Daily Declarations. Every morning upon rising, every evening upon retiring, you will read aloud to yourself a written declaration in which you describe that which you desire as if you already had it. "I have a brand-new, beautiful Rolls-Royce that cost $20,000," you declare as if it were actually in your garage. Next, Joe advises in his book, close your eyes and put yourself in a kind of greed trance in which you "*visualize it completely.* In your mind's eye, *see* the car . . . touch the steering wheel. . . ."

Joe's Rolls was real. So was Joe's yacht club. So was the smile on the face of the hostess who seated us at a table overlooking the yacht basin and told us there would be a "complimentary" fashion show during lunch.

Joe complained a lot during lunch about the "not genuinely rich" guys who were now ripping off his ads to sell success systems to unwary customers, but the thing I recall most clearly about that lunch was the implacable fashion show. Before we could order food, a Japanese woman in a silk kimono sashayed up to the table, whirled about, and said, "Very special fashion show. Are gentlemen interested in beautiful Oriental gifts to take home to ladies?"

"Not today, thanks," Joe said.

She returned while we had chowder. Joe was showing me an imitation of the Lazy Man's Way called "The Easy Road to Riches."

"Look here," said Joe. "He says, 'I have a yacht and four automobiles, two of which are exotic sports cars.' Just like me with my boats and cars. The rest is almost word for word."

The Japanese woman whirled up to the table trailing diaphanous silk shawls. "Shawls make perfect gift," she said.

"Please, we're in the middle of talking," Joe said, sounding a little irritated.

She returned during the main course—apparently making the rounds of each table with each costume change. Joe couldn't stop her. Perhaps she had made her own Dyna/Psyc Daily Declaration about selling shawls this morning. It seemed ironic: Here was this master pitchman, swami of salesmen, ensconced in his yacht club, just a short ride in his Rolls from his hundred-thou house, and the poor guy couldn't get a little peace of mind during a meal precisely because of the pervasiveness of the kind of pitch he was promoting.

Detective Roman and the Disappearance of Dan Brown

Bombs in the mail. Extortion notes. Dark doings at Ezra Pound's mental hospital. A "Defense Committee" with the curious name American Committee for Integrity and Decency (ACID). Twenty-one alleged CIA murders. One genuinely mysterious disappearance.

The strange saga of disappearing Dan Brown and his ultimate get-rich-quick scheme contains heavier elements of mystery and tragedy than are usually to be found in the success-secret subculture.

The curious story first came to my attention a couple of years ago in the pages of *Roman Reports,* a bimonthly publication devoted exclusively to cataloging and evaluating the hundreds of get-rich-quick success-secret schemes advertised each year in national magazines.

Chief investigator and sole proprietor of *Roman Reports* is a dogged amateur detective named Dave Roman. From his base in Maple Heights, Ohio, where he is also a building-materials supplier, Roman clips every coupon he gets his hands on when it promises big bucks fast. When he gets the material, he reads it, digests it for comment in his bimonthly report, returns it, then asks for his money back to check on the money-back-guarantee policy. (Most get-rich-quick schemes sold through the mail make money for their authors because the recipients are frequently too confused or depressed by what they get to ask for a refund when disappointed, or don't want to admit they were taken.)

Reading the wry comments in the pages of *Roman Reports* is like going through a weird rogues' gallery with Roman as a low-key tour guide.

The Belgium Secret is a one page letter that describes one of the gimmicks described in P.O.W.E.R. (previously reported in my reports). It tells you to establish a corporation in a State that doesn't demand proof of capitalization. You buy some cheap plots of land with a down payment for your assets. The idea is to build an inflated financial statement. . . . Don't waste your money on this one. . . .

Big Mac, Inc. . . . is another pyramid scheme. . . . You can join their "Millionaire Apprentice Club" for only $10.

What was appealing about *Roman Reports* was Roman's ability to combine amiable skepticism about most of the material that arrived at his archives with an optimist's faith that somewhere, somehow in his research he'd come across that One Perfect Scheme.

When I came across his first report on Dan Brown's American Trustee & Loan Association (ATLA) operation, I could sense a heightened tone of excitement in Roman's usually unflappable prose.

"This offer costs you $10.95, but is the most unusual information I have ever received bar none!" he exclaimed. According to Roman, Dan Brown II, the man behind ATLA, "is a wealthy man who has his own CIA of sorts. . . . He proposed an economic system that he claimed would have made banks obsolete and make everyone wealthy in a couple of months. He claims this system was used four times in history and each time the banking interests used their wealth and power to destroy it."

So excited was Roman by the prospect of this ultimate get-rich scheme, a scheme so great that it made not just the buyer or the seller but *everybody* rich, that he did something unprecedented—he became a dealer in Dan Brown's book, offering it at a discounted eight-dollar price to readers of the report.

Only one small cloud shadowed the bright, new future that seemed to be dawning in Dan Brown's dream: Dan Brown himself had disappeared. "Dan Brown has been missing since May 9, 1975," Roman reported. "Plus there have been three major resignations on his staff so the organization is a little shaky." Roman promised to investigate for an update.

Explosive developments in the Dan Brown case filled a whole page of the following issue of *Roman Reports*.

"It is a continuing story, and I can't seem to let go of it or find the real truth," Roman confessed, sounding a bit shaken at the news he had to relate. "Dan Brown was jailed because he allegedly tried to send a bomb through the mail to extort $30,000 from the Greyhound Corp." As a get-rich-quick scheme, this certainly was direct, although it did lack the grand vision one had come to expect from the author of the Universal Get-Rich-Quick Scheme.

According to Roman's update, "Dan Brown claims he was framed by the SEC and the CIA. The bomb went off in the post office, but it was a dud and didn't harm a soul. . . . Dan claims he was framed because he released the names of twenty-one CIA murders. . . . The court declared him incompetent and placed him in the psychiatric ward of St. Elizabeth's Hospital in Washington."

St. Elizabeth's, you may be aware, was the place in which that other visionary and monetary theorist Ezra Pound was incarcerated for twelve years. Indeed, Dan Brown's "Christian and patriotic" monetary theories sound suspiciously like Pound's Social Credit scheme for abolishing banking and making everyone prosperous, happy, and tax-free. (Brown and Pound both favor a complex self-devaluating, dated, paper-money system that is supposed to increase the velocity of money and pile it up for people instead of banks.)

Enter ACID to the aid of beleaguered Dan Brown. A group in Washington calling itself the American Committee for Integrity and Decency was formed to defend Dan Brown from "unethical practices and lies" by the government and win his release from St. Elizabeth's. But as this episode of the saga closed, Dan Brown had disappeared again. He had been transferred to a mental hospital outside St. Louis.

Then at last the final report: "Sad news has been conveyed to me and I will pass on the information I have," Roman announced in his November 1976 report. "My investigation of Dan Brown and the American Trustee & Loan Association is at an end." A Mr. George Warix, the founder of ACID, says Roman, "tells me that Dan Brown has been released from the mental hospital outside of St. Louis and was moved back to Washington, D.C., to stay at a halfway house. During the day, Dan was allowed out. . . . August 4 was the last time George saw Dan. I even talked with Dan a week earlier," Roman remarks, but "Dan Brown has not been seen since. George feels the CIA finally got rid of Dan because things were getting too hot and too many people were getting involved in the case. . . . Nothing can be proven, because there is no body. I guess we will all have to come to our own conclusions."

Norvell's Metaphysical Empire

Let me introduce you to the amazing Norvell. The name may sound familiar; you may have seen his ads in *The New York Times* for Sunday lectures on "mind cosmology" and other metaphysical subjects. Norvell—his first name is Anthony, but he prefers the more mystical-sounding solitary name—is a master of merchandising. He's incorporated a whole grab bag of so-called "Secrets of the East" as occult techniques for capturing the cash of the West. Who is Norvell? His publisher, Parker Publishing, has no way to reach him, it said. But from the sketchy biographical details provided by the jacket covers of Norvell books like *Money Magnetism* and *Mind Cosmology,* one can see that we are dealing here with a true child of East and West. He began on the path to enlightenment in Hollywood: "In his earlier years, Norvell was known as the advisor to the motion picture stars of Hollywood, and as an Astrologer, mystic, and psychic with a reputation for being 85 percent correct." Norvell himself claims he transmitted his "magic circle" to such stars as Claudette Colbert, Bette Davis, Clark Gable, Spencer Tracy, Greer Garson, and "about 200 other famous stars" during his Hollywood horoscope heyday.

For some unexplained reason—either a summons to Higher Wisdom from the Cosmic Guardians or perhaps some unfortunate consequences from the 15 percent of his predictions that went awry—Norvell left Hollywood to search for the mystic secrets of the East. Depending on which jacket cover you read, Norvell either "spent years gleaning" his "profound knowledge of the Eastern Mysteries from the Masters of India and the Levant" or conducted "his studies and research . . . in universities and occult libraries in England, India, and Greece." "Most recently, in his quest for truth," one jacket tells us, "Norvell conducted a group of seventy students and lecture members to Egypt where he personally conducted the sacred flame ritual before the Pyramids."

How does a disciple of these mystical practices actually get rich? Well, if you're a follower of Norvell's money magnetism, you spend quite a bit of time each day chanting and magnetizing yourself. You wake up in the morning and polish up your "Golden Nuggets"—chanting ten times a series of statements such as "I will make $100,000 in my own business and be a big success."

Then it's time to read the morning paper and clip out items about rich and famous people for your Golden Hall of Fame and your Scrapbook of Destiny over which you just meditate regularly and say such things as, "I now elevate myself to the Golden Hall of Fame." Before you leave for work you have to read aloud the Millionaire's Secret Vow of Riches ("I recognize there are infinite treasures in the Cosmic Cornucopia of Riches and Abundance. I draw upon the unlimited resources of the universe for my own enrichment"). During the day you must not neglect your "money pump exercise," and chant your money-motivator mantras five times each. All of which is mere preparation for the "magic circle aura ritual to build a million-dollar personality." This involves standing in front of a mirror and declaring: "I now build my magic circle aura of importance and success . . . I am worth $50,000 a year or more and I now project this image of riches and power. . . ."

And if at the end of the day you wonder if it's all worth it, if you wonder why a person with a million-dollar personality spends his day engaging in these practices without any million-dollar reward, well, just look in your wallet. For there, if you've been following Norvell's instructions, you have a check made out to yourself for $1 million. "Sign the check, 'God, the Universal Banker,' " Norvell suggests.* "Every time you see this you will affirm to yourself that God has literally given you a universe . . . it belongs to you as much as anyone else and therefore you already are worth more than a million dollars."

Is There Life Insurance on Other Planets?

If you find this inbreeding of bogus mysticism not quite to your taste, you can blame it on the Babylonians. The whole mystical capitalist tradition in the twentieth century can be traced to one seminal sacred text that appeared in 1926: *The Richest Man in Babylon.* Subtitled in its current edition *The Success Secrets of the Ancients,* this book is the ur-text of the success-secret subculture.** Purportedly drawn from authentic clay tablets unearthed by archaeologists, *The Richest Man* opens with a dialogue between a debt-plagued Babylonian named Bansir the chariot maker and a long-winded know-it-all named Arkad, who tells Bansir the system by which he became "the richest man in Babylon."

The secrets of this system turn out to be little more than keeping a regular

---

*In fairness, I should point out that the actor Jim Carrey claims he walked around for several years with just such a check, made out to himself for ten million, and now he's getting twenty million per picture. So maybe it works—if you have Jim Carrey's talent.

**And *still* popular: As of December 1999 it was number *ten* on the *Los Angeles Times* paperback best-seller list.

savings account and buying insurance, which explains why so many hundreds of thousands of copies of *The Richest Man in Babylon* have been distributed free by savings banks and life-insurance companies. Of course, there weren't any insurance companies in ancient Babylon, but Arkad finesses this problem by *predicting* that in some future age someone will have the vision to invent them. He does this in a passage which will give you the flavor and intellectual force of the "ancient" wisdom that pervades this classic. "In my mind rests a belief," intones the wise Arkad, "that someday wise-thinking men will devise a plan to insure against death whereby many men pay in but a trifling sum regularly, the aggregate making a handsome sum for the family of each member who passeth into the beyond. This do I see as desirable and which I could highly recommend. . . ."

The perversely blasphemous choice of Babylon as ancient city of wisdom (for a devout Bible reader, calling someone the "richest man in Babylon" is no more a compliment than calling him the "grooviest guy in Gomorrah") apparently didn't harm its sales; the book became a well-respected "inspirational classic."

Its success helped enshrine the notion that "the Ancients" (or the sages among them) spent most of their time devising success secrets, leaving unanswered the question of why they weren't smart enough to invent insurance themselves. But once the idea caught on, *The Richest Man* spawned a whole generation of secrets-of-the-ancients-type success books, such as Og Mandino's *The Greatest Secret in the World,* in which we learn of the Ten Great Scrolls for Success of Hafid, the camel boy of Bethlehem.

All of which makes one speculate on the identity of this so-called "Ancient" Arkad. How could he know about life insurance so far ahead of its time unless he was the representative of some vastly superior, but life-insurance-conscious, alien civilization? In fact it is not beyond the realm of possibility that this so-called Arkad was in fact one of Erich Von Däniken's "ancient astronauts" whose many contributions to human civilization are suggested in *Chariots of the Gods.* Certainly the text in *The Richest Man* provides clues that support this notion. Why is Bansir identified as a *chariot maker*? Might he not have been called upon to do some body and fender work on the ancient astronauts' interstellar chariots and been given in return the priceless secret of the insurance industry of the future? Indeed, it would not be surprising in the light of these speculations if we discover that the first alien beings we encounter have not come to redeem or destroy us but instead to sell us a surefire scheme for making big bucks in interplanetary mail order.

The Last Secrets of Skull and Bones

In Which We Contemplate Certain Occult Rituals of the Ruling Class

Take a look at that hulking sepulchre over there. Small wonder they call it a tomb. It's the citadel of Skull and Bones, the most powerful of all secret societies in the strange Yale secret-society system. For nearly a century and a half, Skull and Bones has been the most influential secret society in the nation, and now it is one of the last.

In an age in which it seems that all that could possibly be concealed about anything and anybody has been revealed, those blank tombstone walls could be holding the last secrets left in America.

You could ask Averell Harriman whether there's really a sarcophagus in the basement and whether he and young Henry Stimson and young Henry Luce lay down naked in that coffin and spilled the secrets of their adolescent sex lives to fourteen fellow Bonesmen. You could ask Supreme Court Justice Potter Stewart if there came a time in the year 1937 when he dressed up in a skeleton suit and howled wildly at an initiate in a red-velvet room inside the tomb. You could ask McGeorge Bundy if he wrestled naked in a mud pile as part of his initiation and how it compared with a later quagmire into which he so eagerly plunged. You could ask Bill Bundy or Bill Buckley, both of whom went into the CIA after leaving Bones—or George Bush,* who *ran* the CIA—whether their Skull and Bones experience was useful training for the clandestine trade. (*Spook,* the Yale slang word for secret-society member, is, of course, Agency slang for "spy.") You could ask J. Richardson Dilworth, the Bonesman who now manages the Rockefeller fortune, just how wealthy the Bones society is and whether it's true that each new initiate gets a no-strings gift of $15,000 cash and guaranteed financial security for life.

You could ask . . . but I think you get the idea. The leading lights of the Eastern establishment—in old-line investment banks (Brown Brothers Harriman pays Bones's tax bill), in blue-blood law firms (Simpson, Thacher & Bartlett, for one), and particularly in the highest councils of the foreign-policy establishment—the people who have shaped America's national character since it ceased being an undergraduate power—had *their* undergraduate character shaped in that crypt over there. Bonesman Henry Stimson, secretary of war under FDR, a man at the heart of the heart of the American ruling class, called his experience in the tomb the most profound one in his entire education.

But none of them will tell you a thing about it. They've sworn an oath never to reveal what goes on inside and they're legendary for the lengths to which they'll go to avoid prying interrogation. The mere mention of the words "Skull and Bones" in the presence of a true-blue Bonesman such as Blackford Oakes, the fictional hero of Bill Buckley's spy thriller *Saving the Queen,* will cause him to "dutifully leave the room, as tradition prescribed."

I can trace my personal fascination with the mysterious goings-on in the sepulchre across the street to a spooky scene I witnessed on its shadowy steps late one April night eleven years ago. I was then a sophomore at Yale, living in Jonathan Edwards, the residential college (anglophile Yale name for "dorm") built next to the Bones tomb. It was part of Jonathan Edwards's folklore that on the April evening following "tap night" at Bones, if one could climb to the tower of Weir Hall, the odd castle that overlooks the Bones courtyard, one could hear strange cries and moans coming from the bowels of the tomb as the fifteen newly "tapped" members were put through what sounded like a harrowing ordeal. Returning alone to my room late at night, I would always cross the street rather than walk the sidewalk that passed right in front of Bones. Even at that safe distance, something about it made my skin crawl.

But that night in April I wasn't alone; a classmate and I were coming back from an all-night diner at about two in the morning. At the time, I knew little about the mysteries of Bones or any of the other huge windowless secret-society tombs that dominated with dark authority certain key corners of the

---

*Or George W. Bush, Skull and Bones, 1968.

campus. They were nothing like conventional fraternities. No one lived in the tombs. Instead, every Thursday and Sunday night, the best and the brightest on campus, the fifteen seniors in Skull and Bones and in Scroll and Key, Book and Snake, Wolf's Head, Berzelius, in all the seven secret societies, disappeared into their respective tombs and spent hours doing *something*—something they were sworn to secrecy about. And Bones, it was said, was the most ritualistic and secretive of all. Even the very door to the Bones tomb, that huge triple-padlocked iron door, was never permitted to open in the presence of an outsider.

All this was floating through my impressionable sophomore mind that night as my friend Mike and I approached the stone pylons guarding the entrance to Bones. Suddenly we froze at the sight of a strange thing lying on the steps. There in the gloom of the doorway on the top step was a long white object that looked like the thighbone of a large mammal. I remained frozen. Mike was more venturesome: He walked right up the steps and picked up the bone. I wanted to get out of there fast; I was certain we were being spied upon from a concealed window. Mike couldn't decide what to do with the bone. He went up to the door and began examining the array of padlocks. Suddenly a bolt shot. The massive door began to swing open and something reached out at him from within. He gasped, terrified, and jumped back, but not before something clutched the bone, yanked it out of his hand and back into the darkness within. The door slammed shut with a clang that rang in our ears as we ran away.

Recollected in tranquillity, that dreamlike gothic moment seems to me an emblem of the strangeness I felt at being at Yale, at being given a brief glimpse of the mysterious workings of the inner temples of privilege but feeling emphatically shut out of the secret ceremonies within, the real purpose of which was, from its missionary beginnings, devoted to converting the idle progeny of the ruling class into morally serious leaders of the establishment. It is frequently in the tombs that these conversions take place. Yale itself was a secret society to me, Skull and Bones the secret within the secret.

November 1976: Security Measures

It's night and we're back in front of the tomb, Mike and I, reinforced by nine years in the outside world, two skeptical women friends, and a big dinner at Mory's. And yet once again there is an odd, chilling encounter. We're re-creating that first spooky moment. I'm standing in front of the stone pylons and Mike has walked up to stand against the door so we can estimate its height by his. Then we notice we're being watched. A small red foreign car has pulled up on the sidewalk a few yards away from us. The driver has been sitting with the engine running and has been watching us for some time. Then he gets out. He's a tall, athletic-looking guy, fairly young. He shuts the car door behind him and stands leaning against it, continuing to observe us. We try to act oblivious, continuing to sketch and measure.

The guy finally walks over to us. "You seen Miles?" he asks.

We look at each other. Could he think we're actually Bones alumni, or is he testing us? Could "You seen Miles?" be some sort of password?

"No," we reply. "Haven't seen Miles."

He nods and remains there. We decide we've done enough sketching and measuring and stroll off.

"Look!" one of the women says as she turns and points back. "He just ran down the side steps to check the basement-door locks. He probably thought he caught us planning a break-in."

I found the episode intriguing. What it said to me was that Bones still cared about the security of its secrets. Trying to find out what goes on inside could be a challenge.

And so it was that I set out this April to see just how secure those last secrets are. It was a task I took on not out of malice or sour grapes. I was not tapped for a secret society so I'm open to the latter charge, but I plead guilty only to the voyeurism of a mystery lover. I thought it wouldn't hurt to spend some time in New Haven during the week of tap night and initiation night, poking around and asking questions.

You could call it espionage if you were so inclined, but I tried to play the game in a gentlemanly fashion: I would not directly ask a Bonesman to violate his sacred oath of secrecy. If, however, one of them happened to have fudged on the oath to some other party and that other party were to convey the gist of the information to me, I would rule it fair game. And if any Bonesman wants to step forward and add something, I'll be happy to listen.

What follows is an account of my search for the meaning behind the mysterious Bones rituals. Only information that might be too easily traced to its source has been left out, because certain sources expressed fear of reprisals against themselves. Yes, reprisals. One of them even insisted, with what seemed like deadly seriousness, that reprisals would be taken against me.

"What bank do you have your checking account at?" this party asked me in the middle of a discussion of the Mithraic aspects of the Bones ritual.

I named the bank.

"Aha," said the party. "There are three Bonesmen on the board. You'll never have a line of credit again. They'll tap your phone. They'll . . ."

Before I could say, "A line of *what*?" the source continued: "The alumni still care. Don't laugh. They don't like people tampering and prying. The power of Bones is incredible. They've got their hands on every lever of power in the country. You'll see—it's like trying to look into the Mafia. Remember, they're a secret society, too."

Wednesday Night, April 14: The Dossier

Already I have in my possession a set of annotated floor plans of the interior of the tomb, giving the location of the sanctum sanctorum, the room called 322. And tonight I received a dossier on Bones ritual secrets that was complied from the archives of another secret society. (It seems that one abiding preoccupation of many Yale secret societies is keeping files on the secrets of other secret societies, particularly Bones.)

This dossier on Bones is a particularly sophisticated one, featuring "reliability ratings" in percentiles for each chunk of information. It was obtained for me by an enterprising researcher on the condition that I keep secret the name of the secret society that supplied it. Okay. I will say, though, that it's not the secret society that is rumored to have Hitler's silverware in its archives. That's Scroll and Key, chief rival of Bones for the elite of Yale—Dean Acheson, James Angleton, and Cy Vance's society, among other luminaries of the American foreign-policy establishment.

But to return to the dossier. Let me tell you what it says about the initiation, the center of some of the most lurid apocryphal rumors about Bones. According to the dossier, the Bones initiation ritual of 1940 went like this: "New man placed in coffin—carried into central part of building. New man chanted over and 'reborn' into society. Removed from coffin and given robes with symbols on it [*sic*]. A bone with his name on it is tossed into bone heap at start of every meeting. Initiates plunged naked into mud pile."

Thursday Evening: The File and Claw Solution to the Mystery of 322

I'm standing in the shadows across the street from the tomb, ready to tail the first person to come out. Tonight is tap night, the night fifteen juniors will be chosen to receive the 145-year-old secrets of Bones. Tonight the fifteen seniors in Bones and the fifteen in each of the other societies will arrive outside the rooms of the prospective tappees. They'll pound loudly on the doors. When the chosen junior opens up, a Bonesman will slam him on the shoulder and thunder: "Skull and Bones: Do you accept?"

At that point, according to my dossier, if the candidate accepts, he will be handed a message wrapped with a black ribbon sealed in black wax with the skull-and-crossbones emblem and the mystic Bones number, 322. The message appoints a time and a place for the candidate to appear on initiation night—next Tuesday—the first time the newly tapped candidate will be permitted inside the tomb. Candidates are "instructed to wear no metal" to the initiation, the dossier notes ominously. (Reliability rating for this stated to be 100 percent.)

Not long before eight tonight, the door to Bones swings open. Two dark-suited young men emerge. One of them carries a slim black attaché case. Obviously they're on their way to tap someone. I decide to follow them. I want to check out a story I heard that Bones initiates are taken to a ceremony somewhere near the campus before the big initiation inside the tomb. The Bonesmen head up High Street and pass the library, then make a right.

Passing the library, I can't help but recoil when I think of the embarrassing discovery I made in the manuscript room this afternoon. The last thing I wanted to do was reduce the subtleties of the social function of Bones to some simpleminded conspiracy theory. And yet I do seem to have come across definite, if skeletal, links between the origins of Bones rituals and those of the notorious Bavarian Illuminists. For me, an interested but skeptical student of the conspiracy world, the introduction of the Illuminists, or Illuminati, into certain discussions (say, for instance, of events in Dallas in 1963) has become the same thing that the mention of Bones is to a Bonesman—a signal to leave the room. Because although the Bavarian Illuminists did have a real historical existence (from 1776 to 1785 they were an esoteric secret society within the more mystical freethinking lodges of German Freemasonry), they have also had a paranoid fantasy existence throughout two centuries of conspiracy literature. They are *the* imagined mega-cabal that manipulated such alleged plots as the French and Russian revolutions, the Elders of Zion, the rise of Hitler, and the house of Morgan. Yes, the Bilderberg and George De Mohrenschildt,* too. Silly as it may sound, there are suggestive links between the historical, if not mytho-conspiratorial, Illuminists and Bones.

First consider the account of the origins of Bones to be found in a century-old pamphlet published by an anonymous group that called itself File and Claw after the tools they used to pry their way inside Bones late one night. I came upon the File and Claw break-in pamphlet in a box of disintegrating documents filed in the library's manuscript room under Skull and Bones's corporate name, Russell Trust Association. The foundation was named for William H. (later General) Russell, the man who founded Bones in 1832. I was trying to figure out what mission Russell had for the secret order he founded and why

---

*De Mohrenschildt was the strange czarist exile and adventurer who was a friend of both Jackie Kennedy and Lee Harvey Oswald. (He took Oswald and his Russian wife under his wing when they moved to Dallas.) All of which, needless to say, along with shadowy CIA links, made him, like Mary Meyer, an overdetermined iconic figure in conspiracy-theory literature.

he had chosen that particular death's-head brand of mumbo jumbo to embody his vision. Well, according to the File and Claw break-in crew,

> Bones is a chapter of a corps of a German university. It should properly be called the Skull and Bones chapter. General Russell, its founder, was in Germany before his senior year and formed a warm friendship with a leading member of a German society. The meaning of the permanent number "322" in all Bones literature is that it was founded in '32 as the second chapter of the German society. But the Bonesman has a pleasing fiction that his fraternity is a descendant of an old Greek patriot society founded by Demosthenes, who died in 322 B.C.

They go on to describe a German slogan painted "on the arched walls above the vault" of the sacred room, 322. The slogan appears above a painting of skulls surrounded by Masonic symbols, a picture said to be "a gift of the German chapter." *"Wer war der Thor, wer Weiser, Bettler oder Kaiser? Ob Arm, Ob Reich, im Tode gleich,"* the slogan reads, or, "Who was the fool, who the wise man, beggar or king? Whether poor or rich, all's the same in death."*

Imagine my surprise when I ran into that very slogan in a 1798 Scottish anti-Illuminist tract reprinted in 1967 by the John Birch Society. The tract (*Proofs of a Conspiracy* by John Robison) prints alleged excerpts from Illuminist ritual manuals supposedly confiscated by the Bavarian police when the secret order was banned in 1785. Toward the end of the ceremony of initiation into the "Regent degree" of Illuminism, according to the tract, "a skeleton is pointed out to him [the initiate], at the feet of which are laid a crown and a sword. He is asked *whether that is the skeleton of a king, nobleman or a beggar.* As he cannot decide, the president of the meeting says to him, 'The character of being a man is the only one that is of importance' " (my italics).

Doesn't that sound similar to the German slogan the File and Claw team claims to have found inside Bones? Now consider a haunting photograph of the altar room of one of the Masonic lodges at Nuremberg that is closely associated with Illuminism. Haunting because at the altar room's center, approached through an aisle of hanging human skeletons, is a coffin surmounted by—you guessed it—a skull and crossbones that look exactly like the particular arrangement of jawbones and thighbones in the official Bones emblem. The skull and crossbones was the official crest of another key Illuminist lodge, one right-wing Illuminist theoretician told me.

---

*One wonders—well, I do anyway—how much the contemplation of the skull and the slogan about death abolishing distinctions of rank and renown in this strain of imagery owes itself to Hamlet contemplating the skulls unearthed by the grave digger and wondering which might be "lord such-a-one" or "the pate of a politician." In the early nineteenth century, Germany experienced a great Goethe-inspired vogue for what came to be known as "Hamletism."

Now you can look at this three ways. One possibility is that the Bircher right—and the conspiracy-minded left—are correct: The Eastern establishment is the demonic creation of a clandestine elite manipulating history, and Skull and Bones is one of its recruiting centers. A more plausible explanation is that the death's-head symbolism was so prevalent in Germany when the impressionable young Russell visited that he just stumbled on the same mother lode of pseudo-Masonic mummery as the Illuminists. The third possibility is that the break-in pamphlets are an elaborate fraud designed by the File and Claw crew to pin the taint of Illuminism on Bones and that the rituals of Bones have innocent Athenian themes, 322 being *only* the date of the death of Demosthenes. (In fact, some Bones literature I've seen in the archives does express the year as if 322 B.C. were the year one, making 1977 anno Demostheni 2299.)

I am still following the dark-suited Bonesmen at a discreet distance as they make their way along Prospect Street and into a narrow alley, which, to my dismay, turns into a parking lot. They get into a car and drive off, obviously to tap an off-campus prospect. So much for tonight's clandestine work. I'd never get to my car in time to follow them. My heart isn't in it, anyway. I am due to head off to the graveyard to watch the initiation ceremony of Book and Snake, the secret society of Deep Throat's friend Bob Woodward (several Deep Throat theories have postulated Yale secret-society ties as the origin of Woodward's underground-garage connection, and two Bonesmen, Ray Price and Richard Moore, who were high Nixon aides, have been mentioned as suspects—perhaps because of their experience at clandestine underground truth telling). And later tonight I hope to make the first of my contacts with persons who have been inside—not just inside the tomb, but inside the skulls of some of the Bonesmen.

Later Thursday Night: Turning the Tables on the Sexual Autobiographies

In his senior year, each member of Bones goes through an intense two-part confessional experience in the Bones crypt. One Thursday night, he tells his life story, giving what is meant to be a painfully forthright autobiography that exposes his traumas, shames, and dreams. (Tom Wolfe calls this Bones practice a forerunner of the Me Decade's fascination with self.) The following Sunday-night session is devoted exclusively to sexual histories. They don't leave out anything these days. I don't know what it was like in General Russell's day, maybe there was less to talk about, but these days the sexual stuff is totally explicit and there's less need for fabricating exploits to fill up the allotted time. Most Sunday-night sessions start with talk of prep-school masturbation and don't stop until the intimate details of Saturday night's delights have come to light early Monday morning.

This has begun to cause some disruptions in relationships. The women the Bonesmen talk about in the crypt are often Yale co-eds and frequently feminists. None of these women is too pleased at having the most intimate secrets of her relationship made the subject of an all-night symposium consecrating her lover's brotherhood with fourteen males she hardly knows. As one woman put it, "I objected to fourteen guys knowing whether I was a good lay. . . . It was like after that each of them thought I was his woman in some way."

Some women have discovered that their lovers take their vows to Bones more solemnly than their commitments to women. There is the case of the woman who revealed something very personal—not embarrassing, just private—to her lover and made him swear never to repeat it to another human. When he came back from the Bones crypt after his Sunday-night sex session, he couldn't meet her eyes. He'd told his brothers in Bones.

It seems that the whole secret-society system at Yale is in the terminal stages of a sexual crisis. By the time I arrived this April, all but three of the formerly all-male societies had gone co-ed, and two of the remaining holdouts—Scroll and Key and Wolf's Head—were embroiled in bitter battles over certain members' attempts to have them follow the trend. The popular quarterback of the football team had resigned from Scroll and Key because its alumni would not even let him make a pro-coeducation plea to their convocation. When one prominent alumnus of Wolf's Head was told the current members had plans to tap women, he threatened to "raze the building" before permitting it. Nevertheless, it seemed as though it wouldn't be long before those two holdouts went co-ed. But not Bones. Both alumni and outsiders see the essence of the Bones experience as some kind of male bonding, a Victorian, muscular Christian-missionary view of manliness and public service.

While changing the least of all the societies over its 145 years, Bones did begin admitting Jews in the early fifties and tapping blacks in 1949. It offered membership to some of the most outspoken rebels of the late sixties and, more recently, added gay and bisexual members, including the president of the militant Gay Activist Alliance, a man by the name of Miles.

But women, the Bones alumni have strenuously insisted, are different. When a rambunctious seventies class of Bones proposed tapping the best and brightest of the new Yale women, the officers of the Russell Trust Association threatened to bar that class from the tomb and change the locks if they dared. They didn't.*

---

*It would require some fifteen more years, a wrenching and divisive internal debate, and a secret referendum before Skull and Bones, the last holdout, deigned to admit women.

That sort of thing is what persuaded the person I am meeting with late tonight—and a number of other persons—to talk about what goes on inside: After all, isn't the core of the Bones group experience the betrayal of their loved ones' secrets? Measure for measure.

Tuesday, April 20: Initiation Night—Tales of the Tomb and Deer Island

When I return to New Haven on initiation night to stand again in the shadows across the street from Bones in the hope of glimpsing an initiate enter, it is, thanks to my sources (who insist on anonymity), with a greater sense of just what it means for the initiate to be swallowed up by the tomb for the first time.

The first initiate arrives shortly before eight P.M., proceeds up the steps and halts at attention in front of the great door. I don't see him ring a bell; I don't think he has to. They are expecting him. The doors open. I can't make out who or what is inside, but the initiate's reaction is unmistakable: He puts his hands up as if a gun has been pointed at him. He walks into the gloom and the door closes behind him.

Earlier, according to my source, before the initiate was allowed to approach that door, he was led blindfolded to a Bones house somewhere on Orange Street and conducted to the basement. There two older Bonesmen dressed in skeleton suits had him swear solemn oaths to keep secret whatever he was to experience in the tomb during the initiation rite and forever after.

Now I am trying to piece together what I know about what is happening to that initiate tonight and, more generally, how his life will change now that he has been admitted inside. Tonight he will die to the world and be born again into the Order, as he will thenceforth refer to it. The Order is a world unto itself in which he will have a new name and fourteen new blood brothers, also with new names.

The "death" of the initiate will be as frightful as the liberal use of human skeletons and ritual psychology can make it. Whether it's accompanied by physical beatings or wrestling or a plunge into a mud or dung pile I have not been able to verify, but I'd give a marginally higher reliability rating to the mud-pile plunge. Then it's into the coffin and off on a symbolic journey through the underworld to rebirth, which takes place in room number 322. There the Order clothes the newborn knight in its own special garments, implying that henceforth he will tailor himself to the Order's mission.

Which is—if you take it at face value—to produce an alliance of good men. The Latin for "good men" is *boni,* of course, and each piece of Bones literature sports a Latin maxim making use of *boni.* "Good men are rare," is the way one maxim translates. "Of all societies none is more glorious nor of greater strength than when good men of similar morals are joined in intimacy," proclaims another.

The intimacy doesn't really begin to get going until the autobiographical sessions start in September. But first there are some tangible rewards. In the months that follow tonight's initiation, the born-again Bonesmen will begin to experience the wonderful felicity of the Protestant ethic: Secular rewards just happen to accrue to the elect as external tokens of their inner blessedness.

According to one source, each initiate gets a no-strings, tax-free gift of $15,000 from the Russell Trust Association just for having been selected by Bones. I'd heard rumors that Bonesmen were guaranteed a secure income for life in some way—if only to prevent a downtrodden alcoholic brother from selling the secrets for a few bucks. When I put this question to my source, the reply was that of course the society would always help a downtrodden member with interest-free loans, if necessary.

When I mentioned the $15,000 figure to writer Tom Powers, a member of a secret society called Elihu, he, like members of other secret societies, professed incredulity. But the day after I spoke to him I received this interesting communication from Powers:

> I have checked with a Bones penetration and am now inclined to think you have got the goods where the $15,000 is concerned. A sort of passive or negative confirmation. I put the question to him and he declined to comment in a tone of voice that might have been, but was not, derisory. Given an ideal opportunity to say, "That's bullshit!" he did not.
>
> The interesting question now is what effect the $15,000 report is going to have on next tap day. The whole Bones mystique will take on a mercenary air, sort of like a television game show. If there is no fifteen thousand, the next lineup of tappees will be plenty pissed. I can hear the conversations now: outgoing Bones members telling prospects there is one thing they've got to understand, really and truly—*there is no fifteen thousand!!!* While the prospects will be winking and nudging and saying, "I understand. Ha-ha! You've got to say that, but just between us. . . ."

"If Bones has got a cell in CIA," Powers concluded his letter, "you could be in big trouble."

Ah, yes. The Bones cell in the Central Intelligence Agency. Powers had called my attention to a passage in Aaron Latham's novel, *Orchids for Mother,* in which the thinly veiled version of CIA master spy James Angleton recalls that the Agency is "New Haven all over again. . . . Secret society'd be closer, like Skull and Bones."

"There are a lot of Bonesmen around, aren't there?" asks a young CIA recruit.

Indeed, says the master spy, with all the Bones spooks it's "a regular haunted house."

If you were a supersecret spy agency seeking to recruit the most trustworthy and able men for dangerous missionary work against the barbarian threat wouldn't you want someone whose life story, character, and secrets were already known to you? You'd certainly want to know if there were any sexual proclivities that might make the future spy open to temptation or blackmail.

Now, I'm not saying the CIA has bugged the Bones crypt (although who could rule it out with certainty?). But couldn't the Agency use old Bonesmen to recruit new ones, or might they not have a trusted descendant of a Bonesman—just one in each fifteen would be enough—advise them on the suitability of the other fourteen for initiation into postgraduate secrets?

Consider the case of once gung-ho CIA Bonesman William Sloane Coffin, who later became a leader of the antiwar movement. A descendant of an aptly named family with three generations of Bonesmen, Coffin headed for the CIA not long after graduation from Bones. And the man Coffin tapped for Bones, William F. Buckley, Jr., was himself tapped by the CIA the following year.

In the late summer following his initiation, right before he begins his senior year, the initiate is given a gift of greater value than any putative $15,000 recruitment bonus: his first visit to the private resort island owned and maintained by the Russell Trust Association in the St. Lawrence River. There, hidden among the Thousand Islands, the reborn initiate truly finds himself on an isle of the blessed. For there, on this place called Deer Island, are assembled the active Bones alumni and their families, and there he gets a sense of how many powerful establishment institutions are run by wonderful, civilized, silver-haired Bonesmen eager to help the initiate's establishment dreams come true. He can also meet the wives of Bonesmen of all ages and get a sense of what kind of woman is most acceptable and appropriate in Bones society and perhaps even meet that most acceptable of all types of women— the daughter of a Bonesman.

A reading of the lists of Bonesmen selected over the past 145 years suggests that like the secret society of another ethnic group, certain powerful families dominate: the Tafts, the Whitneys, the Thachers, the Lords, for instance. You also get the feeling there's a lot of intermarriage among these Bones families. Year after year there will be a Whitney Townsend Phelps in the same Bones class as a Phelps Townsend Whitney. It's only natural, considering the way they grow up together with Bones picnics, Bones outings, and a whole quiet panoply of Bones social events outside the campus and the tomb. Particularly on the island.

Of course, if the initiate has grown up in a Bones family and gone to picnics on the island all his life, the vision—the introduction to powerful people, the fine manners, the strong bonds—is less awesome. But to the nonhereditary slots in a Bones class of fifteen, the outsiders—frequently the football captain, the editor of the *Yale Daily News,* a brilliant scholar, a charismatic student politician—the island experience comes as a seductive revelation: These powerful people want me, want my talents, my services; perhaps they even want my genes. Play along with their rules and I can become one of them. They *want* me to become one of them.

In fact, one could make a half-serious case that functionally Bones serves as a kind of ongoing informal establishment eugenics project bringing vigorous new genes into the bloodlines of the Stimsonian elite. Perhaps that explains the origin of the sexual autobiography. It may have served some eugenic purpose in General Russell's vision: a sharing of birth-control and self-control methods to minimize the chance of a "good man" and future steward of the ruling class being trapped into marriage by a fortune hunter or a working-class girl—the way the grand tour for an upper-class American youth always included an initiation into the secrets of Parisian courtesans so that once back home the young man wouldn't elope with the first girl who let him get past second base.

However, certain of the more provincial Bones families do not welcome *all* genes into the pool. There is a story about two very well-known members of a Bones class who haven't spoken to each other for more than two decades. One of them was an early Jewish token member of Bones who began to date the sister of a fellow Bonesman. Apparently the Christian family made its frosty reaction to this development very plain. The Christian Bonesman did not convince his Jewish blood brother he was entirely on his side in the matter. The dating stopped and so did the speaking. It's an isolated incident, and I wouldn't have brought it up had I not been told of the "Jew canoe" incident, which happened relatively recently.

There's a big book located just inside the main entrance to Bones. In it are some of the real secrets. Not the initiation rites or the grip, but reactions to, comments on, and mementos of certain things that went on in the tomb, personal revelations, interpersonal encounters. The good stuff. I don't know if the tale of the brokenhearted token gay and the rotting-paella story are in there, but they should be. I'm almost sure the mysterious "Phil" incident *isn't* there. (According to one source, the very mention of the name "Phil" is enough to drive certain Bonesmen up the wall.) But the unfortunate "Jew canoe" incident *is* in that book.

It seems that not too long ago the boys in a recent Bones class were sitting around the tomb making some wisecracks that involved Jewish stereotypes. "He drives a Cadillac—you know, the Jew canoe." Things like that. Well, one

Jewish token member that year happened to be present, but his blood brothers apparently didn't think he'd mind—it being only in fun and all that. Then it got more intense, as it can in groups when a wound is suddenly opened in one of their number. The Jewish member stalked out of the tomb, tears in his eyes, feeling betrayed by his brothers and thinking of resigning forthwith. But he didn't. He went back and inscribed a protest in the big book, at which time his brothers, suitably repentant, persuaded him not to abandon the tomb.

Outsiders often do have trouble with the Bones style of intimacy. There was, for instance, the story of one of the several token bisexuals and gays that Bones has tapped in recent years. He had the misfortune to develop, during the long Thursday and Sunday nights of shared intimacy, a deep affection for a member of his fifteen-man coven who declared himself irrevocably hetero-sexual. The intimacy of the tomb experience became heartbreaking and frus-trating for the gay member. When the year came to a close and it came time to pick the next group of fifteen from among the junior class, he announced that he was not going to tap another token gay and recommended against gay membership because he felt the experience was too intense to keep from be-coming sexual.

There's a kind of backhanded tribute to something genuine there. The Bones experience can be intense enough to work real transformations. Idle, preppie Prince Hals suddenly become serious students of society and them-selves, as if acceptance into the tomb were a signal to leave the tavern and pre-pare to rule the land. Those embarrassed at introspection and afraid of trusting other men are given the mandate and the confidence to do so.

"Why," said one source, "do old men—seventy and over—travel thousands of miles for Bones reunions? Why do they sing the songs with such gusto? Where else can you hear Archibald MacLeish take on Henry Luce in a soul-versus-capital debate with no holds barred? Bones survives because the old men who are successful need to convince themselves that not luck or wealth put them where they are, but raw talent, and a talent that was recognized in their youth. Bones, because of its elitism, connects their past to their present. It is more sustaining, for some, than marriage."

Certainly the leaders that Bones has turned out are among the more humane and civilized of the old Yankee establishment. In addition to cold warriors, Viet warriors, and spies, there are as many or more missionaries, surgeons, writers (John Hersey, Archibald MacLeish) and great teachers (William Gra-ham Sumner, F. O. Matthiessen) as there are investment bankers. There is, in the past of Bones, at least, an element of genuine missionary zeal for moral, and not merely surplus, value.

It's now a century since the break-in pamphlet of the File and Claw crew an-nounced "the decline and fall of Skull and Bones," so it would be premature for me to announce the imminence of such an event, but almost everyone I spoke to at Yale thought that Bones was in headlong decline. There have been unprecedented resignations. There have been an increasing number of rejections—people Bones wants who don't want Bones. Or who don't care enough to give up two nights a week for the kind of marathon encounter any Esalen graduate can put on in the Bougainvillea Room of the local Holiday Inn. Intimacy is cheap and zeal is rare these days. The word is out that Bones no longer gets the leaders of the class but lately has taken on a more lackadaisical, hedonist, comfortable—even, said some, decadent—group. (I was fascinated to learn from my source that some Bones members still partake in certain sacraments of the 1960s. Could it be that the old black magic of Bones ritual has kind of lost its spell and needs a psychedelic dramatizing these days?)

And the reasons people give now for joining Bones are often more foreboding than the rejections. They talk about the security of a guaranteed job with one of the Bones-dominated investment banks or law firms. They talk about the contacts and the connections and maybe in private they talk about the $15,000 (regardless of whether Bones actually delivers the money, it may deliberately plant the story to lure apathetic but mercenary recruits). Bones still has the power to corrupt, but does it have the power to inspire? The recent classes of Bones just do not, it seems, take themselves as seriously as General Russell or Henry Stimson or Blackford Oakes might want them to.

The rotting-paella story seems a perfect emblem of the decay. The story goes that a recent class of Bones decided they would try to cook a meal in the basement kitchen of the tomb. It was vacation time and the servants were not on call to do it for them. They produced a passable paella, but left the remains of the meal there in the basement kitchen, presuming that someone would be in to clean up after them. Nobody came in for two weeks. When they returned, they found the interior of the tomb smelling worse than if there actually *had* been dead bodies there. The servants refused to cook the meal for the next autobiographical session unless the Bonesmen cleaned up the putrefying paella themselves. The Bonesmen went without food. I don't know who finally cleaned up, but there's a sense that like the paella, the original mission of Bones has suffered from neglect and apathy and that the gene pool, like the stew, is becoming stagnant.

I began to feel sorry for the old Bonesmen: After a few days of asking around, I found the going too easy; almost too many people were willing to spill their secrets. I had to call a halt. In the spirit of Bonesman Gifford Pinchot,* godfather of the conservation movement, I'm protecting some of the last secrets—they're an endangered species. And besides, I like mumbo jumbo.

---

*Yes, Mary Meyer's uncle. See, everything connects!

It's strange: I didn't exactly set out to write an exposé of Skull and Bones, but neither did I think I'd end up with an elegy.

Postscript to "The Last Secrets of Skull and Bones"

A personal postscript. In October 1986 aboard Air Force Two, 35,000 feet over the Carolinas, I asked Vice President George Bush about Skull and Bones. It was probably a bit unfair to choose that particular situation. We were strapped into seats in the forward cabin; if, as legend had it, Skull and Bones members were required to exit a room when anyone pronounced the secret society's name in their presence, here the nearest exit was a seven-mile drop.

I had Bush trapped. (I was covering Bush on assignment for *The New Republic,* to write about a campaign swing.) There were a couple of factors complicating the situation, though. One was named Barbara Bush. She had the window seat next to me in the cabin during the interview, and I couldn't help but notice her expression of disapproval—the knitted brow, the compressed lips—of the kinds of "character" questions I'd been asking her husband even before I got to Skull and Bones.

It wasn't so much her knit brow but her knitting needles I found most disconcerting. I could sense her disapproval with my questions in the stepped-up tempo and, well, pointedness with which she stabbed the needles through the fabric. At this point I can't recall whether it was crochet needles, knitting, or needlepoint; all I remember is the glint of those needles flashing like stillettos as I asked George Bush my Skull and Bones question.

But I had my own reasons for being uneasy about the Skull and Bones question. In a certain sense I felt Bush had suffered a bit unfairly from my story. I had written what I thought of as a story about the *decline* of one of the great mythic emblems of the Yankee Eastern establishment. Indeed, the subtitle of the story when it first appeared was "An Elegy for Mumbo Jumbo."

But, perhaps inevitably, conspiracy-minded right-wing groups had ignored the subtleties in the story and used Bush's Bones connection to *reify* the myth of Bones's occult power. During the crucial 1980 New Hampshire primary, when Bush's first run for the presidency had run aground, the right-wing Manchester *Union-Leader* had aired the Skull and Bones connection, quoting my story; other loony-right (and loony-left) Trilateralist-conspiracy theory tracts had cited my story as proof that Bush was a minion of what was portrayed as a conspiratorial secret society of diabolical internationalist bankers that ruled the world from behind the scenes, Protocols of the Elders of Connecticut–style.

And so it was with a bit of guilt that I asked the then vice president about the influence of his secret society on his life. Did Bones inculcate an ethos of leadership?

"Well, it wasn't about leadership per se," he said, "so much as about friendship." He recited a number of similar platitudes, then he cut it short, nodding to his furiously knitting wife and saying, "We're just not the type who likes to get into all this self-analysis stuff." Barbara Bush nodded vigorously back and returned to her needles.

The most shocking recent development to Bones watchers—the one that, as far as I'm concerned, really rent the fabric of the Bones mystique more than anything I'd done—came during Bush's 1988 presidential campaign. In September 1988, *The Washington Post* published the first installment of a five-part Bob Woodward review of Bush's life and career. The shock in that first installment was that Woodward had interviewed many of Bush's class in' Bones. And that they'd talked. Not merely talked, gabbed. Blabbed. About Bones, about the sexual confessional (they confirmed it), about Bush's experience in Bones, about the midlife crisis Bush was suffering during his vice presidency when he summoned his Bones class to a kind of confessional session and confided in them that he was worried he'd sold his principles in an effort to conform to Ronald Reagan's. I was astonished by the way that— overawed, perhaps, by Woodward or by their sudden closeness to the next president (or both)—Bush's Bones brothers babbled about the very character-analysis issues the Bushes seemed to deplore.*

This, more than anything, was a true measure of the decline of Skull and Bones—when the glamour of the White House overshadowed the mystique of the Tomb.

---

*These indiscretions seemed to have troubled others in the Bones hierarchy or in the Bush hierarchy. The "Who's Who" columnist in the January/February 2000 issue of *The Washington Monthly* reported the following:

"A friend of ours who has a brother who was in Skull and Bones . . . the secret society George W. Bush belonged to, recently got this note from the Skull and Bones command center: 'In view of the political happenings in the barbarian world, I feel compelled to remind all of the tradition of privacy and confidentiality essential to the well-being of our Order and strongly urge stout resistance to the seductions and blandishments of the fourth estate.' Translated we think this adds up to 'Don't go tattle on W.' "

But obviously someone tattled on the anti-tattle edict. Sad. Still you have to love that line about "the barbarian world."

Nonetheless, the presidential candidacy of George W. Bush has renewed my interest in "The Order." And I'm hoping for a response to my recent plea in the pages of the *New York Observer* for further information on its fading secrets.*

---

*Bulletin! This just in. As this book was about to go to press early in April 2000, after review copies had already gone out, I learned some startling new details—and got confirmation of some old legends—from what you might call an outside-inside source. An outsider, a woman who'd been taken inside on an unauthorized tour of the interior of the Skull and Bones tomb by a love-struck initiate who hoped to impress her.

The story came to me in response to a plea I made in the pages of the *New York Observer* for members of the all-girl break-in team, who had penetrated and photographed the interior of Skull and Bones in the late seventies (and who had once shown me the pictures that resulted), to come forward and help demystify the black hole in presidential candidate George W. Bush's biography: the weird, occult group-therapy rituals he participated in down in the crypt of Skull and Bones.

Two weeks later, I received a missive that told the story of someone who didn't have to break in, someone who was invited in (well, was sneaked in) to the crypt, some fifteen years before Bones began to tap women. She provided a convincing corroborating detail: I'd described in my *Observer* story a strange enclosure depicted in the all-girl break-in team photographs, an enclosure I'd described, a bit mockingly, as "The Room with the License Plates of Many States." It seemed to be a silly frat-boy type of thing, but my informant added a detail that made it make sense: She said each of those license plates had the number 322 in it and that, according to her initiate-admirer, Bones members were "supposed to confiscate" any license plate they found with the sacred numbers on it for installation on the wall of the Room of the License Plates in the Bones crypt.

It's an interesting detail if true, when you consider that youths not sheltered by privilege and secrecy often end up doing time in jail for such acts of "confiscation."

But only a prelude to her account of an even more remarkable "confiscation" ritual. She wrote me that she was led into a room festooned with skulls in every nook and cranny and that her admirer proudly showed her one particular skull in a glass bowl filled with turquoise. A skull that bore a plaque that she recalled identified it as the skull of Cochise. (Others have reported it to be Geronimo.)

Whether or not it was truly the skull of the legendary Native American warrior, her besotted initiate explained that, as part of the initiation ceremony, each newly tapped Skull and Bones class is handed the name of a historical personage and told to "confiscate" their skull from their grave and bring it to the tomb for trophy mounting.

If true, it's evidence that one of America's most powerful and prestigious societies has been fostering an ongoing grave-robbing crime wave.

I'm continuing to investigate this allegation, based as it is on credible-sounding but still second-hand testimony of a love-struck swain. I am also investigating a surprising sort of confirmation for a detail I thought I'd been in error on.

Remember the mystery of the $15,000 gift, stipend, or whatever? According to this source, in return for deeding the "Order" a certain portion of their estate after death, surviving Bones members get dividends from the investments made by the Order's corporate shell. The annual dividend, this late-seventies initiate reported to this woman, was some $20,000.

I believe her account, but I'm not sure how to evaluate his—he wavered back and forth, for instance, on whether the confessional sessions were done in the nude, she told me. But the detail about the 322 license-plate "confiscation" rings true. I plan to test it by requesting special 322 SKULL plates and seeing if I can catch them in the act.

The Corpse as Big as the Ritz

In Which We Encounter Sarah Miles, Burt Reynolds,
and the Ghost of the Great Gatsby

Sergeant Forrest Hinderliter of the Gila Bend (Arizona) Police had been up since two in the morning with a dead body and a shaky story. He'd found the body—a black man with a bullet hole in his back—lying on the floor in apartment 44 of the North Euclid Street project at the western edge of town. He'd also found a woman there, and this was her story:

She woke up after midnight to find a man on top of her. She'd never seen the man before. She told him to get off and get out; she warned him she was expecting another man. A car pulled up outside and flashed its lights. A minute later the other man came through the door. Explanations were inadequate. In the scuffle a gun was drawn, a .38 revolver. A shot went off, the first visitor died.

An accident, the woman told Sergeant Hinderliter, the gun had gone off by accident. An accident, the other man, the one who owned the .38, told the sergeant.

Sergeant Hinderliter had the body tagged and carted off to Phoenix for an autopsy. He took statements until six-thirty in the morning, then returned to the station house to check in for his regular Sunday tour of duty.

He was drinking black coffee at Birchfields's café at six minutes past noon when the phone rang. It was Mrs. Steel, the station-house dispatcher, on the line. She had just taken a call from a man at the Travelodge Motel. There was a dead body in room 127, it was reported, an overdose of something.

Up until 1965 Gila Bend showed up frequently in National Weather Summaries as having registered the highest daily temperature in America. One hundred twenty in the shade was not unusual. Occasionally Gila Bend was referred to as the hottest place in America.

It was hot in Gila Bend, but not that hot, the mayor of Gila Bend confided to me one evening at the Elks Club bar. Someone in Gila Bend had been doing some fooling around with the thermometer readings to make Gila Bend look a few degrees hotter than it was. In 1965, the Weather Bureau did some checking and put a stop to the matter. Since then Gila Bend has been just another hot place.

There's an old narrow-gauge railroad that runs south from the town to the open-pit copper mines near the Mexican border. The Phelps Dodge Corporation uses the railroad to run copper anodes from their foundries up to the Southern Pacific freight siding at Gila Bend. Hollywood Westerns occasionally use the railroad's ancient steam locomotive and the cactus wastes surrounding the tracks for location work.

On January 28, 1973, an MGM production company shooting *The Man Who Loved Cat Dancing,* a high-budget, middlebrow Western starring Sarah Miles, Burt Reynolds, and Lee J. Cobb, arrived at Gila Bend. Forty members of the cast and crew checked into the Travelodge Motel on the eastern edge of town.

There was no pulse. The skin had cooled. Pale blotches on the hands, the neck, and the forehead suggested to Sergeant Hinderliter that death had come to the body several hours before he had. Rigor mortis, in its early stages, had stiffened the arms which were wrapped around an empty polyethylene wastebasket. It was 12:30 P.M.

The young man lay curled up on his left side on the floor of the partitioned-off "dressing-room" area of Travelodge room 127. His nose touched the metal strip that divided the carpeted dressing-room floor from the tiled floor of the bathroom. His feet stuck out beyond the end of the partition.

The capsules were big and red. There were about a dozen, and most of them lay in two groups on the floor. Burt Reynolds would later testify he saw pills lying on top of the dead man's arm.

The sergeant wondered why the man on the floor had decided to collapse and die in what was clearly a woman's bedroom: The vanity counter above the body teemed with vials of cosmetics, a woman's wardrobe packed the hangers, a long brown hairpiece streamed across a nearby suitcase. As he stepped out to his squad car Sergeant Hinderliter felt a hand on his arm. The hand belonged to an MGM official.

"He'd been drinking," the MGM man told the sergeant in a confidential tone. "He'd been drinking, he swallowed a lot of pills, he took a bunch of pills, and he was dead. He took an overdose," the man said.

The sergeant asked the MGM person for the dead man's name and position.

The name was David Whiting, he told the sergeant. "He was Miss Miles's business manager. You see, that was Miss Miles's room he was in. It was Miss Miles who found him, but . . ."

"Where is Miss Miles?" the sergeant asked.

"She's over there in 123, Mr. Poll's room, now, but she's much too upset to talk. She's had a terrible experience, you can understand, and . . ."

"Yes, he was my business manager," the sergeant recalls Miss Miles telling him a few minutes later. "He was my business manager, but all he wanted to do was f—— me all the time and I wasn't going to be f——ed by him."

Sergeant Hinderliter is a mild-mannered and mild-spoken cop. He has a round open face, a blond crew cut, and a soft Arizona drawl. His dream at one point in his life was to earn a mortician's license and open a funeral home in Gila Bend, but after four years' study he dropped out of morticians' school to become a cop because he missed dealing with warm bodies. In his off-duty hours Sergeant Hinderliter is a scoutmaster for Troop Number 204. He recalls being somewhat surprised at Miss Miles's language. "Now I've heard that kind of talk sitting around with some guys," he told me. "But I never heard a lady use those words." (Later, as we shall see, Miss Miles denied she had used those words.)

Miss Miles was stretched out on one of the twin beds in room 123, her head propped up by pillows. Her face was flushed, her eyes streaked and wet. She was upset, she told the sergeant, but she was willing to talk.

I might as well tell you the whole story, she said.

The sergeant took notes, and this is the whole story she told that afternoon, as he remembers it:

It all started at the Pink Palomino café. There were a dozen of them there, movie people; they had driven thirty-six miles to the Palomino for a kind of pre-birthday party for Burt Reynolds, who was to turn thirty-eight the next day, Sunday, February 11.

She had driven to the Pink Palomino with Burt Reynolds, but she left early and drove back to Gila Bend with Lee J. Cobb. She had wanted a ride in Cobb's impressive new car—a Citroën on the outside, a powerful Maserati racing engine within. Back at the Travelodge she proceeded to the cocktail lounge. She had one drink. She danced.

It was close to midnight when she started back to her own room. Halfway there she decided to stop by and apologize to Burt for failing to return to Gila Bend with him.

When she entered room 135, Reynolds's room, she found a Japanese masseuse there too. Sarah asked permission to remain during the massage. The Japanese woman rubbed, Sarah talked. Around three A.M. she left and walked around the rear of the building to her own room. As soon as she stepped into the room, she told the sergeant, David Whiting jumped out of the dressing room and grabbed her.

Whiting demanded to know where she'd been and whom she'd been with. She told him it was none of his business. He slapped her. She screamed. From the next room, the nanny Sarah had hired to look after her five-year-old son rushed into Sarah's room through a connecting door.

Sarah told the nanny to call Burt. David Whiting released Sarah and ran outside. Burt Reynolds arrived shortly thereafter and took Sarah back to his room, where she spent the remainder of the morning.

Sometime later that Sunday morning, it may have been eight o'clock, it may have been ten, Sarah left Reynolds's room and returned to the nanny's room, number 126. She spoke briefly with the nanny, reentered her own room to use the bathroom, and found David Whiting's body on the floor. She gasped, ran back to the nanny's room, and told her to call Burt.

Gila Bend Coroner Mulford T. "Sonny" Winsor IV was still in bed Sunday afternoon when the dispatcher called him with news of the Travelodge death. He too had been up all night with the shooting death in the Euclid Street project. He had some questions. Had the dead black man, in fact, been a total stranger to the woman and the man with the .38, or had there been a more complicated relationship?

Coroner Winsor—he is also Justice of the Peace, Town Magistrate, Registrar of Vital Statistics, and a plumbing contractor on the side—wasted no time with the second body, the one he found at the Travelodge. There was nothing in room 127 to suggest anything but suicide. He rounded up a coroner's jury, including three Gila Bend citizens he found eating in the Travelodge Coffee Shop, and took them into room 127 to view the body for the record.

Next Coroner Winsor looked for some piece of identification for the death certificate, some proof that the dead man was in fact David Whiting. He bent over the body on the floor and reached into the pockets of the dark trousers. Nothing. Nothing in the right front pocket. He rolled the body gently over to look in the left front. There: no ID, but a key, a Travelodge key to room 127, Sarah's room, the room in which the young man died.

Coroner Winsor decided to check the young man's own room for identification. He ran back through the rain to the motel office, learned that David Whiting was registered to room 119, and ran back with a key.

He saw bloodstains as soon as he crossed the threshold of 119. There was blood on the pillow at the head of one of the twin beds. There was blood on the bath towel at the foot of the bed. There was blood, he soon discovered, clotted upon wads of toilet tissue in the bathroom. There was blood, he discovered later, on a Travelodge key on the other bed. It was a key for room 126, the nanny's room.

The death of David Whiting suddenly became a more complex affair. Had he been beaten before he died? The coroner called the chief of police over to room 119. The chief of police took one look and decided to call in the professionals from the Arizona State Police. There was the possibility of assault, even murder, to consider now.

Sarah Miles had a boil. The year was 1970 and Sarah Miles had come to Hollywood to do publicity for *Ryan's Daughter*. She had two appointments that afternoon: the first at noon with the show-business correspondent of *Time*, the next at three o'clock with a *Vogue* photographer. It was the *Vogue* appointment that worried her: *Vogue* wanted to feature her as one of the three most beautiful women in the world, and there, on her cheek, was a stubborn boil.

So she was not in an especially good mood as she sat in her bungalow at the Beverly Hills Hotel, waiting for the man from *Time* to arrive. Nor had her mood improved when he finally showed up, thirty minutes late.

He wore a dark, three-piece English-cut suit, a luxuriously proper Turnbull and Asser shirt. He flashed a burnished-gold Dunhill lighter and a burnished-bronze hothouse tan. He removed a bottle from his suit coat, announced that it contained his personal Bloody Mary mix, and began the interview by discoursing at length upon the inadequacies of all other Bloody Marys. His name was David Whiting. He was twenty-four years old.

The subject of Sarah's boil came up. David Whiting confessed that he too had, on occasion, trouble with his skin. However, he told Sarah, he knew the *very best dermatologist in Hollywood,* and knew of an extraordinary pill for boils. Take one and ten minutes later, he promised Sarah, her boil would vanish.

He disappeared for ten minutes and returned with a bottle of the magic boil pills. She took one. The boil lasted much longer than ten minutes. The interview did not. As she went off to be the most beautiful woman in the world for *Vogue,* she assumed she had seen the last of David Whiting.

The next evening they met again. He requested the meeting, but despite his strange performance the first time, she didn't turn him down. She was amused by his pomposity, intrigued by his intelligence. She began calling him "Whiz Kid."

A few days later she was sitting in the V.I.P. lounge of the L.A. airport awaiting a flight to New York when David Whiting showed up and announced that he was taking the same flight. He secured the seat next to her. The next morning in New York he showed up in her suite at the Sherry Netherland. He took a room on the same floor. She never encouraged him, she says, but neither did she tell him to get lost.

Maybe it was the Vuitton luggage.

"He always had to have the best," she remembers. "All his doctors were the best doctors, his dentist was the very best dentist, Henry Poole was the very best tailor in London, everything with David had to be the best. If your agent wasn't the very best agent, then you had to change; if your doctor wasn't right, change, and he couldn't understand me because nothing I had was the best. . . . He'd spend hours at a restaurant choosing the best wines. . . . Suddenly he'd say to me, 'Do you have Vuitton luggage?' and I honestly had never heard of it. I said what was that word, and he said, '*Vuitton!* Come on! Don't pretend with me.' "

She wasn't pretending, she said. "It was funny. He was a *joke* in that he made people laugh. He was the sort of person you could send up. . . . But David was the first person who awakened me to what was the best and what wasn't the best."

Then came the Working Permit Crisis. There was panic in the Sherry Netherland suite. For ten days Sarah had been unable to appear on American television because her working permit had not come through. A small army of MGM PR people scurried in and out of her suite reporting new delays and new failures, receiving scornful tongue lashings from Sarah.

"I began to get quite angry. I remember calling Jim Aubrey, the head of MGM, you know, and telling him this is ridiculous, I've been here ten days, and this is ridiculous, all the money that's being wasted through these silly, interminable delays. And David Whiting was in the room with all these others and he started going, 'What's the matter? What happened? What happened? Working permit? Good God!' And he went straight to the phone and rang up a number and in half an hour my working permit arrived. . . . Literally in one telephone call I had a working permit which these other people hadn't been able to get for ten days. And I sort of thought, hmmmm, that's not bad. . . ."

Then there was the eye infection. "I came up with an eye infection and couldn't go on the Frost show . . . and he said, 'Oh, don't worry, I'll see to that,' and he took me across New York to an eye specialist, who gave me special stuff that cleared up my eyes. He was terribly efficient in certain areas, really terrifically efficient. Then he'd go over the top. Whenever he'd done something good, he'd get euphoric, and he'd suddenly go higher and higher and higher until he suddenly thought he was some sort of Sam Spiegel–cum–President-of-America and he'd go berserk in thinking he was terrific."

He followed her everywhere in New York. He was going to get *Time* to do a cover story on her. He arranged a lunch with Henry Grunwald, editor of *Time,* for her. Things didn't go smoothly. "You f——ed the whole thing up. You f——ed the whole thing," David screamed at her when she reported back to him. He continued to follow her.

A few days later he waved good-bye to her at Kennedy Airport as she took off for England, her country home, her husband, and her child. The next morning he knocked at the front door of her country home in Surrey. He was stopping by on his way to a skiing holiday, he told her. He stayed for a year.

Sergeant Hinderliter didn't see the "star-shaped wound," as it came to be called, the first time he looked at David Whiting's body. Nor had he seen blood. But when he returned to room 127, Sarah's room, he was startled to see a pool of blood seeping out onto the tiles of the bathroom floor. The body seemed to be bleeding from the head.

Sergeant Hinderliter found the "star-shaped wound" at the back of the head, to the right of the occipital point. The wound had apparently stopped bleeding sometime after death, and resumed when the coroner rolled the body over to search for identification.

This "stellate or star-shaped contused laceration one inch in diameter . . . is the kind of injury we frequently see in people who fall on the back of the head," the autopsy doctor would testify at the coroner's inquest.

"This, of course, does not preclude," he added, "the possibility of the decedent having been pushed. . . ."

There were other marks on the body. Two "superficial contused scratches" on the middle of the abdomen. One "superficial contused abrasion" on the lower abdomen. Several scratches on the hands. There were "multiple hemorrhages"—bruises—on the chest and the left shoulder.

"Would those be consistent with someone having been in a scuffle or a fight?" the autopsy doctor was asked at the inquest.

"Yes," said the autopsy doctor.

But despite the suggestive marks on the outside of David Whiting's body, the cause of death, the autopsy doctor concluded, was to be found within.

A CATALOG OF THE VARIOUS DRUGS IN SARAH MILES'S BEDROOM AS COMPILED BY DETECTIVE BARNEY HAYES AND CHEMIST JACK STRONG OF THE ARIZONA STATE POLICE

ITEM ONE: some pills, multivitamin preparation

ITEM TWO: capsules, antibiotic drug

ITEM THREE: capsules, Serax Oxazepan, for treatment of anxiety and depression

ITEM FOUR:	A—capsules of Dalmane, which is a hypnotic, and
	B—some capsules which were not identified
ITEM FIVE:	tablets, Mandrax, which is a hypnotic antihistamine combination
ITEM SIX:	some capsules, Ampicillin Trihydrate, which is an antibiotic
ITEM SEVEN:	some further capsules which were not identified
ITEM EIGHT:	some pills, Compazine, a tranquilizer
ITEM NINE:	A—yellow tablets, Paredrine, which is a hypotensive, and
	B—some gray pills, Temaril, an antipruritic and antihistaminic
ITEM TEN:	tablets of Donnatal, which is antispasmodic and sedative
ITEM ELEVEN:	white tablets, a yeast
ITEM TWELVE:	a liquid, an anticough mixture

One item was missing from the scene. Burt Reynolds told Sergeant Hinderliter that when he had been summoned by Sarah to look at the body, he had noticed a pill bottle clenched in one of David Whiting's fists. He had pried it loose, Reynolds said, and rushed in to Sarah who was, by then, in room 123. He had shown her the bottle and asked her, "Do you know what these are?" She was too upset to reply, he said.

The pill bottle disappeared. Burt Reynolds doesn't remember what he did with it. He might have thrown it away in room 123, he said. He might have had it in his hand when he returned to 127, the room with the body in it. He remembers seeing a prescription-type label of some sort on it, but he doesn't remember what the label said. The pill bottle was never found.

And the pills on the arm: Nobody seems to have explained the pills on the arm. David Whiting may have knocked some pills on the floor, but there would be no easy way for him to knock pills down onto his own arm while lying curled up on the floor. No one else in the case has admitted knocking them down onto his arm, or dropping them there.

There are other unanswered questions about the pills David took on his last night. Item Five on the list of Sarah's drugs is a pill called Mandrax. Mandrax is the English trade name for the formulation of two drugs. One—the main ingredient—is methaqualone, which is described in medical literature as a "hypnotic," and as such occupies the drowsy middle ground between the barbiturates and the tranquilizers. The second ingredient in Mandrax tablets is a small amount of diphenhydramine, which, under the more familiar trade name Benadryl, is marketed as an antihistamine and mild depressant.

American drug companies sell pure methaqualone—without the Benadryl—under several trade names, including the one that had become a household word by the time David Whiting died: Quaalude.

The autopsy doctor found methaqualone in David Whiting's body. (There were 410 milligrams in his stomach, 7.4 milligrams in his liver, and .88 milligrams per hundred milliliters—about 45 milligrams altogether—in his bloodstream.) The doctor also found some Benadryl in his blood, along with half a drink's worth of alcohol and "unquantitated levels" of a Valium-type tranquilizer.

Where did that methaqualone come from? Because of the presence of the Benadryl, it is possible to surmise that the pills David Whiting swallowed were Mandrax, rather than an American version of methaqualone. Sarah Miles would later testify at the coroner's inquest that she "believed" she found "a few"—she was not sure how many—pills from Item Five, her Mandrax supply, missing after David Whiting's death. Sarah would also testify that she believed David Whiting no longer had a Mandrax prescription of his own because, she says, David's London doctor had taken David off the drug. But if David Whiting did take Mandrax that night it still cannot be said with absolute certainty that the tablets he swallowed did come from Sarah Miles's "Item Five."

Nor is there any certainty about the number of tablets David Whiting swallowed that night. Adding up the quantities of methaqualone found in his stomach, blood, and liver, one finds a total of less than 500 milligrams. Since each Mandrax tablet contains only 250 milligrams of methaqualone, it would seem that the residue of perhaps two, and no more than three, tablets was present in David Whiting's system at the time of his death. But there is no data available on how long he had been taking methaqualone before that evening, nor whether he had developed a tolerance or sensitivity to the drug.

Was there enough methaqualone in David Whiting's body to kill him? The autopsy doctor, you will recall, found less than 1 milligram per hundred milliliters in his blood. According to one traditional authority—*The Legal Medicine Annual* of 1970—it takes three times that amount, 3 milligrams per hundred milliliters, to kill an average man. However, about the time David Whiting died, the literature on methaqualone had entered a state of crisis. The Great American Quaalude Craze of 1972 had produced a number of overdose deaths, and, consequently, a number of new studies of the kill levels of the drug. The results of one of those studies—summarized in an article in a publication called *Clinical Chemistry*—was making the rounds of the autopsy world at the time of David Whiting's death. The *Clinical Chemistry* article challenged the traditional 3-milligram kill level, and suggested that less methaqualone than previously suspected could cause death.

The Maricopa County autopsy doctor who first examined David Whiting cited these new, lower figures, plus the combined depressant effect of Benadryl, alcohol, and the "unquantitated levels" of another tranquilizer to explain why two or three tablets' worth of methaqualone could have killed David Whiting. He called the old figures "insufficient and antiquated evidence."

But affidavits from a leading pharmacologist and a leading forensic pathologist introduced at the inquest by David Whiting's mother challenged the certainty of the original autopsy doctor's conclusion, especially his willingness to abandon the traditional authorities. "These reports have not been established in the literature," one of the affidavits said.

So great is the conflict between the new and old figures that a certain small dose cited in the new study as a poisonous "minimum toxic level" qualifies as a "therapeutic dose" under the old system.

These uncertainties placed David Whiting's final Mandrax dose in a disputed netherland between therapy and poison, leaving unanswered the questions of whether he took the tablets to calm down or to kill himself, or whether he killed himself trying to calm down.

SOME ITEMS FOUND IN DAVID WHITING'S TRAVELODGE ROOM (NUMBER 119)

- fifty-nine photographs of Sarah Miles
- a large leather camera bag stamped with a LIFE decal, four expensive Nikons inside
- a six-month-old *Playboy* magazine, found lying on the bottom sheet of the unmade, blood-stained bed, as if he had been reading it while he waited for the bleeding to stop
- a piece of luggage—a medium-size suitcase—lying open but neatly packed on the other bed, as if in preparation for a morning departure and a two-day trip
- two bottles of Teacher's Scotch, one nearly empty, on the night table between the beds, also a can of Sprite
- an Olivetti portable typewriter with the ribbon and spools ripped out and lying tangled next to it
- a book called *The Mistress,* a novel, the film rights to which David Whiting had purchased on behalf of Sarah Miles. He wanted her to play the title role.
- a copy of a screenplay called *The Capri Numbers,* a romantic thriller David Whiting had been working on with an English actor. Sarah Miles was to play the part of Jocylin. In the screenplay's preliminary description of Jocylin we learn that "this story will teach her the meaning of 'there's a vulgarity in possession: it makes for a sense of mortality.' "
- a Gideon Bible

The Bible is not mentioned in police reports, but when I stayed in David Whiting's motel room a month after his death, I looked through the Bible and found three widely separated pages conspicuously marked, and one three-page section torn out.

The upper-right-hand corner of page twenty-three has been dog-eared. On page twenty-three (Genesis 24–25) we read of, among other things, the death and burial of Sarah.

The lower-left-hand corner of page 532 has been dog-eared. It contains Psalms 27 and 28—each of which is headed, in the Gideon edition, "A Psalm of David." In these two psalms, David pleads with God not to abandon him. ("Hide not thy face far from me; put not thy servant away in anger . . . leave me not, neither forsake me.") David declares he wants to remain "in the land of the living" but warns that "if thou be silent to me I become like them that go down into the pit."

The upper-left-hand corner of page 936 has been dog-eared. The Last Supper is over. Christ, alone on the Mount of Olives, contemplating his imminent crucifixion, asks God, "If thou be willing, remove this cup from me." He prays feverishly ("his sweat was as it were great drops of blood"), then descends to his disciples, whereupon Judas betrays him with a kiss.

Torn out of the Gideon Bible in David Whiting's motel room are pages 724 to 730. Consulting an intact Gideon Bible, I discovered that those pages record the climactic vision of the destruction of Babylon from the final chapters of the Book of Jeremiah, and the despairing description of the destruction of Jerusalem from the beginning of Lamentations.

"I shall make drunk her princes and her wise men," says the Lord in regard to his plans for the rulers of Babylon, ". . . and they shall sleep a perpetual sleep and not wake." "I called for my lovers but they deceived me . . . my sighs are many and my heart is faint," says the weeper in the torn-out pages of Lamentations.

Police found no suicide note.

Four months after he moved into Mill House, her country home in Surrey, David Whiting threatened to kill himself, Sarah Miles told me. The threat was powerful enough, she says, to prevent her and her husband from daring to ask him to leave for six more months.

Just what was David Whiting doing, living in the household of Mr. and Mrs. Robert Bolt, Mill House, Surrey, anyway?

At first he was just stopping off on his way to a European ski resort. Then he was staying awhile to gather more material for his *Time* story. His "angle" on this story, he told them, was going to be "the last happy marriage" or something like that. He did not believe in happy marriages, didn't believe they could exist anymore, yet here Sarah and Robert Bolt had what appeared to be a happy marriage and he wanted to find out just what it was they had.

Then David thrust himself into the *Lady Caroline Lamb* project, a kind of family enterprise for Robert Bolt and Sarah. When David arrived in the summer of 1971, *Lamb* was only a screenplay. Robert Bolt—the forty-nine-year-old playwright who wrote *A Man for All Seasons* and several David Lean screenplays—had written it, he wanted Sarah to star in it, he wanted to direct it himself. He was having trouble getting the money for it.

As soon as David arrived he jumped in, started calling producers, money people, studios, agents. He whisked Sarah off to Cannes, rented a villa there for the film festival the better to make "contacts." He went to work on her finances, clearing up a "huge overdraft" in Sarah's account. He talked her into getting new lawyers, new accountants, new agents. He flattered Robert Bolt about his writing, Sarah about her acting. He quit his job at *Time* to devote himself to helping them make *Lamb,* he told them. He persuaded Sarah to make him her business manager, which meant he got 10 percent of whatever she got. He persuaded Robert and Sarah to give him a salaried job in their family film company—Pulsar Productions Ltd. On the Pulsar stationery he became "David Whiting, Director of Publicity and Exploitation."

Lamb is a triangle. A year after he moved in with Robert Bolt and Sarah, David Whiting produced a publicity book about the film. This is how he describes that triangle:

There is Lady Caroline, to be played by Sarah Miles. "On fire for the dramatic, the picturesque . . . a creature of impulse, intense sensibility and bewitching unexpectedness," David wrote. "On those for whom it worked she cast a spell which could not be resisted. . . . Such a character was bound finally to make a bad wife." She ends up dying "for love." "And so at the end of her short life, she achieved the ultimate gesture which all her life she has been seeking."

Then there is her husband, William Lamb, ultimately to become Lord Melbourne, the Whig Prime Minister: "A Gentleman, self-controlled and decent," David wrote. "A capacity for compromising agreeably with circumstance . . . When Caroline threw herself into her notorious affair with Lord Byron, William refused to take it seriously. . . . He detected in Byron all that was specious in the poet's romantic posturing . . . he was not jealous but his spirit was wounded."

And finally there was Byron: "He was a raw nerve-ridden boy of genius," David wrote, "a kind of embodied fantasy . . . emerged from obscurity . . . born to nobility and relative poverty. With his pale face, extreme good looks, and pouting expression . . . the public was entranced with the personality of its twenty-four-year-old author. Nevertheless," twenty-four-year-old David

Whiting added, his "divine fire gleamed fitfully forth through a turmoil of suspicion and awkwardness. His sophistication was a mask for shyness. . . . At the most elementary level he was a poseur."

Halfway into an interview with Sarah Miles I read her that passage about Byron from David's book about *Lamb,* and asked her if that was, perhaps, David Whiting writing about himself.

"I think he got that from Lord David Cecil, actually," she said. "Most of it you'll find is from other books, I'm afraid."

I tried again: "What I mean is, did he see the family he moved into at Surrey as a kind of reflection of the Lamb triangle?"

"The Lamb triangle? I see what you mean. It hadn't crossed my mind until you said it. Maybe you're right. I hadn't thought of it like that at all."

At this point I felt compelled to ask directly, and yet if possible with some delicacy, the question that had been on my mind.

"It seems, uh, a probably fortuitous coincidence that this *Lamb* thing was going on at the same time David was, uh, well, what *was* your, what was his relationship, was he sexually possessive or . . . ?"

"Nope," Sarah interrupted briskly. "Not a bit. You see, this is the area which is weird. He never made a pass at me, he never spoke of me sexually, it was just a sort of"—pause—"I don't quite know how to put it—it seems so self-*brag*ging, you know, to say the things he said—I can't really, because I don't really—I think he, he wanted to put me up *there,* because it would sort of excuse himself from any sort of reality. I think if he had really made an ordinary mundane *pass* and been rejected, it would have ruined this other image that he had. You know what I mean, I mean if at one time we really *had* had an affair, it would have probably been the best thing for David. I mean he probably would have realized that I was just an ordinary girl like the rest of them."

At this point I thought of what Sergeant Hinderliter had told me Sarah had told *him* on the afternoon of the death, about David Whiting "always wanting to f—— me all the time. . . ."

Now that statement did not imply that Sarah Miles had, in fact, slept with David Whiting. It did, however, raise the question in my mind about whether David Whiting had or had not ever made "a mundane pass" at Sarah, and I felt I had to ask her about it.

"Sarah, uh, I feel I have to ask you this, it's, uh, a difficult question," I faltered, toward the close of the interview. "But, uh, this sergeant in Gila Bend told me that you told him that all David Whiting wanted to do . . ." I repeated what the sergeant had quoted her as saying.

She skipped, at most, one third of a breath.

"There have been some *extraordinary* reports from those policemen, I mean there really have." She gave a small sigh. "I mean I don't understand what this is *about*. Well, I went back into the room, well, there's a whole area in there the police were . . . *very odd indeed,* and I don't *understand,* I mean that quote. . . . What time? When?"

I told her when the sergeant said he heard it.

"I mean, can you imagine, can you imagine me saying this to a policeman, that anyone in their right mind could say that. . . ."

"I can imagine you being upset and—"

"But to say *that*! I'm terribly sorry, but I'm not the liar in this case."

It was not sex David Whiting wanted so desperately, Sarah told me, it was family. He'd never had a real family before, he'd told the Bolts. His parents divorced when he was a child, he'd hardly seen his father, who, he said, was some sort of director of Pan Am, a position which gave David the right to fly the world for next to nothing. He'd been a child prodigy, he told them, and his mother had sent him off to one boarding school after another. He'd had some unpleasant years in boarding schools. He was too smart for any of them, but they'd treated him badly. Once he said he had been forced to submit to a spinal injection to cure a "learning deficiency" because he'd been stubbornly pretending he didn't know how to read. So painful was this spinal injection that he'd immediately picked up a volume of Shakespeare and started to perform from it just to forestall repetition of that pain. He'd gone to the finest prep school in Washington, D.C., with the sons of the famous and powerful. He'd become an extraordinary ladies' man among the debutante daughters of the famous and the powerful, he told them. He dropped names of his conquests.

His prep-school classmates thought he would become president, he told the Bolts. But what he wanted to be, he told them, was the greatest producer there ever was. At an early age he had taken off from school to make movies in the Libyan desert and the hot spots of Europe. He had been the youngest man ever appointed full-fledged *Time* correspondent, but he had given all that up for Sarah and Robert and for what they could become under his management. He wanted to make Sarah the greatest star there ever was. He was devoted to them for all that, he told them, but also for their home, and for the feeling of being part of a family at last.

But after three months things started to go wrong in this family. David became dissatisfied with mere "publicity-and-exploitation" duties. He wanted to do more. Nobody understood how good he was, nobody gave him a chance to show how much he could do. He decided to show them. Without the consent of the producer of *Lamb* he arranged a deal to produce a movie of his own— a documentary about the making of *Lamb*. This didn't go over well with the real producer. He made enemies. He started staying up in his room for days at a time, according to Sarah, worrying about his skin problem, his weight problem, his hair-loss problem, claiming all the while that he was working on scripts and deals, but failing to do his publicity work on time. Finally, according to Sarah, he was fired from his publicity job. She was the only one to take his side, she says. She kept him on as business manager, but both she and Robert suggested to David that he might be happier and get more work done if he moved out of their country home into Sarah's London town house.

It was at this point, September 1971, according to Sarah, that David told them that if they ever forced him to leave their family he'd kill himself.

She found it hard to take this threat lightly, Sarah says. Twice before she'd been threatened that way, and twice before she'd ended up with a dead body on her hands. Sarah tells the story of the first two suicides.

First there was Thelma. Thelma had gone through the same exclusive Swiss finishing school as Sarah. Since then Thelma had gone through hard times and electroshock treatment. She'd read a newspaper report that Sarah had taken a townhouse at 18 Hasker Street, Chelsea; she showed up there one day and asked to move in for a while.

Thelma stayed three years. She moved her young son in with her. Sarah gave her a "job" to earn her stay—walking Sarah's Pyrenean mountain dog—but Thelma forgot about it half the time. At night, according to Sarah, "she turned the place into a brothel," admitting a stream of men into her basement quarters. Finally, after Thelma had taken two messy overdoses, Robert Bolt came into Sarah's life and told her she had to get rid of Thelma.

"I told Robert if I chucked her out she'd kill herself," Sarah recalls. "And Robert said, 'Christ, Sarah, grow up. They all say that but not all of them do it.' Robert got to arguing with Thelma one day and said, 'Look, for Christ's sake, Thelma, can't you see what you're doing to Sarah? If you really mean business you'll jump.' "

Sarah asked Thelma to leave. Thelma jumped.

Then there was Johnny. Sarah had been kicked out of her Chelsea townhouse because of the obtrusive behavior of her Pyrenean mountain dog. Sarah and Robert had married and were moving to a country home in Surrey. Johnny came along. He was a landscape gardener and owner of three Pyrenean mountain dogs. "I decided to sublease the Chelsea house to him. I thought it would be a very funny joke, having been kicked out for one, to move in somebody with *three* Pyrenean mountain dogs. That tickled me. I liked that," Sarah says.

Johnny was very well dressed, and told the Bolts he was very well off. "But I let him have it for almost nothing, he was a friend, we'd have him up for weekends, he was a very charming fellow, he was a queer but a very nice man—boy."

After nine months Johnny hadn't paid a cent of rent.

"Robert told me, 'Sarah, you're crazy to let this go on. . . . Go up there and get the money.' So on a Friday I went up. The house looked lovely . . . he had a fantastic deep freeze, fantastic food, new carpets—he lived very high."

She asked him for the money. He said of course he'd give it to her—the very next day.

The next morning, back at her country home, she received a telephone call from a policeman. "He asked me if I were Sarah Miles, and did I own 18 Hasker Street, and I said yes, and he said Mr. Johnny W——— has put his head in the oven, he's gassed himself to death. . . ."

In mid-February of 1972, David Whiting moved into 18 Hasker Street. On the second day of March 1972, David Whiting was rushed to St. George's Hospital, London, unconscious, dressed only in his underwear, suffering from an overdose of drugs. After his release, Sarah and Robert took him back again.

One evening later that year David Whiting was drinking in London with a woman writer who was preparing a story about Sarah Miles. He began confiding in her about his dream. Robert Bolt was nearing fifty, he observed, while he, David Whiting, was only half that age. He could wait, he told her, wait for Robert Bolt to die, and then he knew Sarah would be his at last. The woman writer seemed to think David Whiting was being deadly serious.

Not enough people die in Gila Bend to support a funeral home. So when the autopsy doctor in Phoenix completed his work on David Whiting, he sewed the body back up and shipped it to Ganley's funeral establishment in Buckeye—thirty miles north of Gila Bend—to await claiming by next of kin.

There was some question about next of kin. David Whiting had filled in the next-of-kin blank on his passport with the name "Sarah Miles." No other next of kin had stepped forward. For three days no one seemed to know if David Whiting's parents were dead or alive. Finally on Wednesday the Gila Bend chief of police received a call from a woman on the East Coast who said she had once been engaged to David Whiting. Among other things she told the chief the name of a person on the West Coast who might know how to reach the mother. After several further phone calls, the chief finally learned of a certain Mrs. Campbell of Berkeley, California.

On Thursday, February 15, a small gray-haired woman stepped off the Greyhound bus in Buckeye, Arizona. She proceeded to Mr. Ganley's establishment on Broadway and introduced herself to Mr. Ganley as Mrs. Louise Campbell, the mother of David Whiting. She persuaded Mr. Ganley to drive her into Gila Bend to see the chief of police.

There was trouble in the chief's office that day. As soon as she walked in Mrs. Campbell demanded to know how the chief had located her. No one was supposed to know where she was. She demanded to be told who had tipped him off. The chief asked her about David Whiting's father. She told him they had been divorced long ago. She told him that three weeks before David's death the father had suffered a near-fatal heart attack and was not to be contacted under any circumstances. Her present husband, David's stepfather, was spending the winter in Hawaii for his poor health and she didn't want him contacted either. She said she wanted David Whiting's personal property. The chief told her he couldn't release it to her until after the completion of the inquest, scheduled for February 27. He agreed to allow her to select a suit for David to be buried in.

"The chief opened up the suitcase and she grabbed everything she could and ran outside to the car with it, clutching it in her arms," Mr. Ganley recalls with some bemusement. "Oh, she went running from one room to the other in the police station and finally the chief said, 'Get her the hell out of here, will you?' She grabbed everything she could get before they could stop her. I was picking out certain belongings in which to bury him. She just grabbed them. . . ."

Ten days later, Mrs. Campbell reappeared at Mr. Ganley's funeral home. It was nine o'clock at night. She was accompanied by an unidentified man.

She asked Mr. Ganley to take the body out of the refrigerator. She wanted to examine it, she said.

Mr. Ganley protested, "I said, 'Well, lady, why don't you take him into the County Mortuary . . . we don't like to show a body like this, he isn't clothed, he's covered with, uh . . . he's been in the refrigerator.' She said, 'Well, that's all right.' "

Mr. Ganley took the body out of the refrigerator and wheeled it out for Mrs. Campbell's inspection.

"She wanted to know if all his organs were there," Mr. Ganley recalled. "She said, 'Could you open him up?' I said no, we won't do that. Well, she wanted to know if the organs were there and I said well I presume they are."

A few days later Mrs. Campbell showed up at Ganley's funeral home again, this time with a different man, whom she introduced as a pathologist from a neighboring county. Again she demanded that the body be brought out of the refrigerator for inspection. Again, with reluctance, Mr. Ganley wheeled it out.

Mr. Ganley asked this pathologist if he had any documentary proof that Mrs. Campbell was, in fact, the boy's mother.

"He told me that he just assumed that she was. So I said well, okay, go ahead. So he opened him up and checked the organs, to see if they had all been returned after the first autopsy."

It was during this session, Mr. Ganley recalled, that Mrs. Campbell did some checking of her own. She examined the star-shaped wound on the back of the head and found it sewn up. She complained to Mr. Ganley about that.

"She asked me why we did that, and I said, well, to keep it from leaking all over the table. And she said, 'Don't do anything else to it.' And then she'd probe up in there with her finger."

"She actually put her finger in it?"

"Oh yeah . . . She never expressed one bit of grief except when I first saw her and she sobbed . . . well, one night she kissed him and said poor David or something."

How badly had David Whiting beaten Sarah Miles? You will recall that Sergeant Hinderliter remembers Sarah telling him on the afternoon of the death that David Whiting had "slapped" her. It was the sergeant's impression that Sarah meant she had been slapped just once. He had asked her where Whiting had slapped her. She had pointed to the left side of her head. The sergeant does not recall seeing any marks, or any bruises, or any blood. Eleven days later Sarah told the police and the press that David Whiting had given her "the nastiest beating of my life."

This is how she described it:

"He started to throw me around the room like they do in B movies. . . . This was the most violent ever in my life. I was very frightened because all the time I was saying, 'Hold your face, Sarah, because you won't be able to shoot next day' . . . he was beating me on the back of my head . . . there were sharp corners in the room and he kept throwing me against them . . . I was just being bashed about . . . he was pounding my head against everything he could . . . it was the nastiest beating I've ever had in my life. It was even nastier because it was my friend, you see."

A lot had happened between the Sunday afternoon of February 11, the day the body was discovered, when Sarah told Sergeant Hinderliter about being slapped, and the evening of February 22, when she told the Arizona State Police about the "nastiest beating."

On Monday morning, February 12, an MGM lawyer named Alvin Cassidy took an early plane from L.A. to Phoenix, drove out to Gila Bend, and advised members of the cast and crew of *The Man Who Loved Cat Dancing* that it would not be wise to talk to detectives from the state police without the advice of counsel. MGM people stopped talking.

On Monday afternoon the cast and crew of *Cat Dancing* began checking out of the Travelodge and heading for a new location two hundred miles southeast in the town of Nogales on the Mexican border.

On Monday evening Rona Barrett broke the story on her nationally syndicated Hollywood gossip show.

Rona had sensed something funny going on the night before when she attended the Directors Guild premiere of *Lady Caroline Lamb*. Someone had given Rona a tip that Robert Bolt, who was attending the premiere of his film, had received a "very upsetting phone call."

Monday morning Rona began talking to her sources in Gila Bend. By Monday evening she was able to tell her national audience of a report that Sarah Miles had been beaten up in her motel room by her business manager, a former *Time* correspondent. Rona called it "the alleged beating"—alleged because, according to Rona's sources on location, Sarah Miles was "on the set the next day showing no signs of having been attacked."

On Wednesday of that first week, MGM hired two of the best criminal lawyers in Arizona—John Flynn of Phoenix and Benjamin Lazarow of Tucson—to represent Sarah, Burt, and the nanny.

The MGM legal armada at first succeeded in working out a deal with the detectives. Sarah, Burt, and a few others would tape-record informal, unsworn statements about the night of the death, and answer, with the help of their attorneys, questions put to them by detectives. The detectives and the County Prosecutor made no pledge, but MGM hoped, through this taping device, to avoid having Sarah and Burt and the rest of the cast subpoenaed to testify publicly at the forthcoming coroner's inquest.

These recorded interviews with the detectives, which have come to be known as the "Rio Rico tapes," took place on Thursday, February 22, at the Rio Rico Inn of Nogales, Arizona, where the MGM people were quartered. Sarah's description of the violent, nasty beating, quoted above, comes from one of these tapes.

The deal fell through. Gila Bend Justice of the Peace Mulford Winsor, who was to preside at the inquest, was not satisfied with this absentee-testimony arrangement. He issued subpoenas for Sarah, Burt, Lee J. Cobb, the nanny, and the two other MGM people, commanding them to appear in person in Gila Bend on February 27 to take the stand and testify.

MGM's legal forces promptly went to court. They asked that the subpoenas be quashed on the ground that appearances at the inquest would subject the six people to "adverse publicity and public display."

On February 27, just a few minutes before the inquest was about to open in Gila Bend, Justice of the Peace Winsor was served with a temporary restraining order barring him from calling Sarah or Burt to testify. Justice Winsor decided to proceed with the inquest without them, and called Sergeant Hinderliter to the stand as the first witness.

But the movie company had not counted on the determination of tiny, gray-haired Mrs. Campbell, who turned out to be a shrewd operator despite her fragile, grief-stricken appearance.

Early that morning in Phoenix Mrs. Campbell had hired her own lawyer, presented him with a thousand-dollar retainer, and told him to contest the MGM injunction. Then she caught the first bus out to Gila Bend. On the bus she sat next to a reporter for the London *Sun* who was on his way out to cover the inquest. She introduced herself to the English reporter as a correspondent for a Washington, D.C., magazine and asked him for the details of the case. She wanted to know whether it were possible to libel a dead man.

When she arrived at the courthouse, a one-story, concrete, all-purpose administrative building, Mrs. Campbell began passing out to the press Xeroxed copies of a document that she said was David Whiting's last letter to her, a document which proved, she said, that David Whiting was neither unhappy nor suicidal. (While this "last letter" certainly did not give any hint of suicidal feelings, neither did it give a sense of much intimacy between mother and son. David Whiting began the letter by announcing that he was sending back his mother's Christmas present to him, and went on to request that she send instead six pairs of boxer shorts. "I find the English variety abominably badly cut," he wrote. "Plaids, stripes, and other bright colors would be appreciated, and I suggest you unwrap them, launder them once, and airmail them to me in a package marked 'personal belongings.' ")

Next Mrs. Campbell approached Justice Winsor and asked him to delay the start of the inquest until her lawyer, who she said was on his way, could be present to represent her. She didn't give up when he refused and opened the inquest. She continued to interrupt the proceedings in her quavering voice with pleas for a recess to await the appearance of her lawyer. At one point Justice Winsor threatened to have her removed.

It came down to a matter of minutes. By midafternoon the two men from the County Attorney's office conducting the inquest had called their last witness, and the justice of the peace was about to gavel the inquest to a close and send the coroner's jury out to decide the cause of David Whiting's death. At the last minute, however, the judge received a phone call from the presiding justice of the Superior Court in Phoenix. Mrs. Campbell had secured an order preventing the coroner's jury from beginning its deliberations until a full hearing could be held on the question of whether Sarah, Burt, and the nanny should be forced to appear in person to testify. Justice Winsor recessed the inquest, and Mrs. Campbell walked out with her first victory. She'd only just begun. On March 7, after a full hearing, the court ruled in her favor and ordered Sarah, Burt, and the nanny to appear at the inquest. Finally, on March 14, the three of them returned to Gila Bend and took the stand, with Mrs. Campbell seated in the front row of the courtroom taking notes.

There were strange stories circulating about Mrs. Campbell. There was a rumor that she might not be the boy's mother at all. Other than the "last letter," she hadn't shown any identification to Mr. Ganley. The copy of the last letter she was handing around showed no signature. Mrs. Campbell said she herself had written the word "David" at the bottom of the copy. She had left the original with the signature at home, she said. "Naturally I treasure it . . . that's why I didn't bring it."

Mrs. Campbell refused to give me her home address or phone number. She insisted on keeping secret the whereabouts of both David Whiting's real father and his stepfather, her present husband. She implied that anyone attempting to contact the real father, who was recovering from a recent heart attack, might cause his death: She was protecting him from the news, she said.

She described herself as a freelance science writer, as a former writer for *Architectural Forum,* as a member of the faculty of the University of California at Berkeley, and as retired. She insisted at first that her married name was spelled without a *p* in the middle. Then suddenly she began insisting that it was spelled with a *p*.

She described herself frequently as "a woman without means," and a "woman living on a fixed income," but she hired four of the top lawyers in the state of Arizona to work on the case. She claimed to have flown to England with her aging mother to visit David a few months before he died.

"My only interest in this whole affair is to protect the name of my son," she maintained. "He was not a suicidal type, he was not the type to beat up women."

She was curiously silent about certain areas and curiously ill-informed about others. There was his marriage, for instance. Mrs. Campbell led me to believe that I was the first person to tell her that her son had been married. This revelation took place in the Space Age Lodge, a motel next to the Gila Bend Courthouse building, a motel distinguished by the great number of "life-size" Alien Beings crawling over its roofs and walls. The second session of the inquest—the one at which Sarah and Burt had finally testified—had just come to an end and Mrs. Campbell was seated at a table in the Space Age Restaurant handing out copies of various affidavits to reporters and occasionally responding to questions.

"Mrs. Campbell, has David's ex-wife been in touch with you?" I asked.

"His what?" she demanded sharply.

"His ex-wife, the one who—"

"David was never married," she said firmly.

"What about the London *Express* story which said he was married to a Pan Am stewardess, and that he used her Pan Am discount card to fly back and forth to England?"

"What wife? What are you talking about? Where did you read that? I never heard of any marriage."

(It is possible that she may have been feigning surprise here, although to what purpose is not clear. The mother of the girl he married told me she herself was certain her daughter never married David Whiting. Nevertheless I discovered there *is* a marriage certificate on file with the Registrar of Vital Statistics, Cook County, Illinois, which records the marriage of David Andrew

Whiting to Miss Nancy Cockerill on January 29, 1970. Apparently there was a divorce also, because the wife is now remarried and living in Germany.)

Later that same day I had a long talk with Mrs. Campbell in the coffee shop of the Travelodge Motel, where she was staying during the inquest.

He was born in New York City on either August 25 or 26, she told me. "I'm not sure which is the right one, but I remember we always used to celebrate it on the wrong day." She leaps quickly to prep school. "He did so well at St. Albans that he was admitted to Georgetown University on a special program after his junior year and . . ."

When I asked her where David lived, and where he went to school before prep school, she cut off my question. "I don't see what that has to do with anything. I prefer not to tell you." She proceeded to attempt to convince me to drop my story on David Whiting and instead write an "exposé" of one of the Arizona lawyers hired by MGM, and "how these attorneys use their power and influence in this state." She would give me inside information, she said.

"It was always expected that David would go to Harvard," she began again when I declined to drop the story and returned to the subject of David Whiting. "For a boy of David's ability it was perfectly obvious he was headed for Harvard."

He didn't make it. Something about too many debutante parties, and not quite terrific grades in his special year at Georgetown. David Whiting went to tiny Haverford College instead. He majored in English there and wrote an honors thesis "on F. Scott Fitzgerald or Hamlet, I can't remember," Mrs. Campbell told me.

"There was a line from *The Great Gatsby* I do remember," she told me. "That was David's favorite book, and it's a line I think applies to what I saw here today. It was about the kind of people who always have others around to clean up the mess they leave."

I later checked the Scribner edition of *The Great Gatsby:* "They were careless people, Tom and Daisy—they smashed up things and creatures and then retreated back into their money or their vast carelessness, or whatever it was that kept them together, and let other people clean up the mess they had made."

A Fitzgerald Story of Sorts:

She met him at Mrs. Shippens's Dancing Class. Her name was Eleanor, and she was a granddaughter of F. Scott Fitzgerald and Zelda. He was—well, she never knew who he was, in the sense of family, but it was assumed that the dancing students at Mrs. Shippens's were from the finest families of Washington, Virginia, and Eastern Shore society. He certainly acted the part. His name was David Whiting.

When the male pupils at Mrs. Shippens's reached a certain age, they were placed on Miss Hetzel's list. Miss Hetzel's list was a register of eligible males worthy of being called upon to serve as escorts and dancing partners at the finest debuts and cotillions.

Eleanor met him again at a Hunt Cup weekend. She found him sometimes witty, sometimes amusingly pretentious in his efforts to be worldly. In November 1963, she wrote him inviting him to be her escort at a holiday dance at Mrs. Shippens's. She still has his letter of reply, because of a curious device he employed in it.

Centered perfectly between the lines of his letter to her were the unmistakable impressions of what seemed to be a letter to another girl. This ghostly letter in-between-the-lines was filled with tales of nights of drinking and lovemaking in expensive hotel suites with a girl named "Gloria." Eleanor is certain there was no Gloria, that the whole thing was an elaborate fake designed to impress her, if not with its truth, at least with its cleverness.

"He was always worrying about the way he looked—we'd be dancing or something and he'd always be checking with me how he looked, or giving me these, you know, aristocratic tips about how *I* looked, or *we* looked."

And how did he look?

"Well, he was very fat at first, I think."

"Fat?"

"Oh, quite tremendous. I mean pretty heavy. He'd make jokes about himself. But then all that changed. He spent a summer in North Africa and Libya with a movie production company. He came back from that summer looking much more thin and intense," she remembers. "He came back and all he was talking about was taking over that movie company, and oh, he had great dreams. I remember taking a walk with him—we were at some party and we were both nervous, and we took a walk through this garden and he just went on and on, just—it was the first time I'd seen him thin and he was talking about how he was gonna take over that movie company, and how great he'd been and how he was going to be a producer. . . . He'd always talked about movies, he could name every movie and every movie star that was in them—I mean, some people do that but he was *good,* he knew them *all.*"

She drifted away from him—"He was never my boyfriend or anything," she says pointedly—and didn't hear from him for almost two years when one day she got a phone call in her dorm at Sarah Lawrence.

It was David Whiting, then a student at Haverford. "Well, I hadn't seen him and I didn't know where he was at school, and he said, 'Will you come and see me, I'm at Princeton.' So I took the bus down. I got there I guess about nine in the morning, and called him up and he said could I come over to the room—I didn't know it wasn't his room—so I walked in and he just poured this tall glass of straight gin and no ice and said, 'Will you have some?' And I said, 'No, I don't really think I'm in the mood, I was sort of wondering what we're gonna do today,' and he said, 'Well, I think we'll stay in the room until tonight when we'll go over to some clubs.' I could sort of see the day's program unfolding. . . ."

For the next two hours he tried to convince her to sleep with him. "It could be really boring the way he talked about himself so much and how his ego would be damaged if I didn't sleep with him. I remember it was this scene of me sitting up, you know, every once in a while, and we'd talk and we'd stretch out and I'd say, 'Well, I'm going,' and he'd *throw* me down. And he finally got in a real bad mood, and I went."

"Did he ever admit to you that he was just posing as a Princeton student?"

"Oh yes, at the end I think he did."

"Did he think he could get away with it?"

"Well, I guess if we'd never left the room he could have."

SOME LAST EFFECTS OF DAVID WHITING: AN INVENTORY OF ITEMS LEFT BEHIND FROM HIS EIGHTEEN-MONTH CAREER AS HOLLYWOOD CORRESPONDENT FOR *Time*

- One 275-watt Westinghouse sunlamp. Left in a file cabinet in his old office in the *Time* suite on Roxbury Drive in Beverly Hills, across from the House of Pies. "He used to come in after midnight and sit for hours with the sunlamp on—I don't know if he was working or what," the *Time* switchboard operator recalls. Once he didn't turn it off. "I came in in the morning one day and I smelled smoke, and I checked in David's office, and it was his sunlamp. He'd left sometime early in the morning, and he'd just put it in his drawer without turning it off. It was smoldering in there, he might have set the place on fire."

- One pocket memo book with the notation "Cannes No. 6" scrawled in Magic Marker on the front cover. From the same file cabinet. Not long after he had been transferred to the Hollywood job, David Whiting took off for Cannes to "cover" the film festival. A Paris correspondent for *Time* had been under the impression *he* had been assigned to cover it. There was some dispute. The Paris man filed the story. David Whiting took many notes. Interviews with producers, directors, starlets. Memos to himself. A sample memo to himself from "Cannes No. 6":

> General Memo:
> morn. look good
> pics
> people

- One magazine story, written under an interesting pseudonym, for *Cosmopolitan*. The pseudonym is "Anthony Blaine," a synthesis of Amory Blaine and Anthony Patch, the heroes, respectively, of Fitzgerald's first two novels, *This Side of Paradise* and *The Beautiful and Damned*. The *Cosmopolitan* story by "Anthony Blaine" is about Candice Bergen. He met her in Cannes in 1970. He fibbed about his age to her, he played the worldly bon vivant for her, he followed her to Spain, where she was making a movie, he continued to see her back in Beverly Hills. He was possessed with her, he told friends. He was just a good friend to her, she told me.

- One box kite, still in the possession of Paula Prentiss. David Whiting was doing a story for *Time* about Paula and her husband, Dick Benjamin. The angle was going to be the idea of a happy marriage, he told them. He visited them a second time in their apartment in New York, and "there was a big change from the first time we met him, I could tell something was wrong," Paula recalls, "that he needed something from us. He wouldn't come out and say it, but we could tell, he'd sit and drink martinis and pop pills all the time. But we did have some good moments with him. I remember he brought us a box kite and he took us out on the beach and showed us how to fly it." (The story about Dick and Paula never appeared in *Time*. It did show up in the November 1971 issue of *Cosmopolitan*, this time under David Whiting's real name. *Cosmopolitan* also published a David Whiting story about Sarah Miles, the one he had been "researching" when he began following Sarah around for *Time*. The story, published in December 1971, is titled "Sarah Miles: The Maiden Man-Eater" and the subtitle reads: "She uses words that would make a construction worker blush, but from her they sound refined.")

- One list of all the girls David Whiting had ever kissed. "I walked into his office one day and he had his big debutante album out—it had all his invitations and dance programs, and dashing photos of David and the debs," a woman who writes for *Time* recalls. "And he was working on a list he told me was a list of all the girls he'd ever kissed—just kissed, that was enough—and he was going to add it to the album I think."

- One Bekins Warehouse storage number, the index to the artifacts David Whiting left behind when he left for England. Included are some of his many Savile Row suits he decided not to bring back to London with him. "Let me tell you about his suits," the friend who has custody of the Bekins number told me. "He used to fly to London—on his wife's Pan Am card, of course—fly there on a Thursday to have a fitting done. He'd come back Monday, then fly back again the next weekend for the final fitting and bring back the suit."

- One copy of *The Crack-Up* by F. Scott Fitzgerald, a battered, underlined paperback bequeathed to a woman he knew. Two passages have been cut out with a razor blade. One of the underlined passages: "I didn't have the two top things: great animal magnetism or money. I had the second things, though: good looks and intelligence. So I always got the top girl."

A passage cut out with a razor blade: the fourth verse from a poem called "The Thousand-and-First Ship," a Fitzgerald attempt at a modern version of Keats's "La Belle Dame Sans Merci": "There'd be an orchestra / Bingo! Bango! / Playing for us / To dance the tango, / And people would clap / As we arose, / At her sweet face / And my new clothes."

The endgame began when they checked into the Gila Bend Travelodge on Monday, January 29. At first David Whiting took the room adjoining Sarah's. Hers was number 127, his 126; an inner door connected the two. He didn't last there very long. Rooms 126 and 127 are in the section of the motel most remote from traffic. They could be reached only by walking back from the highway, past the Travelodge bar, past the length of the larger two-story rooming unit, all the way to the rear of the parking lot and around the back of a smaller, single-story row of Travelodge cubicles. The bedroom windows of numbers 126 and 127 face nothing; they look north upon miles and miles of cactus and mesquite waste. Closer at hand to numbers 126 and 127 is the Travelodge garbage shed.

On Friday, February 2, four days after David and Sarah checked into these adjoining rooms, David was forced to move. Sarah's five-year-old son, Thomas, and the nanny hired to care for him were arriving from England that evening. So, on Friday afternoon, nine days before his death, David Whiting moved out of number 126 and into number 119, a room across the parking lot in the two-story motel building.

He seems to have chosen this place of exile with some care. The view, for instance, had two peculiar advantages. For one, the line of sight for someone looking straight out the bedroom window of number 119 runs straight across a short span of parking lot and then directly along the walkway in front of the row of rooms he left behind, right past the doors to numbers 126 and 127. No one entering or leaving Sarah's room could escape the notice of an observer looking out the window of number 119.

The other, more subtle advantage to this observation post had to do with the placement of a staircase. A broad openwork staircase of wood planks and iron bars descends from the second floor of motel rooms above number 119 and touches ground on the sidewalk in front of the room, forming a slanting screen in front of the bedroom window. Outsiders in the Travelodge parking lot can't see through the confusing lattice of horizontal steps, diagonal banisters, and vertical railing supports to the bedroom window of 119 behind it. But someone peeking out from *within* the bedroom window of 119, from behind this sheltering screen, can see quite well, although at first it is something like looking out from within a confusingly barred cage.

Sarah says she never knew where David had moved. She'd never bothered to find out, having no occasion to visit him.

But she knew he was watching her. Keeping track of her movements. She'd return from a day on the set and as soon as she walked into her room, the phone would ring and he'd want to know what she'd be doing that night, and with whom.

He had been acting extraordinarily possessive from the moment they arrived at Gila Bend, she said. She hadn't been prepared for anything quite like it. Before they'd left England he'd seemed in better shape than he'd been in a long time. He'd been working on a screenplay, he'd been going out with women, he'd been less obsessed with managing her personal life.

"But as soon as we touched down in America he was back to square one," she says. "He was the old David again."

Sarah speculates it might have something to do with the way she worked. "When I'm on a picture I'm—see, he had known me as a girl who lived in the country, who loved horses, and who lived a quiet life," Sarah told the inquest. "When I get on a film I like to get to know everybody. The wranglers—I never met wranglers before. Christ, they're marvelous people, you know. I mean I want to spend all my time with cowboys."

So Sarah went out at night. Going out in Gila Bend didn't mean going far. It meant eating at Mrs. Wright's Colonial Dining Room, next door to the Travelodge, then walking back across the parking lot to the Travelodge Cocktail Lounge for drinking and dancing to a country-and-western jukebox. For Sarah—according to Gila Bend locals who hung around with the cast and crew—going out meant dancing a lot, flirting, tossing off four-letter words in a merry way. (A *Women's Wear* profile of Sarah, published a week before David Whiting's death, features a picture of Sarah perched in a sex-kittenish pose on one of the black Naugahyde banquettes in the Travelodge Cocktail Lounge. "The Lady with the Truckdriver's Mouth" is the title of the story.)

Meanwhile, David Whiting stayed in. At first she'd invite him to come to the bar with her, Sarah says, but he'd refuse and stay in his room and watch for her return. He kept to himself, remote from everyone but Sarah, and Sarah began keeping her distance from him. Waitresses at the Travelodge Coffee Shop recall David Whiting coming in alone night after night, sitting at the counter, and ordering, night after night, a shrimp cocktail and a club sandwich.

During the day he'd haunt the shooting set in the desert, a dark and formal figure amidst the real and costumed cowboys and the casually dressed MGM production officials. He'd have one of his Nikons with him, and he'd hover around Sarah clicking off stills. Or he'd have some papers he wanted her to look at, other papers he'd want her to sign. He began getting on the nerves of the MGM people. There are reports he'd been getting on Sarah's nerves.

The first big fight broke out in room 127 on the evening of Tuesday, February 6. The nanny was in the middle of it. Janie Evans is her name, she is twenty-three years old, dark haired, dark eyed, and sultry looking. She had been hired for this Gila Bend trip one week before Sarah and David left England. Sarah had hired her on the recommendation of David Whiting, and there is good reason to believe that David Whiting and the soon-to-be nanny had been seeing each other before the hiring.

In any case David and the nanny had mutual friends in London, and one of them was a woman named Tessa Bradford, and it was a curious story about David and this Tessa Bradford that led to the Tuesday-night fight.

The nanny had been talking to Sarah about David. That winter in London, the nanny told Sarah, David had developed an obsession for Tessa Bradford. He had haunted her house, followed her car, called her at all hours, rented a Mercedes limousine to take her to the theater. After all this Tessa Bradford had dropped him, the nanny told Sarah. She had thought David was crazed.

That Tuesday night in room 127 Sarah asked David about the story. He became enraged, rushed into room 126, dragged the nanny back to Sarah's room demanding that she "tell the truth."

"Why didn't you tell the truth? Why did you say it was a Mercedes when it was only a mini cab? Why did you say I kept phoning her, I only phoned her five times," Janie Evans recalls him yelling.

Then he turned on Sarah. He grabbed her. "He had her—his hand on her neck like this," the nanny testified at the inquest, "wallowing her head backward and forward, and I shouted at him and Sarah pushed at him, and he went through the door and she threw a vase right after him . . . it didn't hit him, it smashed on the concrete outside."

"He got upset that I didn't get upset about him seeing another woman," Sarah explains. "But I couldn't take his private life seriously."

Other things started going wrong for David Whiting. On Wednesday, February 7, the producer of *Cat Dancing,* Martin Poll, approached David on the set. As usual David had been recording Sarah's performance with his Nikon. Poll hinted strongly that David's presence was not entirely welcome.

"He wasn't in anyone's way," Poll told me, "but for myself I like to have a very private set and it was a closed set from the beginning of the picture, and it was distracting to have photographs taken all the time."

"Did you ask him to stay off then, or what was the actual conversation?" I asked Poll.

"I am really not interested in sitting on the griddle," was all Poll answered.

On Thursday, February 8, Sarah saw David Whiting for the next to last time.

"He came into my room that evening and his face was ashen and white, and more sallow than I've ever seen it. And he put the script on the bed and he said, 'I've just read it and it's no good at all. I can't write anything.' "

After that, nobody remembers seeing David Whiting outside his motel room.

On Friday morning David Whiting called the motel manager to complain about the reception on his TV. He was getting sound but no picture, he said. But when the motel manager came to the door of number 119 to see about getting David his picture back, he found the DO NOT DISTURB card hanging from the doorknob. He kept checking, the manager recalls, but the DO NOT DISTURB sign never came down.

There are indications that David Whiting was trying to get out of Gila Bend. Thursday night he placed a call to a woman in Washington, D.C. He talked to her for eighty-four minutes. They had been engaged once. He had continued to confide in her after he left her behind for Hollywood. That night he told her that "the particular situation there in Gila Bend was over for him," she recalls. He didn't sound overjoyed about things, but neither did he sound suicidal, she says. He did say he wanted to see her and talk to her "about this situation in Gila Bend and about him and me." He talked about flying to Washington to see her.

Two nights later, Saturday night, about an hour before midnight David Whiting received a call from a friend in Beverly Hills. The friend wanted to know if David was going to attend the Directors Guild premiere of *Lamb* Sunday evening. "No," David told the friend, "Sarah and I think it will be a bummer."

Nevertheless, David told his friend, he was thinking of leaving Gila Bend for Hollywood sometime in the middle of the next week.

David's voice sounded slurred that night, the friend recalls.

"It sounds like you're into a couple of reds," he told David.

"No," David replied. "Mandrax."

Burt Reynolds wanted a massage. It was close to midnight when he returned from the Pink Palomino, picked up his phone, and asked the desk to ring the room of the Japanese masseuse.

Reynolds was staying in room 135. It was in the same single-story block of cubicles as Sarah's room. The two rooms were no more than six or eight yards apart, almost back to back, in fact. However, as close as they were physically, it was still necessary to go all the way around the building to get from one to the other, and going around the building meant passing directly in front of David Whiting's screened-in bedroom window.

The Japanese masseuse was staying in room 131. Her name was Letsgo (an Americanization of her Japanese first name, Retsuko) Roberts, and she had been summoned to the Travelodge on Friday afternoon to tend to Sarah, who had suffered a bruising fall from a horse. Letsgo and Sarah got along so well that she was plucked from her regular tour of duty at a place called The International Health Spa in Stockdale, Arizona, and installed in a room at the Travelodge.

About midnight on Saturday Letsgo received a phone call from Burt.

He asked her to come over to room 135 and work on him. When Letsgo walked into Burt's room she found Sarah there, she told me. She had the feeling the two of them had been drinking. (Sarah had told Sergeant Hinderliter the masseuse was there when *she* arrived.)

"They were kind of—kind of, you know, not drunk—but kind of happy, you know, after drink," Letsgo recalls.

Burt, attired in a white terry-cloth dressing gown, proceeded to lie on the bed, and Letsgo proceeded to give him a two-hour massage.

Meanwhile Sarah chatted with Burt. She apologized for leaving the party early with Lee J. Cobb. She told him about an old boyfriend of hers. He told her about an old girlfriend of his. Sarah turned on the TV, watched a British film; she ate an apple and banana; she lay down next to Burt on the double bed and dozed off, according to Letsgo.

About two A.M. the masseuse offered to walk Sarah back to her room, but Burt told her he'd see that Sarah got back safely. The masseuse left.

An hour and fifteen minutes later Burt walked Sarah around the back of the building to her room.

Back in his own room, Burt had hardly slipped off his clothes and slipped into bed when the phone rang. It was the nanny. She was saying something about Sarah being beaten up, something about David Whiting. He heard a scream over the phone, Burt told Sergeant Hinderliter the following afternoon. He heard no scream over the phone, Burt testified at the inquest four weeks later.

Scream or no scream, Burt put his clothes back on and headed around the building to Sarah's room. It was at this moment that the paths of Burt Reynolds and David Whiting may have crossed. David's violent encounter with Sarah had just come to an end. He ran out of her room just about the time the nanny called Burt for help. If David Whiting was proceeding to his own room while Burt was on his way to Sarah's, David and Burt might have met in the parking lot at the northwest corner of the building.

When Burt first told the story of the events of that night to Sergeant Hinderliter, he did not mention encountering David Whiting or anyone else on his way to Sarah's room.

Ten days later in the "Rio Rico tapes" and then again on the witness stand at the inquest—much to the surprise of Sergeant Hinderliter—Burt testified that he did see "someone" as he was heading around that corner.

"It was to my left as I came around. . . . I saw someone going in the door, and the door slammed very hard behind him. . . . At the time I didn't know whose room it was, nor could I identify him since I'm not very good at identifying backs, but it looked like a man, and the door slammed behind him. Later I found out, the next day, that that was David Whiting's room."

And then, a few minutes later, leading the wounded Sarah back to his own room, something caught Burt's eye. "As I rounded the corner to go to my room I saw the drapes open and close," in the window of the same room whose door had slammed behind a man a few minutes ago. There was no light on in the room behind the drapes, he told the inquest, a detail which makes his observation of the moving drapes all the more acute, since the window of that room is well-screened from view by a staircase.

At this point, Sarah testified at the inquest, Burt told her, "If I was not as mature as I am now, I would lay him out."

The following afternoon, after the body of David Whiting had been discovered, the masseuse heard this story from Sarah. Sarah and Burt were back in Burt's room. "Mr. Reynolds wanted to go down and fight him, Mr. Whiting, but Sarah, she stopped him. . . ." the masseuse told me. "She told Mr. Reynolds it would cause more trouble."

Sarah testified that shortly after she arrived at Burt's room she became worried about the well-being of the man who had beaten her. She told Burt she wanted to call up David Whiting "to see if he was all right." It was not physical injury she was concerned about, it was injury to David's *feelings,* she says. "Because whenever he has hit me he has always been so ashamed afterward, so remorseful. . . ."

But Sarah did not make the call. Burt advised her to "deal with everything in the morning," and she went to sleep. Had she in fact made that call she might have saved his life.

Not much is known of the movements of David Whiting earlier that night. Sarah did give David a call early in the evening to inform him that Burt had invited her to attend the birthday celebration at the Pink Palomino in Ajo. Sarah says she invited David to come along and that David refused. He was in his room at eleven P.M. calling Hollywood. It is reasonable to speculate that he stayed up waiting, as usual, for Sarah's return. He may have spent these hours peering out from behind his sheltered observation post. In the absence of anyone crossing his line of sight, the picture outside his bedroom window consisted of the empty walkway past Sarah's room and a blank brick wall, the narrow end of the one-story unit containing Sarah's room.

At night the management of the Gila Bend Travelodge switches on an intense blue spotlight implanted among the dwarf yucca palms which line that blank stucco wall. The blue spot illuminates the sharp green spears of the yucca palms and casts confusingly colored shadows of their fanlike arrays upon the wall, an effect apparently intended to create an air of tropical mystery in the Travelodge parking lot.

If David Whiting had been watching at just the right moment, he might have seen Sarah cross the parking lot from the Travelodge Cocktail Lounge and head toward Burt Reynolds's room.

Three things are known for sure. Sometime before three-thirty A.M. David Whiting entered Sarah Miles's bedroom. Sometime after she encountered him there, he returned to his own room, where he left bloodstains. And sometime before noon the next day, he returned to Sarah's room and died.

He had a key to Sarah's room. "I kept on saying, 'David, are you taking my keys, because they're not here anymore,' " Sarah told the inquest. "And he said, 'I don't need to take keys. You know me, I can pick a lock.' He was very proud of the fact that he could pick locks." Nevertheless a key to Sarah's room, number 127, was the only item found on him after his death.

The only witness to the goings-on in room 127 was the nanny, Janie Evans. "I think you'll find that the nanny is the key to this whole thing," Sarah's lawyer in the case, Benjamin Lazarow of Tucson, Arizona, told me, as he slipped a tape cassette—one of the "Rio Rico tapes"—into his Sony. "You listen to this cassette with the nanny on it. Listen to how scratchy and worn out it sounds. You know why? It's because the detectives kept playing it over and over again. They were *very* interested in the nanny's story."

The first thing she saw in room 127 that night, says the nanny, on the tape, was Sarah lying on the floor with David Whiting on top of her bashing her head on the floor. "That'll teach you!" David was yelling at Sarah, the nanny says. (Ten days before the Rio Rico tapes, on the afternoon following the death, the nanny had told Sergeant Hinderliter that Whiting had slapped Sarah, but that she didn't know if she had actually seen it or not.)

The nanny ran over and tried to pull Whiting off Sarah, she said. She failed, and finally, responding to Sarah's plea, picked up the phone and called Burt.

When Burt arrived, the nanny returned to her bed in room 126. Twenty minutes later she was dozing off when she heard noises in Sarah's room. It sounded like someone opening and closing a drawer in there, she says. She called out, "Sarah?" but no one answered. This led her to assume that David Whiting had returned. "I was scared. I mean, he had been violent. I didn't want to see him so I didn't say anything more."

She went back to sleep, she says.

After he finished playing the Rio Rico tapes, Attorney Lazarow took out a tape he had made on his own of an interview with the nanny. At the end of the interview, Lazarow suddenly asked her a peculiar question:

"Did you hit David Whiting over the head with anything?"

She did not, she replied. I wondered what had prompted Lazarow to ask the question in the first place.

"Oh, I don't know," Lazarow said. "Maybe I was just trying to shake her, see if there was something she was leaving out of her story. We were trying to figure out how he might have gotten that star-shaped wound, and we figured maybe it happened when the nanny was trying to pull Whiting off Sarah during the fight, but both she and Sarah said no."

The star-shaped wound on the back of David Whiting's head has yet to be explained away.

An MGM lawyer attempted to explain it away by suggesting that in a fit of rage David Whiting simply smashed the back of his head against a wall. Others suggest that David Whiting was, literally, starstruck that night, and that Burt Reynolds was the star. Reynolds had a reputation in Hollywood for an explosive temper and an itch to fight. Before the death, he regaled Gila Bend locals with tales of past punch-outs, adding that he had decided to leave that part of his life behind now that he had become a big star. A woman who knew Reynolds intimately for years told me that he used to blame it on his spleen. His spleen had been removed after a high-school football injury, and ever since then he'd been unable to control his violent temper because, he said, the spleen had something to do with controlling the rush of adrenaline. All of which helps explain why Reynolds became such an obvious target for suspicion; none of it is evidence.

Spleen or no spleen, if Reynolds *had* lost control of his temper and given Whiting a beating, it seems likely that the body would show more evidence of violence than it did.

According to Dr. Robert Wright, who performed autopsy number two on the body of David Whiting, the most violent interpretation that can be made from a reading of the marks left upon the body is this: Someone grasped Whiting firmly by the shoulders, shook him, and either shoved him back against a wall, causing him to hit his head, or threw him down causing him to strike his head on the ground.

State police crime-lab people found no evidence on either the walls or the bathroom floors of rooms 119, 126, and 127 to suggest that a bloody bashing had taken place in any of those rooms. (The bedroom floors are carpeted.)

The parking lot outside is covered with asphalt. If it happened, it could have happened out there in the parking lot. But a hard rain swept through Gila Bend in the early morning hours of that Sunday. Any bloodstains that might have been left upon the parking-lot asphalt would have been washed away. The mystery of where and how, and by whose hands, if any, David Whiting received his star-shaped wound remains unsolved.

Does it matter? Dr. Wright thinks it matters. Dr. Wright is a forensic pathologist for the Coroner's Office of the City and County of San Francisco, and a professor of forensic pathology at the University of California Medical Center. He was called upon by Mrs. Campbell, David's mother, to perform an autopsy after she had the body shipped out of Arizona and installed in the refrigerator of a funeral home in Berkeley, just one day before the third and final session of the inquest.

"The force of the impact to the head," Dr. Wright declared in his autopsy summary, "could well have caused a temporary loss of consciousness (a brain concussion), and may have caused him to behave in a stuporous fashion, and to be unmindful of his subsequent acts."

He could have been knocked silly, in other words, and in that state of silliness taken two or three too many pills, killing himself unintentionally. It was a borderline overdose. David Whiting might have been unaware he was crossing the border.

Dr. Wright's conclusion must, of course, be weighed against the milder conclusion of the original autopsy doctor who had not been selected by the boy's mother. But his report does give some substance to something the mother said to me in the coffee shop of the Travelodge.

"The horrible part is, severe-intoxication doses of this drug can produce deep coma. And the horrible thing is if these people thought he was dead—the pulse would have been faint—they could have been drunk or high, suppose they didn't know how to take a pulse—they could have sat around for hours, while his life ebbs away."

The nanny woke up at seven-thirty in the morning, she said. She was very cold. She walked through the connecting door into Sarah's room and found the outside door wide open to the chill morning air. She shut the outside door and headed back for the inner door into her own room.

The nanny said she never saw a body in the course of this little expedition. When Sergeant Hinderliter came upon the body about twelve-thirty he found the legs from the knees down sticking out beyond the end of the dressing-room partition. Walking back from closing the outside door that morning, the nanny was walking straight toward the end of the dressing-room partition and, presumably, straight toward the protruding legs of David Whiting. There was light: The lights were still on in the room from the night before. But she was drowsy, the nanny said, and she saw no body.

This means one of three things:

The body was not there.

The body was there and the nanny did not, in fact, see it.

The body was there, dead or alive, the nanny saw it and went back to sleep without reporting it. Or else she reported it to someone, and that someone waited four hours before reporting it to the police.

Which leads to another unresolved question: How long before she reported it did Sarah find the body?

"At one time she told me she went back to her room at eight o'clock in the morning," Sergeant Hinderliter told me, recalling his interview with Sarah the day of the death. "And the next time she turned around and said it was ten o'clock. I didn't question her on the time at that time because she was upset, and because at the time of my interview I was just working on a possible drug overdose."

Eleven days later, in the Rio Rico tapes, and then again at the inquest, Sarah said it was around eleven fifteen when she returned to her room and found the body.

Sarah was on the witness stand. The deputy county attorney had just led her gently through her account of the night of the death, eliding over any discussion of her stay with Burt Reynolds.

Now came the moment many of those following the case closely had been waiting for. The deputy county attorney seemed to be approaching, gently of course, the subject of Sarah's Sunday-afternoon statement to Sergeant Hinderliter. People wanted to know, for instance, whether Sarah had been slapped or beaten.

"Now, do you remember talking to the policeman that came the next morning?" the deputy county attorney asked her, meaning Sergeant Hinderliter, and afternoon, not morning.

"Well, I was terribly shook up the next morning. Do you mean the policeman?"

Yes, said the deputy county attorney, he meant the policeman.

"By the time I saw the policeman I had heard that Mr. Whiting was dead," Sarah replied. "This was when I was in a bad way."

"Do you recall that conversation with the officer at all?" the deputy county attorney asked.

"No. I just told him what had happened."

"But you remember what you told him at this time?" the deputy county attorney persisted.

At precisely this point Sarah burst into tears.

"The truth," she sobbed urgently. "The same as I'm giving you now, I think."

The courtroom was silent. At his desk, the deputy county attorney looked down at his hands as if in remorse for having trespassed the bounds of decency with his ferocious questioning. From his bench, the justice of the peace leaned over toward Sarah and patted her hand comfortingly. When Sarah had wiped the tears from her eyes, the deputy county attorney started an entirely new line of questioning and did not venture near the subject again.

There was one final moment of high melodrama at the inquest. The questioning was over, and Sarah, face flushed and stained with tears, asked to make two final statements. First, she declared, she had never resisted testifying before the inquest. "I was bulldozed by my husband, producers, Burt Reynolds, MGM," she said. "I wanted to go as soon as I could . . . and I was not allowed to do this and for this I feel a grudge."

And second, she said, there was the matter of David Whiting's body, still languishing at that time in Mr. Ganley's refrigerator wrapped up in a sheet. (As of this writing, about three months after his death, the body is still languishing unburied in the refrigerator of the Bayview mortuary in Berkeley, "awaiting further tests" and further word from Mrs. Campbell, who hasn't been heard from in some time, an employee of the mortuary told me.)

"I hear from my attorney," Sarah told the Gila Bend courtroom, "that somebody doesn't want to bury this boy and that the state is going to bury him."

Sarah rose up in the witness stand, eyes wet. *"Well, I would like to bury him!"* she cried. With that, she rushed from the courtroom.

Sarah Miles never contacted him, Mr. Ganley told me. "No sir. I've never heard from Miles or anyone of that type. In fact," said Mr. Ganley, "they weren't even interested in David Whiting after his death."

I asked him what he meant by that, and he told me this story.

It was the afternoon of the death. Mr. Ganley was in room 127 with the body of David Whiting, helping the investigators prepare it for shipment to the County Morgue in Phoenix for an autopsy.

"Miss Miles was in the room next door, and she sent word over she wanted to come in and get a dress because they were having a party up at the bar and she wanted to get up there. And the investigators wouldn't let her have the dress. They told her when they were through with the room she could get anything she wanted out of it."

"But that was what she wanted—a party dress?"

"Yeah, she wanted to go to the Elks Club, they were having a barbecue for Reynolds's birthday," Mr. Ganley said.

Meanwhile, Burt Reynolds was in his room talking with a couple of his friends, trying to decide whether to go to that Elks Club party or not. The party was for him, of course, and he would disappoint a lot of the Gila Bend people if he didn't show up. But then, there had been that unfortunate death, and that made it hard for him to feel like celebrating.

Finally, according to one of the people in the room with Burt, the decision came down to this. "Burt said something like if it had been an accident, that was one thing, then it was tragic, you know, and it was no time to party. But if it was suicide, if this guy was so worthless he didn't have the guts to face life, then why spoil the party?"

Burt went to the party.

Whipple's Last Squeeze

In Which We Excavate the Origins of the
Most Reviled Ad in History

One of the more curious of the recent Charmin toilet-tissue TV spots gives us a rare glimpse of supermarket manager George Whipple in a reflective, even tender, mood. Quite uncharacteristically, this particular Charmin commercial takes us far from the familiar setting of the series—the paper products aisle of "Jerry's Supermarket"—where we are accustomed to see Whipple engaged in one after another frustrating struggle against Charmin-squeezing housewives. No, in this spot we find ourselves in the untroubled interior of Whipple's own home as George, surrounded by wife and children, reflects on how it all began.

"There I was, a young man just starting out," Whipple says. "Had my own store."

"Did you stop the ladies from squeezing the Charmin, Dad?" young Whipple Junior asks.

"You betcha!" Whipple recalls proudly.

Then one day, Whipple continues, a bit dreamily now, he saw a special woman in the toilet-paper aisle. She was squeezing, like the others, but somehow she was different from all the others.

"I was about to tell her, please don't squeeze the Charmin, when I took one look at her and fell in love."

Romantic music swells in the background. The family Whipple grows misty-eyed. "And you let me squeeze the Charmin, didn't you, George?" says Mrs. W.

"Yep," Whipple tells the kids. "And until this day your mother's the only one I've let squeeze the Charmin."

More is going on here than the obvious allegory linking Charmin and sexual fidelity. There's turmoil in toilet-paper marketing these days, turnover in toilet-tissue ad campaigns. There are signs—the unusual Whipple-family-at-home spot, just one of many—that the uncertainties of the marketplace are beginning to affect one of the single most successful, most notorious, and longest-running ad campaigns ever to appear in any medium. There are even intimations that, after a full decade on the air, George Whipple's days in the toilet-paper aisle are numbered. Perhaps there's a foreshadowing of this in Whipple's sentimental journey into the past. Maybe it's time to take a look at the media phenomenon the Charmin campaign has become, focusing first, like Whipple, on how it all began.

The time had come to kill off Gentle the Dog. The year was 1964. For two years, Gentle the Dog had been the number one spokescreature for Charmin toilet paper. Commercials for Charmin featured the fluffy animated animal romping around with other gentle animated souls—a gentle juggler who juggled only soft things, a gentle movie star named Belinda Beautiful who played only gentle roles, even a gentle dogcatcher. But the Procter & Gamble people who produced Charmin and the Benton & Bowles people who produced the commercials decided that Gentle the Dog just didn't fit in with the big marketing plans P&G had for Charmin. P&G production people had devised a new toilet-paper-making process, one they felt P&G could use to push its then-tiny Charmin brand into full-scale competition with the giant of the toilet paper industry, Scott. A February 1973 P&G report explains the secret of this history-making toilet paper breakthrough:

> The fibers from which tissue is made enter the paper machines in a very dilute water solution. Nearly all of this water has to be removed. Previously, the only way to remove the excess water from the tissue was to "squeeze" it out [which] compressed the tissue fibers, taking away from their fluffiness and softness. . . . [T]he solution was relatively simple—eliminate as much of the physical pressing as possible and substitute a flow of hot air [which] would actually "fluff it up." . . . This allows for a deeper, more cushiony texture. An added benefit . . . is that less wood fiber per roll is required to make the same amount of this improved tissue.

In other words, in this new process, each square of one-ply Charmin toilet paper had less paper in it, but *looked* softer. (Whether it *felt* more "cushiony" is a hot dispute we will get into later.) The master marketing strategists at P&G thought this process could give them the opening they wanted in their plot against Scott: They could position this fluffed-up, cheaper tissue between the rougher low-cost one-ply papers (dominated by Scott tissue) and the softer, more expensive "facial-quality" two-ply tissues (dominated by Scott's "Soft-Weve"). Thus they would be offering greater fluffiness to the one-ply buyers and lower price to the two-ply people, thereby taking the trade of both away from Scott and making big money because they use less pulp per sheet. It would take just the right ad campaign to introduce this fluffed-up Charmin into big-league competition, and it looked as if Gentle the Dog couldn't hack the new responsibility. P&G needed a barker of a different sort. Oh, they gave the fluffy mutt a chance. They experimented with an ad in which Gentle trots into a courtroom, asks a judge to have his name changed from "Gentle" to "Gentler," and explains to the puzzled magistrate that new Charmin toilet tissue is "Gentler than ever." This commercial had the effect of putting many people to sleep. Also one dog.

So in the summer of 1964 Benton & Bowles assigned a three-person creative team to come up with a brand-new concept for selling Charmin. The job that faced creative director Jim Haines, group supervisor Flora Fifield, and junior copywriter John Chervokas is generally considered one of the toughest in the ad business because of certain built-in limitations on toilet-paper advertising. Obviously you can't do on-camera comparisons. No before-and-after demonstrations. In fact, at one time toilet-paper people had a rough time convincing broadcasters toilet-paper commercials should even be permitted on home screens because of their inherent indelicacy. So from the beginning toilet paper was soft-pedaled on TV, and most toilet papers found a thousand and one indistinguishable ways to peddle themselves as soft.

Charmin started at a bit of a disadvantage in the soft parade, because for a long time it was one of the few tissues that hadn't cultivated a soft image. And with good reason: It wasn't that soft. When P&G acquired the Charmin tissue-making factory in Green Bay, Wisconsin, back in 1957, Charmin tissue was sort of a rough-hewn, backwoods toilet tissue, sold mainly in rural north country counties. (Skeptics at the time of the purchase, unaware of Charmin's place in P&G's grand design, wisecracked that the main reason for the acquisition must have been to get season tickets to Packers games for executives from P&G's Cincinnati headquarters.)

In keeping with the rough-and-ready quality of early Charmin, the pre-P&G ads for the brand featured a crude, euphemistic absorption test. "They dropped two tissues into a pot of water to see which one sunk first," is the way

Jim Haines recalls an early Charmin turkey. (Since similar tests usually advertise the toughness of heavy-duty paper towels these days, one can speculate on what Charmin felt like back then.) The first series of P&G-produced commercials deemphasized the stiffness but still gave the impression that it was a heavy-duty, institutional, even *outdoorsy*-type toilet tissue: There were endorsements from the housekeeper of an alpine chalet-inn and the housekeeper of a riverboat.

It didn't take P&G's market-research people long to establish that there was a great hunger in the growing American middle class for more softness in their toilet tissue, that there was a correlation between moving up in economic class and moving "up" from one-ply to two-ply tissue, because two-ply was soft, and for one reason or another—advertising being one big reason—soft white tissue was an emblem of the soft white-collar life. But it wasn't until 1960 that P&G production people had softened up Charmin enough to bring Gentle the Dog and his gentle friends to announce that Charmin was "fluffed, buffed, and brushed," presumably like Gentle the Dog's fluffy coat. But comparing a toilet tissue to dog's hair is risky business considering the popularity of wire-haired terriers.

And in any case *gentle* is still not *soft*. *Gentle* still has a residue of averted pain in it (as in "Don't hurt, please be gentle"). *Gentler* is not soft, either. Even *soft itself* wasn't enough for the brand-new ad P&G and B&B wanted from the creative team they assigned to the Charmin account. Everyone was soft already. And Scott's "Soft-Weve" had already beaten everybody to "Softer than soft." Had the whole soft thing reached a dead end, or was there some way to say *softer than softer-than-soft,* and to say it in a way that made a shopper, sated by so many similar softs, select it from the shelf?

There are two versions of the moment of discovery. There may be a third. Flora Fifield, the only one of the Benton & Bowles creative trio no longer in advertising, is reportedly living somewhere in Vermont teaching school, and I was unable to locate her. (Both Procter & Gamble and Benton & Bowles, interestingly, claimed no memory and no records of the three people who created the momentous Mr. Whipple campaign and offered no help in finding them, or in supplying storyboards.)

Jim Haines, the creative head of the trio at the time, is now a partner in an ad agency in Johannesburg.[1] I spoke to him during one of his visits to New York. The way he remembers the big moment, it began with the three of them

---

[1]Among other things, he's in charge of advertising a South African toilet-tissue brand called "Cushy." The campaign for Cushy features, as I recall Haines's description, an Afrikaner grandmother who is so obsessed with squeezing soft Cushy that she takes it to her bedroom with her; her family is constantly finding itself without tissue in time of need and pleading the brand's slogan, "Please keep the Cushy in the loo."

crammed into copywriter Chervokas's cubicle at Benton & Bowles's Fifth Avenue office, tossing a roll of toilet paper to and fro. They were at their wit's end, none of the ideas they'd tried had worked. They had run out of new ideas and they were running out of time. "It was one of those grade-B-movie situations," Haines recalls. "We were having a think session, you know, a frustration session and we were not only kicking ideas around we were tossing the roll around, and we started to get the giggles." The Muse must have kissed the airborne Charmin in midflight because suddenly, "John [Chervokas] caught the roll and started to squeeze it and somebody said, 'Don't squeeze it' and John said, 'Please don't squeeze it' or 'Please don't squeeze the Charmin' and it just happened. The thing just rolled off his tongue. . . ."

The way John Chervokas tells it there was no roll of toilet paper in the air. "I don't remember tossing any roll around, no," Chervokas told me when I spoke to him in his big new office at the Warwick Welsh & Miller agency. Chervokas has just received another of the many promotions that have marked his career since the Charmin creation, the latest being a move from creative director at William Esty to senior vice president/creative director at Warwick. Back in 1972 Chervokas wrote for *Advertising Age* a tongue-in-cheek "confession" about his key role in writing Mr. Whipple into advertising history, but he concedes the Charmin conception has "definitely been a plus" in his career.

Like Haines, Chervokas sets the scene of the historic discovery in his junior writer's cubicle at Benton & Bowles, but Chervokas recalls a more elaborate operation of the creative process. Chervokas says the discovery grew out of their feeling that instead of just *saying* soft, or *showing* soft people and things, they should figure out a way to *demonstrate* soft. What follows is Chervokas's reconstruction in *Ad Age* of the free-association process that led to the birth of Whipple:

> How to demonstrate softness? A feather is soft, but suggests tickling. A baby's behind suggests softness, but that's "too restrictive." Silk is soft, but comparing Charmin to silk risks "over promising." What about a fall? A soft fall. A fall on a pillow? Hugging a pillow? Squeezing a pillow? Squeeze a banana!?
>
> Wait a minute. Here was something. What does a woman do in a supermarket? She squeezes melons, tomatoes, bread . . . Squeeze *Charmin!*

There it was. Just one hitch remained, according to Chervokas, and in the ingenuity of its solution was the birth of George Whipple. Someone pointed out that if the ad told women to squeeze Charmin in the store, "supermarket managers will go crazy. The answer is to tell them *not* to squeeze it." But how to tell them not to squeeze it? You have a crazy supermarket manager tell them not to squeeze it, that's how. "In an hour and a half," Chervokas wrote,

"America's most universally despised advertising campaign became a reality."

Unlike the physicists working on the Manhattan Project, who knew the magnitude of the terror they were about to unleash upon the world, the three people in that cubicle were unaware of the advertising explosion they had on their hands. According to Haines, "We were having a lot of laughs and we thought this was just another laugh until the substance of it was allowed to sink in." They liked the don't-squeeze idea, but the idea of the supermarket manager obsessed with protecting his Charmin from squeezers seemed a bit madcap at the time, particularly for a relatively cautious and conservative client like Procter & Gamble. The higher-ups at Benton & Bowles were a little nervous about it, too. "We encountered some abrasion," Haines recalls. "It may have been inside the agency. They considered it terribly harebrained; it took a lot of convincing inside to get them to convince Cincinnati to test the thing. Somebody had to go out there to fight tooth and nail for the campaign."

Even when P&G executives in Cincinnati grudgingly agreed to shell out for production of three sixty-second sample scripts of the "Don't squeeze" concept, there was no guarantee any one of them would ever make it on the air. Everything depended on the execution, as they say in the ad business, and the success of the execution, most everyone agreed, depended on how successfully the slightly mad character of the supermarket character could be brought off. According to Haines, Chervokas "had a very definite brief in mind. He wanted a Milquetoast character, a bit, I suppose, effeminate in his way, nervous, intimidated, but a champion of Charmin." Chervokas remembers, "I was originally thinking of an Edmund Gwennish kind of character—you know, *Miracle on 34th Street*—you know, a lovable little fraud, maybe a little dumpy . . ." Whoever it turned out to be, they needed just the right actor to do it just the right way. The agency put out a casting call to both coasts and started compiling a reel of filmed auditions for the part.

Most comedy drunk acts these days are gassy drunk acts—the loudmouth, the weeper, the burper. But the classic drunk acts of the golden age of vaudeville were the dancer acrobatic drunk acts. That's what Dick Wilson, the man who plays Mr. Whipple, told me. He was a dancer acrobatic drunk act. This meant he'd go up on a tightrope and make all sorts of funny, heart-stopping, drunken near falls. "I worked with tails. I was classy, a lot of class, but a drunk," he said. He toured the best Canadian and English vaudeville circuits, played drunks for Olsen and Johnson, and ended up in America after the war. TV was good to him. "I must have done over three hundred and fifty TV shows as a drunk. I'm the drunk in *Bewitched,* I was the drunk on *The Paul Lynde Show,*

I did a lot of Disney's drunks." He almost got his first big break in a nondrunk part when some TV people were all set to cast him as the sidekick of *Sergeant Preston of the Yukon*. At the last minute, however, the part got written out and Sergeant Preston was given a dog named King as a substitute sidekick. "I was supposed to be the dog," Wilson said.

Despite these and other disappointments in nondrunk parts, Wilson knew he was capable of more in show business. Maybe he wouldn't play Hamlet, but he wouldn't be satisfied with just playing drunks. He'd begun doing some freelance stage-show producing in 1964. That summer he was in Las Vegas producing a Shirley MacLaine revue at a place called The Kings Road Tally Ho when he got a call from his agent. "He asked me: 'What do you think of toilet paper?' " Wilson recalls. "And I told him I think everybody should use it." "No, no, no," the agent said, according to Wilson, who I suspect has polished this Big Break scene into a little routine over the years. "I'm asking you how would you like to do a commercial for toilet paper, there's an audition tomorrow." "How do you audition toilet paper?" Wilson asked. And his agent said, " 'Please go and take a screen test,' and I said a screen test would be a permanent record. But I went and they liked me because five days later we were making the first Charmin commercial in a supermarket in Flushing."

"Dick Wilson was kidding me when he says you made the first ones in Flushing, wasn't he?" I asked Howard Magwood, the man who directed them.

"No, no, no. It was Flushing," Magwood insisted.

"It wasn't Flushing," says John Chervokas, who was there to watch the filming of his scripts. "I think it was Astoria."

By the time director Magwood and his ten-person production crew set up for shooting in the Flushing or Astoria market, the original scripts drawn up at Benton & Bowles had undergone two interesting modifications. The name George Whipple, for instance, was a late change. I had always harbored a suspicion that it was no accident that "Whipple" sounded like a sinister fusion of *whip* and *nipple,* and that perhaps some devious motivational-research person had created the name as an emblem of a submerged sadomasochistic element in the relations between Whipple and the housewives who risk his punishment for the pleasure of a squeeze.

Alas, the true story seems more innocent. I was able to acquire a copy of a hand-sketched storyboard draft of one of those original Charmin scripts, this one dated September 24, 1964, and entitled "Digby to the Rescue." In this draft, the store manager is named, not Whipple, but "Edgar Bartholomew," a far less provocative choice. The switch to Whipple was made, according to Chervokas, not to make the name more kinky, but because a real Edgar Bartholomew could not be found to sell the rights to his name. (When an ad agency gives commercial characters names, it makes a point of finding real persons with that name and persuades them to sell the use of their name for a token fee, so that *other* real persons with that name won't have legal standing to argue that *their* name is the one being used.) Back in 1964 the public relations director of Benton & Bowles was a well-liked man named George Whipple. Whether or not the hints of whip and nipple had anything to do with it, the creative people liked his name as a replacement for Bartholomew and the real George Whipple sold his agency the use of his name for one dollar.

There *is* one kinky aspect of the first-draft sketch of "Digby to the Rescue" that never made it into the final shooting script. It's the bit in which Digby the cop sticks his nose into the core of the toilet-paper roll. The way it happens in the draft I have, store manager Edgar Bartholomew finds himself so overwhelmed with Charmin-squeezing women that he summons the local cop, Officer Digby, to restore order. The women insist that Digby give the Charmin a squeeze himself to see why they find it so irresistible. Over Bartholomew's protest ("You're on duty!") Digby takes a squeeze. He's visibly impressed, but the women insist that he sniff it, too. (P&G had been perfuming the cardboard core of Charmin rolls for some time.) The sketch calls for the fully uniformed cop to unwrap the paper and plunge his nose into the scented core, take a deep sniff, say "Ummmm . . ." and come up for air totally won over to the Charmin ladies' cause. The big sniff was eliminated from the final shooting—at least on camera. In the storyboard made from the final filmed version of "Digby to the Rescue" the camera tactfully shifts away from Digby as he checks out the fragrance.

Despite this evidence of concern for taste, the original Flushing/Astoria Charmin commercials are not without some less than chaste moments. One script, entitled "Mrs. Logan," has a hidden Whipple staring at a certain Mrs. Logan squeezing tomatoes, melons, and, finally, Charmin, at which point Whipple exposes himself to view and bursts out with the familiar admonition, "Please don't squeeze the Charmin." Then Whipple sneaks off by himself and chortles, "If you only knew, Mrs. Logan. I can't resist it myself. I like to sneak a squeeze on the sly."

"Wasn't that a bit of an innuendo?" I asked John Chervokas.

"No, those were pre-innuendo days," Chervokas maintains, innocently. However, it seems clear that one advantage of pre-innuendo innocence was that admen could get away with saying some very blatant things without the advertising acceptability departments imagining anyone would be dirty-minded enough to think of its innuendo implications (viz. the cigarette ad "It's not how long you make it, it's how you make it long").

Maybe you don't immediately think of Shakespeare when you watch a Charmin commercial, but according to director Howard Magwood it was the

Bard himself who suggested the solution to the single most perplexing problem in producing the original Charmin dramas. "It was a theatrical problem," says Magwood, who left a theatrical career to become a successful commercial director. "The problem was how to play the Charmin-squeezing women. These three broads had to be believable. We'd turn people off if they looked too stupid. The audience has to believe it's fun, crazy, but you can't have actors gagging it up, you have to believe it's real when you do it."

Out in Flushing/Astoria that day, the actresses Magwood had cast for the Charmin squeezers were having trouble *believing* in their part. There were repeated run-throughs where Wilson/Whipple was fine, but the ladies just weren't right. Suddenly the Shakespearean solution suggested itself to Magwood. "I told them, 'Try to think of this as the three witches in *Macbeth,* because they're kind of wild and crazy,' and they said 'Oooh, that's *it.*' "[1] They fell to their frenzy with immediately successful and believable results—all too believable, perhaps, in the long run, because the demented witchlike quality of their behavior has earned the Charmin campaign considerable hostility from the women's movement.

Even when the three original Charmin spots were finally "in the can," as they say in the film business, not many people believed they'd get out for long until the astonishing statistics from the first recall test came back. Procter & Gamble believes in careful testing before committing itself to a campaign. The company gave the Charmin spots a tryout then known as the Burke Recall Test. Benton & Bowles quietly slipped a sample sixty-second Charmin spot, reportedly "Digby to the Rescue," into the regular TV programming in a selected midwestern market. The following day, a consumer research firm called a sample of home viewers and asked them what they watched the day before and if they remembered any particular commercials.

Previous tests of other concepts for a new Charmin campaign had produced recall scores ranging from a mediocre twenty-seven to a humiliating two, according to Chervokas. Then one day that winter in another grade-B-movie development, junior writer Chervokas (the Charmin campaign was his first assignment at Benton & Bowles) got a call from a big shot. "Sit down, John," he said, Chervokas recalls. "Your Charmin commercial scored fifty-five." That was a record smasher, the highest recall score of any commercial tested up until then.

---

[1]They're not talking about tissue wound on a roll, of course, but at one point in *Macbeth* the three witches cry out in unison, "The charm's wound up!" Perhaps the real Shakespearean parallel, if one is to be made at all, lies in the structural similarity of the Charmin commercial to the plots of the "problem comedies," such as *Measure for Measure,* in which hypocritical tyrants who make and enforce decrees against sexuality end up getting caught sneaking a squeeze on the sly themselves.

The Wall Street Journal (October 20, 1971) described the marketing mayhem that followed the full-scale debut of the new Charmin campaign as "the great toilet-paper war" of the sixties. The *Journal* recognized the importance of Mr. Whipple, calling him "no mere foot soldier" in the war, but gave chief credit for P&G's stunning victories over Scott to P&G's big battalions—the billion-dollar company's "awesome marketing muscle" and its "sales force like an invading army." The P&G battle plan was to conquer the country with Charmin one region at a time. First the Midwest, then south to Texas, finally around 1970 attacking the East Coast and the Southwest, and not until 1975 moving its troops across the Rockies into California. The strategy in each region was to soften the territory up with massive air strikes—in 1970 P&G spent $2 million on airtime for Whipple spots—then bring the "invading army" into the supermarkets with marketing muscle to command big displays and premium shelf-space placement.

It worked. By 1970 Charmin had gone from nowhere to equality with the market share of ScotTissue, the largest selling one-ply in the country. Not only that, Charmin began to steal customers away from Scott's "Soft-Weve" and other two-ply tissues. In the five years between 1969 and 1974, production of two-ply tissue increased by only 7 percent, or 36,000 tons, while one-ply production went up 160,000 tons, nearly 20 percent. The growth of Charmin was responsible for much of that increase. Charmin was changing the nation's toilet habits.

Meanwhile, a whole other war broke out in the advertising industry over the *meaning* of it all. At first Whipple had the worst of it: The new, hip wildman-genius types, and the cerebral, sophisticated, creative types all attacked the Charmin campaign and made it a symbol, a catchword, for all that was stupid, degrading, and meretricious about the old-fashioned hard sell, particularly the hard-sell school that believed simple irritation and reiteration were the key to consumer recall. "If I ever get a chance to meet the man who did those godawful, terribly bad, 'Don't Squeeze the Charmin' commercials—and he turns out to be small—I just may slug him," said outspoken ad whiz Jerry Della Femina. (According to John Chervokas, who is not small, they've never met.)

But lately the tables have been turned on the critics. Charmin and Whipple have been around so long, have been successful so long, that admen of the old school are beginning to use the campaign against the clever young wiseguys, rubbing their noses in Charmin, chortling that the Whipple pitch proves that the so-called creative, softer-than-soft-sell stuff may win praise and awards but the old-fashioned abrasive hard sell makes the big bucks for the client. Just this year, Benton & Bowles took a big ad in *Advertising Age* to push this theme. It featured a sketch of Whipple looking far more censorious and mean-spirited than he ever does in the actual commercials, almost as if he were sneering triumphantly at the hippie malcontents who criticize his ad. IT'S NOT CREATIVE UNLESS IT SELLS, the big type boasts.

It sells, but why? Arcane alternatives to the Simple Irritant Theory abound. The Sex in the Supermarket Theory advanced by Faith Popcorn, for instance. Popcorn, currently president of BrainReserve, an agency that makes use of some advanced new creative techniques, attributes the success of Charmin to the sensuality of the squeeze: "It established tactile contact between the consumer and the product, which is very rare in television. It lets you experience the product right there in the store. It's the old 'Lemme feel the material' thing, like people used to feel cloth before they bought it. Just that they let you squeeze it and touch it is a very sexy thing," she says. "Very, very sexy."

Then there's Professor Wilson Bryan Key, who thinks the whole secret is "soft stool." Professor Key is the author of a strange book called *Subliminal Seduction* in which he allows that almost all print advertising is "embedded" with obscene words and pictures. "Mr. Whipple, with his bow tie and his effeminate mannerisms, is almost a perfect anal stereotype," Professor Key told me on the phone from Ontario, where, he claimed, the University of Western Ontario had just fired him because of pressure from advertising agencies enraged at his book. "Go back and look at Freud's description of the anal personality. The idea of squeezing the tissue is the soft-stool syndrome."

Dick Wilson has some less portentous theories about Whipple's phenomenal success. First of all, he rejects the idea that the Whipple series is old-fashioned and abrasive. He cites one TV breakthrough Whipple made in 1965. "Back then I was the first one to wear a mustache in a commercial." And he insists, "The stuff we do is not nauseating, it's cute." But the secret of Whipple's success, according to Wilson, is in the careful delineation of his character: "The director and I worked out his character between us, and we guard him very well. We'll try something and then say, 'No, no, Whipple wouldn't do that.' For instance we never let him be nasty. He's not nasty. He's prissy but he's not nasty."

Wilson himself is a likable character, with the dignity of a vaudevillian who has aged well. I reached him by phone at a hotel in Kansas City where he was rehearsing a production of *The Unsinkable Molly Brown*. "I just finished making eleven new Charmin spots in L.A.," he said. "Four of them in Spanish, where I'm Señor Whipple. That makes two hundred and four in all, although we've remade some of them every once in a while." Charmin has been good to Dick Wilson. He's a certified celebrity now. "I get instant recognition everywhere I go. I have these cards I hand out that have a picture of me and say, 'Don't Squeeze the Charmin. Squeeze Me.' And they do. I get a lot of squeezes that way." Procter & Gamble certainly squeezes the most out of Whipple. They pay him to travel around to supermarket openings, sales conventions, warehouses, and factories to boost sales and morale. They even sell Whipple T-shirts.

However, a new round of escalation in the toilet-paper war is just beginning, and the possibility must be considered that P&G will come to consider Whipple a liability in the heat of the coming battle. He has his enemies out there. Feminists attack the Charmin commercial for degrading women; NOW pickets at a recent P&G shareholders meeting called on the company to "Squeeze out Mr. Whipple." A nun in Wisconsin who relentlessly monitored 150 hours of soap-opera programming to prepare an analysis of P&G's treatment of women for a shareholders group doesn't find Whipple nearly as degrading as some other P&G ads, "merely asinine," but Whipple has become an emblem of all that critics find wrong with P&G, with advertising in general, with American culture. Mr. Clean doesn't get that kind of bad press.

Meanwhile, other brands have been taking aim at Charmin, homing in on certain vulnerabilities Whipple can't camouflage. First, there was Scott's "roller derby" commercial, which pictures a "race" between two frantically unwinding rolls of tissue: Scott and a roll identified as "the other leading brand," clearly Charmin. Scott always loses the "roller derby" because, the spot points out, ScotTissue has a full 1,000 sheets to unwind from its roll while the other leading brand has only 650.

While Scott was skillfully exploiting Charmin's short-sheeted disadvantages among one-ply tissues (Charmin claims it can't fit as many sheets on a roll without the roll swelling to monstrous size because each of its sheets is fluffier than ordinary one-plys), an aggressive East Coast two-ply tissue named Marcal was attacking the apparent flimsiness of one-ply Charmin in comparison with a good two-ply. The Marcal spot mentions Charmin by name and consists of a demonstration in which a sheet of Charmin held up in front of a candle flame is found to be so diaphanous as to be almost transparent, while a sheet of Marcal virtually blocks the light with its staunch two-ply thickness.

Nor were the Whipple commercials responding effectively to these challenges. In fact, they seemed to have lost direction in the past couple of years. There were excursions into Whipple's home life that seem designed to lay to rest suspicions that there was something deviant about his devotion to Charmin. Not all these efforts to promote Whipple's wholesomeness were totally successful. One short-lived spot introduced us to Whipple's own mother, who was played by Wilson himself in Whipple drag: "I shaved my mustache off, dressed in girl's clothes and a white wig and high-heeled shoes and everything else that went with it," Wilson recalled. "They pulled that off the air fast. It was cute but a little grotesque." Then in early 1974 the copy line for the spots underwent an odd change. A Charmin storyboard filed with the FTC and dated December 1, 1973, describes Charmin as "Deep Down Squeezably Soft." Now I'd never been able to figure out deep down *where* it was squeezably soft, but the new copy line is even more puzzling. It describes Charmin's softness as "rich and fluffy"—language whose evocation of taste would be more appropriate to an Oreo creme filling than to a roll of toilet tissue. And in some of the more recent commercials, strange things are seen to be going on within Whipple's own psyche.

"Whipple's Dream" opens with Whipple and three ladies flagrantly squeezing Charmin together, with Whipple brazenly declaring "Charmin's so rich and fluffy it's irresistible," as he squeezes away. Well, it turns out Whipple's actually at home in bed with his wife, who shakes him into realizing this debauch is only a dream. "Ooh, that explains it," Whipple says. "I'd never squeeze Charmin while I was awake." "Certainly not, George," says the wife, who then reveals that Whipple has taken a roll of Charmin to bed with him to squeeze. "Whipple's Temptation," dated January 1 in the FTC files, presents Whipple vigorously urged by a devilish figure to go ahead and squeeze the Charmin, while a haloed Whipple conscience feebly opposes the squeeze. Whipple succumbs, right before our eyes.

Does this new predilection of Whipple for fevered religious visions and erotic dreams reflect a psyche under severe strain after all those years of repression and guilt over forbidden pleasures? Why was Whipple doing things like taking rolls of tissue to bed with him? Why was he permitted full frontal squeezes rather than the sneaky ones on the sly? The answer, I'm afraid, is that Whipple may be going through the same last-chance testing period they gave Gentle the Dog. Because a decade has passed and all signs indicate that Procter & Gamble is getting ready to introduce another toilet-paper development that may equal or exceed the hot-air fluffing that Whipple made famous. At this very moment in certain sections of America, P&G is slipping onto supermarket shelves a new-new Charmin that represents a whole *new* concept in softer-than-softer-than-soft.

It's a tricky new marketing ploy, so try to follow closely. New-new Charmin takes the same weight of paper pulp as old-new Charmin to make a roll. However, a roll of new-new Charmin has only 500 sheets, instead of the 650 in old-new Charmin. That means there is more paper pulp per sheet on each of the 500 sheets than before this improvement. So each sheet is somewhat thicker and the hot-air blower dryers have even more pulp fuzz to puff up. So what results is 500 extra-fluffy, plush, feather-pillow-type sheets of tissue, but 150 fewer sheets for the money. In some markets—northern California, Oregon, and St. Louis, among others—P&G is reportedly testing an extra-extra-plush sheet of toilet tissue with only 400 sheets of plumped-up, pulpy tissue per roll.

The object here is to convince the consumer that fewer plush sheets will last just as long as more, flimsier sheets. P&G refuses to discuss marketing strategy, but a spokesman for Scott, which is also coming out with an extra-plush one-ply to be called "Cottonelle" (soft as cotton), puts it this way: "The assumption in all these new tissues is that people grab off what feels right in their hand, so if you have thicker sheets you have a thicker feeling in your hand from fewer sheets and you won't use as many."

A consumer affairs commissioner in New York's Suffolk County, where some of the new plush Charmin is being tested in the supermarkets, claims that Charmin's explanation of the reduction in sheet count was just a lot of hot air and pulp. "If they did do market research I would like to know the parameters they used—used sheets?" says Commissioner James Lack, who threatened to take civil action against Charmin for misleading the public. "I maintain people use the same number of sheets that they started to use when their toilet habits were born," Lask said. "My staff researched this on an informal basis and the number of sheets doesn't change. I don't like corporations hiding misleading facts." Whatever the facts, if P&G does decide to go full force into the plush and extra-plush toilet market it's going to be a tough advertising job.

Does P&G think that Whipple, with all his notoriety, his enemies, and his ten-year-old pitch, can handle the new responsibility? There's one spot being tested on the air right now which already seems to be easing him off center stage. The people at the Television Monitoring Institute of Huntington Station, Long Island, brought it to my attention. (They make their living taping TV commercials and programming 'round the dial 'round the clock, often for ad agencies who want to know what their competitors are putting on.) This new spot plugs the new plush Charmin being introduced into Long Island supermarkets with a promise never before made in toilet-paper advertising: "You can *hear* the difference in New Charmin." (Since you can already smell it, feel it, see it, and it's so "rich" you can almost taste it, what was left but to hear it?)

But even more interesting than the sound of the roll is the size of the role they've given Whipple. The ladies in the market take up the opening moments of the spot chatting about New Charmin and listening to it. Whipple comes on to deliver a rather perfunctory version of his litany: "Ladies, I don't care if you can see, hear, feel, or smell the difference, but please don't squeeze it." His only line in the spot, barely a walk-on. He's not given the opportunity to deliver his customary soliloquy on the squeeze; instead, a peremptory voice breaks in, says "Excuse me, Mr. Whipple," cuts him off, and takes over the difficult job of explaining the improvement in the new plush product. Whipple merely seems to be in everyone's way. And if this indignity is not enough, I've heard reliable reports that in one spot being tested the script actually calls for Whipple to *urge* the ladies to squeeze the Charmin.

When I heard that sad bit of news, I began to wonder seriously if Whipple was on the way out. If he's not there to tell people *not* to squeeze, any jerk can tell them to *listen* to the toilet paper or whatever the client wants. I wondered if P&G was testing to see if anyone noticed, if anyone cared anymore that Whipple *didn't* care if they squeezed. I called up Whipple, I mean Wilson, in California, and asked if it were true that in a new spot he actually does urge the women to go ahead and squeeze.

"Yes it's true," he said, "but it's only a test, it's only one spot."

I hope so. After all these years, I'd hate to see Whipple go the way of Gentle the Dog.

Postscript to "Whipple's Last Squeeze"

In fact, Whipple did disappear for roughly a dozen years, only to return with a vengeance at the butt end of the millennium in a series of new spots that somehow attempts to elide the fact of his disappearance. In the two I saw, friends and colleagues are holding retirement parties for Whipple—as if he hadn't been retired involuntarily for a dog's age already—but he bursts in to say, no, he's changed his mind. "I can't retire now, I have to show folks about how they've improved new double-roll Charmin." He gets in his car, about to drive off. Is it just me or did some sly fellow at the ad agency slip a tongue-in-cheek double entendre into Whipple's last words in the ad: "Gotta go"?

Part Two

THE
EIGHTIES

The Connoisseur of Scoundrels

In Which Murray Kempton Tries to Find "the Finger of God" in the Fumblings of Man

The scene: an informal dinner party on the rooftop of a brownstone in the East Seventies. The people (with one exception): congenial, civilized, charming. The conversation: charming, civilized, congenial.

Until . . . until someone makes the mistake of asking me what contemporary writers I like. This is a mistake other people at other parties have lived to regret. Because I can be, well, a little fanatical on the subject.

Particularly (as was the case that evening) when I try to explain to people that Murray Kempton is the best writer of prose in America, and I get blank stares from half the group and someone from the other half says something like "Murray Kempton? You mean the newspaper columnist?" with a maddening mixture of incomprehension and disdain. To me it's akin to some late-sixteenth-century twit saying, "Thou meanst William Shakespeare, the *theater* person?"

At that point, with the evening irretrievably ruined for me, I proceed to ruin it for everyone else by launching into a long feverish disquisition on the indispensability of reading Kempton; on the indispensability of reading Kempton to any literate human who cares about the pleasures and possibilities of the

English language; on the indispensability of reading Kempton to any student of human nature who seeks to understand the way the passions of the human heart shape and subvert the pageant of public events.

In fact, I conclude, you can't pretend to understand life in New York City, indeed the whole drama of American civilization, without Kempton's vision and insight: He's nothing less than *our Gibbon*.

For a moment after I conclude with this ringing declaration, there is silence on the rooftop, nothing but the faint rumbling of air-conditioning exhausts on the windows of the adjacent building. I begin to feel I've succeeded in sweeping away all possible objections with this final hammer blow, that my oratory has shamed the assembled company into silent contemplation of the insufficiencies of their lives. I am particularly pleased with myself for the finale, the "*our Gibbon*" line.

And then a voice pipes up, breaking the silence: "Uh, Art Gibbon—isn't he that sportswriter?"

Oh, well. I guess I deserved that. But Kempton doesn't. He deserves better of us. Yes, he got a long-overdue Pulitzer Prize a couple of years ago; but here he is, appearing four times a week on almost every newsstand in New York now (in *New York Newsday*), and yet the recognition and appreciation he gets is so incommensurate with what his astonishing achievements deserve that it constitutes a major injustice, a disgraceful city scandal.

That night, the night of the Art Gibbon debacle, I vowed I was going to do something to correct this injustice. First thing the next morning I would gather up all the scattered Murray Kempton columns I'd been tearing out and stashing all over my apartment; I'd call up Kempton and arrange an interview; and I'd whip out a story that would prove to the doubters, to the Art Gibbon types, to the pseudosophisticates who look down their noses at "newspaper columnists," just how essential regular reading of Kempton is to anyone who pretends to be civilized.

I thought it would take me a couple of weeks. In fact, it's taken me more than a year since the Art Gibbon incident.

I have some excuses. I know you don't want to hear them, but I don't care, they're important. First of all I decided that, in order to do justice to Kempton, in order to support the grand Gibbonian claim I was making on his behalf, I needed to reread Gibbon's *History of the Decline and Fall of the Roman Empire* in its entirety. Believe me, that ate up a lot of time, even skimming, as I'll admit I did, some of Gibbon's extended accounts of the succession of the late emperors of the East, whose interminable intrigues were profoundly—and literally—Byzantine.

But in the course of rereading *The Decline and Fall* for the first time since college, I made two surprising discoveries. Gibbon is much better than I remembered. And in some respects Kempton is better than Gibbon.

The thing I never realized about Gibbon in the miserable circumstances of my sophomore year was what a terrific—and wicked—sense of humor the guy has. For sheer black humor nothing beats his ostensibly polite efforts to explain the "reasoning" behind the early church councils' distinction between orthodoxy and heresy. His account of the persecution of the heretics is amused and detached on the surface, but beneath the elaborately counterpoised antitheses of his prose there is a stirringly passionate disgust. Kempton has that quality too. The baroque civilities of his notoriously knotted sentence structure are capable of concealing and revealing passionate responses to events.

What makes Kempton's achievement so remarkable is that Gibbon was writing with, for the most part, ten centuries of hindsight. Kempton somehow manages, four times a week, on deadline, to give events just a few hours old a focus that seems to reflect a thousand years of accumulated wisdom and perspective. He is this city's single most underappreciated asset.

This has been a particularly good year for reading Kempton because if he can be said to have a specialty, it is as a connoisseur of scoundrels. And this past year—which began with Donald Manes and the city corruption scandals, which featured four simultaneous major Mafia trials, which yielded up Dennis Levine,* who yielded up Ivan Boesky, and which followed that up with Iran-contra—has given Kempton a joyful surplus of rogues to write about.

What he's always done best is make distinctions between degrees of scoundrelhood. Consider, for instance, his take on the investment banking scandals. Rather than merely rail against corruption and immorality in the abstract, he distinguishes between the social productivity of the robber barons of a century ago and the comparative sterility of contemporary corruption.

Of Dennis Levine, Kempton writes:

> Everything in Levine's history would seem to illustrate the splendid freedom from conscience that made giants of the robber barons but in his case most painfully illustrates the social decline that becomes irreversible when commercial immorality abandoned all productive functions.
>
> A hundred years ago Levine . . . would have gone to engineering school and emerged to flog Chinese laborers at the rail spike, bake Slovaks at the blast furnace . . . hang Molly Maguires or shoot Wobblies at the pit face.
>
> Deeds of this description have the inescapable odor of the foul, but when they were done we had the Union Pacific, Pittsburgh, and Detroit to show for it.

And here's Kempton on another unappetizing scoundrel, Donald Manes's bagman-turned–state's witness, Geoffrey Lindenauer. He quotes a bribe-trial witness's description of Lindenauer oozing around to put the touch on him.

*The first major insider trader of the eighties to be caught.

Kempton then asks "Breathes there a man with a soul so dead that his dignity would not revolt when the likes of Lindenauer call out, 'Hi, partner'?"

On the exposure of Roy Cohn's affectional preference: "Roy went astray in no end of ways, but I had always thought of him as the last of ambulant creatures to be misled by moonlight and the rose."

Again on the declining productivity of contemporary corruption: "The difference between then and now is in the erosion of greed's social utility, dreadful as it inarguably was . . . the robber barons sacked the earth and flayed the toiler, but they left mines and mills and railroads behind them. Their greed was the terrible engine of progress. Ours is only the bedizened fellow traveler of decay."

And striking a Gibbonian note on observing the prison-thin figure of Mafia don Anthony "Fat Tony" Salerno: "He has come to look like some bust in the old Roman style, toppled over somewhere in the decline and then salvaged from the ruins of the empire."

But as I was reading over a year's worth of Kempton columns in preparing for my conversations with him, I noticed another theme emerging with unexpected frequency: passionate, almost chivalric, defense of women in trouble. Some of his finest columns have been about women—from his defense of murdered teenager Jennifer Levin against the insinuations of her murderer, Robert Chambers, to appreciations of political women from Bella Abzug to Nancy Reagan. He can go from commiserating with Geraldine Ferraro ("the troubles of Geraldine Ferraro commence to break the heart . . . and yet [she displays] an inflexible gallantry") to a sympathetic account of Joey Heatherton's legal troubles over the passport-clerk–head-whipping incident. Joey, he tells us with great delicacy, is "a young woman who has not been too well used by life and, it must be conceded, has not always used life impeccably in return."

The latter is a perfect example of Kemptonian observation: Utterly aware of the flaws in the fallen nature of his subject and yet good-naturedly tolerant of them, he passes a sentence that combines both judgment and absolution as, I suppose, the best of the bishops from whom he's descended would.

His affectionate reverence for women can be seen in his sly tribute to the powers of Victoria Gotti, the reputed Godfather's formidable wife. Kempton attends the jury-selection phase of the Gotti trial and notes that while most of the prospective male jurors have been giving fearful excuses for not sitting in judgment on Gotti, the prospective women jurors have not.

Probing this mystery, Kempton notes various publicly reported instances of Victoria Gotti's wrathful temperament: "Gotti may or may not have been too loose in his trifling with law and order, but he has to know better than to trifle with her." The women jurors haven't missed this aspect of the alleged Godfather's marriage, Kempton suspects: "There are particular things that only women know, and we can with reason surmise that they have noted on John Gotti's countenance the marks of the henpecked husband invisible to his fellow man. No wife can fear even the most dangerous of men once she suspects he fears his own wife."

Kempton's even able to summon up sympathy for Lillian Goldman, the aggrieved wife of Sol Goldman, who is "almost the grandest, if not quite the gamiest, of our realtors," as Kempton delicately puts it. Kempton's column about their complicated separation and reconciliation litigation is a classic for the hilarity he evokes with his bone-dry deadpan account of this domestic comedy. It seems that under their separation agreement, husband Sol provided an apartment in the Hotel Carlyle for wife Lillian. When he sought a reconciliation (the motive for which, Kempton suggests, may have been less romantic longing than concern about the loss of half his billion-dollar empire, which a divorce would entail), Sol encouraged Lillian to move back in with him by threatening to cease paying her rent at the Carlyle.

"This may of course have been the only way a landlord knew for saying how much he wanted a lost one to return to his bosom," Kempton observes dryly. "But, if that were the case, Lillian Goldman remembers no other sentimental touch except the moment when he held up their joint tax return for 1985 and said, 'See, you're still my wife.' "

Kempton's chivalric exertions have been most passionate in the columns he's devoted to the Jennifer Levin case. He's bitterly outraged by the way her accused murderer Robert Chambers has attempted to save his skin by blighting Levin's reputation. And, again, in the most dry and deadpan way, he introduces a facet of the case that could have a devastating impact on Chambers's fate: "There is, to be sure, gossip, however unsubstantiated, that Chambers took Jennifer Levin's earrings with him before departing, which were it true, might hint faintly at susceptibility to tokens of sentiment, but there is otherwise no expression of Chambers's that does not smoke the fuels of hatred."

It's probably safe to say that Kempton is being wickedly ironic when he suggests Chambers took Levin's earrings as "tokens of sentiment." In fact, he seems to be suggesting Chambers stole them off her dead body, a suggestion that, if true, might tend to undercut Chambers's assertion he was an innocent victim of Levin's "rough sex" ardor.

Kempton closes this column with a melancholy peroration on the decline of chivalry: "Men and, to a lesser degree, women have always had too much trouble keeping their tempers in each other's company; but before chivalry passed into the grave there was some respect for duty to the fiction that they cared about the weak and vulnerable. But now all men are free, which means that any number of them are lost."

I ask Kempton if he considers himself a romantic.

"I hope I consider myself a gentleman," he amends. "Women don't have to have chivalry. . . . Chivalry's a male virtue. I think there's an awful lot of misogyny loose, . . . so someone's got to stand up for them."

Kempton is descended on his mother's side from one of the most illustrious of the First Families of Virginia (the Masons—several men on his father's side were Episcopal bishops of Virginia).

Does your concern for chivalry stem from your descent from Southern aristocracy? I ask him.

"My family *was* very Confederate," he says. "And I always had a kind of Confederate view of everything. Losing-side consciousness is very important. For instance, it explains the Miranda decision."

How so?

"Hugo Black came from the only county in Alabama that stood by the Union. Earl Warren's father was a railroad striker in the Debs strike. He was blacklisted and he spent two years in—"

Really?

"It's fascinating. The losing side—if you don't get too excited about the possibilities of ever being the winner it's a very good way to grow up. I'd recommend it. I sort of grew up on the losing side. It didn't do too much for my character, but there are people whose character it's improved."

And yet, despite his Confederate background, Kempton was doing dangerous civil-rights work in the rural South in the thirties. After we ordered dinner (we met in an Italian place called Poletti's near Kempton's West End Avenue apartment), I mentioned to Kempton I'd just come across a reference to him in a fascinating book (*Song in a Weary Theme* by Pauli Murray, a black woman who was an early civil-rights activist). She describes traveling through the mean backwoods of rural Virginia in the late thirties and working with "a freelance journalist named Murray Kempton" on a pamphlet in defense of a black sharecropper condemned to die because he allegedly shot his landlord. How did a scion of Confederacy end up doing that? I asked Kempton.

He says his involvement in radical politics grew out of a quixotic impulse to go to sea because his cloistered college life at Johns Hopkins didn't seem "real" enough to him at the time. "When I was in college I went to sea, which is about 1936, but while at sea I joined the Communist party. I didn't join it with anything of idealism, as I remember it. The thing was . . . I needed a job and the so-called rank and file of the [Seafarers International Union] went on strike, and I was doing publicity, and—" he adds with typical self-deprecating irony—"it's important to remember, there *was* a time in the United States when you joined the Communist party to advance your career. No, it wasn't much of a career, granted, but the entire membership of the Port of Baltimore was the Communist union. [There was] a thing called the Travelers' Club, which was very important in the movement."

The Travelers' Club?

"The Travelers' Club. Everybody went around saying—about as authentically as Lillian Hellman saying she was able to carry underground messages to the German Resistance—they were 'traveling' which I never did. . . . Very romantic organization." He quit the party after about a year.

"I was sort of unhappy about the Moscow trials. I was unhappy with their position on the war, of course. So I quit. Then I joined the Socialist party, that is, the Norman Thomas Socialist party, and then I resigned and I worked for an organization called the Workers' Defense League and got involved in the Waller case, the sharecropper who shot his landlord."

Kempton wrote a book about that era, about contemporaries both famous and obscure who had joined the party and left, and the varying paths their lives had taken in the disillusioned aftermath. The book is called *Part of Our Time* and it's probably the only piece of twentieth-century American political writing on that subject that can stand unashamed next to Orwell. I know it changed my life. The summer of my junior year of high school I was taking remedial driver's ed, and in the course of haunting an empty school library, I came across *Part of Our Time;* it was a sudden revelation that writing about "current events" didn't have to partake of the terminal boredom of civics classes, that at its best, political writing can partake of the drama, the passion—and the methods—of great novels. It also was an introduction to irony, paradox, and a tragic, loser's-side sense of history, to a sense of the Kemptonian complexity of life.

Kempton now looks back with a mixture of affection and sadness for the people who shared the excitement of that era.

"I used to know a guy named Paul Hall [head of the Seafarers International Union, whose progress from radicalism to respectability Kempton chronicled]. And Paul used to have the most wonderful expressions, and he'd always say of somebody, 'You know I always got along with him—I rode a lot of wild horses with him.' "

He speaks a bit sadly of the people he rode wild horses with in the 1930s, people whose tragedy it is "to have your history remembered only by the likes of me, who, if you committed a bank robbery, would probably be more admiring and appreciative. But people ought to remember people who rode wild horses."

Speaking of bank robbers, another recurrent—and controversial—theme of Kempton's journalism has been his ability to find a kind word to say for the Mafia dons and organized criminals he's come to know in the course of covering their courtroom travails.

I ask him about that and he tells me he has no special reverence for them.

"People are very romantic about these guys, but the only thing I've ever learned is that if you talk to gangsters long enough, you'll find out they're just as bad as respectable people."*

Still, the theme of much of his coverage of the "Commission" trial—of the CEOs of the five big Mafia-family corporations—has been the decline in standards in the boardrooms of organized crime.

He compares the elders of the Cosa Nostra with their uncivilized successors.

"Gotti does not measure up, for my taste. . . . He's not open to the maturing experiences that bring a gangster to the proper sense of his dignity. Gotti's a repellent punk and always will be. He's a mean man. Whereas Persico—I mean, if we're going to compare homicidal maniacs, Persico has every advantage. . . . He's a man who felt there are things one does not do. One does not beat up a woman even to collect a debt."

This ability to see a chivalric streak in even "Carmine the Snake" Persico is a reflection of a key Kemptonian concern: making distinctions among scoundrels. He has a remarkable ability to see the human virtues in those who are ideological enemies and moral pariahs to conventional liberals.

There is Roy Cohn, for instance, with whom Kempton had a sporadic friendship and constant fascination. In a recent column Kempton quotes from a letter Fat Tony Salerno wrote to him. Fat Tony, displaying the courtliness Kempton prizes in these guys, introduced himself by saying, "Roy Cohn . . . always stated that you were an honorable man."

I ask Kempton what his assessment of Cohn is now.

"I never got over my ambivalence about Roy. . . . The world is full of people who are torn between the need to be loved and the need to be feared. Now, usually, really bad guys settle for the need to be feared. I mean, if you didn't like Jimmy Hoffa, he set out to scare you. There are guys like that. But Roy never made peace with those two impulses, never discarded the desire to be loved. . . . You know what baffles me? I don't know what people want out of life. More and more, I don't understand what people want out of life. I don't know what Roy wanted. He obviously wanted experiences of danger where there was no peril. . . . But I'm just sorry Roy was ever born. I'm sorry anybody that unhappy was cast upon the sands of life in America."

There are, however, certain figures Kempton finds utterly without the redeeming virtues of mere scoundrels. These he calls "muckers." Every once in a while he'll write a column finally reading them out of his life because they've offended his sense of dignity too gravely. He did this last fall to Ed

*Is that brilliant time-delay irony or what? Still perhaps my favorite Kempton line.

Koch. The occasion was Koch's gloating, graceless post–World Series comments upon winning his bet with the mayor of Boston and demanding that Boston city hall fly the New York Mets' flag. "Boston today is a city in subjugation," Koch exulted with the overdramatized glee of the ersatz fan.

Kempton found it a sickening spectacle, an offense to the glory and dignity of the athletes of both sides in that beautiful seven-game struggle. Kempton's farewell to Koch is a magnificent display of eloquent rage:

"He has made his duties subordinate to his vanities; he has bullied the ill-fortuned and truckled to the fortuned; to walk in his wake has been to stumble through a rubble of vulgarities and meanness of spirit."

But this last act, seeking to make the beaten but heroic Boston grovel, is just too much:

"The mayor has become a piece of civic property of whom we can no longer speak without apologizing to our fellow countrymen. Still it remains possible to pity him a little. He does not know what it is like to be Pete Rose in the 1975 World Series and go to the dressing room after Carlton Fisk has beaten you with an extra-inning home run and say you don't care who won because it is simply an honor to have played in a game like that one.

"Koch may not care to learn how a gentleman bears himself from examples like Pete Rose's, but there are many—most, I think—New Yorkers who have profited from that lesson and we are not in the main muckers. Still we can hardly acquit ourselves of all the fault in the possession of a mayor who is irretrievably one."

Another personage Kempton finds utterly without redeeming ambivalences is City Comptroller Harrison Goldin.

You reserved some of your most intensely distilled anger for your last column on Harrison Goldin. What is it about him that so particularly arouses this feeling? I ask him.

"Well, for one thing, he's just an awful guy. . . . I don't write about Goldin anymore, because my theory is that when you really get to dislike a man that much, you shouldn't write about him. I mean, a scoundrel without dignity will—I mean, I'm sorry to say it, but they are the ones who simply do not finally justify writing about."

"Your best columns often are ones about scoundrels *with* dignity. I'm thinking of the ones on Carmine Persico and Stanley Friedman.* What is it about scoundrels with dignity that—?"

"Maybe it's not the scoundrel. Maybe it's the dignity I'm celebrating wherever it may happen to exist. It's not a matter of condemning or not condemning scoundrels. . . . It's how people act when the worst things happen to them.

*Democratic party big shot who became embroiled in the city scandals of the eighties.

"I mean," he continues, "I wouldn't call myself a connoisseur of rascals. I've known a lot in my time and I've learned a little bit about how to calculate them. . . . I'm not sorry for Stanley. I'm sorry *about* Stanley."

What was it about his scoundrelhood that appealed to Kempton?

"I don't know. It's very funny. I never in life have seen a job that was perfectly awful and disgusting and degrading that didn't have a good man engaged in it. . . . There are a lot of rotten jobs that men can fall into at an early age, and when the time comes, when they're caught, they'll act decently. You know, it's probably the good man in the bad job who's my favorite subject."

He talks about making distinctions in the kind of corruption one encounters in the city. Worse than the Stanley Friedman bribe-corruption scandals, he feels, are the investment-banking scandals: "At least, at some point, somewhere down the line, there has to come a time when there is a product, that computer they were paying everyone off to finance, while insider trading produced no useful product but paper." And even lower than the investment-banking scandal is the scandal in the Seventy-Seventh Precinct where cops were taking money to protect crack dealers.

"It took me a while to discover this," he says, "but the biggest mistake you can make is to follow your ideas to their logical conclusion. That's the only real mistake you can make with assurance. You can make a lot of others, but every now and then you can be right. But when you follow your ideas to their logical conclusion, you are always wrong. The cop who says to himself, 'Well, if I'm taking money from the numbers runner, I might as well take it from the street dealer,' has followed his ideas to the logical conclusion. . . . But there is a fundamental difference in the kind of corruption that appalls me when people ignore it. It's scary."

Scary?

"Scary when any society loses all sense of comparative decency. What's the moment between Pollard giving secrets to the Israelis because he is intense in believing in Zionism and the moment when he takes the money for it? What's the difference? What's the difference, when you take the insider-trading cases, between the time when a guy says, 'I need this to keep my portfolio up for the office,' and the moment when he goes into business as a tipster for Boesky? . . . There is a difference. I can't say what it is, but there is a difference. And what fascinates me is, why doesn't anyone know the difference? I mean, were there some high tribunal to judge the sins of journalists, I can assure you that there would be a number of things that I'd have to say: 'Well, okay, I did it; I thought it was right at the time.' But how can anybody think that selling crack on the street is right at the time?"

And, speaking of investment bankers and crack dealers—I ask Kempton about a column he'd written a few days earlier in which he took Mario Cuomo to task for a speech he delivered to a group of investment bankers. Cuomo's flattering platitudes, Kempton said, failed to hold their feet to the fire or even take note of the current scandals.

Kempton says Cuomo called him up to protest that column: "He was complaining that I didn't give his investment speech enough credit. . . . I get postcards from him all the time saying, 'I'm glad to have you around to straighten me out or to tell me what I ought to do.' But then he goes back and does the same thing the next day. He just doesn't understand."

What is it he doesn't understand?

"Well, I vastly like him . . . but I have a theory that the trouble with America is we don't have a Whig party. When we made the president of the United States king, in some curious way . . . if everybody was open to running for king . . . the job [that] people closed off was the opposition. I mean, if you could be king, why belong to the opposition? So no one in America has ever understood, in my lifetime, at least, the role of the permanent opposition. If you take Burke and Fox, neither of them could ever be king; consequently they were able to carve out a position. They managed to make this position of being the voice of reproach, what the Whigs used to call 'the good old cause.' If Cuomo decides not to run for president, then the other job open to him is to represent the good old cause. . . . Cuomo doesn't understand that. He doesn't know the specific. . . . And you've got to get off abstractions; you've got to think about people. The greatness of Burke was that whenever he was abstract, he was always shit. Whenever he was concrete and talked about real toads in real gardens, he was wonderful. Cuomo doesn't understand that. You could go through your life, you can end up—if you understand the idea of opposition, you can be Norman Thomas. Is that so bad? You're not president of the United States. A few people will remember you for what you were. He doesn't understand that."

An example of the kind of real toads in real gardens Kempton feels Cuomo fails to understand is the Mary Beth Whitehead case.* Kempton was, I believe, the first reporter to publish the actual details of the Whitehead contract—the mandatory abortion requirement and other barbarities. He's been witheringly scornful of the way the natural mother has been treated by the courts and the lawyers for the Sterns because of her inferior-class background.

"Cuomo is so messed up," Kempton says, "with getting perfectly ready to walk down in St. Patrick's Cathedral and nail up the ninety-five theses on the wall that he doesn't understand that's not what it's about. . . . One of my few virtues is that I find something totally fascinating every three weeks, but this happens to be it. And Cuomo doesn't know, he doesn't react. I talked to him

---

*Whitehead was the surrogate mother who decided she wanted to keep her child, rather than give it to the parents who contracted for it.

on the telephone yesterday and he was kind of complaining. And I said to him, 'Do you understand that to you the Catholic Church is as bad as it is to Jerry Falwell?' I mean, you know, every now and then they're *right*. And this was what Cuomo could be talking about. I mean, he talks about values and why the four children committed suicide in New Jersey. . . . I'm angry with him; I'm sorry to say it. I'm very angry at him because I think he should understand these things and say them. . . . If a politician is not campaigning for something, then I think we ought to ask him to talk about choices that a society might make, and he's not doing that."

I ask Kempton, as a connoisseur of scoundrels, what he thinks of the city's chief scourge of scoundrels, Rudy Giuliani.

"I think he's a bigot."

A bigot?

"A bigot. I don't mean he hates Jews, Negroes, or Italians. I mean, bigotry is the feeling that people need to be hounded off the face of the earth. You can be a bigot if you're a liberal and you're talking about the Republican leader of the House of Representatives. Bigotry is not prejudice; it's a commitment to erase from the face of the earth people that you don't happen to like."

He cites Giuliani's most recent series of indictments (of Bronx congressman Mario Biaggi, and Brooklyn boss Meade Esposito, and of Bronx Borough President Stanley Simon) as examples of prosecutorial zealotry exceeding the bounds of reason.

"Stanley Simon . . . strikes me as the American Dreyfus," he says, laughing. "These aren't scandals. You know, Manes is a scandal, Stanley Friedman is a scandal . . . but a guy getting a job for his brother-in-law?"

Among current corruption prosecutors, a breed of whom he's evidently not too fond, Kempton expresses a marginal preference for Brooklyn's Diane Giacalone, John Gotti's prosecutor.

"When I first met her, she said to me, 'Are you going to compare me with Robespierre?' So I said, 'What do you mean?' And she said, 'When you called Rudy Giuliani "a sea-green incorruptible." ' Now, what fascinated me was, how did she know where that came from? I mean, this is a city of eight million people. There could be no more than twenty who ever read all the way through Thomas Carlyle's *French Revolution,* which, by the way, is the most wonderful book I've read in years. Anyway, she knew where this remark came from. . . . Now, if you say to Giacalone, 'I think the witness you've served up is absolutely repellent to every civilized man,' she will say to you, 'All right, but where else can I get a witness?' But if you say to Giuliani—I remember, he said to me during the Friedman trial, 'What did you think of Lindenauer?' And I said he was so awful that I had been saving a line for ten years, and that was, 'I have read Louis-Ferdinand Céline and I have communed with Roy

Cohn and I will say to you that he is the worst ambulant creature that I have ever seen. Period.' Now, I'm not proud of that line because it's stolen from Disraeli, who said of somebody, 'I have known Bulwer-Lytton and I have read Cicero and I will tell you that he is the most conceited man I have ever known.' Giuliani said to me, 'How could you say that? He [Lindenauer] is very sorry for what he did.' Now I'll give Giacalone one credit. She knew these guys weren't the *least* bit sorry for what they did. They were in a jam; they turned in their friends. But Giuliani *believes* this, he really does believe in the shriven soul, in the penitent. Such men pile the faggots under the feet of anybody who comes into their path."

Would you say he's an example of someone who follows his ideas to their logical conclusion?

"He's 'a sea-green incorruptible,' " Kempton says, returning to Carlyle's phrase for Robespierre. "I just don't like him. I don't like his pale face, his pale eyes. And I don't like him. I don't think anybody goes to glory if Giuliani wins a case."

Since Kempton is quoting historians, I decide to ask him if I was right in thinking Gibbon was his stylistic, if not conceptual, model. "I don't write like Gibbon," he says. "The models that move me most—the prose that touches me most is not eighteenth-century prose but seventeenth-century prose. I mean, it would be ridiculous to say that Clarendon's *History of the Rebellion* is better written than *The Decline and Fall of the Roman Empire*. Well, nothing is better written than *The Decline and Fall,* except possibly Gibbon's autobiography. But there is a line in Clarendon that I don't think Gibbon could have written, and it does define what I would like to do. Do you know anything about Clarendon?"

I confess my ignorance and Kempton fills me in on Clarendon, a man who, in the course of shifting allegiance during the civil wars of the mid-seventeenth century, unfailingly chose the losing side.

"He was a man named Edward Hyde who went into exile in opposition to Cromwell. Then he became lord chancellor for Charles II after the Restoration, and he became Lord Clarendon, and then Charles II couldn't stand him anymore and he threw him out. He was always on the losing side, but he was a towering spirit. I once called [William F.] Buckley because he had this great connection with [publisher] Henry Regnery. And I said, 'You know what I'd like to do? I'd like to spend about six months and do a series of books that were histories of revolutions by the losers. Well, my losers. I mean de Tocqueville in 1848, that's a loser. And one was Clarendon.' And Bill said, 'I've never heard of Clarendon.' "

Kempton returns to the lines in Clarendon that he found most resonant with his own work.

"There are two lines in it that I've never forgotten, that stuck in my mind. In the introduction to his book, he said that his purpose was 'to appeal, if not to the conscience, at least to the curiosity of mankind.' And I thought that's what I'd like to do."

And what was the other line from Clarendon he found so memorable?

"There was one sentence in which he said, 'There is the whole finger of God in these events.' Now, you know Gibbon wouldn't have done that. I mean, Gibbon, you know—what's the point of *The Decline and Fall* except that people who act as though there were such a thing as God are out of their fucking minds? Which is why I like the seventeenth century. I mean, the idea of 'the whole finger of God,' the idea of finding the finger of God in events."

Kempton makes himself sound like a lapsed Episcopalian ("I haven't been in a state of grace for many years" is the way he puts it), but every so often in his columns, the faith makes itself felt.* When he spoke of the finger of God, I immediately thought of an uncharacteristically direct example of this: Kempton's column last spring about Bishop Tutu. It's one of the most simple and powerful pieces of inspirational prose I can recall reading, daringly naked in its soul-baring emotional appeal. I remember beginning to read it on the West Fourth Street subway platform and finding, by the time I finished, my eyes blurred so much I couldn't tell if the incoming local was the K or the E. I tore it out and have carried a yellowing copy of it around with me for nearly a year now.

When I ask Kempton about that column, he dismisses it as nothing special. And on the surface, its subject is slight. Its subject is Bishop Tutu's silliness; at least, it begins with that.

"The most touching thing about Tutu to me is that he is so ridiculous," Kempton tells me. "He is probably the most ridiculous great man I have ever seen. I mean, he's a dithering Anglican bishop from *Masterpiece Theatre*. I mean, you expect whenever you see him to have Alistair Cooke explain to you that this curious sort of phenomenon existed in *Barchester Towers* at one particular point. The giggling that goes on. And that's what makes him so moving."

Somehow Kempton's column manages to capture the silliness and the heroism, and the fulcrum of it is his evocation of the power of fear.

He quotes Tutu telling his Wall Street congregants: "God has set His church, weak, and vulnerable, and fragile as we are, between South Africa and disaster. . . . 'Ha, ha,' God has said to us, 'you guys in South Africa are going to help Me liberate South Africa.' "

"Man's recent history," Kempton writes, "however otherwise graceless, has

---

*In fact, despite his misleading modesty about his state of grace, in the last decade of his life (he died in 1997) he was a faithful churchgoer.

been wonderfully graced by churchmen—by the homely Tutu in Cape Town, majestic Wyszynski in Poland, the subtle Sin in Manila, the murdered Romero in San Salvador, each interposing in his different fashion the reproach of eternal good to transient evil."

And then, two paragraphs later, Kempton does something I've never seen him do before. He shifts abruptly from prose to a kind of heightened preaching. The text of his sermon is fear.

The lives of these churchmen, he writes,

instruct us to cast away fear. . . .

Fear is the infection that sets us ravening and quavering.

It is to the god Fear that we bow down when we pop pills or drink ourselves numb . . . and yes, when we worship the gun.

And Desmond Tutu travels about, not so much defying, as laughing and almost dancing in the shadows of his peril.

No guards surround him, no guns shield him, he is naked to every wind and missile of malice; and he tells pawky little Episcopal jokes and chuckles while he implores. . . .

Lives like his are our redemption, not because they make us holy . . . but because they can teach us to be unafraid.

When I ask Kempton what was responsible for this uncharacteristically direct and heartfelt inspirational shift, he tries to dismiss it.

"I don't know. Maybe I had nothing to write that day and I was straining. . . . There's always a moment when you get into the middle of a piece that is explained not so much by divine inspiration but the fact that you've run out of quotes from the other guy."

Yes, that's true, but it is also at those moments that—with the mask of the quotes from "the other guy" removed—the true face of the self may be most truly revealed. The Episcopal Church lost a brilliant inspirational preacher when Kempton fell from grace to become a newspaper writer.

For he is capable of seeing in the meanest of human impulses the fingerprint, if not the finger, of God. For me, the most inspirational moment in my conversation with Kempton came at the very end of dinner, his response to my final question to him. The subject was the perennial American tragedy of race and its most recent manifestation in Howard Beach.*

I ask Kempton if he is gloomy about the future of race relations in the city, and he invokes Menachem Begin as a source of inspiration on the subject.

"I've always been gloomy, I think, about what I guess I would call the fail-

*The predominantly white neighborhood in Queens where a bat-wielding gang of white youths chased a black teenager onto a highway, where a car struck and killed him.

ure of the sense of community. You know it's very strange. . . . If you can get this into the piece, it's the only wisdom I've learned. . . . There's only one man I've ever met in the course of my entire existence who I thought had a very clear sense of what a community means, and that was Menachem Begin, whose feeling was, if you're Jewish, there's nothing that you don't deserve—whether you're Sephardic or Ashkenazi, it makes no difference. . . . If you're Jewish it's enough. . . . Now, granted, he didn't extend this view to all humanity. But to begin by saying, 'If you're Jewish it is enough,' is something. And the thing that—I wouldn't say it breaks my heart, but certainly *abrades* it considerably—is that with all our quarrels in the United States, nobody ever says, 'If you're American, nothing is too good for you.' . . . Very few of us understand it. Very few of us understand that Michael Griffith [the Howard Beach murder victim] . . . standing in that place was someone to whom, as an American, we owed something. . . . I guess maybe there's something about being Southern and race that goes to that. It is always a feeling inside, awful as it was, that we're all Southerners. . . . There was a sense of recognition, if you were both lost in the North together that—colored guy or yourself—you were both Southerners. It's insular and it's regional, but I don't think you can have a sense of brotherhood and humanity unless you first have a sense of insularity."

God's Fillin' Teeth!

In Which We Watch a Dental Faith Healer
Prospect for Gold

*Exclusive! 9 p.m. Sat.: Rev. Willard Fuller, spiritual healer credited with
25,000 dental healings such as poisonous silver-mercury fillings changing
to gold, new teeth growing in, cavities filled, crooked teeth straightening,
etc. Open-ended lecture and healing session. Separate admission $10.*
—flyer announcing the 1981 Health/Nutrition Victory Conference

Will God fill teeth tonight in the banquet room of the Howard Johnson Motor
Lodge here in Crystal City, Virginia? Will He turn dirty gray fillings to gold?
Will it happen to me? Will I get a "mouthful of miracles" when the Reverend
Willard Fuller, dental faith healer, grabs my jaw and prays for my dental
needs?

An excited crowd is surging up against the as-yet-unopened doors of
HoJo's banquet room, anxious not to be shut out when the divine dental fire-
works begin. Most of them are middle-aged and middle-class and—from the
way so many of them nervously touch their jaws—victims of a lifetime of
dental sorrows. Many of them have been attending the weekend Health/Nutri-
tion Victory Conference at HoJo's, sponsored by the Arlin J. Brown Information Center, a Virginia-based clearinghouse for "unorthodox" healing
methods. The Reverend Fuller is the conference's Saturday-night headliner.

Before we go any further, let me assure you that this Reverend Fuller fellow is a real person. He is not a character out of some Southern Gothic comic
novel; he is not—intentionally—a satirist of the spiritual-healing profession.

He is, in fact, a growing sensation on the healing circuit, electrifying gatherings of both old-time religionists and New Age holistic-health worshipers with dental miracles. He could be the next Oral (!) Roberts.

Already, there's an entire book about his "dental ministry" (entitled *Can God Fill Teeth?*), admiring chapters about his mouth miracles in two other books, articles in *Fate* magazine and the *National Examiner.* From his Jacksonville base, the sixty-five-year-old Reverend Fuller travels the land, bringing his message—"The Lord's out there fillin' teeth"—to scores of dentally troubled gatherings each year.

Clearly—whether you believe in miracles or not—the Reverend Fuller is a phenomenon to be reckoned with. Because, if the Lord is not fillin' teeth at the Reverend Fuller's dental revival meetings, something is going on that's causing large groups of people to *think* He is. And so, if the Reverend Fuller is not a divinely sanctioned healer, he is—at least—an extraordinary master illusionist or a mass hypnotist of some stature. Or, perhaps, a monumentally self-deluded, God-crazed fanatic with an amazing amount of courage. Yes, courage. To go before group after group of people, tell them that you're going to pray for them and God will fill their dental needs, and then have *nothing* happen takes guts. I felt somehow *something* would happen tonight.

Just a few hours before the Reverend Fuller takes the stage in HoJo's banquet room, he's up here in my motel room, trying to explain to me the many mysteries of his dental ministry.

The mystery of "God's gold," for instance: the divine dental substance that is said to suddenly flower in fillings after the Reverend Fuller has touched and blessed a cavity-plagued jaw. In one of the glowing profiles of him that the Reverend Fuller had referred me to, he is quoted as saying, "Professional men all report that even though it looks like gold or silver, it is a metal unlike anything known to science today."

This afternoon, however, he tells me that "we've had metallurgist reports, and they say that the gold is the purest form of gold that they find in use."

Is it possible? Could I be sitting in the presence of a man to whom God has given the gift so long dreamed of throughout the ages—the power of the Philosopher's Stone to transmute base metals into gold? Was the Reverend Fuller the punch line of some divine joke on sages from Pythagoras to Newton who had sought to enrich themselves with such a power? Sure the power exists, the Lord is chuckling, *but it only works in rotten teeth.*

Many are the mysteries of the Reverend Fuller's dental ministry, not the least of which is his ability to accomplish healings through the mail. He consented to this interview only on the condition that I print his mailing address in Jacksonville, Florida (Post Office Box 16131); so that even if I turned out to be a skeptic (or, worse, a spy for his dental-establishment enemies), believers would still be able to send to him for a mouthful of miracles through the mail. He asks no payment for these mail-order miracles.

"I get their letters describing their dental needs, and pray for them, and miracles happen," he says with a shrug. "I am not a healer. I pray for people in the name of Jesus, and God does the healing."

The Reverend Fuller seems to be an intelligent fellow possessed of all the usual faculties (in addition to graduating from a Baptist seminary, he's got a degree in electrical engineering to his credit), and he's not unaware that, by proclaiming "God's fillin' teeth" at gatherings, he's inviting doubt from even the devout.

In fact, the Reverend Fuller confides, the fear of ridicule is a factor that has kept more dental healers from emerging in America. There are other dental healers abroad in the land—or at least people with the potential to do it—but many are afraid to come out and declare their dental gifts, because, the Reverend Fuller says, "they're afraid people will be saying, 'Who's this nut runnin' around sayin' God's fillin' teeth?' "

At first even the Reverend Fuller "lacked the necessary courage" to do the dental work for which he was gifted. The holy cavity-filling mission was thrust upon Fuller, he says, by a kind of dental-healing John the Baptist who came before him.

It happened back in 1960 down in Shreveport, Louisiana. Then, the Reverend Fuller was just beginning to develop his gifts as a Pentecostal-type healer. He'd do grave illnesses—cancers, ulcers, failed sight, you name it— but no one ever asked him to "call upon the Lord for dental needs." But on that fateful day in Shreveport, Fuller attended a healing session hosted by the Reverend A. C. McKaig, who, alone among men, had the conviction to publicly pray for dental miracles.

Well, the instant McKaig laid his hands on Fuller, something happened. According to Fuller, the Holy Ghost began speaking through McKaig, addressing himself directly to Fuller on the subject of dental healing: *"Think it not strange, my son,"* Fuller recalls God telling him, *"that I do these things* [dental healings] *through my servant* [McKaig]. *Because all the things thou hast seen me do through him, I shall do through thee, and greater things shall I do through thee than thou hast seen me do through him."*

Think it not strange, indeed. Sure, we are a nation peculiarly plagued by plaque panic, decay distress, drill phobias, and other dental fears, and, yes, it's a wonder that someone hasn't come forward before to minister to the torment that afflicts our teeth. But, still, sitting here with a man credited with 30,000 dental healings is *strange.* After all, why teeth? Why, with all the suffering, wounded, weeping people in the world, is God doing all this dental work?

"Oh, man, I've been trying to figure it out for twenty-one years now," the Reverend Fuller tells me. "It's still bewildering to me why it happens."

Yet, he has a tentative theory. You might call it the Theory of Testimonial Drama or God's Guerrilla Theater. "Something visible has an effect on you," he explains. "I mean, you'll see it tonight—people get excited about it."

It's true that with other well-known, heavily televised healers, all you see are the supplicants getting touched, falling back in a faint, then rising up and declaring themselves cured. We have to take their word for it that they were really blind or crippled before they "got healed." But with the Reverend Fuller's dental miracles, you don't have to believe what people *say;* you *see* silver turn to gold right before your eyes, he claims.

"After all, if you look with your eyes on the handiwork of God, it's got to have some effect on you," says the Reverend Fuller. "I've had people who have come to me sayin', 'I have nothing particularly wrong, but I have no gold in my mouth.' Then I say, 'Lemme take a look in there,' and there's two gold fillin's, five gold fillin's. They get amazed."

This kind of miracle is what has the Reverend Fuller speculating on God's sense of showmanship in some of His dental work: "Possibly what's happenin' is that someone will have a deteriorating fillin' that needs to be repaired. If God were to repair it to exactly the same shape it was in the beginning, that person might not even know it was changed. Wouldn't have anything to show someone else. So I find that, many times when God repairs a fillin', he'll change the substance from silver to gold, gold to porcelain, or sometimes a whole new tooth. So, when a fillin' changes, it must be for testimonial effect. If you yourself never had gold in your mouth, and you get in line tonight, and I pray for you, and you get a gold fillin', you'll have something to talk about."

In fact, I don't have any gold in my mouth at the moment, I disclose to the Reverend Fuller. "Okay, I'll go for the gold tonight," I tell him. "Will I be able to see it happen?"

"We've never had a failure," he tells me. "We've never had a meeting where it didn't happen for someone."

A mixture of nervous anticipation and uneasiness fills the air of HoJo's banquet room as the Reverend Fuller takes the stage. Close to 150 dentally troubled souls fill the rows of folding chairs that face him. They've come from up and down the East Coast, some from as far away as San Antonio, to get their gums blessed tonight.

Most of them are not Holy Roller types, for whom miracle services are a matter of course. Many of them are from the various holistic and New Age health-worship sects; some are far-right-wing "unorthodox cancer-cure" crusaders; others are cynical but dentally tormented souls who have allowed themselves to be dragged here by friends or family members because they're desperate enough to try anything.

Bestriding the stage in a lustrous blue suit, silver hair ashimmer in the bright glare of the banquet room, the six-feet-four Reverend Fuller is a formidable presence and, it turns out, a dynamite performer. In forty minutes, he has the entire room, skeptics and believers alike, rising en masse and shouting out, "I BELIEVE GOD FILLS TEETH!"

How does he do it? No Holy Roller hysterics, no Marjoe-like emotional manipulations. No, he starts off quietly telling us the tale of "How I Got the Power," entrancing us with the sheer storybook enchantment of a Strange Gift saga. Magic beans, X-ray eyes, you name it. Everybody loves to fantasize about what would happen if somehow someone gave him one weird power.

The Reverend Fuller skillfully disarms us of our disbelief by inviting us to share in his own incredulity when he had first heard about his mentor, McKaig: "People said he prayed for them, and God filled their teeth and met their dental needs. *I had to see that.*"

For weeks after his Shreveport anointing, he tells us, he was afraid to try out his prophesied power for fear of ridicule and failure. Finally, a man he cured of a bleeding ulcer at one of his prayer meetings—this kind of healing was no sweat for him, he assures us—reappeared the next night and challenged the Reverend Fuller. He had a bad tooth, and if God could heal his stomach, what was to prevent Him from taking care of a man's teeth?

Well, there it is. Twenty years and 30,000 dental healings later, the logic is unchallengeable: If you believe in a God who created heaven and earth, mountains and molars, it's impossible to deny He has the ability to fill teeth. You could argue with His priorities (what's He gonna spring on us next, faith-healing podiatrists?), but who can question His powers?

Building upon this unshakable foundation of faith, the Reverend Fuller begins to fire up the temperature of his dental-healing discourse. He takes off his jacket and begins "braggin' on the Lord," as he calls it, telling tale after astonishing tale of miracles wrought in the mouths of those whose jaw He touched. There is the seventy-year-old grandmother who kept complaining about increasing pain underneath her dentures. Says the Reverend Fuller: "She takes those dentures out one morning and finds she's cuttin' new teeth like a baby."

Then there is the woman who was walking by her local Kresge's a few days after a Reverend Fuller session. "She looks in a mirror in the window, and that tooth that troubled her just filled right up before her eyes."

Now the Reverend Fuller is heading into the homestretch of this prehealing psych-up. He goes off on a dizzying little diversion into scientific mysticism—all matter is just patterns of energy, energy is spirit, and with the power of spirit we can rearrange the polarities of molecular spin—but he's got the whole room with him now, everybody buoyed up by his energy as he sweeps us into rhythmic responses to his heated challenges:

"Do you believe in God?"

"YES!"

"Let me hear you. DO YOU BELIEVE IN GOD?"

"YES!"

"Do you believe all things are possible with God?"

"YES!"

"Do you believe God can fill teeth?"

"YES!!"

"Stand up and say it now, say 'I believe God can fill teeth.' "

Everybody in the room rises. "I BELIEVE GOD CAN FILL TEETH."

"Say it louder," the Reverend Fuller commands.

"I BELIEVE GOD CAN FILL TEETH!"

"I think it's time," the Reverend Fuller says. "I think it's time to call upon the spirit."

He lines us up row by row, and we proceed to pass before him. As each of us pauses in front of him, he leans down from the stage, quickly cups the proffered jaw with his hand and prays, "In the name of Jesus, be thou every whit whole."

He says it fast, he says it nearly two hundred times in one uninterrupted mantralike intonation. It is an impressive vocal achievement, especially since, the Reverend Fuller says, he had to conquer a crippling stutter as a child. There is no fainting or shrieking. None of the hysterical swooning and twitching that are the trademark special effects of TV healers like Ernest Angley. I personally feel nothing special, not even a tingle in my jaw, as I return to my seat. And neither, judging from the looks of quiet bewilderment on the faces of many in the room, does anyone else feel anything special.

So here we are: a roomful of people sitting around with mouths closed, secretly running our tongues over our teeth to see if anything new has made its presence felt. There are sidelong glances to see if miracles might be flashing from nearby mouths. Finally, there are a few people opening up and checking out one another's mouths. My wife, Caroline, and I also do this and find that nothing has changed.

Nor does anyone else shout "Eureka!" or "Gold!" Perhaps, I think, my expectations have been raised too high by a chapter about the Reverend Fuller in a paperback called *Psychic Healers* that recounts many noisy and showy miracles: new teeth exploding into existence with "the sound of popcorn popping"; a "golden beam of light" focusing on the mouth and turning a silver filling to gold. No popcorn, no gold beams tonight in HoJo's banquet room. And—*wait just a minute here*—no Reverend Fuller anymore.

He'd said something about "going to get a flashlight" and then wandered off somewhere. Suddenly, a blinding flash of paranoia and anger seizes me. The whole thing has been a hoax, a joke perpetrated by an antireligious prankster preying on the prayerful. He's probably just slipped off into the night, chuckling gleefully to himself at the gullible gums left behind.

I am just beginning to appreciate the satiric genius of the stunt when the Reverend Fuller reappears from the side of the stage with a black briefcase and a solemn expression. Extracting a silvery flashlight, a long-handled dental mirror and a small pocket-size vanity mirror, he proceeds to lead us into the final phase of the healing session—prospecting for God's miraculous gold.

"I have here a flashlight. An ordinary flashlight," he says, brandishing an ordinary-looking flashlight. "I bought it at Parsons Optical Company in San Francisco. The reason I talk about it in this detail is there are those who say these are tricks. Gimmicks. Trickery. That inside the little lens, the man has a little gold spot, and that makes it look like there's a gold fillin' in the tooth. Now take a look at this," he says.

Next, he displays his long-handled dental mirror. "People have said there's a long tube in here filled with putty, and that I somehow inject it into a tooth when I'm looking in your mouth." He goes on to reassure us about the innocence of the simple hand mirror he also carries and the beaker of sterilizing solution borne by his attractive young wife.

Then, he points to someone, a woman just a few rows ahead of me. He comes down from the stage followed by his beaker-bearing wife. He asks the woman what she's asked from God tonight. She tells him about a facial tumor she has, and about a broken tooth. He asks her to open her mouth. He shines his flashlight in there, he pokes around with the dental mirror. He holds up the hand mirror at mouth level so that it reflects to her eyes what appears in the dental mirror.

THE REVEREND FULLER: Tell me, how much gold do you have in your mouth? No gold. I'm asking the lady what kind of work's been done. I asked her if she had any gold in there. She said no. Everybody knows if they've had the gold—they can feel it in their wallets. The reason I ask that question is that many times, I'm finding that people who have a need for a repair in a filling, well, if God fixed it back just like it was, why the person might not even know; they certainly couldn't show anybody else, so I find that many times, as the repair work's begun, the substance will change. Let me take a look. Yes, you've had a lot of work in there—that's the one that broke off, and that buddy is still broken off. Now, let's take a look. Amalgams—dark composition material—that's just about as it was. But now, on second thought—second sight, you might say—look in my mirror, and we see *a white spot.* Are you able to see? At the place where it's broken off. A white spot. Now, there's one on the other side. There're two of them.

WOMAN: That was never there. . . . I'm getting nervous.

FULLER: Many times this is the way they fill. They begin to fill from the sides. We look at a cavity, and it's a dark hole, and then white begins to appear, and it'll just keep on growin'. Now, down in here, we have one that's a different color.

WOMAN: Huh.

FULLER: See, this is the color of silver, and this is the color of this one.

WOMAN: *It's turning gold!*

FULLER: Well, praise the Lord.

WOMAN: It's getting brighter!

She clutches her mouth and shrieks. A crowd pushes around her. All of them, including my wife, see the gold. By the time I reach the woman, the Reverend Fuller has passed on to prospect for the next miracle with his flashlights and mirrors. The woman looks pale, almost in shock.

Was she a ringer? I got her phone number and called her up a month later. Surely by then, I thought, any flashlight, mirror tricks, or mass hypnosis that might have produced the gold that night would have worn off. But, as she told me, "the tooth's still gold."

Her name is Marjorie Bamont, she lives in Philadelphia, and she'd come down to Virginia at the urging of her sister, who, unlike her, was a believer in spiritual healing. "I had an open mind," she said, "but no idea something like this could happen."

She told me that she "did feel something from his hands" when the Reverend Fuller touched her. "It was like a shaking-type thing going through me—a vibration—on the tooth that was chipped," Mrs. Bamont said. "It did feel like it was coming up and up, but I did have it fixed at the dentist before my operation."

But, I asked her again, the gold tooth is still there?

"Yes, the one on the bottom is the one that's still gold. Not a *brilliant* brilliant gold, but that's the one."

Do the nonbelievers in her family see it too?

"My son says it's a trick, that he sprayed something in my mouth. But I would have felt it if he sprayed something."

The second "miracle" is even stranger than the first. Another curious manifestation of God's metal, this time a delicate rivulet of gleaming gold inlay appearing in the back teeth of a Maryland gentleman on the right side of the banquet room.

Once again, the Reverend Fuller has singled him out, manipulated the two mirrors to give him a look. Unlike Mrs. Bamont, who seemed frightened by the dental metamorphosis, this man looks pleased as punch. After the commotion around him subsides and the Reverend Fuller moves on to other examinations, he is smiling and opening wide to give everybody a good look. At last, I get my first glimpse of God's gold.

This particular manifestation of gold is especially dramatic: The lower-right back teeth have a thin, dirty gray river of dental amalgam running down the center between the cusps; the lower-left back teeth have a similarly shaped rivulet, but it is a gleaming ribbon of what appears to be freshly poured gold.

"You didn't have any gold in your mouth before tonight?" I ask the man.

"No," he says. "No gold before now."

I took his phone number and called him a month later. "It's still there, still gold," he reported. His name is Aubrey Patterson, and he's an aerial photographer. He wasn't completely surprised by the appearance of the phenomenon. He thought it was "a psychic manifestation" somehow summoned up by the Reverend Fuller. "Not an illusion, though?" I repeated. "It's really gold on one side and gray on the other?"

"That's right," he confirmed.

Not everyone gets God's gold. Many show no visible change. To them, the Reverend Fuller gives reassurance that healings often happen gradually, overnight, even days after the meeting. He also dispenses homespun advice on preventive dental care, on brushing the gums back into health with baking soda and salt solutions—general dental encouragement. He finally gets around to checking out my mouth with his flashlight but finds nothing unusual.

It takes a while before the final miracle of the night occurs. The banquet room has almost emptied when I come upon him, the man with the brass-bullet teeth.

The strange thing about this case of God's dental work is that it is . . . well, so crude, so amateurish and temporary-looking. But here is a man with three brass-colored fittings on his upper-right bicuspids, a trio he claims didn't exist before tonight. He is a Philadelphia business executive, and he didn't know what to make of what happened. (I was unable to reach him later for a checkup.)

Well, that's all I have to report. Frankly, I'm mystified by the whole thing on several levels. Was I witness to three miracles that night in Crystal City? I don't think it was a joke. I don't think the people I spoke to were ringers. Some kind of mass hypnosis, a long-lasting magic trick? Perhaps. I just don't know.

Yet, if they were genuine miracles, I think there's a deeper and more disturbing question: Just what is God doing filling teeth in a HoJo's banquet room when there are bellies to fill in Bangladesh? I think He owes us an explanation. The only one I can think of is the one offered in Stanley Elkin's remarkable novel of life in Hell, *The Living End.* At the end of *The Living End,* Elkin's tormented hero finally gets to confront God and ask Him to explain His behavior: why He lets people suffer, why history seems so madly unjust, why human life is so weird *"Because,"* Elkin's God answers, *"it makes a better story."*

Postscript to "God's Fillin' Teeth!"

Recently, I checked with CSICOP (the Committee for the Scientific Investigation of Claims of the Paranormal), publisher of the valuable magazine *The Skeptical Inquirer,* which devotes itself to exposing claims of supernatural powers. I'm not an absolute skeptic myself, but I believe rigorous investigative skepticism can clear away false claims and suggest what the truly interesting unsolved mysteries—such as why there is Something rather than Nothing at all in the Universe—are. Anyway, CSICOP (think of them as the real X-Files unit) sent me a thick file on the "Lively Stones" ministry, as Rev. Fuller had taken to calling his dental healing crusade. It appears for a while he'd taken his show international, got into some trouble in Australia in the mid-eighties for advertising himself as a "psychic dentist," then seemed to have allied himself with New Age types, to the consternation of anti-cult Christians.

The CSICOP spokesman told me they'd tried to explain why people seemed to see gleaming new dental work in their mouths. Often, he said, people forget where they have fillings; often, the gleam comes from the light shining on otherwise occluded metal in the mouth; sometimes the "gold" turned out to be tobacco stains. Plus, he added, some people don't need much encouragement to want to think they have a miracle in their mouth. As I observed in my investigation of the cancer-cure subculture, "false hope springs eternal." So, too, it seems, do false teeth.

Turn On, Tune In, Drop Dead

In Which We Look into Elisabeth Kübler-Ross's
Torrid Love Affair with Death

The curious tale of the Queen of Death and the lustful "entities" of Escondido
is one of those little disturbances of man you may have missed if you haven't
been tuned in to developments in the fast-growing "death awareness" movement. The scandal that developed over the erotic escapades of the "entities"
represented a serious image crisis for the movement. Defenders of death
awareness feel that the incident is merely an aberration being used unfairly by
the medical establishment and its pawns in the press—servile minions of the
"cure-oriented," "interventionist," "high-technology life-prolonging" old
regime—to discredit the work of the dedicated devotees of death and dying.
But a case can be made that intercourse with entities—okay, let's call it sex
with the dead—is not an aberration but a summation, a consummation, of the
whole misbegotten love affair with death that the movement has been promoting.

The Queen of Death, of course, is Dr. Elisabeth Kübler-Ross, who reigns over
a mountaintop "Death-and-Dying Center" in Escondido, California, whose
work single-handedly created the death-and-dying movement, and who, until
recently, endowed it with respectability.

Author of *On Death and Dying, Living with Death and Dying, Questions and Answers on Death and Dying,* and *Death: The Final Stage of Growth,* recipient of twenty honorary degrees, Kübler-Ross is now taught, in her estimation, in 125,000 death-and-dying courses in colleges, seminaries, medical schools, hospitals, and social-work institutions. She has come to be regarded as the last word on death. Not only do "death professionals"—hospital and hospice workers, clergymen, and psychiatrists—get their basic training from Kübler-Ross in order to counsel the dying, but her books are so widespread that most people who *die* these days are familiar with her "five stages of dying."

Kübler-Ross's thought has given birth to whole new academic industries—"thanatology" and "dolorology"—helped create the hospice movement, "Conscious Dying Centers," and, more recently, an increasingly cultlike exaltation, sentimentalization, and even worship of death.

In the past, like most sensible people, I've been content to leave strenuous thinking about death in the capable hands of others. Somehow I assumed from all the acclaim from varied quarters that Kübler-Ross couldn't be *too* foolish, assumed that she embodied the typical post-Enlightenment secular consensus on the subject: awareness of death giving an urgency and intensity to life, etc. Probably sensible, caring, and boring. But I have a feeling that we're beginning to see the consequences of not looking more closely at Kübler-Ross's "science." Because something's gone awry with the death-and-dying movement Kübler-Ross helped create. Things have gotten out of hand: Kübler-Ross herself has become the guru to a nationwide network of death 'n' dying centers called Shanti Nilaya; the Conscious Dying movement urges us to devote our life to death awareness and also opens up a "Dying Center"; a video artist kills herself on public television and calls it "artistic suicide"; the EXIT society publishes a handy, do-it-yourself Home Suicide guide that can take its place next to other recent Home Dying and Home Burial Guides; a pop science cult emerges around the "Near Death Experience," which makes dying sound like a lovely acid trip (turn on, tune in, drop dead); attempts at two-way traffic with the afterlife abound, including a courier service to the dead using dying patients and even phone calls *from* the dead; belief in reincarnation resurfaces as "past lives therapy."

Is this multifaceted flirtation with death and suicide—you could call it the Pro-Death Movement—some self-regulating, population-control mechanism surfacing as the baby-boom generation gets older, the better to thin its ranks before its numbers begin to strain nursing-home and terminal-ward facilities? And how did Kübler-Ross—saintly, respected, a *Ladies' Home Journal* "Woman of the Decade" for the 1970s—end up running a dating service for the dead in Escondido? Part of the problem may be heroin. Not Kübler-Ross's problem, but the problem in the very origins of her American death-and-dying movement. You see, Kübler-Ross and the American death-and-dying movement took their inspiration from the British "hospice" idea but neglected to import one crucial ingredient that made it work.

The hospice movement in Britain was a practical, no-nonsense alternative to the increasingly complex, painful, and isolating process of death in modern hospitals, where, in the hectic process of prolonging life with tubes and machines, patients aren't able to enjoy peace and quiet and the company of friends and relatives as they die. The British movement offered instead cozy, small "guest houses" for the terminally ill, with a sympathetic staff and medical treatment designed to ensure comfort, dignity, and alertness rather than an artificially prolonged life.

But your basic British hospice was able to offer its dying "guests" one thing American hospices could not, one thing that made these hospices more than merely pleasant places in which to expire without the aid of "high-technology life-prolonging intervention." The attraction of British hospices, the *sacrament,* in fact, that made them so popular, was the special painkilling mixture they dispensed, a potion described by some as the most powerful euphoriant experience available to the human senses: the "Brompton's Cocktail."

A combination of equal parts of pure heroin and pure cocaine, with a dash of chloroform in an alcohol-and-cherry-syrup base, Brompton's Cocktail became legendary for its ability to bliss out patients suffering from pain so intractable that no amount of mere morphine was able to subdue it.

Not surprisingly, dying hospice patients who were fortunate enough to receive the soothing sacrament were known to make all sorts of warm and endearing remarks when in its embrace; words of wisdom and spirituality and love that hospice professionals tended to attribute to the "caring and sharing" environment of their cozy death hotels, and to the visionary insights unique to the dying process, but which probably owed more to the elation and euphoria of the heroin-cocaine combo.

The problem was that while the "caring and sharing" ideas of the British movement could be imported, the drug laws in this country made it impossible to prescribe heroin for even the most terrorizing bone pain. In addition, the use of cocaine as a euphoriant is discouraged. So as a substitute for the real Brompton's Cocktail, American hospice doctors have concocted a bizarre and stunted version of that sacrament: a combination known as "Hospice Mix," which substitutes morphine for more potent heroin, and frequently uses the powerful immobilizing anti-psychotic drug Thorazine instead of cocaine.

For all their ostensible reverence for the wisdom of the dying and the integrity of the dying process, American hospices that use Thorazine in their "mix" are treating dying patients as if they were psychotics. Unable to offer their dying clients the kind of truly effective and humane pain relief available to the British, American death professionals seem to have overcompensated for this failure by subjecting their dying clients—and afflicting us all—with massive injections of sentimentality, a syrupy overdose of sanctimony about the "beauty" of the dying process, about "learning from pain," to use some typical clichés, and about the wonderful wisdom that makes dying the "final stage of growth."

In doing so, the death-and-dying people have elevated the terminally ill into a new sort of oppressed class—oppressed by "inhuman, cure-oriented" doctors who don't recognize that dying is something to be *celebrated* for its intrinsic worth rather than feared and fought. Death professionals have begun attributing to the dying all the qualities of instinctual wisdom, primitive visionary insight, spontaneous vitality, and organic closeness to the ground of being with which oppressed classes are condescendingly endowed by their more privileged supporters.

"Many Native Americans died with great clarity," declares the codirector of a group called the "Dying Project," a statement that embodies perfectly the identification of the dying with a persecuted minority and, in its lofty condescension, is not far removed in spirit from "The only good Indian is a dead Indian."

While this billing and cooing about death did not originate with Kübler-Ross—the cult of "the Beautiful Death" is a recurrent one in stagnant societies—she did come up with one concept that single-handedly revolutionized and *restructured* the worship of death in America and gave it an up-to-date "scientific" foundation: the "five stages of dying."

Dividing dying into stages was a stroke of genius. Kübler-Ross brought forth her five stages at just about the time when people were dividing life into "passages," stages, predictable crises. Getting dying properly staged would bring every last second of existence under the reign of reason. As every student of elementary thanatology soon learns, the famous five stages of dying are: denial, anger, bargaining, depression, acceptance.

What's been lost in the general approbation of Kübler-Ross's five stages is the way her ordering of those stages implicitly serves a *behavior control* function for the busy American death professional. The movement from denial and anger to depression and acceptance is seen as a kind of spiritual *progress,* as if quiet acceptance is the most mature, the highest stage to strive for.

What Kübler-Ross calls bargaining, others might call a genuine search for reasons to live, to fight for life. But she has no patience with dilly-dallying by the dying. She disparages "bargaining" that goes on too long, describes patients who don't resign themselves to death after they've gotten the extra time they bargained for as "children" who don't "keep their promises" to die.

Yet by "acceptance," Kübler-Ross means the infantilization of the dying: "It is perhaps best compared with what Bettelheim describes about early infancy," she says. "A time of passivity, an age of primary narcissism in which . . . we are going back to the stage we started out with and the circle of life is closed."

Certainly this passivity makes for a quieter, more manageable hospice. Crotchety hospice guests who quixotically refuse to accept, who persist in anger or hope, will be looked on as recalcitrant, treated as retarded in their dying process, stuck in an "immature" early stage, and made to feel that it's high time they moved on to the less troublesome stages of depression and acceptance.

Now let's look at the practical effect of this premium on passivity on an actual encounter between a dying person and a "death professional." Let's look at a little hand-printed pamphlet entitled *It's Been a Delightful Dance:* the story of Ellen Clark as told in a sermon by Dr. Richard Turner.

This is an account of the therapeutic relationship between Turner and Clark, who was dying of cancer when she approached the Cancer Project of "Life Force," Turner's therapy organization, for counseling.

The California-based Life Force was one of several holistically oriented therapy groups that specialize in what has come to be called "cancering." Turner charged forty-five dollars an hour for such counseling.

I came across Turner and his group in 1980, in the Grand Ballroom of the Ambassador Hotel in Los Angeles, at a convention of the Cancer Control Society, a national organization that supports scores of "unorthodox" and forbidden cancer "cures"—everything from apricot kernels and coffee enemas to secret-formula serums and salves. I was somewhat puzzled to find someone like Turner speaking here, since the acceptance-oriented death-and-dying rhetoric in his speech contrasted with the feverish never-say-die, last-minute, miracle-seeking emphasis of the unorthodox-cancer-cure movement. "With certain patients I've counseled it becomes clear that at some level they are ready to die," Turner told me, when I questioned him after his talk. "They've made their choice, they feel they've lived their life. There was one patient of mine who'd done the holistic cures. But as I counseled her on her dying experience, it was as if this was what she wanted, it was as if she was releasing all her barriers and becoming fully human for the first time. She turned into a living, beautiful person so that by the time she died she'd done all her life's work in her last few weeks. Her name was Ellen Clark. In fact I wrote up my experience with her in a sermon I delivered. It's in our literature."

Reading Turner's description of the progress of his therapy with the late Ellen Clark, it's impossible not to notice the influence of Kübler-Ross in the way he idealizes the progressive infantilization of the dying.

The big breakthrough that Ellen Clark achieves as she's wasting away with cancer is, according to Turner's sermon, that she "develops a childlike transparency." How does Turner deal with this in his counseling session? He's eager to encourage it, eager to "reinforce those feelings that we were like children in kindergarten." His technique for reinforcing this? He responds completely only to Ellen's "childlike," "magical" looks; even when she's trying to tell him something in adult sentences he makes sure that "only part of my attention went back to what she was saying. . . . The result was that heavy subject matter such as life and death and problem-solving progressively lost its dominance and an air of lightness pervaded our meetings."

No wonder. Dealing with an adult who's been turned into a happily compliant child is much more fun for friends and family than facing the complexities presented by a stubborn adult who's frantically fighting to live.

As in other tales in the contemporary Beautiful Death literature, an element of parasitism seems to creep into the stories told by the selfless survivors. Turner tells us that after Ellen became the "transparent child," *he* really started getting off on the sessions. He reports feeling "light and alive" after each session. "I was gaining as much from our meetings as her." (Maybe he should have been paying *her* forty-five dollars an hour for the privilege.) Ellen's friends also "reported quite consistently being touched and healed in her presence." Touched and healed: The magical powers of the dying are frequent causes for amazement in the literature.

By turning herself into an agreeable, transparent, loving child with Turner's encouragement, by refusing crankily to seek out some new cure or make a desperate gamble for her life, Ellen made it easy for people to be around her and feel loving. The message for dying patients in Turner's sermon is, to revise Dylan Thomas, "*Do* go gentle into that good night."

And then the climax of the *Delightful Dance* sermon: "The morning after I heard about Ellen's death I went out for my daily jog," Turner tells us. "A beautiful orange butterfly landed in front of my foot. I immediately felt *as if I knew this butterfly,* and apparently it had this same connection with me. . . . The butterfly and I were doing a get-acquainted dance. . . . I felt I was doing a get-acquainted dance with the butterfly within me. I feel I am ready to let go of being the caterpillar. . . . I am more ready to dance with my life. . . ."

And so, according to Turner, Ellen's pretty little death turned out to be a plus for everyone: Ellen got to be a butterfly and he got to dance during his daily jog. The whole thing sounded like a dance of death to me.

This is only the beginning, this reverence for the life-giving holiness of the compliantly childlike death object. It's a long way from there to going to bed with the dead, but the route is direct, and after reading the recent profusion of death-and-dying literature, I've divided it—in homage to Kübler-Ross—into five stages:

Stage 1: worship of the dying;
Stage 2: longing to *be* dying;
Stage 3: playing dead;
Stage 4: playing *with* the dead;
Stage 5: going to bed with the dead.

We've already seen Stage 1, with its reverence for the wisdom of the terminally ill. In Stage 2, death 'n' dying is seen to be an attractive option for healthy people. Why let the dying get all the benefits of facing death? To maximize the high of the dying experience when it comes, healthy people are urged by Stage 2 literature to devote their life to preparing for a beautiful death. Stage 2 advocates range from the Conscious Dying movement and its subsidiaries, the Dying Project and the Dying Center in New Mexico, to the "rational suicide" advocates. The London-based EXIT group is only one of several that put out practical do-it-yourself guides to painless suicide; other books tell you how to arrange the particulars of your death or burial at home. The late Jo Roman, evangelist of "creative suicide," went one step further—she did it on TV.

Stage 2 advocates tend to be the nags of the death-and-dying movement. Since we are not fortunate enough to be terminally ill, they tell us, we must make strenuous efforts to overcome our handicap by concentrating our lives on death and suicide.

It is never too early to start. "Should schoolchildren be asked to write essays on 'How I Would Feel if I Had to Die at Midnight' or compositions envisaging why and in what circumstances they propose to end their lives?" asks Mary Rose Barrington, past chairman of EXIT. "The answer may well be that they should," says Mary Rose, who, oddly enough, is also "Honorary Secretary of the Animal Rights Group." (Do they favor the right to suicide for parakeets?)

Missing out on early childhood death education is no excuse to avoid the subject now. And that means today. Tomorrow may be too late if you believe the nagging of Stephen Levine, director of the Dying Project. "Tomorrow," he points out, "could be the first day of thirty years of quadriplegia. What preparations have you made to open to an inner life so full that whatever happens can be used as a means of enriching your focus?" The first day of thirty years of quadriplegia. It's a particularly ironic formulation of the challenge because Levine and the Dying Project, and the Dying Center (where people check in to check out) are spiritual descendants of ex-Harvard professor and psychedelic pioneer Richard Alpert (now Ram Dass), and thus of a brand of spiritualism that expressed its incurable optimism with the slogan "Today is the first day of the rest of your life." Sure, but tomorrow the wheelchair and the catheter. Such a shift says something about this branch of the Pro-Death movement—either they've run out of good acid and have been dipping into the melancholy Hospice Mix, or, as they grow older, they're suddenly scared of death and afraid to admit it.

If you read Levine's testament, *Who Dies?,* a bible for the Conscious Dying movement, you begin to suspect he's trying to smother his fear of death in protestations of his devotion to it. He's constantly hectoring the reader for having failed to do his death homework: "If you should die in extreme pain how will you have prepared to keep your mind soft and open?" he scolds. "What have you done to keep your mind present, so that you don't block precious opportunity with a concept, with some idea of what's happening, open to experience the suchness, the living truth, of the next unknown moment?"

You could dismiss this scolding as mere schoolteacherish sanctimony, or life-insurance-salesman scare tactics (buy my theory of dying now or you'll be condemned to die inauthentically), but there's something more frightened and frightening in this prose. I think it comes out in the Dying Project codirector's description of the ideal Conscious Dying movement–approved death:

> I've been with people as they approached their death and seen how much clarity and openheartedness it takes to stay soft with the distraction in the mind and body, to stay with the fear that arises uninvited, to keep so open that when fear comes up they can say, "Yes, that's fear all right." But the spaciousness from which they say it is not frightened. Because the separate "I" is not the predominant experience, there's little for that fear to stick to. Clearly a useful practice would be to cultivate an openness to what is unpleasant, to acknowledge resistance and fear, to soften and open around it, to let it float free, to let it go. If you wrote down a list of your resistances and holdings, it would nearly be a sketch of your personality. If you identify with that personality as you are, you amplify the fear of death; the imagined loss of imagined individuality.

This is metaphysical heroin, a Brompton's Cocktail of the mind, the same basic anodyne for the tears of things that all Eastern cults offer: If you detach yourself and experience all passion at one numb remove, in the context of the infinitude of being, nothing hurts as much. If you go the whole route and cease being a person—that "imagined individual" Levine disparages—then you won't even die because there won't be a you to die. You'll never be a person afraid of death because you won't be a person. You'll be, instead, "the spaciousness" that is not frightened. Nonbeings can't cease being. If you make life as spacious and empty as death, you won't notice any transition between living and dying; you might as well be dead.

Which is exactly what the "creative suicide" people say. Or they might call it "CREATING ON MY OWN TERMS THE FINAL STROKE OF MY LIFE'S CANVAS," as video death artist Jo Roman wrote in her last letter to friends. ("By the time you read these lines I WILL HAVE GENTLY ENDED MY LIFE on the date of this letter's postmark," she announces with typical gentleness.)

Roman's trendsetting originality, of course, was not in her committing the act or justifying it on artistic grounds. It was in doing it so publicly. Suicide-proud self-murderers have in the past been content to have their feverish last thoughts and justifications publicized. But Jo Roman insisted on making a federal case of the act itself and the whole tearful "dying process," summoning friends and forcing them to grovel at the altar of her honesty while the videotape cameras rolled. She made the additional breakthrough of claiming for suicides the status of an oppressed *lifestyle* group in need of televised validation: "I want to share it with others in order to raise consciousness. Also, and importantly, because I am averse to demeaning myself by closeting an act which I believe deserves respect."

Of course, creative suicide is not the exclusive province of exhibitionistic video artists. There were the healthy young teenagers in Seattle, a boy and a girl, who, inspired by the transcendent optimism about the indestructibility of the soul in *Jonathan Livingston Seagull,* proceeded to get into a Pontiac and drive it at eighty miles per hour flat out into a stone wall, in order to ensure they spent eternity together.

Suicide and suicide pacts are a predictable enough consequence of the death 'n' dying movement. By romanticizing dying, by making death more "authentic" than life, suicide is made to seem an attractive, artistic, even heroic choice.

Another way of promoting the attractiveness and allure of death is through the creation of an inviting, reassuring, sugarcoated vision of the afterlife. Which brings us to Stage 3 in the development of contemporary death worship: the romance of the Near Death Experience (NDE), or playing dead.

At first the NDE seemed to be a freak, based on a few isolated reports. People who had been pronounced "clinically dead," people who "died" on the operating table, in the ambulance, or the intensive care ward, whose heart and vital functions ceased for ten, twenty minutes, would sometimes, after miraculous "resurrections," tell tales of leaving the body and traveling through a remarkable, otherworldly realm.

Aside from the *National Enquirer* ("DEAD MAN" SPEAKS!), no one paid much attention to these isolated reports until a philosophy professor named Raymond Moody compiled 150 of them into a book called *Life After Life,* which was published in 1975 with an endorsement by none other than Elisabeth Kübler-Ross, who claimed that she had been doing exactly the same kind of research and that Moody's findings duplicated hers.

The "NDE" became the semiofficial afterlife vision for the death-and-dying religion. It was appealing because it made death seem like something to look forward to. Hamlet's "undiscovered country from whose bourn no traveller returns," whose mysteries had long terrified the human imagination, now seemed, from the reports of Raymond Moody's travelers, to be about as frightening as a day trip to the Jersey shore.

Let's look at Moody's "theoretically complete model" of the life-after-life experience, which I have here divided into seven easy-to-follow steps.

1. *A streetcar named death:* Our traveler hears himself pronounced dead. Next he hears "a loud ringing or buzzing and at the same time feels himself moving very rapidly through a long dark tunnel."
2. *The fly on the wall:* "He suddenly finds himself outside of his own physical body. . . . He watches the resuscitation attempt from this unusual vantage point . . . in a state of emotional upheaval."
3. *Family reunion:* "He glimpses the spirits of relatives and friends who have already died."
4. *The heavenly customs inspector:* He meets "a loving warm spirit of a kind he has never encountered before—a being of light. . . . This being asks him a question, nonverbally, to make him evaluate his life. . . ."
5. *The highlights film:* The "being of light" helps him along by "showing him a panoramic instantaneous playback of the major events of his life."
6. *Heaven can wait:* "He finds himself approaching some sort of barrier or border apparently representing the limit between earthly life and the next life. Yet, he finds that he must go back to the earth, that the time for his death has not yet come."
7. *Deportation:* "He is taken up with his experiences in the afterlife and does not want to return. He is overwhelmed by intense feelings of joy, love, and peace. Despite his attitude," though, he's forced to rejoin the unpleasant world of the living.

Of course, it's possible that this pallid panorama of sweetness and light may actually *be* the afterlife and the ultimate riddle of existence has been solved. There are certainly millions of people who would like to believe its reassuring, nondenominational, downy-soft delights: Moody's book and his sequel *Reflections on Life After Life,* and its paperback rackmates *Life Before Life* and *Reliving Past Lives,* have all become big dime-store and drugstore bestsellers, creating a popular NDE-based cult.

The only stumbling block that prevents the NDE from becoming the center of a new popular religion for the living has been that the actual ecstatic death trip experience seemed to be restricted to those privileged few whose heart, breathing, and vital functions had ceased for a certain period, or who were fortunate enough to be nearly killed in a plane crash, car wreck, or other near-death trauma.

Enter the ever helpful Elisabeth Kübler-Ross, who not only endorsed Moody's NDE but took the NDE cult a crucial step further by staking out that bright landscape and its loving beings of light for routine visits by the living—those among the living who learned the correct way of *playing dead.*

She discovered this pastime from her own travels in that realm of bright beings, she says. Her first "out-of-body experience" came at a time when she was, if not near death, at least by her account, dead tired from several years of exhausting nonstop travel, lectures, seminars, and workshops promoting death 'n' dying awareness. Drifting off into a trancelike sleep, she says,

> I saw myself lifted out of my physical body. . . . It was as if a whole lot of loving beings were taking all the tired parts out of me, similar to car mechanics in a car repair shop. . . . I experienced a great sense of peace and serenity, a feeling of literally being taken care of, of having no worry in the world. I had also an incredible sense that once all the parts were replaced I would be as young and fresh and energetic as I had been prior to this rather exhausting, draining workshop. . . . Naturally I associated this immediately with the stories of dying patients who shared with me their near death experiences. . . . Little did we know then that that was the beginning of an enormous amount of new research, which ultimately led to the understanding of death and life after death.

While this first experience was involuntary, she discovered, after hooking up with some out-of-body occultists in Virginia, that she could learn to repeat it at will. She could play dead. Whenever her bodily vehicle needed a tune-up, whenever she wanted to set back the old odometer, rejuvenate the spark plugs, she could take a revitalizing dip into death, that refreshing fountain of youth.

But Kübler-Ross did not stop there. She sailed right on into Stage 4: playing with the dead.

Remember that benevolent "being of light" who greets you when you alight from the streetcar named death? Well, he has friends up there. Plenty of them. Spirit guides. Guardian angels. The enlightened "afterlife entities."

The way Kübler-Ross describes it now, all the while she was garnering her honorary degrees, her acclaim from clergy, shrinks, and academics for working with the dying, she was spending an ever-increasing amount of her time playing with the dead. She made her own decisions only in consultation with her guardian angels and spirit guides. She counseled the living to make their decisions based on the guidance of entities from the Other Side.

In Stage 4, the implications of the previous stages become explicit: *Death is much more wonderful than life,* the dead are much wiser, and, since two-way communication with the Other Side is now possible, it's better to consult with them about the tiresome business of getting through life. By Stage 4, the dead are not really "dead" at all. They're more alive than we, the living, can hope to be. They're not even called "dead" anymore. For Stage 4 death worshipers they are "afterlife entities"; by the time we reach Stage 4 there is no such thing as death.

This was another Kübler-Ross discovery, I learned from her "media person" in Escondido. "Elisabeth doesn't like the term 'near death experience,' " he explained to me, "because she doesn't believe that death exists."

Doesn't believe in death?

"No such thing," he said. "She believes there are just . . . transitions. So it's not a near death experience because it's available to normal living people every day if they tune in to it."

Turn on, tune in, drop dead.

Playing with the dead has become a rapidly expanding national pastime. Spirit guides and guardian angels are becoming for many adults the comforting imaginary playmates they had to abandon as children, the perfect loving parents they never had. This two-way traffic takes some curious forms. According to a *Washington Post* story (apparently not a hoax), a California company has hired a number of terminally ill patients who will, for a fee, act as couriers, memorizing messages to be delivered to the dead as soon as they arrive on the Other Side. A whole new category of spiritualist phenomena is chronicled in the book *Phone Calls from the Dead,* which cites reports that phones all over America are practically ringing off the hook as chatterbox "entities" from the Other Side pester their friends and relatives among the living. (These days they're probably jamming the switchboards to find out if they can get a date for the next Kübler-Ross "workshop.")

We're also witnessing a revival of the old-fashioned table-rapping spiritualist epidemic that swept America in the mid-nineteenth century. The modern version, which dispenses, for the most part, with tables and props, is known— appropriately enough for the TV age—as "channeling," and this narrowcasting from the Other Side is growing as fast as cable TV. And, like cable, it's a franchising operation. I discovered this when a woman announced to me on the phone that she'd "finally gotten her channel." It seems that she'd been a paid student of a medium who was a "channel" to an afterlife entity somehow related to "Seth," the extremely popular, extremely long-winded afterlife entity whose empty maunderings somehow mesmerize middle-class airheads with pronouncements such as: "For in the miraculous spontaneity of the sun there is discipline that utterly escapes you."

After paying the Seth-related medium for months of trance training, this woman had finally been granted an authorized, franchised "afterlife entity" of her own, which would speak through her when she went into a trance and which would allow *her* to charge others for the privilege of getting its utterances on their problems.

I witnessed one such channeling session in a SoHo loft, and a sad spectacle it was. The woman seemed to have been granted a channel with very poor reception, or else there was an exceptionally thick-headed entity in the control room on the Other Side. After ten minutes of "going into trance," complete with head rollings, eye rollings, and all the most clichéd eyelid-batting expressions of the stage spiritualist, the woman finally snapped to and began speaking in the voice of her "channel" (a voice barely distinguishable from her own). But the hapless entity couldn't answer a single question she posed. I'd never seen an entity hem and haw so haltingly and ignorantly. Apparently, the slick and accomplished spiritualist franchiser who sold this gullible woman her channel hadn't even bothered to polish the entity's act enough to make it a good investment for the franchisee. It's probably a common spiritualist scam, taking advantage of such blind devotion to the wisdom of the dead to dump defective entities on the market the way swindlers sold underwater swampland lots in the Florida land boom.

Considering this feverish eagerness to be in touch with entities one way or another, it's not surprising that some death 'n' dying cultists have carried worship of the dead to Stage 5: going to bed with the dead.

It seems as if there has always been a subtext of eroticism in the growth of the death 'n' dying movement. Take the story behind Kübler-Ross's first big break into the national awareness.

"She was doing her seminars with dying patients virtually unnoticed in Chicago," her media person told me over the phone. "But then *Life* magazine heard about her and was going to send someone to see if there was a story in her work. There was this elderly man dying who was going to be the subject of the seminar when *Life* was there, but the old man died the night before."

There followed a hasty search for an understudy dying patient, and what happened next was in the best Broadway tradition: "They found a beautiful young girl to replace the old man." She was twenty-four or twenty-six, the media person told me. "And then *Life* knew they had a story. A real heartthrobber." It was this dying-heartthrob story in *Life,* he said, that made Kübler-Ross a sudden national sensation and enshrined her as Queen of Death.

If the dying can be heartthrobs, if the afterlife entities can be warm and loving and intimate with the living, why would anyone hesitate to go to bed with the dead?

By the time the sexual scandal broke in 1980, Kübler-Ross seems to have been bewitched into buying every last spiritualist trick in the book. She had no less than four personal entities—she called them "Mario," "Anka," "Salem," and "Willie"—attending her. She now believed in reincarnation and claimed to have memories of being alive in the time of Jesus. Where once her seminars had helped the dying, their friends, and their relatives live with despair, she now offered them a grab bag of Big Rock Candy Mountain fantasies of "life after life" to escape from life. And, finally, she'd allied her personal organization with a local sect that called itself the Church of the Facet of Divinity, hailing its minister, faith healer and medium Jay Barham, as "the greatest healer in the world."

Although accounts differ as to who actually did what to whom, allegations of seductions by entities did not arise until the merger with Barham's church. According to one report, "Barham regularly conducted seances in which he acted as a medium to communicate with what he called 'afterlife entities.' At many of these sessions, the former female members of the group asserted, they were instructed to enter a side room where they were joined a few minutes later in the dark by an unclothed man who talked convincingly of being an 'afterlife entity' [who] . . . then proceeded to convince the women that they should engage in sex with him. . . ."

According to another report, the seductive entity mispronounced certain words in a manner remarkably similar to that of Barham. Some of the women began to suspect that the aroused afterlife entity had earthbound limitations when five of them came down with the same vaginal infection after being closeted with him. And then there was the woman who actually turned on the light in the entity-visiting chamber and claimed to see Barham, naked except for a turban.

Barham had a wonderful explanation for his resemblance to the turbaned apparition. He denied engaging in sexual activities with any of the women but said that in order to materialize, certain entities might have *cloned themselves* from Barham's cells, which would explain how they might resemble him in materialized form.

Believe it or not, Kübler-Ross seems to have bought that too. For a year after the "entities" conned and abused her acolytes, she defended Barham and continued to work with him, franchising death, dying, and entity-encounter sessions throughout the country. She now insists, however, that she was no fool, that nobody had pulled the wool over her eyes, that unbeknownst to everyone "I have been conducting my own first-person investigation of . . . Barham." This investigation, which she must have pursued with all the stealth of Richard Nixon's personal "investigation" of the Watergate cover-up, finally uncovered unspecified conduct by Barham that "did not meet the standards . . . of Shanti Nilaya."

None of this substandard behavior, she insisted, took place on her premises or involved her workshops. The clincher in her investigation, Kübler-Ross told a writer, was her decision to have a doctor "measure" Barham's faith-healing power. This test, whose exact nature she did not disclose, revealed to her that his healing skills had declined measurably and that the decline was proof of his misuse of his powers.

"There are those who might say this has damaged my credibility," she conceded. "But it's not important whether people believe what I say. . . . I'm a doctor and a scientist, who simply reports what she sees, hears, and experiences."

Although Kübler-Ross has consistently stonewalled all inquiries about her reported presence at the scene of the assignations with the aroused afterlife entities, there is every indication that her disillusion with Barham has not diminished her swooning worship of death.

In a copyrighted interview with sympathetic questioner Joan Saunders Wixen, Kübler-Ross brushes off the Barham activities and instead boasts of some new benefits troubled people can look forward to as soon as they die. Death is a cure-all, the ultimate panacea: "People after death become complete again. The blind can see, the deaf can hear, cripples are no longer crippled after all their vital signs have ceased to exist."

If this encouragement to euthanasia as a quick solution to all physical imperfections were not so stupid and dangerous, it would be an occasion for regret: Death has claimed another victim, the mind of Kübler-Ross. Another sad but predictable triumph of death over reason, another case of an interesting mind committing suicide. It begins to seem that thinking about death is, like heroin, not something human beings are capable of doing in small doses and then going about the business of life. It tends to take over all thought, and for death 'n' dying junkies, the line between a maintenance dose and an O.D. becomes increasingly fine. When Kübler-Ross finally makes her "transition," I'm certain all her nagging physical ailments will clear up, just as she says, but when she gets to the Other Side they'll have to mark her mind D.O.A.

The Frantic Screaming Voice of the Rich and Famous

In Which We Witness the Blossoming of Nouveau Journalist Robin Leach

Could you do me a favor? It's important—I wouldn't ask you otherwise. Before you get comfortable, before you read any further, could you just run out to a bookstore and pick up a copy of the paperback edition of the new Wallace Shawn play *Aunt Dan and Lemon*?

Don't worry. I'm not going to ask you to read the whole play, at least not now. But I would like you to read the eighteen-page appendix Shawn calls "On the Context of the Play." Trust me on this: It's the single most provocative piece of writing I've come across on New York in the eighties and the rich and famous consciousness of our time. And frankly I'm just not sure I can communicate with anyone who hasn't read it yet.

Because it is in this essay that Shawn gives a beautiful name to the most emblematic personality-change process of the eighties: *blossoming*. What est was to the seventies, blossoming is to the eighties.

Now please don't go confusing blossoming with "fluffing out." Fluffing out is something entirely different. "Fluffing out" (according to a *New York Times* report on executive woman culture) is the term used by hard-nosed career-conscious women to describe less single-minded women who have allowed themselves to drift behind the career curve, a character flaw fatally signaled by the telltale choice of fluffier "pussycat" bows over simple silk-band executive bow ties.

Blossoming is not for pussycats. Blossoming is for tigers of both sexes. Blossoming is—well, this is how Shawn describes blossoming:

> As I write these words, in New York City in 1985, more and more people who grew up around me are making this decision; they are throwing away their moral chains and learning to enjoy their true situation: Yes, they are admitting loudly and bravely, we live in beautiful homes, we're surrounded by beautiful gardens. . . . And if there are people out there who don't seem to like us . . . well, then, part of our good fortune is that we can afford to pay guards to man our gates and keep those people away. . . . The amazing thing I've noticed about those friends of mine who've made that choice is that as soon as they've made it, they begin to blossom, to flower. . . . They develop the charm and grace which shine out from all people who are truly comfortable with themselves. . . . These are people who are free to love life exuberantly.

Blossoming is seductively beautiful to behold, Shawn writes, but he finds something more than a bit sinister about all these people blooming all around him—something that suggests to me the sinister, soul-stealing blossoming of the pod plants in *Invasion of the Body Snatchers.*

As his friends blossom around him, Shawn confesses a longing to succumb, to blossom himself—"a fantastic need to tear that [childhood moral] training out of my heart once and for all so that I can finally begin to enjoy the life that is spread out before me like a feast. And every time a friend makes that happy choice and sets himself free, I find that I inwardly exult and rejoice, because it means there will be one less person to disapprove of me if I choose to do the same."

Welcome, then, to the blossoming world of the rich and famous.

The Cross-Promotional Hotel Deals of the Rich and Famous

When I asked Robin Leach to choose his absolute, ultimate favorite lunch spot for an interview, his reply, through his publicist, was: Nicole's at the Omni Park Central.

Nicole's at the Omni Park Central?

Yes, that's his very favorite place, she assured me.

Did I miss something? Why is it I can't recall Nicole's at the Omni Park Central being mentioned in the copious chronicles of the rich and famous in the same breath as Mortimer's and Le Cirque? Had Nicole's blossomed overnight? Or could it be that Nicole's at the Omni Park Central was one of those fabulous secret *hideaways* of the rich and famous? One of those incredibly unassuming places they seek out to escape the glare of publicity (with the possible exception of Robin Leach and his camera crew, who are allowed in to document their "passion for privacy").

Well, Nicole's at the Omni Park Central turns out to be a pleasant enough place. Although it's tucked into the Seventh Avenue and Fifty-sixth Street corner of the Omni Park Central, it's not exactly a hideaway kind of place, and there don't seem to be any rich and famous customers in evidence. Still, there is a sign announcing WE HAVE BEAUJOLAIS NOUVEAU!

Could that nouveau touch be why Robin Leach chose this place? *Lifestyles of the Rich and Famous* might be said to have given birth to the successor to the New Journalism: the Nouveau Journalism.

But, no, actually there's a more complicated reason why we're at Nicole's at the Omni Park Central, Leach tells me.

"See, in January we're doing a show, not really a *Lifestyles* but a two-hour special I'm involved in called *SuperModel of the World.* And Phillip Georgeas, who used to be the manager of the Berkshire Hotel, which is right near our office, is now the manager of the Omni Park Central, and he's agreed to put up the models from around the world who are going to be in the pageant, and so he's told me to make use of this place for everything. I'm a great believer in loyalty and—"

"Now *SuperModel of the World.* Just what is—?"

"Eileen and Jerry Ford have done this *Face of the '80s* thing for the past three years through Telerep, which is my producer and syndicator, and in a sense what we're doing with *SuperModel of the World* is—if 'rich and famous' has become a generic expression—we're going to rich-and-famous-up the *Face of the '80s.*"

The Network Rip-offs of the Rich and Famous

Think about that: *We're going to rich-and-famous-up the* Face of the '80s.

In fact, he's already done it. Robin Leach has succeeded in rich-and-famousing-up the face of the decade. Certainly the face of the eighties as seen through the eyes of the Nouveau Journalism's shameless imitators in the Infotainment World.

The Sunday night before my lunch with Leach, I watched *60 Minutes* and *Lifestyles of the Rich and Famous* in succession and the comparison was not flattering to *60 Minutes,* whose centerpiece segment that night was a seemingly endless Harry Reasoner report from the Palace Hotel in St. Moritz.

This consisted mainly of extended footage of Harry Reasoner sitting in expensive old rooms telling us how old and expensive they were, how many rich and famous old people stayed in them. He couldn't seem to get over how old and famous and rich everything was. It was very sad and it lacked the nouveau vigor of a Robin Leach segment.

I asked Leach what his reaction to this inept copying was.

"I'm not arrogant," Leach begins, "but I am *overjoyed* that some of the techniques that we use on *Lifestyles of the Rich and Famous* have been adopted by *20/20, 60 Minutes,* and particularly the Barbara Walters specials."

He believes he blazed a path, a clearing in the national consciousness that permitted Rich and Famous Journalism to blossom.

"We took the rich out of the closet. It was now respectable to talk about wealth. And having us be the pioneer in making it respectable, it appears that a lot of other shows on television had to devote a segment within their programs to the rich and famous but without calling it such."

Still, Leach's pride as a craftsman is offended by the failure of his network imitators to *understand* the editing concepts of the Nouveau Journalism.

"I have the greatest respect for Don Hewitt and the *60 Minutes* gang," Leach avers. "But I honestly think we did a better job with our Donald Trump piece than they did, because we had the inside of the house in Connecticut and they just had him in his suit and tie *outside* the house. We actually had the tour inside."

He's critical of *60 Minutes'* ponderous TV technique, too. "I don't know the shooting ratio that *60 Minutes* uses on its pieces, but there is a rule in *our* office that I like to see the visual of what we do change every three seconds. My idea of a dream piece is never to see a shot of people talking, and if you can, do a five-minute piece where you never see the face of the person talking in a close-up, except maybe once. So in terms of the Palace in St. Moritz I can only assume that we would have shot far more than they did, and we probably would have done it with a celebrity, like we did with Loretta Swit in Portofino. You'll find, Ron, as you get to know me through this lunch," he confides, "that I am very, very serious and very, very diligent about what really is bubble gum and bubble bath and froth."

But before we got any deeper into the serious techniques of the Nouveau Journalism, I wanted Robin Leach to clear up a mystery that had the whole town talking that month. Just what treasures were concealed in . . .

The Lost Briefcase of the Rich and Famous

The mystery announced itself overnight when big bold REWARD! posters suddenly appeared—practically blossomed—all over midtown. Robin Leach's briefcase was missing. Reward. No questions asked.

But of course questions *were* asked. Questions were asked by those for whom watching *Lifestyles* was a secretive, shameful vice, by those for whom it was a camp cult classic. And the questions were, of course: What fabulous secrets of the rich and famous, what absolute ultimate inside dope on their intimate doings in those hideaways of theirs, could have occasioned the feverish high-profile search for the lost briefcase?

What *was* the story of the missing briefcase? I asked Leach after we'd placed our drink orders (a Bloody Mary "very spicy with not much vodka" for Leach, a beer for me).

"It's more than a briefcase, really," Leach explains of the purloined satchel. "It's halfway between a briefcase and a small suitcase—it was the whole contents of my desk, which I'd taken to Connecticut for the weekend. Monday morning I took a taxi to work and stopped at a newsstand to pick up the *News* and the *Post*—I never read the *Times*—and regrettably, as we found out afterward, the cab driver had recognized me, and when I got out of the cab she just took off with it, with the briefcase inside."

"She probably thought she was getting the priceless secrets of the rich and famous," I suggest.

"I have no idea. But she would have got the private phone numbers of everybody in the world and a lot of plans and story ideas."

What a haul: the private phone numbers of everybody in the (rich and famous) world. Instant access to the ears of the rich and famous speeding away in the back of a cab. Into the hands of who knew what kind of terrorist or opportunistic insurance salesman. No wonder the all-out campaign to get back the briefcase of the rich and famous.

"I hired a private detective," says Leach. "It took us eight days and—*whoa, excuse me, love*—"

This latter is to the waitress passing by.

"They have the new Beaujolais," he tells me. "*Whoa*—we've got to try the new—sweetheart, instead of the Bloody Mary could I have a glass of the new Beaujolais? Would you like to try it?" he asks me.

"I'll stick with my Heineken."

"Well, then," he says cheerily, "I shall make up for both of us."

Leach returns to the quest for the lost briefcase of the rich and famous. "The private detective managed to find the cab and the cab driver, and he met her on Eighth Avenue and Forty-fourth Street. As she told the story afterward, within ten seconds of taking off with it she didn't want to carry on with what she'd done—she was from Ecuador and she must have panicked about getting arrested. But instead of coming back, she took it home and put it in her bathroom and never opened it."

Listening to this tale left me with an image of that lost briefcase standing there unopened in the bathroom of the frightened Third World immigrant—an obscure object of desire plucked from the inner sanctum of the First World, seductive but too threatening to touch. Clearly the woman was just not ready to blossom.

Our waitress arrived with a glass of the Beaujolais Nouveau.

"Good health, Ron," says Leach pleasantly. "This is my first glass of this." He sips. Appraises.

"It's nice," he says. "Certainly better than last year's. . . ."

The Pornographic Exploitation of the Rich and Famous

I was walking down Broadway in the Forties a week or so before my lunch with Leach and I passed a porno theater marquee promoting, with lavish displays of bare flesh, a movie called *The Decadent Lifestyles of the Rich and Famous*. The subtitle promised to take you "Inside Beverly Hills." Or maybe that was the title, and *The Decadent Lifestyles of the Rich and Famous* was the subtitle. But you get the idea.

I asked Leach if he'd seen the film. It came as a surprise to him. He was visibly disturbed.

"Oh, we have to stop that," he says quickly, taking out a notepad to jot down a reminder. "Thank you very much. Is there really?"

"Yes," I assure him.

"No," he groans. "It hasn't been advertised in any of the papers because we'd have caught it. It's for the lawyers."

"It's amusing though, isn't it?" I ask.

He doesn't look amused. He's even less amused at my next question.

"Don't you feel that in some ways *Lifestyles* is a little bit like porn for the wealth-obsessed, the way—"

"Oh no," he says, shocked at the notion. "Now, Ron, let's be friends. How can you ask that question?"

"You don't think so?"

"No, come on. How could you describe anything that we do as even edging toward that? Where's the tease?"

"Well, isn't it a sort of voyeurism, getting to see forbidden—"

"Well, you can't say it's forbidden. You can say private, yes. It's not forbidden. And we are *so* mom and apple pie on the show. I mean, yes, we had the Playmate of the Year because she just picked up a hundred thousand and there's a little bit of bare shoulder—"

I try to explain to Leach that I'm not accusing him of literal sexual pornography but the pornography of wealth.

"When people say they watch *Lifestyles,*" I explain, "they almost always say, 'I have a shameful confession to make: I never miss *Lifestyles.*' But they say it as if they were confessing to watching an X-rated movie."

Leach groans. I continue to try to explain the porn comparison.

"See, they confess it like it's a forbidden pleasure because there's that strain in the American character that disapproves of lust for possessions, lust for material goods—there's always that tension between the Puritan side and the expansive side, right? So when people say they like your show, they tend to say it like they're confessing a forbidden lust."

Leach is still not buying this argument.

"That doesn't make it pornographic by any stretch of the word."

"Not in the sense of sexual or perverse but in the sense of dealing with forbidden lust, see—"

"What's the definition of pornography?" he asks me.

"Arousing, provoking lust. How about that?"

"Arousing, provoking lust. If we do that, I'm the happiest man on earth. Do you really think we do that? No."

"Lust for beautiful homes. Lust for expensive—"

"There is no avarice," Leach says. "There is no avarice. We are the Gray Line bus tour and we don't cheat you, because when you take the Gray Line bus tour you see the stone wall, you don't go over the top of it. We take you through the front door. There's nothing more than that. We've taken the rich out of the closet. It's no longer wrong to be rich. When Ronald Reagan came back into the White House, there was a certain amount of glamorous life clinging about again. Remember that came about more or less in the same time as shows like *Dynasty* and *Dallas* were creeping on to television. . . . That's why I always describe *Lifestyles* by saying, if the script writers of *Dynasty* and *Dallas* merged those two shows, they couldn't come up with the wealth that we have on our show every week, because real-life wealth completely overshadows what Hollywood could create. So we made rich people respectable, but our viewers do not watch this with lust, which might be your definition of pornographic. There is no lust in watching this."

The Secret University of the Rich and Famous

Leach is continuing to refute my porn analysis of *Lifestyles*.

"We get odd letters from people who say, 'When you were covering Cher's house, there was a shot of a coffee table.' Or, 'Could you please send us the name of the company that manufactures the wallpaper in Donald Trump's apartment?' Now I don't think that's lust. And that's certainly not avarice. That's somebody that wants to go out and buy the same kind of wallpaper. I'll tell you a story, a story that does my heart good because there's a little bit of the moralist in me."

This tale of the morally improving value of *Lifestyles of the Rich and Famous* begins in a liquor store near Leach's little house in L.A. (he says he rents it for $550 a month). Leach goes there, he says, because he gets a good price on Cristal champagne—his only conspicuously rich and famous personal taste.

"One day when I was at the checkout with my wine for a Saturday night dinner, the manager came over to me and said, 'Mr. Leach, I just want to thank you because you've changed the Saturday nights in my house, and I can't tell you how grateful I am.' He said that he had two teenage boys, and until the time *Lifestyles* went on the air, 'I despaired of those boys.' He said, 'They never did their homework, they were out on the streets Saturday night. And I knew sooner or later they were gonna wind up in trouble.' "

But instead, says Leach, they wound up in front of the TV set absorbing the secrets of the rich and famous.

"He told me, 'Those two boys of mine started watching *Lifestyles* and now they don't go out. They sit there with two notepads. Those two kids of mine have decided they've got somehow to get to Brown University.' And I said, 'Why Brown University?' And he said, 'Because they found out that's the major common denominator of all the rich people. So they figure if they work hard at school now and they got to Brown University, they would get an education that would enable them to live like this.' "

Despite this heartwarming evidence of his salutary effect on the youth of America, Leach disclaims any sweeping mission of social improvement.

"If we've provided the little bit of impetus for somebody to better themselves, then socially we've done something. But we're not in it for that. Our mission in a given hour is to entertain. To make people feel good. . . . I mean it never rains on *Lifestyles.* We—"

"It never rains?"

"We'll show snow," he says. "But we prefer sun because it makes people feel better. But it never rains. The roses are always in full bloom. . . ."

The Rich and Famous Parties of the Rich and Famous

But don't get the idea that the poor and aspiring are the only ones who watch *Lifestyles of the Rich and Famous.*

The rich and famous watch it too! They love to see each other blossom.

"I was on a flight back from shooting [Adnan] Khashoggi's fiftieth birthday party this summer"—an event he describes as "the single most momentous party in European history"—"and a passenger from London told me he'd enjoyed a show he'd seen in New York. He told me that David Rockefeller watches it every Sunday night with a gaggle of friends."

"David Rockefeller has *Lifestyles of the Rich and Famous* parties?"

"Yes," claims Leach. "He gives little cocktail parties and then everybody toots into the television room to watch the show. Then they all go to dinner."

The Sad Mercedes Dealer in the Totally Nouveau Nation of the Rich and Famous

When I asked Leach about his most satisfying Nouveau Journalism coups, he cited his hour-long special on the high-flying life of Adnan Khashoggi, once reputedly the world's richest man. And he was particularly pleased with *Lifestyles'* videotaped raid on the kingdom of Brunei, home of the current world's richest man, the sultan of Brunei. Oil discoveries in this tiny Malaysian principality have given the sultan a reputed income of $55 million per day. And the trickle-down from that has made most of the other two hundred thousand inhabitants pretty wealthy (per capita income of a million dollars or so per year).

For some reason the sultan refused *Lifestyles* an interview. Perhaps he was holding out for Portofino with Loretta Swit—who knows? But Leach was undaunted. He just hopped ashore with a camera crew and did a profile of Brunei itself, a tiny nation that is totally rich and totally, unashamedly nouveau.

"What I found amusing," Leach tells me, "is that Brunei is a country that just ten or eleven years ago, before they discovered oil, exported bat droppings as fertilizer to Australia."

"Bat droppings?"

"Suddenly they found oil and gas. So the sultan's new in those terms. It's nouveau riche."

How nouveau? So nouveau it almost sounds like a parody of nouveau-ness.

"This is an extraordinary place to go," Leach tells me, "because you can't imagine—I mean to me the fun part was interviewing the Mercedes-Benz dealer, who was the unhappiest man in the place."

"Why was he unhappy?"

"Well, you see, everybody there buys Mercedes and there's no place to drive them. There's only one road in the whole country, which is mainly a clearing in the jungle. So they buy them not to drive but as status symbols to put in their front gardens. They stack them on top of each other. Like lawn ornaments. You know, they have four of them, they need five. They have five, they need six."

Sounds like the perfect country for Robin Leach, doesn't it? Or does it just sound like Beverly Hills?

"But how could the Mercedes dealer be unhappy?"

"Because," Leach says, "he's on a strict allocation from the factory in Germany and he can't get any more cars."

The Highbrow Literature of the Rich and Famous

I asked Leach to give me an assessment of his rivals and imitators in Nouveau Journalism.

"I think *People* magazine does a very good job, but I think it's too highbrow for the audience it's after," he says.

"*People* too highbrow?"

"The quality of the writing is above the audience, a little too artsy-craftsy. *US* magazine, on the other hand now, has the graphics, the punch, the color, the look that really appeals to that audience. Still, however, any way you cut it they're both glossy versions of what the *Star* is. The *Star* to me is more honest. But these are the growth vehicles of the publishing industry, let's be honest."

The Germ in the Mind of the Rich and Famous

The product of a lower-middle-class family in the non-U section of Harrow, Leach got his start in the Nouveau Journalism covering garden shows.

Of his horticultural coverage Leach says, "I know you'll find the analogy in here somewhere, and it's not quite true. But I would focus on the biggest squash. I would focus on the biggest cauliflower because I really believed that that's what people wanted to read about."

He went on to write gossip for Fleet Street tabloids and then came to America and soon got himself the prized post of gossip columnist for Murdoch's *Star.* His place in history as an auteur of infotainment culture, however, was assured by his participation in the creation of *Entertainment Tonight* and his four years as *ET*'s showbiz gossip correspondent.

I'd read somewhere that Leach had left *ET* over "philosophical differences" with then executive producer and fellow infotainment auteur George Merlis (The Man Who Created *Good Morning America* as We Now Know It). You could think of Leach and Merlis as the Leibniz and Newton of their genre, simultaneous inventors of the calculus of infotainment. In the same way that profound philosophical differences over the nature of nothingness (the concept of "the infinitesimal differential") divided the inventors of the calculus, so too is the difference between Leach and Merlis an unbridgeable gulf.

"I disagreed with the whole direction of *ET* under Merlis," Leach tells me. "They wanted to cover the business side of show business. My belief is that the viewer does not want to understand the box-office take for the week and how it affects the corporate boardroom of the motion picture studio."

And what does the viewer want?

"The viewer wants to see the stars partying with champagne."

The schisms behind the scenes at *ET* still rankle Leach. "Do you know there was a memorandum sent around by one of the executive producers that stopped party coverage?"

"Really? *ET* stopped party coverage?"

"For a short period of time. Then that was followed by a short period of time when they said, 'You don't eat the shrimp when you go to cover a party. . . .' "

The shrimp ban was only a symptom of a deeper philosophical difference. Like the failure of *ET* to understand the importance of furniture shots.

"My real difference occurred—the reason that *Lifestyles* began as a germ in my mind was that it used to greatly aggravate me that we would be able to go off and do wonderful interviews in people's houses and we would never see the chair they were sitting on."

This absence of furniture shots may not seem like a fundamental philosophical inadequacy to you, but to Leach it's a vitally important issue. He wanted to do fewer close-up head shots of movie stars talking about their "commitment to the work." He wanted more of their fabulous lifestyles and expensive furniture.

"If you see a blond bombshell in a bubble bath," Leach sums up, "I think it's far more believable than her claim she wants to do Shakespeare down the road."

The Intimate Floorplay of the Rich and Famous

"What about the sex lives of the rich and famous?" I finally got around to asking. "Is sex better when you're rich and famous?"

"Is sex better when you're rich and famous?" Leach considered. I thought he'd probably have a lot to say on the subject, but unfortunately he seemed to interpret my question as another go at the pornography issue.

"We really don't get into sex on our show, contrary to what everybody might think, including you."

"Well, there are a lot of hot-tub shots."

"That's not sex," Leach says. "Sex is—be it in the bedroom, or on the living-room floor, or in the mink coat—the act of making love. That's what sex is all about. There's a lot of intimate floorplay—foreplay—on *Lifestyles* and Cristal champagne and romantic candlelight. I don't think because we show people in hot tubs or people in the bubble bath that's done for sexual reasons. That's done because that reflects their lifestyle. Movie stars *do* take bubble baths. Movie stars *do* study scripts in their bathtubs. Movie stars *do* like to ease their tensions by going into the Jacuzzi. Whether that's sexual I don't know."

Did you catch the Freudian slip Leach made in the middle of his defense of Jacuzzi Journalism? He said "floorplay" for "foreplay."

What's fascinating about this slip, what's so perfectly rich and famous about it, is the hierarchy of urges it seems to reveal. Usually in a Freudian slip a sexually charged word subverts an "innocent" everyday word, revealing the deep and turbulent tide of the unconscious beneath the surface of the stream of consciousness. But in Robin Leach's slip—"floorplay" for "foreplay"—furniture-related urges (floors, floor plans, home furnishings) appear to be far more primal than those of sex.

The Main Fear of the Rich and Famous

"One of the reasons that *Lifestyles* works," Leach is telling me, "why it isn't the show that people hate, is our writing. Our writing is—"

"Did you say why it *is* the show that people hate?" I ask, mishearing him.

"Why it isn't. My main fear was that it would be the show that everybody hated. What I had to do was kick it off at the very beginning to make it the show people *love* to hate, *then* the show that they loved. And the trick is—there are two tricks. First of all, in all of our pieces there is a *story*. A beginning, a middle, and an end. We look for heroic rags-to-riches sagas. We're subtly not selling but subtly carrying out the legend of the American dream and I feel very strongly about this in America. It was true in my case and it was true in a lot of people's cases. You do not have to be born with a silver spoon in your mouth to make it in this country. I come from a country where you have to be born on the right side of the tracks. . . . You don't in America. So within all the sugar of what *Lifestyles* is all about, there is a little pill in there and that little pill says: 'You must keep this. You must maintain what we have in this country. There is everything right about free enterprise. There is everything right about capitalism.' "

Sure, *if* you can get into Brown University.

The Ten Commandments (or Whatever) of the Rich and Famous

Leach has lost track, in the course of this passionate homage to his adopted homeland, of the other trick, the other one of the two tricks he said make *Lifestyles* the show you love to hate instead of the show you just purely hate.

"The reason the show works and the reason people don't get jealous and don't become envious or all the other commandments—thou shalt not avarice, thou shalt not covet, and thou shalt not whatever—is because there is a little tongue-in-cheek humor in the writing."

It is in this tongue-in-cheek tone, particularly the hyperinflected servile ingratiating tone of *voice* that verges on self-mockery in its overawed statements that is Leach's greatest creation. I think he wants me to believe that it's intentionally *ironic* and therefore "subtle," a favorite self-descriptive word he likes to bestow on his work.

The Subtle Journalism of the Rich and Famous

Toward the end of our meal (Leach had the steak tartare, I had the cassoulet), Leach turned to me and asked me with heartfelt seriousness: "Do you sense as a journalist that there is a subtle journalism in *Lifestyles*?"

"Well," I began, judiciously weighing my words, not wishing to offend Leach, who is, with his low-key Fleet Street sense of humor, a likable guy. "Well, you do get access to worlds that are little seen, so in that respect it's *interesting* journalism. Interesting anthropologically, in a sense. I also sense there is a kind of tongue-in-cheek distancing in the voice and the writing—a kind of deliberate overstating for effect. Is that what you mean—?"

"Mmm," he says, and proceeds to tell an anecdote that I believe is meant to illustrate the subtle journalism to be found on *Lifestyles*.

"I remember getting excited when we were doing Princess von Thurn und Taxis* and I said, 'By any chance does the butler deliver the helmet for your motorcycle on a silver tray?' She said yes, and I got it and I loved it. Do you know in Redondo Beach in California on Saturday nights it is de rigueur to watch *Lifestyles,* dressed in tuxedoes and fancy long gowns in your hot tub?"

"In the hot tub?"

"They wear the tux and long gowns in the hot tubs and they hire butlers to bring them little snacks. It's sort of like the *Rocky Horror Picture Show* cult."

And speaking of *Rocky,* don't you think someone should introduce these West Coast party animals to David Rockefeller?

The Frantic Screaming Voice of the Rich and Famous

But we were talking about Robin Leach's voice, I think.

"The reason for the frantic screaming voice," he tells me, "which has been described as halfway between the adenoids and the Atlantic, is because, just as the picture changes every three seconds, I want double the amount of copy in there to cover it. That was a conscientious decision to wall-to-wall it with copy—instead of the normal thirty words a minute I try to get sixty words a minute. That's how we decided to write it, to help drive the pictures. I mean there are two Robin Leaches. There's the man that's having lunch with you today and then there's the man who's selling washing machines on television Saturday nights."

At this point the waitress—a pleasant middle-aged woman—returns with my credit card receipt.

"Come back real soon," she says, lingering.

---

*Fans of Thomas Pynchon's novel *The Crying of Lot 49* will recognize this name.

"We will," says Leach cheerfully.

"Thanks again," she says again, eyeing Leach.

"I don't talk like I sound on television," Leach is telling me, apropos the two Robin Leaches.

"You're a celebrity, aren't you?" the waitress asks Leach.

"No," he says modestly.

"You're an actor?"

"No."

"You *are*," she insists.

"Do you watch *Lifestyles of the Rich and Famous*?" he asks her.

"Yes," she says, scrutinizing him.

"You do? Well, that's me."

"Oh yeah," she says. "The voice. Oh, very sexy voice you have."

"It must be the English accent," says Leach.

"Yes," says the waitress. "*The Equalizer.* I like him, too."

The Passions of Mario Cuomo

In Which the Governor Sends a Mickey Mouse Watch to
Roy Cohn and Calls Ed Koch a Pelagian Heretic

Who is that tall, spectral figure haunting the gloomy halls of the state capitol
building today? Who is that silver-haired, patrician wraith with the lines of a
shattered past engraved on his face?

Could it be—yes—*it's John Lindsay.*

Once the Great White Hope of American liberalism, the shining paladin of
urban progressivism—what's he doing here in the lobby of Mario Cuomo's
statehouse office?

What Lindsay's doing in the lobby is, in fact, lobbying. The former mayor
is here today as a lobbyist for Drexel Burnham Lambert. The high-flying
"junk-bond" financiers have hired Lindsay to importune the governor to veto
the anti-takeover legislation now on his desk.

Some might relish the ironic appropriateness of this apparition, this Ghost
of the Fiscal Crisis Past. After all, here's Lindsay, whom many blame for turning New York City's credit obligations *into* junk bonds, now a paid hireling
for the junk-bond kings of the private sector.

Some might relish it, but I don't. Coming upon Lindsay on my way to sit
down with Cuomo was like seeing a sad, cautionary specter. Once, in college,

from a distance, I'd believed in the shining promise of the Lindsay crusade, believed that he might be the one to translate the ideals of the civil-rights movement into workable realities on the streets of the cities of the North. And then, as a reporter during the dying days of the second Lindsay administration, I'd seen at close hand exactly why Lindsay came to be called the Man Who Gave Good Intentions a Bad Name.

Would it be different with Mario Cuomo? After his electrifying, impassioned keynote speech at the 1984 Democratic National Convention—the one he'd called "A Tale of Two Cities"—Cuomo succeeded to that place in the hearts of the hopeful that Lindsay once had. Only the thought was, the hope was, that Cuomo's different: He's not another Lindsay. He's got the passion for the old ideals, but he knows how to make them work. He's got a kind of passion for perfecting the mechanical details of governing that make the difference between mere good intentions and successful results. Unlike Lindsay, he's got a way with people that turns them on rather than off to his ideals.

And there was something else about Cuomo that encouraged the hope he wouldn't end up like Lindsay: his reputation as a killer debater and a go-for-the-jugular politician. This was the Cuomo who took apart first Ed Koch and then Lew Lehrman in the '82 campaign debates, the Cuomo who's not afraid to trade head shots with Reagan's designated hit man, Pat Buchanan. The guy who took on his own archbishop on theological grounds at Notre Dame.

If Reagan has adopted Rambo as his role model, Cuomo makes you think of the Clint Eastwood character in *Pale Rider:* the mysterious stranger in the clerical collar folk call the Preacher. He speaks in parables of love, but when he runs into resistance from the greedy, land-raping federals, the Preacher's eyes gleam and he takes great pleasure in blowing the feds full of holes.

Has the phrase *linebacker's eyes* ever been applied to Mario Cuomo? It's used to describe the gleam of passionate intensity that certain souls on fire, like Jack Lambert and Jack "Hacksaw" Reynolds, evince in the anticipation of cutting halfbacks in half.

All I knew about Cuomo's brief career as a minor-league baseball prospect was something I read about a fistfight he'd had with a catcher in the Class B league. But I have the feeling he might have chosen the wrong sport: He could have been a linebacker.

This afternoon as he barrels into the conference room in which I've been waiting, he manifests the burly, aggressive physical presence of a crack linebacker. When he sits himself down, he doesn't really sit. He crouches over the table, shoulders hunched forward, elbows advanced, looking like a roverback hanging over the gap at scrimmage, eager to nail an errant ballcarrier behind the line.

And when he senses intellectual error Cuomo shows you those linebacker's eyes. They gleam with pleasure as he blows holes in arguments and demolishes confused lines of thought. I found Cuomo thoughtful, introspective, compassionate, all those things, and he's got a great stern-but-kind-teacher side to him. But when he spots a mistake he's more like Hacksaw Reynolds than Mr. Chips.

In fact the first thing he wanted to do in our conversation was correct a mistake I'd made about him some months ago. Actually it was a mistake Roy Cohn made.

"Cuomo's tough," Roy had told me during my interview with him. "I saw one thing he did that *scared* me."

What was it that scared Roy, a guy who prides himself on not scaring easily? It was a devastating debating move Cuomo pulled on his hapless gubernatorial opponent, Lew Lehrman, in the climactic debate of the '82 campaign—a one-line remark that shocked Lehrman out of his red suspenders and left him for dead in the debate.

But, Cuomo tells me, Roy Cohn's account of that particular Cuomo moment got it wrong.

"Roy is saying 'Cuomo is one guy I'm afraid of because he went charging over to Lehrman, grabbed his wrist—some bellicose gesture like that—and said to Lehrman, *'My, isn't that an expensive watch.'* ' Well, that didn't occur at all."

What then did happen?

"What occurred was, we were standing side by side debating and Lew was trying to interrupt my answers. Apparently he had some kind of *strategy* in mind," says Cuomo, barely suppressing his evident contempt for the strategic genius behind this tactic, "and at one point he leaned right over in front of me while I was speaking and jammed his watch in my face. He said 'Look at the time.' And I never even touched him. I looked at the watch and I said, *'My, that's an expensive watch.'* And the place broke up.

"So it wasn't me going over to Lehrman," says Cuomo, intent on setting the record straight. "It was Lehrman coming over to me. It wasn't me grabbing his wrist. It was Lehrman thrusting his watch in my face."

He pauses and smiles with satisfaction. "It was, however, I who said, *'My, that's an expensive watch.'* "

The distinction seems important to Cuomo: He didn't hit Lehrman with a low blow—it was a counterpunch.

Not that Cuomo takes the whole thing *that* seriously. It was, after all, Mario Cuomo, he reminds me, who sent Roy Cohn a Mickey Mouse watch after reading Cohn's "Cuomo scares me" comments.

"Can you get the note to Roy Cohn about the Mickey Mouse watch?" the governor calls out to his secretary.

The note that Cuomo sent to Cohn along with the Mickey Mouse gift reads:

"I would never be unwise enough to debate you as a politician. But when finally the public drives me back to the practice of the law and I find myself head to head against you, wearing this will protect you from the kind of attack I made on Lew."

Setting aside the exact circumstances of the expensive-watch attack, what is it with these tough-guy Republicans like Roy Cohn and Pat Buchanan, the most recent victim of a Cuomo counterpunch? Why, I ask the governor, are these GOP street fighters frightened of Mario Cuomo?

"Because they're making a mistake," he says. "Because they misperceive me. Because they don't know me. I'm the easiest opponent they could have, I'm sure. They just don't know me."

"And what is the misperception they have?"

"They're confused. They think because I stood up and spoke about family and speak about law and order without surrendering to the death penalty, because I can balance a budget and still give more money to people in wheelchairs—they're confused into thinking that because I can do all of these things, which is exactly what they say Republicans are supposed to do, that means I'm going to run for president and then for sure they'd lose."

"And why are they wrong in—"

"Because I'm not running for president," he says. "If they knew the truth, which is, all I'm planning is to run for governor, they could all be relieved. They wouldn't bother with me—they'd go beat up Gary Hart."

"Why have you decided not to run for president?"

"I haven't decided not to run for president," he says, correcting me. "I said I'm planning to run for governor. They think I'm planning to run for president."

And of course an answer like that will not do much to change their minds, if you ask me.

But rather than get into that game, there's someone I'd like to introduce you to now. Someone you'll undoubtedly be hearing more about if Cuomo does run for president. Someone you probably need to know to understand Cuomo as a person and a politician.

Maybe you know about this guy already: the French paleontologist and Jesuit priest whose attempts to speak of spirituality in Darwinian and Einsteinian terms were suppressed by the church until after his death in 1955.

I'm speaking, of course, of Pierre Teilhard de Chardin, Mario Cuomo's spiritual mentor.

I'd been surprised to find that nothing I'd read about Cuomo had focused attention on the importance of Teilhard to him. There had been no mention of Teilhard's inspirational work *The Divine Milieu,* which, Cuomo told me, he'd read "a hundred times."

Cuomo's published *Diaries* hint strongly at the centrality of Teilhard to him. In one typical passage from 1981 he finds himself worrying about money: His wife's unhappy with him for not having gotten bigger bucks out of his law practice, and he's unhappy that the political career he sacrificed the big bucks for isn't really doing much to make the world better.

"I wonder what Teilhard would say about this kind of thinking," Cuomo writes. "Is it a form of weakness? How do I deal with what he would call the diminishments of my own spirit and the diminishments imposed by the world?"

Before going up to Albany to sit down with Cuomo, I brushed up on Teilhard, having been impressed by his speculative evolutionary theory in *The Phenomenon of Man* in college, but being kind of rusty on the details. *The Divine Milieu* is far more explicitly devotional and Catholic: It's an impassioned, inspirational work that takes off from the thesis that the universe of matter and energy revealed by contemporary subatomic physics and astrophysics is not a challenge to faith, but rather further revelation of the glory of Created Being. Yes, we are living in a material world, Teilhard says, anticipating you know who. But the material world (including human nature) is interpenetrated with divine potential—it's a "divine milieu," the way energy is the "milieu" of matter in relativistic physics.

I was curious to find out just how important this vision was to the governor. And surprised at just how passionate he was about it.

Our conversation about Teilhard, which somewhat incongruously followed the one about Roy Cohn and the Mickey Mouse watch, began, nonetheless much like that one, with Cuomo correcting another mistake I made.

This time it was my misreading of a passage in *The Divine Milieu* that I had been certain was a key to Cuomo's character development.

The passage I got wrong comes from Teilhard's introduction, in which he's describing the particular kind of person *The Divine Milieu* will have the most meaning for: "A certain kind of human spirit known to every spiritual director."

What is it about this certain kind of spirit? He's the kind of person who has a taste for the life of this world but a "higher Will" to withdraw from what he sees as the sinful confusion of the fallen world in search for the purity of loving God alone. Someone, in other words, who might be drawn to the priesthood or the monastic life for reasons of self-sanctification but who would be better off, Teilhard wants him to know, embracing rather than rejecting the world.

Is that you? I asked Cuomo.

Right doctrine, wrong guy, he replied—in essence. But before refuting my conjecture about his character he reproved my obvious quick-study job on *The Divine Milieu*.

"If you read it only once, then you are missing all the joy of reading it a hundred times as I have," he told me, "because as you know, it's poetry, a kind of intelligent emoting."

Then he got down to the task of setting me straight on the nature of its importance to his personal development.

"First, let me tell you what I think Teilhard is saying," Cuomo begins. "He devotes the book 'to those who love the world.' What he really says is, God so loved the world that he made man. Now it's very important to remember the context. He was banned. The reason he was banned is that before Vatican II it was common to interpret the Catholic theology in this country as saying this world is an evil place. A series of moral obstacles. The best you can do is repair to the monastery and weave baskets. Monks weave baskets to give their hands something to do in the grim interval between birth and eternity. Teilhard was a reaction to all that. Teilhard was saying that *debases* God. That *demeans* God. God didn't make us to get ready for the next world. He made us to be involved in this world. What he is saying to people like me is: The world is good, involvement is good, pain is good, sorrow is good—Being is good. It's very important to somebody raised in the Jimmy Breslin era, when if girls wore patent-leather shoes the nuns got upset that boys would look under their skirts by the reflection. So what kind of spirit am I?" Cuomo asks, coming back, now that he has defined my terms more precisely, to my original question.

"I'm not a spirit, I'm a struggler, a confused human who knows way down deep that there's something immensely beautiful about this world and who, when he comes across a Teilhard, says, 'Hallelujah! Prayers have been answered,' because Teilhard is one who as a scientist, a paleontologist, was able to say to you with perfect theological probity, 'You're right, Mario. I don't understand it either and I'm smarter than you, but I know that it's beautiful and I know you ought to stay with it and I know the more deeply you get involved in it, the more deeply you become a part of it, the more beautiful it gets and we are building up.' We diminish physically to build up spiritually, and when it's all over it just begins, so it's—"

"So it wasn't that you were tempted by renunciation," I say, interrupting Cuomo as the distinction he is making finally dawns on me. "It's the opposite: You found in him a vindication for a temperamental preference for this world."

"This world has a significance better than the significance taught by the old—" He searches for a word for the antiworld Catholic thinkers. "They weren't theologians because they didn't understand the theology. They were good religious people," he says, finally coming up with a charitable formulation for the error he sees in their ways. "Good religious people who concentrated on sin instead of opportunity."

I hadn't planned to get as deeply into theological questions as we did, but I think you get a sense of Cuomo's thought process at its most unmediated—in every sense of the word—when he's talking about such questions as the nature of hell and the continuing mystery of the origin of evil.

We got into hell and evil when I once again strayed into error—this time in my interpretation of a particularly cryptic reference to Teilhard in Cuomo's *Diaries*. Amidst the chaos of his primary campaign against Ed Koch, Cuomo found himself "thinking through the Apostles' Creed in my mind, the old creed that said, 'He descended into hell.' Matching it up to Teilhard." I had a theory about what that passage was *really* about, which I tried out on the governor:

"I wondered whether you were comparing your entering New York State politics to Christ descending into hell?"

"Oh no. No, not really. No," Cuomo says, "because that's inconsistent with believing as I do that almost all of involvement is good. So all the pain of politics and all the disappointment of politics, all the imperfections of politics, that's part of living and experiencing."

What was it then that he was speculating about in that passage when he talked about matching up the old Apostles' Creed with Teilhard?

The theology of hell is "still kind of bothersome" to him, Cuomo says. "If you look at the old Apostles' Creed and you compare it to what's said as a creed now—one of the principal differences is that they leave out of the present creed the portion that says Christ descended into hell."

So?

"I concluded from much analysis while jogging that what they're really saying in the new creed is, hell is the *void*. But the old creed suggested there was a *place,* an existence beneath us the way the world is a place. The new creed suggests that the real hell is a nothingness and a vacuum. And that's a colossal step forward. What Teilhard, I guess, would have said is there is a heaven but there is no hell in the sense of punishment."

Questions of hell and punishment lead him to leap to the theological controversy over the nature of evil.

"There is no explanation for evil, obviously, and Teilhard is very clear on that, too, but—"

"No explanation for evil in Teilhard?"

"I don't think anywhere really. There isn't sufficient understanding allowed us to be able to explain evil—I mean not sin, but unexplained pain to children sitting in Vietnamese villages who got their eyes blown out of their heads by explosions they didn't know were coming and that they had nothing to do with. The mother losing four children in a row, the apparently senseless tragedy. My brother's son freezing to death in the backyard at age five out in Copiague. How do you explain that? The apparent injustice. You can't. You read McBrien's two volumes on Catholicism, which is now all the rage theologically for Catholics—he says there's no point in giving a lot of pages to the subject of evil because we don't *have* an explanation."

Returning to Teilhard, I wondered if there might be something more about him that Cuomo identified with. Perhaps the way his heretical tendencies got him in trouble with his religious superiors might have fortified Cuomo in his outspoken disagreement with Archbishop O'Connor over abortion rights.

"Teilhard was a heretic, right?" I began. "He was condemned for—"

"No, no, he was not," Cuomo corrects me heatedly. "No, sir, there was nothing heretical about Teilhard."

"What about pantheism?" I suggest. "Pelagianism?" (The translator's footnotes to my edition of *The Divine Milieu* are replete with cautionary explanations of certain passages of Teilhard that, he says protectively, might *sound* pantheist, or hint at Pelagian tendencies, but are really okay in context. Pelagianism is the early church heresy that suggests that Adam's original sin does not necessarily taint all succeeding generations of mankind—that human endeavor has a potential for good in this world.)

Cuomo is particularly sensitive to my imputation that his spiritual mentor was a Pelagian heretic.

"Oh no, no, no, no," he says, quadruply negative. "He wasn't a Pelagianist either."

If he seems particularly upset about the imputation of Pelagianism, it may be because it's a particularly intriguing heresy to Cuomo. And one he will soon accuse Ed Koch, of all people, of adhering to.

But meanwhile he wants to correct my misuse of the word *heretic* in its application to Teilhard:

"The harshest criticism he got from the church was not that he should stop believing what he believed—he was just told that he was to stop publishing. It was John XXIII, that magnificent contribution to our humanity, who freed him from that and allowed him to publish, but just to seminarians where they could control it with guidance and understanding. And then eventually to the world at large. But he was never declared a heretic. He was to be read with caution."

"I guess what I was getting at is, you've had this public battle with your bishop. Do *you* feel at all like a heretic?"

"If you don't mind, my *cardinal*," he says.

"Your cardinal now. Do you feel at all like a heretic?"

"No. I will be precise on this subject, and it's a great relief to be able to be. I wrote the Notre Dame speech [on his abortion position] only because the archbishop in one of his early appearances was asked on a television show whether I should be excommunicated, and my wife and son were together with me watching the show at the time, and I have never had a more painful moment than the moment of the archbishop's hesitation in answer to that question."

He pauses, a pained expression on his brow. "The archbishop has since many times, not once or twice but many times, made clear that that wasn't his intent, et cetera. But too late. The damage was done and I felt it was time therefore to write my own apologia, which I did with the help of a number of theologians. When I say the help, I wrote it and then distributed it to theologians whom I trusted. I was absolutely certain that I was right theologically, and since then in *America* magazine a couple of the leading theologians, or at least one in the country, have written that my position, whether they agreed with it or not as a matter of prudential judgment, was perfectly sound theologically, so I have no doubt that my position is sound theologically. My difference with my archbishop, now cardinal, is on a political judgment, agreeing that in my own personal life I would instruct those who wished my instruction that abortion was undesirable. What do you do about that politically? Do you try to pass a constitutional amendment which won't pass and which wouldn't do any good if it passed, or do you try to work affirmatively to convince people that there's a better way than abortion? I chose the latter. That's purely a matter of politics and I said so in the speech, and I'm right and I'm sure I'm right."

An admittedly irreverent thought strikes me at this point. How does a guy so concerned with theological correctness react to being named by *Playgirl* as one of its "Ten Sexiest Men"? A bit later I ask him what he thought of the accolade.

"Thank God John Candy made the list too," he says, laughing. "That way I won't take myself too seriously."

"What *is* your attitude toward sexual revolution or whatever you want to call what's gone on for the last twenty years? How traditional are you? Do you disapprove of permissiveness or—?"

"It's not for me to approve or disapprove," he says, criticizing my question before giving a surprisingly impassioned answer. "I don't judge people's conduct that way. I think from society's point of view it would be better if we were less open about sex. I believe we have profaned it. I believe sex is a beautiful gift of God, or whatever, fate, nature. It is a magnificent opportunity to express real feeling. It is God's device for regeneration. It is a lot of beautiful things. It is not improved by the way in which we as a society are dealing with it publicly. I think we fail to teach the reverence for it that we should. I think we have debased it and that's unfortunate. I think we're all losers as a result of that. It means less to this generation than it might have.

"It's a very personal thing. Some people are married and are frequently involved in sexual encounters, some people very infrequently. It's a personal thing. I do think from society's point of view it would have been better if we had not profaned it the way we have. But aside from that, I think as a people it would be better for us if we were more consistent in keeping violence out of our public exhibitions than sex, for all that I've said about the profaning of sex. Even worse is what we've done with violence, and popularizing violence is one of the great social sins of our time. I think those societies, I guess like Scandinavian societies where they allowed people vast freedom when it came to sexual preferences but were assiduous about trying to keep violence out of movies and publications, et cetera, where they can—that was probably a more intelligent judgment than the one we've made as a society."

Moral seriousness of this sort can be a bit of a problem with some. Recently I had dinner with a college friend and his wife who confessed their Cuomo Problem to me. They weren't the first. I'd found a number of Big Chill types who'd opted for the fast lane a bit resentful, hostile to Cuomo for reminding them of ideals—or, they'd say, illusions—they'd left behind.

Whatever was behind it, the way my friend's wife expressed her Cuomo Problem to me was: "I'd be more comfortable with Cuomo if I knew he had some really human faults, you know, even if it was that he binged on cookies at three in the morning without transforming it into a spiritual lesson."

I ask Cuomo if he would help her out by confessing to me some cookie-binge-type faults. He isn't very forthcoming.

"I have all the faults that everybody has," he insists, "all the appetites that other people have. We control them, each of us, in various ways, but we each sin seven times a day."

Somehow I don't think that was the kind of answer she had in mind, so I try to approach the virtuousness problem from another direction.

"There was something Murray Kempton said—did you read his review of your book?"

"I never understand what he's saying but I love everything he writes," Cuomo avers.

"Well he was very admiring of you in the review, but he also seemed to suggest that in your diary entries you were putting forward your humility in a somewhat prideful way."

Cuomo laughs. "See. I told you I had faults."

"Would you say it's true, though?"

"If Murray said it, I'll accept it."

I begin to shift the subject when Cuomo interrupts, not content to let Kempton have the last word on his pride/humility quotient.

"I'll say this about Murray: He has a little bit of pridefulness about the way he writes about *my* pridefulness."

Do I seem a bit captious about Cuomo here? Perhaps because we're coming to a subject upon which I find his views genuinely admirable, and I don't want to seem like an uncritical sensibility when discussing them. The subject is racial justice, and I admire Cuomo because I think he's one of the few powerful politicians in America who still takes the unfulfilled goals of the civil-rights movement seriously. Not only takes them seriously but takes seriously the task of making them work in a society that wants to ignore the past by calling itself "postracist," as the fashionable phrase goes.

You can hear how impassioned Cuomo is on the subject of race when I ask him how he would have handled racial relations in New York City differently from Ed Koch.

"There *is* a difference, I think, between the mayor and me," Cuomo says. "I think he uses the notion of *evenhandedness* where I would use the notion of *equity*. I have heard him say, 'I treat blacks and whites the same way.' That can be misunderstood at a time when disproportionate numbers of blacks are vulnerable. Then people might mishear you and think that what you're really saying is 'I don't care if you're in trouble, I'm going to treat you like the people who are not in trouble.' Now that doesn't make any sense. That's what Marie Antoinette said: Let them all eat cake. So he puts a greater stress on pure equality. I think more about trying to even up the competition. There are some who are left behind through no fault of their own, who need extra help, and I think we should give them the extra help. The analogy I have used is a family with two children, one in a wheelchair, one wins medals for track. That creates a whole series of situations where the one in the wheelchair should get a little more help than the one who can win medals at track. That's not even-handedness. So there is that difference. And I think when the mayor talks about equality a lot of blacks like it, the ones who are making it, et cetera. But the ones who are at the bottom, who are vulnerable, who are out of work, who are dropouts, think, 'You oppressed us for a couple of hundred years, you enslaved us, you debased us, you tried to dehumanize us, and then you release us and say, "Now you're like everybody else. I'm going to treat you even-handedly." But that's not right because for two hundred years you created a negative. Now you're going to have to do at least two hundred years of positive to make up for it.' I think that's the attitude that some have that the mayor doesn't successfully respond to."

Did you catch the shift Cuomo makes in the midst of this response? I could hear it in his voice, but you can see it on the printed page, too. He begins with semantic distinctions and argumentative analogies (Marie Antoinette, the family with the kid in the wheelchair) to make his point intellectually.

Then something happens to his voice. He stops speaking in his own first-person voice and begins speaking *in the voice of the victims* of racism ("You oppressed *us* for a couple of hundred years, you enslaved *us,* you debased *us . . ."*), a voice that takes on tones of genuine pain and anger, not just abstract empathy.

In that astonishing 1984 Democratic convention keynote address, Cuomo called on Americans not to cease "to feel one another's pain."* That can be an empty rhetorical formulation. But in Cuomo's case, I get a feeling it's a *description* of a kind of spiritual discipline he practices in his approach to political problems.

There's a fascinating, characteristically Cuomoesque postscript to our discussion of Koch and race, one that provides another revealing glimpse into the governor's thought process. And one that gives me an opportunity—at last—to correct an error Cuomo made, in theological reasoning no less.

I don't know whether or not it was prompted by my mention of Pelagianism in connection with his spiritual mentor, or whether Cuomo just has Pelagianism on his mind these days, but a week after our conversation in Albany a quote from Cuomo appeared in print that accused Ed Koch of "Pelagianism."

When I say "a quote from Cuomo" accused Koch of Pelagianism, I may be on shaky ground, because the quote wasn't directly attributed to the governor. The quote appeared in a Ken Auletta *Daily News* column on Koch and race; Auletta attributes the quote to "a thoughtful public official." Judge for yourself if you think I'm rash in concluding it's Cuomo speaking here:

"The core difference between Koch and, say, Governor Cuomo," the "thoughtful public official" says, "is that Koch is a Pelagian. . . . If a kid from the ghetto can't make it, the Pelagian says it's their responsibility. The fact that God placed that kid in the ghetto, gave him no father, and that he was raised poor, that's of no concern."

While I agree with Cuomo on the merits of the equality argument (if somebody can prove to me it wasn't Cuomo speaking, I promise to enter a Trappist monastery and take a vow of silence), nonetheless I think the "thoughtful public official" has made an error in the logic of his heresiology.

His comparison of Koch to the Pelagians does a disservice to the Pelagians, who were far more generous in their view of human nature than Cuomo's analogy would imply. After all, the heresy of the Pelagians was their rather optimistic belief that natural man was not inevitably corrupted by original sin and was capable, in fact, of moral good and spiritual improvement. It is the gloomy predestinarian Augustine (who believed natural man, as such, was beyond hope and who in fact was chief scourge of Pelagianism in the church) to whom Koch is more aptly compared.

---

*Okay, Bill Clinton ran this into the ground. But Clinton's meretricious use of the phrase shouldn't necessarily discredit the sentiment entirely.

And, in fact, I'd say that both Cuomo and his mentor, Teilhard, are closer in spirit—on the doctrinal spectrum that runs from Pelagius to Augustine—to the Pelagians, in their love of this world and belief in the possibility of spiritual evolution, than they are to Augustine. Indeed, there's a technical term Protestant theologian Paul Tillich uses that, although Cuomo would probably deny it, fits both Teilhard and Cuomo: "semi-crypto-Pelagians." (Here's an issue the newly Catholicized Lew Lehrman could really run with next time he debates Cuomo: Okay, it's an expensive watch, but my opponent is a semi-crypto-Pelagian.)

At this point I decided to see what Cuomo's views were on a different kind of heresy. A political heresy. About the lesson of the New York fiscal crisis. The orthodox establishment theology on this point, even among "responsible" New Yorkers, is that New York sinned, that New York and New Yorkers deserve the blame for our plight because our profligate bleeding-heart compassion was blind to hard-headed reality—and the rest of the country shouldn't be taxed to support our profligacy.

The first hint I had that Cuomo didn't buy the self-hating logic of the Blame New York First crowd was that stinging "share the derelicts" wisecrack he had delivered down in Washington a week earlier.

The governor was testifying before a House committee on his opposition to the Reagan tax plan's elimination of state- and local-tax deductibility—a complex, eye-glazing issue no Democrat wanted to touch, but which Cuomo seized on and turned into a moral crusade. One he seems to be winning.

Anyway, an earnest Republican House member from New Hampshire somewhat patronizingly suggested to Cuomo that the committee might deign to offer New York and other high-tax states with large social-service budgets "a portion" of the deductibility they wanted.

Fine, said Cuomo, and we'll send New Hampshire "a portion of our derelicts, our homeless, our illegal aliens, and drug addicts."

I thought that raised an important question the Blame New York First crowd has ignored. "Isn't it true," I ask Cuomo, "that the plight of the northern cities is not due to their immorality but to the costs they incur caring for the victims of southern racism, the vast migration of southern blacks who have sought refuge here?"

"I put it a little differently," Cuomo says, "but I made the same point and that is, we bear burdens that are basically national in their genesis and in present responsibility. Welfare, everybody knows, is a national problem. It's not ours. Not all the welfare cases are indigenous. They can travel here from any part of the country. That's the Constitution."

"Don't you think that in the way the fiscal crisis has been written about, New Yorkers have been unfairly portrayed as immoral and wasteful . . . ?"

"There is a regrettably prevalent view of us," Cuomo says, "as not just wasteful but as loud, even debauched, unpleasant, crude, indifferent to other people. I mean, it's a terribly harsh judgment. And again, it's not everybody of course, but too many people feel that way about New York. There may even be a little jealousy in it because of the spectacular quality of New York City, the bigness of it and the largeness; there may be a resentment about that. There is an intimidation factor as well. People are intimidated by the speed that they see here, the pace that they equate with frenzy. The president was aware of it, and the Republicans were aware of it and played to it by starting their whole campaign for this [tax plan] running against New York. In the president's first speech, he took the opportunity to refer to New York specifically. We're the only state he mentioned."

The talk turns to Forest Hills—and John Lindsay.

Cuomo says he met with Lindsay earlier today about the takeover bill, but sitting across the table from him, he couldn't help but think of Forest Hills.

"We didn't talk about Forest Hills," Cuomo says, "but I can't look at John without thinking of it."

Forest Hills was the beginning of the end for John Lindsay and the beginning of the beginning for Mario Cuomo.

Forest Hills—the revolt of the middle-class Queens community against the Lindsay administration plan to stick high-rise, low-income projects for ghetto dwellers in their midst—was, of course, what brought Cuomo into public life. His ability to "feel the pain" and fears of the angry white residents of Forest Hills enabled him to gain community acquiescence to a scaled-down integrated project that salvaged a workable reality from the blundering, self-destructive good intentions of the Lindsay administration.

"What's the Forest Hills project like now?" I ask Cuomo.

"It's beautiful," he says. "I went back there with Harry Reasoner a little bit ago to do *60 Minutes*. We walked the grounds. Every time I go home to Queens I go past it. I stopped by there the other day with somebody in the car just to show it to them."

"You wrote in your Forest Hills *Diary,*" I say, "that toward the end you thought it might be a turning point away from the attempt to integrate housing or, on the other hand, it might be a turning point for the better where communities are consulted, et cetera. Which do you think it has been?"

"It helped end housing programs," says Cuomo. "The Nixon impoundment was in '72, and we never had another large public-housing program. Forest Hills helped produce a political environment that allowed the federal government to walk away from its obligation for low-income housing, and they have ever since."

"Would you favor a return to some kind of attempt to . . . ?"

"I certainly would, but I'm not going to wait for it. That's why Mayor Koch and I have put together the biggest housing program in the history of the state. It would mean seventy-five thousand units if we could get the legislature to adopt the legislation we need to spend the Battery Park and Port Authority monies."

"You know Democrats have a reputation for being antibusiness. Are you antibusiness?"

"I couldn't be if I cared about those people in wheelchairs and the people out of work, because the place they're going to get a job is in the private sector. You can't make it with the public payroll. You just can't put enough people to work. It costs you too much. So if there's any hope for those eight hundred thousand or so AFDC [Aid to Families with Dependent Children] people, it's in the private sector. That means business. So I'm not only not anti-business, I am pro-business. Not so that they can all drive Rolls-Royces and wear pinkie rings but so that we can create the base we need to do the things we need for people who aren't given the chance to work because they're too old or too weak or because there simply is no job. So yes, I'm very much pro–private sector strength."

By now time was running out, and so I tried to ask the governor one last question that had been on my mind. But first I had to go through one last corrective struggle:

"Last question," I begin.

"You said that already," Cuomo snaps.

"No, I said *two* more questions."

"No, you didn't, you said two more questions *two* questions ago."

"No, no, no."

"Yes, you did."

"We'll go back to the tape."

"When you play the tape you'll see what a good lawyer I am."

Okay, it turns out he was right. But I'm still right about his semi-crypto-Pelagianism. And he let me ask my final question anyway:

"I was struck as I arrived today," I begin, "seeing John Lindsay down there with some other lobbyists waiting in line. Here was the guy who was the great hope of American liberalism and now he's a high-paid lobbyist for Drexel Burnham. Do you think you'll ever end up as a high-paid lobbyist for corporations?"

"Hmm. I don't know. I kind of doubt it. The only reason I could possibly do that would be for the money, and I hate to say this, but money has never meant everything to me that it should have. If I were a little more careful about money, I would have had a lot more of it, and I would have had a lot more freedom and probably could have done a lot more things than I have. But now

I have a son who I am sure is going to get rich if he keeps his health, and I've told him to go into the law practice. He wants public life. He never said that. He won't say it to me but I know it. He's my blood and he wants public life. But first, I told him, go and make money so they can't commandeer you. You see, if you come to this business needing the job then there is the temptation to do things you otherwise might not if you were secure. So I said, build yourself a secure niche. He'll be rich in no time. Honestly. My daughter, my first, is a doctor. My two girls after Andrea are so beautiful and so bright that they're going to make it.

"Money now means something because it keeps you free to be a public servant. I can settle for one hundred thousand dollars. I don't need two hundred fifty thousand. So I doubt very much that I would wind up that way. I'd like to wind up as a judge, a teacher maybe. Not with a lot of classes. That's too hard. I would like to wind up being free to read, being free to listen to music. So anyway, no, I don't want to be a lobbyist. No. I don't want to finish that way."

He pauses. Suddenly a new notion strikes him: "I want to die sliding into third base." Then his eyes light up: "No, throwing a hook shot. I think ideally I'd like to die with the ball just hitting the net, probably a left-hand hook shot off the back wall."

Cuomo gets up and demonstrates his form for that Final Shot.

"It just hits the net," he says with a smile of triumph. "The bell goes off. That's it."

Tales from the Cancer Cure Underground

In Which We Encounter Modern-Day Alchemists, Prophets,
Healers, Herbalists, Biomystics, Doctors of Metaphysics,
and Doctors of Medicine in a Quest for the Cure

> *. . . terrible apprehensions were among the people.*
> —DANIEL DEFOE, *A Journal of the Plague Year*

The Captain rapped on the door of my hotel room promptly at 6 A.M. He was eager to get this expedition under way. He had a decision to make, and his time was running out.

First of all, just thirty hours remained on his VA hospital pass. If he didn't make it back in time, they might find out about this peculiar below-the-border mission. Worse, they might search his room and confiscate whatever magic potion he managed to bring back.

And the time was fast approaching when they were scheduled to do that CAT scan on the Captain's liver, get a picture, give a local habitation and a name to that vexing shadow on his last X ray. They had already cut a malignancy out of his intestines—this shadow could be the dread metastasis.

"No use pretending you're brave or whistling past the graveyard," the Captain told me as we headed south on 405. "I know I've got it again."

But this time the Captain was going to be ready with a plan of his own. That's why he'd asked to hitch a ride with me on my exploratory trip to the cancer clinics of Tijuana. There were at least a half dozen establishments down there offering every kind of exotic therapy and esoteric substance driven below the border by U.S. authorities—everything from the mysterious decades-old Hoxsey elixir to coffee-enema cures, fetal sheep–cell injections, and three varieties of metabolic enzyme treatments. The Captain wanted to scout them all so he'd have his escape route ready when the CAT scan delivered its diagnosis.

"I know surgery is not the answer," the Captain declared. "I can say that from experience. I took chemotherapy and it was rough. I couldn't take it anymore, and from experience, from the statistics, I know it doesn't work. So they told me, 'Why don't you try immunotherapy?' That was equally rough. They inject dead cells in an alcohol base into your back. I still have the scars. Devilish rough. You can see it in the doctors' eyes—they know they're up against something they can't beat."

The Captain does not say the word *rough* from the perspective of a man who's lived a life of ease. Not counting his wartime Marine Corps service, he's spent most of his sixty years working as a mining geologist in one rough place or another, prospecting for platinum in the Bering Strait, seeking rare earths and precious metals in the feverish interiors of Central America. The Captain never minded the physical privations of the prospector's life, he told me—it was malignant fate that had treated him roughly.

"Had a reef of platinum off the Aleutians," he sighed. "Would have made my fortune. I was back in the States getting ready to sell shares of it when a goddamn earthquake wiped it out."

The same thing happened down in Yucatán, the Captain said. Titanium this time, a sizzling vein of it. Another earthquake and it was gone.

These reverses left the Captain—who has no fortune or family to fall back on—at the mercy of the VA when the malignancy first showed up. He complains bitterly of the degrading, no privacy, prisonlike confinement at the hospital, but he has nowhere else to go.

Still, circumstances have not deprived the Captain of his drive, his prospector's instinct, and this time he is on the trail of something more valuable than any of the precious metals he sought in the past. This time the Captain is prospecting for a cancer cure.

So are we all, of course. Who hasn't felt the crablike pincers of cancer panic? In Defoe's time those who spotted the first deadly tokens of the plague on themselves ran madly through the streets shrieking their despair. In our time cancer patients commit suicide on public TV.

While cancer itself is not contagious, the fear is. Defoe's plague year narrator reports that the weekly bills of mortality often featured two or three unfortunates whose cause of death was inscribed: "*frighted,* that is, frighted to death. But besides those who were so frighted as to die upon the spot, there were great numbers frighted to other extremes, some frighted out of their senses . . . and some out of their understanding."

Yes, cancer is just another disease, as Susan Sontag strenuously reminds us in *Illness as Metaphor.* We shouldn't attach any special mystery or dread to it. But we do. And until our medicine men can come up with the magic bullet to kill it, we can't help thinking about it as something more than a disease— some dark curse in the chromosomes, perhaps the symptoms of original sin let loose at the cellular level, a clue to the bittersweet mystery of life.

There would be less temptation to indulge in such speculation if medical science were offering us evidence of inexorable progress toward a cure, or at least an explanation. But while cure rates (actually five-year survival rates) have risen for certain types of cancers—some childhood leukemias and certain localized tumors—two out of three stricken with cancer still die of the disease when treated with what the American Cancer Society calls "proven methods" (surgery, radiation, chemotherapy). And many people suffer more from the side effects of these proven methods of treatment than from the disease. Even the American Cancer Society concedes that "standard management . . . unfortunately may be so fearsome in itself that many people are strongly tempted to seek unproven methods of treatment."

Unproven methods: Defoe's narrator reports that in those plague years, when people despaired of their physicians, they turned to "charms, philtres, exorcisms, amulets and I know not what preparations . . . as if the plague was not the hand of God but a kind of a possession of an evil spirit."

Today, again, the fear of evil spirits—those insidious, invisible carcinogens that possess our precious body fluids—is upon the land. The faith of the people in the cathedrals of orthodox cancer cures is falling away, and thousands are turning for exorcism to the heresies, the sects, the cults, the curious theories of unorthodox cancer cures.

We're not just talking about laetrile here, we're talking about a whole subculture that has existed in this country for at least the century and a half since "Doctor William A. Rockefeller, the Celebrated Cancer Specialist" set himself up for business in the 1840s and sold some black viscous gunk that he claimed would result in "all cases of cancer cured unless too far gone, and they can be greatly benefited." (Doc Rockefeller never made his fortune from his cancer cure; it was only when his son John D. Rockefeller found other uses for the black gunk that petroleum made a little money for the family.)

Still, the popular impression about the unorthodox cancer cure world is that it is composed mainly of cash-hungry charlatans and snake-oil salesmen eager to make an easy killing off the sufferings and hopes of cancer victims. In fact, among the healers, the prophets, and the alchemists, you find less greed than evangelical fervor—the rapturous conviction of religious visionaries. Most healers have their own biomystical theology, a eucharist that may be apricot kernels or sheep cells, their own vision of the nature of the beast, of the evil spirits that possess the flesh and ravage the body with tumors. Cancer cure prophets portray themselves suffering the sublime torment of having absolute knowledge of the secrets of life and, yet, being disbelieved. Let me cite, for instance, the agony of the author of *The Grape Cure.* This book, still sold in health food stores, was first published in the 1920s by a South African immigrant named Johanna Brandt. Unable to convince stiff-necked doctors that a diet of grapes and water would cure cancer she cries out: "To hold the key to the solution of most of the problems of life and to have it rejected untried as worthless, that is to pass through the dark night of the soul. . . . To offer the gift of deliverance from pain . . . and to see it spurned—that is crucifixion—Calvary."

But wait. There's one kicker to this, to gazing condescendingly at the cancer cure subculture as a case study in the anthropology of religion: One of them might be right. What if one of the alchemists or biomystics in this murky netherworld may have somehow stumbled on to something that has eluded the one-track minds of orthodox cobalt and cyclotron technology? We all know the French Academy laughed at Pasteur and his ridiculous "invisible organism" theory of disease.

Even the American Cancer Society concedes that there is something going on with "unproven methods" of cancer management: "A common pattern is that of the proponent who has tried a remedy in several people with what seems to be good results." The American Cancer Society disparages such good results as "often based entirely on the subjective response of the patient, which may result from the false hope instilled in him."

Whatever the explanation, false-hope cures seem to spring up and sweep the nation like religious revivals, a new one at least every decade. In the twenties it was Coley's toxins and Koch's glyoxylide injections; in the thirties it was the Coffee Humber extract and Hoxsey's herbs; in the forties, the Gerson coffee enema and liver extract regimen; in the fifties orgone energy and Krebiozen. The sixties saw the birth of the laetrile apricot pit cure, the seventies, the Wobe-Mugos and other metabolic enzyme cures, and the eighties seem to be headed for a revival of mind cures—some synthesis of self-hypnotic visualization and psychic self-healing techniques—but who knows what's next?

The natural history of these cancer cure cults is, curiously, not unlike the natural history of the tumors they attack. First they swell rapidly with the revivalistic fervor of the faithful and the testimonials of the cured, then they undergo fierce attacks from orthodox medicine. But at a certain point—just as a malignant growth succeeds only in destroying itself when it kills its host—these cults either collapse of their own pathology or go into remission, shrinking and retreating to below-the-border clinics, surviving or providing in their demise a fertile subculture of unorthodox adherents ready to nourish the next eruption.

Although relations between rival healers within the subculture are frequently characterized by fierce infighting and subtle character assassination, they tend to suspend their intrigues once or twice a year and assemble for mass ecumenical rallies of the unorthodox believers, gatherings that are part therapy theory tournaments, part Renaissance Faire, and part revival crusades for the cancerphobic faithful.

And so it came to pass that on the Fourth of July of this plague year, I joined more than a thousand pain-filled pilgrims, healers, herbalists, alchemists, doctors of medicine, and doctors of metaphysics converging on the Ambassador Hotel in Los Angeles for the eighth annual convention of the Cancer Control Society, one of the leading unorthodox alliances. It was there that I met the Captain and we made our plans for a caravan to the clinics below the border.

The L.A. Convention: Bad Thoughts and Cosmic Kicks

The Ambassador ballroom: It's hard to forget the look of the place from all those clips of Bobby Kennedy at the podium delivering what were to be his last words. But I'm early, and the action isn't around the podium. The action is around the vast gold-draped periphery of the near empty ballroom, where exhibitors are rushing to unpack the wares they'll display for the next three days of the show.

At the back of the ballroom, in a prime position for crowd flow, I spy a big banner pinned to the wall proclaiming the availability of Betty Lee Morales "Signature Brand" Supplements. And there, below the banner, I spot Betty Lee herself, a large, jolly, but formidable woman, president of the Cancer Control Society, our hostess for this convocation.

Betty Lee is busy helping her husband unpack the Signature Brand samples he will be taking orders for during the convention. Betty Lee has put her personal signature on her spouse as well as her vitamins—both she and her husband are wearing identical bright-blue Polynesian-style shirts. Betty Lee designed these matching husband-and-wife outfits, a different one for each day of the convention.

Of course, Betty Lee and her husband are not the only entrepreneurs busily setting up wares to display for the health seekers now streaming into the ballroom for the opening session. Along the three sides of the ballroom and spilling over to two adjoining indoor and one outdoor room you can find tables and booths offering the following goods and services, to name a few: Lone Star Cancer Only Life Insurance Policies, Cancer Book House, air ionizers, water distillers, Vit-Ra-Tox Seven-Day Cleansing Program, Gerovital (GH3) Romanian rejuvenation tours, Novafon Ultrasound vibrators, DMSO, Hydrazine Sulfate, three kinds of laetrile, Vita Florum healing water, Polarity Therapy, Computer Nutritional Analysis from Donsbach University, Wheat Grass Therapy at the Hippocrates Health Institute, Biomagnetic Therapy in Puerto Rico, two clinics from Tijuana, trampolines ("rebound physiology energizers"), slanted posture beds, Selenium, Iridology, Holistic survival food, Moksha Prem (massage and polarity specialist), Dr. Cayenne (laxative specialist), Silica B-15, Bee Propolis, Gerson Therapy, and Life-Force.

This Bartholomew Fair atmosphere is a little confusing to the newcomer. Betty Lee Morales's remarks from the podium this morning concede that the unorthodox forces don't present the seeker with any single answer. "You'll hear contradictory advice in the next few days," she tells the thousand or so people gathered for the opening. "You'll hear some people say low protein is the only way, others will say it has to be high protein, same with vegetarian and nonvegetarian." But Betty Lee, whose Signature Brand vitamin line happens to include animal gland extracts, has a peppery piece of advice for puritanical veggies who speak of the sacredness of animal souls. "I'd advise you to read *The Secret Life of Plants,*" she says. After reading about the terror and anguish plants feel at being plucked, you'll never again blame yourself for taking the life of an animal, she tells us.

Terror and toxicity, anguish and blame are the recurrent themes of the morning's program, which concentrates on the prevention of cancer rather than the cure. Betty Lee strikes the keynote of blame when she says, "Our hearts go out to those who have already produced cancer in their bodies." If you've got it, it's your fault—you produced it.

Some even go so far as to say you're practically seducing an otherwise innocent carcinogen into performing an unnatural act within your flesh. Thelma Arthur, a little gray-haired M.D. who's spent forty years advocating mass screening of the population with her controversial Arthur Metabolic Immuno-Differential, describes the seduction this way: "A wandering little carcinogen happened by your system. He wasn't strong, but you were weak. He looked around for some real estate. Found a place to build a cocoon." He's just a cuddly little creature until he's turned into an insatiable beast by your own sinful toxicity.

Whence comes this shameful toxicity? For years the constipated colon has reigned supreme in the realm of the unorthodox as chief seat of the carcinogenic enemy within, and colon-cleansing advocates are out in strength at this year's convention.

"You don't read much in the newspapers about bowel movements," Dr.

Harold Manner, keynote speaker at the CCS banquet, tells us in the middle of our meal. "But it's not really true that you are what you eat. You are what you digest, assimilate, and properly eliminate."

While the late Freudian heretic Wilhelm Reich had been ridiculed for his assertion that regular orgasmic spasms of sufficient potency are essential to preventing cancer, are the connection to the healing rhythmic energy of creation, the current cancerphobic fanatics seem to have regressed in asserting that intestinal peristalsis is the central rhythm of life and the key to curing cancer. I think my appreciation of one of the world's great paintings has been forever besmirched by the colon-connected comment Count Anton Schenk makes at this convention. The count specializes in fetal lamb–cell cancer cures. Nevertheless, he feels compelled to go into a panegyric on the central importance of colon cleansing to human happiness, concluding, "When I see the famous picture of the Mona Lisa . . . the reason she seems to smile so, I think I have found it. She must have received a successful enema."

But there are signs of a shift lately, signs that the new locus of terror will not be the bowels but the brain, the new focus of cure will not be the cleansing of the colon but of the cortex—brainwashing, some might say. There's a terrifying new enemy in the unorthodox cancer world—*bad thoughts*. Our own thought processes may be as deadly as processed foods. Guilt, repression, anxiety not only make you a drag at parties, but these negative emotions also add up to a vaguely defined "carcinogenic personality." To be healthy one must think healthy thoughts all the time or face dire physiological consequences. This analysis has opened the way for all sorts of New Age shrinks, encounter-group therapists, meditation, visualization, and hypnosuggestive healers to enter the cancer cure field. One of the most sophisticated syntheses of all these approaches is represented at the convention by a group called Life-Force, whose cancer project offers psychotherapeutic counseling to cancer patients.

One of the leaders of Life-Force, a charismatic minister and psychotherapist named Dr. Richard Turner, goes so far as to tell the cancer conventioneers that even when one does contract cancer, one should not allow oneself bad thoughts about the diagnosis. One should, instead, welcome it, embrace the malignant growth as an opportunity for personal growth. Dr. Turner cites one client who came to him for counseling after a cancer diagnosis and "realized it gave her a cosmic kick!" Another Life-Force cofounder explains, "When you have cancer you can do anything you want!"

Of Fathers and Sons and Apricot Kernels

During the intermission following the first block of speakers, thousands of conventioneers and scores of cancer-cure subculture celebrities mingle amidst the exhibits and swirl through the corridors with the noise of ionizers, massagers, juicers and food millers buzzing away in the background.

It's late morning, and in the midst of the corridor swirl I am privileged to witness the grand entrance of Ernst T. Krebs, Jr. Krebs bears himself with the immense dignity of a hereditary prince in exile come to survey the squabbling disarray of his émigré rabble. He glows with a grandiose serenity that is, in part, a hereditary legacy. Krebs and his father, E. T. Krebs, Sr., were the first to apply an apricot kernel extract called amygdalin to the cure of cancer. Krebs's father's father was a German *Apotheker,* and both son and grandson inherited the magisterial dignity, the imperious certitude of that elite class of chemists.

Now, at last, thirty-five years after father and son collaborated on the discovery that led to laetrile, several states, including California, have legalized the apricot kernel compound, and four of the nation's top cancer centers— Mayo Clinic, Memorial Sloan-Kettering, UCLA, and University of Arizona— are, under the auspices of the National Cancer Institute, administering it to human cancer patients in controlled clinical trials. The patients are mostly terminal cases on whom orthodox therapies have failed. If there are any positive results, Krebs may well be elevated to the instant sainthood status of great healers like Jonas Salk. The man who cures cancer will stalk the earth like a colossus, and strong men will weep to see him as he passes by.

If the tests go badly Krebs will be condemned to spend the rest of his life at conventions like this, a pretender to the throne recognized only by terminal true believers.*

Krebs radiates total confidence of vindication. A large man with luminous straw-colored hair, pale jowly flesh encased in a luminous blue suit, he exudes a combination of W. J. Bryan's passion (thou shalt not crucify mankind on a cross of carcinogens) and W. C. Fields's imperious grandiosity. Buoyed by the prospect of imminent transfiguration Krebs's voice swells as he describes his father's and his discovery of B-17 as "a Copernican revolution" in the biological sciences. "Laetrile offers hope for not just cancer but for the entire range of degenerative diseases that affect mankind." The discoveries of the Krebs family will return human health to what Krebs claims was once, long ago, an Edenic state.

There is a whole theology of a Fall implicit in Krebsian biology. Once, Krebs tells the throng around him in the corridor of the Ambassador Hotel, once, long ago, "the flesh of all the fruits we know today contained sufficient quantities of B-17" to prevent the development of the diseases that plague us today. But civilization and hybridization tainted these trees of life and the fruits thereof, driving the redeeming biochemical essence deep within the ker-

*None of the trials gave the laetrile believers the scientific validation they'd hoped for.

nel, inaccessible to the bite. The final fall came with the Romans, says Krebs. "When they grafted the sweet almond shoot onto the bitter almond root, the last dietary source of laetrile was lost because the bitter but not the sweet almond kernel contained B-17." The fall of Rome followed soon thereafter.

Not until 1,500 years later did Krebs's father rediscover that which had been lost, and he died without seeing his healing vision fulfilled. The son has dedicated his life to liberating the promise of redemption encapsulated in the kernels and to restoring to mankind this enzymatic eucharist that has the power to transubstantiate tumors and make possible the remission of civilization's carcinogenic original sin.

If you think I am exaggerating the religious dimension of the laetrilists' cause, that's obviously because you haven't read a book called *Thank God I Have Cancer!* It is the work of the Reverend Clifford Oden of Garland, Texas, who says he cured his colon cancer with laetrile but whose more important contribution is to make explicit the religious righteousness of the theory of laetrile cytochemistry.

The Reverend Oden argues that since God created all flesh, benign and malignant, cancer cannot be bad. God made cancer. It must have a meaning, a purpose. A malignancy is, in fact, a message from God embedded in the flesh.

In the midst of Krebs's triumphant laetrile litany, a short, intense, dark-eyed figure persists in interrupting him with a passionate and unorthodox dissent from Krebs's own unorthodoxy. He says that the laetrile of the father hath not the magic of the laetrile of the son, that the son has betrayed his father's legacy.

The dark-eyed dissenter is a naturopath from Pasadena named Richard Barmakian, and his story of a lost laetrile formula clearly disturbs Krebs's serenity. Barmakian describes a quest he went on when "a dear friend of mine was dying of cancer." It took him down below the border to Tecate, Mexico, to see a man he regarded as a kind of wizard of unorthodoxy. Tracking the wizard to his Tecate lair, thirty-four miles east of Tijuana, Barmakian begged him to reveal "anything he knew about curing cancer that I didn't because I just wasn't going to let my friend die. I was determined to save her.

"He was very hesitant to come out with this information. It took him over an hour before he finally opened up and began to explain certain things to me. He told me how when he had lung cancer he had gone to see Krebs Sr., who gave him some little tiny capsules. In very short order his lung cancer disappeared. This was the original effective product with all the enzymes in it. Finally he opened up and told me the story of the real product versus the so-called laetrile of today." Unfortunately Barmakian left Tecate empty-handed; the wizard had none of the real stuff left.

As soon as he got back Barmakian "called a source I knew in Krebs's lab.

The source was reluctant to talk, and when he finally realized I knew what I was talking about he yelled, 'How did you hear about this?'

"After much persuasion he sent me two vials, one of which I sent to my friend airmail special delivery. In three months' time—she'd already been taking laetrile, the present kind, for her adenocarcinoma without results—she recovered."

In the corridor I ask Krebs whether his product differs somehow from his father's potion. "No," Krebs the younger thunders. "No. I have never deviated one micromilligram from the original formula my father and I perfected."

Still, Krebs acknowledges the confusions about real laetrile and false laetrile. I ask Krebs as he makes his way, throng in tow, into the ballroom, which of the laetrile brands is the best. He frowns. "The question is which is the worst."

Missing Persons at the Feast

There is a ghost hovering over the great Cancer Control Society banquet, haunting Dr. Ernesto Contreras even as the smiling Tijuana clinician steps forward to accept his Humanitarian of the Year award at the climax of the ceremonies in the Ambassador's Coconut Grove.

No one at the banquet has the bad taste to touch on the troubling presence of the phantom at the head table. But the death of little Chad Green has cast a shadow on the humanitarian aura surrounding the Humanitarian of the Year. Chad Green had become a cause célèbre in the unorthodox cancer cure subculture when his parents refused the conventional chemotherapy Massachusetts doctors prescribed for his leukemia because they wanted to treat him "holistically." When the state took them to court and a judge ordered them to submit Chad to the conventional chemo regimen recommended by his doctors, the Greens took Chad and fled the country, crossed the border to Mexico where he was admitted to the Tijuana clinic of Dr. Contreras, sometimes known as the godfather of laetrile. The Greens instantly became unorthodox outlaw celebrities, their cause taken up by the curious alliance of New Age and old right-wing defenders of "freedom to choose." The story did not have a happy ending, although the causes of Chad's subsequent death are still the subject of bitter controversy.

At the convention this year, every effort has been made to spare Dr. Contreras, Humanitarian of the Year, the indignity of having to confront questions about Chad's death. During last year's convention, by contrast, Chad's name had been on everyone's lips and everyone loved and blessed the brave little boy in his struggle. This year, Chad's inconvenient death makes his name something of an embarrassment. He's no longer a live martyr, no longer a dead person. He's become a virtual nonperson.

Nor have Chad's parents, Jerry and Diana Green, been made to feel particularly welcome anymore. While the convention program had promised their appearance, they turned out to be no-shows—and under puzzling circumstances at that. Jerry and Diana Green had been scheduled to speak just prior to Contreras's presentation. It turned out that the young couple could not afford travel expenses to the convention, and the CCS declined to help, forcing them to cancel. Bitter acrimony, angry charges, and countercharges broke out between Contreras and the Greens when Chad died. Even the actual cause of the child's death is still a subject of dispute between the doctor and the parents.

Contreras sheds no new light on this mystery during his appearance at the convention. He never once mentions Chad's name. But three days later, below the border at Contreras's clinic, we would confront the godfather of laetrile with the ghost of Chad.

The Mexican Connection: Goat Glands and Horse-Sore Salves

It was on the final afternoon of the convention that the Captain and I made our connection with the woman who would guide us on our Tijuana odyssey. Her name is Marilyn Merrill, and our first stop the next morning was her home in Laguna Hills, where we were scheduled to rendezvous with the other pilgrims and curiosity seekers who would make up our border-crossing caravan.

As we took a Laguna Hills exit off 405, the Captain was in the middle of telling me a surprising story about the premedical uses to which the legendary Ernst T. Krebs the elder had applied apricot kernels. It seems that back in the twenties, before Repeal, the Captain's father was running a small distillery and sought out Krebs in San Francisco.

"That's when I first met Krebs," the Captain explained. "He was supplying apricot kernel extract, essentially amygdalin, to bootleggers."

"Why would bootleggers want laetrile?" I asked.

"This was before it was laetrile," the Captain said, before it became a cancer cure. "Back then it was just an apricot pit extract they used to improve the taste of bootleg liquor. Took the edge off."

Although fashions in prohibition have changed—with liquor now legal and laetrile bootlegged—a Prohibition atmosphere still prevails in the cancer-cure world with the prohibited elixir the object of smuggling, adulteration, and intrigue. In its *Unproven Methods* pamphlet, the American Cancer Society warns darkly against "the 'underground railroad' whereby cancer patients from all over the United States are directed to Mexico . . . for treatment with worthless or unproven methods." Reading that, I had visions of frightened cancer patients crouching in dank basements, moving only at night, the FDA hot on their heels.

But there were no dank basements in Laguna Hills, a prosperous Orange

County suburb. In fact, the gathering of patients and guide at this "underground railroad" way station looked more like an angry suburban kaffeeklatsch.

They were angry because we were late. When the Captain and I pulled into the driveway we found that our fellow pilgrims—two women cancer patients, the husband of one of them and a New Age journalist, Peter Chowka—had been pacing around for an hour, impatient to get our Tijuana safari under way. Our schedule called for us to see no less than five clinics in a single day and, considering the difficulty of finding one's way below the border and the urgency that the possibility of redemption on the journey promised, they were in no mood to waste any more time.

Indeed, there was some grumbling as efforts to consolidate cars into a more compact caravan caused confusion. All this and an unexpected seat switch caused one of the eager pilgrims, a pleasant middle-aged woman we'll call Renee, to burst into tears.

None of this seemed to faze our jolly guide, Marilyn, who finally got us straightened out and under way. How did Marilyn get into her strange business of being travel agent for the underground railroad?

It began with the phone calls. A few years ago, when she became head of the Orange County chapter of the International Association of Cancer Victims and Friends, she began to get calls from time zones all over the world, sometimes in the middle of the night. They were pleas from cancer patients eager for something to hope for below the border, fearful of the unknown, asking her, "What's it really like *down there* on the other side?" not just "Will this save me, or my mother?" but "Is it safe? Is it clean? Is it for real?"

She began ferrying friends across the border to see for themselves. When some local clubwomen asked her to take the whole club, Marilyn rented a bus. It became a regular practice, then a kind of business: bus-along tours to the Tijuana cancer clinics with Marilyn acting as tour guide, speakers from the cancer cure subculture, lunch at the Gerson clinic, chats with patients and doctors. Marilyn's theory about the cures people report from unorthodox treatments holds that those who go below the border with the will to fight will come back up with a greater chance to live regardless of which therapy they choose: It's the border-crossing process itself that is decisive—the decision to go beyond the bounds of the death-sentence certainties of orthodox medicine.

Still, Marilyn is, in effect, a connoisseur of cancer clinics, and I was eager to find out from her which one she'd choose if she faced a personal emergency. While she wouldn't commit herself unequivocally, she did confide that when her mother was diagnosed with skin cancer Marilyn wasted no time in dragging her down to the Hoxsey clinic in Tijuana, where, Marilyn said, the Hoxsey tonic cured her. She'd go there herself, Marilyn said, if she had a similar malignancy.

I was somewhat taken aback: The Hoxsey cure is—especially when considered in light of all the sophisticated, holistic, enzymatic, crypto-scientific cures and prevention regimens mushrooming in the alternative cancer-cure world—the oldest and purest throwback to the age of magical elixirs, secret potions, snake-oil peddlers with cancer salves. I wasn't even aware a Hoxsey clinic existed anymore, although I had read something of its colorful, controversial history.

The legend of the Hoxsey elixir takes us back to the 1840s, when "celebrated cancer specialist" Rockefeller was still selling his cancer salves at medicine shows. The Hoxsey cure had an even humbler origin: as a horse-sore salve.

Great Grampa Hoxsey had this prize stallion, you see, who developed a big cancerous growth on his hoof. He put him out to pasture to die. Well, suddenly, the story goes, the old stallion started to get better. The tumor shrank, and Grampa Hoxsey decided it was because of something the horse had been eating out there in the far pasture. He watched what herbs he went for, compounded them into a salve and started to treat other farm animals with it.

The formula stayed in the family as a horse cure until Harry's father began to try it out on human cancers with amazing results. When the father died the story takes a kind of biblical turn. Seventeen-year-old Harry was the youngest of twelve children, and because he was his father's eager assistant in the cancer salve business, it was to him that the dying old man passed the birthright for the secret formula. He made him memorize it. Later the other brothers and sisters greedily tried to wrest the rights to the formula from Harry, but it existed only in his head—and he kept it there.

Harry Hoxsey built his birthright into a headline-making healing empire. His clinics swelled with devotees claiming cures every place he set up shop, but Hoxsey never bothered to get an M.D. degree and ended up in fractious litigation with the AMA wherever he went, eventually making his last stand in Dallas. Hoxsey won most of his legal battles—including a sensational slander suit against AMA spokesman Morris Fishbein—but eventually the fierce struggles took their toll, and after two heart attacks he moved his clinic below the border in the early sixties and put it in the care of his longtime chief nurse, Mildred Nelson. Now on a hilltop in Tijuana, she presides over a little adobe house that is the shrunken remnant of the once vast Hoxsey empire. It was to be, Marilyn told me, our first stop.

Marilyn is worried about Nurse Mildred's situation, she told me. She's worried about the whole future, in fact, of what remains of the Hoxsey enterprise. Unlike Harry Hoxsey, Nurse Mildred isn't evangelical. She's content to cure whoever happens to come to her. She doesn't have promotional booths at the cancer cure conventions the way the other unorthodox healers do. The only pamphlet she's printed up is primitive compared with those of other clinics.

There are some clinics inside and outside the United States that peddle what they purport to be Hoxsey elixir, but according to Marilyn only Mildred has possession of the original formula. Marilyn fears for the preservation of the true Hoxsey formula in Mildred's fragile exile outpost.

Just before we reached the border our cancer cure caravan stopped to re-group in the parking lot near Motel 8 in San Isidro. This particular Motel 8 has become a popular way station and outpatient residence for cancer victims. They go for below-the-border treatments during the day and return for a good old-fashioned cheapo American motel at night. Motel 8 offers shuttle-bus service to most of the clinics, some of them driven by the Jehovah's Witnesses, who for religious reasons prefer the unorthodox treatments.

In the parking lot Marilyn opened up the back of her car and offered sandwiches, coffee, and snacks from the massive supply she'd packed. The Captain emerged from the black Cadillac he'd switched to and offered a selection of the plastic, foil-sealed, watery fruit juices he brought from his VA hospital stash. Across the parking lot, across a mile or so of scrub, the hills of Tijuana rose in a jumble ahead of us, a maze of crooked streets and alleys covering their contours.

For years Tijuana and other Mexican border towns have been a refuge for an extraordinary array of health dissidents and quacks whose prescriptions and procedures had gotten them in trouble with U.S. authorities. First and still perhaps the strangest of the border-town healers is the notorious Dr. Brinkley who pioneered the goat gland operation and built up a huge medico-populist following in the Midwest and South during the thirties, twice coming within a few votes of getting elected governor of Kansas.

Dr. Brinkley's goat gland operation—he actually transplanted the testicles of goats into the scrota of men for what he claimed were curative and rejuvenative effects—never really went over big with established U.S. medical men. So he was forced to pioneer some of the border-town clinical protocols that cancer cure dissidents would later emulate, using one of the ultrapowerful clear channel X stations based below the border to evangelize half the nation with his messianic medical messages, thus attracting attention to the clinic in a way FCC and FDA authorities couldn't control.

Forbidden cures, like forbidden thrills, have become an enduring part of the lore and the lure of border towns in the popular imagination. Since things have loosened up above the border these days, there aren't too many fantasies or forbidden visions—give or take a donkey or two—you need to go to Tijuana to fulfill, and cancer cure cults are the last refuge of the strange and forbidden exoticism that once seduced people below the border.

In Which We Get to Taste the Tonic

We got lost for about five minutes after we crossed the border. The route to the Hoxsey clinic goes through a part of town that has no street signs, and none of the passersby we asked knew the way to General Ferreira Street. Marilyn usually has a hired Mexican driver for her bus-alongs who knows the way. "I'm facing backward giving the lectures, so I never know the route except from the back," she said, explaining her difficulty. But she's a remarkably calm pathfinder, and, suddenly, as we struggled up a crooked road whose potholes seemed to have been the work of land mine blasts, we crested a hill, and she shouted, "There it is."

There it was, indeed. Not an impressive edifice from the outside, certainly not when compared with the huge Hoxsey clinic in Dallas. Marilyn recalled that when she first took her mother to the modest adobe-and-stucco building with the chipped and peeling exterior, the poor woman burst into tears and sobbed, "Why have you brought me *here*?" She changed her tune, said Marilyn, as soon as she met Nurse Mildred.

Inside, three or four patients sat in the rather dilapidated waiting room, which is graced only by a small black-and-white portrait of the late Harry Hoxsey, the vigorous hatchet-faced healer in his prime. Nurse Mildred was in the middle of a diagnostic conference with the Mexican doctors when we arrived.

While we waited for her I spoke with one patient in the waiting room. His name is Mr. Thomasina, he said in the accent of his native Greece. He lives with his wife in Canoga Park, California. His case history in brief: a diagnosis of prostate cancer with pelvic bone metastasis. "They wanted to operate," Mr. Thomasina said, "but they didn't give me much hope. I knew somebody who'd been cured by Hoxsey back in the fifties. So I came down here instead. That was last spring. I'm in good shape again. Take the tonic four times a day, come back every six months for a checkup."

I was talking to another patient who'd come all the way from Canada to get a lump in her breast treated when Marilyn appeared in the waiting room and told us that Nurse Mildred Nelson would see us now.

She was not what I'd expected. By this time I thought I'd run into just about every variety of cancer-cure person you could imagine—the pseudoscholarly didact, the charismatic mystic, the martyred medico. I thought I'd heard every possible sophisticated, holistic, anticancer, megavitamin, nutritional-supplement rap going.

Yet here on a hilltop in Tijuana was an old-fashioned nurse with an old-fashioned tonic—a tall, angular Texas woman who said she'd cured 80 percent of her cancer patients. She projected no charismatic healer vibes, she didn't even feel it necessary to attack the claims of rival cures ("They may be doing good for people for all I know"). She just sat next to her battered metal file cabinets ignoring the paint peeling from the ceiling, the ringing phones and the chatter of the Mexican doctors scurrying back and forth, and told us how back in the year 1946 she'd left her quiet life as a practical nurse in the tiny west Texas prairie town of Jacksboro and gone to work for the notorious Harry Hoxsey.

Her mother had cancer, and her father devised a plan that he wanted to hide from his practical nurse daughter. "My dad was haulin' heavy machinery into Dallas a lot so I didn't think too much of it when he asked me to bring Mom in on one of the trips," Mildred recalled. "Then he tells me about this new doctor we're goin' to see, and we'd already been to every doctor far as San Antone, but when he starts describing this Harry Hoxsey, I said, 'You're going to a quack.' " She spit out the word "quack" with severe west Texas contempt.

She had no hesitation telling the great Hoxsey himself "You're a quack" when he handed her mother his bottle of tonic. She was stunned when Hoxsey responded amiably by offering her a job in his clinic. "He said, 'If I cure your mother's cancer, will you come work for me?' " He did. She did.

At first, Mildred said, she couldn't believe some of the results she was seeing. "Harry was quite the talker, you know, and he'd tell me one after another, each bigger than the next, and I wouldn't believe it. Took me a year working there to get my feet on the floor, see the improvement month by month in the people coming in before I'd begin to believe it."

The memory of the late irrepressible founder brought some warmth to her eyes, and the severe chief-nurse frown softened. But then I asked what seemed to be *the* wrong question around the place, and she snapped at me like I was some fool patient who couldn't keep his mouth shut on the fever thermometer. "Isn't one of the criticisms of the Hoxsey therapy that the formula's a secret?" I asked. "What happens if, uh, you should pass away without—I mean, might it end up being lost to the world?"

"That's not true," she snapped at me. "For the longest time we've printed the ingredients right on the bottle. And that has been published a number of times."

So would it be possible for someone to formulate it on their own?

"No, I have to put it together in a particular way," she said.

"Well, what will happen if—"

"I'll have someone right here who will do it. That's in the works right now. When Harry died five years ago I wasn't responsible for it, but at his death I became responsible for it."

"Why has it been the feeling that the process should be kept a secret?" Peter Chowka asked.

"He wanted them to recognize it, and then he would turn it all loose."

"So, you feel that because it hasn't been subjected to a fair test, there's no reason to let anyone know how it's prepared?" Chowka asked.

"Right. Not only that, there are a number of them today who will tell you, 'We're using the Hoxsey medicine,' and they know nothing about it. There are herb places that tell you they have the Hoxsey formula, but it isn't the Hoxsey formula."

Mildred's assurances about the preservation of the genuine formula left me feeling uneasy. Was it in a safe-deposit box somewhere or still in her head while the transition was "in the works"? So powerful is the aura of integrity of this woman, yet so strange and fragile the circumstances in which she works, that I found myself terribly worried that this elixir might be lost to the world. The impulse to believe or to suspend disbelief is that strong below the border. Perhaps it's the Lourdes, the pilgrimage effect. You've come all the way to a strange place and you're more likely to experience a miracle here than in Elm City General Hospital back home.

Well, at least I wouldn't die without a taste of the real thing, because at that point Mildred was called away to another room, the Captain and Renee disappeared, and Marilyn emerged from another part of the clinic brandishing a big bottle of brown liquid.

"Want to taste?" she asked, removing the cap and giving me a sniff.

It smelled like cough medicine, the awful elixir terpin hydrate my parents had to force down my throat.

At last, a taste. Marilyn took my palm and turned the lip of the bottle over onto it. I hesitated, looking at the ring of sticky residue she'd left. I took a lick.

It was bitter like elixir terpin hydrate, strong like cough medicine. Not *too* bitter, on the other hand. I was finishing up the last sticky bit when the Captain and Renee emerged from a back room, their faces red, their hands clutching brown paper bags. Mildred wasn't anywhere to be seen.

Marilyn told us all it was time to move on to the next clinic if we wanted to finish by midnight. It wasn't until we were back in her car bumping down the hill that she told me what happened in the back room.

"Mildred is terrific, isn't she?" said Marilyn. "Did you see what she did for those two people?"

"What?" I asked.

"She gave them the medication. It was amazing. She took them into the back room and asked them what they'd been through, and they just burst into tears. They were sobbing and showing her their scars. Then she gave them each a supply of the standard medication and told them to call her and come back free of charge."

A Loyal Daughter and Her Coffee Enema Crusade

Before we'd left the Hoxsey clinic Nurse Mildred had given us directions to our next destination. We were bound for La Gloria. That's the name of the onetime resort hotel that has been converted to the Gerson coffee-enema cancer-therapy clinic.

To get to La Gloria we had to make our way through the maze of streets that surround the Hoxsey hilltop. Our directions called for us to look for a dead end and turn right before we hit it, but every street looked like a dead end, then turned out to be something else. Finally Marilyn asked a passerby for La Gloria, and we were on our way. "Everybody knows La Gloria," said Marilyn as we emerged at last on the Old Ensenada Road, which took us there.

One glance at La Gloria and you feel as if you're in a tropic deeper than Tijuana. Set back from the road, the well-trimmed lawns and the wide verandas reminded me more of a colonial planter's outpost—a German coffee plantation in southwest Africa, perhaps.

Charlotte Gerson Straus is the youngest daughter of the late Dr. Max Gerson. A tall, blue-eyed Rhine maiden, she could well have played the part of the wealthy planter's wife as she formally welcomed us into the clinic's spacious dining room for a late lunch. In the cool, tasteful interior with its polished wood floors servants brought us soup, salad, and a carrot-liver juice concoction, part of the clinic's therapeutic diet. It sounds terrible, but it didn't taste as bad as the Hoxsey tonic.

Dr. Max Gerson was a German-Jewish physician who originally specialized in detoxifying dietary cures for tuberculosis. One of those he cured of TB was Albert Schweitzer's wife. The saintly doctor became Gerson's advocate ever after, calling him "one of the most eminent geniuses in the history of medicine."

Gerson fled Europe in 1936 with his three daughters and soon after set up practice on Park Avenue in New York City and began applying his theories to a cure for cancer. In 1958 he published *A Cancer Therapy: Results of Fifty Cases* and then made what turned out to be a fatal mistake. He accepted an invitation to discuss his therapy on *The Long John Nebel Show,* the pioneer midnight-to-dawn radio talk show that specialized in UFO contactees and bee venom arthritis cures, among other arcane phenomena. Immediately following that appearance, the AMA accused him of "advertising" and expelled him from its ranks. He died little more than a year later of chronic pneumonia.

What was Gerson's cancer cure secret? In the chapter of his book entitled "The 'Secret' of My Treatment," he says, "Of course, there is none!" But, of course, there is. Not a secret physical formula or elixir but a secret metaphysic that fairly sings out the influence of German romanticism.

The opening chapters of his book are a hymn to "the harmony in the metabolism . . . which reflects the eternal mystery of life," to "the Eternal Life" force, to "the concept of totality," to "the whole in its infinitely fine order." Cancer, he tells us, is not a disease of the particular organ or whatever part it first appears in, but of the whole individual; it merely shows up first as a localized tumor. Gerson believed, along with Einstein, that other romantic German-Jewish scientist, in a "unified field theory"—his of health and disease. One can treat the tumor mass only by restoring the total metabolism, the wave of being that washes through the whole body.

But why coffee enemas? According to Gerson the caffeine absorbed by the hemorrhoidal vein travels directly to the liver, where, he said, it stimulates bile secretions to detoxify first the liver and then the rest of the body. The restored metabolism, boosted by massive infusions of raw vegetable and liver juices, then gets rid of the tumor without the aid of drugs.

It's all there in Gerson's book, but I was still a little shaken, as Charlotte Gerson led us on a tour of the clinic's rooms to come face-to-face with an item of furniture she calls "the enema bench."

Somehow the wooden severity of the enema bench reminded me of public stocks, the punitive confinement inflicted on those who fell from grace in early Puritan settlements. The secret of the continuing popularity of the Gerson therapy in the unorthodox world, despite competition from easy-to-take potions and pills, may be precisely due to the arduous, humiliating discipline it subjects the patients to—a testament to the ingrained assumption we inherited from Puritan forefathers and Jewish grandmothers that no redemption, whether from sin or sickness, can be achieved without suffering.

In Max Gerson's case the healer, too, had to suffer for his cure. But his daughter Charlotte has made the redemption from that suffering, the vindication of her father's visionary legacy, a lifetime crusade. In fact, the only time I heard Charlotte abandon her demeanor of icy certitude, the only time she seemed to show any emotional excitement, was when she was describing a moment of symbolic vindication.

It was a particularly significant moment because it had taken place on a radio talk show, a West Coast version of the show that had doomed her father to persecution and fatal suffering. On this show, though, Charlotte said the climate had changed and she was on the offensive. She took the opportunity of the airtime to deliver devastating attacks on the orthodox establishment that had expelled her father. "I really let loose at them," Charlotte said, a triumphantly Gersonian way of putting it.

Somewhat fearful of her severe Germanic demeanor and her icy blue eyes, I decided to test her goodwill by asking her about one old and one new controversy the Gerson method had aroused. First there was the *Death Be Not*

Proud loss of John Gunther's sixteen-year-old son after a seeming remission under Gerson's care back in the forties. And then there were the news stories about deaths caused by coffee enema O.D.s just last year.

The John Gunther, Jr., story is one she's particularly passionate about because, she claimed, her father went to his grave wrongly blaming himself for the boy's death. As you may have read in Gunther Sr.'s *Death Be Not Proud,* Gunther Jr. was brought to Dr. Gerson after he'd been given up for dead by orthodox doctors who had failed to stop the growth of a massive brain tumor. According to Gunther Sr., Gerson's treatment stopped the tumor from growing and enabled the boy to get off his deathbed and go back to school. Everything was going well until, Gerson said in his book, he made one fatal mistake: Against his better judgment he allowed another doctor to treat young John with pituitary hormones for a case of eczema he'd developed. "Six weeks later the tumor grew. [After he died] the disaster threw me into a deep depression," Gerson wrote. "I almost lost the strength to continue this cancer work."

Poor Papa. Only after Gerson's death did the true story come out, daughter Charlotte claimed. "He took the blame—wrongly. The thing that had destroyed Johnny's body was the experimental nitrogen-mustard chemotherapy" the conventional doctors had failed with before they gave him up to Gerson.

"Johnny was the first person my father had treated after chemotherapy, and he wasn't aware that after chemotherapy the body is so destroyed it cannot heal. It took me more than twenty-two cases of healing after chemotherapy—with the same results—to find out that it's too late then."

The new controversy involved reports of coffee enema–related deaths, which had appeared on the television news.

"The news reports were very much distorted," she declared. "It was the case of a lady who had had some chemotherapy. We didn't want to accept her in the first place, but she begged us. The doctors had given up. She came to the clinic, and we put her on a very mild therapy so as not to reactivate the chemotherapy—we'd had bad experiences with that. She did fairly well and went home. About six weeks later she said she wasn't doing well, her glands were growing again. We said that we would need to put her back on a very strict therapy for at least a few weeks if we could, without reactivating the chemotherapy. She thought she could do it at home, and just as we've discovered, the healing reactions after chemo can be very violent, very toxic. She went into a coma. Patients often get low in chlorides, their potassium and sodium levels are okay, but down in Mexico we give them an IV with potassium chloride to build the chlorides right up. At home there's no doctor who knows to do this. Finally, she found a doctor, but she died in the waiting room.

"The health inspector went to her house and found she had been using coffee enemas and put that on her death certificate—'Death by coffee enemas.' The autopsy doctor indicated in his findings that she had widely disseminated cancer with liver metastasis, of which she died. Her husband wanted them to change the death certificate to 'Cancer.' But by the evening news it went out that not one patient but two or three had died of coffee enemas.

"Nothing but lies," she said. "Half truths and lies. Anybody is welcome to come to the clinic and see that we have a twenty-four-hour professional staff of doctors who know how to react. They should come, talk to the doctors, talk to the patients. My father always said . . ."

As we left La Gloria, neither the Captain nor any of the other cancer patient pilgrims looked excited about returning. They were respectful. Impressed. But none seemed eager to return for prolonged stretches on the enema bench.

A Tale of Two Families

We are in another part of Tijuana now, far from the jumble of streets, the tumbledown reupholstery shops, and the skeletal shells of the cars that are stripped and serviced there. We are close to the ocean, and across the broad plaza of Ernesto Contreras's Centro Medico Del Mar we could see the sunset-singed whitecaps. Here, in what one pro-laetrile magazine calls "balmy Playas del Tijuana," we are also close to the most expensive residential district in Tijuana, immense, tastefully landscaped haciendas, the homes of many of the prosperous doctors on the Contreras clinic's large professional staff.

The clinic is a multilevel, luxury, mall-like affair with a facade dominated by a huge tile mosaic of a heroic nude in mortal combat with a zodiac-like crab. It looks like a close contest.

Dr. Contreras has come a long way since the mid-1960s, when he moved into a small furnished apartment so he could turn his own home into a tiny hospital to treat cancer patients with laetrile. The early missionary struggles are far behind him now, but the size of an enterprise like this full-scale ultramodern hospital, clinic, pharmacy, motel complex by the sea entails other problems—problems of empire and succession, and among them, it seems, is another one of those perplexing father-son struggles that plague the prophets of cancer cures.

Jerry and Diane Green weren't aware of any of this when they arrived in Tijuana with their leukemic child in January 1979. For the fugitive family who'd fled in disguise from court orders that their child be force-fed state-sanctioned medicine, for an earnest but innocent couple in their mid-twenties whose convictions had led them to risk their child's future on an underground railroad ride into the unknown, the first sight of Contreras's deluxe clinic complex, this Memorial Sloan-Kettering of the laetrile world, must have been reassuring.

And so, it seemed, was Dr. Contreras. He appeared to believe in all the holistic therapies they did, and he had the facilities to put them into practice. There were even soundproof, plush carpet, "white noise" rooms where oceanic waves of hypnotically soothing static wash over the consciousness of tranced-out cancer patients in visualization therapy as they imagine the white knights of their immune systems slaying cancer cell dragons in dream dramas.

Shelter at last from the storm, thought the Greens, a place for their child to heal. But there was something else available in this holistic heaven—the poison fruit that caused the postmortem trauma: chemotherapy.

The basic situation was this: When three-year-old Chad arrived at Contreras's clinic in January, his leukemia was in a state of remission. He had been taking both chemotherapy (a court-ordered treatment) and laetrile obtained from underground sources.

No one could say for sure which one had induced the blessed remission, but the Greens were eager to get Chad off chemotherapy: They saw it as only a source of suffering, not as a cure. According to them Contreras agreed to "taper off" the chemotherapy for a few months and, if Chad's blood count and bone marrow levels remained stable, to cut it off altogether.

"He even encouraged us in our desire to take Chad off it," Jerry Green told me when I finally reached him in his sad Nebraska exile. "He told us the story of a young girl, a similar case, he had treated eleven years ago who was still alive."

And then, according to the Greens, there came a crucial consultation in July in which Contreras told them that their son was stable and agreed to cut off chemotherapy completely.

Then when Chad died in October, his parents, still stunned by the sudden death of their child, were further shocked to find that Contreras had held a postmortem press conference denouncing what he called *their* decision to cut off the chemotherapy.

In effect, Contreras was saying: Don't blame laetrile, don't blame me or my clinic, I warned those wayward parents against the choice they made. The resultant publicity did go beyond blaming laetrile—the Greens were singled out in their grief for going against the advice of their own doctor. One Boston newspaper referred to the parents as "this wicked couple."

Jerry Green is still trying to figure out Contreras's behavior. He hinted at "vested interests," fear of the power of orthodox medical wrath, even certain "villainous influences" on Contreras, certain powers behind the family throne the doctor couldn't control.

As our contingent of pilgrims filed in and seated itself facing Contreras across his desk, we were all struck not by the sad-eyed drooping figure who feebly gestured us welcome but rather by the dramatic life-size portrait of a young, stunningly beautiful Mexican girl arrayed in a vibrantly colored off-the-shoulder Second Empire gown.

"My wife," Contreras said modestly, "when she was on the stage. As you can see," he added proudly, "she has Napoleonic and Indian blood."

Flanking this commanding vision were smaller snapshots of Contreras's children, a daughter and two proud-looking sons. According to what I've been able to piece together it's the two sons and their concern with the survival of the healing empire they stand to inherit that lie beneath Contreras's contradictory behavior toward Chad's family. The way I heard it Contreras sent his two sons off to the finest medical schools in Mexico City, hoping not only that they would return to stand by his side but that their obvious intelligence and sincerity would make them apostles of his cause even in the temples of the nonbelievers.

"Ernesto, Jr. has been trained as an internal medical oncologist," Contreras said proudly. "He went into the lion's den and is winning over orthodoxy." Others told me that the son went into the lion's den and came out a lion, that he and the other son returned to Tijuana as converts to the temple of orthodoxy, that his allegiance was not to their father's amygdalin therapy but to the chemotherapy and radiation the holistic movement dreaded.

What was a father to do? He'd built his empire on the faith of thousands fleeing orthodoxy in search of "a place where holistic therapy is a reality." Yet the father's empire is fragile if founded only on amygdalin, if subject to sudden shifts in official favor, if a case like Chad's is allowed to "raise a stink." What interest should the father have put first when the spotlight was focused on him by such a case—the legacy he would leave to his sons or the sensibility of Chad's father?

Things seemed, well, melancholy in Contreras's office late that afternoon. The doctor displayed a disarming eagerness to please, but his eyes were mournful and his drooping jowls seemed to register tremors of sadness as he spoke. I had the feeling that he was suffering from a sense that his time of glory had passed and that he envied the rise of ambitious rivals on the metabolic cancer-cure scene. He spent considerable time sniping at their methods, disparaging their lack of orthodox credentials.

"They are not trained oncologists. One is an allergist. Cancer is cancer. It should be treated by people who know it, by an oncologist, like my son Ernesto who is trained in this, at a place where they know how to handle all eventualities, not at one of those little clinics."

Contreras claimed that only at a comprehensive center like his could a patient get "the best of both worlds"—both chemotherapy and metabolic treatment, that they are not contradictory, that, in fact, he was getting exciting results combining laetrile with low-dose chemotherapy.

It was in the midst of Contreras's unexpected hymn to low-dose chemotherapy that I decided to ask him the big question about the disputed consultation and the death of Chad. Without the slightest hesitation he repeated the account the Greens had called "bold-faced lies." He insisted he had never agreed with their desire to stop Chad's chemotherapy. "I told them, 'Why don't we keep him as it is?' After all, there's nothing that beats chemotherapy in childhood leukemias. Children, for some reason, tolerate it, and I won't risk the life of a child to prove a point."

That last little barb—the implication that the parents were out to "prove a point" about holistic therapy rather than to save their child's life—is particularly galling to the Greens. They claimed Contreras stretched the bounds of accuracy in his autopsy of Chad to prove his own point. Contreras claimed his postmortem examination found Chad had died of "a massive involvement of leukemia." But an autopsy by the parents' American pathologist, Dr. Frank Raasch, found no conclusive signs the death had been caused by cancer, no conclusive cause of death at all.

The Greens, with the backing of Frank Sullivan, the former chief psychologist on Contreras's staff, claimed that Chad died because of the trauma of his state-enforced exile, that he longed so badly to return to his Massachusetts home that he just lost the will to live any longer in Tijuana, that the subtle sickness that killed him was homesickness. Sullivan even claimed that in the absence of other causes Chad's must be called "a psychologic death."

The Greens put it more simply. His father said, "Chad died of a broken heart."

He and his wife are left to live with theirs. For parents in their position, fleeing orthodox medicine, faced with life-or-death choices for their son as soon as they cross the border, the unorthodox world, like the streets of Tijuana, offers few reliable signposts. Some are crooked, some lead to dead ends, only a few insiders know the intrigues behind the treatments, whom to trust for what.

When at last we emerged into the sunset-lit plaza of the Contreras complex, gloom seemed to shadow the faces of the pilgrims in our caravan. Dr. Contreras graciously offered to show us the psychotherapy wing in the basement of the clinic—the one with the white-noise rooms. But we all declined, too depressed, too hungry. For the cancer patients it was not so much what Contreras had said in his office, it was the long walk to and from that office—the corridors lined with gleaming hospital machinery.

The Captain explained his feelings: "He seems like a fine fellow, this Contreras, but to me this was too much like a hospital. Nobody who's been in a cancer ward likes going back, even for a visit. It was different at that woman Mildred's establishment." He was still clutching the brown-bagged bottle of Hoxsey tonic Mildred had slipped him two clinics ago. "She had a humanistic touch," the Captain said.

Stone Dragons and Metabolic Technicians

We were late. It was past sunset and our last destination was a good forty miles down the coast just north of Ensenada. That last destination would turn out to be, by far, the strangest and, for me, the most bewildering.

The new Ensenada road is an unlit, two-lane blacktop. Our caravan seemed to be the only travelers on the road after sunset. We could hear the ocean off to our right, but we couldn't see it. In the darkness Marilyn unfolded the weird history of the place we were heading for.

She said the clinic there now—a luxurious, state-of-the-art establishment—is not the first to occupy Plaza Santa Maria, the breathtaking cliff overlooking the Pacific. Several strange and questionable health practitioners had come and gone before the present people took over.

In fact, said Marilyn, the legend goes that the site originally served as sacrificial killing grounds for the Aztecs. "Supposedly," she said, "it's meant to be a healing place so it can overcome the karma of its past."

Unfortunately, this karmic realignment did not have an auspicious beginning. The first place built there was "a fabulous health resort," Marilyn told me. But it failed. "Part of the legend," said Marilyn, "is that the spirits that guard the place will make sure that anyone who tries to pull a shtick will fail."

And, in fact, said Marilyn, Plaza Santa Maria has seen a succession of failed healers and clinic promoters who went a little weird. One disappeared completely. Then there was another one who arrived with a reputation for medical brilliance and took over the clinic for his version of cancer therapy.

"He'd dazzle you with this aura he had and brilliant medical talk, and then he'd whisper to some people he was a reincarnation of God or Christ and tell others that he was sent here from another galaxy."

Marilyn thought there was merit to his therapy. "But I began hearing from people that he'd examine them and tell them that for, say, seven thousand dollars he'd make them completely well; for four thousand dollars he'd get you better but not all the way, that sort of thing."

"What happened to him?" I asked Marilyn.

"Well, he disappeared. I think he may be practicing in Ohio now."

And the people there now?

"Kelley's people are down there now," Marilyn told me. Kelley's people are the newest mass movement in the cancer-cure world, perhaps the wave of the future. Kelley's people claim they've treated no less than fifteen thousand people (although they say a fire in 1975 burned most of their records before that year).

Kelley's system—with its ultrasonic spectrograph blood analysis, its computerized diagnostic gimmicks, its metabolic subgroup typing—is the most sophisticated new synthesis of unorthodox techniques around. Some say Kelley lifted a lot from Gerson and others. But Kelley's got his own "original shtick," as Marilyn described it.

It's a clever one. He believes all people can be classified as one of ten metabolic subtypes, which are sort of the astrological signs of personal biochemistry. Of course, you have to fill out Kelley's three-thousand-question questionnaire and submit it to him or one of his franchise operators to feed into his computers before you can know your sign. Along with your sign, Kelley's computer analysis will tell you where you have undetected malignancies or are in a "pre-malignant" state and what vitamins and raw gland extracts a person of your sign need take to prevent or cure it.

"Halting malignant growth is relatively simple," Kelley declares. All you have to do is take the approximately $400-a-month worth of supplements the Kelley computer prescribes for you—and which Kelley's people will be happy to sell you.

Still, for all the coziness of this computer cancer cure-cum-vitamin franchise operation, Kelley's people have had some trouble finding a safe haven for their central headquarters. Dr. Kelley started out as an orthodontist first in Fort Worth and then in Grapevine, Texas, with a theory he claims cured his own cancer and which he synthesized into "an ecological approach to the successful treatment of malignancy." After he came up with his theory of metabolic subtypes and the computer capacity to market it, mounting controversy over his methods drove him to move his operation to Winthrop, Washington. He also tried to create a Nutritional Academy in Illinois (basically the Hamburger University for the counselor franchisees of the Kelley therapy) and still maintains an International Health Institute in Dallas.

But there were limits to what Kelley's people could do in the United States. An invitation from the proprietor of the Plaza Santa Maria General Hospital to set up a treatment center offered Kelley's people the chance to work with exotic substances, esoteric procedures not permitted above the border, gave them a chance to get out from behind the computer terminals and really get their hands on cancer patients. We were unaware at the time of our visit that Steve McQueen, on his own unorthodox pilgrimage, would become, that very month, one of those patients, that McQueen would become, for better or worse, once it became public, Kelley's Chad.

By the time we pulled up to the high iron gates guarding the Plaza Santa Maria clinic it was nearly ten P.M. and the sentry had to be stirred from a nap.

"Dr. Kelley here?" Marilyn called out.

"He leave today," the sentry said.

"What about Dr. McKee," Marilyn asked. "We called ahead; he's expecting us."

The sleepy sentry mumbled something that sounded like "2001."

"Cottage 2001," Marilyn said.

We started winding around a smooth graveled drive, and even in the darkness I could tell the place was huge. We passed what looked like a small stadium sunk in cliff rock and surmounted by some spooky stone statues. "That's supposedly the site of the Aztec rituals," Marilyn told me. Past their stony scrutiny we wound around through several beautifully landscaped and terraced levels of cottages. The lights were off inside them. From the sound of distant breakers below it seemed we passed near a cliffside ocean overlook, then curved around and up to a cluster of cottages and parked by the only one with a light on inside.

We climbed out of the car, and I could make out the sound of voices and laughter inside. I could make out the number 2001 on the doorpost, and I could see shapes passing behind the curtains. A woman's face parted the curtains, peered out and withdrew. Marilyn mounted the porch and rapped on the door.

From behind the window a man's voice said, "We're all off duty for the night."

Marilyn was not one to be denied so easily.

"Is Dr. McKee in there? We spoke before. These people have come all the way from L.A."

There was a long pause. Finally a sleepy-eyed, slightly built figure emerged.

"I'm Dr. McKee. Please lower your voices. The patients . . . they're all asleep . . . it's too late. We all have to be up early for rounds."

"We came all the way," Marilyn repeated. "These people have been looking forward to seeing the Plaza. They've been to all the other clinics."

Dr. McKee—a licensed M.D. who would later be identified as the "metabolic technician" supervising Steve McQueen's treatment and who is referred to by Kelley's own people as "a genius" surpassing even the founder in his mastery of metabolic wizardry—gazed down at our motley crew with a certain amount of wariness. We'd clearly intruded on something. He was not pleased.

Marilyn started toward the door.

"Out there," he hissed angrily. "We'll do it out there. In the amphitheater. Wait outside."

He disappeared. Several other figures appeared, stalked angrily out the door, stamped down the porch steps and into the night.

At last the good Dr. McKee emerged again and led us off on a trek to the stone amphitheater. There was a chill in the air, and not all of it was coming from the Pacific breezes.

We seated ourselves on the stone steps beneath the stars and the fierce stares of the stone statues. Dr. McKee rubbed his eyes and then—as if he'd switched on some Kelley program computer terminal that works in his sleep—he began to rattle off what kinds of things they do to patients. It was the most astonishing agglomeration of unorthodox cancer-cure techniques I'd ever heard. This place was the Alice's Restaurant of cancer clinics. You can get anything you want.

What a rap. Dr. McKee started off with some Kelley terminology about individuation of metabolic subtypes and temporo-mandibular adjustments. Then he got down to the menu. In addition to the massive doses of raw gland supplements, "we're still in the process of gathering our immunostimulants, but we can offer three different kinds of laetrile, using applied kinesiology to decide which is best for the individual patient. Then we have DMSO, GH3 from Romania, superoxide dismutase. We have three different strengths of mistletoe extract, we've got the Muriana vaccine from Japan, which is a variation of BCG immunotherapy. Then, of course, we've got a full program of EDTA chelation, if vascular treatment is indicated. Let's see, oh, yes, the oxidated catalysts of the Koch remedy. We have quite a bit of those.

"We also offer the virostats for viral-related diseases, lymphomas, some melanomas, also plasmaphoresis, electrophoresis. We use applied kinesiology to discover reactions, then back in the metabolic area we also have live cell therapy, which is guided by Dietmar Schildwaechter, who has experience applying live cell techniques to degenerative diseases and cancer as opposed to mere rejuvenation. We give all the cancer patients here an injection of live thymus cells and an injection of a mixture of reticulo-endothelial cells. These are live fetal cells, deep-frozen and shipped under the same conditions as sperm for artificial insemination. The reticulo-endothelial mixture has thymus, Kupffer cells from the liver, spleen, bone marrow, placenta, and umbilical cord. . . ."

Dr. McKee paused to yawn, rub his eyes, and shake himself awake. "Then, of course, for crisis situations we have allopathic treatments together with supportive biological treatments. For instance, if I'm giving penicillin, I'm also giving propolis and extra thymus, extra vitamin C, and replacing intestinal flora. After I finish, I give an appropriate dose of homeopathic penicillin to clear the disturbance. . . . We use castor oil packs to open up lymphatic drainage over, say, the axilla in breast cancer or over the liver. We have acquired a magnatherm unit, which is a radio frequency diathermy machine that functions as a form of localized hyperthermia, can heat tissue to a depth of four inches front and rear. Heating makes the tumor more sensitive to other modalities."

Pause. Yawn.

"Pain is a situation I'm interested in dealing with more holistically down line"—Kelley people tend to use computer management jargon like "down line." "I'd like Norm Shealy to come in and teach us all the ins and outs of his dolorology program. At present we're using some acupuncture techniques, some neuropathy techniques, which involve subjecting local anesthetics to dermal acupuncture, injecting procaine in trigger areas. We also have a full program of massage therapy, psychotherapeutic emotional release, and we do use surgery in some situations."

"Is that all there is?" I was tempted to ask. Dr. McKee's presentation is impressively slick and encyclopedic even in his sleep. And yet there was something slightly horrifying about that rapid-fire roll call of unorthodox remedies. Was there anything they wouldn't try here?

I remember what one of the Life-Force leaders had said about "the cosmic kick" for cancer patients: "When you have cancer you can do anything." Could it be that there's an equivalent cosmic kick for the unorthodox doctors at a place like this—when a patient has cancer you can do anything *to* them?

I asked Dr. McKee how much the clinic charged. "Eight thousand dollars a month," he said. "The live cell treatment is an optional extra—a full set of fresh live cells runs about four thousand dollars complete," although you can apparently order certain organ cells à la carte.

Finally, someone asked Dr. McKee what the daily schedule for the cancer patient is at this clinic. I listened in disbelief: "They get up at seven in the morning for a coffee enema, followed by a rectal enzyme implant, followed by breakfast, followed by their intravenous. While they're on IVs, I have group rounds with them, which are finished by eleven, when there's a patient education class. Then at one they have lunch. In the afternoon there's chiropractic and splint-balancing classes, massage therapy, psychotherapy sessions, work with the metabolic technician on whatever's going on. At four o'clock most of them take another coffee enema followed by another rectal enzyme implant, dinner at six, after which we have two of the metabolic technicians play music three nights a week, plus a video thing we're developing. At three-thirty in the morning they get up and take another rectal enzyme implant, and they take oral enzymes at the same time.

"Then they're up at seven for a coffee enema. Cancer patients stay on this schedule for an average of a month. Of course, we handle all the other degenerative diseases, arthritis, arteriosclerosis, multiple sclerosis. . . ."

Midnight at the Border: Marilyn's Dream

It was close to midnight when we left the stone dragons and the metabolic technicians in peace and started north for the border. I decided to leave it up to the Aztec gods to decide what the Kelley people were doing for the karma of the place, whether they were "pulling a shtick," as Marilyn had put it. My brain felt like it had had an enzyme implant from all the cancer-cure theories it had been stuffed with in the past four days. There was one more clinic we'd been scheduled to see, a newly established rival laetrile/metabolic clinic in Tijuana. When we passed through the sleepy town at one A.M. the indefatigable Marilyn offered to get out and wake up everyone at that clinic and take us around, but we declined in favor of a fast border crossing.

It was a tense one too. Not for me. I was at the wheel and merely sleepy. But for the two cancer patients in the backseat it seemed a matter of life and death. There had been another complicated seat switch in the caravan. Marilyn's food chests had been transferred to her trunk for the ride back so the Captain and Renee could sit in the back. As we approached the customs booth they tried to stash their brown paper sacks containing the Hoxsey elixir bottles in some inconspicuous place amidst the empty fruit and sandwich bags.

Marilyn cautioned us that it would be a mistake to volunteer to the customs inspector that we'd been to the cancer clinics. Every time she'd done that they'd taken her out of her car, given her and the vehicle a long and thorough search.

This kind of harassment arouses Marilyn's outrage—and her organizing instinct. She has an "I have a dream" vision of an all-out cancer patient revolt against the medical orthodoxy that drives them below the border in search of the hope it cannot offer. Marilyn thinks that cancer patients are restive, ready to coalesce into a civil rights—or terminal rights—movement, ripe for open revolt.

"My dream is," she told me, "if each cancer patient in the world would go down to Mexico to get the medicine of his choice, then come to the border and hold up for them to see whatever it was he thought was curing him of his cancer, whether it was Hoxsey or laetrile or whatever. Held it up in full view of everyone and said, 'You may shoot me if you like, but you're not going to take this away from me.' What does any one of them have to lose? If they'd only wake up to the knowledge that they are invulnerable."

"Invulnerable?" I asked.

"Yes!" she said. "Of course. They have nothing to lose. They'll come to the border and say, 'If you want to take this medicine from me, you're going to have to shoot me first. Your doctors say I'm going to die anyway, so go ahead and try to stop me.' "

Marilyn's extraordinary vision reminded me of a conversation I had once with a radical lawyer who was close to the Weather Underground. He recalled that back in the days before they went underground, one particularly fanatic Weatherperson was constantly urging his collective to start recruiting terminal cancer patients to the fight against the beast. "They'd make the perfect guerrilla warriors," he'd argue. "They'll do anything, take any risk; they have nothing to lose."

"They're waking up now," Marilyn said. "Once they do, once they make that basic commitment to fight for their lives, once they realize that if they gave the disease to themselves they can take it away from themselves—it matters not what kind of therapy they try, they've got a chance to make it."

Our border crossing turned out to be anticlimactic and uneventful. The customs man waved us through. However alien I felt by that time, we didn't look like illegal aliens. The Captain and Renee sighed and reached down below their seats to reclaim the precious tonic bottles they'd stuffed down there. On the long drive back up to Laguna Hills, Marilyn fell asleep in the front seat, I struggled to stay awake behind the wheel, while in the back the Captain and Renee were pumped up by their successful Mexican mission. Clutching their tonics, they chattered away comparing notes on possible next moves.

I have set this particular down so fully, because I know not but it may be of moment to those who come after me, if they come to be brought to the same distress, and to the same manner of making their choice . . .

—DEFOE

If, as Marilyn says, it's the decision to fight one's cancer, not the theory one fights it with, that is decisive, one still has to choose some theory; one can't be what Marilyn calls a "shopper" forever. And so, after my marathon immersion in the cancer cure subculture, what's this shopper's favorite theory?

The theory that intrigues me most is less a cancer cure theory than a theory about the theories themselves, a meta-theory about the phenomenon of unorthodox cancer cures. Something has to explain the anecdotal evidence, the dozens of people at the convention who told me face-to-face the stories of their cures—often by therapies with completely contradictory explanations of the disease. Something has to explain the stories told by the people on the Cancer Control Society's *White Sheet,* a list of scores of people who had all different kinds of cancer and who claim to have been treated with all different kinds of unorthodox therapies. Get the *White Sheet* yourself and call these people up (they've given the CCS permission to publish their phone numbers and invite people to call). You figure it out.

The only way I can figure the phenomenon out, my meta-theory, might be called the Modified False Hope Cure Theory. I picked it up from the American Cancer Society while reading their *Unproven Methods of Cancer Management* pamphlet. I couldn't get over their outright concession that some quacks get "what seem to be good results." Sure, the American Cancer Society goes on to say these good results "are often based entirely on the subjective response of the patient, which may result from the false hope instilled in him" by self-deluded cancer cure prophets.

Well, so what? Does it matter how you're cured if you do get better? I'm willing to be gulled out of a malignancy by unorthodox healers if that's what it takes to get rid of it when orthodox medicine gives up hope. Problem is, we run into a Catch-22 situation here. False hope cures only work if you believe they're true cures. You can't say to yourself, "I'm going to set out to fool myself into being cured." You have to *be* fooled. But now that I know that, and now that I've told you, have I ruined it for us all? Can we ever again hope to be innocent beneficiaries of a false hope cure?

Fortunately, from the evidence of the cancer cure subculture, from the evidence of my journey into the Tijuana clinic scene, it seems clear that false hope springs eternal.

In cases where orthodox medicine fails, perhaps there's a role for the deluded dreamers, the biomystic visionaries, the masked microbe detectors, apricot pit alchemists, mind cure mesmerists—all who keep supplying us with theory after elaborate theory about the elusive malignant plague. Perhaps the periodic transfusions of false hope that the cancer cure cults produce serve a purpose. Some of us may need a Tijuana of the mind, a border to cross to smuggle back some illicit hope when our own world doesn't offer much, a fertile poetics of faith and fraud to fool ourselves into fighting for our lives.

Oswald's Ghost

In Which We Enter the Lonely Labyrinth

Dealey Plaza. It's a hot morning in August, and motorists whizzing down Elm Street are witnessing a curious, if not sinister, phenomenon. Three people have gathered around a manhole at the foot of the famous grassy knoll. There's an attractive young blond woman, a spry, grizzled older fellow in a Coors cap, and a guy in his thirties with a tape recorder. The older guy is bending down and—demonstrating remarkable vigor—pulling the hundred-pound manhole cover out of its recess in the sidewalk.

Then he stops. Waits for a Dallas Police Department squad car to cruise by and disappear into the darkness of the Triple Underpass. At last he has yanked the massive iron seal clear of the opening that leads down to the storm sewer system honeycombing the underside of Dealey Plaza.

Then he does something really strange. He walks out into the middle of Elm Street traffic, heads uphill between two lanes of oncoming cars, and plants himself in the middle of the road about twenty-five yards upstream.

"Okay now, Ron. I'm standing right where the president was when he took the head shot. Now I want you to get down in that manhole," he yells at the younger guy, who, not to be coy, is me. "Elaine," he calls out to the woman, "you show him how to position himself."

So here I am, out in the midday sun, lowering myself into this manhole. It's kind of cool down here, though some might call it dank. While it is nice to escape the pounding of the direct sunlight, this is not my idea of summer fun.

But this is no ordinary manhole. This is the historic Dealey Plaza manhole that a certain faction of assassination buffs—led by Penn Jones, Jr., the guy in the middle of Elm Street—believes sheltered a sniper who fired the fatal frontal head shot on November 22, 1963. This manhole is the first stop on a grand tour of Dallas assassination shrines, during which, among other things, Penn has promised to show me the exact locations from which, he says offhandedly, the nine gunmen fired at John F. Kennedy that day. Sort of the Stations of the Cross Fire in conspiracy-theory gospel.

You remember Penn Jones, Jr., don't you? The feisty, combative country editor of the *Midlothian Mirror.* Author of the four-volume (so far) privately printed series called *Forgive My Grief,* the continuing account of his JFK-assassination investigation, which focuses on the deaths and disappearances of the 188 witnesses (so far) who Penn contends knew too much about the assassination conspiracy to be permitted to live.

Well, Penn Jones, Jr., is still on the case. He has retired from his editor's post to a farmhouse in Waxahachie, where he lives with his disciple and research associate, Elaine Kavanaugh, and publishes a monthly assassination newsletter, *The Continuing Inquiry.*

"Elaine," Penn yells out, "get Ron to back up against the wall there. Then he'll know what I mean."

I think Penn has sensed that I have some reservations about his Manhole Sniper theory, and this elaborate positioning is designed to address my doubts. In fact, I am skeptical.

Not the least of my problems with the Manhole Sniper theory is that it requires the putative manhole assassin to have popped up the hundred-pound manhole cover at just the right moment, fired a shot, then plopped it down over his head without any of the surrounding crowd taking notice of his activity. But Penn is determined to set me straight on this misapprehension.

"Okay now, Ron, you've got to move back so's your back is touching the rear of the hole there," Elaine says.

I follow her instructions and find myself completely under the overhang of pavement. In total darkness, except . . . well, damned if there isn't a perfect little rectangle of daylight coming through an opening in the pavement right in front of my eyes, and damned if Penn Jones's face isn't framed right in it.

"That's the storm drain in the curb side you're lookin' out now," says Elaine.

"See what a clear shot he had?" Penn Jones yells out. "Okay, Elaine, now pull that manhole cover back over on top of him. Ron, you'll see that even in the dark you'll be able to feel your way to one of those runoff tunnels he used to squirm his way under the plaza to the getaway."

Elaine begins to lug the heavy seal over the hole. Over me.

"Well, actually, Elaine, I don't think that'll be necessary. I get the picture," I say, hastily scrambling out, visions of the glowing eyes of sewer rats sending shivers through me.

Penn Jones hustles over, dodging traffic, and drags the cover back into place. He gives me a look that says, "Uh-huh—another one not prepared to follow the trail all the way," and then he sets off on a trot up the grassy knoll to what he says is the next point of fire.

But before we follow Penn Jones up the grassy knoll, before we get any deeper into the labyrinthine state of the art of JFK-assassination theory, let's linger a moment on the manhole demo, because it can serve as a metaphor for my own stance in relation to the whole web of conspiracy theories that assassination buffs have spun out over the past twenty years. A metaphor that can be summed up by saying: I'll go down into the manhole with them, but I won't pull the cover over my head.

When you're dealing with the tangled thicket of theory and conjecture that has overgrown the few established facts in the years since the events of that November 22, you need someone who can distinguish between the real investigators still in the field and the poets, like Penn Jones, whose luxuriant and flourishing imaginations have produced a dark, phantasmagoric body of work that bears more resemblance to a Latin American novel (Penn is the Gabriel García Márquez of Dealey Plaza, if you will) than to the prosaic police-reporter mentality I prefer in these matters.

You need someone with something akin to what Keats called negative capability—the ability to abide uncertainties, mysteries, and doubts without succumbing to the temptation of premature certainty. You need someone like me. I rather fancy myself El Exigente of conspiracy-theory culture, like the "Demanding One" in the TV coffee commercial. I've covered the buff beat since the early seventies—you might call me a buff buff—since the time, before Watergate, when everybody laughed at the idea of conspiracies.

So with El Exigente here as your guide, let's look at who's still on the case after twenty years and whether they have anything worth saying. What are the real mysteries left, and is there any hope we'll ever solve them?

Remember the way the residents of the little coffee-growing village in the Savarin commercial gather, buzzing nervously around the town square, awaiting the arrival of El Exigente, the white-suited coffee taster whose judgment on their beans will determine the success or failure of their entire harvest?

Well, the buff grapevine had been buzzing furiously for days before my departure for Dallas. Cross-country calls speculating about the nature of my mission. My past writings on the subject extricated from files, summoned up on computer screens, and scrutinized suspiciously. Indeed, angrily in some cases, as I learned the morning of my departure, when I received an irate call from newly ascendant buff David Lifton, author of the most successful of the recent buff books, *Best Evidence.* He accused me of plotting to trash his cherished "trajectory-reversal" theory.*

As I set out for Dallas on the eve of the twentieth anniversary of the Dealey Plaza shooting, I was aware that I was heading into a buzz saw of buff factionalism. Long-festering rivalries and doctrinal disputes were dividing the Dallas-area buffs after years of beleaguered unity. Some of the bitterness can be attributed to the aftermath of the British invasion of Dallas-area buff turf in the past decade. First there was British writer Michael Eddowes with his KGB-impostor theory: The Oswald who returned from the Soviet Union in 1962 wasn't the same Lee Harvey Oswald who defected to the USSR in 1959 but instead was a clever KGB impostor who used the name "Alek Hidell" (one of Oswald's aliases in Dallas and New Orleans). A few years later British writer Anthony Summers came to Dallas to research his theory that Oswald was not a Russian but an American intelligence operative. Both writers swept through town, wined and dined the local buffs, wrung them dry of their files and facts, and departed to publish completely contradictory conspiracy theories.

Eddowes's book, *The Oswald File,* left the most lasting legacy of divisiveness; it launched the epic embarrassment of the Oswald exhumation controversy. Eddowes maintained that his KGB-impostor theory could be proved by examining the body buried in Fort Worth's Rose Hill Cemetery under Oswald's name. Dental and medical evidence would show that the body belonged to an impostor, he said.

A number of Dallas buffs invested a lot of credibility in the exhumation crusade. Mary Ferrell, for instance. The great archivist. For years she had labored diligently to collect and index everything ever written about the assassination, every document, every clipping, every scrap of potential evidence. Her husband built a room in their backyard to hold the ever-expanding files. They bought two German shepherds to protect their stock. And for all those years, unlike the publicity-happy buffs who used her work, she had never sought to publish a theory of her own, had never abandoned her archivist's neutrality, had just gone on compiling her ultra-authoritative, supercomplete name index

*"Trajectory reversal" posits that, in addition to the assassins who fired at JFK from the front, from the grassy knoll, the conspiracy included coffin snatchers and autopsy doctors whose job was to surgically alter the dead president's wounds in order to make it look like he'd been shot from the *back* (thus, "trajectory reversal") in order to frame Oswald. The book was a best-seller.

to the JFK assassination. Sample entries from the name index indicate its comprehensiveness:

Boyer, Al. Hairstylist. He accompanied Josephine Ann Bunce, Jayme Bartlett, and Bonnie Cavin to Dallas from Kansas City, Missouri. Warren Commission, vol. 22, p. 903.

Boykin, Earl L. Wife, Ruby O. 1300 Keats Drive. Mechanic at Earl Hayes Chevrolet. Probably the same as Earl Boykin, who gave his address as 1300 Kouts at the Sports Drome Rifle Range one of the days Oswald was allegedly there. *Texas Attorney General's Report.*

But then this dashing Englishman swept into town and away went her meticulous scholarly neutrality. "This Eddowes was some character," one rival buff remarked. "He had his own Rolls-Royce flown over from England. He'd chauffeur Mary around. Then she'd fly over to England, and he'd drive her around London in Rolls-Royces."

It was the old story. Mary Ferrell ended up enlisting in the exhumation cause, drawing a flotilla of Dallas buffs behind her. They were all convinced that the authorities would never let the body be exhumed because of the terrible dual-identity secret it would reveal.

Then in 1981 Oswald's wife, Marina, was somehow enticed into the exhumation battle, and it was Marina's lawsuit that finally opened the tomb. And so out they went to Rose Hill Cemetery with cape and shovel to see just who was buried there.

To the dismay of the impostor theorists, the body they dug up seemed to have Oswald's teeth—the American Marine Oswald's teeth—down to the tiniest detail. The medical examiner said that the Oswald buried in Oswald's grave was the same Oswald who had been in the Marines before he defected to Russia. The second-body buffs weren't satisfied, of course (they're still demanding a reexhumation), but the credibility of the whole Dallas buff community went right down the tubes.

I arrived in Dallas with a suitcase full of current buff literature, most of it newsletters. I've got the *Grassy Knoll Gazette,* put out by Robert Cutler. I've got Penn Jones's *Continuing Inquiry.* I've got Paul Hoch's *Echoes of Conspiracy.* And I've got *Coverups!* from Gary Mack of Fort Worth.

The last is new to me. But buried in a buff gossip column, there's a tip-off that it too is a product of Dallas-buff fratricide: "Gary Mack and Jack White were dismissed by Penn Jones as consultants to *The Continuing Inquiry.* No explanation was given."

I've heard a lot about Gary Mack. He is the industrious young turk of the new generation of high-tech audiovisual-aids buffs who have supplanted the old-style document-indexing types. Over the years, they've blown up, enhanced, and assiduously analyzed every square millimeter of film and tape taken that day in Dallas, and they've discerned, lurking in the grainy shadows, shapes and forms they say are gunmen. Leafing through Mack's newsletters, I come upon a fascinating photomontage of Grassy Knoll Gunmen on the front page of *Coverups!* There is Black Dog Man—I've seen him before—and a new one to me: Badge Man. I am familiar with various suspicious characters of their genre, such as the Babushka Lady and the Umbrella Man, to whom the photographic buffs have attributed various mysterious roles. I decide to call Gary Mack and check these guys out.

Black Dog Man. At first he was a furry shadow on top of the concrete wall behind the grassy knoll. Certain audiovisual-aids types saw in blowups of that furry shadow a manlike shape. In some blowups, they said, they could see a man firing a gun. Skeptical photo analysts on the staff of the House Select Committee on Assassinations thought that the furry shadow looked more canine than conspiratorial and dubbed the dark apparition Black Dog Man.

And there he is on the front page of the October issue of Gary Mack's newsletter. Next to Black Dog Man is Badge Man; an extreme blowup of a tiny square of what seems to be a tree shadow is accompanied by a visual aid, "a sketch of what he might look like if this photo is computer-enhanced." And suddenly—in the sketch at least—Badge Man leaps out of the shadows and takes explicit human form. He's a man in the uniform of a Dallas police officer, complete with badge and shoulder patch. He appears to be firing a rifle concealed by what looks like a flare from a muzzle blast. In the foreground of the Polaroid from which this blowup was made, the Kennedy limousine is passing the grassy knoll and the president is beginning to collapse. It is less than a second after the fatal head shot. Am I watching Badge Man fire it? The House Select Committee photo panel reported, "Although it is extremely unlikely that further enhancement of any kind would be successful, this particular photo should be reexamined in light of the findings of the acoustics analysis," which placed a gunman behind the grassy knoll.

What does your guide, El Exigente, make of Black Dog Man and Badge Man? Much as I would like to have an enhanced portrait of the assassin at the moment he fired the fatal shot, I'm afraid my instinct is that these photos must be classified as an artifact of the Beatles-in-the-trees variety. Some may recall that when Bob Dylan's *John Wesley Harding* album came out—the first one after Dylan's near-fatal motorcycle accident—there were stories of cryptic messages embedded in the album-cover photograph. There was supposed to be a group shot of the Beatles—their four heads anyway—hidden in the shadows of the trees. I saw the Beatles in the trees once they were pointed out to me. But I don't think they were there, if you know what I mean. The same can be said for the thereness of Black Dog Man.

When I reach Gary Mack, he says he has something exciting to show me if I visit his Fort Worth home and investigatory headquarters: a beautiful blown-up enhancement of the Bronson film.

The Bronson film. The last, best hope that we'll get a motion picture of the "other assassins." Sort of the Shroud of Turin of the buff faith. Dallas onlooker Charles Bronson was taking home movies in Dealey Plaza that day. He caught the assassination in color. Showed it to the FBI. Nothing of interest, they said. Fifteen years later an assassination researcher named Robert Ranftel came across an FBI report, buried in one hundred thousand pages of declassified documents, about this film. Dogged Dallas assassination reporter Earl Golz tracked down Bronson—now in Ada, Oklahoma—checked out the film, and discovered something no one noticed before. Up there in the left-hand corner of the frame, the Bronson camera had caught the sixth-floor windows of the Texas School Book Depository. Not just the sniper's-nest window on the corner where Oswald was said to be perched but also the two adjacent windows. It's those two windows that Gary Mack wants me to see.

He also fills me in on his continuing struggle to rescue the Dallas police tape from being reconsigned to the dustbin of history. Gary thinks he can save it. I'm not so sure. For a glorious period of about three years, the Dallas police tape represented a triumphant official vindication of everything—well, almost everything—assassination buffs had been saying since 1964. The tape (actually a Dictabelt made of transmissions from a motorcycle cop's open mike to police headquarters on November 22) was excavated from a box in a retired police intelligence officer's closet in 1978, after Mary Ferrell reminded the House Select Committee of its possible existence and probative value.

Acoustical analysis of the sound patterns submerged in the static on the police tape led the House Select Committee to the spectacular conclusion that "scientific acoustical evidence establishes a high probability that two gunmen fired at President Kennedy" and that the assassination was "probably a result of a conspiracy."

Not only that. The highly respected acoustics scientists who analyzed the tape concluded from their reconstruction of echo patterns and test firings in Dealey Plaza that the second gunman was actually on the grassy knoll. Yes, the much-ridiculed assassination-buff obsession, the grassy knoll. The longest, most thorough official government investigation of the JFK assassination concluded that the buffs were right all along.

The vindication was short-lived, though. In 1982 a new panel of acoustics experts, this one convened at the request of the Justice Department by the National Academy of Sciences and known as the Ramsey Panel, blasted the police-tape findings out of the water. Its determination was that the so-called shots heard on the Dictabelt, including the grassy-knoll shot, took place a full minute after the shootings in Dealey Plaza that day and thus couldn't be shots at all.

And so we're back to square one. The acoustical evidence doesn't rule out a grassy-knoll gunman or a conspiracy or even the nine gunmen Penn Jones posits. But the mantle of scientific proof the buffs had donned now seems to be in shreds.

Not so, says Gary Mack. "Are you familiar with automatic gain control, Ron?" he asks me, and he launches into a highly complex, technical critique of the Ramsey Panel critique of the House Select Committee acoustics report. The Ramsey Panel misinterpreted automatic gain control in their re-timing thesis, he says. They neglected to analyze the sixty-cycle power hum to see if the Dictabelt in question had been rerecorded. They neglected certain anomalies of the Dictabelt that could be cleared up by further analysis of echo-pattern matching—and corroborated by a more precise jiggle analysis of another gruesome home movie, the one taken by Dallas dressmaker Abraham Zapruder.

Gary sounds like he knows what he's talking about, and perhaps he can make his case. But listening to his technobuff talk, I get a distinct sinking feeling that the Dallas police tape—like almost every other piece of "definitive" evidence in the case—is now forever lost in that limbo of ambiguity, that endless swamp of dispute that swallows up any certainty in the Kennedy case.

This morass of technobuff ambiguity leaves me utterly exhausted and depressed, but Gary Mack shifts the conversation to a missing-witness story. It isn't the greatest missing-witness story I've heard. Nothing like the classic Earlene-Roberts-rooming-house story. Nothing like the second-Oswald-car-salesman story. But it has enough of that *misterioso* provocativeness to give me a little thrill of that old-time buff fever and remind me why the whole hopeless confusing case has continued to fascinate me for two decades.

This particular missing-witness story concerns Oswald's whereabouts at the time of the shooting. No witness has ever placed him on the sixth floor any later than 11:55 A.M., thirty-five minutes before the gunfire. Oswald maintained that he was on the first floor throughout the shooting. And one witness, Bonnie Ray Williams, who was eating fried chicken on the sixth floor, stated that as late as 12:20 P.M. he was alone up there, that there was no Oswald on the sixth floor. Where was Oswald? The Warren Commission implied that he must have been hiding on the sixth floor in his sniper's nest from 11:55 on, while the Fried Chicken Man was chomping away.

But Gary Mack tells me about a witness, never questioned by the Warren Commission, who contradicts that hypothesis. She is Carolyn Arnold, now a resident of Stephenville, Texas. Back in 1963 she was executive secretary to the vice president of the Book Depository. She knew Oswald well by sight. She says that she came upon Oswald sitting alone, eating a sandwich in the employees' second-floor lunchroom at 12:15, just ten minutes before the motorcade was scheduled to pass the building. Her timing of this sighting has been corroborated by other employees, who noticed when she left her office to go to the lunchroom.

If Oswald was planning to assassinate the president from the sixth floor, what was he doing calmly eating lunch four floors below, right before the president was supposed to come into view? Could he have been that hungry, that calm? And if that was Oswald in the lunchroom, who were the figures spotted moving around on the sixth floor by witnesses across the street from the building at just about that time?

Whatever the significance of the Carolyn Arnold story—and perhaps it can be explained by eyewitness error—just listening to Gary Mack tell it brings me back to that peculiar sense of dislocation that attracted me to the JFK case in the first place. That frisson of strangeness.

Bring up the *Twilight Zone* theme. It's summer 1964. I'm seventeen, and I'm in a small crowded theater in New York's Gramercy Park section. A fierce man strides across the stage with a pointer, gesturing contemptuously at a huge blown-up slide projection of Lee Harvey Oswald. It's the famous *Life* magazine cover photo, the one with Oswald posing in his backyard with a rifle in one hand, a copy of the Socialist Workers Party paper, the *Militant,* in the other. He's got that weird, glazed, grim-faced grin.

But there's something else going on in this picture, the man with the pointer is saying. Something going on with the shadows. Look at the direction of the shadow of the gun, he commands us. Now look at the direction of the shadow cast by Oswald's nose. Different angle. Something's wrong. This picture has been faked. It's part of the frame-up. That's Lee Harvey Oswald's head but someone else's body. The man with the pointer is, of course, Mark Lane. He has just come from Washington, where he has been representing Oswald's side of the story before the Warren Commission at the request of Oswald's mother, Marguerite. And investigating the case himself. Already he has turned up some stories the authorities don't want us to hear, he says. Stories that suggest deep currents of complicity between the Dallas police and the conspiracy to frame Oswald.

The Earlene Roberts story, for instance. Roberts was the landlady of Oswald's shabby Oak Cliff rooming house. She recounted an incident that occurred a half hour after the shooting. Oswald had returned home and disappeared into his bedroom, and she was sitting in her parlor watching coverage of the assassination on TV when a Dallas police squad car pulled up in front of her place. The car paused, then honked its horn twice and left. Shortly thereafter, Oswald emerged and headed off in haste, only to be intercepted—accidentally, according to the Warren Commission—by Officer J. D. Tippit, who was shot dead while attempting to apprehend him. Was Tippit sent to eliminate Oswald to silence him or set him up?

The police department denied that any of its vehicles passed or stopped at Oswald's address. The only car in the vicinity at the time, they said, was driven by none other than Officer Tippit. Just what was going on between Oswald and Tippit?

Whoa. *Twilight Zone* again. Most Americans remember exactly where they were and what they felt when they first heard that John Kennedy had been shot. I'm no different; I do, too. But I have to confess that I remember even more vividly where I was and what I felt when I first heard the Earlene Roberts story. I remember feeling a chill, feeling goose-bumps crawling up from between my shoulder blades. There was a kind of thrill too, the thrill of being let in on some secret reality. Shadowy connections, suggestions of an evil still at large that ordinary people were not prepared to deal with. Dangerous knowledge.

That Earlene Roberts story certainly struck a nerve. And not just with me. Brian De Palma's second film, *Greetings,* while ostensibly about the draft, featured a character obsessed by Kennedy's assassination and by the Earlene Roberts story in particular. This guy was convinced, as is Penn Jones, that Earlene Roberts's death, before she was able to give testimony to the Warren Commission, was the work of the People Behind It All.

Dangerous knowledge. It's the recurrent theme in almost all the assassination-conspiracy films that followed De Palma's first. In Alan Pakula's *The Parallax View,* in William Richert's *Winter Kills,* in Michelangelo Antonioni's *Blow-Up,* in De Palma's later *Blow Out,* the hero begins by investigating the death of a Witness Who Knows Too Much, and soon he becomes a Witness Who Knows Too Much himself. His attainment of a darker, more truthful vision of the way things really are makes him a target for assassination. A way, perhaps, for us to approach the horror of being assassinated, the unassimilable horror of what JFK experienced at Dealey Plaza.

Let me return to 1964, because in the fall of that year, just two months after hearing the Earlene Roberts story, I was fortunate enough to get to know the assassination researcher whose methods and judgment I still respect above all others in the field. His name is Josiah Thompson, and he was my freshman philosophy instructor at Yale. At the time I knew him, he was becoming increasingly preoccupied with two mysteries: the often misinterpreted nature of the mind of the gloomy Danish anti-rationalist philosopher Søren Kierkegaard and the numinous hints of an alternate interpretation of the truth lurking in the shadows of the Warren Commission's twenty-six volumes.

His investigation of Kierkegaard resulted eventually in a highly acclaimed biography and a study of Kierkegaard's pseudonymous writings called *The Lonely Labyrinth*. His investigation of the teeming labyrinth of the Kennedy case took him into the Warren Report, then out into the world and down to Dallas, where he reinterviewed the witnesses, reexamined the evidence, and found new witnesses and new evidence. He produced what many regard as the most scrupulously researched and carefully thought-out critique of the official conclusions, a book called *Six Seconds in Dallas: A Micro-Study of the Kennedy Assassination*.

And so with Thompson as my exemplar, I came to think of critics of the Warren Report—the best of them, anyway—as intellectual heroes, defying conventional wisdom and complacency to pursue the truth. I had lost track of Thompson during the past ten years, and I was having trouble tracking him down to see what he thought of the JFK case after twenty years. It wasn't until I got to Dallas that I heard a strange story about him from one of the West Coast buffs who had found me in my hotel room through the buff grapevine. He'd heard that Thompson had abandoned his tenured professorship of philosophy and chucked his whole academic career to become a private eye somewhere on the West Coast. What the hell could that mean? Had he become a casualty of dangerous knowledge? Or had he fallen in love with it?

Next morning. Rendezvous with Penn and Elaine at the Book Depository for the grand gunmen tour. The Texas Historical Commission plaque at the base of the building still astonishes with its frank rejection of Warren Commission certainty. This is the building from which "Lee Harvey Oswald allegedly shot and killed" JFK.

"You ever been in the military, Ron?" Penn Jones is asking me. We've moved to the top of the grassy knoll, and Penn is pointing out snipers' nests in the buildings surrounding the killing ground down below.

There was hardly a building or tree that hadn't bristled with guns that day, according to Penn's vision of things. There were gunmen on top of the Dal-Tex Building, gunmen in the Records Building, even gunmen up in the skies.

"Look over there," Penn says, pointing toward the top of the Post Office Annex. "That was an observation post. They had a man there overlooking things so he could assess the damage done" by the first nine gunmen in Dealey Plaza. If they failed, Penn says, he could alert the multiple teams of backup gunmen farther along the parade route. Or if necessary call in the airborne team.

"They," for Penn, is the military. He believes that the military killed

Kennedy. Not the Mafia, not the CIA, not Cuban exiles, not some of the fusions of all three currently fashionable among buff theorists.

"Why the military?" I ask Penn. "Because they thought he'd withdraw from Vietnam? Or—"

"Shit, no. So they could take *over*," he says.

Penn was in the military, a World War II transport officer in the North African campaigns. In some ways Penn is still in the military. Only, he's a general now. A master strategist. As he surveys the landscape of Dealey Plaza, pointing out the teams of gunmen, as we retrace the motorcade route through the streets of Dallas, examining the locations of backup gunmen teams, Penn is like a general reviewing his troops, a battlefield strategist pointing out the logic of his deployments.

Of course, Penn's army of gunmen doesn't spring entirely from his overactive imagination. We're standing on the railroad tracks now, the ones that cross over the Triple Underpass. Penn points out the famous railroad signal-tower perch of the late Lee Bowers. Up there on November 22, 1963, Lee Bowers had a clear view of the area behind the stockade fence that crests the grassy knoll. Right about here, where Penn, Elaine, and I are standing, police officer Joe Smith stopped a man who was exiting the scene with suspect haste, as Smith testified before the Warren Commission. The man showed Secret Service credentials to Smith. The Secret Service says that none of its agents could have been there at that time.

As for the late Lee Bowers, it was his "mysterious death," shortly after his Warren Commission testimony, that set Penn off on his twenty-year chronicling of deaths and disappearances of witnesses with dangerous knowledge.

"Lee Bowers was killed in a *one-car accident* in my hometown of Midlothian, Texas," Penn tells me, his drawl just crawling with embittered sarcasm. "The doctor in Midlothian who examined him told me that when he admitted him, Bowers was in some sort of strange shock."

And we cruise by the site of the old Highlander Hotel in Highland Park. Now replaced by some big new condo tower: "The paymaster stayed here," Penn tells me. "It's also where the gunmen stayed the night before. They tore it down completely. I think it's significant that all these buildings were torn down."

Penn is fascinated by the first-class treatment the gunmen got before the day of the shooting.

"They treat the gunmen real well, *before*," he tells me. "They're mighty important. Every wish of theirs must be complied with."

Almost wistfully he describes the wish-fulfilled life of the gunmen in the secret safe houses he says they occupied the nights before the Night Before.

"There was one up in Lake Lugert, Oklahoma," he says. "That was some damn place. They had anything they wanted. Gambling, women. Lobsters flown in *daily. Shee*it."

Of course, Penn says, things changed for the gunmen the Day After.

"They loaded them in the two getaway planes and then just blew up the planes—one of 'em over the Gulf of Mexico, the other one down there in Sonora Province, old Mexico."

Not every shrine has been torn down. Some have been quietly disintegrating. The Oak Cliff sites. The Earlene Roberts rooming house to which O. returned shortly after the shooting. The house, where he and Marina had lived as their marriage disintegrated that year. Jack Ruby's raunchy apartment and motel pads. The Texas Theater, where O. was finally cornered.

"They just let this area decay," Penn says—as if even the inexorable organic breakdown of wood fiber is due to a conscious decision *they* made.

I'll never forget pulling into the driveway of this Oswald-and-Marina abode. It isn't so much the shock of discovering around back the hauntingly familiar-looking outside staircase that served as a background for the controversial O.-with-rifle-and-nose-shadow pix.

No, it is the expression on the face of the ancient Mexican man who apparently lives in the decaying shrine now. Evidently Penn is a regular, fairly well tolerated visitor here; when we arrive, the man—who is sitting on the sagging, splintered front porch with a child who appears to be his grandson—waves familiarly at Penn. But as we pass, I notice a deeply puzzled expression come over his face. Why do these crazy Anglos keep cruising my driveway? What kind of satisfaction is it they're after, that they never get?

But the thing I'll remember most about our tour this day is not the haunted landmarks or the ghostly gunmen they conceal. The thing I'll never forget, for its intensity and authenticity—an intensity that explains the shadowy world they've created—is the grief of Penn and Elaine.

Actually, it's Elaine's grief. I already know about Penn Jones's grief. It is all there in *Forgive My Grief,* his saga of murdered witnesses to the truth. The title is from Tennyson, by the way, from a passage of *In Memoriam* addressed to God, who took away the poet's closest friend:

> Forgive my grief for one removed,
> Thy creature, whom I found so fair.
> I trust he lives in thee, and there
> I find him worthier to be loved.

Elaine's involvement in this whole thing is hard to figure out, though. Why would a bright, young, attractive woman—young enough to have hardly known who JFK was when he was shot—why would she immerse herself in the buff biz after two decades, when it doesn't look like the case is on the verge of being cracked and all Penn offers is the despair and futility of mourning one lost witness after another?

I begin to get a clue to what might be motivating Elaine during the course of the tour, on our way back from the Oswald-and-Marina house, when Elaine spots a fat woman on the street.

"That looks like my stepmother," she says. "God, she was unfair to me. Every time I see a fat woman, I think of her and how unfair she was."

"Look at that concrete bridge abutment up ahead," Penn is saying. "That's where William Whaley [the taxi driver who took Oswald from downtown to Oak Cliff] died in a crash just after he tried to testify about Ruby and Tippit."

"My mother died when she was twenty-five," Elaine says. "Most of the rest of my close relatives are dead now. All I have left is my grandmother."

And so it continues as the tour winds down, a counterpoint of Penn's public grief and Elaine's personal grief.

Later, after the tour is over and we are cooling off with some beers, Elaine tries to explain why she has made Penn's project her life's work.

"From the moment I met Penn, I knew that's what I was gonna do—work on the case with him," she tells me. "And when I started, I was so excited."

"What happened?" I ask.

"Then I met all these people, and I saw there was no hope."

"Which people?"

"The other people on the case." She reels off a list of prominent buffs.

"What's wrong with them?" I ask.

"They none of them really *loved* John Kennedy. I remember meeting David Lifton and asking him point-blank, 'Did you love John Kennedy?' And he wouldn't give me a direct answer. And that's the real question: Did you love the man? If you didn't love him, why work on the case? Then it's just a hobby or some kind of excitement.

"We're down to two hundred subscribers now," she says. "And most of them are old. Pretty soon they'll die, and in a few years we'll be down to fifty. And that's what we have to look forward to. In two more years it'll be all over.* It's pretty sad."

But Elaine isn't going to give up.

"You get used to people laughing at you. You get used to the scorn and the ridicule. You put up with it because if you really believe in something, you don't stop, no matter what. It's like a religion."

---

*Needless to say, Elaine's pessimism (this was 1983) proved unjustified, although it took another decade and Oliver Stone to exhume conspiracy theories as fanciful as Penn Jones, Jr.'s. In his film *JFK*, Stone discredits the most plausible conspiracy theory, the Mob hit version endorsed by the House Select Committee, and opts for a maximalist military-coup fantasy much like Penn's.

She and Penn drift into a talk about religion, specifically about Thomas Merton, the Trappist monk and philosopher, Penn's idol.

"When Penn's gone, I'm gonna become a hermit like Merton," Elaine says. "Why should I bother with people anymore? I've lost everyone I loved except my grandmother and Penn. When they're gone, there won't be anyone.

"But I guess you've got to keep up the fight," she says, rather unconvincingly. "Still it's pretty sad. It's heartbreaking, depressing. There are days when Penn and I both weep over it. We both grieve over it."

"Over it?" I ask. "You mean—"

"It's sad for the state of the country. But really it's more sad for John Kennedy. That's what we can't get over."

It is then that I realize that these people are not buffs. They are mourners. Their investigation of the assassination is their way of mourning, a continuation of his last rites that they can't abandon. Unlike the rest of us, they haven't stopped grieving.

While the poets peopled the world of that November 22 with a grief-generated galaxy of hostile ghosts, the official investigators narrowed their focus to one man. Somehow lost in the controversy over the acoustical evidence is the fact that the House Select Committee actually came up with a prime suspect. A candidate for the Man Behind It All. And testimony to back that up. It all comes down to what you think of the tail-and-the-dog story.

The tail-and-the-dog story is at the heart of the hottest area of assassination theory still thriving after all these years: mob-hit theory. In the past few years, mob-hit theory has succeeded in shouldering aside such other rival contenders as CIA-anti-Castro-hit theory, pro-Castro-hit theory, and KGB-complicity theory and in pushing itself to the forefront of consideration.

The rush to the mob-hit judgment began in 1979 with the publication of the final report of the House Select Committee. Written by organized-crime expert and chief counsel Robert Blakey, the committee report comes within a whisker of calling the events of November 22, 1963, a gangland slaying and within a whisker of a whisker of pinning the contract on New Orleans mob boss Carlos Marcello.

"The committee found that Marcello had motive, means, and opportunity to have President John F. Kennedy assassinated, though it was unable to establish direct evidence of Marcello's complicity," the report states. "The committee identified the presence of one critical evidentiary element that was lacking with other organized crime figures examined by the committee: credible associations relating both Lee Harvey Oswald and Jack Ruby to figures having a relationship, albeit tenuous, with Marcello's crime family."

The key here is Oswald's uncle Dutz. Ruby's organized-crime ties—to teamster thugs connected with Jimmy Hoffa, to Sam Giancana and guys like John Roselli who were in on the CIA-mob plots to assassinate Fidel Castro—had long been known. What the House Select Committee established was an Oswald organized-crime connection: his uncle Charles "Dutz" Murret, of New Orleans, whom the committee described as both "a surrogate father of sorts throughout much of Oswald's life in New Orleans" and "an associate of significant organized crime figures affiliated with the Marcello organization."

The abstract connections are all there. We know that Marcello hated the Kennedy brothers with a deep bitterness that grew out of much more than fear of the threat that Bobby Kennedy's organized-crime prosecutions posed to his billion-dollar racketeering empire. Marcello had experienced the kind of physical humiliation at the hands of Kennedy justice that can brew a passion for revenge surpassing mere calculation of profit and loss.

Just two months after John Kennedy's inauguration, Marcello was virtually kidnapped in New Orleans by immigration officers acting at the direction of Bobby Kennedy's Justice Department. Arrested, handcuffed, he was dragged without a hearing to a Border Patrol plane and, according to Robert Blakey, "flown 1,200 miles to Guatemala City and dumped there, without luggage." When his presence became known to the authorities in Guatemala, he was expelled and "unceremoniously flown to an out-of-the-way village in the jungle of El Salvador, where [he and his lawyer] were left stranded. Salvadorian soldiers jailed and interrogated the two men for five days, then put them on a bus and took them twenty miles into the mountains. . . . They were hardly prepared for the mountain hike, as they were dressed in silk shantung suits and alligator shoes. . . . Marcello fainted three times. . . . During a downhill scramble, Marcello fell and broke two ribs" before reaching an airstrip and managing to reenter the United States illegally.

Indubitably, in all this unaccustomed humiliation at the hands of the Kennedys, the motive is there.

But where is the direct connection? That's where the tail-and-the-dog story comes in. The teller of the tale is Ed Becker, whom Blakey describes as "a former Las Vegas promoter who had lived on the fringe of the underworld."

The scene is Churchill Farms, Marcello's plantation outside New Orleans. It is September 1962. Becker is there to discuss a business proposition, but the talk turns to the Kennedy campaign against organized crime. The mention of Bobby Kennedy's name drives Marcello into a rage. "Don't worry about that little Bobby son of a bitch," he shouts, according to Becker. "He's going to be taken care of."

How? Becker testified before the House Select Committee that the plan was to "take care of" Bobby by "taking care of" his brother and that Marcello "clearly stated that he was going to arrange to have President Kennedy murdered in some way." Becker said that Marcello compared Bobby to the tail and his brother Jack to the whole dog, citing a proverb: If you cut off the tail, the dog will keep biting; but if you chop off the head, the dog will die, tail and all.

The committee took a lot of time painstakingly and convincingly corroborating the circumstantial details of the story. Then they called Marcello in to testify about it. He denied it. But he also testified before the committee in executive session that he made his living as a tomato salesman, testimony that his recent Brilab* conviction calls into question.

The tail-and-the-dog story may not be enough evidence to indict or convict, although I have been told that the committee staff forwarded its Marcello material to the Justice Department in order to encourage it to do just that. But Becker's story takes mob-hit theory a step beyond motive, means, and opportunity in the abstract.

That night. Back in my hotel room after Penn Jones's tour, recovering from the plunge into undiluted grief. I continue calling my buff contacts across the country. A long midnight talk with Bay Area buff Robert Ranftel is the most provocative.

Ranftel is a codiscoverer of a fascinating new piece of information about the case. The Gillin story. The Psychedelic Oswald theory.

Don't laugh. It's based on careful research, and it addresses perhaps the most enduring and perplexing mystery remaining in the case: the mind of Lee Harvey Oswald.

Because, after all these years the question for most researchers is no longer whether Oswald was involved but who he was. Was he KGB? CIA? Was he a pro-Castro partisan infiltrating anti-Castro groups, or was he an anti-Castro activist setting up false pro-Castro fronts? Was he informing for the FBI or being informed on? Did he support JFK or hate him? There is convincing evidence on both sides of each of these questions. How could one man have created so much ambiguity about his true identity in so short a time? And why? Was he just confused? Or was he out to confuse?

Ranftel unearthed a clue to this dilemma in an episode that took place during Oswald's mysterious sojourn in New Orleans the summer before the assassination. The Gillin story first surfaced in a document that wasn't declassified until 1977, an FBI memo about an interview with a New Orleans assistant district attorney named Edward Gillin. On the day Oswald was killed, Gillin phoned the FBI to report a strange encounter he had had in the

---

*Brilab was the FBI name for a major labor and political-corruption investigation.

summer of 1963 with a man calling himself Lee Oswald. How this skinny guy named Oswald had come into his office and started talking about a book he'd read by Aldous Huxley. A book about psychedelic drugs. "He was looking for a drug that would open his vision, you know, mind expansion," Gillin recalled. He had come to the assistant DA, Oswald said, because he wanted to know if such drugs were legal. And how to get them.

Oswald and Aldous Huxley.* What a bizarre meeting of minds. Oswald and psychedelic drugs. What a combination of ingredients. And yet Ranftel and his coauthors, Martin Lee and Jeff Cohen, reported in a *Rolling Stone* article that there were several other periods in Oswald's career during which the psychedelic connection might have been made.

The U-2 base in Atsugi, Japan, for instance. Where Oswald served as a Marine Corps radar operator before he defected to the Soviets. Ranftel and company discovered that during the time Oswald was stationed there, Atsugi base was a storage and testing facility for the drugs used in the CIA's Operation Artichoke. Artichoke was the forerunner of Operation MK-ULTRA, the CIA's search for a foolproof truth serum—at first called the Twilight Zone drug—which led to the testing of LSD, often on unsuspecting military personnel. Ranftel and his colleagues located a Marine who was stationed at Atsugi at the same time as Oswald who says that he was given LSD and other psychedelics.

And then there was Oswald's curious bad-trip episode at Atsugi. As Ranftel, Cohen, and Lee described it, "While Oswald was on guard duty, gunfire was heard. He was found sitting on the ground, more than a little dazed, babbling about seeing things in the bushes . . . what in the Sixties would become known as a bad trip."

Ranftel and company point to the widespread suspicion that Oswald's defection to the Soviet Union may have been staged with the connivance and encouragement of the CIA or military intelligence, both of which were at the time repeatedly trying to plant "defector" operatives inside the USSR. They cite CIA sources revealing that agents dispatched into situations with the potential for hostile interrogation—including the use of psychedelic interrogation aids—were often exposed to such drugs before setting out on those missions, so they would be able to recognize and cope with the effects of the drugs. People so exposed were known in the intelligence world as "enlightened operatives."

Oswald an enlightened operative? Oswald a Huxleyan psychedelic mystic? For one thing, as Ranftel remarks tonight, "it might explain that strange, quizzical smile you see on the guy's face in so many of his pictures."

---

*As it turned out, Aldous Huxley died on the same day as JFK, November 22, 1963. No connection, I think.

What was going on behind that smile? The Psychedelic Oswald hypothesis, however far-fetched, is a response to, an attempt to reconcile some of the intractable contradictions he left behind. CIA or KGB? Pro-Castro or anti-Castro? Perhaps the answer is neither and both. Perhaps the answer is that he enjoyed the game of posing as both, of playing at infiltrating one side on behalf of the other, of playing both sides against the other, the pleasures of the enlightened operative. We know that as a boy Oswald's favorite TV show was *I Led Three Lives*. Had Huxleyan drugs given a psychedelic twist to the solemnity of that classic of role playing?

The Huxley-Oswald hypothesis might go a long way toward explaining some of the mysteries of Oswald's strange summer in New Orleans—those months before the assassination when he began playing the dangerous game of pro- and anti-Castro politics and which climaxed with his mysterious pre-assassination trip to Mexico City.

New Orleans. The French Quarter's decaying fringe. 544 Camp Street, to be specific. The most intriguing address in the whole JFK case. Only it's not here anymore. I came all the way to this steamy, sweaty late August swamp of a city to enter the building at 544 Camp Street because some buff or other told me it was still here. Because, of all the shrines in the story of O., this one might hold the clue to what was going on in his mind in the summer of 1963, when he fled Dallas, arrived here, and began to act weird.

One thing almost all conspiracy theorists, even Warren Commission defenders, agree on is that though the assassination was an act executed in Dallas, it was conceived in the contagion of intrigue that infected the mind of Oswald that August in New Orleans.

The mind of Oswald. I'm beginning to feel some inkling of the turmoil therein as I stand before the curious sculpture that has replaced the now-demolished building at 544 Camp Street.

I fled Dallas yesterday, sick of brain and body. A bad case of food poisoning got to my body. So bad that for a while I thought I'd end up as number 189 in Penn Jones's list of suspicious casualties of the case.

But it was Gary Mack's assassination film festival that got to me. Drove me out of town. Not the goat's-head hypothesis, not the eyestrain from the Bronson-film blowups. No, it was the Oswald craniotomy controversy that took me out of the merely maddening world of *Blow-Up* right into *Texas Chainsaw Massacre* territory.

Should I tell you about this experience, or will you think it too ghoulish, too gruesome?

Notes on the assassination film festival: Arrived Gary Mack's lovely suburban Fort Worth tract home. Eager to see the Bronson film, but first there was Gary's critique of the goat's-head hypothesis.

The goat's-head hypothesis is the official explanation of the most horrible moment in that horror-filled home movie known as the Zapruder film. The moment when the fatal head shot appeared to slam the president back into the seat of his car as though it had been a frontal hit.

Gary ran and reran that moment for me on his home projector and screen set.

Not that I objected. After all, it could be argued that if you haven't seen the Zapruder film, you haven't actually experienced the assassination. You know a president was shot, an office vacated, but you haven't seen the man's head brutally blown apart, you haven't seen John Kennedy die, and so perhaps you haven't had a chance to confront the loss.

It was the sudden appearance in the seventies of bootleg copies of the Zapruder film and the showing of high-quality copies to congressmen that did more than anything to get the Senate and the House to launch their own investigations of the shooting.

Because, watching that shot knock Kennedy backward, all the senses cry out that it came from the front. But Oswald, we know, was behind. Which would mean a second gunman and therefore a conspiracy.

And yet from a re-study of the autopsy evidence the House Select Committee concluded—just as the Warren Commission had—that the head shot was fired from behind.

"How could that be?" I asked Gary Mack.

"Well, they cited the films of the goat's-head tests," Gary said. "Back in 1948 the Army did filmed studies of the impact of bullets on goats' heads that demonstrated what they called a neuromuscular reaction, which in certain circumstances will cause a backward motion even with a shot from behind."

"And do you accept that?" I asked.

"Well, the thing they fail to take note of," he told me, "is that in the neuromuscular reaction, the extremities are supposed to go rigid. Now if you look closely at the president at the moment he's hit—here, I'll slow it down so you can see that doesn't happen to Kennedy; he's all loose and wobbly."

Next, the Bronson film. Real *Blow-Up* stuff. There was the limo turning the corner onto Elm Street right below the Book Depository, beginning to head downhill toward the Triple Underpass and the spot a hundred yards farther down Elm, where the shots would hit. The real mystery of that particular moment, a mystery that becomes apparent once you've walked the motorcade's route in Dealey Plaza, past the Book Depository and down toward the fatal spot, a mystery neither the official inquiries nor the amateur critics have satisfactorily explained or even addressed, is this: Why didn't Oswald, or whoever was up in the Book Depository, shoot the president when he was coming right toward the sniper's-nest window, when he was heading down Houston Street straight into his gunsight, a mere thirty yards away? Why did the assassin wait until the president's car turned the corner onto Elm Street and began pulling away? Was there an inner struggle, some crisis of conscience going on in the assassin's mind? Did he almost decide to let his target slip away unharmed?

The Bronson-film blowup that Gary Mack showed me that afternoon did not address that question. The Bronson film was really a kind of ghost story. Because in the early footage, six minutes before the limo reached the fatal turn onto Elm Street, there, up in the corner of the frame, in the windows six floors above the street, pale, ghostly, evanescent shapes flickered.

Gary had blowups of the crucial frames. They showed dim gleams of shadowy shapes in the corner sniper's-nest window. And pale, ghostly presences moving, blotches and blurs, in the two windows next to that. Windows that should have been empty at the time of the shooting, according to the lone-assassin theory.

Assassins? Or artifacts in the photosensitive emulsion?

Gary Mack thinks they're men wearing pale green and magenta shirts. They could be. They could be John, Paul, George, and Ringo, for all I can tell. As a matter of fact, does anyone know exactly where the Fab Four were that day? If we go by the *cui bono,* or who-benefits, theory of the assassination, the finger of guilt could well swing toward the lovable Liverpudlian lads, since it's always been my belief that the Beatlemania that swept America just eight weeks after the assassination was really a hysterical transference of repressed JFK-assassination shock and grief. The link being the hair—both John Kennedy and John Lennon being loved for the look of their locks.

I refrained from exploring this theory with Gary, but he had convincing technical answers to my other objections. He was certain that he had prima facie evidence of conspiracy right there on his screen, the kind of evidence no goat's-head shoots can refute, and that costly computer enhancement, which he can't afford, might even show us human features as well as the shirts of the assassins.

But scientific evidence alone is not enough here. This case requires what Kierkegaard called a leap of faith. The existence of God, K. argued, can never be proved by constructing a scaffolding of rational argument. Faith can only come through a leap from that scaffolding into the realm of what he called the absurd. And El Exigente here is not ready to make that leap. He is troubled also by the question of what happened to the green and magenta men and, if they were up there shooting, what happened to their rifles and bullets?

No leap of faith required in the craniotomy controversy, though. No, this one requires a leap back into the grave. Oswald's grave. Or, as Gary prefers, the grave of Oswald's impostor. Because Gary had new evidence that very well might be enough to cause people to open up Oswald's grave *again.* That's right. Just two years after the notorious Eddowes-Marina exhumation seemed to establish that Oswald was the guy buried in Oswald's grave, Gary came upon a key discrepancy in the exhumation evidence.

He began to explain the thing to me in great and gruesome detail, a tale that might be called the Clue of the Assassin's Skull.

To understand the importance of his new discovery, Gary said, you have to know what they did to Oswald's skull during his first autopsy back in 1963.

"It's part of the record they did a craniotomy on him, back then," Gary told me. "They sawed off the top of his skull with a power saw. They reached underneath the brain, cut it off, and lifted it out, and they noted in the official record that a craniotomy had been done.

"Now, when they did the exhumation this time, no mention was made of a craniotomy. And then Paul Groody, the mortician, said it had suddenly struck him after they had reburied the corpse that he hadn't noticed that a craniotomy had been done on the skull of whoever it was buried in Oswald's grave. The skin had rotted away, leaving a naked skull. But with a craniotomy, the top of the skull should have fallen off. It didn't. In fact, there are videotapes of the exhumation showing them handling the skull, even holding it upside down, and nothing falls off. And at one point they severed the head and placed it on a metal stand. Somebody bumped it and it rolled onto the table, but the top still didn't fall off. Which proves that it can't be Oswald's skull down there, that it must be an impostor. Wouldn't you like to see that tape, Ron?"

At that point I made an excuse and fled town.

And so I am here at 544 Camp Street. Trying to forget about Oswald's skull. Trying to get inside his head. Let me explain why this particular address is so important.

Shortly after Oswald arrived in New Orleans in April 1963, he embarked on a mystifying campaign of dangerous and duplicitous political intrigue whose motive is still obscure. One of his first acts was to contact the national headquarters of the pro-Castro Fair Play for Cuba Committee (FPCC) to get a charter to set up a New Orleans chapter. He gave the name "A. J. Hidell," one of his false identities, as president and only member of the chapter.

At the same time, he was approaching anti-Castro Cuban-exile groups, declaring that he shared their feelings, boasting of his marksmanship and his Marine training in guerrilla warfare, and telling them that he wanted to be sent on a paramilitary mission to Cuba.

Then, in August 1963, one of the anti-Castro activists he had been soliciting came upon Oswald distributing pro-Castro pamphlets in his role as one-man Fair Play for Cuba Committee. A fight ensued. Oswald was arrested and jailed. Demanded to see an FBI agent. Told the bureau he was willing to inform on the pro-Castro movement.

Just what was he up to? And on behalf of whom? That's where that address 544 Camp Street becomes so interesting. It's at the heart of the paradox of O.'s simultaneous pro-Castro and anti-Castro activity. The address first surfaced in the case when it was found rubber-stamped on one of the pro-Castro tracts Oswald was handing out. It identified 544 Camp Street as the headquarters of the Fair Play for Cuba Committee. And yet not only did the building at that address never house the FPCC but it also swarmed with right-wing anti-Castro groups and was the headquarters of a right-wing ex-FBI agent named Guy Banister, who was that very summer recruiting people to infiltrate pro-Castro movements.

What was Oswald up to? As far back as 1964, Warren Commission staffers were scratching their heads over that and writing memos to each other about the possibility that Oswald's paper pro-Castro group was a front set up to infiltrate the pro-Castro movement on behalf of the anti-Castro group based in 544 Camp Street.

They never were able to resolve it. When the staffers presented their memo on Oswald in New Orleans to the harried chief counsel of the Warren Commission, it came back with these words scrawled on it: "At this stage we are supposed to be closing doors, not opening them."

Subsequent Senate and House assassination investigations tried to reopen the doors to 544 Camp Street but found only doors within doors.

"We have evidence," then-Senator Richard Schweiker declared, "which places at 544 Camp Street intelligence agents, Lee Oswald, the mob, and anti-Castro Cuban exiles."

Yes, behind those doors Oswald had gotten himself entangled in some of the darker strands in the fabric of American life. And yet what does it all prove? Perhaps there is a clue behind another set of doors—*The Doors of Perception.*

Consider this passage from Huxley's classic account of the psychedelic experience, based on his mescaline trips:

> The schizophrenic is like a man permanently under the influence of mescaline . . . which, because it never permits him to look at the world with merely human eyes, scares him into interpreting its unremitting strangeness, its burning intensity of significance, as the manifestations of human or even cosmic malevolence, calling for the most desperate countermeasures, *from murderous violence at one end of the scale* [italics mine] to catatonia, or psychological suicide, at the other end. And once embarked upon the downward, the infernal road, one would never be able to stop. . . .
>
> If you started the wrong way . . . everything that happened would be a proof of the conspiracy against you. It would be self-validating. You couldn't draw a breath without knowing it was part of the plot.

This last paragraph strikes me as a good description of the mind of the assassination buff as well as of the assassin.

Up until now there have been three theories relating to Oswald's strange immersion in the subcurrents swirling around 544 Camp Street: (1) he was a pro-Castro activist infiltrating anti-Castro movements on behalf of Cuban agents, (2) he was an agent of anti-Castro forces using a pro-Castro front to infiltrate Cuba, perhaps to kill Castro, and (3) he was a pro-Castro activist being cultivated and set up as a patsy by sinister anti-Castro-mob-intelligence-world operatives.

These contradictory theories have one thing in common. They all make Oswald a pawn in someone else's game.

If, however, we go through the doors of perception and look at New Orleans through the eyes of an "enlightened" O., another way of thinking about the ambiguities suggests itself.

Look at New Orleans through the eyes of an O. whose favorite TV program as a child was *I Led Three Lives*. Who may have absorbed the dark conspiracy-obsessed consciousness of that Huxley passage. Someone who has been a U.S. Marine, then a Soviet citizen, then a U.S. citizen again. Someone for whom change of identity has become second nature, someone who has seen the world from both sides and been disillusioned by both. Someone who—with his doors of perception opened—thinks he sees through it all. Someone for whom the only pleasure now is in the posing, the plotting, and the counterplotting. Look at O. as a pre-assassination assassination buff. Not a lone nut but a lone mastermind, deploying identities the way Penn Jones deploys gunmen. What a paradise New Orleans would have seemed that steamy summer to someone like that, with its murky web of plot and counterplot.

How convenient 544 Camp Street would have been. So many strands of intrigue so close at hand, so many strings so easy to pull.

How inconvenient for my purposes that 544 Camp Street has disappeared from the face of the earth. How I wanted to walk its halls and get a feel for its atmosphere. But the building was torn down some years ago to make way for a new federal court building. The old building's exact location at the corner of Lafayette Street is now a concrete plaza empty except for a large, abstract, federally subsidized sculpture.

And yet that sculpture . . .

The best way to describe the sculpture would be to call it a sixteen-foot twisted helix of black painted steel. Military-industrial-complex-size *damaged chromosomes.* Its title: *Out of There.* Hard to believe its creator did not know the significance of the place in which his work was installed. A better monument to the tortuous helical doubling and redoubling of the mind of Lee Harvey Oswald could not be imagined.

I wander south on Camp Street, passing comatose derelicts, disintegrating warehouse buildings, and dingy rooming houses. Come upon the Crescent Street Garage, where O. used to drop in and read gun magazines in the office. Next to the Reily Coffee Company, where he was employed, greasing coffee-grinding machines. The garage was also, according to the testimony of a mechanic, a depot for unmarked FBI and Secret Service cars. The mechanic said that he saw envelopes pass between agents in unmarked cars and Oswald.

Back up the street, past *Out of There,* to the all-night drugstore on the corner of Canal. Another O. hangout that summer. Horrible glaring fluorescents that must have been around since that summer, truly a depressing place, the nature of whose clientele can be surmised from a scrawled sign over the prescriptions counter: "Due to Uncertainties All Drug Sales Are Final."

Due to uncertainties. I push through the sweaty atmosphere back toward my hotel, mired in the maze of uncertainties surrounding O.'s Camp Street summer. His sojourn there suggests everything, proves nothing. Provides support for almost every conspiracy theory; proves none.

And so there it is. After all these years. Theories, uncertainties, possible connections, suspicious coincidences. Yes, the Warren Commission investigation was inept and incomplete, relied on information supplied by agencies with a stake in covering up their failures. And yet, twenty years later, several minor and one major congressional inquiry down the line, there is only more uncertainty.

I speak to Robert Ranftel again. This time about the dismaying question of whether it is time to call it quits, admit defeat, and give up the whole intractable case. Perhaps even concede that—in the absence of any proven alternative—Oswald may have acted alone; the Warren Commission, for all its bungling, might have gotten it right after all.

"What about the mob-hit theory," I ask Ranftel. "Isn't there any hope for that? I mean the House Committee pretty much endorsed it?"

"Well, mob-hit theory is where the action is now," Ranftel says. "Everybody's writing their mob-hit book. Did you see the latest—*Contract on America* [by David Scheim, subtitled *The Mafia Murders of John and Robert Kennedy*]?"

"Do you think mob-hit theory is just another buff trend?"

"I think the organized-crime theory is sort of a halfway house out of the Kennedy case for a lot of buffs," he says.

"A halfway house?"

"Well, it solves a lot of problems. You look at the typical mob hit. It's a murder that goes unsolved. And the people who did it typically never talk. So you can almost use the fact that the JFK case remains unsolved as evidence it was a mob hit. It allows a lot of people to walk away from the case and say we've brought it as far as it can go. You see a lot of assassination buffs now turning into organized-crime buffs."

A halfway house out of the case. Ranftel's phrase suddenly clarifies for me a persistent subtext I thought I'd been picking up in my conversations with some of the best of the buffs. Take Paul Hoch, for instance. Almost universally regarded as one of the most careful and meticulous researchers in the game. A computer programmer by profession, he specialized in looking into an area of ambiguity and searching the thousands of cubic feet of declassified documents in the archives until he found the single document that clarified the point in question. He was still working on the case—publishing his *Echoes of Conspiracy* newsletter—but his work now was filled with echoes of echoes. Reports of reports. Clippings. There seemed to be no edge, no direction, no sense that any of this was leading to anything.

"I get the impression that you're shifting from being an assassination investigator to something more like a commentator," I told Hoch.

"I think that's true. A historian might be more accurate. I try to keep the record straight."

"But what about solving the case?" I asked.

"I just don't know," he said. "I just don't know if it's too late now."

Too late? Would it matter if it weren't? Maybe that's the real question. Maybe, after all, there's no big secret, no clandestine conspiracy there to uncover. Immersed once again in the frustrations of the case, the frequent foolishness and apparent futility of the buff biz, I find myself almost longing to succumb to the simplicity and conventional comfort of lone-assassin certainty. To be able to stuff all the seething ambiguities, strange coincidences, provocative hints, all the suggestions, implications, curious connections, and mysterious sightings that the critics have turned up, just stuff them all in a drawer and say, "Case closed."

Before I do that, though, there is one man I want to track down and talk to. A private eye. My one-time philosophy prof–turned-buff-turned-shamus: Josiah Thompson. What will the author of *The Lonely Labyrinth* have to say about the JFK case now, after twenty years, when it has grown more labyrinthine—and lonelier?

I have some misgivings about calling him. Afraid, I guess, that he has become another casualty of the case. Picturing him in some seedy Sam Spade–like office, embittered and cynical over his failure to crack the JFK case, trudging through the fog, doing divorce work or something similarly dispiriting. But after the first five minutes on the phone with him I know that Thompson is just the person I am looking for. He has emerged from the maze with his lively intelligence, judicious wit, and wry humor intact. And his private-eye work has given him new insights into the problems of the Kennedy case.

He begins by explaining why he chose to make the switch from professor to private eye. After the publication of *Six Seconds in Dallas,* after serving as a consultant on the evidence for *Life* magazine's JFK reinvestigation in 1966 and 1967, he returned to a prof job at Haverford College, disillusioned by the fiasco of the Garrison investigation.

"Garrison just blew the critics out of the water," Thompson tells me. "So I sort of gave up for a while in the late sixties."

After completing his Kierkegaard biography in 1973, he turned his attentions to the complexities of that other twisted and tormented late-nineteenth-century thinker, Friedrich Nietzsche.

While he was on leave out in San Francisco writing a biography of Nietzsche, he had dinner with famed private investigator Hal Lipset. At the time, Lipset was being considered as a possible chief investigator for the newly formed House Select Committee on Assassinations. But Thompson found himself enthralled by Lipset's discussion of his own cases.

"Just on a lark I hit him for a job," Thompson tells me. "And he gave me one. Before I knew it, I was working for five dollars an hour doing surveillance in Oakland."

He was good enough that when Lipset's partner David Fechheimer formed his own firm, he asked Thompson to come to work for him and gave him a murder case for his first assignment.

"I started working on a really great case," he tells me. "And I couldn't give that up. It was too much fun."

In a short time, it seems, he turned into an absolute ace of a private eye.

There's one case in particular that pleases him. A Korean-born prisoner. Jailed for five years on a murder rap. Thompson reinvestigated the original case. Got it overturned. Got his man out of jail.

"He didn't do it," Thompson tells me. "I know who did it."

Interesting: He got an innocent man off, and he knows the identity of the real killer, who is presumably still walking around.

Dangerous knowledge. It is gratifying to find that Thompson hasn't fled from the frustrations of the seemingly insoluble but has instead embraced them. I envy him; I am tempted to hit him up for a private-eye job myself. But first I want to get his private eye–philosopher's assessment of the state of the art of the JFK case.

A few years ago it looked as if Thompson might get credit for cracking that one too. When the House Select Committee came out with its report on the acoustical analysis of the Dallas police tape, it placed a gunman behind the stockade fence on the grassy knoll, exactly the spot Thompson pointed to in his book.

But, refreshingly, he's willing to concede that the acoustical evidence that once promised such certainty now looks muddied.

"Uncertainty has replaced clarity," he says wistfully. "We're back in the swamp. Back in the morass again."

"The lonely labyrinth?" I ask.

He just laughs.

And refreshingly, considering that he was one of the original Warren Report critics, he is prepared to concede that in crucial aspects of the case, further investigation has proved him wrong and the commission right.

The much-ridiculed single-bullet theory, for instance. The whole lone-assassin theory depends in complex but definite ways on the Warren Commission's belief that one bullet went through JFK's body, smashed through John Connally's fifth rib and wrist, and emerged unscratched. I have actually handled that so-called pristine bullet myself in the National Archives, felt how smooth and unmarked its surface is, and scoffed at the idea that it could have emerged so utterly unscathed.

But, as Thompson points out, recent neutron activation analysis of the bullet and the tiny fragments left in Connally's wrist make it almost a scientific certainty that they came from the same bullet.

"That's very powerful evidence that the single-bullet theory is correct," he says. "It absolutely astonishes me, but you gotta look at what the evidence is. One thing I've learned from these years of being a private investigator is that I no longer place much faith in most eyewitness testimony to prove anything. If you're gonna rely on anything, it's the physical evidence and photographs. Another thing I've learned is that it's a waste of time to try to prove anything with government documents, the endless nit-picking that was done by the critics in the JFK case comparing discrepancies in what a witness said to the police or the FBI in a deposition and what they testified to later. You learn that the police get it wrong all the time and that nit-picking doesn't get you closer to the truth."

The truth. What *does* Thompson think is the truth in the JFK case? Is he actually leaning toward accepting the Warren Commission verdict that Oswald acted alone?

No, Thompson says. In fact, he still doesn't think the evidence adds up to Oswald's firing *any* shots that day.

"I think it's maybe sixty-forty that he didn't," Thompson tells me. "Although I can see reasonable men taking the other position."

"What, then, do you think Oswald's role was that day?" I ask him.

"I've stayed away from analyzing," he tells me. "What you have when you look into him is puzzle boxes within Chinese puzzle boxes. In the logic of intelligence circles, anything can mean anything. I think he was scheming in ways I don't understand, and finally, when the president was shot, the curtain opened and he recognized a lot more was going on than he knew."

And who does he think O. was scheming with? Thompson leans toward the mob-hit school of thought because of the new evidence developed by the House Select Committee about Ruby's connections and movements. "If Ruby was given access to the jail, if Ruby was *stalking* Oswald, as it seems they've demonstrated, one has to ask the question, why? And you have to look at the statistics on organized-crime prosecutions and how they dropped off after the assassination. One thing you can say about the assassination is that it's been enormously *effective*. It worked. They blew his head off, and they got away with it."

They?

"Why has nobody broken? And what group can enforce that kind of discipline? Nobody's turned. Of course, maybe there's nobody to turn."

Is there anything his private-eye's instinct tells him about the case that might solve it or explain why it's unsolved?

"That goddam bullet," he says, "that bullet just doesn't fit. You have to consider the possibility that evidence was tampered with. I know when I was working on the *Life* project they left me alone with that bullet for fifteen minutes. I could have done anything with it. But once you raise that possibility— that some pieces of the puzzle have their edges shaved off or pieces never in the puzzle have been brought in—you're never gonna put that puzzle together. In my heart of hearts, that's what I believe happened. And since we no longer have objective criteria of physical evidence, we're left with an epistemological conundrum."

An epistemological conundrum. Yes, that's what it has always seemed like to El Exigente. Somehow the JFK case is a lesson in the limits of reason, in the impossibility of ever knowing anything with absolute certainty. Gödel's Proof and Heisenberg's Uncertainty Principle all wrapped into one. That's why El Exigente has tried to stay above the battle, observing the foibles of the buffs from a position of amused detachment, resisting the impulse to become obsessed with knowledge maddeningly dangerous for its unknowability. I've seen too many brilliant people—some of them my friends—self-destruct in the attempt. I've always been too cautious to risk becoming a passionate casualty of the case.

But now Thompson, El Exigente's mentor, turns the tables on the Demanding One. In his modest but insistent Socratic way, he demands to know what I think.

I tell him I've gone into this most recent journey through the state of the art with the vague feeling that the mob-hit theorists probably have come closest to the truth of the case, but I've come out of it feeling that they have failed to nail it down. That the tail-and-the-dog story is as close as they'll ever come but it falls short of being proof, and that the rest is all the usual suggestive connections of the sort that can support any number of unproven theories.

And, I tell Thompson, I find myself longing—because of the advent of the two-decade anniversary—to come to some conclusion instead of suspending judgment on the crime of the century forever. And that although I am resisting it, to my dismay I find myself tempted after all these years to give in and embrace the Warren Report conclusions.

"You're right to say the conspiracy explanations are unsatisfying," he replies. "And you're right to recognize the urge to push it all into one pattern or the other for the satisfaction of having a conclusion. But," he adds, "you're also right to resist that temptation."

Postscript to "Oswald's Ghost"

Two decades after my inconclusive conclusion to this story, it seems fair to say that conspiracy theorists have failed to make a convincing case, but that shouldn't necessarily warrant smugness on the part of lone-gunman partisans. One mystery of the assassination continues to deepen, the mystery of Oswald. If it's hard to deny he fired those shots, it's still hard to understand why, what motive, what influence, what Oswald was behind them. He may have been a lone gunman, but there was never a lone Oswald: It was crowded inside that head, a labyrinth but not a lonely one. Despite the heroic efforts of people like Norman Mailer (who wrestled with Oswald's Ghost in *Oswald's Tale*), the picture just doesn't seem to come into focus. As a character, he has become one of the enduring American enigmas. Perhaps the closest we'll ever come may be the fictive Oswald Don DeLillo gives us in his brilliant, pitch-perfect novel, *Libra*.

Link Founding Father to Sleaze King

In Which We Entertain an Argument on Behalf of
Certain Tabloid Stories

It's time someone said a kind word for cheap sensationalism, lurid headlines, tabloid shockers, the much-maligned *New York Post,* and tabloids in general. It's amazing how many people there are who somehow think that by making sharp satiric sallies against tabloids they thereby establish themselves as lofty Gibbon-like intellects able to sort out the *truly serious* things in life from the distractions that cloud the minds of others.

The presumption is that the subjects of the typical tabloid headlines—the love-triangle slayings and other crimes of passion, the drug-bigs-slain-in-posh-pads, the psycho-killers, the coeds feared missing, the honeymoon murders, the newlywed deaths—are somehow self-evidently not serious because of the size of the front-page type in which they're heralded. While the subjects on the front page of "serious" papers, the budget battles, disagreements of White House advisers on tax policy, the MX-basing-mode review, the fate of the Mexican peso—are self-evidently more significant, presumably because they are actions, however crazed or maniacal, taken by established institutions rather than by unbalanced individuals.

But I believe the people who unthinkingly make fun of tabloids and their concerns are the victims of a serious intellectual misconception, a kind of knee-jerk gentility, a schoolmarmish mentality that sees the only fit subject of "investigative reporting" to be official misconduct, bureaucratic sins as opposed to those of flesh and blood.

The controversy surrounding the acquisition of the *New York Post* by Australian press lord Rupert Murdoch and the partisanship of its political coverage have obscured the serious argument to be made in favor of "sensationalism" in general and the *Post*'s front page in particular.

In fact, I would not merely defend the *Post*'s choice of headline material but champion it as a continuation of the robust American tradition of civic discourse initiated by *The Federalist Papers,* whose chief ideologist, Alexander Hamilton, I need not remind anyone, was also founder of the *New York Post.*

This is a particularly good time to put to rest the anti-sensationalist fallacy, because it's been an extraordinarily fertile period for *Post* headline writers.

In the space of just one month this fall the *Post* has treated us to the palimony scandal surrounding White House "kitchen cabinet" confidant Alfred Bloomingdale, whose ignominious end the *Post* climaxed with:

VICKI: BLOOMIE
'BURIED LIKE A DOG'

Then there is the continuing saga of newspaper heir Peter Pulitzer, his wife, Roxanne, and their Palm Beach friends, which featured:

SEX-TRIAL SOCIALITE'S
SHOCKER:
'I SLEPT WITH A
TRUMPET'

Equally fascinating but more confusing was the Transsexual Slay Case, in which a man who became a beautiful female model after undergoing a sex-change operation was shot in the head, first by her (his) new husband, then by his (her) old girlfriend, provoking a trial story that began:

NEW TRANS-SEX SLAY
TRIAL SHOCKER

That very same month also brought us the story of the drug suicide of the lover of a corrupt ex-congressman, which involved a

LOVE NOTE ON
DEAD MAN'S CHEST

Needless to say, *The New York Times* did not front-page these stories. On the same day that the *Post* headlined

MANIAC BLASTS 2
IN HOSPITAL

on its front page, the *Times* ran a sober below-the-fold report that the AIR FORCE ALTERS ITS MX BASING PLAN, which claimed that "strategic planners" have decided their dubious "Dense Pack" clustering of doomsday machines* would be guaranteed to self-destruct. It would be more appropriate, more accurate in a larger sense, for the *Times* to run that story in *Post*-size type as

MANIACS IN CRAZED
BLAST PLOT

Which brings us to what might be called the Cumulative Higher Accuracy Defense of sensationalism. Look at the number of madmen, maniacs, weirdos, crazed lovers, berserk slashers, and outright fiends stalking across the front pages of the *Post*. (The most telling distinction between the *Post*'s worldview and that of the more traditional moderate tabloid, the rival *Daily News,* can be seen in these two heads. From the *News:* VANDALS DERAIL TRAIN; from the *Post:* FIEND DERAILS TRAIN.) It is the apprehension of a world of utterly unredeemable fiends and beyond-the-bend berserkness that characterizes the *Post*. But can we be certain this is a less accurate picture of the world than the one presented by the gray, orderly confederation of carefully ruled and fitted boxes of bureaucratic news that make up the front page of "respectable" papers?

Still, you may wonder how stories headlined

STOVETOP
EXORCISM

500-POUND
SEX MONSTER
GOES FREE

---

*A short-lived scheme that envisioned bunching our most massive nuclear missiles in close-packed clusters. I can't recall (or imagine) the initial rationale, but it was abandoned when it was pointed out that a hit on one missile silo might set them all off in an apocalyptic conflagration.

PULITZER'S NIGHTS OF
DRUGS AND DISCO

contribute to the health of the Hamiltonian republic.

Well, let's look at *The Federalist Papers*. Let's look first of all at Hamilton's "Federalist Number Six," his wise and useful meditation on the ineradicable corruption of human nature, which relates the dark passions, the "inflammable humors" within the individual body, to the factional passions that inflame the body politic and threaten the possibility of self-government.

"Has it not been found," Hamilton asks, "that momentary passions . . . have a more active and imperious control over human conduct than general or remote considerations of policy, utility, or justice?"

You bet it has, says old Alex, citing a very *New York Post*–like story out of Plutarch in which Pericles, of all people, that noble champion of the *polis* of reason, was so intoxicated by the wiles of the prostitute Aspasia that he launched Athens into a stupid and murderous war against some kingdom she took a whimsical dislike to and wouldn't stop pouting over. Talk about BLOOMIE BURIED LIKE A DOG.* Of course, anyone who's read Suetonius on the Twelve Caesars knows how lurid and sensational good history can be, but it's doubtful that knee-jerk critics of the tabloids have read Suetonius, or that their anti-sensationalist stand is anything but a temperamental preference for a more orderly world.

Any attempt at self-government, if it's to have a chance of survival with liberty, Hamilton argues, must take into account the powers of "momentary passions" and "inflammable humors" over its citizens and leaders alike, must make an assessment of the "impulses of rage, resentment, jealousy, avarice, and of other irregular and violent propensities." If such sensational and lurid propensities lurking within the human heart cannot be contained by checks and balances within the individual, is it possible for any scaffolding of checks and balances within the government to survive the inflammations of factional strife, the momentary passions of passing majorities? What is the relationship between government of the self and self-government?**

These are not questions that can be answered in the abstract. And the answers one finds are only provisional: Each sensational story chronicled in the

---

*Talk about *Wag the Dog*. Clinton and Pericles: compare and contrast.

**It occurs to me now that one of the most notorious *Post* headlines of all time, one that appeared after this piece was published, one that is considered the *ne plus ultra* signature of the tabloid headline art—HEADLESS BODY IN TOPLESS BAR—also reflects a Hamiltonian preoccupation. It can be seen as a meditation on the age-old philosophic question known as "the mind-body problem"—the split between reason and passion, sensuality and sensibility. Jane Austen would have understood as well.

Post offers an opportunity to challenge and reassess one's sense of the balance between passion and self-restraint, between impulse and reason within oneself and one's fellow citizens. Each classic *Post* story is a reenactment of the drama of self-government that goes on within every fallen soul. Each offers us clues to the secrets of the human heart that cannot be gleaned from poring over the "in-depth" polls that are the "respectable" papers' halfhearted attempts to approach these mysteries.

Now I'm not claiming that all *Post* headlines are probes into the inner depths. There is genuine sensationalism, and a false or made-for-TV sensationalism, *Good Morning America*–level sensationalism—the Liz Taylor divorces, the celeb journalism, the royal anythings. As we all know, even Homer nods, and the tame caperings of Prince Andrew that the *Post* trumpeted as

THE PRINCE AND
THE PORN STAR

and (accompanied by a bare-chested photo of Andrew and erstwhile porn star Koo Stark)

ME TARZAN,
YOU KOO!

are not up to the *Post*'s standards. There were no great emotional stakes or unplumbed depths of passion there, none that would exceed the capacity of a couple of life-insurance salesmen on a Club Med vacation.

Compare these tame goings-on with the cornucopia of excess, decadence, death threats, betrayal, greed, lust, sloth, jealousy, socialites and servants, psychic fraud, champagne, cocaine, vengeance, and deeply disturbing karmic manifestations that characterized the Palm Beach custody divorce trial of Peter and Roxanne Pulitzer.

The *Post*'s Pulitzer trial headlines have been the true summa of the art, a dazzling, shameless display of virtuosity topped, of course, by the justly famed

SEX TRIAL SOCIALITE'S
SHOCKER:
'I SLEPT WITH A
TRUMPET'

Even though this shared a front page with the provocative

JUDGE BOOTS
BLOOMIE LOVER

the Trumpet Shocker pretty much booted the Bloomie head into invisibility.

For those of you too preoccupied by more serious matters to have paid attention to the story so far, the *Post* offered this Cast of Characters list along with the trumpet story:

- PETER PULITZER: 51, grandson of newspaper magnate Joseph Pulitzer. His wife says he committed incest with his daughter when she was a teenager and has smuggled drugs.
- ROXANNE PULITZER: 31, his attractive wife who seeks a divorce. She admits she routinely went to bed with a three-foot trumpet as part of a bizarre psychic ritual. Her husband says she had lesbian affairs and committed adultery.
- JACQUELINE KIMBERLY: wife of James Kimberly, who controls the Kimberly-Clark Kleenex tissues fortune. Pulitzer said she had an affair with his wife. Mr. Kimberly denies the claim, saying the Pulitzers are out for publicity.

What's wonderful about this story is how provocative it is on so many levels of discourse. The Hamiltonian implications are obvious. To anyone who's read *The Federalist Papers,* the Pulitzer marriage is a maimed *confederation,* the exact embodiment of Hamilton's dark vision of the strife, jealousy, anarchic self-destructive collapse that would be the fate of the states under the Articles of Confederation should they not adopt the binding union the new constitution offered.

On a less overtly political level the Pulitzer marriage seemed to be a contribution to the debate over the redemptive possibilities of romantic tragedy. "The road of excess," Blake claimed, "leads to the Palace of Wisdom." After the evidence of the Pulitzer trial, it's impossible not to revise that to: "The road of excess leads to further excess." Or, the road of excess leads to the driveway of the Pulitzer place in Palm Beach.

But there's another more provocative question raised by the Pulitzer trial, a genuine mystery: *Just what is it about these newspaper heirs anyway?* Sure, Patty Hearst was kidnapped, but did she have to turn into machine-gun-toting Tania on top of that? When the Scripps-Howard heir in Colorado started to snort cocaine, why did he have to develop a full $6,000-a-week habit and make a public spectacle of himself? And then there was the Knight-Ridder heir who got fatally involved with a homosexual slasher to the tune of sensational headlines. Were the Pulitzers jealous of the attention, the front-page headlines, the circulation boosts the other heirs were grabbing? Or is there some darker, almost biblical mark of Kane being meted out over generations to the pulp-sensation tycoons: their children recycled into the tragic headlines they built their empires on? Could it have been the spirit of old Joe Pulitzer himself speaking through the trumpet in Roxanne's bed, urging her on to headline-making exploits? Or, darker thought: Might it have been William Randolph Hearst carrying on his vendetta with the Pulitzers from beyond the grave?

A story as grand as the Pulitzer trial naturally leads one to speculations about the workings of fate, and leads me to what might be called a Miltonic defense of sensationalism. As we know, the grand task of *Paradise Lost* was not to retell the story of the Fall but to "justify the ways of God to men."

And there is a kind of Miltonic genre of *Post* front-page story that continually provokes us to take up that task. In that category we should place such stories as

NEWLYWED JAIL
MATRON SLAIN

and

HONEYMOON
LOVERS SLAIN

Why them? Why then? These are the sensationally excessive ironies, the peak of happiness and the utter depth of sorrow, the cruel twists of fate, that make us wonder who's doing the twisting and why. Along with these we can file the for-want-of-a-nail stories:

FIVE DIE BECAUSE
THIS TINY WIRE
FRAYED

Can such cruel ironies have any redemptive meaning? These are the kinds of truly interesting questions not likely to be raised by even the most perceptive analysis of the Senate Republicans' strategy in the upcoming budget battle.

But the best way of disposing of the anti-sensationalist fallacy is to expose the shabby totalitarian roots of its intellectual origin. The *locus classicus* for the case against sensationalism is Plato's grim and dreary totalitarian utopia, *The Republic,* in which he argues—in perhaps his most shameful passage—that the guardians of his republic would ban the reading of Homer and cast *The Iliad* and *Odyssey* outside the walls of the city because his sullen citizens shouldn't be exposed to certain lewd and sensational stories about the conduct of the gods.

In fact *The Republic* singles out as the prime example of Homeric sensationalism a love triangle, that much disparaged *Post* headline specialty. This one, the most celebrated

LOVE TRIANGLE
OF THE GODS

is the Homeric version of the Aphrodite/Hephaestus/Ares triangle, in which the clubfooted Hephaestus, the Olympian smith, traps his wife and her god-of-war lover in a tricky, benetted bed he's constructed to keep them captive till he gets home from the forge. It is the kind of story the *Post* would have headlined

CLUBFOOT HUB
TRAPS LOVE GODDESS
IN NET OF SIN

Homer and Joyce would have understood. They knew that the Trojan War began with a crime of passion.

It's too bad that the "serious" dailies tend to leave regular reporting on crimes of passion and the mysteries of the human heart to the tabloids. But for now the *Post* is all we have regularly serving us up Homeric themes, however raw. I think people should be more appreciative.

Perhaps the single most unappreciated effort of the *Post,* the one on which the verdict of history has been unanimously—and unjustly—negative, is the notorious

SAM SLEEPS

headline. I know. All it was was a bootlegged photo of the pale, bloated body of psycho killer David "Son of Sam" Berkowitz lying on a cot in a mental ward. Sleeping. For some reason this image drove otherwise rational people to almost psycho-killer excesses of condemnation. Why? I think it was because of the very frightening, *genuinely* sensational implication behind the deceptive blandness of SAM SLEEPS.

The very fact that he looks like some ordinary citizen sleeping is disturbing. It raises the question: How do we know that any of us ordinary citizens—looking just as ordinary on the surface as Sam there—might not be harboring a Sam sleeping within us? SAM SLEEPS might be the single most grim and poetic summation of the horror of the whole case. Alexander Hamilton would have understood.

Postscript to "Link Founding Father to Sleaze King"

I still get into arguments about the *Post* and about tabloids in general, and I still think the conventional critique of tabloids misses an important point: that some, not all, tabloid stories offer windows into the secret parts of the human heart. It seems to me no accident that love-triangle tragedies, for instance, have been the genesis of great literature from the *Oresteia* to *Anna Karenina*. As for the *Post* specifically, I believe you can disagree with its partisanship in politics and still admire just how smart its pure tabloid instincts are. There's no reason you couldn't have a liberal tabloid just as good.

Or is there? I was discussing that question with my friend Stanley Mieses, a writer who sandwiched a ten-year stint as a *New Yorker* staff writer between work on both Murdoch and non-Murdoch tabloids. He raised the question whether the absence of a good liberal tabloid might have something to do with a certain puritanical mentality on the left. I wonder if it might have something to do with the fact that liberals tend not to believe in sin, and to think they've got human nature figured out—the causes and cures of tragedy analyzed down to rational causes and social conditions. While tabloid stories often suggest an irreducible mystery and unpredictability, a darkness at the heart of human nature, secret parts that elude rational analysis or reform.

Back on the Watergate Case with Inspector RN

In Which the Ultimate Watergate Buff Closes in on Mr. Big

"I am aware," H. R. Haldeman writes, "that there is a cult of people in this country who collect every scrap of information about Watergate because of its many fascinating mysteries." He's more than aware: His memoir, *The Ends of Power,* is a seething nest of almost every conceivable scrap of Watergate conspiracy theory developed to date. The Democratic Trap Theory, the CIA Trap Theory, the Blackmail Demand Theory: You name it, H. R. Bob buys it. Indeed, the former chief of staff is nothing if not a buff himself, and he spices his book with tantalizing buff-to-buff hints for further investigation of the "fascinating mysteries." "I'll only pause to bring out one more fact about the $350,000," he teases, "this one for the Watergate buffs. . . ."

Although such recognition is welcome, the tone of the reference is regrettably uncharitable. By calling serious students of Watergate a "cult" of "buffs," he is, of course, lumping us with the much-abused "assassination buffs" and the aura of bad taste and futility that is associated with their efforts.

But there is a difference between these two domains of buffdom. Perhaps because—as Nixon partisans like to remind us—"nobody drowned at Watergate," the conjectures and conspiracy theories that have sprung up in its wake lack the taint of ghoulishness that has continued to plague grassy knoll theories, the most recent example of which (David Lifton's *Best Evidence*) insists on conjuring up a gruesome postmortem surgical alteration of the fatal wounds to fit a favored bullet trajectory theory. Although certain Watergate theorists venture equally far into fantasy (I have in my Watergate collection a curious vanity press volume called *The Journal of Judith Beck Stein,* written by a former patient in the Chesnut Lodge sanitarium, which seems to allege that the entire Watergate conspiracy and cover-up was engineered to cheat her out of a legacy and silence her exposure of the banking system), the eyes of Watergate buffs tend to twinkle rather than stare. Ours is a civilized passion.

Who, then, are the Watergate buffs? Not, as you might expect, a coterie of Nixon haters still savoring each delectable detail of his demise, "wallowing in Watergate," as the ex-president put it. No, many of the most relentless and dedicated Watergate buffs are pro-Nixon revisionists determined to prove that the whole episode was a dirty trick perpetrated upon, rather than by, Richard Nixon. (Reed Irvine's *Accuracy in Media* newsletter has tirelessly pursued the Democratic Trap Theory for many years now.)

Some of us are reporters who were stationed in Washington for the thrilling Final Days, and have developed a lasting taste for the arcana, however tangential, of the case. I, for example, can claim credit for being the first to uncover both a prophetic mention of Watergate in the Bible and an anticipation of the Plumbers Squad in the historical etymology of the *Oxford English Dictionary*. In the Book of Nehemiah (8:1) the people of Israel gather after their return from Babylonian exile to hear the prophet Ezra read the law of Moses to them for the first time since they regained their freedom. Where do they gather to hear the Word? At the entrance to Jerusalem known as "the Watergate." And the *O.E.D.* offers an eerie foreshadowing of the substance of the twentieth-century scandal in the eighteenth-century usage of the verb *watergate: to void urine.* That is, in effect, *to leak.**

Though studies of this sort may seem inadmissibly mystical to some, there are hard-nosed investigators among the buffs as well: former prosecutors, Congressional staffers, politicians—even an ex-president, the greatest buff of them all, Richard M. Nixon. All are united by undiminished delight in the

---

*It might be worth explaining, at this late date, why leaks were at the heart of the Watergate scandal: The elaborate and illegal cover-up of the Watergate break-in itself was contrived not so much because of the seriousness of the "third-rate burglary" and bungled bugging but because exposure of the principals behind the bugging (Howard Hunt and Gordon Liddy) would have exposed the so-called Plumbers Squad, the "dirty tricks" team originally formed to "plug leaks"—the operation responsible for "White House horrors" more scandalous than bugging. Hunt blackmailed the White House to maintain silence on the Plumbers, and it was those blackmail payoffs that were at the heart of the impeachment resolutions the House Judiciary Committee voted, the ones for which Nixon resigned rather than stand trial.

"fascinating mysteries" to which H. R. Bob refers. And in fact there *are* genuine gaps in our knowledge that are more extensive than anything any eighteen minutes of tape could supply. There are obvious questions (quick: Who ordered the break-in?) and subtle ones (just what was missing from the "Bay of Pigs report" that Richard Helms finally turned over to Richard Nixon, and how did it shape the outcome of the CIA cover story fabricated in the famous "smoking gun" tape?). And there are more esoteric excursions into the ambiguities of the evidence. Did the White House tamper with the birth certificate of the alleged "love child" of George McGovern? Who was private eye Woolsten-Smith's source of information in the November Group? And what was the mysterious "red box" the president keeps harping on in his September 15, 1972, talk with John Dean? ("What is the situation on the little red box?" asks P. "Have they found the box yet?" Could this be a childhood toy—Nixon's Rosebud?) Finally, of course, there are the larger motivational questions: Was the downfall of the president pure self-destruction, or was he undermined by subterranean power struggles which have yet to be fully analyzed?

Some buffs will stop at nothing in an effort to find some rational explanation for the actions of Richard Nixon. Consider the heroic efforts of Professor Douglas Muzzio, author of *Watergate Games,* an attempt to translate major Watergate turning points into mathematical game theory decision matrixes. Game theory proves, according to Muzzio, that far from acting as he did "because he was 'mad' or 'needed to fail,' " RN "acted rationally in response to events and actions by other Watergate players." Even if the professor's "pay-off matrixes" and "decision trees" fall short of convincing us of that conclusion, he is an extraordinarily well-read buff, and his analysis of the other "Watergate players" is often illuminating. Take, for instance, the game theory rationale he constructs to rehabilitate the much maligned original Watergate prosecutor, Earl Silbert. Muzzio claims that a Silbert prosecutorial "ploy"—tricking Dean into believing Liddy was already talking—was the key to cracking the case. If you find that hard to believe, just study Professor Muzzio's chart.

While such reductionist efforts are good for a chuckle, the idea that all Watergate mysteries were solved by the "smoking gun" is no less laughable. In fact (and this is what raises Watergate cultists from buffdom to scholarship), there is still uncharted territory to be explored. With that in mind, let's take a brisk tenth anniversary wallow in the muddied fields of Watergate theory and survey the state of the art in the kingdoms of conjecture built by the buffs.

Foreknowledge Theory, in its many forms, has been a consistent growth area of buffdom over the past ten years—a steady performer compared to, say,

Deep Throat Theory, which proceeds by fits and starts of guesswork. Fore-knowledge Theory has blossomed into a major revisionist heresy. In its "Dem-ocratic Trap" variation, it's become a vehicle for the quest of die-hard Nixon loyalists for historical vindication. Trap Theory traces its origins to seven vol-umes of executive session testimony taken by Howard Baker's minority staff of the Senate Watergate committee. (The seven volumes, which have come to be known among foreknowledge buffs as "The Seven Volumes," are not to be confused with "The Baker Report," a separate minority staff investigation which, when reinvestigated by the Nedzi Committee of the House, developed into the CIA Foreknowledge Theory.) The Seven Volumes tell a provocative and fairly well-corroborated story of Watergate-eve intrigue among RN's en-emies. The story begins with a British-born, New York–based private eye named A. J. Woolsten-Smith, who came to Kennedy Democrat William Had-dad in April 1972, two months before the Watergate bust, with what he said was reliable information that the Republicans had targeted a sophisticated spy operation against the Democratic National Committee. Haddad introduced Woolsten-Smith to Larry O'Brien's DNC deputy and to Jack Anderson. In conversations with them, specific tips about the Watergate target and the Cuban composition of the break-in team were passed along. It also happened that Jack Anderson was an old friend of Frank Sturgis and ran into him at Washington's National Airport the night before the break-in, just as Sturgis was arriving from Miami with the Cubans in order to make their second entry into O'Brien's Watergate office—the one that would end with their arrest and the beginning of Richard Nixon's fall.

At this point, the foreknowledge scenario becomes more speculative. The man who led the cops into Watergate to arrest the burglars, one Officer Shof-fler, is said to have signed up for an unusual second eight-hour tour of duty that night. Shoffler turns out to be the closest cop to the Watergate when the guard, Frank Wills, called police headquarters. An acquaintance of Officer Shoffler, one Edmund T. Chung, testifies that in a post-Watergate dinner con-versation he got the "impression that Shoffler had advance knowledge of the break-in." According to the Trap Theory, the Democrats learned about the first, May 27, break-in and bugging after it was over and contrived a plan to lure the Committee to Reelect the President (CREEP) team back into Water-gate on June 17, at which point they tipped off the cops. How did they lure them back in? With the malfunctioning bug on Larry O'Brien's phone. Ac-cording to Reed Irvine, that bug "may not have died a natural death." In other words, the Democrats exterminated the bug to lure the CREEP repair team back to be trapped in the act.

Other possible tipsters to Officer Shoffler postulated by other variations of

Foreknowledge Theory include Jack Anderson; the CIA; Howard Hughes's p.r. man, Robert Bennett; or a double agent on the break-in team itself (usually identified as James McCord). If all the people with alleged foreknowledge *had* actually decided to tip off the cops and trap the burglars, you'd think at least one of them would have been able to get through to Officer Shoffler. But Shoffler flatly denies being tipped off, and there is no smoking gun to contradict him. Foreknowledge Theory, in consequence, has bogged down in fanciful embellishments of the supposed Democratic (or CIA or Jack Anderson) conspiracy to trick Dick Nixon. For the most part, foreknowledge has degenerated into inconclusive foreplay.

One person who hasn't given up on foreknowledge, however, is Richard Nixon. In *RN: The Memoirs of Richard Nixon,* a volume which is unquestionably the masterwork of Watergate buffery, RN claims that shortly before he resigned he became aware of "new information that the Democrats had prior knowledge and that the Hughes organization might be involved. . . . And there were stories of strange alliances" between his enemies and moles within the White House. It is easy to see the appeal of Foreknowledge Theory for Nixon. It's the embodiment of the darkest Nixonian fantasies: A hideous congeries of his hypocritical enemies uses dirty tricks to lure him into essaying a dirty trick himself, then stumble over themselves in the shadows in their haste to call the cops.

In fact, the more you pursue Foreknowledge Theory, the more it begins to seem as if Richard Nixon was the only person in Washington who *didn't* know about the break-in ahead of time. Which brings us to a surprisingly stagnant and neglected subdivision of Foreknowledge Theory, the Richard Nixon Foreknowledge Question: Did RN order the break-in or approve it in advance?

Of course, we have RN's word for it that he didn't. Moreover, RN claims that this has been *proved conclusively.* How so? The release of the White House edited transcripts back in 1974, he writes in *RN,* "proved conclusively that I had not known about the break-in in advance." In other words, because RN is not heard *confessing* to ordering the break-in on tape, because he denies it several times (when he knew he was being recorded), it's been proved that he didn't do it. RN frequently shores up this "proof" with copious citations from his "diary entries" immediately after the break-in. Time after time, it seems, he confided to his diary his total bewilderment at the strange and unexpected news that anyone would want to bug the Democratic National Committee.

Most Watergate investigators have been content to let RN by with this Big Surprise version of his reaction, there being no concrete evidence to the contrary. Neither the Ervin Committee, the Impeachment Committee, the Woodstein team, nor the Special Prosecutor's office had evidence or belief enough to conclude that RN knew in advance. The only Watergate observer to take an unequivocal *Guilty! Guilty! Guilty!* stand on Nixonian foreknowledge has been Mary McCarthy. Why so shy, the rest of them? Perhaps they don't want to be perceived as knee-jerk Nixon haters eager to believe the worst about RN. Perhaps everyone is still waiting for another smoking gun to surface.

Well, another smoking gun *has* surfaced, it just hasn't been obtained yet. I came across a clue to its existence and whereabouts in Haldeman's book. If Haldeman is to be believed, the decisive testimony on the RN Foreknowledge Question may be on tape—but not a White House tape. Haldeman writes that he learned of this potentially explosive tape from Ken Clawson, the former *Washington Post* reporter who'd become an aide to Chuck Colson and later was promoted by RN to head the White House p.r. operation during the Final Days. According to Haldeman, an anguished, conscience-stricken Clawson came to him in May 1973, shortly after the chief of staff was forced to resign by RN, and told him: "Chuck Colson is blackmailing Nixon. He's got Nixon on the floor. Nixon didn't know that Colson was taping all of his telephone calls with Nixon *before and after* Watergate happened. He's got on tape just what Nixon said all through the whole Watergate mess."

Now, the novelty of this putative evidence is not in the blackmail revelation (everyone in the White House was blackmailing everyone else by that time), nor is it in the fact there are tapes of Colson and RN. It is that, unlike the thousands of pages of White House tapes we already have, RN *did not know his Colson calls were being taped.* He made four calls to Colson from Key Biscayne in the twenty-four hours after he learned about the break-in arrests: Nearly two hours of talk with Colson would be on these Colson tapes, but not on the White House tapes. RN tells us that, according to his "diary," Watergate was not discussed in those four calls. He and Colson talked about George Meany. About the polls. About the press. He just can't recall anything about Watergate. "Watergate," RN writes, "was the furthest thing from my mind."

If Colson did make tapes of those calls, and if he didn't destroy them as a relic of his sinful past when he got religion, then it's safe to assume they're stashed in a Colson-controlled safe-deposit box somewhere. The contents of that safe-deposit box would probably prove in his own words whether RN had that all-important foreknowledge, and how actively and immediately he collaborated in the subsequent cover-up. It would change our entire understanding of the internal dynamics of the collapse of a government.

Among the delights of buffdom are the unexpected discoveries one makes about apparently unrelated Watergate mysteries while tracing a single strand of the tangled web. And so it was that, while pursuing the question of Clawson's motives in telling the Colson blackmail story, I came across a surprising Clawson reference in *All the President's Men* that seemed to clinch the case for Clawson as the elusive Deep Throat. To all but the most deeply versed initiates of Deep Throat mysteries, the passage was an innocuous bit of background on Clawson: "Wallace had been shot by Bremer about four P.M.," Woodward and Bernstein write. "By 6:30 a *Post* editor had learned the name of the would-be assassin from White House official Ken Clawson."

This sent me searching madly for *Washington Post* (and Woodstein) editor Barry Sussman's book *The Great Cover-up,* where, I recalled, Sussman provides the only intra-*Post* clue to Deep Throat's identity. I found it. It looked like the clincher at last: "On May 15, 1972, hours after George Wallace was shot," Sussman writes, "we at the *Post* had not learned the name of the man who shot the Alabama governor. Woodward mentioned to me that he had 'a friend' who might be able to help. As we began to get into the Watergate scandal, 'my friend' as Woodward called him, came to play a mysterious, a crucial role. Over the months, 'Bob's friend' became more and more important to us and Howard Simons gave him a new name: 'Deep Throat.' "

It looked as though I'd cracked the Throat case: Clawson was the guy who got Bremer's name for a *Post* editor. Woodward's editor says the source from whom Woodward got Bremer's name for the *Post* later became known as Deep Throat. In the movie version of *All the President's Men,* which was made in close consultation with Woodward, Robert Redford appeals to Deep Throat by reminding him, "You helped me out on the Wallace thing."

I was ready to tell the other Deep Throat theorists to close up shop. But I still had just enough doubt—Clawson had a reputation as an unusually rabid Nixon loyalist—that I decided to violate a cardinal rule of buffdom: I made some phone calls. (Buffs, unlike mere reporters, do not make phone calls except to other buffs. They are content with the pleasures of the text, the wealth of resonances already in the literature.)

When I tried to track down Clawson through fellow RN loyalist Victor Lasky (author of *It Didn't Start with Watergate*), I learned that Clawson had fallen ill several years ago and Lasky had lost contact with him. Lasky thought my clue intriguing but had his doubts about Clawson as Throat. "He was one of the last ones to go down in the bunker," Lasky told me. "He was defending the Old Man right down to the last minute. It makes no sense to me—*unless he was putting on the act of acts. . . .*" (My emphasis.)

At the *Post,* Barry Sussman confirmed that Woodward had turned to his "friend" for help with the Bremer name, but wouldn't say for sure that "Bob's friend" had actually been the one to *succeed* in getting the Wallace suspect's name—in other words, Deep Friend wasn't necessarily Clawson.

What about the line in the movie: "You helped me with Wallace"? Sussman thought that the director of the movie, Alan J. Pakula, might have gotten that detail from Sussman's own book rather than from Woodward. Or that he might have been wrong about the Bremer source being one and the same as Deep Throat. Sussman didn't like the Clawson theory at all. Of course, Sussman would not *want* it to be true, wouldn't want the clinching clue to have come from a slight detail he inadvertently let slip in his book. He did tell me that the only other person who had ever delved deeply enough to ask him about the relationship between the Bremer passage in his book and the Wallace line in the movie was John Dean. Dean has been a longtime Deep Throat buff, Sussman said, and in fact had called him recently to speculate about a new suspect.

"Oh, I know, Dean's candidate is Dave Gergen," I said smugly, recalling that Dean's ghostwriter, Taylor Branch, had written about Dean's Gergen theory back in November 1976. Not anymore, Sussman told me: Dean has switched suspects, but not directly from Gergen. There was another intermediary suspect before he settled on his brand-new tenth anniversary Throat candidate. (Sussman didn't tell me either one.) I sympathize with Dean. Before I came upon the Clawson clue, I'd been working the Henry Petersen angle, and I'd never *really* given up my lingering Leonard Garment and Seymour Glanzer suspicions. It was comforting to know that Dean too suffered from similar Throat-switching tendencies. It seems that after ten years his wily ex-antagonist is destined to continue to elude definite detection.

Some suggest that after ten years the real mystery of Deep Throat is his continued silence. "If he's such a big national hero, why doesn't he step forward and claim all the credit?" Victor Lasky asks. "I'll tell you why," Victor Lasky answers. "Because there is no Deep Throat." One possible explanation for the silence of Throat—and it does lend support to the Henry Petersen theory—is that if Throat were, like Petersen or Glanzer, part of the Justice Department prosecutorial team, the disclosure of his identity might give all the Watergate felons cause to petition for a reversal of the verdicts on the grounds of prosecutorial misconduct. Who knows, they might have to restage all the big Watergate trials. As John Dean said, "What an exciting prospect."

In defense of the nondottiness of Deep Throat speculation, let me point out that Watergate and its aftermath was a subterranean war of leaks, of attempts by one faction or another to divert press and prosecutorial attention to rival power centers. Several significant civil wars within the White House and within the bureaucracies and agencies acted themselves out in deep background attacks. Deep Throat might have been a conscience-stricken loner seeking absolution in underground garage confessionals. But he also might have been a cynical game player trying to use *The Washington Post* for some factional gain. Without knowing his identity, our understanding of Watergate history will be incomplete, although I have a feeling we all prefer the continuing mystery to the inevitable disappointments of certainty.

RN certainly does not consider Deep Throat speculation an idle question. He's as big a buff as anyone on the subject. Haldeman gives us fascinating glimpses of RN and his ex–chief of staff batting around Deep Throat theories in buff-to-buff chats. According to Haldeman, RN's personal Deep Throat candidate is Robert Bennett, the Hughes p.r. man who was Howard Hunt's boss in a p.r. firm that also served as a CIA cover. According to Bennett's CIA case officer (cited in the Nedzi Committee hearings), Bennett boasted that he was feeding Bob Woodward information and that Woodward was "suitably grateful," a quote which has become the basis for entire Robert Bennett theories of Watergate, some of them spread by Chuck Colson and all of them, I believe, misguided.

As a buff, however, I find it troubling to see fellow buff RN mired in the dark ages of Deep Throat speculation. All serious analysts of the question have long since abandoned the Bennett-as-Throat hypothesis. Bennett was a source for Woodward, but a source he acknowledges on the record in *All the President's Men*. In fact, J. Anthony Lukas, who boomed Bennett as Deep Throat in a *New York Times Magazine* article, abandoned him and switched to lukewarm endorsement of Mark Felt (Edward Jay Epstein's candidate), the deputy FBI director who was feuding with RN's pet, Pat Gray.

Haldeman's own candidate is Fred Fielding, the former John Dean deputy who later served President Reagan as White House counsel in charge of ethical questions. There's a wonderful description of ethics counsel Fielding in John Dean's book that depicts the future arbiter of integrity drawing on "rectal gloves" in order not to leave fingerprints on the potentially incriminating contents of Howard Hunt's safe.

Of course, no survey of buffdom is complete without an appreciation of the achievements of *RN: The Memoirs of Richard Nixon.* Only fellow buffs can appreciate the indomitable, never-say-die spirit of buffery in this work. If the White House transcripts are the Bible for buffs, *RN* may be considered the Gnostic Gospels, the great heretical reinterpretation of the central sacred texts. One thinks of comparable heroic acts of misinterpretation—William Blake's notion that Milton's Satan is the true hero of *Paradise Lost* comes to mind.

But for the most precise literary antecedent to *RN,* we must consider nothing less than Vladimir Nabokov's *Pale Fire;* for the best parts of *RN,* like Nabokov's novel, take the form of an obsessive, elaborate explication of an established text. In *Pale Fire* we have a mad professor misinterpreting his murdered friend's poem to fashion himself the central character. In *RN* we have a defrocked president doggedly taking on the tape-recorded text of his own words and, with a heroic act of the explicative imagination, transforming guilt-laden utterances into evidences of utter innocence, raising explication to the level of high art.

Consider the balletic leaps of ratiocination he takes with the notorious "I don't give a shit what happens, I want you all to stonewall it, let them plead the Fifth Amendment, cover up or anything else, if it'll save it, save the plan" passage in the tapes. It emerges from the smithy of RN's art as "my oblique way of confronting the need to make a painful shift in our Watergate strategy."

Then there's his marvelous explication of the famous March 21 "cancer on the presidency" talk with Dean, the one in which he repeatedly insisted he wanted to pay a million-dollar hush-money bribe to keep the cover-up going. This, he explains, was his way of ensuring that the truth would come out "in an orderly and rational way."

But RN is not content with exegetical virtuosity. He has brand-new theories to offer buffs. Take his fascinating suggestion about the real culprit in the creation of the eighteen-minute gap. He knows that his explanation of the erasure is a kind of command performance. He knows we're expecting a dazzling effort from him on this one. But he's confident: "I know my treatment of the gap will be looked upon as a touchstone for the candor and credibility of what I write," he begins. It's a breathtaking gesture, almost like Babe Ruth pointing to the stands. He's convinced he can pull it off and make us believe that neither he nor his secretary, Rose Mary Woods, had anything to do with erasing that tape.

What he delivers is less an explication than an epic innuendo implying extended Secret Service conspiracy and treason within the White House:

> I think we all wondered about the various Secret Service agents and technicians who had had free daily access to the tapes, and even about the Secret Service agents who had provided Rose with the new but apparently faulty Uher tape recorder just half an hour before she discovered the gap. We even wondered about Alex Butterfield, who had revealed the existence of the tape system. . . . But it would have taken a very dedicated believer in conspiracies to accept that someone would have purposely erased eighteen and a half minutes of this particular tape in order to embarrass me.

Of course, RN is just such a dedicated believer, and the more you study *RN*, the more you realize just how dedicated he is. He suspected Watergate was a setup from the first. Barely two weeks after the break-in, he was entertaining "the possibility that we were dealing with a double agent who purposely blew the operation."

Indeed, RN is so preoccupied by the idea that he is the *victim* of the break-in and bugging of his opponents that he repeatedly fantasizes that his own party headquarters were bugged. He attributes to Haldeman, in one of his "diary" entries right after the June 17 arrests, the story that "one of Chotiner's operatives had said that a McGovern aide had told him that *they* had our committee rooms bugged." Curiously, he deletes from his diary citation the name of this "Chotiner operative" and that of the McGovern aide who confessed to a Watergate-like crime against RN. RN seems to have an exclusive on this bombshell.

RN's greatest strength as a buff is his generosity as a guide to future 'Gate revelations—the ones destined to keep buffs busy for the next ten years of wallowing. RN's clues to what's in store take the form of elaborate denials of things he hasn't been accused of yet. When one comes across one of these in the text of *RN,* one senses that RN is signaling that there's a truly delicious incriminating morsel on a tape he fears might be released in the foreseeable future.

One of the best of these coming attractions is the passage in which RN attempts to deny offering clemency to Jeb Stuart Magruder about a year into the cover-up. It's April 1973. RN is in the middle of his famous "personal investigation" of Watergate following Dean's "cancer on the presidency" talk. Magruder is about to go back before the grand jury he lied to the summer before. If he tells the truth, he can put all the president's men in jail and make a liar out of RN. Assured of clemency, however, he might be willing to risk continued protective perjury. And so, lurking behind RN's unusually detailed account of a chat with Ehrlichman back then, there must be a heretofore unnoted offer of clemency to Magruder; and it's possible to glimpse in the pale fire of his preemptive interpretation the reflected glare of the guilt he's trying to eclipse: "I had been thinking the night before about Magruder's young children," RN tells us, sawing away at the heartstrings, "and about his wife. 'It breaks your heart,' I said. I thought back to Haldeman's comment two weeks before on how pathetic Magruder had been with his plea for clemency. I told Ehrlichman that this was a painful message for me: 'I'd just put that in so that he knows that I have personal affection,' I said. 'That's the way the so-called clemency's got to be handled.' "

The single most tantalizing of these peeks into future revelations, however, is RN's teasing suggestion that he's got a hitherto unknown break-in in store for us, one that he personally ordered, presumably on tape. RN tells us that on Wednesday, June 21, 1972, with the cover-up still in its embryonic stage, he came up with a bold counterattack proposal: "I said that every time the Democrats accused us of bugging we should charge that we were being bugged and maybe even plant a bug and find it ourselves!"

He seems to have been mulling this idea over for ten days when, in a conversation with Colson for which RN feels compelled to offer a preemptive pre-tape-release explanation, he makes it sound as if he gave a definite go-ahead order: "Colson and I talked about the exaggerated publicity that was being given to the break-in. In sheer exasperation I said it would help if someone broke into our headquarters and did a lot of damage—then we could launch a counterattack. Colson agreed. . . ."

This sounds like the authentic RN. Two weeks after the Watergate break-in, he's champing at the bit to order a break-in on himself to prove that his break-in on his enemies was retroactively justified by the one he'd blame on them. Of course, no such break-in at RN's campaign headquarters has been reported. But would RN have brought up the subject in his memoirs and tried to excuse it ("in sheer exasperation") in advance if the order did not sound serious on the yet-to-be-released tape?

And it happens that not long after this conversation, a break-in took place at the Long Beach office of RN's former physician, Dr. John Lungren.

According to RN, "No money or drugs were taken but my medical files were removed from a locked closet and left strewn about the floor of the office." Note that RN's medical records were not removed from the office. And if the Lungren break-in team had merely wanted to photograph the records, why leave them so conspicuously scattered around? From the description RN provides, it seems as if the only purpose of the Lungren break-in was to advertise the fact that RN was the target. Such advertising comes in handy to RN. He cites it later as evidence that his enemies used the same tactics against him as he did in having his men break into Daniel Ellsberg's psychiatrist's office. The symmetry is so pleasing to RN that one wonders if he had a share in shaping it. RN seems not at all outraged that damage was done to his doctor's office, only that just one network carried the news of the Lungren break-in while all three made a big deal over a 1973 report of a break-in into JFK's doctor's office during the 1960 campaign (another RN job?).

Yes, while other investigators have retired from the field, RN is still probing these baffling break-ins. Haldeman provides us with a fascinating glimpse of Inspector RN at work on the Ellsberg break-in case. Shortly after the November 1976 election (which would soon put a Democratic administration in charge of the disputed storehouse of White House tapes), RN summoned Haldeman to San Clemente "to probe my memory," Haldeman says. According to Haldeman, Inspector RN has been toying with the hypothesis that he—RN himself—ordered the break-in: "I was so damn mad at Ellsberg in those days. And Henry [Kissinger] was jumping up and down. I've been thinking—and maybe I did order that break-in."

But Inspector RN is not completely satisfied with this deft solution to the Ellsberg case. He'd called in Ellsberg operations chief Egil Krogh, and Krogh told him *he* didn't remember the president ordering him to do it. "Again and again that afternoon Nixon returned to the subject," Haldeman recalls. "Finally he said, 'I'm just going to have to check it out further.' "

Surprisingly, Haldeman has doubts about the good faith of Inspector RN's continuing investigation:

> And then I realized the situation. If Nixon had ordered the break-in while in the Oval Office his order was preserved on tape. And those tapes might well become public some day. Nixon was debating whether to reveal what he had really said in that office about the break-in or wait it out. It might be years before that particular tape was unearthed.

Now, it seems to me that this is an extremely uncharitable interpretation of Inspector RN's motives. If you recall, RN has told us that as soon as he heard the shocking news of a cover-up in the White House from John Dean back in March 1973, he proceeded to launch his own intensive investigation of the entire affair. So this account of RN probing to see whether anyone remembered *him* ordering the Ellsberg job is just another indication among many that after ten years, RN *is still on the case.* And, at long last, he may be closing in on Mr. Big.

Postscript to "Back on the Watergate Case with Inspector RN"

It's still remarkable to me that the original Watergate burglary remains unsolved. In the sixteen years since *The New Republic* asked me to do this piece for their tenth anniversary Watergate issue, we still lack a definitive solution. As Stephen Ambrose's biography *Nixon: The Rise to Power* reminds us, "Nobody was ever prosecuted for ordering the Watergate break-in, only for participating in it, or conspiring to cover it up."

But I believe I can point to a couple of new and intriguing clues to the crucial unresolved question I call attention to in that story: Did Richard Nixon give the order for the Watergate break-in, the crime that resulted in his resignation and changed the course of U.S. history, a crime that has not been definitively solved? Did Nixon give the order—was he at least cognizant of it—or did he merely participate in the cover-up afterward to protect himself from the embarrassing consequences of the mistakes of misguided subordinates, as he maintained till the day he died? Was he in effect as much a victim of Watergate as perpetrator?

I've criticized what seems to me the poorly examined consensus among journalists and historians, liberal and conservative, a consensus which takes at face value Richard Nixon's argument of "sophistication" on the question: that he was shocked, *shocked* when he heard about the break-in, shocked not so much by the action as the target—that a savvy pol such as himself would have known better than to seek political intelligence at Democratic National Party Headquarters (in the Watergate). Political sophisticates such as himself know that the really worthwhile intelligence is to be found rather in the (quite separate) presidential *candidate*'s headquarters.

It should be recalled that this is not an idle dispute but the most fundamental question to be asked—and to leave unanswered—about an event which changed the course of history for America and doubtless for the rest of the world as well (considering what Richard Nixon might and might not have done in the final two thirds of his second term at the height of the cold war). And so I think it worth recounting here the clues on two newly released White House transcripts (not available until 1997 when they were published by Professor Stanley Kutler), which shed new light on the question of who ordered the break-in.

First, there is a previously unreleased (and still largely unnoticed) conversation recorded on June 20, 1972, three days after the break-in, a conversation in which Richard Nixon tells his *consigliere,* H. R. Haldeman, how shocked he was at the choice of target, the party committee headquarters at the Watergate: "My God," Nixon says, "the committee isn't worth bugging in my opinion." And then he adds an astonishing admission about this rationale: "That's my public line."

The implication is that the private truth on the matter is different from the "public line." The private truth is that he knows very well there *was* a reason why the Watergate Democratic Party Headquarters was "worth bugging." It's an implication that seems to be confirmed by Haldeman, who responds by saying it wasn't worth bugging "except for the financial thing. They thought they had something going on that."

This exchange not only seems to give the lie to the argument of sophistication, that the whole thing was shocking to Richard Nixon because the target was inexplicable to a savvy pol such as him. It also tends to confirm a line of speculation about the motive for the break-in—another of the unresolved questions that still hang over the Watergate break-in nearly three decades after its commission.

The "financial thing" Haldeman refers to has been further elucidated by Jeb Magruder, the key middleman—the one who got the heat from higher-ups to get the burglars and buggers into the Watergate. Magruder has since confirmed to J. Anthony Lukas that the reason the Watergate Democratic National Committee offices were targeted was because it contained the offices of Democratic Party Chairman Larry O'Brien and "the primary purpose of the break-in was to [find out what] information [O'Brien had] about Howard Hughes' illicit cash transfers to Nixon and friends."

Magruder is the focus of the second striking clue to the break-in order in the tapes released in 1997. This can be found in a conversation some nine months after the break-in when the cover-up was crumbling and the middlemen like Magruder were heading back to the grand jury to tell the truth for the first time, a prospect most unpleasing to the presidential ear.

Haldeman tells Nixon that he's heard Magruder is going to say "that what really happened on the Watergate was that all this planning was going on. . . . They had the plan all set but they were not ready to start with it, and then [Haldeman's aide Gordon] Strachan called [Magruder] and said: 'Haldeman has said that you cannot delay getting this operation started any longer, and the president has ordered you to go ahead immediately and you're not to stall any more, you're to get it done.' "

The president has ordered you to go ahead. It is a second- or thirdhand report, but it sounds like the explicit presidential order to break in to the Watergate that Richard Nixon denied to the day of his death. In my *New Republic* story, I suggest that "knowing whether or not Richard Nixon was the one who ordered the break-in would change our understanding of the internal dynamics of the collapse of an elected government." I would add now, in the wake of Nixon's death, that it would change as well our understanding of the internal dynamics of Richard Nixon himself, one of the great complex, tormented, enigmatic American characters. In his repeated apologies and mea culpas in the wake of Watergate—apologies for the cover-up, not the break-in order— did he finally come clean in a soul-cleansing way? Or did he carry a final lie to his grave? The clues on the newly released tapes suggest that the comfortable split-the-difference consensus adopted by most historians who accept the pose of sophistication—the self-exculpating assertion that Nixon was shocked, shocked by the break-in—must be reconsidered.

Jack Nicholson: The Devil and the Details

In Which We Learn Some Tricks of the Trade

Jack Nicholson is singing "Three Blind Mice" for his visitor. Actually, singing might be the wrong word for the eerie droning intonations he's producing; it sounds more like ritual chanting.

Nicholson is emitting these strange sounds while standing in the middle of the living room of his home on top of one of the Hollywood Hills—a hilltop he shares with Marlon Brando, although Brando's house is on somewhat higher ground.*

In order to generate these particular noises, Nicholson has assumed a posture that suggests his post-shock-treatment mode in *One Flew Over the Cuckoo's Nest*. His arms hang limply at his sides, his shoulders droop into a

---

*I can count on the fingers of one hand the number of film-star stories I've done; this is the only one of those fingers (so to speak) I've wanted to include here. (I'm not counting Troy Donahue as a "film star.") I don't regret the others, it's a part of existence worth a peek at if not much more. What made the Nicholson story different to me was, in part, the circumstances: *The New York Times Magazine* was running a series on the creative processes of various artists, writers, and thinkers, and the point of the story was to talk about his craft rather than his star power or his relationships. Of course, all too many actors can ramble on about "the work," but Nicholson is not just a genuine madman devotee of the method of his art, he also has the raw gift and the remarkable body of work that make his disclosures of his tricks and secrets, as he calls them, worth attending to.

posture that verges on the simian. His jaw is slack, his face drained of expression. To his left, out beyond the glass wall of his living room, the canyons of Hollywood are beginning to redden with the sunset. To his right, on the opposite wall, is one of his Picassos—an early Cubist work that looks to be a painting of a painting of a woman. And from Nicholson's middle comes pouring out, in deep, resonant, utterly uninflected, cello tones:

THREEEEEEEEEEEEEEEEE . . .

BLIIIIIIIINNNNNNDDDDD . . .

MIIIIIIIIIIIICCCCCCCCCE . . .

He is not, of course, attempting to impress his visitor with heretofore hidden talents as a crooner. He says he's demonstrating a Method acting exercise he learned from his second acting teacher, Martin Landau.

"I sang 'Three Blind Mice' for two years in his class," Nicholson says, grinning with a mixture of pride and rue. "It's an exercise Lee Strasberg invented, the song exercise, and the purpose of it is what's known as 'diagnosis of the instrument.' The job is to stand relaxed in this position, look directly at the class, and sing a song, preferably a nursery rhyme, in such a way that you make each syllable have a beginning and an end. You just do the syllable, not the tempo of the song or the meaning. And you *elongate*. The idea is to get the physical body, the emotional body, and the mental body into neutral. Then you should be able to hear through the voice what's actually happening inside. I'm sure you heard some *changes* in my voice—it's a way of locating the tensions, the tiny tensions, the problems with your instrument that get in the way of getting into a role." He reaches back and grabs his buttocks with both hands. "One of the main ones everyone's got is"—he grins—"*heinie* tension. It's an indescribable kind of thing, this exercise, but I guarantee I can tell you what kind of actor you are from hearing you do 'Three Blind Mice.' "

In fact, it is possible to say something about what kind of actor Jack Nicholson is from hearing him perform "Three Blind Mice." He's one of those fanatic believers in the method and mystique of the craft of acting, an actor who, even during the dozen lean years in Hollywood when he was doing only B pictures, D pictures, biker epics and schlock, would nonetheless devotedly go from acting teacher to acting teacher seeking truth the way others of his generation would go from guru to guru or shrink to shrink.

The tendency of those who watch Nicholson on screen and read about his colorful private life is to see him as an "instinctual" actor, as opposed to, say, Dustin Hoffman, Nicholson's chief rival for recognition as premier film actor of his era, who is known for his methodical, cerebral approach to a role. While Hoffman has become known as some kind of demon for actorish preparation, Nicholson is merely seen as some kind of demon.

He jokes about it. "I've been studying to play the Devil," he says of his next project, the role of John Updike's Mephistophelean rogue, Darryl Van Horne, in *The Witches of Eastwick.* "Of course, a lot of people think I've been preparing for it all my life," he adds with a suitably demonic grin.

Still, the view of Nicholson as an instinctual, easy rider of an actor relying on some high-octane-powered "natural gift" misses an essential element of his creative identity: the side of him that would sedulously sing "Three Blind Mice" for two years, that is constantly "diagnosing his instrument." This is a man who still analyzes his roles in terms of Strasbergian "polarities," who, during those lean years, would sit around in Los Angeles coffeehouses for hours discussing Stanislavskian metaphysics with similarly inclined cinema theorists, who would use their meager earnings from biker epics like *Hell's Angels on Wheels* to support themselves while making austere Beckett-like *nouvelle vague* "westerns."

If Nicholson's film persona tends toward world-weary disillusion and cool cynicism, Nicholson himself is still the kind of excitable acting-theory enthusiast who is capable of great earnestness on the subject; capable, for instance, of suddenly pushing back his dining-room chair and leaping up from the table to paraphrase Camus on the actor's life:

"The actor is Camus's ideal existential hero, because if life is absurd, and the idea is to live a more vital life, therefore the man who lives more lives is in a better position than the guy who lives just one."

He's also capable of confiding to an interviewer that he believes "the actor is the *littérateur* of his era," meaning that the actor is capable of "writing," even shaping the inner history of his age through his choice of roles and how he plays them.

And a case could be made that Nicholson has inscribed an idiosyncratic character on the face of our age, one that has reflected and shaped the contemporary personality in the way that only a very few film actors have. "There is James Cagney, Spencer Tracy, Humphrey Bogart, and Henry Fonda," says director Mike Nichols, who worked with Nicholson on *Carnal Knowledge* as well as *Heartburn.* "After that, who is there but Jack Nicholson?"

In the same way that men of earlier generations imitated Cagney and Bogart, incorporated their mannerisms and attitudes into a version of the American male personality, few men between the ages of twenty-five and fifty in America today have not delivered a line with some imitation or caricature of Nicholson's trademark, mocking, deadpan drawl. You can also see his influence in William Hurt's disenchanted character in *The Big Chill* and, more remotely, in David Letterman's acid deadpan demeanor.

In part, it's been a matter of timing, a confluence of the content of Nicholson's roles with the concerns of the baby-boom generation growing out of adolescence into adulthood. While Marlon Brando's and James Dean's naive rebelliousness could be models for teens in the silent generation of the fifties, Nicholson's characters embody the modulations those adolescent attitudes must undergo to survive the disillusion of adulthood.

Nicholson is aware of the fortuitous timing that brought the roles he created into sync with the generational realities.

"Right about the time of *Easy Rider*," he says, "I had gotten myself locked right into the sociological curl—like a surf rider—and I found I could stay right in there, ride this, and cut back against it."

Staying ahead of the sociological curl means the search for projects in which he can play what he likes to call "cusp characters."

"I like to play people that haven't existed yet, a future something, a cusp character. I have that creative yearning. Much in the way Chagall flies figures into the air—once it becomes part of the conventional wisdom, it doesn't seem particularly adventurous or weird or wild. . . ."

And it can be argued that the particular cusp Nicholson's characters are most frequently found on is that painful one between illusion and disillusion. His most memorable characters are fallen angels of one sort or another, whether in the guise of a grounded astronaut *(Terms of Endearment)*, disenchanted Don Juans *(Carnal Knowledge* and *Heartburn)*, self-destructive artists *(Five Easy Pieces* and *Reds)*, defeated rebels *(Cuckoo's Nest* and *Easy Rider)*, disaffected writers *(The Shining* and *The Passenger)*, or various embittered romantics. Of the latter, his role as J. J. Gittes, the disillusioned private investigator in *Chinatown*, may have the most lasting resonance. The shattering discovery Gittes makes at the end of the movie—that beneath the deepest levels of political corruption is something even darker and more frightening, the ineradicable corruption of the human heart—gave that 1974 film the added dimension of being a kind of farewell to arms for sixties' idealism.

Stanley Kubrick has said of Nicholson that he brings to a role the one unactable quality—great intelligence. And it was fascinating in the course of visiting Nicholson and discussing his work to see that intelligence at work preparing for one of his greatest challenges, playing the ultimate fallen angel, the Devil himself.

"Take a look at this," he demands, shoving a huge, musty tome into my hands. He takes it back and opens it up.

"It's Dante's *Inferno*, and these are the original Gustave Doré illustrations. Look at that," he says pointing to an etching of a bat-winged demon tormenting a soul in some lower circle of hell.

He's been immersing himself in the subject: "Aquinas and all those people discuss this, but they never arrive at a definition of evil, which I found interesting. The only thing they could come up with was that you couldn't define the principle because it was always a paradox of opposites."

He has fairly high ambitions for his performance. "When I played *Carnal Knowledge,* I knew that women weren't going to like me for a while. That was a given. I'm going to play the Devil, and I don't want to play him safely. I want people to think Jack Nicholson *is* the Devil. I want them to be *worried.*"

A bit later he takes up the *Witches* screenplay and opens to a passage of dialogue to explain how he breaks down a script. The page of dialogue he opens to is a seduction scene between his character, Darryl Van Horne, and one of the witches, to be played by Michelle Pfeiffer. Nicholson has affixed numbers from 1 to 4 along the margins of this particular page, and he explains that each number represents a single "beat," or moment of response, in a scene. The first thing he does with a script is divide it up into "beats and measures"—a measure being a sequence of beats—to get at the fundamental rhythm of the part before playing it in rehearsals.

Beyond breaking down the script, what Nicholson is also doing at this point is looking for some "secret" to the role, some inner emotional dynamic, a prop, a piece of business, that captures for him the essence of his character's nature.

"I have secrets in all these parts," he says. In fact, he's particularly pleased with himself today because he thinks he has made a breakthrough to the secret in *Witches.*

"I've come up with a dynamic I think is devilishly clever," he says, a dynamic that has to do with his relation to his three co-stars, Michelle Pfeiffer, Cher, and Susan Sarandon. "I'm going to impregnate this artificial world we're creating with that dynamic."

Asked to get more specific, he starts to, then has a change of heart and demands that this secret not be divulged. "I'll feel revealed. . . . That's a very primary thing I was taught—you never give these secrets out, certainly not before you've done the thing, because you'll feel exposed, the mystery. . . ."

Well then, he is asked, what about revealing some "secrets" of previous roles?

"All right. The secret to *Cuckoo's Nest*—and it's not in the book—my secret design for it was that this guy's a scamp who knows he's irresistible to women and in reality he expects Nurse Ratched to be seduced by him. This is his tragic flaw. This is why he ultimately fails. I discussed this with Louise," he says, referring to his co-star, Louise Fletcher. "I discussed this only with her. That's what I felt was actually happening with that character—it was one long, unsuccessful seduction which the guy was so pathologically sure of."

It's a particularly interesting "secret" because what seems distinctive about Nicholson's Oscar-winning performance in *Cuckoo's Nest,* what distinguishes his Randle Patrick McMurphy from Ken Kesey's hero, is the suggestion of a dark side, a pathological impulse behind the drive for pure liberation, a self-absorbed quality that ignores the destruction that "liberation" can bring upon more fragile souls.

"One of the secrets of *Chinatown,*" says Nicholson, continuing, "is that there was a kind of triangular offstage situation. I had just started going with John Huston's daughter, which the *world* might not have been aware of, but it could actually feed the moment-to-moment reality of my scene with him."

"Are you sleeping with her?" intones Nicholson, in an unmistakable imitation of John Huston's line from that scene.

Nicholson shifts again: "Throw me another picture."

"What about your Eugene O'Neill in *Reds*?"

"One of the keys that unlocked O'Neill for me was the fact that he couldn't write with anything but a pencil. He couldn't adapt to the typewriter. He couldn't dictate." And so, Nicholson says, when O'Neill came down with a degenerative disease, "he literally couldn't hold the pencil. I mean, there's something very sensual about lead coming off the pencil. It's one of the purest feelings."

Impure feelings entered into his O'Neill characterization also. "I'll tell you another secret from *Reds*. That poem I gave to Miss Keaton. I wrote a real poem that was extremely revealing." The scene is a climactic one between Nicholson and Diane Keaton, who plays Louise Bryant. He gives her a poem in an envelope only to hear that she's abandoning him for John Reed, played by Warren Beatty. Nicholson's poem was "in that envelope when I gave it to her on camera. It's the kind of thing no one else sees, but you know it's there. And believe me, I did not misplace that prop.

"Here's another example. No one knows it, it didn't matter to the character, but I wore the exact same glasses that my father wore for that part in *Easy Rider.* It's not necessarily meant for a result but for what it does for you."

What it does for you: Only a slight knowledge of Nicholson's family background is required to guess at what seeing the world through his father's glasses might do for him emotionally. The person he knew as his father was a bright, gentle man who pickled his early promise in alcohol, not unlike the good-natured but weak Southern lawyer, George Hanson, who comes to such a brutally disillusioning end in *Easy Rider.*

"What about *Prizzi's Honor*?" Nicholson is asked.

"Well, *Prizzi*—what I recall to be the secret there is actually something more that you hope to get across by inference. It's a kind of observation that I've made about the difference between a street mentality and a jail mentality. People talk about—'Oh, he's a street person, he can get along. . . .' But the difference between the street mentality and the jail mentality is that street mentality gets eaten alive in jail. And jail mentality—that covers like a blanket the mind of a killer. That slightly deeper level of reality. You know there's no angels in there to save you. And if you're in that head and someone else is *not*—well, they're like under a magnifying glass," he says, holding out an imaginary specimen and regarding it with the dead, cold stare of his Charley Partanna character in *Prizzi*.

"You can't help sit here and wonder and say"—he drops into his Charley Partanna Brooklynese—*"Who cares so much about this?"*

"You know, the first thing that John Huston said to me on this was"—and now he's doing John Huston's voice—" 'It seems to me, Jack, everything you've done is informed by intelligence. And you can't have that with this film. It's got to be dumb, very dumb.' He said, 'I've got an idea. I think you should wear a wig, a bad wig.' "

Nicholson resisted the bad wig idea but, "I took a certain level of intelligence away from the character."

"Tell me about *Five Easy Pieces*. What was the hidden dynamic there?"

"Well, the fact that I was playing it as an allegory of my own career is the secret there: 'Auspicious beginnings.' "

Those words are from the famous scene in which Nicholson's character has a final conversation with his stroke-paralyzed father. He's trying to explain to his father, who can't speak (making it a wrenching, one-sided conversation), the mess he's made of his life, why he abandoned his promising early career as a classical pianist to play Prince Hal among the rednecks on the oil rigs of Bakersfield, California.

"I guess you're wondering what happened to me after my auspicious beginnings," he says to his father, and suddenly begins to sob.

It was undoubtedly Nicholson's breakthrough scene in a leading role, and it's a particularly interesting one because that dialogue doesn't exist in the shooting script of *Five Easy Pieces,* the 1970 film directed by Bob Rafelson. In fact, in Nicholson's copy, I found a whole different speech, which he had energetically crossed out. In the margin, he had scrawled: *"Something else?"*

He tells the story of the search for that "something else." There was a crisis on the set the morning the scene was to be shot, he recalls. "I'm in conflict with Rafelson, because he fears my lacking 'sentimentality.' He's always afraid I'm going to make the character too tough and too unapproachable for an audience. So we were down to a few scenes and he was nakedly now saying to me, 'Hey, I want you to cry in this movie.' Now that's one thing, as an actor, you never say. You don't go for an emotion—or one doesn't if they work the way I do. And this is the last kind of direction you want to hear. But," he sighs, "everything is not class. This is the professional game.

"So we were out on the field where we shot it, and I wrote it that morning.

I tried to get all of what I thought—as you know, I've been a writer also, I know why writers fear the thematic scene, and so I tried to get it down to the least amount of verbiage. And that phrase *auspicious beginnings* is what I thought the guy was all about."

The crisis produced what he recognizes as one of his finest moments, something more than an auspicious beginning. "On take one, away I went. And I think it was a breakthrough. It was a breakthrough for me as an actor, for actors. I don't think they'd had this level of emotion, really, in almost any male character until that point. You know, an actor hears the difference where an actor touches that level of emotion for real."

In fact, it's such a strong memory for him, "I can see the grass on the hill and I know what the air was like and I can remember that day and what happened after we went on."

Jack Nicholson is playing the violin. Here again, "playing" is a bit misleading. He's sawing away at his instrument under the intermittent guidance of a violin teacher he's hired. It's part of his preparation for playing the Devil, who in *Witches* displays mesmerizing skill on the violin, among other accomplishments.

In the film, of course, the violin music will be dubbed over, but Nicholson has been studying the motions so he'll be able to make it look like he's playing. The lesson is taking place in the smaller building on the Nicholson compound, a combination guest house and rec room dominated by a massive array of weight-training equipment. (Nicholson has been on a health kick recently, employing a personal trainer.)

The sound of Nicholson sawing away on the fiddle has brought his dog trotting out to sit at his feet, gazing up at the source of the sounds in a rapt parody of the "His Master's Voice" look. Nicholson, sensing a more appreciative audience than the humans present, has begun playing to the attentive dog. He's found that by sawing away up toward the fretwork he's able to make the dog suddenly sit up at attention and cock its head to one side as if transfixed by beauty and wonder. By sawing away lower down on the instrument, he can drive the dog to dive suddenly to the rug, curl up and assume a hopeless and mournful look.

Nicholson is taking great delight in using his primitive powers over the instrument to drive the hapless dog through this limited but pronounced range of responses, all the while flashing various parodic versions of demonic grins at the human audience in the room. It's a hilarious performance and in some ways a self-portrait of an actor in love with the pure pleasure of manipulating an audience—any audience.

"I was always a fantasist," Nicholson says later, apropos of his childhood in

Neptune, New Jersey. "I always wrote my way out of trouble in school. I had to stay after class every day my sophomore year, and they would assign you to write a thousand-word essay, and I'd write thousands of words. By the time I knew no one would be reading, I'd slip in all sorts of mean comments about the people who ran the school. I developed these two characters, a genie and his boy. It's one of the few things I wish I could actually recover. A genie and his boy—God knows what was influencing me at the time."

Nicholson's complicated family life may well have influenced his genie fantasy. The man he knew as his father would often be spirited away by the bottle-genie of alcohol. This difficult family situation took a dramatic new turn in the mid-seventies, when Nicholson learned that the woman he had thought was his older sister was actually his mother, and the people he thought were his parents were in fact his grandparents.

"I hitchhiked everywhere," he says, continuing to describe his origins as an entertainer. "And, you know, I was forever making up things while waiting for a ride. I taught myself to juggle while I hitchhiked, and the camel walk. . . ." At his visitor's request, he gets up and demonstrates the camel walk, a kind of weird shuffle dance step that seems to anticipate the "King Tut" moves of certain break-dancers.

"And of course," he says, "I was a tremendous movie fan. I mean I got insane over *Thunderhead*, which was the sequel to *My Friend Flicka*. I mean, me and my two guys—my mom kept a box of pennies and I used to reach in there and take a handful and we went every day. That picture got me. I always loved movies."

In his last year in high school, Nicholson says his classmates voted him Class Optimist *and* Class Pessimist, an uncanny foreshadowing of his ability to embody the cusp between illusion and disillusion. That same year he took off for Hollywood. It was supposed to be a brief visit to Los Angeles before college, but he never came back. After a couple of years of odd jobs, acting classes, and occasional stints on *Divorce Court,* his career had its first—false—auspicious beginning.

A one-time member of Nicholson's first acting class, Roger Corman, soon to be known as "King of the B pictures," gave Nicholson the lead role—a troubled teen driven to desperation—in an earnest low-budget production called *The Cry Baby Killer.*

It was 1958, Nicholson was twenty-one, and it was the kind of role that could have made him a contender for the much-sought-after status of the next James Dean.

But it didn't. In fact he didn't get another part of any kind for nearly a year, and after that he was mainly offered "character" roles in such Corman schlock as *The Raven* and *The Terror.*

Frustrated and disillusioned in his acting ambitions, Nicholson continued to "diagnose his instrument" in acting classes but also turned his attention to the offscreen creative positions in the filmmaking business. He began to write screenplays; first Corman-style knockoffs like *Thunder Island* and *Flight to Fury,* then the more ambitious *nouvelle vague* western *Ride in the Whirlwind* (in which he also starred as the existential gunman) and the McLuhan-influenced sixties' fantasies *The Trip* and *Head.*

The difficulty of writing left its mark on Nicholson. He would later play writers in four films (Antonioni's *The Passenger,* Kubrick's *The Shining,* Beatty's *Reds,* and Mike Nichols's new movie, *Heartburn*), and no actor has captured so well the dark side of the writer's disposition, the special bitterness and melancholy, even horror of it. There is one scene in particular in *The Shining*—an underrated film that is the first horror movie *about* writer's block—which is treasured by every suffering writer who has seen it, because it comes closest to the awful truth of creative frustration.

In that scene, Nicholson proceeds, in the space of a few lines, to move from a slow burn to a veritable *meltdown* of poisonous rage that captures for all time, with horrifying verisimilitude, the impotent fury of the blocked writer.

"That's the one scene in the movie I wrote myself," Nicholson confides. "That scene at the typewriter—that's what I was like when I got my divorce. I was under the pressure of being a family man with a daughter and one day I accepted a job to act in a movie in the daytime and I was writing a movie at night and I'm back in my little corner and my beloved wife, Sandra, walked in on what was, unbeknownst to her, this *maniac*—and I told Stanley [Kubrick] about it and we wrote it into the scene. I remember being at my desk and telling her"—he shifts into the hate-filled unctuous voice of that character—" 'Even if you don't *hear* me typing it doesn't mean I'm not *writing*. This *is* writing. . . .' I remember that total animus. Well, I got a divorce."

Of all his offscreen roles in the moviemaking process, directing has been Nicholson's greatest source of satisfaction and disappointment. He speaks proudly and protectively of his two directing efforts as if they were beloved but misunderstood children, and he's touchingly eager to explain their unappreciated virtues.

Drive, He Said, made in 1970, was not a commercial success, but it exemplifies Nicholson's ongoing interest in cusp characters, in this case college revolutionaries on the cusp between rebellion and madness. But he's particularly proud of *Goin' South,* a 1979 film he both directed and starred in. Although it aroused little enthusiasm among audiences or critics, Nicholson claims the film has developed a fanatic cult following. "The fact that *Goin' South* fans are the closest thing in the world to Boston Celtics fans is kind of satisfying," he says.

He feels everyone else missed the thematic subtext of the film, a western farce about a drifter who marries a widow with a gold mine. *He* sees it as a film about post-revolutionary disillusion.

"No one extracts the serious plot from *Goin' South*," he complains. The characters, he says, "were once all members of Quantrill's raiders, the original guerrilla warfare unit in America. And what do you do with these people once they're now home? The fact that this wasn't even touched on critically was disappointing to me."

"Are you saying it's a story of our time?"

"Oh, absolutely," he says. "It's about gender conflict, too."

Gender conflict: It's been the source of some of Nicholson's best—and most controversial—work. When it comes to male-female relationships in his movies, Nicholson likes to say he tries to "press on the nerves."

It's an interesting choice of phrase, "press on the nerves," because depending on the context it can imply pleasure or pain, and Nicholson uses it mainly to imply pain. Describing the way he intends to play the male-female dynamic in *The Witches of Eastwick,* Nicholson says, "I want to drip acid on the nerves with this role."

The phrase comes up again when he's discussing his performance in *Heartburn.* The surprise of that performance, the surprise of the movie, is how sympathetically Nicholson plays a character who's pretty much an unmitigated rat in Nora Ephron's novel of the same name—a philandering husband who chooses his wife's pregnancies as opportune times to cheat.

The very tenderness, charm, exuberance, and sympathy Nicholson brings to the role are what make it so problematic.

"If the guy is so charming and lovable as you genuinely make him seem, what makes him do this fairly rotten thing to her?" he is asked.

"Well, here's where you press on the nerves," Nicholson says. "Are we all rotten? Because surely, you have friends and you know half of them, say, are capable of this behavior. And I don't think that you think that half your friends are rotten. That's where you press on the nerves. That was what was delicious about the part. My first acting teacher, Jeff Corey, used to say that all art really can only be a stimulating point of departure. You can't change the world, but you can make the world think."

Mike Nichols believes it's precisely Nicholson's ability to be a loving devil's advocate for his characters, his sympathy for the devil in them, that gives them their corrosive power, or what Nichols calls their "specific gravity."

"Jack's gift is his generosity of spirit," says Nichols. "The self-parodying self-hatred of Jonathan in *Carnal Knowledge* becomes a Dostoyevskian thing—and it can only be acted with a positive feeling toward the character.

This is what I always felt about Jonathan—that Jack's generous nature was spilling over the side of Jonathan. . . . Over and over, Jack plays a character that ends up with more specific gravity than anyone would have guessed from reading the screenplay. Many of the ways he does this are unknowable, but one of the things that makes it weigh so much is that generosity—that throwing away of vanity . . . with both hands. . . . Look at what he did in *Terms of Endearment* with that stomach hanging out," he says of Nicholson's role as the former astronaut, Garrett Breedlove.

"One of the things that motivated me with that character is that everyone was starting to make a total cliché out of middle age," says Nicholson, himself now on the cusp of fifty. "Everybody was supposed to have a middle-age crisis, they were dissatisfied, they hated their job. I just went against the grain of the cliché. I just wanted to say, 'Wait a minute, I happen to be this age and I'm not in any midlife crisis. I'm not an object of scorn and pity by anybody ten years younger than me. There's got to be other people like me, so I'd like to represent that in this movie.' "

Nicholson can be passionately earnest about his belief in the mission of the actor to subvert the conventional wisdom of his age.

"You once quoted Chekhov to the effect that the purpose of the theatrical enterprise should be to undermine the assumptions of middle-class institutions—is that what you mean by pressing on the nerves?" he is asked.

"Yeah, I think that's it," he says. "There are these pre-digested images, these preconceived concepts of how things are. I suppose I'm still crying out for people to try and face the immediate facts of understanding. Get to clarity before you get to power. It becomes weighty and pretentious to say this, but you know, you have to reach beyond yourself. You have aspirations—you just do—and I guess everybody who works at what I do, they're all hoping to make the world better in some way—and that's what pressing on the nerves is about."

The impulse to disrupt the old order of things, to remake the world, is perhaps responsible for Nicholson's continuing fascination with the character of Napoleon. He's been interested in the idea for at least ten years, ever since Stanley Kubrick wrote a screenplay for a Napoleon movie with Nicholson in mind. (It never got off the ground.) Nicholson himself paid $250,000 for rights to a book called *The Murder of Napoleon*. He says he hasn't decided if he wants to play the role or just produce and direct the film.

"I've invested a lot in the subject," he says, meaning more than money. "I sort of look at it like Shaw, Nietzsche, those kind of thinkers did, who consider Napoleon *the* man.

"When I was thinking about him, I got a feeling of autobiography about it—again, in terms of poetics—in the sense that he was a man who conquered the world twice. And became a symbol for the Devil. That's the way they described him in England. But he was ultimately the man who overthrew feudalism, after all. . . . Up until that time, it was all about family. And now, after him, you could just be who you are. . . ."

Nicholson sounds like Napoleon in a besieged mode when he discusses the forces arrayed against creative projects in Hollywood these days. He complains about "conglomeration" narrowing the studios' vision.

"Do you feel like a creative person trapped in an uncreative age in the industry?"

"Well, you know, last night I saw—what's that movie—*Ferris* something?"

"*Ferris Bueller's Day Off*?"

"Well, that movie made me feel totally irrelevant to anything that any audience could want, and 119 years old."

He sighs deeply. "Believe me, everyone else watching it liked it. And you know, I literally walked out of there thinking my days are numbered. These people are trying to *kill* me."

Despite this dispirited view, Nicholson has his eye on the next cusp in the development of his work. "You know, they say it takes twenty years at a minimum to make an actor, a full actor, and that's the stage I'm talking about," he says. "After you've got some kind of idea of how your instrument is, after you have developed some kind of idea thematically of what you think you're about, after you've got some kind of ease with the craft, then possibly you might have some style. And that's a later stage. I know an awful lot about filmmaking and I also know less is more. And that a lot of things you learn, you have to forget about so that it's fresh now. And because of this paradoxical thing, what I seek *now* is naïveté."

Henry: Portrait of a Serial-Killer Hoax

In Which We Investigate One of the Most Successful Liars in American History

Face-to-face with Henry Lee Lucas—the man who is either the worst killer or the best liar in American history—one naturally looks into his eyes for a clue.

I watched Lucas's eyes as he told me his version of the whole strange and bizarre saga. How he went about creating a monstrous myth about himself—the myth of Henry Lee Lucas, the Grim Reaper of Road Kills, an insatiable serial killer ceaselessly scouring the interstates for drifters and strays, enticing them into his car, then leaving their slaughtered, violated bodies behind in ditches beneath the exit ramps.

It's the myth you see embodied with utter credulity in the newly released docudrama *Henry: Portrait of a Serial Killer.* It's the myth that earned him international serial-killer celebrity in the mid-eighties, as he jetted around the country like a rock star on tour, descending on towns with his entourage of Texas Rangers, "singing" for his supper: solving long-unsolved murder cases for local detectives by confessing to the killings himself.

He became the perfect incarnation of a new kind of specter haunting America in the eighties—the serial killer who struck with motiveless malignancy and chilling casualness, who didn't need to feel the apocalyptic delusions of a

Manson to prompt him to kill, who felt, in fact, next to nothing at all. "Killing someone is just like walking outdoors," Henry Lee Lucas liked to say. And unlike Ted Bundy, who denied all till the very end, Henry was *happy* to confess, happy to chew the fat with the shrinks who flocked to him to confirm their theories about serial-killer psychology.

And then, suddenly, Lucas tried to kill off the myth, recant, retract it. It's been investigated, "exposed," and some have believed his retraction. But not enough: Lucas still has a Texas death sentence and the equivalent of nine life sentences for murder stacked on top of that.

It's a myth that will not die—indeed, one Lucas may die for. Later this year, the long-smoldering Lucas controversy is likely to flare up again when Florida authorities put him on trial and seek to stick him with three or more death sentences, for killings they say he confessed to, he says he didn't commit.

Here on death row in Huntsville, Texas, condemned men are separated from visitors by wire-reinforced glass. But even through the glass it doesn't take long to see there *is* something unusual about Henry Lee Lucas's eyes, something that would have made his gaze an asset to either a killer or a liar—a mask to conceal his true intentions. It's got something to do with the fact that one of Lucas's eyes is glass. But it's not just the glass eye that makes Lucas's gaze so unfathomable. It's that the other one, the real one, is so blank and apparently emotionless it's often disconcertingly difficult to distinguish the real from the false orb, much less the real from the false sentiment behind them.

It makes you realize how much the ability to read emotion in someone's gaze depends on the effect created by two eyes in tandem; to look into Lucas's half-glazed gaze is to experience the visual equivalent of the famous "sound of one hand clapping." There's no *there* there.

Indeed, the whole strange Lucas saga is one in which reality and myth, truth and falsehood, have continued to abide side by side—like Lucas's eyes, challenging those who would seek to distinguish them definitively.

I'd set out to see Lucas, half believing the myth. The half that believed had been influenced by a conversation about necrophilia with a true believer in the Lucas myth. This Dallas-based forensic psychiatrist, who'd examined Lucas in the past, cited him as a prime example of the propensity of serial killers to sexually assault the bodies of their murder victims.

But wait, I'd said, hadn't I read something about Lucas having recanted his confessions?

Yes, he replied, Henry had recanted but he still believed Lucas had killed "around sixty," if not the six hundred he'd claimed at one point.

I wrote to Lucas down on death row in Huntsville, scheduled an interview with him. But after reading over the clipping file, I decided that a detour to El

Paso would be necessary first. The file indicated that doubts about the Lucas serial-killer myth were far more serious than I'd gathered from the psychiatrist. It wasn't merely that Lucas himself had recanted his confessions, but that they'd been investigated by the Texas attorney general's office, which had called the Lucas confessions "a hoax" and cast doubt on all but two of the more than six hundred murders Henry had once claimed responsibility for.

The file indicated that a kind of range war had broken out between rival branches of Texas law enforcement, with the Texas Rangers—who'd recouped some of their former glory by managing the Lucas confessions—sticking to their guns, blasting the attorney general's hoax claim, insisting Lucas was the real thing, thus leaving the truth in official limbo.

The file pointed to a mid-1986 El Paso court hearing as a kind of High Noon showdown between believers and debunkers of the Lucas myth.

Down in El Paso, I found a gold mine of astonishing and scandalous testimony about the Lucas confessions. At issue at the hearing was the legitimacy of just a single Lucas confession—to the ax murder of an elderly El Paso woman. But Lucas's intrepid El Paso attorney, Rod Ponton, had taken on the Texas Rangers and put the entire confession process, the entire Lucas myth, on trial. I spent a week immersed in the six-thousand-page hearing transcript and then, in Rod Ponton's basement storage room, I came across a major find: the confession tapes. Hour after hour of Lucas on videotape confessing to murder after murder to team after team of homicide detectives from all over the country.

By the time I settled in to watch the confession tapes, I'd already become far more skeptical. It wasn't merely the El Paso hearing record—which was devastating in itself—but also a long conversation over dinner with the judge who had presided over the hearing, Brunson Moore. A fiery jurist who was still fuming over what he had seen exposed in his courtroom, Moore was outraged that the Texas Rangers had refused to admit they were wrong, refused to go back to police departments all over the country and tell them that Lucas was a fake, that the real killers in all those murders Lucas had confessed to were still at large.

"You're talking about hundreds of murderers let off the hook," Judge Moore told me, "and what have they done? Nothing!"

Watching the confession tapes, I found myself fascinated with the mechanics of the Lucas con game, with the elaborately choreographed dance of deceit and self-deception going on between Lucas and the detectives he was psyching out. Here was Henry Lee Lucas, one of the Great Pretenders of the eighties, one of the classic American con men of all time, in fact, doing his act before my eyes.

There was one moment in particular of all I'd seen and read that lingered in my mind. The "barbecue sauce" line. It was a joke of sorts, but one that let the mask slip and seemed to reveal what was really going on behind Lucas's eyes: a black-humored cynicism, chilling in its contempt for the credulous, one that seemed to find its deepest psychic satisfaction in seeing just how much shit he could get them to swallow.

The moment came in the midst of one of Lucas's discourses on the Hands of Death. This was the purported Satanist ritual-murder cult into which he claimed he'd been recruited by his serial-killer partner in crime, Ottis Toole. Lucas was explaining how, at the behest of the Devil-worshiping Hands of Death, he would often crucify his victims—after which Ottis Toole would often barbecue and *eat* them.

He himself, Lucas said, never joined Ottis in these unholy feasts.

Why not? he was asked.

"I don't like barbecue sauce," he said.

The Lucas I came face-to-face with at Huntsville was strikingly different from the Lucas I'd seen on the confession videos. Back then, five years ago, at the height of his serial-killer celebrity, Lucas was a leaner, meaner, more threatening-looking figure. His dark wavy hair and that inscrutable stare made him look like one of those gaunt, dangerous characters John Garfield played in forties *films noirs*. These days Henry's pudgier; he's kept the weight he put on during the confession spree, when he was rewarded with a strawberry milkshake for each new murder he agreed to confess to. Now fifty-four and graying, Henry looks less like John Garfield than, say, Carroll O'Connor—certainly less like a killer than he once did.

But in fact he is a killer. Even those who believe his confessions were all lies concede he killed one person, perhaps three. And even Henry willingly admits he's responsible for one death. He's already done time for it. It was the murder of his mother, and one of the first things I asked him was how he came to kill her.

"I was brought up like a dog," Lucas told me that morning we first met on death row. "No human being should have to be put through what I was." And the facts (the following account has been independently corroborated except where noted) are fairly appalling.

Henry's stepfather was an alcoholic double amputee who had lost his legs in a railroad accident. "My mother was a prostitute who brought home men, and I was made to watch sex," he said.

They lived in a fairly primitive log-cabin-like dwelling in an isolated backwoods county in western Virginia, the kind of hillbilly milieu that produced the predators of *Deliverance*. His mother dressed him up in girls' clothes, beat him when he rebelled against it, sent him out to sell moonshine. When he was seven years old an injury to his left eye caused him to lose the orb.

Henry left home early, and for a while it seemed he'd escaped the baleful effects of his upbringing. He met a girl named Stella. "She was a factory girl, a hard worker, you know. And I fell in love with her and wanted to get married."

He visited his mother, who now lived in Michigan, to tell her about Stella. They went out drinking. His mother indicated she didn't approve of the marriage.

"I went home with her and I was laying there in bed and all at once I felt something hit me upside the head. She took a broom handle and, boy, she wore it out on my head. And I jumped up, you know, I swing and I don't know whether I had something in my hand or not, but they say I did. And she was hit on the neck or chin or somewhere and I killed her."

In 1960, Lucas was convicted of second-degree murder in the stabbing death of his mother. He still disclaims any memory of the use of a knife.

"At the trial," he said, "I told them I did hit her, I says, 'I guess you could say I'm guilty.' Well, they charged me with second-degree murder, and give me twenty to forty."

On the morning of August 22, 1975, Michigan authorities released Henry Lee Lucas from state prison at Jackson. It is at this point that the Lucas story bifurcates into two radically different, contending narratives. If you believe the narrative compiled by the now defunct Henry Lee Lucas Homicide Task Force based on Lucas's confessions—let's call it "Version A: Henry, Serial Killer"—the moment he got out of prison, Lucas met the man who would become his accomplice in murder, Ottis Toole, and the two of them took off like a shot, driving thirty hours south to Lubbock, Texas, where they broke into the home of nineteen-year-old newlywed Deborah Sue Williamson and stabbed her to death, thereby inaugurating their nonstop marathon of murders. It would continue for eight years and claim 160 or 360 or 600 more victims (depending on when you asked).

There are some problems with Version A, not the least of which is that, by most accounts, Lucas and Toole didn't *know* each other in 1975, didn't meet until 1979. But let's set that aside for a moment and proceed to the alternative scenario, which might be called "Version B: Henry, Hapless Drifter and Bum." Version B does have the advantage of being corroborated by work records and the recollections of neighbors, relatives, and coworkers.

In Version B, Lucas spent the night he was supposedly murdering Deborah Sue in Lubbock at his half-sister's home in Maryland, beginning to attempt to adjust to post-prison life. It would not be easy. Lucas was a thirty-nine-year-old ex-con with a glass eye and an adjustment problem, and even if he was not a serial killer, he was certainly no saint.

"I didn't have the outlook that normal people have," Lucas says. "I'd call myself abnormal because of where I'd been and what I'd been through. It took me a long time after I got out of prison to adjust, you know, to society."

But, he contends, "eventually I adjusted pretty good." For a while, at least. He moved to Maryland, where his half-sister lived. Through her he met a woman named Betty who took a liking to him, and they got married. "I married him for companionship," she'd later say. And Henry Lee Lucas did seem to have a talent for companionship. He was a drifter, not much better than a bum, but people always seemed to be taking him in, offering a place to stay, work, friendship.

But the stretches of settling down, making friends, never lasted long for Lucas. Something always seemed to bring them to an end; there would be misunderstandings, "false accusations," he says—that's what happened to end his year and a half of married life in Maryland.

"I tried to live the right type of life. I seen that the kids [his wife's three daughters by a previous marriage] were provided for. I got them a home, where they didn't have one before. And I worked as a roofer, paid the rent, did everything possible. And the more I'd done—" He breaks off and then resumes bitterly, "It didn't mean *nothing*."

"What do you mean by that?" I ask him.

"My wife accused me of having sex with her kids, and when she accused me of that I said, 'No more,' I couldn't take no more. That tore me apart. I just left and never came back."

He took refuge with his half-sister, but once again, he says, a "false accusation" of molestation drove him out. He hit the road—and the road hit back, hard. By February 1979, Lucas was down and out, seeking succor at a relief mission in Jacksonville, Florida. It was there, according to the Texas attorney general's investigation, that he first met Ottis Toole, a six-foot-tall occasional transvestite and arsonist with a build like a linebacker's and a voice like Truman Capote's.

"Ottis looked to cruise the mission, pick up men, have sex with them, and then beat them up," Lucas recalls. Though Henry indicated a lack of enthusiasm for sharing this experience, Toole took a liking to him anyway, invited him home to meet his mother, offered Lucas a place to stay, got him a job with the roofing contractors he worked for. According to Lucas, he and Ottis were running buddies, pals; they never had a sexual relationship. (Toole indicated otherwise to me in a subsequent interview.) He stayed in the Toole household, he says, because it became the family he'd never had. Indeed, before long, two children arrived: Toole's niece and nephew Becky and Frank Powell, twelve and nine. Both of them would have fateful roles to play later on in the Lucas saga.

But it didn't last, this idyllic period. Nothing good in Henry Lee Lucas's life did. Toole's mother died and a squabble between Toole and his brother resulted in Henry and Ottis's being kicked out.

Soon they banded together with Frank and Becky, along with a Chihuahua, a cat, and some parakeets, in Henry's ancient, broken-down Oldsmobile. They hit the highway, heading west to join the dispossessed of the earth.

"That began my travels," Lucas says of the period when he began roaming the interstates, looking, he says, for some place to call home.

By Lucas's account it was a pathetic odyssey. They were so poor he had to go from town to town selling his blood to blood banks in order to pay for the gas to keep going. When the car broke down, they'd hitchhike, hop a sooty freight car, split up, double back to Florida, and take off again, generally getting nowhere and accomplishing nothing. Except perhaps one hundred murders: According to the Henry Lee Lucas Homicide Task Force (and Lucas's original confessions), this was when Lucas and Toole were at the height of their serial-killer mayhem—sometimes killing two or three people a week, picking them up on the highway or brazenly breaking into their homes, robbing them before raping and murdering them. All of this with two kids in tow.

According to Lucas, the only deaths that occurred in these travels were those of the Chihuahua and the cat, who didn't survive the heat. (He sold the parakeets "to a man under a bridge" for gas money.)* As he points out, and as investigators later verified, blood-bank records in places like Houston and New Orleans verify that Lucas had been selling pints of blood for seven to ten dollars every week or so. "If we were doing all those robberies and burglaries, why would I be selling my blood for a few bucks?" he asks.

Selling blood or spilling blood, this period of Henry's travels finally came to an end in May 1982, when he and Becky—who'd split off from Ottis and Frank—were out hitching by a truck stop near Wichita Falls, Texas, and caught a ride with the Reverend Ruben Moore, a roofer and lay preacher who offered them shelter at his nearby religious refuge, the House of Prayer. Developments there would soon bring Henry Lee Lucas to the attention of the world.

The House of Prayer was a spooky place, something out of Flannery O'Connor: an abandoned chicken ranch consisting mainly of long, low chicken-coop sheds that had been subdivided into residences for the drifters and lost souls who found shelter there.

Henry and Becky moved into one of the abandoned chicken coops, Henry using his roofer's skills to turn it into a cozy apartment for the two of them.

Once again, for a while at least, Henry Lee Lucas had found a place of

---

*I don't know why, but the image of this imprecisely recalled transaction somehow stays with me: Who buys a parakeet "under a bridge"?

refuge. Henry and Becky became part of the community of wayward souls, even attended the Sunday-night prayer meetings, where the sound of speaking in tongues was heard within walls once accustomed to the clucking of hens.

But before long, Becky, who by now was fifteen, began getting restless in this bleak prairie setting. She talked about going back to Florida. Henry thought it was a mistake. They quarreled. When Becky announced she was going to hitchhike to Jacksonville by herself, Henry set off, determined, he says, to hitch with her to Florida, see that she got there safely.

Henry now says he last saw Becky at a truck stop in Alvord, Texas. He'd gone into the truck-stop café to see if any drivers were heading to Florida. When he turned and looked out the window, he says, he saw Becky getting into a Red Arrow truck.

"I run out of the truck stop and started back down the hill a-hollering and they slammed the door and took off. And here was my bag sitting by the road, you know. They took everything except my bag. Left my bag sitting on the road. I didn't know she was gonna run off from me."

Henry returned to the House of Prayer, and Becky hasn't been heard from since. Some, even those who don't believe Lucas is a serial killer, believe this is one further murder he did commit. The summary of a lie-detector exam administered on behalf of the Texas attorney general's office in 1985 (after Lucas recanted his serial-killer confessions) indicated that Lucas "caused the death of not more than three people"—and that he "repeatedly indicated deception" when he denied involvement in the murder of Becky Powell.

He also "repeatedly indicated deception" in denying involvement in one other murder, that of a woman who lived not far from the House of Prayer, an elderly widow named Kate Rich. It was, in fact, suspicion of Lucas's involvement in the death/disappearance of Kate Rich (her house had burned down, her body had not been found, Lucas says he visited her on the day of her disappearance) that brought Henry into the purview of the local sheriff, W. F. "Hound Dog" Conway.

And it was the aptly named Hound Dog's zeal in pursuit, Lucas says, that gave rise to his whole false-confession spree. Hound Dog first pounced on October 18, 1982, arresting Lucas on suspicion of the murder of Kate Rich, putting him in the Montague County jail, and holding him incommunicado, Lucas says, for two weeks. He was released without being charged, but, Lucas says, Hound Dog kept bird-dogging him, "harassed" him for seven months, until finally arresting him on a gun-possession charge.

This time, Lucas says, Hound Dog put the screws to him, locked him naked in an "ice-cold cell" furnished with only a bare steel bed frame. It was the cold that pushed him over the edge, he says; even though it was spring outside, a big industrial-strength air-conditioning unit in the cell blasted him with freezing air twenty-four hours a day, giving him shivering fits. He claims he was told it would go on like that, without access to counsel, without a scrap of clothing or a blanket, until he confessed. (In sworn testimony at the El Paso hearing, Sheriff Conway denied any impropriety in his treatment of Lucas.)

Everything that happened next, the whole twisted saga of the serial-killer confession spree, with all its bizarre and disturbing consequences, was the product of the desperation engendered, Lucas says, by that cold-cell "torture."

That's how he explains why he started confessing—"I did what I had to do to get out of that cell." But two confessions would have been enough for that; the hundreds that followed, he says, were payback. Paying lawmen back: For a lifetime of "false accusations," he'd give them a lifetime of false confessions. The lifelong victim of authority would now victimize the authorities, put them to shame.

That's Lucas's explanation, based on his insistence now that he didn't kill Becky Powell or Kate Rich. But, in fact, if we believe he *did* kill Becky and Kate, the fake-confession spree makes more sense: Knowing he was going to be nailed for two, he'd have much less to lose confessing to hundreds. And he might have something to gain. The false confessions, once exposed, might throw a cloud of doubt over the two murders he did commit.

Whatever the complexities of his motives, his initial efforts to portray himself as a serial killer ran into trouble almost immediately. Indeed, the story of Henry Lee Lucas's serial-killer confession spree is really the story of Lucas's evolution from a crude and unconvincing confessor whose act almost folded at the start to a brilliantly inventive con artist, the Olivier of the false confession, who learned how to analyze and play to the psyches of the lawmen he gulled into complicity in his charade.

Here's how it began. On the night of June 17, 1983, Lucas called out to his jailer and announced that he had something to say. He proceeded to confess to the murders of Becky Powell and Kate Rich. He threw in some horrifying details, claiming the reason Kate Rich's body had never been found was that he'd chopped it up and burned it down to ash in the wood-burning stove at the House of Prayer.

But he didn't stop there. He told local Texas Ranger Phil Ryan, who'd been following the case (these days the Rangers function as a kind of elite band of super–state troopers, often stationed in small counties to lend criminal-investigation expertise to local sheriffs), that he'd killed at least a hundred more. Ranger Ryan asked Lucas to write down the details of all those murders. The document he produced almost ended the whole business then and there. It was a three-page, primitively scrawled list of seventy-seven people he'd supposedly killed. There were childish, cartoonlike "sketches" of the victims' faces, accompanied by disjointed descriptions:

Junction, Plainview, 1-10. Date, 1979. Death, cut head off, knife. Started strangling, stab back, white female, 20, medium, red hair, lots of makeup, five-two,
135, pretty. Picked up, put head in sack, dropped in Arizona, body.

The key to all that happened later, Lucas says, was that the word went out
before any proof came back. "The sheriff went in front of the press immediately," he recalls, "and said that I'd killed hundreds."

The Henry Lee Lucas traveling circus had begun in earnest.

"They were flying in from all over the country," he says. "Helicopters,
everything else flying into that tiny town. Lawmen, news media, writers . . ."

Perhaps if word hadn't gotten out so fast, if lawmen hadn't found themselves committed so soon to the proposition that they had a serial killer confessing in their custody, they might not have been so committed to the
proposition when the problems began to develop.

They did very early on. There were problems with that first list of seventy-
seven victims. As the Texas attorney general's review of the case states, law-
enforcement officers began to investigate and "recognized immediately that
Lucas's description of the abduction/murder of a juvenile female *had never
taken place*." (Italics are mine.) Several other places where he'd claimed to
have buried bodies, including an abandoned chromium mine in Pennsylvania
called the Bottomless Pit, were thoroughly searched and turned up no bodies.
Indeed, *none* of those seventy-seven claimed kills was ever linked to a real
body.

When you think about it, it's not that easy to convince the world you're the
greatest serial killer in American history just on your own say-so. The confession spree couldn't have continued with Lucas just making up murders and
sending people looking for bodies that weren't there. He needed a score. The
key to his first success, the key to all the successes that followed, is evident in
Lucas's description of that first big score: *reversing the information flow.*

That first score, Henry says, involved a murder in Conroe, Texas, north of
Houston.

"Sheriff Corley from Conroe, he sent his deputies up to Montague and they
showed me all the pictures of the murder victim right off."

Henry said, sure, he remembered her—that was one of his kills.

"Then they said, 'We want to take you down there and let you point out the
crime scene to us.' And they drove down there and drove me around everywhere and I couldn't find it."

"You couldn't find it?"

"Until they pointed it out to me."

"Let's get this straight. They stopped by the crime scene and said, 'Here we
are, Henry . . .'"

"Yes: 'Does this look familiar?' "

"You learned to pick up on cues?"

"On what they wanted."

(Sheriff Joe Corley insists that—while he was suspicious of some of the cases Henry tried to take credit for in his county—the two that he *did* clear with Lucas were genuine. He denies that he or his men gave Lucas any details about the crimes in advance.)

Reversing the flow: Instead of Henry making up bodies, lawmen would bring bodies, pictures of them, to Lucas. Sometimes they'd play a kind of reverse Twenty Questions in which he would cannily use trial and error to "remember" a description of his victim ("Yeah, I had one up near Lake Michigan—she was a blonde girl about twenty. . . . Oh, she wasn't blonde? Could've been light-brown, brownish hair. I got so many I get 'em confused"). When he finally guessed right, the lawmen and Lucas would pile into a car, and again by means of trial and error, mostly error, and by picking up often unsubtle clues, he'd "find" the crime scene. Afterward, detectives would announce that Lucas's confession had been verified because he "supplied officials with details only the killer could have known, and led them right to the crime scene."

Or as the Texas attorney general's report summarized, "Lucas would use information provided him during questioning by law enforcement personnel to fabricate confessions."

The next key turning point in Lucas's rise to world-class serial-killer status was the "Orange Socks" confession. It was the Orange Socks confession that got him the death penalty in Texas, that left him truly with nothing to lose. And the Orange Socks confession brought him into the jurisdiction of the lawman who was to become Henry's father confessor, his father figure, the man in whose custody he would become an industrial-strength dynamo of a confession machine: Sheriff Jim Boutwell.

Orange Socks was the name given to a young woman whose unidentified body was found in a ditch off a lonely stretch of Interstate 35 in Williamson County, Texas. Her body was nude except for a pair of bright, fuzzy orange socks. In a way, Orange Socks was typical of the kind of victim Henry Lee Lucas would most successfully claim as his. Probably a hitchhiker (no local people recognized her). Probably an outcast of some kind (nationwide circulation of her picture produced no grieving family to claim her). A four-year-old unsolved homicide with no suspects, no leads, until Sheriff Jim Boutwell visited Lucas in jail and asked him if Orange Socks was one of "his."

Boutwell brought Lucas to his jail in Georgetown, Texas, a small town half an hour north of Austin, after the Orange Socks confession and kept him there. Kept him there and got a special appropriation from the Texas Department of

Public Safety, with the governor's blessing, to establish a Henry Lee Lucas Homicide Task Force, to be jointly administered by Boutwell and the Texas Rangers.

"Things really skyrocketed in Georgetown," Lucas says. "I went from one [confession session] a day or twice a day to seven days a week, probably five or six officers a day came in there."

Lucas certainly seemed to be driven to increase his productivity under the influence of the sheriff. As the attorney general's report notes, Lucas had started with those seventy-seven claimed kills, but "while talking to Sheriff Boutwell on June 22, 1983, he increased the tally to 156. His final estimate [under Boutwell's supervision] was over 600." (Boutwell, a courtly former Ranger and legendary Texas lawman, insisted to me that the 160 or so Lucas confessions actually cleared under his supervision were all properly handled, solid cases.)

The Texas Rangers were the outside men for the task force, the link to state and national law enforcement. They booked detectives who signed up two and three months in advance for appointments with Lucas; they organized "Lucas seminars" to share their serial-killer expertise under the prestigious auspices of the Regional Organized Crime Information Center.

And Lucas had good reason to keep increasing his numbers for the task force. The more cases he confessed to, the more rewards of milkshakes and jail perks he received. He was living high off the hog in Georgetown, better in his carpeted jail cell, he says, than he'd ever lived "outside" in his entire life. He'd been a drifter and a bum living in a chicken coop; now he was an international celebrity, entertaining Japanese camera crews, talking to sympathetic Christian broadcasters about the Devil-worshiping sect that programmed him to kill, making book and movie deals for his life story. And there were deep psychological satisfactions: The ex-con lowlife who'd been pushed around by lawmen all his life was now manipulating the hell out of lawmen, making them dance to his tune, and laughing behind their backs. Toward the end he was almost testing them to see how much they'd swallow, how outlandish the stories could get: claiming to have bumped off Jimmy Hoffa for the mob and to have flown the poison to Jonestown in Guyana.

Like the con-man hero of Gogol's *Dead Souls*, who goes around buying title to dead serfs in order to inflate the value of his estate and social position, Henry Lee Lucas rose by taking title to the dead. The ever higher numbers ensured his stay in the Georgetown jail, where he'd taken up oil painting when he wasn't watching premium cable channels like HBO and Playboy on his personal color set, or ordering in his favorite take-out foods from the Sonic drive-in and other local eateries he preferred to the jail kitchen.

The higher the numbers, the longer he'd enjoy his perks. And when he stopped confessing? As Texas Ranger Bob Prince, co-chief of the task force, put it in an adulatory profile in *Law Enforcement News,* "When [Lucas] gets to the point where he has no more information or he doesn't want to talk with us anymore, death row is waiting for him down there at the penitentiary."

Or, as Lucas put it to me, Prince "said my goose would be cooked."

In fairness to the lawmen far and wide who fell for his confessions— despite the dearth of physical evidence linking him to the crimes (not a single fingerprint, for instance)—there was one confessional ploy of Lucas's that succeeded spectacularly well. He came up with an eyewitness to attest to his killings. Not merely an eyewitness, but an *accomplice.* He came up with Ottis Toole. He and Toole were a killing team, he said, from the beginning. Toole had recruited him into the Hands of Death Satan-worshiping cult. Toole was, if anything, even more bloodthirsty than he (the barbecues).

The astonishing thing was that, as ludicrous as these stories sounded, Toole cheerfully *confirmed them all.*

Lucas says it "came as a surprise" to him when he heard that Toole was backing him up on these tales.

"I didn't expect him to take the cases," Lucas says.

But fate, which had separated the two men back in 1982, had landed them in similar desperate situations in late 1983, when Lucas started including Toole in his confessions. Toole by then was also in jail, facing the death penalty in Florida for an arson-murder rap (he had been convicted of burning down a rooming house, a fire in which an old man died). Toole, like Lucas, had little to lose. And he still had a kind of romantic devotion to Henry; in his own way the Florida firebug was still carrying a torch for Lucas. The transcript of a November 14, 1983, phone call between Lucas and Toole, shortly after they joined forces in the confession spree, reveals the dynamic of their relationship. Toole reproves Lucas for breaking his word "never to run off." Lucas says something sentimental about the two of them "being together" in the hereafter. And Toole, with only the slightest reluctance (he worries about the barbecuing tales: "Wouldn't that make me a *cannibal?*"), enthusiastically backs Lucas up on everything.

Later I asked Toole, who is still serving time in Florida State Prison (his death sentence reduced to life imprisonment), what he had thought when he first heard Lucas was claiming they'd killed hundreds together.

"I said, 'Well, shit, he wants to make himself a pig, goddamn, I'll help him out.' I said, 'I'll pump it all in for him.' I said, 'Fuck it, I got nothing to lose.' "

"I said [to Toole], 'Let's go for it,' " Lucas told me.

"I said, 'Fire away with hell for nothing,' " Toole recalled.

And so they did. Toole's "eyewitness" corroboration became a big asset in selling the legitimacy of the Lucas confessions.

Lucas's Hands of Death ploy—attributing his entire career as a serial killer to his recruitment by Toole into a Satanist ritual-murder cult, i.e., The Devil Made Me Do It—served a shrewdly calculated purpose in his serial-killer impersonation. It was part of Lucas's growing effort to portray himself as a Man of Faith on a Mission from God.

It wasn't long before Lucas was claiming to have been "saved" by his spiritual counselor, "Sister Clemmie"—a devout religious layperson who ran a jail ministry in the Georgetown jail. Clemmie hit the religious-radio-talk-show circuit describing how she'd brought a serial killer to the Lord. Lucas would go on those shows offering pious "advice to Christian youth," from his reformed-serial-killer perspective, on how to avoid the snares of Satanism. He'd even tell his radio audience that God Himself had appeared as a bright white light in a corner of his cell and spoken to him, urging him to keep confessing all his murders, "for the sake of the families"—the families of the victims he'd slain. If he confessed everything, Lucas said God told him, He would help Lucas remember where all the bodies of his victims were, "so they could be given a proper Christian burial."

Sure, it sounds like bunk in retrospect, but Lucas was playing to a powerful emotional dynamic in the hearts of the murder victims' families—the need for some finality, some fitting closure to their suffering, the primal urge to solemnize death with certainty. The horror of the unmarked grave is an ancient theme going back to the age of *The Iliad,* whose final books are devoted to the struggle to obtain the return of Hector's body, give it the proper burial that in some fundamental way separates civilization from savagery.

For hundreds of families across America, Henry Lee Lucas became the great solemnizer of unsolved-murder victims' fates.

But finally, doing it "for the sake of the families," became Lucas's undoing. Because finally there was one family that looked a little more closely than most at what Lucas was "doing for them," a family that wouldn't be satisfied by the consolation of false certainty—if it meant letting the real killer off the hook.

A sudden Texas hailstorm is rattling down on the roof over the boat dock. We're on the shore of a lake somewhere in Texas. Exactly where, I've been asked not to disclose.

Under the thin corrugated-tin shelter, Bob Lemons is telling me, "We don't want to be portrayed as the grieving family everyone should pity. Do you understand? We weren't just passively grieving, we took action. We did the kind of investigation that put the task force to shame. For a while there we were unstoppable. We stopped the whole damned thing in its tracks."

It almost seems as if the Lemonses' collision course with the Lucas task force was fated. Their nineteen-year-old newlywed daughter, Deborah Sue Williamson, was supposedly the very first of the hundreds of victims Lucas killed when he got out of prison in 1975.

And of all the families of victims afflicted by the Lucas confessions the Lemonses had perhaps the most urgent reason to want to believe that his confession to the murder of their daughter was true. Because in the aftermath of the killing, their own son had at first come under suspicion. Although he was later cleared, a Lucas confession certainly would have eradicated any lingering doubts about their son. But the Lemonses smelled something wrong about Lucas's confession from the beginning.

For one thing, the first time Lucas was shown Deborah's picture, he said he'd never seen her, never been to Lubbock in his life. But, Bob Lemons tells me, a year later, "we got a phone call from a detective in Lubbock and he told me that it had been determined, that they'd had Henry to Lubbock, that he had confessed to having murdered Debbie and the case was closed. They had charged him and he would be indicted, which he was. Joyce and I, immediately upon receiving that information, went to Lubbock to hear and see what he said."

They found out Lucas had a *lot* of information about Deborah's murder, but "the problem was the information he was giving them was totally wrong," Bob Lemons says. "He had the description of the house wrong. He had the murder happening inside the house instead of outside. He had the description of Deborah wrong."

Particularly unconvincing, Lemons says, was the portion of the confession tape in which Lucas is supposedly "leading" lawmen to the crime scene.

"They took him to the house and asked him three or four times, 'Now, are you *sure* you don't remember something about this particular place? You know, and particularly out here in back in the patio area?' And he finally caught on to the fact that this [the patio] was where he was supposed to have [killed her]."

The Lemonses went back to the Lubbock detectives. "We tried to tell them, 'This is wrong, we need to put this case back into the open file. The murderer is still loose.' And they were just furious with us."

Doubts were not welcome. But doubts were driving the Lemonses crazy. They couldn't live with the notion that a false confession let the real murderer of their daughter go free.

They decided the only way to resolve their doubts was to launch their own private investigation into Henry Lee Lucas and his travels. They set off on a journey into Lucas's past, eventually selling their house to raise cash for their investigation.

They received the help of a sympathetic state trooper in Maryland, Fran

Dixon, who'd had doubts of his own about the Lucas confessions he'd looked into. "He took us to Henry's half-sister, to his relatives," Lemons recalls. "And we began talking to these people and began comparing what we had with what they had on his whereabouts, and we commenced to all of a sudden realize that when Henry was supposed to be killing somebody in Texas or California he was actually in jail in Maryland or at work in Pennsylvania or living at home with someone.

"It became obvious that this whole thing was a farce," Bob Lemons says.

Before they were through, their private investigation had produced enough documents and eyewitness accounts concerning Lucas's whereabouts to discredit scores of his murder confessions. But, once again, when they sought to bring the results of their investigation to the attention of the Lucas task force, their proffer was rejected out of hand.

By this time the Lemonses weren't alone in bringing doubts about Lucas to the attention of the task force.

There was a veteran journalist in Dallas named Hugh Aynesworth. He'd cowritten a book about serial killer Ted Bundy *(The Only Living Witness),* and originally he'd believed Lucas was a serial killer of even greater magnitude. He planned to do a biography of Lucas. But, Aynesworth says, Lucas confided to him early on that he'd only "done three" (his mother, Becky Powell, and Kate Rich). Aynesworth then began his own investigation of the Lucas-Toole travels, which ended up discrediting dozens more confessions in a *Dallas Times Herald* exposé.

Even Sister Clemmie, the truest of true believers in Lucas and his mission from God, began to have her doubts when Lucas started complaining to her that the task force was asking him to "take cases" that even he found objectionable. (Clemmie has remained loyal to Lucas after the shock of his recantation, and believes he's telling the truth now.)

One case Henry resisted—at first—involved the son of a lawman in a southern state. He'd been convicted of killing a convenience-store clerk and was already serving a murder sentence when Henry's confession sprang him from jail, got him a new trial and eventually an acquittal. The prosecutor who convicted the lawman's son would later testify in the El Paso hearing to his outrage and bewilderment; the prosecutor believes a false Lucas confession helped a real killer walk free.

Then there was a young crusading DA in Waco, Texas, named Vic Feazell, who was troubled by the way Lucas's confession to the murder of a prostitute had blown his chance to get a genuine suspect to confess. In trying to check out that one prostitute-murder confession, Feazell turned up serious problems with about a dozen other Lucas confessions. He, too, put himself on a collision course with the Lucas task force, and touched off what was to become a bitter civil war between branches of Texas law enforcement—a war which began with a showdown over possession of Henry Lee Lucas's body. The showdown resulted from Feazell's efforts to bring Lucas before his grand jury in April 1985 to testify about his confessions. The Lucas task force was extremely unhappy about this.

Feazell sent his men down to the Lucas-task-force lair at the Georgetown jail. "They went down there and pretty much intimidated the Georgetown boys into releasing him and letting us bring him back to Waco," he recalls.

When the task force learned that its chief asset was in the hands of the enemy, it convened an emergency late-night strategy session and decided to call in the feds to get Lucas back.

"The next morning," Feazell recalls, "two FBI agents showed up in my office around seven, seven-thirty, demanding to see Lucas, right before he was to testify before the grand jury."

Feazell ordered his men to hold off the agents, and called for reinforcements. He called in Attorney General Jim Mattox. "He just hit the roof. He told them [the feds] it was obviously a conspiracy because nothing but the murder of a president gets the FBI out at seven A.M."

It was a tense standoff between armed men. "They were pretty upset," Feazell recalls. But he won the tug-of-war, held on to his controversial prisoner—although he paid dearly for that victory later on.

There followed a dramatic recantation scene. What finally brought Lucas to that moment in Waco when he disavowed the whole serial-killer charade? If you listen to Lucas now, it was the mind-numbing horror of the actual confession process.

"I got so sick of looking at those pictures—it was pathetic," he tells me in Huntsville.

"What kind of pictures do you mean?"

"Naked women, murder victims, people cut up in pieces. It was just sickening. You know, it was just sickening."

It would go on twelve hours a day, five, six, seven days a week, looking at hundreds, thousands, of mutilated corpses. "And the more I would try to get away from it, the more they wanted to show me. I told Clemmie, 'I can't take looking at these pictures.' "

At first, he says, he rebelled in a kind of covert, subversive way, deliberately "going wild" with the ever-inflating magnitude of his confessions to everyone and everything. After he raised his claimed-kills total to six hundred in the United States, he casually added that he'd "done about a thousand in Canada." Began claiming he'd kidnapped more than five hundred U.S. "milk carton" children on behalf of the Hands of Death and "sold them into slavery in Mexico." Threw in Jimmy Hoffa and Jonestown.

But none of these claims seemed to prompt the task force to examine any of his more mundane murder confessions, and Lucas realized, he says now, that he'd have to expose his whole act to end it. In addition, he concedes he'd begun to get the feeling the jig was up—he knew Feazell, Aynesworth, and the Lemonses had been investigating him, poking holes in his story. And so, when he walked into Vic Feazell's office prior to testifying to the grand jury, "I asked them, 'What would it be if I told you that I didn't do the crimes?' And they said, 'Well, we know you didn't,' and I said, 'If I tell you that I didn't do the crimes, now they [the task force] would kill me before I got back to Georgetown.' And they said, 'What if we can give you protection?' And I said, 'I don't think you can do it.' They said, 'We'll get the attorney general up here.' So they called me in to talk to [Attorney General Jim Mattox] and he said, 'I guarantee they won't get anyone near you.' And I said, 'Well, I'll tell the truth, then.' And I said to them, 'There's some other people that deserve to know the truth.' "

"What did you mean by that?" I ask him.

" 'The Lemonses,' I said. 'I want them told the truth.' They said, 'The Lemonses already know the truth.' "

Lucas then went before the grand jury in Waco, recanted his confessions, and exposed the techniques of his hoax.

But what Lucas and the Lemonses and DA Feazell and the Texas attorney general didn't realize was that merely exposing the hoax confessions wasn't enough.

"Henry thought that by just telling the truth he could undo everything he'd done," Joyce Lemons says. "It was too late for that."

By the time Lucas had recanted, the machinery of the criminal-justice system had already locked in his lies and given a number of powerful law-enforcement institutions a stake in keeping them locked in. As Joyce Lemons says, "Henry had been everybody's ticket to glory, there were all these book contracts."

As soon as Lucas recanted, the task force had to fold up its tent, and he found himself quickly packed off to death row to await execution in the Orange Socks case.

One year later, in April 1986, Texas attorney general Jim Mattox issued his "Lucas Report." In addition to casting serious doubts on all but two of the Lucas confessions (Becky Powell and Kate Rich), the Lucas Report directly took on the task force and the Texas Rangers: "Those with custody of Lucas did nothing to bring an end to his hoax. Even as evidence of the hoax mounted, they continued to insist that Lucas had murdered hundreds of persons."

But partisans of the Lucas task force weren't taking this assault on their efforts lying down. According to a sworn affidavit from Sister Clemmie, shortly after the 1985 Waco showdown, Sheriff Boutwell told her, "By the time we finish with Vic Feazell, he will wish he'd never heard the name Henry Lee Lucas." (Sheriff Boutwell denies ever making that statement.)

And, in fact, before long a U.S. attorney was spearheading a full-court-press corruption investigation targeted against DA Vic Feazell, an investigation that resulted in Feazell's indictment and arrest on bribery charges on the eve of his reelection campaign. Feazell filed court motions portraying the indictments as "retaliatory prosecution" for his role in exposing the Lucas hoax and putting the prestige of "the law enforcement brotherhood" in question. Feazell fought back, won reelection, and won acquittal from a jury which deliberated for only six hours before rejecting the accusations on the first vote. The Dallas *Times Herald* later called Feazell's ordeal "a vendetta directed at a prosecutor whose major transgression appeared to be that he held the Texas Rangers and lawmen across the country up to public ridicule by helping expose the hoax of Henry Lee Lucas, a confessed serial murderer who turned out to be nothing but a serial con man." Vindicated, Feazell nonetheless had faced eighty years in prison for his attempt to get to the truth about that prostitute murder, and his promising political career was derailed.

El Paso judge Brunson Moore—the man who presided over the final Texas courtroom battle over a Lucas confession and threw it out of court in December 1986—contends that there's "not one guy who's stood up to the task force" who hasn't suffered retaliation from the law-enforcement brotherhood. What disturbs Judge Moore at least as much is the failure of the criminal-justice system to follow up on the hoax revelations and reopen all those murder cases closed by Lucas's confessions.

A particularly dramatic example of this came to light just two days after my second visit with Lucas on death row in June.

An A.P. dispatch in a Dallas paper datelined Salt Lake City reported that "police say the books will stay closed on three Utah murders attributed to Henry Lee Lucas even though . . . a 1986 Texas attorney general's report—*which Utah lawmen say they didn't know existed*—contains evidence which conflicts with information Lucas gave Utah lawmen. [Italics are mine.]

"In one of the [1978] murders," the story continues, "Lucas claimed he was assisted by Ottis Toole although the attorney general's investigation shows that Mr. Lucas didn't meet Mr. Toole until February 1979."

Investigator Mike Feary of the Texas attorney general's office, who worked on the A.G.'s 1986 investigation, was quoted saying, "Nobody should clear a case solely on a Lucas confession. They should ignore it, and see what else they have."

I called Investigator Feary and asked him if somebody in Texas law enforcement didn't have a responsibility to make sure the 150 or so police departments all over the U.S. who have Lucas's confessions still on the books had at least read the attorney general's report. "There may have been some obligation on our part to contact every agency," Feary conceded. Although his office sent out copies of the Lucas Report to lawmen nationwide, he said, it was the Rangers and the task force who knew which police departments cleared which cases—and they weren't sending out the report to *anyone*.

They still aren't. In a phone interview Texas Ranger Bob Prince, former co-chief of the Lucas task force, estimated there were upwards of 150 cases around the country that had been cleared "with different degrees of certainty" by Lucas confessions. But Captain Prince told me that the Rangers themselves hadn't actually cleared the cases, they'd just booked the teams of local detectives in to see Lucas. Therefore it wasn't the Rangers' responsibility to reexamine the evidence. Nor did he express any doubt that Lucas was a genuine serial killer.

The Lucas case is one in which the facts seem fated never to catch up to the myth. Not only are the Lucas confessions embedded in the legal system, they've found their way into the dicey "science" of serial-killer psychology. A 1988 book by a Ph.D. in psychology, *Serial Killers: The Growing Menace,* acknowledges charges that Lucas was a hoax but goes right ahead and includes him in its profile of the serial killer's psyche, then uses the fact that Lucas fits the profile as support for the belief he really is a serial killer.

The newly released film *Henry: Portrait of a Serial Killer* is another case of the media perpetuating the myth without regard to the facts. The film is not a documentary, but it opens with a statement that it is "based on the confessions of a person named Henry, many of which he later recanted." Despite those weasel words, the film—which also features characters named "Otis" and "Becky"—clearly endorses the view that the "person named Henry" was the real thing: the soulless serial killer of the myth. The mostly respectful reviews, and laudatory articles about the film's insight into the American psyche in places like *Film Comment,* seem either unaware or unconcerned that the Lucas confessions might be a hoax and that the film serves the propaganda interests of the Texas Rangers.

Was it all a hoax? Or is it possible that, even if hundreds of the Lucas-Toole confessions were bogus, they may have killed several more people than the two that most students of the case credit Lucas with? When I learned of the new Florida murder cases against Lucas and Toole, set to come to trial this year, it seemed at first as if they might be just as much an anachronism as *Henry: Portrait of a Serial Killer.* But in fact at least one of the Florida prosecutions promises to offer something entirely new: a Long-Silent Witness, one who might be able to pin more murders on Lucas and Toole.

Florida lawmen refuse to talk for the record about the new murder cases or the Long-Silent Witness, but affidavits they filed in the Lucas extradition hearing in Huntsville in 1989 tell a fascinating story.

This climactic chapter of the Lucas saga begins with Ottis Elwood Toole. Toole has always been something of a loose cannon in the Lucas saga. Some of his confessions surpassed even Lucas's in spectacular improbability. There was, for instance, his confession to the murder of young Adam Walsh. He was the six-year-old Florida boy who disappeared in 1981, the son of John Walsh, who later became the celebrated host of the crime-stopper television series *America's Most Wanted.* At one point, when Adam was the object of a highly publicized search, Toole announced that not only had he kidnapped and killed Adam but he had *eaten* him, which was why the body couldn't be found. When the body *was* found, Toole didn't allow it to daunt him. And, unlike Lucas, Toole never officially recanted any of his confessions under oath. He still gets visits from investigators from all over the country, still "takes cases," although business is not as brisk as it was before the Adam Walsh fiasco.

On June 7, 1988, according to court papers, an investigator from the Florida Department of Law Enforcement visited Ottis Toole in Florida State Prison. The investigator was working on the unsolved 1981 murder of a northern-Florida woman named Jerilyn Murphy Peoples, who was shot dead in her house upon returning from a grocery-shopping trip.

According to the Florida affidavit, Toole "advised" the investigator that "Peoples was carrying bags of groceries and that she was shot with a rifle, thereby taking responsibility for her death along with Lucas. Toole also verified that [his nephew Frank] Powell was present when this occurred."

What's surprising is what happened next in the Florida investigation. On June 30, 1988, an investigator took a sworn statement from Frank Powell III, who "advised that he was present during the burglary of the Peopleses' home. Powell further stated that Lucas and Toole are responsible for Peoples's death inasmuch as Peoples surprised Lucas and Toole during the burglary."

This is the potential bombshell in the Florida cases: the emergence of the Long-Silent Witness, Frank Powell III, the younger brother of Becky Powell. As an eleven- and twelve-year-old, he accompanied Lucas and Toole on their travels. Some of their confessions place Powell at the scenes of their crimes, but Powell has never appeared in any judicial forum to confirm or deny what he's said to have seen, never made a sworn statement in any of the Lucas cases until now. With his sister Becky dead or disappeared, Frank Powell III is the only witness to the Lucas-Toole travels, the only one whose testimony has not been heard.

Throughout the years of the Lucas-Toole confession circus, court orders reportedly obtained by Powell's state guardian had prevented any investigating authority from questioning him about what he may or may not have seen. In 1988, however, when Powell turned eighteen, the protective order no longer applied and Florida lawmen moved in with alacrity to get him on the record. (Powell declined a written request from me for an interview.)

There are a number of questions raised by the outlines of the case against Lucas and Toole as adumbrated in the Florida extradition affidavits. For one thing, school records obtained by the Texas attorney general's office indicate Frank Powell III was recorded "present in school" in Jacksonville on the date of the Peoples murder. It's not impossible that he could have slipped away from school to join his uncle Ottis, Henry, and Becky for a four-hour drive to the Florida-panhandle killing site—but it's not clear if Florida investigators were even aware of the problematic school records when they questioned Powell. Nonetheless, armed with the Toole and Powell statements about the Peoples murder, the investigators proceeded to death row in Huntsville. There, they maintain, on July 7, 1988, long after he'd stopped confessing to all other crimes, Henry Lee Lucas proceeded to confess not only to "involvement" in the Peoples killing but also to involvement in two other unsolved Florida murders within a three-month span in the same northern-Florida area.

This, on the face of it, is a shocking turnabout. Down on death row I asked Lucas, "What gives here, Henry? I thought you'd stopped confessing, but here in these affidavits they say: Henry Lee Lucas has given admissions about details of this crime that only the killer could have known."

"I gave them no confessions, no details whatever," he said flatly. "I am not guilty and I will prove it in court."

And then there is Ottis Toole. Curious about where Uncle Ottis stood on these and all the other Lucas cases, I decided to try to speak to him. I wrote to Toole and asked him if he'd agree to be interviewed. What followed was one of the most bizarre encounters I've ever had.

Florida State Prison at Starke (an hour west of Jacksonville) is a forbidding place; it was in the news most recently as the site of an electrocution malfunction, the one where flames shot out from the condemned man's head. I had to pass through four sets of gates before being led to the small conference room where I was to meet with a handcuffed Ottis Toole.

Toole is a formidable-looking fellow—a gaunt, cadaverous six-footer—who appeared, on the surface, menacing enough to be the top-dog serial killer he claimed to be, until halfway into our interview, when he recanted all those claims. The fact that Toole speaks in a lisping, Capote-like southern drawl doesn't detract from the peculiar aura of menace about him. Quite the opposite.

The turning point in my talk with Toole was something I read to him—a passage from a book called *Hand of Death: The Henry Lee Lucas Story*. It's a schlocky "authorized" biography written at the height of the confession spree, and it recounts with complete credulity all the most ludicrous Satanist-cult ritual-murder and cannibalism tall tales Lucas was peddling back then.

"If I had the book I could tell you what-all was what about Henry Lee," Toole told me at the beginning of our interview.

Now, as it happened, I had acquired a copy of *Hand of Death* from Sister Clemmie—to whom it was dedicated and who is mortified by its semi-porno sleazoid style.

I decided to ask Toole some questions about the book.

This is how it went at first:

"Was there a Hands of Death cult, Ottis?"

"Yeah," he said with a big, disingenuous grin.

"Did you commit killings for it?"

"Something like that," he said with that same grin.

"Did Henry commit killings for the Hands of Death?"

"Yeah." Grin.

"How many?"

"Quite a bit." Grin.

"And how about you?"

"Quite a bit."

He stuck to that line until I quoted something from the book about the fate of his niece, Becky Powell.

"The book says you cut up the body of Becky."

"And ate her?"

"Did you?"

"No."

"So that's a lie?"

"Yeah."

My next question about the Hands of Death seemed to be a turning point.

"Did you ever go to a Satanist assassination training camp in the Everglades?"

"Yeah."

"You did?"

"Really," he said, suddenly shifting. "That whole fucking book is lies."

"So what is the truth?"

"What is the truth?"

"Yeah."

"There ain't no murders," he said, laughing.

"No murders?"

"I dug up all the information playing them, digging all the information out of them."*

---

*Some investigators have told me that this recantation helped derail the last gasp of the Lucas-Toole hoax prosecutions. Getting Toole to recant probably had less to do with any Perry Mason skills of mine than with the fact that Toole's desire to perpetuate the hoax was weaker than his longing to claim credit for what turned out to be one of the great con games in American history.

"How would you do that?"

"A lot of [investigators] just walk in and throw the shit in front of you."

"So these Florida murders, they're lies, too?"

"Uh-huh, they're lies, too."

"How come you kept confessing?"

"I . . . I . . . said, 'The hell with it, I ain't never gonna get out—[I've got] twenty-five mandatory years.' "

"Why did you suddenly decide to give them [the Florida cases] up? Was it because no one had come to you for a while?"

"It was the way we could play."

"You guys did play with the system."

"We had the whole United States in an uproar, the biggest uproar in history," he said, recalling the heyday of the Lucas-Toole serial-murder circus. "We was carrying all of them on a wild-goose chase seeing how much money we could get them to spend on it in all the states."

Toole chuckled merrily over the tales of cannibalism and necrophilia they'd told.

"We threw in the filth; filth is what makes the books sell. They say I eat people, I fucked the dead."

In addition, he told me he had lied when he claimed he'd met Henry in 1975—it wasn't until 1979, he said—which would invalidate once and for all the Lucas-Toole confession to the murder of the Lemonses' daughter in 1975. He also indicated that he and Lucas were actually at work in Jacksonville, a thousand miles away, when they were supposed to be murdering "Orange Socks" in Texas—a killing Lucas may yet be executed for. He said he was going to tell the truth from now on.

Needless to say, Toole's statement alone, sworn or unsworn, about anything has little compelling probative value at this point. Press reports, citing Florida officials, indicate he's recanted before. As Texas investigator Mike Feary says of all cases involving a Lucas-Toole confession, "They should ignore it, and see what else they have." Florida investigators claim to have something else in one of the three upcoming murder trials of Henry Lee Lucas: the Long-Silent Witness, Frank Powell III. Whether he will be enough to resolve the question remains to be seen.*

But what about all those other Lucas cases—will they ever be resolved? What about all those murders in places like Utah, where obviously false Lucas-Toole confessions remain on the books and local authorities don't know or don't care that the hoax has been exposed?

I put that question to a "major-case specialist" within the FBI who was

---

*Nothing came of the alleged "new" Florida evidence, and Ottis Toole died in prison.

familiar with the Lucas affair. Shouldn't action be taken to reopen those cases?

Exactly, he said. If the attorney general's report is valid, then what's happening is that there are murder cases out there that are not being investigated, and the perpetrators are going free.

But, he added, the FBI has no jurisdiction to intervene in local investigations of murders. The only remedy, he suggested, lies with the attorneys general of those states that have Lucas confessions on the books—they *could* take responsibility for undoing the damage on their turf and reopen the cases. But he didn't sound optimistic about that prospect.

In fact, the only hope of ever setting the record straight may lie in a suggestion Joyce Lemons made to me: the families. If the families of the victims in Lucas-confession cases were to pressure local detectives and state attorneys general the way the Lemonses did, then, case by case, truth might be separated from falsehood. (The Lubbock police department has reopened its investigation of the Lemonses' daughter's murder.)

But, Mrs. Lemons told me, she'd often found herself shocked when she'd tried to enlist other families in pressing for the truth about the murderer of their loved ones.

"You know what they'd say?" she asked me. " *'It doesn't matter.'* "

"It doesn't matter that the real killer's gone free?"

" 'It doesn't matter. It won't bring our child back.' For God's sake, I know I'm not going to get *my* child back, but I want the person who *really* killed her to be the one to pay. After all, he's . . . these people are still *out there*. And they'd just say. 'Well, it's over.' "

She'd put her finger on the nature of the staying power of the Lucas myth, the reason, after repeated exposures, it just will not die.

"It's over." The relief in those words, the inexpressible comfort of closure—even by a false confession—is something the families, and the lawmen who originally closed the cases, cling to with a death grip when confronted by the alternative: a reopened case that may never be closed, a reopened wound that may never heal, a death unsolemnized.

Henry Lee Lucas filled a lot of needs with his confessions. Indeed, the serial-killer myth offers a perverse kind of comfort, however false, to the national psyche. It offers a vision of America in which Lucas, the lone slayer of, say, 350 innocents, is safely locked up, heading for a date with the executioner. Which is far less threatening than the vision of America without the Lucas myth: an America in which 350 vicious killers are out there on the loose, with one free murder already under their belts, cruising the highways even now, looking to see if they'll get lucky again.

Postscript to "Henry: Portrait of a Serial-Killer Hoax"

In retrospect, Henry Lee Lucas's fake confessions can be looked at as a prototypical eighties phenomenon. The criminological equivalent of junk bonds. But more enduring: As late as 1998, Henry Lee Lucas was about to be executed for the "Orange Socks" killing, one of the hundreds he'd fraudulently confessed to. More than a decade after the Texas attorney general's investigation exposed the massive hoax, the myth won't die, although Henry was about to. The reason: the Texas Rangers' shameful refusal to admit they'd been gulled, conned, and made to look ridiculous by a one-eyed, no-hope drifter. When Governor George W. Bush asked the state parole and pardon authorities to look more closely into the "Orange Socks" killing Henry was about to die for, the Rangers and their powerful supporters continued to perpetuate the myth, hoping perhaps that by killing Henry they could kill off the memory of their shame. At the last minute, Governor Bush, acting on the basis of a review of the Lucas affair, commuted the execution to life imprisonment, a courageous act in the context of the Rangers' political power but one that fell short of addressing the legacy of lies—and the real killers let off the hook by the Lucas confessions still on the books.

But clearly something more than the Texas Rangers' wounded vanity is responsible for prolonging the Lucas hoax. I'd suggest it has something to do with a deeper longing to believe in the figure of the serial killer as the signature icon of evil, a longing responsible for the popularity of *The Silence of the Lambs* and all the innumerable derivative film and TV serial-killer plots that make it seem as if the highways are teeming, the landscape of America is swarming with them. A longing to ascribe all the inexplicable violence and tragedy in contemporary life to inhuman alien monsters, cold-blooded killing machines, rather than the warm-blooded people we live and work with, the "intimate homicides" as the criminologists call them—killings by those closest to us—that make up the majority of murders. Serial-killer culture also perpetuates the myth of the wizardry of FBI "profilers"—the self-promoting practitioners of serial-killer pseudoscience who, despite being almost invariably wrong (about the Unabomber, about Richard Jewell, etc.), have continued to profit from the myth created by *The Silence of the Lambs,* the myth that they have some special insight into the heart of darkness. Again, it's a consoling myth: Serial killers may seem very scary, but Reason and Goodness in the person of the "scientific" profiler has their number. Would it were true.

Part Three

THE NINETIES AND AFTER

Three Intriguing
Archival Mysteries

The Great Ivy League Nude Posture Photo Scandal

In Which a Cunning Pseudoscientist Catches the Elite with Its Pants Down

One afternoon in the late 1970s, deep in the labyrinthine interior of a massive Gothic tower in New Haven, an unsuspecting employee of Yale University opened a long-locked room in the Payne Whitney Gymnasium and stumbled upon something shocking and disturbing.

Shocking, because what he found was an enormous cache of nude photographs, thousands and thousands of photographs of young men in front, side, and rear poses. Disturbing, because on closer inspection the photos looked like the record of a bizarre body-piercing ritual: sticking out from the spine of each and every body was a row of sharp metal pins.

The employee who found them was mystified. The athletic director at the time, Frank Ryan, a former Cleveland Browns quarterback new to Yale, was mystified. But after making some discreet inquiries, he found out what they were—and took swift action to burn them. He called in a professional, a document-disposal expert, who initiated a two-step torching procedure. First, every single one of the many thousands of photographs was fed into a shredder, and then each of the shreds was fed to the flames, thereby ensuring that not a single intact or recognizable image of the nude Yale students—some of whom had gone on to assume positions of importance in government and society—would survive.

It was the Bonfire of the Best and the Brightest, and the assumption was that the last embarrassing reminders of a peculiar practice, which masqueraded as science and now looked like a kind of kinky voodoo ritual, had gone up in smoke. The assumption was wrong. Thousands upon thousands of nude photos from Yale and other elite schools survive to this day.

When I first embarked on my quest for the lost nude "posture photos," I could not decide whether to think of the phenomenon as a scandal or as an extreme example of academic folly—of what happens when well-intentioned institutions allow their reverence for the reigning conjectures of scientific orthodoxy to persuade them to do things that seem silly or scandalous in retrospect. And now that I've found them, I'm still not sure whether outrage or laughter is the more appropriate reaction. Your response, dear reader, may depend on whether your nude photograph is among them. And if you attended Yale, Mount Holyoke, Vassar, Smith, or Princeton—to name a few of the schools involved—from the 1940s through the 1960s, there's a chance that yours may be.

Your response may also depend on how you feel about the fact that some of these schools made nude or seminude photographs of you available to the disciples of what many now regard as a pseudoscience without asking permission. And on how you feel about an obscure archive in Washington making them available for researchers to study today.

While investigating the strange odyssey of the missing nude "posture photos," I found that the issue is, in every respect, a very touchy matter—indeed, a kind of touchstone for registering the uneven evolution of attitudes toward body, race, and gender in the past half-century.

Up Your Legs for Yale

I personally have posed nude only twice in my life. The second time—for a John Lennon and Yoko Ono film titled *Up Your Legs Forever*, which has been screened at the Whitney—I was one of many, it was Art, and let's leave it at that. But the first time was even more strange and bizarre because of its straitlaced Ivy setting, its pre-liberation context—and yes, because of the metal pins stuck on my body.

One fall afternoon in the mid-sixties, shortly after I arrived in New Haven to begin my freshman year at Yale, I was summoned to that sooty Gothic shrine to muscular virtue known as Payne Whitney Gym. I reported to a windowless room on an upper floor, where men dressed in crisp white garments instructed me to remove all of my clothes. And then—and this is the part I still have trouble believing—they attached metal pins to my spine. There was no actual piercing of skin, only of dignity, as four-inch metal pins were affixed with adhesive to my vertebrae at regular intervals from my neck down. I was positioned against a wall; a floodlight illuminated my pin-spiked profile and a camera captured it.

It didn't occur to me to object: I'd been told that this "posture photo" was a routine feature of freshman orientation week. Those whose pins described a too violent or erratic postural curve were required to attend remedial posture classes.

The procedure did seem strange. But I soon learned that it was a long-established custom at most Ivy League and Seven Sisters schools. George Bush, George Pataki, Brandon Tartikoff, and Bob Woodward were required to do it at Yale. At Vassar, Meryl Streep; at Mount Holyoke, Wendy Wasserstein; at Wellesley, Nora Ephron, Hillary Rodham, and Diane Sawyer.* All of them—whole generations of the cultural elite—were asked to pose. But however much the colleges tried to make this bizarre procedure seem routine, its undeniable strangeness engendered a scurrilous strain of folklore.

The Mismeasure of Man

There were several salacious stories circulating at Yale back in the sixties. Most common was the report that someone had broken into a photo lab in Poughkeepsie, New York, and stolen the negatives of that year's Vassar posture nudes, which were supposedly for sale on the Ivy League black market or available to the initiates of Skull and Bones. Little did I know how universal this myth was.

"Ah, yes, the famous rumored stolen Vassar posture pictures," Nora Ephron (Wellesley '62) recalled when I spoke with her. "But don't forget the famous rumored stolen Wellesley posture photos."

"Wellesley too?"

"Oh, yes," she said. "It's one of those urban legends."

She can laugh about it now, she said, but in retrospect the whole idea that she and all her smart classmates went along with being photographed in this way dismays her. "We were idiots," she said. "Idiots!"

Sally Quinn (Smith '63), the Washington writer, expressed alarm when I first reached her. "God, I'm relieved," she said. "I thought you were going to tell me you found mine. You always thought when you did it that one day they'd come back to haunt you. That twenty-five years later, when your husband was running for president, they'd show up in *Penthouse*."

*Most Wellesley photos were taken seminude, in bra and panties.

Another Wellesley alumna, Judith Martin, author of the Miss Manners column, told me she's "appalled in retrospect" that the college forced this practice on their freshmen. "Why weren't we more appalled at the time?" she wondered. Nonetheless, she confessed to making a kind of good-natured extortionate use of the posture-photo specter herself.

"I do remember making a reunion speech in which I offered to sell them back to people for large donations. And there were a lot of people who turned pale before they realized it was a joke."

Distinguishing between joke and reality is often difficult in posture-photo lore. Consider the astonishing rumor Ephron clued me in to, a story she assured me she'd heard from someone very close to the source:

"There was a guy, an adjunct professor of sociology who was working on a grant for the tobacco industry. And what I heard when I was at Wellesley was that, using Harvard posture photos, he had proved conclusively that the more manly you are, the more you smoked. And I believe the criterion for manliness was the obvious one."

"The obvious one?"

"I assume—what else could it have been?"

In fact, the study was real. I was able to track it down, although the conclusion it reached about Harvard men was somewhat different from what Ephron recalled. But, clearly, the nude-posture-photo practice engendered heated fantasies in both sexes. Perhaps in the otherwise circumspect Ivy League–Seven Sisters world, nude posture photos were the licensed exception to propriety that spawned licentious fantasies. Fantasies that were to lie unremembered, or at least unpublicized until . . .

The Return of the Repressed

It was Naomi Wolf, author of *The Beauty Myth,* who opened the Pandora's box of posture-photo controversy. In that book and in a 1992 op-ed piece in *The New York Times,* Wolf (Yale '84) bitterly attacked Dick Cavett (Yale '55) for a joke he'd made at Wolf's graduation ceremonies. According to Wolf, who'd never had a posture photo taken (the practice was discontinued at Yale in 1968), Cavett took the microphone and told the following anecdote:

"When I was an undergraduate . . . there were no women [at Yale]. The women went to Vassar. At Vassar they had nude photographs taken of women in gym class to check their posture. One year the photos were stolen and turned up for sale in New Haven's red-light district." His punch line: "The photos found no buyers."

Wolf was horrified. Cavett, she wrote in her book, "transposed us for a moment out of the gentle quadrangle where we had been led to believe we were cherished, and into the tawdry district four blocks away, where stolen photographs of our naked bodies would find no buyers."

Cavett responded, in a letter to the *Times,* by dismissing the joke as an innocuous "example of how my Yale years showed up in my long-forgotten nightclub act."

Wolf's horrified account attests to the totemic power of the posture-photo legend. But little did she know, little did Cavett know, how potentially sinister the entire phenomenon really was. No one knew until . . .

The Nazi-Posture-Photo Allegation

This is where things get really strange. Shortly after Cavett's reply, George Hersey, a respected art history professor at Yale, wrote a letter to the *Times* that ran under the headline A SECRET LIES HIDDEN IN VASSAR AND YALE NUDE "POSTURE PHOTOS." Sounding an ominous note, Hersey declared that the photos "had nothing to do with posture . . . that is only what we were told."

Hersey went on to say that the pictures were actually made for anthropological research: "The reigning school of the time, presided over by E. A. Hooton of Harvard and W. H. Sheldon"—who directed an institute for physique studies at Columbia University—"held that a person's body, measured and analyzed, could tell much about intelligence, temperament, moral worth, and probable future achievement. The inspiration came from the founder of social Darwinism, Francis Galton, who proposed such a photo archive for the British population."

And then Hersey evoked the specter of the Third Reich:

"The Nazis compiled similar archives analyzing the photos for racial as well as characterological content (as did Hooton). . . . The Nazis often used American high-school yearbook photographs for this purpose. . . . The American investigators planned an archive that could correlate each freshman's bodily configuration ('somatotype') and physiognomy with later life history. That the photos had no value as pornography is a tribute to their resolutely scientific nature."

A truly breathtaking missive. What Hersey seemed to be saying was that entire generations of America's ruling class had been unwitting guinea pigs in a vast eugenic experiment run by scientists with a master-race hidden agenda. My classmate Steve Weisman, the *Times* editor who first called my attention to the letter, pointed out a fascinating corollary: The letter managed in a stroke to confer on some of the most overprivileged people in the world the one status distinction it seemed they'd forever be denied—victim.

My first stop in what would turn out to be a prolonged and eventful quest for the truth about the posture photos was Professor Hersey's office in New

Haven. A thoughtful, civilized scholar, Hersey did not seem prone to sensationalism. But he showed me a draft chapter from his forthcoming book on the aesthetics of racism *(The Evolution of Allure)* that went even further than the allegations in his letter to the *Times*. I was struck by one passage in particular:

> From the outset, the purpose of these "posture photographs" was eugenic. The data accumulated, says Hooton, will eventually lead on to proposals to "control and limit the production of inferior and useless organisms." Some of the latter would be penalized for reproducing . . . or would be sterilized. But the real solution is to be enforced better breeding—getting those Exeter and Harvard men together with their corresponding Wellesley, Vassar, and Radcliffe girls.

In other words, a kind of eugenic dating service, *Studs* for the cultural elite. But my talk with Hersey left key questions unanswered. What was the precise relationship between theorists like Hooton and Sheldon (the man who actually took tens of thousands of those nude posture photos) and the Ivy League and Seven Sisters schools whose student bodies were photographed? Were the schools complicit or were they simply dupes? And finally: What became of the photographs?

As for the last question, Hersey thought there'd be no trouble locating the photographs. He assumed that "they can probably be found with Sheldon's research papers" in one of the several academic institutions with which he had been associated. But most of those institutions said that they had burned whatever photos they'd had. Harley P. Holden, curator of Harvard's archives, said that from the 1880s to the 1940s the university had its own posture-photo program in which some 3,500 pictures of its students were taken. Most were destroyed fifteen or twenty years ago "for privacy scruples," Holden said. Nonetheless, quite a few Harvard nudes can be found illustrating Sheldon's book on body types, the *Atlas of Men*. Radcliffe took posture photos from 1931 to 1961; the curator there said that most of them had been destroyed (although some might be missing) and that none were taken by Sheldon.

Hersey insisted that there was a treasure trove of Sheldon photographs out there to be found. He gave me the phone number of a man in New Mexico named Ellery Lanier, a friend of Sheldon, the posture-photo mastermind. "He might know where they ended up," Hersey told me.

Going from Hersey to Lanier meant stepping over the threshold from contemporary academic orthodoxy into the more exotic precincts of the Sheldon subculture, a loose-knit network of his surviving disciples. A number of them keep the Sheldon legacy alive, hoping for a revival.

Lanier, an articulate, seventyish doctoral student at New Mexico State, told me he'd gotten to know Sheldon at Columbia in the late 1940s, when the two of them were hanging out with Aldous Huxley and Christopher Isherwood and their crew. (Sheldon had a prophetic mystical side, which revealed itself in Huxleyan philosophic treatises on the "Promethean will." Sheldon was also, Lanier told me, "the world's leading expert on the history of the American penny.") At that time, Sheldon was at the apex of his now-forgotten renown. *Life* magazine ran a cover story in 1951 on Sheldon's theory of somatotypes.

While the popular conception of Sheldonism has it that he divided human beings into three types—skinny, nervous "ectomorphs"; fat and jolly "endomorphs"; confident, buffed "mesomorphs"—what he actually did was somewhat more complex. He believed that every individual harbored within him different degrees of *each* of the three character components. By using body measurements and ratios derived from nude photographs, Sheldon believed he could assign every individual a three-digit number representing the three components, components that Sheldon believed were inborn—genetic—and remained unwavering determinants of character regardless of transitory weight change. In other words, physique equals destiny.

It was the pop-psych flavor of the month for a while; *Cosmopolitan* magazine published quizzes about how to understand your husband on the basis of somatotype. Ecto-, meso-, and endomorphic have entered the language, although few scientists these days give credence to Sheldon's claims. "Half the textbooks in [his] area fail to take [him] seriously," remarked one academician in a 1992 paper on Sheldon's legacy. Others, like Hans Eysenck, the British psychologist, have suggested that Sheldon wasn't really doing science at all, that he was just winging it, that there was "little theoretical foundation for the observed findings."

Nonetheless, in the late 1940s and early 1950s, Sheldonism seemed mainstream, and Sheldon took advantage of that to approach Ivy League schools. Many, like Harvard, already had a posture-photo tradition. But it was at Wellesley College in the late 1920s that concern about postural correctness metamorphosed into a cottage industry with pretensions to science. The department of hygiene circulated training films about posture measurement to other women's colleges, which took up the practice, as did some "progressive" high schools and elementary schools.

What Sheldon did was appropriate the ritual. Lanier confirmed that the Ivy League "posture photos" Sheldon used were "part of a facade or cover-up for what we were really doing"—which would make the schools less complicit. But Lanier stoutly defended "what we were really doing" as valid science. As part of his Ph.D. project, he has been examining Sheldonian ecto-, meso-, and endomorphic categories and the "time horizon" of the individual.

"Conflicting temporal horizon can account for all the divorce we have today," Lanier said. "The Woody Allen/Mia Farrow-type thing."

Huh? Woody and Mia?

"I'm trying to find some clue to the breakup because of the discrepancies between their time focus," Lanier said.

"Well, Woody's certainly ectomorphic, but . . ."

"No, let me correct you," Lanier said tartly. "Woody Allen creates an *illusion*. He puts on a big *show* of being ectomorphic, but this is all a cover-up because he's quite mesomorphic."

"I think he would be surprised to hear that."

"I know," Lanier said. "He wouldn't want to admit it, but the only way you can know this is by looking at photographs very carefully."

Lanier also filled me in on the cause of Sheldon's downfall: his never completed, partly burned *Atlas of Women*. In attempting to compile what would have been the companion volume to his *Atlas of Men*, which included hundreds of nude Harvard men to illustrate each of the three-digit body types, Sheldon made the strategic mistake of taking his photo show on the road.

What happened was this: In September 1950, Sheldon and his team descended on Seattle, where the University of Washington had agreed to play host to his project. He'd begun taking nude pictures of female freshmen, but something went wrong. One of them told her parents about the practice. The next morning, a battalion of lawyers and university officials stormed Sheldon's lab, seized every photo of a nude woman, convicted the images of shamefulness and sentenced them to burning. The angry crew then shoveled the incendiary film into an incinerator. A short-lived controversy broke out: Was this a book burning? A witch hunt? Was Professor Sheldon's nude photography a legitimate scientific investigation into the relationship between physique and temperament, the raw material of serious scholarship? Or just raw material—pornography masquerading as science?

They burned a few thousand photos in Seattle. Thousands more were burned at Harvard, Vassar, and Yale in the 1960s and 1970s, when the colleges phased out the posture-photo practice. But thousands more escaped the flames, tens of thousands that Sheldon took at Harvard, Vassar, Yale, and elsewhere but sequestered in his own archives. And what became of the archives? Lanier didn't know, but he said they were out there somewhere. He dug up the phone number of a man who was once the lawyer for Sheldon's estate, a Mr. Joachim Weissfeld in Providence, Rhode Island. "Maybe he'll know," Lanier said.

At this point, the posture-photo quest turned into a kind of high-speed parody of *The Aspern Papers*. The lawyer in Rhode Island professed ignorance as to the whereabouts or even continued existence of the lost Sheldonian archives, but he did put me in touch with the last living leaf on the Sheldon family tree, a niece by marriage who lived in Warwick, Rhode Island. She, too, said she didn't know what had become of the Sheldon photos, but she did give me the name of an eighty-four-year-old man living in Columbus, Ohio, who had worked very closely with Sheldon, one Roland D. Elderkin—a man who, in fact, had shot many of the lost photos himself and who promised to reveal their location to me.

The Mystery Solved

With Roland D. Elderkin, we're now this close to the late, great Sheldon himself. "There was nobody closer," Elderkin declared shortly after I reached him at his rooming house in Columbus. "I was his soul mate."

Elderkin described himself a bit mournfully as "just an eighty-four-year-old man living alone in a furnished room." But he once had a brush with greatness, and you can hear it in his recollection of Sheldon and his grand project.

To Elderkin, Sheldon was no mere body-typer: He was a true philosophe, "the first to introduce holistic perspective" to American science, a proto–New Ager. Elderkin became Sheldon's research associate, his trusty cameraman and a kind of private eye, compiling case histories of Sheldon's posture nudes to confirm Sheldon's theories about physique and destiny. He also witnessed Sheldon's downfall.

The Bonfire of the Nude Coed Photos in Seattle wasn't Sheldon's only public burning, Elderkin told me: "He went through a number of furors over women. A similar thing later happened at Pembroke, the women's college at Brown." In each case, the fact that female nudes were involved kindled the flame against Sheldon. Toward the end, Sheldon became a kind of pathetic Willy Loman–esque figure as he wandered America far from the elite Ivy halls that had once housed him, seeking a place he could complete the photography for his *Atlas of Women.*

Rejected and scorned, out of fashion with academic officialdom, Sheldon is still a hero to Roland D. Elderkin. And so when Sheldon died in 1977, "a lonely old man who did nothing his last years but sit in his room and read detective stories," Elderkin said, "there was nobody else to carry on." It fell to Elderkin to find a final resting place for the huge archives of Sheldon's posture nudes.

It wasn't easy, he said. Elderkin went "up and down the East Coast trying to peddle them" to places like Harvard and Columbia, which once welcomed Sheldon but now wanted nothing to do with nude photos and the controversy trailing them. "That's how I found out about the burning at Pembroke," Elderkin recalled. "I was trying to get someone at Brown to accept them, and he said, 'That filth? We already burned the ones we had.' "

"And you know where they are now?" I asked incredulously. "Hersey and Lanier said they didn't know."

"Sure I do," he said. "I was the one that finally found a home for them."
And then he told me where.

Before we proceed to the location of the treasure itself, it might be wise to pause and ponder the wisdom of opening such a Pandora's box. With scholars like Hersey alleging eugenic motives behind Sheldon's project, with the self-images of so many of the cultural elite at stake, would exposure of the hidden hoard be defensible? Is there anyone, aside from lifelong Sheldon disciples, who will step forward to defend Sheldon's posture photos?

Of course there is: Camille Paglia.

"I'm *very* interested in somatotypes," she said. "I *constantly* use the term in my work. The word *ectomorph* is used repeatedly in *Sexual Personae* about Spenser's Apollonian angels. That's one of the things I'm trying to do: to reconsider these classification schemes, to rescue them from their tainting by Nazi ideology. It's always been a part of classicism. It's sort of like we've lost the old curiosity about physical characteristics, physical differences. And I maintain it's bourgeois prudery.

"See, I'm *interested* in looking at women's breasts! I'm *interested* in looking at men's penises! I maintain that at the present date, *Penthouse, Playboy, Hustler,* serve the same cultural functions as the posture photos."

With these words ringing in my ears, I set out to see if I could open up the Sheldon archives.

The Secret Is Bared

Down a dimly lit back corridor of the National Museum of Natural History in Washington, far from the dinosaur displays, is a branch of the Smithsonian not well known to the public: the National Anthropological Archives.

Although it contains a rich and strange assortment of archival treasures, it's particularly notable for the number of Native Americans who travel here to investigate centuries-old anthropological records, poring over them in a cramped, windowless research room whose walls are hung with stylized illustrations of tribal rituals painted by one Chief Blue Eagle. It was here that my quest for another kind of tribal illustration—the taboo images of the blue-blood tribe, the long-lost nude posture photos—culminated at last.

In 1987, the curators of the National Anthropological Archives acquired the remains of Sheldon's life work, which were gathering dust in "dead storage" in a Goodwill warehouse in Boston. While there were solid archival reasons for making the acquisition, the curators are clearly aware that they harbor some potentially explosive material in their storage rooms. And they did not make it easy for me to gain access.

On my first visit, I was informed by a good-natured but wary supervisor that the restrictive grant of Sheldon's materials by his estate would permit me to review only the written materials in the Sheldon archives. The actual photographs, he said, were off-limits. To see them, I would have to petition the chief of archivists. Determined to pursue the matter to the bitter end, I began the process of applying for permission.

Meanwhile, I plunged into the written material hoping to find answers to several unresolved mysteries. Although I did not find substantiation in those files for Hersey's belief that Sheldon was actively engaged in a master-race eugenic project, I did find stunning confirmation of Hersey's charge that Sheldon held racist views.

In Box 43 I came across a document never referred to in any of the literature on Sheldon I'd seen. It was a faded offprint of a 1924 Sheldon study, "The Intelligence of Mexican Children." In it are damning assertions presented as scientific truisms that "Negro intelligence" comes to a "standstill at about the tenth year," Mexican at about age twelve. To the author of such sentiments, America's elite institutions entrusted their student bodies.

Another box held clues to the truth behind Nora Ephron's tale about smoking and "manliness." It turned out to be true that a research arm of the tobacco industry had sponsored studies on the relationship between masculinity and smoking, and that the studies had involved Sheldonian posture photos of Harvard men—although there is no evidence that the criterion of masculinity was the "obvious one" referred to by Ephron. I located a fascinating report on this research in a December 1959 issue of the respected journal *Science,* a report titled "Masculinity and Smoking." According to the article, and contrary to the rumor, it is "not strength but weakness of the masculine component" that is "more frequent in the heavier smokers." Here, perhaps, is the most profound cultural legacy of the Sheldonian posture-photo phenomenon: the blueprint for the sexual iconography of tobacco advertising. If, in fact, heavy smokers looked more like Harvard nerds than Marlboro men, why not use advertising imagery to make nerds *feel* like virile cowboys when they smoked?

Finally and most telling, I found a letter nearly four decades old that did something nothing else in the files did. It gave a glimpse, a clue to the feelings of the subjects of Sheldon's research, particularly the women. I found the letter in a file of correspondence between Sheldon and various phys-ed directors at women's colleges who were providing Sheldon with bodies for the ill-fated *Atlas of Women.* In this letter, an official at Denison University in Granville, Ohio, was responding to Sheldon's request to rephotograph the female freshmen he had photographed the year before. Something had apparently gone wrong with the technical side of the earlier shoot. But the official refused to allow Sheldon to reshoot the women, declaring that "to require them to pose for another [nude posture photo] would create insurmountable psychological problems."

Insurmountable psychological problems. Suddenly the subjects of Sheldon's photography leaped into the foreground: the shy girl, the fat girl, the religiously conservative, the victim of inappropriate parental attention. Here, perhaps, Naomi Wolf has a point. In a culture that already encourages women to scrutinize their bodies critically, the first thing that happens to these women when they arrive at college is an intrusive, uncomfortable, public examination of their nude bodies.

Three months later, I finally succeeded in gaining permission to study the elusive posture photos. As I sat at my desk in the reading room, under a portrait of Chief Blue Eagle, the long-sought cache materialized. A curator trundled in a library cart from the storage facility. Teetering on top of the cart were stacks of big, gray cardboard boxes. The curator handed me a pair of the white cotton gloves that researchers must use to handle archival material.

The contents of the boxes were described in an accompanying "Finder's Aid" in this fashion:

BOX 90 YALE UNIVERSITY CLASS OF 1971
Negatives. Full length views of nude freshmen men, front, back and rear. Includes weight, height, previous or maximum weight, with age, name, or initials.

BOX 95 MOUNT HOLYOKE COLLEGE PHOTOGRAPHS
Negatives. Made in 1950. Full length views of nude women, front, back and rear. Includes height, weight, date and age. Includes some photographs marked S.P.C.

Among the other classes listed in the Finder's Aid were: the Yale classes of '50, '63, '64, '66, and '71; the Princeton class of '52; Smith '50 and '52; Vassar '42 and '52; Mount Holyoke '53; Swarthmore '51; University of California '61 and '67; Hotchkiss '71; Syracuse '50; University of Wisconsin '53; Purdue '53; University of Pennsylvania '51, and Brooklyn College '51 and '52. There were also undated photos from the Oregon Hospital for the Criminally Insane (which I could not distinguish in any way from the Ivy League photos). All told, there were some 20,000 photographs of men—9,000 from Yale—and 7,000 of women.

In flipping through those thousands of images (which were recently transferred to Smithsonian archives in Suitland, Maryland), I found surprising testimony to the "insurmountable psychological problems" that the Denison University official had referred to. It took a while for the "problems" to become apparent, because, as it turned out, I was not permitted to see positive photographs—only negatives (with no names attached).

A fascinating distinction was being exhibited here, a kind of light-polarity theory of prurience and privacy that absolves the negative image of the naked body of whatever transgressive power it might have in a positive print. There's an intuitive logic to the theory, although here the Sheldon posture-photo phenomenon exposes how fragile are the distinctions we make between the sanctioned and the forbidden images of the body.

As I thumbed rapidly through box after box to confirm that the entries described in the Finder's Aid were actually there, I tried to glance at only the faces. It was a decision that paid off, because it was in them that a crucial difference between the men and the women revealed itself. For the most part, the men looked diffident, oblivious. That's not surprising considering that men of that era were accustomed to undressing for draft physicals and athletic-squad weigh-ins.

But the faces of the women were another story. I was surprised at how many looked deeply unhappy, as if pained at being subjected to this procedure. On the faces of quite a few I saw what looked like grimaces, reflecting pronounced discomfort, perhaps even anger.

I was not much more comfortable myself sitting there in the midst of stacks of boxes of such images. There I was at the end of my quest. I'd tracked down the fabled photographs, but the lessons of the posture-photo ritual were elusive.

"There's a tremendous lesson here," Miss Manners declares. "Which is that one should have sympathy and tolerance for respectable women from whose past naked pictures suddenly show up. One should think of the many times where some woman becomes prominent like Marilyn Monroe and suddenly there are nude pictures in her past. Shouldn't we be a little less condemning of someone in that position?"

A little less condemning of the victims, yes, certainly. (I speak as one myself, although it turned out that my photo was burned in the Yale bonfire of the late 1970s.) But what about the perpetrators? What could have possessed so many elite institutions of higher education to turn their student bodies over to the practitioners of what now seems so dubious a science project?

It's a question that baffles the current powers that be at Ivy League schools. The response of Gary Fryer, Yale's spokesman, is representative: "We searched, but there's nobody around now who was involved with the decision." Even so, he assures me, nothing like it could happen again; concerns about privacy have heightened, and, as he puts it, "there's now a federal law against disclosing anything in a college student's record to any outsider without written permission."

In other words, "We won't get fooled again." Though he is undoubtedly correct that nothing precisely like the posture-photo folly could happen again, it is hard to deny the possibility, the likelihood, that well-meaning people and institutions will get taken in—are being taken in—by those who peddle scientific conjecture as certainty. Sheldon's dream of reducing the complexity of human personality and the contingency of human fate to a single number is a recurrent one, as the continuing IQ controversy demonstrates. And a reminder that skepticism is still valuable in the face of scientific claims of certainty, particularly in the slippery realms of human behavior.

The rise and fall of "sciences" like Marxist history, Freudian psychology, and Keynesian economics suggests that at least some of the beliefs and axioms treated as science today (Rorschach analysis, "rational choice" economics, perhaps) will turn out to have little more validity than nude stick-pin somatotyping.

In the Sheldon rituals, the student test subjects were naked—but it was the emperors of scientific certainty who had no clothes.

Postscript to "The Great Ivy League Nude Posture Photo Scandal"

A minor furor errupted upon publication of this story in *The New York Times Magazine,* with alumni of all the implicated colleges besieging their alma maters with demands to know the disposition of their posture nudes. Within a week, *The Washington Post* reported that the Smithsonian had come to an agreement with Yale for the swift incineration of the nearly ten thousand Yale photos I'd uncovered. In a flash, they were reduced to ashes. When I relayed this news to a cynical friend of mine, his reaction was, "When does the federal bureaucracy *ever* take swift action? Everything, no matter what, no matter for whom, takes forever. But when a few Yalies get their naked butts exposed. . . ."

The Riddle of the Scrolls

In Which We Listen for the Roaring Breath of God

The Judaean desert. Remember that "voice crying in the wilderness" in the Scriptures? This is that wilderness, God's proving ground. This is the place where many believed the Messiah would materialize. The place where the End would begin.

This vista of ancient barren hills inhabited mainly by scorpions and vipers (and a few scattered Bedouin shepherds living in tents like Abraham's) is arguably the most terrifyingly bleak landscape on the face of the earth. And—perhaps because of that—the most productive of fevered, world-shaking visionary encounters with God and the Devil. It was here that Elijah heard the Voice of the Lord while being kept alive by ravens. Here Jesus was tempted by Satan with visions of the power and glory of a worldly kingdom. Here John the Baptist lived on locusts and honey and decided the End was coming.

Beneath the limestone cliffs where the desert hills drop down to the sterile salt flats of the Dead Sea shore, at a place called Qumran, lie the crumbling, unroofed ruins of a two-thousand-year-old "monastery" and the unmarked graves of its long-dead inhabitants. Here, in this sun-blasted wasteland, the lowest point on earth, the sunken navel of the world, we're trudging through a dusty graveyard in the ovenlike heat. My companions, a small group of American Christian scholars, are making a pilgrimage to the last resting place of the Dead Sea Scroll writers—the long-extinct, still-enigmatic sect of dissident Jewish visionary writers and biblical exegetes (ancient Harold Blooms!) who, some believe, were the Jews who invented Christianity.

The now-anonymous writers in the graves beneath our feet managed to defy their hellhole setting to create a body of literature that would endure the world's most dismal publishing history for nineteen centuries. And then would—after a sudden, sensational, mutilated resurrection—demonstrate an extraordinary power to haunt, obsess, and torment those who sought to divine their meaning.

The Qumran writers vanished from the face of the earth, or at least from the pages of history, sometime around A.D. 70, but, perhaps sensing their end was coming, they went to some trouble to see that their visions survived. They rolled up their scrolls in linen and sealed these mummified manuscripts into three-foot-high clay jars they stashed in caves in the cliffs above us. Hoping perhaps to return from exile—or the grave—to unroll the Scrolls in the presence of the Messiah in the New Jerusalem at the End of Time, which they thought was just a moment away. Instead, their work stayed buried until the spring of 1947, when, on the eve of the creation of a new Jerusalem in a new Israel, a Bedouin shepherd stumbled onto some of those jars in a cave—and the trouble began.

Part of the trouble was the product of secrecy: A small clique of scholars who came to control the eight hundred or so Scrolls in the 1950s kept many of them under wraps and out of sight for years while slowly issuing annotated editions that advanced their academic careers—a policy that engendered wild rumors about Suppressed Secrets of the Scrolls, Vatican conspiracies to cover up bombshell revelations about Jesus, and the like. The unpublished Scrolls became the focus of the same secrecy/paranoia dynamic that grew up around the unreleased JFK files, only the purported stakes were even higher: not the identity of an assassin, but the identity of the Messiah.

But beneath the sensationalism, the sudden appearance of the Scrolls did pose a potentially serious challenge to the official versions, both Christian and Jewish, of that moment when what we now know as Judaism and Christianity turned against each other with centuries of tragic consequences. Were the Scroll writers Essenes, a pacifist, separatist, celibate sect, as scholarly and spiritual orthodoxy prefers to believe—relatively irrelevant to the life of Jesus? Or were they the heretics who taught "Christianity" to Christ?

Until now the debate has been handicapped by the inaccessibility of hundreds of fragmentary Scroll texts kept from view by the scholarly "cartel" that monopolized them. But last year an open rebellion by outside scholars led by heretical biblical studies Professor Robert Eisenman and Hershel Shanks, crusading editor of *Biblical Archaeology Review,* "liberated" the unpublished Scrolls—brought out a comprehensive edition of bootlegged photographs of the long-unseen fragments. And this month, with the first book of English translations being rushed into print by Eisenman, the Long Lost Secrets of the Dead Sea Scrolls will become public and the Final Battle will begin—over what they really *mean.*

In fact—although I can't disclose this to my companions, having been sworn to silence by Professor Eisenman—I'm carrying on my person transcripts of his first translations of some of the most significant "unpublished" Scroll texts. As the first nonscholar to read these fragments of the Qumran legacy in 1,900 years, I'd felt it somehow appropriate to bring the newly liberated works back to the graves of their long-silent authors.

Because beyond my interest in their work as explosive ammunition for theological and historical debate, I'd found myself, in the course of reading the Scrolls, compelled to respect these writers for the power and the pathos of their poetry and prose, to admire them as *writers.*

Their pathos: You can feel it in this graveyard.

"Look at the way they buried their dead," says one of my companions, James Tabor, professor of religious studies at the University of North Carolina at Charlotte. Tabor points down at the faint but regular depressions in the stony dust of the burial ground. "See the way the graves are lined up in a north-south direction." He gestures toward the heat shimmers in the distance. "The way they interpreted the prophetic texts, they thought the Messiah would appear north of here and wake them from the dead on the Day of Judgment. If they were buried facing north, the first thing they'd see when they awoke from the grave would be His face."

The current consensus has it that they'd fled what they regarded as the impurities defiling temple worship in Roman-controlled Jerusalem to live here in purity and prepare for the Day of Reckoning. They called themselves the Children of Light, wore only white garments, and devoted themselves to a life of rigorously devotional communal living, the better to bring on the Messiah and the Final Battle with the Evil Ones, the Children of Darkness. They died before it happened, but went to their deaths certain they'd wake up to glory one timeless moment later, when the graves beneath us would burst open, the dry bones jump up and clothe themselves with flesh to greet the Messiah.

It didn't happen that way. This is the historical pathos of the Qumran writers, one that may be at the heart of their power to appeal to us: the urgent sense in their work of *belatedness,* of being—like us—in an apocalyptic holding pattern at the End of History, trapped in a premillennial moment, helplessly enduring the cruel reign of the Children of Darkness, sensing that God is late, or worse, has fled. Leaving them to pine desperately for the End.

They're still waiting, these bones in the graveyard, the last prayer on their lips before they died a refrain familiar to us: the first-century equivalent of *Apocalypse Now!*

Hiking up the dry, rock-strewn ravine known as Wadi Qumran that afternoon, Jim Tabor pointed out a cleft in the cliff above, which looked like it might be a newly opened cave. There was a dicey moment as one of our party made a risky climb up the cliff wall to see if he could reach it. We all watched nervously from below, holding our breath as the climber inched his way toward the tantalizing cleft: The closer he got to it, the more he kept losing his footing, slipping perilously, desperately trying to grip the cliff face, only to find it crumbling to dust in his hands. Finally, just a few feet short, he had to abandon the effort without resolving whether he'd uncovered a new Dead Sea cave or just a dead end.

We were witnessing, of course, a metaphor for the quests the Dead Sea Scrolls have inspired over the last half-century: The high stakes and the profound frustrations, the uncertain foundation the Scroll fragments give to those who seek the fingerprints of God in them.

In the four decades since they surfaced, the Scrolls have driven a remarkable number of scholars, mystics, seekers, Messiah theorists, and apocalypse freaks (and some who are all of the above) to make some remarkable claims about "explosive" discoveries. But few so literally explosive as the discovery announced to the world here at the Qumran cliffs in May of this year [1992] by Dr. Vendyl "Indiana" Jones.

Dr. Jones is the flamboyant sixty-two-year-old, Texas-born preacher-turned–biblical archaeologist whose quest for the legendary Lost Ark of the Covenant predated (and postdated) Steven Spielberg's Indiana Jones character. Although Vendyl Jones doesn't exactly say Spielberg lifted his life for *Raiders of the Lost Ark* (and the evidence suggests he didn't), he's not been shy about pointing out the parallels between Indy Jones and "Vendy" Jones, as he's sometimes referred to. While Indy went on to pursue the Holy Grail, Vendy is still on the trail of the Lost Ark. The Ark, you'll recall from the biblical legend, was the physical repository of the Ten Commandments, the tablets Moses brought down from Sinai. The Ark was also, some said, the locus of the very Presence of God Himself.

Vendy Jones believes he can find the Lost Ark using the Copper Scroll, a highly anomalous Dead Sea Scroll, not only because it's the only one inscribed on metal but also because it seems to be less a theological document than some kind of treasure map. Some scholars believe that the Copper Scroll's cryptic directions to vast quantities of precious metals—tons of gold and silver—are descriptions of metaphorical treasures. But Jones, following in the footsteps of one of the first great Scroll heretics, Oxford's John Allegro, is convinced the Copper Scroll is a map of *real* treasures—the treasures of the Second Temple hidden by the high priests before the Romans sacked it in A.D. 70. And, more important, a map to the sacred vestments, ritual implements, and relics of priestly worship stashed away against the time when the Temple would be rebuilt to greet the Messiah in the New Jerusalem.

In May, Jones summoned the international media to a dramatic dawn press conference in the mouth of a Dead Sea cave he believes is the "Cave of the Column," as described in the Copper Scroll. And they came. Vendy had some credibility going for him on the basis of a previous find: *The New York Times* had front-paged a 1988 discovery at one of his nearby digs, a jug of anointing oil that dated back to the time of the Second Temple. And so CNN, CBS, and the European media all trekked out to Qumran at dawn to witness the bald, sunburned, drawling Texas preacher in pith helmet and desert gear emerge from the cave with his hands full of a "fine reddish-brown powder" and proclaim his momentous find: the ritual incense of the Second Temple. The sacred substance priests burned to perfume and purify the Holy of Holies. Furthermore, he told reporters, the find led him to believe he was closing in on the Ark of the Covenant itself.

It was, by all accounts, a strange press conference. Jones offered handfuls of the purportedly sacred substance for reporters to smell. Told them he'd come upon nine hundred pounds of it in a man-made chamber fourteen feet beneath the cave floor. Gave them a chemical analysis on the stationery of Israel's famed Weizmann Institute of Science/Department of Nuclear Physics, and issued a press release quoting the analyst to the effect that the "atomic fingerprints" of the elixirs of the Temple incense—the frankincense, myrrh, saffron, and spikenard—were present in the powder.

Yes, *on the stationery* of the Weizmann Institute. As we'll see, there were some problems there, but nothing compared with the problems Vendy Jones suddenly got from the Israeli authorities.

Vendy later conceded to me that he knew why he'd made the Israelis nervous: In the powder-keg context of Arab-Israeli relations, Vendy's magic powder had explosive potential. The discovery of any alleged relics of the Second Temple has the power to feed the flames and the fantasies of fundamentalist fanatics, some of whom believe they can prepare the way for the Messiah by replicating and reconstructing every last feature of the Second Temple, from the precise kind of thread woven into the vestments of the priests to the exact chemical composition of the sacred incense. The problem is that the hilltop site of the Second Temple (known as Temple Mount) is now occupied by the third-holiest Muslim shrine in the world, the Dome of the Rock, the promontory from which Muhammad is said to have ascended to heaven. In the mid-eighties there were spectacular arrests of bomb-carrying Messiah fanatics determined to begin rebuilding the Temple even if it meant blowing up the

Dome of the Rock and touching off a holy war—indeed, *because* such a conflagration might bring the Messiah sooner for the Final Battle.

Which may explain why Israeli authorities showed up at the Cave of the Column the day after the press conference and yanked Jones's dig permit.

Vendy packed up and left, but he vows he will return. From his headquarters at the Institute of Judaic-Christian Research in Arlington, Texas, Jones, a former Baptist who now calls himself a "non-Jewish believer in Judaism," tells me he's raising money for a new expedition. Last time, he says, he was *this* close to the Ark itself. At the time the Israelis closed down his dig, he and his crew had explored "six of the seven underground chambers in the Cave of the Column." He's convinced from the decryptions of the Copper Scroll made by his Israeli wife, Zahava, that the Ark must be there, in the seventh chamber.

But if it's not *there,* he assured me, he knows where it's *got* to be. Using what he calls "remote sensing technology" applied to aerial photographs of the Dead Sea wilderness site of Gilgal, he believes he can pinpoint another possible hiding place for the Ark. Remote sensing devices, he explains, can pick up things like "compression of dirt and traces of ancient trails" in a desert wilderness. He starts telling me about the time the Ark was seen at Gilgal: when the people of Israel gathered there for a mass circumcision before crossing over to the Promised Land. "They didn't circumcise in the wilderness," Jones says. "And there were over six hundred thousand circumcised at Gilgal."

"So you're saying you'll find the Ark by looking for the heavy, compressive tread of hundreds of thousands of men trudging toward adult circumcision?" I ask.

"Well, we don't expect to find the *foreskins,*" he says merrily, "but there's a joke you must have heard: You know why foreskins make good purses? Because you stroke 'em, they turn into suitcases!" He laughs uproariously. "You gotta have a sense of humor about these things," he adds. When I say goodbye he's still laughing, a swashbuckling Texan apparently unconcerned by the notion that he is playing with fire in the Holy Land.

My companions at Qumran tell me they're skeptical about Vendy's "atomic fingerprints" claim, but interested enough to investigate further. They invite me to accompany them when they pay a visit to an influential Messiah-theorist rabbi who'd been at Vendy Jones's dawn press conference and acclaimed the find as important. And who has his own stash of the sacred substance.

That evening, in one of the strangest moments of my reporting experience, the rabbi emerged from the kitchen of his suburban-Jerusalem home bearing a silver salver filled to the brim with the "fine reddish-brown powder." And there it was in front of us, the powder—it looked like gourmet chili powder—that some believe is the very perfume of the apocalypse.

"Rub it between your fingers, then sniff it," the rabbi suggested. "Taste it." I did all but the latter. It smelled, well, like *dirt* to me, although I must admit I wouldn't have recognized the atomic fingerprints of frankincense even if they had been there. But were they there? After we sniffed the incense, the rabbi himself admitted he had some questions about Vendy Jones's claim. It wasn't just that most academic archaeologists dismissed it. It was the problem with the Weizmann Institute scientific analysis. The institute, when called by reporters, claimed no connection with the report by the man who signed himself "chemical consultant" and who used some curious locutions for a scientist (a random sample "amazingly weighed exactly 26.0 grams"). Jones insists the tests themselves vindicate his find, regardless of the stationery question.

But doubts haven't dampened the rabbi's enthusiasm for the quest. He, too, had a theory about the Ark. He knew someone, he said, who had already located it. He told us about another rabbi he knows who was with a group of seekers when they secretly tunneled beneath the Dome of the Rock to explore the ruined foundations of the temple upon which the Muslim shrine rests. They were stopped mid-dig by Israeli authorities, but what's not generally known, what's only whispered about among the cognoscenti, is what happened just as they were halted.

They said they'd come within inches of breaking through a final layer of mortar to a still-intact chamber they were certain was nothing less than the secret compartment where the Ark had been hidden.

The authorities prevented them from breaking through, but the rabbi in the lead claimed to have heard—dimly but unmistakably—through the fragile subterranean masonry, an awesome *roaring* sound like a fierce wind. A sound he said he knew for sure was the roaring breath of God.

Part Two:
Entering "a Very Dark Hole"

In Which a Learned Man of God Speaks Gravely
About "the Curse of the Scrolls"

East Jerusalem. The courtyard garden of the palace of Pasha Rabbah Effendi el Husseini, now the American Colony Hotel.

Graham Greene stayed here, and one suspects Graham Greene would have loved the Reverend Dr. James Charlesworth and his obsession with his White Russian. You see, Reverend Charlesworth is accustomed to having his White

Russians concocted in a certain, *special* way by Ibrahim, bartender and long-time fixture of this Arabian Nights scene, which has hosted eminences from Lawrence of Arabia to Glubb Pasha. But Ibrahim is mysteriously absent tonight, and so, in the flickering candlelight of the courtyard garden, Reverend Charlesworth—Methodist minister, scholarly luminary of the Princeton Theological Seminary, and pillar of the Dead Sea Scroll establishment—has been trying, without much success, to explain to the new Arabic-speaking waiter exactly how to prepare White Russians, Ibrahim-style.

When the somewhat confused waiter departs, Reverend Charlesworth and I return to our conversation about Scroll scholars and their curious behavior. I ask him about the dark side of Scroll study. What might be called Scroll Scholar Syndrome. In reading the literature, I tell him, I was struck by the number of *calamitous* episodes that have befallen those who have gotten too deep into Dead Sea Scroll studies.

Consider the first unfortunate soul to bring forth ancient manuscripts from the Dead Sea shores, back in the late nineteenth century, a man named Shapira. He saw his find "declared a shameless forgery" by experts who denied any genuine manuscripts could have survived the harsh climate for two thousand years. Shapira, "the luckless purveyor" of the "forgery," was "hounded to a lonely and despairing suicide," according to one historian. Indeed, Shapira "blew his brains out in a Rotterdam hotel," *Biblical Archaeology Review* editor Hershel Shanks told me.

What is it about the Scrolls that brings misfortune to scholars? I ask Charlesworth.

He laughs. "Well, one *could* write a whole article about the Curse of the Scrolls. I've seen it since the fifties. There *is* something about the Scrolls. Let's just be objective: Some of the people who have worked most intensely on the Scrolls have either gone crazy, have suffered from severe alcoholism, have had nervous breakdowns, or have had the most *horrible* lives of confusion, lack of happiness, loss of self-identity. . . ."

An amazing summation, particularly coming from a scholar not otherwise prone to melodrama. In fact, one might say the lives of the Scroll *scholars* have been as gravely marked by messianic expectations and bitter disappointments as those of the Scroll *writers*.

Much of the drama has swirled around the members of the Scroll editorial team in Jerusalem, the elite group of scholars who hoarded the secrets of Qumran for four decades. It was King Hussein's government in then Jordanian East Jerusalem that initially gave the Scroll team its stranglehold on the manuscripts in 1953, naming a Dominican scholar-priest, Roland de Vaux, to head the team. They had full power to limit access to the texts to themselves and whichever favored few graduate students and acolytes they blessed with a precious fragment. Privileged access became the basis of lifelong academic careers, scholarly empire building—the Scrolls were the hot center of contemporary biblical studies and Scroll scholars became powerful, globe-trotting academic superstars.

It's hard to overestimate the atmosphere of acute anxiety at the time the Scroll team began its translations. Would the New Testament have to be rewritten because of the new testimony? It's true that most of the Scrolls proved *not* to be controversial—many of the relatively intact identifiable texts found were multiple copies of already well-known books of the Old Testament and the biblical Apocrypha. (A few scholars have argued that the Qumran corpus was actually a "library" collection of Scrolls written elsewhere.) The source of the nervousness, the potential shock value, was the so-called Sectarian texts, the ones that appeared to have been composed by the Scroll Sect writers themselves, the ones that analysis of scribal handwriting styles had placed in the period shortly before the time of Christ.

There were psalms, hymns, beatitudes, and liturgies of worship. But there were also detailed rules of communal living that emphasized common possessions, baptism, and a shared meal of bread and wine, and suggested to many a proto-Christian worship. There were earnest, painstaking reinterpretations of the prophetic books of the Bible, exegeses that made it seem that the prophecies were about *them,* about the community of the New Covenant, as they called themselves (shortly before the Christians used the term and long before Bill Clinton). And about the shadowy leader of the sect, a messianic figure they called the Teacher of Righteousness, who was preparing the way of the Lord in the wilderness. And about the enemies of the Righteous Teacher, the allegorically named Wicked Priest; the Spouter of Lies; and ancient slick-politician types they called the Seekers After Smooth Things.

It wasn't long before the trouble started: In 1956, John Allegro, one of the original members of the Scroll team, an Oxford-trained Hebrew scholar, gave a sensational interview to the BBC in which he argued that the Dead Sea Scrolls would make the Gospels look derivative if not obsolete. He claimed they showed that the Scroll Sect's Teacher of Righteousness had been crucified one hundred years before Jesus, and implied that the Gospel crucifixion story was at best a mythologized, hand-me-down version of the Dead Sea Scroll original—that the Righteous Teacher was the "real" Jesus.

Whatever the merits of Allegro's claim—and almost all of his Scroll-team colleagues denounced it as unsupported by the texts—there was something so megalomaniacal about his anti-Christian ambition that it went beyond an intellectual position. In a letter to his Oxford colleague John Strugnell, later to become editor in chief of the Scroll team, who'd been considering a career as a theologian, Allegro proclaimed that "by the time I've finished, there won't be any church left for you to join."

"Allegro had a fixation with finding the nontruth of Christian crucifixion," Strugnell says.

Allegro wanted, in other words, to be the Messiah of Atheism. He was treated like the Anti-Christ. Not till a decade later, when John Lennon declared that the Beatles were "more popular than Jesus," did a remark on the subject of religion cause more of an outcry. His mainstream colleagues ostracized Allegro, but he was a man possessed by Scroll Fever. He struck back with an even more blasphemous theory in 1970, when he published *The Sacred Mushroom and the Cross*. A book which advanced the outré thesis that there was *no* historical Jesus, that the name Jesus in the Gospels was a code word for the psychedelic mushroom *Amanita muscaria,* which, Allegro claimed, was the original sacrament of Christianity. Allegro, roundly ridiculed, went off to live in self-imposed exile on the Isle of Man.

Allegro's outbursts and, to a lesser extent, Edmund Wilson's more sober speculations in *The New Yorker* (he publicized the more moderate interpretation of the French scholar André Dupont-Sommer, which maintained that the Righteous Teacher had developed doctrines Jesus later popularized) gave birth to a torrent of popular mystical apocalyptic fantasies about the Dead Sea Scroll Sect, the Righteous Teacher as a yoga master–Jesus who learned the secrets of godhood during his Lost Years in India.

"By now," says Hershel Shanks, "there's a whole fantasy literature about what's in the Scrolls, with the supermarket tabloids talking about finding the cure for AIDS and the date of the Second Coming. It's even infected semischolarly work. You've probably seen this new work by Australian scholar Barbara Thiering, who claims Jesus was crucified at Qumran, kept alive with some snake poison, and later went to a Mediterranean island where he and his wife had two children, before he divorced, remarried, and died in Rome."

But by the mid-eighties the mainstream scholarly consensus on the Scrolls had solidified—and consigned the Scroll writers to a much less central role. The consensus had it that the authors were the Essenes, and though their teachings may have been part of the ferment Jesus absorbed, they were too far removed to have played an important role in His life. The Dead Sea Scrolls and Dead Sea Scroll studies had become a kind of Dead End.

But then, two years ago, Scroll Fever broke out of its Scroll-team quarantine and onto front pages worldwide. The Scroll team itself became the focus of a best-selling conspiracy theory: *The Dead Sea Scrolls Deception,* by Michael Baigent and Richard Leigh, charged that the committee was the cat's-paw of a Vatican cover-up suppressing bombshell Scroll texts.

Meanwhile, in Jerusalem, John Strugnell—the august head of the Scroll editorial team, the potentate of Qumran, the man who kept the Scrolls' secrets under his thumb—was self-destructing in a spectacular blaze of infamy, driven from his throne by a furor over remarks he allegedly made to a Tel Aviv newspaper calling Judaism a "horrible religion" that should have died out after Jesus appeared.

Strugnell: They were still talking about his fall in Jerusalem with a mixture of wonder and awe. If the Reverend Charlesworth is a pillar of the prestigious Scroll-scholar establishment, Strugnell was its *pinnacle*. He was a scholarly Master of the Ancient Universe with a degree from Oxford and a professorship at Harvard who had reigned over the international Scroll team since 1987. Hershel Shanks recalls Strugnell making an appearance at a U.S. conference of biblical scholars in the mid-eighties, bestriding the halls like a colossus, "dispensing new texts as if he were dropping crumbs from his table, everyone scrambling for them, feeling gratitude on the outside, rage within."

But with his reign threatened, Scroll Fever raging around his head, and his head about to roll, the besieged scholar king began spreading the word that if only he were left alone to *operate* he'd have a shot at bringing to light an unimaginably precious treasure. Yes, he was close to getting his hands on a long-rumored but never seen Qumran Scroll, the Aramaic Book of Enoch, the visionary, apocryphal account of the secrets of the angels, holy and fallen.

The surfacing of an original Book of Enoch would be a sensational coup, and Strugnell, burdened, as he now concedes, by drink and manic-depression, was spinning a sensational story about how he proposed to pull it off.

Something about a wealthy Kuwaiti who owned the Scroll but wanted to clandestinely liquidate this most priceless of assets in the wake of the Iraqi invasion. The piquant detail of this purported intrigue, the one that had people who heard it buzzing, was that the Kuwaiti had proposed smuggling a microfiche photo of the Scroll into Israel (for Strugnell to authenticate) by concealing it in the vagina of a Jordanian prostitute who would then stroll across the Allenby bridge, past the Israeli border police, and deliver it to Strugnell. The Book of Fallen Angels secreted inside a fallen angel. It was almost biblical, although probably apocryphal.* (Hershel Shanks says the way *he* heard the story, it was two prostitutes and they approached Strugnell in Bethlehem with, presumably, a two-part microfiche.)

The details are less important than the dramatic transformation in Strugnell: from a mild-mannered scholar of esoteric biblical philology into a swashbuckling adventurer, a veritable Vendyl Jones.

Shapira lost his life, Allegro lost his head, Strugnell lost his job and, for a while, his reason. What was it about the Scrolls that was responsible for this pattern of peculiar behavior Charlesworth called "the Curse of the Scrolls"?

In an uncharacteristically spooky footnote to his landmark Scroll work, Ed-

---

*An almost too literal embodiment of "the secret parts of Fortune."

mund Wilson made mention of what he called an ancient local superstition about some kind of "mysterious agency" that haunted the Qumran cliffs and repulsed unsuitable supplicants to the community there. And there is a parallel Jewish legend about the Evil Ones, fallen angels who haunt the wilderness there.

Reverend Charlesworth has a less supernatural explanation of the "curse": When scholars go into Scroll study, he tells me in Jerusalem, "we enter into a very dark hole. . . . Some of these men are geniuses, *extremely* brilliant people. . . . But to work intensively, from five in the morning through to three the next morning without a break, trying to piece together—"

At this point our waiter returns to set the long-awaited White Russian down in front of Charlesworth.

Who stares at it with a *deeply* pained expression.

"Can you put it in a bigger glass?" he asks the waiter. "And I need it, I need it to be *stirred*."

The waiter mumbles something sadly and walks away.

"Ibrahim's not here," Charlesworth tells me mournfully. "And I need it in a bigger glass," he says, calling after the waiter. "Ibrahim puts it in a *square* glass. And it needs to be *stirred*."

Ah, yes: the strain. Charlesworth goes on to attribute the breakdowns, the madness, the "horrible lives," not to a supernatural agency but to the sheer brain-burning mental strain of Scroll scholarship. Particularly on the impossibly fragmented Scrolls from Cave Four, the jigsaw puzzle from hell:

"I want you to put together six *hundred* jigsaw puzzles," he commands me as if I'm a Scroll-scholar initiate. "I'm giving you 100,000 *fragments*. Cave Four literally had 100,000 fragments. Some of the fragments are from documents thirty feet long; the fragments may be three feet apart. They are written by hundreds of different scribes . . . most of them you cannot read. Go: That's your instruction. Where would you begin? The first thing you start doing is shaking. And the more you look at it, the harder you work, the more intense it is. It would drive you *crazy*, the demands upon your mental powers."

Terrifying as it is, however, Charlesworth's mental-strain analysis of Scroll Scholar Syndrome neglects a more soul-wrenching dimension of the phenomenon: the spiritual stakes, the kind of Higher Instability of Faith that Scroll scholars seem to fall victim to. A remarkable number of the best and brightest of them have flickered back and forth from belief to unbelief to a new kind of belief. There have been losses of faith and leaps of faith, conversions and reversions. Twentieth-century Christians becoming first-century Jews: Professor James Tabor, raised an Evangelical Christian, gave that up in graduate school and found a new version of his faith in Scroll study—he now describes himself as a sort of modern "Ebionite," after the adherents of a long-extinct sect of Jewish followers of Jesus who Tabor believes were the spiritual heirs of the Qumran sect. Oxford Scroll mandarin Geza Vermes was born Jewish, raised Catholic, then returned to Judaism. Preeminent Israeli biblical scholar David Flusser is a Jew who has become such a champion of Christ's spiritual message that one sharp-tongued critic calls him "Mr. Jesus."

Why this Higher Instability? Because Scroll study forces one to focus with fierce intensity on that moment when Christianity and Judaism converged and diverged, when the membrane between the two was never more permeable. In a provocative recent essay called "Through That Glass Darkly" (in *Salmagundi*), George Steiner speaks of the historical moment of the Scroll writers as a period when apocalyptic, messianic longings "burnt a fever in time itself." An epoch whose remoteness from us—we have almost nothing firsthand *but* the Scrolls— obscures the answer to what Steiner calls a momentous question, one "almost wholly unexplored, in some Freudian sense perhaps suppressed: . . . [why] the core of Judaism rejects the messianic claims and promises put forward by Jesus of Nazareth."

That "very dark hole" the Scroll scholars enter: It's really that murky gap between the Old Testament and the New, the time when the two religions defined themselves against each other and changed the world forever. The real curse of the Scrolls may be a kind of spiritual Heisenberg uncertainty principle: The more microscopically one focuses on a few fragmentary texts, the more feverishly one attempts to find historical answers to spiritual questions, the more one tries to find, in effect, the fingerprints of God on a few tattered scraps of ancient fabric—the more uncertain one becomes, not just of what one's looking for, but of who one *is*.

Part Three:
In the Hall of the Heretic King

In Which We Hear About "a Staggering Discovery" and Stumble on the Seventh Seal

Huntington Beach, California. Orange County's original "Surf City," home to the International Surfing Museum. And home base to embattled Scroll dissident Professor Robert H. Eisenman, chairman of the Religious Studies Department at Cal State Long Beach, who from his academically unfashionable perch overthrew the monopoly of his Oxford-Harvard arch-rival, John Strugnell, liberating the Unpublished Corpus from the Scroll-team stranglehold.

Eisenman lives a few miles inland from the ocean, in a split-level suburb on La Batista Avenue. But don't try to make any ironic remarks to Eisenman about his living on "The Baptist" street. Don't portray him as a voice crying in the wilderness. He doesn't like the implication of isolation and doom, the rebellious prophet's bloody head on the plate.

He knows he has enemies. "I'm beset by Lilliputians! By people who are putting darts in me like idiots!" he tells me in one of his many rants against his antagonists in academic orthodoxy. "They're absolutely, totally *blind,* like the people in Plato's cave, who see no light and have not even a vague comprehension of these things."

And don't, says the very spin-conscious scholar, make any facile comparisons between him and his famous deconstructive architect-theorist brother, Peter Eisenman. (I'd made the mistake of remarking that one brother deconstructs the orthodoxy of form in Western culture, while the other disassembles the orthodoxy of spirit, the architecture of faith.)

"I think my brother purposely does things that are fun," Eisenman says, frowning, "and he likes to be naughty." He adds, a bit unnecessarily, "I'm not about 'naughty.' "

What is he about, this obsessed scholar-crusader? During the intense five-day stretch I spent with him, I found myself fascinated with the enigma of Eisenman, a smart, humorous, modern man, a good-natured husband and father of four—good-natured, that is, on any subject but his Scroll theory. On which he becomes a furious, evangelical zealot, a virtual incarnation of the Righteous Teacher, cursing his enemies, cursed by his obsession.

Now, the value of a scholarly theory should stand or fall on the character of the evidence, not on the psychology of the theorist. But it's almost impossible to discuss Eisenman's Scroll heresy without examining his "family secret." A secret which, depending on your point of view, either has given him the special kind of insight he needed to unlock the true secret of the Dead Sea Scrolls or has led him to project his personal history onto the Scroll texts and make them into a mirror of his own mind. "Did Eisenman tell you about his family?" Jim Tabor asked me when we were out at the Qumran caves. "It's pretty amazing when you think about it, the connection to his theory."

Eisenman did tell me, one evening in Huntington Beach. He'd been a whiz-kid physics student at Cornell in the mid-fifties, a classmate of Thomas Pynchon, exhibiting only a mild foretaste of his later rebellious temperament, when he took part with Pynchon in a student march on the president's house. Then, just as he was about to leave for Israel for the first time, to work on a kibbutz, Eisenman learned a secret about his family that, he told me, was "one of the eye-openers of my life."

It had to do with the hidden paternal side of his family. Eisenman's mother came from a German-Jewish family that had arrived in the States in the 1830s and was proud of its assimilated Americanness. So proud, according to Eisenman, that they displayed a snobbish disdain for his father's Russian-Jewish immigrant family, who'd arrived a half-century later.

"But just at the time I was going to Israel," Eisenman told me that night as we were cruising up the Pacific Coast Highway in his ancient gray Mercedes, "suddenly my father appeared and said, 'Uh, son, you know you have a family in Jerusalem.' "

It turned out much of his "Russian" family was actually living in Jerusalem. But his father had concealed their existence from him. "And there I was, twenty-two, twenty-three years old, and up to that time he had never breathed a word that we had a family in Jerusalem."

Eisenman still seems astonished by his father's complicity in this effort to conceal what his mother's family regarded as a literally unspeakable side of his identity: its unassimilated Jewishness.

And then when he went to Jerusalem he made a further discovery: "It was absolutely staggering. . . . It wasn't just a *family* in Jerusalem. It turned out my great-grandfather had come to Jerusalem at the time the Turks settled there. . . . He'd founded a religious hospital, the Bikur Holim. . . . They were in *everything* there. They were in the electric company, the law courts, the Jewish Agency. And when I came there I was treated like royalty returning—and in all the twenty-two years in America no one breathed a word about it!"

I was treated like royalty returning. The fantasy that one is actually the secret heir to royalty raised incognito by an ordinary family until destiny calls was dubbed "the Family Romance" by Freud. But, for Eisenman, *his* royal family was a reality—repressed by Jewish self-hatred.

The eureka moment for Eisenman, the one that linked his family romance to his Scroll theory, came in 1976, he told me, when he was teaching a New Testament class and rereading the New Testament Epistle of James, the brother of Jesus. That work and certain Epistles of Paul, like Galatians, speak of a time in the immediate aftermath of the crucifixion. When James, presiding over something referred to as "the Jerusalem Church"—the mostly Jewish nucleus of apostles and disciples of Jesus—came into conflict with the apostle Paul, who was traveling in the north making converts among the Gentiles.

The Epistles depict Paul getting into a serious dispute with James's Jerusalem Church. Would the new converts have to follow the strictures of Jewish Law, including, for instance, adult circumcision (James's position), or could they win salvation just by faith in Jesus and his New Covenant alone (Paul's more accessible view)?

Eisenman was struck by how much the theology, the imagery, of James, particularly in the matters of strict observance of the Law, resembled the beliefs, the language and imagery, of the Scroll Sect's Righteous Teacher in *his* dispute with his enemies, the Seekers After Smooth Things, the Spouter of Lies. And how the debate between James and Paul was the genesis of a centuries-long split in the early church between the "Judaizers" and the "anti-Judaizers."

The more Eisenman looked into the neglected figure of James, and the other members of Jesus' family (he had four brothers according to one Gospel), the more he began to believe that the Jewish family of Jesus had been deliberately erased from history by anti-Judaizing editors of the New Testament. That the importance of the Jerusalem Church of James—first-century Jews for Jesus—had been edited from collective memory the way Eisenman's Jewish family in Jerusalem had—and for the same reason: The heirs were embarrassed by their unassimilated Jewishness.

Although the full truth about the shadowy Jerusalem Church may have been obscured by the victorious anti-Judaizers—whose zeal Eisenman blames for the horrors of Christian anti-Semitism—Eisenman believes we can recapture the spirit, the soul, of James's "original" Jewish Christianity by looking at the Dead Sea Scroll Sect. The more extreme formulation of his theory—that James actually *was* the Scroll Sect's Righteous Teacher—has come under withering fire from academics who dismiss it as impossible on the basis of paleography (the dating of ancient documents through scribal handwriting) and carbon 14 dating, both of which Eisenman deems too imprecise for certainty within a hundred years.

But under attack Eisenman tends to fall back to a more moderate position: that James and his Jerusalem Church were a direct outgrowth or branch of a broader messianic movement that included the Scroll Sect.

In a recent issue of Hershel Shanks's *Biblical Archaeology Review,* James Tabor and University of Chicago professor Michael Wise, Eisenman's co-translator, argue that the language in one previously unpublished Qumran fragment, which Shanks colorfully describes as "the Cosmic Messiah Text," explicitly foreshadows the description of Jesus that appears in Luke 7:22—a Messiah who heals the sick, raises the dead, and preaches glad tidings to the poor. "It's perhaps the strongest, most specific linguistic link so far between Qumran and Christianity," Tabor told me.

And there are signs that some more mainstream academics—like NYU's Lawrence Schiffman—are also questioning the orthodox view that the Qumran sect were pacifist, irrelevant Essenes.

But don't try to tell Eisenman his views may finally be gaining some acceptance. They're coming around, he says, but they're not giving him credit, because they're "low, extremely ungracious, in fact, cowardly, servile," he tells me. Schiffman, he adds, is "a running dog of the Establishment." (Schiffman denies his work owes anything to Eisenman. "His wild theories are totally unsubstantiated," Schiffman fires back, "and he misrepresents the true significance of the Dead Sea Scrolls as ancient Jewish texts.")

Still, Eisenman says, he's not bitter. He takes satisfaction in having already achieved some stunning victories: After all, he points out more than once, "I'm just about *solely* responsible for getting the Scrolls opened up."

Opening up the Scrolls: This summer in his office on La Batista Avenue, Eisenman afforded me an exclusive look at the first translations of the Unpublished Corpus he and Wise are rushing into print.

It was thrilling to read them aloud into my tape recorder (Eisenman wouldn't allow a single slip of paper out of the house for fear of a leak) and hear the words of writers who'd been silent for so long. Although, after a while, I did find myself a bit oppressed by Eisenman's insistence on leaning over my shoulder and stabbing his finger at the page whenever he found any imagery he felt vindicated his theory against the Lilliputian enemies besieging him.

Still, reading the long-silent texts aloud gave me a feeling for the cumulative power of the Qumran writers, a passion that came through even in these badly fragmented, conjecturally reconstructed texts. Indeed, Eisenman was a bit taken aback at my enthusiasm, particularly for texts which *he* didn't consider decisive for his embattled polemic, but which I liked for their forceful poetry. However, a few weeks later he called to tell me that, influenced by my reaction, he'd changed the provisional titles he'd given to some of the fragments to reflect the drama (or melodrama) I'd been responding to. Thus, "A Fragmentary Apocalypse" became "The Tree of Evil (A Fragmentary Apocalypse)"; "Beatitudes" became "The Demons of Death." And the ultra-dry-sounding "A Record of Sectarian Discipline" became the semi-gross "He Loved His Bodily Emissions (A Record of Sectarian Discipline)."

There is one text that he'd originally titled "The Messiah at War" that's already put Eisenman at war. This fragment, which has been popularly known as the "Slain Messiah" text, was the first bombshell Eisenman brought forth from the liberated texts and hurled into the popular press, earlier this year— one which subsequently blew up in his face. Eisenman's discovery was a cryptic reference to a "slain" or "pierced" messiah. A reference predating Christ which seemed to be a sensational challenge to the uniqueness of the Gospel crucifixion story. But an onslaught of orthodox scholars led by Oxford's Geza Vermes charged that Eisenman and his co-translator had made a glaring grammatical mistake, mistranslating what was really a reference to a messiah who *slays his enemies*. While Eisenman defends his interpretation, saying the text can be read both ways, at the very least he was left looking like he'd unwisely rushed to judgment.

The temptation to jump the gun, to find *something* in these maddeningly teasing fragments is a seductive and perhaps dangerous one (think of all the blood that's already been shed arguing over interpretations of ambiguous ancient texts). I felt a touch of this Scroll Fever one afternoon while I was racing through Eisenman's translations of the Unpublished Corpus. It happened when I was reading into my tape recorder one of the more exotic texts, a forty-two-line fragment that Eisenman had called "Stories Concerning the Adventures of Jews at the Court of the Persian Kings."

It's an atypical Scroll text, more fabulist than religious, suggestive of a novelistic imagination—all that's left of a lost Jewish *Arabian Nights.* The passage that struck me reads, "Among the books was found a cer[tain] scroll [sea]lled by seven seals (impressed by) the signet ring of Darius."

"Could this be the source of the seven seals in the Book of Revelations?" I asked Eisenman.

"It probably has something to do with it," he said dismissively.

Those who remember the Seventh Seal passage from the Book of Revelations (or the Bergman film) recall that after the climactic opening of the Seventh Seal, all hell will literally break loose, bloody plagues from the bottomless pit will be unleashed upon the earth in the final apocalyptic holocaust.

It struck me what's unleashed upon the world when the seventh seal in the Persian-court text is opened is a *scroll*—perhaps a metaphor for the havoc unleashed when the jars that contained the Dead Sea Scrolls were unsealed.

But I couldn't get Eisenman interested in my Seventh Seal conjecture. It just doesn't show up as a blip on his radar. Which is now focused with laser-like intensity on an "absolutely staggering" discovery that he says will be the big news in his forthcoming book of translations. This one, he says, "will force us to rewrite the entire raison d'être of Christianity as we know it. Just *mind-boggling.*"

The fragment he's referring to is No. 4Q266, one he entitles "The Foundations of Righteousness (The End of the Damascus Covenant: An Excommunication Text)." What he's found the fragment to be, he says, is, in essence, a *curse.* Not a curse of the Scrolls, a curse *in* the Scrolls: an elaborate formal communal curse he believes to be the excommunication sentence read to those who transgressed the strict commandments of the Qumran sect. Here in the Eisenman-Wise translation is how the curse reads:

> His soul has rejected the Foundations of Righteousness.
> For rebellion, let him be expelled from the presence of the Many. . . .
> 'Boundary markers were laid down for us.'
> Those who cross over them,
> You curse . . .

What makes it so staggering, he claims, is that the cursing language used seems to be mirrored by the language Paul uses in Galatians when he describes his split with the Jerusalem Church of James. The Jamesians censured Paul because he dismissed the importance of fidelity to Jewish Law. Paul responded by proclaiming that the Jewish Law was "a curse" that Jesus had redeemed mankind from.

Eisenman calls Paul's inversion of the cursing language in the Qumran excommunication text, and his turning the curse against the Jews, "the fundamental basis of Western religious expression." Paul, says Eisenman, "turns this around, and then all Jews ever after are hanged . . . have to go around as the enemies of the whole human race. And that, of course," Eisenman concludes, "ends up in the Holocaust."

This is a lot of weight for a connection based mainly on the similarity of language structures to bear. It is, I believe, an example of the way Eisenman's hostile obsession with Paul as the source of Christian anti-Semitism—Paul as the villain in the "family romance" of Jewish Christianity, Paul as the archetypal self-hating Jew—has become the lens through which Eisenman looks at the evidence now. This is his version of the Scroll curse: It's cursed his ability to look at the texts objectively, and often has *him* cursing those who don't accept his theory as insufficiently opposed to the anti-Semitism he says is inherent in the New Testament.

On the other hand, it must be said that in his arch-rival, John Strugnell, Eisenman found someone who fills that bill precisely, the perfect enemy—the Wicked Priest to his Righteous Teacher, the Paul to his James.

Strugnell, disgraced and deposed, is still a sore point with Eisenman. A very sore point, one that can be traced back to a remarkably dramatic showdown—a real *mano a mano* duel between him and Strugnell one wild night in Jerusalem.

One evening over dinner at their favorite Italian place in Huntington Beach, Eisenman and his wife, Heather (a Scottish-born convert to Judaism), paint the duel in dramatic detail for me. The year was 1986. Eisenman had been awarded a National Endowment for the Humanities fellowship to pursue his Scroll studies in Jerusalem. There was one part of the Unpublished Corpus he particularly wanted to examine: the so-called Zadokite fragments of the Damascus Document, including that very same 4Q266 fragment, he says, which would later turn out to contain the Excommunication Curse he showed me.

They wouldn't let him see it. The Scroll team, including Strugnell, wouldn't cooperate at all, he says. But one night in Jerusalem not long after this rebuff, Eisenman found himself face-to-face with Strugnell at a Scroll-scholar soirée.

It was an uneasy encounter from the beginning, one he later chronicled in *Midstream,* a monthly Jewish affairs magazine. According to Eisenman and his wife, as the evening wore on, Strugnell grew more and more spirited and attentive toward Mrs. Eisenman, questioning her at one point about why she'd converted to Judaism and married a Jew. Strugnell then suggested that they take a drive out beyond the gates of the city to greet the dawn over Moab from the top of the Mount of Olives. "My presence was immaterial to him," Eisenman recalls laconically.

In the event, dawn found all three of them drinking together when the duel began. Strugnell "proposed a curious toast," Eisenman recalls in *Midstream*. "Turning to me in the lucid way some alcoholics have, he asked whether I was prepared to drink to anyone he proposed."

Intrigued, Eisenman assented.

"Thereupon he raised his glass and said he wanted to drink 'to the greatest living man of the latter part of the twentieth century.' " Strugnell then pronounced his choice: "Kurt Waldheim."

"I drank and quietly replaced my glass," Eisenman writes, "searching my mind for a name that would cause him as much distress as he had caused me."

At last Eisenman came up with just the name: Orde Wingate, the English general famous for leading "Wingate's Raiders" in World War II Burma. More to the point, Eisenman explains, Wingate was "an ardent Zionist from his days in Palestine in the thirties. He had been the pro-Jewish T. E. Lawrence of that time. . . . He had laid the foundation for the Israeli army and trained all of Israel's future military leaders of the next generation. . . .

"I therefore said to Strugnell, 'I drank to whomever you asked, will you now drink to whomever I ask?' He nodded his head: Certainly. 'All right,' I said, 'I want to drink to Orde Wingate. . . .' "

According to Eisenman, "Strugnell was mortified: He knew who Wingate was. A wave of trapped anger swept across his face. '*No,*' he said, slamming his glass on the table. 'I will not drink to that traitor!' "

(Strugnell, now dismissed from his eminence, in exile up in Cambridge, Massachusetts, told me there was "some conversation" about Waldheim in which he criticized Israeli "intervention" in Austrian politics over the issue—but he denied any competition of toasts, and denied he *believes* Waldheim was "the greatest man," etc. Eisenman and his wife insist their version is faithful and there could be no mistaking the thrust of the remark.)

That one moment, Eisenman now says, impelled him to launch his crusade, against Strugnell, against what he calls "the Strugnell mind-set," which ruled the Scrolls and kept the Unpublished Corpus under wraps.

In that moment, he feels, Strugnell's mask of scholarly objectivity slipped off, long before he told the world Judaism was a "horrible religion." "Here I am, faced with the situation that the Israeli authorities are giving *this* person total control of the Scrolls. . . . *That's* what set me off."

Part Four:
A Visit to a Fallen Angel

*In Which We Learn About the Enoch Intrigue and
the True Meaning of the Word "Horrible"*

He won't be there. In August the Annenberg Research Institute in Philadelphia convened a yearlong colloquium of some of the world's leading Scroll scholars, an ambitious attempt to define the state of the art of Scroll scholarship in the face of the unruly outbreak of Scroll Fever among the masses.

But John Strugnell, once the chief luminary of the Scroll-scholar world, won't be there. Instead, he'll most likely be *here* in Cambridge, in an ancient top-floor flat across the street from the Harvard Divinity School. He'll be here, painfully ascending the creaking stairs of the walk-up with a cane, shuffling from bookshelf to bookshelf in the small apartment stacked to the ceiling with the lifetime's worth of books and papers he brought back from Jerusalem, seeking to pluck some reference or other for the memoirs he's writing. Memoirs he hopes will set the record straight on what he calls his "calamities."

"What do they say of my calamities in Jerusalem?" Strugnell queries wistfully when I call him up to arrange a visit to his place of exile.

Depends on who you ask. Both Magen Broshi, head of Jerusalem's Shrine of the Book—the museum that now has physical possession of most of the intact Scrolls—and Hebrew University scholar David Flusser spoke warmly if sadly about Strugnell as a colleague and asked me to give him their regards. Both attributed his "Judaism is a horrible religion" remarks to his "sickness," the drink and manic-depression he was suffering from in the final years of his reign over the Scrolls. A sickness which, Strugnell tells me, he now has under control, but only after his children briefly committed him to Massachusetts's famed McLean Hospital, the recovery retreat of choice for distressed Harvard geniuses dating back to Robert Lowell.

Is he a fallen angel, or, as Eisenman sees him, a kind of Wicked Priest?

Strugnell evokes a humbler image these days: "A squeezed orange."

It is an image he employs in response to my citation of Reverend Charlesworth's "Curse of the Scrolls" litany.

Strugnell doesn't like the supernatural, Mummy's Tomb connotation of *curse,* but he agrees there is a tremendous *strain* in Scroll study. "I mean, obviously when you look so closely into the origins of Christianity and Judaism—the texts that we are specializing in are the *only* new texts that we have or we're likely to have. And the only way to get anything out of it is like an orange. To squeeze harder and harder, and make sure you get the maximum." He pulls himself forward in his rickety old swivel chair with the aid of his cane. "And there is a danger of excess there. That you squeeze *too* hard . . ."

He's speaking of squeezing the texts, but the subtext—the squeezing of John Strugnell—is not far from the surface.

It started shortly after his ascension to Scroll editorship, one of the most prestigious posts in the world of international scholarship. A day-school student at St. Paul's in London, Strugnell went to Oxford with thoughts of studying for the Presbyterian ministry, but got caught up in the excitement of Scroll scholarship, going to Jerusalem to replace John Allegro on the Scroll team. Although Strugnell is known for editing only one major Scroll text, hymns of praise he entitled "An Angelic Liturgy," he made his bones as a Scroll scholar in a kind of avenging-angel role: publishing a savage 114-page "correction" of Allegro's alleged translation errors.

Strugnell, who took charge of the Scroll editorial team in 1987, defends his stormy tenure by blaming the glacial pace of publication on the regime of his predecessor, the Dominican Father Benoit. Indeed, as far back as 1977, in Benoit's reign, Oxford's Scroll expert Geza Vermes had warned that the delay in releasing texts was "likely to become the academic scandal *par excellence* of the twentieth century." Strugnell claims that when he took over he was energetically trying to squeeze the recalcitrant scholars into emitting more texts from the Unpublished Corpus—*had* them on a speeded-up schedule. But by then it was too late; *New York Times* coverage of the "scandal" lit a fire under the Israeli authorities, who began squeezing Strugnell. Who admits he was in a state of collapse around the time he gave the interview that got him fired.

As for that "horrible" interview, with Avi Katzman in *Ha'aretz,* the Tel Aviv newspaper, Strugnell insists at great length to me that his remarks were taken out of context, that the interviewer had asked him to address the question of a historian's objectivity. And that in explaining how a conscientious historian had to be vigilant about his subjective biases, he'd instanced his own Catholicism (he converted in the mid-seventies), and what he called "the classical Christian theological argument" that Judaism's Old Covenant had been *replaced* by Christianity's New Covenant, making it obsolete. As for using the word *horrible,* he insists that he was using it in the Miltonic sense ("I went to Milton's school," St. Paul's). *Horrible* in the Miltonic sense means "deplorably in antiquity," Strugnell tells me, in the sense of a religion that depends on primal awe, horripilation.

The *Oxford English Dictionary* does cite *horrible* in the sense of "inspiring awe and dread." It describes the usage as *primarily* "of things objectionable, but often without such qualification." Still, Strugnell would have to be "deplorably in antiquity" himself not to know that the use of the word *horrible* to characterize someone's religion would offend people, regardless of Miltonic connotations.

While he denies any personal animus against Jews, he does say he objects to Israeli policies toward the Palestinians. And in fact, he says, his sympathetic relationships with Arab and Palestinian sources are key factors that put him in a unique and indispensable position to be the intermediary between the shadowy possessors of the Unseen Scrolls and the outside world. The Unseen Scrolls: not the Unpublished Corpus, which are now out, but the Scrolls that have *never* been read, some of them never even *unrolled*.

Which brings us to the intrigue over the Enoch Scroll. Not only does it exist, Strugnell says, it's the tip of the iceberg. There are no fewer than *four* intact Scrolls out there, he claims—a sensational story if true, even more sensational if they could be brought to light.

Which is what he was working on when he was deposed, he says. What he's still working on now, he implies.

"If he can really come up with Enoch," James Tabor tells me, "it would be incredible. We only have Enoch in Ethiopic," he explains, and the earliest extant version is a fourteenth-century copy, done after Enoch was excluded from the canon by the early church. Most scholars suspect the Enoch we have was heavily censored by church copyists over the centuries. "When you go from the Old Testament to the New Testament," Tabor says, "the single book that really fills you in on this whole world of religious development is Enoch, which has angels in heaven, all the stuff that is mostly passé in the New Testament outside Revelations. You think, Where the hell did this kind of Jewish occultism, cosmic speculation, come from? And Enoch is the book."

The prospect of finding an Original Enoch is particularly enticing because of its bearing on what, to me, is the most interesting aspect of the Scroll Sect's theology: the way they wrestled with the problem of evil and the role of the angelic Watchers.

Wrestle is literally the word here. I mentioned to Strugnell what Israeli biblical scholar David Flusser calls "the Dark Side" of the Scroll Sect: their invention of a radical predestination doctrine known as the Two Spirit Theology. In which one's soul is said to be fated for all eternity, blessed or cursed as the result of a kind of angelic wrestling match between two of the "Watcher" spirits (as they're called in Enoch and Scroll texts): a Good Angel and an Evil Angel, who struggle for possession of your soul *long before the creation of the world,* while God looks on, a kind of Watcher of the Watchers Himself, a passive spectator to this Cosmic Wrestling Federation Soul Slamathon.

But Strugnell spoke quite lucidly about more subtle aspects of the Two Spirit Theology: The Scroll writers are not always rigidly consistent on predestination. Some texts indicate that one's *own* struggles with good and evil can influence the outcome of the angelic wrestling match; others suggest the struggle was not decided *before* the creation, but is still going on *within us* now.

One can certainly sense the Two Spirits struggling within Strugnell (apt name, is it not?) as he hints at how he thinks the Enoch intrigue might be consummated: He'd like to surface the Scroll, but he'd like to make sure it surfaces as *his* Scroll.

He tells me that because of "questions of high finance and Jordanian law" he's "not at liberty to tell you [anything more] except that it exists." But he goes on to hint strongly that he could still play an important role in bringing the lost Book of Angels to light.

"*When* the owner wants to get rid of it, and there is a public library willing to buy it, under all the conditions of international law and Jordanian law and so on—at *that* time," he says, choosing his words carefully, "I could certainly suggest, you know, who would be the best scholar to edit it." After all, he adds, "that used to be my job."

That used to be my job. What he's hinting at here, it seems, is more than the resurfacing of the Enoch Scroll, but a resurfacing of John Strugnell, reascension to his lost preeminence. Perhaps the curatorship of a well-endowed institute exclusively dedicated to the New Finds?

The timing is right. The last secrets of the known Dead Sea Scrolls—the Unpublished Corpus texts—are finally out. New unknown Scrolls would cause a sensation. Perhaps the Lost Aramaic Book of Angels will yet serve to resurrect *this* fallen angel.

Part Five:
A Vision of the King of Evil

In Which We Watch the Watchers Wrestle for Our Souls

One night two thousand years ago, one of the initiates at the Qumran monastery had a very bad dream. "The Testament of Amram," one of the most striking visionary works in the Dead Sea Scrolls, has the unmistakable feeling of a real nightmare. Or worse, perhaps it wasn't a dream—perhaps it was a waking vision, something chilling he encountered one night outside the walls beneath the cliffs of the Judaean desert.

It was a vision of the very face of the Evil One wrestling for possession of his soul.

The next day, one may conjecture, the writer sat down and unrolled a length of scroll, dipped his sharpened quill into his inkwell in the monastery's scriptorium, and inscribed the text that has come down to us—in fragmentary form—as "The Testament of Amram." Much of it has been lost, but not the power of the following glimpse of the face of Evil. Here is the Eisenman-Wise translation of the vision:

[I saw Watchers] in my vision, the dream-vision. Two (men) were fighting over me . . . holding a great contest over me. I asked them, "Who are you, that you are thus empo[wered over me?" They answered me, "We] [have been em]powered and rule over all mankind." They said to me, "Which of us do yo[u choose to rule (you)?" I raised my eyes and looked.] [One] of them was terr[i]fying in his appearance, [like a s]erpent, [his] cl[oa]k many-colored yet very dark. . . . [And I looked again], and . . . in his appearance, his visage like a viper. . . . [I replied to him,] "This [Watcher,] who is he?" He answered me, "This Wa[tcher . . .] [and his three names are Belial and Prince of Darkness] and King of Evil."

Okay, it's a bit literal-minded in a surreal way. One wishes that all the Evil Ones of the world were as readily identifiable by their telltale writhing viper faces as this Watcher was. Or as happy to identify themselves—*Please allow me to introduce myself*—as the King of Evil.

But there's more to it than that. There's a deeper anxiety beneath the surface horror show in the text, one that reflects better than almost any other Scroll vision the tension in the Two Spirit Theology over God's role in the persistence, the apparent *triumph,* of evil in the world—a question that still torments theologians and the millions of troubled people who buy books like *When Bad Things Happen to Good People.*

The Scroll Sect doesn't have the kind of consoling answers of the sort that the book does. The Scroll writer who calls himself "Amram" seems to be offered a choice of which Watcher, Good or Evil, he wishes to be ruled by, but the subtext here is the conspicuous *absence* of God in the decision-making process: He appears to be just a passive watcher of the Watchers, apparently uninvolved in the outcome of the struggle between Good and Evil, helpless to affect the decision.

Yes, it's true "The Testament of Amram" (in the Vermes translation) concludes with the obligatory affirmation that ultimately, finally, "the Sons of Darkness will be burnt" and sent to "perdition." But it sounds like whistling past the graveyard: All around them the Scroll Sect writers could see the innocent being slaughtered; not the wicked but the righteous were being burnt; the Messiah was late, or never coming; God seemed to have abandoned the field to the grappling of the Watchers; the thrice-named Evil One in the vision of Amram comes across as far more formidable than the Good Angel.

In a Jerusalem study lined with books in a dozen ancient languages, David Flusser, professor emeritus at Hebrew University and biblical scholar extraordinaire, tried to convince me that the Scroll Sect had the answer to the paradox of God's role in the persistence of evil. Assuming the voice of a Righteous Teacher, he declaimed, "Evil exists by the *decision* of God. It exists because God decided that the struggle against it will help you [in your spiritual evolution] and you will recognize the truths, and at the end the wickedness will disappear as smoke, and the world will be as full of the truths of God's grace as of the sun." Flusser concluded triumphantly: "Despair is the thing against which you must *fight* to be purified."

An impressive rationale for the riddle of evil, but it still seems to put God in the position of being a kind of cruel aerobics instructor of the soul—pumping up its spiritual strength by forcing it to "feel the burn" of suffering, defeat, and despair.

Which is a little too pat to be entirely consoling. I have to give Eisenman credit: Although I have my doubts about his heretical Scroll theory, he is one of the few Scroll scholars who seem to have a real feel for the inconsolable, indeed heroic, pathos of the Scroll Sect's doomed followers.

"They're watching a moment when everything is falling apart around them," Eisenman told me. "You would weep because they know everything is being destroyed around them. They *know* that they're losing everything."

We spoke about the comparable position of pre-Holocaust European Jews, unable to believe God would allow them to perish and evil to prevail. The Scroll Sect, Eisenman said, "never stopped thinking God will not forget His people. That's why I say this is an extremely poignant moment," the eve of their destruction.

"But He *did* abandon them, didn't He?" I suggested. "They lost, they disappeared."

"But they didn't lose hope. They went to their death believing. They had no reason to keep believing, but they did, and they were ready to die for their beliefs. I have to admire them for that."

No one knows exactly what happened to the Scroll writers, exactly how they perished. Some say they fled the monastery under Roman assault, having first hidden their sacred texts in jars in the caves for the day when they'd return to greet the Messiah. Others believe they may have been among those who held out until the end at Masada during the final Jewish revolt, and chose suicide over surrender there. Still others believe they died out quietly somewhere in the desert wasteland on the other side of the Dead Sea.

We have no account of their last days. They bequeathed us a mystery and, it seems, a curse upon all who pretend to be able to solve it on the basis of the fragmentary evidence left behind.

Do not understand me too quickly, André Gide implored his readers. After two thousand years it may still be too soon to understand the Scroll writers. Or, worse, too late.

In the Nabokov Archives

In Which We Trace Certain Patterns on Wings

Needless to say, I pounced on the *Pale Fire*s first. Not one, but several editions inscribed with the cryptic annotations of the Master himself. There was, in fact, a veritable treasure of other never-before-seen-in-public, personally inscribed Nabokov editions piled up before me in the East Seventy-sixth Street premises of Glenn Horowitz Bookseller. Nabokov annotating Nabokov!

But first, *Pale Fire:* that stunning novel in the form of annotations on a 999-line poem in heroic couplets is a singular obsession of mine, one of my great loves in all of literature. One that I feel is a kind of *test,* in the sense that I'm just not sure I can trust those who resist it.

This is not an elitist sentiment: I swear I got into an argument about the *Pale Fire* narrator question (was it V. Botkin, as certain clues in the unreliable index suggest, was it John Shade, as the so-called Shadeans insist, or is the question meant to be infinitely reflexive, ultimately undecidable?) at a high-stakes poker game last month. Okay, the poker player happened to be a Harvard comp lit major who'd been unduly influenced by fashionable aporist postmodern theory in his argument for undecidability; but we conducted the argument between hectic rounds of seven-card stud, so don't call us effete esthetes. It's an important issue!* And poker is not irrelevant.

Important because it bears upon the powers and limitation of the creative imagination as embodied in the mind of Vladimir Nabokov, who authored a parallel world that rivals, in its unique beauty and complexity and sadness, the Creation brought into being by that other Supreme Esthete, God. Was the man who was perhaps the supreme aesthetic intelligence of this century a believer in ultimate coherence, or incoherence? In a God who played poker and rolled dice, or one who performed exquisitely beautiful card tricks?

In any case, the *Pale Fire*s I pounced on were part of an extremely unusual collection of books culled from the personal library of the Nabokov family. Unusual, because these were, in effect, the Nabokovs' *lares* and *penates,* the family's household gods. After VN died, his beloved wife Véra kept them with her wherever she traveled. There are, in particular, his personal copies of his own books, ones that over the years he inscribed with sometimes surprising, sometimes cryptic, sometimes revealing annotations and emendations. Reading through them was for me, a lifelong VN devotee, something akin to being at play in the fields of the Lord. In addition, there are presentation copies of books he gave to Véra, many of them inscribed with beautiful hand-drawn figures of butterflies, the expression of his lifelong obsessive love of lepidopterology.

---

*For those who care (and I hope you do) but don't recall the details, the novel begins with that 999-line poem, the last, unpublished work of a recently murdered (fictional) American poet, John Shade. The poem is now in the hands of a strange, self-proclaimed close friend of the murdered poet who made off with it. Holed up in a tourist cabin, he has produced some two hundred pages of Commentary, keyed like footnotes to the line numbers of the poem. This expansive Commentary constitutes the bulk of the novel, and just who wrote the Commentary is the heart of the argument over *Pale Fire* (well, one of the arguments). The author of the Commentary says his name is Charles Kinbote but discloses that his secret, true identity is "Charles the Beloved," the exiled king of Zembla, "a Northern land," who lost his throne to a revolution and has come to roost on the faculty of the college where Shade taught. The agenda of his sometimes mad, sometimes bad, sometimes both sad and brilliant Commentary is to convince the world that this last work of Shade's genius is really about *him:* that although it seems to be centered around Shade's loss of his daughter, Hazel, it's really about his, Kinbote's, loss of his kingdom.

But who really is Kinbote? Suggestive clues in the Commentary's Index, and in notes found in Nabokov's papers, have led many to believe the real author of the Commentary is V. Botkin, a minor figure in the novel. But a whole school of partisans known as "Shadeans" have adopted the argument made by Nabokov's most comprehensive biographer, Brian Boyd: that both the poem *and* the Commentary were written by one person, the poet, Shade, who invented a mad Russian commentator on his poem. I've cared enough to devote four *Observer* columns to arguing that Boyd's position was unnecessarily—and un-Nabokovianly—reductive. The aporists, like my Harvard friend, believe it is a mystery designed not to be solved but to deepen with its own undecidability. The latest development, in Brian Boyd's new book on *Pale Fire*, is Boyd's abandonment of his long-held Shadean position—and his adoption of an even more esoteric theory: that the real author or "inspirer" of the Commentary was the ghost of John Shade's dead daughter, Hazel, sending muselike messages from beyond the grave. *Pale Fire* scholars share some of the, well, intensity, of Dead Sea Scroll scholars.

In fact, for me perhaps the single most thrilling object in the collection, one of the single most thrilling graven images I've encountered, the one book in the collection that most seemed to *speak* from beyond the grave and the graven realms, was a unique Nabokov book, one he created himself by hand, one never before seen by the world, and one that I believe discloses an important secret about his esoteric passion.

In the rare book trade, this sort of one-of-a-kind volume is known as a "nonce," a near-archaic term for a book that has not been published in multiples but was handmade, created in lonely splendor, once and once alone. This particular nonce, bound in tan cloth covers, was a gift of love VN gave to Véra, a kind of distillation of the other great passion of his life. It is, this nonce, a carefully stitched-together collection of ten of his favorite lepidopteral studies. Some were never reprinted after their initial appearance in such arcane publications as Harvard University's *Bulletin of the Museum of Comparative Zoology* (which devoted an entire issue to VN's "The Nearctic Members of the Genus Lycaeides . . ."), *The Lepidopterists' News,* and the wonderfully named quarterly of butterfly studies, *Psyche.*

Some have seen VN's lepidopteral obsession as a kind of eccentricity, if not an affectation. (He devoted seventy years to collecting and classifying specimens, becoming a highly regarded figure in the field, in particular for his extremely fine-tuned sensitivity to intraspecies variations—distinctions based on exquisitely calibrated descriptions of wing markings and the subtle morphological variations in male genitalia.) But as one astute bibliographic note on his lepidopteral publications points out, VN once declared that "My passion for lepidopterological research . . . is even more pleasurable than the study and practice of literature, which is saying a good deal."

Saying a good deal indeed, but in some way not saying quite enough. I found myself mesmerized by the butterfly nonce, mesmerized by it as a numinous object, spellbound, as well, by the fearsomely dense thickets of VN's lepidopteral prose. When he tells us that "clues provided by aberrational individual [butterflies] and certain ontogenetic data suggest that the maculation [colored spotting on the wings] of a given interspace develops phylogentically in result of a series of recurrent waves or rays of pigment"—what is he *really* talking about? What mystery are the "clues provided by aberrational individual[s]" really clues to, beyond patterns of pigment on a butterfly wing?

After hours of immersing myself in this dense prose, only occasionally illuminated by flashes of Nabokovian wit, I felt it begin to disclose to me a kind of clue, a glimmer of the nature of the luminous bond between VN's literary and lepidopteral passions. I'll get to the butterfly secret, as I've come to think of it, but I want to at least touch on a few of the treasures to be found in the rest of the VN archives, some of which I suspect I'll return to in the future.

In particular—in light of the multiplicity of butterflies, hand-drawn, intensively studied, and lavishly described by VN in these volumes—I'd like to dwell upon the one *caterpillar* rendered here. It can seem, if you think about it, that VN's lepidopteral obsession, the profusion of butterflies on his pages, does seem to slight the lowly caterpillar from which they all are engendered: the mundane crawling creature whose spinning of a translucent cocoon and transformation into a delicate winged being seems an implicit metaphor for the trance-spun spell of art, the metamorphosis of earthbound reality into winged beauty.

But, in fact, there *was* a caterpillar, one caterpillar (that's all I found at any rate), a graceful, hand-drawn, one-horned caterpillar that crawls across the top of a page in one of the extraordinary series of heavily hand-revised sections of VN's autobiography, *Speak, Memory*.

Glenn Horowitz, and his senior cataloger, Sarah Funke, who are preparing—with the blessing of VN's son and translator, Dmitri—a sale catalog of the collection, recalled for me that *Speak, Memory* went through a remarkable number of stages of creation and re-creation, as VN created and re-created his past. Appearing first as *Conclusive Evidence* in 1951, it was republished in England as *Speak, Memory,* then that work was translated into Russian by VN, and subsequently heavily revised and re-created, even renamed as *Speak Memory: An Autobiography Revisited.* He was continually spinning a cocoon of silken lines around his past, and the VN archives contain each successive version in the staged metamorphosis. Curiously (or not so curiously, as it turns out), the lone caterpillar drawing makes its appearance on a heavily marked-up copy of *Conclusive Evidence*'s reincarnation as *Speak, Memory* before the "revisitation." It's a particularly fascinating volume because pages and pages of Nabokovian memory, of stunning, stirring, evocative prose about his past, are apparently being expunged before our eyes, much of it never to be seen by the world again.

The caterpillar drawing crests a page which is entirely crossed out with a big bold VN "X," a page in which VN is in the midst of describing a dreamy childhood memory. It's a childhood, you'll recall, that began as a beautiful Russian idyll of art, love, and beauty, only to be shattered by ugly politics, by the assassination of his father—a liberalizing aristocrat under the czar—by proto-fascist, anti-Semitic fanatics, an assassination that is echoed in transfigured form in the murder plot embedded in the annotations of *Pale Fire.*

In any case, the excised page surmounted by the caterpillar contains a particularly plangent account of the child VN, cocooned in the heavy blankets of a sleigh on a snowy St. Petersburg night, entering into a kind of dream realm, "the almost hallucinatory state that our snow-muffled ride engendered." He dreams of the dueling deaths of his beloved Aleksandr Pushkin and Mikhail

Lermontov, but beneath the dreams of poets dying is a nightmarish foreshadowing. "Behind it all there was yet a very special emotional abyss that I was desperately trying to skirt, lest I burst into a tempest of tears."

And yet when he describes the "abyss," it scarcely sounds nightmarish on the face of it. It was, he writes, "the tender friendship underlying my respect for my father; the charm of our perfect accord." He goes on in the original text to note some embodiments of that perfect accord: "the butterflies we discussed, the chess problems we solved, the Pushkin iambics that rolled off his tongue. . . ." But curiously (although he later reinstated much of the dreamy sleigh ride he had excised), he heavily crossed out one clause from that list: "the butterflies we discussed." And then he crossed out the final term that sums up the list of father-son accords, one that reads in the original, "the habitual exchange of homespun nonsense and private jokes which is the secret code of happy families."

The secret code of happy families: crossed out, but why? Because he thought the echo of Leo Tolstoy's opening to *Anna Karenina* ("All happy families are alike . . .") too hubristic a literary allusion? Or was the memory of that lost idyll of family happiness too unbearable to recapitulate in light of its foreshadowed end, the "abyss" to come, the metamorphosis from happy to unhappy family? It's a metamorphosis reimagined, reembodied in the caterpillar crawling across the crossed-out page toward its unimaginable destiny— crawling above the expunged lines about butterflies and the deleted reference to the secret code, the lost language of happiness. It's his own metamorphosis from cocooned child to melancholy artist.

And speaking of secret codes, the VN archives contain several instances of the magician disclosing some of his card tricks, decoding certain of his most recherché anagrammatic encodings, his literary sleight of hand. These can be found most frequently in the margins of his copy of *Ada*. One of the delights of that amazing work, one almost biblical in its radiant genesis of an alternate Creation, is VN's confection of an alternate literary canon composed of hybrids of writers and book titles from this world. Some of them are not hard to decode (T. S. Eliot is given the Jewish name Beckstein, a karmic payback, perhaps, for his most singularly anti-Semitic poem, "Burbank With a Baedeker: Bleistein With a Cigar."). And some might discern in the name of a patent medicine in *Ada*—"Mr. Henry's oil of Atlantic prose"—a reference to Henry James, although VN makes it explicit here with a penciled "Henry James" in the margins. But what about a novel described in *Ada* as "*The Puffer* by Mr. Duke"? We might still be in the dark, if not for VN's penciled marginal note which identifies this as "Saul Bellow's *Herzog*" (Get it? Bellows equals puffer; Herzog, in German, equals Duke).

Why decode these minor, if not trivial, allusions (Martin Amis calls Nabokov and Bellow the two great Russian novelists of our era) and not others? Did VN decode it because he felt that after his death, it would be too obscure for posterity ever to get? For his own benefit, in case he forgot it in its obscurity? Or just for the eyes of Véra and Dmitri?

I'll mention only one further decoding here among the many, because it yields a beautiful, melancholy reward. Next to a passage in *Ada* in which there's a reference to a work called "The Weed Exiles the Flower," published by "Melville and Marvell," he's added a penciled marginal note referring us to line 6 of a poem by Herman Melville, "The Ravaged Villa," a poem I raced to look up. "The Ravaged Villa," previously unknown to me, turns out to be a kind of meditation on a shattered Keatsian Grecian urn, on the broken fragments of a painted pastoral idyll scattered across the floor of the "ravaged villa." A chilling vision of de-creation, one that might have struck a chord in VN—particularly the line about the weed exiling the flower—as an emblem of the shattered aristocratic idyll of his childhood and the melancholy exile to come.

I'm going to limit my comments here on the cryptic underlinings in VN's *Pale Fire* to permit me further study. But I can't resist pointing out one intensely suggestive correction to an apparent misprint in an annotation *about* misprints in the epic footnotes of *Pale Fire*. Because it bears upon the question of ultimate coherence or incoherence *Pale Fire* raises. Does art create order out of disorder or merely mirror, at best transfigure, a fundamental disorder in creation?

At the close of one of the funniest and most touching passages in *Pale Fire,* a misconceived passage about misprints by the mad annotator Charles Kinbote, there is a parenthetical cross-reference that reads, in the published version: "for other vivid misprints, see line 802." In his personal copy of *Pale Fire,* VN has crossed out the 2 in 802 with a penciled slash and substituted below it the numeral 3, making it read 803.

Is this some private joke, or could there actually have been a galling publisher's misprint in the footnoted cross-references to a *further* footnote about misprints? Is this the place where the cosmic comic incoherence of creation shows its seam, the flaw even, in the shimmering fabric of *Pale Fire*? Is it a flaw that discloses a higher transfigured coherence, or is it a token of the triumph of incoherence? Is God playing dice with the universe, or is VN loading the dice? I think I need time to think about this, but, meanwhile, let me return to the butterfly secret and to what I believe may be a not widely recognized coherence between VN's love of literature and his love of lepidopterology.

What they have in common, I came to realize, is that they are both, the literary and the butterfly work, about *language*. What VN was doing in his lovingly obsessive study of wing-marking patterns and genital morphology was an act of *reading;* he was reading and translating the language, the esoteric genetic poetics of butterfly markings. It's something I began to get an amorphous feeling for from a close reading of the lepidopteral monographs. I came upon an explicit clue at the close of VN's major work on the butterfly genus *Lycaeides,* one he'd devoted much of his life to limning. Summing up his incredibly painstaking, dizzyingly detailed attempt to describe and categorize the variety of wing patterns of *Lycaeides,* to find meaning in the subtle shifts in the pigmentation of the tiny "maculations," he adds, "In conclusion, a few words may be said concerning the specific repetition, rhythm, scope and expression of the genetic characters supplied by the eight categories discussed."

Repetition, rhythm, scope, and expression: These are the terms of prosody, the study of poetic metrics (one of the volumes in the VN archives is his *Notes on Prosody*), and I'd suggest VN devotes the same reverent attention to resonant minutiae in the rhythmic configurations of butterfly "characters" as he does to the configuration of characters—letters, sounds, and syntax—in the language of poetry. VN is famous for his synesthesia, of course, in which letters were colors to him; in butterflies, colors were letters.

I have little other experience of lepidopteral literature (although I loved an exchange VN includes in the nonce with a censorious Mr. Brown, whom VN accuses of failing to understand his poetic, "qualitative"—as opposed to quantitative—lepidopteral methods) but it seems to me the continuing preoccupation, the quest in VN's lepidopteral prose, is to distinguish meaningful genetic utterances from transient aberrations. To distinguish signal from noise and decide which new patterns of characters deserve to be incarnated as a subspecies, *given a name.* And I could be projecting here, but I sense beneath VN's fascination with the pure language of lepidopterology an enchantment with a particular *kind* of poetry being inscribed upon the butterfly wings: an erotic drama about beauty and desire, about the way certain patterns of color, the poetry of genetic utterances in pigment, become eroticized in the vision of the butterflies. The way the beauty of these markings might inspire butterfly lust, mating and then new hybridized languages. The way the grim, brutal Darwinian struggle for the survival of the fittest is sublimated into an erotic, aesthetic struggle—the survival of the most beautiful in the drama of mating and morphology.

But there is another kind of drama being played out in his butterfly prose: a drama about the limits of language, limits which VN is constantly testing in his effort to read and translate into human language the expressive hieroglyphics inscribed on butterflies. One senses that when he is translating the esoteric language of butterflies, he is paying tribute not to blind chance and genetic mathematics, but to a rival creator of beauty. It's a kind of duel between poets, VN's tribute to the lepidopteral prosody of God the Esthete, who discloses His secret coherences in the signs inscribed on butterfly wings.

The Secret Parts
of Certain Icons

Mr. Bill's House of Horror

I don't want to sound alarmist or paranoid, but I have reason to believe Bill Gates has been the victim of a fiendishly elaborate computer-hacker scheme that may have been masterminded by the Unabomber. That's the only way I can explain the content of "Inside 'The House,'" a devastatingly wicked satire of a pompous high-tech guru's pretentious futurism that unaccountably appeared *under Bill Gates's byline* in the otherwise respectful recent cover story in *Newsweek*. I just can't believe Mr. Gates himself could have written this embarrassing parody, and so I'm forced to conclude hackers must have somehow intervened in the production process and substituted a hostile caricature of the software billionaire's thought process and prose.

It just can't be the real Mr. Gates who wrote this breathless, glowing description of the deeply disturbing Orwellian entity he's building, the one modestly referred to as "*The* House." It can't be Mr. Gates because the enthralled media has told us he is a deep-thinking genius; scores of admiring profiles have hung on his every electronically transmitted word as if they were carved in stone rather than ether.

But this piece of writing in *Newsweek* (posing as an excerpt from Mr.

Gates's new book) could only have been penned by an enemy trying to make Mr. Gates and all his techno-futurist ilk look silly. Which is why I think the Unabomber must have linked up with subversive anti-technocracy hacker-punks to pull off this daring prank. Of course, the same crew seems to have inserted the exact *same* language in the section on "The House" that appears in Mr. Gates's book. So perhaps it actually is Mr. Gates, and this rhapsody to his ridiculously cumbersome robotic house is further proof of the neo-Veblenian sociological axiom that reads, as I recall, "When a given CEO's net worth passes the billion mark, *nobody will tell him how silly the house he's building is.*" Mr. Bill has built himself the Emperor's New Home.

The excerpt, which is billed as "a guided tour of the *super-high-tech* home [Mr. Gates is] building near Seattle," begins with some hilarious gee-whizzing over the pathetically trivial achievements of his high-tech lighting system. Not only will lights come on when you enter a room but, Mr. Gates boasts, *"unoccupied rooms will be unlit."* Makes you wonder how we ever managed *that* before the advent of Windows 95.

The portrait that emerges of Mr. Gates—or the Unabomber *posing* as Mr. Gates, let's call him Una-Bill—as he gushes over his house would be sad if it weren't scary: Una-Bill seems utterly oblivious to how closely the house he's building resembles a high-tech prison.

"First thing, as you come in, you'll be presented with an electronic pin to clip to your clothes," Una-Bill enthuses. And while the stylish pin is a slight improvement over the obtrusive electronic anklet worn by federal felons under house arrest, the function is roughly the same. Una-Bill *says* the pin will be used to serve your needs, so you can program in your entertainment preferences. But it's repeatedly described in terms of its surveillance function: "It also allows the house to *track* a resident's location." And the pin is only the start. Una-Bill says he's working on even better surveillance technology for his lucky guests: "a camera system with visual recognition capabilities" that would enable "The House" to know whether you're being naughty or nice.

It sounds a little better than living with a 7-Eleven felony-cam watching you, but not much.

And, to continue the charming prison motif, remember the spotlights that swept the Yard in the Big House movies? In Bill Gates's Big House, that pin you're forced to wear will "cause a moving zone of light to accompany you through the house" at night.

But the real horror—and hilarity—comes with the Una-Bill vision of virtually enforced entertainment: the Pod System. The idea is that you program your electronic pin with your tastes in entertainment—what movies you want to watch, what music you want to hear—and then everywhere you go in the house the walls turn into screens, the ceiling into speakers, so you're constantly surrounded with a moving envelope of nonstop entertainment; your traveling pod.

But what happens when you actually meet another *person* in the house? What happens, in other words, *when pods collide?*

Mr. Gates tries to gloss over the problem: "If you and I are enjoying different things and one of us walks into a room where the other is sitting, the house might continue the audio and visual imagery for the person who was in the room first, or it might change to programming both of us like."

Notice that he doesn't even consider the possibility of the two pod inhabitants *actually having a conversation,* but forget that, let's consider the problem posed by Mr. Gates's pod-collision scenario. I'm walking down the hall surrounded by, say, *Chinatown* in my pod, and Bill's coming toward me watching, say, *The Sorcerer's Apprentice* (that fable of Faustian techno-horror) in his pod. Is Bill's house really going to shut Bill's pod off just when Mickey is overwhelmed by all those little broomsticks, and switch Bill to Roman Polanski cutting off a piece of Jack Nicholson's nose? Not if the house knows who's paying the bills. Or is it going to annoy us both by switching us to "programming [it thinks] both of us like"—and we end up watching *Surf Nazis Must Die?*

Bill's traveling pods will turn his house into a comic nightmare with all the inhabitants doing their best to avoid *any* interaction to prevent their pods from colliding.

The really scary thing about the picture of Mr. Gates that emerges from this "guided tour" of his house (and, in effect, his mind)—and the thing that convinces me it can't be the real Mr. Gates, it's gotta be the Unabomber's caricature—is that we get a glimpse of someone who's gotten as far as he's gotten without developing the *slightest* appreciation, apparently not even the slightest conception, of the values of privacy, autonomy, and hospitality—*even in his own home.* Una-Bill exhibits the distinctive feature of the totalitarian mind; the inability to distinguish between the private and the public spheres. It suggests this isn't just the way he wants to run his house, it's the way he wants to run the *world:* total surveillance, enforced entertainment, everyone isolated in programmable pods.

I've always felt the Unabomber's hostile analysis of the techno-mind was as extreme and unwarranted as his methods. But the "Gates" who authored this guide to "The House" seems to confirm all the Unabomber's paranoid assumptions about cyberculture. Which is why I think the Unabomber really *is* "Gates." Unless perhaps Mr. *Gates* is the Unabomber. Can he have created his own evil-genius persona to do Manichaean battle with himself? Now *that's* paranoid.

Fear and Loathing in the Zagat Guide

A specter is haunting the models of New York: the revolt of the resentful restaurant eaters. It is one of a number of disturbing revelations an examination of the 1996 Zagat guide yields.

I've been trying to figure out why I find so many of the quotes in the Zagat guide so irritating. Yes, I know, the Zagat serves a useful function; many swear by it. But there's always been something annoying to me about the mind-set of the Zagat survey respondents cited in the capsule summaries of each restaurant. Not just their many strained efforts to get labored imitations of "colorful" restaurant review prose into print. No, there was something *else* about the tone of certain respondents that rubbed me the wrong way. But I couldn't put my finger on just what it was until I read the very first entry in the 1996 edition—on Abyssinia, an Ethiopian restaurant in SoHo. Toward the end of a decidedly mixed review, one survey respondent is quoted as disparaging what he or she calls the "one-car garage" ambience of the place.

That was it right there, that one-car garage sneer: the distillation, the quintessence of suburban snobbery. A sensibility that sees the world through the narrow lens of profoundly petty class distinctions, like the one between those poor benighted souls condemned to languish in the dimness of dwellings equipped with one-car garages, and the enlightened and worldly elite of landed gentry who learned about fine dining in their two-car garage, split-level estates in Hewlett or Short Hills.

Of course, you don't have to live in the suburbs to exhibit suburban snobbery. A number of Zagat respondents prove that by demonstrating another key distinguishing characteristic of the mind-set: the strenuous effort to show off one's profoundly with-it worldliness, a worldliness that is at once acutely aware of every seismic tremor of trendiness, but pretends to be beyond caring in a deeply Zen way. Thus we have, later on in the guide, ostentatiously blasé put-downs of places sneered at as "last year's model hangout," or "the kind of place where people still wear black." They don't really care about trendiness, they just *happen* to be more acutely trend-aware than the city folk who do.

If it's this status-obsessed mentality that makes some (not all) Zagat surveyors so irritating, what makes them perversely pleasurable to read is the regularity with which they give themselves away in their sad efforts to prove to us how truly hep to the jive they are.

Consider the comment, also on the very first page of the 1996 guide, in the entry on the Acme Bar & Grill, which one Zagat surveyor assures us is a "rocking hip" place.

Rocking hip? It sounds like a geriatric orthopedic problem. As someone who admits to being out of touch, even I could tell you that a person who uses the phrase "rocking hip" is unlikely to be your most reliable guide to what is really "rocking hip" in the Platonic sense of the phrase.

Don't think I'm relying only on the first page for these observations. In fact, I've read through the entire guide twice, but the entries on the first page did turn out to be a treasury of clues to patterns that emerge in the later pages. Let's linger for a moment over the Zagat guide's Ethiopian problem, for instance. For some reason, they go out of their way (in this case the Zagat writers, not the survey respondents) to add gratuitous insults to *all three* of the entries on Ethiopian restaurants in the book. In the entry on Abyssinia, they actually characterize the cuisine as "resembling dog food."

And they don't stop there. Not content to let one of their respondents disparage the "one-car garage" ambience of Abyssinia, the Zagat writers go out of their way to add their own belittling remarks about the décor in each of the other two Ethiopian places. "N.B.," they append to the review of Ghion, an Upper West Side Ethiopian place, "Authentic Ethiopian décor will never make the pages of *Architectural Digest*." How painfully provincial can you get—judging an exotic culture's décor by the standards of the bible of suburban snobbery? And if that's not enough, in the third Ethiopian place they describe, they make a point of taking another cheap shot at the décor, telling us "this is one place that benefits from getting a dash [i.e., being too new to be rated] for décor." Could it be, one begins to wonder, that someone has a *problem* with African culture (which—N.B.—didn't evolve for millennia with the sole aim of qualifying for a spread in *Architectural Digest*)? Just asking.

And to return for a moment to that "rocking hip" place, the Acme Bar & Grill, we have, in this entry, the first hint of what will become a recurrent subtext in the rest of the guide: Fear. Fear stalks the pages of the Zagat guide, Fear sneaks into the quotes in various guises. One of them being Fear of Food. The Acme entry contains the first of what will be a series of leaden cholesterol or heart-disease witticisms, more sclerotic than any blocked artery. The big question about the Acme food (standard Southern fare), one of the respondents tells us, is "whether you want your food served 'with or without angioplasty.' " You can just see the table of suburban cardiologists busting a gut over that sally, which is followed later on in the guide by other tiresomely repetitive quips on artery hardening that the Zagat respondents evidently feel are the epitome of sophisticated food wit. As in "you can hear your arteries clog as you eat," and "A must once a year, if your cardiologist approves in writing."

Fear of food exhibits itself also in the exaggerated clichés about the supposedly fearsome size of steaks and lobsters. The 1993 edition of Zagat describes the steaks at Smith & Wollensky as "elephant-sized." By 1995, they've mushroomed to "brontosaurus-sized." Then, in keeping with the prehistoric colossus imagery, in the new 1996 guide they're "mammoth" size.

Now, I've actually had the steaks there; they're at most twenty-four ounces (or thirty-six ounces for two)—great steaks, but hardly meriting the Jurassic hysteria expressed by the respondents. The same with lobsters which are described as "Tyrannosaurus rex"–like or "the lobster that ate New York" when these are at most four- or five-pound creatures being eaten by 200-pound people. We're bigger!

In fact, some of this hyperbole reflects what is, to my mind, the real flaw of the Zagat ratings: Its surveyors seem to see things through the lens of already established cliché and hype. Steakhouses are known for big portions, so regardless of the actual portion size, the raters dutifully replicate the cliché by raving about being served "the whole cow," etc.

The same goes true, I believe, for the way they end up slavishly worshiping all the usual suspects of endlessly hyped expensive food shrines: the Temple of Bouley, the Church of Le Bernardin, the Cathedral of Le Cirque.

But the note of fear in the hysteria over steak size (and the Freudian terror in the clichés about seafood freshness: "so fresh it swims in your mouth," "so fresh the soft-shell crab bit me") is echoed in other fearful aspects of the Zagat Zeitgeist. Fear of food is only surpassed by Fear of Foreigners—unless you count Fear of Models—but let's consider Fear of Foreigners first.

It manifests itself in the warnings about the presence of Europeans at certain New York restaurants. Often, those warnings take the form of sneering at "Eurotrash." An epithet that implies the sneerer himself has a kind of Henry Jamesian discernment, the ability to distinguish truly worthy Europeans from trashy pretenders: an epithet that, in the Zagat raters' lexicon, seems to have become an indiscriminate term of opprobrium applied to just about all well-dressed foreigners.

What's peculiar about the use of the Eurotrash epithet is the raters' paradoxical delight in bragging about their own European experiences, laboriously insinuating boasts about their well-traveled worldliness into their restaurant remarks: "Feels like Siena," they'll say, or "gives you the impression you're still in Capri," "gelati like Florence," and, of course, the endless "like dining in Paris" clichés. My favorite is "Up to the quality of Indian restaurants in the U.K."(!)

You're left with the impression of a group of people who like to boast about going to Europe, but can barely stand being in the same room with actual Europeans. It seems like what would please them most would be if they could visit a Europe entirely depopulated of Europeans—a vast, continent-size Euro Disney.

But the most insidious and debilitating fear of the many fears that haunt the Zagater mind is the fear of—and consequent anger at—models. Consider the way the very presence of models, indeed, of any woman they fear *might* be a model or might *want* to be a model, runs rampant in the respondents' replies:

"last year's model hangout"
"attitudinally 'model staff' "
"model wannabe staff"
"going downhill faster than you can say 'model' "
"snotty service for nonmodels"
"black leather, artists, model wannabes"
"staff thinks they're models"
"Is it a restaurant or a modeling agency?"

Who knew that models were such an oppressive, threatening presence? Is their beauty that disturbing, that deeply fearsome? I suspect that what's going on here is that Fear of Models is really an expression of the deep-seated Fear of the City Itself that is buried deep in the suburban mentality. Models are the symbolic urban Delilahs who can delude you with their charms into missing the last train back to Larchmont, seduce you into those dens of iniquity where people "still wear black."

What I want to say to the Zagaters is: Get over it. The distractions of models are one of the hazards of urban life. If you can't handle it, go back to Short Hills or Shaker Heights.

What I want to say to the models is: I'm *concerned.* Next thing you know, this irrational prejudice will result in restaurateurs seeking the approval of the Zagat crowd by offering, in addition to No Smoking sections. No Model Rooms. Perhaps with one of those international negativity symbols to mark them: a red circle with a slim silhouette inside, slashed through by the red bar that proclaims: No Models Allowed.

Well, I, for one, wish to assure the models of New York that I will stand by them in solidarity against the oppressive antimodel forces that seek to persecute them. If you are driven out of New York restaurants by the churlish antimodel movement, *I'll cook for you.*

My Theater Problem—and Ours

I'm still not sure it wasn't a practical joke—the strange thing that happened to me when I went up to Lincoln Center to see the new Spalding Gray performance. But it *was* pretty funny.

I'd asked my editor at *The Observer* to see if she could get me press tickets to see the new Gray monologue. I'd had a reasonably good time at his early performances, although I worried he was commodifying himself into shtick. So I was interested in where he'd go with the potentially trite midlife-crisis, new-baby stuff I'd heard the new monologue dealt with.

There seemed, however, to be some difficulty getting the tickets. Apparently, the p.r. man for the Vivian Beaumont made a pointed reference to someone at *The Observer* not writing with sufficient enthusiasm about a past Gray performance; my editor, Deirdre,* who usually works wonders with the most recalcitrant types in the world, was ready to give up, and seats for the public were sold out. But then, finally, she told me they'd come through; I was to show up in the lobby of the Vivian Beaumont and pick up the tickets from the press person there on Tuesday, December 3.

---

*The whip-smart Deidre Dolan, whose dedication I'll always be grateful for.

That evening we got the tickets: My companion and I settled into our seats; she leafed through the *Playbill* (this detail becomes important later) as I studied the typically bare Spalding Gray stage set. All seemed in order.

It was a bit surprising, I admit, when the lights went down, and a mass of green foliage descended from the ceiling and splayed out into an entire tropical jungle that covered the stage; when snakes made of painted cardboard or papier-mâché began to writhe amidst the undergrowth. And when a full-size papier-mâché jaguar stalked out, it seemed like an odd introductory touch for a Spalding Gray performance. As was the Latinate, funereal chanting music that filled the hall. But I thought to myself, Well, there's a midlife crisis theme, maybe what's going on is a reference to the famous opening lines of the *Inferno* where Dante, "in the middle of this life we lead," finds himself lost in an allegorical woods. Doesn't he run into a big black leopard at some point? Perhaps Spalding is making a pretentious (or, better, self-mocking) dramatic allusion to eternal themes of death and midlife contemplation.

But then *another* jaguar came out and started *fucking* the first jaguar. Hmmm, I didn't recall that from the *Inferno*. But hey, he's entitled to take modernist liberties with classic themes, and it does introduce the whole sex-and-death dynamic, right? Then, a hunter figure with a giant wooden East Asian–type mask on top of his head stalked into the jungle, and I did begin to think to myself something to the effect of: "Gee, Spalding must not really be *confident* his monologues can carry an evening alone anymore, if he's got to tart it up with all these silly allegorical trappings."

About this time, a New Orleans–style funeral band dressed in black top hats appeared and trudged mournfully across the stage playing a dirge. Also, some guys in skeleton costumes had started capering around the jungle, a woman in a rustic cabin seemed to be breast-feeding a puppy dog, although it later turned out to be a baby jaguar. So it all did seem to fit into the midlife fear-of-death and new-baby themes.

Oh, I get what's going on, I thought to myself: Maybe he got some big genius grant, and he was generously giving jobs and exposure to his downtown performance-artist friends and their clichéd takes on "primitive" rituals. About that time, some of the skeleton guys set up a bedsheet, lit a torch behind it and put on an Indonesian-type puppet skit about a shoemaker who gets eaten by a jaguar, who then shits out one of his boots. I recall wondering at that point if, generosity aside, Mr. Gray was really *wise* to give so much creative control—and *time*—to his faux folk-art friends. But then someone came out with an object that looked like it had sparkling candles on it. Aha! I said, a birthday cake. *Here's* when all the scenery disappears, Spalding Gray comes out on the bare stage, and delivers the punch line: All of that—the funeral dirge, the jaguars fucking, the chick breast-feeding the dog, whatever—it was all going on *in his head* the night before his fiftieth birthday; it was a visual *allegory* of his midlife crisis.

But *noooooo* (as John Belushi so memorably put it). The cake disappeared, and the hunter with the big wooden mask was thrashing around through the jungle and, at this point, I turned to my companion and said, "Uh, could I see your *Playbill*?" I still couldn't quite believe there was anything amiss because, after all, she'd been reading the *Playbill* before the performance. When it turned out there was no sign of Spalding Gray on the *Playbill* cover (although there was a guy in a mask), I began to think something *might* be wrong. But I held out a kind of last-ditch hope that the hunter guy would take off his mask, and *that* would be Spalding. The ability of the mind to rationalize is a beautiful and scary thing.

Yes, it's true the title on the *Playbill* did say *Juan Darién: A Carnival Mass.** But as my companion (who, in fairness, I should mention graduated from Harvard *with honors*) later said, she thought perhaps it might be a generic cover for the whole Vivian Beaumont subscription series that included both Spalding and *Juan Darién*.

It took a while before she came around to my point of view that we were in fact at the wrong play. We were not seeing Spalding Gray, but some pretense at folk art—although the "folk" in question seemed to be not so much the people of the Third World from whom its motifs had been appropriated, but rather the kinds of "folk" who people the Bennington and Oberlin dance departments, and certain precincts of SoHo.

Later on, the p.r. person who'd provided me with this experience insisted that it was *not* a practical joke to punish *The Observer* for not being reverent enough about Spalding Gray in the past, but rather just a mixup in his office that resulted in our being handed an envelope with the wrong tickets. And even if it had been a practical joke, I'd still be more grateful than offended. Because I came to see it as a perfect allegory—not the pretentious Joseph Campbellesque allegory of *Juan Darién*—but an allegory of my entire experience of the theater in New York City.

Because in one way or another, I *always* seem to find myself at the wrong performance. I always seem to be seeing plays that seem utterly unlike what everyone else seems to have seen. I'm forever going to things that have been raved over by critics, chattered about by the chattering classes, awarded prizes and grants, and finding myself thinking—in those moments when I can keep myself awake from the industrial-strength tedium they induce—that this is the most clichéd, empty, contrived piece of ranting I have ever seen. Afterward,

---

* A misguided mélange by Julie Taymor, who later went on (after *The Lion King*) to make a brilliant film version of Shakespeare's *Titus Andronicus*.

I'd find myself wondering, Is it possible I went to the *wrong* theater; this second-rate, self-satisfied, soporific contrivance *can't* be the same stuff that people are taking seriously, can it?

My growing sense that I was seeing the Emperor's New Play over and over again began to crystallize a few years ago after I'd been stunned by the emptiness of an evening spent watching the almost universally rhapsodized-over *Dancing at Lughnasa*. Another leaden celebration of the virtues of "ordinary folk" which—to me—radiated a contempt for the poor folk it so condescendingly sought to empathize with, while smugly celebrating its own faux-Chekhovian compassion for their emotionally repressed plight.

The audience, which suffered in expectant silence for much of the dull proceedings, had been prepped for the *big* moment in the play (in which one of the emotionally repressed sisters in the poor Irish family gets up and does a jig on a table) by a rave Frank Rich review that spotlighted this allegedly liberating breakthrough moment as a peak experience in the theater. At last, when the moment came and she started her earnestly emotive dance, you could feel the palpable relief, the virtual *earthquake* of *kvelling—This* is *Theater!—* going on around you.

It was at that moment I came to fully appreciate the tragic heroism of Frank Rich (and of any theater critic with more than half a brain). Here was a guy who was forced to sit through stuff like this (and worse!) *every night*. Who was clearly smart enough to see through it all, and yet—perhaps because he was constantly under attack as a "butcher" by the powerful owners (and advertisers) who purveyed this sort of product, for trying to tell the truth about it—any time he came across anything with the *slightest* glimmer of life, you couldn't blame him if he tried hard to rave about it to show he had a heart.

But it seems to me that the disparity between what's lauded as greatness in the theater today and the reality of the product is far greater than in any other art form. Don't get me wrong. It's not that I don't like or haven't seen good theater. I'll see any Shakespeare; you learn something even from bad performances. I was blown away by the film of *Vanya on 42nd Street;* in fact, I think it proves my point. The breathtaking level of intelligence in the acting and staging was so far above almost anything I've seen on Broadway or Off-Broadway in memory. I defy you to rent the movie of *Vanya* and tell me anything that comes *close* to it on the boards today.

Why is this? One explanation was suggested by Peter Brook, a director I've always admired (I saw his *Midsummer Night's Dream* twice, and I think it changed my life, and ruined me for anything less). In a devastating aside in *Looking for Richard*, Mr. Brook pointed out that contemporary theater has never solved the technical (and artistic) problem of theatrical ranting: the meretriciousness that infects the attempt to communicate inner life with words and gestures that must resound to distant balconies. It's particularly a problem for the misconceived naturalism of most "good drama" on Broadway and Off. But I think the larger problem might have to do less with the writing and the acting and the ranting than with the complacency of the audience. With the fact that theatergoing today seems to have less to do with the rituals on stage than the rituals in the seats. With the self-validating function it performs in conferring Culture, like a medal of valor, on the audience: The pain and tedium they suffer through has won them the right to believe they are participating in an important cultural ritual. And it's rarely felt as pain. It's felt as resounding waves of self-*approbation,* a folk mass of self-satisfaction. Who was it that said that religion is really about the sanctification of wealth? New York theater, the secular religion of the city, is really about the sanctification of self. At the close of most performances, I'm convinced the audience is not applauding the play they've seen or the actors, but applauding *themselves* just for being there.

This was a theory I developed while attending a performance of *Mrs. Klein,* the play about Melanie Klein (the British Freudian savant) and her daughters. The audience at the Lucille Lortel theater in the Village seemed equally divided between *identically dressed* psychoanalysts (hello, "Henry Green"!)— who made you fear for their clients—and swooning actor-director devotees of the star: acting-teacher guru and theater diva Uta Hagen.

Both halves of the audience worshiped every breath taken, every word spoken with a frightening intensity. For the shrinks, every trite Freudian reference (e.g., "I'm going to put that in my *id* drawer") in the dialogue was the occasion for ostentatiously knowing, often explosive guffaws ("We're shrinks, we know what *that* means").

Meanwhile, every time the great lady of the theater paused for effect (and there were *many* pauses for effect, believe me) in an attention-getting way, all the actor-director types practically went into cardiac seizures at the genius supposedly on display. It wasn't a bad play, but the quality of whatever was going on on stage was irrelevant. The audience was celebrating itself.

Oh, well, I'm probably just going to the wrong plays. I finally do have tickets for Spalding Gray, though. I'm just a little worried that if it doesn't feature jaguars fucking in the first few minutes, I'm going to be *real* disappointed.

The Emperor's New Logo

∽

I love a mystery, and Lucent Technologies Inc.—the new multibillion-dollar high-tech spin-off of AT&T—has given us, in its expensive new corporate-identity ad campaign, a truly profound, deeply emblematic, multilayered enigma: What the hell does the Big Red Zero they've chosen as their corporate logo really mean?

I've always been fascinated by the mystique surrounding logo science itself, a glamorous esoteric mystique that seduces—some might say suckers—huge bottom-line corporations into lavishing astonishing sums on big-time logo gurus in the belief that they hold the key to the Deep Sell, a profound, pre-verbal way to reach You, the Consumer, on some primal mythic level that words cannot express. A level that only the Zen-like, psychographic visual-symbol geniuses of logo science can fathom.

Clearly, Lucent Technologies (formerly Bell Labs) has bought into the mystique. But what have they gotten for their money? What have the logo gurus brought forth from the mythic realm of the collective unconscious to symbolize the new company? A symbol that may mean many things, many, many *deep* things to Lucent, but which looks, to the casual observer, like a Big Zero. A flaming red goose egg.

You must have seen the corporate identity ads Lucent has been running on TV and in print since mid-April. Everything about them bespeaks state-of-the-art, cyber-era advertising deep-think. The ads go to great lengths to establish an aw-shucks, studied-casual approach: They take the form of low-key, lower-case, e-mail-like communiqués—a computer keyboard tapping out words on a screen, in a carefully calculated informal style that tries a bit too hard to look like on-line Beat poetry:

> *invented*
> > *dial tone*
> > *(ALSO phone, transistor, laser, Telstar satellite, fiber-optic cable, cellular and voice mail)*
> > *Have won awards (Nobel, etc.)*
> > *Specialize in making things that make communications work . . .*

They specialize in the "things that make communications work," and clearly a *lot* of work has gone into thinking about how they communicate who they are. The name Lucent, for instance: a name devised, it turns out, by the same people who devised the Big Red Zero. You have to give them credit for what seems like an inspired choice with the name at least, suggesting as it does lucidity, clarity, a kind of luminiferous glow (although it does sound very close to "loose end," which has some unfortunate connotations).

But that symbol? I have the feeling they got *so* lost in logo deep-think, they lost track of the obvious. The first time I saw it, it looked to me like some scary, sadistic grade-school teacher had scrawled a big red grade of zero on their ad. And that's the *nicest* interpretation that suggests itself, judging by the response I got from several friends. The flaming red circle brought out some associations I feel Lucent was *not* reaching for:

"It's an inflamed orifice," suggested one. "Could it be a subliminal safe-sex thing?"

"It's designed to link oral, genital, and anal longings to Lucent products in a subconscious way," theorized another.

"It could have been designed by the Unabomber," said another. "Its hollow center symbolizes the emptiness and nothingness of technological culture."

Don't you wish you had been there in the Lucent boardroom for the Emperor's New Clothes moment when the logo gurus unveiled their creation to the befuddled Lucent big shots?* More than a century of high-tech, cutting-edge physics and communications breakthroughs, innovations that have linked the world into a brave new virtual community in the brave new realm

---

*Okay: I know I'm perhaps overly fond of the Emperor's New Clothes trope—cf. The Emperor's New House and the Emperor's New Play, among other references. But only, I'd say in my defense, because I keep finding icons for whom the nude wardrobe fits.

of cyberspace, all summed up by . . . a Big Red Zero? A bloody goose egg? A scarlet letter implying nothingness? Didn't anyone have the temerity to question whether an inflamed zero—red ink!—was the right message they wanted to implant deep in the pre-verbal brain of you, the potential buyer, when you thought of Lucent? Was everyone too intimidated to speak up in the presence of the Emperor's New Logo?

I decided to investigate. I wanted to find out what the flaming goose egg meant to the Lucent people, or, at least, what it was *supposed* to symbolize. I had an open mind; I was willing to be blown away by the blinding logic of logo gurudom.

It took a while to get an official statement on the meaning of the scarlet O from Lucent. The operator I reached at their 888 number didn't know. One p.r. guy said my message got "lost" in his in-box. He did, finally, get back to me, to inform me that what I thought of as the flaming goose egg, *they* called "the Innovation Ring." And, he added, "an important part of the story is that it's red and that it's a hand-painted brush-stroke." He handed me off to another p.r. person, who, when I asked *how* a red circle symbolized innovation, told me she "couldn't give me that" herself; I'd have to go to the source—to the logo gurus in San Francisco—for the answer.

And finally, from the logo gurus I got a faxed page entitled "The philosophy behind the new identity." After a discussion of the name came the following logo deep-think explaining *"What does the symbol mean?"*:

> Historically the circle has represented universality, knowledge and perfection. The circular shape . . . embodies these qualities, while the energetic brush-stroke style provides the sense of innovation and human energy upon which the company is based . . .
>
> *The symbol is about knowledge.* This bespeaks the knowledge of the company and its people . . . gained through years of experience unequaled in the industry.
>
> *The symbol is about innovation.* Innovation is a product of knowledge—applying knowledge in creative ways. The expressionistic rendering of the symbol conveys the innovative spirit of the company.
>
> *The symbol is about perfection.* The perfection of the symbol does not lie in technical symmetry, but rather in perfectly capturing the spirit of the company in a single, masterful brush stroke.

It goes on to explain that red was chosen because "it is a powerful, confident color . . . it represents the entrepreneurial energy of the new company." I don't know. I read all that, and I look at the Innovation Ring, and I *still* see a big fat zero.

But I particularly like "the symbol is about perfection" paragraph. The symbol is "about perfection" because it perfectly captures the spirit of the company. By that line of reasoning, *I* am perfection, because only *I* perfectly capture the spirit of me. (You are perfection, too, don't worry.)

But if the Lucent logo were *really* perfect, wouldn't it perfectly communicate only what it *wants* to communicate? If it were really perfect, would it conjure up other decidedly unpleasant competing associations: grade-school martinets scrawling zero for conduct on one's permanent record? Inflamed bodily orifices? Big red-ink, bottom-line zeros? Cosmic emptiness? Or is it just me and my disaffected friends? (But we're perfect in being that way, don't forget.)

I felt I had to ask someone at Lucent actually involved in the decision. Didn't anyone in all their focus groups, their in-depth study of the question, raise the Emperor's New Logo question: Why are we branding ourselves with a big zero?

Finally, I reached a polite and earnest Lucent executive who was involved with the decision. He was telling me how carefully they'd vetted the "Innovation Ring" symbol for possible offensive meanings. "We took a lot of focus-group input in and out of the company to develop it; we didn't ask whether people *liked* it, but we did a lot of linguistic checks, cultural checks, things to ensure that our mark was not—worst case—offensive to anyone," in a foreign language or culture.

But what about its connotation in plain old English? I felt bad, but I had to ask it: "Was there any concern that a red circle could be interpreted as a zero?"

"Uh, no," he said, sounding a bit taken aback. "Because it's not a *precise* mark. It's a hand-drawn, artistic—" he paused. "Had we gone with a very precise mark, perhaps so, but the artistic and hand-drawn nature—we didn't feel it at all depicted *that*."

Well, history will be the judge of how it's ultimately perceived. Perhaps America will embrace the Flaming Red Zero as its new symbol of perfection and innovation—although isn't there an inherent conflict in those qualities? Innovation thrives on *imperfection,* while perfection needs no innovation. Clearly, I can't think like a logo guru.

Chaplin and Benigni:
The Arrogance of Clowns

Herewith a report on my trip to Cambridge, to the Harvard Film Archive, shrine to cinephilia, to denounce one of the icons of all cinephiles as "an arrogant clown."

The Harvard Archive and the Harvard Book Store had invited me to speak about my book and about Chaplin's Hitler spoof *The Great Dictator* in conjunction with a screening of the film. Which forced me to do two things I wouldn't otherwise have done: see the Chaplin film again. And see *Life Is Beautiful*, which I'd been resisting like crazy because I sensed the rage I'd feel about the self-congratulatory Italian clown and his feel-good fable of the Holocaust might be unbearable. And it was. It still is. But I'll get to that in a moment. I want to speak first about the Chaplin film, which—in giving us a feel-good fable about Hitler that glorifies its self-aggrandizing clown–hero maker—might be called *Life Is Beautiful, The Prequel*.

The Great Dictator is one of those rarely questioned classics given knee-jerk obeisance because the film buffs dictate to us that we should revere it. It's Chaplin, after all! The Little Tramp takes on Hitler! How could you not love it?

Well, let me count the ways.

Let me begin by talking about the inadvertent—and perhaps tragic—consequences the comic persona of Charlie Chaplin may have had on real-life history for the crucial decades (1920 to 1940) *before* the October 1940 release of *The Great Dictator.* Tragic consequences Chaplin could have addressed and redressed in *The Great Dictator,* a film he wrote and financed as well as directed and starred in, giving him total creative control. Tragic consequences which he instead compounded, out of vanity and arrogance—the arrogance of clowns—the arrogant assumption that even the most intransigent evil can be dissolved in the mocking laughter of the triumphant clown. Tragic consequences because of a terrible missed opportunity to *really* take on Hitler in a scathing, satiric way at a time when a still-neutral America was deciding whether to assist those at war with Hitler. A missed opportunity the dimensions of which are signaled by the little-known fact that Chaplin was lionized for *The Great Dictator* by the right-wing, isolationist, "America First" Daughters of the American Revolution for its "antiwar" message, one that served the interests of the Hitler appeasers at the time. The knee-jerk Chaplin-worshiping film buffs either don't know—or don't want to remind anyone—that their hero got a D.A.R. award for *The Great Dictator* at a time when the D.A.R. was trying to cripple FDR's efforts to aid those fighting the Führer.

In any case, in my talk at the Film Archives, I began by tracing the origin of these tragic consequences to its comic source: the mustache. No less a personage than H. R. Trevor-Roper (now Lord Dacre), the dean of the Oxbridge historians' profession, author of one of the first—and still one of the most influential—postwar visions of Hitler *(The Last Days of Hitler),* reached for the mustache when seeking to explain to me, one evening in London, the tragic underestimation of Hitler in the 1930s: "The conventional wisdom about Hitler was always—before the war at least, till Munich—he was taking off from the Music Hall, he looked ridiculous—he had the Charlie Chaplin mustache. . . ."

That 'stache: It was Chaplin's first, before Hitler's; Chaplin adopted a little black crepe blot beneath the nose for his Mack Sennett silent comedies after 1915, Hitler didn't adopt his until late 1919, and there's no evidence (though some speculation) that Hitler modeled his 'stache on that other actor's.

More important was the relationship, the tale of two mustaches, that developed after they both became international sensations, global media stars in the 1920s. More important was the way Chaplin's mustache became a *lens* through which to look at Hitler. A lens, a glass, in which Hitler became *merely* Chaplinesque: a figure to be mocked more than feared, a comic villain whose pretensions would collapse of his own disproportionate weight like the Little Tramp collapsing on his cane. Someone to be ridiculed rather than resisted. No, I'm not saying the mustache was the *cause* of the tragic underestimation of Hitler, but it fed into and embodied a deeply flawed vision. A predisposition not to explain Hitler but to explain him away.

Of course, the relationship, the similarities between Chaplin and Hitler went deeper than the mustache, as others have pointed out. Both in their formative years had been lonely outsiders, homeless tramps for a time. Both were at times rumored to be Jewish, both thought of themselves as artists (while Hitler failed in his conventional ambitions as artist he succeeded in turning the Nazi project into what the philosopher Berel Lang has called a consciously sculpted "art of evil"). Both were powerful actors—manipulators of mass audiences and mass emotion and sentiment. And both specialized in one emotion in particular: self-pity. They were both *geniuses* of self-pity, Chaplin wringing self-congratulatory tears from millions for his self-pitying "Little Tramp." Hitler whipping millions of Germans into frenzies of self-pity with his vision of their victimization by Jewish, Communist conspiracies to immiserate them.

I suspect the power of self-pity has been vastly underestimated as a factor in history. But there's another quality they shared, one mixed somehow inextricably with the self-pity: arrogance. An arrogance less obvious on the surface in Chaplin than Hitler, but still quite profound. It was after seeing Mr. Benigni's feel-good fable of the Holocaust, with its Death Camp Lite setting and its cheap, insulting optimism about physical and spiritual survival, a vision of the Final Solution that amounts to an aesthetic version of Holocaust denial, that the phrase first occurred to me: the arrogance of clowns. An arrogance of clowns that for some reason seems to feed on the Final Solution. Jerry Lewis's long-unreleased fable of a clown in a death camp, *The Day the Clown Cried,* makes Mr. Benigni's the hat trick of the clowns 'n' genocide genre. (I can't resist quoting National Public Radio critic Elvis Mitchell calling Mr. Benigni "the Patch Adams of the Holocaust." It is a film so self-congratulatory, so self-reverential about its star's puny posturing, it ought to be called not *Life Is Beautiful,* but *I Am Beautiful.*)

Don't get me wrong—I have nothing against clowns per se, although the thought of watching *Patch Adams* makes me break out in a rash. But there is something grating about their arrogance: Perhaps it's the insecurity and self-pity it masks. If you have to apply grotesque smears of greasepaint to your face to get a laugh, you can't have much confidence in your native endowment of humor. And clowns are, in a way, if not great dictators, then petty ones: You *must* laugh. I *am* funny. I'm a *clown.* (To me the emblematic clown in American culture, the one that exposes the true horror of clownhood, is John Wayne Gacy, the serial killer who dressed up as a clown at children's parties when not viciously throttling to death his scores of victims.)

The only clowns I really like are the growing genre of *anti-clowns* the culture has spawned in reaction to in-your-face clowning: the brilliant, incomparable Krusty the Clown on *The Simpsons;* the late, lamented Homey the Clown from *In Living Color;* and, of course, Shakes the Clown from the Bobcat Goldthwait movie of that name, which has been called "the *Citizen Kane* of alcoholic clown movies."

Let's look at the arrogance of clowns, and the form it takes in the Holocaust Lite hat trick, as I think of *The Great Dictator, Life Is Beautiful,* and *The Day the Clown Cried.* (Isn't it fascinating—well, pathetic, self-pitying, and arrogant—the way clowns assume their tears are so *special?* Gee, a clown cried! How *ironic.*) At its heart is the belief that clowning reigns supreme, that clowning can overcome, transcend the most intractable evil and that clowning, clowns are somehow in *themselves* triumphs of the human spirit. One of the most offensive things Mr. Benigni has done in his intoxication with the unmerited success of *Life Is Beautiful* is to claim Primo Levi, the great Holocaust writer and thinker, as his inspiration. The self-infatuated clown has distorted some remark Levi made about a moment in Auschwitz that felt dreamlike into a license to flog the meretricious moral that make-believe can triumph over the death camps. If only the Jews in the camp had a sense of humor about their situation! If only they had Mr. Benigni's brilliant and profound vision to turn it all into a game! If only they didn't act so depressed, most of them would have survived, as they do in *Life Is Beautiful.* Life is beautiful, yes, for Mr. Benigni, now that he's become the grandiose prophet of death-camp fun.

Chaplin's arrogance in *The Great Dictator* is manifested in what might be called a grandiose act of intellectual laziness. Given a chance to take on Hitler, to do something genuinely scathing, something that might cut deep (as, for instance, the brilliant satires on Hitler penned by the brave, doomed anti-Hitler Munich editor Fritz Gerlich), he took the lazy clown's way out. His Hitler is a harmless schlemiel who falls down stairs. No need to resist someone who will probably collapse of his own accord. His Hitler is, beneath the bluster, a wistful Chaplinesque dreamer, especially in that famous, overrated (and deeply misleading) dance with a globe balloon, no more truly menacing than, say, Dabney Coleman as the mean boss in *9 to 5.*

I could cite ten more things I hate about *The Great Dictator.* The way Chaplin both stereotypes and blames Jews for their plight. His Hitler figure only turns on the Jews after a Jewish banker turns him down for a loan. Hitler's anti-Semitism then is just an opportunistic tool, not a deep genocidal hatred; treat Hitler a little better, Patch Chaplin seems to say, and the Jews will be fine. All dictators are just "unloved." Get Hitler some serious nooky and he won't have time to hate. Then there's his vision of the Hitler henchmen—at worst, harmless buffoons out of the Bowery Boys comedies, at best noble protectors of Chaplin's little Jewish barber character. And the storm troopers: Hey, they're human, they respond to *beauty.* When Paulette Goddard, the little Jewish laundress with the prettily smudged face who's initially insulted by the storm troopers, gets a beautifying makeover and gauzy lens treatment from Chaplin (as barber and director), suddenly the storm troopers are super-*polite* to her. See, if only the Jews had cleaned themselves up a bit, no Third Reich.

Why have the Chaplin worshipers continued to celebrate this offensive piece of tripe? In part, I think, because many of them are tunnel-vision film buffs who have aestheticized themselves into insensibility. One member of the audience at my Harvard Film Archive talk opined that *The Great Dictator* wasn't about Hitler at all, that it was *really* about Chaplin's dissatisfaction with the shift from silent to sound films. (He seemed to believe that Chaplin's childish mangling of the German language—Ha! Ha! The Germans talk funny! *That's* what's wrong with Hitler!—was an attack on language itself, thus a searing comment on the talkies. What a waste of a brain.)

But the true locus of the disgraceful failure of the film is its final six-minute speech in which Chaplin—perhaps aware of how grotesquely inadequate his clowning has been—speaks directly, out of character, as himself, to the camera.

Here, given the opportunity to take on Hitler directly, before an audience of millions at a crucial moment in history, he never mentions Hitler's name, never mentions Nazism. Instead, he gives the world rambling, incoherent effusions on peace and love and can't we all get along. Effusions that some have called the product of the Hitler-Stalin Pact and the Communist Party line of that moment: that the working classes of the Western democracies shouldn't resist Stalin's ally Hitler because the struggle against Hitler was a misguided "capitalists' war." Effusions that won Chaplin the enthusiastic plaudits of the right-wing pro-appeasement lobby as well. The only people the arrogant clown managed to "bring together" then with his foolish and damaging feel-good fantasy were the Stalinists and the Hitler appeasers. Oh, and yes, that other arrogant and ignorant clown Roberto Benigni, so vocal in claiming the Chaplin mantle. Wear that mantle like a shroud, Roberto. Life is beautiful for *you,* but not for the dead you insult.

Two Faces of Paranoia

Kim Philby: The Spy Who Created the Cold

The Strange Death of Danny Casolaro

Kim Philby: The Spy
Who Created the Cold

In Which We Sort Through the Last Effects
of the Third Man

The presence of the Philby papers in London was still a closely guarded secret when I stumbled on them through an inadvertent slip by Graham Greene's nephew. I'd found him, the nephew, in the cluttered basement of his Gloucester Road Bookshop, where he'd been preparing for the imminent sale of the late novelist's personal library.

I'd come to see him about one volume from that library in particular, Greene's copy of *My Silent War,* the memoirs of Kim Philby, the spy of the century. It had been reported that Greene had made some cryptic annotations in the margins of the Philby book, and I hoped they might provide a clue to the strange story I was pursuing. A story about a possible deathbed revelation Graham Greene had had about Philby. A story that epitomized the maddening elusiveness of the man: the way those who felt they knew Philby, who thought they'd finally penetrated to the truth beneath the masks, could never be sure they'd known him at all.

Greene had first come to know Philby when the two were working for the British Secret Intelligence Service during World War II and Philby was the brilliant, charming counterintelligence specialist who disguised his intellectual arrogance with a disarming stammer.

Later, Greene would learn that Philby was disguising a lot more than that: that he'd been Stalin's secret agent, burrowing his way into the upper reaches of the British establishment since the 1930s. And still later—after Philby had been exposed as a long-term Soviet mole, indeed the ur-mole, the legendary Third Man, the most devastatingly effective double agent ever exposed, after Philby had surfaced in Moscow in 1963, a hero of the KGB—Greene and Philby had struck up a peculiar and controversial friendship.

They'd become correspondents, confidants, and—after perestroika had permitted them face-to-face reunions in Russia—something like soul mates. Greene seemed to pride himself on being the one Westerner who truly understood the endlessly enigmatic Philby; knew him with all the masks off.

But then, in 1991, as Greene lay dying of a blood disease in a Swiss hospital, a letter reached him throwing all that into question. It suggested Philby had a wild card up his sleeve he'd never disclosed.

The provocative new take on the ambiguity-riddled Philby question came in the form of a letter from Greene's biographer Norman Sherry, who'd been researching Greene's Secret Service connections. Pursuant to that, Sherry had been conferring in Washington with Anthony Cave Brown, the espionage historian then researching a forthcoming Kim Philby biography. Cave Brown was the intrepid spy sleuth who'd first revealed (in *Bodyguard of Lies*) the details of the elaborate D-day deception strategy—the way the Allies used the "double-cross system" to blind Hitler to the truth about the Normandy landing.

Cave Brown had put forth a startling proposition to Greene's biographer: that Kim Philby might have been part of an even more complex deception operation than anyone had imagined—a *double* double-cross.

It had been whispered about before in the West; it had been debated (we now know) in the inner sanctums of the KGB itself. But the theory the two biographers were weighing was deeply shocking: Kim Philby, famous for deceiving the British by posing as a loyal agent of the Crown while really working for the KGB, might actually have been deceiving the *Soviets* by posing as their agent on behalf of the Brits. Could it be, Sherry wrote Greene, that Philby, regarded as the most destructive and demoralizing Soviet penetration of the West, was actually a Western agent penetrating the KGB's Moscow Center?

It's a notion that I suspect might have been extremely galling to Greene. After all, he had risked his reputation as a judge of human character (a matter of pride to most novelists), as a man able to see into "the heart of the matter," by writing an extraordinarily sympathetic introduction to Philby's 1968 KGB-blessed memoir, *My Silent War,* an introduction that touched off a bitter row in Britain about the meaning of loyalty and treason.

Greene's introduction portrayed Philby not as a cold and ruthless traitor with the blood of betrayed colleagues on his hands (as most in Britain saw him) but as an idealist who sacrificed his friendships to a higher loyalty. A man whose belief in Communism Greene memorably—and maddeningly to many—compared to the faith of persecuted Catholics in Elizabethan England, who clandestinely worked for the victory of Catholic Spain. Greene portrayed Philby as someone who served the Stalin regime the way "many a kindly Catholic must have endured the long bad days of the Inquisition with this hope . . . that one day there would be a John XXIII."

Many in Britain have never forgiven Greene his defense of Philby, still an unhealed wound in England. Some speculate his pro-Philby stand cost Greene a knighthood and a Nobel Prize.

Imagine Greene's distress, then, at the possibility that Philby had been not a Soviet double agent but a British triple agent. Greene had gone out on a limb to portray Philby as a passionate pilgrim, a sincere devotee of the Marxist faith—radically innocent rather than radically evil. But if, in fact, his friend had all along been an agent of the Empire, *a hireling of Colonel Blimp,* it would mean that Philby had been laughing at Greene. Not merely laughing at him, but *using* him, using him as *cover.* Graham Greene would turn out to be Kim Philby's final fool.

"As a matter of urgency," Cave Brown told me, "Greene summoned up enough energy to send for his papers, for all his literature relating to Kim and certain letters from him."

Cave Brown believes that Greene spent those last hours playing detective, sifting the literature and his memories of Philby for clues to the hidden truth about the role the ultimate secret agent played in the secret history of our century. And that Greene was preparing to respond to Sherry's query with his last word on the Philby case. It would have been Greene's summa, his ultimate espionage thriller. With little time left to live, Graham Greene was in a race against the clock.

The Original Disinformation Virus

Why does Kim Philby continue to cast such a dark spell over the imagination? Why is Philby such a magnetic specter to novelists like Greene and John Le Carré (whose *Tinker, Tailor, Soldier, Spy* enshrined the Philbian mole Bill Haydon at the dark heart of cold-war literature), to playwrights like Alan Bennett and poets like Joseph Brodsky (the Russian exile laureate whose rage at the sight of Philby's face on a Soviet postage stamp inspired a magnificently vicious ten-thousand-word tirade in *The New Republic*)? In part, it's the same sort of horrified fascination that fueled the sensation over Philby's mercenary successor mole, Aldrich Ames of the CIA: a fascination with the primal act of betrayal itself. Dante reserved the Ninth Circle of Hell for the Betrayer. Even in an age jaded by serial killers, the crime of treason still has a primitive power to shock, treachery a still-compelling ability to mesmerize.

The mole, the penetration agent in particular, does not merely betray; he *stays*. He doesn't just commit a single treacherous act and run; his entire being, every smile, every word he exchanges, is an intimate violation (an almost sexual penetration) of all those around him. All his friendships, his relationships, his marriages become elaborate lies requiring unceasing vigilance to maintain, lies in a play-within-a-play only he can follow. He is not merely the supreme spy; he is above all the supreme *actor*. If, as Le Carré once wrote, "Espionage is the secret theater of our society," Kim Philby is its Olivier.

And, like only the very best actors, Philby didn't merely hold up a mirror to human nature. He revealed dark shapes beneath the surface only dimly glimpsed before, if at all—depths of duplicity, subzero degrees of cold-bloodedness that may not even have been *there* until Philby plumbed them. Once in an interview on another subject, the essayist George Steiner made the provocative suggestion to me that the nightmare world of the death camps might not have been realizable had not Kafka's imagination first embodied their possibility in his fiction. I have a similar feeling that the Age of Paranoia we've lived in for the last half century—the plague of suspicion, distrust, disinformation, conspiracy consciousness that has emanated like gamma radiation from intelligence agencies East and West, the pervasive feeling of unfathomable deceit that has destabilized our confidence in the knowability of history—is the true legacy of Kim Philby. One that might not have been imaginable had Philby not pushed the permutations of doubleness—double identities, double meanings, and double-crosses—into triply complex territory, into the bewilderment of mirrors we're still lost within. He's the high priest of the Age of Paranoia, the original disinformation virus, and we're still only beginning to learn how much of the secret history of the century bears Philbian fingerprints.

Unlike the spy scandals of the 1940s and 1950s, the Philby case has been a slow-motion series of revelatory detonations stretched out over decades. One reason the truth has been so slow in emerging is that it's just so embarrassing. Even before James Bond, the spymasters of the British Secret Service enjoyed a worldwide reputation for infinite subtlety, invincibility, and aristocratic élan. Philby made them seem like bumbling fools who were so blinded by class prejudice they couldn't imagine that a man from all the right schools and all the right clubs could betray his blue-blood legacy.

Indeed, the deeply chagrined British government clamped such a tight lid on the Philby case that it took nearly five years after he defected to Moscow in 1963 for the most embarrassing truth to come out (in a groundbreaking *Sunday Times* of London investigative series): that Philby was no ordinary midlevel spy; that, in fact, he'd been one small step away from being named to one of the most powerful posts in the Western world at the height of the cold war—Chief of the British Secret Service. (Although British officialdom pooh-poohed this assertion at the time, it was confirmed to me in London this spring by Sir Patrick Reilly, the former head of the Joint Intelligence Committee, the board of spy mandarins that oversees the selection of "C," the chief of the British Secret Intelligence Service.)

Philby was no less a nemesis of the American spy establishment. In the final act of his active duty career in the West, before the spotlight of suspicion fell on him in 1951, Philby was stationed in Washington, where, as chief British liaison with American intelligence agencies, he charmed the CIA's deepest secrets out of his principal contact, James Jesus Angleton, the man who would go on to become legendary as the CIA's chief mole hunter. This shattering betrayal left behind a destructive legacy of distrust and paranoia in Washington—principally in Angleton's mind—reverberations of which would come to plunge the CIA into civil war for decades afterward.* And in an incredible final act that closed the circle of deceit, in what may have been his last operational mission, Philby indirectly collaborated with Aldrich Ames in solving a high-level mole case for the KGB.

But these spy dramas only begin to capture the extent of Philby's role in the secret history of our century, the extent to which he was far more than a cold-war spy—he was a secret shaper of the very landscape of the cold war.

We know, for instance, that Philby was, in effect, talking to Stalin throughout World War II. Stalin considered reports from Philby "particularly reliable," writes the intelligence historian John Costello, the first Westerner to get access to Philby's operational files.

What is less well known is that Philby was, in effect, talking to Hitler, too. Cave Brown recalls a memorable conversation he had with Sir Ronald Wingate, a key member of the secret Churchill Cabinet department that formulated elaborate strategic deceptions like the one that kept Hitler guessing wrong about the D-day landing.

"You were talking directly to the Devil himself, weren't you?" Cave Brown asked Sir Ronald while they were out on a pheasant shoot.

"We could have a message on Hitler's desk within a half hour," Wingate replied. "Sometimes fifteen minutes at the right time of day."

Then Cave Brown learned the name of the man who was one of the chief conduits in these conversations with the Devil: Kim Philby.

As head of the Iberian section of MI6 counterintelligence, Philby was run-

*The definitive account of the self-destructive effects of Angleton's paranoia over Kim Philby can be found in *Cold Warrior: James Jesus Angleton, the CIA's Master Spy Hunter* by the British writer Tom Mangold.

ning agents in Madrid and Lisbon who were so highly trusted by the Nazis that the words he fed to them for transmission to the Abwehr would be whispered to Hitler almost at once.

In *Catch-22,* Joseph Heller memorably envisioned all the mighty forces of World War II, Allied and Axis, manipulated by a single low-level communications specialist, ex-Pfc. Wintergreen, an all-knowing, wise-guy protohacker of the war's information flow. In fact, Kim Philby was the *real* ex-Pfc. Wintergreen—talking to Stalin, talking to Hitler, *listening* to Hitler through his command of the Ultra Secret, the code-breaking material produced by the famous "enigma machine" that read the ciphers of German military intelligence. And just to complete the circle, Philby was also influencing Churchill. Every day the Prime Minister would eagerly await his briefings by Philby's MI6 boss, Stewart Menzies, who would bring Churchill a digest of Hitler's secrets, some of the choicest bits prepared by Kim Philby. Similarly, Philby could manipulate FDR as well, through whatever he chose to pass on to his junior partners in U.S. intelligence.

Without a doubt, the mind of Philby was a key junction box, a node, a filter through which some of the most secret messages of the war were routed. But the question remains: Was Philby merely a courier or was he a creator?

That question, I believe, is at the heart of the continuing fascination with Philby: We're still not sure whose game he was playing, or what his own game really was. He remains a one-man enigma machine whose true aims and motivations have yet to be fully decrypted.

The Notional Philby

I'd first written about Philby some ten years ago* in the context of his complex duel with CIA mole hunter Angleton and the espionage equivalent of three-dimensional chess that the two men seemed to be playing with phantom moles, false defectors, and putative penetrations. I'd advanced a kind of Philbian solution to the still-unresolved mole hunt controversy—the "notional mole" gambit. Angleton had turned the CIA inside out looking for the American Philby. I suggested the possibility that there never was a real mole, not of the stature of Philby, not while Angleton was there, anyway. But that Philby had deliberately planted the false suspicion in Angleton's mind that the KGB

---

*In "The Shadow of the Mole," *Harper's,* November 1983. It was in that piece that I reported on post-facto efforts by Angleton partisans in the Mole War that followed Philby's betrayal, who sought to insinuate that Philby had been their dupe. I reported on this speculation not because I endorse the idea Philby was a triple agent but as an instance of the final irony of the Philby affair: that he was unable to escape the shadow of paranoia, the miasma of mistrust, he had so ingeniously engendered: Elements within his own KGB suspected him of a double double-cross.

had a mole within the CIA (thus the phrase "notional mole" coined by Philby's Double Cross colleagues of World War II) in order to provoke the disruptive and destructive mole hunt that followed—one that paralyzed the agency with paranoia and ultimately claimed Angleton himself as a suspect and victim.*

What struck me in looking back on it, in reviewing the vast Philbian literature and mole war chronicles, was that, like many writers on the subject, like James Angleton himself, I had been seduced on the basis of fragmentary evidence by the image of another kind of Notional Philby: an image of Philby in his post-1963 Moscow period that Philby himself had assiduously cultivated in his memoirs and correspondence with Westerners. An image of Philby as the peerless mastermind, the Ultimate Player in the East-West intelligence game, always operating one level deeper than anyone else. It was a romanticized, almost cinematic image: Philby still the unflappable Brit aristo waiting for the cricket scores to arrive at the Moscow post office, then returning to the KGB's Moscow Center to run a few more rings around the best intelligence minds of the West.

How much truth was there in it? In the aftermath of the collapse of the system he sold his soul for, with the opening of the KGB archives and the loosening of the tongues of the former KGB men who were his colleagues, we suddenly have a wealth of new information about Philby's career since 1963, when he first reached Moscow. We have more information, but do we have more answers? In the hopes of sorting out the new clues to the mind of Kim Philby, I undertook an odyssey into the infamous "wilderness of mirrors" he'd bequeathed us, talking with spooks and spymasters in Washington, London, and Moscow, with some of Philby's victims and bewildered successors; trading theories with mole war chroniclers like Cave Brown, Nigel West of Britain, and Cleveland Cram of the CIA. It was an odyssey that led me eventually to the bookshop basement in South Kensington and the tip-off about the hush-hush cache of Philby papers in London.

I'd asked Greene's nephew about the cryptic marginal annotations in Greene's copy of Philby's memoirs, thinking they might contain a clue to Greene's deathbed detective work. The nephew, a friendly, intelligent fellow named Nicholas Dennys, confirmed that the annotations consisted of passages that had been suppressed in the British edition of the book by the British Of-

---

*In a passage I regret having had to cut for space, I had constructed a kind of genealogy of paranoia: Angleton's paranoia after the Philby betrayal led to destructive excesses of suspicion, which in turn begat an overreaction against even legitimate vigilance, which begat Aldrich Ames, the real mole who benefited from the way Angleton's paranoia about a notional mole had discredited virtually *all* suspicion. A subsequent independent history of the affair by Cleveland Cram confirmed this dialectic of paranoia Philby's betrayal initiated as the origin of the Ames affair.

ficial Secrets bureaucracy but had survived in the American edition. And that they'd most likely been made long before Greene's final days.

A false trail perhaps, but then Dennys let slip a clue to a real one.

Why, he asked, had I chosen this time to come to London to pursue a Philby story? Was it because of the papers?

What papers? I'd asked him.

The Sotheby's consignment, he replied offhandedly. It seemed that Philby's Russian widow, Rufina (his fourth wife), had gathered up all the manuscripts, books, and memorabilia he had left behind in his Moscow apartment after his death and had engaged Sotheby's to put them all on the block.

But when I called Sotheby's to inquire about the Philby papers, there was nothing offhanded about their reaction. How did I find out? Who had I talked to?

It seems that they'd promised a world exclusive to a British journalist whose wrath they feared. In addition, they were nervous about reception of the news of the Philby sale—scheduled in London for July 19—about charges of profiting from the fruits of treachery. (And, in fact, when word of the sale did become public, the heat from the Tory press was so great the auction house decided to withdraw some of the more frivolous Philby items, among them his pipes, homburg, and martini shaker.) But confronted with a fait accompli, the Sotheby's people agreed to let me study the Philby documents, provided I didn't break the embargo.

What I found, when I got to see the consignment from Moscow, was a strange mixture. There were letters, diaries, memoranda, a secret speech to KGB spy luminaries. There were tributes and tacky trophies from KGB and Eastern European spy fraternities; posthumous tributes to Philby's father, the famed Arabian explorer St. John Philby. There were photographs of Philby on safaris to Siberia and Cuba; Philby with the East German spymaster Markus Wolf, the crafty intriguer often identified as the model for George Smiley's arch-nemesis Karla in the Le Carré novels. There was correspondence between Philby and Graham Greene, filled with catty comments about Brit Lit contemporaries like Malcolm Muggeridge and grandiose geopolitical pipe dreams the two old spies cooked up, most notably a Greene scheme for a joint U.S.-U.S.S.R. commando raid to free the Ayatollah's hostages in Iran. And a detailed request to a KGB protégé in London for special English brands of coarse-cut orange marmalade and lime pickle.

And then there was the unfinished autobiography. Five chapters in manuscript pages whose publication the KGB had apparently prohibited.

A fairly safe general rule when reading Philby's prose is to assume he's lying or distorting—and then try to divine the truth the lies are attempting to conceal. It's a tricky game, but there were some moments, particularly in the childhood memories he recounted in this autobiographical fragment, when I felt the real Philby, or perhaps more accurately, the original Philby, seemed closer to the surface.

One moment, one childhood memory in particular, stood out from the rest. A moment I came to think of as a kind of metaphysical Rosebud of the Philby psyche. A moment of communion between Philby and his colorful, eccentric explorer father. One that probably leaped out at me because fresh in my mind was a remarkable vision of Philby and his father in the flesh that had been vouchsafed me shortly before I left for London.

The Two Philbys

Beirut, 1959. Dawn outside the Kit-Kat Klub. Anthony Cave Brown, then a correspondent for *The Daily Mail,* is gazing out from his hotel balcony.

"I'll never forget that morning," Cave Brown told me, with characteristic melodramatic color, "because at that hour of dawn the entire sky was suffused with a dramatic ocher color—threatening, ominous, mystical. It was the *shamal,* the wind from the Arabian desert."

Then he heard voices filtering up from the Avenue des Français, home of the Kit-Kat Klub and other seedy belly-dance lairs. And out of the ocher mists of dawn, staggering up the street came the two Philbys, arm in arm, singing an obscene song.

There was Philby the Elder, Harry St. John Bridger Philby, then near seventy, "potbellied and satanic looking," Cave Brown recalls. Soon to die but still a living legend, St. John was one of the great Arabian explorers and intriguers, a more successful rival to Lawrence of Arabia (St. John bet on the Saud family, the ones who now rule Saudi Arabia) and the first Westerner to have traversed and mapped the vast, forbidding, and forbidden Empty Quarter of the Saudi interior. Adventurer, scoundrel, convert to Islam, St. John had turned against the Empire during World War I, when the Brits backed the puppets of his rival Lawrence against Philby's patron Ibn Saud; bitter over this loss, he'd then avenged himself on the Crown by helping to spirit the Saudi oil concession out of British clutches and into the hands of American oil companies. At the time of the Kit-Kat Klub sighting, St. John, known then as Hajj Abdullah, was living in a villa in a mountain village with his Saudi harem-girl, still up to his neck in Mideast intrigue.

As was his son. Nicknamed Kim by his father (after Kipling's boy-spy who played a part in the Great Game of intrigues between the Brits and Russians in nineteenth-century Central Asia), Harold Adrian Russell Philby had gone on to play an even greater game of his own. He'd followed in his father's footsteps onto the imperial playing fields of Westminster public school and Trinity College, Cambridge, and then into the Imperial Secret Service, which he would, like his father, betray.

At that point in Beirut, Kim Philby was living in the strange shadowy limbo he'd been condemned to since 1951, when he'd come under suspicion of being the Third Man in the great Burgess and Maclean spy scandal. (Guy Burgess and Donald Maclean, two highly placed British diplomats who were Cambridge classmates of Philby and recruits to his Cambridge "Ring of Five" spies, defected just before Maclean was to be arrested on suspicion of espionage. Part of the subsequent sensation over these "spies who betrayed a generation" was the suspicion that a mysterious, unidentified Third Man in high places had tipped them off.)*

Forced to resign (under suspicion) in 1951, Philby had been subjected to repeated interrogations without cracking. Publicly cleared in 1955 but still suspected privately by Western security services, Philby had been sent to Beirut by the Brits in 1956 to pose as a journalist—in part to spy for them, in part to see if he'd continue to spy for the Russians. Of course, he did both, playing and being played in a doubly complicated game in which he served as a two-way conduit for disinformation.

It's hard to imagine a father-son team causing the Crown more trouble. That eerie ocher dawn in Beirut, the two Philbys were walking, staggering arm in arm, but were they working hand in glove?

They were, in any case, harmonizing together that morning on an old R.A.F. dirty ditty, one that lamented the passing of a lady of the night named Lulu. "What shall we do," the song asks, for—well—carnal delight, "when Lulu's dead and gone?"

I suspect it was an emblematic moment for Cave Brown, this vision of the two Philbys. He calls his Philby biography *Treason in the Blood,* and what distinguishes it from previous works on Kim Philby is the extent to which it's a father-son story. Cave Brown sees a historical, even genetic link in their taste for treachery. Reading Cave Brown's manuscript, one comes away with

---

*The relationship between that phrase for Philby, "the Third Man," and *The Third Man,* the Graham Greene–written film that appeared in 1949 (two years before the phrase was used in the Philby case) is complex and fascinating. In the second volume of his *Life of Graham Greene,* Norman Sherry discusses a minor but persistent mystery in the Secret Service career of Graham Greene, who served under Philby in MI6 when Philby ran the Iberian desk. In 1944, when Philby was given a promotion to head of counterintelligence and offered Greene, his protégé, a promotion to his old post on the Iberian desk, Greene refused the promotion and abruptly transferred out of MI6 entirely. It was an act that Philby himself professed to be mystified by ever after. Sherry offers the following speculation: "Perhaps Greene, always intuitive, resigned because he suspected that Philby was a Russian penetration agent. Greene once told me that if he had known Philby was a Soviet counterspy, he might have allowed Philby 24 hours to flee as a friend, 'then reported him.' " In fact, in the relationship of the naive writer Holly Martins in *The Third Man* to his close friend (who turns out to be a loathsome racketeer) Harry Lime, Greene may well have been working out the conflicts of loyalty to friend, country, and conscience he felt about his friend Philby, whose first name, Harold, happens to be the same as that of Harry Lime. In *The Third Man,* the great spy novelist of the century may be wrestling with his feelings about the spy of the century who soon became known as "the Third Man."

an impression of the two of them as a kind of family firm of global trouble-makers whose self-aggrandizing game-playing transcends any loyalties they might have had to lesser entities East or West.

But there's something primal, indelible about that image of father and son in the Levantine dawn. The empire, like Lulu, might be dead and gone, but the two Philbys survive, two successful predators sending out an obscene howl of triumph and defiance before setting off in search of fresh treacherous plea-sures.

Spy Glass Hill

Where does the Philby story really begin? Previous Philby literature has fo-cused almost microscopically on the cloistered quadrangles of Cambridge in the 1930s, on the hothouse Marxist cells that flourished amidst the sherry par-ties and secret societies, on the overlapping erotic and political relationships amongst the privileged upper-class youth who were seduced by one another and by canny Russian case officers into what became known as "The Ring of Five," perhaps the single most devastating spy ring in history.

Cave Brown's biography differs from Cambridge-centered Philby studies in that he finds the true locus of origin of the Philby mystery in the Middle East, in the father's formative ventures into espionage, which, he says, set the pattern for the son. Indeed, he goes further, asserting in his book that Philby the Elder, regarded by most until now as far right politically, may have been recruited by Soviet intelligence in the Red Sea port of Jidda shortly before his son was approached in England. Cave Brown says he was told by a former KGB official, Oleg Tsarev, that St. John Philby was a "Soviet asset." Cave Brown also raised the possibility with me that the father's contacts with the KGB in the Mideast may have led to the son's being targeted for recruitment. He almost goes so far as to suggest the father was *running* the son, that Kim was *his* agent.

I've come to believe rather that if St. John Philby did recruit his son into the Great Game, it was more a metaphysical than literal recruitment, and I'd put it much farther back in time and place, not in the Middle East itself but in a *map* of the Middle East.

In the opening pages of his unpublished memoir,* Philby depicts himself as a wistful loner of a child—collecting butterflies, spending long hours drawing imaginary maps. Map making was his only real passion. Not ordinary atlas-type maps, but "maps that could be invented," Philby writes. "This discovery resulted in [my drawing] a long series of imaginary countries with compli-

---

*Which has, since the auction, disappeared into the hands of a private collector.

cated promontories and inlets and improbably situated hills. My grandmother criticized me for calling all of them Spy Glass Hill."

Perhaps, in some sense, the young Kim Philby was drawing maps of his own lonely island psyche. But the true apotheosis of his map-making obsession, the moment that blissfully, sublimely united him with his long absent father, came on the occasion of St. John's return from one of his fabulous Arabian expeditions. This, Kim says, was his first conscious memory of his father:

> I remember he took me through Kensington Gardens to the Royal Geographical Society. There, in an upper room, he sat me on a stool beside a huge table covered with large sheets of blank paper, ink bottles, pens, and a lot of pencils sharpened to the finest point imaginable. My father was drawing a map, and, as far as I could see, an *imaginary* map at that because he had no atlas to copy from.

He was, most probably, filling in the blank spaces in the notorious Empty Quarter, giving reality to what was until then a largely imaginary landscape. Kim admits to two feelings about this spectacle: first "admiration" and then "wonder" that this was his father's *work*. To Kim, it was the supreme form of play.

A fierce debate has long raged in Philby literature over the question of his true motivation: Was he driven solely by sincere dedication to the cause of the oppressed proletariat, as he claimed to be? Later on in the autobiographical manuscript, Philby gives us this pious version, perhaps designed for the eyes of his ultimate editors, the KGB.

From the earliest age, he says, he felt "a sympathy for the weak" and the underdog. The plight of the poor lepers. "Why," he says he wondered at an early age, "did Jesus cure only *one* leper when he could have cured them all?"* Skepticism of this sort led him to question other established notions—of nationhood and empire—and, he declares, he "became a godless little anti-imperialist by the age of eight."

Perhaps this is true. But reading the yellowing typescript of the unpublished autobiography in Sotheby's London offices, I became convinced that the map-making imperative is the telltale heart of the matter. That, for Kim Philby, espionage, on the grand geopolitical scale he came to practice it, *was* a kind of map making, or map remaking, a way of creating the conceptual landscape of the world, the contour lines of desire and hostility, trust and distrust, power and weakness.

In a sense, then, Philby was not an anti-imperialist, but a *personal* imperialist, an imperialist of the self, who used his power to impose his own vision on the globe, to make the Great Powers navigate by his charts. To make his own mischief on a grand scale. To make his own map.

---

*Philby's treachery by this account is traceable to a question of theodicy.

The Black Bertha File

Consider, for instance, the new information about Philby's role in the Hess case. It's hard for those of us born afterward to recapture the kind of world-wide sensation made back in May 1941 by the news that Hitler's faithful No. 2, Rudolf Hess, had parachuted into the Scottish countryside on some kind of peace mission. Imagine, for comparison, the headlines Dan Quayle might have made if, at the height of the Gulf War hostilities, he'd parachuted into Baghdad on a self-proclaimed mission to talk peace with Saddam.

Many questions about the Hess flight have yet to be answered with assurance, because, as espionage historian John Costello puts it, "the British Government seems more determined than ever to keep the final truth of the Hess affair locked in the closet of official secrecy." Another historian I spoke to claimed that the Royal Family itself ("I suspect it's the Queen Mum") had been the real source of objection to releasing what's left, perhaps because embarrassing evidence of the Windsor family's sub rosa contacts with the Third Reich over a separate peace might be disclosed.

Whatever the case, the 1941 Hess flight came at a pivotal moment in the war and a pivotal moment in Philby's career as a spy. Seven years earlier, Philby had left Cambridge to go to Vienna, where, with other Oxbridge leftists like Stephen Spender, he'd participated in the doomed struggle of the Socialist workers against the proto-Fascist Dollfuss regime. It was there in Vienna he first found the heady thrill of being in the white-hot crucible of history in the making, of fighting the advance guard of Hitlerism, if only as a fringe player. He became a courier in a Communist underground network and lost his virginity in the snows of the Vienna woods, to an Austrian Communist Jew whom he then hastily married to help her escape the police.

When he arrived back in London, he was ready. A Soviet intelligence officer made an approach on June 1, 1934, in Regent's Park. His name was Arnold Deutsch and, fifty years later, in his autobiography, Philby seems still under the spell of Deutsch's magnetism, an almost sexual seductiveness. Not surprising, perhaps, because Deutsch was a charismatic former sexologist, originally a follower of Wilhelm Reich, the Freudian Marxist schismatic who made healthy orgasms the key to personal as well as societal revolution. (The lingering influence of this doctrine on Philby may be glimpsed in a not entirely facetious inscription in a book that turned up in the Sotheby's auction consignment. The book was a gift to Melinda Maclean, the wife of his fellow spy, Donald; Philby betrayed his own wife to woo her away from his friend. The inscription to Melinda reads: "An orgasm a day keeps the doctor away.")

Deutsch painted a romantic picture for Philby: The struggle for the future was being waged all over the world. The Soviet Union was alone in resisting

Hitler; the British Secret Service was forever scheming to destroy the world's only Socialist state; the Soviets needed someone sympathetic within the citadel of these incessant schemers. That would be Philby's long-range penetration mission: do anything he could to get inside the British Secret Service. In fact, he came close to becoming *head* of it.

But it was slow going at first; Philby publicly ditched his left-wing politics, and soon his left-wing Austrian wife. For several years, he posed as a pro-German sympathizer, then used his right-wing contacts to make his way to Franco headquarters in Spain in the midst of the Civil War. Originally sent there as an advance man for a possible Soviet-sponsored assassination attempt on Franco, he bootstrapped his way into a position as a London *Times* war correspondent, eventually receiving a prestigious decoration, the Red Cross of Military Merit, from the dictator he'd originally been sent to kill.

Finally, in 1940, shortly after the fall of France (which he covered for the *Times*), he got the invitation he'd been hoping for, an invitation to join the British Secret Service. He'd begun in guerrilla training operations and was just about to transfer to the true brains of the outfit, the foreign counterintelligence department of MI6, when Rudolf Hess fell out of the sky.

At that moment, huge forces in the world were on the verge of momentous shifts. Hitler was about to make apparent his fateful choice between an invasion of England in the West and an attack on his then-ally in the East, the Soviet Union. There were factions in both Britain and Germany hoping to arrange a peace between the two "Aryan" powers to free Hitler's hand for an attack on the Bolsheviks. Stalin suspected a deal was being made behind his back, and Hess's flight seemed to confirm his suspicion. He lashed his intelligence chiefs into finding out what was really going on, who was betraying whom.

After fifty years, we still don't really know for sure, but what we do know now is what Philby *told* Stalin was going on. This came to light three years ago when the successors to the KGB released the contents of its "Black Bertha" file on Hess ("Black Bertha" was reportedly Hess's nickname in the homosexual underground of Weimar Germany), a file containing the texts of Philby's reports to Stalin on the Hess Affair.

How reliable were they? On the basis of Philby's reports, Stalin came to believe the most paranoid interpretation of the Hess flight that (as John Costello describes it) "Hess had been lured by an MI6 deception to fly to Scotland. He apparently had not only done so with Hitler's knowledge but with a genuine offer of a final peace deal before the impending attack on the Soviet Union."

There are some who believe there really *was* a plot by MI6 to lure Hess to England for one reason or another. Most, however, take the position of the Cambridge historian Christopher Andrew and his coauthor, former KGB

Colonel Oleg Gordievsky: that Philby was innocently in error in his reports to Stalin, "that he jumped to the erroneous conclusion that [Hess's flight] was evidence of a deep laid plot between appeasers in high places and the Nazi leadership."

But was it just a mistake? There is another, more sinister interpretation to be made of Philby's reports to Stalin. An interpretation that suggested itself to me after a conversation with James Douglas-Hamilton, the son of the Scottish peer Hess had ostensibly come to England to see and the author of a respected book on the case based on his father's private papers.

Douglas-Hamilton, now an M.P. for Edinburgh, told me that, from his study of the Black Bertha file, he'd concluded that Philby hadn't made an innocent error but rather "he *lied.*"

He lied, Douglas-Hamilton says, "by claiming that he was present at a dinner in Berlin when my father supposedly met Hess—which never happened. My father never met Hess." Douglas-Hamilton believes Philby lied about that detail and others in his report to exaggerate his knowledge of the affair, to bolster the credibility of his report to Stalin that the Hess flight was part of a plot by the Bolshevik-haters in the British Secret Intelligence Service to unleash Hitler on the Soviets.

We know the effect of Philby's reports: Andrew and Gordievsky conclude that "contributing to Moscow's distrust of British intentions was to be one of Philby's main achievements as a wartime Soviet agent."

Stalin's paranoia over the Hess case never diminished; he berated Churchill about it as late as 1944. And Philby's interpretation of the Hess affair planted bitter seeds of suspicion and distrust that would bear fruit in the swift shattering of the wartime alliance after 1945 and in the Iron Curtain landscape of postwar Europe.

Of course, there were real enough reasons for distrust between Moscow and London, but it appears that what Philby did was not report but deliberately *distort,* add fuel to the fires of mutual distrust.

To what end? Later, in his Moscow years, Philby liked to portray himself as a faithful servant of the Soviet people and the cause of proletarian internationalism. But it seems that, in the Hess case at least, he was using the immense leverage of his pivotal position to serve his own interests, play his own game—make his own map. An agent of neither West nor East but, more than anything, an agent of chaos.

By the end of the war, Philby would take the game to an even more dizzying level of complexity and power. By 1945, he had engineered a spectacular coup within MI6 that got himself promoted to head of the newly created Russian section. He was then the man simultaneously responsible for telling the Brits what Stalin thought and telling Stalin what the Brits thought. In this unique Janus-faced position at this critical moment, he was perhaps the ultimate intelligence player, a key conceptual map maker of the postwar world, perfectly placed to make the colossi of East and West dance to his tune.

This is not the only interpretation of the Philby enigma, of course. There are still those who come forward to say that Kim Philby was really dancing to *their* tune—that Philby was "as much pawn as player."

Some die-hard supporters of James Angleton, for instance, claim *he* was playing a "deep game" with Philby all along, deliberately feeding him disinformation—a proposition vigorously denied to me by the mole war historian of the CIA, Cleveland Cram, one of the few men who've read every single secret CIA file on Philby, even those the agency denies exist.

And Cave Brown's forthcoming biography entertains a provocative variant on the Philby-as-pawn hypothesis, that Philby was used by "C"—Sir Stewart Menzies, the legendary head of the wartime Secret Intelligence Service—to play disinformation games with the Soviets during the war (a fact reported by none other than the former CIA head Allen Dulles). And that "C," knowing of Philby's early Communist background, may have known about, and used, Philby's relation with the Russian intelligence services for his own "deep game," a game that may have been played out even after Philby arrived in Moscow.

Support for this seemingly far-fetched triple-agent hypothesis, the one that triggered Graham Greene's deathbed summons for his Philby papers, comes from an unexpected source. The newly opened KGB files on Philby reveal that at least some elements in the KGB were as paranoid about Philby's all-powerful, unfathomable deceptiveness as James Angleton was.

Cave Brown's manuscript quotes at length one senior KGB colleague of Philby's, Mikhail Petrovich Lyubimov, formerly of the KGB's British section:

> When I read Kim's files to prepare myself for work as the deputy chief of the British Section, I found a big document, about twenty-five typewritten pages, dated about 1948, signed by the head of the British Department, Madame Modrjkskaj, who analysed the work of Philby, Maclean, and Burgess. And she came to the conclusion that Kim was a plant of the M.I.6 working very actively and in a very subtle British way. The deputy chief of Smersh, General Leonid Reichman, a friend of mine and of my father, told me only four years ago: "I am sure that [Philby, Burgess, and Maclean] were British spies."

Just how subtle was Kim Philby? Could he have been a British spy when he arrived in Moscow? Those who argue the case—on both sides—focus on one of the single most mystery-shrouded episodes in the whole Philby saga: the moment in Beirut when he was literally between two worlds. The moment in 1963 when one of his closest Secret Service colleagues confronted him with evidence that he was a Soviet agent in a dramatic, face-to-face showdown. The showdown that resulted in Philby first confessing and then double-crossing his confessor by slipping out of Beirut to the safety of Moscow.

Windows into the Soul

London, 1994. The old spy was dying fast. His breath was coming in gasps over the phone. In three days he would be dead. This was, I believe, the last interview he gave. He couldn't talk for long, he told me, but there were still some things he wanted to say about Kim Philby, some myths he wanted to put to rest. He was still haunted by Philby. Still plagued by the rumors and whispers about his showdown with Philby that night in Beirut in 1963.

The dying spy was not the only one haunted. The events of that night in Beirut have plagued and disrupted the spy establishments of the United Kingdom for the past quarter century—Kim Philby's parting black valentine to those he betrayed. The belief that Philby was tipped off by a high-placed mole to the coming confrontation, that the "confession" he gave was an artful sham, disinformation designed to buy time to execute his escape plan—a belief still held by many in the spy business—was directly responsible for the twenty-year-long mole hunt in Britain that culminated in the famous "Spycatcher" controversy.

"It's nonsense," the dying spy insisted to me. Philby was *not* tipped off he was about to be confronted. Philby walked into it unawares. "He wasn't ready at all. He was simply asked to come to an apartment by his [MI6] contact in Beirut. He didn't know who he was going to meet. Instead of finding our man in Beirut, he found me."

The man Philby found, the spy speaking to me, was Nicholas Elliott, the perfect embodiment of the blue-blood, playing-fields-of-Eton establishment Philby arose from and betrayed. After serving in a number of top MI6 posts, he eventually became Margaret Thatcher's personal intelligence adviser on Soviet affairs. A cultivated bon vivant who also reportedly possessed an inexhaustible store of filthy jokes, Elliott had become close to Philby during their wartime service in MI6. So close, in fact, that at one time Philby disclosed something to Elliott he'd disclosed to no one else—the shattering secret of his marital life. A secret that (Elliott argues in his memoirs) revealed that "the arch-deceiver had himself been deceived, the arch-liar had been tricked for so many years."

It wasn't sexual infidelity. Rather it was his wife's failure to confide the nature of the secret life *she* was living—and Philby's ten-year failure to penetrate her deception.

In 1948, Aileen (second of his four wives) came down with the latest in a succession of mysterious illnesses. Philby begged his friend Nicholas Elliott, then MI6 station chief in Bern, to find a Swiss doctor who could get to the bottom of Aileen's problem. After flying Aileen to Bern for treatment, Philby was devastated to learn from a psychologist there that ever since her teens, Aileen had been afflicted with a severe compulsive disorder that caused her to cut and mutilate herself and to inject herself with her own urine.

"It was an intense affront to Philby's pride," Elliott writes, that his wife had been able to hide a secret self from him.

Perhaps the fact that Elliott had that glimpse of the deceiver deceived explains Philby's peculiar conduct toward him in that Beirut showdown in 1963.

In describing that moment in Beirut to me, Elliott was at great pains to insist that he was in command. In the last year of his life, controversy over the Philby confession had broken out anew in the London *Times*'s letters column; Elliott had been accused of "bungling" the job.

Elliott insisted to me he had taken Philby by surprise and that Philby was "shaken."

"Very simply, I told him, 'I know you're a traitor and you'd better admit it, if you're as intelligent as I think you are,' " Elliott said. " 'And we'll both try to work something out.' "

Elliott offered Philby full immunity from prosecution, if he'd return to England and provide the intelligence services with a complete damage assessment—a deal similar to the one that would later be accepted by Philby's fellow "Ring of Five" mole Anthony Blunt. "That was the point of it all—the damage assessment," Elliott told me.

Philby later told Phillip Knightley, author of a groundbreaking biography, that the deal had been unacceptable to him. Because it would have involved naming names—other KGB moles—"that was no deal at all." But Elliott contended to me that Philby had, in fact, accepted the deal. Elliott believed then, and continued to believe till the end of his life, that Philby had been ready to give up and go home.

Of course, it didn't happen that way. Philby returned with a typewritten confession and then asked for more time to arrange his affairs. Elliott returned to London with the confession, apparently trusting Philby to keep his word about coming home. Philby instead chose another home. Within a week, he'd disappeared from Beirut and, before long, showed up in Moscow, mocking the men he'd betrayed.

From out of the murk of this exceedingly murky episode have emerged several conflicting theories of what was really going on:

1. Philby had cracked: Tired and shamed by Elliott, he wanted to accept the deal and go back to Britain. But, Elliott told me, when the KGB learned of

what had gone on between him and Philby, "it caused consternation" and Philby practically had to be kidnapped at gunpoint and shanghaied off to Moscow.

2. Then there are those, like the author of *Spycatcher,* Peter Wright, and the espionage historian Nigel West, who think Philby *was* tipped off by a highly placed British mole (the Third Man's Third Man) and his "confession" was all an artful con, Elliott a gull for believing him. (Former Secret Service mole hunter Wright's obsessive search for the man who tipped off Philby spread the same kind of suspicion and paranoia that Angleton's mole hunt did in the CIA—which might have been Philby's objective in hinting to Elliott that he had been warned.)

3. A third school argues that Elliott's real mission was not to persuade Philby to come back home to England at all but to pointedly hint Philby would be better off if he repaired to Moscow, sparing his old colleagues the embarrassing prospect of Philby at large in the United Kingdom, free to broadcast humiliating details of his successes in conning everyone.

4. Finally, there is an even more conspiratorial school that believes it was at this point that Elliott "turned" Philby from Soviet double to British triple agent and that the whole confrontation had been nothing but a charade to convince the KGB that Philby had to be brought back to Moscow, where he could serve as a British penetration of Moscow Center.

In the course of my odyssey through the Philbian cosmos, I came upon two extraordinary documents that throw new light on this mysterious episode.

The first is a memo that contains a purported account of a confession *about* Philby's confession. A purported account of Nicholas Elliott's deathbed confession about that Beirut encounter—the notional shrive.

It contends that sometime in the seventy-two hours between the time I spoke to him and his death, Nicholas Elliott was "shriven"—his confession was taken according to the rites of the Anglican church. What is said in a shrive is meant to be between the dying man, his confessor, and his God.

The memo on the alleged shrive was sent to me by E. J. Applewhite, the CIA station chief in Beirut during Philby's last days there. It records Applewhite's conversation with a spook in London whose name Applewhite has blotted out in the copy he sent to me.

The memo, entitled "Elliott and Philby Confrontation," begins as follows:

[Name blotted out] says he has learned from several old hands from his tour in the U.K. that, shortly before Nicholas Elliott died in London of cancer of the liver, Elliott was "shriven" by one Canon Pilkington. The canon was on the point of telling [the] informant the nature of Elliott's final confession, but he was interrupted. The informant said no matter: I know what Nick's confession would have been—that in that final climactic confrontation with Philby in Beirut, the dictates of patriotism and duty were strained to the breaking point by bonds of friendship and class loyalty to Philby, and that in the event it was Elliott's great lapse that he had tipped Philby off and had "permitted him to fly the coop." That was what was weighing on the Elliott conscience.

Applewhite, distancing himself from the informant's story, calls it "an oversimplification." But I think it's more than that. It sounds to me like a sophisticated disinformation operation on the part of the informant, one worthy of Kim Philby himself.

Note that the "informant" tries to give the impression that Canon Pilkington betrayed the sanctity of the confession, when in fact the informant only conjectures what the canon *might* have told him, had he not been "interrupted." And, in fact, when I reached Canon Pilkington, he denounced the story colorfully as "a load of codswallop." Pilkington said he and Elliott had had "a few words" on the subject of Philby, but that there was no formal shrive and no deathbed remorse about Philby.

Who might have been the source of the disinformation? I'd suggest it's a manifestation of the undying bitterness over the Philby affair between the gumshoes of MI5 (the British equivalent of our FBI) and the old-school-tie aristocrats of MI6, equivalent to our CIA who were thought to have protected Philby as one of their own.

What's shocking here is the lengths to which the partisans in the never-ending Philby wars will go: A notional version of a dying man's final rites is used to accuse him of collaborating in the escape of a traitor.

Still, there *was* something about that confession drama in Beirut that tormented Elliott until the end. And if it did weigh on Elliott's conscience, might it also have weighed on Philby's? Did Kim Philby have a conscience?

Here the second revealing document to surface has particular relevance—a memorandum in Philby's own handwriting that I found myself fixated on while going through the Philby papers in Sotheby's London offices. If espionage, as defined by Sir Francis Walsingham, the sixteenth-century founder of the British Secret Service, is the effort to "find windows into men's souls," I found this document to be, if not a window into Philby's soul, then a glimpse of his own chilling soullessness.

It's a nine-page memorandum in Philby's tiny, precise handwriting, a memo that seems to have escaped the KGB sweep of his apartment after his death. (His wife, Rufina, claims it only recently turned up, perhaps stuck in the back of a file drawer.) As such, it may be the only manuscript from Philby's Moscow years not read, pored over, and vetted by his suspicious spymasters. All we have of the uncensored Philby.

The subject of the memo is one that was obviously close to Philby's heart: the psychology of interrogation and confession; how a spy should behave when he's confronted and accused of treason. The memo seems to have been drafted for a KGB training course for agent handlers. But it also may have been Philby's indirect way of confronting KGB suspicions about his behavior in Beirut.

Philby opens the memo with a "syllogism" on confessions:

1. Giving information to the enemy is always wrong.
2. Confession is giving information to the enemy.
3. Therefore, confession is wrong.

This is a pretty audacious ploy. After all, Philby himself had supposedly *confessed*—he certainly gave *some kind of* information to the enemy, his friend Nicholas Elliott. Was it all disinformation and black valentines?* Could the KGB be sure? It seems possible Philby is attempting to counter suspicion of him with *this* syllogism:

1. Philby is said to have confessed.
2. Philby says all confession is wrong.
3. Therefore, Philby could not have (really) confessed.

Whatever the ulterior purpose of Philby's syllogism on confession, something else emerges in the remainder of the nine-page memo, the painstaking analysis he devotes to the interrogation-confession dramas of two KGB atom spies of the late 1940s, Klaus Fuchs and Alan Nunn May, who faced the same kind of tense inquisitions Philby had but who cracked under pressure.

With the eye of an expert who's seen such battles of will, both as interrogator and as suspect, Philby takes us inside the give-and-take of the atom spy confrontations and concludes that in both cases the seemingly confident interrogators were actually in a desperately weak position. They knew that the sort of evidence they had was either too vague or too explosively secret to be used in court.

The interrogators were therefore "bluffing desperately," Philby says, and the suspects were in a far stronger position than they knew: If they had held out and refused to confess, "they'd have remained free men."

Free men! His use of the term is doubly ironic. He'd just enumerated all the obstacles the interrogators faced from the due-process, civil-liberties protec-

---

*Black valentines: spycraft jargon for praise designed to poison. Philby's disingenuous praise for Angleton in his 1968 memoir, for instance.

tions afforded by Western democracies—the right to a public trial, to confront accusers, to the protection against self-incrimination that shielded the suspected spies from the tortured "confessions" and summary executions the Soviet system routinely used for those suspected of treachery.

I found something particularly repellent about Philby's smug dissection of the weaknesses of Western interrogators, inhibited by the protections afforded the weak and the underdog—something almost willfully *unconscious*. Why, one wants to ask him, dedicate oneself to destroying *this* system, for the sake of one that he knew had arbitrarily murdered its most naively idealistic operatives on the basis of mere suspicion?

Philby writers often cite the doggerel verse from Kipling's *Kim* about the qualifications of a successful spy, as a way of explaining this kind of moral schizophrenia:

> *Something I owe to the soil that grew—*
> *More to the life that fed—*
> *But most to Allah, Who gave me two*
> *Separate sides to my head.*

But schizophrenia doesn't really explain Philby so much as excuse him. The disease metaphor suggests he was a victim and not responsible for his thought processes and the acts that grew out of them. Unfortunately—in some cases, certainly—he was.

The Great Pretender

The former spy was talking about Kim Philby's love letters. His courtship style. He was attempting to counter a tale told by another spy suggesting that Philby was bisexual.

No, this spy said, that wasn't Philby. He'd never thought Philby was homosexual, he insisted, but there *was* something peculiar about the nature of his heterosexuality, something that revealed itself in his love talk.

"What I never understood is the way he used language," the former spy said. "He would describe himself as deeply, utterly devoted from almost the first moment, as if the last woman had never existed, even though he'd professed himself deeply, eternally devoted to her. Those letters to Eleanor . . ."

Eleanor Brewer was the married woman Philby wooed away from her husband, a *New York Times* correspondent in Beirut. In *The Master Spy,* his book on Philby, Phillip Knightley describes the "tiny love letters written on paper taken from cigarette boxes," which Philby would send to Eleanor several times a day:

Deeper in love than ever, my darling. . . .

XXX from your Kim

To be followed later the same day by

Deeper and deeper my darling. . . .

XXX from your Kim

Of course, it was more than just little love notes that won Philby the affection—and, amazingly, the enduring loyalty—of his women. In *The Spy I Loved,* Eleanor's memoir of their affair, their marriage, and her brief sojourn in Moscow with Philby (before he left her to take up with Melinda Maclean), Eleanor describes her first impressions of Philby in Beirut:

> His eyes were an intense blue. I thought that here was a man who had seen a lot of the world, who was experienced, and yet who seemed to have suffered. . . . He had a gift for creating an atmosphere of such intimacy that I found myself talking freely to him. I was very impressed by his beautiful manners.

Many men, as well, found themselves "talking freely to him," much to their regret. For Philby, intimacy was his special espionage talent.

When the former spy finished his disquisition on Philby's all-or-nothing-at-all love rhetoric, I asked him if he thought there was an analogy between the kind of near-religious conversion experiences Philby underwent in his romantic life and the blind romanticism of his ideological conversion.

He smiled and asked me, "What do you think?"

It may strain the analogy a bit, but after a lifelong romantic affair with the image, the fantasy of Soviet Communism, Moscow was still a mail-order bride for Philby until he came face-to-face with her in 1963.

Up until then, he'd enjoyed the best of both worlds. He could wallow in decadent bourgeois freedoms while maintaining a surreptitious self-righteous superiority over others who did, keeping pure his devotion to the promised bride. Then, in 1963, after his flight from Beirut, he arrived in Moscow and saw with his own eyes the ugly reality of the love object he'd worshiped from afar.

Not just the grim, disillusioning reality of Soviet life, but the shocking truth about his own status in the organization he'd dedicated his life to, the KGB.

"They destroyed him," the former KGB man told me over the phone from Moscow. The man speaking, Mikhail Lyubimov, was among Philby's closest KGB colleagues, the one who perhaps knew him best, the one with whom Philby shared the depths of disenchantment and doubt he'd successfully concealed from journalists and friends in the West up until the moment of his death.

Before speaking to Lyubimov, I'd listened to some twenty hours of tapes made in Moscow by Cave Brown. Tapes, for the most part, of interviews with key figures in the KGB orbit around Philby's apartment on Patriarch's Pond in Moscow, men who'd shared his hospitality, his secrets, and his doubts.

It's astonishing at first to hear these men, once possessors of the most closely guarded secrets of the century—the secrets of the inner sanctum of the KGB, secrets men were murdered for knowing or seeking to know—discussing them so freely, so offhandedly with a journalist. Astonishing to hear these men casually dissecting the Philby persona.

One can hear in their voices different degrees of affection, admiration, sadness, and anger at the treatment of this man, who had come to be such a highly charged symbol. But the common thread running through all their memories and reflections about Philby was *deception*.

Not deception in the sense of the grand game of global psych-out that Philby's enemies envisioned him playing. "This is rubbish!" Lyubimov told me. It's a judgment former KGB General Oleg Kalugin (Philby's boss in Moscow from 1970 to 1980) concurs with on Cave Brown's tapes. It's also one that the writings of Oleg Gordievsky, the British mole within the KGB, reflect: Philby wasn't running deception operations in Moscow. He was the *victim* of one, of a Soviet deception about the kind of life he'd be leading once he came in from the cold.

According to Lyubimov, this deception began in Beirut just before his escape to Moscow. While Philby was weaving a web of deceit around Nicholas Elliott, he was unaware of the one being woven for him. "When he was leaving Beirut, he was told he would be in Lubyanka," Lyubimov told me, referring to the Lubyanka headquarters building of the KGB, not the infamous prison in the basement known also by that name.

Others have reported that Philby expected to be made a KGB general, that he expected to be named head of the KGB's England division. But, in fact, when he arrived, he found he'd been deceived in several ways: He was told that he was not and never would be a KGB officer of any kind; rather he was an "agent," a hireling—a lack of respect that never ceased to rankle him.

Not only didn't Philby get a rank, even more humiliating, he didn't even get an *office*.

"Any normal man who'd accomplished the feats Philby had would think he'd get his own study, his own telephone, a desk," Lyubimov told me. "It never happened. Nothing happened. He became a sort of a little beggar somewhere in a little apartment. It was three rooms but very small."

In fact, Philby's first seven years in the Soviet Union were almost a form of house arrest. Again a victim of deception: "The KGB told him they were afraid the British MI6 was going to try to assassinate him, so he had to have guards all the time, close surveillance," Lyubimov said.

But the real reason was the Soviets didn't completely trust him not to bolt for home. "They were afraid something would happen. And he would end up back in Britain or even America."

"Did he know they didn't trust him?"

"Oh yes, he knew."

But it didn't take long after he arrived in the Soviet Union for Philby to realize he'd been the victim of another kind of deception, an even more profound one.

From the first, he felt "a complete disillusionment from Soviet reality," Lyubimov says. "He saw all the defects, the people who are afraid of everything. That had nothing to do with any Communism or Marxism which he had a perception of."

The Marxism that Philby "had a perception of" before his arrival was a variety Lyubimov characterizes as "the romantic Marxism of the Comintern agents of the 1930s." Of the daring "illegals," like the sexologist Deutsch, who thought of themselves as fighting fascism for the sake of the future but rarely had to endure the reality of the future as it was embodied in Stalinist rule—until Stalin brought them back to be murdered in the Purges.

The reality of Brezhnev's Russia, with its slow-motion Stalinism, was deeply demoralizing to Philby. According to several of the KGB men Cave Brown interviewed, Philby was often dangerously outspoken in his open contempt for the Brezhnev regime. But was this because Philby was morally outraged by the system or because he wasn't given the place in it he thought he deserved?

Lyubimov, who tends to romanticize Philby, believes his distress was genuine. "The idea of the absence of freedom—he couldn't understand it," Lyubimov told me. "He began to see it with how they treated Solzhenitsyn—which he called disgusting. That was the beginning of his dissidency. Once we had a quarrel about the treatment of writers. Kim was shouting, 'Who is responsible?' And I was saying: 'Well, it's not my department [of the KGB]. I'm not responsible.' And he said: 'No! You *are* responsible! We are *all* responsible.' "

Kim Philby dissident? Cave Brown tends to believe, based on his conversations with the former KGB men around Philby, that he may have played a role with other liberal elements of the KGB in making Gorbachev's success possible. He suggests that Margaret Thatcher's early embrace of Gorbachev in 1984 ("We can do business together") might even have been prompted by information about Gorbachev's intentions passed to her Soviet affairs adviser, Nicholas Elliott, by Philby—through Graham Greene's British intelligence contacts. Cave Brown advances the argument that, toward the end of his life, Philby was seeking "redemption"—that fostering a Thatcher–Gorbachev rapprochement might have been the means for a reconciliation with the England he betrayed.

Cave Brown hedges his bets on whether Philby was doing so on behalf of his homeland, as an actual British triple agent, on behalf of reformist factions in the Soviet Union, or on behalf of himself. The perennial Philby mystery again.

My belief is that while Philby may have hedged *his* bets in some ways, it's unlikely he was a triple agent. Indeed, he was extremely sensitive about being called even a *double* agent. Hated it, in fact. The way he saw it, a double agent betrays one master for another, while he, Philby, had only one master all along: the Soviet Union. He had no loyalty to the Brits to betray.

But I also believe Philby *was* engaged in an elaborate and desperate deception operation during his Moscow years, his last great intelligence operation. This was his campaign to conceal from those in the West just how badly he'd been deceived about the Soviet system.

One thing we learn from a study of Philby's Moscow years is that for all his contempt for the capitalist world, he had a pronounced, even unseemly, eagerness to be respected by the West, particularly by his fellow Brits. One thing he was not going to do was give them the satisfaction of seeing how badly the betrayer had been betrayed. Not while he was alive.

"He had a natural desire to have a pretense, to have a facade," Lyubimov told me.

The deception-disinformation operation began with Philby's book *My Silent War,* a masterpiece of overstatement through deceptive understatement. In it, Philby created a picture of himself as a cool, daring, nerveless, unflappable operator, who used only the driest deadpan understatement to describe his hairbreadth escapes, ingenious stratagems, and clandestine coups. The conspicuous absence of boasting accomplished what boasting itself could not. And along with casually dropped references to "my comrades," his unfailingly brilliant and loyal KGB collaborators, he painted a portrait of espionage superheroes, a team that had accomplished far more than he could ever speak about.

The truth was, he really wasn't on the team at all anymore. Occasionally, the KGB took pity on him, because it looked as though he was drinking himself to death in his despair, and gave him some quasi-operational tasks. For a few years, he taught an informal seminar on England to fledgling KGB officers about to depart for Albion to try to recruit the next generation of Philbys.

Still, there was at least one instance when Philby's talents were brought into play. In the late 1970s, Philby, who never lost his nose for sniffing out a mole, was called in to assess a KGB intelligence disaster in Norway, a key agent blown. Given a sanitized version of the files to analyze, Philby contended he knew what went wrong: The Brits must have a mole in the KGB who blew the cover of the Norway agent. In fact, he turned out to be right. There really was a high-level mole in the KGB, Oleg Gordievsky, although the Soviets were unable to pinpoint him until years later when, Gordievsky believes, Aldrich Ames provided information that clinched the case. Gordievsky barely escaped with his life.

But for the most part, Philby was frozen out, his suggestions ignored. "The KGB was too stupid and impotent to make use of him," Lyubimov reiterated to me. "This destroyed him. This ruined his life."

And, in fact, the book *My Silent War,* which had been one of the chief vehicles of Philby's deception of the West, became one of the chief instruments of torture the KGB used against him. Philby desperately wanted the book, which came out in 1968 in the West, to be published in the Soviet Union—to give him the heroic status with the Soviet public his vanity thought he'd earned.

"All this time, he wanted to be a hero of this country," Lyubimov says. "But they did everything to prevent him from this."

It took twelve years of delays, of brutal editing, of bad translations for Philby to get a mutilated version of *My Silent War* into print in Russian.

And even then, Lyubimov says, "It wasn't really published. A little edition, just distributed to the Central Committee, the military." It was, adds Lyubimov, "almost a *confidential* publication. He was *killed* by this."

And yet you wouldn't know it from the way Philby bragged about his book to Phillip Knightley in 1988: "It was an enormous success and sold more than 200,000 copies. The trouble was that I hadn't foreseen that it would sell so well. It was only in the bookshops a few days and then it was gone. So I didn't get enough copies for myself."

This is fairly pathetic, but at times Philby's desperation to be thought of as a success by his British peers reaches comedic levels. To Knightley, he described his Order of Lenin decoration as comparable to "one of the better Ks" (degrees of knighthood), sounding like a pseud out of Evelyn Waugh.

And there was one point at which Philby's image-building campaign seemed to go beyond deception to an astonishing level of self-deception. The former CIA chief Richard Helms is fond of telling a story about an exchange between Philby and an American reporter in Moscow. The reporter told of a projected film about his life. Philby asked who was going to play him.

"Michael York," replied the reporter.

Philby recoiled, as if slapped. *"But he's not a gentleman,"* he said.

Perhaps the single most telling instance of Philby's last great disinformation operation can be found in correspondence between him and Graham Greene over Greene's novel *The Human Factor.* It was a book Greene wrote in the 1960s but didn't publish until the late 1970s because it came so close to the Philby affair.

Many found resemblances to Philby and his predicament in Greene's protagonist, a midlevel mole named Castle. Apparently, Philby did too. Greene had sent him a copy of the manuscript before publication, and Philby had made particular objection to one passage, at the very close of the book, when Castle, like Philby, has escaped to Moscow and is trying to adjust to his ambiguous position there.

The passage Philby objected to depicts Castle in a tiny, depressing apartment, amid stained, secondhand furniture, insisting over his malfunctioning telephone to his wife in London that he's quite content: "Oh, everyone is very kind. They have given me a sort of job. They are grateful to me. . . ."

Philby wrote to Greene urging him to change this impression. It was misleading, melancholy. And, by implication, not at all like *his* circumstances in Moscow. Greene wrote back thanking Philby for the helpful suggestion, but he would not change the bleak mood.

Greene must have had the novelist's sixth sense from this exchange that the melancholy portrait of the lonely mole in his Moscow apartment, vainly boasting how "grateful" everyone was, had struck home with Philby. That there was a truth to it Philby recognized, a truth about himself that all the tacky ribbons and trophies he gathered from his "grateful" fraternal KGB comrades could not obscure.

Shortly after Graham Greene's funeral, his biographer, Norman Sherry, visited the room where Greene had died. On a table next to the empty bed, he found the letter he'd written to Greene, the one asking for his final thoughts on Philby. Members of Greene's family said that they had found no reply.

If Greene took a Philby secret to his grave, it might have had nothing to do with whether Kim was a double or triple agent. It might have had everything to do with the lonely man in the Moscow apartment.

Perhaps Greene saw through Philby's last great lie, but—unlike Kim—he wouldn't blow a friend's cover.

The Strange Death of Danny Casolaro

In Which a Golden Boy Is Strangled by an Octopus

One of the first stories I heard about Danny Casolaro's funeral was the five blondes at the grave site. Five stunners ranging in age from twenty to forty, all dressed in black, all weeping copiously.

I was feeling pretty bad about Danny myself, for my own reasons. I'd been thinking: Maybe I shouldn't have yelled at him the last time we spoke. Maybe I shouldn't have been so harsh, shouldn't have told him, "Danny, you've got to get *ruthless* with yourself."

I'd been feeling that way ever since the morning of August 13, when I was idly flipping through *The Washington Post* and froze at the headline: "WRITER PROBING INSLAW CASE FOUND DEAD—Freelancer Was in West Virginia to Meet Source, Friends Say."

Friends were saying more than that. Friends and family were disputing the local coroner's hasty preliminary verdict of suicide, a verdict issued before the locals learned about who Danny was and what kind of story he'd been looking into. About the death threats and warnings he'd told them about in the final weeks before he was found with his wrists sliced open with an X-Acto-type blade in a bloody motel-room bathtub. The friends were saying that

Danny was hot on the trail of the long-sought Missing Link between the scandals that had been convulsing Washington—B.C.C.I.,* the October Surprise, and Iran-contra—and that he was killed to keep him quiet.

And it wasn't just friends saying that; a former U.S. attorney general, Elliot Richardson, the ordinarily circumspect Brahmin, was calling for a federal investigation, and suggesting Danny "was deliberately murdered because he was so close to uncovering sinister elements in what he called 'The Octopus.' " Was this another Silkwood case? Was Danny murdered because he was "The Man Who Knew Too Much," as *Time* put it?

But at that point I wasn't thinking murder. I was thinking guilt—my own. I'd had several phone conversations with Danny about his Octopus idea in the weeks before he died, and I'd been pretty skeptical: A lot of it sounded like a rehash of familiar conspiracy-theory connections. That's what I'd meant when I raised my voice and enjoined him to be "ruthless" with himself: slash away the underbrush, so that whatever he had that was new would emerge. Still, when someone you've yelled at to be ruthless with himself is found dead with his wrists slashed, it makes you wonder if he took your words too much to heart.

Which is why I had to go down to West Virginia. Which is why I'm sitting fully clothed in an empty bathtub in the motel room just across the hall from the one in which Danny died, here at the Sheraton Martinsburg ("where meetings and fitness are our business"). Staring up at the cheap cottage-cheese-textured ceiling of the bathroom, perhaps the last sight Danny Casolaro saw.

I've spent the past ten days immersing myself in Danny's world, retracing his steps from the fragments and pieces of the puzzle he left behind in his notes, trying to reconstruct the vision of the Octopus that led him to meet his death here. To see if I could find out, to my own satisfaction, the answer to the murder-or-suicide question: Did Danny Casolaro die because he was, in some sense, too ruthless with himself? Or because someone got too ruthless with him?

> *"Danny, this story isn't fun, it's no adventure. It's traumatic, it's a disease, it's like going into the depths of insanity. . . . It [the story] is the Octopus."*
> —Danny's friend Ann Klenk, summer 1991

I didn't know the guy well. Met him about a dozen years ago down in D.C. I was doing a story about revisionist Watergate theories for *The New Republic* and someone had referred me to Danny as a guy who was pursuing the "Dem-

---

*The Bank of Credit and Commerce International, prosecuted in the late eighties for a variety of arms-dealing, money-laundering operations, including the Iran-contra affair.

ocratic trap" theory—the idea that shadowy figures in the intelligence community hostile to Richard Nixon actually set up the Nixon White House for the Watergate bust.

What I remember most about that evening was not so much the mysteries of Watergate as the mystery of Danny.

The Arabian horses, for instance. Not many investigative reporters I knew raised thoroughbred Arabians in the heart of Virginia horse country. Danny did. Good-looking, good-natured, golden-haired Danny looked less the ink-stained wretch most investigative reporters are than a Fitzgerald golden boy. I was left with a hazy impression of a Gatsbyesque horsey-set dabbler in the arcana of right-wing conspiracy theories.

In fact, it turns out Danny did have a kind of Gatsby fixation, one that apparently persisted until the final hours of his life. One of the last people to report seeing him alive was a waitress at a Pizza Hut, the one that shares a parking lot with the Sheraton Martinsburg. She describes Danny as flirting with her in a lighthearted way on the Thursday afternoon before his body was found. She says that Danny, apparently in high spirits, was quoting to her some lines from a favorite poem, the one about the "gold-hatted, high-bouncing lover" that Fitzgerald used as the epigraph to *The Great Gatsby.*

According to Wendy Weaver, an attractive blond ad exec who was Danny's steadiest girlfriend, Danny was a romantic who loved to quote those particular lines, because it was how he saw himself. Once, Wendy told me, "he painted a tin hat gold, and came into a restaurant that I was in, wearing a tuxedo and carrying roses."

Had Danny struck gold in his Octopus investigation or was he just gilding tin? What was the grail he died trying to find?

He started calling me last winter—I hadn't heard from him in years—first to ask for a copy of a story I'd done about "the Blond Ghost," the legendary ex-CIA-covert-operations mastermind Ted Shackley.* He was pursuing some leads concerning Shackley, he said. Danny wouldn't tell me anything more at that point than that he was working on "something really big," that there was a Shackley angle to it, and that he was reluctant to elaborate ("It would take hours").

Then, this past summer, two months before he died, he started calling me again, asking me for advice on a proposal for a book, a book he wanted to call *The Octopus,* about a shadowy group of rogue intelligence operatives who, in a Ghostly way, were linked to spectacular covert-world-generated scandals from the Bay of Pigs and Watergate to Iran-contra, B.C.C.I., and the October Surprise.

---

*"The General and 'The Blond Ghost,' " *Vanity Fair,* January 1990.

I liked the guy, but when I tried to cut through the thicket of conspiracy-theory connections he was reeling off for me, I just couldn't get a clue to what he might have that was new.

And there was something in Danny's tone of voice that disturbed me, something I'd heard before: that note of smug, condescending certainty that begins to creep into the voice of those who feel they have it All Figured Out and are quite beyond the need to document and substantiate. Later he left a message on my answering machine thanking me specifically for the advice to be ruthless. It was the last I heard from him.

And so as I headed down to Washington and West Virginia to begin retracing the last journey Danny took, I was so skeptical about the Octopus murder theory that I even harbored a suspicion that Danny might have *staged* his own death. That, while his friends were saying it was murder disguised to look like suicide, maybe it was really a suicide staged to provoke suspicion of murder. That by killing himself and leaving enough ambiguities to raise the possibility of murder Danny would make his own death the sensational final chapter of the book he never wrote—the one thing that would validate the seriousness of the quest he was on. It would be the Gatsbyesque thing to do.

But now I think I may have wronged him in at least one respect. By the time I got to the motel here in Martinsburg—after spending hours immersed in his notes, days talking with his friends, nights having strange conversations with his sources—I still didn't believe in the Ludlumesque Octopus conspiracy Danny hyped up for his book proposal. But I now believed that he was onto *something,* that his investigations were real, and that, in the months before his death, they were taking him into areas that involved dangerous knowledge and dangerous characters—one of whom had already been convicted of "solicitation of murder."

> *"Will you kiss me when I'm dead?"*
> —Danny Casolaro to Ann Klenk
> three weeks before he died

The line that best characterizes the kind of journey Danny Casolaro was on in the months before his death was one I found on a scrap of paper amid the literally thousands of sheets and scraps of notebook paper, envelopes, and cocktail napkins I'd been studying. (Was the "Denise" whose number is written on a cocktail napkin from a bar in Tacoma, Washington, a key source or a waitress he was trying to pick up?)

Five big file boxes of Danny's Octopus-investigation notes were retrieved from his basement office by his close friend Ann Klenk, who raced over there as soon as she got the news he was dead.

"He'd told me several times that summer that if I heard he met with an accident, make sure I got that shit out of there," says Klenk, an attractive ex-girlfriend who stayed close to him for twelve years after they broke up. Over dinner at a place near her CNBC office, where she works as a producer for Jack Anderson, she told me that, toward the end, a change had come over Danny. That his obsession with the story had become grim and all-consuming and that one evening at her place he'd turned to her and asked, "Will you kiss me when I'm dead?" (Danny's brother Dr. Anthony Casolaro also reports that in the last couple of months Danny warned him "not to believe it" if he died in what was reported to be an "accident.")

Anyway, there it was on a scrap of notepaper in Danny's files, that line, written in his cheap ballpoint, probably the best testimony to how he had come to see his quest:

> In the middle of the journey of our life, I found myself in a dark wood, having lost the straight path.

It is, of course, the opening of the *Inferno,* the description of Dante's state of mind when he came upon the hole in the world that led down to the gates of hell.

Danny Casolaro's dark wood was a bizarre, tangled lawsuit involving a computer-software company called INSLAW; unfortunately, his guide was not exactly the wise Virgil figure who took Dante in hand. Danny's guide—some would say his Svengali—was a Machiavellian rogue scientist who wove the web Danny was tracing from a jail cell in Tacoma. And the hole in the world Danny fell into was a sunbaked Indian reservation located, appropriately enough, a few hours south of Death Valley as the buzzard flies.

Before plunging into that dark wood, it might be useful now to fill in the picture of the pre-Octopus Danny. He'd always been a restless soul. The son of a successful obstetrician, he grew up to be an affable, athletic six-footer, a boxer with a touch of the poet, searching for something more than his suburban-Virginia setting offered. At age sixteen, his brother Tony remembers, "Danny got it in his head to go down to Peru to look for the lost Inca treasure." Tony recalls he got only "as far as Ecuador, where he ran into some rich guy" who distracted him into a scheme to ship corbina fish to the United States.

Danny's first brush with a mysterious death came when his younger sister died in San Francisco's Haight-Ashbury in the late sixties. It was never certain whether it was an accidental death or suicide. But friends say the traumatic effect of the death on his family made Danny, a Catholic, even more adamantly anti-suicide.

After graduating from Providence College in 1968, Danny began a writing career that shifted fitfully back and forth between fiction and nonfiction. In a ten-year-old résumé I dug out of the file boxes retrieved from his house, Danny informs us that

> in 1969, I wrote two books and authored the initial treatment for *Rain for a Dusty Summer,* a film starring Ernest Borgnine.
>
> From 1970 to the present [circa 1982], I've been a Washington correspondent, contributor, columnist, editor for national magazines, daily newspapers, weekly newspapers, professional journals, and trade journals including *World News, National Star, London Sun, Sydney Daily Mirror, National Enquirer . . . El Dorado News Times, Home and Auto, Washington Star, American Paint Journal . . . Media Horizons* magazines . . . *Washington Crime News.*

A mixed bag, perhaps skewed a bit toward the supermarket tabs, but Danny goes on to claim:

> During these years my investigative work included reporting on some of the most important stories of the decade. In 1970–71 I was one of the first journalists to expose the renewed Soviet Naval presence in Cuba, prompting U.S. government official warning statements. . . . In 1971 I was one of the first U.S. journalists to uncover the makeup and composition of the Castro intelligence network in the U.S. . . . In 1972–3 I was the first journalist to expose how the Chinese Communists were smuggling opium into America. In 1973 to 1974 I was the first journalist to expose and document the "prior knowledge of Watergate" story, a major breakthrough showing an untold side of the Watergate Scandal.

In fact, there's some doubt about where his investigative output on some of these stories appeared. Reed Irvine, the chairman of the right-wing watchdog group Accuracy in Media, recalls that Danny came to talk to him about his revisionist Watergate theory. "But he never wrote anything for us and I never saw anything on the subject he ever wrote," Irvine told me. "I think he was one of those guys who liked to talk big but never delivered."

What's interesting about Danny's investigations is that they all had a definite right-wing agenda. Subversive Castro spy networks, sinister opium-peddling Red Chinese, Soviet naval nukes in Cuba—these suggest Danny had a pipeline into right-wing intelligence networks, or at least hard-right propagandists. It's ironic that Danny's Octopus conspiracy theory has been picked up by the left-leaning Christic Institute.* A close reading of his book proposals makes it clear that Danny viewed the Octopus as something that *subverted* the right-thinking, anti-Communist covert operations he believed in, like the Bay of Pigs.

---

*A Washington think tank of sorts that went from being pro-Sandinista to purveying vast global CIA/right-wing conspiracy theories.

By the end of the seventies, Danny's life changed in a couple of important ways. His ten-year marriage to his wife, Terrill, a former Miss Virginia, came to an end. She moved to Florida; their son, Trey, stayed with him. It was, by all accounts, a shattering breakup. "He loved her deeply, very deeply," Ann Klenk told me. "He even started writing a book about her. It was a romantic novel, he called it *Pursuit*."

Around that time, Danny dropped out of journalism and became a kind of entrepreneur. He started working for, then acquiring, a series of computer and data-processing trade journals. He began making good money, but with daily and weekly deadlines, he had little time for the kind of investigations he once boasted of. By the mid-eighties, after playing the field with a succession of what his friends invariably describe as remarkably beautiful women, he entered into a long-running relationship with Wendy Weaver.

"It was love at first sight for me," says Wendy, still very starry-eyed about Danny. "He was magnetic, charming, charismatic."

But then, at the end of the decade, just when it seemed he'd settled down into a comfortable, early middle age, he found himself adrift. He'd decided to sell his chain of computer publications, but according to friends and family, "Danny was really out of his league making the deal. He just didn't have a business sense." He walked away with a sum not commensurate with the sweat equity he had put in over the years.

Another friend says that Danny's bitterness over the deal marked the beginning of "a clear deterioration in his morale. He was not the kind of guy to run around bitterly raging. Danny just internalized. He felt under pressure to make something of himself in a highly achievement-oriented environment."

His friends recall an enormously generous guy who'd throw them surprise bon voyage parties and write them soulful birthday poems. "He was someone with an incredible ability to give love, but he had trouble taking it in," another ex-girlfriend told me.

Clearly, something was missing. And so, in the spring of 1990, Danny set out to settle the score with fate by bagging that One Big Story, the contemporary equivalent of the lost treasure of the Incas he'd sought as a teenager.

> *"This story killed my friend, and I want very simple questions answered. . . . These people who were jerking him around—whether he killed himself or he was killed—I still hate them."*
>
> —Ann Klenk

It was Danny's computer-world contacts that brought him to the INSLAW case, and it was INSLAW that brought him into the ambit—some would say under the spell—of the rogue scientist/weapons designer/platinum miner/alleged crystal-meth manufacturer who sent Danny off on the quest for the grail he was to die seeking.

The INSLAW case alone is enough to drive a sane man to madness, if not suicide. The INSLAW lawsuit has devoured the lives of those involved the way the all-consuming *Jarndyce* v. *Jarndyce* Chancery suit devoured its progeny in *Bleak House*. If they ever make a movie of the INSLAW suit, it could be called *Mr. and Mrs. Smith Go to Washington and Meet Franz Kafka.*

The Mr. and Mrs. Smith in question are Bill and Nancy Hamilton, an earnest, dedicated St. Louis couple who went to Washington and, in the early seventies, began working on the high-tech side of the war on crime. INSLAW, the software company they built, designed a breakthrough program for use by U.S. attorneys in administering the crime war: It tracks cases, ranking their priorities and helping allocate resources to them. It put INSLAW on the ground floor of a potential quarter-billion-dollar market.

Then, the Hamiltons claim, their company became a crime *victim*. They charge that elements within the Justice Department—cronies of Reagan attorney general Ed Meese's—plotted to sabotage their contract with Justice, drive the company into bankruptcy, and steal the valuable software for their own profit. Far-fetched as that might sound, back in 1987 a federal bankruptcy judge ruled definitively in favor of Mr. and Mrs. Hamilton, declaring that the Justice Department had used "trickery, fraud, and deceit" to misappropriate the software and then tried to drive INSLAW out of business. (The decision was reversed on appeal. Elliot Richardson took the case to the Supreme Court for review; it refused to hear it.)

But this victory was merely the cue for the real Kafkaesque weirdness to begin. Suffice it to say that the Hamiltons, struggling desperately to escape from bankruptcy, began to suspect there was something larger going on behind the scenes that accounted for what they saw as a pattern of mysterious interventions and string pulling directed against them.

Then along came a master conspiracy theorist who confirmed their darkest suspicion: that they weren't in the world of Kafka but that of Robert Ludlum. That the alleged theft of their software by Reagan-Meese Justice Department cat's-paws was actually a key element in the hottest new conspiracy theory of them all. He told them that their case was, in effect, the grassy knoll of the October Surprise plot.

His name is Michael Riconosciuto, and he's the rogue scientist and self-proclaimed former covert operator who became the Hamiltons' tutor and Danny's Svengali. (It should be noted that the person who brought Riconosciuto to the Hamiltons' attention was a key lieutenant of conspiracy-cult leader Lyndon LaRouche; LaRouche intelligence reports were also found in Danny's files.)

In May 1990, according to the Hamiltons' internal "Memorandum for the Record" I found in Danny's files—a memo which became a road map for Danny's fatal journey—Riconosciuto gave the Hamiltons the following account:

That in October 1980, Riconosciuto was serving as director of research of a weapons-design project operating out of the sparsely populated Cabazon Indian Reservation in the California desert (there were only twenty-four actual Cabazons living there at the time). That Bill Casey—then Reagan's campaign director, later CIA head—hired Riconosciuto and a Reagan confidant, Earl Brian, to undertake a secret mission to Iran.

Riconosciuto told the Hamiltons that he "did the electronic funds transfer" to convey a payoff of more than $40 million to "certain elements in Iran" to "prevent a deal with the Carter Administration to release the American hostages prior to the election."

Riconosciuto added that Brian's reward was a kind of license to grab the Hamiltons' lucrative software, with the help of Reagan's Justice Department minions. Riconosciuto further told the Hamiltons that he "saw documents" in the law offices of a former U.S. senator in which the INSLAW-related October Surprise payoff was "chiseled in stone." (Brian denies all these charges and any connection to the INSLAW case.)

Enter Danny Casolaro. In the summer of 1990, shortly after Riconosciuto had disgorged the details of this story to the Hamiltons, Danny showed up in their offices on K Street in downtown Washington, expressing interest in doing some kind of story on the INSLAW case. And at some point that summer the Hamiltons made available to Danny their twelve-page Riconosciuto memo with its profusion of suggestive and seductive leads, its wealth of references to code names, cover-ups, corporate fronts, cutouts, and covert ops— all of which show up in the notes Danny left behind, many of which go far beyond the October Surprise.

The moment he got his hands on that maddening memo, with its maze of illusion and reality, was the moment Danny's life changed and he began his descent into the obsession that would lead to his death. He was slowly, then rapidly, sucked into a kind of covert-ops version of Dungeons & Dragons, with that memo as his guide and Michael Riconosciuto as his Dungeon Master.

> *"Stop it, Danny. Just stop it! Get a job. Just let this goddamn story go."*
>
> —Ann Klenk

In Danny, Riconosciuto found the perfect audience. The spook and the journalist have always shared an affinity: each thriving in a realm of secrets and lies, cover-ups and cover stories, sharing the romance of the covert mentality, with its thrilling sense of being privy to the secret heart of matters undreamt of by the ordinary, CNN-watching citizen. And both Casolaro and Riconosciuto were in a similar position: lone operatives freelancing on the fringe, longing to be at center stage.

The turning point in their relationship came when a dramatic prediction Riconosciuto made seemed to come true. In February 1991, he told Danny, a high-ranking Justice Department official had warned him not to give a deposition to House Judiciary Committee staffers investigating the INSLAW controversy or he'd end up in jail. Several weeks later, federal agents arrested Riconosciuto on charges of distributing speed. (Riconosciuto, who did talk to Judiciary Committee staffers, insists the chemicals were actually being used in an innovative process for refining platinum ore; the Justice Department official has denied making any threat.) As soon as he got news of the arrest, Danny hopped a jet and flew all night cross-country to Tacoma, where he spent ten days working as an unpaid, unofficial investigator of the Riconosciuto "frame-up"—and of the endless tangled tales of intrigue and dirty tricks this imprisoned Scheherazade of the spook world had to tell.

"Danny said that when he started out he only believed 5 percent of what I was saying" and doubted 95 percent. "But by the end," Riconosciuto boasted to me from jail during one of *our* marathon conversations, the ratio was reversed.

I'd still put his credibility at Danny's original figure of 5 percent—but even so, the 5 percent that does check out makes Riconosciuto one of the more remarkable characters I've encountered in years of debriefing spook types. If he's a liar, he's not your ordinary liar. He's extraordinarily skillful at weaving fact and fiction into a seamless web of seductive intrigue. And he did direct Danny down some dark paths in which he came into contact with some seriously dangerous dudes.

> *"These people in the desert were murdered. Murder, dope, government. That's dangerous. Think about it, Danny."*
>
> —Warning from "Clark Gable"

It was a whipsaw, a psychological whipsaw, Danny Casolaro got caught in. A cruel game of paranoid psych-out played with Danny's head. The players batting him back and forth were Michael Riconosciuto and his longtime shadowworld nemesis, the man we'll call, for reasons to be clear soon enough, "Clark Gable."

But it was no game, it was a long-distance duel. In fact, the only thing the two men agree on is this: Danny's death was murder. And each implies the other may well have had something to do with it.

Let's look first at Riconosciuto. Here are some of the things he told Danny—and me—about himself:

That he was a child prodigy who developed a powerful argon-based laser, then went to work in the lab of a Nobel Prize–winning scientist at Stanford at age sixteen. That his grandfather was a top military aide who worked with an early CIA chief, General Walter Bedell Smith—family connections, he said, "opened a lot of doors for me."

That from Stanford he went on to Haight-Ashbury in the sixties, where he was responsible for an underground-newspaper spread in which, he said, "we published pictures of narcotics agents," including one "showing [an agent] having sex with these underage girls that we took from a rooftop."

Ultimately, Riconosciuto told Danny and me, vengeful narcs engineered his "frame-up" on charges of manufacturing psychedelic drugs.

In Danny's notes I found evidence that he'd checked out these claims, even getting Riconosciuto's grades and IQ from a parochial school he attended: The IQ was a somewhat-less-than-prodigy-level 124; the story about building the argon laser is true. But Danny dug up clips that tell a somewhat different version of the narc-sex-vengeance "frame-up." They report that Riconosciuto was arrested in Seattle in September 1972 by "federal narcotics agents who say they have had the defendant under surveillance off and on since 1968." What Riconosciuto said back then at his trial was that sinister drug people tried to force him to make psychedelic drugs, threatening to kill him if he didn't do their bidding. They'd already been "responsible for fourteen murders," he told the court.

That figure—"fourteen murders"—rang a bell. In my first conversation with Riconosciuto, I was exploring some cryptic but provocative notes I'd found in Danny's files about "biological warfare" projects. The notes made references to the possibility of manufacturing "slow-acting brain viruses" such as "Mad Cow Disease" which could be slipped into "meat pies." (Hey, I'm just reporting what the notes said.)

Riconosciuto was reluctant to talk about the germ-warfare leads. "It's a real *Dr. Strangelove* tale," he said. "But it's obviously real enough that anybody who's ever come near it has gotten killed. And Danny was starting to make progress."

When I asked him to elaborate on the germ-warfare story, he uncharacteristically—or perhaps theatrically—clammed up. "I really don't want to be the one to say, you know, because I know of fourteen people that are dead that have tried to come out publicly on this."

While it's clear Riconosciuto has a special affection for the figure of fourteen deaths, that's only a fraction of the mortality rate around him, he said. "That's only on the 'bio-tech,'" as he called the germ-warfare stuff. "There's almost fifty dead total that have been connected with me in one way or another since the early eighties."

While this claim captures the paranoid flavor of conversations with Riconosciuto, it's deceptive in one sense. Because, while there may not have been fifty, or even fourteen, there were some real, documentable murders happening around him, particularly after he arrived at the Cabazon Indian Reservation in the early eighties and became involved with "Clark Gable" and "Dr. John."

The whole Cabazon-reservation maze Danny was pursuing is further proof that the reality of the covert-ops shadow world will always out-invent the clichés of a Tom Clancy. It is also, to my mind, the strongest barrier to believing Danny's death was a simple suicide. Regardless of what money problems he had, or book-proposal rejections he suffered, he was really onto a *story* here.

Evidence that Danny was onto something real can be found in a front-page, three-part investigative series in the *San Francisco Chronicle* that appeared three weeks after Danny died and that was inspired in part by his probe into the Cabazon-reservation enigma.

"Just fifteen years ago," *Chronicle* reporter Jonathan Littman begins, "a handful of Cabazon Indians barely scratched out a living on their reservation in this tumbleweed desert just north of the Salton Sea," near Indio, California. But since a "mystery man," Dr. John Nichols, took control of their affairs as the "administrator" of the tiny tribe, a staggering *quarter-billion* dollars has been poured into projects based on the reservation.

What Nichols did was leverage the one asset of the woebegone Cabazon band—their "sovereign status" as a quasi-independent nation, which allows them to build casinos and enter into joint ventures with corporations. Such joint ventures are shielded to some degree from the usual legal and regulatory scrutiny, making the reservation extremely attractive to the kind of enterprise that prefers to operate in the shadows. In fact, Dr. Nichols (the doctorate is of divinity) seemed to have close contacts with CIA and military-intelligence operatives (according to the *Chronicle*, he would tell some that he'd had a hand in the CIA assassination attempts on Fidel Castro and Salvador Allende). Contacts which attracted to the desolate reservation what the *Chronicle* called "a maze of politicians, military officers, organized crime figures, intelligence agents, foreign officials ranging from Saudi sheiks to Nicaraguan contras."

One of the people who materialized in this maze is our friend Michael Riconosciuto. He claimed he'd spent the years since his psychedelic-lab bust as a government informer on the antiwar movement and as a covert CIA operative in South America (where he says he first met Dr. Nichols) infiltrating the liberation-theology movement. Back in the States, Riconosciuto then became the "technical adviser" to mystery man Dr. Nichols on the reservation. Before long, Riconosciuto says, he began to learn about some "horrible things" going on out there.

This is the labyrinth Riconosciuto was leading Danny into—the one he died in. The *Chronicle* reporter tells us that, "just days before his death," Danny Casolaro "planned to visit the Reservation. . . . Although he did not divulge what role the Cabazons may have had in the conspiracy [he was investigating], Casolaro . . . recently told this reporter that one of the titles he was considering for his [Octopus] book was *Indio*."

It would have been a more accurate title. Indeed, the grandiose "Octopus" of Danny's maladroit, overhyped book proposal was—to continue the piscine imagery—a red herring. But there *was* a lowercase octopus out there in the desert beyond Indio.

Riconosciuto himself, the resident demon of this labyrinth, supports the more modest, lowercase characterization of the octopus: "Danny's theory was different" from the typical megaconspiracy theory, he told me. "Danny was dealing with real people and real crimes."

One of the crimes was murder. Several murders, all unsolved. One victim was Michael Riconosciuto's "business partner," a man named Paul Morasca, whom he candidly describes as a money launderer. Morasca was found hogtied and asphyxiated in a San Francisco apartment. One of the initial suspects in the murder was Michael Riconosciuto himself, and he says the accusation shocked—*shocked*—him, and motivated him to spill the beans on all the dirty deeds done on the reservation.

He claims he was responsible for pinning a "solicitation of murder" charge on Dr. Nichols for trying to hire a hit man to kill some casino associates on the reservation. (Nichols pleaded no contest and served sixteen months' jail time on the charge. A Cabazon spokesman has said, "There's nothing sinister going on at the reservation. It's just a very successful operation.")

Anyway, it was in the midst of this film noir intrigue out there in the sterile desert flats that Riconosciuto first encountered the man who would become his partner, his target, his obsession, and, ultimately, the second pole of Danny's Octopus investigation: the man we're calling Clark Gable.

We're calling him Gable for two reasons: first, because those among Danny's friends who met this mysterious figure when he flew into D.C., to warn Danny his life was in danger, invariably describe him as "looking just like Clark Gable, only without the big ears," and, second, because his real name is Robert Booth Nichols, and there already is a Nichols (Dr. John, no relation) in this story.

The circumstances in which Riconosciuto and Gable met are in dispute. But it seems that for a time they planned some R-and-D ventures for high-tech hardware behind the shield of the Cabazons' sovereign status. Gable admits to being the head of a holding company, one of whose subsidiaries has licenses on the prototype for an automatic weapon. But he won't say much more about his business. When I finally reached him at a California number I'd found in Danny's notes, he denied any involvement in improper activities. He told me his falling-out with Riconosciuto began at the reservation when he caught the self-styled scientist in "lies" about his esoteric inventions. He blames Riconosciuto and others who have been "Michaelized" for peddling dark tales about him. He hedged when I asked him about intelligence-world connections. "I have been involved in sensitive activities. That's the only way I can describe it," he said. And while he denied being *in* the CIA, he said he'd "been involved with a lot of people who tell me they are in the CIA, although I have no way of substantiating it."

What is certain is that Michael Riconosciuto has it in for Gable, and that he began pointing Danny in Gable's direction, filling his head with allegations of Gable's sinister, international covert-world connections. Indeed, he began to paint a picture of Gable that linked him to very big, very dangerous organized-crime syndicates, including the feared Japanese Yakuza and the fearsome Gambino crime family of John Gotti. That linked him in addition to various CIA and British intelligence plots, because Gable was the friend of a legendary Bondish Brit known as "Double Deuce." (Are you beginning to get a feel for the texture of Danny Casolaro's world by now?)

In fact, Riconosciuto attempted to convince Danny, with some success for a while, that this man Gable was the key to what Danny was starting to call the Octopus.

According to an ex-FBI man who was a source for Danny in his final weeks, Danny began rashly and unwisely calling Gable himself about these allegations. "Danny began getting into areas that were dangerous, very dangerous," the ex-FBI guy told me. "This is dangerous work. He was warned. You know. Gable warned him."

A Visit from Clark Gable

I have the details of the strange encounters between Danny and Gable from three different sources, none of whom was eager to be the sole source.

Because all recalled them as chilling. The exotic quality of those meetings is captured by one of Danny's friends, who had lunch with Danny and Clark Gable. Gable had flown into Washington, D.C., on a weekend about a month before Danny's death, was staying at the top-bracket Four Seasons Hotel in Georgetown, and seemed to have little business other than to spend time with Danny Casolaro.

The friend, a well-connected player in Pacific Rim politics who requested that his name be withheld, said Gable was "very slick, very civilized-appearing. Danny used to say he had the manners of a gentleman, but underneath he was a thug."

The friend recalls Gable "doing that thing that guys do on bar stools the world over. He looks at you with that wink and says, 'You know, I'm *not* in the CIA.' "

When the three of them finally sat down to lunch at Clyde's in Tyson's Corner, the friend says, Gable promptly informed them he'd "just taped a radio broadcast as the incoming minister of state security in Dominica, and was preparing a coup that 'some bimbo in the CIA' was asking him about. But he was actually at a higher level than the 'bimbo.' " (The island of Dominica, which figures heavily in Danny's notes, is an impoverished flyspeck in the Caribbean that has been characterized as "the Third World's Third World." Gable says he was asked by the leader of the opposition party on the island if he'd become security minister, should an election bring it to power; he says he cleared this with the State and Justice departments. He also denies any CIA coup plot and says the broadcast was an interview about economic development.)

Danny's friend says he "never witnessed a performance" like the one that ensued. "[Gable] had this story that they were going to turn Dominica into a CIA base, had plans for a desalination program, and pulled out this design drawn by a French architect of a dome the size of Texas Stadium that was half underwater. Really, the whole thing reminded me of Ernst Stavro Blofeld [the Bond villain]. I mean, good Lord, you could just see James Bond swimming out there with a *babe*. I excused myself at this point. I really didn't want to hear anything more after seeing Blofeld's underwater lair."

"Did he come across as a con man?" I asked Danny's friend.

"It's funny," he said. "It was like he was real slick, really *like* Clark Gable, and there were nuggets of truth. The guy just oozes intrigue." (Gable told me he was exploring plans for exploiting the island's heavy rainfall to export purified water, and denies anything improper about it.)

Then, the friend says, Danny showed him a side of Gable he didn't want to know about.

"After lunch Danny pulls me aside and pulls out this purported FBI wiretap summary on [Gable], and it showed how [Gable] is connected. It linked him to the Yakuza and to the Gambinos as a money launderer. And that widened my eyes. I said, 'Danny, I'm gonna take you out back and whip your ass! You just put me in a meeting with this man and didn't tell me what the hell—why didn't you tell me before?' And Danny was kind of, 'Oh, I don't know. I wanted to see how [Gable] would react.' In other words, he gaffed me with a hook and tossed me in the water to see if the Octopus would move!"

Gable says the suggestion that he's involved with the Yakuza and the Gambinos is "totally false." It's "absolutely ridiculous" to link him to "the *Gambia* family," he told me, conspicuously mispronouncing the name. He traces the trouble to an FBI misunderstanding of his screenplay career. He says he was introduced to a high-level executive of MCA several years ago at a coffee shop. When the MCA man encouraged him to turn some tales he'd told him into screenplays, they became friends and, briefly, business associates. Unknown to him, the MCA man was the subject of a full-court-press FBI investigation for being a key organized-crime link to the entertainment industry. And so, Gable says, his voice was picked up by taps on the MCA man's phone. The bureau misinterpreted their conversations as containing code words for illegal activities, turned around, targeted him, and slandered him to his business associates. In fact, Gable's company is suing an FBI man for libel and slander. He says that the "wiretap summary" was part of the FBI man's affidavit in the Gable slander suit.

In addition to the dispute over the wiretap affidavit, there's also a dispute over the nature of the warning Gable gave Danny. Riconosciuto, who wasn't there, tries to portray it as a personal threat from Gable. But others recall that it was Gable warning Danny against Riconosciuto.

Danny's girlfriend Wendy Weaver, for instance, spent a long, strange evening with Danny and Gable and has an indelible memory of the warning.

"It was a weird night, so weird," she recalls. "We met at the Four Seasons [bar]. He was pretty well lit when we got there. He was very charming, very handsome. When I tried to find out who he really was, he really didn't give me an answer. He just started these warnings. . . . He kept saying, 'You don't know how bad this guy Riconosciuto is. Tell Danny to stay away.' He said, 'Riconosciuto—he might not get you today, he might not get you next month. He might get you two years from now. If you say anything against him he will kill you.' "

He repeated it several times, Wendy says. "At least five times."

Later in the evening, Wendy reports, there was a heated altercation with "this Asian-looking guy, who apparently insulted me in some way. And Danny was scared. After we got rid of [Gable], Danny goes, 'Wendy, this guy is scary.' That's the first I heard him say that."

While Gable was trying to warn Danny about Riconosciuto, Riconosciuto, for his part, was desperately trying to warn Danny about Gable. Or so he says. "I was absolutely frantic trying to warn him," Riconosciuto told me.

It was Danny's habit of "bouncing" Riconosciuto's stories off Gable that put him in peril, Riconosciuto says. One of the things he was supposedly "bouncing" involved what Riconosciuto said was a major heroin-related sting. (Gable denies any involvement in drug traffic. "I hate narcotics," he told me.) Another involved Riconosciuto's claims about an effort by the Cali cocaine cartel to derail the extradition of an alleged Colombian kingpin called Gilberto.

Gable just "went ballistic," Riconosciuto says, when Danny bounced this Gilberto matter off him. "But by the time I heard about it, there was nothing I could do, you know, except to warn Danny.

"And I called from that day on—it was on a late Monday—Tuesday, Wednesday, all the way through the weekend when they found Danny. Every day I was calling the Hamiltons, asking if anybody had heard from Danny. And I was *frantic*."

Mad Cow Disease and a Blaze of Glory

What was going on in Danny's head as he was being whipsawed between these two shadowy operators and their death warnings?

There was one point in my immersion in Danny's mental world when I felt a flash—a brief, chilling, but illuminating flash of what it must have been like for him when he got in too deep. It came in the course of a phone conversation I had with Ann Klenk, who was not only one of Danny's oldest and closest friends but also the one whose skeptical perspective on his obsession I'd come to rely upon.

She was telling me of her surprise and puzzlement over something she'd just learned: that not long before his death Danny had approached a nurse he knew and questioned her closely about the symptoms of multiple sclerosis and brain diseases.

This was particularly pertinent to the murder-or-suicide question, because an autopsy examination of Danny's brain revealed possible symptoms of M.S. Initially, his friends and family had dismissed this as irrelevant—it couldn't be a motive for suicide, because Danny had never complained of symptoms or, to their knowledge, known of the disease.

Then I mentioned to Ann the cryptic notes I'd found in Danny's files: on germ warfare, on slow-acting brain viruses like Mad Cow Disease, about targeting people with them by slipping them into meat pies.

That's when it struck me. "Oh, God," I said to Ann, "Danny's asking a nurse about brain disease—maybe he thought *he'd* been targeted."

Had he gone that far, or was *I* now too far gone down the road to paranoia that he'd traveled?

A few days later, I happened to mention the report of Danny's seeking information about brain-disease symptoms to Michael Riconosciuto. Who promptly said, "Oh, yes. He, uh, was *concerned*. And that was one of the reasons he had such an obsession [with this story]. Because he felt he had been hit by these people."

"Hit by them?"

"He confided this to me to try to get me to talk further" about biological-warfare projects he'd discovered, Riconosciuto explained. He'd been warning Danny that he wasn't appreciating the danger his investigation was exposing him to. "I told him, 'You can't envision your own death. Why would you want to do this [kind of reporting]?' And he finally came out and said, 'I'm going to die anyway and . . . I want to go out in a blaze of glory and take them with me.' "

What did he mean, he was going to die anyway? I asked Riconosciuto.

"He suspected that he had been, you know . . . a source told him that he, among others, had been targeted with this sort of [slow-acting virus] thing."

This was too much even for Riconosciuto. "I told Danny, 'Look, the paranoia will consume you. You need to go and get tests.' And Danny went and got tests and they were inconclusive. Now, what he probably had was the genesis of a naturally occurring ailment."

The paranoia will consume you. This exchange marks the moment when Danny's conspiracy-obsessed imagination surpassed even that of his most inventive source. In fact, the definition of terminal paranoia might be the point where Michael Riconosciuto says you're too paranoid for him.

And yet, there's something in Danny's reported remark that caught my attention: Riconosciuto's recollection of Danny's saying, *I want to go out in a blaze of glory.*

Certainly, as it turned out, Danny went out in a blaze of *publicity.* The networks, the magazines, the mainstream reporters who had given him the brush-off in the weeks before he died, gave him star treatment as a corpse. ABC's *Nightline* and CNN assigned SWAT-team investigative squads to follow the leads in his notes. He couldn't have had it better if it had been scripted.

Could he have scripted it?

More than anything, it's the conspicuous theatricality of Danny's behavior in the last ten days of his life—when he suddenly went into his "I've cracked the whole case" mode—that led me to reluctantly revive consideration of what might be called "the Gatsby scenario": that his death was a final act of self-creation.

What ultimately led me back to the Gatsby scenario was the inadequacy of *both* the case for murder and the case for simple suicide.

One can certainly understand why almost every one of Danny's friends and family leans toward the murder theory. (His mother's first reaction when she heard the news: "They've killed him!") They knew he'd been getting warnings. They knew he'd been getting threatening phone calls. On the Monday before the Saturday he died, he told his brother, "I'm getting these strange phone calls saying, 'You're gonna die.' " Also that week, shortly before he left on the fatal journey to that West Virginia motel, the neighbor who looked after his house reported answering Danny's phone and hearing a voice saying, *"You're dead."* She reports a similar "You're dead, you son of a bitch" call hours after his body was found—which rules out Danny himself as a possible source of the alleged threats against him.

And then there was the unmistakably clear—at least on the surface— prophecy to his brother: *If anything happens to me it won't be an accident.*

With admirable dedication, Danny's younger brother Dr. Tony Casolaro has made it his mission to ensure that if there is any truth to this he will make certain it gets out. Which has resulted in this soft-spoken, reserved specialist in pulmonary medicine—quite the opposite of the extroverted, gung-ho party dude Danny was—plunging into his dead brother's world.

He's talked to Clark Gable. He's even taken collect calls from Michael Riconosciuto in which Danny's jailbird Svengali spun out his "fentanyl" theory: that Danny was immobilized by the powerful synthetic heroinlike drug fentanyl, and then, in a state of compliant, semiparalyzed alertness, was forced to cut his own wrists.

After spending weeks on his brother's case, Tony Casolaro is torn. He can't believe it's suicide, because his brother was so excited and upbeat about his investigation on that last Monday he saw him.

Tony is also troubled by a number of facts. Papers and files Danny had been seen with up in West Virginia were missing from his motel room. Stolen by his murderers? (Of course, if Danny wanted to create doubt he could have made a point of "disappearing" the papers before killing himself.) Then there are the still-unexplained phone calls from people who seemed familiar with the implications of Danny's death before even the police knew. There was the hasty embalming, the cursory look at the death scene by the cops, who made an initial judgment of suicide. (The reinvigorated Martinsburg police investigation—ongoing as of this writing—has been far more thorough, but perhaps too late.)*

But, on the other hand, Tony knows the actual scenario for murder is "kind of Tom Clancy–ish."

"The way I envision it could have happened," Tony told me over dinner one night in downtown Washington, D.C., "someone stands over him and says, 'You write this suicide note or my partner who's standing with your son will, you know, [kill your son].' And Danny would just go, 'Fine.' "

Danny was a big, tough guy, a boxer, fearless, Tony says. But if he felt his son's life was being threatened, "he wouldn't be someone who would resist that kind of pressure."

---

*The new investigation added to the detail but didn't dispute the suicide verdict of the first.

Having written the suicide note, this murder scenario goes, Danny would then have run the bath, gotten undressed, gotten in, and started carving up his wrists with the blade his captors provided him.

The reason his friends and family, all solid-citizen types, could believe in such a far-fetched scenario is precisely that Danny made such a big point of telling each of them in the week before his death that he was on the verge—or *over* the verge—of the big breakthrough he'd been looking for. That he was about to go to West Virginia to "wrap it up," to get the final piece of the puzzle, to nail it once and for all. He told one friend he was going to West Virginia "to meet the head of the Octopus." He told another he was going to West Virginia to "bring *back* the head of the Octopus."

The exact nature of the breakthrough he was trumpeting seemed to vary. He told three people he had finally solved the whole insanely complicated INSLAW mystery. He gave two other friends the impression that he'd gotten the goods on the October Surprise case and linked it to B.C.C.I. He told a source he met in West Virginia that he'd just "gotten enough information on B.C.C.I. to hang Clark Clifford." He went through an elaborate charade with the two friends— showing them a key document that he said tied it all up. The document was a photocopy of a $4 million check signed by Adnan Khashoggi, the Saudi arms dealer who's been linked to Iran-contra. The check, copies of which I found in his files, is made out to Manucher Ghorbanifar, the shadowy Iranian exile arms dealer who played a mysterious role in the Iran-contra deal.

"He was really excited when he got that," Danny's friend Ben Mason told me. "It was like, 'This is it!' "

Was this the magic document/smoking gun of the whole October Surprise/B.C.C.I./Iran-contra megaconspiracy?

That's what Danny implied to his friends. Mason, a musician who wrote songs with Danny, is still under the impression that the discovery of the check was a scoop, a Danny Casolaro exclusive. But, as it turns out, the check had been made public by the congressional Iran-contra committee in 1987 and was well known to reporters in the field.

Ben Mason says that the real bombshell significance of the check is in its link to another document Danny showed him on the eve of his West Virginia trip: a passport photo of an Iraqi named Hassan Ibrahim, a reputed arms dealer. There are those who say that it was Ibrahim whom Danny was going to meet in West Virginia, that it was most likely Ibrahim who was the mysterious "Middle Eastern–looking man" Danny was seen with in the bar of the Sheraton Martinsburg the day before he died. But thus far nothing solid has turned up to suggest the whole magic "Missing Link check" act was anything other than a creative leap of speculation by Danny—if not a deliberate charade.

It should also be recalled that Danny was a novelist. And that he'd spoken to a number of his friends about possibly telling the whole Cabazon-Octopus story as a novel. His theatrical "I cracked the case" declarations in that final week suggest the thriller-novelist imagination at work, setting the stage for the obligatory mysterious murder essential to every spy thriller—in this case, his own.

The timing for all this is notable. The sudden flurry of melodramatic "I cracked the case" calls began at the end of July, shortly after Danny's nonfiction Octopus book proposal was rejected by the first mainstream publisher he sent it to, Little, Brown. One friend Danny called that final week remembers him "planting the seeds" earlier that summer. "Danny began telling me about these death threats he was getting on his answering machine," the friend says. "And I said, 'Look, Danny, the telephone company can find ways to trace these calls.' And he got very embarrassed."

Meaning he faked it? I ask.

"Right." This friend's theory is that Danny knew he was suffering from some progressive debility, like M.S.—there'd been several "accidents" involving Danny's muscle coordination. That Danny knew he wouldn't or couldn't ever get his book written, in part because he wasn't sure what he really *had*. "What he did is throw a whole issue up against the wall so that it would be sorted out in some fashion." The friend believes that if Danny staged his death to look like murder, it would be "tragic," but also a "very wild, courageous," desperate attempt to get the truth out.

Then why leave a suicide note? Ann Klenk asked. It's a cogent objection. If he'd left no note, or, she suggests, if he'd driven his car off a cliff, or jumped off a building, *then* people would be more likely to speculate he'd been run off the road like Karen Silkwood, or he'd been pushed off the building he "jumped" from. She thinks if it *was* suicide it may well have been because "Danny finally found it all a crock," because the whole thing was "LaRouche sickthink, doublethink," and disinformation.

Some, however, cite the note itself as a clue to the murder. The note read, "To those who I love the most: Please forgive me for the worst possible thing I could have done. Most of all I'm sorry to my son. I know deep down inside that God will let me in."

Several of Danny's friends have told me emphatically that that last line— "God will let me in"—is the tip-off. That Danny, a Catholic, knew that suicides could not be "let in" to the Kingdom of Heaven. And that by including that line, by saying he would be "let in," he was signaling—under the noses, or under the guns, of his captors—that his death was *not* suicide.

Perhaps. But the best response to Ann Klenk's contention that he wouldn't have left a suicide note if he had wanted people to think he'd been murdered is, well . . . the actual reaction to his death. A VICTIM OF "THE OCTOPUS"? asked *Newsweek* in a full-page takeout. THE MAN WHO KNEW TOO MUCH? asked *Time*. CLOUDED IN MYSTERY, *People* said darkly two months after his death.

And that's only the mainstream media. Among the conspiracy theorists it's already an article of faith that Danny was assassinated. "A government-sanctioned hit," declares Virginia McCullough, a California-based October Surprise–conspiracy specialist who exchanged notes with Danny before he died. She says Danny was just the latest of several reporters murdered because of their October Surprise investigations—all "government hits." Riconosciuto has added Danny's body to the fifty he says were murdered because of their proximity to him and his schemes. Danny's missing files have already begun to assume the all-purpose, prove-anything status of such other totems of con-spiracy theory as the eighteen-minute gap on the Watergate tapes, the stolen papers of Howard Hughes, and the missing diary of Mary Meyer (the mur-dered JFK mistress).

And Danny himself—the reality of who he was and what he was really after—has begun to be subsumed by his enshrinement in the rolls of the mar-tyrs to the great Octopoidal conspiracy in the sky.

That evening, in my room at the Sheraton Martinsburg, I climbed out of the bathtub. You stare too long at that cottage-cheese ceiling and you begin to see patterns coalescing in the pockmarked surface.

I sat down at the functional desk, trying to ignore the heavy-handed irony of the hotel's promotional card in front of me. It showed a picture of a knotted rope being stretched taut between two fists. *This trip probably has you tied up in knots. . . . If you're at the end of your rope, give us a call.* It was an ad for the hotel's massage service.

I tried to imagine Danny Casolaro at the end of his rope, stretched to the breaking point by his two sources, staring at that knotted cord.

For about the tenth time in the past twenty-four hours, I opened up Danny's last surviving notebook, one of those cheap composition notebooks with a speckled black-and-white cover. On the inside cover was a date: August 6, four days before Danny died. Wendy Weaver had just located it and supplied it to me, along with ten loose pages of notes which had not previously surfaced.

The notebook itself had only one page written on by Danny. There was only one substantive note:

Bill Hamilton Aug. 6
M.R. . . . also brought up Gilberto.

This is an apparent reference to the alleged Cali-coke-cartel kingpin who figured in the last murky Michael Riconosciuto quest Danny was pursuing.

What caught my attention were the two names and phone numbers on that page, above the note, under the heading "To Call."

One name was "Jonathan," apparently Jonathan Beaty, the reporter who broke *Time* magazine's story on alleged B.C.C.I. hit squads.

The other was "Ron." Followed by my phone number.

He didn't call, but I suspect that if he'd reached me in the forty-eight hours before he left for Martinsburg he might well have told me some version of the "I finally cracked the case" riff. And I suppose if I'd heard it, it would have had the same effect on me: I would have been far more predisposed to believe the murder theory.

There is, of course, a legitimate, even compelling reason to pursue every piece of missing evidence, every discrepancy, every unexplained circumstance surrounding Danny's death—the reason Jack Anderson, dean of investigative columnists (who believes it's likely that Danny was murdered), gave: "Anytime a reporter is found dead while covering a story, it's a threat to all of us until the truth comes out." I don't think we should close the book on Danny Casolaro until we rule out the murder theory. Just as maybe a disturbing 5 percent of what Michael Riconosciuto says is credible, I'd say there's still a disturbing 5 percent chance that Danny Casolaro was murdered.

But I do have my own theory about what really killed Danny Casolaro. And the larger lesson his death has for us.

I believe that, in a sense, Danny was correct when he worried he might have been "targeted" with a "slow-acting brain virus." Not exactly the organic virus he worried about, not Mad Cow Disease or multiple sclerosis. Rather, I believe what destabilized Danny was an extremely virulent strain of the *information virus* we're suffering from collectively as a nation: Conspiracy Theory Fever. A slow-acting virus that has infected our ability to know the truth about the secret history of our age.

Don't get me wrong: I believe there *are* real conspiracies—Watergate was one; Iran-contra and CIA/Mafia plots against Castro were others. But those in the grip of Conspiracy Theory Fever seem compelled to believe that (to paraphrase the Flannery O'Connor title) *everything that conspires must converge.* That all conspiracies are tentacles of one big Octopoidal conspiracy that contains and explains everything.

The chief symptom of slow-acting brain viruses like Mad Cow Disease is that the brain becomes "spongiform," riddled with holes. The chief symptom of Conspiracy Theory Fever is that the brain becomes too *spongelike,* too absorbent, indiscriminately accepting all facts and conjectures as equals, turning coincidence into causality, conjectures into certainties, however riddled with holes they might be.

It's clear that toward the end Danny Casolaro fell victim to this kind of fever. He couldn't be content with the lowercase octopus of the Cabazon-reservation maze. He somehow had to convince himself and the rest of the world that he'd come upon the mega-conspiracy that explained everything. Even if he died trying.

Certainly a share of the blame for conspiracy fever must go to spooky sources like Riconosciuto and Clark Gable, to the LaRouchians, to paranoids-in-power like CIA counter-intelligence guru James Angleton, to the overly credulous Christic Institute types. And to the mainstream media, whose inadequate performance on the key scandal nexuses of our time have left the field open to the paranoids and opportunists who populate it with phantom Octopi.

Still, I think of Danny Casolaro not as a paranoid or opportunist but as a kind of Gatsbyesque conjurer, a feverish romantic illusionist. Gatsby gazed with longing at the glow of the green light across the water that separated him from his lost love.

The far-off glow Danny Casolaro yearned for was the illusory Ultimate Story, the one that would illuminate the source of the ongoing American nightmare. It was an illusion Danny loved so much he may well have given his life to make it seem true.

Some Literary Investigations

To the Shores of Light—Or, My First Latin Lesson

Much Ado about "Nothing"
in Two New Translations of Genesis

Floored by Dickens and *Dombey*

An Ode to Helen Vendler, Goddess of Keats's "Autumn"

Hart Crane's Hieroglyphs: The Unmentionable Truth

Dr. Borges and Dr. Ron Solve the Problem of
Memory and Regret

To the Shores of Light—
Or, My First Latin Lesson

Actually, it's not my *very* first lesson, it's my first since my freshman year at
college when—after five years of Latin—I hit the wall. Gave up, frustrated by
the conflict between my awareness of the dazzling, voluptuously seductive
beauty of the elegies of Propertius and Tibullus, my awe at the incomparable
works of Catullus, which ranged from obscene and bitter love lyrics to his
thrilling epic on the marriage of Peleus and Thetis—and my own clumsy and
inept translation skills. The Latin was so intense and lovely but so hard to
reach and render. It didn't come naturally to me, and I resented those for
whom it did. So I quit just when I should have pressed ahead, something I've
always regretted, although I've continued to read and reread the Latin poets I
left behind, in translation. To me, the Silver Age of Latin literature surpasses
any comparable period in English literature, although it evokes (and probably
inspired) the era of the seventeenth-century Cavalier lyric poets I love.

And recently, my regret at leaving Latin behind has been exacerbated by
my growing fascination with the great poet-philosopher Lucretius, author of
De rerum natura (On the nature of things), an amazing visionary epic about
the nature of the universe that ranges from the bonds of attraction between in-

finitesimal atoms to the erotic bonds that bind—and torment—men and women.

I've cited Lucretius in recent columns as a reproof to the hubristic pretensions of "inflationary universe" theorists like Alan Guth. Lucretius is perhaps most renowned in philosophic literature for his dictum about creation: *nullam rem e nilo gigni divinitus umquam,* or "No power, however divine, can create something from nothing." Mr. Guth actually claimed he'd refuted Lucretius: He boasted that he'd proved how the entire universe was created from nothing. Only he cheated: Mr. Guth's "nothing" turns out to be a variety of somethings—"quantum fluctuations" in a "false vacuum," an extremely small "seed" from which the universe grew—a vindication rather than a repudiation of Lucretius.

Beyond that, though, I sensed in my readings of Lucretius, through the scrim of the translation, the presence of the kind of inspired vision that reaches from the origins to the furthest limits of the universe, that links the hearts of men to the heart of creation, the kind of vision of ultimate mystery one finds in the cabalists, whose metaphors for the opening moments of creation ("the breaking of the vessels" and the like) seem to anticipate the most sophisticated contemporary conceptions of the formation of matter in the moments after the big bang.

I felt I wanted to get closer to Lucretius, to the mind of the man whose words, even in translation, had such remarkable resonance for me. And that the only way to do so would be to go back to the Latin and translate it myself. A task that seemed hopeless—until I saw a tiny ad in the *Observer* classifieds:

Hoc Legere Potesne? *If you don't know the answer, then you need a Latin tutor!*
Oxford/Wellesley grad teaches all levels. Very patient & expd. Flex rates

The person behind the ad turned out to be the extremely bright and (as I was to discover) extremely patient Beatrice Cody. To my delight and good fortune, it happened that she'd specialized in Lucretius (as well as Virgil and Ovid) at Oxford. I told her I wanted to begin by focusing on the first thirty lines of *De rerum natura,* the famous and controversial (well, famous in *some* circles) invocation to the goddess Venus. An invocation to Venus both as the traditional goddess of love and as a figurative representation of the binding attractive, even erotic force that gives the atomized universe its coherence in Lucretius's cosmological vision—the ruling principle of being.

The reason the invocation to Venus is controversial among Lucretius scholars and those others of us who care is that Lucretius claims to have written his entire seven-thousand-line epic poetic vision to *disprove* the existence of gods and goddesses, to free men from the superstitious awe and worship of the classical deities by giving us a vision of creation in which all the wondrously complex and awe-inspiring phenomena of life can be explained by the combinational coherence, the invisible choreography of atoms. (Yes, Lucretius, following Democritus and other Greeks, had a prescient vision of the atomic structure of the universe.)

But if that's true, if Lucretius was seeking to discourage superstitious awe of the powers of the gods, what's he doing opening his poem with a hymn to a goddess? Is he merely poetically personifying an abstract power into an embodied metaphor for the binding force of attraction that creates from atomic chaos coherent matter and beings? Or is he making some kind of *exception*—out of awe or fear—for the goddess of love, seeing her as a supreme being with real, personified Being? Inquiring minds want to know!

I use the tabloid catch-phrase here deliberately because there is a sensational, tabloidlike story (or slander) attached to Lucretius by later tradition that may bear some relation to his attitude toward Venus. If you believe the lore about Lucretius, he died an unusually, ironically Venusian (venereal?) death: His wife poisoned him with an aphrodisiac. The details in the sources are hazy. In one version it is in the throes of the later-fatal toxic love-drug that Lucretius conceived the vision and penned the verses of his Venus-ridden creation epic *De rerum natura* (check out Tennyson's long poem about the affair, "Lucretius"). But there are those who say that this whole fatal-aphrodisiac story was invented by early Christian authorities to discredit Lucretius's godless vision of creation—the love poisoning as poetic justice for the poet-celebrant of unleashed Venus.

I meant to ask my tutor what contemporary Oxford scholars thought about the scurrilous story. (As it turned out, she said some believe it's really a story about the orgiastic gourmand Lucullus, falsely ascribed to Lucretius.) But first, before we set about the hard work of translating the opening hymn to Venus, I wanted to get her view on a phrase that appears there and recurs later in Lucretius: "the shores of light," or, as the Latin has it in line 22, *"dias in luminis oras."*

The shores of light—I love that phrase. Perhaps because I'm rereading it and writing this column on the Bainbridge Island ferry, which plies the shores of light off Seattle. Shores gleaming with light, the light that glows in the incandescent foam of a shore-breaking wave, the diamonds of refracted sunlight flickering on the peaks of the waves—"shores of light" is a powerfully evocative phrase. I should point out that the literal translation of the Latin phrase is more on the order of "the border regions of light." The venerable Loeb Classical Library edition Englishes it as "the shining borders of light." But the learned and judicious commentary my tutor Beatrice brought with her, by P. Michael Brown of the University of Glasgow, suggests that "borders" here means not so much a well-defined bright line, but a region of transition from darkness to light, more metaphorically a transition from uncreation, *precre-ation*, to creation. Which is why I love "shores of light," suggested in a new translation of Lucretius by Anthony M. Esolen (Johns Hopkins University Press).*

"Shores of light" suggests a dawn region, that moment when the sun's glowing reflection is seen before the sun itself. "Shores of light" evokes the process of creation, gestation itself, evokes—as my tutor Beatrice helpfully suggested—the mythical birth of the goddess Venus from the foam of the sea.

It is here that Lucretius is at his most hauntingly visionary. You feel the entire epic was inspired by a powerful, personal vision, almost a visitation by Venus on the shores of light. But Lucretius at his most mystical is also somewhat mystifying: He insists that nothing can be created from nothing, and that everything is created from atoms (and returns to atoms when destroyed). But he never explains how atoms were created from nothing. A slight flaw in the logic there, but one that perhaps didn't seem a problem to Lucretius, possessed as he was by some soul-changing vision of the shores of light foaming into being from the ocean of nothingness.

But to return from the shores of light to my own murky grapplings with the dark difficulties of translating Latin poetry: I did make a couple of illuminating discoveries in my painstaking, tutor-assisted efforts. It wasn't easy. By the end of nearly two hours devoted to translating a mere twenty-two lines with her help, I felt smoke coming out of my ears from the burning circuits of a brain trying to come to grips with Latin sentence structure after all these years.

This will sound obvious to Latin scholars but only now dimly dawned on my shores of ignorance: The great Latin poets achieved some of their subtlest and most resonant effects through the pictorial deployment of word array in a sentence. Latin gives poets far more freedom than English to dissolve and divide phrases in a sentence without regard to links of meaning. Word array, the physical juxtaposition of not necessarily related words, achieves effects like those of Georges Seurat in juxtaposing points of color.

Take this example from the opening passage of Lucretius's hymn to Venus. It's the line that goes: *"tibi suavis daedala tellus / Summittit flores."*

Translating by word order, it would go: "for you delightful inventive earth sends forth flowers." But the useful complications of Latin case and declension signal that the meaning is: "for you [Venus] the inventive earth sends forth delightful flowers."

"Inventive earth" sends "delightful flowers," rather than delightful, inventive earth sends forth flowers. But look at the physical array, the flower

*Edmund Wilson used the phrase earlier as a title for a collection of essays.

arrangement of the line: The phrase for flowers, *suavis flores,* is divided (parted like petals, Nabokov might say) to enclose, embrace the words for inventive earth.

Looked at another way—from within the bouquet of delightful flowers—the globe of the inventive earth is sending forth, gestating, radiating from within (within the heart of the sentence as well) the flowers that crown and cling to its outer surface.

The use of *daedala* as an adjective seems no accident, either, conjuring up as it does Daedalus, the great artificer of labyrinths who sent forth his own first flower, his son Icarus, from the surface of the earth—the earth to which he tragically fell when the sun melted his wings. Compressed within this word array, then, is the double-edged resonance of creation: nature sending forth joyful flowers; human nature sending forth a soul to suffer a tragic fall.

Such is the multiple resonance of Lucretian creation, generating shifting structures of meaning the way Lucretius's monistic atoms generate the pluralistic phenomena of the world from differential spatial arrays. The multiple effects Lucretius achieves from the array of words in his sentences are an embodiment of his quantum vision: Words are the quanta of language, the way they're arrayed determines different meanings.

It's worth mentioning that the earth-flowers phrase is followed by one about the power of Venus to make the wild ocean laugh and the stormy heavens grow peaceful. A postcoital vision of the terrors of nature tamed, soothed by the goddess of love.

But it should be pointed out that the goddess Venus in Lucretius is herself two-faced: a soother of creation and a tormentor of men, as Lucretius's brilliant, lascivious ode to the cruelty of Venus, to the madness she inspires in her prisoners of love, will demonstrate later on in *De rerum natura.* I'll save that for my next Latin lesson.

Much Ado about "Nothing"
in Two New Translations of Genesis

❧

I've been thinking a lot about Nothing lately. Not the trivial "nothing" *Seinfeld* bores are forever citing to defend the emptiness and vacuity of that painfully overrated sitcom. ("It's about *nothing*!") Not that puny nothing, not the nothing that is the temporary and contingent absence of Something. No, I'm thinking of the Nothing that is the absence of Everything; the Nothing that came before Anything. The Grand Nothing. The Big Nada. The Nothing that is More (and less) than zero. The *Really* Big O.

I'm speaking of the Nothing that came before Creation Itself, the Nothing that is glimpsed in the first verse of Genesis. An ultimate Nothing that may not even exist, according to some, but a Nothing that is at the heart of the single great metaphysical challenge to the pretensions of both science and religion: the eternal, unanswerable (or as yet unanswered) question, Why is there Something—anything—instead of Nothing?

What led me into this hopeless quest for Nothing?

Well, recently, I found myself fascinated by the experience of reading and thinking about two new translations of the book of Genesis—in particular, the very first "in the beginning" verses. Fascinated by the way subtle shifts in emphasis between the version by Everett Fox in the new Schocken Bible and the version by biblical literary scholar Robert Alter in his translation of Genesis raise thought-provoking questions about the very process of Creation—and the nature of the Nothing that came before it.

You know, of course, the King James version:

> *In the beginning God created the heaven and the earth. And the earth was without form, and void, and darkness was upon the face of the deep. And the spirit of God moved upon the waters. And God said, "Let there be light . . ."*

Now consider Everett Fox's Schocken Bible version. Mr. Fox, inspired by the German translation of Martin Buber and Franz Rosenzweig, has sought to return to what he sees as the disturbing *strangeness* of the original Hebrew, to jolt us out of singsong familiarity and, in this case, make us experience the act of creation as if it hadn't happened before, as if it were almost inconceivable:

> *At the beginning of God's creating / of the heavens and the earth, / when the earth was wild and waste, / darkness over the face of Ocean, / rushing-spirit of God hovering over the face of the waters— / God said: Let there be light!*

But now take a look at what Robert Alter—who believes Mr. Fox has gone *too* far back toward strangeness at the cost of the incantatory power of Genesis—does with the same passage:

> *When God began to create heaven and earth and the earth then was welter and waste and darkness over the deep and God's breath hovering over the waters, God said, "Let there be light."*

There are a couple of things that struck me in hovering over these two passages. First, there is a critical difference between "God's breath" in Mr. Alter's verse and the "rushing-spirit" of God in Mr. Fox's. A difference between a more personalized Deity in Mr. Alter, a Being at least metaphorically in our image, one who, in some remotely analogous way, "breathes." As opposed to the more impersonal, inhuman, slightly scary "rushing-spirit"—one with an undefined, perhaps indefinable form, if not exactly chilling, then certainly less warm.

Then there are the subtle differences in the nature of the "hovering" each translation attributes to God in the moment before Creation. Mr. Fox has that moment of Nothingness before Something as "the rushing-spirit of God hovering over the face of the waters." A far more dramatic onrush of God's presence than in the calmer King James version, in which "the spirit of God" merely "moved upon the waters." One a thrilling onrush, the other a stately royal progress.

Mr. Alter, on the other hand, has an image that expresses less forward progress than the stasis implicit in "hovering" itself, in "God's breath hovering *over* the waters." He didn't have to rush there or move there, He *was* there.

Mr. Fox's, then, is a more dramatic, a more active vision of the moment before creation. His translation of *ruah,* the Hebrew word in that opening verse—which he says could mean "both spirit and wind"—as "rushing-spirit" inevitably suggests a kind of temporality to the moment before Time began. A rush from one *place* to another, from one moment *forward* to another, a kind of initiating rush, one perhaps connected with the initiating words, "Let there be light." Is this perhaps the rush that stirred Nothingness to readiness to become Something—God's foreplay with Non-Being?

But Mr. Alter offers a provocatively different vision of the nature of God's hovering, of what He was *doing* while He hovered in wait to create.

"The verb attached to God's breath-wind-spirit *(ruah),*" he tells us in a footnote, "elsewhere describes an eagle fluttering over its young and so might have a connotation of parturition or nurtur[ing] as well as rapid back-and-forth movement."

What we realize now is that these two gifted translators have subtly endowed or en-gendered their respective visions of God "hovering" in nothingness before creation, with masculine and feminine connotations.

Mr. Fox's "rushing-spirit" has a more masculine, intrusive narrative feel—the phallic shape and direction of time's arrow. While Mr. Alter glosses his hovering God as explicitly *maternal*—a mother bird hovering over a nest of eggs or hatchlings. Hovering, in Mr. Alter's version, is suggestive of motion, yes, but not of direction—of motion back and forth in which neither "back" nor "forth" is a start or beginning but a designation for indistinguishable poles or points. No arrow rushes from one to another (unless it's an arrow with two heads and no tail).

But Mr. Alter's nurturing maternal image does something more than hover: It seems to be gestating, suggesting that Being is not brought out of nothingness with a flip of the Let There Be Light Switch. Rather, it develops, evolves from a kind of loving, maternal hovering over Non-Being. His Nothing is pregnant with Something that needs hovering attentiveness to be brought to term. It seems to forge or imply a continuum between Non-Being and awakening, stirring Being.

There is something about the image of hovering—the suggestion of pulsation, of flickering in and out of phase, in and out of Being at any one point, that powerfully evokes the contemporary quantum-Uncertainty vision of the being of a particle: a hovering cloud of probability-waves, a flickering in and out of being on the face of a sea of Nothingness.

Read strictly, there does not seem to be in either translation (nor in most others) any necessary connection between the process of preliminary hovering and the subsequent moment of Creation. But Mr. Alter's maternal image suggests there is one: as if Being were being *gestated* by God out of Nothingness, had to be quickened with His breath before the Cosmic Egg could be hatched, as if words alone—"let there be light"—were not enough to create something out of nothing.

Which raises the metaphysical chicken-and-egg question: What *was* that something which God's breath, his rushing-spirit, whatever you want to call it, hovered *over* in the timeless moment before creation? And if God created that which he hovered over before Creation, when and why did He do it? And if He didn't create it, who did? How did it get there, to become the Nothing out of which creation was brought to light?

Hovering over these two translations of Genesis reminded me of how much of *something* there was in the nothingness before creation. There was, arguably, a landscape, at least a seascape: There was an "earth" and a "deep." However "void" and "without form" they may have been in the King James version, it was a *something* that lacked form. "Wild and waste," Mr. Fox calls that something. "Welter and waste and darkness" Mr. Alter calls it. *Tohu-bohu* the Hebrew calls it. Chaos, yes, but chaos is a disordered Something. Not quite Nothing.

Again, there are subtle differences: Mr. Fox separates the "darkness" over the water from the "wild and waste" of the formless earth. Mr. Fox glosses *tohu-bohu* as mere "emptiness" in his footnotes, but Mr. Alter goes further in saying *tohu-bohu* connotes "emptiness or *futility* [emphasis mine], and in some contexts is associated with the trackless vacancy of the desert."

Mr. Alter has, in effect, *emotionalized* his empty landscape of nothingness. The "futility" of this void almost seems to express a longing, a dream of the coherence it can't imagine but knows it is not.

The more you think about it, the more the Nothing before the Creation takes on a somethingness, if not a life of its own. The landscape of Nothing begins to look like Lear's turbulent heath in the storm, rather than a primordial Nothing, utterly empty of phenomena. One comes away from these translations of Genesis with a sense that neither science nor the Bible offers us a vision of absolute Nothing. Of a nothing before even wild and waste and welter, before earth and ocean deep, before *tohu-bohu* came into being. It raises impossible questions of the sort that got medieval theologians in trouble when they wondered what God was doing before the Creation. (Or, scientifically, what was Nothing doing before the Big Bang?) To take it one step further, what was He doing before *tohu-bohu* was created? Certainly He had to preexist even formlessness and chaos, or we must imagine *they* came into being through some other means without His agency.

Which may leave embedded in Genesis a deeper mystery than creationists realize: the mystery of the *pre*-Creation creation. If God didn't create it, who did? And if He did, what purpose did it serve? And, finally, is there—can we imagine—something more like Nothing than the nothingness before Creation? An utter absence not only of form and void, but of *any* aspect of Being?

I know I probably spend more time thinking about these questions than is strictly practical. But I'm not alone in my preoccupation with the question of utter Nothingness, as I was relieved to learn recently when I came upon a remarkable essay by a brilliant American philosopher attempting to prove that Nothing, strictly speaking, cannot exist. A 1721 essay penned by one of the least-known, most powerful, and original thinkers in American history: Jonathan Edwards. He's the Yale-based theologian most remembered for his religious writing, especially some terrifying attempts to imagine the nature of Hell and conjure up the painful texture of eternal torment. But his work as a metaphysician and philosopher has earned him lasting and increasing respect outside of strictly theological circles.

And here, in an astonishing paper deceptively entitled "Of Being," he takes on the entire notion of *Non*-Being, the idea of an ultimate Nothing, the really big O, and claims to prove there is no such thing as Nothing.

I feel I have a kind of notional relationship with Jonathan Edwards, having spent three undergraduate years living in the residential college at Yale named after him. But I hadn't read him in a long time, probably not since I was an undergraduate, when I came across, in a New Haven bookstore, an extremely valuable new edition of Edwards's philosophic and theological writings, *A Jonathan Edwards Reader.* It was put together by three professors who are now engaged in the monumental task of producing a complete edition of Edwards's works at Yale, John E. Smith, Harry S. Stout, and Kenneth P. Minkema.

The more I studied Edwards's "Of Being," the more I found myself grateful that, in that vast output, they had selected this particularly powerful and imaginative philosophical effort, Edwards's disproof of Nothingness. It seems intuitively wrong, the notion that Nothing does not exist. But for two weeks now, I've struggled through physical and metaphysical fevers, trying to contend with the tricky arguments Edwards was making against Nothing. And I haven't found a way around them. If he hasn't proven Absolute Nothing does not exist, he's gone a long way toward proving that it's literally *inconceivable,* beyond the power of the mind to imagine, principally because we cannot conceive of removing space itself from existence.

Here, *you* try to refute Edwards on the removal of space from existence: We can conceive, he says, of a universe from which all objects are removed. But, he insists, the man who tries to imagine removing space from existence "contradicts himself," because we can't remove space from *itself:* "When we go about to form an idea of perfect nothing, we must shut out . . . of our minds both space that has something in it, *and* space that has nothing in it. . . . When we go to expel body out of our thoughts, we must be sure not to leave empty space in the room of it; and when we go to expel emptiness from our thoughts, we must not think to squeeze it out . . . but we must think of the same that the sleeping rocks dream of, and not till then shall we get a complete idea of nothing."

Not till then: in other words, never. The sudden resort to poetic absurdity, the idea "that the sleeping rocks dream of" is almost shocking in the context of such abstruse metaphysical speculation, and gives a dreamy spin to what might otherwise seem an exercise in cold logic. It almost seems to preserve the absurd possibility of a Nothing that exists in a noumenal, inaccessible dream realm beyond comprehension or conception, but not necessarily beyond existence.

But with no access to the putative dream world of sleeping rocks, an imaginary Nothingness is as self-contradictory and inaccessible to human conception as Stephen Hawking's controversial concept of "imaginary time." Edwards goes on to declare, "There is no other way, but only for there to be existence; there is no such thing as absolute nothing."

Why this impassioned attack on the notion of absolute Nothingness? We know "nature abhors a vacuum," but why does Jonathan Edwards? He gives the game away and discloses his hidden agenda when he returns to the impossibility of imagining removing *space* from existence. And here he pulls the divine rabbit out of his hat, the obscure object of his desire to disprove the possibility of Absolute Nothingness.

"That space," he tells us, the space that can't be removed from existence, from itself, that space that is the ground of being, "That space is God . . . indeed, it is clear to me that all the space there is not proper to body [i.e., not taken up by objects], all the space there is without the bounds of the creation [in other words, we might say, the space the expanding universe is expanding *into*], all the space there was before the creation, is God himself."

It's a radical, even heretical idea of what God is, at least on the face of it. It's seems like a remarkably disembodied, emptied-out, depersonalized deity, a surprising vision from the same impassioned preacher famous for graphically envisioning "sinners in the hands of an angry God." If God is nothing but space, whence come those hands with which he dangles sinners over the flaming pit of Hell?

But, as Jonathan Edwards scholar Kenneth Minkema of Yale pointed out to me when I called to discuss the question, it could just as well be seen as a radically *intimate* notion of God, a God not separate from, but inextricable from, immanent in, the very fabric of our bodily being, not just the warp and the woof of the fabric, but the physics of space through which the tissue of flesh is woven.

Edwards's conjecture might be a brilliant way of killing two birds with one stone (or dreaming rock), one metaphysical, one theological: He disproves the possibility of Absolute Nothingness that has tormented metaphysicians, and simultaneously comes up with the proof for the existence of God that has eluded theologians—by calling God, in effect, the Being of Nothingness.

At the very least, it's a concept that's difficult to disprove: It's hard to answer an argument that calls that which appears to be Absolutely Nothing in fact Absolute Being.

Must we give up the idea of Nothingness? I tracked down someone I thought might be able to help me answer Edwards, my favorite writer on arcane questions of metaphysics and science, Jim Holt. His brilliant essays (in *Lingua Franca, Harper's,* and *The Wall Street Journal*) on the realms of thought where philosophy, physics, and metaphysics converge have validated for me my own untutored passion for such questions. Mr. Holt was in fact the author of a memorable *Harper's* essay ("Nothing Ventured," November 1994), in which he defended the validity of the "Why is there Something rather than Nothing?" question first posed by Leibniz and explored the efforts of the physicists known as "nothing theorists" to provide an answer.

When I reached him, I was delighted to learn Mr. Holt was taking his pursuit of Nothingness the next logical step up the ladder to Being: He was contemplating writing a book on what he feels is the remarkable, overlooked cultural and political influence of the concept of "the infinitesimal"—the notion of that which is precisely *next* to Nothing.

And while he wasn't familiar with Edwards's refutation of Absolute Nothingness in "Of Being," he was some consolation to me in my despair over refuting its premise. No one, Mr. Holt said, no philosopher, no physicist, not even the ablest of the "Nothing theorists," had been able to conjure up a vision of what Absolute Nothingness would be. Even the nothing theorist he admired most, a physicist named Alex Vilenkin, postulated an idea of absolute nothingness in which the laws of quantum physics would somehow exist and obtain. (Exist where? In whose mind? In what sense of "existence"?) It was a nothingness in which a profusion of laws governing somethingness were somehow present, but that sounds like something rather than nothing to me.

I had long had a sneaking suspicion that some recent partisans of "something from nothing" among astrophysicists were talking through their hats. Mr. Holt is conversant with the mathematical physics of the sort Stephen Hawking and Alan Guth (author of the "inflationary universe," something-from-nothing theory) use to cloak their metaphysical speculations. And so I ventured to ask him the emperor's-new-clothes question about Mr. Guth in particular: "Guth's inflationary universe theory, where he argues that the universe bubbles into being from 'fluctuations in a vacuum,' doesn't really explain how something came from nothing, does it? Because those fluctuations in a vacuum—he admits it's not a real vacuum but a 'false vacuum'—those fluctuations are something generated by the presence of quantum phenomena, right? It's sophistry, isn't it—he doesn't explain where quantum phenomena came from."

To my surprise and relief, Mr. Holt agreed. He spoke highly of the physicist Edward Tryon, the first of the nothing theorists, whose "fluctuations in a vacuum" idea was adopted by Mr. Guth, but he conceded that, by assuming quantum fluctuations, as Mr. Tryon does, you're not getting something from nothing, you're starting with *something*.

But listen to the way Mr. Guth, in his book celebrating his self-proclaimed discovery of the secrets of the universe, *The Inflationary Universe,* claims to have solved the something-from-nothing question. Listen to the hubris of his boast that he has refuted the dictum of the great Roman poet-philosopher Lucretius who said *nothing can come from nothing:* "After two thousand years of scientific research," Mr. Guth grandly announces, "it now seems that Lucretius was wrong. Conceivably, *everything* can be created from nothing . . . In the context of inflationary cosmology, it is fair to say that the universe is the ultimate free lunch."

I don't think so. It's only in the context of inflationary self-esteem that Mr. Guth can claim to have refuted Lucretius, a far greater visionary. Because Mr. Guth relies for his "refutation" on the pitifully inadequate notion of "vacuum fluctuations" that precede the Big Bang, quantum flutterings in the void which refute the notion that the void is a void.

"The inflationary theory can explain how the universe might have evolved from an initial seed as small as Tryon's vacuum fluctuations," Mr. Guth says.

Hello, Mr. Guth? You're not describing how something came from nothing. You're describing how something came from a very small *seed,* a far less impressive achievement. An achievement that amounts to just about nothing—any third-grader can explain how really big things can come from really tiny seeds, but that's not the same as explaining how something came from nothing. It's amazing how Mr. Guth can get away with such guff, another symptom of America's knee-jerk reverence for the high priests of science.

It's another instance of the fact that the real problem in American culture is not too little self-esteem, but rather too much. A little humility might have prompted Mr. Guth to question whether he'd inflated his inflationary universe concept beyond its capacity to challenge truly great thinkers like Lucretius and Leibniz and Jonathan Edwards. Clearly, Nothing deserves more respect. Nothing isn't going to go away that easily. Nothing just isn't going to disappear.

Floored by Dickens and *Dombey*

Let me begin with an apology to the many friends and collaborators whose calls and letters I haven't returned in the past ten days.

I've been lost in a fever, possessed by a nine-hundred-page nineteenth-century novel that has left little room for anything else in my life: Charles Dickens's *Dombey and Son*.

This is not the first time I've been overcome by a spell of Dickens madness, but it hasn't struck for some time now. I thought it might have run its course. I went through a three-year-long prolonged siege of it in the seventies that changed my life, but it seems like a fever dream now. An epic, mesmerizing, spellbinding enthrallment, but also, in some powerful way, a transformative spiritual experience, a kind of possession by another Being.

It's been succeeded by subsequent, more temperate enthusiasms for Jane Austen and Anthony Trollope and Wilkie Collins, but I still find it a bit annoying having to explain or justify my Dickens possession to devotees of Austen or Trollope. (Wilkie Collins enthusiasts understand, but they're sadly few and far between.) It's still galling to have to endure the polite condescension of those who see Austen or Trollope as more sophisticated artists, when in fact Dickens contains, subsumes, and fuses within his great novels all the excellences of Austen, Trollope, *and* Collins. And while they are crystalline tributary streams, his is a primal oceanic cosmos, one of the only bodies of work in the language to rival Shakespeare's in depth, power, and complexity.

And so I say to those of you who have had Dickens ruined for you by high-school English teachers and have done nothing to remedy your loss; to you half-bright intellectuals, unable to see the depth of an artist without Jamesian and Joycean signposts of modernist portent to rely upon (and reassure you, This is *Art*!), you'll never know what you're missing.

I wouldn't even bother to try to breach your wall of insularity if it weren't true that I, too, was once like you. I, too, was once snobbishly condescending about Dickens in a benightedly sophomoric way. At least throughout my undergraduate years when I dwelled serenely in the empyrean realms of pre-eighteenth-century poetry; practically sneered at anything couched in mere prose; couldn't bring myself to take modernism and postmodernism seriously because their ironies had all been anticipated and executed in an inimitably dazzling way in *Tristram Shandy*. Well, I still think *that's* true. But I changed my mind about Dickens, or had my mind, initially, changed for me.

As I reflect upon my benightedness, I see that it was in part an immature inability to separate Dickens's dark art from the cheery, plum-pudding enthusiasm of the sentimental Dickensians, the encrustations of overfamiliarity, wholesomeness, and caricature that obscure for many the dizzying labyrinth of strangeness and madness, the landscape lit by lightning illuminating the inextricable embrace of love and terror at the heart of his work.

I, too, was a willing stranger to all that until a life-changing encounter with a friend who found a way to crack the facade of my complacent disdain. A few years after I graduated, I was having lunch with Steven Weisman, a friend I knew from a notoriously intense college seminar on Milton and the Metaphysical poets. Weisman, now of the *New York Times* editorial board, had a habit I regarded as a bit peculiar of reading nine-hundred-page Dickens novels like *Little Dorrit* not only with pleasure, but with deep regard for their artistic seriousness. What struck me on this occasion was something he said he noticed while rereading *David Copperfield*—that ultimate plum-pudding-encrusted chestnut. When he saw my raised eyebrows, he suggested I look at something that succeeded in subverting my misguided snobbery: the Miltonic dimensions of Dickens's major works. "Look at Uriah Heep, all that serpentine wringing of hands, that coiling and writhing—he's Milton's Satan!"

That was all it took to get me started, the imprimatur of high art I needed to get me to see past the low-mimetic surface of Dickens's prose and plunge into its Miltonic depths. Aided, I should add, by the encouragement of another wise *littérateur,* Ross Wetzsteon of *The Village Voice,* who called my attention to Vladimir Nabokov's intense response to *Bleak House* (in his *Lectures on Literature*) and Edmund Wilson's seminal essay on "The Two Scrooges," a sophisticated, post-plum-pudding appreciation of Dickens's depths (don't quote me the superficial carpings of lesser lights like Oscar Wilde and G. K. Chesterton until you've read Nabokov and Wilson, please).*

And so it began—my three-year immersion in Dickens's realm, beginning with the ones I'd never read, like *Bleak House* (the one you should begin with if you've only read obvious high-school choices like *Great Expectations* and *A Tale of Two Cities:* You can't call yourself literate in English-language fiction if you've read *Middlemarch* but not *Bleak House*). Then on to the later nine-hundred-page masterpieces like *Little Dorrit* and *Our Mutual Friend* (which features Riah, Dickens's transfigurative spiritual Jew, his moving attempt to atone for Fagin). Then back to the beginning, to *The Pickwick Papers* and *Nicholas Nickleby* (I'm still crazy about the Crummles theatrical troupe, and every other instance of Dickens's lovingly caustic satire of theatricality and the performing self). To *Martin Chuzzlewit* and *Hard Times* (my least favorites). Next, *The Old Curiosity Shop* (forget Little Nell, Quilp is a mesmerically fascinating monster, Dickens's gothic response to Richard III; remind me to tell you sometime my theory about the ghostly presence of Shakespeare that haunts all Dickens novels, manifests itself in subtle analogues and sly caricatures of Shakespearean characters—a persistent, echoing, referential Presence that suggests Dickens's conscious awareness, both competitive and reverent, for the rival cosmologist in the language). Then back to the familiar classics with a sense of the radical strangeness fresh eyes bring to their radiance and their darkness. Finding that *A Tale of Two Cities,* with its vision of the "Terror of History," left *Great Expectations* feeling lesser by comparison. But then—in the sense that a woman I know once declared "I *am* Rosanne Cash"—*I* am Sydney Carton (in the doomed, self-pitying, romantic, melancholy sense, rather than the selfless heroic sense, I should add).

Finally, there was only one of the major works (yes, I even plowed through *Barnaby Rudge*) I hadn't finished: *Dombey.* One I'd left off reading with maybe 150 of the 950 pages left to go. One I'd left off reading in the first instance not because I wasn't loving it, but perhaps because I was loving it too much. Because it affected me all too powerfully and personally at the time. I recall getting all bent out of shape by the hypnotic, incantatory evocation of Death beckoning in a chapter called "What the Waves Were Always Saying." It was about the death of a child, little Paul Dombey, the son and heir, but it was more than that. More than a resonant piece of visionary literature about

---

*The Wilson essay can be found in *The Wound and the Bow.* The best study of Dickens for skeptics is *The Violent Effigy* by Oxford's John Carey.

the death of one being, but a glimpse of the death of *all* Being, when "the wide firmament is rolled up like a scroll." The end of all Being imagined metaphorically as the end of all *reading*! Perhaps it was the anxiety about the end of all reading, the end of reading all Dickens all the way through—although I must admit, on a less purely spiritual level, there was a woman involved: Another reason I refused to finish reading *Dombey* was that I'd been reading it along with a woman I was parting from, and one of *Dombey*'s subplots involves a young couple separated by an ocean, as we were to be. I had a sense the novel would bring them the reunion that I would be denied—I couldn't bear the disparity finishing the book would bring.

And so I left it; went on to *Our Mutual Friend* or *Little Dorrit,* didn't come back to finish *Dombey.* For more than twenty years now, I'd left the end unread. I think it's that, in addition to not wanting to have to reexperience parting with the woman in question, I didn't want to part with Dickens. Didn't want to experience, to admit the finality that having finished every last chapter of the major works would bring. Perhaps that's why I subsequently came to focus so obsessively on the mystery left behind by the unfinished manuscript of Dickens's last work, *The Mystery of Edwin Drood,* the novel Dickens never completed because death intervened. I even devoted a fevered subplot of a novel I wrote to the quest to solve the mystery of *The Mystery of Edwin Drood*—the secrets Dickens might have disclosed, not just the puzzle of who the guilty party was. (Edmund Wilson believed it was Dickens's divided soul that made the completion of *Drood*—like the completion of himself—impossible.) But perhaps I was savoring in *Drood*'s incompleteness the sense that Dickens's oeuvre never really comes to a dead end.

Whatever the reason, it's been two decades, and I never felt compelled to return to finish *Dombey* until two weeks ago. I think what tipped the balance was coming across Daniel Pool's entertaining new introduction to the world of the great Victorian novelists, *Dickens' Fur Coat and Charlotte's Unanswered Letters,* which reminded me of *Dombey*'s pivotal role in the evolution of Dickens's compositional technique. Published serially in 1847, the same year as *Vanity Fair, Dombey* was the first of his serialized novels Dickens had the time and the money to plan out completely before serialization began— rather than unfolding it on the fly, like a scroll unrolling the firmament.

It occurred to me that finally finishing *Dombey* might be an opportune way of assessing the transformative three-year Dickens fever dream I'd gone through two decades ago, reassessing my feeling about Dickens and myself after successive subsequent immersions in Austen, George Eliot, Trollope, and Collins. And so I began it again. Began it as a kind of test—to see if I was still susceptible to the kind of Dickens frenzy that had once consumed me.

To see if I were still capable of being *floored* by Charles Dickens. I use the word *floored* advisedly; I've always felt it was in some way *the* key Dickensian word because it embodies the signature Dickensian emotional response: a kind of *violent awe,* a veritable fit of thunderstruck wonder, a physical transport of amazement. Powerful enough to fling one bodily to the floor, to cause one to throw *oneself,* literally awestruck, to the ground. It is, I believe, Dickens's defining stance, his violent, florid (floor-ed) response to the theatrical pageant of life; it is my violent, florid response to the theatrical pageant of Dickens.

Floored: It's a word that first struck me forcefully when I came across it in a memorable moment in the opening chapters of *Bleak House.* The moment when young Esther Summerson first finds herself in a coach with a stranger who will turn out to be her guardian (and, later, more)—the outspoken Mr. Jarndyce. He sees she's alone and upset, he offers her sweets and sweetmeats, "the best plum-cake that can be got . . . sugar on the outside an inch thick like fat on mutton chops. Here's a little pie . . . Made in France [from] livers of fat geese. There's a pie!" He offers her, in other words, prototypical Dickensian riches.

She rejects them. "They are too rich for me," she says. "Floored again!" says Mr. Jarndyce. He takes the sweets and throws them out the window.

Think about that all too easily taken for granted word, *floored.* Simple meaning: thrown to the floor. It's a word that *The Oxford English Dictionary* citations suggest had more of a literal than metaphorical meaning until Dickens took it up. A word used to describe equestrians thrown to the ground by their horses in Byron. What Dickens did was popularize what we might call total metaphysical or spiritual flooring, the same transition the phrase "knocked out" went through in the past few decades in America, from the athletic to the aesthetic, from being knocked out by a boxer to being knocked *out* by an object of art or love, violently transported to an ecstatic state in a way that suggests the violent transport of a conversion moment in a revival meeting when frenzied worshipers are floored by the Spirit.

Watching this seizure of amazement on Mr. Jarndyce's part is terrifying at first to young Esther. It's not a warm fuzzy thing. But consider a bit more closely what goes on in that exchange. He's floored by her refusal of his gifts but not angry at *her;* he's struck with wonder by her and turns on the *food*—flinging it out the coach window for its failure to floor her. He's a man of florid temperament, generous enough to feel that her failure to be floored may be the fault of the (flawed) offerings, ones he then abolishes from existence with a violent, awed deference to *her.*

Am I making too much of this? I don't know; after coming upon a couple further "floored" expostulations in *Dombey and Son,* I decided to check out my memory of one of the most notoriously florid characters in Dickens's work, Betsey Trotwood, David Copperfield's choleric great-aunt. Look at the description of her reaction when young Copperfield shows up unexpectedly.

"If you please, Aunt," Copperfield says, introducing himself to a woman who hasn't seen him since his birth.

"EH?" exclaimed Miss Betsey, in a tone of amazement I have never heard approached. (!)

"If you please, Aunt, I am your nephew."

"Oh Lord!" said my aunt. And sat down flat in the garden path.

Catch that: She sat down flat—floored!

Let me proceed now to enumerate a few things that floored me about *Dombey and Son*.

1. Edith Dombey and the sensationally powerful critique of marriage as sexual slavery she embodies. Edith is the most full-blooded and fully sexual woman in Dickens's work. And *blood* is the operative word. While *Dombey* is Dickens's most radically feminist novel, the only one I recall that explicitly mentions "Women's Rights," it doesn't speak with the language of a tract; it speaks with the language of Edith Dombey's blood.

Let me explain. Edith Dombey is a beautiful widow of thirty from a fallen aristocratic family whose impoverishment, or that of her giddily desperate mother, forces her into a marriage transaction she finds repellent. A marriage to the majestically self-absorbed, magisterially self-infatuated, and terminally wooden patriarch of a powerful London investment banking firm that bears his name, Paul Dombey of Dombey and Son. She lets herself be bought: It's a sacrifice, a submission Edith makes unwillingly for her mother's sake, one exacerbated by the sublimated prurience in the ostensibly flattering attention of Dombey's unctuous but predatory business manager, Mr. Carker. One of the great Dickens villains, Carker is a powerfully, repellently sexualized, infinitely more sophisticated and insinuatingly creepy analogue of Uriah Heep's serpentine loathsomeness.

While Dombey is too thickly swaddled in his pride to be aware of how repugnant and degrading Edith finds the courtship and the marriage, Carker misses no opportunity to inflame Edith's consciousness of the kind of slow-motion, socially legitimized sexual violation it represents. There's a shocking intensity to this sick sub-rosa sexuality, a deeply disturbing, lascivious sophistication unlike anything else in Dickens, unlike just about anything else I've come across in Victorian fiction; it has a kind of twisted modernity to it.

Which makes Edith's fiery defiance all the more stirring. A defiance she expresses at first—inscribes on her body—with her blood. Blood that races hotly to her face, signaling in florid red her disdain, disgust, and self-mortification at every moment of her courtship and marriage transaction. Blood that flashes in her eye in the sensationally dramatic showdown moments in which she de-fies her husband's demands for deference and submission in public social intercourse (and, we suspect by elision, in private sexual intercourse). Blood she finally spills in a moment of near self-destructive madness when—after Mr. Carker has lubriciously kissed her hand—she smashes the knuckles violated by his lips into a wall, forcing her to bandage the bleeding.

But the stunning turnabout in *Dombey,* the ultimate reversal I hadn't reached when I stopped reading it two decades ago, is the way Edith finally inscribes her defiance not in *her* blood, but in that of Mr. Carker. The way she shifts from passive defiance to aggressive vengeance, stage-managing Dombey's disgrace, Carker's fall, living to see Carker (whom she's contrived to convict as an adulterer without surrendering more than a single loathsome kiss) driven to his death beneath the wheel of a locomotive. Leaving little left of him but blood on the tracks. Blood that is lapped up by "some dogs . . . that sniffed upon the road, and soaked his blood up, with a train of ashes."

2. That image of an adulterer's blood on the tracks. Did Leo Tolstoy lift the notion of the locomotive annihilating an adulterer at the close of *Anna Karenina* from the final chapters of *Dombey and Son,* published three decades earlier? We know that Fyodor Dostoyevsky was a devotee of Dickens's work in translation (the smart way to read Dickens is to find the proto-Dostoyevsky beneath the plum pudding; come to think of it, the smart way to read Dostoyevsky is to find the Dickens within *him*). I'm not sure about Tolstoy, but both images of locomotive annihilation and adulterer's self-immolation fuse death, desperation, and desire into a shrieking, roaring climax. And, by the way—I know we're getting a little far afield now—but that image of blood on the tracks, could *that* be where Bob Dylan got the image for the title of his adultery album, *Blood on the Tracks*? I'd always envisioned an animal that had torn its limb out of a hunter's trap, fleeing through the snow, leaving blood on its tracks, with an allusion perhaps to the "tracks" of an album, each of them infused with the emotional bloodshed in the songs. But I like the idea of tracing *Blood on the Tracks* back to *Anna Karenina* and even further back to *Dombey and Son.*

And—stop me, somebody, before this train of allusion runs me over— remember Edith Dombey's bloody bandage? The one she uses to cover the self-inflicted wound on her knuckles when she smashed her hand against the wall to annihilate the sexual suggestiveness of Mr. Carker's kiss: Does *that* have a later echo in the bruise on the back of Daisy Buchanan's knuckle at the beginning of *The Great Gatsby*—one of the most powerfully compressed erotic images in modern fiction, one that slyly alludes to the brutality of her sexual relationship with Tom? (Implicit is Daisy's hand being smashed back against the headboard of a bed.) Just asking.

3. Finally, the thing that may have floored me the most: That damn Dickens, he got me sobbing again. I'm bitter about it. I thought I could resist it this time, that it was an artifact of my impressionable, emotional youth, when I'd have these exhausting, cathartic sobbing sessions at certain moments in the novels. Not the oft-caricatured death of Little Nell, thank you, but, say, the reunion of Esther and Mr. Jarndyce after she'd been ravaged by smallpox. I can't even *think* of that without welling up, much less read it again.

No matter how much I resisted—and I *did*—just about every novel sneaked in under my emotional radar and floored me in a sobbing fit. Occasionally to my great embarrassment: I remember emerging from the nine-hour Royal Shakespeare Company production of *Nicholas Nickleby* with my then-wife, tears still streaming down our faces on the sidewalk outside the theater and running into Harold Hayes, the brilliant former *Esquire* editor and a onetime mentor. I remember him gazing at me curiously, and the only thing I was able to stammer out was *"The death of Smike!"* (a famous tear-jerker moment in *Nickleby*). I think he kind of understood.

Anyway, up till the very end, I thought I had gotten through *Dombey* clean. Yes, the death of the child, little Paul Dombey, early on, the visionary language of love and death in the chapter called "What the Waves Were Always Saying" had me going. But in a more spiritual than emotional way; it left me moved but dry-eyed. In fact, so had the whole novel—exhilarated, mesmerized, back in a Dickens trance again—but still dry-eyed. Until page 975 of 976, when he sneaked up and *got* to me once again after all these years. It was kind of a cheap trick, although one grounded deeply in the 974 pages that preceded it. I'm not going to describe it because I don't want to deprive you of the moment, if you get that far. I'll just say it involves the invocation of the name of the young, ingénue heroine in the novel, Dombey's long-neglected and -rejected daughter Florence. A name which, come to think of it, is a cognate of "floored," isn't it? (Floor-ence.) Damn it: *floored* again.

An Ode to Helen Vendler, Goddess of Keats's "Autumn"

The brilliant critic Christopher Ricks, the Oxbridge-bred explicator of both T. S. Eliot and Bob Dylan, is perhaps best known for his earlier work on John Keats, the one with the peculiar title *Keats and Embarrassment*. A work inspired in part by the profusion of blushing in Keats's poetry. And embarrassment, I blush to say, has certainly been a key component of my own Keatsian obsession.

He's one of those poets, after all, for whom professing a passion can seem—to some, anyway, to those who can't get deeper than the encrustation of conventional reverence—an embarrassingly obvious preference, close to cliché. Keats conjures up febrile, neurasthenic undergraduates trying to seduce Radcliffe girls by reading aloud the "Ode on Melancholy" with special sensuous attention to the embarrassing, sexually suggestive lines about the "globed peonies" and bursting "Joy's grape against his palate fine." ·

This stereotyped view of Keats neglects, of course, his authorship of one of the most piercingly stringent, unsentimental, and skeptical observations about the way the mind works in trying to give coherence to an incoherent reality: the concept—which every self-aware journalist and historian takes to heart—of "negative capability." A kind of Ockham's razor, with its caution against the "irritable reachings" after unfounded certainty in the presence of ambiguity.

Still, embarrassment dominates my personal Keatsian past. There is, for instance, a fond but embarrassing memory of leaving Swinging London to drive southwest in a rented Austin Mini to Winchester, to gaze out, on the very same hour of the very same day (sunset, September 19), to take in from the same vantage point as Keats the painfully beautiful vista that he describes in perhaps his greatest ode, "To Autumn." The better to see through his eyes the way the "barred clouds bloom the soft-dying day, / And touch the stubble-plains with rosy hue."

I wanted to see that light, that "soft-dying" reddening glow reflected on the stubble field of felled stalks. Hoping that the experience might throw some light on the mysteriously seductive power the poem has held over me ever since I first read it. Pretty embarrassing! But I don't care. It helped. Nothing had changed in a century and a half, and I'll never forget that thrilling autumnal light.

So let's talk about the ode "To Autumn." It *is* autumn now, come to think of it (a peg at last!). And it's one of those poems I've returned to repeatedly regardless of season, always feeling it more deeply, always feeling, also, that something about its appeal has eluded me or eluded articulation. For a long time it appealed to me because of its implicit darkness, the way the apparently placid scenes of post-harvest ease—an almost postcoital drowse of rural beauty—concealed dark lacunae, suggesting, evoking finality, closure, and death.

I recall defending, at a graduate seminar at Yale, Harold Bloom's already unfashionable conjecture about the bleating of the lambs "from hilly bourn" in the final stanza of the ode. Mr. Bloom argued that the bleating was a foreshadowing of the death cry of the lambs when they had their throats slit at approaching slaughter. A slaughter slyly, subtly, almost unnoticeably signaled by the description of them as *"full-grown"* lambs.

You can find such autumnal intimations of coming wintry death lurking beneath the surface throughout the poem without looking too hard. It's a kind of blissfully sublimated meditation on melancholy and death, on the urgency mortality lends to life, that one can find in more florid dramatic form in Keats's "Ode on Melancholy."

But recently I've had a renewed experience of wild surmise with the ode to Autumn. That breathtaking phrase "wild surmise" needless to say comes from the close of Keats's great sonnet "On First Looking into Chapman's Homer." Wherein Keats compares his first reading of George Chapman's Elizabethan translations of Homer to Cortés's first vision of the shocking immensity of the Pacific Ocean, a vision Cortés experienced "upon a peak in Darien" (that's not a line from *The Ice Storm* but a place in Panama).

Actually—and this is important—it's not Cortés staring at the Pacific with "wild surmise" as I've inaccurately recalled it on occasion (I blush to say). As I see the poem, Cortés (in fact, historically it was Balboa) reaches the summit, sees the Pacific first, turns back to his men who have yet to get a glimpse; it's *they* who stare with wild surmise at Cortés's face as he registers the disturbing immensity of the Pacific vista. The wild surmise line then depicts the discovery of the Pacific as an act of *reading:* They're reading his face. In fact, it's a metaphor of breathtaking precision because the wild surmise is more than the act of reading; it's specifically an act of translation (like Chapman's). Cortés's men are translating what they read on Cortés's face—the look in his eyes—into a surmise about what he's seen of the Pacific. All great poetry is translation from one realm of vision to another.

Where was I? Oh yes, my own recent parallel experience of wild surmise. One that conjures up the opening lines of "On First Looking into Chapman's Homer," in which Keats tells us that "Much have I travell'd in the realms of gold"—but never has he, in previous voyages into Homer's work, been able to "breathe its pure serene / Till I heard Chapman . . . / Then felt I like some watcher of the skies / When a new planet swims into his ken."

Well, in a similar sense, much have I traveled in the realms of lit crit, having—since I fled grad school—maintained a horrified fascination with the bombastic jargon that has possessed so many of its practitioners. Much have I traveled, but not till I read Helen Vendler's sixty-page essay on the ode "To Autumn" have I felt the poem swim into my ken like a new planet once again.

It's embarrassing to admit that this is the first time I'd read her essay, which first appeared in 1983 in her book on *The Odes of John Keats*. It has a reputation among the cognoscenti, but in some ways I guess I feared reading it, not that it would disappoint, but that it would be too good, that it would take possession of my experience of the poem. That it would be too rich, in the sense so much of Keats is almost unbearably rich. For years, for instance, I found it impossible to get all the way through "The Eve of St. Agnes" because it was too exquisite, the force-fed foie gras of Keatsian genius.

But hey, life is short. And so at last I plunged into Professor Vendler's essay on "Autumn." It was, if you'll forgive me for harping on a theme, an *embarrassment* of riches. Particularly embarrassing to me on the very first page. On one of the most basic issues of reading the poem, it looked as if I'd been off by a full 180. God, this is a difficult confession to make, one I utter only because I'm not 100 percent certain I'm wrong. So let me just come out and say, blushingly, that I've always thought the figure of Autumn was a guy!

I mean not an ordinary guy, but a male figure, some drowsy rural Bacchus type watching "the last oozings" of a "cyder-press," intoxicated by the prospect of the wine of apples. But in the second sentence of her wonderful essay, Helen Vendler tells us, "Once again Keats must find a female divinity to worship, and we ask whether it will be a classical goddess like Psyche. . . ." In other words, she's certain Autumn is a babe!

I'm sure she must be right, but ever alert to what one of the later New Critics called "conspicuous irrelevance," it does seem a bit odd to me that the figure in Keats's "Autumn" *could* be read as either gender. There are no primary, secondary, or even tertiary sexual characteristics explicitly alluded to unless you count the hair "soft-lifted by the winnowing wind." But then again, the hair is not explicitly characterized as a woman's hair or even long hair. I'd always imagined the tangled locks of a lazing satyr.

The sexuality of Autumn is not embodied in the gender of the figure of Autumn so much as it is in the generalized sexuality of the harvest season all around it. In the way Autumn will "swell the gourd, and plump the hazel shells / With a sweet kernel." But each of these two images could be read either as feminine fertility or male tumescence. It would almost seem as if some effort has been made to exclude gender definition from the figure of Autumn, but I could be wrong.

Setting aside that initial embarrassing (to me) difficulty, I found in the rest of Professor Vendler's essay on "Autumn" a Chapman-like oceanic power that swelled every sentence that followed. I found myself thinking of Helen Vendler herself as something like the figure of Autumn in the ode, who conspires with the sun "to load and bless / With fruit the vines that round the thatch-eves run." In the sense that Professor Vendler loads and blesses not the vines but the lines of the ode that round the stanzas run, blesses them with a harvest of resonant insights.

She "set[s] budding more, / And still more" allusions and inclusions till, like the honeycombs of the harvesting bees in the poem, she's "o'er-brimmed" it with the distillations she's extracted from Keats's efflorescence. But she does something more in this amazing essay than bring the ode to fruition. She cracks open—finds within its shell—a "sweet kernel" of signification, a brilliant "wild surmise" about its true subject, one I curse myself for not having seen before: the sense that in "Autumn" Keats is contemplating not merely the harvest in the stubble fields but the harvesting of his own field of consciousness, of his ripening genius, his own poetic fruits. A harvest in two senses: the process of harvesting the fructifying conceptions of his own brain, of giving to his inchoate thoughts and visions a local habitation and a name, incarnating, making the insubstantial word flesh—or at least ink—in the lines of his verse. There's that harvest, yes, but then there's another, darker harvest in prospect she suggests: the shadow of the Reaper whose scythe Keats could already sense (he would soon die of tuberculosis), the final autumnal harvest of his own being.

I find it an utterly persuasive surmise that, as she says, " 'Autumn' is Keats's most reflective view of creativity and art." I would only add (my embarrassingly humble contribution to this conjecture) that confirmation of it can be found in the image of the figure of Autumn, a lazy reaper, mesmerized by a "cyder-press" watching the "last oozings" of apple juice trickle from it. Isn't there, in that figure of a watcher mesmerized by what issues from a *press,* a partially submerged image of a reader-reaper transfixed by the spell of the poetry that issues from a printing press?

Let's dwell for a moment on that reaper who's too "Drows'd with the fume of poppies" to cut down the next swath. Because Professor Vendler's footnote to that phrase raised once again the one matter on which I depart from her reading—the gender of the Autumn figure. In tracing the origin of the "fume of poppies" phrase, she cites John Dryden's *Virgilian Pastorals.* "In the sixth of these," she tells us, "two satyrs find Silenus [a Pan-like pastoral figure] lying on the ground 'Dos'd with the fume of poppies.' Keats, who had been reading Dryden . . . first wrote in the draft of 'To Autumn' that autumn was 'Dos'd with red poppies'; he must have heard the echo of Dryden's intoxication."

It also seems likely to me that Keats's Autumn figure was inspired by Dryden's lazy male satyr. Professor Vendler, apparently to counter this natural supposition, cites, as the model for Autumn, John Lemprière's figure of the harvest goddess Ceres holding up the poppy sacred to her. But Keats's second-stanza Autumn figure sounds more like a lazy *guy* than a productive female goddess. He's too tired and/or intoxicated to continue the harvest; he's a *slacker.* It could be we're both reading into the Autumn figure images of ourselves: I see a lazy guy who'd rather dream and drowse; she sees a productive, redemptive goddess. Of course, she's far too modest to think of herself as a goddess, but after reading her stunning essay on "Autumn," I do.

Hart Crane's Hieroglyphs: The Unmentionable Truth

The lost language of Crane: I love the sound of that phrase (its resonance indebted to the David Leavitt novel title). I'm speaking of the lost language of Hart Crane, to my mind *the* great American poet of the twentieth century, inventor of a unique ecstatic poetic language that is at once maddeningly elusive and crazily exhilarating, a language I can't always decipher but one that always speaks to me, a haunting, cryptic poetic rhetoric, a supremely literate glossolalia, a speaking-in-tongues that registers on levels of intelligibility both deeper and more elevated than quotidian speech.

Why celebrate and seek to retrieve Hart Crane's lost language now? In part because immersion in the highly charged language of Keats's ode "To Autumn" sharpened my appetite for the difficult pleasures offered by the idiosyncratic speech certain great poets invent to embody the unspoken and the unspeakable. In part also because a new edition of Crane's letters (*O My Land, My Friends;* Four Walls Eight Windows) reproduces at full length one of the most remarkable clashes in the tormented history of the relationship between literature and literary criticism—a clash over the lost language of Crane.

Do I need to introduce Hart Crane? Probably not to most readers, although

I fear most know him mainly for his somewhat overblown epic poem, *The Bridge,* his rhapsodic tribute to the structure that links Brooklyn to Manhattan. It's a celebration of the possibility of finding linkages, coherences, bridges between the apparently meaningless chaos, the traffic noise, of American life and the realm of poetic transcendence. It's a poem Crane designed as a kind of "answer song" to T. S. Eliot's *The Waste Land* and its despair at the fragmentary incoherences of modern existence.

But I've always felt that *The Bridge,* breathtaking as it is in places, is not the true locus of Hart Crane's genius, that it suffers from the strains of its didactic mission. And that the pure distillation of Crane's astonishing gift, the grammar of the lost language he invented, can be found in the collection of poems he published shortly before *The Bridge;* the one he called *White Buildings.*

There, in one astonishing poem after another—"At Melville's Tomb," "The Wine Menagerie," "For the Marriage of Faustus and Helen," "Voyages," and all the rest—Crane created his private lexicon of ecstatic apprehension, a witchy alchemy of sound and signifier both seductive and frustrating. A language somehow teasingly just short of yielding itself up, supremely intelligent but just shy of complete intelligibility, neither opaque nor transparent, a kind of crystalline translucency. I can't get enough of the *White Buildings* poems; lately "For the Marriage of Faustus and Helen" has possessed me, sent me back to Ben Jonson's dazzling seventeenth-century play *The Alchemist* to trace Crane's alchemical inspiration to its source.

But I want to focus here on "At Melville's Tomb" since it's the subject of that remarkable clash over poetic language I spoke of.* On the surface, it is an encounter between a poet and a critic, but on a deeper level it's the encounter

---

*I love this poem so much, I want you to read it, the better to follow the argument about it as well.

AT MELVILLE'S TOMB

> Often beneath the wave, wide from this ledge
> The dice of drowned men's bones he saw bequeath
> An embassy. Their numbers as he watched,
> Beat on the dusty shore and were obscured.
>
> And wrecks passed without sound of bells,
> The calyx of death's bounty giving back
> A scattered chapter, livid hieroglyph,
> The portent wound in corridors of shells.
>
> Then in the circuit calm of one vast coil,
> Its lashings charmed and malice reconciled,
> Frosted eyes there were that lifted altars;
> And silent answers crept across the stars.
>
> Compass, quadrant and sextant contrive
> No farther tides . . . High in the azure steeps
> Monody shall not wake the mariner.
> This fabulous shadow only the sea keeps.

between the poet and the critic *within* Hart Crane—one of the few illuminating instances in which a truly great poet reads, interprets, and explicates himself for us. Decodes his private language.

It's illuminating because it's about the eternal mystery of what makes some language poetry, what makes poetry more than themes and ideas—what poetry can do that prose doesn't.

Here's the situation: Back in 1926, Crane submitted "At Melville's Tomb" to Harriet Monroe, editor of the influential magazine *Poetry*. Monroe found its language too recalcitrant, too opaque, too hieroglyphically indecipherable, but she agreed to publish it, albeit—and this is pretty amazing—along with a kind of admonitory letter from her to Crane telling him his poem was too hard to understand.

"Take me for a hard-boiled unimaginative unpoetic reader," she begins, obviously convinced that no one could take *her,* august editor of *Poetry,* as anything of the sort. She goes on, in effect, to ask him, "What the hell are you talking about in this poem?" Attacking Crane's key images, she asks "how dice can bequeath an embassy (or anything else); and how a calyx (of death's bounty or anything else) can give back a scattered chapter, livid hieroglyph; and how, if it does, such a portent can be wound in corridors (of shells or anything else)." She also questions how "frosted eyes" can lift "altars."

She sounds like she believes these are questions for which there could be no good answers. Crane's reply must have surprised and stunned her, but she was smart enough to publish it, though it appeared in a later issue.

In what still remains one of the great acts of literary criticism by a poet, Crane sent her a long letter explaining exactly how dice can bequeath an embassy, exactly how a calyx can give back a chapter, exactly how portents can be wound in corridors of shells. How in fact, his language was not unintelligible, just not intelligible to her until he explained it. But in doing so, in introducing his specific acts of explication, he also penned one of the most intelligent contemporary exemplars of the "Defense of Poetry" tradition, in which poets (like Sir Philip Sidney) have tried to explain to the literal-minded the value of poetic language. One in which Crane introduces his own notion of the power of the elided, of the unspoken key to the spoken—what he calls "the unmentioned."*

He disputes Monroe's reductive mind-set—the belief that a poem is "about" what a paraphrase of its language reduces it to, and that its language should obey the dictates of ordinary logic. He argues that poetic language is not necessarily "illogical" but rather that it pursues "another logic" in pursuit

---

*Dare I say the "secret parts" of his poems?

of which a poet can take "certain liberties which you claim the poet has no right to take." To deny these liberties "is to limit the scope of the medium so considerably as to outlaw some of the richest genius of the past."

He cites a line from William Blake—"a sigh is a sword of an Angel King"—as one that has a power beyond pure logic. And then he tosses off a brilliant bit of explication of his respected rival Eliot, adducing the logic beneath the apparent illogic of the line in Eliot that goes, "Every street lamp that I pass beats like a fatalistic drum." He asks Monroe to reconsider the apparently illogical relationship "between a drum and a street lamp—via the *unmentioned* throbbing of the heart and nerves in a distraught man which tacitly creates the reason and 'logic' of the Eliot metaphor."

Beautiful: the unmentioned throbbing of the heart beating like a drum, rhythmically dimming the light by means of the unmentioned pulsing of blood in the eyes. With the mention of "the unmentioned," Crane proceeds to elucidate the unmentioned elements in his own poem that supply the esoteric logic to the images Monroe objected to. Before getting into Crane's recovery of the Lost Language of the poem, consider something he fails to mention—or perhaps thinks so obvious that even Monroe doesn't need to be told. As I see it, the clue to the Melville poem is the way it's haunted by the unmentioned spirit of Ariel's song in *The Tempest,* the elegy to the drowned sailor—a lyric that haunts Eliot's *Waste Land* as well. The famous lines, "Full fathom five thy father lies; / Of his bones are coral made; / Those are pearls that were his eyes." A painfully beautiful lyric in which death is transfigured by (into) art.

If she'd sensed this, Monroe might have had less trouble with the "dice of drowned men's bones" bequeathing an embassy. Or as Crane patiently explains it to her in his letter: "Dice . . . being the bones of dead men who never completed their voyage, it seems legitimate to refer to them as the only surviving evidence of certain messages undelivered, mute evidence of certain things, experiences that the dead mariners might have had to deliver."

Swiftly he moves on to the "calyx of death's bounty." And explains to Monroe that "the calyx refers in a double ironic sense both to a cornucopia and the vortex made by a sinking vessel. As soon as the water has closed over a ship, this whirlpool sends up broken spars, wreckage, etc., which can be alluded to as livid hieroglyphs, making a scattered chapter so far as any complete record of the recent ship and her crew is concerned."

And finally, frosted eyes lifting altars? "Refers simply to a conviction that a man, not knowing perhaps a definite god yet being endowed with a reverence for deity . . . postulates a deity somehow, and [lifts] the altar of that deity by the very action of the eyes lifted in searching."

I found Crane's explication of his poem a tour de force that left me satisfied, yet also longing for more. Longing for him to be my Virgil, my guide to the unmentioned depths of *all* his poems. It's frustrating because he's both demonstrated the possibility of finding the "other logic," the lost language of his poems, and left us desolate without the Rosetta stone to the rest of his hieroglyphs. One of my fantasies of the afterlife is finding and button-holing Hart Crane and getting him to elucidate the unmentioned secrets of all his other poems. In some of them I still find myself as much at sea—although not as disapprovingly—as Harriet Monroe. (In fact, we should all be grateful she had the curiosity and the temerity to draw Crane out so eloquently.) What the hell is the "tooth implicit" in "The Wine Menagerie," for instance? The truth implicit? Help me, Hart.*

Finally, there is one other unmentioned aspect of "Melville's Tomb," one almost unmentionable in its sadness. The sense that in it Crane was writing his own epitaph, inscribing his own tomb. Do I need to mention the fact that on April 27, 1932, Crane plunged to his death from the stern of a freighter that was carrying him back from his beloved tropics to New York? Most chose to believe his death was a deliberate suicide, although there is some ambiguity over whether it could have been a drunken fall. In a sense this poem may be the unmentioned clue to the deliberation behind Hart Crane's death by drowning, to the moment he chose to become one of those "dead men who never completed their voyage," as he describes the drowned sailors in "Melville's Tomb."

Needless to say, the poem is not set at Melville's *actual* tomb—a stone slab in a cemetery in the Bronx—but rather it conceives of the vault of the ocean itself as Melville's true resting place: "This fabulous shadow only the sea keeps." I don't think it was an accident that Crane himself chose to end his life by burying himself in Melville's oceanic tomb. A fabulous shadow himself, Crane's poems became the "calyx of [his own] death's bounty" leaving scattered chapters, livid hieroglyphs for the living to decipher. Leaving us the lonely but exhilarating task of recovering his lost language on our own.

---

*It subsequently occurred to me that the "tooth implicit" might be a comic way of talking about a *missing tooth*. A gap that implies a loss.

Dr. Borges and Dr. Ron Solve the Problem of Memory and Regret

I blame Arturo Pérez-Reverte, you know, the Spanish novelist. If I hadn't de-rived so much pleasure from his diabolical literary detective novel *The Club Dumas,* I probably wouldn't have felt the fatal lure of the Borges labyrinth again. Because Mr. Pérez-Reverte is a kind of contemporary avatar of the spirit of Jorge Luis Borges—who appears in the epigraph to *The Flanders Panel,* the first of Mr. Pérez-Reverte's novels published here. Both novels aroused my longing for the real Borgesian thing again.

It's a seductive and dangerous taste, Borges. Once you've allowed yourself to be enticed into his garden of forking paths, you can't be sure you'll emerge the same, you can't be sure you'll emerge at all. It's happened to me before. In fact, I'm retracing one particular Borgesian excursion here in part as a cau-tionary tale—too much Borges can be hazardous to your metaphysical stabil-ity. And in part because I still *kind* of believe this particular Borgesian thought-experiment—the one about dinosaur bones—really has some genuine therapeutic potential. And if I can help just one person . . .

Of course it helps if you're a little bit familiar with the inimitable Borgesian sensibility, the *frisson* of sudden dislocating strangeness his fiction induces. And if you're not by now, why not? Trying to explain to you what you're missing is like trying to explain in words the taste of chocolate or garlic, the flavor of Chekhov or Kafka. There is nothing *like* the way Borges can reveal the shadowy lacunae in the sunlit surface of reality, the way obscure and arcane bookish speculations can suddenly open trap-doors beneath the apparent solidity of the ground beneath your feet—or escape hatches into the hidden attics of single-story homes.

This peculiar Borgesian odyssey of mine began with a passage in a little-known essay in one of Borges's lesser-known—and now out of print—collections of sly speculative essays called *Other Inquisitions*. It may be hard to find; in fact, I can't find my *own* copy now, but it does exist, I swear: Borges loved the idea of reviewing and commenting on books that had never been written, citing imperfect editions of encyclopedias that never existed, but *Other Inquisitions* is *real,* however fantastical the speculation about dinosaur fossils may seem.

What Borges loved to do is to take up some odd, heretical, apparently illogical bit of theory that had some singularly provocative, irritating quality. He liked to prod it, poke it, even torture the notion (he called the book *Inquisitions,* after all) until it yielded up some unexpectedly dislocating dimension.

In this case, he began with the silly-sounding argument made by a nineteenth-century theologian who was trying to come up with a novel refutation of Darwin's theory of evolution. A refutation that would take into account recently discovered fossil evidence, such as dinosaur bones, which seemed to confirm Darwin's view that the earth was far older than the conventional biblical timetable (which placed the week of Creation in Genesis in the year 4004 B.C.). Certainly, it *looked* like far more time was required than six thousand years for species like dinosaurs to thrive, grow extinct, and then fossilize in the earth's crust.

Not necessarily so, this Victorian writer (I *think* it was Philip Gosse)* argued: God could still have created the world in 4004 B.C. and—as part of His creation—implanted the bones of apparently extinct species in the newly created earth's crust in order to make it *appear* that the world was older, the better to tempt and test believers to deny His Word, to separate the truly faithful sheep from the skeptical goats.

Borges doesn't *really* take this seriously as science or theology (although I kind of like the idea of a God who'd play that elaborate a practical joke on His human creations), but Borges likes one thing about it a *lot:* He likes the idea that it's impossible to *disprove.* And that *it* seems to disprove Time itself. Forget about the fixation on the year 4004 B.C., how can we be sure, Borges asks, that the world wasn't created just *two minutes ago*? That we were brought into actual being two *seconds,* one *instant* ago—complete with the memories of an

---

*In fact, the title of the essay is "The Creation and P. H. Gosse."

illusory past planted within us like so many dinosaur bones? Both theologians and physicists insist that Something was created out of Nothing. If you believe something as improbable as that, the belief in an illusory implanted past is not much more of a leap.

For all we know, for all the certainty we have of the "real" world, the external world you think you've been living and breathing in all your life might only have come into existence a couple of minutes ago when you began reading this column. (I'm not claiming the column *caused* it to come into being.) And what you feel as a past you've lived through is just an illusion, a false memory, a fiction you arrived complete with when you came into being a little while ago. And if you can imagine the world created two minutes ago, why not two seconds ago, two instants, why not one, why not none? There's no way to prove that the *entire* past, one's own, the world's, is not illusory.

This is what Borges is *really* after. He has this peculiar crusade against Time itself, a running argument that the past is a fiction, which can be found throughout his work. He doesn't think Time exists, not in the sense of a continuity at *all*. You can see it in his heretical interpretation of Zeno's Paradox, the one about Achilles and the tortoise: how the fleet-footed Achilles can never catch up with a slow-moving tortoise who has a head start on him. Because as fast as Achilles goes, he will have to cross an infinite number of points to reach the tortoise and, even if it takes only an infinitesimal moment to cross each of the infinite number of points, that still means it requires an infinite amount of time. In fact, Borges argues, extrapolating from Zeno, Achilles never can actually move at *all,* motion itself is an illusion, as is Time, because there is always an infinite gulf of infinite points in time and space between any one point and the next.

Borges makes a more systematic, philosophic argument against Time in a difficult but provocative essay called "A New Refutation of Time" (which appears in Grove's edition of *A Personal Anthology*), an essay that attempts to extend Berkeleyan Idealism's refutation of Matter and Space to Time. You can—almost—visualize Borgesian Time (or non-Time) if you think of a strip of 35-millimeter film. When you speed it up through a projector, it *looks* like there's real continuity: One person is walking through space and time, say. But in fact every single frame is utterly separate, utterly unconnected. What is depicted is not one continuous person, but twenty-four different people, twenty-four *different* present moments per second. In fact, Borges believes only *one* frame, the frame of the Present, is real. The past frames are a dinosaur-bone fictional memory; the future, a dream of the person in that one present frame.

Now me, I'm a practical guy. While I find all this heretical metaphysics intriguing, I also found myself wondering *why* Borges was so intensely interested in proving the fictive nature of the Past, the lie of Time. What was in it for him? Could it have something to do with his lifelong encroaching blindness, did he wish to render the past visual reality he was losing nothing but a fiction, anyway?

And what was in it for *me*, for us? I think what this thought-experiment offers us is a tortuous Western way of arriving at a moment of Eastern detachment: a moment of consoling detachment from the regrets of the past, both personal and historical; a therapeutic way of dealing with the crippling effect of painful memories, loss, regret; a way of believing in the possibility of that most elusive precious delusion: the fiction of a fresh start.

Think about it: If you indulge yourself in the thought-experiment, the illusion, the fantasy, however brief, that the world was created in an instant or two ago, then memory and history are just fictions you have to live with, a novel you've been written into as a character, but a character whose past acts you don't have to feel responsible for. All those misdeeds, missed opportunities, those regrets you feel etched in stone upon your consciousness, the hurt you've felt, the hurt you've inflicted—for a moment or two, you can imagine they're just the cards, the illusory dinosaur bones you've been dealt. You're entering into a *role,* perhaps you're entering into the role of a fuck-up, but at least the past fuck-ups are not really *your* responsibility. *You* don't have to stagger around with the crushing burden of them weighing you down with a crippling bitterness that will inevitably cause you to repeat or recapitulate the suffering that's twisted you. I mean, sure, you *do* have to stagger around with it, but every once in a while you can metaphorically unburden yourself, imagine a metaphysically irrefutable way of conceiving every next moment as a fresh start.

I think that's what Borges was looking for in refuting Time, a way to escape the prison of regret that is the past. I know I am.

Does this sound like the basis for a self-help philosophy or what? "The Power of Borgesian Thinking"? I'm joking, sort of, but when you think about it, aren't all the great, serious therapeutic systems attempts to come to terms with the devastating consequences of excessive self-lacerating suffering over the past, over history and memory? The best to be hoped for from psychoanalysis, Freud memorably conceded, was to shift from excessive neurotic misery into ordinary unhappiness. I think Borgesian Metaphysical Therapy (as I plan to call it in my Tony Robbins–like infomercial) can accomplish that at least as well. I've actually tried it out on several people I've known who were caught in a vicious cycle of regret and self-laceration. Taken them through the dinosaur-bone thought-experiment to the possibility of conceiving a fresh start. And I think it helped. I remember several years ago trying it out on an angry, despondent guy in a bar in Montana. Guy named Ted something. Kasynovski, maybe? Said it helped him, although he never wrote to thank me.

But, seriously, even if you distrust Dr. Ron's Borgesian Metaphysical Therapy, don't let that put you off reading Borges. Start with *Ficciones* and *Labyrinths,* but don't miss "A New Refutation of Time." (If you can refute the Refutation, I'd like to see it.) And if anyone can find me another copy of *Other Inquisitions* with the dinosaur-bone essay, I would be grateful, just so I can be sure it wasn't something I dreamed up by myself from a fictive past.

Two Home Visits

The Catcher in the Driveway

Long Island, Babylon

The Catcher in the Driveway

In Which We Visit J. D. Salinger's Property Line and Hear
the Sound of One Hand Clapping

There is no name on the mailbox at the bottom of the driveway. It's the only mailbox on the route with no name. The house above the driveway is screened by a slope of trees, several of which brandish glaring neon-pink NO TRESPASSING signs. Signs that, in addition to specifying NO HUNTING, TRAPPING, FISHING in big black capitals, proceed further to emphasize the sweeping metaphysical inclusiveness of the prohibition by adding OR TRESPASSING OF *ANY* KIND.

 Just being here, at the bottom of the driveway, just beyond the verge of the property line, feels like a trespass of *some* kind. This is not just private property. It is the property of the most private man in America, perhaps the *last* private person in America. The silence surrounding this place is not just any silence. It is the work of a lifetime. It is the work of renunciation and determination and expensive litigation. It is a silence of self-exile, cunning, and contemplation. In its own powerful, invisible way, the silence is in itself an eloquent work of art. It is the Great Wall of Silence J. D. Salinger has built around himself.

 It is not a passive silence; it's a palpable, provocative silence. It's the kind of silence people make pilgrimages to witness, to challenge. It's a silence we both respect and resent, a lure and a reproof. Something draws us to it, makes us interrogate it, test it.

There's a line in *Mao II,* Don DeLillo's novel about a Salinger-like reclusive writer who wonders: Why are so many so obsessed with my invisibility, my hiddenness, my absence?

"When a writer doesn't show his face," he answers himself, "he becomes a local symptom of God's famous reluctance to appear."

The silence of a writer is not the *same* as the silence of God, but there's something analogous: an awe-inspiring creator, someone we believe has some *answers* of some kind, refusing to respond to us, hiding his face, withholding his creation. The problem, the rare phenomenon of the unavailable, invisible, indifferent writer (indifferent to our questions, indifferent to the publicity-industrial complex so many serve), is the literary equivalent of the problem of theodicy, the specialized subdiscipline of theology that addresses the problem of the apparent silent indifference of God to the hell of human suffering.

And when a writer won't break his silence, we think of ways to break into it. We think of knocking on his door or leaving messages in his mailbox.

S.'s two mailboxes beckoned to me as I stood at the bottom of his driveway. The gray metal U.S. Postal Service box was shut with a rusty hasp. But next to it stood a forest-green, open-ended mailbox with the logo of a local paper, West Lebanon's *Valley News,* on it. Empty, except that stuck in the back was a single piece of printed matter that looked as if it had been orphaned there for some time. Someone else's message for S.? It turned out to be a junk-mail flyer, perhaps the single most misdirected piece of junk mail in America.

GET ON TARGET! the flyer shrieked in hyperventilating three-inch-high type. It was a junk-mail flyer advertising customized promotional junk-mail flyers—*meta* junk mail. LET US HELP YOU ADVERTISE YOUR BUSINESS! it urged J. D. Salinger.

America's self-promotional culture reaching out to target the last private person left.

It made me think twice about leaving a letter there, a message for S. It made me think more than twice about what I might say, or whether I should just depart and leave his silence in silence.

I knew I had to consider my next move carefully, because I could end up doing something I might regret for a long time.

The Season When the Silent Speak

The night before I set out for New Hampshire, I heard a strange tale about J. D. Salinger's Wall: the Fake Wounds Story. It came up after I'd mentioned my fascination with S.'s Wall in a talk I'd given at Harvard's Nieman Fellows house. Hoping I might smoke out some arcane lore about S. from the ace reporters in my audience, I told them about my concept for the expedition: I would be heading up to Cornish, the tiny, hilly hamlet eighteen miles south of Hanover that has been S.'s place of silent retreat for the past forty-four years. Not to disturb S., not to knock on his door or wait on his doorstep. No, I told them, what I most wanted to do was gaze at S.'s *wall*. This was at least partially true. If S. *were* to emerge from behind the wall and engage me in a discussion about "the sound of one hand clapping," I would not decline. But I did not expect this would happen. My idea was that S.'s Wall itself—not just the physical wall of wood or stone I'd heard he'd built around his house but the metaphysical Wall, the Wall of Silence he'd built around himself, around his work—was in a way his most powerful, most eloquent, perhaps his most lasting work of art. I explained my notion of the Party of Silence: how writers like Salinger and Thomas Pynchon and William Wharton and to some extent Don DeLillo (less silent than publicity shy) constituted a small but powerful minority caucus in American culture. They are less a party than a loose-knit group of kindred spirits whose varieties of conscious silence range from writing but not publishing (S.) to publishing but not appearing (Pynchon) to publishing under a pseudonym to avoid publicity (Wharton) to publishing but not actively publicizing himself (DeLillo). Their varieties of reticence and concealment and self-effacement cumulatively constitute a provocative dissent from the culture of self-promotion that has swept contemporary publishing, a reproof to the roaring "white noise" (a DeLillo-novel title) of the publicity-industrial complex that dominates contemporary celebrity culture.

And suddenly this season, it seemed that the silent—in their own idiosyncratic gestural ways—had begun to speak! In January, a report stunned the literary world to the effect that S. had made a small but significant reversal, a slight opening, if not a breach, in the Wall. He had inexplicably, quixotically granted permission to a small-press publisher (Orchises Press in Alexandria, Virginia, which specializes in little-known contemporary poets) to issue a hardcover edition of his last published story, "Hapworth 16, 1924," which had first appeared in the June 19, 1965, issue of *The New Yorker* and survived mainly in faded nth-generation photocopies.

This was a surprising and puzzling reversal because S. had declined for three decades to permit the story to be issued in book form (as he had his other long *New Yorker* stories like "Franny" and "Zooey"). And he'd made it his practice to unleash from behind his wall attack-dog legal assaults on unauthorized publication of other uncanonical works (early uncollected short stories; personal letters a biographer found in university archives). He'd even succeeded in suppressing quotations from *already published* works: Late last year, his agents forced a nonprofit website run by a fan of *The Catcher in the Rye* to cease offering inspirational quotations from the novel to other fans.

The "Hapworth" development wasn't earth-shattering on the face of it: S.

wasn't releasing the rumored novel or novels he's been working on for the last three decades—the ones that, according to some reports, will continue to gather dust in a safe somewhere until (at least) after his death. He wasn't going to tour behind the "Hapworth" story or visit Oprah's Book Club. But against the background of the Wall, the monolithic, uncompromising Wall of Silence he'd erected around himself, the decision seemed to portend something more than the mere reprint of a magazine story.

S. turned seventy-eight this year;* he'd been off for decades on what many supposed was some kind of spiritual quest, seeking something that demanded isolation and silence, a quest that had to be shielded by the Wall. Had he decided to compromise the strictness of his silence because of his awareness of mortality—the onrushing, unbreakable silence to come? Or had his quest at last produced some *answer* he wanted to begin to communicate? Was there something buried in the "Hapworth" story, some clue, some key to his silence, that he wanted to remind us of? Since it was S., now more mythic presence than real person, the speculations were tinged with a kind of millennial urgency—the promised return of a prophet.

What gave the Salinger announcement additional impact was that it came close upon the disclosure that his fellow pillar of the Party of Silence, Thomas Pynchon, was about to publish a new novel, *Mason & Dixon,* his first in seven years. And Pynchon would be followed, later this year, by a much-anticipated new DeLillo novel, *Underworld.*

Pynchon's silence had been a different sort of silence from S.'s, more moderate in one respect: Unlike S., he'd never ceased to publish out of principle. But more extreme than S.'s in another respect: S. had, in the postwar era, cut quite a public figure in the New York literary world—dining at the Stork Club with his British publishers, playing poker with writers and editors, lunching with urbane *New Yorker* wits like S. J. Perelman—before he suddenly exiled himself, silenced himself as a public persona, retreated behind his Wall, and stopped publishing, if not writing.

Pynchon, on the other hand, had almost from the very beginning refused to play the literary game: He'd *always* been an absence rather than a presence. He's been a stealth writer from the moment the publicity-industrial complex first tried to fix him on its radar screen. Legend has it that Pynchon was living in Mexico at the time his remarkable debut novel, *V.,* was about to appear in 1963 and that when he discovered that *Time* magazine had sent someone down there to photograph the new sensation, "he just got on a bus and disappeared," as one of his associates told me. Ever since, for thirty years, he's been

*1997.

a wraith, a rumor with no known address. (At least with Salinger, we knew what state, what town, he lived in.)

Pynchon's legendary invisibility had been so complete for so long that back in 1976 one imaginative author (John Calvin Batchelor) had even written an extremely clever mock-scholarly essay arguing the half-serious conjecture that Thomas Pynchon *was* J. D. Salinger, a Salinger who had been evading (or protecting) his Wall of Silence by publishing under cover of the Pynchon pseudonym. Others have suggested that the man behind the pseudonym William Wharton was actually Salinger incognito.

The accumulation of comic exotic speculations about Salinger and Pynchon is testimony in a way to the compelling hold their forms of silence still have over us. In a publicity-mad, celebrity-crazed culture, they have become in effect the Madonna and Michael Jackson of Silence, celebrities for their reticence and their renunciation of celebrity, for their Bartleby the Scrivener–like great refusal, the resounding echo of their silent "I would prefer not to." You can gauge the continuing totemic power of Salinger's name in the zeitgeist-sensitive film *Jerry Maguire,* in which Tom Cruise compares the unadorned reticence of the cover of his idealistic "Mission Statement" (the critique of go-go materialism that gets him fired from his sports-marketing agency) to the purity of the cover of *The Catcher in the Rye.*

Of course, within the Party of Silence, there is not one silence but many varieties and degrees of reticence. Literary history has given us *burning silence,* perhaps the most extreme and heartbreaking case being Nikolai Gogol's feeding the second part of his comic masterpiece *Dead Souls* into the flames of a wood-burning stove in the throes of a spiritual crisis or nervous breakdown. There is the *silence of low self-esteem:* Emily Dickinson's not believing her works were truly worthy of ever appearing. There is the *enforced silence* of censorship, the *internal silence* of crippling writer's block. But the silence one confronts in S.'s driveway is the silence whose power is most compelling: the deliberate silence that represents some kind of spiritual renunciation, what the Trappist writer Thomas Merton called *elected silence.* "The withheld work of art," someone says in a DeLillo novel, "is the only eloquence left."

Trying the Patience of a Saint

To return to the Fake Wounds Story: Just as I'd hoped, one of the Nieman Fellows approached me after my talk with a fascinating story about S. He had a friend, he said, who, as a youth, had made the Pilgrimage to Salinger's House, a journey that is the closest thing a secular literary culture has to a religious ritual, a rite of passage. It is a pilgrimage S.—much to his regret, one must suppose—seemed to encourage with a famous passage in *The Catcher in the*

Rye in which Holden Caulfield describes the powerful connection he feels with writers whose work he loves and how that kind of connection makes him want to call the writer up. He doesn't say *look* the writer up, but few pilgrims make that distinction because few have his phone number anyway. (I have a number for him. I just haven't used it.)

The Pilgrimage to S.'s House, to the shadow of his Wall, has itself become part of American literary myth, most prominently in W. P. Kinsella's *Shoeless Joe,* in which an Iowa farmer sets off for New Hampshire with a plan to kidnap J. D. Salinger and take him to a baseball game because a Voice has given him the mission to "ease his pain." The Fake Wounds Story turned out to be a kind of inadvertently parodic inversion of the ease-his-pain injunction. That night in my hotel room in Cambridge, I was able to track down the guy that the Nieman Fellow had told me about, the one who'd made the fake-wounds pilgrimage.

The way he told it, back in the sixties, when they were teenagers, he and a couple of similarly Salinger-obsessed buddies had hatched what they thought was a fiendishly clever plan to lure Salinger out from behind his Wall. The plan was to drive to Cornish and locate the Salinger house, at which point he planned to tear up his clothes and cover his head and body with ketchup to simulate blood—to make it look as if he'd been badly beaten up. They'd screech up the driveway to the walls of S.'s house, toss the "victim" out of the car, roar off, and leave him there moaning. The idea was that S. would then *have* to emerge—he couldn't resist the cry for help of a man who might be bleeding to death on his doorstep. S. would have to come out from behind his Wall, take the fellow in, and ease *his* pain.

In a slapdash way, it was a plan to try the patience of a saint, because embedded in it was an ethical/spiritual dilemma: The ketchup-smeared kid would not be just another feckless adolescent fan or a doorstepping journalist but a suffering human being in need of help. Could S. refuse?

And so they did it—smeared the ketchup, dumped the body out right in front of the Wall. The kid began moaning in pain from his fake wounds and waiting to see whether S. would appear to help heal them.

A brief digression might be in order here on S.'s Wall, the theories of its origins and true purpose, including its possible genesis in the Girl Reporter Betrayal Story. A digression I make in the spirit of Thisbe's plaintive apostrophe in the Mechanicals' play in *A Midsummer Night's Dream,* the one that she addresses to the actor playing "Wall": *"O Wall, full often hast thou heard my moans."*

The most convincing account of the first appearance of S.'s Wall can be found in the only serious Salinger biography in existence, *In Search of J. D. Salinger,* by Ian Hamilton. It's a book whose tortured history is in a way monument to, and victim of, S.'s silence, one that bears real wounds, gaping holes in it from its encounter, its painful collision, with the Wall.

Hamilton, the respected British biographer of Robert Lowell and himself a poet, set out to write a life of S., knowing it was unlikely S. would cooperate. But Hamilton could not have expected the veritable war S. eventually waged against his book, a war to force Hamilton to rip out from his manuscript quotations and paraphrases from some private letters of S.'s he'd located.

Still, the wounded version of the Hamilton book that survived S.'s legal attack contains some surprising material, none more so than his account of the origin of the Wall.

According to Hamilton's chronology, S. moved to Cornish in January 1953. Then thirty-four, he was a success both critically and commercially from the 1951 publication of *The Catcher in the Rye* but not yet a cult figure. His hegira to the mountain fastness of the North must have helped contribute to the cult—he was no longer a New York writer, however special; he was now the Man on the Mountaintop. In fact, the property occupies a hilltop, albeit one that is almost invariably referred to as a hilltop "with a view of five states" (perhaps because of the implicit spiritual resonance of *states*).

Most accounts agree that S.'s retreat had *something* to do with the spiritual transformation he was undergoing. An increasing preoccupation with Eastern spiritual disciplines—particularly Hindu Vedantic philosophy, with its emphasis on karma and reincarnation, and Zen Buddhism, with its stress on the abandonment of ego—began showing up in his short stories in the early fifties. But Hamilton reveals that S.'s moving to Cornish didn't initially mean embracing a solitary spiritual life. At least at first, S. led a very active social life, both with adult neighbors in Cornish and (more curiously) with a crowd of high-school youths in Windsor, the larger town across a covered bridge in Vermont. According to Hamilton, who tracked down some of S.'s high-school pals, "He used to be a ball of fun," as one of them put it. "He was forever entertaining the high-school kids—he bought us meals and drinks. He was very interested in the basketball and football games. . . . After the Spa [an after-school hangout], we used to pile into his jeep and go up to his house. It was always open house up there." "We all looked up to him," recalled another, "especially the renegades."

But then came the Betrayal, the original media sin. Apparently, one of the Windsor High School students asked S. for an interview for the high-school page of a local paper. He gave her the interview, but the paper, the Claremont *Daily Eagle,* ran it like a scoop. According to a *Life* magazine account of the episode quoted by Hamilton, " 'The next time a carload of them drove up to Salinger's home, he did not seem to be at home. . . .' When they tried again, they found the house 'totally hidden behind a solid, impenetrable, man-tall, woven wood fence.' " Interviews interfere with his mission, S. told a photographer at the time. No more "until I've completed what I set out to do."

The Era of the Wall had begun. For S. within his Wall, it was a period of increased preoccupation with spiritual questions, signaled in the famous epigraph about silence he added that year to the hardcover edition of his first short-story collection, *Nine Stories:*

> *We know the sound of two hands clapping.*
> *But what is the sound of one hand clapping?*
>
> —*A Zen koan*

It all added to the mystique: What was going on behind the Wall, what kind of silent quest? The Wall excluded the world but lured it, too, inspiring quests of its own, wild speculations. In one of his later stories, S.'s narrator/alter ego speaks of the rumors that he spent "six months of the year in a Buddhist monastery and the other six in a mental institution."

There were many indications of rural normality as well: There was marriage to a young Englishwoman, Claire Douglas; there were children, Matt and Peggy; there was a yearlong live-in liaison* with a young writer, Joyce Maynard; and then another marriage. The man wasn't a complete hermit or a monk. But there was a growing sense that the Wall that kept the world out had somehow succeeded in imprisoning S., walling him in. In DeLillo's novel about the Salinger-like novelist, there's an implicit parallel between a poet held hostage by terrorists in some basement in Beirut and the novelist held hostage in his little room, hostage to the terror of celebrity—or to the terrifying magnitude of his own vision of perfection.

In Which S.'s Healing Philosophy Is Disclosed

At the very least, it seemed increasingly to wall in his work. In the dozen years after he built the wall in 1953, he published just four short stories; then came "Hapworth" and thirty-two years of silence. There was a growing sense among readers and critics that he was walling himself in imaginatively as well, writing with increasing obsessiveness about the insular inwardness of the Glass family (the Corleones of the sensitive contemporary-lit set), a big New York family whose seven children are haunted and tormented in various ways by the enigmatic spirituality—and mysterious suicide—of the firstborn, Seymour. Guru, poet, avatar, former child prodigy and quiz-kid celebrity, Seymour, we learn in the "Hapworth" story (which takes the bizarre form of a

---

*Not by her recently published account an exemplar of "normality."

twenty-thousand-word-long letter from an impossibly precocious seven-year-old Seymour writing home from summer camp), is himself haunted by visions of his past lives—his previous incarnational "appearances," as he calls them. And by a premonition of his own death, the gunshot suicide described cryptically in "A Perfect Day for Bananafish"—a story, a suicide, that has launched a thousand term papers and dissertations all attempting to explain why Seymour silenced himself.

Was S. committing slow artistic suicide within the Wall, silencing himself within the glass house of his Glass family chronicle? Or had he achieved some strange new level of spiritual or artistic transcendence—writing that no longer required the ego validation of publication or readers, at least within his lifetime? Or—horrible thought—was he writing now only for God's eye and planning to pull a Gogol: feed the work to the flames before he died?

Those of us who cared rushed to rustle up faded Xeroxes of the "Hapworth" story and search it for clues, once the announcement was made of S.'s decision to permit the story a life beyond the Wall again. At one point in "Hapworth"—S.'s most hermetic and self-referential work—little Seymour Glass seems to offer some signals about the silence of his creator.

In speaking of the karmic homework he needs to do, Seymour mentions the need to "move as silently as possible" and then cites an Eastern sage, Tsiang Samdup (in a way that presumes we are, of course, familiar with his authority), on Silence: "Silence! Go forth, but tell no man," the estimable Samdup enjoins us, according to little Seymour. Which hints at what S. might be doing: continuing to *go forth* with his writing but *telling no man*—not publishing what he's written. Until perhaps he's well on his way to the next incarnation.

The "Hapworth" story also offers us a tantalizing preview of the *next* never-seen Salinger story—the one he may have written but shown only to God, or perhaps the one he's been writing and revising, unable to finish. For all we know, it might be the story that silenced him. We know about this story, or we think we do, because seven-year-old Seymour in "Hapworth" foresees both the event that occasions it and the story that his brother Buddy, Salinger's alter ego, will write about the event. Is it just an accident that this story, the story that may have silenced S., is a story about a Temptation and a Fall into Celebrity? About the sudden celebrity that the Glass family children fall into as wunderkind stars of a radio quiz show called *It's a Wise Child.* An exposure to publicity that would leave them all scarred and wounded in various ways. The putative post-"Hapworth" story can be seen as an allegory of the wounds S. himself experienced in his sudden transformation into a wunderkind celebrity.

Wounds, yes: Let us return again to the Fake Wounds Story, in which a possibly wounded S. inside his wall is confronted by a fraudulently wounded seeker moaning outside the wall. What happened, the somewhat chagrined fake-wounds victim told me, was that soon after he was dumped off, ketchup-smeared, moaning, the lights came on in the house behind the wall "as if someone was watching." And then, after a while, the lights went off. Then nothing. Silence. No one came out. Eventually, his friends returned, and they all slunk off. They didn't come away from it thinking S. was cruel or heartless. Rather, they got the feeling that the fake-wounds thing had been tried before: that it had become a regular *routine* for seekers to bear wounds, both real and false, to the wall. That S. had somehow developed the ability to diagnose the difference between blood and ketchup, between real pain and its simulation. This jibes somewhat with the story Jonathan Schwartz, the writer and radio personality, told me about a woman he knew who'd made the pilgrimage with her five-year-old child. She'd gone as far as knocking on S.'s door, and when he wouldn't let her in, she told him she had a tired, ailing child in her car. At that point, S. became enormously solicitous, invited them both in, and fed and played with the child for hours while they all watched the Marx Brothers' *Monkey Business* and an episode of *I Love Lucy*.

Saint Francis of Assisi or Michael Jackson? The saint and the strangely reclusive celebrity both draw the wounded. The Fake Wounds Story has stayed with me because it seems to explain the powerful attraction of the Wall, the compelling seductiveness of the silence a writer like S. surrounds himself with. The power that lures us, either in person or metaphorically, to S.'s Wall is a feeling that the silence betokens some special knowledge, some wisdom, the penetration of some unutterable mystery beyond words, beyond speech, expressible only in silence. The Wall he's built is, metaphorically, a place where we can bring our *real* wounds to be examined, healed—the wounds, the holes in our soul, the empty places eaten away by a sense of inauthenticity, by the ravages of celebrity culture.

Which brings me to the rather extraordinary discovery I made about S. as a healer in the course of pursuing various inquiries about the Man Behind the Wall—something I believe has never been reported before. It's a revelation I was led to very indirectly by a chain of random connections and one that contradicts the conventional wisdom of an S. utterly in thrall to Eastern religious disciplines. While it's true that Eastern disciplines have their appeal for him, in fact the healing discipline that, for a time, at least, most appealed to him, one he also expounded upon to others, is a far more down-home, Western system of healing: homeopathy. Yes, homeopathy, the heretical alternative system of diagnosis and healing invented by the German physician Samuel Hahnemann in the late eighteenth century, one long dismissed by mainstream medicine, one taken up again by New Age healers, one reportedly still relied upon by the British Royal Family, among others.

Why homeopathy? Part of the appeal might lie in the way the German Romanticism of Hahnemann's healing system offered a bridge between the physical and the metaphysical, transcended the dualism of mind and body that S.'s child avatars like Teddy in *Nine Stories* and Seymour in "Hapworth" railed against. Homeopathy is all about the interpenetrating resonance of the two realms. Setting aside the question of its scientific validity, one can find a metaphoric poetry in homeopathy's attempt to explain itself that I'd suggest would resonate with S.'s solitary absent presence.

Old Samuel Hahnemann believed in treating similars with similars: that an infinitesimal dose of what was making you ill could make you better. If, for instance, you were vomiting, homeopathy prescribed tiny doses of nausea-inducing herbs. More peculiarly and controversially, Hahnemann believed that the more he diluted his remedies in distilled water, the more powerful they became. This has led critics to claim that at their "highest potency," i.e., their greatest dilution, his homeopathic remedies were diluted to the point of *invisibility* and that homeopathic doctors were essentially prescribing nothing *but* distilled water to their patients. To which homeopathic defenders poetically reply, It's not the presence of the curative herb in the water but the "potentizing" imprint the once-present, now-absent dose has left on the molecular-level configuration of the fluid. A memory of an encounter, now somehow inscribed in water.

I'm not defending the science, just admiring the poetry of a healing system in which absence and memory have more power than presence—and suggesting that somewhere in this homeopathic rhetoric there is a metaphor for S.'s own absence and invisibility in our culture: that the *withdrawal* of his presence has left his memory, his influence, perhaps even his healing power *more* potent than an undiluted presence would be. That his silence is a kind of homeopathic remedy for the disease of noise we all suffer from.

I learned some other surprising things about S. in the course of my inquiries. I learned that in addition to the Glass family chronicle, he has also written a screenplay, a draft of some kind, in which his faithful Glass family narrator and alter ego, Buddy, is forced to confront criticism of the increasingly murky and mystical turn S.'s later Seymour-obsessed Glass family stories have taken. (I'd pay to see that.) I've also heard, though I'm less sure of this, that he may have written some film scripts under a pseudonym for European producers.

I learned that he's not a Howard Hughes–like recluse, that he has traveled here and abroad, that he's tuned in to the culture around him, hasn't walled himself off from it.

And finally, I learned what his favorite junk food is. I learned this from a friend who happened to find herself standing behind S. at a deli counter where he's a regular. S. was complaining about the way his *soppressata,* a rustic salami, was sliced (he likes it "thinly sliced and layered," like the prose in his early *New Yorker* stories), a concern that may be a tribute to his late father, Sol, a meat and cheese importer. I asked my friend to speak to the deli clerk and found out the astonishing fact that S.'s favorite junk food is (I swear) *doughnut holes*!* The pastry equivalent of the sound of one hand clapping.

But of all these revelations, the one about homeopathy strikes me as the most powerful truth about who S. is: if not a healer then an investigator of illness in the largest sense of the word, a literary diagnostician of the sickness, or slickness unto death, we suffer from as individuals and as a culture.

His remedy? I learned that S. had a particular interest in a homeopathic remedy called lycopodium, a variety of club moss, diluted to near invisibility, of course. A quick check of the homeopathic literature produced the fascinating disclosure that there is among Hahnemann disciples something known as "the lycopodium personality." Described by one British practitioner as "diffident, conscientious, meticulous but self-conscious . . . [lycopodians] *dislike public appearances* [italics mine] and may take offense easily. . . ."

I had an uncanny feeling that in reading the homeopathic literature about the lycopodium personality, I was glimpsing at one remove the way S. diagnoses his own persona. And perhaps a clue to his decision to release the "Hapworth" story. A medicine for melancholy from Dr. S., a tiny but highly potentized dose of his presence injected afresh into the bloodstream of the culture, an infinitesimal opening in the Wall around himself, in the hope of evoking, in homeopathic fashion, a Presence, a memory of an Absence—lycopodium for the soul, ours and his.

The Catcher in the Driveway

As I crossed the border from Massachusetts to New Hampshire, heading northwest on a wintry-bright, sudden-thaw late-February morning, I found myself haunted by several questions about my pilgrimage to S.'s Wall.

First, would I find the place at all? Not having the address, I was depending on the kindness of strangers to guide me there, although I'd heard that the flinty New Hampshire townspeople in Cornish were not known for their kindness to strangers seeking S. Of course, in a way I almost hoped I *wouldn't* be able to find the place: It would mean that S.'s neighbors had, in effect, built a wall *around* the Wall.

I took the exit off Route 89 at West Lebanon and headed south toward Cornish on a rural route that clung to the banks of the icebound Connecticut River, having no idea what to do once I reached Cornish.

---

*In case you are unfamiliar with them, doughnut holes are the small sugared balls of fried dough that, *conceptually* anyway, are the holes punched out to make doughnut rings hollow.

After a recent *New York* magazine story disclosing Pynchon's location, or at least his neighborhood, S. may be the last private person left in America. I wanted to find the place, but I *feared* finding it—feared that (even if I would never publish the address or the directions there) I might pose a threat, however symbolic, to that last preserve of privacy, an endangered species of privacy now nearly extinct. I feared also the questions I'd have to face if I did find it, questions about myself, what I'd do facing S.'s Wall. Interrogating S.'s silence, facing his Wall, would inevitably entail interrogating, facing, a side of myself I might not want to see.

But, as fate would have it, a half hour after arriving in Cornish, I found myself at the bottom of S.'s driveway, gazing up at the NO TRESPASSING signs, considering my next step and the ethical, literary, philosophical dilemmas it posed.

I found this place fast—not because it is easy to find but because I was lucky. That it was blind luck was something I confirmed in the two days I spent in Cornish afterward, testing the townspeople and the wall around the Wall; asking them to lead me to S.'s place and getting turned down. Some told me they didn't know the way; some told me they didn't know who S. was; some told me they wouldn't tell me if they *did* know; some told me they did know but wouldn't tell me; some told me, "The gentleman likes his privacy" or variations of that sentiment. At one general store, a guy told me that college students from Dartmouth still came regularly looking for it, but "folks don't tell" and he wouldn't. At another general store, I was told, with a disapproving sneer, "We don't give out that information."

So there *was* a wall around the Wall in S.'s adopted hometown. But not an impregnable wall.

In the parking lot of one of the general stores, after being sent off with a discouraging, disparaging "folks don't tell," I chanced upon an elderly couple in an aging pickup truck. I told them, "My boss sent me up here to find J. D. Salinger's house, you know, just the house, not to bother him. Any chance you could help me?" The old fellow in the pickup-truck cab started giving me elaborate directions that ended vaguely: "Follow the road to the top of the hill; then it kind of gets complicated to describe. You'd better just ask some people when you get up there."

That didn't sound too promising to me, asking people around there. But I was able, with some difficulty, to persuade the guy to let me follow him in my car as he drove to the place. And so we set off. I'm going to cover my tracks at this point. Let's just say that after a long drive and a long stretch of road that a sudden thaw had turned into hubcap-deep mud, the truck stopped at a driveway featuring the only mailbox on the route that had *no name* on it.

I got out of my car and went up to the cab of the truck.

"Is this it?" I asked the ancient one.

"This is it," he said, gesturing up a driveway that slanted up a wooded slope to a house heavily screened by trees—a house on a hill that, even from below, one could see, could well offer the proverbial "view of five states."

"You're sure this is it?" I said.

He nodded and waited, watching, I think protectively, to see what I'd do. He seemed to satisfy himself that I had no plans for an actual intrusion and drove off.

Of course, it is marginally possible that he was part of S.'s roving disinformation squad, specifically detailed to mislead strangers in town seeking S., directing them to a designated false S. address. But that sounded more Pynchonesque in its paranoia than Salingeresque.

I looked for other signs. The driveway slanting up the slope to the tree-screened house matched others' descriptions. The existence of a second, older building on the property matched accounts of S.'s building a new structure in the late sixties after a divorce. I didn't see a physical wall, but I later learned that when S. built the new structure on his property, the old Wall was replaced by the now-tall stand of trees that screened and guarded the place. I was pretty confident this was the place. The orphaned GET ON TARGET! junk-mail flyer in the *Valley News* mailbox seemed ironic, poetic confirmation.

Assuming this was S.'s abode, assuming I had the right target in sight, what were my options? I could:

1. Violate the NO TRESPASSING sign, violate my own previously established ground rules, violate S.'s peace by going up the driveway and knocking on the door. But I just couldn't do that. I remembered the hunted, haunted, trespassed-and-violated look on S.'s face when a paparazzo caught him by surprise nearly ten years ago. Don DeLillo told me it was the sight of this terrified photo that inspired him to write *Mao II,* his meditation on a reclusive writer and the terror of celebrity. I felt bad enough just being here, felt that my presence outside his driveway was already a kind of karmic violation I would have to pay for with several unpleasant future lives. I could not take that step. I would not knock on his door.

2. Wait here long enough and hope to find S. coming or going. Which would amount to staking him out, or "doorstepping" him, as the Brit-tab phrase has it. I couldn't do that.

3. Just soak in the silence surrounding S.'s abode. Pay my silent respects to the Wall and go. When I'd confided to Jonathan Schwartz my misgivings about actually going up to S.'s place, he'd dismissed my hesitation. He had thought of it often, he said. He would not hesitate to do it, "just to breathe the same oxygen." So I breathed in the springlike oxygen and tuned in to the sounds of S.'s silence, tuned in to the sound of a rushing rivulet of thaw-melted snow burbling down the slope from S.'s house to the road. A distant bird cry. The deep, soulful soughing of the wind through S.'s trees.

A man passed by, walking a dog.

"This is the Salinger house, isn't it?" I said.

He smiled in a friendly way but said, "I can't answer that."

I listened to the silence. S.'s silent presence is like an unvoiced koan, a trick question that forces one to question oneself. I meditated upon S.'s silence, upon the absence of it in my life, upon all the other absences in my life. I began to feel very sad; I began to feel S.'s sadness, his sorrow and pity for a world filled with unenlightened souls like mine.

But then I thought about the famous Fat Lady passage in *Franny and Zooey*. You recall: the one in which Franny, the oversensitive, spiritually obsessed youngest sister of the departed guru Seymour, is suffering a nervous break-down because she can't take the insensitive and hypocritical chitchat of the be-nighted souls that surround her in her tony college. She wants to withdraw from the world, find a pure communion with Jesus through incessant prayer, prayer so incessant that after a while it becomes the pure, silent language of the heart.

Zooey, one of Franny's brothers, brings her out of the spiritual crisis by re-minding her of the Fat Lady. When they were all quiz-kid celebrities and got tired of performing for the unseen multitude of geeks and rubes in their audi-ence, the sainted Seymour would tell them to do it "for the Fat Lady." And each of them would think of some overweight woman out there in the radio audience, maybe swatting flies on her porch while listening to the show. Don't look *down* on such people; do the show out of *love* for the Fat Lady, Seymour urged them. "But I'll tell you a terrible secret," Zooey tells Franny. *"There isn't anyone out there who isn't Seymour's Fat Lady. . . . Don't you know who that Fat Lady really is? . . .* It's Christ Himself. Christ Himself, buddy."

A beautiful sentiment: Love every soul on the planet, however alien, for being an embodiment of godhood. But hasn't S. *rejected* that sentiment in withdrawing from the world, in disdaining contact with the perhaps foolish fans who love his work, in fleeing from the inept, excessive ways in which the world expresses its love for a writer? Isn't S., like Franny, spurning the Fat Lady? Aren't I, in some way, the Fat Lady on his doorstep? Shouldn't S. love *me*, welcome me, like the Fat Lady?

I listened to the Wall of Silence. And decided just listening wouldn't be enough. I decided on a fourth option. I would write S. a letter and leave it in one of his mailboxes.

Easy to say, but after all this time, after all these years, what did I have to say to S.? What one thing would *you* say, dear reader, given a chance to com-municate with the strange, silent, spiritual artist behind that Wall, the last pri-vate person in America?

I decided I needed to think about it overnight. I checked into a nearby coun-try inn (where the proprietor said S. had held an anniversary party with his third wife a couple of years back).

Back at the inn, I checked my answering machine in New York to find an anguished message from Jonathan Schwartz about a just-published attack on S.—well, on "Hapworth," but one that extended to S.'s entire Glass family oeuvre—by a major critic. Jonathan was sure that S. would see the attack; he thinks of S. as *very* tuned in to the literary world despite the impression of spiritual detachment. (He reminded me that when his friend and her five-year-old watched *Monkey Business* with S., the woman noticed stacks of *New York-ers* and *New York Times*es in S.'s house. Jonathan believes that many are misled by S.'s unworldly spiritual preoccupations and miss out on the mordant comic observations of worldliness his best work displays.) He was afraid the attack would embitter S. and convince him to alter his plans for letting "Hapworth" (and perhaps himself) out into the world again.

I suddenly had an image of S. as Punxsutawney Phil, the well-known groundhog of Groundhog Day. Of S. poking his ever-so-sensitive, twitching nose outside his burrow of silence, seeing his Shadow—sniffing the hostility—and deciding that it wasn't worth it. Returning to Silence forever.

I decided that maybe what I needed to do in the message I was drafting was—in my own ego-bound way—to try to "ease his pain." A kind of homeopathic remedy: a message from a single stranger to a man who feared the great mass of strangers. I say "ego-bound" because the method I chose could not be said to be free of self-serving vanity. I think that at the core of every pilgrimage to S. is the belief of each pilgrim that in his heart he *understands* the object of the pilgrimage better than anyone else—and the concomitant hope that S. will *recognize* that, validate that. In some way, he will acknowledge that *you,* you out of all of them, have penetrated to the heart of the Mystery: At last, I've found someone who *knows* me.

This plays into my own special vanity about my talent for literary exegesis. And so I started composing a letter on a yellow legal pad that began on an "ease his pain" note but shifted, I'll admit, rather rapidly, to a plea for Recognition.

Dear Mr. Salinger, I began. *I hope you won't mind if I pass along this appreciation of your "Hapworth" story.* [I was planning to include in the envelope an explicatory essay on "Hapworth" I'd published recently in *The New York Observer.*] *I thought you might get a chuckle out of my conjecture in there about the sound of one hand clapping. . . .*

This is where my very un-Zenlike vanity announces itself. It was more than a "conjecture": I thought I'd *nailed* that supposedly unanswerable one-hand-clapping koan. See, I once had a conversation about it with a fellow who'd spent seven years in a Zen monastery. He told me what he claimed was the spiritually "correct" answer to the question—that is, the answer an enlightened person would *spontaneously* come to if he was *truly* enlightened.

When asked by a master, What is the sound of one hand clapping? the enlightened initiate would just *know* not to reply in words but, in solemn silence, to raise just one hand from his side and wave it toward the center of his chest *as if* it were meeting the other hand for a clap. The sound of one hand clapping is the sound of that silent wave, the sound of an absence, the absence of the noise ordinarily made by the collision of two hands. The sound of one hand clapping is the silence one tunes *in* to in that absence, the resonant silence of the rest of creation, the vast Oneness of Being one absorbs in the absence of that narrowing clap.

That koan about the sound of one hand clapping appears, of course, as the epigraph at the opening of S.'s first collection, *Nine Stories*. My exegetical revelation was the discovery that if you turn to the first page of the text and begin reading "A Perfect Day for Bananafish," the famous story of Seymour Glass's suicide, you will find a rather astonishing image, a secret, surprising image of the sound of one hand clapping embedded right there. It's there in the description of Seymour's wife, Muriel, drying the lacquer on her nails in their Florida beachfront hotel room. It's there in S.'s description of Muriel waving one hand, "her left—the wet—hand back and forth through the air," to dry her nails. Making the gesture of one hand clapping.

I concluded by telling S. I was writing a story praising the art, the example, of his silence and that if he *had* anything to communicate (e.g., *Yes, Ron, you alone have understood me*), I would be honored to hear from him.

Was my message a product of mixed motives, both selfless and selfish? Yes, it was. But I never claimed to be as spiritually advanced as S. And I *have* shown restraint; I haven't used the telephone number I have for him.

The next morning, early, I drove back to S.'s driveway. Found the Sunday paper nestled in a U-shaped fold in the *Valley News* mailbox. I put my note and my "Hapworth"/one-hand-clapping essay in an envelope and slipped it into the fold. Stayed a moment to appreciate the silence, then drove off to have breakfast at a Denny's in nearby West Lebanon.

I could have left town then. Perhaps I *should* have left town then. But instead, I decided to go back. The way I rationalized my return was that I was going back only to see if the letter had at least been taken in with the Sunday paper. And in fact, when I arrived back, the paper was gone, and so was the envelope with my letter. Mission accomplished.

Again, I should have gone then. But there was a magnetism to the place. To S.'s invisible Wall. To the echoing silence that seemed to emanate from S.'s abode. If it *was* S.'s place. As long as S. remained invisible up there at the end of the driveway behind the NO TRESPASSING signs and the no-name mailbox, it didn't really matter if it was or it wasn't. I could be paying tribute to S.'s silent invisibility *anywhere* he was invisible.

But I thought I would make one final gesture before heading home, one final tribute to S.'s silent presence or absence. I thought I would make the sound of one hand clapping. And so, facing up to the house, I made the silent one-handed wave. I tuned in to the resonant, silent sound of creation that enveloped me and S., tuned in to all five states of being. I was the Catcher in the Driveway.

And then, to my horror, I heard another sound—the sound of a car engine starting up, the sound of a car heading down the driveway toward me!

Would S. be at the wheel? My whole life passed before me in review. I had fantasized S. reading my letter and my appreciation of Muriel's one-handed wave and silently saying to himself, "At last. Someone who truly understands me and my work."

But I hadn't imagined S. finding me on his doorstep, looking like a doorstepper.

The car reached the bottom of the driveway. I was positioned next to my car, about twenty feet to the right. Because of the light, I couldn't see if there were two figures or one in the front seat or what they looked like.

The car paused at the bottom of the driveway. Seemed to take in my presence. And—if it could ever be said it was possible for a *car* to look furious—*this* car looked furious. Then roared off to the left, in the opposite direction from me, spraying mud.

In the silence left behind, I felt terrible. I felt a wave of remorse strike me. I had wanted to be known to S. as a serious pilgrim, someone who understood him and his silence, someone who respected his silent privacy—but perhaps someone he might *want* to speak to (because of my exegetical insights, of course). But now I felt that, inevitably, it *looked* to S. as if I were a doorstepper. I felt my intrusive driveway presence might inadvertently change S.'s mind about releasing "Hapworth," about releasing anything—that I might have thus ineradicably altered the course of literary history. If S. was Punxsutawney Phil, *I* was his Shadow. He'd retreat into his burrow; his wintry silence would never end.

I waved after the car. With one hand. Feeling devastated. For God's sake, reader, don't try to follow my path. My only consolation is to hope to hell I had the wrong house.

Postscript to "The Catcher in the Driveway"

The publication of *Gone,* Renata Adler's memoir of *The New Yorker,* brought with it a startling detail that seemed far more significant than the question of who stabbed whom in the back alleys of West Forty-third Street. According to Adler, Salinger told her that the real reason he'd stopped publishing in the magazine was that he was too solicitous of the modesty of *New Yorker* editor William Shawn to ask him to read (much less publish) the kind of writing Salinger had been doing, writing that involved sex. Was he being serious? Actually, I hope so; I'd love to read Salinger on sex. He is, after all, the writer who managed to turn an inventory of a woman's medicine cabinet into a veritable Arabian Nights' fantasy. And it's more hopeful than the "ethic of silence" Adler said some of Shawn's writers adopted, whereby it was somehow a spiritually superior thing not to write.

It was in part to combat the almost universal negativity that had been projected upon Salinger's silence (as terminally eccentric, as vanity, even as pathology) that I'd initially undertaken this story. I wanted to make the case that his silence, whatever its source, had become something more than a negation, that it's become a kind of positive statement or at least a heroic critique of the publicity-industrial complex from which he'd withdrawn.

Yet I still feel conflicted about the story. I'm not sure whether it's possible to pay tribute to a writer's silence by going up to but not over his wall, without intruding on it. I'd argue that a story *about* these conflicts and doubts was worth doing: I was a surrogate for a public both respectful of and drawn to test Salinger's silence. And besides, shouldn't he love me like he loves "the Fat Lady"?

Long Island, Babylon

In Which We Seek the Source of Longing in Long Island

It would be foolish to believe that a single story could sum up the entire range of bizarre and sensational behavior that is Long Island Babylon. Particularly a story that doesn't even mention Amy or Sol, Joey or "Joel the Ripper," little Katie Beers or Howard Stern, much less the "Homeroom Hit Man," the "Angel of Death" nurse, the Islip Garbage Barge or Geraldo Rivera.

Nonetheless, I feel that the story of the unprintable Satanist Ritual Killing Ground Photo comes close.

Some years ago in Northport—not far from the birthplace of Thomas Pynchon, who is, far more than the frequently invoked F. Scott Fitzgerald, the true literary avatar of the Long Island soul—two allegedly angel-dusting, devil-worshiping teenagers were branded as "ritual cult murderers" of another teenager in the Aztakea woods.

It was one of the first such episodes in what would become a national trendlet, and perhaps the first signal that something sinister was stirring out there behind the split-level shutters of Long Island's suburbs. But this particular story about the unprintable photo, one I heard from a former *Newsday* editor who swears it's true, isn't about the killing itself; rather about something that happened the night after the death became public.

It seems the paper had dispatched a photographer to get a nighttime shot of the supposedly spooky, satanist ritual killing ground out there in the woods, something that would capture the diabolical horror of it all. But when certain pictures came out of the darkroom, they just weren't . . . suitable. Unusable. Not because they were too terrifying (at least not terrifying in a Luciferian way). But because many photographs of the alleged cult coven's killing circle prominently featured a large boulder, across the face of which was scrawled the following somewhat-less-than-terrifying cult slogan:

SATIN LIVES!

A check with the *Newsday* photo library disclosed that contact sheets of all unpublished photos had been discarded.* Nonetheless, ten years later, it can be said with confidence: Satin *still* lives on Long Island. No, Satin flourishes. Satin rules. Satin lives in Joey Buttafuoco's auto-body shop, Satin lives in Sol Wachtler's Manhasset town house, Satin lives in the recurrent reminder that even when we try our hardest to be sensationally bad, we often wind up just a little bit off—as much embarrassing as menacing.

I say "we" because, while I was born in Manhattan and have lived most of the latter half of my life there, I grew up on Long Island, and I'm resigned to the fact that in some essential, irrevocable way I'll always be a Long Islander. Resigned to the fact that, whenever I tell someone my hometown was Bay Shore, I feel compelled to add, preemptively, "Yes, that's right, that's the home of Katie Beers's dungeon."** Resigned to the fact that every mush-mouthed hayseed in America feels he has the right to say, condescendingly, "Oh, you're from Long Island, you mean *Lawn Guyland*"—as if everyone there spoke that way and he was establishing a Henry Higgins–like sophistication by comparison.

Resigned to the fact that while people from New Jersey, the second most maligned and unfashionable place to come from in America, at least have native son Bruce Springsteen to transmute their state's toxic wastelands into a kind of doomed romantic grandeur, those of us from Long Island have . . . Debbie Gibson and Billy Joel.

Resigned to the fact that while the image of Long Island was once merely unfashionable, uncool, the epitome of Plastic Suburbia, a Levittown of the Mind lampooned by sixties folkies for its cookie-cutter "Little boxes made of

---

*My source, the photo editor, remembers it clearly. So does a second person in the art department. The top editor, however, insists that it's an apocryphal story, a kind of newsroom (sub)urban myth. I believe my sources, but even apocryphal stories can illustrate underlying attitudes, here an attitude toward Long Island as a place where hapless would-be Satanists haven't learned to spell the name of their Dread Lord right.

**A briefly famous tabloid shocker in which a kidnapped ten-year-old girl was—after a long search—discovered locked in a high-tech "dungeon" beneath the floor of a split-level house in Bay Shore owned by an adult male "family friend."

ticky tacky," suddenly in the past few years the Guyland (as we expatriates like to call it) has turned into a veritable tabloid pandemonium, no longer just tacky, but spectacularly mortifying, ludicrously, demonically possessed—possessed by Satin.

Resigned, yes, but also lately, I must admit, perversely proud. Suddenly my background, my hometown has become tremendously exotic, the object of awe and wonder, not just snickering. Perversely proud but also profoundly puzzled. What the hell *happened*? What happened to the incredibly boring place I grew up in, where I swear *nothing ever happened*? What happened to turn it into this charnel house of sensational spouse slayings; fatally attracted judges posing as low-life, blackmailing private eyes sending condoms to mistresses' daughters; cold-blooded, steroid-juiced young killers; kidnappers with dungeons; horticultural serial killers? A veritable Babylon, and not the colorless stop on the L.I.R.R. right after Amityville, Copiague, and Lindenhurst, but a Babylon out of the Book of Revelation, the blood-drenched Mother of Abominations.

I was thinking about all this rather gloomily the other day. I believe it was the week after the story of the obsessed tennis coach and dungeon builder, Gary Wilensky (who wanted to make his teenage tennis student Jennifer Rhodes *his* Katie Beers), broke, and *Newsday* printed his high-school yearbook photo that revealed—wouldn't you know it?—he came from Roslyn, Long Island. About the same time, a local television station ran a scare story about a so-called Cannibal Killer, a former schoolteacher who had killed and eaten a student and who was about to be granted weekend furloughs from the psych ward so he could return to his parents' home in—you guessed it—Melville, Long Island.

I found myself staring resentfully at a recent Dewar's profile ad that featured a cheerful achiever whose hometown was Chicago. Under the rubric "Home: Chicago, Illinois," the Dewar's ad quoted her saying: "Toddlin' Town? Up and running's more like it!"

Bleakly, it occurred to me that just about every other place in America can find something to be perky and boosterish about. Death Valley, the Great Dismal Swamp, despite the names, are natural wonders. Feisty Cleveland, battling back from its toxic river-on-fire image, has the Rock-and-Roll Hall of Fame under construction at last.

But Long Island . . . what can you say in a Dewar's ad these days?

Home: "Long Island. *Plenty of sleazy spouse murders and more to come!*"

Or

Home: "Long Island. *When better dungeons are built, our psychos will build them.*"

Or perhaps something a bit more hopeful: *"We've already been through our Satanist phase."* Or *"When* you *get three TV movies of the week,* then *you can criticize."*

So what is it about the Guyland, anyway? Yes, I know there are sensational tabloid crimes everywhere and the closeness to the Manhattan media nexus tends to magnify everything. But even so, that was always true. There's just no denying that *something* has changed in the past decade, that, as our bard Billy Joel sings on his new album, there's "lots more to read about Lolita and suburban lust."

But why? Why is this Island different from all other islands? And why are so many Long Islanders suddenly running amok?

The question of Long Island uniqueness was posed in a particularly acute way by one of the characters on one of those three Amy Fisher–Joey Buttafuoco made-for-TV movies.

The scene: The interior of Joey's Complete Auto Body Shop. One of Joey's employees is theorizing about the deep, underlying source of the love triangle shooting. He's obviously given some thought to the vexing question, attributing it to "Mid-Island Syndrome."

"It's the wires," he declares. "The wires weren't buried underground like in other parts of the country, so with all this electricity in the air, it fries some people's brains."

Now there are some practical objections to this theory. A Lilco spokeswoman, after checking with the Long Island power company's electric service operations department, insisted that Long Island does not differ from the rest of the nation in the way it deploys its high-tension lines and that, in fact, more are buried than exposed. Still, the power-line explanation at least attempts to offer a unified field theory of Long Island mania. And even the Lilco spokeswoman, perhaps attempting to divert attention from the power lines, offered an implicit endorsement of the quest for *some* explanation.

"Now the water—that's another story," she said.

But before we get deeper into a consideration of Long Island theories, we have to do some surgery. We have to define exactly what we're talking about when we talk about the Guyland.

First, let's slice off Brooklyn and Queens at the Nassau County line. Now let's excise the Hamptons and Fire Island, which are really Manhattan transfers. I'm tempted to chop off Great Neck, a kind of transplanted Upper West Side, but if I did we'd lose one of the genuine culture heroes of the Guyland, the Great Neck native Andy Kaufman, the inspired madman comic recently memorialized anew by R.E.M.'s beautiful song "Man on the Moon."

Still, when we look at the results, we're left with something, well, very cut off, all stump: the *Boxing Helena* of islands.

Which brings us to the first General Theory of Long Island I want to consider: Gullah Theory—People who think of Long Island as mainly a bedroom suburb of New York City don't grasp just how cut off much of the island really is, how isolated, how strange. Once you get out beyond Huntington on the North and Massapequa to the South, you're not dealing with city commuter culture, you're dealing with Long Island *lifers,* a different breed altogether.

"When people write about Long Island," the novelist Richard Price once observed, "they write about Fitzgerald's West Egg, but they don't think about places like Freeport." And the further out you go, the less has been written, the less is really known by most New Yorkers whose experience with *this* Long Island—the Guyland of Freeport and Hicksville and Wyandanch, of Brentwood and Farmingville and Nesconset—consists of a few conversations with locals in diners off the Long Island Expressway or the occasional trip to the supermarket in Bay Shore before catching the ferry to Fire Island.

As someone whose miserable summer job experience as a teenager consisted mainly of holding down positions in the supermarkets of Bay Shore (the low point was a hot-asphalt summer retrieving shopping carts on a vast King Kullen parking lot), I can assure you day-trippers, you sophisticated graduates of Riverdale and Stuyvesant, you street-smart urban boys and girls from the city hoods, you don't realize what a different world you glide through in your air-cooled jitneys.

You day-trippers and weekend Hamptonites tend to forget the islandness of the Guyland. But the fact is, the only link to the mainland of America from the 516 area code are the ferries to New London and Bridgeport: *Nothing goes through Long Island to get to somewhere else.*

That is *very* cut off. There are virtues to being so cut off—closeness, cohesiveness, and a sense of commonality. But there are also problems—a kind of inbreeding, spiritual if not physical, and, frequently, the development of an idiosyncratic dialect that separates, even alienates, native speakers from mainstream culture. The classic instance is the "Gullah" spoken by the descendants of West Africans, who've lived for centuries on certain sea islands off the Georgia and Carolina coasts, almost completely in isolation from the mainland. The famed Guyland dialect, so alien and untuneful to outsiders is, in effect, *our* Gullah.

Being this cut off has made the Guyland a laboratory for more than just language, made it, in effect, a kind of Plum Island of culture. You recall Plum Island, don't you—the little island off the tip of Long Island's North Fork, the one marked on maps "Animal Disease Laboratory (Restricted)" because it's the site of top-secret, heavy-security, infectious-disease research labs. Let's not even get into the indignity of this situation: Of all the pork barrel projects, boondoggles, and federal plums to be plucked, *we* get Plum Island.

Still, it makes one wonder: There's been trouble at Plum Island lately. Recent power failures and evacuations raised questions about the possibility that the almost unbelievably virulent strains of microbes (like Rift Valley Fever) supposedly sealed up on the island, have escaped. Questions that were not put to rest by reports of jerry-built attempts to resterilize a sealed laboratory by vaporizing formaldehyde in ninety-seven electric frying pans. Could it be that Mid-Island Fever is actually the result of the escape of an experimental *behavioral* virus from Plum Island? Is *that* what's in the water?

I'm not persuaded it's the wires or the water. Such theories don't approach the heart of the matter—that Long Island something in the *soul*. Which brings us to what might be called *Great Chain of Wanna-Being Theory.*

I had an epiphany on this subject in the aftermath of a fascinating conversation with Rob Weiss, the twenty-six-year-old, first-time director of the recently released *Amongst Friends,* a sort of Five Towns *Mean Streets.* Weiss's film is the first I know that actually dares to let Long Island be Long Island. Previous films, like Hal Hartley's *The Unbelievable Truth,* praised by outsiders for its strong authentic Guyland flavor, actually seem, to this native son, to shy away from showing the Uncongenial Truth of the real thing, to attenuate raw Guyland vitality for fear perhaps it would overwhelm the uninitiated. (And nobody in Hartley's film speaks with a real Long Island accent.)

Amongst Friends doesn't shrink from strong Guyland flavors and accents. Weiss revels in them, wallows in them with, yes, a kind of perverse pride. Indeed, his film may represent the opening shot in a counteroffensive against the prevailing derisive suburb-from-hell light in which the Guyland has been seen lately. An up-front, in-your-face, yes, we're-a-suburb-from-hell-and-we-like-it-like-that attitude. Long Island Pride at last.

And just in time. One gets tired of Long Island serving as a whipping boy, the archetype of uncool for the self-proclaimed hip. As in this recent exchange between the comedian Rosie O'Donnell (from Commack) and Madonna in this month's *Mademoiselle:*

MADONNA: You know, Ro, you're the only person I know from Long Island who's funny.

O'DONNELL: Not true—Jerry Seinfeld.

MADONNA: Well, *I* don't think he's funny.

While I agree with Madonna about Seinfeld, it's unfair to blame Long Island. Even if he is from Massapequa and acts like he's from the Five Towns.

The Five Towns—those enclaves of wealth, notorious for nouveau riche attitude—are really a kind of test for the rest of us from Long Island, a challenge to the inclusiveness of Long Island Pride: Do we disown them or defend them? And *which* Five Towns are they? As long ago as 1963, in his first novel, *V.,* Thomas Pynchon raised the question of the Phantom Fifth Town. One of his characters, Rachel Owlglass, a Bennington hipster chick, "came from the Five Towns on the South Shore of Long Island," Pynchon wrote. "An area comprising Malverne, Lawrence, Cedarhurst, Hewlett, and Woodmere, and sometimes Long Beach and Atlantic Beach, although no one has ever thought of calling it the Seven Towns."

In fact, indignant Five Towners have told me Pynchon made an egregious error in this list: Inwood, not Malverne, they insist, belongs in the magic circle of the inner five. Perhaps, at last, *here* is the explanation for Pynchon's legendary reclusiveness: For the last thirty years he has been so ashamed of this mistake he's never dared show his face again. (Could it be that he's hiding in Inwood, the town he erased from his list?)

Amused and a little bit bitter about the Five Towns the way most Long Islanders outside them are—the Five Towns are *Long Island's Long Island*—Pynchon depicts them as a kind of fairy-tale kingdom of sheltered princesses, "like so many Rapunzels within the magic frontiers of a country where the elfin architecture of Chinese restaurants, seafood palaces and split-level synagogues is often enchanting as the sea. . . . Only the brave escape."

Rob Weiss speaks as someone who's looked at the Five Towns from both sides now. He grew up in middle-of-the-middle-class Baldwin, but his father made enough money (organizing gambling junkets to Atlantic City) to enable Weiss to transfer from Baldwin High to Woodmere Academy, the haute Five Towns private day school. Weiss told me that although he'd seen it from the outside, once inside the heart of the beast he still was shocked by the frenzied conspicuous-consumption culture among his Benz- and Beamer-driving fellow students at Woodmere. In Baldwin (home of Joey Buttafuoco's Complete Auto Body Shop), Weiss says, "you had an identity, you were a jock, you were a brain, whatever you *were,* you *were.* At Woodmere, it was what you had, what brand, it was a whole wannabe scene."

The Phantom Shifting Fifth Town Problem seems to grow out of the wannabe syndrome. Weiss and I were talking about the difficulty—even natives have it—of recalling exactly *which* five towns were *the* Five Towns. How people who live near the Five Towns frequently seem to blur the boundaries by including their own little hamlet among the fab five. In the course of one of several exploratory trips to the Guyland recently, I found myself discussing the Five Towns with a waitress in a diner in Baldwin (the one where Joey Buttafuoco eats breakfast, she boasted). "I'm from the Five Towns," she said. When I asked her which one, she said, "Oh, Lynbrook," which is close geographically but not otherwise. In addition to Pynchon's Phantom Fifth Town wannabes, Atlantic Beach and Long Beach, I've also heard residents of Oceanside and all the Hewlett clones—Hewlett Harbor, Hewlett Bay Park, Hewlett Neck—include themselves in. (There's even a "Five Towns College" located in . . . Dix Hills.)

On the other hand, those actually in the Five Towns, if you believe Weiss's film, all want to be somewhere else—or some*one* else. He gives us Jewish gangster wannabes, blunt-spoken, blunt-smokin' Bugsy Siegels "walking the killer streets of Hewlett Harbor," as one character's girlfriend sarcastically observes. He gives us "sixteen-year-old Jewish kids thinking they were Flavor Flav" (the Public Enemy rap star who was in fact a Freeport native). Everyone else wants to be a player in Manhattan or Hollywood. Weiss, who just moved to Los Angeles himself, told me he's "amazed at how much Hollywood *is* Five Towns" and cites players like Scott Rudin and Brandon Tartikoff as Five Towns transplants. (Tartikoff corrected the record, saying people "automatically assume I'm from Great Neck or one of the Five Towns, but I'm really from Freeport"; he credits his middle-of-the-middle-class Freeport roots for his legendary ability to feel the pulse of the suburban, baby boomer, TV generation. Rudin is actually from Baldwin.)

After talking with Weiss, I was left with this vision: everyone outside the Five Towns wanting to be inside and everyone inside wanting to be something, somewhere, someone else.

The intellectual historian Arthur O. Lovejoy characterized the central hierarchical metaphor of Western thought as the "Great Chain of Being," one that links the lower realms of imperfection and error upward to ever purer regions of divine perfection. What we have on the South Shore of Long Island is a Great Chain of *Wanna-Being,* a series of communities linked together by longing to be something else, something more. Indeed, suddenly the true meaning of the "Long" in Long Island, the secret hidden in the name itself, blazed forth: it stands for *longing.*

Longing. Amy longed. Sol longed desperately. Joel longed murderously. Walt Whitman longed lustfully. Walter Hudson, all 1,200 pounds of him, longed hungrily. It's the soulful longing you hear in doo-wop songs, always and forever popular on Long Island.

The locus classicus of Long Island longing, of course, is that image of Gatsby, the eternal iconic wannabe, standing on the West Egg pier, yearning for the green light of East Egg—a cosmic longing that is both romantic and real estate–driven. One that unites him with the Roslyn resident longing to live in Roslyn Harbor and the Baldwin body shop owner longing for the forbidden Merrick princess.

But I prefer a more humble, more grungy than Gatsbyesque image of Long Island longing. Not someone stretching out his arms to a mansion across a moonlit channel, but the orphaned Islip garbage barge searching the oil-slicked waters of America's coastline, forlornly longing for a place to unload its cargo, a home for the wretched refuse of Long Island's shores.*

---

*For some reason, a barge full of Long Island refuse chugged around the coast of North America for months without finding a landfill willing to take its cargo.

As someone who grew up within the boundaries of Islip Township, watching weeks of coverage of this epic odyssey of humiliation and rejection, I found it hard not to identify with the brave little barge as it was turned away from landfill after landfill all down the Atlantic coast and across the Gulf of Mexico. North Carolina, Florida, Alabama, Mississippi, Louisiana, Texas— all turned it away; then Mexico, Belize, the Bahamas: No one would take Long Island's garbage! It was hard not to feel that what was being enacted was a metaphor, a dramatization of the disdain mainland culture had for Long Island itself.

I came to admire the plucky, never-say-die spirit of the barge. And felt a perverse kind of vindication that amazing week not long ago when three national television networks devoted their primest of prime time to two-hour telefilms about the Amy and Joey story: At last Long Island trash had found a home.

A unified field theory of longing would go a long way toward explaining what sometimes seems like an epidemic of desperate—and often desperately incompetent—spouse-murder plots on the Guyland. Recently I immersed myself in some ten years of tabloid clippings on sensational Long Island homicides and came away with two powerful impressions. First, that the most sensational ones were almost always intrafamily homicides or spouse slayings. Now it's true that, cross-culturally, homicides among intimates occur more frequently than "stranger" homicides. But in another sense of the word, there's no doubt Long Island has some of the *stranger* family homicides, stranger and more desperate. That was the second impression I had from study of the tabloid clips: The desperate longing to get the deed done—however bizarrely, incompetently, or self-revealingly—often proved to be the undoing of the doer.

Consider this 1988 *New York Post* story, not one of the most sensational but representative of the broad midrange of Long Island spouse slayings. It appeared under the headline:

ACCUSED HUBBY-KILLER'S HUNT FOR HIT MAN

The trial testimony therein described a woman who might be called the Ancient Mariner of Spouse Slayers—she soliciteth one of three:

"A Long Island housewife on trial for arranging her husband's murder openly sought a hit man several times, witnesses testified."

The key word here is *openly*. She "tried to hire a fellow church member, a county official, and an undercover cop to kill [her husband] prior to his November 1986 bludgeoning death."

"Are you connected to the mob?" she asked a county official with an Italian surname shortly after meeting him. "I'm looking for someone to kill my husband."

Yes, surely this goes on in the rest of America, but not, I feel, with the urgency Long Islanders bring to it. One gets the feeling reading the clip file that on any given night the landscape of Long Island is crowded with bars where husbands and wives are overtly, ineptly, longingly seeking someone to kill their spouses. Although it seems that husbands come more naturally to it, are more likely to employ a do-it-yourself approach than a hired gun.

Consider the recent case of Dr. Robert Reza, a distinguished Bayport pulmonary specialist who was having an affair with the organist at his church. (Hadn't he ever heard of the Massapequa church secretary Jessica Hahn, Jim and Tammy Faye Bakker's nemesis?) So badly did the doctor long to kill his wife, he concocted a scheme to shoot and strangle her, then raced down to Washington to establish an alibi. Where he was shocked, *shocked* (he told police) when he learned his wife had been murdered by an "intruder" in his absence. All the while leaving a paper trail of travel times that succeeded in proving he and only he could have committed the crime.

The classic Guyland twist to this story is that when the doctor's alibi began to crumble, he confessed—and switched to what might be called the Guyland Defense, which, as I recall from watching the trial on the Court TV channel, amounted to asking the jury to decide that *living on Long Island itself* was enough to engender a homicidal depression severe enough to be exculpatory. (The jury declined to accept this novel courtroom stratagem.)

If we accept for the moment that it is not the power lines, not demonic possession (despite four sequels to *The Amityville Horror,** which as we all know was "based on fact," I remain unpersuaded that the literal Gate to Hell is located a few blocks south of Montauk Highway; the Gate to *Heck,* maybe)—that it's *longing* that makes Long Island Long Island, then what is the source of that force field of yearning that seethes beneath our stony topsoil? (Another injury to a Guylander's self-esteem: to learn as early as ninth grade that Long Island is geologically "terminal moraine," the refuse left behind by the melting of the last glacier—in effect, the dumping ground for the last garbage barge of the ice age.)

One cannot ignore the role of class and status in fueling the engine of longing. The fact is that almost all of Long Island—if one sets aside the old money Locust Valley Gold Coast on the North Shore and scattered enclaves of poverty—can be said to be middle class. Which only proves how little is said by saying "middle class." Long Island is an elaborate, exquisitely hierarchical

---

*About a Long Island house just a few miles from mine that was the real-life scene of a bloody family slaying and—according to the films—concealed the secret entrance to Hell.

status structure *within* the middle class. The more fine the gradations, the more subtly demarked the differences, the more totemic power each gradation is invested with; the more fiercely each step up is coveted and flaunted. Perhaps beneath it all are the imperatives of real-estate rhetoric, designed to generate profits by creating largely metaphysical status distinctions among otherwise indistinguishable entities like Hewlett, Hewlett Harbor, Hewlett Neck, and Hewlett Bay Park.

I know I was not immune to the pervasive inculcation of status distinctions. I recall in high school being made acutely aware of my family's precise position on the Great Chain of Car Model Status. The fact that we owned a Chevrolet Bel Air, which in the early sixties was one painful step *below* the top-of-the-line Impala and one deeply relieved step *above* the bare-boned generic Biscayne, signified more than the ludicrously insignificant threefold variations in exterior chrome trim. They represented three distinct *worlds*.

While I could see through the shallowness, the falseness of those distinctions, I can't deny that, even so, they got to me: Every once in a while I found myself, shamefully, wishing we *had* the damned Impala.

The obverse side of the longing for the status rung just out of reach is the fear of slipping down. Barbara Ehrenreich once made a pretty persuasive argument that the epidemic of spouse violence on Long Island, the number of orders of protection violated by homicidal husbands stalking their exes, might have at its source the desperation of the declassed: the men who, because of a long-stagnant economy, lash out in panic at the sight of the rungs ripping out of the ladder below them, a process made more painful by the hyperacute consciousness of class on the Guyland.

A shockingly different and rather more cold-blooded explanation for the spouse-murder syndrome comes not from sociology but sociobiology. Call it Selfish Gene Demolition Derby Theory.

A researcher brought to my attention a rather astonishing study that appeared in a 1988 issue of the respected journal *Science*. Entitled "Evolutionary Social Psychology and Family Homicide," the study exhibits the remarkable cold-bloodedness of the sociobiological perspective that explains human behavior as a product of the drive by the "selfish gene" to maximize its posterity by any means necessary, however amoral. The authors refer to infanticide, for instance, as a strategy for maximizing the efficiency "of lifetime parental effort" in multichild families.

And most cold-blooded of all, they argue on the basis of diverse cultural studies (ranging from the Ache Indians of Paraguay and tribal horticulturists to Australian baby batterings and North American spouse killers) that family homicides of the type Long Island has become famous for are *adaptive*. In other words, a neo-Darwinian rationale for intrafamily murder! Parents who kill unhealthy or maladaptive (or adoptive) children, men who kill unfaithful wives are driven to it by the deeply rooted longing of the selfish gene to triumph in the reproductive derby of evolution. By weeding out the weak links on its own genetic team and cutting down the competition, these murderers maximize the proliferation of their own genes.

Murdering a wife can be counterproductive for a husband's short-term prospects in the reproductive derby, the authors concede, but this "hardly gainsays its candidate status as a masculine psychological adaptation." By this logic, the more sensational, the more attention-getting the murder, the more it serves this loathsome "masculine psychological adaptation" by terrorizing women into remaining faithful.

While this thesis confirmed my skepticism about the value of sociobiological thinking, it had a deeply disheartening effect on me. The good news is that some scientists believe Long Island may be on the very cutting edge of the evolution of the species. The bad news is that it's because of our penchant for killing those closest to us in attention-getting ways.

I couldn't help it: Something about the savage sociobiological vision of this "Devolution Derby" made me think of the Islip Speedway, a now-defunct motor-racing arena in my home township, the one that gave birth to the Demolition Derby, perhaps the signature contribution of the Guyland to American popular culture.

Invented in 1958 by a flamboyant Long Island promoter named Larry Mendelsohn—who later went on to dream up the even more suicidal and still popular "Figure-Eight Racing" course (think about it)—the Demolition Derby cannot be topped as Long Island spectacle, and metaphor.

What you had in the Demolition Derby was a couple dozen standard American road-hog sedans that would, when the gun sounded, begin to ram into each other viciously, with intent to maim, cripple, and destroy. Until, after hours of screeching, smoke-belching, metal-ripping collisions, the last carcass still moving . . . won.

Oh yes, there was one crucial twist that made the event even more bizarre and emblematic: The rules required the drivers to smash into each other *in reverse.* Which made the spectacle a kind of parable of Darwinian evolution by annihilation; postindustrial America on rewind to self-destruct; Gatsby's boats "beating backward" against the tide of time.

The speedway is gone now, although the Demolition Derby as a concept has gone national, according to Marty Himes of the Himes Museum of Motor Racing Nostalgia, which is operated out of Himes's house and grounds in my hometown, Bay Shore. Himes added a curious, chilling footnote to Speedway lore. After the death of the Demolition Derby inventor, Mendelsohn (suicide, says Himes), the new operators of the Speedway, Barbara and Jim Cromarty, moved into a house on the South Shore that they'd purchased from a savings bank. The Cromartys knew the house they were moving into had been the site of the bloody DeFeo slayings of 1974 (a son had slaughtered his parents, as well as his two sisters and two brothers). What the Cromartys didn't know was that the previous owner of the Dutch Colonial house, George Lutz, was about to release a book, to be followed by a movie, that identified the Speedway operators' new place as home to . . . the Amityville Horror!

There was something appropriate about this figure-eight convergence of Guyland myths that linked, however tenuously, the Demolition Derby to the Gate of Hell. And made me wonder: Why had *this* ritual, this spectacular enactment of the longing for self-destruction sprung up in *my* backyard, of all places? It was so boring and uneventful, so *generic,* when I was growing up. But maybe that was it—the generic rather than the genetic explanation.

The Guyland has long seemed to suffer from the curse of genericism. Consider the very name itself. Couldn't they have taken a little more *time,* come up with something a little more colorful, expressive. Or was it just, "What shall we call this long island off the coast here?"

"Let's call it *Long Island.*"

And so, rather than a name, it was a category, a generic creature from the word go.

Perhaps we can take some comfort in believing that we are the true originals from which generic American culture has been generated. I know my former employer, King Kullen, always boasted it was the *first* supermarket in America. We had the first Levittown. California may not have been far behind, but its suburbs, its split-levels and ranch houses, are indisputably modeled on ours.

There is a nice resonance to Pynchon's line about ranch houses and split-levels lacking "a second story," lacking, in other words, another dimension, lacking mystery, secrets. Driving some to inscribe secretive second stories on the landscape—or on their fellow citizens—in whatever sensational way they can. I know I can recall feeling the contraction of my horizons when my family moved from a big old three-story Bay Shore place my grandmother once operated as a boarding house and that housed three generations of our extended family to a brand-new nuclear-family-only generic ranch house in neighboring Brightwaters, with its single inescapable story. It was a kind of sensory deprivation that, I'm sure, drove me to the sensation-seeking culture of journalism. I'm sure that his adolescence in nearby West Babylon helped make Geraldo Geraldo. ("Esthetically speaking, growing up on Long Island sucked," Geraldo declared elegantly in his autobiography, *Exposing Myself.*)

It also explains the sensational effect Pynchon's second novel, *The Crying of Lot 49,* had on me when I discovered it in high school. I remember going around and inscribing on phone booths graffiti in the shape of the "muted post horn"—the novel's symbol for a centuries-old, conspiratorial secret society operating even now in Pynchon's tract-house suburbs. Here, at last, was the longed-for "second story" to suburban reality, however paranoid. And I remember thinking when I first read Pynchon's description of the "ordered swirl" of suburban tract-house patterns seen from above as a kind of "printed circuit," one that revealed "a hieroglyphic sense of concealed meaning"—*finally* someone understands.

But I didn't really understand until I'd spent some time in the ordered swirl of Levittown, researching a story about the ur-burb's creator, Bill Levitt. In order to see the fabled circuit board tracts from the inside, I'd posed as a prospective home buyer and let a gold-jacketed Century 21 realtor show me through Levittown homes for sale.

What I saw was a revelation. Most people's image of Levittown has been formed by the famous photos taken immediately after it became notorious in the late forties. Aerial photos showing an endless grid of treeless streets lined with bare, stencil-faced boxes, houses for pod people, breeders of conformity: Soulless generic housing, social critics said, would produce soulless generic burb clones.

Seeing Levittown firsthand four decades later was something of a shock. The place has grown positively *hairy* with a veritable frenzy of individuation.

Each of the original cookie-cutter homes had sprouted dormers, add-ons, extensions, carapaces of nearly baroque, Dickensian singularity. The interiors I saw were virtual Old Curiosity Shops of built-ins, floor-to-ceiling trellises of shelves, knickknack-crammed nooks and crannies—a thousand different do-it-yourself fantasies. Levittown turned out to be not the epitome of suburban self-abnegation but a tribute to the ineradicable drive for self-expression. A drive that can sometimes turn weird: I think it's no accident that Levittown gave birth to Bill Griffith, the talented creator of the subversive comic cult figure Zippy the Pinhead, an unshaven, befuddled, and demented clown who wanders the suburban landscape issuing mutant aphorisms from a mall-damaged brain.

If there can be said to be a Long Island psyche, perhaps it has something of the contours of those Levittown houses, the product of that same intense longing to inscribe an individual identity on a generic one-story setting, something that has grown hairy, gnarly, idiosyncratic, eccentric, and many-storied in reaction. Something like serial killer Joel Rifkin's garden.

I believe Howard Stern was the first to take note of how truly strange Joel's garden was; Howard called it "that Edward Scissorhands garden." There have been conflicting reports about whether Joel or his mother designed the garden in front of the East Meadow house they shared, or whether it was a collaboration. And perhaps no one would have paid much attention to this horticultural extravaganza had it not sprouted, blossomed, in front of the home of a horticultural serial killer who had been planting bodies all over the landscape as well. But spooky television news clips of that garden at night made it seem as if it, too, was a product of that same desperate frenzy for individuation, here turned sinister.

Instead of the standard, featureless suburban lawn, one glimpsed a complicated jumble, if not jungle, of bushes and hedges; thorny, briary shapes that, in retrospect, can be seen as a self-portrait of his own state of mind. Joel Rifkin's garden as the internal landscape of the Long Island psyche, barely kept in trim, only provisionally under control.

But wait. Let's not end this in Joel Rifkin's garden. Not without giving some thought to the positive redeeming qualities of Long Island. I could talk about the beaches. I could talk about the diners (I *love* the diners). I could talk about the peace of mind the lawns and trees brought to people like my father, who grew up in Brooklyn, lived through the Depression and the war, and found the American dream on the same streets that became a nightmare of boredom to me.

But I believe the truly redemptive Long Island qualities can be found in some of the darkest, most unlikely places—for instance, Howard Stern's sense of humor and Katie Beers's dungeon.

What Howard Stern epitomizes at his best is Long Island's militant irreverence. The way Guylanders (the lifers, not the wannabes) refuse to be impressed by celebrities, dignitaries, airs and names of the sort so dear to New Yorkers, Manhattanites in particular.

We know them too well, is the Guyland attitude. We've witnessed their slavish, degrading status-crazed behavior in the Hamptons. We know they're no different, certainly no better, than us. And they hate us for it. They hate us because they know we know. Which goes a long way to explain why Long Island's crimes and misdemeanors have been so magnified by the media lens of nearby Manhattan to look even more monstrous than they are.

And what about Katie Beers's dungeon? Reading over accounts of her imprisonment, watching news clips of her release, I found myself genuinely moved by the courage and spirit of the ten-year-old; by the matter-of-fact cheerfulness that carried her through her ordeal and saw her emerge from her dungeon smiling bravely—even willing, in that very moment, to make a gesture of comfort to the sobbing figure of her captor as he was led away to *his* imprisonment.

Long Island is like that in this sense: Consigned in the mind of America to a dark place not unlike Katie Beers's dungeon, locked up there by the media, the Guyland, like little Katie, has learned to smile through the abuse and persevere. Perhaps because it knows a secret, a secret about the future.

. . .

The Spaceplex, St. James, Long Island. This towering pinball inferno, this laser video-game pandemonium the size of a rocket hangar, this Gothic cathedral of a cyberpunk sensorium, is stuck out in the middle of the middle of the central-island midlands, somewhere between eerie Lake Ronkonkoma (the pervasive local folklore held that Ronkonkoma was "the only lake in the world with no bottom," which gave rise to rumors of creatures haunting the bottomless nether regions) and the scarily generic Smithhaven Mall.

The Spaceplex was a favorite haunt of Katie Beers, who was something of a pinball wizard in her own right. The Spaceplex was where she could lose herself, or at least distract herself from the warring dysfunctional families who were pinballing *her* back and forth between them. The Spaceplex was where Katie thought she was going when she was kidnapped by her "family friend," John Esposito, and where he told police she'd disappeared from, after he'd locked her into the dungeon he'd built beneath the floorboards of his Bay Shore home.

The Spaceplex is an awesome vision of a run-down–*Blade Runner*ish future, unlike anything to be found anywhere else in America—yet. Entering the thirty-foot-high, 45,000-square-foot rocket hangar is like going through the Gate of Heck. This is Satin's realm: A long, black strobe-lighted Techno-throbbing tunnel leads to a soaring, inky dark, cathedral-like *cave,* its hollows filled with the echoing caterwauling din of a million boops, beeps, boinks, and bong-bong-bongs; its blackness flickering with the reflections of a million flashing sensors, registering a billion acts of virtual violence. The official name is the Spaceplex Family Fun Center. It is really Long Island as the virtual future.

Not that I didn't have a great time there. I rediscovered the joy of pinball ten generations more advanced than the games I played at Katie Beers's age. Ten generations more violent and deranged: I played Blasteroids, Road Riot, Spy Killer, Cabal, Martial Combat, Time Killers, Laser Ghost, Robotron, Rampage, Line of Fire, Lethal Enforcers, Sky Shark, and Black Knight (my favorite).

After a while, communing with the pinballs in the enveloping Spaceplex darkness, I felt a kind of mind-meld with my Guyland past—the eternal search for distraction, the trench warfare against tedium. But there was something about the Spaceplex that reminded me of another place, another run-down future place: the Space Coast. That's what Cocoa Beach and the other towns along the Canaveral coast of Florida took to calling themselves during the space boom, when we were still going to the moon, when it looked like the Space Coast might be the Homeport, the Spaceplex for a Trekkie-like Federation of the Planets in the not-unforeseeable future.

They were still calling it the Space Coast some years later when I spent some time down there covering a shuttle launch in the aftermath of the boom, after the Space Goldrush. When the only vibrant optimism about the power of space imagery was pretty much limited to a topless joint in a strip mall that advertised "topless space suit strippers." When the Space Coast was on the verge of becoming the first Space Ghost Town.

There's that same unmistakable sense of a lost future in the Long Island Spaceplex, a peeling-vinyl, soiled-Astroturf, diminished vision of the future that is so much less than the one we were promised, the one we longed for. A sense of the aimless derangement that disillusion over a lost future produces.

I think that's why that beautiful, wistful R.E.M. tribute to Andy Kaufman should qualify as the true Long Island anthem. The song conjures up both the suburban rec-room-in-the-finished-basement past ("Let's play Twister, let's play Risk. . . .") and that sense of an abandoned future, too. I'd wondered at first what the meaning of the refrain in the song—"If you believe they put a man on the moon"—meant, until I saw the Spaceplex and understood. The future as ghost town: The age of heroic futurist odysseys is so far past, it seems only a rumor they put a man on the moon. Laser Ghost and Blasteroids are the only legacy of the lost illusion.

Long Island, after all, was supposed to be the future *before* the future. We always had a head start on the life cycle of suburban baby-boom culture because we were the firstborn burbs of the baby boom; a burbland created almost all at once, very fast and virtually ex nihilo, right after the war, a self-contained social organism. An organism whose sociobiological clock started ticking a little earlier than subsequent burbs, and whose shrill alarms now seem to signal that it has raced through its mature stage and is now rocketing headlong into the social-organism equivalent of senile dementia.

And so the America that laughs at Long Island's nonstop Satinist Demolition Derby, the America that looks down on Long Island as something alien, some exotic, carnivalesque pageant separable from its mainstream because it's separate from the mainland, may have to think again. May have to learn to say of this unruly island what Prospero said of the unruly Caliban at the close of *The Tempest:* "This thing of darkness I acknowledge mine."

Because when America laughs at Long Island, it's laughing in the face of its own onrushing future.

Some Contemporary Contentions

The Pissing Contest

Oliver Stone versus Quentin Tarantino

Oliver Stone *versus* Quentin Tarantino? Pitting writers against each other as if they were professional wrestling stars in a grudge match is not considered sophisticated literary practice, although it *is* true that the man who is regarded as perhaps the single most prodigiously learned man of letters in the language, George Steiner, once wrote an entire volume dedicated to putting two mad Russians into *mano a mano* competition. He called it *Tolstoy or Dostoevsky?* and there was blood on the floor before referee Steiner gave Foaming Fyodor the edge.

And for a long time, American fiction has been ruled and riven by the war between the rival sensibilities of Hemingway and Fitzgerald. A somewhat artificial but nonetheless instructive distinction between archetypal poles: Mythic Macho Outdoor Man of Nature versus Aesthete Analyst of Indoor Intrigue and Internal Self-Consciousness. Categories that are descendants of the Great Divide in American literature, the one between what Philip Rahv called "Redskins" and "Palefaces": wildman nativists versus Euro-influenced aesthetes; in the nineteenth century, Mark Twain versus Henry James. (Philip Roth famously disrupted the duality by declaring himself neither Redskin nor Paleface but rather a wildly, embarrassingly, self-conscious "Redface.")

I'm not sure you could find any such stark two-person polarizations among American *novelists* today (mostly, sadly, because people don't care about literary fiction as they once did)—no two well-defined sensibilities that divide and influence readers the way Hemingway and Fitzgerald once did. But I think there are a pair of *writers* whose distinctive voices define conflicting American visions, both of which reflect the divided consciousness of our culture. I'm thinking of Oliver Stone and Quentin Tarantino, respectively chief Redskin and primo Paleface of the cinema. For better or worse, they are the Hemingway and Fitzgerald of our time.

I know they're looked upon primarily as directors—as film people, not word people—but I believe a strong case can be made for recognition of both of them as American *writers*. I've read their screenplays, dozens of them. At their best, they're works that would have powerful validity on the page, regardless of what they became on the screen. (Stone has just published a novel, *A Child's Night Dream,* something he wrote as an adolescent. He would have been smarter to have published his collected screenplays, which show his real strength as a writer and the seductive power of a well-written screenplay as reading matter, not just as a blueprint for the screen.)

I think they've both suffered because their onscreen violence can obscure the more subtle concerns of their sensibilities, particularly Tarantino's. I've argued, for instance, that beneath the profane raillery in which the Cheeseburger Royale discussion in Tarantino's *Pulp Fiction* is couched, one can discern a philosophic argument over nominalism and epistemological relativism cloaked in the apparently trivial chitchat about the names used to designate Quarter Pounders with Cheese here and in France.

But I also feel I understand a dimension of Oliver Stone's work, perhaps better than he understands it himself. I think that's what's behind our bitter Dual Urinal Pissing Match. The dramatic Dual Urinal Piss-Off took place in the men's room at some charity benefit a couple years after I'd interviewed Stone for a piece in *Vanity Fair.* A piece that I thought was sympathetic and admiring but that he hated with a passion, in part, I believe, because I'd recorded him giving vent to his mad vision of existence, the Meat Stew/Writhing Anaconda Panorama.

Stone had been fairly indiscreet in the piece, it's true, raging at the heads of the seven major Hollywood studios, calling them "cocksucker vampires." But after the piece came out, his rage turned on me, and he fired off angry salvos protesting his portrayal. The rage had not abated, as I learned when I found myself standing at a urinal during a break at the benefit as Oliver Stone walked in, took up a position at the urinal most distant from me, unzipped his formal wear, and started denouncing me in an exchange that went something like this:

ME: Hi, Oliver.

O.S.: I *hated* that piece.

ME: You didn't *understand* that piece—it was an appreciation of your work as a writer.

O.S.: *You made me look like a fucking lunatic!*

This was one of those occasions in life when you wish you'd said what you thought of saying later. I *should* have said:

"Oliver, you *are* a fucking lunatic, and that's what I *like* about you."

Because I do admire his work; I admire the manic, even psychotic, energy his films express. Instead, I let him get the last word. After he'd zipped up and was exiting the men's room, he turned back and sneered: "Taking a *long time,* aren't you, Ron?"

I loved that. I still haven't quite figured out why he thought he was one-upping me with that remark—an imputation of prostate trouble? A faster-is-better, macho peeing ethic? (But couldn't it just as easily have been said that I had *more to give*?) Who knows—but clearly *he* thought this was a devastating exit line. A coup de grâce in our personal war.

It was a great Oliver Stone moment, because it reflects the essence of his vision that all life *is* constant war—the war of all against all. All life is a pissing match. A vision nowhere better expressed by Stone than in his Meat Stew/Writhing Anaconda Panorama, which he had expounded to me over lunch in Santa Monica, at a restaurant near the pier. It was a particularly inspired Stonian effusion that is probably the reason he accused me of making him look like a "fucking lunatic" in my *Vanity Fair* piece—although it's all on tape:

He'd been talking about life being a "continual conflict . . . a raging sea. . . . It's a war! . . . There's a psychological war all around us," he told me, gesturing toward the seemingly placid palm trees.

If you were God looking down, what you would see would probably blow your mind out. I don't think you'd live. It's like one acid trip to the millionth degree. I mean, there's murder going on *now,* there's fish eating each other in the sea, there's pythons, there's anacondas swarming in the depths of some Brazilian river. There's mugging, there's a rape, there's a woman dying. *Tortures!* Eyeballs being pulled out in Guatemala probably right now as we speak. Babies are dying, babies are being born, people are fucking in motel rooms across the hall. The world is very rich . . . it's like a meat *stew.* It's all a war. It's raging. This woman putting lipstick on at the next table, where does that lipstick come from? *What got mashed up* to make that lipstick?

Thus, the Stonian vision: a Hemingwayesque world of primal nature, total war; of writhing, swarming snakes in a bubbling meat stew of ceaseless violence. It's powerful, primal, and, above all, *earnest* as well as Ernest. Earnest in the sense of being nonironic, heartfelt, passionate, balls-out bleeding heart on the sleeve. So earnest it risks being called square, in the way Stone's Jim Morrison movie was: the squareness of a latecomer to the sixties who takes its prophets a little too seriously, a little more seriously than they took themselves.

But the Meat Stew/Writhing Anaconda vision serves to define Quentin Tarantino's work as well—and to distinguish it from Stone's. Both men are lumped together for their over-the-top violence. But Tarantino's vision is very different, far more aesthetic and ironic. Because to Tarantino, the meat stew is not nature but *culture:* the writhing anacondas not real snakes but writhing, swirling *images* on screens—in a virtual jungle of pixels rather than a real one of pythons.

If you watch Tarantino's films, if you read his screenplays, all that writhing and stewing of images is not so much war as *dance.* "To me, violence is a totally aesthetic subject," he once said. "Saying you don't like violence in movies is like saying you don't like dance sequences in movies."

His tough-guy act, his tough-guy actors, and his blam-blam moments may disguise it, but Tarantino is an *aesthete,* a dandy, a Fitzgeraldian observer of the delicate dance of social interaction. For him, the violence of the writhing anacondas is *choreography* to be savored and analyzed.

Think about it: The great defining moments in Tarantino films are almost always moments of *literary criticism.* The defining moment of *Reservoir Dogs,* the first film he directed (as well as wrote), the scene that instantly distinguished it from all other violent gangster films ever made before, is the opening scene, in which his bank robbers are gathered around a breakfast table at a pancake house, *deconstructing a Madonna song.* Arguing over the subtextual meaning of "Like a Virgin."

Oliver Stone, given that same group of murderous thugs, would have them facing off over urinals, comparing how long it took each to pee. Tarantino isn't afraid to depict *his* gangsters talking *almost* as if they were cultural-studies majors.

And again, in *Pulp Fiction,* what's the defining moment? It's when Jules and Vincent (Samuel L. Jackson and John Travolta), two hit men, are analyzing the philosophical implications of the way brand names for burgers—designations of values—shift in different linguistic frameworks. In his heart, Quentin Tarantino is an English major. In *his* heart, Oliver Stone is a Green Beret major.

And the two of them came together (and came apart) for a major, *major* war over the movie that Tarantino wrote and Stone took away from him to direct—*Natural Born Killers.* A true pissing match if there ever was one, some revealing details of which have emerged in a new book on the making of the movie. Jane Hamsher's *Killer Instinct* tells the story of how Oliver Stone managed to end up appropriating the Quentin Tarantino script for *Natural Born Killers* for his own purposes, and how Tarantino cried foul but Stone crunched ahead and made his movie anyway. There's one curious omission in the Hamsher book: Nowhere are we given an intimation of how Stone *feels* about taking a rival director's vision away from him. Hamsher doesn't even see it as an issue. What she neglects, what no one but me (and probably Oliver Stone) seems to have noticed, is the pissing-match element: Stone's payback for Tarantino's mocking treatment of him: his creation of creepy Oliver Stone caricatures in two of his scripts.

Remember, in *True Romance* (a Tarantino script directed by Tony Scott), there's an unpleasant Hollywood character called Lee Donowitz. Pretty instantly recognizable: He made an Oscar-winning Vietnam combat movie, *Coming Home in a Body Bag,* which sounds like an amalgam of Stone's *Platoon* and *Born on the Fourth of July.* In Tarantino's script, "Lee" is a pompous, vain poseur who acts ineptly like a big-time outlaw.

And if that's not bad enough, there's even an Oliver Stone–like figure in the original Tarantino script for *Natural Born Killers,* a character who was, needless to say, cut from the Oliver Stone rewrite. Here, once again, the character is a pompous director of violent but "issue oriented" films, in this case a film about serial killers Mickey and Mallory Knox called *Thrill Killers.* In fact, the film Stone directed turned out to be not far from the one Tarantino parodied in that script: what's been called an exploitation of violence posing as an exploration of it. Just listen to Tarantino's Stone figure, Neil Pope, as he dispenses papal bull:

> It is my belief that Mickey and Mallory Knox are a cultural phenomenon that could only exist in our sexually repressed society. A flower that could only bloom amidst a grotesque fast-food culture. . . . Yet amidst the violence and murder and carnage, you've got the structure of a Wagnerian love story.

It's a dead-on caricature of Stone and a pretty good description of the actual movie he went on to make: *Natural Born Killers* is a "Neil Pope" film at heart, complete with the heavy-handed psychologizing Stone used to mark Tarantino's script as his territory.

It's an unfair rap to reduce Stone to earnest or Ernest Hemingway–esque moralist. He's more a reckless antinomian visionary who deserves credit for the courage of his excess, even in pissing matches. The unfair rap on Tarantino is that he's an *amoralist,* an artist content to float in the stew of cultural images, a Warholian collagist, cutting and pasting pop signifiers.

But, in fact, I think that completely misunderstands Tarantino, misapprehends the originality of his talent. Because, at his best, in the interludes between the blam-blam, he's a genuinely curious philosophic investigator of manners and morals, more akin to a novelist of manners such as Jane Austen, say, than even to Fitzgerald.

Quentin Tarantino as Jane Austen? Consider one of the longer scenes in *Pulp Fiction,* a six-page scene in the screenplay in which Jules and Vincent are discussing—really getting *deep* into—all the ramifications for manners and morals of giving a foot massage to the boss's wife. A discussion that considers reflectively the differential gender frameworks in which the meaning of foot massages is construed, the social construction of sensual acts versus their intrinsic or essential effects, and the unspoken messages a foot massage conveys.

And though the language may not be the sort Jane Austen resorts to when making these fine distinctions ("Is it as bad as eatin' her out?" Jules muses. "No, but you're in the same fuckin' ballpark"), these minute acts of social discrimination—and the way they reflect, microcosmically, tensions in the macrocosmic fabric of a society—are pure Jane Austen territory.

My favorite line in all Tarantino's work—perhaps his funniest, most profound line—comes in the midst of the Socratic discussion Jules and Vincent have about why Jules won't eat pigs, why he respects dogs more than pigs even though dogs (like pigs) eat their own feces.

It's because "a dog's got personality," Jules says.

"So by that rationale," Vincent replies, "if a pig had a better personality, he'd cease to be a filthy animal?"

Jules's comeback is the signature Tarantino line: "We'd have to be talkin' 'bout one motherfuckin' CHARMING pig. It'd have to be the Cary Grant of pigs."

The Cary Grant of pigs. I'd argue that it's an image Jane Austen would appreciate. Because, despite surface appearances and the Merchant-Ivoryizing of her work, if you know it well, you know Austen has a *very* dark vision of human nature. Not dark in a spectacularly showy, blam-blam underworld way like Tarantino's or Stone's writhing meat stew; but she has a vision of a society filled with snakes, stewing with the depredations of emotional outlaws—a vision of human nature in which men are not far above swine. But she also has an appreciation for those who can rise above their swinishness, redeem their piggy nature through civility and charm, and become—in Tarantino's emblematic image—the Cary Grants of pigs.

Charles Portis and
the Locked Trunk Secret

Listen, I bow to no one when it comes to expertise on the myth and reality of secret societies in America, in distinguishing the dark nimbus of paranoia and conspiracy theory surrounding them from the peculiar human truths at their heart.

As the author of the still-definitive study of America's ultimate secret society, Skull and Bones, I have been shown the much-whispered-about photos that the all-woman break-in team took of the interior of the Skull and Bones "Tomb"—complete with its candid shots of that sanctum sanctorum of America's clandestine ruling-class cult: the Room with the License Plates of Many States. I could tell you the secret Skull and Bones nicknames of the class year of D_{154}, in the coded Skull and Bones calendar of the years. (Let's give a shout out to good old J. B. "Magog" Speed, for instance.)

I say I bow to no one, but that's not true. When it comes to knowing and limning the heart of the heart of the secret-society-esoteric-knowledge-weird-nickname-ancient-mysteries-of-the-East racket, I bow—*we should all bow*—to one man, one novelist. Not Pynchon or DeLillo or any of the other usual suspects on the secret-society subject, but a maddeningly underappreciated

American writer who in a brilliant and shockingly little-known novel has somehow captured more of the truth about this aspect of America, about the longing for Hidden Secrets, the seductions of secret societies, than all the shelves of conspiracy-theory literature. The only man to penetrate the true heart of dimness. I'm speaking of Charles Portis and his now-almost-impossible-to-find novel (suppressed by You Know Who?), *Masters of Atlantis.*

It's an indictment of the dimness of our culture that the film *Conspiracy Theory* made millions while *Masters of Atlantis* languishes in the recesses of secondhand-book stores, out of print, not even in paperback, and Portis gets neither the popular nor the literary-world acclaim that he deserves. In a way, Portis has not helped matters; he lives off the beaten path down in Arkansas with an unlisted phone number, doesn't do publicity, has never networked, and refused, politely but firmly, to talk to me for this piece.

Who is this man Portis? His is not a Salinger-like antisocial reclusiveness, more a kind of publicity-shy modesty. And we do have a few clues about his past. We know he grew up in a tiny town near the Arkansas-Mississippi border. We can guess from a recent short story he published in *The Atlantic Monthly* that he served as a marine in the Korean War. We know that he was a rising star at the legendary writers' newspaper *The New York Herald Tribune,* eventually heading its London bureau, and that he departed abruptly in the mid-sixties to return to Arkansas to start turning out a remarkable series of novels, beginning with *Norwood* in 1966.

Meanwhile, Portis has become the subject of a kind of secret society, a small but fanatic group of admirers among other writers who consider him perhaps the least-known great writer alive in America. Perhaps the most original, indescribable sui generis talent overlooked by literary culture in America. A writer who—if there's any justice in literary history as opposed to literary celebrity—will come to be regarded as the author of classics on the order of a twentieth-century Mark Twain, a writer who captures the soul of America, the true timbre of the dream-intoxicated voices of this country, in a way that no writers-workshop fictionalist has done or is likely to do, who captures the secret soul of twentieth-century America with the clarity, the melancholy, and the laughter with which Gogol captured the soul of nineteenth-century Russia in *Dead Souls.*

Tom Wolfe once spoke about the way city-born creative-writing types go directly from East Coast hothouse venues to places like Iowa City, where "they rent a house out in the countryside, and after about their fifth conversation with a plumber named Lud, they feel that they know the rural psyche."

Charles Portis is the real thing to which these grad-school simulacra can only aspire in their wildest dreams. He is a wild dreamer of a writer, and I don't want you misled by the references to Mark Twain into thinking he is some kind of regionalist or humorist. Nora Ephron, one of the founding members of the Portis Society (as I've come to think of the circle of devotees), compares him in scope, sophistication, and originality to Gabriel García Márquez. "He thinks things no one else thinks," she says.

For some members of the Portis Society, an appreciation of his work is a matter of life-and-death urgency. Roy Blount, Jr., has written of Portis's third novel, *The Dog of the South,* "No one should die without having read it." And that's not even his favorite (although it is mine). He's partial to *Norwood* and speaks of those for whom Portis is a kind of life-and-death *test* of human beings. How a fellow Portis Society member couldn't decide whether to marry the woman he loved until she read *Norwood.*

It's funny: Before I spoke with Blount and learned of his "Don't die until you've read *The Dog of the South*" pronouncement, I'd used the rhetoric of imminent death in my appeal to Portis for an interview. I'd tried to explain in a letter to him how much his work mattered to me by telling him that if I had to choose any one section of any one novel to be read aloud to me on my deathbed in the hours before expiring, to remind me of the pleasures that reading had brought me during my lifetime, it would probably be certain passages in *The Dog of the South* involving one of Portis's inimitable, seedy-but-grandiose con men, Dr. Reo Symes.

I'll try to explain why those passages in particular fascinate me, but first I need to discuss the initiation rite to the Portis Society, the barrier you literary sophisticates must be able to get past (or limbo beneath) if you are to show yourselves worthy of Portis's genius. A kind of test of true—as opposed to surface, image-conscious—literary sophistication.

The test is a novel Portis wrote before *The Dog of the South, Masters of Atlantis,* and *Gringos,* his great dreams-of-secret-knowledge trilogy. A novel that was—I hesitate to use the word, it's so deeply shaming in literary terms—too *popular* for its own good. A novel whose title I almost dare not utter to the uninitiated, because it may completely throw you off the scent of Portis's greatness. (Not because there's anything wrong with it in itself, but because of its image.) A novel whose title I'm therefore going to disguise and not utter for the moment. Or maybe I'll give it a more inoffensive (at least in this context), substitute title, say, *Necrophilic Whores of Gomorrah.*

Well, admit it, you'd probably be more receptive to my case for Portis's greatness if he'd written some Burroughsian necrophilia novel rather than the all-too-fatally popular novel he *did* write, whose title is, I blush to say, *True Grit.* Yes, he's *that* guy, and they made a movie out of it that won John Wayne his only Oscar. Now, get over it and let me get back to Dr. Reo Symes. He's the greatest in a great gallery of Portisian talkers: brilliant and garrulous con artists, deliriously gifted fabricators, delusional mountebanks, disbarred lawyers, defrocked doctors, disgruntled inventors, dispossessed cranks, and disgraced dreamers who crawl out of the cracks and crevices of Trailways America with confident claims that they have the Philosopher's Stone, the key to all mysteries. Or, more often, that they had it and lost it, or had it stolen from them but are close to getting it back.

This Dr. Symes is quite a character himself. No longer a doctor—he lost his medical license over some trouble with a miracle arthritis cure he was peddling called "the Brewster Method." ("You don't hear much about it anymore but for my money it's never been discredited," Symes says.) Lately, he's been involved in a scheme to manufacture tungsten-steel dentures in Tijuana (the "El Tigre model," he calls it), and he seems to be on the run from some scam involving "a directory called *Stouthearted Men,* which was to be a collection of photographs and capsule biographies of all the county supervisors in Texas." Somehow, the money collected from the stouthearted supervisors is missing, although Symes insists, "It was a straight enough deal."

But when he runs across Portis's narrator, Ray Midge, an Arkansas guy who's retracing the steps of his runaway wife by using credit-card receipts, all Dr. Symes can talk about is the mysterious, elusive John Selmer Dix, a writer of inspirational books for salesmen. Symes is obsessed with Dix's greatness, with the idea that in his last days Dix had somehow broken through to some new level of ultimate revelation that tragically was lost to the world with his death, when the trunk in which he carried his papers disappeared.

"Find the missing trunk and you've found the key to his so-called 'silent years,' " Symes tells Ray Midge. Symes is fixated on what might be false sightings of Dix and what seems to be a proliferation of Dix impostors. He knows of only one man who claims to have seen Dix "in the flesh . . . in the public library in Odessa, Texas, reading a newspaper on a stick.

"Now the question is, was that stranger really Dix? If it was Dix answer me this. *Where were all his keys?*" (The keys to his trunk of ultimate secrets, of course.) "There are plenty of fakers going around. . . . You've probably heard of the fellow out in Barstow who claims to this day that he *is* Dix. . . . He says the man who died in Tulsa was just some old retired fart from the oil fields who was trading off a similar name. He makes a lot of the closed coffin and the hasty funeral in Ardmore. He makes a lot of the missing trunk. . . . There's another faker, in Florida, who claims he is Dix's half brother. . . . They ran a picture of him and his little Dix museum in *Trailer Review.*"

Dr. Symes's delirium rises to a pitch of inspired madness tinged with an element of Oliver Stone paranoia ("the hasty funeral in Ardmore"), a poetic desperation that makes you intuit that it's not the reality of Dix that obsesses him but the *idea* of Dix—of someone somewhere who Had It All Figured Out but who disappeared in a Trailways haze. What Portis is getting at is the deep longing, the profound, wistful desperation in the American collective unconscious, to believe that somehow things do make *some* kind of sense, that life is not all chaotic horror and random acts of cruelty by fate, that there is an Answer, even if it's locked in a trunk somewhere and we've *lost the keys.*

The search for the lost keys is at the heart of Portis's subsequent two novels as well. In *Masters of Atlantis,* a secret society founded by a con artist and his gullible dupe comes to be a source of genuine meaning and faith for half a century of devotees (with the suggestion that all secret societies pretending to esoteric knowledge, from Skull and Bones to the Masons to the CIA, are the products of collective self-delusions). In *Gringos,* a beautiful, intense, comic-phantasmagoric novel, it's the search for the Inaccessible Lost City of Dawn somewhere in the Mayan rain forests that draws, like a magnet, all the lonely and dispossessed, the mad romantics and con artists of the States, to seek out what is missing from their lives by going Below the Border to search for the indecipherable truths encoded in the Mayan hieroglyphics.*

Rereading Portis is one of the great pure pleasures—both visceral and cerebral—available in modern American literature. Except it's really *not* available to those who aren't Portis Society initiates (who have squirreled away multiple copies of *Masters of Atlantis* in locked trunks to ensure a lifetime supply). It is a crime and a scandal, it's virtually clinically *insane,* that Portis's last three books are out of print and not in paperback—almost as inaccessible as the lost works of John Selmer Dix. Some smart publisher will earn an honored place in literary history and the hearts of his countrymen by bringing out a complete and accessible edition soon—now.

Meanwhile, I can't stop thinking about Dr. Symes and Dix. What *is* it with all those Dix impostors, those shadowy half brothers with their little Dix museums in *Trailer Review?* Are they real or figures of Symes's Dix delirium? Is the proliferation of Dixes a way of expressing the notion that we're all, in some way, Dixes, hauling around locked trunks containing the inaccessible, unimaginable secrets we hide from one another? Perhaps Portis could tell, but Portis isn't talking, at least not to me.

---

*Not unlike the guests of the cancer cure mystics of Tijuana, come to think of it.

Postscript to "Charles Portis and the Locked Trunk Secret"

As a direct result of the plea expressed herein, the people at Overlook Press, Tracy Carns and Peter Meyer, have begun bringing out a complete trade-paperback edition of the out-of-print Portis backlist. I won't, at his request, disclose anything about the time I finally got to meet the reclusive writer at the Waffle House at the Little Rock, Arkansas, airport, except that we both shared a fondness for the country and western–type odes to breakfast items on the Waffle House jukebox, including my favorite, "The Hash Browns at the Waffle House Are Out of This World."

Is Thomas Pynchon "Wanda Tinasky"?

Wanda who? you ask. A good question. "Wanda Tinasky" was the pseudonym of the unknown author of a mysterious series of some eighty letters to the editor of a couple of northern California weekly newspapers in the 1983–1988 period, primarily to Mendocino County's *Anderson Valley Advertiser*. The letters caused a stir back then among the culturally literate back-to-the-land bohemians, Earth Firsters, fugitives from the sixties, poets, hemp growers, eccentrics, and paranoids in that little community. Caused a stir because the letter writer, who described herself as a homeless bag lady living under a bridge, displayed a remarkable combination of arcane literary erudition, sly pop culture savvy, in-jokey intimacy with radical history, and idiosyncratic gnostic speculations about literature and culture.

Then in 1990, two years after the pseudonymous Wanda Tinasky stopped sending letters to the *Anderson Valley Advertiser*, Bruce Anderson, its editor, picked up a copy of Mr. Pynchon's just released novel *Vineland*, one rooted deep in the countercultural subcultures of northern California counties like Humboldt and Mendocino, one that made it sound like the elusive Mr. Pynchon had been living there in the eighties while writing the novel. Reading

Mr. Pynchon's *Vineland* suddenly conjured up a name from the past in Mr. Anderson's mind, an unsolved mystery: Wanda Tinasky. Had Mr. Pynchon himself been writing those Pynchonesque letters while living anonymously, pseudonymously among the denizens of the Emerald Triangle whose culture he'd chronicled in *Vineland*?

When I first read about the Wanda Tinasky claim in a provocative essay by Pynchon aficionado Charles Hollander in *New York Press* two years ago, I was skeptical but intrigued, although not intrigued enough, for some reason, to try to get hold of the letters and evaluate them myself. But a couple months ago, in the aftermath of my column anticipating the themes of *Mason & Dixon,* Bruce Anderson sent me the rather wonderful and endearing book that has resulted from the Wanda Tinasky mystery, *The Letters of Wanda Tinasky.*

The book not only reprints all the Wanda letters, but accompanies them with a smart and extensive annotated guide to all the arcane literary and local references in them (much like the Martin Gardner *Annotated Alice*–type books); includes the letters from *Advertiser* readers responding to Wanda and provoking her responses, along with prefatory essays by Mr. Anderson, Pynchon scholar Steven Moore, and writer T. R. Factor (who did the annotations). Which makes the book as a whole more than merely an "Is She or Isn't She Pynchon?" debate, but a funny, literate, weirdly touching portrait of an unusual community obsessed by a literary mystery, a shadowy Visitation—in a way, a literary ghost story.

But if it's a ghost story, was the specter Thomas Pynchon? Or a remarkably sophisticated but reclusive writer with a Pynchonesque range of allusion and interest, a Pynchonesque feel for the arcana of High and Low culture, a Pynchonesque fondness for ampersands, someone who deployed unmistakably Pynchonesque clues (like "Wanda's" claim to have worked for Boeing Aircraft) who happened to be writing in the Emerald Triangle in the period Mr. Pynchon was living there—but who was *not* Mr. Pynchon.

Mr. Pynchon's agent (and wife) Melanie Jackson has flatly denied he wrote the Wanda Tinasky letters, although it's possible to conceive that she is carrying out his wishes in maintaining pseudonymity for his Wanda guise. Columbia University English professor Edward Mendelson, one of the nation's foremost Pynchon scholars (he's also W. H. Auden's literary executor), told me that he was carried away with the Wanda letters' Pynchonesque qualities when he first read them, but subsequently decided, mainly on the basis of external factors, that Mr. Pynchon did not write them. Professor Mendelson claims that comparison of the typography of the typewritten Wanda letter reproduced in *The Letters of Wanda Tinasky* with other extant Pynchon letters shows a key discrepancy: Unlike Mr. Pynchon, Wanda places commas and other punctuation *outside* quotation marks (the English style) rather than inside them. Professor Mendelson also argues, from what he says are "very reliable" sources, that while Mr. Pynchon *did* sojourn in the Emerald Triangle, the years of his stay did not coincide with the period of Wanda's letter writing, and that *Vineland* is set more in the more northerly Humboldt County, rather than in Wanda's Mendocino.

These seem to be strong but not necessarily definitive refutations of Pynchonian authorship of the Wanda letters. I find myself unable to make up my mind, but I'm fascinated with Wanda, whoever she or he is. If she isn't Mr. Pynchon, she's still a wonderfully engaging voice whose prose gives, at the very least, some of the surface pleasures of Mr. Pynchon's, and occasionally some of the deeper ones. So I think what I'm going to do is enumerate some of the most Pynchonian passages in Wanda's letters, some of the most Pynchonian clues, for your consideration. Not so much to prove Wanda *is* Mr. Pynchon, but to explain why I like Wanda, *whoever* she is. To explore what we talk about when we talk about the "Pynchonesque."

1. The Cap/Cape of Invisibility Riff. This appears in Wanda's "Open Letter to Gary Snyder," the West Coast Beat poet icon, and seems to arise from a dispute over a Snyder reference to a line from Anacreon, the sixth-century B.C. Greek lyric poet. Consider the strangeness of a letter to the editor of a local weekly on the California coast beginning, out of the blue, apropos of nothing that appeared in the paper:

"Re: The line, 'Anyone can tell a Parthian by his turban,' in *Versions of Anacreon* (from John Taylor's literal interlinear [translation])."

Wanda doesn't like the translation. "Might *anyone can tell a Parthian by his cap (or headgear)* be better? Reminds me of the 'cap of weaselskin' (i.e., sable) worn by the nightspy in the *Iliad,* Chapman's printer making cap of cape and subsequent editions faithfully repeated the error down through the centuries, giving rise to the 'Cap of Invisibility' of the literary fairy tales et al."

Of course, we know that resonant misprints in texts play an important role in the Pynchon oeuvre, particularly in *The Crying of Lot 49,* when the subversive Tristero conspiracy uses obscure misprints on stamps (like "Potsmaster" for "Postmaster") as the signature of its underground communication system. And doesn't a meditation on invisibility inevitably conjure up thoughts of Mr. Pynchon's own invisibility? If it *is* he, in fact, who is Wanda's ghost, then the Wanda guise is *his* cape of invisibility.

2. The riff on "reverse *Schadenfreude*." While *Schadenfreude* is the perverse feeling of joy at the suffering of others, "it came to me," Wanda writes in another letter, "that the reverse of *Schadenfreude* would be *Glückschmerz,* i.e., a feeling of pain at someone's else good fortune* (someone's else is correct English grammar, someone else's is incorrect)," Wanda helpfully adds. Very Pynchonian: He loves to extract wit from ponderous and cumbersome

---

*Admit it: *Glückschmerz* is a comic-genius concept, certainly worthy of Pynchon.

Germanic aesthetic terms. Wanda herself cites Bertolt Brecht's famous *Verfremdungseffekt*—alienating theatrical artifice—"used," Wanda explains, "to break the spell as it were, & remind the audience that what they are watching was not real." Wanda's letters are wonders of *Verfremdungseffekt*.

3. **Explicit Pynchonian biographical references.** Wanda claims to have worked at Boeing Aircraft in the past, as did Mr. Pynchon. She claims to be working on a romantic novel involving local Emerald Triangle characters (as was Mr. Pynchon); she speaks of trips she's made to New York to consult with publishing industry figures and laments the disappearance of Maxwell Perkins–type editors (Wanda jokes "Perkins used to drink champagne out of my slipper"). It could, of course, be the case that Wanda was just a well-read Pynchon fan, planting suggestive but false clues. Still, that makes it a rather remarkable coincidence that the *real* Mr. Pynchon happened to be her virtual neighbor, doesn't it?

4. And speaking of coincidence, consider **Wanda's suggestive meditation on the medieval metaphysician Nicholas of Cusa,** who expressed his vision of God's infiniteness as "the coincidence of contradictories" that vanquishes Reason—a veritable theology of Coincidence, long a Pynchonian preoccupation.

5. **The use of the ampersand and "Yr. Ob'd'nt Servant."** Both Mr. Pynchon and Wanda *love* ampersands, I believe for the archaicizing effect (cf. the title *Mason & Dixon*), and Wanda signs many of her letters with the deliberately antiquated salutation "Yr. Ob'd'nt Servant." The one tiny, pre-publication disclosure I'll make about *Mason & Dixon* (a disclosure more of typography than substance) is that in addition to the prolific use of ampersands in the new novel, there is, very early on, a letter signed "Y'r ob'd't s'v't." Not decisive, since it is an eighteenth-century letter, but interesting.

6. **Explicitly Pynchonian literary (self?) references.** In her first letter to the *Anderson Valley Advertiser,* Wanda suggests the *Advertiser* change its name to *The Boonville Bugle*—the bugle, as many have already noted, being a possible reference to the central Pynchon icon, "the muted post horn" in *The Crying of Lot 49.* There is also a repeated reference to the proverb "Waste not, want not"—W.A.S.T.E. being the cryptic acronym of the Tristero conspiracy in that novel.

7. **An explicit Pynchon invisible ghostwriter-impersonator reference.** In a postscript to one of her letters, Wanda states flatly: "The novels of William Gaddis and Thomas Pynchon were written by the same person." She's referring elliptically to a fairly obscure rumor in the seventies that Mr. Gaddis, the author of the massive cryptic epic *The Recognitions,* was the "real" author of the massive cryptic epic *Gravity's Rainbow.* Displaying a suspiciously acute awareness of arcane Pynchon lore, she seems to be suggesting the reverse: that "Pynchon" might have written "Gaddis," or that they were *both* pseudo-

nyms of someone else. A few offhand words creating a dizzying labyrinth of impersonation possibilities in an (almost) inimitably Pynchonesque way.

8. The almost impossibly arcane Joycean reference (traced by annotator Factor to an obscure bit of litigation James Joyce was involved in during his stay in Zurich) that prompts Wanda to wonder, "Do you think anyone but me appreciates this sort of thing?" (I do, Wanda, I do.)

9. The riff on the Rosenbergs. I've always wondered why more attention hasn't been paid to the heavily shadowed but highly suggestive vision of what really went on between the Rosenbergs and the couple that betrayed them, as seen through a fictive glass darkly at the close of E. L. Doctorow's *The Book of Daniel.* Wanda is the first I've seen to illuminate the way, as she puts it, "Mr. Doctorow gives you a little tiny tickle of something . . . & this thing grows through the book, until it's a big black 'reality.'" I won't go into further explication of Wanda's theory of Mr. Doctorow's theory, but I have to say, it's an impressive explication of a little-understood but resonant passage, one that reflects Wanda's highly developed feel for lefty historical controversies (like the one over Lenin's New Economic Policy). Again, very Pynchonian.

10. Wanda's Luddite disposition, reflected in disparaging remarks about "the Cathedral of Science" as the church of our age—in a 1983 letter written less than a year before Mr. Pynchon published his brilliant essay "Is It O.K. to Be a Luddite?" in *The New York Times Book Review.*

11. The possible clue buried in the *name* "Wanda Tinasky." I know this will sound far-fetched to some, but there's a well-known passage in *V.* in which one of the characters spins out an old shaggy-dog-story joke about a guy born with a golden screw in his navel. How for years he couldn't figure out what it was for until finally one day he decides to remove the screw. At which point, his ass falls off. I think in *V.* it's an allegory for the way self-consciousness undoes the coherence of the self, something like that. But think about the name *Tinasky:* Break it down to *tin ass key.* A tin key that unlocks the ass, a golden screw that holds the ass on. Coincidence? I'm not sure. I can't make up my mind. But I do know that if Wanda is not Mr. Pynchon, she or he, whoever she is, ought to step forward to be honored for capturing, in a playful, original way, the spirit of Mr. Pynchon in her prose. It makes you wonder why whoever Wanda is *hasn't* come forward—unless it *is* the Man himself. And so I'll close with this plea:

Dear Wanda,
  Whoever you are, wherever you've Wanda-d, write *me* a letter, I can keep a secret.

Yr. Ob'd'nt S'v't.

Ecstatic Mortification:
The Self-loathing Spirituality
of Martin Amis

Despite being an obsessed reader, I almost never go to *readings*. Some terror of being trapped and bored even by writers I admire, some resentment, I'm sure, at the reversal of the power relationship in the public reading process—reading a book privately you control *exactly* how much you can and want to absorb, when to start and stop, who's in *charge*.

Not so when you're at the mercy of the writer, the fidgety wait, the often unsatisfying selection of passages, either too cryptically truncated or irritatingly overfamiliar or overlong. And then, of course, the presence of Other People often eager to demonstrate how deeply they *understand* with sighs and whispers and preening *moues* of self-satisfaction. You know what I mean.

But when I heard that Martin Amis would be reading from an unpublished work, in the basement of a Benetton, of all places, I felt compelled to brave the heat and what I was certain would be a mob of snotty literati, to get a preview of a forthcoming novella called *Night Train*.

I was prepared for a crowd, but I must admit I was unprepared for both the size and character of the wall-to-wall crush that jammed the basement coffee bar, backed up the stairs, and spilled out into the sportswear aisles above.

And that was a full half hour before the scheduled starting time. It wasn't just the size of the crowd that surprised me as I squeezed my way down through the bodies thronging the stairs, so much as the conspicuous absence of, well, the usual suspects, I guess you'd say: the snotty literati who were either away in the Hamptons or way too cool to arrive early enough to find a place. Instead, the crowd was like a mass casting call for the cast of *Friends,* clean-cut, clear-skinned, fresh-faced, young publishing types, it seemed.

It made me wonder whether Mr. Amis is no longer taken as seriously by snotty literati types as he once was, whether the whole controversy over money, agentry, literary celebrity, and expensive dental reconstruction that blew up a couple years ago around the publication of *The Information* had somehow eclipsed or obscured what it was that made him so compelling as a writer—why it was worth caring about his work rather than merely chattering about his advances and his teeth.

As more and more bodies crammed themselves into the sweaty mosh pit of the Benetton basement, and the wait for the now overdue author went on, I began revolving around in my mind a theory about Mr. Amis's work, why exactly I find his vision so powerful. Why it represents to me something more than addictively entertaining, acidly sophisticated dark comedy. The way it seems to me to embody as well a perversely spiritual vision, a brilliant heretical counterstatement to the Grand, Overinflated secular religion of our culture: the Religion of Self-Esteem. What Mr. Amis does is counterpose to the doctrine of self-esteem as the be-all and cure-all of the human condition what might be called the Virtue of Self-Loathing, the spiritual Discipline of Self-Disgust.

Mr. Amis's work constitutes a provocative dissent to a therapized culture utterly dominated by an almost utterly unexamined assumption, one that you find at the heart of all pop psychology, self-help, New Age, recovery movement literature: that the root of all human evil, the Original Sin of self and society, the source of all civilization's discontents is the *lack* of self-esteem, the inability to love ourselves *enough.*

Well—just as a thought-experiment, just for a moment—consider the possibility that what we're really suffering from is rather *too much self-esteem.* That instead of flogging ourselves into liking ourselves more, instead of all the brainwashing school programs, seminars, self-help books, and home-study courses hectoring us to love ourselves more, to "find the greatest love of all inside of me" as Whitney Houston wails, it might be far more salutary all around to take a good hard look at how genuinely loathsome human nature really is. Start to love ourselves a little less.

I mean, I don't know about you, but I don't often run into people who suffer from too *little* self-esteem; on the contrary, I see many more suffering from a choking overstuffed surplus of it practically oozing out of their mouths and trickling down their chins like melted butter from the maw of a fat guy gorging on lobster. It's kind of ridiculous, when you think about it, to realize that the official ideology of contemporary culture is that we don't think highly *enough* of ourselves. I mean, look at history, look what we've done to ourselves and others; has this ceaseless chronicle of tragedy and depredation really been caused by shrinking violets afraid to love their inner child? I don't think so. Wouldn't it be more accurate to say it's the product of self-aggrandizing madmen who love themselves, esteem themselves and their self-serving delusions way beyond any sane estimation of their self-worth?

That's why I find Martin Amis's work so appealing, such a powerful, caustic corrective. He is the muse of rhapsodic self-loathing, the magus of vertiginous self-disgust, the high priest of humiliating self-mortification. A loathing and disgust that takes on a spiritual dimension, because it inspires a kind of meditative introspection of the sort that religious initiates undertake, the soul-searching self-examination that, if conducted with the proper degree of scathing Amisian skepticism and self-contempt, can result in a salutary *loss* of self-esteem: the rarely experienced, almost forgotten state that once was known as humility.

A state, humility, sometimes only attained through the purgatory of humiliation, the underworld of hellish self-torment Mr. Amis's characters inhabit or descend into. It's there in *Success,* it's there in my sentimental favorite, *Money,* the epic chronicle of the slow-motion self-destruction of the blithely self-hating John Self, who raises comic self-abasement almost to the level of spiritual self-realization. It's there in *London Fields,* in the virtuosity with which the inimitable Nicola Six transforms the promised bliss of sexual longing into a fiendishly articulated chronicle of male humiliation. And, of course, it's there in perhaps its most wickedly distilled form in *The Information,* a novel about writers humiliating each other (and themselves), because, as everyone knows, writers have refined the art of self-torture to its absolute peak; writers are the connoisseurs, the *scientists* of self-loathing. And even the rewards of literary celebrity, the ostensible subject of *The Information,* are just more instruments for ratcheting up the dialectic of envy and humiliation, as Mr. Amis himself learned when his conspicuous success subjected him to an ordeal by bad publicity. (At the Benetton reading, he winced briefly during the question period when a well-meaning reader asked him whether he still had nightmares about his teeth—an intended reference to the bad dental dreams that figured prominently in *Dead Babies.* But he seemed to think the questioner was alluding to his expensive American dental reconstruction that angry and envious British literati made into the symbol of his alleged abandonment of loyal agents, friends, and publishers for bigger advances.)

In a certain sense, the ritual of humiliation in Mr. Amis's work can be seen as serving the kind of self-mortifying function of the memento mori, the grinning skull that monks and anchorites kept ever before their eyes to remind them of the transitory insubstantiality of the flesh that briefly clothes and disguises the walking death sentence of human existence.

That's there at the heart of Mr. Amis's work, the skull beneath the skin, but with a difference that distinguishes it from the dry-as-a-bone, monastically disciplined kind. Amisian self-loathing is, well, wet. You know, *juicy,* almost joyous in its feverish degradation, a kind of floridly fulminating decay. One that finds its most acute embodiment, the ultimate Amisian objective correlative, in John Self's bad tooth. The painful, decayed, and badly abscessed molar he is perpetually touching and testing with his tongue when it's not sending explosive bursts of nerve pain direct to his brainpan to remind him of his impending physical and moral implosion. That inflamed molar is a private, inner memento mori within the skull to remind him, us, of the inexorable rottenness of human Being, of being human.

And, really, aren't we better off acknowledging it than denying it? There was an image that seemed to express that sentiment in something Mr. Amis read that night in the Benetton basement. In addition to reading some all-too-brief but tantalizing excerpts from *Night Train,* a novella about a homicide detective and the forensic metaphysics of suicide, he also read the entire text of a short story published that week in *The New Yorker.* A story whose preoccupations with mortality and denial are embodied in the image of a little sprat (a bait fish) a kid named Pablo takes home from the shore to keep as a (soon dead) pet in his room. When someone asks him how he'll prevent it from rotting and decaying, he replies: "Fish cream," he'll slather it with "fish cream."

Fish cream: It's as good a metaphor as any for the self-esteem therapy we're urged to slather over the decay within ourselves, to conceal rather than acknowledge it. A cosmetic cover-up that can mask the sight, but not the stench of corruption and mortality.

But the most remarkable moment in the reading, for me anyway, came at the very end when Mr. Amis took a few questions, and someone asked him about the way his novels often pair conspicuously successful and mortifyingly failed figures, and what that said about his own anxieties on the subject. I'll quote his answer at length because I think it illuminates his belief in self-laceration, the Way of Humiliation as the way to spiritual revelation:

"I think failure is an infinitely more interesting subject" than success, he said. "Success is always the same, success is the subject of trash fiction. Failure is paradoxically rich and complex and fascinating. And I also think that we *live* in our failures. We don't go around congratulating ourselves for our successes. It's those terrible gaffes, those terrible flops that make our hands fly to our faces, that make us stop dead on the street and babble to drown out the memory."

Ecstatic mortification! That babbling is the self-loathing equivalent of speaking in tongues. The amazing grace of utter disgrace.

The Hidden History
in Ben Hecht's Suitcase

I've been thinking about Ben Hecht a lot lately, thinking about the amazing trajectory of this bitter, brilliant cynic of genius, now fading into cultural forgetfulness. Remembered by the general public, if at all, for *The Front Page* and, to a lesser extent, for *Twentieth Century*. Remembered by film buffs and historians of Hollywood for being a screenwriter of such profligate talent and prolific output that scholars are still identifying dozens of scripts he wrote and rewrote without ever bothering to put his name on—in addition to the obvious ones he's credited for, including *Underworld, Gone With the Wind,* and *Wuthering Heights.* (Run out and rent *Twentieth Century* if you haven't seen it; it's deliriously funny and one of showbiz culture's great satires of its own meretricious theatricality.)

I've been thinking about Ben Hecht in part because I happened upon a melancholy piece in *Biblio,* the magazine for book and manuscript collectors, on the fading of the Hechtian literary reputation, once on a par with H. L. Mencken's. And because by coincidence on the very same day, while shifting some books out of boxes into storage, I came across a cache of my Ben Hecht books and found myself plunging once again into Hecht's 1954 *A Child of the Century,* still one of the great American memoirs.

What struck me in particular on this reading was a section I'd dog-eared and marked with exclamation points years ago when I first read it. It's a story Hecht tells about an absolutely astonishing episode that took place in Munich in 1919 when Hecht was serving as foreign correspondent for the *Chicago Daily News;* when Hecht's trajectory as a journalist intersected with that of history (and that of Hitler) in ways that had unfathomable consequences.

Rereading it, I suddenly understood it in a new way: as a clue to a mystery about Hecht, about the extraordinary turn his life took in 1942 when he suddenly suspended his lucrative Hollywood screenwriting career to become the first mainstream American writer (one of the first writers of any kind, anywhere) to speak out, to cry out, to try to alert an indifferent world to the Holocaust then in progress.

To put this remarkable 1919 Munich episode in perspective, let's briefly review Hecht's career before and after it. *A Child of the Century* is, like Charles Dickens's *Sketches by Boz,* the kind of book that—if you have any life left in you—will make you wish you'd been a journalist back when that did not mean mainly doing profiles of celebrities dictated by the schedules of movie studio publicists. Hecht recounts, with the pure storytelling brio he is unequaled for, the breathtaking exhilaration and the breathtaking cynicism of Chicago journalism at its insanely competitive peak. (His first regular newspaper job was "picture chaser"—a proto-paparazzo—lifting photos of accident victims from the living rooms of the bereaved to give the paper an exclusive on the dead.) A cynical frenzy Hecht captured beautifully in *The Front Page,* but which he tops in some of the newspaper tales in *A Child of the Century.*

Hecht rose (or fell) from the manic frenzy of street reporting to the realm of literature through the influential *Chicago Daily News* column he developed in which he reinvented the *feuilleton*—the Continental tradition of literary essays in daily newspapers—for a fabulist-inclined American audience. Samples of his best work in that vein can be found in a collection called *1001 Afternoons in Chicago.* Those afternoons, those columns, made Hecht influential enough to be considered a founder of what came to be known as the Chicago Literary Renaissance, along with Theodore Dreiser, Sherwood Anderson, and Carl Sandburg. After which he moved to New York, where he wrote for Mencken's *Smart Set* and *Vanity Fair* and became one of the least overrated among the vastly overrated Algonquin wits. All the while writing bitter, tormented, self-conscious novels of unfathomable cynicism with titles like *A Jew in Love* and *The Kingdom of Evil.*

Later on in the twenties, he followed some of the Algonquin types out to Hollywood. Indeed, it was Hecht to whom Herman Mankiewicz wrote that famous telegram from the Coast: MILLIONS ARE TO BE GRABBED OUT HERE, AND YOUR ONLY COMPETITION IS IDIOTS.

Hecht became, in fact, a kind of idiot savant of screenwriters, famously dictating two or three at a time for insane fees that deepened his cynicism and self-loathing as they fattened and inflated his bank account.

But nothing in his Hollywood period prepares you for the turn Hecht's life took after the war began, when he was approached by members of the Zionist underground in Europe (later founders of Irgun) and asked to help tell the world—which didn't want to hear—what was happening to the Jews of Europe.

Hecht's efforts, in his widely read column in the legendary New York afternoon daily *P.M.*, were climaxed by a now-famous public memorial rally in Madison Square Garden, in March 1943, a Hecht-produced pageant which broadcast nationally the truth about the slaughter to a still indifferent world. Many credit Hecht's impassioned plea in print for the victims ("Remember Us" in the February 1943 *Reader's Digest*) as the first, most visible, and—as Hecht's biographer William MacAdams calls it—"the most powerful, most historically important statement to call America's attention to the mass slaughter of Jews by Nazis."

Later in the postwar years, Hecht went on to become one of the most visible, vocal American supporters of the Irgun underground in its armed struggle to found the State of Israel. But his role as the first Cassandra-like prophet of the Holocaust in process should alone, if there were any justice, secure Hecht an honored place in the century's history.

In rereading Hecht's chronicle of this remarkable odyssey once again, a couple of mysteries about him finally seemed to resolve themselves. First was the question of Hechtian cynicism: a bleak black hole of cynicism, beyond mere surface wise-guy cynicism, a cynicism about himself, about all of Being that prevailed in his work even before Hollywood, even before the Holocaust. And then there was the question of why Hecht, almost alone of all writers, was receptive to the story of the ongoing mass murder of the European Jews—at a time when governments, media, and populaces throughout the world turned a deaf or disbelieving ear to the reports of the horror filtering out from the death camps.

Perhaps the answer may be found in that incredible episode in Munich in 1919, the same Munich to which Hitler returned from the war, the Munich that would soon become the stage for Hitler's rise to power.

Hecht arrived in defeated Berlin in January 1919, just a couple months after the German surrender. With the help of his American dollars (he bought the services of two Luftwaffe aces who fought in Baron von Richtofen's squadron; they stole a decommissioned bomber that they used to ferry Hecht over the landscape of vanquished Germany), and with his invaluable Chicago newspaperman's instinctual ability to smell a rat, Hecht was soon onto the story most of the international press was missing: the devious maneuvering by the German General Staff to retain its weapons and its power in German politics. Scheming which gave rise to, among other things, the "Stab in the Back" myth, one of the Big Lies Hitler rode to power.

By maneuvering the hapless socialist government, which had been left holding the bag when the Kaiser fled, into responsibility for signing onerous armistice (and later, peace treaty) terms with the Allies, the German Army set itself up to claim forever after that it was never really defeated, but only "stabbed in the back" by the treacherous civilian authorities, the "November Criminals," as Hitler called them (after the November 1918 armistice).

The other aspect of the game the German Army generals were playing—the other rat Hecht smelled—was the way the army seemed to him to be tolerating, if not encouraging, local outbreaks of Red-led revolutionaries, the better to convince the Allies that Germany still needed a well-armed military force to suppress and prevent Bolshevik revolutions from sweeping the nation.

Here's where the suitcase comes in. In a remarkable chapter of *A Child of the Century* called, laconically, "Concerning a Suitcase," Hecht tells the story of how he abandoned his journalistic neutrality to play a role in this complicated game, how he became no longer a mere observer, but an active participant in the making of history.

He describes how he was approached in Berlin by a well-known Bolshevik agent who asked for a lift (in Hecht's bomber) to Munich, where a revolution had broken out against the old regime. He's also asked for a lift on the same flight by the head of Germany's Anti-Bolshevik League and two high-ranking aides to the German General Staff. Bolsheviks and anti-Bolsheviks sit calmly in the cabin of Hecht's bomber, playing poker on top of a suitcase as a remarkable transaction concerning the suitcase plays itself out.

In front of the pistol-equipped anti-Bolsheviks, the Bolshevik agent asks Hecht if he can carry the suitcase, filled with one million gold marks in hard currency, past airport security. The money is meant to be used to bribe the military garrison in Munich not to oppose the Bolshevik revolutionaries. Hecht takes the suitcase and carries it off the plane through security, knowing that the armed, anti-Bolshevik army men "had only to draw a gun and put an end to this Lenin-Trotsky plot."

Yet they did nothing, Hecht claims, because the short-term success of the Munich revolution was in the long-term interests of the military in making the case to the Allies for maintaining their armaments. Hecht finds the Bolshevik agent equally cynical—knowing he is being used to stir up a revolution that will eventually be brutally crushed, but allowing himself to be used because a local success, however short-lived, serves *his* long-term international interests as well, regardless of how many comrades are killed in the undertaking.

It's an amazing story, and we have only Hecht's word for it that it's true, although he's not alone in his *analysis* of the cynical maneuvering behind the scenes in that period. I'm inclined, with some reservations, to believe it, although I'm not sure I completely credit Hecht's own account of its effect on him. He says the episode "left me with a permanent cynicism toward history" and that "the cynicism of the [Munich suitcase episode] was beyond anything I had as yet seen in the world."

This may be true, as far as it goes. But I suspect it may have left him with something more than cynicism. I suspect it *might* have left him with a legacy of guilt. Because the consequences of this episode, the consequences of the cynical maneuvering in which he and that suitcase had played a part were not negligible, may have been incalculable. Whether or not a million marks smuggled by Hecht into Munich made a difference, the revolution in Munich *did* succeed for a short time, a brief, violent flowering followed by a far more savage reconquest of the city by the army—and the subsequent installation of a right-wing nationalist Bavarian regime that proved itself hospitable to the rise of Hitler and his party.

One respected historian* has recently gone so far as to argue that it was Hitler's horrified reaction to this Bolshevik revolution in Munich back then in 1919 that precipitated his entry into (literally) reactionary politics. It's a minority view (not one I share), and Hecht is unlikely to have gone so far as to have held himself responsible for Hitler. But by entering into history, by playing the game as he did—even with the result of clarifying history and exposing the game—he might have felt himself at least partly responsible for setting the stage in Munich, a stage Hitler seized for his own purposes. It might give Hecht's abandonment of Hollywood for the stage of history in the early forties, for his heroic role as the Cassandra-like herald of the Holocaust, an even more personally tragic dimension: He might well have seen his own suitcase as Pandora's box.

*John Lukacs in *The Hitler of History*.

Two Singers

A (Modest) Proposal to Rosanne Cash

Elvis, Healer

A (Modest) Proposal
to Rosanne Cash

I don't want you to get the wrong idea if I begin what is meant to be a celebratory column on what might seem to be a dark note—with a reference to a poem
about suicide. But my concept for this particular column comes from a poem,
actually a *title* I came across in a Beat anthology I picked up as a teenager. I
forget the author, I forget the poem, but the title (or some approximation of it)
has stayed with me: "Preface to a Forty-Volume Suicide Note."*

It could just be me, but I've always found the idea of a forty-volume suicide
note to be a perversely upbeat, life-affirming concept: Any guy who's projecting a forty-volume suicide note is never really going to check out voluntarily,
because there's clearly just *so* much to say, so many scores to settle, so much
to set straight. With, inevitably, more and more material accumulating in the
time it takes to do justice to what's come before. Like Tristram Shandy's famously impractical project for a journal in which he planned to devote a year
to *really* capturing the truth of each new day—with each successive day of
diary writing thus requiring another full year to chronicle—"Preface to a

*It was by Amiri Baraka, at the time LeRoi Jones.

Forty-Volume Suicide Note" was not about ending things, but about expanding them to infinitude.

It is in this spirit that I now present *my* fantasy epic, my "Preface to a Forty-Volume Marriage Proposal to Rosanne Cash." Forty volumes could not even begin to scratch the *surface* of my awestruck admiration and devotion, which continues to grow even as I write this and listen to *The Wheel* over and over for maybe the forty thousandth time.

I know, I know: She's married again now, it's not a very practical project, you'll say, probably hopeless. But it's a work in progress I've been drafting in my mind for several years now, ever since I learned she'd been divorced from the extremely talented but obviously foolish songwriter Rodney Crowell. (I would *never* make her unhappy.) I feel I made a strategic mistake by waiting too long to publish at least my preface, if not the entire forty volumes, until it was too late and she got married again. I don't intend to make that mistake again.

Of course, I don't want to wish her any unhappiness with her new husband, who, I'm sure, is a splendid fellow, but let's face it: Judging from her heart-wrenching songs, the men in her life have not always been the most reliable (as I *would* be, I swear). And after seeing Rosanne perform live at the Bottom Line recently, I am hopelessly under her spell again. It was one of the most intense and emotional evenings of music I've ever experienced—and that night I decided that, however quixotic it might seem, I really *should* go ahead and publish the preface to my forty volumes, if only as a way of paying tribute to her talent, to her persona, to *her,* without risking breach-of-promise litigation.

And so, herewith, my preface, in the form of a direct appeal: The Top Ten Reasons Why You Should Consider My Proposal:

Reason No. 1: I really understand how brilliant your work is. Oh yeah, a lot of guys will *say* they understand you, but I really, *really* appreciate what a great songwriter—what a great writer, period—you are. I really, *really* get that breathtaking fusion of grace and urgency in your voice, the offhand, tossed-off killer lyrics that cut straight to the heart like a cardiac surgeon.

Consider the new issue of *Granta*. Have you, has anyone, actually read the work of these twenty "best young novelists"? So much earnest, labor-intensive striving for novelty, for intensity, for effect. And yet, with a few exceptions (the peerless Lorrie Moore, for one), I could name twenty of your songs, Rosanne, that just blow them all off the *map,* songs that display writing at such a far higher level of inspiration and intensity—writing that radiates the kind of compelling urgency that should cause the *entire Iowa Writers' Workshop* to implode with envy and shame. In fact, if *Granta* was smart and not so sedulously intent on reifying conventional literary hierarchies, it would devote an entire issue to contemporary songwriting *as* literature, because that's where the real excitement in American writing lies now.

Reason No. 2: I completely agree with your critique of men. There's a great song on your very intense and beautiful new album *(Ten Song Demo)* called "If I Were a Man" in which you play with the idea that you could do better at being a guy than guys do. That you wouldn't be so stupidly wayward and untrustworthy and (let's face it) doglike as almost all men are. (But not me!)

Reason No. 3: I really, *really* understand certain of your songs in ways that even *you* might not—yet. As proof of this, I cite "Sleeping in Paris," one of your most haunting, almost supernaturally lovely, and yet somehow disturbing lyrics. It's a song about the pain of separation between two people who both love and distrust each other intensely, a song with a brooding, incantatory refrain—"Soon we'll be sleeping in Paris"—that seems to imply more than a trip through the Chunnel. There's something grave, uncanny, premonitory about the way you sing that phrase—"sleeping in Paris" always seemed to me to be a euphemistic metaphor for death, for the Big Sleep that will finally, truly unite the two divided lovers in the permanent embrace that has eluded them in life. A love suicide pact? I don't know, but this song ain't no stroll by the Seine, if you ask me.

"I think it's got to be about death," I said to the woman I attended the Bottom Line concert with, as we awaited the late show.

"I think it's about drugs," she said. Maybe it was about death *and* drugs, we speculated—like the ending of *Romeo and Juliet*.

And then about halfway through the set, you, Rosanne, introduced "Sleeping in Paris" by saying, "This is a song about a happy couple."

Yeah, right. I don't think so. Like Tristan and Iseult were a happy couple, like Romeo and Juliet had a happy ending (it could have been called "Soon We'll Be Sleeping in Verona"). The rest of the audience seemed to take your "happy couple" line at face value. But *we* knew you were being deeply ironic in a way that conjured up the great tragic and romantic myths of the past, in which happy couples were united only in the Big Sleep of death.* Of course, I could be completely wrong, but you have to admit it would be hard to find anyone in the world who *cares* more about your songs than me. (Except perhaps for my friend Betsy, who once announced to me, "I *am* Rosanne Cash.")

And, speaking of death, this brings me to *Reason No. 4* why you should marry me: In practical terms, the marriage probably wouldn't take up too much time in your life, anyway. Certain of your songs are so deeply engraved on my heart—like postoperative scars—that if you ever granted me the supreme privilege of singing one of them to me face-to-face, I can just about guarantee the medical certainty that I would expire on the spot from a heart at-

---

*I should mention that in the letter Ms. Cash wrote the *Observer* in response to my column, she confirms, "my intro to 'Sleeping in Paris' *was* ironic. There is something foreboding in blind hope." Blind hope springs eternal!

tack. Then, after a brief but respectful interval, you could go back to the unreliable-type guys you write your songs about.

Reason No. 5: Our backgrounds are not as dissimilar as they might seem. I've always felt there was a special affinity between Jews and Southerners (my first wife was a Texan): Both have histories of sorrow and spirituality; both are tuned in to the wail beneath the world. That's what country music and the Delta blues are about. And then, in your new album, I discover you've written a song about—of all things—the Wailing Wall in Jerusalem! ("Western Wall") Which I feel is no accident, perhaps even a secret *signal* to encourage me.

Reason No. 6: I feel I would fit in with the Cash family. One day in Nashville, I had a memorable encounter with a couple of them. I'd been traveling through the South in Willie Nelson's tour bus, working on a story about the aftermath of his IRS troubles, following Willie as he went about the business of auctioning off all the remnants and mementos of his eventful life. We'd been poking around the storeroom of the Willie Nelson Museum in a Nashville mall. Willie was taking one final look at what was left of his past when Carlene Carter, one of your half sisters and, like Crystal Gayle, another half sister, a strong singer in her own right (but not a songwriting genius like you), stopped by with Larry Gatlin of the Gatlin Brothers, to schmooze and sympathize with Willie. Who was stoic but still a bit stunned by his reversal of fortune. Carlene and Larry started telling the story of how they'd just recently been at the deathbed of Mama Cash, your stepmother, and how she'd been struggling and suffering trying to "pass over" (another Jewish reference?) until at a certain point she was ready to go, and the whole assembled Cash family joined hands around her bedside and "sung her into heaven."

It sounds a bit corny, I know; maybe you had to be there, but there was something very real about it; it seemed to lift Willie's spirits. It may have been designed to: It was a story about an extended family closing a circle around one of its wounded (around Willie as well), an unbroken circle, a circle of song, and it got to me. I liked the Cash family for that. Plus, I know I could get along with your father, Johnny Cash, because I like to wear black, too.

Reason No. 7: I would understand the necessity of tolerating your memories of Rodney Crowell. The dude is a talent; I'll be the first to admit it: Like you, he's a wildly talented songwriter, and you had a long, stormy, wildly intense marriage. So I wouldn't try to fight the past; I would even encourage you to record again with him. I would probably be insanely (but not quite homicidally) jealous, but I would kill to hear the songs that resulted.

Reason No. 8: I would try to be unreliable and Bad if that's still important to you. (But I would always treat your daughters worshipfully because I know nothing—no guy, no song—matters more to you.)

Reason No. 9: Interiors and *Seven Year Ache* and the urgency you bring to singing "Runaway Train" and the infinite tenderness with which you sang "Wouldn't It Be Loverly?" to close out your second encore that night at the Bottom Line.

Reason No. 10: The Wheel over and over and over again.

Postscript to "A (Modest) Proposal to Rosanne Cash"

In an *extremely* good-natured response to this hyperbolic but not *entirely* metaphoric proposal, Rosanne Cash wrote, in a letter published in the *Observer,* "I plan on hanging Ron Rosenbaum's 'marriage proposal' [column] in a prominent place. Should my husband begin to take me for granted, he will be reminded that I am not without options." But I'm not holding my breath. In fact, I must admit that after three years of all-too-contented silence from Ms. Cash, I wrote another column withdrawing my proposal and directing a new plea, this time to Margo Timmins of the Cowboy Junkies. False hope springs eternal. . . .

Elvis, Healer

In Which the Hurt, the Lame, and the Tenured Seek
the Graceland Within

It's Death Week here in Memphis, the week leading up to the mass veneration
of Elvis Presley's grave, and the signature sound in the ambient soundtrack is
a song called "Hurt." The city is swelling with pilgrims from all over the
world. Tens of thousands of mourners, fans, impersonators, icon sellers, former Elvis entourage members, and hangers-on are flooding into this oven-
baked Egyptian-named Mississippi River metropolis, the place that midwifed
the birth of the blues on Beale Street and bore witness to the death of Elvis on
his Graceland toilet. For days, a *Canterbury Tales*–like fusion of carnival and
spiritual impulses has been building toward the convergence on the grave in a
climactic ceremony referred to simply as "Candlelight." It's the central ritual
in Elvis Culture, a phenomenon that has lately transcended the familiar contours of a dead celebrity cult and has begun to assume the dimensions of a redemptive faith.

It began, the veneration ritual, with small gatherings at the gates of Graceland in the first few years after Elvis's death on August 16, 1977. A few hundred fans lighting candles on Death Night has mushroomed to tens of
thousands now. Despite the oppressive August heat in Memphis, the death

ceremony eventually dwarfed the January birthday remembrance on the Elvis liturgical calendar and began expanding from a single night to a full weeklong pilgrimage and pageant. The corporate headquarters of Elvis Presley Enterprises at Graceland (representing the Estate, which is owned by Elvis's daughter, Lisa Marie) prefers calling it Elvis Week to Death Week and schedules a busy round of upbeat celebratory concerts, dances, and the like. But for the deadly serious mourners who make the pilgrimage here from all continents (and from all age brackets), the central focus is on loss, on hurt, on the moment of grieving communion at the grave.

On the evening of the fifteenth of August, when the last light fades from the sky, the gates of Graceland will part and a solemn throng of worshipers bearing burning tapers will begin slowly flooding through the entrance to the estate, climbing the hill toward the grave site, dripping paraffin wax and tears in their wake, as they wind their way up to the Meditation Garden, circle around to the flat bronze grave marker and pause there to commune with the spirit of the departed King.

I'd been hearing about the Death Night ceremony, about the way it's grown into a must-see *sui generis* American folk ritual, a fusion of our longing for spirituality and our lust for celebrity. Witnessing it will be, for me, the climax of two weeks' total immersion in Elvis Country (as the Mississippi-Tennessee realm of Elvis shrines is called) and in the larger domain of Elvis Culture. An odyssey that took me and the photographer James Hamilton south from Graceland to the birthplace shrine in Tupelo, Mississippi; then to the cemetery in nearby Priceville, where we searched for the unmarked grave of Elvis's stillborn twin; next, west to Oxford, Mississippi, for a weeklong encounter with academic theories of Elvis at the University of Mississippi's first International Conference on Elvis Presley, and finally, north on Highway 61 through the Delta and back to Memphis for Death Week.

One thing I've learned is that—dramatic as it is—Death Week is but the tip of the iceberg of Elvis Culture, a phenomenon whose dimensions can only be incompletely hinted at by citing numbers. According to Paul Williams, the vice president for Presley Affairs (among other things) at RCA, Elvis recently passed the *half-billion* mark in record sales, and the release next month of a new boxed set of his seventies' recordings (which contains some stunning and heartbreaking reflections of the pain of his final years) will only add to this number, one that perhaps no artist in any medium has ever attained. The number of visitors making the pilgrimage to Graceland every year has climbed to three-quarters of a million—making it, Graceland officials like to boast, the single most visited home in America, save for the White House. A White House, it hardly needs mentioning, now occupied by a sometime Elvis impersonator.

And speaking of impersonators—the lay priests of the Elvis religion—this peculiar phenomenon has become a remarkably pervasive fixture of the iconography of American culture. There are tens of thousands of amateur and professional impersonators belting out sweaty versions of "Viva Las Vegas" in gem-encrusted white jumpsuits all over America. A figure rivaled only, perhaps, by the number of reported appearances the real Elvis seems to be making—the "sightings," as they're called in Elvisian literature.

But more to the point than the quantity of Elvis manifestations is the quality, the intensity, of the posthumous devotion he inspires—the number of people who have "Elvis shrines" and "Elvis rooms" in their homes, who trade in icons like vials of Elvis sweat, buy and sell his hair and warts. It has become a truism that the three most identifiable names in the whole world are Jesus, Coca-Cola, and Elvis. What's more remarkable is that, to some, Elvis has come to seem less like the soft drink—just another commodity—and more like a savior. Greil Marcus, the cultural critic who has long been the most prescient observer of the Presley phenomenon, has written (in *Dead Elvis*) that "the identification of Elvis with Jesus has been a secret theme of the Elvis story at least since 1956." While Elvis himself disclaimed the comparison ("There is only one King," he piously averred), what he seems to offer to those who revere him is some kind of healing. Not necessarily physical healing (although there are reports of that) but healing for emotional travail. And not just for stereotypical Elvisians.

The sea change in the perception—and the demographics—of Elvis's spirituality can perhaps be traced to the release of Paul Simon's hugely successful *Graceland* album of 1986. That haunting title song—about a pilgrimage by an urban sophisticate in pain, a guy who's "blown apart" by the loss of love, going to Graceland with "the child of my first marriage," seeking some kind of secular spiritual succor for his pain at the place where the pain-racked body of Elvis Presley finally came to rest—suggested that the grace of Graceland was something accessible to all.

Similarly, Elvis culture has transcended the camp ridicule, the kitschy condescension, the hostile tell-all bios (whose portraits of a burned-out wreck of a hunk of burning love, crucifying himself with pills and self-pity, only fueled the compelling power of his suffering savior image). The pilgrimage to Graceland has become a way for all kinds of Americans to come to terms with all kinds of pain and loss.

I witnessed a particularly dramatic instance of the way this worked on the penultimate night of Death Week, when I attended an Elvis memorial dinner at the grand old Peabody Hotel. It was a charity benefit run by Marian Cocke, Elvis's onetime private nurse, one of the few people in the world to see at close hand just how badly hurt Elvis was at the end. (She was there at the hospital when he was pronounced dead.) You can tell instantly why Elvis would have called on Nurse Cocke when he was in pain: She radiates a kind of healing warmth that extends to all in her orbit. She told me something about the last few times Elvis had summoned her for help in the final days. Tormented by an inability to sleep that no amount of drugs could assuage, he'd asked her up to his bedroom suite. "He just wanted me to sit with him and hold his hand until he could fall asleep," she told me. And so she'd sit for hour after hour. It wasn't physical pain, Nurse Cocke told me, it was a deeper hurt, one that had been with him all his life, one that no amount of pink Cadillacs, gold records, or little yellow pills could alleviate.

Nurse Cocke's memorial banquet featured a beautiful candlelight ceremony, but it was a moment during the entertainment afterward that crystallized for me my sense of the pain-filled transaction going on between Elvis and the Elvisians. Two highly professional Elvis impersonators sang, and what struck me most forcefully about their performances was the one song they both did that just stopped the show. It's a song not very well known to the casual Elvis observer like myself—I'd been hooked the first time I heard "Heartbreak Hotel" as a kid, but like many I'd lost interest by the time the Beatles arrived—a song Elvis recorded just a year before his death. But it has become one of those secret shared passions that mark a true Elvis initiate. A song that Elvis did in his most melodramatic quasi-operatical all-out soul-baring hold-nothing-back style. A song called, simply, "Hurt."

"I'm *hurt*," he sings over and over. It's a hurt that seems to transcend the petty betrayals of the woman in the song. It's a bigger hurt: his own naked, personal pain.

So powerful, so popular was the song among the Elvisians at Nurse Cocke's banquet that it evoked an extraordinary outburst: The first impersonator did "Hurt" to cries and screams and whistles and then the second impersonator got up and—toward the end of his set—announced that he, too, had planned to do a version of "Hurt," but that since the previous impersonator had done it, he'd close with a different number.

Not a chance: A cry began to build from the audience. A few yelled: *No! No! Do Hurt!* But most simply cried out, *Hurt!* A chant began to build: *Hurt! Hurt! Hurt!* And it continued until he relented and sang it.

Hurt! Hurt! Hurt! It was a demand, a song request, yes, but in a sense it was more than that: It was a self-diagnosis. It was Elvis fans expressing what they, commoners, shared most deeply with the King: hurt. The pain of their lives, of life itself, a pain that was acute and unappeasable, whether experienced in Graceland or a trailer park; the kind of pain that pills and religions seek to minister to, the kind of pain that is the true source of the growing reach of the Elvis faith.

Elvis Has a Risin'

I wasn't sure I'd heard the word correctly. *Risin'*? There was a suggestiveness to the word Sam Phillips used—connotations both sexual and spiritual—that was characteristically Elvisian. But I didn't understand what he was getting at at first. Phillips—legendary to some as the Man Who Discovered Elvis, to others as the Man Who May Have Invented Rock and Roll Itself—had been telling me about the time back in '56 when Elvis, then twenty-one, appeared here, in Phillips's Memphis living room, in a state of acute terror. Elvis was then a fledgling superstar who'd only recently left Sam's nest—Sun Record studios, where he'd cut his first hits under Sam's supervision—to cast his fate with the wily Colonel Parker and RCA's major-label operation. But, Sam says, Elvis would still come to him for advice on personal matters. Which was why he'd appeared in Sam's living room that afternoon to drop his pants and ask Sam about the "risin' " that, as Sam recalled it, "scared him half to death."

"I want to tell you Elvis Presley believed every damn thing I told him," Sam told me. "He literally did." Which shouldn't come as a surprise: In the emerging Gospel of Elvis, Sam is the John the Baptist figure. He is the one who heard a sound—a sound that had never been heard before, the musical equivalent of the voice crying in the wilderness—before Elvis appeared to embody it. He was the one who prophesied, dreamed of a sound that could unify black and white music, even black and white souls in a rock-and-roll embrace. He was the one who famously said, "If I could find a white boy who could sing with a black sound," he could conquer the world.

He heard that sound one afternoon in his Memphis studio when a nervous Elvis was fumbling his way through his first recording session and suddenly broke into an inspired rockabilly version of a bluesy R & B number called "That's All Right (Mama)." It was inspired on Elvis's part to integrate previously segregated musical sensibilities; it was inspired on Sam's part to recognize it, and nothing was the same afterward.

At seventy-two, Sam Phillips is still very much the evangelist, the rock-and-roll prophet, black brows and burning eyes, the cadences of the preacher-cum–all-night-clear-channel-DJ on his lips, his words racing like a Rocket 88. Sam had been tracing for me the genealogy of that sound he'd heard, the one that eventually changed the world—tracing it back to a sound he first heard in his childhood, the sound in the voice of his spiritual godfather, an old blind black man afflicted with syphilis, a man named Silas Payne. Sam's family, struggling farmers in the Deep South town of Florence, Alabama, had taken Uncle Silas, as he came to be called, into their home as a charity case, and it was from him, Sam told me, he first came to love the sound and the soul of black folks, came to love them in a way only certain white Southerners can—

with a love that longs to make itself burn away the sins of the White South. A longing that can't help but fail, but is even more intense for knowing it will. A love tormented with guilt—a very Faulknerian love—gave birth to the sound Sam Phillips sought and found in Elvis.

The specter of syphilis recurs again in the story of the risin'. After a terrified Elvis showed up here in Sam's living room and dropped his pants that afternoon, Sam saw the object of Elvis's dread:

"He had a big risin' just above his pubic hair."

"A big what?" I asked.

"Risin'. It was a big carbuncle-type boil—he had had that thing for a month and Elvis thought he had syphilis. And he came out here and was sitting over there," Sam said, indicating where I was sitting. "And he said, 'Mr. Phillips, I got somethin' I'm just worried to death about.' And he was just kinda like a little kid showin' his daddy. And he showed me, and I said, 'Elvis, that's a damn risin', man, that's a carbuncle. How long you had it?' He said: 'Three to four weeks, and I just kept thinkin' it would go away. You don't think I've got somethin'?'

"He didn't say syphilis, but in his mind he was absolutely mortified. I said, 'Elvis, let's just go down to the hospital and have that boil lanced.' "

Sam wound up his story: "I had to go in with him. Anyway, finally the doctor lanced the thing with his scalpel and that thing shot up like two feet, I'm not lyin'. It surprised the doctor. Doctor thought it was gonna ease out, but that thing was so deeply embedded."

What I love about this story is that it's such a revealing glimpse of the young Elvis, still a scared kid mystified by what has suddenly become of him. It's almost a metaphor for Elvis confronting the mystery of himself: a risin' that shot up from some deeply embedded place on the pelvis of the body politic.

Elvis was a risin', Elvis still *is* a risin', although now Elvis culture is risin' like a vast tidal swell. Yet it's a risin' that still raises the same divisive question: Is the shooting up of this deeply embedded phenomenon therapeutic, an expression of healing, or an eruption of disease?

Parchman

The Mississippi State Penitentiary in Parchman is everything the legend prepared you for: Set amidst broiling flat fields once worked by convicts under the discipline of the whip, the brick-oven cell blocks still breed riots in the heat (one nasty one just a month or so before we arrived); the Abandon All Hope gates still radiate grim menace.

Parchman. For decades, the name alone could send a shiver of fear through

Mississippians. It was the spectral enforcer of the harsh police-state-like system the poor of both races labored under, the hell within the hell of sharecropper misery, a theme of the dirgelike Delta blues, many of which were born as convict songs on Parchman's prison farms.

Parchman was the Presley family secret. It was to Parchman that Elvis's father, Vernon, was consigned in 1938 when Elvis was but three. Vernon's crime? Altering a $4 check—the proceeds of a desperate Depression-era sale of the family pig—to read $14. By all accounts, the trauma of seeing his father taken away and caged was one Elvis never really recovered from, one he managed to keep a deep, dark family secret till the day he died.

There have arisen in the growing field of Elvis studies a number of theories about the primal origins of Elvis—of the talent, the charisma, and the pain. Earlier this month, for instance, a clinical psychologist, Peter Whitmer, delivered a paper at Harvard on Elvis as a "Twinless Twin," his take on the thesis that the primal defining event of Elvis's life occurred in the moments before his birth, when his twin, Jesse Garon Presley, emerged stillborn, leaving Elvis a lifelong legacy of loss, pain, and survivor guilt. Some say Elvis would "talk to" Jesse for the rest of his life. And that every song he sang was really a duet—with the ghost of his dead twin. (Other "twinless twins," according to Whitmer: Liberace, Diego Rivera, Thornton Wilder, Philip K. Dick, and—yes—Ed Sullivan.)

Others argue that it was Elvis's overly intense relationship with his mother, Gladys, that shaped him. That she was *the* love he lost when she died shortly after he joined the Army—and that every love song he ever sang was really sung to Gladys.

But I prefer what I'll call my Parchman Hypothesis: The trauma of his father's confinement initiated a lifelong dialectic, a gyration between confinement and liberation that would define the Presley psyche. A repressed childhood gave way to the liberating sound and fury of his music (like "Jailhouse Rock"), a liberation stifled when Elvis found himself imprisoned again in the Army. (Elvis died the day he entered the Army, John Lennon contended.) An incarceration followed by his release and the licentiousness of his Hollywood years; a period succeeded by the self-imprisonment of his last decade, in which he turned his own flesh into his final penitentiary, escaping the Parchman within only in death—the final jailbreak.

Indeed, probably the very last song Elvis sang, on the day of his death, was a prison lament: "Unchained Melody."

Leg Wiggle Revisionism

Confinement, of course, can take many forms. But suddenly, last summer, the possibility arose that eighteen years after his jailbreak from life, Elvis would face a form of confinement he could never have imagined: enshrinement in academia. The announcement that the University of Mississippi's highly regarded Center for the Study of Southern Culture was cosponsoring what it intended as an annual conference of "Elvis scholars," a conference that would, moreover, feature Elvis impersonators, gospel preachers, and "Memphis mafia" types touched off a brief firestorm of national controversy. While semiotic papers on Madonna have been a fixture of university "cultural studies" programs for some time, many found that the notion of Elvis scholarship transgressed the boundary between academic self-parody and outright scandal.

For the most part, the arguments that raged about the Elvis conference's right to exist were about the wrong questions. It all began as an attack by Faulkner people on Elvis people. Oxford, Mississippi, is the home of Faulkner's Rowan Oak homestead and of an annual genteel scholars' conference on his legacy at Ole Miss. Faulkner partisans denounced the university's decision to hold an Elvis conference as an act of lowbrow lèse-majesté to their high culture icon. Elvis conference organizers like Bill Ferris of the Southern Culture Center fired back—accusing the Faulkner people of the same "class-based snobbery," the prudish genteel contumely that Elvis had endured when he burst upon the scene.

The fallacy on both sides was to insist that studying the Elvis Presley phenomenon meant equating "Hound Dog" with *Light in August*. While some Elvis scholars at the conference were perfectly prepared to do just that, it's not the necessary consequence. A better way of looking at it is this: Few serious scholars would look askance at a conference of classical scholars on the subject of the Eleusinian Mystery Cults and their influence upon the reception of Christianity in the Hellenic world. And yet what were the Eleusinian mysteries but the equivalent of ecstatic rock-and-roll rites whose wild Dionysian chants, while not perhaps as elegant as Sophocles' choral laments, may have had more influence on Western culture. Just as Elvis's lyrics, while less sophisticated than Faulkner's prose, may—for better or worse—have had a more profound influence on our culture.

In fact, I found the Elvis conference itself a fascinating cultural barometer, in part because of the striking new image of Elvis that emerged from it: an Elvis who is no longer the victim of pathology as in the tell-all bios. The scholars' Elvis has more in common with the one the fans cry out to: the Healing Elvis. This is Elvis as racial integrator, as gender-liberating sexual healer. The Multicultural Elvis is an even grander figure than the one the fans conceive of—an Elvis who heals not just personal pain in individual souls but painful rifts in the nation's soul, rifts not only between black and white but between sex and spirituality in America.

I began to detect the emerging contours of the Multicultural Elvis, the King as Martin Luther King, in my conversations with an Ole Miss English professor, Vernon Chadwick, about the conflicting theories of Elvis's sexuality—or what might be called the Leg Wiggle Controversy. Chadwick was the guiding spirit of the Ole Miss Elvis conference. As perhaps academia's foremost Elvis scholar, Chadwick is an interesting combination of good-natured, native-Mississippi good ol' boy and up-to-the-second Yale-lit-bred academic. He can deploy jargon du jour like *bricoleur* to describe Elvis as an assembler of clothing "signifiers," yet still get down with sublimely nonacademic Elvis devotees like the father-son impersonator team Paul and Elvis Aaron Presley MacLeod, who have turned their home in Holly Springs, Mississippi, into a shrine called Graceland Too, open to the public twenty-four hours a day (my personal favorite stop in Elvis country).

Chadwick's academic exploration of Elvis grew out of his study of Melville. He told me about a paper he'd published on Melville's Polynesian romances (*Omoo, Typee,* etc.) as the forerunners of Elvis's cinematic Hawaiian trilogy *(Blue Hawaii, Girls! Girls! Girls!,* and *Paradise, Hawaiian Style)* in their shared preoccupation with transgressive interracial, multicultural, social, and sexual intercourse. Chadwick sees Elvis, in his Hawaiian oeuvre, as "the deconstructor of civilized prejudices and prohibitions," reenacting "the anthropological function of the 'taboo man' first delineated by Melville in *Typee.*" The taboo man being, like Elvis, a healing figure with "a special license . . . to cross boundaries—geographical, cultural, sexual, spiritual—otherwise inaccessible to the ordinary tribally regulated man."

But while Chadwick pays obeisance to Elvis as a sexual figure, his stance on the Leg Wiggle Question suggests that he and other Leg Wiggle Revisionists are not completely comfortable with Elvis's sexuality qua sexuality.

Exhibit A is Chadwick's defense of Elvis against what he regards as the Northern misperception of the Leg Wiggle. Reviewing Peter Guralnick's excellent book on the early Elvis, *Last Train to Memphis,* Chadwick wrote: "With astonishing cultural illiteracy, New York critics of the 1950s (as xenophobes still do today) mistook Elvis Presley's leg-shaking rock and roll as an obscene striptease, when in fact his moves stemmed from the provincial subworlds of Southern gospel, country, and blues that combined spiritual exaltation with bodily release." Chadwick is here following Guralnick in situating the source of the famous leg-shaking gyrations in a spiritual rather than sexual context—that is, in the frenetic, spasmodic, possessed-by-the-Word bodily movements of the Pentecostal preachers and white gospel singers of Presley's youth.

In describing Elvis's movements as only incidentally erotic, Chadwick plays down the explicitly sexual character of the pelvic thrusts and hip swivels that made teenage girls shriek. (Were those teenyboppers really responding to

Elvis's gospel roots?) You might even go so far as to say that in insisting that Elvis's sexuality is spiritual, that his groin is really responding to the gospel, Chadwick is doing to Elvis posthumously what Ed Sullivan did to him on TV:* He's cutting off his sexuality at the waist in order to sanctify him. Chadwick is, in effect, saying what Sullivan so condescendingly said about Elvis after he'd emasculated him: "This is a real decent, fine boy."

Do we really want a completely decent Elvis? I confronted Chadwick with that objection at a reception on the opening night of the Ole Miss conference. The scene was Oxford's Southside Gallery, which was hung with the works of the Reverend Howard Finster, the apocalyptic folk artist who had come to the conference to deliver "an Elvis sermon." Finster had disclosed to me his theory of the Leg Wiggle earlier that day, a far more sacralized version of it than even Chadwick adhered to. For Finster, a self-proclaimed "man of visions" who says he's been visited himself by an angelic vision of Elvis, the Leg Wiggle was on a Mission for God: "Elvis was sent by God to revive sex," he told me, to "stimulate sex and nature" at a time America needed to raise its reproduction rate. Elvis was, although the reverend didn't put it this way, a fertility totem, the baby maker of the baby boom. (Presumably that's why, when God saw the population rising *too* rapidly, He sent us The Captain and Tennille.)

"I'd defend myself this way," Chadwick said in response to my view that spiritualizing Elvis's sexuality was doing an Ed Sullivan job on him. "In Southern spirituality, spiritual exaltation is close to bodily release, and that bodily release implies as well a healthy spiritual and sexual concept."

Again the emphasis on wholesomeness, on health, on Elvis as a kind of singing Bill Moyers–Joseph Campbell figure. God forbid Elvis should be allowed to be purely sexy or—horrors—frankly and joyfully "dirty."

But Chadwick has even more grandiose claims to make on behalf of Elvis's sexuality—as a kind of profound nationwide sexual healing force.

"In his second preface to *Leaves of Grass,*" Chadwick told me, "Whitman directly targets American popular culture and literature and says it must be more accurate to the true nature of sexual experience and have a strong sexual content. I see Elvis as the Second Whitman, the second stage of the Whitman sexual revolution."

I wondered at the importance Chadwick and other Elvis scholars at the conference attached to the wholesomeness of Elvis's sexuality—the tendency to see him as a saintly figure. (Or more: Chadwick even went so far as to tell a conference audience that Elvis's "Don't Be Cruel" was analogous to the Sermon on the Mount! Even academics can't resist the Elvis-Jesus analogy.) In part, I think it has something to do with the importance Elvis has for Southern

---

*Sullivan made sure his TV cameras showed Elvis only from the waist up.

liberal scholars seeking a redemptive vision of their native region, eager to find a source of health in a culture widely stereotyped as "redneck"— particularly on the even more contentious and significant question of race.

Death Night: The Hour of the Great White Hurt

The whiteness of Elvis culture: It's not the first thing you notice on Death Night, but it's something you can't help seeing. While some black musicians like James Brown and B. B. King have paid tribute to the way Elvis opened up mainstream opportunities for them, judging by the crowds during Death Week the black public is comparatively indifferent.

Certainly, you notice other things on Death Night: the wheelchairs, for instance, the clutch of crippled Elvis pilgrims, many from overseas. Their passage here had been paid for by fan clubs who give Graceland-trip scholarships to the handicapped in search of healing for the soul, if not the body. And, yes, you notice the impersonators, many in father-son pairs. Then you notice the tears, the way the flickering candle flames are reflected in the tracks of the tears running down the faces of the pilgrims patiently standing in that serpentine line up the driveway to the Meditation Garden and the grave—the Elvis fan's stairway to heaven.

And you notice certain people you've seen before. The blond middle-aged woman you'd seen at the Ole Miss Elvis Conference, not an academic but a dedicated acolyte. She'd become an Elvis fan, she had told me down there, not because of his music but because of his pain.

She'd identified with Elvis, she said, because she saw him—as she saw herself—as the victim of a dysfunctional alcoholic family. "If you study the family history," she told me, "you'd see: It was passed down." But unlike Elvis, she'd rescued herself, she said, with a twelve-step program. And now by getting into Elvis's pain, she was somehow mourning her own and forgiving herself. I found her on Death Night lingering at the Meditation Garden after she'd knelt by the grave, her cheeks still streaked with tears, lingering there crying, she said, because she was feeling his pain. It's an example of how exposés of Elvis's sins and vices, like his gargantuan prescription-drug abuse problem, often have the effect—particularly in a twelve-step recovery and redemption-oriented culture—not of repelling but of drawing fans closer to him as fellow victim and sufferer.

You also notice the silent communion at the grave marker. The way so many stopped and seemed to engage in some kind of intense communication with the man buried there. They don't think he's alive. I found very few who bought into the Elvis-faked-his-death-and-can-be-seen-buying-Big-Gulps-at-Kalamazoo-7-Elevens theory. But they do think he's some kind of Living

Presence. While it's true that many were just fervent fans paying their respects to a man whose music moved them, many more spoke of him as a kind of higher being, "up there in heaven," who hears their prayers, who understands them the way no one on earth could.

What kind of being are they talking about or talking to? I had an illuminating conversation on that question with Charles Reagan Wilson, professor of history at Ole Miss and author of a forthcoming book, *Judgment and Grace in Dixie: Southern Faiths from Faulkner to Elvis.* Wilson says that for Elvis's religiously inclined followers, he occupies a kind of intermediary realm that "blurs the boundaries between the supernatural and the sacred, something like the way UFOs do for believers." That Elvis is a figure more than human, less than divine, with elements of St. Francis of Assisi and E.T.

Certainly, you can be impressed with the sincerity of the devotees and admire the improvisational rituals people devise to find ways of healing themselves. But you still can't help wondering at how few black faces there are. In the nearly four hours we spent drifting up and down the serpentine trail of tears—it was long after midnight when we left—we saw only one black family.

This is not to say that Elvis culture is racist, or that Elvis was racist. But it does make one skeptical about some of the more extreme claims made for the Multicultural Elvis of the Ole Miss conference, particularly the claim that Elvis had been the medium, the medicine man, through which black sexuality cured the pathologies of the white race.

Such was the expansive visionary claim made by one of the most eloquent speakers at the conference, Jon Michael Spencer, professor of music and American studies at the University of Richmond. Spencer, who is black, began his talk with a witty deconstruction of the Elvis scenes in *Forrest Gump.* If you'll recall, the young Elvis is a boarder in the Gump home at the time Forrest is forced to wear complicated leg braces. Braces that force Forrest to walk in an elaborately syncopated knock-kneed fashion, a fashion that the young, pre-stardom Elvis takes careful note of.

Professor Spencer sees the Gump version of Leg Wiggle theory as an appropriation, an erasure of the culture that was the true origin of Elvis's gyrations: "Those syncopated leg and body movements are not attributable to Forrest Gump but to the rhythms that underlie African-American music. . . ." He will not even permit the Chadwick-Guralnick attribution of the Leg Wiggle to white gospel. No, Spencer insists: "What Elvis loved in white gospel was the rhythms of *black* gospel."

Spencer insists that it was a specifically black sexuality that Elvis displayed, that Elvis became the channel for, that Elvis broadcast to white America. That what Elvis accomplished was "the sexual seduction of whites into blackness." And that it was emphatically a therapeutic seduction—the Sexual

Healing of White America. It's a healing Spencer describes in Jungian terms: "Elvis's injection of black rhythms into mainstream American culture accomplished the reconciliation of the unnatural binary oppositions between body and soul, flesh and spirit, spirit and nature."

But if white America was so profoundly and thoroughly healed by exposure to Elvis's black sexuality, would we really be as socially segregated a society as we still seem to be? On the way from the Elvis conference back to Memphis for Death Week, we'd driven up Highway 61, the blues highway (and the apocalyptic killing ground of the civil-rights era in the famous Dylan song), in order to make a special pilgrimage to the place I thought of as the real Heartbreak Hotel, the place where Bessie Smith died. It's now called the Riverside Hotel, but when the great blues lady was brought there after a car wreck on Highway 61 it was "a colored hospital," a place she bled to death in.

It was a sobering experience to see firsthand the appalling, unabated black poverty of the Delta. And it left me wondering about the optimistic vision of Spencer and the other academics at the Ole Miss conference. If Elvis so profoundly healed and integrated America, that Heartbreak Hotel where Bessie Smith died should have been as grand and as splendid a shrine as Graceland.

Healing with Vegas Soul

More curious and notable perhaps than the whiteness of the faces of Elvis culture is the whiteness—for want of a better word—of the music at its heart. Very early on, Elvis discovered that the power of big, bland ballads—weepy, syrupy crooner vehicles of the sort Pat Boone sang, songs like "Love Me Tender" and "Can't Help Falling in Love"—was far greater than the power of breakthrough rockers like "Mystery Train" and "Good Rockin' Tonight." That the power of the Leg Wiggle was exceeded by that of the tear jerk. And after 1958, with some exceptions (the brief "Suspicious Minds/Burning Love" period), it was sentimental, soap-operatic ballads like "Are You Lonesome Tonight?" and "Unchained Melody" that became the heart of his work and the soul of the Elvis cult.

It was these songs, weepy, blatantly sentimental sobbers like "You Gave Me a Mountain" and "Solitaire," that you heard pumped out over the speakers in the Memphis strip malls and souvenir shops during Death Week. It's these big broad Vegas soul ballads as suety with emotion as Elvis's peanut-butter-and-bacon diet, that the hard-core worshipers want to hear.

Vegas soul: It's a much-despised, even oxymoronic notion to some. But it's a powerful presence in mainstream American lives. While I never saw Elvis in Vegas, I once spent two weeks trying to figure out Wayne Newton's appeal there, watching two shows a night at the Aladdin Casino showroom and learning what Wayne had learned from Elvis. (Wayne has said he considers himself

Elvis's true successor in Las Vegas.) What I learned from studying Wayne was the spell those big, shamelessly sentimental Vegas ballads cast over real people. Hard-bitten couples who'd been through a marriage or two, through rocky times—cheating, money trouble—and survived to celebrate, and after a few drinks and a few songs like "Lady," "My Way," and "The Impossible Dream," they reached an emotional communion that would inscribe these songs in their souls forever. Vegas soul is not the kind of breakthrough soul that rock critics rave about, but these people don't live rock critics' lives, and, for them, it works; it heals.

It is this Elvis, the Vegas Healer, not the Young Elvis, who is at the heart of the posthumous cult. America put the Young Elvis on its postage stamps; as the novelist Kay Sloan put it at the Ole Miss conference, it was the Young Elvis who empowered her generation of women to become "romantic revolutionaries," but it is the Late Elvis—the old, fat, sweaty Vegas Elvis—that America has taken to its heart.

Dramatic confirmation of this can be found in Elvis impersonator culture, which I've come to believe is the key to understanding the mystery and power of the Elvis religious experience.

I had spent considerable time talking to impersonators in the course of my journey through Elvis country, and what I found reversed my preconceptions. I'd assumed impersonators would be thuggish exhibitionist types, the kind of obsessives you'd want to avoid like a plague. But I came away impressed by how many of them were remarkably gentle fellows, soft-spoken, good-humored, and—surprisingly, considering their stage act—shy. They're dreamers: I remember the father in a father-son impersonator pair from Dubuque telling me an elaborate fantasy (although I'm not sure he realized it was) about running into Lisa Marie Presley on the grounds of Graceland on Death Night a year ago. "She was disguised as a security guard," he assured me. And he, of course, was disguised as Elvis. "But when she saw me, it was like she was sure she was seeing her father. She didn't want to let on, but we both knew." It was a lovely, almost Shakespearean fantasy of communion through double disguises, a tribute to the way Elvis liberated his imagination.

Another impersonator complained to me about how the judging in the increasingly professionalized impersonator contest network is prejudiced, if not rigged. This guy, who's a Jersey cop in his day job, had recently come in second in an important regional contest wearing the white jumpsuit and rhinestone-studded belt of the Vegas Elvis.

"Why only second?" I asked him.

"What you find is that a Young Elvis will almost always take first place— guaranteed," he said with a trace of bitterness. "It's the athleticism they get to display. But where it counts, on stage, the people love the Late Elvis best."

There are those who argue that the communion between "the people" and the Late Elvis impersonator is at the very heart and soul of the healing power of Elvis spirituality. Mark Gottdiener, for instance. Gottdiener is chairman of the department of sociology at the State University of New York at Buffalo, and his talk at the Ole Miss conference had been billed with the unfortunate title "Elvis as a Sign System." But Gottdiener proved to be a keen observer of the dynamics of Elvis culture.

For one thing, he offered a provocative new take on the Elvis-Jesus question, a revision of Greil Marcus's view. Gottdiener suggests that Elvis doesn't function *as* Jesus in Elvis culture; rather, Elvis is "the other Jesus."

The other Jesus is the permissive savior, the indulgent, carnal, materialistic object of worship. Gottdiener argues that while "commodification" of the real Jesus can border on the blasphemous, Elvis gave permission for his celebrators to wallow in glitzy, even sleazy paraphernalia. Elvis liquor decanters, for instance, swept the South in the seventies and are now prized icons in Elvis culture, but one can hardly imagine Jesus liquor decanters. What the other Jesus has in common with the real one, Gottdiener argues, is that he gives his celebrants permission, encouragement, to express love.

Here's where the impersonators come in. Gottdiener sees the impersonator experience as the central communion, the agape, or love feast, of Elvis spirituality, an emotionally liberating opening to a feeling of intimacy. The impersonator gives permission in his hokey setting for people to invoke love, the emotion, the feeling of intimacy that they might not give in to otherwise.

If this sounds abstract, I have to admit something very much like it happened to me the night during Death Week that I saw Duke Mason, a four-foot-tall Elvis impersonator, rock the house with his rousing version of "Viva Las Vegas." Okay, maybe I'd spent just a little too much time in Elvis country—perhaps the cultural equivalent of the Stockholm syndrome had set in—but I found myself genuinely moved by the way the pint-size, pompadoured impersonator took the stage and transformed himself into a giant. I'd been resisting the pervasive sentimentality of Elvis culture, but couldn't help feeling a welling affection, not just for Duke but for Elvis. For having the power from beyond the grave to create this bizarre but touching moment.

But if Gottdiener sees the impersonators primarily as figures of love, he doesn't neglect what seems to me a more potent factor in the posthumous Elvis cult: pain. In fact, Gottdiener came up with a striking parallel to the impersonator phenomenon in the scary cult of the Penitentes. The Penitentes were a sect of American Indian converts to Christianity who once flourished in the Southwest. The centerpiece of their frightening rituals is the Good Friday reenactment of the crucifixion—in which one of their members is literally nailed to the cross, while others scar and mutilate themselves in the pattern of Christ's wounds. They are, in a sense, Jesus impersonators who carry the Imitation of Christ to a bloody literal conclusion.

Gottdiener sees Elvis impersonators as Penitentes, but I'd suggest that Elvis *himself* was the chief Penitente—a Pain Artist, exhibiting his suffering the way Kafka's Hunger Artist made his starvation a spectacle. Elvis crucifying himself with needles rather than nails, Elvis making a Penitente-like spectacle of his self-destruction. You can hear it in the pain-filled lyrics of his last songs, see it in the tapes of his final performances. That pain, as much as love, is the medium of communion between him and his posthumous cult, the sense that by immersing themselves in Elvis's pain, by feeling his pain, they're somehow healing their own.

Still, the question remains: What was the source of that hurt?

Pay No Attention to the Man Behind the Curtain

When you think about it, the whole slick and professional Graceland tour is really structured around an elision, an omission, a single forbidden vista: the room Behind the Curtain, the Death Room. You barely even get a glimpse of the curtain on the tour. But if you look straight up as you enter the front door, if your eyes follow the carpeted staircase leading to the second floor, your gaze ends abruptly at a thick, dark blue curtain—the Dark at the Top of the Stairs that shuts off the bedroom suite where Elvis died.

The tour doesn't go there. Virtually no one goes there. "The family," meaning Elvis's ex-wife, Priscilla, and his daughter, Lisa Marie, have declared it off-limits to the Graceland tour, which one can understand. But curiously they've decreed that the suite be kept exactly as it was the day Elvis died, almost as if they were keeping it ready for his return. Almost as if by keeping it unchanged, it might still be possible for fate to change its mind and take a different turn. (Or perhaps they're keeping it closed off to give unofficial license to the notion that he's still alive, he's still up there.) Whatever the motive, it's a bit of showbiz worthy of Colonel Parker.

One night in Graceland after the tours and the staff had left, I found myself virtually alone with the forbidden vista, unable to take my eyes off the curtain at the top of the stairs. The security guard told me that although he'd worked at Graceland for more than ten years, he'd never himself had a glimpse of what was behind the curtain. Only a few trusted cleaning people were permitted back there.

"There's millions of people who would give their right arm for one look up there," he told me.

"What is the biggest mystery about Elvis to you?" I'd asked him.

He had no hesitation. "What was it he was going through the last six months, what was going through his head."

Or to put it another way, what kind of pain was he wrestling with?

I spoke to many Elvisian figures in search of an answer, even Colonel

Parker himself. But the most provocative explanation emerged in a conversation I had with Larry Geller, Elvis's former hairdresser and spiritual adviser. A highly controversial figure in Elvisian literature dissed by some rivals in the entourage for leading Elvis astray, Geller has led a fascinating life in the penumbra of stardom. A onetime associate in the Hollywood salon of Jay Sebring, the *Shampoo*-like stylist to the stars who was murdered by the Manson family, Geller left Sebring in 1964 to become Elvis's full-time hair-care guy. A position that grew into spiritual confidant as he initiated Elvis into a hodge-podge of esoteric mystical and theosophical books and systems—most notably a perennial metaphysical chestnut called *The Impersonal Life,* a tome that Elvis would enthusiastically press upon the cast and crew of *Tickle Me* and other Hollywood classics he was working on.

Elvis was far more intellectually curious and spiritually aware than many give him credit for, Geller insists—a genuine seeker, desperate to find an answer to the question, "Why me?" Why on earth had an obscure truck-driving teenager been singled out for the kind of renown few saints and prophets had ever known? He was sure there must be a reason, he must have a mission to fulfill—a reason for his risin'—and he was insatiable in his search for it.

Perhaps feeling that Geller's influence threatened the cash cow they relied upon, certain members of Presley's entourage tried to turn Elvis against Geller. Geller resigned, and shortly thereafter Elvis and Priscilla proceeded to ceremonially burn all Elvis's mystical books. (The Bonfire of the Inanities?) But, according to Geller, Elvis summoned him back to Graceland shortly before he died and the two made ambitious plans to make a film of Kahlil Gibran's *Prophet*. On the day of Elvis's death, Geller says, he gave Elvis the book he was reading in the bathroom when he died: *The Scientific Search for the Face of Jesus.*

Geller's account gives us a picture of a more complex and self-aware Elvis than either the hagiographies or the hostile tell-alls. And a more interesting explanation for the pain: Burning those books left him with a hunger for spiritual sustenance, a void within as big as the cosmos, a hole in his soul he couldn't fill with peanut butter or bacon. (Although he clearly tried.) Geller gives us Elvis: Victim of Existential Pain.

The question remains, though, what is it about the pain of the Man Behind the Curtain that Americans continue to be drawn to? One answer suggested itself to me in a conversation at the Sun Studio Cafe. This is the low-key, funky eating place next door to the now legendary hole-in-the-wall recording studio where many say rock-and-roll itself was invented by Sam Phillips, the place where Elvis was discovered or invented when Sam coaxed a sound out of him that hadn't been heard before. Sun is still a working studio (U2 made a pilgrimage to record there some years ago), as well as a shrine, and it has a kind of vitality that the mausoleum-like Graceland lacks.

A couple of pilgrims at the Sun Cafe were discussing the difference. "This is a place of life," one woman was saying, "while Graceland—I was just over there and it's so *sad*."

"Sad because of what became of him?" I asked her.

"No," she said, "sad because of what became of *us*."

But that's precisely why America has come to love and embrace the Late, Fat, Pain-Racked, Self-Destructive Elvis. It's a way of coming to terms with our own sense of loss, with what's become of us as a nation—the transition America has made from the young, vital, innocent pioneer nation we once were (the young, vital Elvis we put on our stamps) to the bloated colossus we feel we've become: the Fat Elvis of nations. For America, finding a way to love the fat, sweaty figure Elvis turned into, the heartbroken, pain- and pill-filled impersonator of greatness, may be our way of finding, in our *own* fat fate, some forgiveness, some humor, even some healing.

Some Personal Matters

Victims of The Dance

The Unbearable Sadness of Tear Gas

Spiritual Lessons from L.A.

Stumpy versus Lucille: The Great Pet Debate

Victims of The Dance

For some time now, I've wanted to write a kind of tribute to that elite group of beautiful tragic souls who more than any other group define the uniqueness of New York. Whose presence and numbers distinguish this city from all the other great cities in the world. Those lovely intense spirits I think of as Victims of *The Dance*.

All those brave, limber, fiercely idealistic young women who come to New York from all over the world, drawn by the mystique of The Dance. The ones who, like beautiful doomed mayflies, burn out their brief youth with the frightening intensity of their devotion to an elusive, impossible ideal of spiritualized aesthetic transcendence. The ones who slave themselves into near-starvation, refine their bodies and souls into a state of impossible purity in order to serve the dictates of demented choreographers, and mad dance savants. Who sacrifice all the other more practical paths in life for a few brief moments on some bare, drafty stage in a badly lit SoHo loft, their finely honed limbs often tormented into impossibly pretentious, neo-expressionist or emptily minimalist postures, hoping to salvage from the dross and fakery of so many contemporary productions one pure moment of rapturous communion with the elusive evanescent—perhaps nonexistent—Spirit of *The Dance*. Before . . .

Before what? Before reaching twenty-seven or maybe thirty and realizing the cruel fleeting grail of The Dance has robbed them of their youth, left them like the victims of *"La Belle Dame Sans Merci,"* "alone and palely loitering," looking through the temp ads in their organic cafés, wondering what's left in life that could possibly compensate for what they sacrificed, what they've lost, what they loved.

I was reminded of the tragic plight of Victims of The Dance, I was reminded how much I, too, am, in a way, a collateral Victim of The Dance (well, of the dancers who caused me so much splendid misery) by something I noticed on a recent visit to Dance Theater Workshop. A small notice on a bulletin board offering "Therapy for Dancers seeking to make 'career transitions.' " A euphemistic way of saying transition out of The Dance, the transition from the realm of the sublime to the realm of the mundane and the ridiculous the rest of us occupy.

It was the first time in a while I'd ventured into a venue like Dance Theater Workshop. Places like that tend to bring back too many memories of my first years in the city when I was always under the spell of one Victim of The Dance or another. But some friends had an extra ticket to the drag Joni Mitchell performance—you know, that guy John Kelly who "channels" Ms. Mitchell's spirit with an eerily near-identical approximation of her singing voice and her folky bohemian moves. I was skeptical, but it turned out to be not some camp oddity, but what I thought was a brilliant piece of theater. A funny, touching, *thoughtful* meditation on the fine line between sensibility and sentimentality. One that allowed you, through the distancing scrim of drag, to really experience Joni Mitchell afresh again beneath the stylistic tics, the accretions of cliché her imitators have inscribed on her image.

I found myself responding to songs such as her amazing, haunting Amelia Earhart ballad from *Hejira* (that refrain *"it was just a false alarm"* still kills me) in a way I hadn't in years. It brought back the Joni Mitchell who's fascinated artists as disparate as Prince and Bob Dylan (who once revealed to me, in an interview, that he wrote the song "Tangled Up in Blue"—one of his all-time greats—after spending a lost weekend playing Joni Mitchell's *Blue* album over and over and over again).

The whole thing put me in an enormously sentimental mood, made me think of the dancers I'd known—their brave Amelia-like adventurousness, their leg warmers, their fifty-pound sacks of millet.

I think it's the millet that says it all. I was fortunate when I first came to New York to find myself a dancer girlfriend; she'd come from Wisconsin to study with Merce Cunningham, Alwin Nikolais, and other downtown luminaries; she'd gone mushroom hunting with John Cage! She found us an apartment—one handed down to her from other dancers—a real treasure, she said, just over the bridge in Brooklyn, although it turned out it was about a forty-minute IRT ride way out to the heart of Crown Heights in a large apartment building where we were the only white people. In other circumstances, we might have been looked upon as intruders, but somehow her dancer's aura, her exotic dance rehearsal clothes and the fifty-pound sacks of millet won us the protective respect accorded to the truly mad.

The millet was basically what she and her dancer friends seemed to live on year in year out, a way of reducing expenses for sustenance to the point of nothingness in order to support their art. Really, they all seemed to live on air, but every now and then they'd pool their resources and lug huge sacks of the cheapest raw grains home from some wholesale organic market and spend hours, weeks, boiling and boiling and boiling the stony millet until it softened sufficiently to serve as porridge or be mixed with the dried lentils that were forever soaking in huge pots.

Someone should do a study of dancers' diets, which often seem to be artfully sublimated, aestheticized versions of anorexia. There was one particularly intense dancer I knew in SoHo who seemed to live on nothing but the pickled ginger she cadged from the Sushi Boutique (as we used to call it) on West Broadway and Prince Street. It was scary the ways they'd find to mortify the body, the better to serve the spirit.

The millet was a symbol of their power to transubstantiate the most recalcitrant earthiness into the pure energy of the spiritual sublime. It was, I finally realized, more than an art they were engaged in, it was a religious vocation, one to which they brought an ascetic, spiritual devotion, one from which they derived a St. Teresa–like ecstasy that was both sensual and soulful. I was always immensely in awe of it: of the clear-eyed transformative radiance that set them apart from all others.

Indeed, that night at Dance Theater Workshop, as we awaited the performance, my friends and I found ourselves spotting them, scattered among the audience (and especially among the staff): these rare creatures with the unmistakably distinctive dancer aura. It had something to do with the posture and the gaze. The posture that suggests less an osseous spine like the rest of us, but a bolt of pure energy animating their being, shining out from their eyes. The brilliant clarity and directness of dancers' eyes is almost painful to look at by those of us who see the world through a bloodshot fog. Their eyes are inextinguishable beacons of that rarest of rare qualities in this city: non-ironic hopefulness.

It's the posture, the eyes, yes, but also the walk. Philip Greenberg of *The New York Times* recently did a photo feature (called "If It Walks Like a Duck . . .") in which he approached women in the street just on the basis of their walk and asked them if they were dancers, found he was almost invariably able to spot the ones who were. It's more than a matter of ballet turnout. That can be a give-away; but even nonclassically trained dancers have a walk like no other walk. A radiant resilient walk that I'd argue is one of the most distinctive, attractive, unique assets of New York as a cityscape. The fact that here in New York, far more frequently than in any city in the world, on almost any block, at almost any moment, one can run into one of these Ariel-like sylphs bestowing on the drab concrete sidewalks and streets, on the fear- and angst-crazed faces of its citizens, the benefice of their Higher Mode of Dancer Being—it's one of the things that makes this city civilized.

The street is their stage. Those who may not star in some pretentious postmodern-minimalist, foundation grant–supported, neo-expressionist loft-theater vanity production, still get to star every day on the streets they illuminate with their inimitable presence. They perform for all of us just by passing by.

Which brings me to that notice on the bulletin board at Dance Theater Workshop. The one about "career transition" therapy for dancers who pass the cruel cutoff age of twenty-seven to thirty. The dark side of the dance fantasy. The moment that comes so soon for so many of them, when the choreographers avert their eyes because they've become too old, too familiar, yesterday's news. Victims of The Dance.

The moment when they realize that if they don't have the money to fund their own company or get funded as choreographers, they're on their way out of the cruelly Darwinian dance world. They'll have to face joining the faceless crowd of strivers, the throng of the earthbound. Usually without having developed any of the practical skills necessary to survive, much less thrive on more than millet for the rest of their lives.

Life is unfair, yes, but it's *more* than unfair for them to have to bear the burden alone. After all, they sacrificed their youth for *us,* to illuminate *our* dreary lives by their very presence in the streets. Don't you think we owe them?

The notice on the Dance Theater Workshop bulletin board turned out to be the phone number for a program called Career Transitions for Dancers, organized by the Actors Fund of America. There's another program, called the International Organization for the Transition of Professional Dancers, which gives scholarships to dancers (both men and women, I should point out) who want to resume their dance-interrupted college educations. The latter group administers a scholarship program funded by Caroline Newhouse, a sculptor and painter who is generously looking out for these lost Victims of The Dance. A *Times* piece on the scholarship program poignantly noted that "to qualify for help, dancers must be over twenty-seven years or unable to perform because of injury." Over twenty-seven years! But the magic, the walk, doesn't die at twenty-seven. It can illuminate the space around us all for long after.

I'd suggest that supporting Victims of The Dance should be a task for all of us, as a city, to undertake in a serious way. If the city funds an expensive landmarks-preservation program, aren't these living, breathing landmarks, the ones who animate our streets and sidewalks with their very walk, at *least* as worthy of serious municipal protection? I almost feel that dancers shouldn't *have* to go back to school and learn some boring trade, some pathetic, meretricious profession. They'd lose the magic! They deserve better than that! I believe the Giuliani administration should seriously investigate my modest proposal: that dancers who no longer can find work in some little SoHo company or other shouldn't have to become bank clerks or computer programmers. They should be subsidized by the city—with money and plenty of millet—*just for being among us,* just for walking around, just for illuminating our lives with their aura, their eyes, their graceful spirituality, and their stride.

The Unbearable Sadness
of Tear Gas

As the Democrats gather to nominate a president in Chicago for the first time since 1968's riot-torn, tear gas–saturated, head-banging, history-changing, election-losing, whole-world-is-watching apocalyptic debacle; as the debate over the larger meaning of 1968 has been raised to world-historical status by Paul Berman's provocative thesis (in *A Tale of Two Utopias*) that the spirit of 1968 was *really* what brought down the Wall in 1989; as the whole idea of the sixties has devolved into a deadly serious scholarly debate (see *Lingua Franca*'s recent "Who Owns the '60s?" issue); I feel justified at last in sharing with a waiting world my own, more modest, more Forrest Gump–like experience of Chicago 1968. An experience that nonetheless changed my life and turned me into a journalist. An experience whose most vivid memories now seem focused on the twin themes of tear gas and apocalyptic euphoria.

I suppose I should begin by putting my pitifully naive 1968 self in perspective. I had just graduated college that spring; I had very little to shield me from the Vietnam draft beyond a one-year Carnegie fellowship in the Yale English department, a place where I'd spent the previous four years burrowing away from the twentieth century back into the seventeenth, into the world of the metaphysical poets.

I loved it, but I was feeling an itch to be part of my own century again. (The only demonstration I participated in was to protest the denial of tenure to a metaphysically inclined philosophy professor ousted by the hard-line Analyticals.) I *had* spent one weekend as a volunteer for Eugene McCarthy's antiwar primary campaign in New Hampshire (lured there by a bohemian Smith girl who wore a *Bonnie and Clyde* beret). And when, following McCarthy's surprise showing in the primary, President Johnson promptly announced he wouldn't run for reelection, I had a sudden heady seizure of feeling (however unrealistic) that I had participated in the overthrow of a government.

And then, on the awful morning of June 6 when I awoke to discover Bobby Kennedy had been assassinated, I decided I had to be there in Chicago, be there at ground zero for what was looking to be a bitter, violent end to the whole apocalyptic drama of 1968.

At the time, I had no experience as a journalist, but I managed to convince the editor of a soon-to-fold Long Island daily, *The Suffolk Sun,* to give me an assignment letter; and I set out for Chicago in a hand-me-down '61 Chevy Bel Air, which coated the interstate with the oil it was leaking.

Then when I got to Chicago, I got two lucky breaks: First, they gave me a press credential, the first one I had ever had. A really low-status press credential, to be sure; in fact, I think it was called, insultingly, a "Peripheral Pass," but it permitted me access to press conferences in the convention hotels, allowed me to experience for the first time that completely delicious press-pass mode of being—in it, but not of it, able to cruise through chaos and tragedy looking sympathetic but knowing all the time that it's ultimately all *great material.*

My second lucky break involved housing. I had virtually no money and no place lined up to stay, so—on the strength of my strenuous weekend of doorbell ringing with the Smith girl in New Hampshire, which brought down the government—I applied at McCarthy-for-President headquarters for free housing with one of the liberal families in Chicago who were helping the cause by offering guest rooms to volunteers. It wasn't a complete scam; I thought maybe I'd put in some time helping the McCarthyites out although, in fact, I never got around to it. But it turns out I lucked into an assignment to an extremely well-connected family who gave me a big guest room in their elegant town house. And invited me to what would turn out to be *the* wicked media-politico party of the convention week, one of whose wicked highlights took place in my bedroom.

But first, a digression on tear gas. I got gassed the first night I got to Chicago, and several nights thereafter, but there's nothing like the first time. It was a Sunday night, I believe, the papers were filled with screaming headlines about the Soviet invasion of Czechoslovakia, adding an international dimension to the tension over the antiwar movement's invasion of Chicago. One of the brilliant Yippie agitprop masters had rechristened Chicago "Czechago" in an attempt to link the onrushing confrontation with the Chicago cops to the worldwide clash between authority and dissent. Paul Berman has, with good-natured hindsight, adumbrated the ideological confusion in the linkage: The Movement was in Chicago to protest a war against a Soviet-style state (North Vietnam) that was supported by the same Soviet police state that was crushing our supposed allies-in-dissent in Czechoslovakia. But as Mr. Berman also points out, for better or worse, 1968 was not so much about ideological consistency as it was about the spirit of rebellion—at its best, anarchic, antinomian, even Blakean in its radical innocence, on the side of dissent in general against oppressive authority in general. At its worst, misguided, sectarian, and willfully ignorant, but certainly no more willfully ignorant than those sending hundreds of thousands to die in a misguided war.

The impossibility of having the right historical perspective, the long view, in the short-fused heat of the moment, is part of the tears of things, the part one always learns too late. In the heat of the moment, there is only the tear gas of things. In any case, that night, the first night of "Czechago," was the first time I heard the crack of tear gas–grenade launchers, the vicious hiss and sizzle as the canisters landed, as a mass of Chicago cops beat and gassed the gathering protesters out of their encampment in Lincoln Park.

Although I've been tear-gassed covering riots a half dozen times since then and had gotten to the point where I could savor the fine distinctions between the pure elixir of tears and the advanced pepper gas variations, the experience still has a kind of absurdity to it that has rarely been remarked upon. It's almost like some Kurt Vonnegut riff: The Evil Planetary Warlords decide "We're gonna defeat the rebel forces by making them unbearably *sad.*" It's almost as if today's psychologically sophisticated FBI were to try lobbing George Jones and Tammy Wynette tapes into David Koresh's Waco compound, blasting Emmylou Harris weepers to the Montana Freemen.

Yes, I know, tear gas at first only creates the physiological simulacrum of sadness. But if you're surrounded by hundreds of people with hot tears streaming down their faces (some laced with blood), believe me, it makes you feel *genuinely* sad. The forcible irritation of the tear glands can compel the emotional effect to follow. Only in the twentieth century would authority manifest itself as *emotional* terrorism. Perhaps some of the sadness I felt had something to do with the problematic emotional memories any kind of enforced gassing can evoke in this century. Or perhaps it afflicts those naturally predisposed to tune in to the tears of things.

But Chicago introduced me to another paradoxical effect of tear gas: tear gas as an aphrodisiac. Perhaps it was the synergistic effect of tear gas and adrenaline on the nervous system, perhaps it was something physical—irritants coursing through the bloodstream. Or something as complex and metaphysical as the feeling Milan Kundera conjures up in his account (in *The Unbearable Lightness of Being*) of the feverish air of Prague that very weekend in 1968: "The Russian invasion was not only a tragedy; it was a carnival of hate filled with a curious (and no longer explicable) euphoria."

A carnival of hate, filled with a curious erotic euphoria. It's rarely been reported and, as Mr. Kundera says, it's not really explicable, but it was going on: People were getting *busy,* knocking boots all over Chicago, one of the places being, as it turned out, my guest bedroom. It was something I discovered not long after I returned from the Lincoln Park riot to find that wicked party I spoke of reaching a peak, as people came in from all over the city, buzzed and jazzed by adrenaline and the gas vapors still clinging to their clothes. There was a sizable literary contingent there, Styron, Mailer, Jean Genet, network people, antiwar-movement figures, liberal politicos and, I seem to recall, Abbie Hoffman put in an appearance. Certainly his absurdist spirit was everywhere that week.

Everybody at the party was feeling doubly buzzed, not just from the whiff of the gas but from the whiff of the apocalypse in the air, a sense that we were witness to a moment when familiar things were about to spin out of control, perhaps forever. Still, I had a deadline to meet; I had to file my first dispatch for *The Suffolk Sun* the next morning, so I reluctantly left the party and made my way up to my second-floor guest bedroom to work on a first draft I'd left lying on my typewriter.

Curiously, I found the door closed and locked. I knocked, heard some stirring inside, and then suddenly the door burst open and a man and a woman, faces flushed with excitement, rushed past me out the door.

I'm disguising some details here, but let's just say the guy was a well-known cultural figure, and the woman was the wife of a different well-known cultural figure. Now it's *possible* they were flushed and excited from having stumbled on the first draft of my *Suffolk Sun* story, carried away with the breathtaking prose.

However, I suspect something more was going on, that they'd both been swept away by the immanent spirit of '68-ness, which imprinted itself on the lives of just about everyone who was there in Chicago that week.

But it wasn't until a full twenty years later that I realized how deeply imprinted it was on all three of us. Because two decades later, I had a fascinating encounter with the two of them. Had not seen them since, although I had heard through the grapevine that, not long after that night in Chicago, their first night together, they'd left their respective spouses, gotten married and stayed together ever since. That euphoric tear gas night in 1968 had changed their lives forever the way Chicago changed a *lot* of lives with, I'm sure, no shortage of tears as well as euphoria in consequence.

We were, the three of us, getting our coats at the end of some end-of-the-eighties New York party; we all looked at one another curiously. They introduced themselves. I remember one of them saying something like "Haven't we met before?" and the other saying "You look *very* familiar."

Really, they didn't know me from Adam; but my features, now twenty years older, still registered from that one intensely imprinted instant at that bedroom door.

I wasn't sure how to respond: Something told me *not* to make explicit their vague recollection, that it would be somehow intrusive to remind them how we'd first met. I don't think they quite believed me when I said I didn't think we'd met before. Or maybe they knew I knew, and we all let the moment pass without the need to speak of it. Because we shared an understanding beyond words, the shared sense of having been part of the secret society of that year, that night.

Spiritual Lessons from L.A.

I get a little irritated at the knee-jerk anti-California attitudes of a certain kind of New Yorker, the type who feels he can establish his intellectual seriousness by putting down Los Angeles.

As for me, I love L.A., not in a Kandy Kolored Randy Newmanesque way, but in a noirish, Raymond Chandler, *Chinatown,* Rickie Lee Jones/Tom Waits, bitter-romantic, seedy-disillusioned, Sandra Bernhard/Bruce Wagner, melancholy-dreamer way. *The Pat Hobby Stories** as opposed to *The Last Tycoon.* Aldous Huxley in the hills, Krishnamurti in the Canyons, David & David on the speakers, getting in touch with my inner Jackson Browne, the one that loves romantic sleaze, the emotional spectrum from *Day of the Locust* and *The Long Goodbye* to *Late for the Sky.*

And I think the anti-L.A. poseurs are missing something; either they've never really been there, or they're too intellectually insecure to realize that L.A. is a great place for Learning; the city has much to Teach. I feel I've

The Pat Hobby Stories are Fitzgerald's underappreciated last works, bitter comic tales of a desperate over-the-hill hack screenwriter, Fitzgerald's self-mocking vision of his own L.A. crack-up.

learned something new, something revealing about America, about myself, every time I've been there. I was reflecting on the kinds of spiritual lessons I've learned from the City of Angels the other night at the Screening Room party for the Chateau Marmont *Hollywood Handbook*. A party filled with beautiful L.A. types and New Yorkers muttering about how superficial they all were (not me: I knew they were spiritual teachers in disguise). The Hotel California affair made me realize how many of my L.A. memories, the lessons I learned, were hotel-haunted. Although not the first one, the radiant first time I arrived in the city and learned the meaning of "high on the hog."

I'd been up in San Francisco researching a story for Harold Hayes at *Esquire* on the spectacular but doomed black prison revolutionary movement centered around Angela Davis and George Jackson. The mother of a defendant in a Soledad prison murder trial—a fascinating woman who'd just made the curious choice to join the Communist Party, but who (perhaps even more curiously) had a thing for Carole King's *Tapestry* album (something to do with the sentimentality at the core of the Party and the music?)—asked me to drive her and a friend down to L.A. I leaped at the excuse; I'd never been there before.

We drove all night down the fast but treacherous central route known as "the Grapevine," the mountainous road that was shrouded to the point of invisibility by an opaque fog, intermittently pierced only by the reflective squares of the midline, which floated up toward you through the thick white cotton as if you were cruising dreamily through the clouds—occasional gleams of reality that were barely enough to keep you from plunging down a ravine.

As dawn broke over the Bakersfield flats, the C.P. mom guided us straight into Watts, to an amazing place called Ray's. It was a Saturday night turning into a Sunday morning, so there was a clash of resplendently arrayed crowds—late-night partygoers and players winding down, and early-morning churchgoers firing up. To thank me for driving, she bought me the supreme Ray's treat, maybe the best breakfast I've ever had, something the menu called "High on the Hog," a mountain of savory scrambled eggs crowned with a succulent golden-fried pork chop encircled with bright yellow cheese grits.

It was in Ray's that I was clued into the true historical origin of the phrase "high on the hog" in the hierarchical economy of slave plantation culture. In which the best, choicest cuts of a slaughtered porker, the ones literally higher up on the hog, were reserved for the white masters, while the slaves were left to make do with the lower parts, the feet, the belly, the offal, and the innards.

That was my introduction to L.A. as a learning experience: the disciples of the sacred and the profane chowing down together in the heart of Watts, to the sounds, both sacred and profane, of Sam Cooke on the jukebox, a sweet spiritual vision of a city where all America came to live high on the hog.

Next time in L.A.: Oscar night at the Beverly Hills Hotel. Another spiritual lesson. Two of my friends had just won gold statuettes for a joint project. I'd been sitting right next to them in the Dorothy Chandler Pavilion when they were called up to accept the award. Back at the Beverly Hills Hotel, after a late-night toast in the Polo Lounge to their win, to their romantic relationship, I left them to return to my dive, the Continental Hyatt House (of *Fear and Loathing* fame), then came back to retrieve a jacket or something. And froze when I saw the two of them, two talented, brilliant people who'd just celebrated a fairy-tale triumph, standing in the cool floral-papered corridor off the hotel lobby, each holding an Oscar in one hand, each pointing a finger in the other's contorted face, in the midst of a vicious destructive fight that—it turned out—they'd never get over.

Next memory, next hotel, this one a motel way lower down the food chain than the Hyatt. A Motel 6, I think it was, on Sunset and Vine, a kind of safe house where I'd registered under a false name along with producer Michael Shamberg, who later did *The Big Chill* and who was then fronting a cleverly subversive video documentary group called TVTV. The two of us were holed up anxiously awaiting contact from what we thought was the Weather Underground collective that would soon be blindfolding us and taking us on a wild ride to a secret rendezvous with then federal fugitive Abbie Hoffman. Looking back on it, I may have missed the *real* story, which was right there in front of me at the Motel 6 on Sunset and Vine. A kind of bivouac of broken dreams for the transients, the hustlers, the lost, the disillusioned, and the demented among Hollywood wannabes. The ones who'd fallen off the Hog, or never gotten a taste of the choice cuts, but still believed they were destined to be stars. If I'd paid more attention, I might have suspected then the real reason for the failure of the Revolution the Weather Underground never figured out. The Motel 6 at Sunset and Vine was the Winter Palace; however angry and dispossessed they felt, the bitter losers within were too attached to their broken dreams to rise up against the dream machine.

Cut to a different kind of underground scene, a different hotel, the Sunset Marquis, whose confusing internal views give one the sense that one is living in a leafy and landscaped underground cavern. I was stuck there living a hermetically sealed existence—broken only by visits to the surface to gorge on the green-chili-cheese omelettes at the Ben Franks on Sunset. A hermetically sealed, supreme test of my hermeneutic talents: I'd been scheduled to interview Bob Dylan for *Playboy* in connection with the coming release of his self-produced, sixteen-hour-long film-and-nervous breakdown called *Renaldo and Clara*. Well, actually, by the time I got to the Sunset Marquis, Dylan had been persuaded to edit it down to a slim four-and-a-half-hour version. But the word I got was Dylan was *concerned*. That the film was so complex and deep that he didn't want to talk to anyone who didn't *really* understand it.

So I went up to the Burbank studio lot where Dylan was struggling to edit his tormented vision and saw the tangled, self-referential four-and-a-half-hour epic twice (insanely great music from the *Rolling Thunder* period, laden with incredibly heavy-handed visual allegory). Then returned to the Sunset Marquis to apply my English-major skills to explicating the film's allegories in relation to the complicated imagery of Dylan's song lyrics. After several disembodied Sunset Marquis nights and vivid green-chili-cheese nightmares, I'd nailed it. I'd figured it all out. When I walked into Dylan's trailer on the Burbank lot, I took the arrogant approach. I told him, "I don't think there's any point in our talking at *all* unless we're on the same wavelength about the film, so let me tell you what I think is going on." Frankly, by this time, I thought it was a test for *him;* if he didn't get what I'd gotten out of it, he wasn't worthy to discuss his work with *me*.

So I launched into a twenty-minute disquisition focusing on fat English-major targets in the film like the iconography of the *transparent mask*. When I came to a stop, I could see he knew that I got it, but he was a bit annoyed about that. Maybe he'd made it *too* transparent. He wasn't gonna give me credit.

Sneering in classic Dylan fashion, he said, "You talk to *Ginsberg* or something?" Like I'd *cribbed* it from his Talmudic Beat poet friend! I wanted to strangle him, but I had to laugh. There in that "Positively 4th Street"-type put-down line—not in the silly transparent mask stuff—was the wicked soul of the artist I loved.

Last L.A. learning experience for now. This time I was staying at one of my favorite places, the low-key Westwood Marquis. And learning a double-leveled lesson about the Tragedy of Good Intentions and the Meaning of Art. See, I'd met this brilliant black homicide detective in the course of reporting a story in which he was a subsidiary character. I'd been deeply impressed by this guy, who was a legend among homicide cops. A legend for a special talent: getting confessions, getting murder suspects to "give it up." Loosening the tongues of some of the most menacing characters around, not by force, but by convincing them he was saving their *souls*. He was the detective as con man and preacher: in fact, in real life, a lay preacher in a charismatic speaking-in-tongues congregation. He was an inspirational figure in the community, and I got together with a couple of guys I know who were marginally "in the industry" to try to get someone to make a film based on him. We got the detective a little money to start (none for us) and went out West to pitch the project to a few people.

We had some good response at first, but the producers all wanted to meet the cop to seal the deal. The only problem was that—just as we checked in to the Westwood Marquis—we got some bad news. Our guy, this hardworking cop who'd rarely taken much of a vacation in twenty years on the force, had taken some of his movie-rights money and taken his girlfriend and taken a trip to the Virgin Islands. The problem was with what he *hadn't* taken. Before he left, he went off his blood pressure medication to (do I have to spell it out?) enjoy the trip more fully. You guessed it: In the midst of his holiday, living high on the hog at last (and deservedly so), he suffered a serious stroke and he still hasn't recovered.

The project hasn't, either. But there was one moment in the course of pitching it that will forever be enshrined in my memory as the ultimate summation of state-of-the-art L.A. wisdom, or at least attitude. A vice president of production at a now-abolished subdivision of a major studio delivered it. He was a state-of-the-art Hollywood player: faded jeans and a cashmere sweater with no shirt, an expensive Armani jacket and lots of L.A. art on the wall. He got into a name-dropping L.A. art-scene conversation with one of the guys I was pitching the homicide cop project with, an actor who matched him with cool artist name-drops, till the studio guy gestured at the pieces on his office wall, sighed and delivered himself of the ultimate Hollywood philosophical summa:

"Ah yes, Art," he said, "Art is what we do, now that they tell us we can't do drugs and fuck strange women anymore."

But don't get me wrong. Like I said, I love L.A.

Stumpy versus Lucille: The Great Pet Debate

⚬

I want to pick a fight over cats and dogs. Cats *versus* dogs. A response to an intriguing new phenomenon on the literary horizon: the smash success of the sensitive, well-written I-really-really-*really*-love-my-dog book *Pack of Two: The Intimate Bond Between People and Dogs,* by Caroline Knapp, author of the widely praised memoir *Drinking: A Love Story.* Okay, maybe I'm jealous. I was talking with my friend Susan Kamil, the editorial director of Dial Press, which published Ms. Knapp's memoir. Ms. Kamil asked after the health of my beloved cat Stumpy (who suffers from a chronic heart condition) and then spoke glowingly about Ms. Knapp's new book, which chronicles the way she traded her obsessive love of intoxicating spirits for the intoxicating love of her spirited new dog, Lucille.

Listening to this praise, I found myself growing indignant. What makes *her* dog more special than my cat and *our* relationship? How could she even compare the love of a mere dog to that of a cat (to that of *my* cat)? Don't dog owners realize how deluded they are in thinking that the love of their dogs is meaningful, that it really says something beautiful about *them,* that it says anything about them?

Now I don't mean for this to devolve into a "My cat is better than her dog" thing. Not right away, anyway. Before getting to that level, I feel it's important to address the more general delusion dog lovers suffer from, one that is evident from a quick glance at Ms. Knapp's book. It's a lively and affecting personal memoir which I urge all impassioned dog lovers to buy. But it's a lively and affecting chronicle of a delusion.

Ms. Knapp spends enormous amounts of time wondering if her dog loves her, how much her dog loves her, obsessing over all the little signs of love and affection, explaining to us how much it means to her own sense of self-worth, self-esteem, and self-respect that her dog really, really, *really* loves her.

Her dog, she says at one point, "became an emblem of my wish for an emotional sure thing . . . This is why I was so profoundly possessive of her, so jealous of her affection. She was the one creature on the planet I loved without reservation, and I had to have *all* of her love in return, for the alternative, I believed, was to be left with nothing."

It's an interesting notion of love: "an emotional sure thing." (Cats are never a sure thing.) Is "sure thing" love a higher love or just a surer, more comforting one? It suggests a longing for a creature who will love you regardless of who you are, what you do, what you become, how you act. But can the love of the dog really do that for you? Is the love of a dog a sure thing, a real thing, in the first place? Is the love of a dog really about a searching affirmation of your soul, or is it more about a steady supply of dog food?

I hate to break the news to Ms. Knapp and her fellow dog-love junkies, I hate to be the bearer of bad tidings, but the "love" of dogs means nothing. Zero. Dogs are the slavering sycophants, the slobbering indiscriminate flatterers, the bootlickers, the pathetic transparent brownnosers of the domestic animal kingdom. Dogs are skilled at sucking up, creating the pathetic illusion of love, but it has nothing to do with how lovable you actually *are*. Dogs will slaver over anyone who gives them food and security. Dogs will suck up to serial killers, dogs will make goo-goo eyes at child molesters, dogs will fawn and whimper over mass murderers. (I cite a certain German shepherd named Blondi who shamelessly sucked up to Hitler himself. The Führer rewarded Blondi's devotion by testing out his cyanide death pills on the doomed sycophant dog.)

In one of the only great cat books ever written, *The Cat Inside* by William Burroughs (yes, *that* Burroughs, it's the only work of his I really admire aside from *Junky*), Burroughs went into a brilliant anti-dog rant which culminated in his characterization of dogs as "the grinning slavering rednecks of the animal kingdom." They are that *inside* (and to all humans they don't feel the need to suck up to for food), but the *public* face of dogs is even worse: grinning, groveling little con artists scamming their love-starved masters and mistresses into believing that it's really about *them,* how special they are rather than about Ken-L Ration tender beef chunks and how special *that* is.

Don't tell me I'm speaking as someone who doesn't know dogs. I grew up with dogs, loved dogs, but never was deluded enough to think that my dogs loved me because of my great personality or any special attainment of heart and soul as *some* dogs have conned some masters into believing.

This is the key difference between dogs and cats. A dog, as someone said, always acts like he's afraid he's going to lose his job. A cat acts like the employer, you're the ranch hand—and you're always in danger of losing *your* job. A cat's vast sense of entitlement may be delusive, but at least it's honest: A cat does not fake orgasms of affection the way dogs do, a cat is not an easy lay emotionally. If you win the love of a cat you have something meaningful, you have something that can genuinely increase your self-respect.

This is not written out of boastfulness: After eleven years, I'm still not sure if I *have* the love or respect of my cat, Stumpy. I'd like to have it, I'd like to be assured of it, but I'm not going to found my entire sense of self-worth on its presence or absence. What's more important—and more selfless, I'd suggest, than the needy, greedy Fido-loves-me rapture of dog lovers—is that I love and respect *him.*

That old saying, "Want a friend, buy a dog" could have been coined by a cat. You can buy a dog's friendship, but with a cat a lifetime of devotion might, only *might* qualify you for some visible signs of affection. And then again, it might not. But it seems to me that even the slightest intimation of affection from a cat like Stumpy means far, far more than the slobbering flattery of some brownnosing dog.

Okay, this may be true of cats in general versus dogs in general, you might say, but what makes your cat, Stumpy, so special, so exceptional? I should note at this point that I am not alone in this view, that I have a number of sophisticated and otherwise world-weary witnesses to testify to this. How is Stumpy special? Let me begin to count the ways:

1. *The still shadowy, deeply mysterious circumstances under which he lost his tail.* All we know for sure is that Stumpy, an orange marmalade–colored alley cat about a year old was found on a street near the Brooklyn waterfront with a severe injury of unknown origin: His tail had been half bitten, torn, or cut off by parties unknown. After he was taken to a local vet by a Good Samaritan cat-rescuer, it was found necessary to amputate most of the tail, leaving the eponymous Stump. Put up for adoption in the window of a Brooklyn Heights pet store, he was brought to my attention by Liz Hecht, the fiery red-haired animal rights activist and founder of Citizens for Alternatives to Animal Labs. Few people know cats the way Liz does and she assured me that Stumpy was special.

But Stumpy's never spoken of the circumstances of his waterfront injury. True, he's dropped occasional hints that it was mob-related—although at other times he's indicated "national security" was involved. (I believe he's holding out for a movie option before he'll tell the full story.) But it has been suggested that there was a woman involved. I'm inclined to believe the latter because . . .

2. *Stumpy's Skill with the Ladies* is a key aspect of his exceptionalism. Women are *fascinated* with him. I still get calls from some who have no interest any longer in me, but desperately want to know how Stumpy is. Someday, I feel I could write about Stumpy's Rules for winning over women. One chapter would have to do with . . .

3. *The Wink.* He never does this for me, but he will walk right up to a woman visitor he considers worthy and give her a frank, confidential, one-eyed wink. Most of them profess they've never seen a cat do this, and they find it both unnerving and stunningly seductive. But it's just one of the repertoire of guilefully charming behaviors he displays only for women he fancies. Including . . .

4. *Direct Conversation.* Again, he never does this for me, however much I implore, imitate cat sounds, make little meows until I'm hoarse. But he will talk to certain women. One special favorite just has to start making cat language sounds and he becomes a regular chattering Noël Coward, answering back with alacrity and responsiveness. When I try to join in, he gives me a disdainful glance and a wall of silence goes up; it's like, "Dude, don't try to cut into my time."

5. *Stumpy's Heart Condition.* I don't want to turn this section of the column into too much of a tear-jerker, but you have to admire the courage and pluckiness of this marmalade-coated little guy. Shortly after he arrived at my place, not long after his tail stitches had finally dissolved, he displayed panting and respiratory symptoms that were quickly diagnosed (with the help of high-tech, state-of-the-art echocardiography) as cardiomyopathy, a valve defect that had caused his valiant little stray cat heart to enlarge and overstrain itself. Fortunately, the condition has been controllable with twice-daily doses of Inderal (a beta-blocker pill) or relatively controllable, considering Stumpy's predisposition to climb to great heights in whatever apartment he occupies. Once he ascended an extremely tall ladder that some workmen had left behind and was in the process of making a risky leap to the top of a bookshelf when he caused the ladder to collapse, causing himself to fall and suffer a mild "cardiac decompensation," as the vet called it, a cat heart attack.

He recovered, yes, but the fact that he has stared death in the face and can still wag his stump at life's little pleasures—a catnip mouse, a fresh can of Fancy Feast—is a clue to his most touching and soulful asset. . . .

6. *Stumpy's Zen-like Tragic Sense of Life.* This is what you see in his eyes, the tragic awareness one finds in the final poems of William Butler Yeats: "Cast a cold eye / On life, on death. / Horseman, pass by!" The flicker of a smile on that ancient Chinese jade mask of tragedy. Stumpy has looked at life from both sides now, very little impresses him, few of the ordinary urgencies, the little disturbances of man so many of us use to distract ourselves from the contemplation of the Big Questions have any charms for him. (Although Whisker Lickin's tuna flavor cat treats will occasionally return him to more earthly concerns. That and the occasional pigeon that zooms past our window and arouses his primitive hunting instincts.) But otherwise he sees through the petty, needy concerns that preoccupy human beings. He has a job to do, patrolling the apartment, supervising me, and making sure that he gets his daily twenty or so hours of sleep so that he can maintain maximum alertness for these taxing tasks. It is the aura of grave seriousness with which he carries out his patrol duty responsibilities that might be the source of his most distinctive quality. . . .

7. *His Comic Genius.* It has something to do with the way he walks around with the air of a guy who's got Everything Figured Out. I think he must be doing a deliberate parody of that human tendency to act as if we know what's really going on—that we have things under control—when we don't have the slightest clue about the Larger Mysteries of Existence. I mean, Stumpy's a guy who doesn't have much of a clue about what goes on right outside our apartment. He'll fight like a crazed maniac, virtually give himself a heart attack resisting a trip outside because his medical experiences have led him to believe that the entire world outside our door is the vast waiting room of a sadistic catheter-wielding veterinarian. (Come to think of it, there's a kind of metaphoric truth to this vision.) But despite his ignorance, he stalks around like he's king of the jungle with an invincible sense of entitlement and self-importance and a secure sense of his preeminent place in the order of the universe. It's a hilarious send-up of the comic pretensions of human beings to believe they've got things figured out—or that they ever could. It's endlessly hilarious.

So there's that, and there's the way he wags his stump when he's happy. Also hilarious, just like a dog in a way. But better.

Postscript to "Stumpy versus Lucille: The Great Pet Debate"

Nearly a year after this column appeared, *The Atlantic Monthly* published a cover story entitled "Why Your Dog Pretends to Love You" (by Stephen Budiansky), which offered apparent scientific validation (from the field of evolutionary genetics) for an argument I'd initially made mainly in jest: that dogs are false flatterers, Darwinian con men: "Just as we are genetically programmed to seek signs of love and loyalty, dogs are genetically programmed to exploit this foible of ours," Budiansky wrote. Nonetheless, I want to reemphasize something that might have gotten lost in the comic belligerent tone of my column: *I love dogs.* I grew up with three wonderful dogs: Tiger, a Boston terrier; Skipper, a spaniel mutt; and Loki, a golden retriever–cocker spaniel mix whom I believe a truly Enlightened Being. This is not really an argument about cats and dogs so much as one about *humans,* the way certain humans can project too much meaning onto the love of their dogs.

Still, I'll admit I'm prejudiced. I can't resist appending what I think may be the most lovely evocation of self-absorbed cat affection in literature. It's the epigraph to my favorite twentieth-century novel, *Pale Fire,* which Nabokov took from Boswell's *Life of Samuel Johnson:*

> This reminds me of the ludicrous account [Johnson] gave Mr. Langton, of the despicable state of a young gentleman of good family. "Sir, when I heard of him last, he was running about town shooting cats." And then in a sort of kindly reverie, he bethought himself of his own favorite cat, and said, "But Hodge shan't be shot: no, no, Hodge shall not be shot."

Hitler, Singer, Pharaoh, and Shakespearean Romance

⸎

Explaining Hitler

Singer's *Shadows:* Footnotes to Hitler

Explaining Pharaoh

This "Rarest Dream": The Final Affirmation of
Shakespearean Romance

Explaining Hitler

In Which We Assess the Inexplicability of Horror and the
Horror of Inexplicability

In the realm of Hitler explanations, it's come to be called "the survival myth,"
and, though no one believes it now, it struck a chord in the postwar popular
imagination. The image of a Hitler who had escaped—escaped the Berlin
bunker, escaped the flames that were said to have consumed him, escaped
judgment—turned out to be a perversely seductive one, inspiring fantasists
from the lowbrow (the legendary *Police Gazette* "Hitler Is Alive in Argentina"
series) to the highbrow (George Steiner's challenging parable *The Portage to
San Cristóbal of A.H.*). These days, as it becomes ever more difficult to imagine that a centenarian Hitler still lives, popular culture has given us *parts* of
Hitler escaping; the final sentence of the 1994 best-selling thriller *The Day
After Tomorrow,* for instance, breathlessly revealed that Hitler's "severed,
deep-frozen head" had survived in the hands of neo-Nazis, who wanted to rebuild him from the top down.

Hitler may not have escaped us physically, as the survival myth has it, but
in certain important respects he has eluded us. We know where the head is
now, or think we do. As the fiftieth anniversary of Hitler's death approached,
a sudden flurry of reports in British and German publications debated a new

claim that four curved fragments of bone now reposing in a Moscow archive were part of Hitler's skull. But the obsession with the whereabouts of Hitler's remains may be a symptom of a more disturbing truth: Regardless of where the skull is, a sure sense of Hitler's mind, of his psyche, has escaped us.

To spend time, as I have for the past several years, with historians, psychologists, psycho-historians, philosophers, and theologians who have devoted themselves to the task of explaining Hitler is to realize how pervasive is the feeling of something still missing, something still inexplicable. "For all the harsh obviousness of his impact on history," Hugh Trevor-Roper (now Lord Dacre), one of the most influential postwar Hitler explainers, maintains, "his character remains elusive." More than elusive, Trevor-Roper elaborated in a conversation with me: "It remains a frightening mystery." Alan Bullock (now Lord Bullock), the Oxford historian and conceptual rival of Trevor-Roper in postwar Hitler-explanatory literature, summed up his frustration after a lifetime of study: "The more I learn about Adolf Hitler," Bullock told me, "the harder I find it to explain."

Is the real survival story, then, Hitler's escape from explanation? Is meaning itself Hitler's final victim? The problem is, first, that the available evidence on key questions is maddeningly incomplete. A half century after Hitler's death, some of the basic facts of his life—from his ancestry (who was his paternal grandfather?) to his last moment (did he die a "soldier's death," by shooting himself with his own gun, or a "coward's death," by biting a cyanide capsule?)—are still the subject of sometimes bitter controversy. Nor can any consensus be found on such fundamental questions as the origin of Hitler's anti-Semitism (and the source of its unique virulence), or the nature of his sexuality and its relation to his political pathology. Missing most of all is a satisfactory sense of Hitler's psychological evolution, his apparent metamorphosis from human being into incarnation of evil. Something that will explain Hitler's baby pictures.

Those baby pictures: They have become a symbolic focus of a fascinating debate not only over the very possibility of attempting to explain Hitler but over the morality of such an attempt. Claude Lanzmann, who directed *Shoah,* the nine-and-a-half-hour documentary about the Holocaust, is the most prominent member of a growing faction of intellectuals who believe that any attempt to understand Hitler inevitably degenerates into an exercise in empathy with him. To understand all is to forgive all, and to Lanzmann even the first steps down the slippery slope to understanding are impermissible.

Lanzmann rhetorically flourishes Hitler's baby pictures as icons of his crusade against what he calls "the obscenity of the very project of understanding." There is a famous baby picture, taken when Hitler was about a year old, that shows a round-faced, chubby-cheeked child, a mildly pensive cherub.

One could, considering what one knows of his fate, "backshadow" into his dark eyes and parted lips a melancholy, or even a haunted, expression—the stirrings of some deep disturbance. But one could just as easily see there not incipient demonism but a kind of gentleness.

The point Lanzmann wants to make is that this is Hitler as an innocent— Hitler before he became *Hitler.* "There are some pictures of Hitler as a baby," he has said. But you can't *"engender* the killing, the mass murders, the destruction of six million people" from those pictures. No finite number of explanatory facts—psychological traumas, patterns of bad parenting, political deformations, personal dysfunctions—can add up to the magnitude of the evil that Hitler came to embody and enact. No explanation or concatenation of explanations can bridge the gap, explain the transformation from baby picture to baby killer, to murderer of a million babies. It is not just a gap, Lanzmann argues. It is "an *abyss.*"*

In surveying the landscape of explanation, Lanzmann echoes a line from Primo Levi's memoir *Survival in Auschwitz:* "There is no why here." It is a line—a decree—that was delivered to Levi by an SS death-camp guard. A line that has led another Auschwitz survivor—the psychoanalyst Dr. Louis Micheels—to an impassioned dissent. It is wrong, Dr. Micheels told me, to adopt an SS decree in a death camp as the final verdict on our quest to understand Hitler. "There *should* be a why," he insists. "There must be a why."

The five decades since Hitler's death have seen a wild profusion of whys, a proliferation of competing Hitlers. Following upon the founding, and clashing, visions offered by Hugh Trevor-Roper and Alan Bullock in Britain—the possessed, demonic, true-believer Hitler versus the cynical, scheming, opportunist Hitler—popular biographies like those of John Toland, in this country, and Joachim Fest, in Germany, have added a wealth of new details from the loosened tongues of the last surviving Hitler contemporaries—details that have tended to deepen the mystery rather than bridge the abyss Lanzmann spoke of. As the tide of fresh facts began to ebb, wave after wave of theory arose. The psychoanalytically oriented school of "psycho-history" plumbed Hitler's murky unconscious for primal scenes and inner Jews. The ideological school plumbed the equally murky depths of his prose and claimed to find in

---

*Further testament to the disturbing power of the Hitler baby picture could be found in the reaction of foreign publishers to the original cover of my book *Explaining Hitler* (this *New Yorker* story, revised and expanded, became part of the manuscript for the book). The cover of the American edition featured a blowup of the baby picture Lanzmann referred to. But out of some dozen foreign editions now, in eleven different languages, all but one (the Israeli edition) refused to feature the baby picture in full. Most preferred to go with fist-waving, *sieg-heil*ing images of Hitler. Somehow the baby picture is more threatening. Perhaps because it asks the question: Was Hitler was one of us? Could a child that looks as innocent as that—as one of our own—turn into a Hitler?

his feverishly logorrheic discourse an intellectual coherence, a serious Weltanschauung that was the true engine of his murderous acts. The last decade has seen the rise of "historicizing" modes of Hitler interpretation, in which Hitler is viewed less as a prime mover than as a product of deep currents in European history—a logical culmination of Western culture rather than an aberration from it.

The multiplicity of theoretical Hitlers is echoed in the multiple Hitlers of popular culture, which range from Chaplin's laughable caricature to drooling psychopaths, from occult satanists to Alec Guinness's more genuinely terrifying "human" Hitler in the 1973 film *Hitler: The Last Ten Days*.

What one discovers from an immersion in the postwar Hitler literature and from conversations with leading Hitler interpreters is that Hitler explanations often tell us as much about the explainers as they do about Hitler. That, in a sense, when we talk about who Hitler is, we are talking about who we are—and who we are not. We project upon the inky Rorschach of the evidence an image of our anti-self. Hitler theories are cultural self-portraits in the negative—ways of distancing ourselves from him. And ways of protecting ourselves. Another thing that becomes evident from an odyssey into the realm of Hitler explanations is a deeper need: explanation as consolation; explanation, however meretricious, as a shield against having to face the horror of inexplicability, the inexplicability of horror.

Consider, for instance, a little-known Hitler explanation that emerged in Germany in the 1980s—the tale of the billy-goat bite. It's an explanation that, in its yoking together of high tragedy and low barnyard comedy, represents both a reductio ad absurdum of more high-minded attempts to explain Hitler and a prime example of explanation as consolation.

Sometime in mid-1943, after the tide had turned decisively against Hitler on the eastern front, German Army authorities arrested an obscure Army private named Eugen Wasner and shipped him back to Berlin to face a special court-martial and the guillotine. While the formal charge against Wasner was "maliciously slandering the Führer," the actual crime for which he faced beheading was his embarrassing explanation of Hitler.

Private Wasner's account was an extremely bloody variant of what might be called the genital-wound school of Hitler interpretation, a mode of thought that has at various times been employed to elucidate the prose of Henry James and the sanguinary appetite of Jeffrey Dahmer. It has led some to look for the source of Hitler's evil or pathology, whichever you choose to call it (and the choice is a hotly disputed one), in a putatively absent left testicle or in the deranging effects of a dose of syphilis. Some might say that it's the ultimate act of phallocentric thinking to insist that whatever was wrong with Adolf Hitler had to originate with his genitalia. But genital-wound explanations of Hitler have been rattling around in "Hitler studies" (as Don DeLillo dubbed the field in his novel *White Noise*) for decades. Wasner's story first came to light in 1981, in a memoir published in Germany under the title *Tödlicher Alltag,* or "Deadly Routine." Its author, Dietrich Güstrow, who was then a prominent attorney in the Federal Republic, and whose book was widely and respectfully reviewed, tells us that in 1943 he served as Private Wasner's defense counsel before the secret military tribunal that tried the soldier for slandering Hitler and sentenced him to death.

According to the lawyer's memoir, the occasion of Private Wasner's slander was a barracks bull session in which Private Wasner boasted that as a youth he had attended the same school as Adolf Hitler, in Leonding, Austria. Bitter about recent defeats on the eastern front, the private told his buddies, "Adolf has been warped ever since a billy goat took a bite out of his penis."

Wasner proceeded to give a graphic description of the bloody consequences of young Adolf's attempt to prove he could urinate in the mouth of a billy goat. A preposterous story on the face of it. And yet Güstrow declares forty years later, "Regarding the truth of Wasner's report, I never had any doubts." But Güstrow goes further than merely vouching for the truthfulness of the story. He makes explicit the implication of Wasner's report: the traumatic billy-goat bite as an explanation for Hitler's subsequent derangement. To Güstrow, that billy-goat bite was—like the single "shudder in the loins" in Yeats's "Leda and the Swan," like the single bite of the apple in Genesis—an act of blind appetite from which whole histories of sorrow and tragedy would ensue. In a sense, Güstrow's own appetite—his desire to find in this incident a single satisfying explanation for Hitler's psyche—is more revealing than the negligible value of his theory. It's an example of the appetite for single-pointed explanation—the yearning to find some decisive turning point in Hitler's biography that can explain Hitler and "engender" the Holocaust from his "craziness." A yearning that tells us as much about the explainer as about Hitler. For Güstrow, believing that a billy-goat bite explains Hitler, that a preposterous mishap created Nazi Germany, can be seen as a way of absolving German society—and himself—of implication in Hitler's crimes. The billy goat becomes the *scapegoat* upon which he projects—and thereby purges—German guilt.

One paradox in attempting to explain Hitler is that there are already too many explanations. A tour of the literature of Hitler theories—both high and low—can yield the impression that Hitler's crimes were the most overdetermined events in history: that his life was an unending series of traumas, turning points, tragic twists of fate, metaphorical billy-goat bites; that epiphanies, awakenings, transformations, moments of metamorphosis are thick upon the ground at every stage of his existence.

Was it, in fact, the very ground itself that distorted him? Sir Isaiah Berlin, in *Against the Current,* has advanced a thought-provoking borderland theory of charismatic political leadership which attributes the maniacally aggressive nationalism of such figures as Napoleon, Stalin, and Hitler to their geographical origins—their birth on the outlying marches, the borders of the empires they will later come to command and expand. (Hitler was born in 1889 in Braunau, an Austrian town just across the river from southern Germany.)

If it wasn't geography, was it genealogy? Did Hitler somehow learn during his childhood in Austria a "terrible" family secret: that his father had actually been fathered by a Jew? Several postwar psychoanalytic Hitler explainers (among them Robert Waite, a Williams College emeritus professor of history) have seized upon this recurrent rumor to suggest that Hitler's torment over the possibility that he was "tainted," "poisoned" by Jewish blood, was the secret engine of his anti-Semitism.

If it wasn't genealogy, was it chemotherapy? In 1907, Hitler, then eighteen, witnessed the agonizing death from cancer of his mother, who had been unsuccessfully treated by a Jewish doctor with the caustic chemical iodoform. Rudolph Binion, a professor of history at Brandeis, contends that Hitler's repressed anger at that Jewish doctor was the genesis of his hatred of Jews.

If it wasn't chemotherapy, was it pornography? Some historians, among them Alan Bullock, believe that there was "something sexual" to the highly charged quality of Hitler's anti-Semitism. As evidence of this, Robert Waite has pointed to an unusual interest Hitler seems to have developed in Vienna during his lost years (1908–1913), after his mother's death and the failure of his artistic ambitions had plunged him into the lower depths of the city's homeless shelters. At some point in that period, Hitler appears to have become enamored of a lasciviously illustrated, semi-pornographic, anti-Semitic publication called *Ostara,* which was edited by a self-styled Aryan mystic named Lanz von Liebenfels. The American biographer John Toland and other writers argue that Hitler's own peculiarly sexualized variety of anti-Semitism was in part derived from Lanz's (and *Ostara*'s) obsession with tales of lustful Jews defiling Aryan maidens. This obsession, they say, may have imprinted itself on the youthful Hitler's psyche and can be found echoed in passages of *Mein Kampf* redolent with sexual hysteria. "With satanic joy in his face," Hitler writes, "the black-haired Jewish youth lurks in wait for the unsuspecting girl whom he defiles with his blood."

If it wasn't pornography, was it hypnotherapy? There were many thousands of anti-Semites in Europe in those years, but only one became Adolf Hitler. Much postwar scholarship has been devoted to uncovering the event that transformed Hitler from ordinary anti-Semite to single-minded murderer of millions—the moment that convinced him he must make extermination of the Jews his mission. In the late seventies, two writers—Binion and Toland—independently advanced a startling hypothesis about the origins of Hitler's murderous ambition, focusing on an incident that took place five years after Hitler left Vienna. (Hitler had migrated to Munich in 1913 and enlisted in a Bavarian regiment of the German Army when the First World War broke out, in August of 1914.) They pointed to an episode at the very end of the war—one that Hitler himself described in *Mein Kampf* as a life-changing experience. Blinded by a poison-gas attack on the western front, Hitler was admitted to a military hospital in October of 1918. He appears to have recovered his sight for a while and then suffered a relapse—perhaps a form of "hysterical blindness"—when the news of Germany's humiliating defeat reached him.

To others, Hitler described what happened next as a kind of miracle. In his blind, bedridden despair, he received a vision (or had a hallucination), heard a voice from above summoning him to a great destiny—to save Germany. It was then, the story goes, that he miraculously recovered his sight and vowed to devote himself to avenging Germany's defeat. Binion contends, however, that the voice Hitler heard was not a voice from above, as Hitler believed; it was the voice of a hypnotist. His name was Dr. Edmund Forster, and he was the ranking psychiatrist at Hitler's hospital. That much has been confirmed. Binion suggests, on the basis of fragmentary sources (a naval-intelligence debriefing of an Austrian psychiatrist and a thinly fictionalized account by a friend of Franz Kafka's), that Dr. Forster cured Hitler's blindness by using then fashionable mesmeric techniques to put him in a trance and implant the belief that his beloved Germany needed him to recover his sight in order to serve the cause of national resurrection. In this view, Dr. Forster's spell worked all too well: In trying to cure Hitler, he transformed a previously obscure corporal into a monster.

Like the Jewish-blood and bungling-Jewish-doctor hypotheses, the mesmeric theory has come under fire. Waite, for one, argues that the sources are too vague and inadequate to sustain such a conjecture and that no records survive which prove that Dr. Forster attended Hitler. (Forster, though, seems to have claimed, shortly before committing suicide, in 1933, that the Gestapo was pursuing him for those very records.)

The hypnotist theory is perhaps the most sophisticated exemplar of a long-enduring quest in Hitler interpretation for some mesmeric secret: the key either to Hitler's own transformation or to his hypnotic power over his audiences. An enduring apocryphal tradition attributes that power to some occult initiation. Hitler himself invoked metaphors of hypnotic trance when he described himself as someone who moved inexorably toward his goals with the "precision and security of a sleepwalker."

The search for the hypnotist who created a mesmeric Hitler may reflect our own longing to understand not just his mesmeric power over Germany but the distressing way he continues to mesmerize us—yet another instance of how Hitler explanations hold up a dark mirror to our own anxieties.

Consider, in this light, two particularly revealing explanatory patterns that have emerged in the past two decades, patterns that constitute two remarkable reversals: the tendency to see Hitler as a victim, and the apparent need to find a Jew to blame. Recently, I came across on TV an arresting example of Hitler seen through the lens of American popular culture in the nineties, Hitler integrated into the explanatory framework of pop victimology: Hitler as a serial killer suffering from low self-esteem.

In November of 1991, *Unsolved Mysteries,* the enormously popular "reality" television series, devoted a "special edition" to a topic that was something of a departure from its usual fare of UFO sightings and psychic-healer probes—an hour given over entirely to "Diabolical Minds: Case Studies." What this turned out to be was a series of portraits, including brief segments about Ted Bundy, John Wayne Gacy, and Adolf Hitler. Grouped with the others in this way, Hitler becomes just another serial killer, the most prolific one of all time, yes, but basically a kind of workaholic Hannibal Lecter—a figure explicable in the psychobabble of serial-killer pseudoscience as the victim of a dysfunctional family. Of Hitler's father, the narrator tells us, "Many believe his physical and emotional abuse virtually destroyed his son's self-esteem." Had there been more time, perhaps problems with Hitler's "inner child" might have been invoked. But the real explanation turned out to be that terrifying contemporary plague: poor self-image. Thus, the segment on Hitler concluded that "he felt compelled to subjugate millions to avenge his own deep feelings of inferiority."

Absurd as this theory sounds, it does offer a kind of consolation on a couple of levels. For one thing, the explanation makes Hitler a more familiar figure. We know serial killers, or think we do by now. We've met their families on Geraldo's and Maury's shows, and we know they don't just spring from some primordial ooze. Some of us are even charmed by Hannibal Lecter: If you set aside the cannibalism, he can be good company. Though Hitler was far worse, *Unsolved Mysteries* suggested, we know his type. That alone—that he is a familiar type, not a revelation of some new, previously unfathomed depth of evil in human nature—may to some degree be comforting.

We can laugh at *Unsolved Mysteries,* and yet two purportedly more sophisticated psychological interpretations of Hitler, by renowned psychoanalytic savants, also ask us to empathize with Hitler: One calls him a victim of an abusive father, the other of an overindulgent mother.

The principal champion of the abusive-father theory is the psychoanalyst Alice Miller, the author of *The Drama of the Gifted Child* and *For Your Own Good*. In the latter work, which argues that the corporal punishment of children is the root of all evil, Miller presents us with a fifty-five-page Hitler explanation that could be entitled "The Drama of the Poor Abused Child Adolf." Miller declares, on the basis of sketchy evidence, that his father, Alois, beat him violently, and, on the basis of even sketchier evidence, that Alois's brutality stemmed from his rage at his origins—from the rumor that Alois was the bastard son of a Jew who had seduced Alois's unmarried mother, Maria Schicklgruber. One can understand Miller's desire to advance her worthy child-centered agenda through Hitler: If she can prove that this embodiment of evil was created by childhood beatings, the proof will buttress her brief for abolishing punishment for children. But there are times when her analysis amounts to special pleading on behalf of the child Adolf. Consider the shocking way she deals with objections from some historians that Hitler's father was not the child beater that Hitler later portrays him as. To which Miller replies: "As if anyone were more qualified to judge the situation than Adolf Hitler himself." Yes, and who more worthy of our trust and the presumption of honesty? Because Hitler was once a child, Miller seems to be saying, he cannot tell a lie about his childhood. Believe the children, even if the child was Adolf Hitler.

An inadvertently parodic counterpoint to Miller's demonization of Hitler's father can be found in the work of Erich Fromm, an equally respected and even more renowned psychoanalytic thinker: He singles out not Hitler's father but his mother, Klara. Fromm's version of Alois is not the abusive monster Miller portrays. Fromm assures us that Alois was a well-meaning, stable fellow, who "loved life," whose devotion to his honeybees was admirable, and who was "authoritarian" but "not a frightening figure." Instead, Fromm tells us, Hitler's mother, Klara, was the catalyst of his neuroses. In his retrospective psychoanalysis of Hitler (published in his 1973 book, *The Anatomy of Human Destructiveness*), Fromm confidently assures us that Hitler can be explained by Fromm's own "necrophilia" theory, which postulates a love of death and dead bodies and, consequently, the inclination to commit mass murder. Fromm asserts that this "necrophilous character system" had its origins in the "malignant incestuousness" of Hitler's attachment to his mother. "Germany became the central symbol for mother," Fromm writes. Hitler's fixations, his hatred for the "poison" (syphilis and Jews) that threatened Germany, actually concealed a deeper, long-repressed desire to destroy his mother.

Fromm's serene confidence in these grandiose abstractions and his unsupported leaps of logic based on them are breathtaking as he proceeds to his conclusion: Hitler's deepest hatred wasn't Jews—it was Germans! Germans embodied his highly fraught relationship with his mother. He made war against the Jews because his real goal was to ignite a worldwide conflagration in order to cause the destruction of Germany.

Theories of Hitler as the unfortunate victim of bad parenting (the Menendez defense of Hitler, one could say) are just a subset of a whole litany of attempts to explain (or explain away) Hitler as suffering from mental illness—an explanation that tends to exculpate him on the ground of what the courts call "diminished capacity," an inability to know right from wrong.

To these mental-illness theories can be added a strain of explanation that attributes Hitler's state of mind to a physical illness, thus removing him even further from conscious culpability. One of the most curious and revealing of these germ theories of Hitler has been Simon Wiesenthal's persistent, if quixotic, quest to explain Hitler's psyche as the by-product of a case of syphilis. Wiesenthal, long known as the pre-eminent hunter of Nazi war criminals, has been trying to track down—with the same determination he has applied to hunting escaped SS men in South America—the spectral spirochete that he believes was responsible for deranging Hitler.

Wiesenthal's devotion to this, of all possible Hitler-explanation theories, is certainly puzzling at first glance. The syphilitic-Hitler theory had been a feature of prewar rumor but had fallen into neglect until Wiesenthal attempted to revive it in the late 1980s. Puzzling also is the particular variant of the Hitler-syphilis story he has chosen to promote—a version in which the putative source of Hitler's infection was not just a prostitute in the Viennese lower depths (as in some versions) but specifically a Jewish prostitute. Her Jewishness then becomes Wiesenthal's explanation for the elusive grail of Hitler studies—the origin of his anti-Semitism. And the syphilis—the mentally deranging effects of the final stage of the disease—exacerbated his paranoia about Jews. Wiesenthal's syphilis theory becomes then a prime example of both the Hitler-as-victim trend and the concurrent misguided tendency to seek a Jew to blame. The prostitute joins a roster of Jewish "suspects," which by this time includes the Jewish doctor who treated Hitler's mother, the rumored Jewish seducer of Hitler's unmarried grandmother, and the rumored Jewish seducer of Hitler's half niece, and perhaps lover, Geli Raubal.

But Wiesenthal, now eighty-six, seems deadly serious in his quest for confirmation of this theory, despite the fact that evidence for the existence of a Jewish prostitute who had sex with Hitler (evidence for the existence of *anyone* who had sex with Hitler) is negligible. Despite the lack of evidence, it's clear that Wiesenthal wants to believe in this Jewish succubus. But why? What's the explanation for his explanation? Even if he found her, and somehow identified her as the bearer of the germ of Hitler's anti-Semitism, what could be the point? Wouldn't it inevitably tend to do something utterly unjust: make it seem as if the whole weight of the Holocaust should come down on the fragile shoulders of one poor woman of the streets?

One possible answer is that for someone like Wiesenthal, who has personally experienced the horror of the death camps, felt the hatred that killed millions all around him, it might in some way be preferable to have an unjust explanation of that hatred than an inexplicable hatred. Bad logic to explain an unimaginable tragedy is preferable to no logic. The Jewish-prostitute story may be cold comfort but better that than no comfort at all.

What has been lost, of course, in the search for a scapegoat is a sense of Hitler's own responsibility. Hitler disappears from these explanations, and is replaced by the person or the disease that "caused" him. Hitler also disappears in recently fashionable Great Abstraction theories, which argue that Christian anti-Semitism or capitalism or European racism or modernism produced Hitler. Here, too, explanation serves as consolation. If Hitler was an inevitable result of these larger forces, then nothing could have prevented the war or the genocide. If these larger forces would have produced a Hitler anyway, then Hitler's personal motives become irrelevant. The disturbing alternative is to believe that a single individual possessed the intent, had the will to bring about the horror—a notion some might find incomprehensible, and possibly unbearable.

But Great Abstraction theories have themselves aroused an impassioned counterreaction—a call for a return to a focus on the person of Hitler, summed up by the title of an influential 1984 essay in *Commentary* by the scholar Milton Himmelfarb: "No Hitler, No Holocaust." Himmelfarb's target is the Great Abstraction theory that singles out Christian anti-Semitism as the true source of the Holocaust. He argues that traditional anti-Semitism alone is not sufficient: "All that history . . . could have been the same and Hitler could as easily, more easily, not have murdered the Jews. He could more advantageously have tightened the screws of oppression," as anti-Semitic tyrants had done in the past, without attempting complete extermination. That decision was Hitler's alone, Himmelfarb insists: Hitler murdered the Jews not because he had to, not because he was being dictated to by abstract historical forces, but "because he wanted to."

He wanted to. It's remarkable that the decisiveness of Hitler's desire should have become so controversial. But, as with such other paradoxical reversals as Hitler-as-victim and the search for a Jew to blame, the debate over the very nature of Hitler's desire has become emblematic of the uncertainties that still cloud the whole enterprise of Hitler explanations.

There was a moment during my conversation with Emil Fackenheim, the foremost "theologian of the Holocaust," as *Commentary* has called him, that epitomized for me how sharp are the schisms over the fundamental nature of Hitler's desire. Fackenheim is famous for arguing that Hitler cannot be explained by the existing methods and theories of history and psychology—that his evil is so extreme that it is not even on the same continuum as the rest of humanity. For Fackenheim, Hitler represents an evil that only theology can explain.

It was a hot June afternoon two years ago in Jerusalem. Out on his little patio, Fackenheim, an energetic sixty-seven, dressed in a polo shirt, Bermuda shorts, and sandals, was telling me that he had made a close study of the explanatory literature before concluding that explanation had failed. He had some strong feelings about certain aspects of the conventional wisdom. Fackenheim recalled something once written about Hitler's final words, his deathbed testament. "You know Robert Waite's book?" Fackenheim asked, referring to Waite's psycho-historical study *The Psychopathic God: Adolf Hitler.* "It's a very good book, but I think he made a few mistakes: One thing Waite says is 'Nobody goes to his death with a lie.' " (What Waite actually wrote is that the deathbed testament is "quintessential Hitler.")

In Hitler's last words to the world—in the midst of the destruction he'd brought upon his own people with his war against the Jews—he exhorted the German government and people to continue the battle to the death with the Jews, the "universal poisoners of all nations."

"Waite believes that since Hitler went to his death with his famous testament of hating Jews, that must have been the true Hitler," Fackenheim said. "But it's completely false! Hitler, who posed all his life, who could never believe anything until he had the crowd before him to cheer him, went to his death like an actor. For posterity."

In other words, Hitler's deathbed testament was a fraud, a piece of deception designed to maintain his act as a crusader who died for the "great cause" of anti-Semitism. Fackenheim's view implies that Hitler was, first and last, an opportunist, who believed in nothing but his own ambition and used anti-Semitism only to advance it. "Look at his marriage," said Fackenheim, who later told me he had no doubt that Hitler was "a strange sexual pervert." "His wedding"—to Eva Braun—"just before his death. What does that mean? It was all a performance."

I asked the obvious question: "Are you saying he didn't even believe in his anti-Semitism?"

"I don't think he knew the difference between acting and believing," Fackenheim replied, and then added a devastating fillip: "Of course, it's a shocking thing to consider that six million Jews were murdered because of an actor."

But it seemed to me that there was something more than bitter irony behind the black humor of that remark—that it represented Fackenheim's ultimate effort to rescue Hitler from the sinkhole of explanation, to preserve him from mitigation, to assign to him the highest degree of evil. By characterizing Hitler's apparently implacable hatred of Jews as merely an actor's trick, by thus denying him the "virtue" of passionate sincerity (or the pity perhaps due to a victim of a pathological mental illness), Fackenheim deflects, even derails, the entire project of Hitler explanation. Most explainers have focused on finding the source of the pathological fury of Hitler's hatred of the Jews—a hatred that Fackenheim suggests was not pathology but pure, cold-blooded calculation.

And thus all the more evil. Evil for evil's sake, evil inexplicable by illness or ideology and all the more inexcusable. "Radical evil," a term Fackenheim uses to define a phenomenon that goes beyond the number of the victims—a new category of evil. While it might seem at first glance not terribly controversial to call Adolf Hitler evil, Fackenheim has in fact put his finger on another fault line in Hitler explanation—the surprising reluctance of some of those who have written about Hitler to consider him *consciously* evil rather than someone who perpetrated evil acts in the sincere belief that he was doing good.

It is precisely this question—whether Hitler was cynical or sincere—that is at the heart of the great divide between the two most influential Hitler explainers in the English-speaking world: Hugh Trevor-Roper and Alan Bullock. While thousands upon thousands of books and monographs have followed, it is their two seminal works, written shortly after the war—Trevor-Roper's *The Last Days of Hitler* (1947) and Bullock's *Hitler: A Study in Tyranny* (1952)—that have defined the poles of a fundamental debate about Hitler that continues to this day.

The death threat was postmarked Lisbon. Hugh Trevor-Roper remembers that detail well. Recalling it this autumn evening, in front of a roaring fire in a common room of the Oxford-Cambridge Club in London, he treats the threat, which he received shortly after the publication of *The Last Days of Hitler,* as an amusing footnote now, although he seems to have taken it seriously at the time.

"It was from the Stern Gang," Trevor-Roper recalled, referring to the Jewish underground guerrilla group in Palestine, which had demonstrated its willingness to engage in political assassination. The death sentence, Trevor-Roper says, was the Stern Gang's way of expressing its disapproval of his vision of Hitler in *The Last Days.* But it was more than a footnote. It was an early signal of how highly charged Hitler explanations would become in the postwar world, and of what was really at stake—the nature of Hitler's posthumous survival.

Trevor-Roper's *The Last Days of Hitler* was not only one of the first Hitler books but one of the most famous and influential. (It is still in print, a million copies and forty-eight years later.) The book reflected Trevor-Roper's strength as a historian (the meticulous scholarship that would eventually enable him to rise to perhaps the most illustrious post in the profession, Regius Professor of Modern History at Oxford) and as an intelligence operative (he distinguished himself during the war as an MI6 counterintelligence specialist). As a title, *The Last Days of Hitler* is somewhat misleading. While Hitler's final weeks in the Berlin bunker are the focus of the book, it is more than a study of his end; it is a full-blooded evocation of who he was and of the power of his charisma.

The book began as an intelligence mission. In June of 1945, Soviet officials deliberately started spreading the lie that Adolf Hitler was still alive, and being harbored in the British zone of occupation in Berlin for nefarious joint operations against the Soviet Union. To find out the truth about Hitler's fate, British Intelligence dispatched Trevor-Roper to Berlin. Once there, he threw himself into the task, descending into the bombed-out, waterlogged ruins of the bunker; tracking down and interrogating Hitler's officers, aides, secretaries, and flunkies (including those who'd soaked their leader's dead body with gasoline and set it on fire). By the time he was through he'd precisely documented Hitler's whereabouts, moment by moment, from April 20, the Führer's last birthday, through April 30—the day of his suicide.

The irony of Trevor-Roper's intelligence mission is that, while he succeeded brilliantly in establishing the fact of Hitler's physical death, the book he later wrote played an important role in Hitler's metaphysical survival—gave him a kind of life after death. The source of this resurrection was something he hadn't expected to find—a deeper mystery than whether Hitler had physically survived: the survival of the Hitler spell. While one might have expected to encounter the power of that spell when Hitler was a demagogue on the rise or after he'd become the triumphant Führer, Trevor-Roper was surprised at the extent to which, even after ignominious defeat, the spell still held sway among those in Hitler's inner circle.

"Even in the bunker, when all the buildings of Berlin are falling down on top of him, even when he was dead they carried out his wishes," Trevor-Roper told me, still fascinated by the phenomenon. "They stayed behind! They stayed there until he was dead, and when he was dead they exposed themselves"—to bombs—"and carried out Hitler's last wishes."

"People have described this as mesmeric power—do you think it's literally mesmerism?" I asked.

"He certainly had an extraordinary power," Trevor-Roper replied. "When he wanted to mesmerize, he did have this effect. It didn't work on everyone.

It didn't work on—to put it crudely—aristocrats or on people who were sensitive to the vulgarity of his behavior."

It is hard to imagine Trevor-Roper—in every respect the embodiment of the waspish don, from his Oxbridge tweeds to the bone-dry ironies of his speech and prose—succumbing to the spell of a dead dictator. But, as he wrote in an essay revisiting *The Last Days* in a 1989 issue of *Encounter,* "I have been accused of having exalted Adolf Hitler and having created a public image of him as the genius of National Socialism. Indeed, of being the prime author of that myth, almost a positive successor to Dr. Goebbels."

If the Stern Gang was Trevor-Roper's most menacing critic, his most thoughtful one has been Professor Alvin Rosenfeld, the director of the Jewish Studies Program at Indiana University and the author of a 1985 study of postwar Hitler fiction and fantasy entitled *Imagining Hitler.* Trevor-Roper was not writing fiction, of course, but his spellbinding, cinematic vision of Hitler, Rosenfeld argues, became the defining image, the ur-Hitler for the decades of pulp fiction and film that followed.

The essence of Rosenfeld's critique is that in attempting to describe Hitler's spell Trevor-Roper fell under it—and that his book perpetuated it. In trying to explain how this happened to the respected Oxford scholar, Rosenfeld himself seems drawn to a subdued version of the occult rhetoric of possession he criticizes in Trevor-Roper. Rosenfeld says that when Trevor-Roper wrote about Hitler "the fiction writer within the scholar seemed to come alive," as if some dark being within Trevor-Roper had been awakened by exposure to Hitler's spell, to take possession of the otherwise scrupulously rational scholar.

Rosenfeld cites, in particular, Trevor-Roper's description of Hitler's eyes, which concludes, "The fascination of those eyes, which had bewitched so many seemingly sober men. . . . Hitler had the eyes of a hypnotist which seduced the wits and affections of all who yielded to their power. . . . This personal magnetism remained with him to the end; and only by reference to it can we explain the extraordinary obedience which he still commanded in the last week of his life."

It is Rosenfeld's thesis that Trevor-Roper's resort to "the special language of the occult sciences," his use of words like "wizard" and "enchanter," gave birth to the occult-messiah version of Hitler that became a fixture of postwar literature. And yet despite the criticism that he mythologized Hitler, Trevor-Roper has never backed down from his belief that there was something irrational at the heart of Hitler's appeal, "a frightening mystery" not explicable by the traditional tools of historical and psychological analysis. Rather, the thrust of Trevor-Roper's defense against the criticism—at least, in my conversation with him—consisted of a counterthrust: an attack on the opposing school of Hitler explanation embodied by his rival Hitler biographer Alan Bullock.

In fact, throughout our talk Trevor-Roper returned repeatedly and vigorously to what he believes is the key inadequacy of the original Bullock vision: the belief that Hitler can be explained in the same terms as traditional historical models, such as Caesar and Napoleon. It's a view that Bullock first advanced in the 1952 *Study in Tyranny*. Bullock's eight-hundred-page biography is more comprehensive than Trevor-Roper's *Last Days* and focuses far more on Hitler's manipulative political skills than on the emotional magnetism that fascinated Trevor-Roper. In a sense, Bullock's concern with the gritty machinations of backroom politics may reflect the class differences between him and the patrician Trevor-Roper. The middle-class Yorkshireman Bullock is impatient with high-flown notions of mesmeric attraction.

"It's a good book," Trevor-Roper said, prefacing his assessment of Bullock with faint praise. What he objects to, however, is Bullock's vision of Hitler—what Trevor-Roper calls the "mountebank Hitler." "This was influential right after the war," Trevor-Roper told me. "And in Alan Bullock's book he described Hitler as an opportunist who was solely concerned with acquiring power."

"Mountebank" is a word little used these days, which is unfortunate, because the word does have an expressive power that conjures up a whole worldview. Derived from the old Italian phrase for "mount-on-bench" a mountebank is described by the *OED* as "an itinerant quack who from an elevated platform appealed to his audience by means of stories, tricks, juggling and the like." A grander figure than a mere con man or charlatan, the mountebank is a figure of public life, often a politician—one who practices his charlatanry from a public platform. At the core of the mountebank characterization is cynicism and manipulativeness. The mountebank may pose as a true believer, as one possessed by a grand mission, but it is all "tricks, juggling and the like." Indeed, this is the actor-Hitler that Emil Fackenheim insists upon. By contrast, the essence of Trevor-Roper's vision of Hitler is that he was not an actor but a true believer, a man of conviction, however wicked those convictions were—not a cynic but, rather, horrifically sincere. It's a position that Trevor-Roper articulated most strikingly when I asked him whether he thought Hitler knew that his actions were evil.

"Oh no," Trevor-Roper said firmly. "He was convinced of his own rectitude."

One has to hear Trevor-Roper pronounce the word "rectitude," with such plentitude of rectitude himself. He almost succeeds in endowing a sincere belief in genocide with a kind of perverse dignity. This is not his intention, of course. He certainly means to say that Hitler was dreadfully, *mistakenly* "convinced of his own rectitude," but that Hitler nonetheless genuinely believed that the Jews were trying to destroy the Aryan race and had to be destroyed—in self-defense.

Trevor-Roper traces the origin of his belief that Hitler was sincere to his own reading of *Mein Kampf,* in German, back in 1938 (before Hitler permitted a full English translation). What *Mein Kampf* revealed to him about Hitler was something that few scholars and political figures took seriously before the war. "There was a powerful and coherent, if horrible, message which he had thought out, a philosophy," Trevor-Roper said. "He obviously took himself deadly seriously. He was not, as Bullock calls him, an adventurer. He considered himself a rare phenomenon, such as appears only once in centuries. It was not a joke that he was selling."

In other words, he was not a mountebank?

"Well, the conventional wisdom about Hitler before the war—at least, until Munich—was that he was a sort of clown, that he was taken off from the music hall. He looked ridiculous. He had this Charlie Chaplin mustache and he made these ranting speeches, and people couldn't take him seriously." He paused. "After Munich, they had to take him seriously."

Again and again, Trevor-Roper returned to the attack on what he insisted was the wrongheadedness of the mountebank-Hitler concept that Bullock bequeathed the postwar world. It was almost as if Bullock's Hitler were the real enemy. "He was not an adventurer," Trevor-Roper reiterated emphatically at one point. "At the end of the war, the Allied line was that Hitler was an adventurer, an irresponsible opportunist."

The mountebank idea still had the capacity to infuriate Trevor-Roper. "The question was why the Germans followed an irresponsible opportunist. But the fact is that he nearly won the war. If he *had* won the war—and it was by a whisker he didn't, I think there were three or four moments in the war when he really could have won it—historians would be saying to you he was, as he saw himself, this great historical figure. I was the odd man out at the time."

I found it fascinating that, at the age of eighty-one, Trevor-Roper could still become so impassioned on this point. For him, it seemed not just an embattled academic position but an article of faith. Indeed, over the years Trevor-Roper's predilection for believing in Hitler's sincerity has been nothing if not consistent. It's certainly there in his most illuminating essay on Hitler, "The Mind of Adolf Hitler," which appeared as the introduction to the 1953 edition of Hitler's *Secret Conversations,* also known as the *Table Talk.*

"You believe that the Hitler of the *Table Talk* is the real Hitler—that he's not posing?" I asked him.

"Oh, it's the real Hitler," Trevor-Roper replied. "Oh yes, oh yes, no doubt about it."

The *Table Talk* dates back to mid-1941, when Hitler established his underground command post for running the war on the eastern front. His nightly routine was highly consistent. After midnight, tea and cakes would be served, and

Hitler would relax with his personal staff, including several young secretaries, a couple of congenial aides, and a guest or two from the outside world. Then, beginning around two A.M., and sometimes continuing until dawn, when he finally went to sleep, Hitler would hold forth to his captive audience for hour upon hour, pontificating upon the world situation, history, art, philosophy, literature, opera, culture, and, above all, his vision of the Brave New Aryan Future.

Prevailed upon by the flattery of his increasingly powerful aide, Martin Bormann, to permit a stenographer to attend these sessions, so that none of the pearls of wisdom he dispensed would be lost, Hitler relished the idea that he was speaking for history. Bormann would take the transcripts from the stenographer and knit together the raw flow of Hitler's words, editing, refining, polishing, constructing a testament to Hitler's thought process—his stream of consciousness as he wanted history to see it.

My own response to the *Table Talk* is far more equivocal than Trevor-Roper's: that, at best, it's the real *counterfeit* Hitler. Even though the words are, for the most part, Hitler's, it's as false a creation as the "Hitler Diaries" of a decade ago. In a sense, the *Table Talk* is Hitler's own Hitler-diary hoax.

Here, for example, we have Hitler on the evening of October 24, 1941, piously declaring, "The Ten Commandments are a code of living to which there's no refutation. These precepts correspond to irrefragable needs of the human soul; they're inspired by the best religious spirit."

Is this a Hitler convinced of his own rectitude or a Hitler *posing* as someone convinced of his own rectitude? Perhaps the best answer to that comes in the *Table Talk* entry for the very next evening, in a revealing discussion of the Final Solution that may be Hitler's consummate lie.

What makes this lie so astonishing is that it's delivered to the two men who are in the best position to know what an enormous falsehood it is—the "special guests" in the command post, the SS and Gestapo chief, Heinrich Himmler, and his chief lieutenant in the SS, Reinhard Heydrich. To them, his closest confederates in carrying out the Final Solution (which in the preceding months had accelerated to programmatic mass extermination), Hitler, in an obviously staged performance, delivers himself of these chilling reflections:

> From the rostrum of the Reichstag, I prophesied [in 1939] to Jewry that, in the event of war's proving inevitable, the Jew would disappear from Europe. That race of criminals has on its conscience the two million dead of the First World War and now already hundreds of thousands more. Let nobody tell me that all the same we can't park them in the marshy parts of Russia! Who's worrying about our troops? It's not a bad idea, by the way, that public rumor attributes to us a plan to exterminate the Jews. Terror is a salutary thing.

This is not the language of a man "convinced of his own rectitude" in exterminating Jews. This is a man so convinced of his own criminality that he must deny that the crime is happening (it's only a "rumor," which, though "salutary," is not true); must surround that backhanded denial with disinformation (we are "parking" the Jews in the marshy parts of conquered Russian territory, not murdering them); must preface that disinformation with a justification for the act disingenuously denied ("That race of criminals has on its conscience the two million dead"—and therefore if the "rumor" were true the killing would be just).

One tries to imagine the glances that Hitler, Himmler, and Heydrich must have exchanged during the orchestration of this elaborate charade. The three Holocaust perpetrators here become the first Holocaust deniers, establishing the pattern for the "revisionists" who followed: The Holocaust didn't happen, but, if it did, the Jews deserved it. If this is "the real Hitler," as Trevor-Roper declares, the realness is to be found in his slippery falseness, not in the "sincerity" that Trevor-Roper persists in finding in him.

Trevor-Roper's credulousness on this question is perhaps what was responsible for getting him into trouble in the 1983 Hitler-diaries affair. In *Selling Hitler,* Robert Harris's account of that fiasco, Trevor-Roper repeatedly professes himself unwilling to doubt the bona fides of the con men peddling the diaries. Asked to judge their authenticity by Rupert Murdoch, who was considering purchasing them for *The Times* of London, Trevor-Roper (by then Lord Dacre) initially pronounced them genuine. But just as *The Times* was about to go to press with the big scoop, Trevor-Roper changed his mind. He quickly called the editor, Frank Giles, to urge him to stop the presses. In Harris's account, another editor reached Murdoch, advised him of Trevor-Roper's qualms, and asked his boss what to do. In one of the legendary moments of contemporary journalism, Murdoch replied, "Fuck Dacre! Publish!"

This propensity to presume the sincerity of characters that others see as mountebanks—from Hitler to the Hitler-diary hoaxers—is surprising in a man of Trevor-Roper's sophistication but may have something to do with his distance from their more plebeian class origins. Yet there's something more to it than that—another instance in which a Hitler explanation tells us something unexpected about the explainer. It's almost as though Trevor-Roper is refusing to entertain the idea of a human soul depraved enough to carry out Hitler's crimes *without* being convinced of his own rectitude. Perhaps Trevor-Roper simply cannot let go of a stubbornly optimistic faith that human nature is incapable of *that* radical an evil.

A noisy chess match in the common room of the Oxford-Cambridge Club had made conversation difficult, and Trevor-Roper was late for his next appointment, yet before leaving he brought up the subject of the *Table Talk* one more time. He was speaking about an error in the initial translation which had Hitler saying, "I feel quite confused." "Now, Hitler was never confused about anything," Trevor-Roper told me. The word should have been *embarrassed.*

What struck me most forcefully about that statement was Trevor-Roper's absolute confidence in his grasp of Hitler's thought world: Hitler was never confused about anything, but he *was* subject to embarrassment.

The issue of Hitler's embarrassment brought to mind one of the most disquieting Hitler stories I'd ever heard, the story of "the newborn babe." Disquieting in part because of its source—David Irving, the controversial historian and Holocaust "revisionist." And disquieting because, despite its source, it seemed to me one of the most chilling portrayals of Hitler's thought world I'd come upon.

In his London study, Irving had been boasting of how he'd penetrated what he called "the magic circle"—that select group of aides who had stayed with Hitler in the bunker to the bitter end. How, late one night, one of those closest to Hitler for the longest period of time, his personal secretary, Christa Schroeder, had disclosed to Irving an encounter with Hitler in the aftermath of the Night of the Long Knives, in June 1934—the night Hitler had his stormtrooper chieftains murdered. "You know he could be quite cruel," Christa Schroeder told Irving. "At the end of this bloody day when they were going to take them all up to prison to be shot, we flew back to Berlin and I'd lost sight of Hitler in the Chancellery for a while. And I went to the cafeteria. You know, it was quite late, but he joined me because we were both vegetarians. He came in an hour later, stood in the doorway, and he says, 'So, Fräulein Schroeder, now I have had a bath and I am as clean as a newborn babe again.' "

" 'Clean as a newborn babe'—meaning from the blood?" I asked Irving.

"That's right," Irving said. "She found it symptomatic of the facility with which he committed mass murder," he added matter-of-factly. "That he just had to have a bath and was as clean as a newborn baby."

"He leaves the blood behind in—"

"Went down the plughole," Irving assented enthusiastically. "Like the blood in *Psycho*."

What struck me about this extraordinary story was the way it spoke to the Trevor-Roper–Bullock dispute. It was Hitler mocking the very notion that he could be embarrassed by the blood on his hands. In depicting himself as a "newborn babe," he is practically flaunting his own baby pictures—those tokens of innocence which Claude Lanzmann finds so troubling. He is laughing at the absurdity of his blood-drenched self as a newborn babe. Rather than being convinced of his own rectitude, he is making an obscene joke of it.

But does it really matter what Hitler thought about what he did? Certainly it does not matter to his millions of victims. The question does matter, however, to the world that survived, because ultimately Hitler explanations are ways of talking about the nature of human nature, the nature of evil.

. . .

"If you ask me what I think evil is," Alan Bullock said to me as we approached the pillared facade of Oxford's Ashmolean Museum, "it's the Incomplete."

"The Incomplete?"

"In the sense that it has a yet-to-be-brought-into-being quality, yes," Bullock replied.

More than anything else about Bullock, this mystical streak surprised me. After all, the hallmark of the work of this octogenarian Oxford historian has been scholarly restraint and modesty, a scrupulous unwillingness to exceed the limits of the available evidence. In his published work Bullock is a scholar who eschews speculation. But in person Bullock is a veritable fount of speculation, ranging from his notion of Hitler's metaphysical incompleteness to rather earthy thoughts about Hitler's physical incompleteness. Or, as Bullock put it, the "one-ball business."

The "one-ball business" had come up in the context of a question I'd asked Bullock about the death, in 1931, of Hitler's young half niece, Geli Raubal. In his biography Bullock had stated his belief that Hitler "was in love" with Geli, that they'd shared a tormented relationship plagued by his jealousy and possessiveness. But Bullock does more than depict Hitler in love with Geli; he asserts that her still puzzling death—an apparent suicide, in her bedroom in Hitler's Munich apartment—was "a greater blow than any other event in his life" (a remarkable statement, considering what that life encompassed). Over a glass of wine in the common room of St. Catherine's College, I'd asked Bullock if he still believed that Geli's death was a moment of transformation for Hitler.

"Well, it seems so—I mean, the keeping of the room, the sentimentality," Bullock told me, referring to a Miss Havisham–like shrine to Geli which Hitler ever after maintained untouched in the room in which she died.

Bullock then turned to the nature of their relationship. "But what did he want her to *do*?" he asked. "What did Hitler want from Geli he couldn't get, or she couldn't give? Did he want her to marry him? Be his mistress? But could he perform? I mean, it was suggested actually, I understand he, sexually—" Bullock appeared somewhat uncomfortable with the subject. "I mean, you come back to the one-ball business."

I asked him whether he believed the 1945 Soviet autopsy report that no left testicle had been found in Hitler's charred body.

"Oh, there's no question," Bullock replied.

In fact, certain questions raised by the Russian autopsy about Hitler's last moment of life have *not* been laid to rest—questions ranging from the one testicle that the Russians claim was missing from Hitler's genitals to the one bullet that passed through Hitler's head. A long-standing dispute between Bullock and Trevor-Roper over the circumstances of Hitler's suicide reflects once again their profound disagreement about Hitler's essential character.

Most authorities agree that on the afternoon of April 30, 1945, with Soviet troops advancing on the bunker, Hitler and Eva Braun entered their private suite with two revolvers and some cyanide capsules. Shortly thereafter, a single gunshot was heard, and Hitler's aides carried the two dead bodies to a bomb crater just outside the bunker, set them on fire, and then buried the charred remains in a shallow grave. A few days later, Soviet troops captured the bunker, dug up the remains, and called in pathologists. With the help of dental records, they identified Hitler's body and performed an autopsy. The results of the autopsy were kept secret by the Soviets until 1968. Before then, almost all historians agreed with the scenario that Trevor-Roper had pieced together from his interrogations and published in *The Last Days*. According to that account, Eva Braun killed herself by crushing a cyanide capsule in her mouth, while Hitler chose the traditional death of a defeated German officer—shooting himself in the head with his pistol. The crux of Trevor-Roper's view of Hitler's death is once again his unshakable faith in Hitler's sincerity. "Of Hitler at least it can be said that his emotions were genuine," he wrote in *The Last Days*—he died a soldier for the cause.

The Soviet autopsy findings, which came to light in *The Death of Adolf Hitler*, a 1968 book by the Russian journalist Lev Bezymenski, told another story. Soviet pathologists reported finding crushed glass shards of a cyanide capsule clenched in Hitler's badly burned jaw, and thus concluded that he had died from cyanide poisoning. Bezymenski argued, on the basis of the pathologists' report and a story attributed to Hitler's valet, Heinz Linge, who was just outside the death chamber, that Hitler died not a soldier's death but a coward's death. According to Bezymenski, Hitler, lacking the courage to pull the trigger on himself, bit down on a cyanide capsule; after his death, Linge entered the death suite and fired Hitler's pistol into his head to create the illusion that the Führer took the soldier's way out.

But Trevor-Roper contends that the Soviet autopsy report shouldn't be taken at face value—that it was a political as well as a medical document, designed to diminish Hitler for history. Seen in that light, the Soviet report of Hitler's genital incompleteness could also have been concocted as a crude way of further derogating Hitler. The missing testicle thus becomes the objective correlative of the lack of manliness that the Soviets imputed to his style of suicide.

Until recently, Bullock has steadfastly adhered to the findings of the Soviet autopsy, in part because they validated his original conception of Hitler as a schemer up until his final moment—an actor even in his final act. But evidence in a new book, *The Death of Hitler*, by Ada Petrova and Peter Watson, caused Bullock to alter his view. "What the book shows is that Linge's story is ruled out," Bullock now says. "This is what Trevor-Roper said from the beginning." Bullock now accepts Petrova and Watson's view that Hitler—almost simultaneously—bit down on a cyanide capsule and then fired a bullet through his head.

Bullock remains fascinated, however, not just with the conclusions of the Soviet autopsy but with the autopsied organs. He told me that he had revised the paperback of his 1991 dual biography, *Hitler and Stalin,* to include an account of the bizarre odyssey of Hitler's organs, based on interviews with the Soviet soldiers who had disposed of Hitler's remains. "On Stalin's orders, Hitler's organs, which had been placed in jars during the autopsy, were removed to the Kremlin," Bullock wrote.

"Stalin had the organs sent to him in Moscow?" I asked Bullock.

"Yes, he had them sent," Bullock replied. "Ah, marvelous! But did he *eat* them is what I want to know!" he asked, grinning, as he conjured up a horrific primal communion between the two dictators. "I'm sure some psychiatrist is going to say, 'Yeah, he ate Hitler's ball.' I must say, his one and only ball. Just think of what they'll make of that one. Poor old Waite—he'd really go overboard on that one."

In *The Psychopathic God,* Robert Waite built an elaborate castle of Freudian interpretative analysis on the slender foundation of Hitler's purportedly half-empty scrotal sac. Bullock doesn't buy the Freudian interpretation of the one-ball business. But in an important sense, the Hitler he gave the world was a significantly deflated figure.

Bullock's quest for the truth about Hitler began, he told me, in the midst of the Blitz. Before the war, he was primarily a historian of ancient wars—a student of the conflicts chronicled by Thucydides and Tacitus. But after the invasion of Poland, in 1939, he turned his attention to the present. "I spent the war in London building up the broadcasting to Europe"—the BBC service to Nazi-occupied nations—"so I was sensitized in a big way to the politics and history of Europe in that period," he said. "I think all historians who were drawn into the war, like Hugh Trevor-Roper and Hugh Seton-Watson, came back with the question: Why? How did this happen?"

Shortly after the war ended, Bullock traveled to Germany, and what he remembers is the silence. "I remember going to the Ruhr—this was the heart of Europe as far as industry was concerned—and there was silence everywhere. There wasn't a single smokestack. There were no cars, no trains. Long lines of foreign workers wending their way home. It was like a remote agricultural country, except for the ruins. I couldn't believe what had happened. I mean, civilization was destroyed. All of us, I think, came back wanting to know why."

What galvanized him to write a Hitler biography was the Nuremberg trials. "There were twenty-six volumes of verbatim testimony from the trials, and I reviewed every one of those," he said. "I became intensely excited about them. From the point of view of the historian, the Nuremberg trials were an absolutely unqualified wonder. I mean, the greatest coup in history for historians. They captured the records of the most powerful state in the world immediately after the event! So I became involved with the publication of those, and then out of the blue came an invitation to write the life of Hitler."

Bullock's massive biography was an instant success upon publication, a best-seller on both sides of the Atlantic. To date, *Hitler: A Study in Tyranny* has sold more than three million copies, and it remains in print in a 1962 revised edition. When first published, the book "struck a chord," Bullock told me, because it dramatically defied the popular conception of Hitler which had taken shape after the war—the demonic-madman Hitler that Trevor-Roper had been instrumental in creating. "I remember very much the reaction in the popular press," Bullock said. "That Hitler wasn't a madman. He was an extremely astute and able politician. I think that really did surprise people."

Bullock's was a decidedly contrarian view. As the terrible dimensions of the Holocaust carnage became more and more a fact of shared consciousness, the figure of Hitler had grown to mythic, horrific proportions. He had become something close to an apotheosis of evil. New words had been employed—"genocide," "Holocaust"—to describe his crimes, and the dimensions of his persona became inflated to match the dimensions of the slaughter. Against the backdrop of Trevor-Roper's messiah of irrationality, Bullock's Hitler was a deliberately diminished figure: a man of shrewdly rational—even petty—calculation; a human-scale schemer, not an all-powerful evil genius who burst the bounds of previous frameworks of explanation.

While Trevor-Roper had stressed how close Hitler came to winning the war, the recurring subtext of Bullock's *Study in Tyranny* is how close Hitler came to failing to reach power. His dramatic reconstruction of the high-stakes maneuvering for the Reich chancellorship, which brought Hitler to power in 1933, subverts the notion of some profound historical inevitability of Hitler by emphasizing the degree to which pure luck and shabby backstage scheming played a role in bringing him to office.

Bullock's *Study in Tyranny* is more than a biography; it's a heroic effort to fit Hitler into the more familiar framework of classical historical portraiture. Fittingly, Bullock affixes to the book an epigraph from Aristotle: "Men do not become tyrants in order to keep out the cold."

"Lovely remark," Bullock told me. "I'm a classics scholar, and Aristotle's *Politics* is a wonderful book that I just thought had to be brought to bear. Men become tyrants because they wish to exercise power. It is not for material betterment or comfort but because they have an itch for power."

"The love of power for its own sake?"

"That was my view of Hitler then. It's changed, you know."

It is rare for a scholar to concede such a dramatic shift in position. While there had been hints of a change in the 1962 edition of *Study in Tyranny*, Bullock had never, as far as I knew, spelled out how profound a revision he'd embraced—nor had he ever mapped out the new model of Hitler's mind he'd developed to replace the original. The first intimation of the direction of that change had come when I mentioned to him the theologian Emil Fackenheim's take on the actor Hitler. I'd told Bullock about Fackenheim's belief that Hitler's hatred of the Jews was, like all his professed convictions, the charade of a cynical actor.

"Ah!" Bullock said. "He was the great actor *who believed in the part.* Absolutely. That's the unique thing about him. He's a great actor but he— There's a wonderful quotation from Nietzsche."

At this point, we were in his study at St. Catherine's, and he drew down from his bookshelf a volume of Nietzsche to read aloud some lines that expressed his own revised view of Hitler's psychology:

> Men believe in the truth of all that is seen to be strongly believed. In all great deceivers, a remarkable process is at work to which they owe their power. In the very act of deception with all its preparations—the dreadful voice, the expression, the gestures—they are overcome by their belief in themselves, and it is this belief which then speaks so persuasively, so miracle-like to the audience. Not only does he communicate that to the audience but the audience returns it to him and strengthens his belief.

The mental process of public figures that Nietzsche is describing here is complicated. It begins with what seems like a cynical calculation: that what is important is not to believe but *to be seen to believe*—that the counterfeiting of belief counts for more than the sincerity of belief. But if there is calculation initially, what follows is the "remarkable process" whereby the actor-deceiver becomes carried away, becomes a believer in his own deception—possessed by himself.

Think of the process beginning with a calculating Hitler—call it Bullock I —then proceeding to incorporate the spellbinding, sincere Hitler of Trevor-Roper, and, finally—through a meshing of thesis and antithesis—coming to a synthesis, the Hitler of Bullock II. The actor who comes to believe in his own act. The mesmerist who mesmerizes himself.

The key change in his thinking, Bullock told me, came as he reinterpreted the role of ideology in Hitler's thought world. "I changed my mind about Hitler, in that I originally took him as solely interested in power," Bullock explained. "I now think the ideology is central. I think it's what armors Hitler against remorse, guilt—anything. Hitler was unmovable on this ideology, this belief he was the man sent by Providence. The belief in himself. I think I have brought that out much more in the second book than I did in the first. In the first, I didn't grasp that." ("Alan admits that I changed his view," Trevor-Roper boasted. And Bullock acknowledges the influence on him of his rival's views.)

I was impressed by Bullock's humility, but wondered whether this more complicated and dynamic model of Hitler's thought process didn't contain a contradiction. "Can one be sincere and insincere at the same time?" I asked him.

Bullock trumped me with a visual metaphor and a story about a funeral. "It's like fast-moving water, isn't it?" he said.

Fast-moving water? I thought of light flickering off the peaks of rapidly moving waves. There was something intuitively convincing about the image, the flickering back and forth of calculation and belief in the fast-moving stream of consciousness.

As for the funeral, it had taken place just that morning, Bullock said. A colleague had drowned in a swimming accident. Bullock had spoken at the service. "I experienced it this morning when I was speaking," he told me. "I was speaking with my whole heart, because I really was very distressed—the wife who had gone through this appalling experience was in front of me, looking at me. And at the same time I was saying to myself, 'Are they listening to me? Am I being a success?' I'm being frank with you. I don't think I'm an insincere man, but I'm perfectly aware of what I do, and I wanted to be a success."

Bullock's new synthesis of Hitler's thought process can sound abstract until he connects it to a momentous turning point in the war, in which Bullock finds the origins of Hitler's defeat. That turning point, Bullock believes, came after his first heady victories on the Russian front, in 1941. Bullock perceives Hitler to have been cautious and cunning before that—ready, for instance, to withdraw immediately if the French had shown any sign of military opposition to his reoccupation of the Rhineland in 1936.

"Up to that point in 1941, he's hesitant—and then he's ruthless," Bullock said. "But, once he gets the attack on Russia, then I think he thinks, you know, This is it."

According to Bullock, the astonishing success of Hitler's June 1941 offensive, the victorious onslaught that brought his armies to the outskirts of Moscow, caused Hitler to become intoxicated with his own powers—so intoxicated that he lost the caution and cunning that had been essential ingredients of his political and military successes. "The man destroys himself," Bullock said. "Which is so interesting. I mean, making the German Army stand in front of Moscow and not retreat"—thus condemning the overextended troops to decimation by the cold and by the Soviet counteroffensives when a tactical retreat might have preserved Hitler's overwhelming strategic advantage.

> If only he'd been flexible, it's quite conceivable Stalin could have made a compromise peace. That's one of the things that's a mystery. But the extraordinary thing about this—and this is where the element of hubris comes into it—is that it's when he gets to the point where he no longer manipulates his image but believes in it entirely, when he drops the manipulation, that he's destroyed. He was destroyed by his own image. As long as he believed and manipulated, he was successful, but when he gets outside Moscow he no longer manipulates. It's will and will alone afterward.

"He loses the pragmatism?"

"All of it. Look, the man could have had half of Russia on his side against Stalin. That's the moment he destroys himself. Oh, it's a very satisfactory Greek tragedy."

Can Hitler be explained by traditional concepts of evil, such as those found in classical tragedy? Or was Hitler an abhorrent anomaly—outside the continuum of ordinary human nature—as Emil Fackenheim believes?

Bullock flickers back and forth on these questions. Shortly after he made his remarks about Hitler's defeat being a vindication of classical Greek tragedy, he raised the issue of whether Hitler explodes the old framework.

I'd asked him if his lifelong study of Hitler had resulted in a change in his view of the potential of human nature for evil.

"A lot," he said. "I mean, if you're brought up as most of us are, we live in a very protective society and we're confronted by . . . I'll never forget coming out of Yad Vashem"—the Holocaust museum in Jerusalem. "I was shattered. Shattered."

"Does it require that we reconsider what the essence of human nature is?" I asked him. "Does there come a point, a critical mass, where quantity of killing matters?"

"I think there's an extra thing that comes into it when you mechanize it," Bullock said. "Then it's suddenly the accountants working on the cost-benefit of this and that method of killing. This is the horror of the German Holocaust. It isn't done in hot-blooded fury of battle or revenge. It's cold-blooded. The Jews were not a military threat. When the Russians committed atrocities—by God, they had provocation. That *was* revenge. This wasn't revenge. This was cold-bloodedness."

So for Bullock, the state of mind behind the killing is a key factor in defining the degree of evil—but not the only factor. He returned to the question of scale.

"It's a difficult one, isn't it? Scale—I'm afraid I think it does matter, but I resist that conclusion. I mean, I feel it's somehow or other morally flawed, that judgment. And yet I do think if you see a million people killed, somehow or other it's worse than if ten are killed."

It was at this point in our conversation that Bullock's mystical streak emerged. We'd left his study to walk from St. Catherine's to the Ashmolean Museum, where Bullock had a trustees' meeting. He'd been discussing the difficulty of defining Hitler's evil in conventional terms. "I must say, I think the mystics have something to say on the question," Bullock told me as he set a vigorous pace across the bridge over the river Isis. Shortly thereafter, he delivered himself of that remarkable statement about evil as Incompleteness.

His voice rose. "The paradox of Jesus embracing Judas!" he exclaimed. "That's fascinating. You read it, your hair stands on end! He kissed him on the lips!"

It took me some time to figure out the relationship between Bullock's vision of evil as Incompleteness, Jesus' embrace of Judas, and Bullock's conception of Hitler. But there is a unity there.

Consider evil as Incompleteness: evil conceived not as an alien, inhuman otherness but as a less highly evolved form of humanness—lower, far lower on the great chain of being but still part of the same continuum of creation that gave birth to us. Thus Judas, the most conspicuously evil figure in the New Testament, can be embraced as a part of creation, albeit the most incomplete part.

Bullock finds in the mystics' love of paradox a validation for his own paradoxical vision of Hitler's thought world—simultaneously sincere and insincere. "Extraordinary," Bullock tells me. "Tao, Sufi, Zen Buddhism, Catholic, Protestant, Blake, Plato, Plotinus—although they're so different, they all loved paradox. That which is and that which is not; that which is wholly united and that which is wholly divided."

It was Bullock's father, Frank, who inspired his interest in the mystical path, and he speaks movingly of his father's unorthodox spiritual quest. "A Unitarian minister, he came to feel after the [First World] War that religion was dying and that there were so many people on a sort of spiritual hunt he couldn't reach," Bullock recalled.

> So, although he continued to preach—and a marvelous preacher he was—he did revive an old tradition, an alternative ministry. He completely severed himself from the church side of things, took a room that had no resemblance to a chapel. There was no ritual, no prayers. And he called his preaching psychology lectures. And he went on for twenty or thirty years. And there he brought home many of his religious beliefs, stated them in some nonreligious terms. A lot of people came to listen to him. Totally without recognition, because this was a town in the north that no one had heard of—Bradford. And he said, "Well, my

luck is to talk to forty or fifty people." And he never complained. I think that in
the nineteenth century he would have been a great preacher. And in the late twentieth century he'd be on television. And—well, he was a lovely man, he really
was.

Could it be that on some level Bullock was juxtaposing his modest, unsung
preacher father with the shameless and malevolent German street preacher he
has spent his life chronicling? Bullock's revised vision of Hitler's thought
world seemed to be yet another instance of the interrelationship of explainer
and explanation. In his new thesis, Bullock was incorporating two sides of
himself, two generations of Bullocks—his own orthodox, classically trained
mind-set and his father's unorthodox, mystical perspective.

As we approached the pillars of the Ashmolean, toward the end of our conversation, Bullock returned to an even more challenging aspect of Incompleteness—the controversial notion of an Incomplete God, a God not
sufficiently omnipotent to prevent Hitler's crimes.

"Some days, I ask God," Bullock told me, his voice dropping to an impassioned whisper, " 'If You were there, why didn't You stop it?' " And then he
added the sad lesson of a lifetime spent attempting to explain Hitler: "Never
believe God is omnipotent."

It was a thesis I was to hear posed in even more dramatic terms from a surprising source in Jerusalem—Yehuda Bauer, a professor of Holocaust Studies
at Hebrew University who is widely regarded as one of the foremost historians of the Holocaust. Bauer had been talking about the tortured attempts by
some theologians to explain Hitler and the Holocaust as "part of God's plan."

It's a problem Fackenheim has wrestled with—one that has led him to re-
define but reaffirm his belief in God. But Bauer believes, in the harsh light of
the Holocaust, that "there's no way there can be an all-powerful and a just
God. If He is all-powerful"—and He did not stop the killing—"He is Satan. If
He is just"—but did not have the power to stop the killing—"He is a nebbish.
I don't need a God like that."

Even for a professed atheist like Bauer, the attempt to explain Hitler entails
an attempt to explain God. But what about the attempt to explain Hitler? I
thought that Bauer, if anyone, would be in a position to answer the question:
Will there ever be a why?

Bauer told me he believes that it is theoretically possible. "But the fact that
something is explicable doesn't say we have explained it," he said.

Bauer is saying that there *is* a why, but it may be too late to find it. There are
too many long-dead eyewitnesses, too many gaps in the documentary record,
too many gaps in the record of memory. But that doesn't mean Hitler is outside human nature. The Holocaust opened up "new horizons . . . regarding the

possibilities, or the capabilities of humans," including capabilities for evil "that were never suspected before," Bauer has written. The reality of these capabilities suggests to Bauer that "such actions are likely or possible by others too."

We may despair of ever explaining Hitler. But we cannot abandon the attempt, because of those "others"—the other Hitlers who may be among us even now.

Singer's *Shadows:*
Footnotes to Hitler

I'm going to try an experiment here, invent or improvise an untried literary form, the serialized literary essay: I'm going to write about a novel in installments *as I'm reading it,* rather than reflect upon it in the tranquillity of completion. While this may seem to have a number of obvious disadvantages conventional reviews do not—writing about the beginning of a book in ignorance of the end, for instance—I believe it can also do something that the review form sometimes can't: capture some of the thrill and immediacy of falling in love with a book, not knowing where the infatuation will lead—to fulfillment or disillusion. Experiencing and recording the excitement as it happens.

It's an experiment made all the more appropriate—or tricky—by the fact it will be performed upon a novel that was itself initially published in serial form, *written* in serial form, written to be read and responded to in installments. It's a novel that I believe demands a novel response, a novel that has seized control of my mind and soul at a time when I have no time for seizures but can't help myself. A novel of almost unbearable intensity (so far), a novel of great beauty and great horror, one that seems in some ways to be about the persistent paradoxical simultaneity in life of beauty and horror. A novel I can only take in small installments, such is its painful intensity and such is my own (paradoxical) wish to prolong the painful pleasure of reading it.

Look how long I've managed to forestall even mentioning the book's title, which is *Shadows on the Hudson,* the astonishing new Isaac Bashevis Singer novel (translated from the Yiddish by Joseph Sherman). New, of course, in the sense that it was only recently discovered among his papers, in its original un-translated Yiddish form. Singer wrote it initially in twice-weekly installments for the Yiddish-language *Forward* in the late fifties. But new also in the way it's caused a new stir about the true character of Singer's work—the degree of darkness at its heart—and evoked wildly divergent responses from reviewers. And new in that it opens up a window on a unique moment in time in which an entire vision of history and human nature had to be invented anew.

I won't deny the possibility that the kind of response I'm having to the Singer book (so far) might have something to do with the circumstances of my own life, the timing of the moment *Shadows on the Hudson* first took posses-sion of me: I started reading it when I was first in the throes of the grueling task of doing the footnotes (endnotes) for my forthcoming book on controver-sies over attempts to explain Hitler. And (so far) among the many things the Singer novel seems to be about, it's about the very *first* postwar attempts to explain Hitler by a group of Jews who escaped him. To wrestle with the inex-plicability of horror and the horror of inexplicability. The very first attempts by the survivors of the community of Eastern European Jews—once lumi-nous, now incinerated—to grope wildly in the darkness for a way of coming to terms with the catastrophe that had consumed most of their families and all of the golden civilization that gave birth to them. The very first attempts to ask the question: Is it possible to go on living lives that are more than footnotes to Hitler?

At least that's what it seemed to be about when I stopped reading on page 160, about a third of the way through, when I had to stop to finish footnoting my Hitler book, and when one of the characters in this Hitler-riddled novel (in every sense of "riddled") tells another, "Time, too, is also a Hitler. It destroys everything." It is this same character who raises the key question of the novel: whether in the shadows of the death camps and those who ran them we have to re-envision the nature of human nature. "[A]nyone who didn't see it with his own eyes doesn't know what the human species really is."

Time, the timing, and the *time-framing* of *Shadows on the Hudson* is cru-cial, it seems to me. The story opens in 1947, yet Singer began writing it in late 1957. It's taken him a decade to come to grips with the travails of those trying to come to grips with the immediate aftershock of the catastrophe, when the ashes of the dead were still warm, the wounds of the living still raw, and Hitler very much the ghost at the feast that opens the book.

About that feast: I don't want to give you the impression that this is some grimly depressing abstract novel of ideas. To me, Singer's *Shadows* is a novel of sensation in both senses of the word, in which speculations both shocking and sensational are embodied in the flesh. In which ideas are felt as sharply as a slap in the face or as urgently as the wicked lick of a tongue (and sometimes both simultaneously). Only Singer (well, almost only Singer) can fuse theodicy and adultery so sensationally. Which is exactly what he seems to be doing in the dazzling dinner party scene that opens the novel. A sensational tour de force in which anguished, urgent talk of God's responsibility for Hitler is subverted by the hothouse flowering of a compelling, compulsive, and destructive adulterous intrigue that forms the core of the novel (so far).

But first let me introduce you to some of the people gathered for this haunted feast, set in a sumptuous Upper West Side apartment in one of those block-long behemoth buildings like the Apthorp or the Belnord. A feast set in a snowstorm that seems to elevate and isolate the dinner party into the lone packet of warmth in an icily hostile cosmos, the way the plague does in Boccaccio's *Decameron,* say. It's more than a snowstorm: As the two potential adulterers stare out a bedroom window while the other guests wonder about their absence, "the sky above the roof was luminous in the glare of New York, half red, half violet . . . as if a cosmic conflagration were in progress. . . ."

Inside, it's one of those gatherings in which Singer conjures up the lost glory of the "golden tradition": the genius-riddled Polish-Yiddish culture consumed by the cosmic conflagration of the Holocaust. Every guest is either descended from wonder-working rabbis, or impossibly brilliant sages, or is one in his own right. An array of extraordinarily prodigal scholars, scintillatingly caustic heretics, and wickedly charming scoundrels. And some who seem to be all those things at once.

One of my favorite figures is a relatively minor character (so far), Professor David Schrage, a mathematical genius descended "from learned and wealthy Warsaw Hasidim" who nonetheless "for the past twenty years . . . had devoted himself to psychic research to which he applied his mathematical knowledge. In Poland for a time he had been closely associated with the famous Madame Kluski . . . [He] had come to America on the eve of the Second World War but his wife Edzhe had died at the hands of the Nazis. To this day he continued to mourn for her and never ceased trying to contact her spirit in the world beyond."

The famous Madame Kluski! Learned and wealthy Hasidim! A math genius who does psychic research and longs to contact his lost wife in the world beyond! What a character, and he's one of the *least* memorable at the dinner party. There is the brilliant Zadok Halperin, "something of a celebrity" for his prodigious learning, "his German works on Kant and Solomon Maimon are cited in philosophy textbooks. His Hebrew monographs were studied at the University of Jerusalem. His proficiency in Talmud and sacred studies knew no limits" even though he "despised religion." He's the one who first utters the name of the ghost at the feast. Abruptly—everyone in this novel plunges abruptly into the most shocking and painful speculations—he declares to his host, Boris Makaver, "Just because Hitler was a maniac, a psychopath, must the world return to the middle ages?" Nothing has really changed, he says. The rules of Euclid's geometry remain the same.

"But now we have another geometry," another formidable guest, a Dr. Margolin, shoots back. He's ostensibly referring to the non-Euclidean geometries of Georg Riemann and Nikolai Lobachevski. But he's really talking about the new non-Euclidean moral geometry of the post-Hitler cosmos.

And then there is the adulterous triangle that emerges that night. At the apex is Anna, the host's vibrant and erotically self-destructive (so far) daughter, who cries out against the talk of God and geometry but has her own post-Hitler geometrical syllogism to offer: "I can't bear to hear about God. After what happened in Europe I don't even dare mention the word God—because if God really does exist and allowed it all, it's even worse than if He did not exist."

It's the primal cry of post-Holocaust theodicy, how to reconcile the existence of an omnipotent and (presumably) loving God with the kind of evil that seemed to prevail in the death camps. It's a question half a century of post-Hitler ratiocination has not answered to anyone's complete satisfaction, but one many have learned to live with. But here in 1947, it's being asked at a time when the question, the wound, was still at its most raw and searing.

It's a question that haunts, stalks, and shadows *Shadows,* pervades every conversation, invades even the comfortable circumstances of the dinner party and harries even the smallest gesture, like the lighting of a cigarette. When the host Boris Makaver complains about the smoke from a cigarette, a woman asks him, "Whom does the smoke harm? There's no danger." And, Singer tells us, "Boris understood what she was thinking. The smoke at Auschwitz had been worse."

To us a half-century later, this might verge on excess, but remember the timing and the time frame, remember Singer is writing what amounts to a historical novel, when the scent of that smoke was still acrid in the nostrils.

In any case, Anna is tired of her husband, a lawyer named Luria, an unprepossessing fellow except for his name. (Is it an accident he bears the name of the founder of the medieval Jewish cabalist tradition, Isaac Luria? I don't know yet.) He's "both violent and sickly, a chronic failure as well as a liar." No wonder Anna seems to be inciting the adulterous attentions of her former tutor, Hertz Greim, another wonder-working prodigy who has squandered his intellectual gifts in favor of exercising his talent with women. He, too, is haunted by Hitler and the question raised by the new geometry:

"Having lost his entire family in Poland, he had ceased to believe in humanity and its moral prescriptions." He keeps a mistress, has lived off his wife, and cheats on both of them as he's about to with Anna.

The night wears on, and the flirtation between Greim and Anna becomes more explicit and shameless. As their lust sharpens, so does the question it raises, at least in Greim's mind: Does his irresponsibility, the pain he'll cause his wife and her husband, matter? Does anything matter, does any sense of responsibility matter when, after all, as he tells himself, "God had abandoned the world. It was once more the domain of idols and idol worship." What force could the commandment against stealing another's wife have anymore? What force do any commandments have in the world of post-Hitler moral geometry?

Someone once wrote that without adultery, there would *be* no novel, and this is a novel that asks whether private lives, the kind of private lives that novels have traditionally been about, can *matter* to a people struggling with the question of whether any kind of life can be lived that is more than a footnote to Hitler.

A question I'll examine further (perhaps I'll even have read far enough to know Singer's answer) in the next installment.

From the Second Installment*

Now, at this point I think I should confess to a truly revealing Freudian slip I made in last week's column. A slip I made in speaking of the adulterer Grein, who may or may not be using Hitler as a meretricious rationale for shameless conduct he'd pursue anyway—God or no God, Hitler or no Hitler. Theodicy as an excuse for adultery.

In any case, in the draft I faxed into the *Observer,* I called him Hertz *Greim,* not Hertz *Grein* and that's the way it appeared in print. Talk about your transparent slips! Think Greim as in *grime.* Think Hertz as *hurts,* which may have been Singer's own semi-transparent piece of Yiddish-English wordplay. Hurts Grime. Grime Hurts. The fact that Greim (Grein) hurts, that he suffers, may be what's (marginally, possibly) redeeming about this character—so far, now that I'm two thirds of the way through the novel.

He hurts, does Hertz. Even as he accumulates grime from his sordid conduct, even as the husband whose wife he steals dies of bitterness and sorrow,

---

*I've eliminated only the "story so far" recapitulation of the first column.

making him virtually a murderer as well as an adulterer. He hurts even as he plunges deeper into the grime of his behavior and the grimy consequences of his act—first in a seedy hot-sheet hotel room, then on a wild adulterous hegira to Miami Beach—a Singer tour de force, Miami conceived as a palm-fringed purgatory. Even there, enjoying the poisoned fruits of his crime, the man undeniably, I think sincerely, *hurts*. That is what makes him a compelling character—the way he's tormented, torn apart by the struggle between self-laceration and self-indulgence, and still can't help himself. *Shadows on the Hudson* is a great title, conjuring up, I think, the flickering shadows cast by the flames of the crematoria that darken the refuge of the survivors. But it could just as well have been called *Grime and Punishment*.

But to say it's Singer's most Dostoyevskian novel doesn't really do justice to the degree of its darkness. There's a far darker vision of the cosmos—in the eyes of certain of his characters, if not in Singer himself—than anything even Dostoyevsky dared imagine. Darker even than the vision of the Grand Inquisitor episode of *The Brothers Karamazov*. Perhaps the darkest vision I've ever come across in literature. One whose darkness I feel I shielded you from in the first installment of this essay, in part because it hadn't completely manifested itself. One whose darkness Singer might well have wanted to shield English-speaking readers from by leaving *Shadows* untranslated. One whose darkness is captured in two incendiary remarks I find myself still hesitant to repeat but ones which, if I omitted, would fail to do justice to the profound depths of bitterness Singer is capturing and recording, if not endorsing, the bitterness of certain of those survivors who first attempted to explain Hitler in the aftermath of the Holocaust.

Here, in these remarks, Singer's characters are going beyond questioning God's goodness, beyond questioning his silence or his existence. They're . . . well, let me let them speak for themselves.

One character who's lost his entire family gives voice to near-ultimate blasphemy when he says if God permitted what Hitler perpetrated, "then it would appear that the Creator Himself is, perish the thought, a Nazi."

Perish the thought indeed, but then another character goes *beyond* near-ultimate, to the ultimate blasphemy:

Grein's mistress, Esther, also a refugee from the Holocaust, tells him: "In the ghetto there was a pious Jew who recited psalms the whole time. They dragged his entire family to the ovens, but he crouched in a hole somewhere and went on praying. You know the justification: God knows what He's doing. We sinned. In the World to come, we will make atonement. For months he sat in that cellar with other Jews, all dying of hunger. Then one day he suddenly grabbed his phylacteries and tore them to pieces. He spat on them and trampled on them and he screamed, 'God, I don't want to serve you any longer! You're worse than Hitler!' "

Now that's dark, that's darker than Elie Wiesel's vision of God in *Night* in which he sees a young boy hanged on a gallows in the death camp and calls that corpse the God that has died to him. The God in Esther's story, not necessarily Singer's God, not necessarily even Esther's God, but the God Esther bitterly conjures up in the words of a maddened Jew whose family and faith have been incinerated, is not dead or dying but alive and malevolent, the ultimate blasphemy, God as Hitler.

How does a novel, how does a novelist, how does a *reader* recover from a vision like that? One suspects that sentence alone might explain why Singer left *Shadows* untranslated as long as he lived. It's not necessarily Singer's sentiment, but he's capturing an abyss of bitterness he watched engulf those who escaped death in the flames but were burned alive with the fires of rage, regret, and revolt, each a burning bush of inextinguishable agony. How does he recover? I'm not sure he will, I'm only two thirds of the way through the novel as of this installment, and things are certainly getting darker for Hertz Grein, whose abnegation before the consequences of his abandoned conduct in what he sees as a God-abandoned world leads him to deeper and deeper depths of self-loathing and self-pity.

His descent culminates in a horrible scene of humiliation and cowardice when he finds himself in the apartment of Stanislaw Luria, the man he's driven to death by stealing his wife. The corpse has barely cooled, and Anna, the woman he's stolen, has accused him (and herself) of murdering the man. And then, in a moment of diabolical farce, when Anna's father, a man who's supported Grein all his life, shows up, Grein doesn't have the courage to face him, even hides in the bathroom hoping to escape the gaze he cannot face, in a farcical echo of Adam attempting to hide from God. And then he descends even further down the rungs of Gehenna (as Hell is called in Talmudic tradition. Grein: "Gehenna is shame"): As his new wife sits *shivah* for the man they, in effect, have murdered, he can't resist cheating on her with his old mistress Esther.

Slowly, Singer's artistic strategy (both aesthetic and theological) in *Shadows* is beginning to dawn on me. Perhaps it's a false dawn, since I have a third of the book still to read, but from the glimmer I get of his challenge to the God-as-Hitler theodicy, he wants to reveal that a world without God is a hell on earth. To live a life as if God abandoned the world, as Hertz Grein does, to reject heaven-and-hell theology, is not to inhabit a world of moral neutrality but a world of hell alone, a world that unleashes the hell, the Hitler-like impulses within human nature, when we make our own commandments—a hell of our own creation.

But something else began to draw me on as I progressed toward the final third of the novel: a feeling that in *Shadows on the Hudson* Singer is vouchsafing to us his personal fiery vision of existence. I'd call it his burning-bush vision, of souls on fire, of blazing simultaneity. It's a vision I'll try to do justice to in the third and final installment of this essay, if the third and final installment of this amazing novel bears it out.

From the Third Installment*

In the last installment of my serialized response to *Shadows on the Hudson,* Isaac Bashevis Singer's long-lost and initially serialized novel, I promised to unveil what I felt was a primal Singerian vision revealing itself in *Shadows,* one I'd referred to as "blazing simultaneity." Beginning with what seems to be, at first, a throwaway passage about a derelict.

It's a passage in which Hertz Grein, the novel's antihero, the former prodigy–turned–prodigal adulterer, simultaneously torn by lust and self-laceration, wanders out of a synagogue where he's made a first hesitant step toward penance for his sins. Emerging from the dim interior into the painfully blazing sun of a Central Park morning, he comes upon a sleeping derelict:

> On the sidewalk, next to a trash can, lay a drunk, his face battered, unshaven, inflamed as though with plague, babbling and slavering while his eyes cried out with the pain of those who have lost all control over themselves. This derelict seemed somehow ignited from the alcohol, as if he might burst into flames at any moment like a paper lantern.

We never meet this derelict again, but in some essential way, he may be the single most emblematic character in the novel. That derelict: He is Grein, seeing himself. He is us seeing ourselves. He is, one senses, Singer's tormented vision of himself and—in another, deeper sense—of the nature of his own fiction.

The paper of the paper lantern metaphor is the hint: What are Singer's fictions if not word-intoxicated inscriptions on the paper lanterns of his pages, inscriptions that ignite and blaze up in our brains? What are Singer's characters but paper lanterns always on the verge of igniting and consuming themselves in the intoxicating fire of their conflicting passions, in the fires of God-intoxicated heresy, of unholy longing and holy remorse simultaneously?

Simultaneity, it seems to me, is the key, the vision of blazing simultaneity at the heart of the heart of human nature in *Shadows,* in Singer's cosmos. As I raced through this amazing novel, reading and writing about it simultaneously, I found myself struck by the recurrence of the word *simultaneous* or *simultaneously* and explicit images of simultaneity.

*Here less than one paragraph of recapitulation has been cut.

Let me begin with the explicit uses of the word. In a dream, Hertz Grein is in a room with a corpse.

> Someone was searching for the corpse, but the person was not dead. He was sitting in a chair in the gloomy daylight, yellow, terrified, his melancholy eyes glazed in unearthly stupor, and Grein was giving him a loaf of bread with an egg. He was simultaneously both the deceased and the mourner. But how was that possible?

How possible? One way, one might suggest, is that the dying corpse in his dream is Grein's own dying soul, the soul he's mourning for. The dream is not surprising in the light of a previous passage, in which he leaves his wife to run off with another woman. Here, Singer tells us, "Grein did things and was astonished at what he did, almost as if he were a being divided into two, with one half watching the other."

Grein is not the only one in the novel who expresses or apprehends simultaneity. The word blazes forth on the paper lantern of Singer's prose in frequent, occasionally unexpected, manifestations. The painter in the novel, Anfang, is "simultaneously smiling and sorrowful." In a cafeteria, Grein finds "a short fat man was simultaneously eating and doing a crossword puzzle," the sensual and the intellectual facilities simultaneously, unconnectedly engaged.

The moral universe that surrounds him is a blazing profusion of simultaneity, but Grein's trouble is his resistance to it. He knows, he says, there's "a Cabalistic teaching that the Evil Spirit bears witness to the existence of God. If a left or dark side exists, then a right or light side must exist also." But Grein, Singer somewhat intrusively reminds us, wants the uncomplicated, nonsimultaneous accommodation to the contraries of life: "What Grein sought did not and could not exist: He wanted the fear of heaven without dogma; religion without revelation; discipline without proscriptions; Torah, prayer, and isolation built on a pure unadulterated religious experience."

But he lives in a realm, this world—an underworld, really—in which nonadulteration is a delusion, and adultery is a metaphor for the moral chiaroscuro of simultaneous good and evil inclinations within us. Not that all simultaneity is exalted for its own sake in *Shadows*. There is a mismatched *meshuga* simultaneity that is a kind of Bizarro version of God's creation. I somehow doubt Singer would have been a reader of the *Superman* comics' Bizarro episodes (my personal favorites as a kid), the ones that featured a parallel Bizarro-world where everything was drawn badly and shakily, everything and everyone, even the Man of Steel himself, Bizarro-Superman, was off-kilter, off-center, just *off*. But there's a similar feel of Bizarro simultaneity in Singer's vision of what I called last week the "palm-fringed purgatory of Miami Beach":

"Everything was jumbled together: day and night, summer and winter, dishabille and elegance . . . The air smelled of oranges and gasoline."

What is going on with these visions of simultaneity, both in the world around us and the realm within us? And how does this vision of simultaneity relate to the blazing ignition of the paper-lantern image? I knew you'd ask me that, and I know some might think it a stretch, but I think it hearkens back to the primal image of blazing simultaneity in the Bible: the burning bush. A living entity simultaneously burning up and remaining unconsumed as it serves as the medium for the voice of the Creator. Blazing into flame but remaining eternally the same. It's the friction of simultaneous contrarieties that ignites the blaze within us; it's the friction of simultaneous contrarieties that sets the fiction—the inscriptions on the paper lantern of Singer's prose—on fire.

Or so it seems until the very end of *Shadows on the Hudson,* when it appears as if Singer collapses the contrarieties, crushes the simultaneities within Hertz Grein and turns him into someone who extinguishes the flame within himself for the sake of his soul. It's an ending—an epilogue, really—that is likely to mislead and displease many because it seems so uncompromising, such a lurch toward ultra-orthodox piety, a lurch not so much from sincere conviction but from weakness, because the alternative—living any longer with the searing blaze of conflicting simultaneity—has become simply unbearable.

I'm not sure the epilogue should be taken as Singer's own final vision. Here's where *The Kreutzer Sonata* comes in. You know *The Kreutzer Sonata,* right? Consider yourself lucky if you don't. It is, in many ways, one of the most repugnant texts you'll ever encounter. It radiates a poisonous distillation of Tolstoy's final bitterness against the world of flesh and sensuality, women and sexuality. At least that's one way of looking at it; it may indeed be *Tolstoy's* way of looking at it, alas. Most interpreters read it almost purely as a screed, knowing how closely the views of the main character—a confessed wife murderer who buttonholes a fellow passenger on a long train journey in order to discourse endlessly about the evils of contemporary sexual mores—reflect Tolstoy's own views at the time.

The train traveler is obsessed in particular with what he regards as the depraved and degrading practice of continuing sexual relations between husband and wife after childbirth. But he goes beyond that to come close to arguing that all sexual relations, *even* for procreation, are deplorable, and that the human race would be better off chastising itself into nonexistence through total chastity. Tolstoy actually seemed to believe in some of these nutty ideas in his later years. He seemed to endorse an utterly nonironic reading of their expression in *The Kreutzer Sonata* in a "postface" (as opposed to "preface") or afterword that he added to *The Kreutzer Sonata* after receiving many letters asking him whether he really believed in what the man on the train was expounding.

But I believe *The Kreutzer Sonata* is better read as fiction than propaganda, that Tolstoy was too much the artist to produce just a tract, that the artist in Tolstoy subverted the propagandist, even if part of him believed the propaganda. I believe one can (in fact one can't *help* but) read *The Kreutzer Sonata* as a story that subverts itself: It's a tale told by a madman so maddened by his own self-loathing and despair at his inability to control his own impulses that he must try to generalize his own pathological state into a disease of all humankind and impose an iron law of chastity on the rest of mankind to make him feel better about his own lack of self-control. He is, in some ways, like the paper-lantern derelict Hertz Grein comes across in Singer's novel, "babbling and slavering with the pain of those who have lost all control over themselves."

And I believe it is in this light we can read Singer's shocking *Kreutzer Sonata*–like "postface" epilogue to *Shadows on the Hudson:* the letter from Hertz Grein to his childhood friend and Holocaust survivor Morris Gombiner. Grein writes the letter from Me'ah Shearim, the ultra-orthodox neighborhood in Jerusalem. He's fled there after his uncontrollable adulterous appetites have left a trail of devastation behind him in America. Ruined the lives of men and women he was close to, ruined his own life.

Now he's cut himself off from everyone he knew in America, cut himself off from his own children, and he's writing a long letter denouncing the secularized lives they all led in America, denouncing himself as well, but also praising himself for the new choice he's made: to become one of the ultra-orthodox in Me'ah Shearim.

There's lots of language about bridling himself with the leather straps of the phylacteries he wears for morning prayers, about the need for the external restraints, the metaphorical bridles, of orthodox garb to curb that which cannot be controlled from within—as a signal to the world that he has rejected the way of all flesh to harness himself to his vision of God's demands. "As long as the other nations" do not harness themselves thus, he writes, "they will remain unbridled beasts and will go on producing Hitlers and other monstrosities. That is now as clear as day to me."

Clear as day? To Grein, yes, but to Singer? Is this his final resolution of what seemed to be his most dark and questioning novel? Just as we shouldn't read Singer's endorsement into the most bitter challenges to God in the novel—the ones that certain of his Holocaust survivors raise, the ones that go beyond blaming God for Hitler to speaking of God as Hitler—we also shouldn't automatically assume that Singer is endorsing the argument Grein makes in the epilogue.

Even though it's Grein's vision that concludes the novel, I'd argue that *Shadows on the Hudson* is an *argument* about these issues that Singer has not resolved in his *own* heart. That he entertains conflicting visions of the question within himself simultaneously. That it's a novel about his own blazing simultaneity. Grein's answer is not necessarily *the* answer, but the answer of someone like that derelict who's abandoned hope of ending the pain of controlling himself, someone like the wife murderer in *The Kreutzer Sonata*. Curiously, more than curiously, I think, Grein actually invokes Tolstoy, the Tolstoy of the *Kreutzer Sonata* period, in his letter. In speaking of the way Orthodox Jewish garb signals a renunciation of the hell on earth he believes this world and its temptations to be, Grein tells his friend, "That's why Tolstoy finally put on a peasant blouse. That piece of clothing was his attempt to separate himself from the corrupt world . . . I'm certain that if Tolstoy had lived longer, he would have turned to Judaism—that is, to the prayer shawl and phylacteries, fringed ritual undergarments . . ."

Tolstoy turning Orthodox Jew? The evidence of his attitude toward Jews recently adduced by Lev Navrozov* suggests otherwise, but the comic extremity of the remark may be Singer's sly way of subverting Grein's grim rant by pushing it just a bit too far to be taken completely seriously, or at least taken as completely Singer's.

Certainly, the evidence of Singer's own life and practices do not bear out an uncritical adoption of Grein's ultra-orthodoxy. On the contrary, to the end he maintained the vision of contradictory simultaneity that is, I believe, the true heart of *Shadows on the Hudson.* He maintains it in one of the last interviews he gave before he died, a fascinating conversation Singer had with writer Norman Green in December 1987, an interview that has yet to be published in English.

It took place on a wintry Friday afternoon as shadows fell on the Hudson, two blocks away from Singer's Upper West Side apartment. Singer was talking about his own continuing uncertainty about the nature of God, the nature of human nature, and the relations between the two. It's "all guesswork," Singer said. "Human nature and nature . . . do not reveal to us any clear way or idea what we should do . . . We are made to guess things." But "much of our morality is built on" going against the impulses of nature God has apparently given us, he added.

The struggle for control of those impulses is a painful one, Singer said. "So in a way, we cannot just all the time give compliments to the Almighty and praise Him . . . We have a feeling of protest. Why has He made this whole or-

*"Tolstoy and the Jews," *Midstream,* November 1997.

deal for us to suffer? So I think that one can admire God, admire His wisdom, and at the same time [simultaneously!] protest His so-called neutrality . . . The great religious leaders were also protesters in their own way. The Book of Job is a book of protest. And so are many great books . . ."

And so is *Shadows on the Hudson,* Isaac Bashevis Singer's Book of Job.

Explaining Pharaoh

What does it mean, why was it necessary, for God to "harden" Pharaoh's heart? That's the disturbing aspect of this week's Torah portion,* which takes us into the final negotiating strategy of God and Moses as they try to force Pharaoh to let the Israelites go. This is toward the end of the plagues: after the hail and before the locusts. And after the locusts and the darkness, of course, is the slaughter of the firstborn of the Egyptians and the Exodus.

In this last series of plagues, God has been upping the ante, heightening the contradictions, however you want to put it. Pharaoh seems ready to make a deal after the hail, but God "hardens his heart," and Pharaoh suddenly sets conditions. Then come the locusts and darkness, and each time Pharaoh seems ready, but God hardens Pharaoh's heart. Then God sets out to shatter

*The *Forward,* Isaac Bashevis Singer's still vigorous newspaper, asked me to write one of their six-hundred-word weekly commentaries on the Torah portion for that week. I was thrilled to be asked, to write anything for Singer's old paper. I'm not sure if they were thrilled at what they got, but it does express in compressed form the mystery of theodicy that still obsesses me.

his heart with the slaughter of tens of thousands of Egyptian children—
the firstborn, children who couldn't be held responsible for Pharaoh's hard
heart.

The way it's depicted, Pharaoh starts off a bad guy, enslaver, tyrant, and all
that, but God turns his ordinary wickedness into adamantine evil, makes it
hard for him to give in, then punishes him for this additional God-given stubbornness by murdering Egyptian children. Whose heart is the real hard one?
Why is it necessary?

God in the passage is pretty candid about this: He did it to make a point, to
show off, to show who's the Boss: "In order that I may display these my signs
[the plagues] among them and that you may recount in the hearing of your
sons and of your sons' sons how I made a mockery of the Egyptians and how
I displayed My signs among them—in order that you may know I am the
Lord" (Exodus 10:1–2).

So, you could argue there was an educational value to all this, not just for
Pharaoh but for the Israelites, who are, throughout the Bible, forever losing
sight of who's the Boss, whoring after Golden Calves and the like. Perhaps it's
wiser to take the passage in a more metaphorical way: "hardening Pharaoh's
heart" was meant to bring to the surface the essential evil, the ineradicable inhuman face of slavery regardless of the temporary moderation that the particular human face heading the system might show.

That works for me, but there are some other metaphoric implications I still
find troubling. Recently, I gave a talk at a synagogue about the question of
Hitler's evil, its origins and uniqueness. After I finished, the rabbi added
some thoughtful words of his own—centered on this very passage: the mystery of God's hardening Pharaoh's heart. This raised the implicit question:
Did God harden Hitler's heart as well; was the Holocaust part of His plan?
There have been ultra-orthodox sages in Israel, for instance, who explain
the Holocaust either as God's justifiable wrath against European Jews for
straying from Orthodoxy—or as part of God's long-range plan to hasten the
creation of the State of Israel to prepare for the coming of the messiah.
The phrase used to make the connection, the phrase that conjures up the rod
Moses used to bring down the plagues on Egypt, is a chilling one: Hitler was
"the rod of God's anger." God hardened Hitler's heart the better to serve
God's plan.

It's chilling but—if you believe everything is part of God's plan, that He
would cause the slaughter of tens of thousands of children to make a point—
who's to say the ultra-Orthodox are not right about such a God?

For me this is one of the passages that sends me back to something challenging that the *Forward*'s own Isaac Bashevis Singer said in one of the last
interviews he gave before his death: "We cannot just all the time give compli-

ments to the Almighty and praise Him. . . . We have a feeling of protest. Why has He made this whole ordeal for us to suffer? . . . The great religious leaders were also protesters in their own way. The Book of Job is a book of protest." I don't think God hardened Hitler's heart; Hitler didn't need help. But if He did, I protest.

This "Rarest Dream": The Final Affirmation of Shakespearean Romance

It's a dream, a nightmare, a hallucination, this play *Pericles*.* A voyage in a drunken boat, a fractured fairy tale. The closest thing to the feel of it in twentieth-century literature may be the magic realism of the "Nighttown" sequence in *Ulysses,* which manages to fuse the Homeric and the phantasmagoric in a peculiarly sinister Periclean way. *Pericles* is Shakespeare's hallucinatory *Odyssey.*

It's a play that opens with a dark riddle** and is itself the opening riddle of the last great phase—the final enigma—of Shakespeare's development as artist and dramatist: the rich and strange period of the Late Romances that begins with *Pericles* and continues with *Cymbeline, The Winter's Tale,* and *The Tempest.*

It's a sudden breakthrough into a realm that's like nothing else in Shakespeare, like little else in all other literature, a far cry from the bitter exigencies of Lear's heath, Elsinore's frozen parapets, and Desdemona's bed. It's a realm

---

*An essay composed for the program of the New York Shakespeare Festival's 1998 production of *Pericles.*

**Pericles' close reading of a riddle recited by his prospective bride reveals a devastating incest secret.

of shipwrecks and pirates, miraculous rescues and resurrections, bodies raised from the dead, gods descending to earth and women ascending from statues, all attuned to the music of the spheres only Pericles (and Shakespeare) have the gift to hear.

Let's linger a moment on the concept of pirates, not the ones who burst into the plot of *Pericles* to rescue his daughter Marina from murder and then sell her to a brothel keeper. Pirates of another kind figure in the history of *Pericles,* the text of which has suffered a fate as mysterious and perilous—and ultimately redemptive—as any of its heroes and heroines.

Pericles first materializes on the stage of the Globe Theatre in 1608 performed by Shakespeare's company. But we no longer have access to the play Shakespeare wrote (or cowrote or rewrote and revised). We only have a maimed and possibly pirated version—the pirates, some scholars argue, being rival theatrical entrepreneurs whose hasty shorthand record of what they heard at the Globe has given us the partly maimed version that is all we have left.

The pirated original shimmers maddeningly beneath the choppy surface of the text we have, like the pearls in the eyes of the drowned sailors full fathom five beneath the ocean in *The Tempest.* But this loss, a loss that has driven scholars to distraction for centuries, has been—like so many losses in the Late Romances—redeemed: Over the centuries it has given license to great players and directors to make of *Pericles* a special subject of devotion. Given them freedom to feel, to intuit, to dream into and under the mangled text and restore what has been lost through a kind of sympathetic magic. To resurrect on the stage what is lost on the page, and to give us, through a glass darkly, a vision that has made *Pericles* a revelation to audiences whenever it is performed.

This theme of the loss redeemed, the wound not just healed but transfigured, is threaded throughout *Pericles.* It finds itself expressed in the figure of the needle and thread, in fact, in the couplet in which the Chorus introduces us to Marina, Pericles' daughter, the posthumous child of a tempest living her life in heartbroken exile, devoting herself, like Odysseus's Penelope, to weaving and threading a tapestry: "She would with sharp needle wound / The cambric, which she made more sound / By hurting it."

It's all there, the needle and the damage done, the needle undoing the damage done. The needle that, similar to the way the point of pen inscribes a story, "writes" by poking holes in the cambric (the fabric) and knitting the holes together into a storytelling tapestry that transfigures the pain of each piercing.

It's a tapestry, *Pericles,* a play that's woven together—if you forget the feckless Pericles—by women. Wounded women, damaged women, imperiled princesses, captured, raptured, restored heroines.

There is incestuous Antiochus's daughter, nameless, virtually speechless, dangerously alluring—"see where she comes apparell'd like the spring"—her face "a book of curious pleasures," her body and soul bound to forbidden ones in a riddling text only Pericles can read.

There is Thaisa, another daughter put up for auction by her father, who chooses Pericles in an act of reading (the battle of the symbolic mottoes), bears his child, and is buried at sea for her pains, only to be resurrected and re-united with husband and child.

(Births and deaths are never ordinary in the Late Romances—all are momentous, mysterious, inextricably linked—as in posthumous children—restoring to us the primal wonder at the miraculous creation and destruction of life.)

And finally there is Marina, one of the most wondrous and mysterious of Shakespeare's women, born at sea, the other side of the sea you might say, wild Neptune's serene child. A woman whose redemptive intelligence and artistry, whose wit and charisma, music and charm weave the raveled strands of the plot together just as she weaves the "sledded silk" into a tapestry. Born "in a tempest when my mother died / This world to me is a lasting storm," she charms the tempests within men with the music of her voice.

Marina is more than Marina. She becomes for us all the lost heroines of Shakespearean tragedy—Ophelia, Desdemona, Cordelia—risen from their untimely graves and given radiant life again. In Marina's first words you hear the echo of Ophelia's last: "I will rob Tellus," the earth, she declares, "of her weed to strew the green with flowers . . . the purple violets and marigolds." Which echoes, reverses, and redeems Ophelia's despairing near-dying words about withered violets: "I would give you violets but they withered all when my father died." Where Ophelia wove garlands of weeds and violets that dragged her down into the watery grave she drowned in, Marina weaves garlands of flowers into a tapestry that turns a grave into a place of rebirth.

Marina has haunted audiences and subsequent poets. In "Marina," T. S. Eliot asks, "What is this face less clear, and clearer . . . more distant than the stars and nearer than the eye?" Nearer than the eye—in other words, she exists somehow inside our heads.

Both less real and more, Marina is a figure or a figment of recompense—all we're given, and more than enough—for the way we're subject to the wayward, even wicked, whims of gods and fate. *Pericles* at its most primal is a meditation about theodicy—how to reconcile the ways of gods to man. Marina is the grace we're given—occasionally, unpredictably, unmeritably—for the fates we're forced to suffer, for the way injustice seems to single out those who most deserve to be blessed. Pericles is Shakespeare's Odysseus but he is also his Job. By the last act he's deepened: Maddened, speechless, ragged, and hirsute, prostrate on a shipborne berth that is virtually a floating bier, he is close to Lear. Indeed, it seems to me that the amazing recognition scene between Pericles and his daughter Marina in the fifth act is Shakespeare's way of rewriting the tragic doomed reunion of Lear and Cordelia before death takes them both. The denouement of tragedy turned into the transfigurative reunion of Romance.

There are the same elements of doubt and wonder and rapture in each reunion scene. Lear awakes from madness and dreams to see his rejected but still loyal and loving daughter before him. Cannot believe he's alive, cannot believe his daughter is not a delusion or a dead visitation: "Pray do not mock me / I am a very foolish, fond old man," Lear pleads. "O I am mocked," echoes Pericles, as recognition dawns that the woman who visits him on his shipboard bier may be his long-lost daughter, Marina. "I am wild in my beholding," he says, doubting his senses. "Thou lookest like one I loved indeed," Pericles murmurs, Lear-like. "Methinks I should know you," Lear says, "yet I am doubtful."

They are duets of doubt and faith between fathers and daughters, these echoing recognition scenes. In *Lear*, of course, the moment of joyful recognition and reconciliation is brutally cut short, the moment snatched away by fate as, in a final cruel twist, even after the tide of battle turns their way again, the order to execute Cordelia by hanging is carried out before it can be rescinded. In *Pericles* the cruel reversal is itself reversed. The reunion holds, the communion prevails, resounds, and astounds: "This is the rarest dream that ever dull sleep did mock sad fools withal." The rarest dream—one whose precariousness and perhaps insubstantial dreaminess cannot be denied, one that beggars and beguiles belief.

Shakespeare seems deliberately to draw out the recognition scene in *Pericles* as the half-mad king requires proof after proof, tests hope against hope, to prolong it, savor it, to wring out every unbearably heartbreaking moment of unbelieving belief, the better to redeem and recuperate the unbearable loss at the close of *Lear*.

"Never, never, never, never, never," a broken and bereft Lear mutters over Cordelia's lifeless, breathless body, a quintuple incantation of the quintessence of tragedy.

"Ever, ever, ever, ever, ever" is the unspoken reply of Periclean Romance.

Sources

The Nineties and After

Acknowledgments

I want to begin by thanking my editor at Random House, Jonathan Karp. I was fortunate to be able to work with Jon on *Explaining Hitler;* his thoughtful and insightful guidance, his remarkable confidence that I would somehow be able to sculpt a book out of a decade's expedition into that heart of darkness pulled me through my own moments of doubt. And Jon is, more than anyone, responsible for the shape (and weight) of *The Secret Parts of Fortune.* I had raised the possibility of a collection of my "Edgy Enthusiast" columns, and he came back with an idea for something far more comprehensive: a kind of mega-tome that would include material never before in hardcover (all of the material in the "Nineties and After," and some of "The Seventies" and "The Eighties") and material that was long out of print, stories I'd forgotten but that he remembered or had been reminded of by other writers. And so I submerged my edginess in his enthusiasm for the idea. It means a lot to me to be able to see these stories given a new life in book form. I'm not going to say much more about Jon's merits as an editor for fear he'll get too popular and won't have as much time to put up with my obsessiveness. Just take my word for it: He's terrific.

I feel the same way about Kathy Robbins, my superb literary agent, whose advice has done so much to make my life as a writer fulfilling: I'm too selfish to want to share her with any more writers than she has already. In fact, I've occasionally had the fantasy of somehow persuading her to give me nonstop advice about *everything,* every minute of the day, Cyrano-style, maybe with some kind of remote headset hookup. But barring that, I have been extremely well taken care of over the years by her and by the smart, good-natured group of people who work at the Robbins office, including, to name just the current crew, Bill Clegg, David Halpern, Heather Holland-Wheaton, Catherine Luttinger, Rick Pappas, Gillian Scott, Robert Simpson, Dori Steele, and Beth Valove.

This is the second book I've done with Random House, and I'm immensely grateful for the care and enthusiasm everyone has brought to my books including, especially, Ann Godoff, Sally Marvin, Paula Shuster, Andy Carpenter, Amy Edelman, Benjamin Dreyer, Evan Stone, and Monica Gomez. I owe special thanks to Timothy Mennel, now senior copy editor, who also worked on *Explaining Hitler* and who represents a rare combination of erudition, humor, and empathy.

I want to thank all my colleagues at the *New York Observer,* a collection of talented people who have made writing for the paper a pleasure. And my *Observer* readers, who have encouraged me to pursue the arcane and difficult regardless of the absence of a peg. I've spoken in the introduction of how much I'm indebted to Peter Kaplan and Eric Etheridge for encouraging me to pursue an unconventional course with the column. My other hero in the start-up was my first editor, Deirdre Dolan, whose patience and wit—and willingness to devote considerable time to poring over multiple revises—gave me the confidence to expand my efforts from brief list-like items of praise to more challenging weekly essays. My subsequent editors there, David Yezzi, Katja Shaye, William Berlind, and most recently the extremely sharp and dedicated Amy Larocca, have all been great, as have savvy *consiglieri* at the *Observer* such as Peter Stevenson, Mary Ann Giordano, Jim Windolf, Lauren Ramsby, Terry Golway, Joe Conason, Brian Kempner, and Renée Kaplan. Arthur Carter deserves special praise for having created a new literate and skeptical voice in New York, a paper I looked forward to reading even before I started writing for it.

Special thanks for their contributions to this book to Errol Morris whose generous words in his foreword mean even more to me because I admire his work so much.

To Robert Vare, distinguished editor and *raconteur,* who was an invaluable adviser as my editor at the *Times Magazine* and *The New Yorker.*

To the talented photographer Nina Roberts, whose skill and sense of mischief made possible the Skull and Bones jacket-cover photo caper.

To all my students at Columbia Journalism School (I wish I'd been a better teacher, but I learned a lot from you).

And to the late Dan Wolf and Harold Hayes, the two inspiring editors who first believed in my work.

Now comes the hard part. Trying not to leave out any of the people—editors, researchers, and friends—who have directly or indirectly made contributions to these stories and to my life as a writer. So here are some of them (please forgive inadvertent omissions), in alphabetical order: Elise Ackerman, Daniel Ahn, Sarah Alcorn, Jane Amsterdam, Faye Beckerman, Dick Bell, Elizabeth Bogner, Susan Braudy, Tina Brown, Dominique Browning, Richard Burling, Nancy Butkus, Peter Canby, Virginia Cannon, Jon Carroll, Betsy Carter, Michael Caruso, Beatrice Cody, Stephanie Coen, Robert Conquest, Cynthia Cotts, Richard Ben Cramer, Stanley Crouch, Greg Curtis, Byron Dobell, George Dolger, Nancy Donahoe, Jan Drews, Mike Drosnin, Emily Eakin, Susan Edmiston, Lee Eisenberg, Abbie Ehrlich, Harry Evans, Ed Fancher, Liz Ferris, David Freeman, Deborah Friedman, Anne Gilbert, Alfred Gingold, Nan Graham, David Granger, Hortense Greenberg, Liz Groden, Amy Gutman, James Hamilton, Linda Healey, Liz Hecht, Virginia Heffernan, Nat Hentoff, Kim Heron, Rick Hertzberg, David Hirshey, Gary Hoenig, Richard Horowitz, Sarah Jewler, Alex Jones, Louise Jones, Susan Kamil, Katie Karlovitz, Craig Karpel, Sarah Kernochan, Noah Kimerling, Michael Kinsley, Waltraud Kolb, Dan Kornstein, Ed Kosner, Sarah and Victor Kovner, Lewis Lapham, Jon Larsen, David Livingstone, Larissa MacFarquhar, Robert Manoff, Bill Marshall, Caroline Marshall, Gerry Marzorati, Lauren Mechling, Charles Mee, Robert Metcalfe, Stanley Mieses, Adrienne Miller, Clio Morgan, Adam Moss, Phillip Nobile, Michael O'Laughlin, Suzanne O'Malley, Kathryn Paulson, Sheldon Piekny, Richard Pollak, Gerald Posner, David Remnick, Helen Rogan, Henry and Evelyn Rosenbaum, Jack Rosenthal, Christine Schoemer, Henry Schroeder, Julia Sheehan, Jesse Sheidlower, Richard Spivak, Dora Steinberg, Mark Steinberg, Alexander Stengel, Sam Tanenhaus, The Dixie Chicks, Lauren Thierry, Josiah Thompson, Jill Tolan, Mary Turner, Ellen Umansky, Jim Watkins, Steven Weisman, Alan Weitz, Peter Wells, Ross Wetzsteon, Carolyn White, Meredith White, Rhoda Wolf, and Rebecca Wright.

For the paperback edition I'd like to thank publishing sage Robert Jones, who was also editor of the HarperCollins edition of *Explaining Hitler*, and Alison Callahan, his extremely able second-in-command.

Index

ABOUT THE AUTHOR

RON ROSENBAUM's work has appeared in *Harper's, The New Yorker, The New Republic, Esquire,* and *The New York Times Magazine.* His book *Explaining Hitler* has been translated into ten languages. He writes "The Edgy Enthusiast" column for the *New York Observer* and is at work on his next book, on Shakespeare scholars. Aware of the controversy over authors posing with their pets on book covers, he has not posed with his soulful cat, Stumpy, whose comic genius is described on pages 702–707 of this volume.

◼ Perennial

Books by Ron Rosenbaum:

THE SECRET PARTS OF FORTUNE
Three Decades of Intense Investigations and Edgy Enthusiasms
ISBN 0-06-093446-8 (paperback)

Forcefully reported, brilliantly opinionated, and elegantly phrased, *The Secret Parts of Fortune* is a vital record of American culture from 1970 to the present. Rosenbaum's intellectual adventure stories take readers on a wildly original tour of the American landscape, deep into "the secret parts" of the great mysteries, controversies, and enigmas of our time.
"A masterly concoction; a blend of boy reporter, Ancient Mariner, lounge lizard . . . ."—*New York Times Book Review*

EXPLAINING HITLER
The Search for the Origins of His Evil
ISBN 0-06-095339-X (paperback)

When Hitler's war ended in 1945, the war over Hitler—who he really was, and what gave birth to his unique evil—had just begun. *Explaining Hitler* is an extraordinary expedition into the war zone of Hitler theories, illuminating what Hitler explainers tell us about Hitler, about the explainers, and about ourselves.
"Brilliant . . . . Restlessly probing and deeply intelligent."—*Time*
"Fascinating . . . . A provocative work of cultural history."
      —Michiko Kakutani, *New York Times*